CAREER
DEVELOPMENT
AND
COUNSELING

CAREER DEVELOPMENT AND COUNSELING

Putting Theory and Research to Work

edited by

STEVEN D. BROWN

ROBERT W. LENT

WILEY

John Wiley & Sons, Inc.

Published by John Wiley & Sons, Inc., Hoboken, New Jersey.
Published simultaneously in Canada.

This publication is designed to provide accurate and authoritative information in regard to the subject matter covered. It is sold with the understanding that the publisher is not engaged in rendering professional services. If legal, accounting, medical, psychological, or any other expert assistance is required, the services of a competent professional person should be sought.

Designations used by companies to distinguish their products are often claimed as trademarks. In all instances where John Wiley & Sons, Inc. is aware of a claim, the product names appear in initial capital or all capital letters. Readers, however, should contact the appropriate companies for more complete information regarding trademarks and registration.

For general information on our other products and services, please contact our Customer Care Department within the United States at (800) 762-2974, outside the United States at (317) 572-3993 or fax (317) 572-4002.

Wiley also publishes its books in a variety of electronic formats. Some content that appears in print may not be available in electronic books. For more information about Wiley products, visit our web site at www.wiley.com.

Library of Congress Cataloging-in-Publication Data:

Career development and counseling : putting theory and research to work / edited by
    Steven D. Brown and Robert W. Lent.
        p.   cm.
    Includes bibliographical references.
    ISBN 0-471-28880-2 (cloth)
    1. Career development.   2. Vocational guidance.   3. Counseling.   I. Brown, Steven D.
    (Steven Douglas), 1947–   II. Lent, Robert W. (Robert William), 1953–
    HF5381.C265373   2005
    331.702—dc22
                                                                            2004042226

Printed in the United States of America.

10 9 8 7 6 5 4 3 2 1

This book is dedicated to the memories of Edward Bordin, Lloyd Lofquist, Frank Parsons, Anne Roe, E. K. Strong, Donald Super, and all the pioneers who paved the way for the science and profession of career development and counseling.

Contents

Preface

THIS BOOK GREW out of our experiences as career development counselors and researchers—and, especially, teachers. In the latter role, we have felt constantly challenged to find a career text that would sufficiently acquaint graduate students with the scientific underpinnings of career development and counseling. For example, for many years, the first editor has taught a graduate-level course on career development and counseling taken by master's students in community and school counseling programs and by doctoral students in counseling psychology; the second editor has also taught and supervised master's and doctoral students in a variety of fields who are learning career counseling. Our common concern has been to help students acquire knowledge critical to becoming informed practitioners—that is, practitioners who base their practices on the best that our science, and relevant research emanating from other disciplines, has to offer. While we intended this book to be helpful to a wide audience of students, practitioners, and researchers, our main goal was to create a text that could be used in graduate-level courses to promote scientifically based career practices—a goal that serves as the organizing scheme for the book.

Scientifically informed practice first requires accurate knowledge of relevant career theories and the research derived from them. The first section of the text provides in-depth coverage of theories of career development, choice, and adjustment. However, as in all helping professions, not all theories generate sufficient research, survive empirical investigation, or are equally useful to practitioners working with diverse clientele. It is also common for once-viable models to gradually fade from use or for their most helpful aspects to become integrated within newer approaches. Instead of providing an encyclopedic collection of career theories, we chose to focus on only those theories that, in our view, have garnered sustained empirical attention, shown promise of evolving into more useful models, or have the clearest implications for promoting optimum career development, treating career-related problems, and preventing future difficulties in the workplace. We were fortunate that in most cases the original theorists themselves agreed to write for the text. Students can, therefore, be assured that they are reading the most accurate and up-to-date statements of the theories and their practical applications.

We also believe that career practitioners require not only knowledge of scientifically supported career theories and their implications for practice but also knowledge of research that may not emanate directly from these theories, or even from our discipline, but is nevertheless important to promoting fully informed practice. For example, students will appreciate, after reading the first section of this text, that several well-researched career theories have important implications for assisting clients with job dissatisfaction and other work-related problems.

However, the knowledge that these theories provide to practitioners is incomplete. Fully informed career counseling also requires that counselors know and use findings from relevant fields such as personality and industrial-organizational psychology. Research from these fields suggests, for example, that basic personality constellations influence peoples' career satisfaction and other workplace difficulties and point to characteristics of the work environment (e.g., supervisor support, work overload, role ambiguity, goal facilitation) that affect adjustment difficulties at work.

In trying to select textbooks for our courses, we found that available texts tend to be somewhat parochial in that they tend to give little, if any, attention to important work from other disciplines that is relevant to career practice. Thus, we think that readers will find this text unique not only for its more focused coverage of theories in Section I but also in its coverage in Section II of relevant research across disciplinary boundaries that has much to say about career development, choice, and adjustment. To facilitate this cross-disciplinary agenda, we invited some superb researchers from both within and outside the career counseling/vocational psychology field (e.g., experts in organizational psychology) to contribute chapters to the book.

The third and fourth sections of the book—Assessment and Occupational Information (Section III) and Career Interventions Across the Life Span (Section IV)—represent mainstays of most career development texts. However, in both sections we asked authors to be selective and scientific in their coverage—to highlight and discuss only those assessment and informational tools and interventions that have garnered some scientific support and have the clearest implications for promoting career development and remediating problems that persons may encounter in developing optimum aspirations, making career choices, adjusting to their workplaces and careers, and achieving a satisfying and successful post-work life.

The final section (Section V, Special Needs and Applications) expands on coverage provided in the preceding sections. The first four sections of the book are based on an assumption that we have as researchers and practitioners—that there are common ingredients, derived from extant theories and supported by interdisciplinary research, that influence the career development, choice, and adjustment of all individuals, regardless of their backgrounds (e.g., gender, race, ethnicity, socioeconomic status, intelligence) or specific presenting concerns. Thus, we think that the material covered in the first four sections provides important insights for working with all persons to promote their career development, help them make work-related choices, and assist them in achieving adjustment (i.e., satisfaction and success) in their work and after-work lives.

However, it is also clear from the extant theoretical and empirical literatures that persons' background characteristics and circumstances have some unique influences that need to be considered to do maximally effective development and counseling work with them. For example, although career interventions with all children and youth have the general goal of helping them eventually to make satisfying and satisfactory work and lifestyle choices, the unique characteristics, experiences, and needs of intellectually precocious children, children from economically disadvantaged backgrounds, and youth with disabilities may require a different, or at least modified, focus of intervention efforts.

Similarly, adults who seek choice-making or job-finding help because they have lost a job, are seeking a new work direction, or are returning to the workforce bring with them some unique needs that first-time choosers or implementers may not have that require attention from counselors. Thus, the chapters in Section V involve special applications of career development services to youth and adult clients—they do not supplant the knowledge that readers gain in the first four sections of the book, but provide information that counselors need to know to fine-tune and improve the services that they offer to the widest array of clients.

We have many people to thank for their contributions to this book. First and foremost, we thank the hundreds of students whose formal and informal input over the past two and a half decades did much to shape our thinking about how to teach career development and counseling. Second, we are grateful for the participation of an extremely gifted and distinguished group of contributing authors. Third, we thank our editor at Wiley, Tracey Belmont, for convincing us to do this book and for keeping us motivated and on-task. Fourth, as always, we thank our family members (Linda, Zack, Kate, Ellen, and Jeremy) for the support and encouragement they gave us throughout this project, for their patience and forbearance, and for their many kindnesses. Finally, we thank in advance those instructors and other professionals who agree that career clients deserve nothing less than services that are based on sound, interdisciplinary science and who decided, therefore, to adopt this text for their courses or to read the book for their own professional development. We hope that the book lives up to your expectations, and we look forward to receiving your feedback.

STEVEN D. BROWN
ROBERT W. LENT

February 3, 2004

Contributors

John A. Achter, PhD
University of Wisconsin–Stout
Menomonie, Wisconsin

Consuelo Arbona, PhD
University of Houston
Houston, Texas

Patrick Ian Armstrong, MA
University of Illinois at
    Urbana–Champaign
Champaign, Illinois

Nancy E. Betz, PhD
The Ohio State University
Columbus, Ohio

Becky L. Bobek, PhD
ACT, Inc.
Iowa City, Iowa

Steven D. Brown, PhD
Loyola University Chicago
Chicago, Illinois

Maria Cristina Cruza-Guet, MA
Lehigh University
Bethlehem, Pennsylvania

Catalina D'Achiardi, MA
Southern Illinois
    University–Carbondale
Carbondale, Illinois

René V. Dawis, PhD
University of Minnesota
Minneapolis, Minnesota

Ellen S. Fabian, PhD
University of Maryland
College Park, Maryland

Lisa Y. Flores, PhD
University of Missouri–Columbia
Columbia, Missouri

Barbara A. Fritzsche, PhD
University of Central Florida
Orlando, Florida

Paul A. Gore Jr., PhD
ACT, Inc.
Iowa City, Iowa

Linda S. Gottfredson, PhD
University of Delaware
Newark, Delaware

Barbara Griffin, PhD
University of Sydney
Sydney, Australia

Jo-Ida C. Hansen, PhD
University of Minnesota
Minneapolis, Minnesota

Beryl Hesketh, PhD
University of Sydney
Sydney, Australia

Jorie L. Hitch, MA
Southern Illinois
    University–Carbondale
Carbondale, Illinois

LaRae M. Jome, PhD
University of Albany, State University
    of New York
Albany, New York

Cindy L. Juntunen, PhD
University of North Dakota
Grand Forks, North Dakota

Nancy E. Ryan Krane, PhD
The Ball Foundation
Glen Ellyn, Illinois

Richard T. Lapan, PhD
University of Missouri–Columbia
Columbia, Missouri

Robert W. Lent, PhD
University of Maryland
College Park, Maryland

James J. Liesener, PhD
Norfolk State University
Norfolk, Virginia

David Lubinski, PhD
Vanderbilt University
Nashville, Tennessee

Matthew J. Miller, MA
Loyola University Chicago
Chicago, Illinois

Rachel L. Navarro, MA
University of Missouri–Columbia
Columbia, Missouri

Tiffany J. Parrish, PhD
University of Central Florida
Orlando, Florida

Susan D. Phillips, PhD
University of Albany, State University
  of New York
Albany, New York

Steven B. Robbins, PhD
ACT, Inc.
Iowa City, Iowa

Jay W. Rojewski, PhD
University of Georgia
Athens, Georgia

James B. Rounds, PhD
University of Illinois at
  Urbana–Champaign
Champaign, Illinois

Joyce E. A. Russell, PhD
University of Maryland
College Park, Maryland

Alan M. Saks, PhD
University of Toronto
Toronto, Ontario, Canada

Mark L. Savickas, PhD
Northeastern Ohio Universities
  College of Medicine
Rootstown, Ohio

Arnold R. Spokane, PhD
Lehigh University
Bethlehem, Pennsylvania

Harvey L. Sterns, PhD
The University of Akron
Akron, Ohio

Linda Mezydlo Subich, PhD
The University of Akron
Akron, Ohio

Jane L. Swanson, PhD
Southern Illinois
  University–Carbondale
Carbondale, Illinois

William C. Tirre, PhD
The Ball Foundation
Glen Ellyn, Illinois

Sherri L. Turner, PhD
University of Minnesota
Minneapolis, Minnesota

Kara Brita Wettersten, PhD
University of North Dakota
Grand Forks, North Dakota

Roger L. Worthington, PhD
University of Missouri–Columbia
Columbia, Missouri

MAJOR THEORIES OF CAREER DEVELOPMENT, CHOICE, AND ADJUSTMENT

CHAPTER 1

The Minnesota Theory of Work Adjustment

René V. Dawis

THE THEORY OF Work Adjustment (TWA; Dawis & Lofquist, 1984) grew out of the University of Minnesota's Work Adjustment Project, a 20-year federally funded research program to study how vocational rehabilitation clients adjusted to work. This research, conducted in the 1960s and 1970s, is reported in 30 bulletins of the *Minnesota Studies in Vocational Rehabilitation* series (Industrial Relations Center, University of Minnesota—Minneapolis) and in several journal articles, book chapters, and books. Since the mid-1970s, the Work Adjustment Project has continued as the Vocational Psychology Research Program of the Department of Psychology, University of Minnesota.

When it started, the Work Adjustment Project attempted a wide-ranging, broad-gauged approach to its research problem (Scott, Dawis, England, & Lofquist, 1960). It collected data on a large number of individuals and on a large number of variables, such as job satisfaction, work attitudes, job performance ratings, work histories, education and training experiences, aptitudes, needs, interests, and personality traits. It quickly became apparent that such a large mass of data could be analyzed in endless ways and that a theoretical framework was needed to narrow down and provide focus for data analysis. TWA was developed for this purpose (Dawis, England, & Lofquist, 1964). Furthermore, TWA was found useful in providing direction for subsequent research. In turn, the ensuing research led to revisions and additions to TWA (Dawis & Lofquist, 1984; Dawis, Lofquist, & Weiss, 1968; Lofquist & Dawis, 1969). For more on the history of TWA, see Dawis (1996, pp. 75–80). As this history shows, many individuals, including some whose names are not mentioned here, contributed to the development of TWA.

THEORETICAL FOUNDATIONS

The Theory of Work Adjustment belongs to a class of theories known as P-E theories (Dawis, 2000), which are about the person (P) in an environment (E) and the fit between, and the interaction of, P and E. There are a variety of Es (physical, school, work, family, home, social, or even one other person); hence, it behooves P-E theorists at the outset to identify and define the E to which they refer. As its name indicates, TWA is about the work environment.

There are P variables and E variables, and these are often used to account for behavior or behavioral outcomes. However, the basic proposition of P-E theories is that the explanation for behavior or behavioral outcomes lies not so much with the P or the E variables, but rather, with the P-E combination. Even if P and E variables contribute to the explanation, it is a particular P-E combination that will best explain the particular behavior or behavioral outcome.

P-E theories use two constructions to denote the P-E combination: fit and interaction. *Fit* refers to the degree to which P characteristics correspond to E characteristics assessed across commensurate (parallel or matching) dimensions. For example, different workers (P) have different sets of skills, and different jobs (E) require different sets of skills. Fit means that some workers have the set of skills that a job requires but other workers do not, or some jobs require the set of skills that a worker has but other jobs do not.

Interaction refers to P's and E's *action on* and *reaction to* each other in a mutual give and take. Workers and work environments are not static, unchanging entities, but rather, they can and do change. For example, dissatisfied workers will "do something" to change dissatisfying work situations, such as complain to management or work even harder to "prove" to management that they deserve better treatment. Management might respond to complaints negatively by laying off workers or respond positively by increasing worker pay. TWA is both a P-E fit theory and a P-E interaction theory.

The Theory of Work Adjustment grew out of the individual differences tradition in psychology (Dawis, 1992). The psychology of individual differences is about human variability, how people differ from one another, as contrasted with general psychology, which is about how people behave on average. Human variability affords a way to describe human individuality. Such individuality may result in different consequences for different people in the same situation. In studying this phenomenon, the psychology of individual differences focuses on variables that are stable over time, the class of variables known as *traits* (as contrasted with *states,* the class of variables that fluctuate over time). TWA adopted the trait concept in its description of P. Furthermore, research on TWA has used the methods of the psychology of individual differences that emphasize quantification (especially the psychometric measurement of stable individual differences) and statistical analysis to account for variance (individual differences), especially through the use of correlational methods (Tinsley & Brown, 2000).

When TWA was first published in 1964, it was presented as a series of nine formal propositions that captured the substance of the research conducted to that date, but it also provided direction for future research. Subsequent research suggested new propositions for TWA. Eight were added in 1984. The list of 17 TWA propositions is shown in Table 1.1, which is presented on pages 20–21 of this chapter.

The Theory of Work Adjustment started out as a P-E fit theory. As TWA was revised and expanded, it developed into an interaction theory—a process model that included the fit (or predictive) model. Before the two models are described, the basic concepts on which TWA is premised are first presented and discussed.

BASIC CONCEPTS

As a psychological theory, *TWA's focus is on P and P's behavior.* However, P does not exist or behave in a vacuum; rather, P always exists and behaves in an E. Any theory about P has to be a theory about P-in-an-E.

The theory of work adjustment begins with the assumptions that (1) as a living organism, P has requirements that have to be met, many or even most of them through E; (2) P has capabilities that enable it to meet these requirements; and (3) much of P's behavior in interacting with E is about meeting these requirements.

Among the most important of P's requirements are *needs:* biological needs that have to do with P's survival and psychological needs that have to do with P's well-being. Needs are presumed to develop from the genetic material inherited by P, conditioned by the many Es to which P is exposed, until some state of relative stability is reached, typically in adulthood.

Many of P's needs in adulthood can be met at work. In TWA, the E of concern is the work environment, which in our contemporary world is effectively the work organization. TWA, then, is about P as worker and employee, and E as work environment and work organization.

As an operating principle, TWA conceptualizes P and E as parallel and complementary. Thus, TWA assumes that E (in parallel with P) also has requirements that have to be met and capabilities that enable it to meet its requirements. Complementarily, some of E's requirements can be met by P in the same way that some of P's requirements can be met by E. Thus, in work, P and E come together because each has some requirements that the other can meet.

Fulfillment of their requirements results in *satisfaction* for P and E. To differentiate E's satisfaction from P's satisfaction, TWA terms E's satisfaction with P as the *satisfactoriness* of P, reserving the term *satisfaction* to denote P's satisfaction with E. The two constructs, satisfaction and satisfactoriness, imply and extend to their negatives, *dissatisfaction* and *unsatisfactoriness.* Thus, at the dichotomous level, there are four possible states in which P can be: satisfied and satisfactory, satisfied but unsatisfactory, dissatisfied but satisfactory, or dissatisfied and unsatisfactory. TWA expects the first state to be conducive to behavior that maintains the P-E interaction (*maintenance behavior*) and the other three states to result eventually in behavior to change the situation (*adjustment behavior*). At the extreme, the P-E interaction may be terminated (P either quits or is fired). But as long as P is tolerably satisfied and satisfactory, P remains in, and is retained by, E. The length of time P stays in E is termed *tenure* in TWA. These three outcomes—the satisfaction, satisfactoriness, and tenure of P in a given work E—are the basic indicators of work adjustment, according to TWA.

As mentioned, P has capabilities, some of which can be used to satisfy E's requirements (or some of them). P's capabilities that matter most to E are P's *skills.* Work skills are drawn from basic human skills: cognitive, affective, motor, physical, and sensory-perceptual. Like needs, basic skills are presumed to originate from P's inherited genetic material and are shaped through learning (experience and training) via exposure to a variety of Es. Though basic skills may reach relative stability (typically in adulthood), P continues to acquire new skills (such as work skills) developed from basic skills all through life.

At work, E's requirements of P are about getting the work done and maintaining or improving the organization. One way to describe E's requirements is to express them in terms of E's *skill requirements* for P, the set of skills P has to have to get the work done and to maintain or improve the organization.

E, likewise, has capabilities, some of which enable it to satisfy P's needs (or some of them). The ones that matter most to P are E's reinforcement capabilities, that is, E's ability to deliver *reinforcers* (borrowing a construct from behavioral psychology) to satisfy P's needs. Some examples of E's work reinforcers are pay, prestige, and working conditions. One way to describe P's needs is in terms of the reinforcers that P requires of E. That is, needs may be viewed as *reinforcer requirements.*

Thus, TWA uses two constructs to describe P: needs (reinforcer requirements) and skills (response capabilities). Two complementary constructs are used to describe E: reinforcers (reinforcement capabilities) and skill requirements (response requirements). That is, the P and E constructs are parallel and complementary.

The central construct in TWA is *P-E correspondence.* P-E correspondence has two meanings in TWA. The first is *fit* between P and E as ascertained across commensurate variables. This is the meaning used in TWA's predictive model, where P's satisfaction and satisfactoriness are each predicted from a P-E correspondence variable. In each case, the P-E correspondence variable reflects the degree to which each meets the requirements of the other.

The second meaning of P-E correspondence is that of *coresponsiveness,* the mutual responding of P to E and E to P, that is, the interaction of P and E. This is the meaning used in TWA's process model.

THEORY OF WORK ADJUSTMENT'S PREDICTIVE MODEL

In TWA's predictive model, P's satisfaction and satisfactoriness are the dependent variables that are predicted from two P-E correspondence variables:

1. The correspondence of E's reinforcers to P's needs (reinforcer requirements) predicts P's satisfaction.
2. The correspondence of P's skills to E's skill requirements predicts P's satisfactoriness.

In turn, P's satisfaction and satisfactoriness (actual or predicted) predict P's tenure in E.

Factor analysis can be used to summarize the large number of needs and skills in a fewer number of factors or reference dimensions. These factors yield scores that have proven to be more stable and more reliable than the need and skill scores and thus are more useful in prediction. Furthermore, factors can be used to estimate needs and skills that P does not have but could potentially acquire, and such estimated scores would be useful in counseling to help clients forecast the types of work that they might do in the future in which they would be most satisfied and satisfactory. These factors are designated in TWA by the terms *values* (for need factors) and *abilities* (for skill factors). That is, in TWA, values are defined as reference dimensions underlying needs, and abilities are reference dimensions underlying skills. Inasmuch as P-E correspondence requires commensurate variables on the E side, parallel reference dimensions underlying E's reinforcers and skill requirements are termed *reinforcer factors* and *ability requirements,* respectively. These four new constructs—values, abilities, reinforcer factors, and ability requirements—were incorporated into the TWA predictive model. Thus, the new P-E correspondence variables are:

1. The correspondence of E's reinforcer factors to P's values.
2. The correspondence of P's abilities to E's ability requirements.

Figure 1.1 diagrams the basic TWA predictive model.

Figure 1.1 shows P Satisfaction as being predicted (solid line with arrow) from E-Reinforcers-to-P-Values Correspondence (*Reinforcer Factors* is shortened to *Reinforcers* for convenience in drawing the figure). P Satisfactoriness is predicted from P-Abilities-to-E-Requirements Correspondence (*Ability Requirements* is shortened to *Requirements*). P Satisfaction and P Satisfactoriness are shown to predict P Tenure through the unobserved (dashed boxes) decision variables of *Remain/Quit* for P and *Retain/Fire* for E.

IMPROVING PREDICTION

Prediction can be improved by the use of moderator variables. Moderator variables are variables that affect (moderate) the correlation between two variables. To improve the prediction of satisfaction and satisfactoriness from P-E correspondence variables, TWA proposes that each moderate the prediction of the other. That is, P Satisfactoriness moderates the correlation between E-Reinforcers-to-P-Values Correspondence and P Satisfaction. This predictive correlation will be higher for satisfactory workers and lower for unsatisfactory workers (or for more satisfactory versus less satisfactory workers, respectively). In like manner, P Satisfaction moderates the correlation between P-Abilities-to-E-Requirements Correspondence and P Satisfactoriness. This predictive correlation will be higher for satisfied (or more satisfied) workers and lower for dissatisfied (or less satisfied) workers.

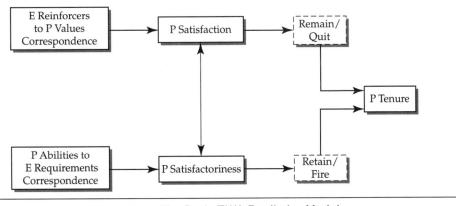

Figure 1.1　The Basic TWA Predictive Model.

The theory of work adjustment further proposes that style correspondence moderates the prediction of satisfaction and satisfactoriness. *Personality style* (P Style) in TWA consists of four variables that describe how P typically responds:

1. *Celerity,* or quickness of response.
2. *Pace,* or intensity of response.
3. *Rhythm,* or pattern of response.
4. *Endurance,* or persistence (length of time) of response.

Parallel variables describe *environment style* (E Style). TWA proposes that P-Style-to-E-Style Correspondence moderates the prediction of P Satisfaction and P Satisfactoriness from their respective P-E correspondence variables. The prediction of P Satisfaction and P Satisfactoriness will be higher for workers with better style correspondence and lower for workers with poorer style correspondence.

Finally, other factors (such as interests and personality traits) that are not included in TWA's P-E correspondence variables can have a bearing on P's satisfaction, satisfactoriness, and tenure. Figure 1.2 shows the expanded TWA predictive model with the moderator variable relationships (shown in broken lines) and "other factors."

Although other factors can also influence work adjustment outcomes (i.e., satisfaction, satisfactoriness, and tenure), research on TWA's predictive model has consistently shown that the P-E correspondence variables are able to forecast work adjustment outcomes with sufficient precision as to be theoretically and practically useful. The TWA predictive model can be used to help people identify and choose among work possibilities that will likely bring them satisfaction, satisfactoriness, and tenure in the future. The predictive model, however, provides no account of the work adjustment process—how P and E achieve correspondence when it is lacking or regain it when it is lost.

THEORY OF WORK ADJUSTMENT'S PROCESS MODEL

The TWA process model was developed to explain how P-E correspondence is achieved, maintained, and reachieved, if necessary. Although TWA provides for both maintenance behavior and adjustment behavior, the focus here is on the

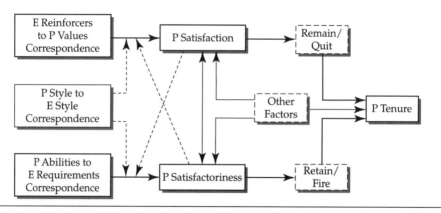

Figure 1.2 The Expanded TWA Predictive Model.

latter because of its implications for working with people who might seek counseling (those who are successfully maintaining correspondence with their environments are unlikely to be seeking counseling). More extended discussion of TWA's process model is provided in Dawis (1996) and Dawis and Lofquist (1984).

The new construct TWA introduces in its process model is *adjustment style*. Adjustment style consists of four variables: flexibility, activeness, reactiveness, and perseverance. Each variable is defined as the process model is being described. In the following discussion, the focus is on P, although a parallel process can be described for E, as well.

The Theory of Work Adjustment's process model describes adjustment as a cycle. The cycle starts when P becomes dissatisfied and initiates adjustment behavior. Recall that dissatisfaction results when P perceives discorrespondence between E's reinforcers and P's needs and values. Different Ps can tolerate different degrees of discorrespondence and dissatisfaction before they initiate adjustment behavior. The degree of discorrespondence tolerated before becoming dissatisfied enough to engage in adjustment behavior defines P's *flexibility*. High levels of flexibility mean P does not easily become dissatisfied; conversely, low flexibility means P is easily dissatisfied.

Once adjustment behavior is initiated, P has two modes of adjustment available. First, P could adjust by acting on E to reduce discorrespondence and, thus, dissatisfaction. P could try to change E's reinforcers or E's skill requirements or both. Thus, for example, P could demand a raise if compensation needs are not being adequately met. This adjustment mode is termed *activeness* in TWA. Second, P could adjust by acting on self rather than E to reduce discorrespondence. P would try to change P's own needs or skills or both. For example, P could use skills better or acquire new skills to do a better job to convince E to improve P's compensation. This adjustment mode is termed *reactiveness* in TWA. These two adjustment modes are seen as uncorrelated; that is, P could be in any of four combinations of dichotomized activeness and reactiveness (high-high, high-low, low-high, low-low).

Finally, people will work only so long at trying to reduce discorrespondence and dissatisfaction before giving up and leaving E (quitting their job). How long P will attempt to adjust before quitting reflects P's *perseverance*. Like flexibility, perseverance differs in levels among different Ps. Less persevering Ps will give up trying to adjust more readily than will more persevering Ps. Thus, the adjustment cycle ends with P becoming either satisfied again or so dissatisfied as to leave E.

Over time, P's adjustment style choices may tend to become more stable. When this happens, we may speak of flexibility, activeness, reactiveness, and perseverance as traits, that is, as typical behavior tendencies. The more pronounced such behavior tendencies are, the more significant they become in counseling people who are trying to adjust in work (trying to achieve or reachieve correspondence with E).

Figure 1.3 is a diagram of TWA's process model. It shows work adjustment as a cycle, with P's adjustment being initiated by dissatisfaction (P Satisfaction: No). It also shows a similar process occurring for E. Thus, P and E could both be in Maintenance Behavior, both in Adjustment Behavior, or one in Maintenance and the other in Adjustment. Figure 1.3 shows graphically why, to be successful, any counseling of P for work adjustment has to take account of E as well.

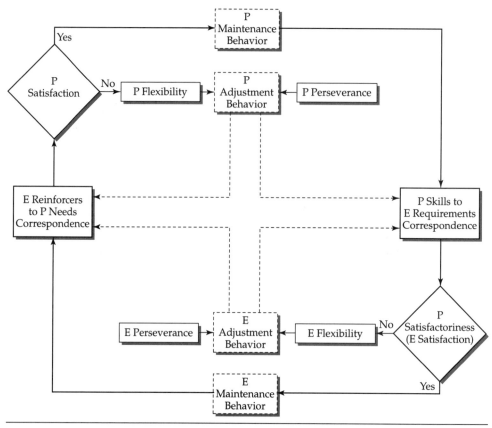

Figure 1.3   The TWA Process Model.

THEORY OF WORK ADJUSTMENT
VARIABLES AND THEIR MEASUREMENT

In this section, the TWA variables are defined in more detail, and conventional psychometric ways of measuring them are discussed. However, TWA variables can be measured in other ways (see Other Instruments and Other Methods section) if the psychometric measures described are not available.

SATISFACTION

In TWA, satisfaction is treated as a state variable, defined as an affective response to the cognitive evaluation of P-E correspondence (perception of how well E's reinforcers correspond to P's values and needs). A positive affective response is satisfaction; a negative one is dissatisfaction.

Satisfaction, so defined, is a variable with many different referents. Work satisfaction has at least three: job satisfaction, occupational satisfaction, and career satisfaction. TWA research has been concerned mainly with job satisfaction, that is, satisfaction with the reinforcers found on the job. However, TWA research has on occasion examined satisfaction with occupational and career reinforcers.

Satisfaction-dissatisfaction is typically measured via questionnaires to elicit respondents' descriptions of their affective responses. Job satisfaction measures are of two types: global and facet. Global measures elicit respondents' overall satisfaction with the job, taking all facets into account. Facet measures elicit respondents' satisfactions for a variety of work facets (such as pay, working conditions, and ability utilization). Facet measures typically report facet scores as well as total scores (sum of facet or item scores), whereas global measures report a single score representing the level of overall satisfaction (see also Fritzsche & Parrish, Chapter 8, this volume).

For its research, the Work Adjustment Project developed a facet measure of work satisfaction, the Minnesota Satisfaction Questionnaire (MSQ; Weiss, Dawis, England, & Lofquist, 1967), with scales yielding scores for 20 facets, two factor-based scores (Intrinsic and Extrinsic Satisfaction), and a total score (General Satisfaction) summed across all items. The 20 MSQ facets are ability utilization, achievement, activity, advancement, authority, company policies and practices, compensation, coworkers, creativity, independence, moral values, recognition, responsibility, security, social service, social status, supervision—human relations, supervision—technical, variety, and working conditions. These 20 facets do not by any means exhaust the domain of work reinforcers, but substantive research on TWA had to begin somewhere, and the 20 facets appeared to be a good place to start. They continue to be empirically and practically useful.

Needs and Values

Inasmuch as TWA hypothesizes that satisfaction is a function of need/value-reinforcer correspondence, a 20-need Minnesota Importance Questionnaire (MIQ; Gay, Weiss, Hendel, Dawis, & Lofquist, 1971) was developed to parallel the MSQ. The same 20 work facets were used in the two instruments, the difference being the question asked of the respondents: "How satisfied are you with this facet?" (MSQ) versus, "How important is this facet to you?" (MIQ).

Several factor analyses of the 20 MIQ need scales showed that a six-factor structure was the best representation. The six factors were termed *values* because response to the MIQ involved a judgment of "importance" (Lofquist & Dawis, 1978). These six MIQ values are achievement, altruism, autonomy, comfort, safety, and status. Each is scored from component need scales, which is why the MIQ is described as "a measure of needs and values" (Rounds, Henly, Dawis, Lofquist, & Weiss, 1981). Values in TWA are considered trait variables, even more so than needs. Rounds and Armstrong (Chapter 13, this volume) describe the MIQ and its uses more completely.

Reinforcers and Reinforcer Factors

These E variables were theoretically required to enable the construction of a P-E correspondence variable as the predictor for satisfaction. To simplify matters, a commensurate approach to correspondence was adopted; it was assumed that each need could be paired with a commensurable reinforcer. The Minnesota Job Description Questionnaire (MJDQ; Borgen, Weiss, Tinsley, Dawis, & Lofquist, 1968) was developed to measure the same 20 reinforcers (work facets) used in the MSQ and MIQ. This time, the instrument question was, in effect, "How much is this facet descriptive of the job?"

The MJDQ was also used to generate Occupational Reinforcer Patterns (ORPs; Stewart et al., 1986). Each ORP consists of a profile of scores, one score for each reinforcer, descriptive of an occupation's reinforcers as rated by either incumbents or supervisors.

The data for a subset of 109 ORPs, selected to approximate the occupational distribution of the employed labor force, were subjected to factor analysis (Shubsachs, Rounds, Dawis, & Lofquist, 1978). The three factors that emerged represented combinations of scales that were parallels of the six MIQ values: achievement-autonomy-status, safety-comfort, and altruism. These were identified as a self-reinforcement factor, an environmental reinforcement factor, and a social reinforcement factor, respectively. Thus, the MJDQ, the MIQ, and the MSQ provided a set of commensurate instruments for reinforcers, needs/values, and satisfaction, all referring to the same 20 work facets. This research also led to the development of the Minnesota Occupational Classification System (MOCS; now in its third edition as MOCS III; Dawis, Dohm, Lofquist, Chartrand, & Due, 1987), which classifies a large number of occupations by the degree to which self, environmental, and social needs and values are reinforced (see Gore & Hitch, Chapter 16, this volume).

SATISFACTORINESS

In TWA, satisfactoriness is actually a satisfaction variable—E's satisfaction with P as worker and employee, and with P's performance in carrying out work duties and P's behavior as a member of the work organization. The Minnesota Satisfactoriness Scales (MSS; Gibson, Weiss, Dawis, & Lofquist, 1970) is a rating instrument that is to be completed by P's employer or employer representative, usually the work supervisor. It consists of 28 items organized into four factor-based scales: Performance, Conformance, Personal Adjustment, and Dependability. A fifth score, General Satisfactoriness, is the sum of all item scores. As a *satisfaction* variable, satisfactoriness is considered a state variable.

SKILLS AND ABILITIES

Skills are repeatable behavior sequences performed in response to prescribed tasks. Skills vary on a number of dimensions: content of the task, difficulty of the task, time needed to do the task (speed), and effort expended on the task, among others. Workers can be categorized by the sets of work skills they possess. (For an extended treatment of skills and abilities, see Lubinski & Dawis, 1992.)

Basic skills consist of a few groups: sensory and perceptual skills, cognitive and affective skills, and motor and physical skills. Higher order skills involve different combinations of basic skills. So-called *ability tests* are tests of higher order skills. When such tests are factor analyzed, a hierarchical factor structure is commonly found (Carroll, 1993). At the top is a general factor, Spearman's *g* or general ability. Next are group factors that typically refer to content (e.g., verbal ability, numerical ability, spatial ability). Below these are specific ability factors (e.g., reading comprehension, vocabulary, knowledge of grammar), each of which may be measured by several skill tests.

Because it was well constructed and available, the General Aptitude Test Battery (GATB; U.S. Department of Labor, 1970; see also Ryan Krane & Tirre, Chapter 14, this volume) was used in TWA research as the measure of skills and abilities. The

GATB consists of 12 skill tests that measure nine ability factors derived from factor-analytic studies of about 100 skill tests. Before the GATB, specific batteries of selected skill tests had to be developed for each occupation for use in the Department of Labor's selection and placement programs. This led inevitably to the accumulation of many skill tests, whereas the GATB, with only 12 tests, could be used for the same purpose for all occupations. It was from this GATB experience that TWA derived the idea of defining *abilities* as "reference dimensions" (factors) in the description (measurement) of skills.

The Vocational Psychology Research Program (Department of Psychology, University of Minnesota) has developed the Minnesota Ability Test Battery (MATB) as a parallel (psychometrically equivalent) form of the GATB (Dawis & Weiss, 1994).

SKILL AND ABILITY REQUIREMENTS

Jobs are typically defined in terms of the work tasks that need to be performed. Because task performance requires skills, jobs can also be described in terms of the skills required to perform the job. To determine skill requirements, the Department of Labor used the *empirical method,* which entailed administering several skill tests to a group of workers in a specific occupation and using the test scores to predict the workers' performance ratings. The skills that predicted performance ratings were taken as uniquely descriptive of the job. TWA adopted this idea of using *skill requirements* to describe occupations (i.e., the E in P-E).

The U.S. Department of Labor used the GATB, in lieu of skill tests, to ascertain the three or four aptitudes (ability dimensions) that characterized each occupation and called the set an Occupational Aptitude Pattern (OAP; U.S. Department of Labor, 1970, Section II). OAPs were determined for hundreds of occupations. TWA research used the OAPs as the data for the theory-required measurements of ability requirements. By using OAPs as ability requirements, a given individual's "aptitude" (predicted satisfactoriness) can be ascertained for any of the hundreds of occupations for which there are OAPs. Furthermore, the OAP data were incorporated into the MOCS system, enabling the classification of hundreds of occupations in terms of both ability requirements and reinforcer systems (see Gore & Hitch, Chapter 16, this volume).

CORRESPONDENCE

Correspondence as *fit* is assessed through commensurate P-E measurement, such as the MIQ and ORPs or the GATB and OAPs. With such commensurate measures, need/value-reinforcer correspondence and skill/ability-requirement correspondence can be quantified for use as predictors of satisfaction and satisfactoriness, respectively.

But even with commensurate measurement, the assessment of correspondence was found not to be straightforward. Rounds, Dawis, and Lofquist (1987) developed 19 different indexes of correspondence that took account of elevation, shape, and scatter (the three independent components of a profile) as well as directionality, zero-point, and importance weighting. Using these 19 indexes, they found a wide range of results for the same data in predicting satisfaction from need-reinforcer correspondence, with the best results overall being obtained with simple correlation as the correspondence index. This simple index is thus used most often in our research on TWA's predictive model.

TENURE

Tenure can be defined simply as length of stay on the job. But even such a simple definition can hide a lot of problems. How are leaves of absence counted? Sabbaticals? Part-time employment? What if the job tasks change? When does it become a new job? What about a transfer to the same kind of job but in a different company? This brings up the question of the different kinds of tenure: position tenure, job tenure, occupational tenure, and company or organizational tenure. Such considerations show that there is no simple or single way to define tenure. It is left for the research investigator to define tenure operationally in each study. In TWA research, the incumbent is asked to give job title, dates of employment, and hours per week, and these data are used to calculate "number of full-time weeks employed" as the measure of tenure (Dawis & Lofquist, 1984, p. 208).

STYLE VARIABLES

Style variables are the newest additions to TWA. They were conceptualized to fill in the gaps left in TWA's account of the work adjustment process. Style variables are construed as traits, defined as stable behavioral tendencies resulting from behavioral experiences over a considerable length of time. Most of the style variables are also construed as time-indexed variables, requiring reference to time in their definition. Thus, for personality style, *celerity* is how quickly P typically responds, *pace* is how much energy P typically expends per unit time, *rhythm* refers to the typical pattern of pace over time, and *endurance* is how long P can typically maintain response.

With respect to adjustment style, *flexibility* refers to how long P typically tolerates discorrespondence and dissatisfaction before initiating adjustment behavior, and *perseverance* is how long P typically persists in adjustment behavior. The adjustment modes are not time indexed, although adjustment occurs over time: *activeness* being P's typical tendency to adjust by effecting change in E, versus effecting change in P (self)—*reactiveness*. Parallel comments pertain to E style variables, as well.

Measures of style variables of adequate psychometric quality (reliability, validity) are not yet available. For the most part, judgment (rating) scales have been used in TWA research (Dawis & Lofquist, 1984, p. 216). Two novel approaches to measurement have been tried with promising results, one using signal detection theory to measure flexibility (Cheung, 1975), and another using items from well-known personality instruments to measure flexibility, activeness, and reactiveness (Lawson, 1991). However, without proven measures of style variables, the style propositions of TWA have not been tested as rigorously as the propositions of the basic predictive model have been.

OTHER FACTORS

Causation in human behavior is both multiple and overlapping: For any dependent variable, there almost always are many *sources of variation* (causes), and these frequently are correlated. Thus, it is not surprising to find other variables besides TWA variables that can predict satisfaction, satisfactoriness, and tenure. One of these is *vocational interests*, one of the oldest, best measured, and most researched variables in vocational psychology. Interests are a robust predictor of satisfaction and tenure, as attested to by an extensive literature. And interests correlate lowly with needs, values, skills, and abilities (Dawis, 1991). Thus, although TWA does not mention it, interests are an important variable to include in any research about work and careers.

Another important one of these "other" variables is *personality* (shorthand for personality traits measured by questionnaires and inventories). Like interests, there is an extensive literature on measured personality traits. Like interests, measured personality traits are well-known correlates of behavioral outcomes, such as satisfaction, satisfactoriness, and tenure. Like interests, personality traits should be included in research about work and careers. For example, conscientiousness, openness to experience, and emotional stability (neuroticism) have been shown to predict adult occupational level and income (Judge, Higgins, Thoresen, & Barrick, 1999).

The theory of work adjustment considers interests and personality traits as higher order, more complex, variables that can be derived from the more fundamental TWA variables of structure and style. This belief has not been tested, but it has been shown that interests and personality traits correlate only modestly (0.20s to 0.30s) with values and abilities (Dawis, 1991).

Yet another set of "other factors" is that of family factors. This includes complex variables such as family culture, family expectations, and family socioeconomic status. Family *culture* is a loose amalgam of variables including family structure (e.g., nuclear versus extended, two- versus one-parent, number of children, decision-making structure, bonding, closeness). Family expectations are by-products of family culture. Family financial status is always an important factor. These family factors find their way directly or indirectly into the causal chain of career development and work adjustment.

A final set of "other factors" is the labor market. Demand and supply of jobs in P's particular occupation is important to consider. Availability of training opportunities, cost of such, *frictional* factors such as discrimination—all of these and many others may be hypothesized to affect the causal chain of career development and work adjustment in important ways and in particular situations.

There may be other factors to consider. Some, or even many, of them may be correlated with TWA variables or may moderate their predictive value. As we found out when we first began our research, one can go on and on postulating independent variables that may have significant effects, but that can easily dissipate one's research efforts—which, in the first place, is where theory comes in—to narrow and limit the focus of research. And that is what TWA did for us.

OTHER INSTRUMENTS AND OTHER METHODS

Much of TWA research has employed the MIQ, MSQ, MSS, MJDQ, and ORPs—instruments developed for TWA. One misconception in the field is that research on TWA can be done only with these instruments. This kind of misconception is held about other theories as well, which is unfortunate because a theory is only about constructs and their interrelations and not about the measures for the constructs. Different investigators can use different instruments for the same constructs and even use different analyses to probe for the presence of the same relations. In fact, support for a theory is more robust when it comes from the use of other instruments and other methodologies and analytic approaches.

Insofar as TWA is concerned, there are many other good instruments available to measure its basic constructs: satisfaction, satisfactoriness, needs, values, skills, abilities. Only the style variables do not have adequate instruments because of their novelty, but, in time, this lack may be addressed.

Theory of Work Adjustment variables may also be assessed by methods other than the use of psychometric instruments. When psychometric instruments are unavailable or cannot be used, counselors can still implement TWA by using other methods of assessment. For example, the method of estimation or judgment by rating or ranking (used with style variables as described previously) may be used to assess needs, values, skills, abilities, and other TWA variables. Ways to ensure validity and reliability of ratings and rankings are described in the literature (e.g., Guilford, 1954).

The method of inference may also be used in conjunction with the corollaries of the TWA Propositions (see Table 1.1 on pages 20–21). For example, Corollary IIA says that if you know the reinforcers of P's previous job and you know P's satisfaction with that job, you may infer P's values—without benefit of direct measurement. Corollary IIB says that if you know P's values and P's satisfaction in a job, you may infer what the reinforcers in that job might be.

RESEARCH ON THE THEORY OF WORK ADJUSTMENT

Chapter limits prevent the presentation of TWA research in detail (for more complete coverage, see Dawis & Lofquist, 1984, pp. 69–94, and Dawis, 1996, pp. 98–102). The research is summarized here.

Support is strong for the first three propositions of TWA (see Table 1.1), which are about the roles of satisfaction and satisfactoriness in work adjustment and the prediction of satisfaction and satisfactoriness. This support comes not just from TWA research but, more convincingly, from the research of many other investigators using instruments other than those developed for TWA research. For example, every validity study of ability tests as predictors of rated performance in any occupation is support for Proposition III, which states that satisfactoriness is predictable from ability-requirement correspondence.

Support for the tenure propositions (VI, VII, and VIII) is also strong and comes from both TWA and other research. The relation of satisfaction to tenure is particularly strong, backed by an extensive literature.

The remaining propositions, especially the style propositions (X–XVII), have not been studied to any great extent. A few studies show some support for the moderator relation propositions (IV and V). Aspects of the style propositions have been studied, with mixed results, the main problem being that of measuring the variables. There is some reason to believe that the measurement of these style variables as traits might lie in personality measurement (i.e., the measurement of personality traits via questionnaires and inventories).

APPLICATIONS OF THE THEORY OF WORK ADJUSTMENT

Theories have a heuristic use; therefore, it helps if the theory is framed in such a way that makes it easy to remember and recall. In this regard, TWA has a mnemonic advantage in the binary symmetry of its constructs: person and environment, correspondence and satisfaction, requirement and capability, response and reinforcement, satisfaction and satisfactoriness, needs and skills, values and abilities, structure and style, maintenance and adjustment, celerity and endurance, pace and rhythm, flexibility and perseverance, activeness and reactiveness, tenure and termination. Moreover, these paired constructs are organized by just two principles: (1) Correspondence makes for satisfaction, and (2) dissatisfaction drives adjustment behavior.

The theory of work adjustment can be used heuristically to organize facts, aid conceptualization, and suggest approaches to intervention. With the TWA constructs as basic conceptual tools, we can tackle a variety of problems, as illustrated in the following discussions about career development, career choice, and career counseling.

DEVELOPMENTAL INTERVENTIONS

Education literally means "bringing out." What is to be "brought out?" From the earliest times, schools have focused on bringing out capabilities, on developing skills and abilities. Only tangentially have requirements been touched on. TWA maintains that a focus on requirements is just as important as that on capabilities. Children have to learn about their needs and values much more explicitly, to the same extent that they learn about their skills and abilities. Learning is acquisition. Hence, TWA proposes that needs and values have to be acquired in the same way that skills and abilities are acquired. And in such learning, we must attend to individual differences, with proper respect for the child and the child's family.

If teachers are to facilitate self-knowledge in children, they first have to be expert at assessing needs, values, skills, and abilities on the fly, that is, on the basis of ordinary information available in the everyday classroom. Standardized instruments can help and are likely to be used by counselors, but everyday observations can be useful and are much less intrusive if teachers are skilled in using them in assessment. Next, teachers and counselors have to know how to teach each child how to assess self, which in turn depends on knowing the child's response capabilities and reinforcement requirements.

But learning about needs, skills, values, and abilities can be problematic and even traumatic to the child who compares self with other children. A possible antidote is to teach children early about individual differences and all its implications and about TWA's message that besides individual differences there are environmental differences and that the optimal environment is different for each child—which might help children become more cognizant and respectful of their own and others' individualities.

In addition to having appropriate skills, teachers and counselors should be aware of their own needs and values, that is, their own reinforcement requirements. They should know how to assess their correspondences with various Es, which in the school setting includes each of their pupils and their parents. Such knowledge might help them understand their differential effectiveness with different children.

One matter TWA addresses explicitly is environments. Each E has distinctive features with respect to skill requirements and reinforcement capabilities. At the start, the child has only a few "salient Es" (Lofquist & Dawis, 1991), but these grow in number as the child grows. Each of the child's Es is constrained to begin with, but enlarges over time. Teachers and counselors have to find out for each child what these salient Es are, how far their boundaries extend, and what their distinctive features are (skill requirements, reinforcement capabilities). This is information that teachers and counselors can use to advantage in helping each child learn how to cope with various salient Es.

Coping with Es means adjustment, which means learning about self and Es in the adjustment-behavior mode. Children must learn not only about their needs/values and skills/abilities but also their adjustment styles. In learning about Es, they must learn, too, not only about skill requirements and reinforcement capabilities but also about environment adjustment styles. Acquiring such knowledge does not need to be all-encompassing all at once. Skillful teachers and counselors can use specific instances to teach about even just one variable at a time, about the variable's features for the P and E involved in the particular instance.

If the preceding prescriptions are pursued, three benchmarks can be used to chart progress along the way: the child's satisfaction, satisfactoriness, and tenure. It is important to ascertain whether a child is happy or unhappy in the school environment. This assessment should be as important as the customary assessment of the child's satisfactoriness—meeting the requirements of school, family, and society. Tenure, staying in a situation or fleeing from it, is the third important indicator prescribed by TWA. In interpreting tenure data, the child's satisfaction and satisfactoriness status should be considered.

In TWA's view, human development is the unfolding of requirements (needs, values), capabilities (skills, abilities), and style. This unfolding depends on the degree of P-E correspondence experienced with every E that P encounters. In turn, the Es that P encounters depend to a significant extent on *opportunity* or lack thereof. Opportunity means access to Es that promote development (i.e., high P-E correspondence). Development, in turn, opens more doors to more Es that promote more development—the virtuous circle. Conversely, lack of opportunity retards development, which perversely shrinks further opportunity, which further retards development—the vicious circle. These are logical outcomes that flow from the TWA process model.

CHOOSING A CAREER

Choosing a career wisely is the first step toward adjustment in work. TWA's prescription is obviously to choose a career wherein an individual can be satisfied and satisfactory. TWA's predictors—reinforcer-value and ability-requirement correspondences—can be used to narrow the world of work to a manageable number of occupations to consider. Then, "other factors" (see previous section) can be used to narrow the list even further. In choosing from among the finalist occupations, an individual must be aware of the trade-off nature of choice, the need to balance between advantages and disadvantages, and finally to decide on the basis of what is most important to the person. Thus, knowledge of an individual's needs, values, skills, abilities, and style characteristics can help in reaching wise decisions, but it also requires knowledge of occupations in complementary terms: reinforcers, skill and ability requirements, and style characteristics.

Theory of Work Adjustment research, as mentioned previously, has developed a taxonomy of occupations to aid in career choice, the Minnesota Occupational Classification System (MOCS). The current edition, MOCS III (Dawis et al., 1987), is organized around two axes, reinforcers and requirements, with three categories of reinforcers (self, social, environmental) and three categories of ability requirements (perceptual, cognitive, motor). Using three levels for each category (high, average, not significant) yields 729 (27×27) possible patterns, termed *taxons*, which can be used to help clients identify occupational possibilities that reinforce their particular patterns of needs and values and make use of their particular patterns of skills and abilities (see Gore & Hitch, Chapter 16, this volume).

IMPLEMENTING CAREER CHOICE

There are three steps to implementing a career choice:

1. Preparing for the career.
2. Finding a starting position.
3. Working up the career ladder.

The theory of work adjustment can be useful in all three steps.

In conventional career preparation, attention is focused on the skills required and on skill acquisition. This may be the most important part of career preparation, but TWA also directs attention to the reinforcers the individual is to encounter in the occupation, which requires preparing for them, also. For example, for first-time wage earners, receiving compensation on a regular basis is a new experience, and some workers may not know how to handle this experience wisely. Working in a team or working under close supervision are examples of other reinforcement conditions that might need attending to in career preparation.

The theory of work adjustment does not have anything to say about finding a starting position or about job finding in general, but it does apply when a person faces a decision about accepting a job offer or choosing from among job offers. Then, TWA can suggest a list of things to consider when reaching a decision. For example, money may not be everything when viewed in the light of a person's total reinforcer requirements. Another use of TWA constructs is considering potential career paths in the work organization when deciding about a first position.

In working up the career ladder, people usually focus on what the succeeding reinforcer structures are bound to be and, presumably, are motivated by these anticipations. TWA reminds them also to consider the skill and ability requirements and the style characteristics and to prepare for these. For example, professional people who move into managerial positions often fail to prepare for the skill requirements (e.g., people skills, decision-making skills) and style requirements (e.g., fast pace, erratic rhythm, high flexibility) of the new managerial positions. Again, TWA can suggest a list of things to attend to as the person climbs the career ladder.

WORK OR CAREER DISSATISFACTION

When experiencing work or career dissatisfaction, people often get carried away by the affect involved and may fail to see things rationally. TWA does provide a way to see things rationally, to get a comprehensive grasp of the situation, and to generate possible approaches to solving the problem. TWA tells the dissatisfied worker to examine both antecedents and consequences, specifically, the antecedent of P-E correspondence and the consequence of P and E behavior. TWA also points to the basic approaches to adjustment open to P: activeness, by getting E to change E's reinforcements and/or skill requirements, and reactiveness, by changing P's need hierarchy and/or skill repertoire.

Although TWA does not mention it explicitly, one problem that has to be resolved when there is dissatisfaction is the question of perception versus reality. TWA's conception of satisfaction makes it clear that perception plays a role in satisfaction/dissatisfaction. Thus, it is important for the dissatisfied worker to test reality in as many ways as possible. One of the better ways to do this is to seek work or career counseling by a competent career counselor, preferably—in TWA's view—one versed in TWA.

A FINAL APPLICATION: FROM THEORY OF WORK ADJUSTMENT TO PERSON-ENVIRONMENT CORRESPONDENCE

The Theory of Work Adjustment refers to one environment encountered by P, but obviously, P encounters many other environments. TWA constructs and relations can be generalized to apply to any environment and has been termed *person-environment correspondence* (PEC) theory. Expositions of PEC theory are given in Lofquist and Dawis (1991) and Dawis (2002), and we recommend these to students interested in helping clients achieve greater satisfaction and satisfactoriness in their family, interpersonal, intimate relations, and other important nonwork environments.

Table 1.1
Formal Propositions of the Theory of Work Adjustment (TWA)

P = Person in an environment (E). The following are restatements of the 17 propositions of TWA presented in Dawis and Lofquist (1984). The revisions are of two kinds: (1) The propositions are renumbered to give priority of place to satisfaction. Thus, for example, Proposition II in the 1984 propositions was about satisfactoriness and Proposition III about satisfaction; here it is reversed; and (2) the variable names are those used in Figures 1.1, 1.2, and 1.3. For example, *satisfaction* in the 1984 propositions is now *P Satisfaction* and *satisfactoriness* is now *P Satisfactoriness*. Otherwise, the content and substance remain the same in this version as they were in the 1984 set.

Proposition I. Work adjustment at any time is indicated by the concurrent levels of P Satisfaction and P Satisfactoriness.

Proposition II. P Satisfaction is predicted from E Reinforcers to P Values Correspondence, provided that there is P Abilities to E Ability Requirements Correspondence.

    Corollary IIA. Knowledge of E Reinforcers and P Satisfaction permits the inference of P Values.

    Corollary IIB. Knowledge of P Values and P Satisfaction permits the inference of E Reinforcers.

Table 1.1 *(Continued)*

Proposition III. P Satisfactoriness is predicted from P Abilities to E Ability Requirements Correspondence, provided that there is E Reinforcers to P Values Correspondence.

Corollary IIIA. Knowledge of P Abilities and P Satisfactoriness permits the inference of E Ability Requirements.

Corollary IIIB. Knowledge of E Ability Requirements and P Satisfactoriness permits the inference of P Abilities.

Proposition IV. P Satisfactoriness moderates the prediction of P Satisfaction from E Reinforcers to P Values Correspondence.

Proposition V. P Satisfaction moderates the prediction of P Satisfactoriness from P Abilities to E Ability Requirements Correspondence.

Proposition VI. The probability that P will quit E is inversely related to P Satisfaction.

Proposition VII. The probability that E will fire P is inversely related to P Satisfactoriness.

Proposition VIII. P Tenure is predicted from P Satisfaction and P Satisfactoriness.

Given Propositions II, III, and VIII:

Corollary VIIIA. P Tenure is predicted from E Reinforcers to P Values Correspondence and P Abilities to E Ability Requirements Correspondence.

Corollary VIIIB. P Tenure is predicted from P-E Correspondence.

Proposition IX. P-E Correspondence increases as a function of P Tenure.

Proposition X. P Style to E Style Correspondence moderates the prediction of P Satisfaction and P Satisfactoriness from P Values/Abilities to E Reinforcers/Requirements Correspondence.

Proposition XI. P Flexibility moderates the prediction of P Satisfaction from E Reinforcers to P Values Correspondence.

Proposition XII. E Flexibility moderates the prediction of P Satisfactoriness from P Abilities to E Ability Requirements Correspondence.

Proposition XIII. The probability that P Adjustment Behavior will occur is inversely related to P Satisfaction.

Corollary XIIIA. Knowledge of this probability associated with P Satisfaction permits the determination of the P Flexibility threshold.

Proposition XIV. The probability that E Adjustment Behavior will occur is inversely related to P Satisfactoriness.

Corollary XIVA. Knowledge of this probability associated with P Satisfactoriness permits the determination of the E Flexibility threshold.

Proposition XV. The probability that P will quit E is inversely related to P Perseverance.

Corollary XVA. Knowledge of this probability associated with P's quitting E permits the determination of the P Perseverance threshold.

Proposition XVI. The probability that E will fire P is inversely related to E Perseverance.

Corollary XVIA. Knowledge of this probability associated with E's firing P permits the determination of the E Perseverance threshold.

Given Propositions VIII, XV, and XVI:

Proposition XVII. P Tenure is predicted jointly from P Satisfaction, P Satisfactoriness, P Perseverance, and E Perseverance.

REFERENCES

Borgen, F. H., Weiss, D. J., Tinsley, H. E. A., Dawis, R. V., & Lofquist, L. H. (1968). The measurement of occupational reinforcer patterns. *Minnesota Studies in Vocational Rehabilitation* (No. XXV), 1–89. Minneapolis: University of Minnesota, Industrial Relations Center.

Carroll, J. B. (1993). *Human cognitive abilities: A survey of factor-analytic studies.* New York: Cambridge University Press.

Cheung, F. M. (1975). *A threshold model of flexibility as a personality style dimension in work adjustment.* Unpublished doctoral dissertation, University of Minnesota, Minneapolis.

Dawis, R. V. (1991). Vocational interests, values, and preferences. In M. D. Dunnette & L. M. Hough (Eds.), *Handbook of industrial and organizational psychology* (2nd ed., Vol. 2, pp. 833–871). Palo Alto, CA: Consulting Psychologists Press.

Dawis, R. V. (1992). The individual differences tradition in counseling psychology. *Journal of Counseling Psychology, 39,* 7–19.

Dawis, R. V. (1996). The theory of work adjustment and person-environment-correspondence counseling. In D. Brown, L. Brooks, & Associates (Eds.), *Career choice and development* (3rd ed., pp. 75–120). San Francisco: Jossey-Bass.

Dawis, R. V. (2000). The person-environment tradition in counseling psychology. In W. E. Martin Jr. & J. L. Swartz-Kulstad (Eds.), *Person-environment psychology and mental health* (pp. 91–111). Mahwah, NJ: Erlbaum.

Dawis, R. V. (2002). Person-environment-correspondence theory. In D. Brown & Associates. *Career choice and development* (4th ed., pp. 427–464). San Francisco: Jossey-Bass.

Dawis, R. V., Dohm, T. E., Lofquist, L. H., Chartrand, J. M., & Due, A. M. (1987). *Minnesota Occupational Classification System III: A psychological taxonomy of work.* Minneapolis: University of Minnesota, Department of Psychology, Vocational Psychology Research.

Dawis, R. V., England, G. W., & Lofquist, L. H. (1964). A theory of work adjustment. *Minnesota Studies in Vocational Rehabilitation* (No. XV), 1–27. Minneapolis: University of Minnesota, Industrial Relations Center.

Dawis, R. V., & Lofquist, L. H. (1984). *A psychological theory of work adjustment.* Minneapolis: University of Minnesota Press.

Dawis, R. V., Lofquist, L. H., & Weiss, D. J. (1968). A theory of work adjustment (revision). *Minnesota Studies in Vocational Rehabilitation* (No. XXIII), 1–14. Minneapolis: University of Minnesota, Industrial Relations Center.

Dawis, R. V., & Weiss, D. J. (1994). *Minnesota Ability Test Battery: Technical manual.* Minneapolis: University of Minnesota, Department of Psychology, Vocational Psychology Research.

Gay, E. G., Weiss, D. J., Hendel, D. D., Dawis, R. V., & Lofquist, L. H. (1971). Manual for the Minnesota Importance Questionnaire. *Minnesota Studies in Vocational Rehabilitation* (No. XXVIII), 1–83. Minneapolis: University of Minnesota, Industrial Relations Center.

Gibson, D. L., Weiss, D. J., Dawis, R. V., & Lofquist, L. H. (1970). Manual for the Minnesota Satisfactoriness Scales. *Minnesota Studies in Vocational Rehabilitation* (No. XVII), 1–51. Minneapolis: University of Minnesota, Industrial Relations Center.

Guilford, J. P. (1954). *Psychometric methods.* New York: McGraw-Hill.

Judge, T. A., Higgins, C. A., Thoresen, C. J., & Barrick, M. R. (1999). The Big Five personality traits, general mental ability, and career success across the life span: Personnel. *Psychology, 52,* 621–652.

Lawson, L. (1991). *The measurement of flexibility, activeness, and reactiveness using an iterative scale construction method.* Unpublished doctoral dissertation, University of Minnesota, Minneapolis.

Lofquist, L. H., & Dawis, R. V. (1969). *Adjustment to work.* New York: Appleton-Century-Crofts.

Lofquist, L. H., & Dawis, R. V. (1978). Values as second-order needs in the theory of work adjustment. *Journal of Vocational Behavior, 12,* 12–19.

Lofquist, L. H., & Dawis, R. V. (1991). *Essentials of person-environment-correspondence counseling.* Minneapolis: University of Minnesota Press.

Lubinski, D., & Dawis, R. V. (1992). Aptitudes, skills, and proficiencies. In M. D. Dunnette & L. M. Hough (Eds.), *Handbook of industrial and organizational psychology* (2nd ed., Vol. 3, pp. 1–59). Palo Alto, CA: Consulting Psychologists Press.

Rounds, J. B., Dawis, R. V., & Lofquist, L. H. (1987). Measurement of person-environment fit and prediction of satisfaction in the theory of work adjustment. *Journal of Vocational Behavior, 31,* 297–318.

Rounds, J. B., Henly, G. A., Dawis, R. V., Lofquist, L. H., & Weiss, D. J. (1981). *Manual for the Minnesota Importance Questionnaire: A measure of vocational needs and values.* Minneapolis: University of Minnesota, Department of Psychology.

Scott, T. B., Dawis, R. V., England, G. W., & Lofquist, L. H. (1960). A definition of work adjustment. *Minnesota Studies in Vocational Rehabilitation* (No. X), 1–75. Minneapolis: University of Minnesota, Industrial Relations Center.

Shubsachs, A. P. W., Rounds, J. B., Jr., Dawis, R. V., & Lofquist, L. H. (1978). Perception of work reinforcer systems: Factor structure. *Journal of Vocational Behavior, 13,* 54–62.

Stewart, E. S., Greenstein, S. M., Holt, N. C., Henly, G. A., Engdahl, B. E., Dawis, R. V., et al. (1986). *Occupational reinforcer patterns.* Minneapolis: University of Minnesota, Department of Psychology, Vocational Psychology Research.

Tinsley, H. E. A., & Brown, S. D. (Eds.). (2000). *Handbook of applied multivariate statistics and mathematical modeling.* San Diego, CA: Academic Press.

U.S. Department of Labor. (1970). *Manual for the USES General Aptitude Test Battery.* Washington, DC: U.S. Government Printing Office.

Weiss, D. J., Dawis, R. V., England, G. W., & Lofquist, L. H. (1967). Manual for the Minnesota Satisfaction Questionnaire. *Minnesota Studies in Vocational Rehabilitation* (No. XXII), 1–119. Minneapolis: University of Minnesota, Industrial Relations Center.

CHAPTER 2

Holland's Theory of Vocational Personalities in Work Environments

Arnold R. Spokane and Maria Cristina Cruza-Guet

EXPLAINING WHY AND how individuals make career and work-related life decisions and assisting clients while making such decisions have been fundamental activities of counseling professionals for more than a century. Western efforts in the early twentieth century were aimed at assisting individual job seekers in an increasingly crowded urban environment (Parsons, 1909). This very practical approach to career decision making was gradually eclipsed by efforts to formulate viable theories of vocational choice and by empirical efforts to describe the characteristics of individual deciders, including, most predominantly, the measurement of vocational interests (see Dawis, 1992, and Tyler, 1995, for thoughtful discussions of the individual differences tradition in psychology, and Hansen, Chapter 12, this volume, for a review of interests and their measurement). Most recently, attention has returned to vocational interventions in response to a widening need for career counseling for a broader array of client populations. The hallmark of Holland's theory of vocational personalities in work environments has been the application of vocational theory to practical client concerns.

The next generation of counselors will assist a progressively more diverse clientele in a global social environment and with improved technology. The cultural validity and utility of the models and methods that we employ, then, will be of increasingly crucial interest to counseling students, practitioners, and researchers. The counseling profession is responding vigorously to the challenge of applying career theory (Lent & Worthington, 2000) and retooling intervention practice (Ponterotto, Rivera, & Sueyoshi, 2000; Spokane, Fouad, & Swanson, 2003) for use across cultural and social boundaries. Fortunately, the multicultural literature relevant to Holland's theory is now considerable and can help to point the way in providing career assistance to these new client groups. This chapter begins with a detailing of the theory, followed by discussion of assessment tools and issues, research on the Holland theory, and how the theory can be used in work with clients experiencing career difficulties.

THE THEORY

John Holland was in 1959 a young iconoclast, schooled in the Minnesota empirical tradition ("If a thing moves, measure it. If two things move, correlate them."), who broke from the dominant approach to the measurement of interests. Dubbed "dustbowl empiricism" for its Midwestern origins, the Minnesota tradition eschewed theory in favor of an atheoretical or empirical measurement method. Holland's creation of a theoretical, but highly practical, self-scoring measure of vocational interests (the Vocational Preference Inventory [VPI; Holland, 1985], followed by the Self-Directed Search [SDS; Holland, Fritzsche, & Powell, 1994]) catalyzed a shift in the counseling profession's emphasis from formulating vocational choice theory back to evaluating optimally useful career assessments and interventions. This shift from the development of competing theories that characterized the late 1900s to the design and evaluation of more effective career interventions completes the cycle of vocational psychology from the practical to the theoretical and back to the practical.

The interweaving of practice and theory has characterized Holland's model since its inception (Holland, 1959). Characteristic of Holland's scientific style, the theory has been tested, revised, and used by a large number of professional colleagues with whom Holland regularly communicates and to whom he provides intellectual support and guidance. The professional following that Holland has created and the practicality of the model and instruments account in large measure for the theory's wide public and professional support.

Holland's (1997) theory describes how individuals interact with their environments and how individual and environmental characteristics result in vocational choices and adjustment. Holland maintains that by late adolescence most people come to resemble a combination of six vocational personality/interest types: Realistic (R), Investigative (I), Artistic (A), Social (S), Enterprising (E), or Conventional (C) in six parallel work environments.

These six types (RIASEC), which are drawn from repeated empirical investigations, are described in Table 2.1, including each type's characteristics, self-descriptions, and occupations. The essence of the theory is the projection of the respondent's personality onto occupational titles.

The theory asserts that most people resemble more than one, and, in many cases, all, of the types to some degree. Thus, an individual's personality is a composite of several of the types—each individual having a unique combination. These types reliably show characteristic behavioral repertoires, patterns of likes and dislikes, specific values, and unique self-descriptions (Holland, 1997). The pattern of an individual's personality scores and resemblances is called a subtype, which is denoted by the first letter of each type in order of magnitude for that individual. For example, a computer programmer who completes one of the Holland inventories might have a full code of IRCAES. Typically, however, the highest three letters of the type code (IRC, called the three-letter code, or summary code) are used in assessment and intervention. Individuals with similar codes typically show similar patterns of vocational preference and generally prosper in similar occupational environments.

The types array themselves in an approximately hexagonal configuration (see Figure 2.1). The hexagon, which has been examined in a large number of empirical studies, is important because it permits the investigation of crucial relationships

Table 2.1
The Six Personality Types

The Realistic type likes realistic jobs such as automobile mechanic, aircraft controller, surveyor, farmer, electrician. Has mechanical abilities, but may lack social skill. Is described as:

Asocial	Inflexible	Practical
Conforming	Materialistic	Self-effacing
Frank	Natural	Thrifty
Genuine	Normal	Uninsightful
Hardheaded	Persistent	Uninvolved

The Investigative type likes investigative jobs such as biologist, chemist, physicist, anthropologist, geologist, medical technologist. Has mathematical and scientific ability but often lacks leadership ability. Is described as:

Analytical	Independent	Rational
Cautious	Intellectual	Reserved
Complex	Introspective	Retiring
Critical	Pessimistic	Unassuming
Curious	Precise	Unpopular

The Artistic type likes artistic jobs such as composer, musician, stage director, writer, interior decorator, actor/actress. Has artistic abilities—writing, musical, or artistic—but often lacks clerical skills. Is described as:

Complicated	Impractical	Open
Disorderly	Impulsive	Original
Emotional	Independent	Sensitive
Expressive	Introspective	
Idealistic	Intuitive	
Imaginative	Nonconforming	

The Social type likes social jobs such as teacher, religious worker, counselor, clinical psychologist, psychiatric case worker, speech therapist. Has social skills and talents but often lacks mechanical and scientific ability. Is described as:

Ascendant	Helpful	Responsible
Cooperative	Idealistic	Sociable
Empathic	Kind	Tactful
Friendly	Patient	Understanding
Generous	Persuasive	Warm

The Enterprising type likes enterprising jobs such as salesperson, manager, business executive, television producer, sports promoter, buyer. Has leadership and speaking abilities but often lacks scientific ability. Is described as:

Acquisitive	Energetic	Flirtatious
Adventurous	Excitement-	Optimistic
Agreeable	seeking	Self-confident
Ambitious	Exhibitionistic	Sociable
Domineering	Extroverted	Talkative

The Conventional type likes conventional jobs such as bookkeeper, stenographer, financial analyst, banker, cost estimator, tax expert. Has clerical and arithmetic ability but often lacks artistic abilities. Is described as:

Careful	Inflexible	Persistent
Conforming	Inhibited	Practical
Conscientious	Methodical	Prudish
Defensive	Obedient	Thrifty
Efficient	Orderly	Unimaginative

Source: Reproduced by special permission of the publisher, Psychological Assessment Resources, Inc., 16204 North Florida Avenue, Lutz, Florida 33549, from the Self-Directed Search Professional User's Guide, by John L. Holland, PhD, Amy Powell, PhD, and Barbara Fritzsche, PhD. Copyright © 1985, 1987, 1994.

between and among the six types that should be similar across social (e.g., men and women) and cultural subgroups. The large body of empirical evidence exploring the structure of interests (see Hansen, Chapter 12, this volume) demonstrates that the arrangement and proximity among the Holland types are consistent across gender and cultural boundaries and can reliably be characterized as hexagonal or, roughly, circular as depicted in Figure 2.1.

Work environments can also, according to Holland's theory and supportive research, be described in commensurate and complementary terms on the basis of

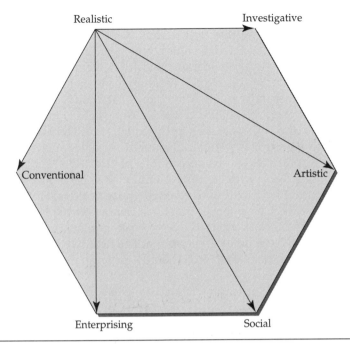

Figure 2.1 The Holland Hexagon. [*Source:* Reproduced by special permission of the publisher, Psychological Assessment Resources, Inc., 16204 North Florida Avenue, Lutz, Florida 33549, from the *Self-Directed Search Professional User's Guide*, by John L. Holland, PhD; Amy Powell, PhD; and Barbara Fritzsche PhD. Copyright © 1985, 1987, 1994.]

the personalities of the people working in them and the types of work activities in which people typically engage. In other words, work environments as well as people can be described with respect to summary codes, permitting the study of the interaction of an individual or group of individuals (e.g., IAS types) with a specific work environment (e.g., ERC).

Now that the key person and environment characteristics of Holland's theory have been described, these elements can be combined to understand how, according to Holland, individuals make the choices that they do. Four theoretically derived diagnostic indicators are central to Holland's theory: congruence, consistency, differentiation, and identity.

The first diagnostic indicator, *congruence,* is Holland's term for the degree of fit between an individual's personality and the type of work environment in which he or she currently resides or anticipates entering. A highly congruent person, for example, is an individual who has a three-letter code of AES, who is considering a career as a film editor (classified on the basis of the Holland types typically found in this occupation as AES). In contrast, an individual with an AES personality subtype who is contemplating becoming a biological scientist would be considering a highly incongruent option. In assessment, counseling, and research, congruence requires the use of one of several mathematical indices (see Brown & Gore, 1994; Camp & Chartrand, 1992; Young, Tokar, & Subich, 1998) to assess the degree of fit between the code of the person and the code of the environment.

Holland suggests that individuals will search for and enter work environments congruent with their subtype that will permit them to "exercise their skills and abilities, express their attitudes and values, and take on agreeable problems and roles" (Holland, 1997, p. 4). A considerable body of evidence confirms that congruence is sufficient, but not necessary, for vocational satisfaction (Spokane, Meir, & Catalano, 2000) and that individuals who change careers typically move in a congruent direction. Further, the ability to make a congruent choice can be mediated by several variables or conditions, such as the importance the individual places on identification with a group, as well as adjustment variables such as anxiety or depression. Research continues in this crucial area of Holland's theory, but it is clear that many persons have a difficult time identifying congruent occupational options, seeking accurate information to evaluate those options, and engaging in effective entry behaviors. Congruence, thus, has important implications for career intervention since counselors typically do not see persons who have been able, without help, to find a congruent career option. The next two concepts, consistency and differentiation, may also affect how readily individuals can make or adapt to vocational choices.

The second theoretical indicator, *consistency,* is a measure of the internal harmony or coherence of an individual's type scores. Consistency is calculated by examining the position of the first two letters of the three-letter code on the hexagon. According to Holland's theory, persons whose summary codes include types that are close to each other (i.e., adjacent) on the perimeter of the hexagon (see Figure 2.1) are more similar psychologically (e.g., Realistic and Investigative) and have more consistent and harmonious personality profiles than do those with subtypes that are opposite each other on the perimeter of the hexagon (e.g., Enterprising and Investigative). Individuals with consistent interest types within their personal three-letter code should feel more at ease with their personality characteristics and encounter fewer choice-making difficulties as a result.

Differentiation refers to the distinctness of the individual's personality profile (i.e., Does the personality profile clearly resemble some types and not others?) and is defined as the highest minus the lowest score among the six types or among the three scores comprising the three-letter code. The highest differentiation possible would be a high level of resemblance to one type alone, whereas the lowest would be a perfectly flat profile with identical scores on all six types. Low levels of differentiation should, theoretically, lead to less clarity and more difficulty in making vocational choices.

A final construct, *identity,* refers to the degree to which the individual has a clear "picture of one's goals, interests, and talents" (Holland, 1997, p. 5). Identity is related to differentiation and consistency in defining the strength of personalities and environments. Identity is measured using the Vocational Identity Scale (VI) from My Vocational Situation (Holland, Gottfredson, & Power, 1980).

The relationships among these four diagnostic/theoretical indicators (congruence, consistency, differentiation, identity) and their use as interpretive ideas as well as organizing or theoretical constructs are described in detail in the Self-Directed Search (SDS) professional manual (Holland, Powell, & Fritzsche, 1994). Other things being equal, a congruent, consistent, and well-differentiated individual should have higher vocational identity and will "probably do competent work, be satisfied and personally effective, and engage in appropriate social and educational behavior" (Holland, 1997, p. 40). He or she should, therefore, be better able to identify congruent vocational possibilities, make career choices and adjustments with less difficulty, and feel more satisfied and successful at work.

Work environments are described in the theory with a parallel or commensurate set of constructs (i.e., work environment consistency, differentiation, and identity). Differentiation and identity of a work setting are calculated by estimating the number of different occupations present in a work setting. For example, an advertising agency might consist of graphic designers, photographers, and audiovisual production specialists whose codes would cluster around A—AER, AES, and so on; account representatives and sales personnel whose codes would cluster around E—ESA and so on; and perhaps several secretaries whose codes would cluster around C—CSA. Such an advertising environment would be highly differentiated, but with a clear identity. Work environments can be classified more formally using the Position Classification Inventory (PCI; G. D. Gottfredson & Holland, 1991), an 84-item assessment of the job requirements, skills, perspectives, values, personal characteristics, talents, and key behaviors.

MEASUREMENT OF PERSONS AND ENVIRONMENTS

Among its most valuable contributions, Holland's theory has generated several practical instruments for assessing persons and environments that can be useful in identifying potentially congruent vocational options (e.g., college majors, occupations). In addition, because of the generativity and popularity of Holland's theory, many extant measures of vocational interests have incorporated scales to measure Holland personality types.

The measure most representative of the theory is the Self-Directed Search (SDS; Holland, Fritzsche, & Powell, 1994). The SDS, one of the most, if not the most, widely used interest inventories, consists of the Assessment Booklet, Occupations Finder, and Interpretive Guide. The SDS was designed to be a self-administering and self-scoring inventory that both assesses Holland type and teaches the respondent about the theory. Originally published in 1971, the SDS has been revised several times, most recently in 1994 (Form R; Occupations Finder updated in 2000), and includes a comprehensive set of user manuals. The SDS is also available in online format at http://www.self-directed-search.com for use by the lay public. A simple graphic of the steps involved in using the SDS is presented in Table 2.2.

Other instruments developed by Holland include the Vocational Preference Inventory (VPI; Holland, 1985); My Vocational Situation and the Vocational Identity Scale (VI; Holland et al., 1980); the Position Classification Inventory (PCI; G. D. Gottfredson & Holland, 1991), a psychometric device for classifying work environments using the Holland system; and the Career Attitudes and Strategies Inventory (CASI; Holland & Gottfredson, 1994). Other widely used vocational inventories and measures that include scales to assess Holland types include the Strong Interest Inventory (SII; Harmon, Hansen, Borgen, & Hammer, 1994); the new Armed Services Vocational Aptitude Battery (ASVAB) workbook, a clever and colorful intervention for students (Department of Defense [DOD], 1993); the Vocational Insight and Exploration Kit (VEIK; Holland, 1992); and other Vocational Card Sorts, as well as the Bolles Party Game (Bolles, 1998). Many of these

Table 2.2

Steps in Using the SDS

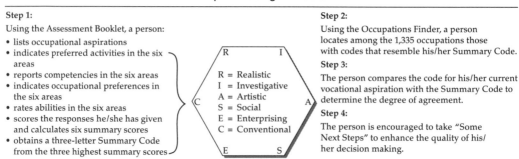

Step 1:	Step 2:
Using the Assessment Booklet, a person:	Using the Occupations Finder, a person locates among the 1,335 occupations those with codes that resemble his/her Summary Code.
• lists occupational aspirations	
• indicates preferred activities in the six areas	**Step 3:**
• reports competencies in the six areas	The person compares the code for his/her current vocational aspiration with the Summary Code to determine the degree of agreement.
• indicates occupational preferences in the six areas	
• rates abilities in the six areas	**Step 4:**
• scores the responses he/she has given and calculates six summary scores	The person is encouraged to take "Some Next Steps" to enhance the quality of his/her decision making.
• obtains a three-letter Summary Code from the three highest summary scores	

R = Realistic
I = Investigative
A = Artistic
S = Social
E = Enterprising
C = Conventional

Source: Reproduced by special permission of the publisher, Psychological Assessment Resources, Inc., 16204 North Florida Avenue, Lutz, Florida 33549, from the *Self-Directed Search Professional User's Guide*, by John L. Holland, PhD, Amy Powell, PhD, and Barbara Fritzsche, PhD. Copyright © 1985, 1987, 1994.

instruments are described in related chapters in this volume (Gore & Hitch, Chapter 16; Hansen, Chapter 12; Ryan Krane & Tirre, Chapter 14).

RESEARCH ON HOLLAND'S THEORY

The acid test of any psychological theory or counseling practice must be the extent to which a model is supported by rigorous scientific evidence. We urge readers to consult the numerous scholarly reviews of the research on Holland's theory in textbooks and professional journals, or better still, to read the original studies before passing judgment on the weight of evidence and support for the theory. The Holland system has been subjected to more empirical tests than any other model of career development. A surprising amount (though certainly not all) of this research has been supportive of the existence of a limited set of types, the underlying circular (or hexagonal) structure of those types, the validity of the instruments to measure types, though not to the same degree for the instruments designed to measure environments, and, to a lesser extent, the interactive proposition of the theory.

Holland's early studies (Holland, 1962) correlated VPI scores with a comprehensive set of self-descriptive adjectives (see Table 2.1) establishing the existence and validity of the six types in large, representative high school samples and in college populations. Similarly, educational environments (see, e.g., Astin & Holland, 1961) and occupational environments using work activities (G. D. Gottfredson & Holland, 1991, 1996; Helms, 1996; Mount & Muchinsky, 1978; Smart & Thompson, 2001; Toenjes & Borgen, 1974) were assessed consistent with theoretical predictions. Later studies explored the overlap between personality and interests (Borgen, 1986; Costa, McCrae, & Holland, 1984; Larson, Rottinghaus, & Borgen, 2002), self-ratings of abilities and skills (Swanson, 1993), and characteristic behaviors (Wampold et al., 1995). Finally, the sizeable set of empirical studies of person-environment congruence has been reanalyzed and summarized on multiple occasions (Assouline & Meir, 1987; Spokane, 1985; Spokane et al., 2000; Tinsley, 2000). The body of literature examining the validity of Holland's theory is the largest and most diverse of any theory in vocational psychology. Because of its importance to the theory, recent evidence for the utility of theory across cultures is reviewed in a later section.

GENDER ISSUES

As Fitzgerald, Fassinger, and Betz (1995) noted, the presumption in person-environment interaction theories of vocational behavior is that when occupational environments support the expression of (are congruent with) personality, positive outcomes such as satisfaction, stability, and achievement occur. Consistent with repeated evidence, when women complete raw score inventories such as the SDS, their scores reflect higher Social and Artistic scores and lower Investigative and Realistic scores than their male counterparts. Further, employment data continue to show that women are concentrated in lower level clerical and service occupations (Fitzgerald et al.). How and why these differences sustain themselves is a vexing problem for all vocational theories. Clearly, women's career development is directed less by personal preference and constrained by more barriers and mediating realities than that of men. Traditionally, women have considered family issues to a greater extent than have men. In addition, gender role socialization contributes to reduced efficacy in activities such as mathematics and science.

Some caution should be exercised, then, when assessing or counseling women who are considering career choices to minimize or counteract the complex constraints on women clients. As Linda Gottfredson (1982) appropriately noted, raw score inventories reflect how interests are, rather than how they ought to be, and thus should be combined with inventories that employ gender norming in counseling and research. These complex issues should be addressed with clients in ways that encourage realistic exploration and occupational entry.

One recent study (Betz & Schifano, 2000) took a more direct approach to this problem and administered either a "neutral" intervention, or a "Realistic" intervention "focused on building, repairing, and construction activities" to 54 undergraduate women. The authors used models to demonstrate the activities, persuaded and supported, and employed anxiety management strategies in a three-session, seven-hour attempt to enhance women's Realistic interests and self-efficacy. Although demand characteristics were a problem in the study design, a sharp increase in posttest Realistic self-efficacy was found even though there was no significant change in Realistic interest item scores. To the extent that self-efficacy limits already-nascent Realistic interests, this finding is important. There is some evidence that underlying interest structures may respond to brief interventions (Malett, Spokane, & Vance, 1978), but vocational interests appear to be enduring dispositions that are resistant to alteration, though the self-efficacy component of interests may respond to interventive modification. In addition to concerns about gender differences, researchers are intensively examining differences in Holland types across cultures.

VALIDITY OF HOLLAND'S THEORY ACROSS CULTURES: EMPIRICAL STUDIES

There is clear evidence of support, as reviewed in the previous section, for Holland's theory. However, another equally important way to judge the scientific merit and usefulness of a theory is in terms of its cross-cultural generalizability and practical utility—Does the theory apply as well with persons from varying cultural backgrounds?—an increasingly important consideration for the counseling professions.

Three culturally related questions seem important in assessing the cross-cultural validity and utility of the theory. First, do the same six types exist across cultures and subgroups, and do they arrange themselves in the hexagonal structure? Second, what, if any, effect does culture have on the outcomes of person-environment interaction? Third, do career assessments and interventions based on the model have cross-cultural utility? We should not presume a theory to be culturally valid or useful until empirical support confirms its utility. Conversely, we should not conclude that a theory is invalid until evidence concerning its invalidity is presented (Lent & Worthington, 2000).

The cross-cultural research on Holland's theory has primarily addressed the first and second questions with studies conducted internationally in China, Israel, France, Nigeria, New Zealand, and Australia. Research has also focused on cultural subgroups in the United States, including African Americans, Native Americans, Mexican Americans, and Asian Americans. This section discusses, selectively, cross-cultural studies addressing these first two questions that have appeared since the last major review of cross-cultural research on Holland's theory (Spokane, Luchetta, & Richwine, 2002).

Seven recent studies (Farh, Leong, & Law, 1998; Leong & Austin, 1998; Leong, Austin, Sekaran, & Komarraju, 1998; Leung & Hou, 2001; Shih & Brown, 2000; Soh & Leong, 2001; Tang, 2001; Zhang, 2000) shed collective light on the cross-cultural validity of the Holland types in Hong Kong, India, and Singapore. Farh et al. (1998) examined 1813 male and female freshmen in science, engineering, and business management. Holland codes were derived from self-reported preferences for occupations and the unisex edition of the ACT (UNIACT) inventory using a combination of English and Chinese items. Findings revealed that students who preferred occupations of a particular Holland type generally had interest scores congruent with that type. Evidence supporting the Artistic and Social types was weaker, which might be expected from the nature of the sample under study (science, engineering, and technology majors). Similarly, Soh and Leong (2001) examined the structural equivalence of RIASEC types drawn from samples in Singapore and the United States. Soh and Leong concluded that there was cultural equivalence for the S and E types and possibly for I types but not for the A and R types. In a third study, Leung and Hou (2001) administered the SDS to 456 female and 321 male Chinese high school students in Hong Kong. Congruence rates for male students were lower than those for comparable U.S. students but were similar for female students (Leung & Hou). The authors concluded that the SDS could be used to differentiate Chinese science and arts students.

Leong et al. (1998) use a modified English version of the VPI and a measure of job satisfaction to examine congruence, consistency, and differentiation in a sample of 172 natives of India. Congruence was minimally related to occupational satisfaction in females ($r = 0.20$) and males ($r = 0.14$). The authors also addressed directly the issue of equivalence of measurement by asking subjects to indicate when they did not understand the meaning of an item (occupational title). Twenty-four percent (14 of 160) of items had 5% or more of subjects indicate that they did not understand the item.

Zhang (2000) administered a shortened form of the SDS to 268 male and 332 female students at the University of Hong Kong. Holland type was related to thinking style, with Social and Enterprising types being related to "external" and "judicial" thinking style. Similarly, Tang (2001) employed a Chinese version of the SII, which has demonstrated a "similar structure" to U.S. versions but in which the RIASEC orders obtained were roughly circular, but flattened, with I and R very closely spaced and S and A reversed. Alternate models were discussed for explaining these differences—for example, Gati (1991). Finally, Shih and Brown (2000) studied 112 Taiwanese students in the United States and found a –0.27 relationship between vocational identity and a measure of acculturation.

In sum, studies in Asian cultures find that the U.S. versions of instruments do readily translate into Asian languages and reveal somewhere between four and six Holland-like types in a roughly comparable (to U.S. samples) circular/hexagonal configuration (see also Rounds & Tracey, 1996). Gender differences in structures persist in Asian samples (see also Hansen, Collins, Swanson, & Fouad, 1993, for U.S. samples), and the I and R types appear to be closer to each other on the hexagon than in U.S. populations (Tang, 2001; Zhang, 2000). The ordering of A and S is less consistent in these studies. These tentative conclusions should be tempered by the likelihood of dramatic sampling differences in U.S. and Asian studies. Finally, congruence appears to be related to theoretically relevant outcomes (Farh et al., 1998; Leong et al., 1998). Identity also seems related to these outcomes (Shih & Brown, 2000).

Three studies conducted in Italy (Lent, Brown, Nota, & Soresi, 2003), Ghent (De Fruyt, 2002), and Iceland (Einarsdóttir, Rounds, Ægisdóttir, & Gerstein, 2002) examined the utility of the theory in non-Asian cultures. Lent et al. (2003) examined the relationship of interest congruence to the occupational choices of 796 Italian high school students and found that interests were strong and significant predictors of occupational choices across all six Holland types. Similarly, De Fruyt (2002) gave 934 Dutch college students the SDS, the NEO-Personality Inventory (NEO-PIR), the PCI, and the CASI. Congruence was modestly but significantly related to job satisfaction (especially for I and C types) in a sample of Dutch village students, as was incongruence, but not to work involvement or perceived stress. In a third investigation, Einarsdottir et al. (2002) administered the SDS to 438 university students and the SII to 449 career counseling clients in Iceland. The underlying circular structure and arrangement of the six Holland types were similar to that found in U.S. samples.

In addition to the preceding cross-cultural studies, several recent investigations tested Holland's theory in subcultural groups within the United States. In a comparison of African American and White college students, for example, Toporek and Pope-Davis (2001) found no significant differences between the two groups of students on vocational identity. Day and Rounds (1998) compared the underlying structure of interests in samples of African American, Mexican American, Asian American, Native American, and Caucasian American groups ($n = 49,450$) using three-way individual difference scaling and concluded that the "groups' responses reflected a remarkably similar underlying structure, consistent with conventional interpretations of vocational interest patterns" (p. 728). The authors noted the problems of differences in sampling but suggested that there may be "universals" in the underlying structure of vocational interests and personality (Day & Rounds).

In sum, the increase in cross-cultural utility and validity studies of Holland's theory is cumulating in a body of evidence from which tentative conclusions can be drawn about the theory's applicability across cultural and subcultural boundaries. Given the early state of research in this area and the array of methodological and conceptual issues that need to be addressed, however, definitive conclusions may be some years away. Comparative studies of measurements and of interventions that include more than one cultural sample are still badly needed. Studies of Asian samples are accumulating, but studies from underdeveloped nations and, especially, studies accounting for the effects of poverty and socioeconomic status are needed. Finally, there have been few cross-cultural intervention studies that compare the processes, strategies, and outcomes of career interventions along the lines of Brown & Ryan Krane (2000) across cultures and subgroups (Spokane et al., 2003).

CASE EXAMPLE

Jennifer, a 37-year-old White female, was referred for vocational counseling by a colleague who had seen Jennifer for about 18 months for a generalized anxiety disorder. Such referrals that blend personal and vocational concerns are common in adult vocational counseling. Initially, the client indicated that she was in "no hurry" and would prefer to wait several weeks until after the holiday season. Four weeks later, Jennifer indicated that she would like to arrange a session quickly because she had just received a layoff notice from her employer, a large insurance company.

The first session centered on the client's background, work history, and present job loss. Jennifer's cultural background emphasized traditional Western values of independence, individualism, and a career success orientation. All three of Jennifer's siblings held professional positions. During this session, the client described a 10-year series of events, including a history of substance abuse during and after college. During her first year at college, she became depressed after an incident in which her father criticized her active social and sexual life. She withdrew from college and went home to work as a bank teller, which she hated. After one failed marriage, Jennifer met her present husband, an independent businessman who owns two family businesses and several properties that he manages. This marriage, by all reports, is solid and supportive for both Jennifer and her husband, who was also divorced.

This case, in addition to being an excellent example of the use of Holland's theory, is a good illustration of the overlap between career and personal issues during career intervention. Following the initial interview, sessions focused on generating and rehearsing possible future scenarios, formal and informal assessments, and discussion of related family and personal issues. Despite her complex personal life, Jennifer completed her BS in accounting (Conventional) and worked for six years as a bookkeeper or accountant. Her ideal day in the future and her present community service reflect a growing interest in artistic and creative endeavors as well as hands-on and practical physical work interests. Early in our discussions, it became clear that Jennifer's vocational interests were complex in nature and might cause difficulty for Jennifer in integrating her diverse interests. This complexity became increasingly clear as we examined the resulting assessment protocols. Jennifer completed multiple inventories to ensure both full coverage of her complex interests as well as gender balance.

After two sessions with Jennifer, we agreed on an intervention and assessment plan. Jennifer indicated that she was considering several options for work-lifestyles and was unsure how to proceed. As a result, we began with a guided fantasy (ideal day/typical day) in which the client imagined several general lifestyle scenarios in the future. In addition, the client completed the Tyler Vocational Card Sort, a Q-sort of occupational titles designed to ascertain a pattern of positive and negative choice constructs being employed by the client (see Spokane, 1991 for a description of these techniques). Because the client expressed an interest in general work-lifestyles, she also completed the 16PF Personal Career Development Profile, which generates personality information as well as information on problem-solving resources, coping patterns, interaction styles, organizational preferences, and career preferences. Finally, Jennifer completed the Self-Directed Search.

The Holland code from the SDS was ACS (see Figure 2.2). ACS is a "rare" code with no occupations listed in the SDS Occupational Finder. Further, the code shows minimal evidence of differentiation—five of the six type scores were within 15 points of one another. The first two letters of the code, C (Conventional) and A (Artistic), are opposite each other on the hexagon (highly inconsistent); the combination with S (Social) is also unusual. There are no occupations listed in the SDS Occupations Finder that were consistent with the code ACS, thus complicating Jennifer's search process.

The Career Interest scale of the 16PF was consistent with the SDS profile and revealed a combination of hands-on orientation with a strong "producing" interest defined in part by mechanical activities and woodworking and a strong creative interest reflected in writing, performing arts, and arts/design. The Personal Lifestyle Effectiveness scale was suggestive of independence and alerted the client to a tendency to overlook her own needs and to focus on practical rather than theoretical activities. The pattern of specific occupational scales was both consistent with the client's background as an accountant and reflective of her expressed interest in urban design and architecture.

The Tyler Q-Sort suggested a negative association with occupations lacking in independence and creativity, a negative reaction to overly scientific and detailed activities, and a dislike for desk-type jobs or those requiring a hard-sell approach. Positive constructs included a blended life and work-style orientation with a fun, down-to-earth component and an interest in historical architecture.

The Typical/Ideal Day Fantasy revolved around the restoration of historical buildings with an independent schedule and a strong family orientation.

Options generated for exploration included:

1. Return to work in an organizational setting using accounting background.
2. Work for a nonprofit organization concerned with urban design and planning.
3. Start small business reupholstering furniture.
4. Start small business development including restoring buildings in her neighborhood for rental.
5. Manage the family business.

Sessions (10) continued until the client concluded that she was happy for the foreseeable future with purchasing and restoring older buildings in her neighborhood for rental and lease. This work has continued for several months resulting in

Occupational Daydreams _____

List below the occupations you have considered in thinking
about your future. List the careers you have daydreamed
about as well as those you have discussed with others. Try to
give a history of your daydreams. Put your most recent
choice on Line 1 and work backwards to the earlier jobs you
have considered.

Occupation   Code

1. *Architect* | A | | I | | R |
2. *Artist (artisan/craftsman)* | A | | S | | E |
3. *Welder (ornamental)* | R | | L | | S |
4. *Actor* | A | | E | | S |
5. *Jeweler (gemologist)* | R | | E | | C |
6. *Photographer* | A | | R | | S |
7. *Musician* | A | | S | | C |
8. *Chef* | R | | A | | S |

How to Organize Your Answers _____

Start on page 4. Count how many times you said L for "Like."
Record the number of Ls or Ys for each group of Activities,
Competencies, or Occupations on the lines below.

Activities (pp. 4–5)	4	2	11	8	2	7
	R	I	A	S	E	C

Competencies (pp. 6–7)	5	1	7	7	3	11
	R	I	A	S	E	C

Occupations (p. 8)	4	0	11	6	4	4
	R	I	A	S	E	C

Self-estimates (p. 9) (What number did you circle?)	4	2	6	5	4	6
	R	I	A	S	E	C
	5	3	3	5	3	6
	R	I	A	S	E	C

Total scores (Add the five R scores, the five I scores, the five A scores, etc.)	22	8	38	31	16	34
	R	I	A	S	E	C

The letters with the three highest numbers indicate your
Summary Code. Write your Summary Code below. (If two
scores are the same or tied, put both letters in the same box.)

Summary Code

A		C		S
Highest		Second		Third

Figure 2.2 Occupational Daydreams and Summary Code from the Self-Directed Search
Protocol. [*Source:* Reproduced by special permission of the publisher and the client, Psychological Assessment Resources, Inc., 16204 North Florida Avenue, Lutz, Florida 33549,
from the *Self-Directed Search Professional User's Guide,* by John L. Holland, PhD; Amy
Powell, PhD; and Barbara Fritzsche PhD. Copyright © 1985, 1987, 1994.]

the restoration of three rental buildings and the purchase of two additional buildings. She also keeps the books for the family business. This integration appears to provide a good combination of hands-on practical work, use of her accounting background, and incorporation of her ACS three-letter code.

The client terminated with the option to return for future sessions, and she appears happy, active, and adapting well to her work and personal lifestyle combination. The anxiety that characterized her early work with my clinical colleague appeared to be well managed and less salient. On follow-up at one and two years, Jennifer was stable in her career, happy, and emerging as a community planner and developer.

PROMOTING CAREER DEVELOPMENT

The consummate counseling psychologist, Holland views human differences as assets and strives to provide practical assistance to a wide array of individuals using the personal and environmental resources available to them (Holland, 1997). Holland reasons that individuals search for occupational environments that are congruent with their vocational personality. A variety of forms of vocational assistance from brief, self-guiding interventions to intensive interactions with a counselor or in a formal class can promote career development by facilitating the search process. Critical ingredients in successful career interventions (Holland, Magoon, & Spokane, 1981) include:

1. Absorption of information about self and the world of work.
2. Acquisition of a realistic and accurate cognitive framework for approaching and understanding the search task.
3. Provision of social support (e.g., from a counselor, coach, or group members).
4. Opportunities to imagine and envision future possibilities.
5. Mobilization of effective exploratory behavior.

These five ingredients are effective across intervention type (Brown & Ryan Krane, 2000; Brown et al., 2003). A fundamental assumption of Holland's theory is that intervention should be geared toward promoting the effective implementation of a reasonably fitting or congruent career option. Thus, studies of the process and elements of career interventions contribute substantially to our ability to assist clients in their search for a reasonably fitting option (Spokane et al., 2000).

WORKING WITH DISSATISFIED AND
POORLY PERFORMING CLIENTS

Successful career search, selection, and entry depend on the client's ability to explore and assess possible career options in an unimpeded manner. Barriers and impediments can be external, such as job discrimination or undue family pressure; or they can be internal, such as anxiety, depression, or psychopathology. Holland's model depends on the client's ability to project himself or herself into vocational options—or in the case of the assessment devices, onto occupational titles to ascertain the potential for positive outcomes (e.g., Physicists are careful, I am careful; therefore, I would make a good physicist.). To the extent that such impediments exist, clients will be less able to execute a successful search and may distort or misconstrue the reasonableness of available options, thereby entering work environments that are incongruent with their personalities. The result, according to Holland's theory, would be a reduced likelihood of finding satisfaction and achieving success. Thus, career interventions with such clients would focus on finding more congruent work environments and overcoming internal and external impediments to entering congruent careers. Career intervention, absent impediments, can be a straightforward process. High levels of anxiety may reduce or limit exploration just as depression may inhibit effective consideration of otherwise appropriate options. Therapeutic interventions may need to shift focus for a time to address such issues to facilitate client progress (Spokane, 1991). Career problems may result from mental health concerns, and mental health problems may exacerbate career concerns. Some evidence suggests that career intervention can alleviate mental health concerns and personal therapeutic interventions can reduce career concerns. Counseling psychologists are uniquely suited to integrate and intervene in these overlapping domains, and Holland's theory can provide theoretical guidance.

SUMMARY

Holland's theory is unique in employing a comprehensive and integrated assessment system of individuals and their work environments based on a theoretical formulation of vocational personalities. The system has been subjected to more tests and analyses than any other model of career development. A surprising amount (though certainly not all) of this research has been supportive of the existence of a limited set of types, the underlying circular (or hexagonal) structure of those types, the validity of the instruments to measure types, and, to a lesser extent, the interactive proposition of the theory. The cross-cultural validity and utility of the model and the interventions that logically derive from it are encouraging, especially in Asian populations. Evidence examining career interventions using the instruments and principles of the theory supports the rigor as well as the practicality of the theory and related assessments and interventions for use in evidence-based counseling practice.

REFERENCES

Assouline, M., & Meir, E. I. (1987). Meta-analysis of the relationship between congruence and well-being measures. *Journal of Vocational Behavior, 31,* 319–332.

Astin, A. W., & Holland, J. L. (1961). The Environmental Assessment Technique: A way to measure college environments. *Journal of Educational Psychology, 52,* 308–316.

Betz, N. E., & Schifano, R. S. (2000). Evaluation of an intervention to increase realistic self-efficacy and interests in college women. *Journal of Vocational Behavior, 56,* 35–52.

Bolles, R. N. (1998). *What color is your parachute?* Berkeley, CA: Ten Speed Press.

Borgen, F. H. (1986). New approaches to the assessment of interests. In W. B. Walsh & S. H. Osipow (Eds.), *Advances in vocational psychology: Vol. I. The assessment of interests* (pp. 83–125). Hillsdale, NJ: Erlbaum.

Brown, S. D., & Gore, P. A. (1994). An evaluation of interest congruence indices: Distribution characteristics and measurement properties. *Journal of Vocational Behavior, 45,* 310–327.

Brown, S. D., & Ryan Krane, N. E. (2000). Four (or five) sessions and a cloud of dust: Old assumptions and new observations about career counseling. In S. D. Brown & R. W. Lent (Eds.), *Handbook of counseling psychology* (3rd ed., pp. 740–766). New York: Wiley.

Brown, S. D., Ryan Krane, N. E., Brecheisen, J., Castelino, P., Budisin, I., Miller, M., et al. (2003). Critical ingredients of career choice interventions: More analyses and new hypotheses. *Journal of Vocational Behavior, 62,* 411–428.

Camp, C. C., & Chartrand, J. M. (1992). A comparison and evaluation of interest congruence indices. *Journal of Vocational Behavior, 41,* 162–182.

Costa, P. T., Jr., McCrae, R. R., & Holland, J. L. (1984). Personality and vocational interests in adulthood. *Journal of Applied Psychology, 69,* 390–400.

Dawis, R. V. (1992). The individual differences tradition in counseling psychology. *Journal of Counseling Psychology, 39,* 7–19.

Day, S. X., & Rounds, J. (1998). Universality of vocational interest structures among racial and ethnic minorities. *American Psychologist, 53,* 728–736.

De Fruyt, F. (2002). A person-centered approach to P-E fit questions using a multiple trait model. *Journal of Vocational Behavior, 60,* 73–90.

Department of Defense. (1993). *Armed Services Vocational Aptitude Battery.* Washington, DC: Author.

Einarsdóttir, S., Rounds, J., Ægisdóttir, S., & Gerstein, L. H. (2002.) The structure of vocational interests in Iceland: Examining Holland's and Gati's RIASEC models. *European Journal of Psychological Assessment, 18,* 85–95.

Farh, J., Leong, F. T., & Law, K. S. (1998). Cross-cultural validity of Holland's model in Hong Kong. *Journal of Vocational Behavior, 52,* 425–440.

Fitzgerald, L. F., Fassinger, R. E., & Betz, N. E. (1995). Theoretical advances in the study of women's career development. In W. B. Walsh & S. H. Osipow (Eds.), *Handbook of vocational psychology* (2nd ed., pp. 67–110). Mahwah, NJ: Erlbaum.

Gati, I. (1991). The structure of vocational interests. *Psychological Bulletin, 109,* 309–324.

Gottfredson, G. D., & Holland, J. L. (1991). *The Position Classification Inventory: Professional manual.* Odessa, FL: Psychological Assessment Resources.

Gottfredson, G. D., & Holland, J. L. (1996). *Dictionary of Holland occupational codes* (3rd ed.). Odessa, FL: Psychological Assessment Resources.

Gottfredson, L. S. (1982). The sex fairness of unnormed interest inventories. *Vocational Guidance Quarterly, 31*(2), 128–132.

Hansen, J. C., Collins, R. C., Swanson, J. L., & Fouad, N. A. (1993). Gender differences in the structure of interests. *Journal of Vocational Behavior, 42,* 200–211.

Harmon, L. W., Hansen, J. C., Borgen, F. H., & Hammer, A. L. (1994). *Strong Interest Inventory: Applications and technical guide.* Palo Alto, CA: Consulting Psychologists Press.

Helms, S. T. (1996). Some experimental tests of Holland's congruency hypotheses: The reactions of high school students to occupational simulations. *Journal of Career Assessment, 4,* 253–268.

Holland, J. L. (1959). A theory of vocational choice. *Journal of Counseling Psychology, 6,* 35–45.

Holland, J. L. (1962). Some explorations of a theory of vocational choicer: I. One and two-year longitudinal studies. *Psychological Monographs, 76*(26, Whole No. 545).

Holland, J. L. (1985). *Manual for the Vocational Preference Inventory.* Odessa, FL: Psychological Assessment Resources.

Holland, J. L. (1992). *Counselor's guide to the Vocational Exploration and Insight Kit (VEIK).* Palo Alto, CA: Consulting Psychologists Press.

Holland, J. L. (1997). *Making vocational choices: A theory of vocational personalities and work environments* (3rd ed.). Odessa, FL: Psychological Assessment Resources.

Holland, J. L., Fritzsche, B. A., & Powell, A. B. (1994). *Technical manual for the Self-Directed Search.* Odessa, FL: Psychological Assessment Resources.

Holland, J. L., Gottfredson, D. C., & Power, P. G. (1980). Some diagnostic scales for research in decision making and personality: Identity, information, and barriers. *Journal of Personality and Social Psychology, 39,* 1191–1200.

Holland, J. L., & Gottfredson, G. D. (1994). *CASI: Career Attitudes and Strategies Inventory: An inventory for understanding adult careers.* Odessa, FL: Psychological Assessment Resources.

Holland, J. L., Magoon, T. M., & Spokane, A. R. (1981). Counseling psychology: Career interventions, research, and theory. *Annual Review of Psychology, 32,* 279–305.

Holland, J. L., Powell, A. B., & Fritzsche, B. A. (1994). *Professional users guide of the Self-Directed Search.* Odessa, FL: Psychological Assessment Resources.

Larson, L. M., Rottinghaus, P. J., & Borgen, F. H. (2002). Meta-analyses of Big Six interests and Big Five personality factors. *Journal of Vocational Behavior, 61,* 217–239.

Lent, R. W., Brown, S. D., Nota, L., & Soresi, S. (2003). Testing social cognitive interest and choice hypothesis across Holland types in Italian high school students. *Journal of Vocational Behavior, 62,* 101–118.

Lent, R. W., & Worthington, R. L. (2000). On school-to-work transition, career development theories, and cultural validity. *Career Development Quarterly, 48*(4), 376–384.

Leong, F. T., & Austin, J. T. (1998). An evaluation of the cross-cultural validity of Holland's theory: Career choices by workers in India. *Journal of Vocational Behavior, 52,* 441–445.

Leong, F. T., Austin, J. T., Sekaran, U., & Komarraju, M. (1998). An evaluation of the cross-cultural validity of Holland's theory: Career choices of workers in India. *Journal of Vocational Behavior, 52,* 441–455.

Leung, S. A., & Hou, Z. (2001). Concurrent validity of the 1994 Self-Directed Search for Chinese high school students in Hong Kong. *Journal of Career Assessment, 9,* 283–296.

Malett, S. D., Spokane, A. R., & Vance, F. L. (1978). Effects of vocationally relevant information on the expressed and measured interests of freshman males. *Journal of Counseling Psychology, 25,* 292–298.

Mount, M. K., & Muchinsky, P. M. (1978). Concurrent validation of Holland's hexagonal model with occupational workers. *Journal of Vocational Behavior, 13,* 348–354.

Parsons, F. (1909). *On choosing a vocation.* Boston: Houghton Mifflin.

Ponterotto, J. G., Rivera, L., & Sueyoshi, L. A. (2000). The career-in-culture interview: A semi-structured protocol for the cross-cultural intake interview. *Career Development Quarterly, 49,* 85–96.

Rounds, J., & Tracey, T. J. (1996). Cross-cultural equivalence of RIASEC models and measures. *Journal of Counseling Psychology, 43,* 310–329.

Shih, S., & Brown, C. (2000). Taiwanese international students: Acculturation level and vocational identity. *Journal of Career Development, 27*(1), 35–47.

Smart, J. C., & Thompson, M. D. (2001). The environmental identity scale and differentiation among environmental models in Holland's theory. *Journal of Vocational Behavior, 58,* 436–452.

Soh, S., & Leong, F. T. (2001). Cross-cultural validation of Holland's theory in Singapore: Beyond structural validity of RIASEC. *Journal of Career Assessment, 9,* 115–133.

Spokane, A. R. (1985). A review of research on person-environment congruence in Holland's theory of careers [Monograph]. *Journal of Vocational Behavior, 26,* 306–343.

Spokane, A. R. (1991). *Career intervention.* Englewood Cliffs, NJ: Prentice-Hall.

Spokane, A. R., Fouad, N. A., & Swanson, J. L. (2003). Culture-centered career intervention. *Journal of Vocational Behavior, 62,* 453–458.

Spokane, A. R., Luchetta, E. J., & Richwine, M. H. (2002). Holland's theory of personalities in work environments. In D. Brown & Associates (Eds.), *Career choice and development* (4th ed., pp. 373–426). San Francisco: Jossey Bass.

Spokane, A. R., Meir, E. I., & Catalano, M. (2000). Person-environment congruence and Holland's theory: A review and reconsideration. *Journal of Vocational Behavior, 57,* 137–187.

Swanson, J. L. (1993). Integrated assessment of vocational interests and self-rated skills and abilities. *Journal of Career Assessment, 1,* 50–65.

Tang, M. (2001). Investigation of the structure of vocational interests of Chinese college students. *Journal of Career Assessment, 9,* 365–379.

Tinsley, H. E. A. (2000). The congruence myth: An analysis of the efficacy of the person-environment fit model. *Journal of Vocational Behavior, 56,* 147–179.

Toenjes, C. M., & Borgen, F. H. (1974). Validity generalization of Holland's hexagonal model. *Measurement and Evaluation in Guidance, 7,* 79–95.

Toporek, R. L., & Pope-Davis, D. B. (2001). Comparison of vocational identity factor structures among African American and White American college students. *Journal of Career Assessment, 9,* 135–151.

Tyler, L. E. (1995). The challenge of diversity. In D. Lubinsky & R. Dawis (Eds.), *Assessing individual differences in human behavior: New concepts, methods, and findings* (pp. 1–13). Palo Alto, CA: Davies-Black.

Wampold, B. E., Ankarlo, G., Mondin, G., Trinidad-Cavillo, M., Baumler, B., & Prater, K. (1995). Social skills and social environments produced by different Holland types: A social perspective on person-environment fit models. *Journal of Counseling Psychology, 42,* 365–379.

Young, G., Tokar, D. M., & Subich, L. M. (1998). Congruence revisited: Do 11 indices differentially predict job satisfaction and is the relation moderated by person and situation variables? *Journal of Vocational Behavior, 52,* 208–233.

Zhang, L. (2000). Are thinking styles and personality types related? *Educational Psychology, 20,* 271–282.

CHAPTER 3

The Theory and Practice of Career Construction

Mark L. Savickas

THE THEORY OF career construction explains the interpretive and interpersonal processes through which individuals impose meaning and direction on their vocational behavior. The theory updates and advances Super's (1957) seminal theory of vocational development for use in a multicultural society and global economy. It incorporates Super's innovative ideas into a contemporary vision of careers by using social constructionism as a metatheory with which to reconceptualize central concepts of vocational development theory. In viewing these traditional concepts as processes that have possibilities, rather than continuing to view them as realities that predict the future, I am certain to alienate both constructionists and positivists who argue that their positions are theoretically incommensurate and that in trying to credential both, I slight each one. Nevertheless, I have been intrigued by viewing conventions in vocational psychology's canon, including Holland's hexagon and Super's stages, as social constructions rather than scientific discoveries.

In addition to advancing vocational development theory by transforming its central concepts, I have tried to integrate its segments. Super formulated his theory by focusing, in turn, on circumscribed segments of vocational behavior, which resulted in a "segmental theory" that is actually a loosely unified set of theories, each dealing with specific aspects of vocational development. Super (1969) hoped to someday integrate the segments into one comprehensive theory. To move toward that goal, in addition to using social constructionism as a metatheory, I adapted the tripartite framework devised by McAdams (1995) to organize personality theories. Using McAdams' general framework as a common theoretical foundation enabled me to progressively incorporate into one overarching theory the three classic segments of career theory: (1) individual differences in traits, (2) developmental tasks and coping strategies, and (3) psychodynamic motivation—or, for short, the differential, developmental, and dynamic views of career (Savickas, 2001). Career construction theory incorporates these three perspectives—representing the what, how, and why of vocational behavior—under the rubrics of vocational personality types, career adaptability, and life themes. Before describing in detail these types, tasks, and themes, I present a brief overview to orient readers to the whole theory before examining its parts.

OVERVIEW

Career construction theory addresses how the career world is made through personal constructivism and social constructionism. It asserts that we construct representations of reality, but we do not construct reality itself. Furthermore, the theory views careers from a contextualist perspective, one that sees development as driven by adaptation to an environment rather than by maturation of inner structures. Viewing careers from constructionist and contextual perspectives focuses attention on interpretive processes, social interaction, and the negotiation of meaning. Careers do not unfold; they are constructed as individuals make choices that express their self-concepts and substantiate their goals in the social reality of work roles.

Career construction theory, simply stated, asserts that individuals construct their careers by imposing meaning on their vocational behavior and occupational experiences. Whereas the objective definition of career denotes the sequence of positions occupied by a person from school through retirement, the subjective definition used in career construction theory is not the sum of work experience but rather the patterning of these experiences into a cohesive whole that produces a meaningful story. Herein, *career* denotes a subjective construction that imposes personal meaning on past memories, present experiences, and future aspirations by weaving them into a life theme that patterns the individual's work life. Thus, the subjective career that guides, regulates, and sustains vocational behavior emerges from an active process of making meaning, not discovering preexisting facts. It consists of a biographical reflexivity that is discursively produced and made "real" through vocational behavior. In telling career stories about their work experiences, individuals selectively highlight particular experiences to produce a narrative truth by which they live. Counselors who use career construction theory listen to clients' narratives for the story lines of vocational personality type, career adaptability, and life theme.

VOCATIONAL PERSONALITY

By attending to individual differences in vocational traits, career construction theory seeks to improve practice in augmenting, not replacing, person-environment fit theories that match people to occupations. The rational model (Parsons, 1909) for matching people to positions has been one of vocational psychology's most significant contributions to the human sciences. This model has been fully explained in the preeminent statements of person-environment psychology presented by Holland (1997) and by Lofquist and Dawis (1991). While career construction theory reconceptualizes some aspects of these foundational formulations about vocational personality types and work adjustment, it really concentrates instead on the implementation of vocational self-concepts, thus providing a subjective, private, and idiographic perspective for comprehending careers to augment the objective, public, and nomothetic perspective for understanding occupations.

It may be worthwhile to compare objective personality traits to subjective self-concepts because some counselors see no difference between the two. Person-environment fit theory attributes recurring uniformities in a person's social behavior to personality structure. The underlying dimensions that structure behavior are called *traits* (which career construction theory prefers to view as *resemblances* and *reputation*). According to R. Hogan (1983), "the primary function of trait ascription is to evaluate other people, specifically, to evaluate their potential as resources for the group" (p. 60). Thus, in a group that divides labor among its members, traits can be used to assign individuals to work roles. For example, a conventional person should make a better banker than an artistic person. Holland's RIASEC (Realistic, Investigative, Artistic, Social, Enterprising, Conventional) model, composed of trait complexes organized into types, offers a useful approach for appraising individual differences and for describing occupational groups. The objective perspective of types and traits does not, however, recognize the significance of subjective experience nor seek to understand behavior from the individual's own point of view. Accordingly, the life theme and self-concept perspectives of career construction theory complement the objective perspective by eliciting and interpreting clients' subjective conceptions of themselves and their world. These personal ideas and feelings about self, work, and life reveal purpose—and purpose rather than traits composes the life themes that control behavior, explain behavioral continuity, sustain identity coherence, and foresee future action.

Life Themes

The life theme component of career construction theory emerged from Super's (1951) postulate that in expressing vocational preferences, individuals put into occupational terminology their ideas of the kinds of people they are; in entering an occupation, they seek to implement a concept of themselves; and after stabilizing in an occupation, they seek to realize their potential and preserve self-esteem. This core postulate leads to the conceptualization of occupational choice as implementing a self-concept, work as a manifestation of selfhood, and vocational development as a continuing process of improving the match between the self and situation. From this perspective on the self, work provides a context for human development and an important location in each individual's life (Richardson, 1993).

Most individuals, regardless of their social-economic status, can find opportunities in their work to both express themselves and matter to their community. However, rather than choose among attractive options, some individuals may have to take the only job that is available to them, often a job that grinds on the human spirit because its tasks are difficult, tedious, and exhausting. Nevertheless, the work they do can be meaningful to them and matter to their community. Working with diverse clients in manifold cultures around the globe, it has been my experience that career construction theory can be used to help most individuals create deeper meaning and broader mattering in their daily work as well as assist them to find better ways to implement their self-concepts and advance their life projects despite painful pasts and social barriers to career adaptation.

CAREER ADAPTABILITY

The third central component in career construction theory is adaptability, that is, the attitudes, competencies, and behaviors that individuals use in fitting themselves to work that suits them. Viewing career construction as a series of attempts to implement a self-concept focuses attention on the sequence of matching decisions. Accordingly, career construction theory focuses on neither the person nor the environment in the famous P–E symbol; instead it focuses on the dash (–), asserting that building a career is a psychosocial activity, one that synthesizes self and society. More accurately, the theory focuses not on a dash but on the series of dashes that build a career. With a changing self (P) and changing situations (E), the matching process is never really completed. The series of changing preferences should progress, through successive approximations, toward a better fit between worker (P) and work (E). The overriding goal toward which career adaptation moves is a situation in which the occupational role substantiates and validates the individual's self-concept.

PROPOSITIONS

The three components of vocational personality, career adaptability, and life themes structure the 16 propositions that appear in Table 3.1. These propositions express the current statement of career construction theory, one that incorporates, revises, and expands Super's initial (1953), definitive (1984), and final (1990) statements of his vocational development theory. For a complete exposition of career construction theory, consult Savickas (2002). Instead of restating the theory herein, this chapter concentrates on how it can inform and improve the practice of career education and counseling.

Table 3.1
Career Construction Theory Propositions

---

1. A society and its institutions structure an individual's life course through social roles. The life structure of an individual, shaped by social processes such as gendering, consists of core and peripheral roles. Balance among core roles such as work and family promotes stability whereas imbalances produce strain.
2. Occupations provide a core role and a focus for personality organization for most men and women, although for some individuals this focus is peripheral, incidental, or even nonexistent. Then other life roles such as student, parent, homemaker, leisurite, and citizen may be at the core. Personal preferences for life roles are deeply grounded in the social practices that engage individuals and locate them in unequal social positions.
3. An individual's career pattern—that is, the occupational level attained and the sequence, frequency, and duration of jobs—is determined by the parents' socioeconomic level and the person's education, abilities, personality traits, self-concepts, and career adaptability in transaction with the opportunities presented by society.
4. People differ in vocational characteristics such as ability, personality traits, and self-concepts.

(Continued)

Table 3.1 *(Continued)*

5. Each occupation requires a different pattern of vocational characteristics, with tolerances wide enough to allow some variety of individuals in each occupation.
6. People are qualified for a variety of occupations because of their vocational characteristics and occupational requirements.
7. Occupational success depends on the extent to which individuals find in their work roles adequate outlets for their prominent vocational characteristics.
8. The degree of satisfaction people attain from work is proportional to the degree to which they are able to implement their vocational self-concepts. Job satisfaction depends on establishment in a type of occupation, a work situation, and a way of life in which people can play the types of roles that growth and exploratory experiences have led them to consider congenial and appropriate.
9. The process of career construction is essentially that of developing and implementing vocational self-concepts in work roles. Self-concepts develop through the interaction of inherited aptitudes, physical make-up, opportunities to observe and play various roles, and evaluations of the extent to which the results of role playing meet with the approval of peers and supervisors. Implementation of vocational self-concepts in work roles involves a synthesis and compromise between individual and social factors. It evolves from role playing and learning from feedback, whether the role is played in fantasy, in the counseling interview, or in real-life activities such as hobbies, classes, clubs, part-time work, and entry jobs.
10. Although vocational self-concepts become increasingly stable from late adolescence forward, providing some continuity in choice and adjustment, self-concepts and vocational preferences do change with time and experience as the situations in which people live and work change.
11. The process of vocational change may be characterized by a maxicycle of career stages characterized as progressing through periods of growth, exploration, establishment, management, and disengagement. The five stages are subdivided into periods marked by vocational development tasks that individuals experience as social expectations.
12. A minicycle of growth, exploration, establishment, management, and disengagement occurs during transitions from one career stage to the next as well as each time an individual's career is destabilized by socioeconomic and personal events such as illness and injury, plant closings and company layoffs, and job redesign and automation.
13. Vocational maturity is a psychological construct that denotes an individual's degree of vocational development along the continuum of career stages from growth through disengagement. From a societal perspective, an individual's vocational maturity can be operationally defined by comparing the developmental tasks being encountered to those expected based on chronological age.
14. Career adaptability is a psychosocial construct that denotes an individual's readiness and resources for coping with current and anticipated tasks of vocational development. The adaptive fitness of attitudes, beliefs, and competencies—the ABCs of career construction—increases along the developmental lines of concern, control, conception, and confidence.
15. Career construction is prompted by vocational development tasks, occupational transitions, and personal traumas and then produced by responses to these life changes.
16. Career construction, at any given stage, can be fostered by conversations that explain vocational development tasks and occupational transitions, exercises that strengthen adaptive fitness, and activities that clarify and validate vocational self-concepts.

In the remaining sections of this chapter, I discuss, in turn, the three major components of career construction theory. First, I briefly discuss how the theory views vocational personality types and the content of their occupations. Then I address the process of psychosocial adaptation by describing vocational development tasks and outlining the coping responses that individuals use to construct their careers. Next, I discuss how an individual's enduring preoccupations and problems, as expressed in integrative and self-sustaining narratives, guide adaptation by negotiating cultural opportunities and constraints. Having described the three major components of the theory, I then present a case study that illustrates the theory's usefulness in helping one client construct her career. With this overview, I turn to the first component of career construction theory, the one focused on the psychology of individual differences.

VOCATIONAL PERSONALITY

Individuals form personalities in their families of origin and develop these personalities in the neighborhood and school as they progress through the growth stage of their careers. *Vocational personality* is defined as an individual's career-related abilities, needs, values, and interests. Before these characteristics are expressed in occupations, they are rehearsed in activities such as household chores, games, hobbies, reading, and studying. The range of personality dispositions, particularly as they relate to work roles, is well described by Holland's (1997) taxonomy. His RIASEC prototypes provide a readily comprehensible and broad-band tool for organizing vocational phenomena into type categories. The types or trait complexes, although decontextualized and abstract, provide extremely useful comparative dimensions for conducting vocational appraisals of individuals and environments. RIASEC types can be used to summarize an individual's dispositional signature, including skills, interests, values, and abilities for enacting work roles. After determining an individual's degree of resemblance to each of the RIASEC types, the resulting three-letter code characterizes that individual's personality organization and work-relevant traits.

Career construction theory appreciates Holland's (1997) explanation that his inventories indicate degree of *resemblance* to protoytpes. In career construction theory, these interest types are simply resemblances to socially constructed clusters of attitudes and skills; they have no reality or truth value outside themselves. The RIASEC hexagon reflects regulated similarities in environments that produce personality patterns of six types among individuals with heterogeneous potentials. Thus, career construction theory views interests as a relational phenomenon that reflects emergent and socially constituted meanings and leads to a person's *reputation* among a group of people (J. Hogan & Holland, 2003). Moreover, interests are viewed as dynamic processes, not as stable traits. Therefore, counselors should not privilege interests above other constructs as predictors of occupational congruence and job success. The idea of shared interest is just one among many important indicators to consider when individuals choose occupations and build their careers. Counselors who use career construction theory occasionally do administer interest inventories; however, they do not interpret the resulting scores as portals on a client's "real" interests. Instead, they use the results to generate hypotheses that are viewed as possibilities, not predictions.

Holland's typology offers a practical structure for identifying the content of a vocational personality, that is, the personological and vocational results of an individual's efforts at self-organization of his or her skills, interests, values, and abilities for dealing with life roles. Another valuable aspect of Holland's theory is that, because vocational personality types congregate to form work environments, the same RIASEC types have been used to characterize the social organization of occupations. Accordingly, Holland's hexagonal arrangement of RIASEC types is used by counselors to teach clients about not only how they organize their interests but also how society has organized macroenvironments such as occupations, college majors, and leisure activities. Thus, Holland's theory serves clients by providing a concise vocabulary for describing both who they are and what they are looking for, as well as by teaching them a simplifying taxonomy with which to organize and store information about the work world. Accepting the preeminence of Holland's typology enables career construction theory to concentrate on bridges between personality and work, especially how individuals build and cross their own bridges. Thus, career construction theory concentrates on self-extension, not on the self-organization reflected in vocational personality types nor on the social organization of occupations.

CAREER ADAPTABILITY

An occupation provides a mechanism of social integration, one that offers individuals a strategy for participating in and sustaining themselves in society. Careers are constructed when individuals extend themselves into these occupational roles. While vocational personality types emphasize the occupational content of career, adaptability emphasizes the coping processes through which individuals connect to their communities and construct their careers. Succinctly stated, career adaptability deals with *how* an individual constructs a career whereas vocational personality deals with *what* career they construct. To elicit career content, the counselor might ask a client, "What occupation interests you the most?" To elicit career process, the counselor might ask that client, "How did you decide on that occupation?" In short, when looking at careers, the content perspective focuses on *making wise choices,* whereas the process perspective focuses on *making choices wisely* (Katz, 1969).

In examining the content of careers using the RIASEC model, we looked from two perspectives—the self-organization of individuals and the social organization of occupations. In considering adaptation, we again take the twin perspectives of self and society. From the social vantage point on adaptation, counselors look at the community expectations being encountered by a client. From the individual vantage point on adaptation, counselors look at how the client responds to these expectations. The next two sections address, first, the major vocational development tasks involved in constructing a career and, second, the adaptive responses that complete these tasks.

Developmental Tasks

Society invites adolescents to extend their personalities into the world and join the workforce. The goal of the school-to-work transition is that emerging adults learn to contribute to society by fitting their personalities into suitable work roles. The social expectation that adolescents seek occupations congruent with their abilities and interests is communicated to them in the form of vocational development tasks. The continuum of developmental tasks, which spans the life cycle, has been divided into five career stages, with each stage named for its principal activity: growth, exploration, establishment, management, and disengagement. Each career stage contains its own set of developmental tasks. While the career stages emphasize change, the vocational development tasks within them detail how stability is reestablished and continuity maintained.

The first career stage centers on the origin and growth of the individual's vocational personality. The growth stage is followed during adolescence and emerging adulthood with exploratory activities that enable the individual to make fitting educational and vocational choices based on self-knowledge and a fund of occupational information. In due course, the tentative choices and trial positions of the exploration stage clarify the situation so that the young adult is ready to stabilize in a certain occupation and maybe a particular job with one employer. Having established a secure job, and perhaps advancing in it, an adult then enters a period where further advancement is unlikely. At this point, the individual manages to hold on to the position by keeping up with new developments and innovating work routines. At some point, the individual becomes ready to leave the job and begins to decelerate activity in it while turning over responsibilities to other workers. During this period of disengagement, the person may grow and explore new interests in other positions and occupations or, if it is later in the life cycle, prepare for retirement. Practitioners and researchers use the activities of growth, exploration, establishment, management, and disengagement to characterize the maxicycle of stages in a career.

The career stages, with their developmental tasks, function as a habitus in supplying workers with meanings they can use to interpret their work lives. *Habitus* means the interpenetration between objective divisions of the social world and an individual's subjective vision of them, causing a correspondence and interplay between an individual's mental structures and a community's social structures (Guichard & Cassar, 1998). Individuals mentally structure the story of their own work life using the social structure provided by society's grand narrative of a career. The narrative frames people's stories of work and its consequences as they think about and take stock of their work lives. Thus, habitus makes an individual's story of personal experience and private meaning comprehensible to others by embedding and systematically organizing it according to a dominant social structure. In addition to providing a commonsense framework, the grand story of career synchronizes individuals to their culture by telling them in advance how their work lives should proceed and prompting them to stay on schedule. Given these scripts, individuals bring to life the grand narrative, or some parts of it, by enacting their unique version of it in a particular historical era, given location, and specific opportunity structure that discriminates by race, age, sex, religion, and class.

The story of the career stages tells a grand narrative about psychosocial development and cultural adaptation. Essentially, the metanarrative of career can be characterized as a progress story. Success in adapting to each developmental task results in more effective functioning as a student, worker, or retiree and lays the groundwork for progressively mastering the next task along the developmental continuum. The key metaphor in this portrayal of the American Dream is climbing a ladder. Incremental progress up the occupational ladder is indexed by increasing wages, benefits, and security. Progress stories do give hope and security to many people; nevertheless, there are many other people whose experience does not fit the story. Instead of progress, some people encounter barriers that force them to regress, drift, flounder, stagnate, or stop. Unable to move ahead on a career path, they drop back, get sidetracked, become stuck in a rut, run into a dead end, or fall by the wayside.

The grand narrative of career tells a story, an account that people use to understand themselves and others. It is not *the* account, it is *an* account of vocational development tasks for one culture in one historical era. It was constructed in the 1950s to depict the then-current corporate culture and societal expectations for a life, especially a male life that privileges the work role over family and friendship roles. Other accounts are being narrated today as the global economy, information technology, and social justice challenge dominant narratives and rewrite the social organization of work and the meaning of career. These rich narratives chronicle untold stories and voice complexity. These new stories, rather than focusing on progress through an orderly sequence of predictable tasks in a maxicycle, will increasingly focus on minicycles by emphasizing adaptability for transitions, especially coping with changes that are unexpected and traumatic. The new job market in our unsettled economy calls for viewing career not as a lifetime commitment to one or two employers but as selling services and skills to a series of employers who need projects completed (Kalleberg, Reynolds, & Marsden, 2003). In negotiating each new project, the prospective employee usually concentrates on salary yet also seeks control of the working environment, work-family balance, and training for the next job.

While the grand narrative changes from stability to mobility to reflect the labor needs of postindustrial society, the activities that characterize the five principal career stages—growth, exploration, establishment, management, and disengagement—are still useful and can be viewed as activities that compose a minicycle around each of the many transitions from school to work, from job to job, and from occupation to occupation. As each transition approaches, individuals can adapt more effectively if they meet the challenges with growing interest, focused exploration and informed decision making, trial behaviors followed by a commitment projected forward for a certain time period, active role management, and forward-looking deceleration and disengagement. For example, a high school graduate entering her first job usually progresses through a period of growth in the new role, including exploration of the nature and expectations of that role. She becomes established in it, manages the role for a long period, and then experiences disengagement if with further growth she becomes ready to change jobs or even switch occupational fields. Similarly, the established worker, frustrated or advancing, may experience growth and explore new roles and then seek to get established in one of them. In postindustrial economies, people may not work at one job for 30 years. New technologies, globalization, and job redesign require workers to more actively construct their careers. They can expect to change jobs relatively often and make frequent transitions, each time recycling through minicycles of growth, exploration, stabilization, management, and disengagement as they move within or across the career stages of the maxicycle.

DIMENSIONS OF CAREER ADAPTABILITY

The attributes that individuals need to successfully engage the tasks inherent in minicycle transitions and maxicycle stages constitute career adaptability. Adaptability involves adjusting to vocational development tasks, occupational transitions, and personal traumas by solving problems that are usually unfamiliar, often ill-defined, and always complex. Career construction theory conceptualizes development as driven by adaptation to an environment rather than by maturation of inner structures. Accordingly, career adaptability differs from Super's (1955) earlier conception of vocational maturity, which refers to an individual's degree of vocational development relative to an individual's peers. Super's view of development assumed that individuals move in an orderly and normative sequence toward a desirable end state of maturity and, in the process, they become more complete as they unfold and elaborate their latent potentials. An individual's vocational maturity can be operationally defined by comparing the developmental tasks being encountered to those society expects an individual to be encountering at a particular stage of life. This view was more useful when society provided stable and orderly environments that fostered some uniformity in development. However, today's turbulent society is unable to prompt orderly development, thus forcing individuals to respond to a wide range of external influences that can push development in various directions (Collin, 1997).

The change from an industrial society emphasizing a factory system to a knowledge-based society emphasizing information technology occasioned the formulation of a new career construct—adaptability. *Career adaptability is a psychosocial construct that denotes an individual's readiness and resources for coping with current and imminent vocational development tasks, occupational transitions, and personal traumas.* Adaptability shapes self-extension into the social environment as individuals connect with society and regulate their own vocational behavior relative to the developmental tasks imposed by a community and the transitions encountered in occupational roles. Functioning as self-regulation strategies, career adaptability enables individuals to effectively implement their self-concepts in occupational roles, thus creating their work lives and building their careers.

The actual strategies involved in career adaptation are conditioned by historical era, dependent on local situations, and variable across social roles. Therefore, researchers can describe adaptive resources and strategies best when they select a particular developmental task or occupational transition and then locate it in a specific social ecology. Nevertheless, for the purposes of career construction theory, I have defined global dimensions of career adaptability and organized them into a structural model with three levels. At the highest and most abstract level, picture four dimensions of career adaptability, each named according to its function: concern, control, curiosity, and confidence. These four dimensions represent general adaptive resources and strategies that individuals use to manage critical tasks, transitions, and traumas as they construct their careers.

At the intermediate level, the model articulates a distinct set of functionally homogenous variables for each of the four general dimensions. Each set of intermediate variables includes the specific attitudes, beliefs, and competencies—the ABCs of career construction—which shape the concrete coping behaviors used to master developmental tasks, negotiate occupational transitions, and resolve personal traumas. The ABCs are viewed as mechanisms for synthesizing vocational self-concepts with work roles. Attitudes are affective variables or feelings that fuel behavior, whereas beliefs are conative variables or inclinations that direct behavior. The attitudes and beliefs dispose individuals to act in certain ways; thus, they form dispositional response tendencies. Although conceptually distinct, it can be difficult to distinguish an attitude from a belief, so treating them both as dispositions, meaning a state of mind or feeling toward something, has practical advantages in devising interview questions and psychometric inventories. The cognitive competencies, which include comprehension and problem-solving abilities, denote the resources brought to bear on making and implementing career choices. The development and use of competencies are shaped by the dispositions. The cognitive competencies, in turn, modulate vocational behavior, which is portrayed at the third and most concrete level in the structural model of career adaptability. Vocational behavior denotes the numerous coping responses that produce vocational development and construct careers.

Having outlined the structural model of career adaptability, I turn to a detailed explanation of the four dimensions of response readiness and coping resources. In career construction theory, adaptive individuals are conceptualized as:

1. Becoming *concerned* about their future as a worker.
2. Increasing personal *control* over their vocational future.
3. Displaying *curiosity* by exploring possible selves and future scenarios.
4. Strengthening the *confidence* to pursue their aspirations.

Career adaptability thus increases along the four dimensions of concern, control, curiosity, and confidence. Each is discussed in turn, with Table 3.2 serving as an overview that summarizes the discussion and allows comparison of the dimensions. The first column in Table 3.2 indicates the career questions that society prompts individuals to ask themselves. The second column lists the career problems arising from negative responses to the questions. The third column lists the adaptability dimension associated with positive responses to the questions. The next columns list the dispositions, competencies, coping behaviors, and relationship orientations that compose each dimension. The final column lists the primary type of career intervention that addresses each career problem and attempts to turn it into an adaptive strength. The first row in Table 3.2 deals with career concern.

Career Concern   An individual's concern about his or her own vocational future is the first and most important dimension of career adaptability. The fundamental function of career concern in constructing careers is reflected by the prime place given to it by prominent theories of vocational development, denoted by names such as Ginzberg's *time perspective*, Super's *planfulness*, Tiedeman's *anticipation*, Crites' *orientation*, and Harren's *awareness* (Savickas, Silling, & Schwartz, 1984). Career concern means essentially a future orientation, a sense that it is important to prepare for tomorrow. Attitudes of planfulness and optimism foster a sense of concern because they dispose individuals to become aware of the vocational tasks and occupational transitions to be faced and choices to be made in the imminent and distant future. Career concern makes the future feel real as it helps an individual remember the vocational past, consider the vocational present, and

Table 3.2
Career Adaptability Dimensions

Career Question	Career Problem	Adaptability Dimension	Attitudes and Beliefs	Competence	Coping Behaviors	Relationship Perspective	Career Intervention
Do I have a future?	Indifference	Concern	Planful	Planning	Aware Involved Preparatory	Dependent	Orientation exercises
Who owns my future?	Indecision	Control	Decisive	Decision making	Assertive Disciplined Willful	Independent	Decisional training
What do I want to do with my future?	Unrealism	Curiosity	Inquisitive	Exploring	Experimenting Risk-taking Inquiring	Interdependent	Information-seeking activities
Can I do it?	Inhibition	Confidence	Efficacious	Problem solving	Persistent Striving Industrious	Equal	Self-esteem building

anticipate the vocational future. Thinking about his or her work life across time is the essence of career because a subjective career is not a behavior; it is an idea—a reflection on the self. Career construction is fostered by first realizing that his or her present vocational situation evolved from past experiences and then connecting these experiences through the present situation to a preferred future. A belief in the continuity of experience allows individuals to connect their present activities to their occupational aspirations and visions of possible selves. This sense of continuity allows individuals to envision how today's effort builds tomorrow's success. Planful attitudes and belief in continuity incline individuals to engage in activities and experiences that promote competencies in planning, which include skill at sequencing their activities along a time line that spans from the present situation to a desired future.

A lack of career concern is called *career indifference,* and it reflects planlessness and pessimism about the future. This apathy can be addressed by career interventions designed to foster a forward-looking orientation and awareness of the vocational development tasks and occupational transitions on the horizon. Career counseling interventions, in general, help people formulate occupational daydreams in which they begin to design their lives. Career indifference is addressed, in particular, by interventions such as the Real Game (Jarvis & Richardt, 2001), the Life Skills Program (Adkins, 1970), time perspective workshops (Whan & Savickas, 1998), and writing future autobiographies (Maw, 1982). These interventions induce a future orientation, foster optimism, make the future feel real, reinforce positive attitudes toward planning, link present activities to future outcomes, practice planning skills, and heighten career awareness. These coping attitudes, beliefs, and competencies strengthen career concern and prompt thoughts about who controls the individual's career.

Career Control   Control over an individual's own vocational future is the second most important dimension in career adaptability. The fundamental function of control in constructing careers is reflected by the vast amount of research on topics such as decision making, assertiveness, locus of control, autonomy, self-determination, effort attributions, and agency (Blustein & Flum, 1999), as well as the widespread advice to younger workers in a knowledge-based society and mobile labor market that they act as "free agents," "independent contractors," and "me incorporated." Career control means that individuals feel and believe that they are responsible for constructing their careers. While they may consult significant others, they own their career. The dominant culture in the United States and those who have assimilated it lean toward independence in balancing self and society. Consequently, the most popular models and materials for career intervention assume that the individual is autonomous in making career choices. Attitudes of assertiveness and decisiveness dispose self-governing individuals to engage the vocational development tasks and negotiate occupational transitions, rather than procrastinate and avoid them. The belief that they own their own future and should construct it by choosing rather than chancing leads individuals to sense that they are responsible for their lives, whether they view themselves from a collectivist perspective or an individualist perspective. Although the range of options in a collectivist context may be narrower, the alternatives still must be explored to avoid losing the "I" in the "they." Individuals who encounter a narrower range of options exercise career control by exploring the limited number of possibilities to make them personally meaningful and by fine-tuning conferred choices to enact them uniquely. Whether individuals take an individualistic or a collectivistic stance, they can benefit from being intentional about what they do and responsible for how they do it. Moreover, counselors must know that the two stances, which seem so different at first look, both enable individuals to strengthen themselves as they strengthen others. Assertive attitudes and belief in personal responsibility incline individuals to engage in activities and experiences that promote decisiveness and competence in decision making.

A lack of career control is often called *career indecision.* The inability to choose can be addressed by career interventions designed to foster decisive attitudes and decisional competencies. Career counseling interventions, in general, help people enhance the ability to decide by clarifying their choices and what is at stake. Career indecision is addressed, in particular, by interventions such as assertiveness training, decisional training, and attribution retraining that build decisional skills, foster responsibility, attribute success to effort, teach time management techniques, and practice self-management strategies. These coping attitudes, beliefs, and competencies strengthen career control and prompt curiosity about possible selves and alternative futures.

Career Curiosity   With a sense of control comes the initiative for learning about the types of work that the individual might want to do and the occupational opportunities to do it. The fundamental function of curiosity in constructing careers is reflected by the extensive coverage given to it by prominent theories of vocational development under the rubrics of exploration and information-seeking behavior as well as in their direct products—self-knowledge and occupational information. *Career curiosity* refers to inquisitiveness about and exploration of the fit between self and the work world. When acted on, curiosity produces a fund of knowledge with which to make choices that fit self to situation. Systematic exploration and reflection on random exploratory experiences move individuals from naive to knowledgeable as they learn how the world works. Attitudes of inquisitiveness dispose individuals to scan the environment to learn more about self and situations. Belief in the value of being open to new experiences and experimenting with possible selves and various roles prompts individuals to try new things and have adventures. Attitudes and dispositions that favor exploration and openness lead to experiences that increase competence in both self-knowledge and occupational information. Individuals who have explored the world beyond their own neighborhoods have more knowledge about their abilities, interests, and values as well as about the requirements, routines, and rewards of various occupations. This broader fund of information brings realism and objectivity to subsequent choices that will match self to situations.

A lack of career curiosity can lead to naiveté about the work world and inaccurate images of the self. This unrealism can be addressed by career interventions designed to provide information. Career counseling interventions in general—especially those involving test interpretation and occupational information—help people learn about themselves and the work world. Career unrealism is addressed, in particular, by interventions such as clarifying values, discussing extrinsic versus intrinsic rewards, engaging in job simulations, shadowing workers, practicing goal setting, learning how to explore, reading occupational pamphlets, working part-time jobs, and volunteering at community institutions. Teaching clients how to use Holland's RIASEC hexagon is an important intervention in its own right because it gives individuals a schema for organizing and remembering the facts found and the conclusion drawn from their exploration (both intended such as systematic information seeking and unintended such as exploratory experiences that occur in classrooms, on playing fields, and during trips). Once individuals form occupational daydreams and envision possible selves, they usually wonder if they can realize their aspirations.

Career Confidence   The fourth and final dimension of career adaptability is confidence. Self-confidence denotes the anticipation of success in encountering challenges and overcoming obstacles (Rosenberg, 1989). Career choices require solving complex problems. It takes confidence to do what is required to master these problems. The fundamental role of confidence in constructing careers is reflected in the extensive scholarship on self-esteem, self-efficacy, and encouragement in theories of vocational development. In career construction theory, confidence denotes feelings of self-efficacy concerning the individual's ability to successfully execute a course of action needed to make and implement suitable educational and vocational choices. Career confidence arises from solving problems encountered in daily activities such as household chores, schoolwork, and hobbies. Moreover, recognizing that he or she can be useful and productive at these tasks increases feelings of self-acceptance and self-worth. Broader exploratory experiences reinforce the confidence to try more things. Individuals who have been sheltered or excluded from certain categories of experience (e.g., math and science) find it difficult to be confident in approaching those activities and, consequently, will be less interested in occupations that require skill at those activities. Mistaken beliefs about social roles, gender, and race often produce internal and external barriers that inhibit the development of confidence.

A lack of career confidence can result in career inhibition that thwarts actualizing roles and achieving goals. Career counseling interventions, in general, build self-confidence through the relationship dimension of counseling. A working alliance with a counselor enhances the client's self-acceptance and self-regard. Career inhibition is addressed, in particular, by interventions designed to increase feelings of confidence (Dinkmeyer & Dreikurs, 1963) and self-efficacy (Betz & Schifano, 2000) through role modeling, success acknowledgment, encouragement, anxiety reduction, and problem-solving training. These interventions create a sense in individuals that they are good enough to deal with the problems posed by life, teach them to focus on *what* they are doing more than on *how* they are doing, increase the courage to try when the outcome is in doubt, and promote skill at problem solving. These coping attitudes, beliefs, and competencies strengthen career confidence and lead directly to engaging and mastering vocational development tasks, occupational transitions, and personal traumas.

PROFILES OF CAREER ADAPTABILITY

In theory, adolescents should approach the tasks of the exploration stage with a concern for the future, a sense of control over it, the curiosity to experiment with possible selves and explore social opportunities, and the confidence to engage in designing their occupational future and executing plans to make it real. In reality, development along the four dimensions of adaptability progresses at different rates, with possible fixations and regressions. Delays within or disequilibrium among the four developmental lines produces problems in crystallizing career preferences and specifying occupational choices, problems that career counselors diagnose as indifference, indecision, unrealism, and inhibition. Moderate disharmony in the development of the four dimensions of adaptability produces individual differences in career choice readiness and explains variant patterns of development. Strong disharmony produces deviant patterns of development. Accordingly, comparing development among the four dimensions is a useful way to assess career adaptability and to understand the antecedents of vocational decision-making difficulties and work adjustment problems. More importantly, it provides a counseling plan with specific goals and associated strategies. For example, if a client shows indifference and lacks career concern, he or she may benefit from interventions that prompt anxiety about the future and then address this anxiety by exercises and interactions that foster planful attitudes, planning competencies, and preparatory behaviors (e.g., see Table 3.2, row 1). In contrast, if a client has a strong sense of concern and control, yet seems unrealistic or unknowledgeable, he or she may benefit more from interventions that foster career curiosity in the form of inquisitive attitudes, exploration competencies, and information-seeking behaviors (e.g., see Table 3.2, row 3).

The schema for assessing career adaptability, as diagramed in Table 3.2, arranges the four dimensions into a structural model that can be used to recognize individual differences in the readiness and resources for making and implementing choices. In applying the model to comprehend the career adaptability of an individual, it is best to use a structured interview (Savickas, 2000). Using the schema outlined in Table 3.2 as a template through which to hear a client's career stories permits a counselor to assess that client's adaptability and, if indicated, offer the client a developmental plan to increase adaptive resources and readiness.

While it is best to assess career adaptability by structured interview, it can also be assessed for purposes of group counseling and career education by instruments such as the Career Maturity Inventory (Crites & Savickas, 1996), which measures attitudes toward career decision making; the Career Development Inventory (Savickas & Hartung, 1996), which measures attitudes toward career planning and exploration, as well as information about occupations and skill at matching people to jobs; the Career Decision-Making Self-Efficacy Scale (Betz & Taylor, 1994), which measures self-confidence about engaging in the tasks of making a career choice; and the Career Beliefs Inventory (Krumboltz & Vosvick, 1996), which surveys conceptions about career construction. Whatever assessment technique is used, the counselor will have some idea of how the client engages vocational development tasks and occupational transitions, a necessary complement to understanding the client's vocational personality. The counselor should next attend to why the client has encountered a writer's block in authoring the next chapter in her or his career story.

LIFE THEMES

The narrative component of career construction theory addresses the subject matter of work life and focuses on the *why* of vocational behavior. Career stories reveal the themes that individuals use to make meaningful choices and adjust to work roles. By dealing with the *why* of a career, along with the *what* and *how*, career construction seeks to be comprehensive in its purview. Although the content and process of careers are both important, studying vocational personality and career adaptability as separate variables misses the dynamics of the open system that cuts across self-organization (i.e., personality) and self-extension (i.e., adaptability) to integrate them into a self-defined whole. The essential meaning of career and the dynamics of its construction are revealed in self-defining stories about the tasks, transitions, and traumas an individual has faced. In chronicling the recursive interplay between self and society, career stories explain why individuals make the choices that they do and the private meaning that guides these choices. They tell how the self of yesterday became the self of today and will become the self of tomorrow. Thus, career tells the story of an individual's dispositional continuity and psychosocial change. From these prototypical stories about work life, counselors attempt to comprehend the motivation and meaning (the why) that constructs careers.

It is critical that neither the counselor nor the client view the stories as determining the future; instead, they should view storying as an active attempt at making meaning and shaping the future. The stories guide adaptation by evaluating opportunities and constraints as well as by using vocational personality traits to address developmental tasks, occupational transitions, and personal traumas. In telling their stories, clients are constructing a possible future. Clients seem to tell counselors the stories that they themselves need to hear because, from all their available stories, they narrate those stories that support current goals and inspire action. Rather than remembering, individuals reconstruct the past so that prior events support current choices and lay the groundwork for future moves (Josselson, 2000). This is an instance, not of the present taking lessons from the past, but of the past taking lessons from the present, reshaping itself to fit current needs. This narrative truth may differ from historical truth because it fictionalizes the past. In so doing, it preserves continuity and coherence in the face of change and allows the person to meet that change with fidelity and flexibility.

Unlike the RIASEC types and adaptability dimensions, career stories fully contextualize the self in time, place, and role. Career stories express the uniqueness of an individual in her or his particular context. Furthermore, the separate career stories told by an individual are unified by integrative themes that arrange the discrete experiences of work life into a plot. By consciously organizing and binding together these discrete experiences, a unifying life theme patterns lived experience with a meaningful coherence and long-term continuity. That pattern becomes a fundamental and essential way of being because it provides a way for individuals to see themselves and what is important in the world. Thus, in career construction theory, pattern is the primary unit of meaning.

IDENTIFYING LIFE THEMES IN CAREER STORIES

In attempting to discern the pattern while listening to clients' career stories, counselors can become disoriented by the numerous particulars of a life. To prevent becoming confused by a client's complexities and contradictions, counselors listen not for the facts but for the glue that holds the facts together as they try to hear the theme or secret that makes a whole of the life. Arranging the seemingly random actions and incidents reported in career stories into a plot can be done in many ways. Career construction theory proposes for this purpose that the counselor listen for the quintessence of the stories a client tells. I approach this task by assuming that the archetypal theme of career construction involves turning a personal preoccupation into a public occupation. As I listen to a client narrate his or her stories, I concentrate on identifying and understanding his or her paradigm for turning essence into interest, tension into intention, and obsession into profession.

I prefer the definition of a life theme provided by Csikszentmihalyi and Beattie (1979): "A life theme consists of a problem or a set of problems which a person wishes to solve above everything else and the means the person finds to achieve a solution" (p. 48). For me, the problem is the preoccupation, and the solution, at least in the work domain, is the occupation. Often, clients' preoccupations are unpleasant, involving difficulty and distress. Yet, some clients' preoccupations are pleasant, involving ease and enjoyment. Thus, when I use the word *problem*, I mean the content of a preoccupation—whether positive or negative—that individuals must address in solving themselves. Career construction revolves around turning a personal problem into a public strength and then even a social contribution. In counseling for career construction, the essential activity entails articulating the preoccupation and discussing possible solutions in the form of occupations. This involves helping a client to construct interests (Kitson, 1942). I believe a counselor should be more skilled at creating interests than at assessing interests with inventories. Many times counselors need to help clients create interest by showing them how a few occupations and avocations directly address their preoccupation and in so doing may resolve their problems. The view that interests originate as solutions to problems is not new. Early in the history of vocational guidance, Carter (1940) concluded that interests are "solutions to the problems of growing up" (p. 187). Interest, in proposing a path from preoccupation to occupation, strives to maintain an individual's integrity by charting strategies for survival and, it is hoped, integrative adaptation and optimal development—the very stuff of life themes.

Common understanding of life themes abounds in our culture. Consider, for example, the following four familiar themes: the sickly child who becomes a champion bodybuilder, the stuttering child who becomes a network news anchor, the shy child who becomes an actor, and the poor child who grows up to be wealthy. These well-known themes express cultural scripts that tell how an individual moves from weakness to strength, from timidity to confidence, from inhibition to expressiveness, and from poverty to affluence. I have never attempted to catalogue life themes, because this would defeat the very purpose of appreciating an individual's unique story. Nevertheless, at the risk of turning this idiographic concept into a nomothetic catalogue, curious readers may wish to review the list of 34 themes identified in a Gallup study of two million people (Buckingham & Clifton, 2001).

Life themes are also about *mattering*. Counseling for career construction aims to help clients understand how their life project matters to themselves and to other people. In career construction theory, the theme is what matters in the life story. It consists of what is at stake in that person's life. On the one hand, the theme matters to individuals in that it gives meaning and purpose to their work. It makes them care about what they do. On the other hand, what they do and contribute to society matters to other people. The belief that what they do matters to others is important to self-concept (Marshall, 2001). Recognition from significant others consolidates identity and heightens the sense of belonging. Josselson (1994) views this mattering as a relational component of identity—a sense of social meaning and relatedness.

COMPARING PERSONALITY TYPES TO LIFE THEMES

It may be worthwhile to compare life themes to vocational personality types because their differences may not be self-evident. The essential difference between the two is that themes focus on uniqueness, whereas types focus on similarity. For example, RIASEC codes represent an individual's similarity to ideal prototypes. A code of RI means that the individual most resembles the Realistic type and next most resembles the Investigative type. In comparison, career stories portray individuals' unique conceptions of their personalities from their own point of view. The narrative lines are not composed of personality traits; instead, lines of need, purpose, and intention draw the self-portrait. Themes reveal why an individual is unique. Thus, objective types focus on *what* interests and abilities individuals possess, whereas subjective themes focus on *why* these characteristics matter. While types have remarkable stability, life themes may be reconstructed to open new avenues of awareness and understanding. Finally, vocational personality theories concentrate on congruence, that is, fitting workers to work to produce success and satisfaction, whereas life theme theories focus on mattering, that is, enabling the workers to use work to produce significance and validation.

Types and themes are complementary perspectives, the objective and subjective, that should be integrated, along with the third perspective of adaptability, in comprehensively understanding an individual's efforts to cooperate with and contribute to society. While career interventions may be conducted from any one of these three perspectives, intervention produces better outcomes when all three perspectives are used together (Savickas, 1996). Multiple perspectives allow a counselor to view the client more completely and thus be more useful to that client. The following case study illustrates the advantages of taking, in turn, all three perspectives on a client's vocational behavior and career construction.

CASE STUDY

I begin counseling for career construction by interviewing a client using a uniform set of questions. The Career Style Interview (Savickas, 1989) is designed to elicit self-defining stories that allow counselors to identify the style that individuals impose on their characters and to understand the resulting thematic unity. Data from a Career Style Interview also clearly manifest a client's vocational personality type and career adaptability, as I have shown in several brief case studies (Savickas, 1988, 1995a, 1995b, 1997, 1998). I now present a more complete case study, first using the results of a Career Style Interview to assess vocational personality type, career adaptability, and life theme and then describing how I used this assessment in counseling to help the client narrate a livable career story that enabled her to make educational and vocational choices and enact roles that were meaningful to her and mattered to others.

MEETING ELAINE

When I first met Elaine, she was a 20-year-old, full-time college student who said that she could not decide on a major, although her mother urged her to declare premed. She lived at home and commuted to campus each day. She guessed she would major in premed and go on to medical school but she was unsure of this right now. She reported that she had been to her college counseling center, yet now feels more undecided after working with a counselor there. She wants me to help her explore whether medicine is the right choice for her. She has just completed the fall semester of her sophomore year and in the spring must declare her major. She sometimes thinks engineering would be good for her, and she took an engineering class during the fall semester. She thought that maybe chemical engineering would be good, but civil engineering is easier. She has requested information from another college that has better integrated computers into its chemical engineering curriculum. She was attracted by computers and liked the idea that if she transferred to that college, she could live in a dorm. I asked her the questions in the Career Style Interview and recorded her responses on the form.

CAREER STYLE INTERVIEW WITH ELAINE

In response to the first question concerning how I could be useful to her, Elaine responded that she did not know why she could not choose a major, she needed help in making a choice, and she wondered whether medicine would be a good choice for her. Next, I asked Elaine to identify and describe three of her role models. She stated that *Ann of Green Gables* has spirit and a temper, set goals and went after them, did what she wanted, has integrity, and has fun. The heroine in the book *Wrinkle in Time* led her friends in a showdown against creatures trying to take over their minds. She thought of ways to stick together and fight the creatures. Laura, in the book *Little House on the Prairie* had wild ideas of things to do and enjoyed competing with and outdoing others. To assess preferred environments, I asked Elaine about favorite magazines, books, and television shows. She likes *Vogue* because it is about fashion, *BusinessWeek* because it is about advertising campaigns, and *Details* because it is about men's clothing. Her favorite television show is *Laverne and Shirley* because they do things off the norm without getting into trouble. Her favorite book is *The Search of Mary Kay Malloy*, which tells the story of an Irish girl and her voyage to America by herself. In response to questions about her hobbies and leisure activities, Elaine said that she likes to go to the movies, shop in thrift stores for fashionable clothes, and talk to people. She also enjoys cross-stitch sewing while watching television because she feels that she is not wasting time and can have a finished product. She also likes to sew because she can make what she wants, not what other people have. Elaine reported having two favorite sayings. The first, by Curious George, was, "I am curious about things." The second was, "Do it well." By "do it well," her parents meant nearly perfectly and they checked it. Do it wrong and you have to redo it until it is right. When asked about high school subjects, Elaine responded that she liked math because you learn the right way to do things and to problem solve for yourself. She hated history and geography because she had to memorize unimportant facts and dates.

Nearing the end of the Career Style Interview, I asked Elaine to report three early recollections, and, after she had done so, I asked her to give each story a headline or title. The three stories with their headlines were:

1. *Little girl annoyed because she must sit still:* Going to Disneyland with grand-parents and uncle and his girlfriend. I was in the back of the camper trying to sing and dance for my grandmother. She told me to sit down so I would not get hurt. I got on uncle's girlfriend's nerves by trying to talk to her. Tried to talk but she did not think I should move around at the same time.
2. *Playful girl dreads speaking with relatives:* I remember a family reunion at Grandma's (the other one). I was playing an old corn thing with my cousin. I did not know who most of the people were. Grandma made me stop play-ing and said I had to talk to the people because they knew who I was. Grandma said, "You kids, behave."
3. *Mischievous child has fun at first or dog plan fails:* This family that my parents met in England came to visit. I teased their son. He made fun of the curlers in my hair. The boy was chasing me all over the yard. So I ran by my dog where the boy could not get me but he threw a stick and hit me in the eye. His mother and my mother took me in the bedroom and cleaned my eye.

To complete the Career Style Interview, I asked Elaine to tell me the part of her life story that is important to her current career problem. She said:

> I was always undecided. In the second grade, I went to get new shoes. After I wore them to school one day, I would take them back and get a different pair. The boy who sat next to me thought I was rich because I had so many pairs of shoes but it was because I could not decide.

Elaine's Vocational Personality, Career Adaptability, and Life Themes

Career construction theory focuses on stories because it views language as the ef-ficient means for building careers out of complex social interactions. In those re-lationships, language and stories are construction tools for making meaning. Storytelling crystallizes what clients think of themselves. Many clients laugh and cry while telling their stories because they see their life themes emerge in the space between client and counselor. It is important that counselors help clients understand the implications of what they have said in telling their stories. This means relating the theme to the problems posed in the beginning of the inter-view. It is also best to use the clients' most compelling metaphors and the words that they have used repeatedly. At the same time, constructivist counseling ex-pands the language that a client has available to make meaning out of experience. It offers clients the logical language of the RIASEC model as well as the dramatic language of stories and the symbolic language of poetry. Helping clients to en-large their vocabulary of self increases their ability to story their experience and to understand and communicate who they are and what they seek.

Every counselor can read Elaine's stories from the perspective of his or her fa-vorite career theory. Herein, I demonstrate my interpretive routine. In particular, I highlight a few representative scenes in Elaine's story to illustrate six tricks of the trade in counseling for career construction. First, I begin to make sense of Elaine's stories by reviewing how she wants to use the counseling experience. Her goals frame the perspective from which to view her stories. In response to my introductory question—"How can I be useful to you in constructing your career?"—Elaine had said that she did not know why she cannot choose a major, she would like help in making a choice, and she wanted to discuss whether medicine would be a good fit for her. This gives us two points of reference. She wants the counselor to help her understand why she cannot choose as well as to move her closer to making a choice, whether it be medicine or something else. Thus, in reviewing her career stories, I attend to her experiences with decision making. I am particularly interested in how decision making relates to her life themes. I also note that in terms of career adaptability, she may benefit from increasing her sense of career control.

Second, I look for the verbs in her early recollections. I start with the first verb in the first story, having learned that this is a particularly important form of movement for the client. In Elaine's first recollection, the first verb is "going." To me, this means that she wants to move, to be on the go, and to travel. I then look in the remaining stories for other evidence to support this idea. I note the phrases "moving around" and "dancing" in the first recollection, and I find further support in her favorite book, which tells the story of a girl's journey to another country. Other verbs in her early recollections stand out by their repetition. "Playing" and "singing" seem important to her. She is enthusiastic about life. Also "try" appears three times in the first recollection, suggesting that she is industrious and persistent in pursuing difficult goals. "Talking" appears in the first two recollections, so she likes to communicate. And finally, in the first two recollections, adult women tell her to sit down and stop playing. I start to see the tension in her life between wanting to be on the go and being told to sit still. There is much more in her stories, but this is enough to get started. It is important to remember that these memories are not necessarily reasons for her behavior; she has constructed them to reflect her current struggle. From the many available stories, each reflecting the same theme, clients tell those that they themselves need to hear.

Third, I look at the headlines Elaine had composed for each of her three recollections. These headlines are rhetorical compressions that express the gist of her story. From Elaine's point of view, she is a "little girl" who is annoyed because powerful others stop her from enthusiastically pursuing her dreams. They want her to stay put where they place her, and she dreads talking to them about her needs. She knows that she can be mischievous and irritate them, yet understands that this negative plan will fail in the long run. It is worthwhile to read these plot lines in two ways. On the one hand, they reveal more about the life theme that will shape her career. On the other hand, they indicate in the here and now the problem she wants to work on during counseling and what she expects from her counselor. She wants a counselor to encourage her movement and her gusto for life, teach her to speak up for herself, and devise a plan that will not fail.

Fourth, I want to understand how Elaine is attempting to solve her problems in constructing a career and how occupations can help her actively master the problems she faces. I seek to draw the line from preoccupation to occupation that is implicit in her stories, and that is the essence of the life theme. To do this, I compare the first early recollection to her role models. The early recollection portrays the pain and problem while the role models propose a tentative solution and display ways to pursue it. In Elaine's case, the first story is about a playful girl being told to sit still and do as she is told. This resonates to her current dilemma—sitting still as her mother tells her to major in premed. The sitting still can be her metaphor for indecision. To see the plan she has in mind, I look to whom she has chosen as models for self-design because they have solved the very problems that she herself now faces. How Elaine describes her role models reveals core elements in her self-concept and articulates goals that she has set for herself. In Elaine's stories, the key figures model spirit, enthusiasm, playfulness, goals, competitiveness, persistence, temper, fighting wrong-headed authority, and enlisting compatriots in these battles. These qualities are reaffirmed in her other stories. She is not frightened by wild ideas and doing things off the norm as long as they are fun and do not get her into trouble. She is curious and definitely a problem solver. She is neat and likes to do things well. She enjoys fashion, but maybe in a conventional and businesslike way.

Fifth, I profile Elaine's career adaptability. After reviewing the coping strategies in her stories, I concluded that she is deeply concerned about the future, shows curiosity about it, and could use a little more confidence in her ability to make it happen—but this is due more to perfectionistic tendencies than to a lack of self-esteem. The major deficiency in the profile is the absence of strong career control. Indecision is her try at wrestling her mind away from powerful others who want to make it up for her. Ownership of her career is at stake, and she is ready to fight for it now. She just needs a plan and some encouragement. I start by trying to help Elaine view her indecision as a strength, not a weakness. It is her way of fighting powerful creatures who are trying to control her career.

Sixth, I appraise Elaine's vocational personality. I do this by looking at her stories through the lens of Holland's RIASEC hexagon. Looking through the six-sided lens, I see that she most resembles the Investigative type (a curious problem solver who likes math and science). She next most resembles the Conventional type (likes teams, partners, caution, cleanliness, norms). In the middle falls resemblance to the Social type (talking, playing with others, taking care of other people). I see less resemblance to the Artistic and Enterprising types, although liking travel, fashion, and adventure suggests their presence. These may represent latent potentials that she will actualize in the future. I see the least resemblance to the Realistic type; actually, I see none but there certainly must be a little there. The lack of Realistic characteristics in her career stories seems strange for someone interested in civil engineering (code IRE); and even medicine has Realistic in its code of ISR.

Having gone through my six-step interpretive routine in a systematic manner, I then summarize my conclusions and prepare to meet the client by doing two final things—crafting a success formula and composing a life portrait. I aim to write a first draft of a success formula that the client and I will edit together until the client finds it accurate and inspiring. Success formulas are an integral part of Haldane's (1975) technique for articulating dependable strengths. I recommend his books and materials highly. To help counselors write success formulas, I devised a handout (Savickas, 1989, p. 312) that lists a set of activities for each of the six RIASEC types. In writing a success formula for Elaine, I selected one phrase each from the three lists that coincide with the RIASEC types that Elaine most resembles (i.e., ICS). From Investigative, I selected *solve problems*; from Conventional, I selected *be part of a team*; and from Social, I selected *help others*. The first draft of her success formula then became: *You feel happy and successful when you are a part of a team that helps people solve problems.* It could just as easily been: *You feel happy and successful when you use logic to provide advice about how to organize things.*

I then move from the success formula to a more comprehensive portrait of the client (Lawrence-Lightfoot & Davis, 1997). I try to draw a life portrait that captures a client's essential character yet lacks the finishing touches that the client must add during counseling. I aim for an honest portrayal of a client's life as a work in progress, a life that is simultaneously predetermined and unpredictable. The portrait includes tentative answers to implicit questions such as, "Who am I?" "What is my quest?" and "How can I grow and flourish?" It also addresses the four questions listed in column one of Table 3.2. I emphasize and repeat the life theme, affirming its significance and validity. Then I use the life theme to unite the meaning of the client's separate career stories into a narrative structure that integrates contradictory views, baffling behaviors, and inconsistent episodes. Most of all, I illuminate the secret that makes the client's life whole. By clarifying what is at stake and the choices to be made, the life portrait will enhance the client's ability to decide. After I have sketched a portrayal that includes a client's personality type, career adaptability, and life themes, I am ready to engage the client in a conversation about the what, how, and why of his or her career.

I start by reviewing the client's response to my opening inquiry about how counseling might be useful to him or her. Then I present the life portrait. I always present the portrait in a way that highlights its developmental trajectory, especially the movement from problem to strength so that clients feel their own movement from tension to intention. In so doing, I act as a storyteller in focusing on dramatic movements, always talking about where the client is headed and asserting the client's agency in directing this movement. Occasionally, I pause to act more like a poet in bringing important details into sharp focus by highlighting vivid expressions of the self in a narrative moment. This is analogous to pausing the movie of the client's life to study a single frame or photograph. These pauses in the action are used to reconstruct old meanings in a way that creates new meanings and opens new avenues of movement. I always restate the obvious in the life portrait in candid language because what is not acknowledged grows bigger than it needs to be. As I present a portrait to the client, I remain curious, never certain. Several times I ask the client if I understand things accurately by inquiring, "What am I missing?" The portrait must be presented as a tentative sketch and, in the end, the validity of my portrayal of a client is arbitrated by its utility to that client.

With Elaine, I started our second meeting by asking her if she had any additional thoughts about her responses during the Career Style Interview or if there were any things she wished to add or clarify. Although she did not, many clients do because they continue to think about the questions and conversation in the hours following the first session. I then reminded her of what she had said in response to my inquiry about how I could be useful to her. Elaine had said that she did not know why she cannot choose a major and she would like help in making a choice. She also had mentioned that she wanted to discuss whether medicine would be a good field for her. This gives us three points of reference in viewing her life portrait: why she cannot choose (i.e., career adaptability), how good a fit is medicine (i.e., vocational personality type), and how to move toward making a choice (i.e., life themes).

I then depicted her life theme as fighting powerful creatures who are trying to steal her mind or, in this particular instance, her career. She is rebelling by sitting still and refusing to decide in their favor while she marshals personal resources and social support to make her own choice. I paused to get her reaction and revisions. We explored her feelings about the portrait, because affect helps to create meaning. We also looked at her strengths, especially the personal characteristics of which she was most proud. We then discussed how the problems she currently faced were really the best solutions that she could come up with so far. For example, I helped Elaine to reconstruct her indecision from being a problem to being the best solution she has found for trying to fight off the creatures who are stealing her career by making her sit still for what they want. In this way, I attempted to help her use language, especially her own favorite metaphors and verbs, as a means of controlling the situation and increasing feelings of agency.

Having thus addressed Elaine's first concern—understanding why she cannot make a decision about her academic major—we moved to her second question— how well a career in medicine would suit her. To address this question, we considered her vocational personality and interests, especially how she proposed to use the world to become more whole. Following career construction theory, I sought to create and confirm interests, not diagnose them, by concentrating on the inner means and outer ways that she could use to position herself in society. We discussed the interests she had formed as being solutions to her problems in growing up. She wants to be independent and on the go, use logic to solve problems, and work as a part of a team. I presented the two success formula variations that I drafted for her. She revised them until she felt pleased with the following success formula: *I feel happy and successful when I am part of a team that uses logic to help people by providing advice about how to solve their problems in an organized way.* Medicine does not seem to fit her plot as well as some other fields. Medicine has a Holland code of ISR, and she does not strongly resemble the Social or the Realistic types. Certainly, she could do medicine, but it may not fully incorporate her self-concept.

We then conversed about her desire for a career in which she could use logic to solve structured problems and be part of a team (IC), not solve the ambiguous, physical problems that patients routinely present to their physicians. I commented that if she were to become a physician, she would probably be attracted to a specialty such as radiology. We also talked about whether the Realistic colleagues and aspects of engineering jobs really appeal to her. We talked about exploring majors in computer science, mathematics, and finance. Next we looked in the *Dictionary of Holland Occupational Code* (Gottfredson & Holland, 1996) to identify occupations that fit her code and found two listed under ICS (immunohematologist and packing engineer) and eight listed under CIS (computer security coordinator, computer security specialist, data processing auditor, foreign clerk, ophthalmic photographer, ophthalmic technician, polygraph examiner, and stress test technician). Most of all, we talked about discovering a way in which she could flourish and places where self-definition and self-determination would be possible.

Having addressed, to her satisfaction, the issue of how well medicine suited her and which other fields merit exploration, we addressed her third question, which was how to move forward toward choosing a major. We discussed ways forward from where she now sits, including alternative resolutions and possible selves. Her indecision is not a weakness; it reflects a potential strength that must blossom, in her case, probably into a talent for solving problems and a lifelong decisiveness. That life must be full of movement, not sitting. I explained that development arises from activity and overcoming difficulties met in the world. We then engaged in a conversation about self-construction activities that might make her feel more whole and move her closer to being the person she wanted to be, such as working at a summer job away from home, living in a college dormitory, taking a workshop on assertiveness, and meeting with a counselor to discuss family issues. She was encouraged by our conversation and felt that looking back over her life had given her the ability to move forward and the resolve to do so. We agreed to talk on the phone in the middle of the next semester and meet again during the summer.

When she visited again, the next summer, Elaine reported that she had taken a continuing education course in assertiveness, worked with a college counselor for five sessions to improve her relationship with her parents and reduce her perfectionism, lived away from home while working a summer job as a ticket-taker at an amusement park, and completed elective courses in computer science and accounting. She was leaning toward declaring a major in computer science but wondered if engineering would be a better fit for her. Thinking that she would prefer to explore this ambivalence in an organized way, I invited her to complete the Incorporation Worksheet (Savickas, 1980). The worksheet lists 12 adjectives, two for each of the six RIASEC types. A client rates three elements, from one to seven, on each of the 12 adjectives. The first two elements are two different occupations being considered, and the third element is the self. As we sat together, Elaine rated on a seven-point scale how well the 12 adjectives describe first a computer specialist, then an engineer, and finally herself. The ratings show her construction of the three elements. Although her perceptions may be inaccurate when compared to objective occupational information and personality inventories, they reflect the conceptions that guide her behavior. If the ratings had seemed grossly inaccurate, we would have discussed them.

In examining her ratings, we first determined a RIASEC code for each of the three elements: ICA for computer specialist, IRC for engineer, and ICS for herself. In terms of RIASEC types, there was a better fit between her and computing than between her and engineering. We then examined how well each occupation incorporated her self-concept by calculating and summing differences between the rating for the two comparisons. The difference between self and computing was 18; the difference between self and engineering was 26. Obviously, Elaine perceived computer science as better incorporating her self-concept. She enjoyed this exercise and felt good about the conclusion she had drawn—to major in computer science.

I next saw Elaine after she graduated with a major in computer science. She told me how much she had enjoyed her courses but detested the sexism exhibited by many of her instructors. To combat their bias, she had organized a club for females who were majoring in computer science. She was proud of what they had achieved in combating sexism. She was even more proud of the occupational position that she had recently secured. In two weeks she would begin a job as a computer systems analyst in a position that required traveling with a team of colleagues throughout the United States to regional branches of a national firm where she would solve their computer problems. Furthermore, Elaine told me that she and her mother were now "friends" and that her mother was proud of her accomplishments and pleased with her prospects. Elaine looked forward to now becoming a woman on the go, one encouraged by a mother who tells her not to sit still. She glowed as she told me how she had used the things that we had talked about to help her roommates and friends make career choices.

SUMMARY

In this chapter, I have tried to convey the excitement that attends helping people construct their careers. Counselors are privileged to be able to invite clients into a safe space wherein they can examine their vocational personalities, career adaptability, and life themes and then edit their narratives to be more livable and to open new avenues of movement. The modern dichotomies between personal and career counseling and between self and society have become integrated in postmodern conceptions of a self that is formed, maintained, and revised through interpersonal relationships and work roles, and which evolves during a life course of contribution to and cooperation with a community. Occupations offer a way forward for individuals who live in a postindustrial society that abjures stable moral meanings and fragments identities. Career offers individuals a way to construct, test, and implement a stable self by choosing disciplined activities and accepting their obligations. Counseling for career construction encourages individuals to use work and other life roles to become who they are and live the lives they have imagined. In so doing, they will become people that they themselves like and that others cherish.

REFERENCES

Adkins, W. R. (1970). Life skills: Structured counseling for the disadvantaged. *Personnel and Guidance Journal, 49,* 108–116.

Betz, N. E. (2000). Self-efficacy theory as a basis for career assessment. *Journal of Career Assessment, 8,* 205–222.

Betz, N. E., & Schifano, R. S. (2000). Evaluation of an intervention to increase realistic self-efficacy and interests in college women. *Journal of Vocational Behavior, 56,* 35–52.

Betz, N. E., & Taylor, K. M. (1994). *Career Decision-Making Self-Efficacy Scale manual.* Columbus: Ohio State University, Department of Psychology.

Blustein, D. L., & Flum, H. (1999). A self-determination perspective of interests and exploration in career development. In M. L. Savickas & A. R. Spokane (Eds.), *Vocational interests: Meaning, measurement, and counseling use* (pp. 345–368). Palo Alto, CA: Davies-Black.

Buckingham, M., & Clifton, D. (2001). *Now, discover your strengths.* Available from http://www.gallupjournal.com/sfCenter.

Carter, H. D. (1940). The development of vocational attitudes. *Journal of Consulting Psychology, 4,* 185–191.

Collin, A. (1997). Career in context. *British Journal of Guidance and Counselling, 25,* 435–446.

Crites, J. O., & Savickas, M. L. (1996). Revision of the Career Maturity Inventory. *Journal of Career Assessment, 4,* 131–138.

Csikszentmihalyi, M., & Beattie, O. V. (1979). Life themes: A theoretical and empirical exploration of their origins and effects. *Journal of Humanistic Psychology, 19,* 45–63.

Dinkmeyer, D. C., & Dreikurs, R. (1963). *Encouraging children to learn: The encouragement process.* Upper Saddle River, NJ: Prentice-Hall.

Gottfredson, G. D., & Holland, J. L. (1996). *Dictionary of Holland occupational codes* (3rd ed.). Odessa, FL: Psychological Assessment Resources.

Guichard, J., & Cassar, O. (1998). Social fields, habitus and cognitive schemes: Study streams and categorisation of occupations. *Revue Internatiale de Psychologie Sociale, 1,* 123–145.

Haldane, B. (1975). *How to make a habit of success.* Washington, DC: Acropolis Books.

Hogan, J., & Holland, B. (2003). Using theory to evaluate personality and job-performance relations: A socioanalytic perspective. *Journal of Applied Psychology, 88,* 100–112.

Hogan, R. (1983). A socioanalytic theory of personality. In M. Page (Ed.), *Nebraska Symposium on Motivation 1982: Personality-current theory and research* (pp. 55–89). Lincoln: University of Nebraska Press.

Holland, J. L. (1997). *Making vocational choices: A theory of vocational personalities and work environments* (3rd ed.). Odessa, FL: Psychological Assessment Resources.

Jarvis, P., & Richardt, J. (2001). *The Real Game series: Bringing real life to career development.* New Brunswick, Canada: National Work/Life Center.

Josselson, R. (1994). Identity and relatedness in the life cycle. In H. A. Bosma, T. L. G. Graafsman, H. D. Grotevant, & D. J. De Levita (Eds.), *Identity and development: An interdisciplinary approach* (pp. 81–102). Thousand Oaks, CA: Sage.

Josselson, R. (2000). Stability and change in early memories over 22 years: Themes, variations, and cadenzas. *Bulletin of the Menninger Clinic, 64,* 462–481.

Kalleberg, A. L., Reynolds, J., & Marsden, P. V. (2003). Externalizing employment: Flexible staffing arrangements in US organizations. *Social Science Research, 32,* 525–552.

Katz, M. R. (1969). Can computers make guidance decisions for students? *College Board Review, 72.*

Kitson, H. D. (1942). Creating vocational interests. *Occupations, 20,* 567–571.

Krumboltz, J. D., & Vosvick, M. A. (1996). Career assessment and the Career Beliefs Inventory. *Journal of Career Assessment, 4,* 345–361.

Lawrence-Lightfoot, S., & Davis, J. H. (1997). *The art and science of portraiture.* San Francisco: Jossey-Bass.

Lofquist, L. H., & Dawis, R. V. (1991). *Essentials of person-environment correspondence counseling.* Minneapolis: University of Minnesota Press.

Marshall, S. K. (2001). Do I matter? Construct validation of adolescents' perceived mattering to parents and friends. *Journal of Adolescence, 24,* 473–490.

Maw, I. L. (1982). The future autobiography: A longitudinal analysis. *Journal of College Student Personnel, 23,* 3–6.

McAdams, D. P. (1995). What do we know when we know a person? *Journal of Personality, 63,* 365–396.

Parsons, F. (1909). *Choosing a vocation.* Boston: Houghton Mifflin.

Richardson, M. S. (1993). Work in people's lives: A location for counseling psychologists. *Journal of Counseling Psychology, 40,* 425–433.

Rosenberg, M. (1989). *Society and the adolescent self-image* (Rev. ed.). Middletown, CT: Wesleyan University Press.

Savickas, M. L. (1980). Leisure in your career: Curriculum ideas for post-secondary school settings. In M. Haas (Ed.), *Expand your alternatives* (pp. 1–3). Washington, DC: National Vocational Guidance Association.

Savickas, M. L. (1988). An Adlerian view of the Publican's pilgrimage. *Career Development Quarterly, 36,* 211–217.

Savickas, M. L. (1989). Career-style assessment and counseling. In T. Sweeney (Ed.), *Adlerian counseling: A practical approach for a new decade* (3rd ed., pp. 289–320). Muncie, IN: Accelerated Development Press.

Savickas, M. L. (1991). Improving career time perspective. In D. Brown & L. Brooks (Eds.), *Techniques of career counseling* (pp. 236–249). Boston: Allyn & Bacon.

Savickas, M. L. (1995a). Constructivist counseling for career indecision. *Career Development Quarterly, 43,* 363–373.

Savickas, M. L. (1995b). Examining the personal meaning of inventoried interests during career counseling. *Journal of Career Assessment, 3,* 188–201.

Savickas, M. L. (1996). A framework for linking career theory and practice. In M. L. Savickas & W. B. Walsh (Eds.), *Handbook of career counseling theory and practice.* Palo Alto, CA: Davies-Black.

Savickas, M. L. (1997). The spirit in career counseling: Fostering self-completion through work. In D. P. Bloch & L. J. Richmond (Eds.), *Connections between spirit and work in career development: New approaches and practical perspectives* (pp. 3–25). Palo Alto, CA: Davies-Black.

Savickas, M. L. (1998). Career style assessment and counseling. In T. Sweeney (Ed.), *Adlerian counseling: A practitioner's approach* (4th ed., pp. 329–360). Philadelphia: Accelerated Development Press.

Savickas, M. L. (1999). The psychology of interests. In M. L. Savickas & A. R. Spokane (Eds.), *Vocational interests: Their meaning, measurement, and counseling use* (pp. 19–56). Palo Alto, CA: Davies-Black.

Savickas, M. L. (2000). Assessing career decision making. In E. Watkins & V. Campbell (Eds.), *Testing and assessment in counseling practice* (2nd ed., pp. 429–477). Hillsdale, NJ: Erlbaum.

Savickas, M. L. (2001). Toward a comprehensive theory of career development: Dispositions, concerns, and narratives. In F. T. L. Leong & A. Barak (Eds.), *Contemporary models in vocational psychology: A volume in honor of Samuel H. Osipow* (pp. 295–320). Mahwah, NJ: Erlbaum.

Savickas, M. L. (2002). Career construction: A developmental theory of vocational behavior. In D. Brown & Associates (Eds.), *Career choice and development* (4th ed., pp. 149–205). San Francisco: Jossey-Bass.

Savickas, M. L., & Hartung, P. J. (1996). The Career Development Inventory in review: Psychometric and research findings. *Journal of Career Assessment, 4,* 171–188.

Savickas, M. L., Silling, S. M., & Schwartz, S. (1984). Time perspective in career maturity and decision making. *Journal of Vocational Behavior, 25,* 258–269.

Super, D. E. (1951). Vocational adjustment: Implementing a self-concept. *Occupations, 30,* 88–92.

Super, D. E. (1953). A theory of vocational development. *American Psychologist, 8,* 185–190.

Super, D. E. (1955). The dimensions and measurement of vocational maturity. *Teachers College Record, 57,* 151–163.

Super, D. E. (1957). *The psychology of careers.* New York: Harper & Row.

Super, D. E. (1969). Vocational development theory. *Counseling Psychologist, 1,* 2–30.

Super, D. E. (1984). Career and life development. In D. Brown & L. Brooks (Eds.), *Career choice and development* (pp. 192–234). San Francisco: Jossey-Bass.

Super, D. E. (1990). A life-span, life-space approach to career development. In D. Brown, L. Brooks, & Associates (Eds.), *Career choice and development* (2nd ed., pp. 197–261). San Francisco: Jossey-Bass.

Whan, K. M., & Savickas, M. L. (1998). Effectiveness of a career time perspective intervention. *Journal of Vocational Behavior, 52,* 106–119.

CHAPTER 4

Applying Gottfredson's Theory of Circumscription and Compromise in Career Guidance and Counseling

Linda S. Gottfredson

AT THE BEGINNING of the twentieth century, 36% of workers were employed in farming, fishing, forestry, and other agricultural work, and only 4% in professional services (United States Census Office, 1902). By the beginning of the twenty-first century, only 2% of the workforce remained in agriculture, with 16% now in the professions and another 15% in management (U.S. Census Bureau, 2002). New technologies in transportation and communication have led to the proliferation of new kinds of work and made it easier for people and jobs to migrate around the nation, even the world.

The full menu of occupations and lifestyles that the modern world offers most individuals is thus far larger than it was a mere 100 years ago. At the same time, American society has tried to make opportunities more equally available to all individuals, regardless of gender, ethnicity, or class. While barriers remain, many have fallen in the past half-century. Both the wider variety of occupations and more equal access to them bespeak vastly expanded vocational options for young people.

But this expanded choice is a challenge, even a burden, for young people. The opportunity to choose is also the responsibility to choose and to choose wisely. Moreover, the occupation an individual holds is increasingly seen as the measure of who he or she is in society. It is no wonder that so many youngsters procrastinate or seem paralyzed by anxiety when required to make vocational decisions. Many just drift or settle for any job that comes their way.

The Theory of Circumscription and Compromise focuses on how young people gradually come to recognize and deal with, or fail to deal with, the array of vocational choices their society provides. After summarizing the theory, I use it to outline a career guidance and counseling system for facilitating growth and reducing risk during the school years. Although not elaborated here, the system can also be used to diagnose and remediate common vocational problems in adolescence and aid adults who wish to revisit their career choices.

THE THEORETICAL CHALLENGE

Imagine 1,000 newborns in their cribs. They know virtually nothing of either the outside world or of themselves, probably not even that the two are distinct. Ten years later, all will know a great deal about both. Within 20 years, all will have made many life-shaping decisions, often without realizing it. At 30, the 1,000 will have spread across a great variety of occupations and social landscapes.

Chance will have played a part in who ends up where, but the pattern of outcomes will hardly be random—or novel. Regardless of their own social origins, all 1,000 newborns will develop essentially the same view of occupations by adolescence. Like adults, they will distinguish occupations primarily along two dimensions—their masculinity-femininity and their overall social desirability (prestige level). They will also share common stereotypes about the personalities of different kinds of workers—accountants versus artists, engineers versus teachers, and so on. Despite their similar perceptions, their occupational aspirations will nonetheless reproduce most of the class and gender differences of the parent generation: Girls will aspire mostly to "women's" work, boys to "men's" work, and lower class youngsters to lower level jobs than their higher social class peers. And yet, not even siblings will be peas in a pod, because their preferred vocational selves and life paths tend to differ, sometimes dramatically (Dunn & Plomin, 1990). As adolescents, perhaps all 1,000 newborns will report wanting jobs in which they can perform the kinds of tasks that interest them, but many will not be able to articulate just what their interests are. Few will know what workers actually do on the job, even in the occupations to which they aspire. Some will be forced to take jobs that are not consistent with their interests, but many will do so by choice.

What explains this somewhat puzzling pattern of aspirations, of knowledge and ignorance, at the threshold of adulthood? The circumscription and compromise theory suggests that four developmental processes are key to understanding it. Each presents different risks that, as discussed later, can be minimized to enhance career development.

THE THEORY: KEY DEVELOPMENTAL PROCESSES, PRODUCTS, AND STAGES

Most vocational theories, including this one, view vocational choice as a matching process, that is, as individuals seeking occupations that satisfy their interests and goals and for which they possess the skills, abilities, and temperament. This process requires that young people first learn the relevant attributes of different occupations and of their own developing selves and then discern which occupations have rewards and requirements that match their still-evolving interests, abilities, values, and goals. Implementing a choice then requires that they identify available options, weigh the alternatives, and find means of entry.

The circumscription and compromise theory suggests that four developmental processes are especially important in the matching process: age-related growth in cognitive ability (*cognitive growth*), increasingly self-directed development of self (*self-creation*), progressive elimination of least favored vocational alternatives (*circumscription*), and recognition of and accommodation to external constraints on vocational choice (*compromise*).

COGNITIVE GROWTH

The matching process is cognitively demanding. The tasks it involves span all six levels of Bloom's (Anderson & Krathwohl, 2001) widely used taxonomy of cognitive tasks in teaching and learning: for example, learning isolated facts (*remember*, Bloom's lowest level), spotting and understanding similarities and differences (*understand*), drawing inferences from and assessing the relevance of information (*apply*), integrating information to assess the pros and cons of a decision or course of action (*analyze*), applying one or more criteria to judge which choices are better than others (*evaluate*), and developing a plan to meet a goal (*create*, Bloom's highest level).

Not surprisingly, the vocational assessment and counseling profession is devoted primarily to helping adolescents and adults improve such knowledge and decision making. Counselees' competent engagement in the process is often labeled *vocational maturity*. However, our 1,000 newborns will begin narrowing their preferences and making other vocationally relevant decisions long before they are cognitively proficient or aware that they are making such decisions. Understanding the impact of preadolescent cognition on vocational development is, therefore, essential for facilitating vocational growth in adolescence and beyond.

Children's capacity for learning and reasoning (their *mental age*) increases with chronological age from birth through adolescence. Children progress from thinking intuitively in the preschool years, to concretely in the elementary years, to abstractly in adolescence; from being able to make only simple distinctions to multidimensional ones. They recognize more similarities and differences, and increasingly abstract ones, which they use to make sense of the diverse phenomena in their lives. In short, with age, children become able to take in, understand, and analyze ever-larger bodies of information of increasing subtlety and complexity. They gradually notice and figure out more aspects of the many-layered world around them.

Same-age children also differ considerably among themselves in the general learning and reasoning ability required to do this. At any given chronological age, some are far above or below their peers in mental age (that is, higher or lower in *general intelligence*). The brighter the child, the more information he or she understands and extracts from his or her surrounds and from direct instruction.

Children's steady growth in mental competence affects their behavior and lives in many ways. In the vocational realm, its two major products are the *cognitive map of occupations* and the *self-concept*. Both are incomplete but organized understandings of the occupational world and of the self that children develop and elaborate with age. Although our 1,000 newborns will all construct essentially the same cognitive map of occupations, they will develop increasingly individualized self-concepts. As we shall see, children's conceptions of people and occupations develop in parallel as they perceive, one, then, two, then more dimensions of difference. The first distinctions that young children draw among both people and jobs involve their most concrete, visible attributes. As detailed later, children's views of both become more complex and nuanced as they become capable of making multidimensional comparisons, inferring internal states, and discerning patterns in behavior.

This progression is so natural and universal that it is seldom perceived as vocationally relevant, if noticed at all. Vocational understanding and decision making tends to garner attention only when its demands crescendo, that is, when adolescents simultaneously realize the full complexity of making life decisions and the imminent need to do so.

Self-Creation

A preexisting occupational world awaits us at our birth. That world is large, evolving, and complex. However simplified and incomplete children's early cognitive maps of it are, it is there to be observed and explored. Children also construct self-concepts, but none is born with an already developed self to observe. Where does that self—the self they will seek to know and implement—come from? Is it fixed in their genes? Is it stamped in by the environments that happenstance thrusts on them? Or, are their selves perhaps just incidental by-products of a contest between the two forces?

The self is none of these things because we are not passive products of either nature or nurture, but active agents in our own creation. Counseling psychology's insight that individuals are both unique and agenic is confirmed by what might seem an unlikely source, behavior genetics. We are unique individuals because we are products of unique genotypes (unless identical twins) and unique experiences. Biologically related individuals who are reared together tend to be similar for both genetic and environmental reasons, but behavior geneticists have been surprised to discover how few and temporary the effects of shared environments are in Western populations studied (Plomin, DeFries, McClearn, & McGuffin, 2001; Rowe, 1994). For instance, the circumstances we share with siblings, such as our parents' education, income, interests, and childrearing style, have little or no impact on our basic (Big Five) personality traits at any age, and their impact on intellectual abilities wanes and, for general intelligence, dissipates altogether by adolescence (Loehlin, 1992; Plomin & Petrill, 1997).

More culture-specific personal attributes such as interests, attitudes, and particular skills are more influenced by shared environments (e.g., Betsworth et al., 1994; Tesser, 1993). Vocational interests are fairly general products of the close partnership between nature and nurture, but their emergence is more culturally contingent and experience-dependent than are the basic personality traits and abilities. In fact, they appear to represent particular constellations or intersections of those fundamental human traits that cultures mobilize for specified ends, such as managing accounts or repairing machines (cf. Ackerman & Heggestad, 1997). These constellations seem to be assembled, like standard toolkits, to accomplish a culture's recurring tasks. The experiences that would activate, exercise, and consolidate them as distinct vocational interests (e.g., in working with numbers versus machines) are not available to people of all ages or in all locales, precisely because they involve specialized realms of cultural activity (e.g., clerical, artistic, scientific, political). Many adolescents, therefore, lack sufficient experience to bring out or verify their more culturally targeted interests, abilities, and values.

To the extent that the slings and arrows of fortune have a lasting influence on our highly general traits, it is mostly the arrows that strike us one at a time (called *nonshared* effects), not family by family (*shared* effects; Jensen, 1997). Even biological siblings reared together become less alike in general ability and personality as shared environmental effects wane relative to nonshared ones. Thus, while both genes and environments make us similar to people with whom we share genes and environments, the unique aspects of both our nature and nurture guarantee that we will be distinct as individuals and become increasingly so with age.

Behavior genetic research also confirms that we help to construct ourselves and determine the form we take. First, we become who we are through experience, that is, by engaging the world around us. Only through repeated experience, for example, do our genetically based temperaments become consolidated (*traited*) as enduring personality traits. For attributes to become traited does not mean that they become fixed in stone, but only that they are now relatively stable manifestations of our individuality across different situations; for example, shy John avoids crowds, cocktail parties, and working in teams, but gregarious Jane loves them all.

Second, we do not just implement a nascent self by stepping out into the swirl of life, as if flipping a switch that initiates a preprogrammed sequence of events. We also affect the direction of our development by exposing ourselves to some formative experiences rather than others. Behavior geneticists first realized that development might become more self-directed with age when they discovered that phenotypic (observed) differences in IQ become increasingly heritable with age. For example, with age, adopted children become less like their adoptive family members but more like the biological relatives they have never met (Plomin et al., 2001).

To explain this startling discovery, since confirmed for academic achievement, too, behavior geneticists have proposed a *genes-drives-experience theory* (Bouchard, Lykken, Tellegen, & McGue, 1996). As children mature, they take an increasingly active and independent role in selecting, shaping, and interpreting their environments. Moreover, when given the opportunity, they select experiences more in line with their genetic proclivities. Each comes into the world with a different internal genetic compass, which causes them to be attracted to or repelled by different kinds of people, activities, and settings. The anxiety-prone will more often avoid anxiety-provoking situations, the emotionally stable will perceive the world as more benign than will the neurotic, and the musically gifted will more often seek opportunities to develop their talent (called *active gene-environment correlation*). People also create different environments for themselves by evoking different reactions from the people around them. The obnoxious evoke more hostile social environments for themselves than do the amiable, and parents appropriately provide different kinds of toys, support, and developmental opportunities to their children when they differ in needs, interests, and talents (called evocative or *reactive gene-environment correlation*). In addition, people differ genetically in their sensitivity to given external influences, such as particular pathogens or kinds of instruction (*gene-environment interaction*).

Therefore, even if we were all provided identical parents, classrooms, and neighborhoods, our personal proclivities would constantly incline us to perceive, provoke, and exploit them differently. As a result, we would eventually come to inhabit different worlds. When and where people are free to do so, genetically unique individuals refashion common environments in ways that reflect, reinforce, and better resonate with their personal tendencies. Environments, therefore, are not just "out there" molding us from the outside in but are themselves partly genetic in origin because we have had a hand in shaping them more in line with our genotypes (Plomin & Bergmann, 1991). Our lives, our close personal environments, are our *extended phenotypes*. The partly genetic origin of environments is confirmed by research showing that the occupations and educational credentials that people obtain, the major life events they experience, the social support they receive, and other important aspects of their lives are often moderately heritable (Bergmann, Plomin, Pedersen, McClearn, & Nesselroade, 1990; Lyons et al., 1993; Plomin, Lichtenstein, Pedersen, McClearn, & Nesselroade, 1990; Rowe, Vesterdal, & Rodgers, 1998).

Our genetic compass constitutes the core of our individuality and, from the deepest recesses of our being, quietly but incessantly urges (not commands) us in some directions rather than others. It competes with a cacophony of signals emitted by our culture, but it operates like a gyroscope, helping us orient ourselves while being pushed this way or that. It contributes some consistency to our myriad daily choices, which cumulate over time to shape a life path. Which forks we take at each stage in life is constrained to the ones that currently exist in our culture, especially for persons in our situation; no one becomes a loan officer or astronaut in societies that do not lend money or send anyone into space. We are also constrained by our past choices—for example, wanting to go into dentistry after having become an accountant or wanting to become a police officer after having disqualified ourselves by committing a felony.

Our genetically conditioned tendencies are not fully fixed, but change somewhat with age as genes turn on or off, puberty being an obvious example. The social environments to which we have access or must move also change with age. Our streams of experience inevitably shift as a result, somewhat altering the contours of our lives and selves in the process, no matter how deeply layered they have become. We are, therefore, to some extent always works in progress, finalized only by death.

Just as our personal traits develop only through experience, we come to know them only while engaging the world. We must infer our personalities and abilities by noticing what we do well, how we typically interact with others, how other people react to us, how we feel about our various experiences. That is, our genetic compasses are made manifest by what we resonate to and what repels us, perhaps especially when their signals conflict with the expectations of family or friends. The *self* resides in these long-term consistencies in behavior, belief, and feeling, and *self-insight* lies in gaining a fuller, clearer-eyed view of them. The *self-concept* derives from our perceptions of this individuated self and what we might want or fear it to be.

When viewed from a life course perspective, the genetically conditioned selection, shaping, and interpretation of our life environments is called *niche seeking* (Scarr & McCartney, 1983). Vocational choice is one particularly important element of it. Niche seeking does not occur in a cultural vacuum, however. Our 1,000 newborns were all born into a social niche, and it is from their social origins that they will view and venture forth into the larger world. Cultures provide or allow only a limited array of niches, but free societies still give their members much leeway to create selves and life niches more in line with their genetic proclivities.

CIRCUMSCRIPTION

As just noted, modern culture provides an extensive menu of occupations and life niches. Our 1,000 newborns will never learn much about most of them or know that others even exist. What nearly all learn, however, is that there are major varieties of work and that these varieties occupy different places in the general social order. We are social beings and, therefore, exquisitely sensitive to where we fit, or would like to fit, into society. Vocational choice is a highly public way of asserting who we are. It is, therefore, the social aspects of jobs that often concern us most and that children consider first.

Vocational choice begins as a process of *circumscription,* of eliminating occupational alternatives that conflict with self-concept. Early in life, children begin to rule out whole sets of occupations as socially unacceptable for someone like themselves as they start to recognize the more obvious distinctions among jobs. They rule out progressively more sectors of the occupational world as they become able to perceive additional, more abstract dimensions of suitability or *compatibility.* Most such circumscription occurs without their knowing, or wondering much about, what workers actually do in the jobs they so peremptorily reject.

All children move through the same four stages of circumscription, shown in Figure 4.1, but some faster or slower than others depending on their cognitive ability. The ages and grade levels associated with the stages are, therefore, only approximate. The stages overlap but coincide roughly with the preschool years, elementary school, middle school, and high school.

Stage 1: Orientation to Size and Power (Ages 3 to 5) Children in the preschool and kindergarten years progress from magical to intuitive thinking and begin to achieve object constancy (e.g., they know that people cannot change their sex by changing their outward appearance). They begin to classify people in the simplest of ways—as big and powerful versus little and weak. They also come to recognize occupations as adult roles and have ceased reporting that they would like to be animals (bunnies), fantasy characters (princesses), or inanimate objects (rocks) when they grow up. As indicated in Figure 4.1, their vocational achievement is to have recognized that there is an adult world, working at a job is part of it, and they, too, will eventually become an adult.

Stage 2: Orientation to Sex Roles (Ages 6 to 8) Children at this age have progressed to thinking in concrete terms and making simple distinctions. They begin to recognize more occupations, but primarily those that are highly visible, either because of frequent personal contact (teachers) or because their incumbents wear uniforms, drive big trucks, and otherwise draw a child's attention. Children also rely on highly visible attributes to distinguish among varieties of people, the most obvious and salient one for them at this age being gender. As concrete thinkers, they distinguish the sexes primarily by outward appearances, such as clothing, hair, and typical activities. Being dichotomous thinkers, children see particular behaviors and roles (including jobs) as belonging to one sex but not the other. Rigid thinking confers a moral status on the dichotomies it creates, and children of both sexes tend to perceive their own sex as superior and to treat sex-appropriate behavior as imperative. Person-job match is, therefore, perceived in terms of sex

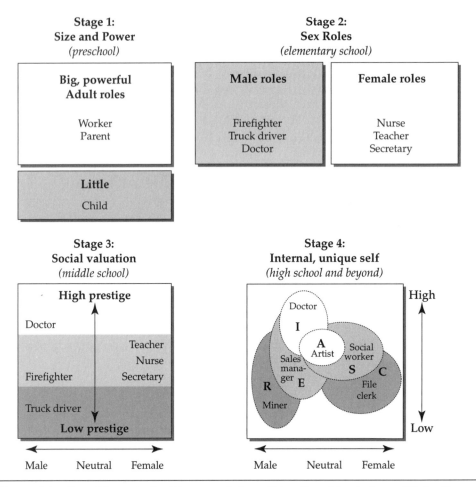

Figure 4.1 Four Stages in the Circumscription of Vocational Aspirations. [*Note:* R = Realistic; I = Investigative; A = Artistic; S = Social; E = Enterprising; C = Conventional.]

role. Although children's views of people and jobs will become more subtle and complex, their naïve early understandings have already turned them toward some possible futures and away from others.

Children are also starting to determine more of their own experiences (choosing friends, play activities, and role models) and thus the direction in which they develop. The cultural menus from which they make such choices also become larger with age. Girls and boys tend to be offered and prefer different experiences. Cultures have somewhat different expectations for the two sexes, and those cultural differentials, whatever they are, may be reinforced by persisting genetically conditioned sex differences in activity, preference, and behavior. Culture alone does not sustain gender differences in occupational aspirations (e.g., working with people rather than things), as any parent who has tried to interest sons in dolls and daughters in trucks is likely to testify. But culture can contribute to sex differences by pushing genetically diverse individuals to adhere to a common average sex type for their sex. Thus, while nature and nurture both affect degree of vocational circumscription by sex type, one-size-fits-all cultural prescriptions encourage many poor person-job fits because the members of both sexes are genetically diverse and, therefore, many do not fit the prescribed average.

Stage 3: Orientation to Social Valuation (Ages 9 to 13)   By Stage 3, our 1,000 children are able to think more abstractly. They recognize more occupations because they can now conceptualize activities they cannot directly see; for instance, people who sit at desks, answer phones, and write things on the computer may be carrying out different economic functions (e.g., secretaries, managers, journalists, and research analysts).

They have also become aware of status hierarchies and more sensitive to social evaluation, whether by peers or the larger society. By age 9 (grade 4), youngsters start to recognize the more obvious symbols of a person's social class (clothing, speech, behavior, possessions brought to school); and by age 13 (grade 8), most rank occupations in prestige the same way adults do. Children now array occupations two-dimensionally, by prestige level as well as sex type. Whereas they had earlier aspired to jobs low and high alike, they now rank those same occupations differently (see Figure 4.1). This shows up especially in boys' aspirations, as illustrated in Figure 4.1, because jobs sex-typed as masculine happen to vary more in social status than do jobs typed as feminine.

Children have, in addition, come to understand the tight links among income, education, and occupation. A job's place in the occupational hierarchy affects how workers live their lives and are regarded by others, and an individual's chances of climbing the hierarchy depend heavily on academic accomplishment. In other words, children see that career choice enters them into a competition to get ahead or at least make a respectable showing.

Children have, therefore, begun to identify floors and ceilings for their aspirations. They cease considering work that their families and communities would reject as unacceptably low in social standing, such as driving a garbage truck. Higher social class families set a higher floor (*tolerable-level boundary*) for acceptability. On the other hand, children seldom aspire to the highest level occupations. Rather, they rule out occupations that are too difficult for them to enter with reasonable effort or that pose too high a risk of failure if they try. They base this *tolerable-effort boundary* mostly on their academic ability. Years of schooling have relentlessly exposed students' differences in intellectual capability and left few with much doubt about their ability relative to classmates and their odds of educational and occupational advancement.

By the end of Stage 3, then, children have blacked out large sections of their occupational map for being the wrong sex type, unacceptably low level, or unacceptably difficult. The territory remaining in the map is the child's zone of acceptable alternatives or *social space*. Figure 4.2 provides two hypothetical examples, one for a middle class girl (Panel A) and one for a working class boy (Panel B). (The occupations shown are a small sample of the common cognitive map that all groups share.) This girl, like most others, has ruled out occupations to the far left of the map as too masculine (engineer, building contractor, hardware sales, police officer), while the boy has ruled out occupations toward the right as not masculine enough (bank teller, librarian, receptionist, dental hygienist, nurse). Being middle class, the girl has also ruled out careers in the lower third or so of the occupational hierarchy because few people in her social circle hold such jobs

Panel A: Middle-class girl

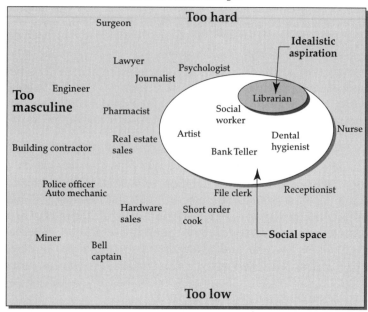

Panel B: Working-class boy

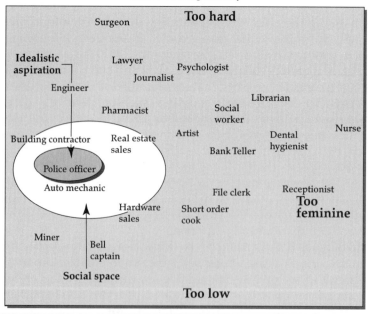

Figure 4.2   Two Hypothetical Children's Self-Defined Social Spaces within the Cognitive Map of Occupations Shared by All Adults.

or consider them worthy careers. In working class neighborhoods, jobs at that level are more common and their incumbents more likely to be thought successes, so it is typical that the working class boy would extend his zone of acceptable alternatives into a lower stratum of occupations. The boy's tolerable-effort boundary may be lower than the middle class child's for two reasons. First, children from lower social class families tend not to be as academically talented as children from higher social classes. Second, they are under less pressure and have less support for aiming as high as their abilities could take them. Therefore, even though this boy may be at least as bright as the middle class girl, he may not see that his talent could open more difficult doors or why he should even make the extra effort. From his social vantage point, jobs need not be as high level to be good enough.

Vocational choice to this point, therefore, seems to be mostly a by-product of wanting to belong, be respected, and live a comfortable life as defined by the individual's reference group. It is not a search for personal fulfillment on the job, but for a job that will provide a good life when not at work. The job sectors that children no longer see as appropriate for themselves become paths closed to them, at least psychologically, even when those occupations might be more congruent with their personal interests. Unless prompted to do so, the children are not likely to seek out or pay attention to information about the options they have peremptorily rejected. While circumscription greatly eases the cognitive burden of vocational choice, it can foreclose the experiences necessary for knowing whether they might, in fact, have the interest and ability for such work. To the extent that individuals' tolerable-effort and tolerable-level boundaries reflect expectations set by their birth niche, irrespective of their own attributes, individuals are less likely to pursue alternatives as far from their origins or as close to their own interests as they might otherwise do.

Stage 4: Orientation to Internal, Unique Self (Age 14 and Older)   Vocational development erupts into conscious awareness during Stage 4. In earlier stages, it has consisted mostly of the preconscious elimination of unacceptable alternatives. Now, however, adolescents engage in an increasingly conscious search among the remainder, the occupations in their social space, for occupations that would be personally fulfilling. That is, they begin thinking about which careers would be compatible with their more personal, psychological selves.

Continued cognitive growth has enabled adolescents to apprehend better the abstract, internal, unique aspects of individuals and occupations, such as the interests, abilities, and values exercised while performing different jobs. They are, therefore, able to distinguish different fields of work and know that both worker personalities and economic functions differ from one field to another. Although the distinctions captured by Holland's typology of personality and work (Realistic, Investigative, Artistic, Social, Enterprising, and Conventional), shown in Figure 4.1, remain somewhat inchoate in their minds, they now become salient factors in person-job match.

The matching process has thereby become more multidimensional, which makes it more difficult. Adolescents must also begin factoring in nonvocational goals and obligations that will affect career planning. Many girls ponder how to balance home and work life, and many boys ponder how to generate sufficient financial support and security for a family. Moreover, many adolescents still struggle to know what their specific vocational interests, abilities, and goals are, partly because many of their vocationally relevant personal attributes are not yet fully formed. As discussed earlier, personal attributes that are directed toward specific cultural ends—including vocational interests, values, attitudes, and special abilities—are less formed by adolescence than are the highly general traits of ability and personality, because the former depend more on specific relevant exposure and experience that are not so universally available.

Career development becomes more difficult and anxiety provoking when our 1,000 adolescents are called on to make vocationally relevant decisions, such as which courses to take and credentials or training to seek. As a result, they must now consider what workers actually do on the job, the qualifications they must possess, and how to obtain them. If prompted, most can name a most favored choice, their *idealistic aspiration*. But the occupations most attractive to them may not be the most readily available. *Realistic aspirations* are the somewhat less desirable but still acceptable occupations that individuals think they could actually get. The difference between idealistic and realistic aspirations is that the latter have been modulated by the perceived *accessibility* of occupations. Both kinds of aspirations tend to change as the adolescent learns more about how compatible and how accessible different occupations really might be. Therefore, any series of expressed aspirations, whether idealistic or realistic, is really just a sampling of the occupations from the individual's social space. Even those named spontaneously as the least acceptable tend to be drawn from—and signal—the individual's social space.

One risk at this stage of development is that young people have not gotten, or will not get, sufficient experience for testing their vocational interests and abilities, especially for occupations they have ejected from their social space long before. Another risk is that, because of either external pressure or ignorance, anxiety, or inaction on their part, they may commit themselves to a choice before they really know the options accessible to them.

COMPROMISE

Whereas circumscription is the process by which youngsters progressively eliminate from consideration occupations they think unacceptable for themselves, *compromise* is the process by which they begin to relinquish their most preferred alternatives for less compatible but more accessible ones. When weighing the relative merits of the more attractive alternatives in the individual's social space, the process is called vocational *choice*. When forced to select among the minimally acceptable, choice shades into *compromise*. When forced to consider unacceptable alternatives, compromise is painful and no longer seems a matter of choice, but of barriers to choice. I focus next on three factors in the compromise process. Why do young people know so little about the accessibility of the work they prefer? How does their own behavior increase or decrease its actual accessibility? And which dimensions of person-job compatibility are they most and least willing to relinquish when they have to settle for less favored or unacceptable alternatives?

Truncated Search, Limited Knowledge   With age, children become increasingly aware of major social and psychological attributes, which they then use to judge the suitability of different occupations for people like themselves. Individuals possess far less knowledge, however, about the accessibility of their preferred alternatives. Indeed, information on which jobs and training programs are available and how to enter them is highly specific to particular times, places, and occupations; time-consuming to locate and learn; and quickly outdated. Gathering that information takes time and effort. People tend to minimize their search costs by seeking information primarily for the occupations that interest them most, only when they need to make a decision, and mostly from sources they already know and trust, such as family and friends.

While cutting search costs, this method also limits the amount and kind of information that young people gather. They tend to know relatively little about the accessibility of different kinds of postsecondary education and work, which limits their options. What they learn is fairly narrow and contingent on the particular people and opportunities in their social circle, making them less likely to move very far from their birth niche, even when that might suit them better.

Bigger Investment, Better Accessibility   Certain jobs simply have not existed in certain times or places, or they have been off limits to certain categories of people. Moreover, there will always be external circumstances, such as the health of the economy or family obligations, that constrain individuals' ability to pursue preferred alternatives. On the other hand, their social niche may also provide special support, which opens or reveals new opportunities, for example, well-connected family members, well-informed compatriots, and ready access to career counseling and information services.

Very importantly, however, individuals' opportunities also depend somewhat on their own behavior. First, jobs and training programs are effectively inaccessible when individuals remain ignorant of openings and how to apply for them. People learn more and expand their options when they are active seekers of information, not just passive consumers of it. Second, jobs can become more accessible when people take action to make themselves more competitive relative to other applicants, for example, by getting relevant experience or additional training. They further increase their opportunities when they actively mobilize support or assistance in pursuing their aims. Seldom are opportunities laid out for us, cafeteria-like. We must often search them out or create them ourselves. Initiative matters.

Thus, the more freedom people have in uncovering opportunities and enhancing their competitiveness, the more that differences in personal skill, initiative, and persistence will matter for opening up options, surmounting barriers, and reducing the need to compromise. The partially self-generated nature of opportunity and constraint is suggested, as mentioned earlier, by the moderate heritability of social support and life events. Individuals who just sit and wait for opportunity to knock are less likely to ever get the knock, and they abdicate much opportunity for directing their own development.

The Good Enough or Not Too Bad   People look for compatible jobs from among those that seem accessible or could be made so. Compatibility rests on people finding jobs that provide a good match with the sex type, level, and field of work they prefer. They seek good matches, not the best possible, because the "good enough" is sufficient, easier to determine, and more feasible to locate.

When good matches are not available, individuals must decide which dimensions of match to relinquish. The dimensions closest to the core of the self-concept seem to be relinquished last. These are also the earliest dimensions of match, with sex type being first, prestige level second, and field of work (clerical, scientific, artistic, etc.) last. When faced with options that are all unacceptable in either sex type, level, or field, those of acceptable sex type (i.e., not outside the tolerable sex-type boundary), therefore, tend to be preferred over those that are not. When all available alternatives are at least minimally acceptable in sex type, people usually opt for an acceptable level of work rather than their most preferred field of work. Only when both sex type and prestige level are minimally acceptable (i.e., the occupations are within their social space) will individuals opt to maximize fit with their vocational interests rather than further enhancing prestige level or sex type.

Stated in reverse, individuals pick a job from their social space that fits their vocational interests, if any is accessible. If not, they shift to a different line of work rather than seek the same type of work outside their social space, that is, one of unacceptable prestige or sex type. People look outside their social space only when they see no accessible options within it. In such cases, they push their tolerable-level boundary further out than they do their tolerable-sex-type boundary. For example, if the girl in Figure 4.2 is unable to implement any of the alternatives in her social space, she is more likely to entertain lower prestige work as a receptionist or teller than more masculine work (engineer, pharmacist) that is comparable in level to her idealistic aspiration (librarian). Likewise, if the working class boy is unable to become a police officer or mechanic, he is more likely to compromise by seeking to be a construction worker or sales representative than to take an office job. Both youngsters are perhaps compromising more than they need to, either because they needlessly circumscribed their choices at an earlier age or because they lack knowledge about the opportunities potentially available to them.

Individuals differ greatly in the personal traits that encourage exploration, optimism, and persistence, especially in the face of opposition and defeat, but all individuals have it within their power to improve their options. In short, the compromise process is another crucible of self-creation, whether through our action or inaction.

EMPIRICAL SUPPORT

The circumscription and compromise theory was derived from synthesizing evidence across a variety of disciplines, primarily vocational assessment, career choice, job performance, status attainment (sociology), mental ability, and behavior genetics. The empirical support for its specific processes and stages is provided in the original statement of the theory, two revisions, and related articles (Gottfredson, 1981, 1986, 1996, 1999, 2002; Gottfredson & Lapan, 1997).

The founding evidence for different aspects of the theory varies in amount and quality, ranging from the much replicated and meta-analyzed (patterns of vocational interests and aspirations, cognitive growth and diversity, heritability of behavior, and social inequalities) to the sparsely reported (priorities in circumscription and compromise). It is the latter elements of the theory that have received the most attention in subsequent tests of the theory (see Gottfredson, 1996, 2002; Vandiver & Bowman, 1996, for reviews). Some researchers have claimed to confirm the theory (mostly concerning circumscription) and others to disconfirm it (mostly concerning compromise). These tests have not been very informative one way or the other, however, because they tend not to assess well, if at all, individuals' self-designated social spaces. To trace either circumscription or compromise, it is essential to know which occupations, sampled from the full range of work, individuals consider unacceptable versus acceptable.

The validity of theories or their specific parts is most effectively assessed when they make *falsifiable* predictions. They receive their strongest support when they suggest novel, *nonobvious* predictions that are subsequently confirmed. Their utility relative to competing theories can be judged by confronting them head-to-head where they make *different* predictions about the same phenomenon, for example, which interventions will be most effective and why.

For instance, my theory predicts that career interventions will effect more change when they target narrow, specific attributes rather than highly general ones. In contrast, social learning theory (Krumboltz, 1994) seems to predict no difference in the effectiveness of teaching general versus specific vocational interests, skills, and attitudes, or perhaps even that teaching the former would be more effective precisely because they are more broadly generalizable. To take another example, to the extent that assessed self-efficacy is malleable, my theory predicts that improving it will depend on improving actual competence; to the extent that it is stable, the measures in question will be tapping an enduring *personality* trait, specifically, positive affect. In contrast, sociocognitive process theory (Lent & Hackett, 1994) appears to conceive self-efficacy as an attribute that can be directly raised without first improving competence but which, after enhancement, will lead individuals to develop more such competence. Were these and other such theoretical contests to be held, they could not only profile the strengths and weaknesses of different theories but also guide intervention strategies.

THE PRACTICAL CHALLENGE

What use, then, can career counselors make of the circumscription and compromise theory? What might it suggest for promoting the future work satisfaction and satisfactoriness of our 1,000 newborns? While the theory seeks to explain demographic patterns in career development, its purpose is to help individual persons, whether singly or in groups. This is the traditional aim of career counseling: to help individuals clarify and implement their visions of a satisfying career life, even if parents or social engineers might prefer something different.

The theory shares many assumptions with other vocational theories (Gottfredson, 1981), so it leads to many of the same recommendations. But it also highlights special challenges that require mobilizing old tools in new ways. For instance, how can we help clients identify genetic resources and constraints that we can never directly observe? How can we help adolescents reexamine the merits of childhood choices they now take for granted, but without seeming to denigrate them? How can we encourage realism in vocational options without quashing hope and opportunity? And how can we provide clients the complex information they need for identifying and implementing good choices without overwhelming them?

Moreover, we lack much evidence about which kinds of career interventions are most effective. There is meta-analytic evidence, however, indicating that interventions are more effective when they require sustained personal reflection and engagement (written exercises); help build a support network; and provide individualized feedback, information about the world of work, and real-life models of effective career-related behavior (Brown & Ryan Krane, 2000). The career guidance and counseling system outlined next, therefore, emphasizes these features.

APPLYING THE THEORY: OBJECTIVES, STRATEGIES, AND TOOLS

Each of the theory's four developmental processes poses special risks and points to a particular class of counselee behaviors that can be optimized to reduce those risks and enhance development. As indicated in Table 4.1, cognitive growth points to effective learning; self-creation, to adequate experience; circumscription, to self-insight; and compromise, to wise self-investment. Two counselor strategies are provided for each of the four behaviors to be optimized. I discuss each strategy's application with students from three age ranges corresponding roughly to Stages 2 to 4 of the theory: elementary, middle, and high school/college. Different interventions are appropriate for the different ages, so cells 1 to 9 in the table sample the sorts of activities and resources that are useful for each stage of development. Counselors should consider others, too (e.g., Niles & Harris-Bowlsbey, 2002; Zunker, 1998).

Effective learning (cells 1 to 3) and adequate experience (cells 4 to 6) are important at all ages because they are the foundation for self-insight and wise self-investment. Self-insight is best addressed beginning in middle/junior high school, when children have developed more capacity for it (cells 7 to 8). Self-insight is essential, in turn, for wise self-investment, which should be stressed beginning in senior high school, when the need for making and implementing decisions becomes urgent (cell 9). Table 4.1 is, essentially, a guide for compiling and deploying a comprehensive counseling and guidance toolkit for different developmental ages.

The theory suggests that effective career counseling provides not only coaching in lifelong self-development and self-agency but also "problem-solving consultants" (Savickas, 1996, p. 191). For reasons of space, I focus here on the system's use in enhancing development and preventing problems during the school years. I limit discussion of its use for diagnosis and treatment in adolescence and beyond (Gottfredson, 2002) to indicating where my eight strategies coincide with the six questions in Savickas's (1996) framework for solving career problems.

OPTIMIZE LEARNING

The major risk that youth face in the cognitive development process is failing to develop adequate knowledge for sound decision making because the cognitive demands for acquiring and integrating it are so high. This leads, in turn, to undue circumscription and compromise—to constricted opportunity. The practical challenge this poses for counselors is, therefore: How can we optimize counselees' learning and use of complex information in complex environments when making career life decisions?

Vocational counseling psychology has always put a high premium on developing and conveying information about self and work. What the cognitive growth process points up, however, is that information and instruction must be kept

Table 4.1

Overview of Aims, Strategies, and Sample Tools for a Comprehensive Career Guidance and Counseling System

Developmental Process	Behavior to Be Optimized	Counselor Strategies	Sample Tools		
			Early Elementary School	Middle/Junior High School	High School and Beyond
Cognitive growth	Learning	A: Reduce task complexity. B: Accommodate cognitive diversity.	1: Information and tasks are discrete, concrete, short, and require only simple inferences (NAEP level: 150–225).	2: Information is lengthier; tasks require relating ideas and making generalizations (NAEP level: 200–275); low-ability students require less complex material (see Cell 1).	3: Information can be somewhat complicated; tasks require some analysis and integration of information (NAEP level: 250–325); low-ability students require less complex material (see Cell 2).
Self-creation	Experience	C: Provide broad menus of experience (intellectual, social, and things-related). D: Promote self-agency in shaping own experience.	4: Field trips, career days, contact with diverse workers, experience kits, personal portfolios.	5: Also—exemplars in novels, biographies, current affairs, and daily life; simple jobs in home or neighborhood, extracurricular activities, hobbies, scouting, school service projects; community visits.	6: Also—broad selection of courses, community service, job shadowing, co-op, extern- and internships, tech-prep, clubs, (J)ROTC, FFA, scouting, student government, sports, construction-repair projects; summer jobs.
Circumscription	Self-insight	E: Facilitate inventory and integration of information about self. F: Promote sound conception of fitting and feasible career life.		7: List tentative life goals, major strengths and weaknesses, family expectations, potential barriers; exercises in identifying role conflicts, job requirements, which occupations they reject and why; simple exercises in setting goals and making decisions.	8: Formal assessments of interest, ability, personality, values; analysis of past activities, support, barriers, effects on others; computerized information on person-job match; exercises in setting and balancing career life goals.
Compromise	Self-investment	G: Facilitate assessment of accessibility of preferred career life. H: Promote self-agency in enhancing self, opportunity, and support.			9: Books and training in writing resumes, interviewing for jobs, skill building and anxiety management; job banks, placement services; aids for identifying best bets and backups, building support system, enlisting mentors.

commensurate with counselees' cognitive capabilities. Attaining commensurability requires appreciating not just that children grow in mental age as they mature, but also that tasks differ greatly in their cognitive complexity and that individuals of the same chronological age differ enormously in mental age. Cognitive differences among both tasks and individuals influence the effectiveness of counseling interventions. Roselle and Hummel (1988) found, for example, that less intellectually able college students used the computerized guidance system DISCOVER II less effectively and appeared to need more structure and discussion with the counselor.

Figure 4.3 illustrates two strategies for dealing with these cognitive constraints.

Reduce Task Complexity   The Y-axis in Figure 4.3 represents differences in task complexity. Cognitive demands are greater when the information to be processed is more voluminous, abstract, multifaceted, ambiguous, uncertain, changing, novel, and embedded in extraneous material. Information processing is also more demanding when it requires more inferences, dealing with conflicting tasks and unclear means-ends relations, identifying which operations to use, and navigating other such complexities (Gottfredson, 1997; Kirsch, Jungeblut, & Mosenthal, 1994). More complex tasks are more difficult to learn and to perform well than are simpler tasks and thus pose a particular challenge in guidance.

The X-axis represents the cognitive differences among children, specifically, in their mental age. As children advance in chronological age, they also grow in mental age (until late adolescence or their early 20s). They thus become able to perform progressively more complex cognitive tasks, as described earlier. The diagonal line stands for the level of task complexity that is best suited, pedagogically, to individuals of different mental ages. The A and C in Figure 4.3 represent individuals confronted with tasks that are, respectively, much too difficult and much too low level to facilitate development. Perhaps person C (mental age 15) has been asked to explain the concept of life goals and person A (mental age 9) to balance conflicting ones. B and D, in contrast, are persons presented with different tasks but ones commensurate with their (different) abilities (mental ages 12 and

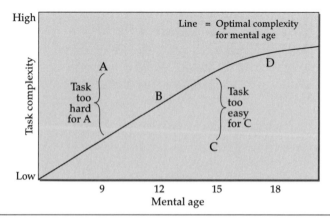

Figure 4.3   Two Variables That Influence the Cognitive Suitability of Counseling Interventions.

18). These two individuals will learn more from tackling their ability-congruent tasks than will A and C from their ability-mismatched exercises.

Counselors cannot raise anyone's mental age (general intelligence level) because no such technologies exist, but they can adjust the cognitive demands of the assistance they provide and offer additional cognitive support when task complexity cannot be reduced. Career information and activities are often inherently complex, such as locating job opportunities and integrating goals to create a career life plan. Career libraries, job banks, typologies of occupations grouped by similarity and difference, and instruction in decision-making strategies are among the many ways long used to reduce the cognitive burden on counselees. Another way to reduce that burden is to provide cognitive scaffolding for accomplishing complex tasks, for example, by breaking tasks such as identifying interests and making decisions into smaller steps, sequencing them across grade levels in an age-appropriate manner, and making the process more concrete and experiential. The lists of behavioral objectives for each grade level in comprehensive K through 12 career guidance programs illustrate this principle, perhaps because they are integrated with academic instruction (e.g., Gysbers & Henderson, 1994, App. A).

A careful analysis of the complexity and comprehensibility of career materials and interventions would likely reveal, however, that some of their complexity is needless. For instance, exercises may be more complicated than necessary, too abstract, or their vocabulary difficult. Health researchers have discovered this to be the case with health education materials, which tend to be written several grade levels above the reading comprehension capabilities of the average person. They have also documented that many patients fail to comply with essential treatment regimens because they do not understand prescription labels, health forms, and physicians' instructions, which failure increases their morbidity and mortality (Gottfredson, 2004). Like health care providers, counseling and guidance personnel need to verify—not presume—that their communications are being understood because clients are loathe to volunteer that they do not understand. Service providers should also take care not to mistake lack of ability for lack of motivation.

General guidance on typical levels of cognitive competence at different grade levels can be gleaned from the National Assessments of Educational Progress (NAEP), especially in reading. The latest NAEP Trend Series data (National Center for Education Statistics, 2000) show that the average American 9-year-old is just becoming able to locate facts and draw inferences from simple written material (mean NAEP reading score of 212); at age 13, the average child is starting to identify facts in lengthy material and to identify main ideas and draw inferences from passages in literature, science, and social studies (mean of 260); and typical 17-year-olds are on the threshold of (but not yet) understanding complicated passages in their school subjects and analyzing and integrating less familiar material (mean of 288). Cells 1 to 3 in Table 4.1 summarize the task complexity level that is appropriate for the average student at each of three broad levels of schooling. They guide the selection of counseling tools for optimizing the three other key behaviors (cells 4 to 9).

Accommodate Cognitive Diversity   Many children are not average, but years behind or ahead of their age-mates in cognitive ability. Consider, for example, that the average NAEP reading gap between 9- and 17-year-olds, 76 points on a scale of 0 to 500, is comparable to the range of scores spanned by the middle two-thirds of students *within* both these age groups (roughly a 2-SD within-age difference). This 76-point mean age difference is also comparable to the reading gap between the 25th and 90th percentiles within all three NAEP age groups, which gaps are, respectively, 185 to 259, 234 to 308, and 261 to 341 for students ages 9, 13, and 17 (National Center for Education Statistics, 2000). Note also that the top 10% of 9-year-olds already read at the 25th percentile for 17-year-olds despite being eight years younger, as does the average 13-year-old (mean score of 260), despite having four fewer years of schooling. Clearly, materials that are ability-commensurate for the average individual will not be effective for the many who are markedly more able or less able than their age-peers. Virtually any school cohort of 13-year-olds spans the entire nine-year mental-age range depicted in Figure 4.3. The range is higher and narrower among college students but still wide.

One-size-fits-all instruction and assistance works no better in career education than in academic, health, or other kinds of education. As documented in both military training and the public schools, less able individuals learn better when the material to be learned is simple, concrete, nontheoretical, complete, step-by-step, highly structured, repetitive, one-on-one, and involves hands-on activities rather than book learning (Snow, 1996; Sticht, Armstrong, Hickey, & Caylor, 1987). However, this kind of instruction impedes learning among more cognitively able individuals, who learn best when material is more theoretical, not so atomized and prestructured, and allows them to reorganize and assimilate information in their own way.

This finding explains why it is so difficult to provide effective group instruction to cognitively diverse individuals. What helps some students will fail to help—or will stifle—others in the group. While schoolteachers can accommodate less able students by omitting or delaying introduction of the most complex tasks in a curriculum (e.g., algebra), the obligations of imminent adulthood (finding a job) afford counselors and their clients no such luxury. Moreover, those obligations come all the earlier for struggling students, because they are more apt to leave school early or not seek postsecondary education. Such students can be provided assistance in a simpler, more concrete, experiential format with additional cognitive scaffolding. They have difficulty generalizing what they learn to new situations, but most can readily learn domain-specific skills and practical knowledge with sufficient practice. Hands-on experience is an important teacher, also, because, as discussed next, no guidance program can teach the intimate personal knowledge to which only the individual is privy.

OPTIMIZE EXPERIENCE

The major risk for youth in the self-creation process is failing to experience a varied enough set of activities, whether directly or vicariously, to develop and know their career-relevant personal traits, particularly their vocational interest and aptitude profiles. As described earlier, people's most general traits of ability and personality are consolidated and known to them via engaging the world in daily life. Designated as P in Figure 4.4, these traits appear to require only universally available experience to emerge. People's more culture- and occupation-specific trait constellations, skills, habits, and attitudes are developed and known, however, only via involvement in relevant, nonuniversal activities, precisely because they are domain-specific and culture-bound. These are the traits (P-E in Figure 4.4) that embed a person in the culture and vice versa. The practical challenge that the self-creation process poses for counselors is, then: How can we increase the likelihood that young people will gain sufficient exposure and experience to know what their career potentials really are?

Provide Broad Menus of Potential Experiences   Counseling interventions cannot create vocational interests or abilities for which there is no genetic support, but they can help young people discover whether they possess those foundational resources. Most important, counselors and guidance systems can provide a broad menu of possible experiences and encourage individuals to sample ones new to them. Children tend to be exposed to somewhat different occupations depending on their birth niche, so systematically exposing all students, from kindergarten on, to all sectors of the common cognitive map of occupations (Figure 4.2) helps to broaden their horizons. In addition, because children tend to ignore information about sectors of work they deem unacceptable, exposing them to the demographic diversity of individuals in those different sectors of work can help to break down self-limiting stereotypes about race, gender, and class.

Many young people continue to make career choices partly on the basis of gender, race, and social class background, but systematic exposure to occupational alternatives and nonstereotypic workers can reduce their unthinking reliance on such criteria. Reliance on social attributes can also be reduced by alerting students to more pertinent bases for choice, namely, the abilities and interests that different occupations require and reward. Students should, therefore, be provided vicarious or direct experience from an early age in all major forms of work activity:

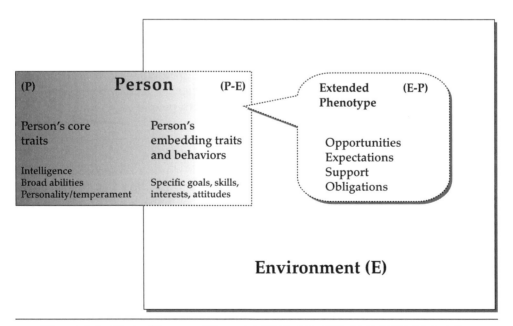

Figure 4.4   Three Classes of Personal Attributes of Persons in Environments.

dealing with data, people, and things. How can such guided exposure and experience be achieved at each developmental stage?

In the early elementary years (cell 4 in Table 4.1), field trips, videos, guest speakers, career days, job experience kits, school projects, regular class assignments, and the like can show students (or remind them of) the great variety of occupations. Such tools can also acquaint young children with the most general features of work: what workers do on jobs, how they get them, the kinds of settings they work in, why they work, and how their jobs affect their personal lives as well as the economy. Children in the early elementary grades orient most to the sex type of work and do not yet grasp the relevance of interests and abilities. Guidance systems neither can nor should instruct students that sex-typed choices are wrong or less worthy, but they can help keep children's sex-type boundaries fluid by providing concrete counterstereotypic examples. Some children resonate to live models of nontraditional career choice (female firefighters and male nurses), and others may at least stop ridiculing such options. Providing both sexes simple experience in dealing with data, people, and things may further inhibit reflexive narrowing of occupational aspirations according to the gender of workers rather than the work they perform.

Guidance activities should be commensurate with young children's mental capabilities: short, elemental, discrete, and concrete. They should also allow personal contact and hands-on participation to the extent possible. For example, observing and speaking with workers in cross-gender jobs will leave a much stronger impression than merely hearing that such people exist. Inferences and connections between ideas must also remain simple and obvious. Children in the early grades have limited capacity for reflecting on and integrating their experience, so multiyear personal portfolios can be used to record growth and experience for review at older ages. Creating such portfolios can also make career-related exposure seem more salient and reinforce learning.

By middle school (cell 5), children are able to participate in a greater variety of in-class, extracurricular, and at-home activities (e.g., service projects, sports, hobbies, family outings). These activities create new opportunities for students to gauge their facility and satisfaction in working with data, people, and things. Academic class work already provides good testing grounds for aptness with data and ideas (reasoning, reading, writing, math, and clerical skills), but schools provide only haphazard opportunities for working with people (e.g., leadership, social skills) and yet fewer for working with things (spatial-mechanical skills). Experimentation in working with people and things need not be extensive, but it is especially important for non-college-bound students.

Because they are now more cognitively able, middle/junior high school students can be asked to deal with somewhat more abstract information and, moreover, to do so in written exercises. Vicarious experience can be gained, for example, by analyzing work and workers portrayed in novels, biographies, and films. To remain effectively experiential, however, such tasks must provide highly personal involvement and individualized feedback. That is, they must be sufficiently engaging to activate and test students' natural proclivities (P traits) and discover which particular domains of cultural activity attract or repel them most (the P-E trait constellations).

Once again, attention to the pertinent bases for career choice can help forestall undue circumscription. At this age, circumscription involves eliminating options that are either too low level or too difficult. However, children may set their tolerable-level boundaries too high or their tolerable-effort boundaries too low relative to their actual abilities. Some will mistake lack of experience for lack of talent. Some will overestimate their intelligence, and others, especially girls, will underestimate it. All are too young, however, for clear profiles of abilities and interests to have emerged. Guided experience in working with data, people, and things at different levels can, however, keep some middle school students from ruling out options that might be especially fitting and feasible for them.

As students enter high school (cell 6), part-time jobs, community service, extern and intern opportunities, job shadowing, and the like provide additional valuable experience. They function like job previews, whereby students can discover firsthand the work activities they do and do not like and which aptitudes they might have. College students can likewise benefit from sampling different extracurricular activities and academic courses, including service learning. Only by directly experiencing different forms of endeavor can they know rather than merely imagine which ones they would like, dislike, and have or not have a knack for. Experience often teaches students what they do not like and would never want to do. They may need to be reassured that such experience is valuable precisely for that reason and is not wasted.

Experience is authentic self-assessment of a sort that no formal assessment can ever provide. Vocational interest inventories, for instance, can only register the trait constellations that experience has already evoked and begun to consolidate.

Promote Self-Agency in Shaping One's Own Experience   Few young people realize the degree to which they direct their own development by daily engaging in some activities rather than others and assuming some roles rather than others. All people, no matter what their genetic and environmental constraints, have the power to mitigate or improve their conditions at all stages of life. That power rests, however, on the active but wise exercise of personal agency.

Counselors can provide experiential lessons in recognizing and beneficially exploiting self-agency. The aforementioned activities for imparting experiential knowledge about self and work can be designed to provide practice in personal agency at the same time. For instance, guidance programs can, in small steps, help elementary and middle school students project themselves into the future, imagine alternative futures, identify their effects on others, and gradually become acquainted with setting and pursuing goals. Such efforts can prime young people to accept rather than avoid developmental tasks and to see themselves as responsible actors rather than passive targets of influence.

Hands-on experience can also help students augment their repertoire of life skills. This, in turn, builds self-confidence because demonstrated competence is the firmest foundation of self-efficacy. It may also help them face the life challenges to come by providing exercises in anticipatory coping (Lazarus, 1980). In short, providing practice in self-agency has the potential to cultivate it as an expectation and habit. People differ greatly in their natural tendency to exercise it, however. Persons with generally negative affect (depressive, pessimistic, etc.) need more experience and support, even to accept that they possess any control over their lives.

Problems in recognizing and wisely exercising self-agency seem to be addressed by the *career education* and *career therapy* questions in Savickas's (1996) framework, because both address problems in personal agency: How do I shape my career? How can work help me grow as a person?

OPTIMIZE SELF-INSIGHT

Formulating career choices that are compatible with an individual's goals, interests, and abilities depends on his or her knowing what the latter are and identifying careers that fit them. As just noted, the major risk for young people when narrowing or circumscribing their choices is prematurely foreclosing good options and otherwise stunting their development for lack of self-knowledge. Experience does not automatically result in insight, so the practical challenge for counselors is: How can we help counselees to gain insight from their previous behavior and experience and then conceptualize a future career life that is both fitting and feasible for them?

Promote an Inventory and Integration of Information about Self   Counselors can elicit and help counselees take stock of what they already know or can demonstrate about themselves. Figure 4.4, introduced earlier, shows the three types of self-knowledge to be sought: the individual's highly stable general traits of personality and ability (P); the individual's more domain-specific, more malleable attributes such as goals, attitudes, interests, skills, habits, and beliefs (P-E); and the external opportunities, expectations, support, and obligations the individual has created or evoked for himself or herself (E-P, or extended phenotype).

By middle/junior high school (cell 7), students have become capable of cataloguing their more obvious personal attributes and of making simple generalizations about themselves, others, and jobs. They already have a store of experience to reflect on, especially if they have been exposed (or exposed themselves) to varied activities. Exercises requiring them to review that experience can help them discern the consistencies in their behavior, including patterns in their choice of activities and friends, reactions to events, and effects on others. Having them identify their major strengths and weaknesses, likes and dislikes, hopes and fears, and accomplishments and goals can also help them recognize that they do, in fact, have enduring traits and potentials to develop (and perhaps proclivities to suppress). These exercises can, therefore, help students understand that they have an internal unique self, even if they cannot yet see it clearly. They can also teach that such attributes—the differences among individuals *within* a gender, race, or class, not the differences *between* groups—are most pertinent in career choice.

Middle school students still define themselves largely by their social attributes, however, and, therefore, still conceive the compatibility of careers largely on that basis. It is thus a good time to have them look at the sorts of occupations they have excluded from their self-designated social space. Structured exercises can expose students' tolerable sex type, prestige, and effort boundaries by asking them to rate the compatibility of occupations sampled from all major sectors of work (e.g., Gottfredson & Lapan, 1997; Lapan, Adams, Turner, & Hinkelman, 2000; Turner & Lapan, Chapter 17, this volume). Their spontaneously generated likes and dislikes will not be sufficient for exposing these boundaries. Having students then explain why they have rejected the occupations they have can reveal beliefs they take for granted but perhaps should not, such as that people with their social attributes (gender, class, religion, etc.) "don't do" that type of work. For example, the hypothetical girl in Figure 4.2 might find that her interests and abilities are compatible with being a journalist, an option that she may have ejected from her social space years before because she had wrongly assumed that it was too difficult or otherwise out of reach for her.

A review of options rejected as too high or too low can also reveal two potential birth-niche problems: underaspiration and the effort-ability squeeze. Children from lower class families tend to be brighter than their parents, but they do not aspire to commensurately more prestigious occupations. Jobs below their ability level are sufficient to be successful in their social circles, causing many to set unduly low tolerable-effort boundaries. Others fear estranging themselves from family and friends by moving, for example, from blue-collar backgrounds into white-collar work (Lubrano, 2003). In contrast, children of high-achieving parents tend to have high aspirations, but they tend not to be as bright as their parents. Many, therefore, feel compelled to seek careers that are near or beyond the limits of their capabilities; that is, their tolerable-level boundaries may bump up against their tolerable-effort boundaries. Both types of children may gain insight into their career choices and anxieties if queried why they have rejected some occupations as too low level and others as too high.

By high school (cell 8), students are both more able and more eager to know their unique internal selves. Self-insight can be fostered by having adolescents generate and review four types of career-related information about themselves: their current abilities, interests, life goals, and impact on their personal environments. Many formal assessment tools are available for measuring personal traits, especially core personality and ability (P) traits and domain-specific attributes such as vocational interests and values (P-E). I am not aware of any assessments of extended phenotypes, at least ones conceived as such, but it is nonetheless essential that young people assess the merits of the extended phenotypes they have been constructing for themselves.

Formal assessments are effective tools, but not the only ones, for uncovering proclivities and potentials. Counselors can structure other opportunities (written exercises on life goals, group discussions of past experience, etc.) to help individuals gain self-insight. Moreover, formal assessments, which deliver ready-made results as if captured by a magic eye, may not be the best means of teaching young people that they are works in progress and that they possess considerable control (and responsibility) over the form they take.

Gathering and integrating information to form an accurate self-concept coincide with Savickas's (1996) *career counseling* question: Who am I? He discusses the variety of tools for addressing such concerns.

Promote Sound Conception of a Fitting and Feasible Career Life   If self-insight is gained by abstracting the self from the flow of daily activities over time and place, then making fitting career life choices is akin to deciding where and how to embed that self in social life. Choosing an occupation is not just picking a job but a *career life,* that is, individuals committing themselves to a way of life, developing a social niche, connecting themselves to the culture in some ways rather than others. Good career decision making, therefore, requires more than ensuring that their interests and abilities are compatible with a job's requirements and rewards. It also requires balancing occupational preferences with other life roles and obligations, current or expected. The aim of such examination is not to identify the one best career (a chimera, in any case), but to set a favorable direction and avoid big mistakes.

Middle/junior high school students (cell 7) can be introduced to such considerations by simple exercises that have them, for example, enumerate the different life roles and life choices they observe, document that jobs in their community require different skills and reward different interests, evaluate the life decisions that literary characters or others have made, and speculate about how workers' jobs and family lives affect each other.

High school and college students (cell 8) need to start constructing tentative career plans while still in school because poor educational decisions can effectively block some paths in life. They have already ruled out many occupations as potential careers for themselves, and they now need to pick one option from their social space. A first step is to identify occupations entailing activities and rewards that would satisfy someone with their interests and then determine whether they have, or can acquire, the abilities and skills necessary to get the job and perform it well.

Vocational psychologists have developed a wide variety of computerized systems (e.g., DISCOVER, SIGI), occupational classifications (e.g., Holland's six-category RIASEC typology), and vocational interest inventories (e.g., Strong Interest Inventory, Self-Directed Search) for matching people's interests to occupations (Gore & Hitch, Chapter 16, this volume; Prince & Heiser, 2000; Ryan Krane & Tirre, Chapter 14, this volume). There are relatively few such tools for assessing person-job match on the basis of abilities (e.g., O*NET, 2004, http://online.onetcenter.org). However, a review of the job aptitudes literature suggests that both people and jobs can be classified in terms of general ability *level* and ability *profile* (Gottfredson, 2003). Jobs requiring only average intelligence (e.g., most crafts, clerical, sales, and protective service work) are distinguished primarily by whether they also draw on mechanical-spatial ability (mostly Holland's Realistic work), extraversion (Social and Enterprising work), or clerical speed and conscientiousness (Conventional work). There is relatively little mid-level Artistic or Investigative work. Jobs requiring above-average general intelligence (mostly college-entry jobs) are distinguished primarily by whether they require an ability profile tilted toward verbal rather than math aptitude (law, the humanities), a tilt toward math (medicine, mathematics, the biological and social sciences), or a tilt toward math plus spatial ability (engineering, hard sciences). These are not independent intelligences, but more like different flavors of general intelligence. As noted earlier, schools provide ample opportunity to gauge intelligence level and certain differences in profile shape (clerical, math, and verbal abilities). Special efforts must be made, however, to ascertain whether students are strong in mechanical-spatial aptitude, which tends to be higher among males.

Not all occupations that are compatible with an individual's interests and abilities necessarily mesh, however, with his or her nonwork life goals and obligations. Although there are no goal-integration algorithms comparable to the RIASEC system for matching interests with jobs, workshops and other aids can provide practice in clarifying goals, opportunities, and barriers; balancing competing goals and needs; compiling a career life plan; and so on (e.g., Zunker, 1998).

Many students become anxious and seek help when they are required to make, not just imagine, career life decisions. Counseling psychologists have, therefore, paid particular attention to helping individuals who are having difficulty making good career decisions or any at all (e.g., undecided students). Helping clients develop a fitting and feasible career life plan is the *vocational guidance* question in Savickas's (1996) framework: What shall I choose?

OPTIMIZE SELF-INVESTMENT

Perhaps the most difficult challenge counselees face is implementing a career choice, that is, locating and obtaining the training or job that will initiate the chosen career life. Success in doing so depends on the accessibility of the preferred option, which depends in turn on many factors in constant motion, including personal qualifications and liabilities, available openings, and competition for them. The preferred career may not be a realistic choice, necessitating compromise. The risk in this process is that individuals will make unnecessary or unwise compromises because they are not aware of, or do not take, opportunities to improve the accessibility of the career lives they seek. The practical challenge for counselors is: How can we help individuals assess and increase the odds of implementing their preferred options?

Facilitate Appraisal of the Accessibility of Preferred Career Life   Implementing a career choice means investing in efforts toward that end. Just as with any other investment, it requires committing time, effort, and material resources to locate good investment opportunities. Any investment also imposes opportunity costs, because resources are finite: Investing in some things means *not* investing in others. Moreover, time and resources will be lost if poorly invested.

Appraising the accessibility of different career options is costly because the requisite information is scattered, constantly changing, multifaceted, and often difficult to interpret. Job banks, occupational projections, catalogs of training programs, and placement services can reduce the cost by providing up-to-date information about openings currently or soon available in different lines of work (cell 9). The foregoing resources can also be used in assessing a client's chances of selection by providing profiles of the entry standards and competitors against which the client will be judged. Realism also requires an accounting of a person's competing obligations, access to social and financial support, and personal risks and tradeoffs involved in pursuing the preferred option. How good a bet is it, *really*? Its relative merits can be judged, and prudence served, by appraising the merits of acceptable back-up or safety-net alternatives. The aim of such appraisal is to have individuals, singly or in groups, identify their constraints. It sets the stage for exploring ways they might mitigate or bypass them.

Promote Self-Agency in Enhancing Self, Opportunity, and Support to Implement Plans
Getting into and succeeding at our preferred career life is rarely, if ever, a sure thing. It is, therefore, prudent to try to increase the odds in our favor, especially when they are low to begin with. This requires enhancing our qualifications, mobilizing support, or creating new opportunities for ourselves.

We cannot expect to change our intelligence, temperament, and other core (P) traits, but we can learn to play to our strengths and avoid situations that bring out our flaws. Our narrower, more specific (P-E) attributes are more malleable, however. We can, therefore, invest in ourselves by developing new skills, beneficial habits, and strategies for coping with specific situations. The same is true of our social circumstances; some are effectively fixed but others can be changed. There is always leeway for shaping the environment, and certainly our own life niche (extended phenotype), by creating new opportunities, generating or defying expectations, building support networks, and incurring or deflecting obligations.

For instance, an inventory of clients' strengths and weaknesses, social advantages, and barriers will identify much that they can highlight, modify, or mitigate. If not very competitive for a particular job or educational program, they can acquire relevant experience and skills training (using the tools in cell 6 of Table 4.1). Counselees can also become more effective applicants by learning how to write good resumes or how to dress and prepare for interviews. They can identify more job opportunities inside and outside their birth niches by consulting career centers as well as compatriots; generate additional emotional, social, and financial resources by seeking out mentors, advisors, and scholarships; gain confidence as well as contacts by getting more work experience, either paid or volunteer; and ease anxieties by developing contingency plans.

Once again, there are large individual differences, this time in seeking and grasping opportunity. Whereas some counselees show initiative, optimism, and energy in seeking good options and overcoming barriers, others let circumstances govern their fate. Whereas some are quick to spot and take advantage of opportunities, others are overwhelmed by the cognitive or emotional demands involved. Counselors need to provide more emotional and logistic support for the latter. They also need to work with some counselees to suppress destructive or distasteful behavior, such as extreme impulsiveness, aggressiveness, hostility, or lying, by encouraging them to get skills training (change themselves directly) or avoid the experiences and settings that trigger the behavior (change their environments).

The foregoing self-investment strategies relate to Savickas's (1996) *occupational placement* question: How do I get a job? When they are used to aid persons already working, they relate to his *position coaching* question: How can I do better?

SUMMARY

Dealing with the barriers in life is difficult, and the freedom to choose can be yet more daunting when stakes are high and conditions uncertain. The gift of occupational choice, albeit constrained, poses big challenges for our 1,000 newborns. Confused or overwhelmed, some drift with the currents of their birth niche, thereby abdicating the opportunity and responsibility to direct their lives. Others gradually exercise control, but too late to avoid irreversible loss of opportunity. Career counselors can help clients use their freedom to answer the challenges it poses. As outlined here, they can first help individuals avoid unnecessary, self-limiting circumscription and compromise. They can then help individuals identify and wisely invest the genetic and social resources at their disposal to fashion gratifying career lives.

REFERENCES

Ackerman, P. L., & Heggestad, E. D. (1997). Intelligence, personality, and interests: Evidence for overlapping traits. *Psychological Bulletin, 121,* 219–245.

Anderson, L. W., & Krathwohl, D. R. (Eds.). (2001). *A taxonomy for learning, teaching, and assessing: A revision of Bloom's taxonomy of educational objectives.* New York: Longman.

Bergmann, C. S., Plomin, R., Pedersen, N. L., McClearn, G. E., & Nesselroade, J. R. (1990). Genetic and environmental influences on social support: The Swedish Adoption/Twin Study of Aging (SATSA). *Journals of Gerontology: Psychological Sciences, 45,* 101–106.

Betsworth, D. G., Bouchard, T. J., Jr., Cooper, C. R., Grotevant, H. D., Hansen, J. I. C., Scarr, S., et al. (1994). Genetic and environmental influences on vocational interests assessed using adoptive and biological families and twins reared apart and together. *Journal of Vocational Behavior, 44,* 263–278.

Bouchard, T. J., Jr., Lykken, D. T., Tellegen, A., & McGue, M. (1996). Genes, drives, environment, and experience: EPD theory revised. In C. P. Benbow & D. Lubinski (Eds.), *Intellectual talent: Psychometric and social issues* (pp. 5–43). Baltimore: Johns Hopkins University Press.

Brown, S. D., & Ryan Krane, N. E. (2000). Four (or five) sessions and a cloud of dust: Old assumptions and new observations about career counseling. In S. D. Brown & R. W. Lent (Eds.), *Handbook of counseling psychology* (3rd ed., pp. 740–766). New York: Wiley.

Dunn, J., & Plomin, R. (1990). *Separate lives: Why sibling are so different.* New York: Basic Books.

Gottfredson, L. S. (1981). Circumscription and compromise: A developmental theory of occupational aspirations [Monograph]. *Journal of Counseling Psychology, 28,* 545–579.

Gottfredson, L. S. (1986). Occupational aptitude patterns map: Development and implications for a theory of job aptitude requirements [Monograph]. *Journal of Vocational Behavior, 29,* 254–291.

Gottfredson, L. S. (1996). Gottfredson's Theory of Circumscription and Compromise. In D. Brown, L. Brooks, & Associates. (Eds.), *Career choice and development* (3rd ed., pp. 179–232). San Francisco: Jossey-Bass.

Gottfredson, L. S. (1997). Why *g* matters: The complexity of everyday life. *Intelligence, 24,* 79–132.

Gottfredson, L. S. (1999). The nature and nurture of vocational interests. In M. L. Savickas & A. R. Spokane (Eds.), *Vocational interests: Their meaning, measurement, and use in counseling* (pp. 57–85). Palo Alto, CA: Davies-Black.

Gottfredson, L. S. (2002). Gottfredson's theory of circumscription, compromise, and self-creation. In D. Brown & Associates (Eds.), *Career choice and development* (4th ed., pp. 85–148). San Francisco: Jossey-Bass.

Gottfredson, L. S. (2003). The challenge and promise of cognitive career assessment. *Journal of Career Assessment, 11,* 115–135.

Gottfredson, L. S. (2004). Intelligence: Is it the health epidemiologists' elusive "fundamental cause" of health inequalities? *Journal of Personality and Social Psychology, 86,* 174–199.

Gottfredson, L. S., & Lapan, R. T. (1997). Assessing gender-based circumscription of occupational aspirations. *Journal of Career Assessment, 5,* 419–441.

Gysbers, N. C., & Henderson, P. (1994). *Developing and managing your school guidance program* (2nd ed.). Alexandria, VA: American Counseling Association.

Jensen, A. R. (1997). The puzzle of nongenetic variance. In R. J. Sternberg & E. Grigorenko (Eds.), *Intelligence, heredity, and environment* (pp. 42–88). New York: Cambridge University Press.

Kirsch, I. S., Jungeblut, A., & Mosenthal, P. B. (1994). *Moving towards the measurement of adult literacy.* Paper presented at the March NCES meeting, Washington, DC.

Krumboltz, J. D. (1994). Improving career development theory from a social learning perspective. In M. L. Savickas & R. W. Lent (Eds.), *Convergence in career development theories: Implications for science and practice* (pp. 9–31). Palo Alto, CA: Consulting Psychologists Press.

Lapan, R. T., Adams, A., Turner, S. L., & Hinkelman, J. M. (2000). Seventh graders' vocational interest and efficacy expectation patterns. *Journal of Career Development, 26,* 215–229.

Lazarus, R. S. (1980). The stress and coping paradigm. In L. A. Bond & J. C. Rosen (Eds.), *Primary prevention of psychopathology: Vol. 4. Competence and coping in adulthood.* Hanover, NH: University Press of New England.

Lent, R. W., & Hackett, G. (1994). Sociocognitive mechanisms of personal agency in career development. In M. L. Savickas & R. W. Lent (Eds.), *Convergence in career development* theories: Implications for science and practice (pp. 77–101). Palo Alto, CA: Consulting Psychologists Press.

Loehlin, J. C. (1992). Genes and environment in personality development. Thousand Oaks, CA: Sage.

Lubrano, A. (2003). Limbo: Blue-collar roots, white-collar dreams. New York: Wiley.

Lyons, M. J., Goldberg, J., Eisen, S. A., True, W., Tsuang, M. T., Meyer, J. M., et al. (1993). Do genes influence exposure to trauma: A twin study of combat. American Journal of Medical Genetics (Neuropsychiatric Genetics), 48, 22–27.

National Center for Education Statistics. (2000, August). Results over time—NAEP 1999 long-term trend summary data tables. Available from http://nces.ed.gov/nationsreportcard /tables/Ltt1999.

Niles, S. G., & Harris-Bowlsbey, J. (2002). Career development interventions in the 21st century. Upper Saddle River, NJ: Merrill Prentice-Hall.

Plomin, R., & Bergmann, C. S. (1991). The nature of nurture: Genetic influence on "environmental" measures. Behavioral and Brain Sciences, 14, 373–427.

Plomin, R., DeFries, J. D., McClearn, J. E., & McGuffin, P. (2001). Behavioral genetics (4th ed.). New York: Worth.

Plomin, R., Lichtenstein, P., Pedersen, N. L., McClearn, G. E., & Nesselroade, J. R. (1990). Genetic influence on life events during the last half of the life span. Psychology and Aging, 5, 25–30.

Plomin, R., & Petrill, S. A. (1997). Genetics and intelligence: What's new? Intelligence, 24, 53–77.

Prince, J. P., & Heiser, L. J. (2000). Essentials of career interest assessment. New York: Wiley.

Roselle, B., & Hummel, T. (1988). Intellectual development and interaction effectiveness with DISCOVER. Career Development Journal, 35–36, 241–251.

Rowe, D. C. (1994). The limits of family influence: Genes, experience, and behavior. New York: Guilford Press.

Rowe, D. C., Vesterdal, W. J., & Rodgers, J. L. (1998). Herrnstein's syllogism: Genetic and shared environmental influences on IQ, education, and income. Intelligence, 26, 405–423.

Savickas, M. L. (1996). A framework for linking career theory and practice. In M. L. Savickas & W. B. Walsh (Eds.), Handbook of career counseling theory and practice (pp. 191–208). Palo Alto, CA: Davies-Black.

Scarr, S., & McCartney, K. (1983). How people make their own environments: A theory of genotype environment effects. Child Development, 54, 424–435.

Snow, R. E. (1996). Aptitude development and education. Psychology, Public Policy, and Law, 2, 536–560.

Sticht, T. G., Armstrong, W. B., Hickey, D. T., & Caylor, J. S. (1987). Cast-off youth: Policy and training methods from the military experience. New York: Praeger.

Tesser, A. (1993). The importance of heritability in psychological research: The case of attitudes. Psychological Review, 100, 129–142.

United States Census Office. (1902). Abstract of the twelfth census of the United States, 1900. Washington, DC: Government Printing Office.

U.S. Census Bureau. (2002). Statistical abstract of the United States: 2002. Washington, DC: U.S. Department of Commerce, Economics and Statistics Administration.

Vandiver, B. J., & Bowman, S. L. (1996). A schematic reconceptualization and application of Gottfredson's model. In M. L. Savickas & W. B. Walsh (Eds.), Handbook of career counseling theory and practice (pp. 155–168). Palo Alto, CA: Davies-Black.

Zunker, V. G. (1998). Career counseling: Applied concepts of life planning (5th ed.). New York: Brooks/Cole.

CHAPTER 5

A Social Cognitive View of Career Development and Counseling

Robert W. Lent

IN MANY WAYS the career development process and the literature devoted to its understanding resemble a giant jigsaw puzzle. The puzzle includes pieces such as genetic endowment, environmental resources and barriers, learning experiences, interests, abilities, values, personality, goals, choices, satisfaction, performance, change (or development) over time, and multiple transitions, such as school-to-work and retirement. Those who are fascinated by this puzzle have had no difficulty identifying and studying its individual pieces. The greatest challenge, as with all jigsaw puzzles, lies in fitting the many different pieces together to form a coherent picture.

But here is where the jigsaw analogy runs into trouble. Jigsaw puzzles per se need only to achieve an aesthetic unity, and they can have only a single solution. The pieces fit together to create a static picture that is pleasing to the eye. Career theories, by contrast, deal with moving pictures. They need to create a framework for understanding complex and dynamic (i.e., changing), as well as relatively stable, aspects of human behavior. They need to assemble the many elements of the career development puzzle into a logical progression (or plausible story), which is not the only version that is possible. They need to be capable of organizing existing knowledge and of generating new knowledge about how people live their work lives. And, typically, we expect them to spawn interventions that will help promote optimal career and life outcomes for as many people as possible.

Social Cognitive Career Theory (SCCT; Lent, Brown, & Hackett, 1994) is a fairly recent approach to understanding the career puzzle. It is intended to offer a unifying framework for bringing together common pieces, or elements, identified by previous career theorists—such as Super, Holland, Krumboltz, and Lofquist and Dawis—and arranging them into a novel rendering of how people (1) develop vocational interests, (2) make (and remake) occupational choices, and (3) achieve varying levels of career success and stability. The primary foundation for this approach lies in Bandura's (1986) general social cognitive theory, which emphasizes the complex ways in which people, their behavior, and environments mutually influence one another. Taking its cue from Bandura's theory, SCCT highlights people's capacity to direct their own vocational behavior (human agency)—to assemble their own puzzle, so to speak—yet it also acknowledges the many personal and environmental influences (e.g., sociostructural barriers and supports, culture, disability status) that serve to strengthen, weaken, or, in some cases, even override human agency in career development.

This chapter contains three main sections:

1. An overview of SCCT's basic elements and predictions.
2. A brief summary of the theory's research base, including study of diverse populations (e.g., people of color, women, persons with disabilities, gay and lesbian workers).
3. Consideration of developmental and counseling applications—that is, how SCCT can be used as a source of ideas for maximizing career options, fostering career choice-making and implementation, and promoting career success and satisfaction.

More comprehensive, technical presentations of SCCT, its research base, conceptual underpinnings, relations to earlier career theories, practical implications, and applications to particular populations can be found in other sources (e.g., Brown & Lent, 1996; Fabian, 2000; Hackett & Byars, 1996; Lent, Brown, & Hackett, 1994, 2000; Lent & Hackett, 1994; Morrow, Gore, & Campbell, 1996; Swanson & Gore, 2000).

SOCIAL COGNITIVE CAREER THEORY'S BASIC ELEMENTS AND MODELS

This section presents SCCT's basic elements, along with a description of how they fit together with other variables to form theoretical models of academic and career interest, choice, and performance.

COMPETING—OR COMPLEMENTARY—SOLUTIONS TO THE CAREER PUZZLE?

Trait-factor (or person-environment fit) career models, as exemplified by Holland's typology (see Spokane & Cruza-Guet, Chapter 2, this volume) and the theory of work adjustment (Dawis, Chapter 1, this volume), tend to view people and their work environments in trait-oriented terms, emphasizing attributes that are relatively global, constant, and enduring across time and situations. Trait models assume that much of what drives career behavior is based on proclivities—such as interests, abilities, values, and personality dispositions—that are largely molded by genetic endowment and early learning experiences. These models have contributed greatly to the understanding of career behavior and to career counseling by highlighting relatively stable features of persons and environments that, if appropriately matched, are likely to lead to satisfying (from the perspective of the person) and satisfactory (from the perspective of the environment) choices.

Developmental career theories (see Savickas, Chapter 3, and Gottfredson, Chapter 4, this volume) tend to focus on more or less predictable challenges that people face on their way to and through adulthood—challenges (such as learning about themselves, exploring the world of work, developing a vocational identity, narrowing career options from the larger fund of possibilities, selecting a career, and adjusting to work) that enable them to take on and (it is hoped) flourish at the role of worker. Certain developmental theories are also concerned with how the worker role relates to other life roles (e.g., parent, leisurite), how contextual factors (e.g., socioeconomic status) affect career trajectories, and—in the case of Savickas's emerging developmental perspective—how people help to construct, or author, their own career/life stories and experiences.

Social Cognitive Career Theory shares certain features and goals with the trait-factor and developmental perspectives, yet it also is relatively distinctive in several respects. For example, like trait-factor theories, SCCT acknowledges the important roles that interests, abilities, and values play within the career development process. Along with developmental theories, SCCT shares a focus on how people negotiate particular developmental milestones (e.g., career choice) and hurdles (e.g., prematurely eliminated options) that have an important bearing on their career futures. At the most general level, all three perspectives (trait-factor, developmental, social cognitive) are concerned with the prediction, understanding, and optimization of career development. They simply emphasize somewhat different processes and predictors, or theoretical mechanisms—differences that may prove to be more complementary and bridgeable than irreconcilable (Lent & Savickas, 1994).

In contrast to trait-factor approaches, SCCT highlights relatively dynamic and situation-specific aspects of both people (e.g., self-views, future expectations, behavior) and their environments (e.g., social supports, financial barriers). While the stability of traits helps in predicting certain outcomes (Dawis, Chapter 1, this volume), traits encourage a focus on the constancy in human behavior—for example, why people and environments remain the same over time. This is an extremely important matter: Part of the success of career counseling lies in its ability to help people forecast the types of careers that they are likely to enjoy and do well in. However, a moment's reflection will reveal that people and environments do not always remain the same; indeed, they sometimes change dramatically. Witness, for example, the huge changes brought about in the workplace by technology, corporate downsizing, and economic globalization—and the consequent demands that such changes have placed on workers to update their skills and cultivate new interests (or find a new home for their old ones).

By focusing on cognitions, behavior, and other factors that, theoretically, are relatively malleable and responsive to particular situations and performance domains, SCCT offers an agenda that is complementary to that of the trait-factor perspective—namely, how people are able to change, develop, and regulate their own behavior over time and in different situations. As a result, SCCT may be able to help fill in certain gaps in trait-factor theories—for example, how do interests differentiate and intensify or shift over time? What factors, other than traits, stimulate career choice and change? How can career skills be nurtured and deficient performance remediated?

The issue of SCCT's differences from developmental theories is a somewhat more complex matter, given the considerable heterogeneity that exists among older and newer (and even just among newer) theories within this camp. However, at a general level, SCCT tends to be less concerned with the specifics of ages and stages of career developmental tasks, yet more concerned with particular theoretical elements that may promote (or stymie) effective career behavior across developmental tasks. For this reason, SCCT may provide a complementary framework from which to address questions that are relevant to particular developmental theories—such as how work and other life roles become more or less salient for particular individuals (Super's theory), how individuals' career options become constricted or circumscribed (Gottfredson's theory), and, perhaps most importantly, how people are able to assert agency (i.e., self-direction) in their own developmental progress (Savickas's theory).

CENTRAL PIECES OF THE PUZZLE, ACCORDING TO SOCIAL COGNITIVE CAREER THEORY

Following general social cognitive theory, SCCT highlights the interplay among three *person variables* that enable the exercise of agency in career development: self-efficacy beliefs, outcome expectations, and personal goals. *Self-efficacy* beliefs refer to "people's judgments of their capabilities to organize and execute courses of action required to attain designated types of performances" (Bandura, 1986, p. 391). These beliefs, which are among the most important determinants of thought and action in Bandura's (1986) theory, have received a great deal of attention from career researchers (e.g., Lent et al., 1994; Rottinghaus, Larson, & Borgen, 2003; Swanson & Gore, 2000). In the social cognitive view, self-efficacy is not a unitary or global trait, like self-esteem (i.e., general feelings of self-worth), with which self-efficacy is often confused. Rather, self-efficacy is conceived as a dynamic set of self-beliefs that are linked to particular performance domains and activities.

An individual might, for instance, hold high self-efficacy beliefs about his or her ability to play piano or basketball but feel much less competent at social or mechanical tasks. These beliefs about personal capabilities, which are subject to change and are responsive to environmental conditions (e.g., How supportive is the piano teacher? How tough is the basketball competition?), may be acquired and modified via four primary informational sources (or types of learning experience):

1. Personal performance accomplishments.
2. Vicarious learning.
3. Social persuasion.
4. Physiological and affective states (Bandura, 1997).

The impact that these informational sources have on self-efficacy depends on a variety of factors, such as how the individual attends to and interprets them. However, in general, personal accomplishments have the potential to exert the greatest influence on self-efficacy. Compelling success experiences with a given task or performance domain (e.g., math) tend to raise self-efficacy in relation to that task or domain; convincing or repeated failures tend to lower task or domain self-efficacy.

Outcome expectations refer to beliefs about the consequences or outcomes of performing particular behaviors. Whereas self-efficacy beliefs are concerned with an individual's capabilities (e.g., "Can I do this?"), outcome expectations involve imagined consequences of particular courses of action (e.g., "If I try doing this, what will happen?"). Bandura (1986) maintained that both self-efficacy and outcome expectations help to determine a number of important aspects of human behavior, such as the activities that people choose to pursue and the ones they avoid. Self-efficacy may be the more influential determinant in many situations that call for complex skills or potentially costly or difficult courses of action (e.g., whether to pursue a medical career). In such situations, people may hold positive outcome expectations (e.g., "A medical career can lead to attractive payoffs"), but avoid a choice or action if they doubt they have the capabilities required to succeed at it (i.e., where self-efficacy is low).

On the other hand, we can also envision scenarios where self-efficacy is high but outcome expectations are low. Such belief patterns may be held by some women or students of color, for example, who are confident in their capabilities in a particular performance domain (e.g., math, science) but who refrain from elective courses or advanced study in that domain because of negative expectations of how they would be treated (e.g., chilly environment, discrimination; see Betz, Chapter 11, this volume). Suffice it to say that both self-efficacy and outcome expectations can influence people's choices, and their relative effects may depend on the person and the situation. People develop outcome expectations about different academic and career paths from a variety of direct and vicarious learning experiences, such as perceptions of the outcomes they have personally received in relevant past endeavors and the secondhand information they acquire about different career fields. Self-efficacy can also affect outcome expectations, especially in situations where outcomes are closely tied to the quality of their performance (e.g., strong performance on a classroom test is typically linked to a high grade, teacher praise, and other positive outcomes), because people usually expect to receive favorable outcomes in performing tasks at which they feel competent.

Personal goals may be defined as an individual's intention to engage in a particular activity or to produce a particular outcome (Bandura, 1986), addressing questions such as, "How much and how well do I want to do this?" Social Cognitive Career Theory distinguishes between *choice-content goals* (the type of activity or career the individual wishes to pursue) and *performance goals* (the level or quality of performance the individual plans to achieve within a chosen endeavor). Goals afford an important means by which people exercise agency in their educational and occupational pursuits. By setting personal goals, people help to organize, direct, and sustain their own behavior, even over long intervals without external payoffs.

Social cognitive theory maintains that people's choice and performance goals are importantly affected by their self-efficacy and outcome expectations. For example, strong self-efficacy and positive outcome expectations in relation to musical performance are likely to nurture music-relevant goals, such as the intention to devote time to practice, to seek performing opportunities, and, perhaps (depending on the nature and strength of their self-efficacy and outcome expectations in other domains), to pursue a career in music. Progress (or lack of progress) in attaining goals, in turn, has a reciprocal influence on self-efficacy and outcome expectations. Successful goal pursuit, for example, may further strengthen self-efficacy and outcome expectations within a positive cycle.

ASSEMBLING SOCIAL COGNITIVE CAREER THEORY'S THEORETICAL FRAMEWORK: THREE SEGMENTAL MODELS

In SCCT, (1) the development of academic and career interests, (2) the formation of educational and vocational choices, and (3) the nature and results of performance in academic and career spheres are conceived as occurring within three conceptually distinct yet interlocking process models (Lent et al., 1994). In each model, presented next, the basic theoretical elements—self-efficacy, outcome expectations, and goals—are seen as operating in concert with other important aspects of persons (e.g., gender, race/ethnicity), their contexts, and learning experiences to help shape the contours of academic and career development.

Interest Model   Home, educational, recreational, and peer environments expose children and adolescents to an array of activities—such as crafts, sports, math, socializing, and computers—that may be harbingers of later career or leisure options. Young people are selectively encouraged by parents, teachers, peers, and important others for pursuing and for trying to perform well certain activities from among those that are available to them. By practicing different activities—and by receiving ongoing feedback, both positive and negative, about the quality of their performances—children and adolescents gradually refine their skills, develop personal performance standards, and form self-efficacy and outcome expectations about different tasks and domains of behavior. For example, rebuke from peers about an individual's athletic skills (e.g., hearing the repeated message, "You stink") is likely to deflate his or her self-efficacy and outcome expectations in this domain.

According to SCCT's interest model, illustrated in Figure 5.1, self-efficacy and outcome expectations about particular activities help to mold career interests (i.e., each person's particular pattern of likes, dislikes, and indifferences in relation to career-relevant tasks). Interest in an activity is likely to blossom and endure when people (1) view themselves as competent (self-efficacious) at the activity and (2) anticipate that performing it will produce valued outcomes (positive outcome expectations). At the same time, people are likely to develop disinterest or even aversion toward activities (such as athletics, in the preceding example) at which they doubt their efficacy and expect to receive undesirable outcomes.

As interests emerge, they—along with self-efficacy and outcome expectations—encourage intentions, or goals, for sustaining or increasing the individual's involvement in particular activities. Goals, in turn, increase the likelihood of activity practice, and subsequent practice efforts give rise to a particular pattern of performance attainments, which, for better or worse, helps to revise self-efficacy and outcome expectations within an ongoing feedback loop. This basic process is seen as repeating itself continuously before career entry. Consistent with the assumptions of trait-factor theories, career-related interests do tend to stabilize over time and,

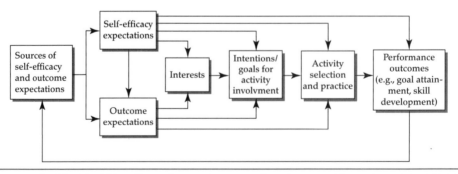

Figure 5.1   Model of How Basic Career Interests Develop over Time. Copyright 1993 by R. W. Lent, S. D. Brown, and G. Hackett. Reprinted by permission.

for many people, are relatively stable by late adolescence or early adulthood (see Hansen, Chapter 12, this volume). In the view of SCCT, however, adult interests are not necessarily set in stone. Whether interests change or solidify is determined by factors such as whether initially preferred activities become restricted and whether people are exposed (or expose themselves) to compelling learning experiences (e.g., childrearing, volunteering, technological innovations) that enable them to expand their sense of efficacy and positive outcome expectations into new spheres (e.g., teaching, social service, computer use). Thus, SCCT assumes that, when they occur, shifts in interests are largely due to changing self-efficacy beliefs and outcome expectations.

Social Cognitive Career Theory also takes into account other aspects of people and their environments that affect the acquisition and modification of interests. For example, abilities and values—staples of trait-factor theories—are important in SCCT, too, but their effects on interest are seen as largely funneled through self-efficacy and outcome expectations. That is, rather than determining interests directly, objective ability (as reflected by test scores, trophies, awards, and the like) serves to raise or lower self-efficacy beliefs, which, in turn, influence interests (Lent et al., 1994). In other words, self-efficacy functions as an intervening link between ability and interests. Career-related values are built into SCCT's concept of outcome expectations. These expectations may be thought of as a combination of people's preferences for particular work conditions or reinforcers (e.g., status, money, autonomy), together with their beliefs about the extent to which particular occupations offer these payoffs (e.g., my beliefs about how much being a professor can offer things that I value in and from work).

It needs to be emphasized that self-efficacy and outcome expectations do not arise in a social vacuum; neither do they operate alone in shaping vocational interest, choice, or performance processes. Rather, they are forged and function in the context of other important qualities of persons and their environments, such as gender, race/ethnicity, genetic endowment, physical health or disability status, and socioeconomic conditions, all of which can play important roles within the career development process. Figure 5.2 offers an overview of how, from the perspective of SCCT, selected person, environmental, and learning or experiential variables contribute to interests and other career outcomes. Given space limitations, I focus on gender and race/ethnicity here.

Social Cognitive Career Theory is concerned more with the psychological and social effects of gender and ethnicity than with the view of sex and race as categorical physical or biological factors. Gender and ethnicity are seen as linked to career development in several key ways—in particular, through the sorts of reactions they evoke from the social/cultural environment and from their relation to the opportunity structure to which individuals are exposed (e.g., the access offered to career-relevant models and performance experiences). Such a view encourages consideration of how gender and ethnicity influence the contexts in which self-efficacy and outcome expectations are acquired. For instance, gender role socialization processes tend to bias the access that boys and girls receive to experiences necessary for developing strong efficacy beliefs and positive expectations about male-typed (e.g., science) and female-typed (e.g., helping) activities. As a result, boys and girls are more likely to develop skills (along with beneficial self-efficacy and outcome expectations) and, in turn, interests at tasks that are culturally defined as gender appropriate (Hackett & Betz, 1981).

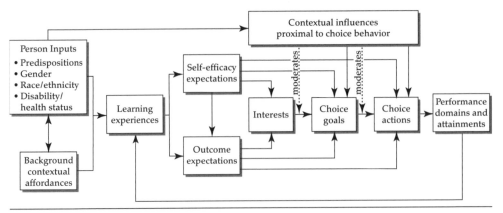

Figure 5.2   Model of Person, Contextual, and Experiential Factors Affecting Career-Related Choice Behavior. [*Note:* Direct relations between variables are indicated with solid lines; moderator effects (where a given variable strengthens or weakens the relations between two other variables) are shown with dashed lines. Copyright 1993 by R. W. Lent, S. D. Brown, and G. Hackett. Reprinted by permission.]

To a large extent, then, variables such as gender and ethnicity may affect interest development and other career outcomes through certain socially constructed processes that, as it were, operate in the background but, nevertheless, can powerfully influence the differential learning experiences that foster self-efficacy and outcome expectations—leading, at times, to skewed conclusions about what interests or career options are "right" for certain classes of persons. At later stages in the career development process, gender, ethnicity, culture, socioeconomic status, and disability conditions may, additionally, be linked to the opportunity structure within which people set and implement their career goals, as discussed next.

Choice Model   Choosing a career path is not a single or static act. As SCCT's interest model illustrates, career choice is preceded by a host of subprocesses—such as the development of self-efficacy, outcome expectations, interests, and skills in different performance domains—that, over time, will leave open and make attractive certain choice paths for a given individual and render other options much less appealing or likely to be considered further. Once initial career choices are made, they are, however, subject to future revision because individuals and their environments are dynamic entities. Events and circumstances may well transpire that could not have been foreseen during initial choice-making or career entry. New paths (or branches from old paths) may open up, barriers (e.g., glass ceiling) or calamities (e.g., job loss) may arise, or value and interest priorities may shift over the course of the individual's working life. Thus, it seems prudent to think of career selection as an unfolding process with multiple influences and choice points.

For conceptual simplicity, SCCT divides the initial choice process into three component parts:

1. The expression of a primary choice (or goal) to enter a particular field.
2. An individual's taking actions designed to implement his or her goal (e.g., enrolling in a particular training program or academic major).

3. Subsequent performance experiences (e.g., exemplary or subpar attainments) that form a feedback loop, affecting the shape of the individual's future choice options.

This conceptual division identifies logical intervention targets for preparing people to make career choices as well as for helping them to deal with problems in choice-making. Throughout the choice process, it is well to keep in mind that people do not choose careers unilaterally; environments also choose people. Thus, career choice (and choice stability) is a two-way street that is conditioned, in part, by the environment's receptivity to the individual and judgments about his or her ability to meet (and to continue to meet) training and occupational requirements.

Similar to Holland's theory (Spokane & Cruza-Guet, Chapter 2, this volume), SCCT assumes that, just as "birds of a feather flock together," people's vocational interests tend to orient them toward choice options that might enable them to perform preferred activities and to interact with others who have similar work personalities. This flocking together works best under supportive environmental conditions. For example, a person whose primary interests lie in the social domain is likely to gravitate toward socially oriented occupations, allowing him or her to work with others in a helping or teaching capacity. However, this process is not always so simple or unencumbered: Environments may not be supportive of individuals' choices, and people are not always free to pursue their primary interests. Choice may be constrained, for example, by family wishes, economic realities (e.g., the need to bring in immediate income, lack of funding for training), and the quality of one's prior education. In such instances, personal interests may not be the prime mover behind an individual's career choice. It is, therefore, important to take into account additional variables that influence the choice process.

Social Cognitive Career Theory's choice model, shown in Figure 5.2, is embedded within a larger conceptual scheme that acknowledges the precursors and sequelae of choices. As described earlier, self-efficacy and outcome beliefs are seen as jointly influencing career-related interests, which tend to foster career choice *goals* (i.e., intentions to pursue a particular career path) that are congruent with an individual's interests. Goals, then, motivate choice *actions,* or efforts to implement goals (e.g., seeking relevant training, applying for certain jobs). These actions are, in turn, followed by a particular pattern of performance successes and failures. For instance, after gaining entry to an engineering college, a student may have difficulty completing the required math and physics courses. He or she may also discover that the work environment and rewards available in engineering suit him or her less well than had been initially anticipated. These learning experiences may prompt the student to revise his or her self-efficacy beliefs and outcome expectations, leading to a shift in interests and goals (e.g., selection of a new major or career path).

Self-efficacy and outcome expectations can affect people's goals and efforts to implement their goals above and beyond the influence of interests (note the separate paths from self-efficacy and outcome expectations to goals and actions in Figure 5.2). This is no esoteric matter: These additional theoretical paths are intended to help explain occupational choice in many real-world instances where people are not simply free to pursue their primary interests. As Bandura once observed (personal communication, March 1, 1993), people are not necessarily drawn to work on assembly lines or in coal mines by a consuming interest in the work. When people perceive the need to make occupational choices that compromise their interests or for reasons other than interests—for instance, because of environmental barriers or limited opportunities—they may choose less interesting options based on what work is available to them, in concert with their self-efficacy (e.g., Do I have or can I develop the skills to do this work?) and outcome expectations (e.g., Are the pay-offs worth it for me to take this job?).

Let us consider some additional ways in which people's environments affect the choice process. Each person derives certain "affordances" from the environment—for instance, social and material resources or hardships—that help to shape his or her career development (Vondracek, Lerner, & Schulenberg, 1986). In SCCT, these contextual affordances are divided into two general types, based on when they occur within the choice process. The first type includes more distal, background influences (e.g., cultural and gender role socialization, types of available career role models, skill development opportunities) that help to shape self-efficacy, outcome expectations, and, hence, interests. The second type involves environmental influences that come into play during the active phases of choice-making. Examples include emotional or financial support for pursuing a particular option, job availability in the individual's preferred field, and sociostructural barriers, such as discrimination. Figure 5.2 includes consideration of these distal (lower left) and proximal (upper right) contextual affordances.

In presenting SCCT's interest model, we had considered the more distal effects of contextual variables on the acquisition of self-efficacy and outcome expectations. We here consider two means by which contextual factors may affect people during the process of setting and implementing their career choice goals, thereby helping to promote or lessen personal agency over their career choices. First, SCCT posits that certain conditions may *directly* affect people's choices or implementation possibilities. In certain cultures, for example, individuals may defer their career decisions to significant others in the family, even where the others' preferred career path is not all that interesting to the individual. People may also encounter environmental supports or barriers in relation to the options that they, themselves, most prefer. Such direct influences are represented by the solid arrows from contextual variables to goals and actions in Figure 5.2.

Second, contextual variables may affect people's ability or willingness to translate their interests into goals and their goals into actions. According to SCCT, career interests are more likely to blossom into goals (and goals are more likely to be implemented) when people experience strong environmental supports and weak barriers in relation to their preferred career paths. By contrast, nonsupportive or hostile conditions can impede the process of transforming interests into goals and goals into actions. In statistical terms, this implies that contextual supports and barriers can *moderate* the goal transformation process (shown by the dotted paths in Figure 5.2). That is, the relations of interest to goals and of goals to actions are expected to be stronger in the presence of favorable versus restrictive environmental conditions.

In summary, SCCT posits that educational and occupational choices are often, but not always, linked to people's interests. Circumstances and cultural conditions sometimes require a compromise in personal interests. In such instances, choices are determined by what options are available to the individual, the nature of his or her self-efficacy beliefs and outcome expectations, and the sorts of messages the individual receives from his or her support system. Environmental factors (supports and barriers) may also facilitate or hinder the choice implementation process, regardless of whether people are pursuing options that are consistent with their primary interests or that they freely chose.

Performance Model   In addition to how interests develop and choices are made, SCCT is concerned with the factors that affect academic and career-related performance. This includes the level (or quality) of attainment individuals achieve in educational and work tasks (e.g., measures of success or proficiency) and the degree to which they persist at particular tasks or choice paths, especially when they encounter obstacles. Persistence can be seen both as a matter of choice stability, involving the decision to remain at or disengage from a particular activity (e.g., educational task, job position, career), and as an indicator of how well an individual is performing at either required or chosen endeavors (e.g., perseverance in problem solving). Thus, SCCT's choice and performance models overlap somewhat in their concern with persistence. From the perspective of educational and work environments, persistence is considered a sign of performance adequacy because it is assumed that competent performers will persist (and *be allowed to persist*) longer, enabling attainment of educational milestones (e.g., high school graduation, college major retention) and job tenure. However, persistence alone is an imperfect indicator of performance adequacy because people often discontinue their involvement in certain endeavors for reasons other than deficient capabilities (e.g., shift in interests, opportunity to pursue new job or career paths, corporate downsizing).

As shown in Figure 5.3, SCCT sees educational and vocational performance as involving the interplay among people's ability, self-efficacy, outcome expectations, and performance goals. More specifically, ability—as assessed by indicators of achievement, aptitude, or past performance—affects performance attainments both (1) directly, for instance, via the task knowledge and performance strategies that people develop and (2) indirectly, by serving to inform self-efficacy and outcome expectations. That is, people base their self-efficacy and outcome expectations partly on their perceptions of the skills they currently possess (or can develop) and of how well they have performed and what outcomes they have received under relevant performance conditions in the past. Self-efficacy and outcome expectations, in turn, influence the level of performance goals that people set

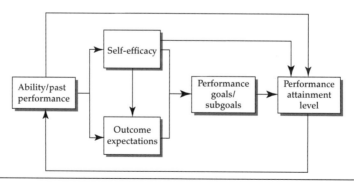

Figure 5.3   Model of Task Performance. Copyright 1993 by R. W. Lent, S. D. Brown, and G. Hackett. Reprinted by permission.

for themselves (e.g., aiming for an A in algebra or a promotion at work). Stronger self-efficacy and positive outcome expectations promote more ambitious goals, which help to mobilize and sustain performance efforts.

Consistent with general social cognitive theory, SCCT posits a feedback loop between performance attainments and subsequent behavior (Bandura, 1986). Several benefits accrue from attempting and succeeding at performance tasks, especially ones that are progressively more challenging. Such experiences provide the opportunity to enhance an individual's task-relevant knowledge and strategies, achieve valued outcomes, and, in turn, promote self-efficacy and outcome expectations within a dynamic, skill development cycle. Although this model details person-level (e.g., cognitive, motivational) processes, it bears repeating that people develop their talents, self-efficacy, outcome expectations, and goals within a larger sociocultural context. As shown in Figure 5.2, the learning experiences to which people are exposed and the performance outcomes they receive are intimately related to features of their environments, such as educational quality, nature of available role models, parenting style, gender role socialization, peer supports, and community and family norms.

It should also be emphasized that self-efficacy is seen as complementing—not substituting for—objectively assessed ability in SCCT's performance model. Complex performances are aided not only by abilities but also by an optimistic sense of efficacy, which helps people organize, orchestrate, and make the most of their talents. What people can accomplish depends partly on how they interpret and apply their skills, helping to explain why two individuals with similar objective capabilities can achieve performances that vary greatly in quality (Bandura, 1986). People who doubt their capabilities may, for instance, be less likely to deploy their skills effectively or to remain focused and perseverant when problems arise.

Might we conclude, then, that higher self-efficacy is always a good thing? In fact, the effects of self-efficacy may depend on how high or low it is in relation to current levels of objective ability. People may encounter problems when they greatly misconstrue their capabilities in either the positive or the negative direction. Self-efficacy beliefs that greatly overestimate current capabilities (overconfidence, in colloquial terms) may encourage people to attempt tasks for which they are ill-prepared, risking failure and discouragement. Self-efficacy that seriously underestimates documented ability (i.e., underconfidence) may interfere with performance by prompting less effort and perseverance, lower goals, greater performance anxiety, and avoidance of realistic challenges. Both types of misconstrual may hamper skill development. By contrast, self-efficacy that slightly overshoots but is reasonably congruent with current capabilities (slight overconfidence) promotes optimal skill use and motivation for further skill development.

RESEARCH ON SOCIAL COGNITIVE CAREER THEORY

The central variables and predictions of SCCT have attracted a good deal of research in recent years. A full-scale review of research generated by, or relevant to, SCCT is beyond the scope of this chapter, though some of the major research trends and findings can be summarized here. Several more thorough reviews (e.g., Bandura, 1997; Swanson & Gore, 2000) and meta-analyses (e.g., Lent et al., 1994; Sadri & Robertson, 1993; Stajkovic & Luthans, 1998) of this literature may be consulted for in-depth analysis of research linking social cognitive theory to career development processes and outcomes. In this section, I first consider the theory's overall empirical status and then discuss selected applications of SCCT to the career behavior of diverse clientele.

LARGER TRENDS AND FINDINGS

A substantial body of findings suggests that social cognitive variables aid understanding of educational and career behavior during the preparatory, transition (e.g., school-to-work, work change), and postentry (work adjustment) phases of career development. Among the social cognitive variables, self-efficacy has received the most attention, with traditional qualitative research reviews concluding:

- Domain-specific measures of self-efficacy are predictive of career-related interests, choice, achievement, persistence, indecision, and exploratory behavior.
- Intervention, experimental, and path-analytic studies support certain hypothesized causal relations among measures of self-efficacy, performance, and interests.
- Gender differences in self-efficacy help to explain male-female differences in occupational consideration (e.g., Bandura, 1997; Hackett, 1995; Hackett & Lent, 1992; Swanson & Gore, 2000).

Meta-analytic reviews provide a helpful, quantitative way to integrate findings from a large number of independent studies, allowing conclusions about the strength of hypothesized relationships across all studies that have addressed particular hypotheses. Several meta-analyses of research, primarily involving late adolescents and young adults, have directly tested a number of SCCT's hypotheses. Meta-analysis of the interest hypotheses, for instance, indicates that self-efficacy and outcome expectations are each good predictors of occupational interests and that, as predicted, the relation of ability to interests appears to operate through (or be mediated by) self-efficacy (Lent et al., 1994; see Figures 5.1 and 5.2). A recent meta-analysis of 53 samples, including more than 37,000 research participants, confirmed that there is a strong overall relationship between self-efficacy and career interests ($r = 0.59$; Rottinghaus et al., 2003).

Meta-analysis of SCCT's choice hypotheses has shown that career-related choices are strongly predicted by interests ($r = 0.60$; Lent et al., 1994). Self-efficacy and outcome expectations also relate to career choice both directly and indirectly, through their linkage to interests (see Figure 5.2; Lent et al., 1994). A recent set of studies has examined the manner in which perceived environmental supports and barriers relate to the choice process. Although this work has not yet been meta-analyzed, the majority of findings suggest that, rather than relating directly to choice outcomes, the primary role of these environmental variables may be to strengthen or weaken self-efficacy beliefs, which, in turn, promote interest and choice (e.g., Lent, Brown, Nota, & Soresi, 2003; Lent, Brown, Schmidt, et al., 2003).

Meta-analysis of SCCT's performance model predictions have focused on the linkage of self-efficacy to various indicators of performance. Findings have shown that self-efficacy is a useful predictor of both academic (Multon, Brown, & Lent, 1991) and occupational (Sadri & Robertson, 1993; Stajkovic & Luthans, 1998) performance and that certain factors affect the strength of the self-efficacy-performance relationship. For instance, self-efficacy tends to be more strongly related to performance in older versus younger students and in low-achieving versus adequately achieving students (Multon et al., 1991). In addition, consistent with theory, ability has been linked to performance outcomes both directly and indirectly, through intervening self-efficacy beliefs (Lent et al., 1994; see Figure 5.3).

Finally, meta-analysis has been used to examine the sources of information, or learning experiences, from which self-efficacy beliefs are assumed to derive (see Figure 5.2). Of the four primary sources (prior performance accomplishments, vicarious learning, social persuasion, physiological and affective states), performance accomplishments (e.g., indicators of a person's previous success or failure) typically show the strongest relation to self-efficacy within a particular performance domain. Self-efficacy is, in turn, a good predictor of outcome expectations (Lent et al., 1994). As discussed in a later section, such findings offer useful implications for the design of interventions to promote self-efficacy and outcome expectations and, in turn, subsequent career outcomes.

Collectively, the meta-analyses are consistent with theoretical assumptions that:

- Interests relate strongly to self-efficacy and outcome expectations.
- A person's ability or performance accomplishments are likely to lead to interests in a particular domain to the extent that they foster a growing sense of self-efficacy in that domain.
- Self-efficacy and outcome expectations relate to career-related choices largely (though not completely) through their linkage to interest.
- Past performance promotes future performance partly through people's abilities and partly through their self-efficacy, which can aid them to organize their skills and persist despite setbacks.
- Self-efficacy appears to derive most strongly from past performance accomplishments but is also responsive to vicarious learning, social encouragement and discouragement, and affective and physiological states.

APPLICATIONS TO DIVERSE POPULATIONS

This section cites examples of work applying social cognitive variables to the career development of women and particular groups of minority persons. Social Cognitive Career Theory was designed to aid understanding of the career development of a diverse array of students and workers, taking into account factors such as race/ethnicity, culture, gender, socioeconomic status, age, and disability status. The earliest effort to extend social cognitive theory to career behavior focused on how the self-efficacy concept might illuminate women's career development. Hackett and Betz (1981) noted, for example, that gender role socialization processes tend to provide girls and young women with biased access to the four sources of efficacy information (e.g., gender-traditional role models, differential encouragement to pursue culturally prescribed activities). Such experiences nurture self-efficacy for traditionally female activities but may limit self-efficacy in nontraditional career domains.

In testing their thesis, Betz and Hackett (1981) found that college women reported stronger self-efficacy for performing occupations that are traditionally dominated by women than by men and that these beliefs were linked to their interests in and consideration of traditional and nontraditional choice options. Other research has shown that self-efficacy beliefs help to explain gender differences in scientific/technical field interests (e.g., Lapan, Boggs, & Morrill, 1989). Studies using general samples of students often find sex differences in self-efficacy as to gender-typed tasks and fields (e.g., mathematics); differences in self-efficacy are less likely to emerge, however, in samples of women and men who have had comparable efficacy-building experiences with such tasks (Hackett & Lent, 1992).

These sorts of findings suggest that women's career pursuits can be constricted or expanded by the learning environments to which they are exposed and, in particular, by the nature of the self-efficacy beliefs that such exposure enables. As Bandura (1997) has observed, "cultural constraints, inequitable incentive systems, and truncated opportunity structures are . . . influential in shaping women's career development" (p. 436). Thus, self-beliefs are embedded within a complex web of systemic processes. While this analysis suggests some daunting environmental obstacles to women's career development, it also implies several developmental and preventative routes for redressing socially imposed limitations. Such routes include, for example, educating parents and teachers about the educational and occupational implications of gender-typed efficacy development and about ways to foster self-efficacy and support systems, thereby enabling children to acquire (and profit from) performance experiences in as wide a range of activity domains as possible. Indeed, consistent with Gottfredson's (Chapter 4, this volume) theory, exposure to and experience with non-gender-stereotypic activities may need to be provided relatively early in children's lives to preserve the maximum number of options for later educational and career consideration (also see Rojewski, Chapter 6, this volume).

Similar social-cognitive dynamics have been discussed in relation to the career development of persons of color. Hackett and Byars (1996) noted, for example, how culturally based exposure to sources of efficacy information (e.g., social encouragement to pursue certain options, experience with racism, role modeling) may differentially affect African American women's career self-efficacy beliefs, outcome expectations, goals, and subsequent career progress. Hackett and Byars suggested theory-based methods, such as developmental interventions, social advocacy, and collective action, to promote the career growth of African American women. In other work, applications of SCCT's basic interest and choice models to Hispanic, Black, and Asian American student samples have found support for the cross-cultural relevance of these models (e.g., Fouad & Smith, 1996; Gainor & Lent, 1998; Tang, Fouad, & Smith, 1999).

Social Cognitive Career Theory has also been extended, conceptually or empirically, to a number of other client populations. For instance, Szymanski, Enright, Hershenson, and Ettinger (2003) considered self-efficacy and outcome expectations as useful constructs in understanding the career development of persons with disabilities, and Fabian (2000) discussed how SCCT could be used to derive career interventions specifically for adults with psychiatric disabilities. Social Cognitive Career Theory has also been suggested as a useful framework for understanding certain career processes in gay and lesbian workers (Morrow et al. 1996). Finally, the theory has been employed in a number of cross-cultural and international applications (e.g., de Bruin, 1999; Kantas, 1997; Lent, Brown, Nota, & Soresi, 2003; Van Vianen, 1999).

In sum, research offers support for a number of theoretical assumptions (from SCCT and from the larger social cognitive theory) about how self-efficacy and outcome expectations function in relation to career interests, choice, performance, and other career outcomes. The applications described in this section also convey SCCT's potential utility in understanding and facilitating the career development of a diverse range of persons. While such applications are exciting in their promise, there is need for additional research that clarifies how social cognitive variables operate together with culture, ethnicity, socioeconomic status, sexual orientation, and disability status to shape the career development of students and workers. Theory-based intervention studies have begun to appear (e.g., Betz & Schifano, 2000; Luzzo, Hasper, Albert, Bibby, & Martinelli, 1999), yet more such work is needed to help strengthen the empirical basis for practical applications of SCCT. Nevertheless, currently available findings may offer valuable implications for career education and counseling practice. We consider such implications in the next section.

APPLYING SOCIAL COGNITIVE CAREER THEORY TO SELECTED CAREER DEVELOPMENT CONCERNS

Social Cognitive Career Theory suggests a host of ideas for developmental, preventive, and remedial career interventions—that is, for promoting development of students' academic/career interests and competencies, for preventing or forestalling career-related difficulties, and for helping people cope with existing problems in choosing or adjusting to work. Suggestions for developmental and preventive applications can be derived from SCCT's basic interest, choice, and performance models—especially from hypotheses about how self-efficacy and the other social cognitive variables develop in childhood and adolescence. In remedial applications, the theory may be used as an organizing framework both for adapting existing counseling methods and for developing novel intervention techniques. In this section, we consider ways in which SCCT may be employed in dealing with selected developmental and remedial career concerns.

PROMOTING ASPIRATIONS AND INTERESTS IN YOUNG PERSONS

From the perspective of SCCT, several key processes occur during childhood and adolescence—within academic, family, peer, and other settings—that set the stage for later choice-making and adjustment. These processes include acquisition of self-efficacy and outcome expectations related to diverse activities, development of career-relevant interests, and formation of career aspirations. (In SCCT, aspirations represent provisional occupational goals or daydreams.) These processes relate to developmental tasks that are prominent during the elementary and middle school years and are continually revisited and refined in high school and beyond (Lent, Hackett, & Brown, 1999).

Young children typically have a very limited grasp of their capabilities, not to mention career activities and paths. Given their limited experience and exposure to career role models, their career-related interests and aspirations are likely to be somewhat stereotypical, narrow, and fluid (e.g., a boy expressing the desire to become a fireman one week and a baseball player the next). Over the course of childhood and adolescence, people typically receive increasing experience with varied performance tasks as well as direct and vicarious exposure to a widening range of career possibilities. These experiences lead to differentiated beliefs about an individual's capabilities in diverse activity domains and an expanded sense of the working conditions and reinforcers afforded by different career options. Emergent self-efficacy and outcome expectations, in turn, nurture career-relevant interests and goals that tend to become more defined and crystallized over time, yet are still relatively modifiable based on additional learning about the self (e.g., personal capabilities, values) and careers (e.g., skill requirements, available reinforcers). In this way, career aspirations gradually (but not invariably) tend to become increasingly stable and realistic—which is to say, congruent with personal interests, capabilities, and values.

This analysis suggests that self-efficacy and outcome expectations—and the information on which they are based—are key to the cultivation of students' academic and career interests and to the range and types of occupational options they are willing to consider. At the same time, students' career aspirations can become constricted either because their environments provide limited or biased exposure to particular efficacy-building experiences (e.g., few opportunities to succeed at scientific pursuits, no gender-similar role models in math) or because they acquire inaccurate self-efficacy or occupational outcome expectations. These observations suggest that developmental interventions to promote favorable self-efficacy and outcome expectations are likely to be most useful during childhood and adolescence, before interests and aspirations become more stable and some options become prematurely foreclosed.

The four sources of efficacy information can be used as an organizing structure for psychoeducational interventions. Personal performance accomplishments are a particularly valuable intervention target, given their potent effects on self-efficacy. Incrementally graded success experiences can foster a sense of efficacy at particular tasks, yet it is also important to attend to the manner in which students interpret the quality of their performances. For example, objective successes may not impact self-efficacy where students attribute their good grades to luck, effort, or task ease. This is a common occurrence in the case of girls' achievements in math, science, and other nontraditional activities (Hackett, 1995). Efforts to modify students' self-efficacy may, therefore, profit from inclusion of cognitive restructuring procedures that encourage students to entertain self-enhancing performance attributions (e.g., a person crediting his or her success to developing personal capabilities, viewing ability as an acquirable attribute rather than a fixed, inborn entity).

Useful intervention elements can also be fashioned from the other three sources of efficacy information. For example, modeling can be used to assist students to explore academic and career domains that they may not have previously encountered or been encouraged to consider. Students are most likely to identify with role models whom they perceive as being similar to themselves along important dimensions, such as gender, ethnicity, and age. Social support and persuasion can be used to encourage students to attempt new tasks, to persist despite initial setbacks, and to interpret their performances favorably, for example, by focusing on skill growth versus ultimate task success. Physiological and affective states may also require attention where, for example, task-related anxiety appears to be diminishing self-efficacy and disrupting performance. Relaxation exercises and other cognitive-behavioral strategies can be used to reduce debilitative anxiety.

Content-specific efficacy beliefs (e.g., in math and other school subjects) need not be the only focus of efficacy-building efforts. It also seems desirable to encourage self-efficacy and skills at larger "career process" domains, such as communication, teamwork, conflict management, leadership, and multicultural sensitivity. Such general skill domains have been seen as integral to students' transition from school to work (Lent et al., 1999). In addition to a focus on self-efficacy enhancement, SCCT would encourage a variety of other developmental intervention targets. In particular, exposure to career information (see Gore & Hitch, Chapter 16, this volume) is key to fostering acquisition of realistic outcome expectations (i.e., beliefs about the working conditions and reinforcers available in diverse occupations). Social Cognitive Career Theory would also encourage age-appropriate interventions designed to help students to explore their emerging interests and the various careers with which they may be compatible (Turner & Lapan, Chapter 17, this volume). Such interventions would best be approached with the explicit understanding (communicated to parents, teachers, and students) that interests, goals, values, and skills are fluid attributes that can change and grow with additional experience. Assessment may, thus, best be viewed as a snapshot at a single point in time, rather than as a reflection of immutable qualities.

Finally, SCCT would encourage a focus on fostering skills such as decision making and goal setting (e.g., breaking larger distal goals into proximal subgoals, locating supports for personal goals). Such skills can be taught by using examples from domains, such as studying or friendships, that are meaningful to young people and that can be generalized to career development. Social Cognitive Career Theory has been used recently as a basis for designing (Prideaux, Patton, & Creed, 2002) and evaluating (McWhirter, Rasheed, & Crothers, 2000) career education programs.

FACILITATING CAREER CHOICE-MAKING AND IMPLEMENTATION

In an ideal scenario, people arrive at late adolescence or early adulthood with:

- A good appreciation of their interests, values, and talents.
- An understanding of how these self-attributes correspond with potential vocational options.
- A clear goal, or choice, that links their self-attributes to a suitable career path (i.e., one that can engage their interests, satisfy their values, and value their talents).
- Adequate skills at making decisions, setting goals, and managing goal pursuit (i.e., self-regulation skills).
- An environment that provides needed support for their goals (e.g., social encouragement, mentors, financial resources) and minimal goal-related barriers (racial discrimination).
- A set of personality traits (e.g., low levels of negative affectivity, high levels of conscientiousness) that can generally aid the process of making and implementing important life decisions by, for example, minimizing chronic indecisiveness and maximizing follow-through with goals and plans.

Those who possess ample amounts of these personal and environmental resources are unlikely to seek the services of a career counselor. Unfortunately, however, problems may occur in any or all of these areas—and various other challenges, such as physical disabilities or difficulties in life domains apart from career choice, may arise as well—that can hamper an individual's efforts at career choice-making and implementation. Adept career counselors are able to assess and treat a wide array of these choice-limiting problems. While a full-scale discussion of career choice problems and solutions is beyond the scope of this chapter, it is possible to highlight a few strategies derived from SCCT that can aid in navigating certain impasses to career choice-making and implementation.

Expanding Choice Options   Like most other approaches to career choice counseling, SCCT aims to help clients select from an array of occupations that correspond reasonably well with important aspects of their work personalities (e.g., interests, values, skills). Some clients are blocked in this effort because their work personalities are not sufficiently differentiated (e.g., measured interests produce a low, flat profile) or because they feel stifled by a constricted range of career options. In such instances, my colleagues and I have found it helpful to explore the social cognitive processes that may underlie choice problems, adapting assessment strategies that are commonly used in career counseling (e.g., Brown & Lent, 1996). An important implication of SCCT's interest model is that people often reject potentially viable career options because of inaccurate self-efficacy and outcome expectations (e.g., a person may believe, erroneously, that he or she does not have the skills to perform effectively in a given occupation or that the occupation does not offer the working conditions that he or she values). By revisiting previously discarded options and considering the reasons they have been discarded, career clients can often clarify their interests, skills, and values—and also expand the range of potentially satisfying options from which they may choose.

We have used two strategies to explore discarded options. In the first strategy, standardized measures of vocational interests, values/needs, and aptitudes are administered, and the results are examined for discrepancies between the occupational options generated by the various measures. We especially look for aptitude-interest and value-interest discrepancies. Instances in which clients appear to have the aptitude to succeed at particular occupations, but where they show relatively low interest in them, may suggest that personal capabilities are being discounted (i.e., that interests may not have developed because their self-efficacy is unrealistically low). Similarly, instances in which a client's values appear compatible with particular occupations, but where the client shows little interest in the occupations, may suggest inaccurate outcome expectations (i.e., he or she may possess limited or biased information about the occupations, resulting in faulty assumptions about its potential to meet his or her needs). Such discrepancies are targeted for further discussion and, possibly, counseling aimed at boosting self-efficacy or instilling accurate outcome expectations.

Our second strategy for exploring foreclosed occupational options uses a modified vocational card sort procedure. We first ask clients to sort a list of occupations into three categories: (1) might choose, (2) would not choose, and (3) in question. We then focus on those occupations that are sorted into the "would not choose" and "in question" categories. The client is encouraged to sort these occupations into more specific categories reflecting self-efficacy beliefs (i.e., "might choose if I thought I had the skills"), outcome expectations (i.e., "might choose if I thought it could offer things I value"), definite lack of interest (i.e., "wouldn't choose under any circumstance"), or other. Occupations sorted into the self-efficacy and outcome expectation subcategories are then explored for accuracy of skill and outcome perceptions. As with the first strategy, further assessment, efficacy-building, or information gathering may then be employed to challenge faulty assumptions about self or career and to maximize the range of possible choice options. (See Brown & Lent, 1996, for case examples of the use of each strategy with adult clients who were considering career changes.)

Coping with Barriers and Building Supports   A key assumption of SCCT's choice model is that people are more likely to implement their career choices (e.g., to translate their goals into actions) if they perceive that their preferred options will be accompanied by minimal barriers and ample supports within the surrounding environment. Conversely, clients who anticipate, for example, that their significant others will disparage their favored path or that they will not be able to access the financial support they need to pursue their choice may be less willing to follow through with their goals. These assumptions have led us to build consideration of potential choice supports and barriers directly into the choice counseling process. In particular, we have developed a set of steps to help clients:

1. Identify and anticipate possible barriers to their choice implementation.
2. Analyze the likelihood of encountering these barriers.
3. Prepare barrier-coping strategies (i.e., methods for preventing or managing likely barriers).
4. Cultivate supports for their goals within their family, peer, and other key social systems.

We have used a modified *decisional balance sheet* procedure to help clients identify potential choice barriers. Specifically, we ask clients to generate both positive and negative consequences in relation to each career option they are seriously considering. We then have them focus on the negative consequences that might prevent them from pursuing each option. Next, the client is asked to estimate the chances that each barrier will actually be encountered, and strategies are developed and rehearsed for preventing or managing the most likely barriers. Brown and Lent (1996) illustrate the use of these barrier-coping methods with a client who had been reluctant to pursue her preferred option because of the fear that it would jeopardize her romantic relationship. After identifying and analyzing this barrier, the client was helped to neutralize it by negotiating a dual-career strategy with her partner, enabling her to preserve the choice option she most wanted to pursue.

In addition to anticipating and preparing to deal with barriers, it can be very useful to assist clients in building support systems to help sustain their choice efforts (Lent et al., 2000). In fact, support-building has been identified as a key element in successful career choice counseling (Brown & Ryan Krane, 2000). Once clients have narrowed their career options, they can be encouraged to consider:

- Steps they need to take to implement their preferred options.
- Environmental (e.g., social, financial) resources that could help them to achieve these steps.
- Resources they could use, specifically, to offset likely barriers to obtaining their goals.

Counselors can also help clients to consider where and how to access needed supports. In many cases, clients' existing support systems can provide resources useful to their goal pursuit (e.g., access to relevant job contacts). In other cases, resources may be obtained by cultivating new or alternative support systems (e.g., developing relationships with peers who will support, rather than deride, their academic or career aspirations).

Clients' families are often central to their career choice-making and implementation efforts, particularly in collectivist cultures. It is, therefore, useful to build into counseling a consideration of how the client's preferred options mesh with the wishes of his or her family (or significant others). Clients sometimes need special assistance in negotiating conflicts between their own goals and others' goals for them. Depending on the cultural context and the client's preferences, family members or other stakeholders can be invited to participate in choice counseling and to assist the client in developing barrier-coping and support-building strategies.

Goal Setting and Implementation   Some clients need additional assistance with the processes of setting goals and managing pursuit of their goals. These processes can be conceived as "career self-regulation skills" that need to be mastered so that clients can create, enact, and alter satisfying career plans, especially in the future, after counseling has been completed. Once decisions have been made and goals have been selected, many factors can affect the likelihood that clients will implement, or follow through with, their preferred choice. We have already considered the possible effects of environmental supports and barriers. Another important factor affecting choice implementation involves the manner in which people frame their goals. It has been found, for example, that larger goals (e.g., becoming a doctor) are more likely to be enacted if they are clear, specific, divided into manageable subgoals (e.g., taking premed courses, applying to medical schools), set close in time to intended actions, stated publicly, and held with strong commitment (Bandura, 1986). By contrast, vague, amorphous, distal, private, weakly held goals (e.g., "I'll probably go for some sort of advanced degree at some point") provide far less reliable guides for action. Clients can, therefore, be encouraged to frame their goals in facilitative (e.g., clear, specific, proximal) terms and to consider specific steps and resources needed to implement their goals. Because not all possible barriers to choice implementation can be anticipated and averted, clients can be encouraged to remain flexible and adaptable in their decisional stance (Phillips, 1994), for example, by preparing backup plans.

PROMOTING WORK SATISFACTION

Social Cognitive Career Theory was originally conceived to help explain the processes of interest development, choice-making, and performance. Although affective processes and outcomes, such as educational or work satisfaction, were not a central concern in the original theory, a social cognitive model of academic/career satisfaction is under construction (Lent & Brown, 2003). Explication of this nascent model is beyond the scope of this chapter. However, it is possible to outline, at least tentatively, the counseling-related tenets of our satisfaction model-in-progress.

The literature on overall life satisfaction and satisfaction with specific life domains, such as work, suggests that certain personality traits (e.g., extraversion, absence of neuroticism) are reliably associated with satisfaction (DeNeve &

Cooper, 1998; Judge, Heller, & Mount, 2002). Thus, to a certain extent, people who tend to be happy and outgoing in general are also likely to be happy in their school and work lives. Such findings do not, by themselves, offer much in the way of counseling implications because personality and affective tendencies are often relatively stable and difficult to change (Brown, Ryan, & McPartland, 1996). However, satisfaction is also, fortunately, linked to several factors that are readily modifiable and subject to personal control. These agentic factors include several of the social cognitive elements.

It has been found, for example, that personal goals are importantly related to satisfaction outcomes (Lent, in press). While several aspects of goals may affect satisfaction within a given life domain (e.g., simply having goals, having self-set goals), making progress toward valued personal goals appears to be a particularly important determinant of satisfaction. Working backwards in the presumed causal chain, people are more likely to make progress on their valued goals and to be satisfied to the extent that they (1) feel self-efficacious, (2) hold favorable outcome expectations, and (3) have access to environmental supports and resources relevant to the pursuit of their goal.

The counseling implications of this brief analysis are reasonably straightforward. If work (or educational) satisfaction results partly from goal progress in work (or educational) spheres, then satisfaction might be promoted by enabling workers (and students) to set and make progress toward valued personal goals (e.g., working toward a hoped-for grade in their major). This focus on goal progress would draw on strategies described earlier. For example, students or new workers can be helped to:

- Set reasonable yet challenging performance goals (i.e., goals that are congruent with current skills but that may promote further skill growth).
- Break complex, distal goals into simpler, proximal subgoals.
- Decide on how goal progress can be measured and what steps can be taken when progress does not meet expectations.
- Focus on and self-reinforce incremental progress and not just ultimate goal attainment.
- Identify and access environmental supports and resources that can aid goal progress.
- Anticipate and prepare strategies to cope with barriers to goal attainment.

This focus on promoting progress toward personal goals may work well as a general guide to prevention of educational or work dissatisfaction as well as a way to promote satisfaction and continued development of skills and interests. For example, more experienced workers may be assisted to ward off burnout by setting and progressing toward new goals or by considering job redesign or restructuring options that can infuse their work with new challenges and opportunities for value fulfillment. Parenthetically, what is called "burnout" may often be more aptly described as "rust-out"—that is, situations in which all work-related goals have been met, skills and incentives have plateaued, and work has, thereby, been divested of much of its interest value and enjoyment. Where work satisfaction cannot be promoted in other ways—or where the work role is not one of the individual's most valued life domains—involvement (and goal setting) in other life domains, such as leisure or volunteer activities, may provide alternative outlets for life satisfaction.

Apart from these preventive and developmental possibilities, remedial applications may profit from analysis of the source and type of dissatisfaction that a client is experiencing. Educational or work dissatisfaction can stem from a number of causes, such as acute or chronic work stresses, job skill requirements that significantly overshoot or undershoot the client's current capabilities, interpersonal difficulties, or discrepancies between personal values and work reinforcers (e.g., inadequate salary). Moreover, work (dis)satisfaction can be divided into more specific components, such as job facet satisfaction and organizational satisfaction (see Dawis, Chapter 1, this volume; Fritzsche & Parrish, Chapter 8, this volume). Appropriate cognitive-behavioral strategies can be derived from social cognitive and related theories to address various sources and types of work dissatisfaction. For example, performance deficits can be remediated by focusing on self-efficacy and skill promotion strategies described in the next section, and interpersonal problems can often be handled through conflict resolution procedures or development of particular interpersonal skills and strategies (e.g., assertion, leadership, collaborative problem solving, cross-cultural communication).

Like person-environment fit theories, an SCCT perspective acknowledges that work dissatisfaction can result from incongruence between personal and environmental attributes and that dissatisfaction can, therefore, be reduced by improving the fit between P and E. For example, value-reinforcer incongruence may be addressed via worker-supervisor negotiation, job restructuring, skill upgrading, or, where necessary, job or career change counseling. One important difference from traditional P-E fit theories, however, is that SCCT accepts that the incongruence (or discorrespondence) can occur along any number of dimensions (e.g., interest, personality, value, skill) that may be salient to the individual. Another difference is the assumption that the subjective perception of P-E fit is often more important than objectively assessed fit in determining an individual's satisfaction with the work environment. For example, dissatisfaction can result from the conviction, accurate or not, that a person's skills considerably undershoot or exceed job requirements or that the job does not adequately draw on or reward his or her primary talents (sometimes referred to as underemployment). These differences call for multifaceted fit assessment and remedial efforts that build on, yet extend beyond, what P-E theories would prescribe. (Brown & Lent, 1996, discuss examples of SCCT-based counseling that had been initiated by clients experiencing work dissatisfaction due to poor perceived fit between their values or skills and the outlets afforded by their work settings.)

FACILITATING WORK PERFORMANCE

Social Cognitive Career Theory offers several implications for efforts to promote academic/career success and optimize performance. The basic hypotheses of SCCT's performance model suggest that self-efficacy beliefs can facilitate attainment in a given academic or career domain as long as an individual possesses at least minimally adequate levels of the skills required in that domain. While this does not mean that every student or worker can be transformed into an Einstein simply by increasing his or her confidence, it does imply, as suggested earlier, that self-efficacy can help people make the most of the skills they have and facilitate further development of their skills, thereby enhancing future attainments. Thus, procedures designed to boost self-efficacy beliefs may be valuable ingredients both in developmentally oriented skill-building programs (discussed earlier in the context of promoting aspirations) and in remedial efforts with persons experiencing performance difficulties.

A basic efficacy-based strategy for improving performance involves exploring possible discrepancies between self-efficacy estimates and data on objectively assessed skills or past performance. Intervention procedures may then be designed that are responsive to the type of discrepancy that is identified. For example, students or workers with weak self-efficacy beliefs but adequate skills in the relevant performance domain may benefit from relatively nonintensive interventions designed to promote their self-efficacy and, possibly, further develop their skills, depending on their current skill level. Those exhibiting both weak self-efficacy and deficient skills, however, may be good candidates for more intensive remedial skill-building efforts that can be organized around the sources of efficacy information.

There may also be occasions where the extent of the skill deficit is very large, the client is unwilling to engage in (or may be unlikely to profit from) remedial activities, or the environment (e.g., college, work organization) is unwilling to support such activities or has decided to terminate the student or employee. In P-E fit terms, such scenarios reflect a serious mismatch between the individual's skills and the skill requirements of the setting. In such cases, educational or career choice (or change) counseling can be offered, with an eye toward identifying suitable, alternative academic or occupational options having ability requirements that are more nearly correspondent with the client's current skills. Social Cognitive Career Theory does not imply that self-efficacy compensates for a lack of requisite skills or that efforts to boost self-efficacy are always indicated—in fact, such efforts seem unlikely to impact performance (and any resulting gains in self-efficacy are unlikely to be sustained) if they ignore seriously deficient skills.

Where the client possesses adequate skills but weak self-efficacy beliefs in a given performance domain, the theory would suggest the value of activities designed to help him or her:

- Obtain personal mastery experiences with progressively more challenging tasks in that domain.
- Review past success experiences.
- Interpret past and present successes in ways that promote, rather than discount, perceived competence.

Similar to earlier suggestions for promoting self-efficacy beliefs, clients can be encouraged to attribute success experiences at skill development to internal, stable factors, particularly personal ability, rather than to internal, unstable (e.g., effort), or external (luck, task simplicity) factors. For instance, as clients succeed at performance tasks or as they review past experiences, they can be asked for their perceived reasons for task success. Nonadaptive attributions can be challenged, for example, by having clients generate and evaluate alternative interpretations for their performance successes (Brown & Lent, 1996).

This focus on providing, reviewing, and interpreting mastery experiences can be augmented by counseling activities that draw on the other sources of self-efficacy. For instance, providing exposure to relevant models, verbal support, or assistance with anxiety coping can help to elevate self-efficacy and, in turn, skill development and performance. In addition, SCCT points to outcome expectations and performance goals as operating, along with self-efficacy, as key motivators of performance. Thus, a comprehensive approach to performance facilitation might also entail efforts to instill beneficial outcome expectations (e.g., accurate knowledge of work conditions and reinforcers) and realistic, yet challenging, performance goals (e.g., goals that are achievable but that can stretch and further refine an individual's skills).

SUMMARY

Social Cognitive Career Theory is an evolving framework that seeks to build on and extend Bandura's (1986, 1997) general social cognitive theory to the understanding of career development processes. This framework highlights social cognitive variables, such as self-efficacy, that enable people to exercise personal agency in their own career development; it is also concerned with the ways in which other person and environmental factors (e.g., gender, culture, barriers, supports) help shape people's career paths. Originally aimed at explaining academic and career interest, choice, and performance processes, the theory is currently being extended to the study of educational and work satisfaction. This chapter overviewed the theory's basic elements, predictions, and research status; it also considered some of SCCT's implications for the design of developmental and counseling interventions.

REFERENCES

Bandura, A. (1986). *Social foundations of thought and action: A socialcognitive theory.* Englewood Cliffs, NJ: Prentice-Hall.

Bandura, A. (1997). *Self-efficacy: The exercise of control.* New York: Freeman.

Betz, N. E., & Hackett, G. (1981). The relationship of career-related self-efficacy expectations to perceived career options in college women and men. *Journal of Counseling Psychology, 28,* 399–410.

Betz, N. E., & Schifano, R. S. (2000). Evaluation of an intervention to increase Realistic self-efficacy and interests in college women. *Journal of Vocational Behavior, 56,* 35–52.

Brown, S. D., & Lent, R. W. (1996). A social cognitive framework for career choice counseling. *Career Development Quarterly, 44,* 354–366.

Brown, S. D., Ryan, N. E., & McPartland, E. B. (1996). Why are so many people happy and what do we do for those who aren't? A reaction to Lightsey. *Counseling Psychologist, 24,* 751–757.

Brown, S. D., & Ryan Krane, N. E. (2000). Four (or five) sessions and a cloud of dust: Old assumptions and new observations about career counseling. In S. D. Brown & R. W. Lent (Eds.), *Handbook of counseling psychology* (3rd ed., pp. 740–766). New York: Wiley.

de Bruin, G. P. (1999). Social Cognitive Career Theory as an explanatory model for career counselling in South Africa. In G. B. Stead & M. B. Watson (Eds.), *Career psychology in the South African context* (pp. 91–102). Pretoria, South Africa: J. L. van Schaik.

DeNeve, K. M., & Cooper, H. (1998). The happy personality: A meta-analysis of 137 personality traits and subjective well-being. *Psychological Bulletin, 124,* 197–229.

Fabian, E. S. (2000). Social cognitive theory of careers and individuals with serious mental health disorders: Implications for psychiatric rehabilitation programs. *Psychiatric Rehabilitation Journal, 23,* 262–269.

Fouad, N. A., & Smith, P. L. (1996). A test of a social cognitive model for middle school students: Math and science. *Journal of Counseling Psychology, 43,* 338–346.

Gainor, K. A., & Lent, R. W. (1998). Social cognitive expectations and racial identity attitudes in predicting the math choice intentions of Black college students. *Journal of Counseling Psychology, 45,* 403–413.

Hackett, G. (1995). Self-efficacy in career choice and development. In A. Bandura (Ed.), *Self-efficacy in changing societies* (pp. 232–258). Cambridge, England: Cambridge University Press.

Hackett, G., & Betz, N. E. (1981). A self-efficacy approach to the career development of women. *Journal of Vocational Behavior, 18*, 326–336.

Hackett, G., & Byars, A. M. (1996). Social cognitive theory and the career development of African American women. *Career Development Quarterly, 44*, 322–340.

Hackett, G., & Lent, R. W. (1992). Theoretical advances and current inquiry in career psychology. In S. D. Brown & R. W. Lent (Eds.), *Handbook of counseling psychology* (2nd ed., pp. 419–451). New York: Wiley.

Judge, T. A., Heller, D., & Mount, M. K. (2002). Five-factor model of personality and job satisfaction: A meta-analysis. *Journal of Applied Psychology, 87*, 530–541.

Kantas, A. (1997). Self-efficacy perceptions and outcome expectations in the prediction of occupational preferences. *Perceptual and Motor Skills, 84*, 259–266.

Lapan, R. T., Boggs, K. R., & Morrill, W. H. (1989). Self-efficacy as a mediator of investigative and realistic general occupational themes on the Strong-Campbell Interest Inventory. *Journal of Counseling Psychology, 36*, 176–182.

Lent, R. W. (in press). Toward a unifying theoretical and practical perspective on well-being and psychosocial adjustment. *Journal of Counseling Psychology.*

Lent, R. W., & Brown, S. D. (2003). *A social cognitive model of educational and vocational satisfaction.* Unpublished manuscript, University of Maryland-College Park.

Lent, R. W., Brown, S. D., & Hackett, G. (1994). Toward a unifying social cognitive theory of career and academic interest, choice, and performance [Monograph]. *Journal of Vocational Behavior, 45*, 79–122.

Lent, R. W., Brown, S. D., & Hackett, G. (2000). Contextual supports and barriers to career choice: A social cognitive analysis. *Journal of Counseling Psychology, 47*, 36–49.

Lent, R. W., Brown, S. D., Nota, L., & Soresi, S. (2003). Testing social cognitive interest and choice hypotheses across Holland types in Italian high school students. *Journal of Vocational Behavior, 62*, 101–118.

Lent, R. W., Brown, S. D., Schmidt, J., Brenner, B., Lyons, H., & Treistman, D. (2003). Relation of contextual supports and barriers to choice behavior in engineering majors: Test of alternative social cognitive models. *Journal of Counseling Psychology, 50*, 458–465.

Lent, R. W., & Hackett, G. (1994). Sociocognitive mechanisms of personal agency in career development: Pantheoretical prospects. In M. L. Savickas & R. W. Lent (Eds.), *Convergence in career development theories: Implications for science and practice* (pp. 77–102). Palo Alto, CA: Consulting Psychologists Press.

Lent, R. W., Hackett, G., & Brown, S. D. (1999). A social cognitive view of school-to-work transition. *Career Development Quarterly, 44*, 297–311.

Lent, R. W., & Savickas, M. L. (1994). Postscript: Is convergence a viable agenda for career psychology. In M. L. Savickas & R. W. Lent (Eds.), *Convergence in career development theories: Implications for science and practice* (pp. 259–271). Palo Alto, CA: Consulting Psychologists Press.

Luzzo, D. A., Hasper, P., Albert, K. A., Bibby, M. A., & Martinelli, E. A. (1999). Effects of self-efficacy-enhancing interventions on the math/science self-efficacy and career interests, goals, and actions of career undecided college students. *Journal of Counseling Psychology, 46*, 233–243.

McWhirter, E. H., Rasheed, S., & Crothers, M. (2000). The effects of high school career education on social-cognitive variables. *Journal of Counseling Psychology, 47*, 330–341.

Morrow, S. L., Gore, P. A., & Campbell, B. W. (1996). The application of a sociocognitive framework to the career development of lesbian women and gay men. *Journal of Vocational Behavior, 48*, 136–148.

Multon, K. D., Brown, S. D., & Lent, R. W. (1991). Relation of self-efficacy beliefs to academic outcomes: A meta-analytic investigation. *Journal of Counseling Psychology, 38*, 30–38.

Phillips, S. D. (1994). Choice and change: Convergence from the decision-making perspective. In M. L. Savickas & R. W. Lent (Eds.), *Convergence in career development theories: Implications for science and practice* (pp. 155–163). Palo Alto, CA: Consulting Psychologists Press.

Prideaux, L., Patton, W., & Creed, P. (2002). Development of a theoretically derived school career program: An Australian endeavor. *International Journal for Educational and Vocational Guidance, 2*, 115–130.

Rottinghaus, P. J., Larson, L. M., & Borgen, F. H. (2003). The relation of self-efficacy and interests: A meta-analysis of 60 samples. *Journal of Vocational Behavior, 62,* 221–236.

Sadri, G., & Robertson, I. T. (1993). Self-efficacy and work-related behavior: A review and meta-analysis. *Applied Psychology: An International Review, 42,* 139–152.

Stajkovic, A. D., & Luthans, F. (1998). Self-efficacy and work-related performance: A meta-analysis. *Psychological Bulletin, 124,* 240–261.

Swanson, J. L., & Gore, P. A. (2000). Advances in vocational psychology theory and research. In S. D. Brown & R. W. Lent (Eds.), *Handbook of counseling psychology* (3rd ed., pp. 233–269). New York: Wiley.

Szymanski, E. M., Enright, M. S., Hershenson, D. B., & Ettinger, J. M. (2003). Career development theories, constructs, and research: Implications for people with disabilities. In E. M. Szymanski & R. M. Parker (Eds.), *Work and disability: Issues and strategies in career development and job placement* (2nd ed., pp. 91–153). Austin, TX: ProEd.

Tang, M., Fouad, N. A., & Smith, P. L. (1999). Asian Americans' career choices: A path model to examine factors influencing their career choices. *Journal of Vocational Behavior, 54,* 142–157.

Van Vianen, A. E. M. (1999). Managerial self-efficacy, outcome expectations, and work-role salience as determinants of ambition for a managerial position. *Journal of Applied Social Psychology, 29,* 639–665.

Vondracek, F. W., Lerner, R. M., & Schulenberg, J. E. (1986). *Career development: A life-span developmental approach.* Hillsdale, NJ: Erlbaum.

INFORMATIVE RESEARCH

CHAPTER 6

Occupational Aspirations: Constructs, Meanings, and Application

Jay W. Rojewski

OCCUPATIONAL ASPIRATIONS HAVE been studied extensively over the past half-century. The topic of occupational aspirations (i.e., answers to the question, "What do you want to be when you grow up?") has probably received as much attention as any other career-related concept and remains important in both the psychological and sociological literature. The attraction of career aspirations for investigators is, no doubt, fueled by familiarity and ease of access. Who hasn't been asked about his or her future work and educational plans? We all have aspirations, and they have helped shape our understanding that adults in our society work and that each of us is responsible for deciding what type of work we would like or expect to do.

Another possible reason for the attention devoted to occupational aspirations is the simple, intuitive logic it offers: The easiest way to find out a person's vocational interests or goals is to ask. It doesn't require lengthy, expensive, or intellectually advanced methods or measures. Anyone can do it; just ask. However, the empirical study of occupational aspirations has revealed that the construct is anything but simple. In fact, investigations reveal a fairly complex construct with relationships to a number of other career development and career behavior constructs that have implications for career counseling and education (Johnson, 1995).

The study of occupational aspirations is intriguing, yet the simple question about work-related goals is not so simple. In fact, aspirations can be an important variable in understanding a person's self-concept, career-related behavior, perception of social forces on the opportunities available, and future educational and career-related choices and attainment. This chapter, then, synthesizes the literature on occupational aspirations and attempts to apply relevant research results to our understanding, theory, and practice. Specifically, I define aspirations, explore the related notion of occupational expectations (*ideal* versus *real* aspirations), summarize several theoretical positions related to the development and shaping of aspirations, and identify the internal and external variables that shape aspirations within a career development context.

DEFINITIONS

Despite considerable study of occupational aspirations in the twentieth and, now, twenty-first centuries, a clear, concise, and consistent definition is still rather elusive. This situation exists not because the concept is too difficult to explain or too mundane to bother. Rather, it seems that many authors simply assume that readers already know what aspirations are and do not need to be reminded. Unfortunately, inconsistent or ambiguous nomenclature, definitions, and measurement can lead to an inaccurate view of the role aspirations play in occupational exploration, choice, and attainment (Johnson, 1995).

So, what are occupational aspirations? Interests? Goals? Plans? Preferences? Choices? All of these? The answer to this question is important since there are subtle, but important, variations in the meanings ascribed to these various terms. In fact, occupational aspirations are an individual's *expressed career-related goals or choices*—Johnson (1995) referred to them as *point-in-time* expressions of occupational goals—although they do not all represent the same degree of commitment. While the term *interest* is sometimes used interchangeably with aspirations, a clear distinction between the two exists. Aspirations represent individual goals given ideal conditions, while interests reflect an individual's emotional disposition toward particular career options.

Research shows that expressed occupational aspirations are equal to or better than interest inventories in predicting future occupational membership (Schoon & Parsons, 2002). In fact, aspirations can provide substantial predictive power for later aspirations—current aspirations are predictive of career-related choices up to 8 to 12 months after first expressed—and, to a lesser degree, careers that people eventually enter (G. D. Gottfredson, 2002; L. S. Gottfredson, 1996; Holland & Gottfredson, 1975; Holland, Gottfredson, & Baker, 1990; Silvia, 2001). The more consistent or coherent aspirations are over time, the greater their prediction accuracy.

Evidence that occupational aspirations can predict future aspirations and choices at least as well as interest inventories, personality, and background characteristics was established by the late 1960s with a number of studies (e.g., Cooley, 1967; Holland & Lutz, 1967; Holland & Whitney, 1968). A decade before these studies, Strong (1953) also considered the validity of using aspirations to predict future occupational attainment. Strong reported an overall *correlation* of 0.69 between the occupational aspirations of college freshman and their occupational attainment 19 years later. (See also early literature reviews by Whitney, 1969, and Dolliver, 1969.) Today, most researchers agree that the occupational and educational aspirations of adolescents are among the most useful predictors of eventual educational and occupational choices made in adulthood (Mau & Bikos, 2000).

While acknowledging that a significant relationship exists between current and future occupational aspirations, L. S. Gottfredson and Becker (1981) challenged the notion that the connections were as strong between aspirations and actual job attainment. Studying almost 1,400 employed males between 15 and 24 years of age, they found that occupational aspirations do have some predictive power. However, they argued that the existing opportunity structure (e.g., availability of and access to jobs or training) both conditioned aspirations to narrow ranges early in life and affected the direction of early career development. Further, the authors questioned the belief that aspirations are solely an indicator of eventual occupational attainment. They wrote:

> A widespread assumption in vocational psychology is that aspirations for particular types of work play a significant role in determining the kinds of jobs people eventually obtain. It may be, however, that vocational aspirations are largely reflections of the kinds of employment experiences and opportunities people have had, and they may not function as important determinants of future behavior. (p. 121)

Thus, according to Gottfredson and Becker, rather than guiding or determining eventual attainment, aspirations are possible reflections of past experience and societal perceptions. Nonetheless, it is clear that early aspirations can be used to predict later aspirations and, eventually, the occupational choices that people make.

While aspirations can inform us about the attraction toward or preference for particular occupations, they may not always accurately reflect the occupations that people realistically expect to enter. In fact, the literature makes a clear distinction between idealized aspirations and realistic expectations. Aspirations are viewed as desired career goals given ideal circumstances and reflect the degree of attraction toward or preference for a particular occupation. Occupational expectations, on the other hand, reflect the perceived likelihood of actually entering a particular occupation.

Knowledge of the congruence or discrepancy between an individual's occupational aspirations and expectations can offer some insight into the processes of compromise and circumscription (i.e., inclusion or exclusion of particular occupational alternatives) in career decision making. For example, adolescents with lowered occupational expectations are more likely to make premature (i.e., anticipatory) educational and career-related compromises. Premature compromise and circumscription is a concern, particularly in early adolescence, because unnecessary or excessive compromise may overly restrict the range of future educational *and* occupational options. Discrepancies may reflect individuals' views toward their particular circumstances, abilities, the likely effects of perceived barriers, and future opportunities (L. S. Gottfredson, 1981, 1996; Hellenga, Aber, & Rhodes, 2002; Lapan & Jingeleski, 1992).

When discrepancies exist, most people expect to enter occupations that require less education and offer lower socioeconomic benefits and prestige (Davey, 1993). Much research has focused on factors that might be related to aspirations—expectation discrepancy and lowered occupational expectations. In general, it appears that aspirations may be compromised when people:

- Do not feel (accurately or inaccurately) that they have the abilities to succeed in their aspired to occupation(s).
- Think that the educational or entry-level requirements are beyond their current resources.
- Are not supported by, or are incongruent with, family and friends about what they should do occupationally.
- Perceive significant community or societal barriers to entry into, or success in, their occupational aspirations (Armstrong & Crombie, 2000; Cook et al., 1996; Davey & Stoppard, 1993; Johnson, 1995; McNulty & Borgen, 1988; Slocum, 1974).

MEASURING ASPIRATIONS

Some criticism exists in the literature about the way occupational aspirations (and expectations) are conceptualized and measured. Johnson (1995) argued that aspirations are multidimensional in nature and influenced by complex personal constructs people hold about their world. She reported four underlying factors or dimensions that influence occupational aspirations:

1. Personal ambitions for autonomy and financial reward.
2. The nature of the work tasks involved.
3. How the work deals with people.
4. The perception of an occupation as being male or female.

Two externally based factors appeared to influence occupational expectations: the perceived degree of occupational training or education and entry-level requirements, and the orientation of the work toward people.

While Johnson's (1995) work points to a multidimensional, complex construct, most research has treated aspirations and expectations as unidimensional in nature. From this perspective, aspirations are often determined by one or two questions that ask respondents to dream or suspend the influence of possible barriers—for example, "If you were free to choose any job, what would you most desire as a lifetime kind of work?" (Curry & Picou, 1971; Walls & Gulkus, 1974). McNulty and Borgen (1988) used a particularly clear question to elicit occupational aspirations from their research participants:

> It is interesting to think about the occupation that would be most desirable to you, without having to consider limiting factors such as money, ability, and talent, opportunities to obtain further education and training, et cetera. This may sound impossible but if you were completely free to choose, what would be your ideal occupation? Be as specific as possible. (p. 220)

Occupational expectations, on the other hand, are assumed to represent occupations that an individual considers to be realistic or accessible (Armstrong & Crombie, 2000; Burlin, 1976; Davey & Stoppard, 1993; Heckhausen & Tomasik, 2002; Hellenga et al., 2002). Again, McNulty and Borgen (1988) provide a good example of the type of question used to solicit occupational expectations:

> What occupation are you most likely to enter? That is, looking ahead into the future from where you are now and what you are doing in school now, what occupation do you think that you are more likely to take up after you have completed your education? Be as specific as possible. (p. 22)

The generally qualitative nature of aspirations is usually quantified for experimental research using some combination of existing occupational categorization schemes. The most common approach is to describe aspirations based on *level* and *field*. The level of an aspiration or expectation reflects a specific occupation or a limited range of occupational goals bounded by (1) time (i.e., short-term or long-term perspectives), (2) idealistic (high) hopes and realistic (lower) expectations, and (3) difficulty of the occupation reflected by the occupational prestige hierarchy (W. H. Sewell, Haller, & Portes, 1969). "As a behavior orientation variable, a person's level of occupational aspirations directs his [sic] behavior toward obtaining an occupation at or near the goal region" (Otto, Haller, Meier, & Ohlendorf, 1974, p. 2). The level of aspirations is reflected by a vertical dimension of classification based on occupational prestige (including average wages, degree of authority, freedom of action, amount of education required, and intelligence). "Prestigious occupations require more education, pay more money, are more complex, exercise authority, and require higher levels of ability, whereas occupations low in prestige require little education, pay poorly, involve simple tasks, are directed by others, and require little cognitive ability" (G. D. Gottfredson, 1996, p. 68). Classification by level provides a ranking scheme that allows occupations to be grouped according to socioeconomic groups (McNulty & Borgen, 1988). Field, on the other hand, is a horizontal dimension that is based on the type of work activities reflected by an aspiration (e.g., tasks, duties, and responsibilities). Adolescents are more likely to shift between fields at the same level than move up or down between levels (L. S. Gottfredson, 1981; Rojewski & Yang, 1997).

The use of prestige scores has enjoyed a long history in the study of occupational aspirations (G. D. Gottfredson, 1996), particularly from a sociological perspective. Several classification options exist for researchers. One option is to use major occupational groupings typically used by governmental agencies such as the U.S. Bureau of the Census and U.S. Department of Commerce (Stevens & Cho, 1985). Large national databases such as High School and Beyond and the National Education Longitudinal Study of 1988 (NELS:88) have employed this strategy by asking respondents to select the occupational area they expect to be employed in at age 30 from a predetermined list of 17 major occupational categories. Further, these broad categories can be collapsed into three groups that reflect high, medium, and low levels of education, prestige, and status attributed to the occupations (Haller & Virkler, 1993; Rojewski, 1996). For example, occupational categories requiring a college degree and providing high prestige typically include high professional (e.g., doctor, accountant, scientist, lawyer), lower professional (e.g., social worker, clergy, registered nurse), schoolteacher, technical occupations (e.g., medical technician, computer programmer), and managerial positions. Moderate prestige occupations requiring a high school diploma or some college education include small business owner and positions in sales, office or clerical, trades (e.g., auto mechanic, baker, carpenter), and military or protective services. Categories requiring less than a high school diploma for initial entry and offering low prestige include full-time homemaker, service positions (e.g., child care, waiter), machine operators (e.g., assembler, welder, bus driver), and laborers (e.g., construction worker).

A second option involves coding expressed aspirations according to a socioeconomic index (SEI). Various researchers (e.g., Blau & Duncan, 1967; Naoko & Treas, 1992; Stevens & Cho, 1985) have calculated occupational prestige scores that reflect the income and educational attributes of occupations found in the total labor force. SEI codes have been widely used as a summary measure of occupational status in empirical investigations, although their use does cast a sociological or status attainment perspective on analysis. Prestige scores are often employed in investigations for several reasons:

- They provide a continuous variable of aspirations that facilitates data analysis.
- Prestige levels influence people's perceptions about the relative worth, power, and status of occupations (Kraus, Schild, & Hodge, 1978).

- SEI codes reflect status expectations and ability estimates that can be used in considering individual and societal constraints on choice (Hotchkiss & Borow, 1996; Saltiel, 1988).

THEORIES

From a theoretical standpoint, the development, expression, and attainment of educational and occupational aspirations and expectations can be explained by several different theories covering psychological (Super's self-concept development theory), social psychological (Social Cognitive Career Theory; Gottfredson's theory of vocational aspirations development), and sociological (status attainment theory) perspectives (Blau & Duncan, 1967; Fassinger, 1985; L. S. Gottfredson, 1981, 1996; Lent, Brown, & Hackett, 1996; Lent, Hackett, & Brown, 1996; McNulty & Borgen, 1988; W. H. Sewell et al., 1969; Super, 1990; Super, Savickas, & Super, 1996). Each of these theories is described in greater detail elsewhere in this volume. Therefore, the purpose here is to highlight aspects of each theory that explain the development and role of aspirations in the career choice process.

Psychological Theory: Super's Self-Concept Developmental Theory

Super's (1990) developmental theory views career development as a series of specific vocational tasks that must be accomplished according to a defined and predictable sequence—growth, exploration, establishment, maintenance, and disengagement. A time of particular importance in developing and pursuing occupational (and educational) aspirations is the exploration stage, which begins around age 14 and is characterized by a progressive narrowing of career options, from fantasizing about possible careers to identifying tentative options, to final decisions about career choice. Super posited that self-concept plays a critical role in career development. In fact, aspirations (career choices) are viewed as a representation of an individual's occupational self-concept. Occupational aspirations can change over time, but they tend to become increasingly stable as adolescents mature.

Social Psychological Theories

Social psychological theories of career behavior emphasize how culture, gender, and life events interact with individual career preferences to determine career aspirations and choice. Unlike psychological theories, which focus on individual attributes like self-concept and role salience, social psychological theories focus on ways that individual attributes are shaped by experiences and surroundings. In this section, two theories—Social Cognitive Career Theory (SCCT) and the theory of career circumscription and compromise—are reviewed.

Social Cognitive Career Theory   SCCT incorporates self-efficacy, outcome expectations, and personal goals with other person, contextual, and learning factors to explain academic and career choices and attainment (Lent, Brown, & Hackett, 1994, 1996). The self-efficacy construct (situation-specific estimates of an individual's ability to successfully perform a task or behavior; Lent, Chapter 5, this volume; Lent & Hackett, 1987) is a central factor that influences career decisions and helps "determine individuals' willingness to initiate specific behaviors, their persistence in the face of obstacles or barriers, and their level of competence in executing the behaviors" (Arbona, 2000, p. 288). Career choice is a dynamic process from the SCCT perspective, one that is being constantly modified by learning experiences and performance outcomes (e.g., academic achievement), as well as "how people read their capabilities and potential payoffs in view of continuous performance feedback" (Lent, Hackett, et al., 1996, p. 11).

Bandura's (1986) *triadic relationship* of personal attributes, environmental factors, and overt behavior explains how individuals actively shape their occupational interests and goals. Social Cognitive Career Theory adds to this explanation by describing the smooth translation of academic- and career-related interests into goal intentions and goals into action (Rottinghaus, Lindley, Green, & Borgen, 2002; Swanson & Gore, 2000). While SCCT does not specifically address the occupational aspirations construct, it most likely reflects goals ("What type of work do you expect to do?"). Occupational aspirations stem partly from an individual's self-efficacy, outcome expectations, and interests and can be important mediators of motivation and development.

SCCT also identifies other person and contextual influences on the general cognitive processes involved in career choice (Lent, Chapter 5, this volume; Lent, Brown, et al., 1996; Lent et al., 1994). For example, SCCT highlights the way that inputs such as gender, race, and socioeconomic status "shape the learning opportunities to which particular individuals are exposed, the characteristic reactions (e.g., support, discouragement) they receive for performing different activities, and future outcomes they anticipate" (Lent, Hackett, et al., 1996). Lent and his colleagues view these variables as socially constructed and conferred aspects of experience that tend to influence the availability of academic and occupational opportunities. Self-efficacy, outcome expectations, and aspirations (goals) are influenced through differential socialization patterns defined by gender or race/ethnicity. Similarly, socioeconomic status influences occupational aspirations in much the same way as other person variables (i.e., through differential access and exposure to skill and efficacy-building experiences).

Finally, SCCT establishes strong ties between academic *and* career interests, choices, and performance. Successive academic attainment provides access to more advanced educational opportunities that, in turn, lead to more prestigious occupational opportunities. Lent, Brown, et al. (1996) proposed that academic interest and ability serve as feedback mechanisms that help shape future career selection. Thus, both educational aspirations and educational performance influence an individual's occupational behavior. This position not only reflects the strong relationship between educational and occupational aspirations (Ma & Wang, 2001; Mau & Bikos, 2000; Rojewski & Yang, 1997) but also provides some explanation about why the relationship exists and how it influences career choice and attainment.

Theory of Career Circumscription and Compromise   L. S. Gottfredson's (1981, 1996, Chapter 4, this volume) theory explains the development of occupational aspirations from a social psychological perspective. Aspirations reflect an individual's occupational self-concept and are defined as the "joint product of assessments of compatibility and accessibility. Aspirations are called expectations or realistic aspirations when they are tempered by knowledge of obstacles and opportunities.

They are called idealistic aspirations when they are not" (1996, p. 187). The theory outlines two processes in the longitudinal development of occupational aspirations: compromise and circumscription. *Compromise* occurs as individuals give up their ideal, albeit inaccessible, aspirations for more realistic and accessible choices. These choices (1) occur within a developmental process, (2) are a reflection of occupational self-concept, and (3) lead to satisfaction when they fit with occupational self-concept.

Circumscription is the process of narrowing (i.e., irreversibly eliminating) occupational options by comparing self-image to images of possible occupations and determining the level of compatibility between the two. This process begins in early childhood and occurs in a series of four stages: size and power, sex roles, social valuation, and unique self (Armstrong & Crombie, 2000). The first stage occurs between 3 and 5 years of age when children develop an orientation to size and power. Stage 2 (6 to 8 years of age) focuses on determining appropriate sex roles. Children use concrete, dichotomous thinking and rule out occupations they deem inappropriate for their sex. Social status comes into play in Stage 3 (9 to 13 years of age) when occupational aspirations are ranked by prestige and social value. During this third stage, adolescents begin to identify ceiling (tolerable *effort* boundary) and floor levels (tolerable *level* boundary) of appropriate occupational aspirations. Finally, in Stage 4, occurring at age 14 and beyond, individuals are oriented toward their internal unique selves. L. S. Gottfredson (1981, 1996) posited that when faced with the need to compromise occupational aspirations, individuals follow a predictable path. Sex type (Stage 2) is least, prestige level (Stage 3) more likely, and field of interest and personality (Stage 4) most likely to be compromised. It is interesting that "most individuals will settle for a *good enough* job rather than the best possible choice" (Swanson & Gore, 2000, p. 242). Further research is required before definitive conclusions can be made about this aspect of the theory (Vandiver & Bowman, 1996).

SOCIOLOGICAL THEORY: STATUS ATTAINMENT THEORY

Status attainment theory views occupational aspirations and choice from a sociological perspective, asserting that social forces are more powerful in determining occupational attainment than personal ones (Fitzgerald, Fassinger, & Betz, 1995; Jencks, Crouse, & Muesser, 1983). Occupational aspirations and attainment reflect the existing stratification of society and are determined by some combination of bias and discrimination, social attitudes, cultural expectations, and stereotyped experiences because of gender, race/ethnicity, or social class (Hotchkiss & Borow, 1996). Negative cultural perceptions or societal expectations may impose lower status and a devalued role on some adolescents, particularly women, minorities, and individuals from lower socioeconomic strata (Hellenga et al., 2002). This may, in turn, result in limited career aspirations reflected by narrow, stereotypical employment possibilities.

Blau and Duncan (1967) first outlined the status attainment model, also known as the *classic* model, in an attempt to explain occupational mobility in the United States. They identified four variables of importance to understanding occupational attainment, including *antecedent* variables (e.g., father's educational attainment and occupational status) and *intervening* variables (e.g., educational attainment and status of first job). Initially, the model posited that the social status of an individual's parents affects the level of education attained, which, in turn, affects the occupational level achieved (Hotchkiss & Borow, 1996).

Sewell and his colleagues (W. H. Sewell et al., 1969; W. H. Sewell, Haller, & Ohlendorf, 1970) refined the original model by incorporating elements of family background and influences of significant others and by reemphasizing the critical role of education in attainment. Of these variables, individual aspirations, significant others, and academic ability and performance are most important in explaining occupational attainment. Aspirations are a central mechanism in determining occupational attainment and are formed through social interaction. Both occupational and educational aspirations are formed at an early age through two feedback mechanisms: evaluations received from significant others and self-assessment of potential based on academic performance (Knottnerus, 1987). Finally, studies using the status attainment framework (e.g., Alexander & Eckland, 1975; Haller & Virkler, 1993; Jencks et al., 1983; Marjoribanks, 2002) have demonstrated a consistent relationship between educational and occupational aspirations and achievement.

Status attainment theory has relied on a functionalist, socialization model to explain lower occupational attainment of disadvantaged groups. However, the model does not work as well with women, persons of color, or people with low socioeconomic status as it does with White males (Alexander & Eckland, 1975; Dunne, Elliott, & Carlsen, 1981; Hanson, 1994; Knottnerus, 1987). Several reasons have been advanced to explain the limited predictive value of the status attainment model for these groups. Hellenga et al. (2002) suggested:

> [I]n an historically White- and male-dominated society, White men are "built into" educational and vocational pathways; their vocational destination will be largely dependent on where they start out—their parents' education, their own socioeconomic status, and abilities. However, for members of groups still overcoming racism and sexism, personal qualities and environmental supports can make the difference between perseverance and acquiescence, success and failure. (p. 210)

Summary of Theoretical Perspectives and Their Role in Understanding Occupational Choice

The four theories reviewed here each present a somewhat different explanation of what aspirations are, how they develop, and the specific role they play in the career development process. While each theory offers certain advantages, no theory is comprehensive enough to address all issues. Therefore, a collective perspective may provide the best way to understand the complexity represented by occupational aspirations.

Super's (1990; Super et al., 1996) developmental self-concept theory explains aspirations from a developmental perspective and sees aspirations as a reflection of occupational self-concept. Positioning aspirations within a developmental framework is important, but Super's theory does not integrate social and environmental factors into its explanation, nor has much research focused on the early development of aspirations (e.g., during the growth stage). L. S. Gottfredson's (1981, 1996) theory of career circumscription and compromise also views aspirations as a reflection of occupational self-concept but extends this idea in several directions. First, Gottfredson emphasizes the early development of aspirations and suggests that individuals use aspirations as a reflection of social value in sex type, prestige, and self-interest. To Super, aspirations are the implementation of an individual's psychological self (occupational self-concept) and reflect "successive approximations of a good match between the vocational self and the world of work" (Swanson & Gore, 2000, p. 240). L. S. Gottfredson, however, sees aspirations first as individuals' attempt to place themselves in a broader social order and only secondarily as the implementation of their psychological self. She also posited that aspirations result largely from the elimination or rejection of options rather than selection or expansion.

The SCCT espoused by Lent, Brown, et al. (1994, 1996) further emphasizes the interaction of person and environment to explain aspirations. From this perspective, however, aspirations reflect self-efficacy beliefs and socialization patterns based on external factors such as gender, race/ethnicity, and socioeconomic status, and the internalization of differential learning experiences. Another important aspect of the SCCT is the strong relationship between academic and career behavior. Lent and his colleagues emphasize both occupational *and* educational aspirations, making a clear connection between academic ability and performance and occupational attainment. Educational performance provides feedback that shapes future educational and occupational behavior and choice. Like SCCT, status attainment theory emphasizes social aspects of aspiration development and the strong relationship between educational and occupational aspirations. However, status attainment theory does not address the role of personal or psychological aspects of career behavior such as self-concept or self-efficacy. Rather, occupational aspirations and attainment are viewed within a broad system of social stratification. From this perspective, career goals are constrained by institutional and impersonal forces beyond individual control. Bias and barriers are erected on the basis of external factors such as gender, race, and social class, often limiting individuals' career alternatives.

RESEARCH ON OCCUPATIONAL ASPIRATIONS

The research summarized in this section supports each of the four theories discussed earlier in this chapter. For example, a psychological perspective is represented by the inclusion of constructs such as self-concept, self-esteem, and locus of control. Social-psychological aspects of aspirations development emerge as individuals interact with significant others in their lives and environments, at home and in school. The very close connection between educational and occupational aspirations is acknowledged. Status attainment theory recognizes how academic achievement affects the opportunities made available or denied to individuals and, in turn, how school-based experiences influence educational and occupational aspirations and attainment. Our understanding would be enhanced from future studies that focus on this connection.

Findings about three social demographic factors that have received attention from all of the theoretical perspectives—gender, race or ethnicity, and socioeconomic status—are also summarized. SCCT acknowledges the role of these background variables in providing context and shaping individual experience and learning. Status attainment theory emphasizes how these factors affect the social stratification process. According to a growing body of literature (e.g., L. S. Gottfredson, 1996; Trice, 1991; Trice & McClellan, 1993; Trice, McClellan, &

Hughes, 1992), these demographic factors have a substantial and direct influence on childhood aspirations, but become more indirect in their influence as mediating variables such as significant others and academic achievement become more important in adolescence.

STABILITY

Currently available theory and research suggests that occupational aspirations are formed in early childhood and that these aspirations tend to become increasingly realistic and relatively stable over time (Armstrong & Crombie, 2000; Rojewski & Yang, 1997; Trice & King, 1991; Trice & McClellan, 1993). The evidence supporting these fundamental assertions was strong enough for Wahl and Blackhurst (2000) to declare that our conventional wisdom about planning for college and setting employment or lifestyle goals may be a case of offering too little, too late:

> A review of theory and recent research related to educational and occupational aspirations reveals that important career development processes may occur well before adolescence. In fact, tentative college plans may be formed in early elementary school with career preferences evident as early as kindergarten. (p. 3)

Evidence suggests that early career aspirations are heavily influenced by prevailing gender and racial stereotypes (Sellers, Satcher, & Comas, 1999; Wahl & Blackhurst, 2000).

Studies showing the stability of aspirations have looked at children as young as 5 and 6 years of age up through early adulthood. Trice (1991) asked 422 children, either 8 or 11 years old, what they wanted to be when they grew up. Approximately one-half of both 8- and 11-year-old respondents expressed stable aspirations in interviews conducted eight months after initial data collection. Aspirations were most often related to their parents' careers and the careers of others in their community.

Changes can and do occur with expressed occupational aspirations and at times (e.g., during the career exploration stage) can occur rather frequently. McNulty and Borgen (1988) found that students shifted their aspirations more often between occupational fields at the same prestige level than moving up or down within a particular field. Changes within similar prestige levels might reflect shifting aspirations from plumber to carpenter or from doctor to lawyer. Less frequently, changes occur between prestige categories (Davey, 1993). Typically, when changes in prestige categories do occur, aspirations are raised to a higher prestige category.

Baiyin Yang and I analyzed the occupational aspirations of students in the NELS:88 database at Grades 8, 10, and 12, finding that occupational aspirations were relatively established by the eighth grade and remained stable (in terms of prestige level) from early to late adolescence (Rojewski & Yang, 1997). In a separate study, I examined the stability of adolescents' occupational aspirations between the 8th and 10th grades (Rojewski, 1997). Typically, adolescence is viewed as a time when decisions about careers may frequently change because of exploration activities and a growing sense of personal abilities, lifestyle needs, and workplace requirements. However, just over half of the students I studied (52.9%) held stable aspirations (for prestige level) from 8th to 10th grade. Females were more likely to aspire to either high- (e.g., accountant, manager, teacher) or low-prestige (e.g., service, machine operator, homemaker) occupations, while more males aspired to moderate-prestige jobs (e.g., sales, trades, military, or protective services). Forty-four percent of the sample reported different aspirations (in terms of broad prestige level) at the two data points. These differences are potentially important because they reflect very different education requirements for entry-level positions, social status, and income. Changes in aspirations also reflect differing perceptions about an individual's occupational self-concept and acceptable social roles.

INFLUENCES

The development of occupational aspirations and expectations can be explained by some combination of background variables, psychological factors, and sociological or environmental influences (Farris, Boyd, & Shoffner, 1985; Fassinger, 1985; McNulty & Borgen, 1988). Factors such as gender (Davey & Stoppard, 1993), socioeconomic status and parents' occupations (Hotchkiss & Borow, 1996; McNair & Brown, 1983), self-concept (L. S. Gottfredson, 1981, 1996; Super, 1990; Super et al., 1996), locus of control (Taylor, 1982), and educational aspirations (Farmer, 1985; Mau, Domnick, & Ellsworth, 1995) have been identified as important correlates of occupational aspirations development. Several of these factors are briefly reviewed here.

Gender   Research over a more than 30-year span has consistently shown gender differences in occupational aspirations. In fact, Sellers et al. (1999) considered gender-role stereotyping and its influence on occupational choice pervasive in our society. Female adolescents are likely to express higher occupational aspirations than their male peers. Male adolescents are more likely to aspire to moderate-prestige occupations, while female adolescents are more likely to aspire to either high- or low-prestige occupations (Apostal & Bilden, 1991; Betz & Fitzgerald, 1987; Davey & Stoppard, 1993; Dunne et al., 1981; Farris et al., 1985; G. D. Gottfredson & Holland, 1975; Haller & Virkler, 1993; Jenkins, 1989; Rojewski, 1996; Rojewski & Yang, 1997). Despite higher aspirations, females tend to restrict their range of potential occupations at an early age and are more likely than males to adjust their narrower educational and occupational expectations downward over time (Hanson, 1994; Wahl & Blackhurst, 2000). Looft (1971) used the term *occupational foreclosure* to describe this process of range restriction in occupational aspirations.

These differences, coupled with lower occupational attainment for females, have led some to conclude that gender is the single most powerful and persistent influence on occupational development (L. S. Gottfredson, 1981, 1996; Hall, 1994). Not only is the influence of gender powerful, it affects children at a relatively young age. Various possibilities have been suggested to explain the differences found between males and females, including possible gender bias in the socioeconomic index scales used to code occupations, rising wages in low-prestige jobs, greater geographic restrictions on females, increasing occupational opportunities for females in high-prestige careers, concerns about balancing career and family/relationships, presence of children in the household, and marital and fertility plans (Apostal & Bilden, 1991; Betz, 1993; Dunne et al., 1981; Fitzgerald et al., 1995; Maxwell & Cumming, 1988).

Other explanations for gender differences in occupational aspirations have also been proposed. For example, Davey and Stoppard (1993) found that females hold a more flexible life role orientation (i.e., family and career salience) than do males. This flexibility can explain the discrepancies often found among female aspirations, expectations, and attainment. Astin (1984) explained that young women might expect to pursue more traditionally female occupations than they desire because they are perceived to be more accessible than male-dominated occupations. Gender self-concept and the sex stereotyping of occupations, described by L. S. Gottfredson (1996), among others, are other possible explanations for observed gender differences. While it is true that both males and females are affected by traditional gender-stereotyped thinking, outcomes usually favor males in terms of job availability and income potential (Dunne et al., 1981). Given that research consistently shows gender differences in occupational aspirations, expectations, and attainment, there is little doubt that the career development and status attainment process of women is more complex than for males (Betz, 1993; W. H. Sewell et al., 1970).

Gender has also been examined as a factor that can affect discrepancies between aspirations and expectations. Arbona and Novy (1991) reported on the occupational aspirations and expectations of Black, Mexican American, and White college freshmen. Contrary to other studies, they found little difference in the degree of discrepancy among college freshmen based on race or ethnicity. However, gender was associated with statistically significant discrepancies in White and Mexican American females, suggesting that these college women aspired to non-traditional (and more prestigious) careers, but did not expect to be able to pursue or attain them.

Davey and Stoppard (1993) also reported that one-third of the female high school students they studied expected to have occupations that were more traditionally female than their most desired occupation. Further, they found that traditional female expectations, regardless of aspirations, were associated with a perceived lack of support from significant others and concerns about the cost of postsecondary education.

Race or Ethnicity   While considerable progress has been made in understanding gender influences on occupational aspirations, limited understanding exists about race and ethnicity (Mau & Bikos, 2000). At present, the role of race and ethnicity in the development of occupational aspirations and expectations is often viewed as being indirect in nature. For example, Super (1990) explained that race and socioeconomic status influence career decision making and attainment by opening or closing opportunities and shaping occupational- and self-concepts. Lent et al. (1994) proposed that race and socioeconomic status affect career choice options primarily through their impact on learning opportunities giving rise to particular types of self-efficacy beliefs and outcome expectations. From a sociological perspective, race is viewed as a stimulus variable that produces reactions from others. The influence of these reactions is often internalized and acted on at an early age (Hotchkiss & Borow, 1996).

The effects of both race or ethnicity and socioeconomic status are not easy to disentangle from other variables (Osipow & Fitzgerald, 1996), resulting in a fair amount of confusion about their respective roles in shaping occupational aspirations. The study I coauthored with Yang (1997) offers some potential insight. We initially hypothesized that gender, race/ethnicity, and socioeconomic status would all have enduring effects on the development of occupational aspirations. Instead, we found that when controlling for the effects of race/ethnicity (categorized as a dichotomous variable, White/non-White) with socioeconomic status, race/ethnicity had very minimal direct influence. In other words, socioeconomic status moderated the effects of, and was more influential than, race/ethnicity on aspirations.

Other studies of race and ethnicity influences reveal more mixed results, ranging from no racial differences (Hauser & Anderson, 1991; Rotberg, Brown, & Ware, 1987; Singer & Saldana, 2001; Thomas, 1976) to higher aspirations for Whites than for racial and ethnic minorities (Bogie, 1976; Curry & Picou, 1971; Hellenga et al., 2002), to higher aspirations for racial and ethnic minorities than Whites (Dillard & Perrin, 1980; Wilson & Wilson, 1992). Arbona and Novy (1991) found no overall differences in the Holland type of the occupational aspirations of African American, Mexican American, and White participants. However, when examined by gender, more White and Mexican American men aspired to, and expected to work in, realistic and investigative occupations than African American men, while a larger proportion of women than men aspired to, and expected to work in, social and conventional occupations. Thus, gender-role stereotypes seemed to have greater influence on occupational expectations than aspirations for African American and Mexican American groups.

Much of the work that has been done on racial influences has looked at African American adolescents and adults. Reviewing this literature, Bowman (1995) claimed that relatively little is known about how race affects the occupational aspirations of African Americans. What the research does show is a tendency for African Americans to have lower aspirations and expectations than their White counterparts (Hellenga et al., 2002; T. E. Sewell & Martin, 1976). Jacobs, Karen, and McClelland (1991) reported moderate differences in aspirations by race. White males were more likely to aspire to professional and managerial occupations, while African American males were more likely to aspire to lower prestige jobs, such as craft and blue-collar occupations. However, it appears that education level may be a moderating variable because when education was held constant, there were no differences between the two groups.

Socioeconomic Status   It is somewhat surprising that the influence of socioeconomic status on career aspirations has not received a great deal of attention in career psychology (Osipow & Fitzgerald, 1996). Yet, despite limited and sometimes contradictory findings (e.g., Rashmi, Kauppi, Lewko, & Urajnik, 2002; Sellers et al., 1999), it seems that socioeconomic status does play some role, either directly or indirectly, in determining occupational and educational aspirations (e.g., Furlong & Cartmel, 1995; Holmes & Esses, 1988; Rojewski & Yang, 1997; W. H. Sewell & Shah, 1968; Wahl & Blackhurst, 2000). Generally, research findings indicate positive correlations between socioeconomic status and occupational aspirations: Individuals from higher socioeconomic status aspire to, expect, and attain more education and more prestigious occupations than individuals from lower class backgrounds.

Schoon and Parsons (2002), for example, found that family socioeconomic status was related to later adult occupational attainment of children. However, more important, they also found that this relationship could be explained by educational aspirations and educational attainments during the school years. That is, children from lower socioeconomic backgrounds did poorer in school and had lower future educational aspirations than did children from higher socioeconomic backgrounds. This, and not their socioeconomic background per se, led them to end up as adults with less prestigious occupations (see also Marjoribanks, 2002).

These are very important findings because they suggest that an individual's future occupational attainment is not an inevitable result of where he or she grows up. Rather, the potential career-limiting influences of socioeconomic status can be reduced by helping children growing up in such family backgrounds to perform better in school and, as a result, develop higher levels of educational aspirations for their future.

How else might socioeconomic status influence aspirations? Status attainment theory studies, in particular, have emphasized how socioeconomic status provides a context for the development of occupational aspirations and attainment (Hellenga et al., 2002; W. H. Sewell et al., 1969, 1970). Friesen (1986) maintained that it is necessary to understand both opportunity and process. In terms of opportunity, higher socioeconomic status brings greater access to the resources needed to finance education, provides special learning experiences, and offers exposure to role models that have high prestige occupations. Conversely, socioeconomic status can also result in bias and structural barriers that negatively affect the aspirations and expectations of those from lower socioeconomic status backgrounds. Knottnerus (1987) explained the importance of social context:

> Aspirations—the central mechanism in the process—are formed in social interaction. Aspirations develop in response to the evaluations one receives from significant others and the self-assessment of one's potential based on academic performance. Assuming that status groups structure social interaction, the implications are that significant others—for example, teachers and peers—tend to be drawn from socioeconomic positions somewhat similar to those of the youth's parents and provide encouragement from a similar value orientation. . . . Thus, aspirations formed at an early age shape educational and occupational attainments. (p. 116)

Other Influences   In addition to gender, race, and socioeconomic status, a number of other variables correlate with occupational aspirations, including personal and psychological characteristics such as self-efficacy, self-esteem, self-concept, and locus of control (Betz & Hackett, 1983; Fouad & Smith, 1996; Lent, Brown, & Larkin, 1986); family variables such as parents' expectations, education, and occupations (W. H. Sewell & Hauser, 1980; Singh et al., 1995; Wilson & Wilson, 1992); and school experiences such as academic achievement and ability (Braddock & Dawkins, 1993; Hossler & Stage, 1992; Majoribanks, 1985; Mau & Bikos, 2000). The influence of significant others on both educational and occupational aspirations has also received attention (Davey & Stoppard, 1993; Knottnerus, 1987; W. H. Sewell et al., 1970). The available literature supports the notion that parents play a primary role in shaping their children's occupational aspirations. Steinberg, Dornbusch, and their colleagues, in particular, conducted a series of investigations that demonstrate the powerful influence of home life on aspirations and attainment. They found that parenting styles and parenting practices shape adolescent academic competence and achievement (Glasgow, Dornbusch, Troyer, Steinberg, & Ritter, 1997). Specifically, authoritative parenting—democratic but with clear firm rules, demanding yet supportive, open communication, and encouragement of independence—has a positive effect on academic achievement across both gender and socioeconomic status. Adolescents with authoritative parents are better able to balance individual and group needs, report higher self-perceptions of ability, and are more self-reliant than other youths (Steinberg, Dornbusch, & Brown, 1992; Steinberg, Lamborn, Dornbusch, & Darling, 1992).

Jodl, Michael, Malanchuk, Eccles, and Sameroff (2001) criticized past literature studying the role of parents on children's occupational aspirations because of the heavy focus on structural attainment features such as socioeconomic status or parental occupations. They argued that *process* variables—parents' role modeling, attitudes, behavior, and related socialization practices—were equally important in understanding the role parents play in their children's occupational lives. Examining two specific domains, academics and sports, parents' values predicted their children's occupational aspirations both directly and indirectly. In the academic domain, a direct path existed between parents' beliefs and practices and their children's aspirations. Conversely, an indirect path existed for the sports domain where fathers' behavior mediated the relationship. The researchers concluded that family plays a primary role in, and establishes a critical context for, career development.

Barber and Eccles (1992) looked at occupational aspirations in light of the effects of divorce and single parenting. They proposed a conceptual model to explain the long-term influences of divorce and single parenting on both family processes and child identity formation. The model included three factors—maternal employment (role modeling, time spent with children, work attitudes), family processes (distribution of family responsibilities), and parental expectations—assumed to mediate or be linked to the socialization of occupational aspirations. These three factors heavily influence adolescents' values, self-concept, and achievement, which in turn are predicted to influence educational and occupational aspirations. Countering long-held beliefs that divorce or single parenting is often negative, Barber and Eccles suggested that there might be advantages for children living with a single parent:

> Children in single-parent, female-headed families may develop a greater sense of personal responsibility and self-esteem, and girls and boys may develop less gender-role stereotyped occupational aspirations ... which could lead to their increased success in the labor market. (p. 122)

IMPORTANT ROLE OF EDUCATIONAL ASPIRATIONS AND ATTAINMENT

As described earlier, a number of authors (e.g., Alexander & Eckland, 1975; Haller & Virkler, 1993; Marjoribanks, 2002; Mau & Bikos, 2000; Mau et al., 1995; Rojewski, 1999; Rottinghaus et al., 2002; Schoon & Parsons, 2002) have concluded that educational aspirations—the impressions formed about academic abilities and highest level of education an individual would like to attain (Furlong & Cartmel, 1995)—and educational attainment are the bedrock of career development and choice. In a thorough review of the literature on the academic achievement-career development link, Arbona (2000) identified a number of predictors of school success—thus, indirectly on educational and occupational aspirations—including socioeconomic status, children's and parents' intelligence, quality of education, parental and peer influences, and motivational factors. Educational aspirations are important because they guide individuals in what they learn in school, how they prepare for adult life, and what they eventually accomplish (Walberg, 1989).

The role of educational aspirations in career attainment is often explained in this manner. Through a complex set of processes and interactions, high educational (and to a lesser degree, occupational) aspirations enhance the opportunities an individual receives to acquire advanced education, which, in turn, allows for greater occupational possibilities in adulthood. In contrast, lowered educational aspirations may lead adolescents to preclude involvement in certain types of academic activities and, thus, limit their future occupationally-related opportunities and experiences. For example, adolescents who do not complete certain academic prerequisites in middle school because of lowered aspirations are often unable to enroll in advanced mathematics and science courses in high school. A lack of academic prerequisites, then, all but eliminates the possibility of attaining a college degree, which, in turn, results in diminished opportunities for attaining high-prestige occupations (Arbona, 2000, Chapter 22, this volume; Betz, 1993; Fitzgerald & Betz, 1994; Lent et al., 1994). Rosenbaum (1979) described this process in terms of a tournament where those ousted from the tournament (in this case, academics) at an early age do not have opportunities to compete for future opportunities.

Indeed, given its cumulative effects, an early lack of academic achievement is progressively more difficult to counteract as children grow (Arbona, 2000). Mau and Bikos (2000) indicated that the single best predictor of occupational aspirations was academic performance. High school academic program (college preparation versus technical preparation), school type, and academic proficiency were other predictors of both educational and occupational aspirations in their study. Academic achievement has also been linked to postsecondary aspirations in a number of other studies (e.g., Bogie, 1976; Hellenga et al., 2002; Lent, O'Brien, & Fassinger, 1998).

Several of my own investigations highlight the prominent role of educational aspirations and academic achievement on the development of occupational aspirations, as well as on postsecondary attainment. For example, Yang and I (Rojewski & Yang, 1997) reported that achievement had a modest positive influence on occupational aspirations that was greatest in Grade 8 and then decreased until high school graduation. Higher academic achievement was positively correlated with higher occupational and educational aspirations. We found it interesting that educational, not occupational, aspirations had consistently higher factor loadings on the occupational aspirations construct we designed. This means that early adolescents' educational aspirations were a more reliable measure for occupational aspirations than occupational aspirations themselves.

Rojewski and Kim (2003) found further evidence for the importance of educational aspirations. We studied adolescents whose status two years after high school graduation was known (e.g., in college, employed full time) and found that educational aspirations in Grade 8 were more accurate predictors of what young adults were doing two years after the completion of high school than were occupational aspirations. We concluded, "Our analysis examined the developmental nature of aspirations in early adolescence through structural equation modeling finding that (1) occupational aspirations are influenced more by academic achievement and expected postsecondary educational attainment than anticipated occupational attainment and (2) that aspirations, identified by prestige level, are relatively stable from Grades 8 to 10" (Rojewski & Kim, 2003, p. 106).

The weight of evidence defining the connection between academic achievement-educational aspirations-occupational aspirations was enough for Ma and Wang (2001) to recommend:

> [T]he focus of educators and administrators should be on improving education outcomes, and they should use factors of educational productivity to promote student career aspiration. In other words, resources for a direct campaign to promote student career aspiration may well be spent in improving the chance of student academic success. (p. 452)

IMPLICATIONS FOR PRACTICE

An important issue about occupational aspirations is that they tend to be relatively established by the eighth grade and remain fairly stable throughout adolescence. A comprehensive, longitudinal, and integrated focus on education, career development, and the direct connection between the two is needed so that secondary (and postsecondary) educational options are not eliminated prematurely (Rosenbaum, 1979) and appropriate career-related choices can be identified, planned for, and attained. Given the considerable influence of social demographic variables such as gender, race or ethnicity, and socioeconomic status on aspirations and the early emergence of aspirations, it appears that the typical practice of introducing time-limited career development interventions for eighth- and ninth-grade students (e.g., conducting a career day or offering an eight-week career awareness unit) may simply be a matter of too little, too late. Specific interventions should begin in elementary school years and be sustained through secondary and postsecondary education. While an emphasis on career education has become an increasingly important part of the elementary and middle school years (Murrow-Taylor, Foltz, Ellis, & Culbertson, 1999), a great deal more needs to be done. Wahl and Blackhurst (2000) indicated that efforts must be started early when impressions are being formed so that realistic information about the world of work can be provided and career stereotypes combated. Rashmi et al. (2002) posited that to be effective, interventions should focus on involving families and supporting positive education values at an early age. Several chapters in this volume also provide a wealth of suggestions about potentially useful interventions, including Turner and Lapan (Chapter 17), Arbona (Chapter 22), Fabian and Liesener (Chapter 23), Juntunen (Chapter 24), and Achter and Lubinski (Chapter 25).

When considering findings about occupational aspirations, it is important to remember that lower aspirations are not by themselves negative. In fact, the labor market does not produce unlimited numbers of high-prestige occupations. Lowered aspirations may reflect an accurate and realistic assessment of an individual's abilities, interests, and skills (G. D. Gottfredson & Holland, 1975; L. S. Gottfredson & Becker, 1981). However, the limiting effect that lowered aspirations have on identifying future goals and establishing initial plans should be addressed by career educators at all levels. Those involved in career guidance and counseling efforts should be aware of the factors that positively and negatively influence aspirations when developing career development programs (Wahl & Blackhurst, 2000).

Aspirations are not always necessarily indicators of eventual attainment. However, they have considerable psychological meaning and predictive value in identifying individuals' future educational and career options (Holland & Gottfredson, 1975). Further, knowledge about the construct provides insight into how personal and social pressures influence career development, the process of career compromise and decision making, and ways that early academic experiences and performance might shape our adult lives. While a great deal is known about occupational aspirations and connections to both educational and occupational attainment, additional investigation is warranted. For example, future research might examine the dimensionality of aspirations (e.g., Johnson, 1995), clarify the longitudinal perspective and role of aspirations in occupational attainment, or refine existing models. Study of the potential of early and sustained school-based career interventions for enhancing the career development of children and adolescents is also needed.

REFERENCES

Alexander, K., & Eckland, B. K. (1975). Basic attainment process: A replication and extension. *Sociology of Education, 48,* 457–495.

Apostal, R., & Bilden, J. (1991). Educational and occupational aspirations of rural high school students. *Journal of Career Development, 18,* 153–160.

Arbona, C. (2000). The development of academic achievement in school-aged children: Precursors to career development. In S. D. Brown & R. W. Lent (Eds.), *Handbook of counseling psychology* (3rd ed., pp. 270–309). New York: Wiley.

Arbona, C., & Novy, D. M. (1991). Career aspirations and the expectations of Black, Mexican American, and White students. *Career Development Quarterly, 39,* 231–239.

Armstrong, P. I., & Crombie, G. (2000). Compromises in adolescents' occupational aspirations and expectations from grades 8–10. *Journal of Vocational Behavior, 56,* 82–98.

Astin, H. (1984). The meaning of work in women's lives: A sociopsychological model of career choice and work behavior. *Counseling Psychologist, 12,* 117–126.

Bandura, A. S. (1986). *Social foundations of thought and action: A social cognitive theory.* Englewood Cliffs, NJ: Prentice-Hall.

Barber, B. L., & Eccles, J. S. (1992). Long-term influence of divorce and single parenting on adolescent family-related and work-related values, behaviors, and aspirations. *Psychological Bulletin, 111,* 108–126.

Betz, N. E. (1993). Basic issues and concepts in career counseling for women. In W. B. Walsh & S. H. Osipow (Eds.), *Career counseling for women* (pp. 1–41). Hillsdale, NJ: Erlbaum.

Betz, N. E., & Fitzgerald, L. F. (1987). *The career psychology of women.* New York: Academic Press.

Betz, N. E., & Hackett, G. (1983). The relationship of mathematics self-efficacy expectations to the selection of science-based college majors. *Journal of Vocational Behavior, 23,* 329–345.

Blau, P. M., & Duncan, O. D. (1967). *The American occupational structure.* New York: Wiley.

Bogie, D. W. (1976). Occupational aspirations–expectation discrepancies among high school seniors. *Vocational Guidance Quarterly, 24,* 50–58.

Bowman, S. L. (1995). Career intervention strategies and assessment issues for African Americans. In F. T. L. Leong (Ed.), *Career development and vocational behavior of racial and ethnic minorities* (pp. 137–164). Mahwah, NJ: Erlbaum.

Braddock, J. H., & Dawkins, M. P. (1993). Ability grouping, aspirations, and attainments: Evidence from the National Educational Longitudinal Study of 1988. *Journal of Negro Education, 62,* 324–336.

Burlin, F. (1976). The relationship of parental education and maternal work and occupational status to occupational aspiration in adolescent females. *Journal of Vocational Behavior, 9,* 99–104.

Cook, T. D., Church, M. B., Ajanaku, S., Shadish, W. R., Jr., Kim, J., & Cohen, R. (1996). The development of occupational aspirations and expectations among inner-city boys. *Child Development, 67,* 3368–3385.

Cooley, W. W. (1967). Interactions among interests, abilities, and career plans [Monograph]. *Journal of Applied Psychology, 51*(2), 1–16.

Curry, E. W., & Picou, J. S. (1971). Rural youth and anticipatory occupational goal deflection. *Journal of Vocational Behavior, 1,* 317–330.

Davey, F. H. (1993). The occupational aspirations and expectations of senior high school students [Electronic version]. *Guidance and Counseling, 8*(5).

Davey, F. H., & Stoppard, J. M. (1993). Some factors affecting the occupational expectations of female adolescents. *Journal of Vocational Behavior, 43,* 235–250.

Dillard, J. M., & Perrin, D. W. (1980). Puerto Rican, Black, and Anglo adolescents' career aspirations, expectations, and maturity. *Vocational Guidance Quarterly, 28,* 313–321.

Dolliver, R. H. (1969). Strong Vocational Interest Blank versus expressed vocational interests. *Psychological Bulletin, 72,* 95–107.

Dunne, F., Elliott, R., & Carlsen, W. S. (1981). Sex differences in the educational and occupational aspirations of rural youth. *Journal of Vocational Behavior, 18,* 56–66.

Farmer, H. S. (1985). Model of career and achievement motivation for women and men. *Journal of Counseling Psychology, 32,* 363–390.

Farris, M. C., Boyd, J. C., & Shoffner, S. M. (1985). Longitudinal determinants of occupational plans of low-income rural young adults. *Journal of Research in Rural Education, 3,* 61–67.

Fassinger, R. E. (1985). A causal model of career choice in college women. *Journal of Vocational Behavior, 27,* 123–153.

Fitzgerald, L. F., & Betz, N. E. (1994). Career development in cultural context: The role of gender, race, class, and sexual orientation. In M. L. Savickas & R. W. Lent (Eds.), *Convergence in career development theories: Implications for science and practice* (pp. 103–117). Palo Alto, CA: Consulting Psychologists Press.

Fitzgerald, L. F., Fassinger, R. E., & Betz, N. E. (1995). Theoretical advances in the study of women's career development. In W. B. Walsh & S. H. Osipow (Eds.), *Handbook of vocational psychology: Theory, research, and practice* (2nd ed., pp. 67–109). Hillsdale, NJ: Erlbaum.

Fouad, N. A., & Smith, P. L. (1996). A test of a social cognitive model for middle school students: Math and science. *Journal of Counseling Psychology, 43,* 338–346.

Friesen, J. (1986). The role of the family in vocational development. *International Journal for the Advancement of Counseling, 9*(1), 5–10.

Furlong, A., & Cartmel, F. (1995). Aspirations and opportunity structure: 13-years-olds in areas with restricted opportunities. *British Journal of Guidance and Counselling, 23*(3), 361–375.

Glasgow, K. L., Dornbusch, S. M., Troyer, L., Steinberg, L., & Ritter, P. L. (1997). Parenting styles, adolescents' attributions, and educational outcomes. *Child Development, 68,* 507–529.

Gottfredson, G. D. (1996). Prestige in vocational interests. *Journal of Vocational Behavior, 48,* 68–72.

Gottfredson, G. D. (2002). Interests, aspirations, self-estimation, and the Self-Directed Search. *Journal of Career Assessment, 10,* 200–208.

Gottfredson, G. D., & Holland, J. L. (1975). Vocational choices of men and women: A comparison of predictors from the Self-Directed Search. *Journal of Counseling Psychology, 22,* 28–34.

Gottfredson, L. S. (1981). Circumscription and compromise: A developmental theory of occupational aspirations [Monograph]. *Journal of Counseling Psychology, 28,* 545–579.

Gottfredson, L. S. (1996). Gottfredson's Theory of Circumscription and Compromise. In D. Brown, L. Brooks, & Associates (Eds.), *Career choice and development* (3rd ed., pp. 179–232). San Francisco: Jossey-Bass.

Gottfredson, L. S., & Becker, H. J. (1981). A challenge to vocational psychology: How important are aspirations in determining male career development? *Journal of Vocational Behavior, 18,* 121–137.

Hall, R. H. (1994). *Sociology of work: Perspectives, analyses, and issues.* Thousand Oaks, CA: Pine Forge.

Haller, E. J., & Virkler, S. J. (1993). Another look at rural-nonrural differences in students' educational aspirations. *Journal of Research in Rural Education, 9,* 170–178.

Hanson, S. L. (1994). Lost talent: Unrealized educational aspirations and expectations among U.S. youth. *Sociology of Education, 67,* 159–183.

Hauser, R. M., & Anderson, D. K. (1991). Post high-school plans and aspirations of Black and White high school seniors: 1976–86. *Sociology of Education, 64,* 263–277.

Heckhausen, J., & Tomasik, M. L. (2002). Get an apprenticeship before school is out: How German adolescents adjust vocational aspirations when getting close to a development deadline. *Journal of Vocational Behavior, 60,* 199–219.

Hellenga, K., Aber, M. S., & Rhodes, J. E. (2002). African-American adolescent mothers' vocational aspiration-expectation gap: Individual, social, and environmental influences. *Psychology of Women Quarterly, 26,* 200–212.

Holland, J. L., & Gottfredson, G. D. (1975). Predictive value and psychological meaning of vocational aspirations. *Journal of Vocational Behavior, 6,* 349–363.

Holland, J. L., Gottfredson, G. D., & Baker, H. (1990). Validity of vocational aspirations and interest inventories: Extended, replicated, and reinterpreted [Electronic version]. *Journal of Vocational Behavior, 37.*

Holland, J. L., & Lutz, S. W. (1967). The predictive value of a student's choice of vocation. *Personnel and Guidance Journal, 46,* 428–436.

Holland, J. L., & Whitney, D. R. (1968). *Changes in the vocational plans of college students: Orderly or random?* [ACT Research Reports (No. 25)]. Iowa City, IA: American College Testing Program.

Holmes, V. L., & Esses, L. M. (1988). Factors influencing Canadian high school girls' career motivation. *Psychology of Women Quarterly, 12,* 313–328.

Hossler, D., & Stage, F. K. (1992). Family and high school experience influence on post-secondary educational plan of ninth-grade students. *American Educational Research Journal, 29,* 425–451.

Hotchkiss, L., & Borow, H. (1996). Sociological perspectives on work and career development. In D. Brown, L. Brooks, & Associates (Eds.), *Career choice and development* (3rd ed., pp. 281–334). San Francisco: Jossey-Bass.

Jacobs, J. A., Karen, D., & McClelland, K. (1991). The dynamics of young men's career aspirations. *Sociological Forum, 6,* 609–639.

Jencks, C., Crouse, J., & Muesser, P. (1983). The Wisconsin model of status attainment: A national replication with improved measures of ability and aspiration. *Sociology of Education, 56,* 3–19.

Jenkins, S. R. (1989). Longitudinal prediction of women's careers: Psychological, behavioral and social-structural influences. *Journal of Vocational Behavior, 34,* 204–235.

Jodl, K. M., Michael, A., Malanchuk, O., Eccles, J. S., & Sameroff, A. (2001). Parents' role in shaping early adolescents' occupational aspirations. *Child Development, 72,* 1247–1265.

Johnson, L. (1995). A multidimensional analysis of the vocational aspirations of college students [Online version]. *Measurement and Evaluation in Counseling Psychology, 28*(1), 25–44.

Knottnerus, J. D. (1987). Status attainment research and its image of society. *American Sociological Review, 52,* 113–121.

Kraus, V., Schild, E. O., & Hodge, R. W. (1978). Occupational prestige in the collective conscience. *Social Forces, 56,* 900–918.

Lapan, R. T., & Jingeleski, J. (1992). Circumscribing vocational aspirations in junior high school. *Journal of Counseling Psychology, 39,* 81–90.

Lent, R. W., Brown, S. D., & Hackett, G. (1994). Toward a unifying cognitive theory of career and academic interest, choice, and performance [Monograph]. *Journal of Vocational Behavior, 45,* 79–122.

Lent, R. W., Brown, S. D., & Hackett, G. (1996). Career development from a social cognitive perspective. In D. Brown, L. Brooks, & Associates (Eds.), *Career choice and development* (3rd ed., pp. 423–475). San Francisco: Jossey-Bass.

Lent, R. W., Brown, S. D., & Larkin, K. C. (1986). Self-efficacy in the prediction of academic performance and perceived career options. *Journal of Counseling Psychology, 33,* 265–269.

Lent, R. W., & Hackett, G. (1987). Career self-efficacy: Empirical status and future directions [Monograph]. *Journal of Vocational Behavior, 30,* 347–382.

Lent, R. W., Hackett, G., & Brown, S. D. (1996). A social cognitive framework for studying career choice and transition to work. *Journal of Vocational Education Research, 21*(4), 3–31.

Lent, R. W., O'Brien, K. M., & Fassinger, R. E. (1998). School-to-work transition and counseling psychology. *Counseling Psychologist, 26,* 489–494.

Looft, W. R. (1971). Sex differences in the expression of vocational aspirations by elementary school children. *Developmental Psychology, 5,* 366.

Ma, X., & Wang, J. (2001). A confirmatory examination of Walberg's model of educational productivity in student career aspiration. *Educational Psychology, 21,* 443–453.

Marjoribanks, K. (1985). Families, schools, and aspirations: Ethnic group differences. *Journal of Experimental Education, 53,* 141–147.

Marjoribanks, K. (2002). Family background, individual and environmental influences on adolescents' aspirations. *Educational Studies, 28*(1), 33–46.

Mau, W. C., & Bikos, L. H. (2000). Educational and vocational aspirations of minority and female students: A longitudinal study. *Journal of Counseling and Development, 78,* 186–194.

Mau, W. C., Domnick, M., & Ellsworth, R. A. (1995). Characteristics of female students who aspire to science and engineering or homemaking occupations. *Career Development Quarterly, 43,* 323–337.

Maxwell, G. S., & Cumming, J. J. (1988). Measuring occupation aspiration in research on sex differences: An overview and analysis of issues. *Journal of Vocational Behavior, 32,* 60–73.

McNair, D., & Brown, D. (1983). Predicting the occupational aspirations, occupational expectations, and career maturity of black and white male and female tenth graders. *Vocational Guidance Quarterly, 32,* 29–36.

McNulty, W. B., & Borgen, W. A. (1988). Career expectations and aspirations of adolescents. *Journal of Vocational Behavior, 33,* 217–224.

Murrow-Taylor, C., Foltz, B., Ellis, M. R., & Culbertson, K. (1999). A multicultural career fair for elementary school students. *Professional School Counseling, 2,* 241–243.

Naoko, K., & Treas, J. (1992). *The 1989 socioeconomic index of occupations: Construction from the 1989 occupational prestige scores* (GSS Methodological Report, No. 74). Chicago: National Opinion Research Center.

Osipow, S. H., & Fitzgerald, L. F. (1996). *Theories of career development* (4th ed.). Boston: Allyn & Bacon.

Otto, L. B., Haller, A. O., Meier, R. F., & Ohlendorf, G. W. (1974). An empirical evaluation of a scale to measure occupational aspiration level. *Journal of Vocational Behavior, 5,* 1–11.

Rashmi, G., Kauppi, C., Lewko, J., & Urajnik, D. (2002). A structural model of educational aspirations. *Journal of Career Development, 29*(2), 87–108.

Rojewski, J. W. (1996). Occupational aspirations and early career-choice patterns of adolescents with and without learning disabilities. *Learning Disability Quarterly, 19*(2), 99–116.

Rojewski, J. W. (1997). Characteristics of students who express stable or undecided occupational expectations during early adolescents. *Journal of Career Assessment, 5*(1), 1–20.

Rojewski, J. W. (1999). Occupational and educational aspirations and attainment of young adults with and without LD 2 years after high school completion. *Journal of Learning Disabilities, 52,* 533–552.

Rojewski, J. W., & Kim, H. (2003). Career choice patterns and behavior of work-bound youth during early adolescence. *Journal of Career Development, 30,* 89–108.

Rojewski, J. W., & Yang, B. (1997). Longitudinal analysis of select influences on adolescents' occupational aspirations. *Journal of Vocational Behavior, 51,* 375–410.

Rosenbaum, J. E. (1979). Tournament mobility: Career patterns in a corporation. *Administrative Science Quarterly, 24,* 220–241.

Rotberg, H. L., Brown, D., & Ware, W. B. (1987). Career self-efficacy expectations and perceived range of career options in community college students. *Journal of Counseling Psychology, 34,* 164–170.

Rottinghaus, P. J., Lindley, L. D., Green, M. A., & Borgen, F. H. (2002). Educational aspirations: The contribution of personality, self-efficacy, and interests. *Journal of Vocational Behavior, 61,* 1–19.

Saltiel, J. (1988). The Wisconsin model of status attainment and the occupational choice process. *Work and Occupations, 15,* 334–355.

Schoon, I., & Parsons, S. (2002). Teenage aspirations for future careers and occupational outcomes. *Journal of Vocational Behavior, 60,* 262–288.

Sellers, N., Satcher, J., & Comas, R. (1999). Children's occupational aspirations: Comparisons by gender, gender role identity and socioeconomic status. *Professional School Counseling, 2,* 314–317.

Sewell, T. E., & Martin, R. P. (1976). Racial differences in patterns of occupational choice in adolescents. *Psychology in the Schools, 13,* 326–333.

Sewell, W. H., Haller, A. O., & Ohlendorf, G. W. (1970). The educational and early occupational status attainment process: Replication and revision. *American Sociological Review, 35,* 1014–1027.

Sewell, W. H., Haller, A. O., & Portes, A. (1969). The educational and early occupational attainment process. *American Sociological Review, 34,* 89–92.

Sewell, W. H., & Hauser, R. M. (1980). The Wisconsin study of social psychological factors in aspiration and achievement. *Research in Sociology of Education and Socialization, 1,* 59–99.

Sewell, W. H., & Shah, V. P. (1968). Social class, parental encouragement, and educational aspirations. *American Journal of Sociology, 73,* 559–572.

Silvia, P. J. (2001). Expressed and measured vocational interests: Distinctions and definitions. *Journal of Vocational Behavior, 59,* 382–393.

Singer, B., & Saldana, D. (2001). Educational and career aspirations of high school students and race, gender, class differences [Electronic version]. *Race, Gender, and Class, 8*(1).

Singh, K., Bickley, P. G., Keith, T. Z., Keith, P. B., Trivette, P., & Anderson, E. (1995). The effect of four components of parental involvement on eighth-grade student achievement: Structure analysis of NELS:88 data. *School Psychology Review, 24,* 299–317.

Slocum, W. L. (1974). *Occupational careers.* Chicago: Aldine.

Steinberg, L., Dornbusch, S. D., & Brown, B. (1992). Ethnic differences in adolescent achievement in ecological perspective. *American Psychologist, 47,* 723–729.

Steinberg, L., Lamborn, S. D., Dornbusch, S. M., & Darling, N. (1992). Impact of parenting practices on adolescent achievement: Authoritative parenting, school involvement, and encouragement to succeed. *Child Development, 63,* 1266–1281.

Stevens, G., & Cho, J. H. (1985). Socioeconomic indexes and the new 1980 census occupational classification scheme. *Social Science Research, 14,* 142–168.

Strong, E. K. (1953). Validity of occupational choice. *Educational and Psychological Measurement, 16,* 11–121.

Super, D. E. (1990). A life-span, life-space approach to career development. In D. Brown, L. Brooks, & Associates (Eds.), *Career choice and development: Applying contemporary theories to practice* (2nd ed., pp. 197–261). San Francisco: Jossey-Bass.

Super, D. E., Savickas, M. L., & Super, C. M. (1996). The life-span, life-space approach to careers. In D. Brown, L. Brooks, & Associates (Eds.), *Career choice and development* (3rd ed., pp. 121–178). San Francisco: Jossey-Bass.

Swanson, J. L., & Gore, P. A. (2000). Advances in vocational psychology theory and research. In S. D. Brown & R. W. Lent (Eds.), *Handbook of counseling psychology* (3rd ed., pp. 233–269). New York: Wiley.

Taylor, K. M. (1982). An investigation of vocational indecision in college students. *Journal of Vocational Behavior, 21,* 471–476.

Thomas, M. J. (1976). Realism and socioeconomic status of occupational plans of low socioeconomic status Black and White male adolescents. *Journal of Counseling Psychology, 23,* 46–49.

Trice, A. D. (1991). Stability of children's career aspirations. *Journal of Genetic Psychology, 152*(1), 137–139.

Trice, A. D., & King, R. (1991). Stability of kindergarten children's career aspirations. *Psychological Reports, 68,* 1378.

Trice, A. D., & McClellan, N. (1993). Do children's career aspirations predict adult occupations? An answer from secondary analysis. *Psychological Reports, 72,* 368–370.

Trice, A. D., McClellan, N., & Hughes, M. A. (1992). Origins of children's career aspirations: II. Direct suggestions as a method of transmitting occupational preferences. *Psychological Reports, 71,* 253–254.

Vandiver, B. J., & Bowman, S. L. (1996). A schematic reconceptualization and application of Gottfredson's model. In M. L. Savickas & W. B. Walsh (Eds.), *Handbook of career counseling theory and practice* (pp. 155–168). Palo Alto, CA: Davies-Black.

Wahl, K. H., & Blackhurst, A. (2000). Factors affecting the occupational and educational aspirations of children and adolescents. *Professional Counseling, 3,* 367–374.

Walberg, H. J. (1989). Student aspirations: National and international perspectives. *Research in Rural Education, 6*(2), 1–6.

Walls, R. T., & Gulkus, S. P. (1974). Reinforcers and vocational maturity in occupational aspiration, expectation, and goal deflection. *Journal of Vocational Behavior, 5,* 381–390.

Whitney, D. R. (1969). Predicting expressed vocational choice: A review. *Personnel and Guidance Journal, 48,* 279–286.

Wilson, P. M., & Wilson, J. R. (1992). Environmental influences on adolescent educational aspirations: A logistic transform model. *Youth and Society, 24,* 52–70.

CHAPTER 7

Job Search Success: A Review and Integration of the Predictors, Behaviors, and Outcomes

Alan M. Saks

JOB SEARCH IS a topic of considerable importance to researchers who are interested in the predictors and consequences of job seekers' job search activities and to practitioners who assist job seekers in finding employment. Many stakeholders have a vested interest in the job search process, including individuals, educational institutions, career counselors, organizations, and society at large. Thus, job search is of relevance to a wide range of individuals, including those who have suffered involuntary job loss, individuals who are entering the workforce for the first time, and individuals who want to change their jobs, organizations, or even careers. Given that workers in the United States are expected to engage in more than a dozen job changes over the course of their work lives, "job search has become an integral aspect of American worklife" (Kanfer, Wanberg, & Kantrowitz, 2001, p. 837).

It is, therefore, of considerable importance to understand how people search for employment, how job search activities influence job search success, and how to assist job seekers in their job search efforts. Fortunately, there has been an increasing amount of research in the past 10 years on job search, including a meta-analysis on the antecedents and consequences of job search behavior (Kanfer et al., 2001).

Although job search research has advanced considerably since Schwab, Rynes, and Aldag (1987) reviewed the literature more than 15 years ago, there remains a need to integrate variables that have often been studied in isolation and in different streams of job search research. For example, one stream of research focuses on the predictors and outcomes of job search (e.g., Saks & Ashforth, 1999; Wanberg, Hough, & Song, 2002; Wanberg, Kanfer, & Banas, 2000; Wanberg, Kanfer, & Rotundo, 1999) while a separate stream focuses on interventions to help unemployed job seekers find employment (e.g., Caplan, Vinokur, Price, & van Ryn,

1989; Vinokur, Schul, Vuori, & Price, 2000). Clearly, these are two areas that should inform each other. That is, the findings from research on the predictors and outcomes of job search should be used as a foundation for the development of job search interventions.

A second area where integration is lacking exists within the literature on job search predictors and outcomes. The problem stems from studies that focus on particular job search behaviors. For example, some studies focus exclusively on the sources that job seekers use to find employment (e.g., Huffman & Torres, 2001; Leicht & Marx, 1997), while others focus on job search intensity (e.g., Wanberg et al., 1999), networking intensity (Wanberg et al., 2000), and assertive job-seeking behaviors (Schmit, Amel, & Ryan, 1993). Thus, there is a need to integrate these various forms of job search behavior into a unified and integrated framework.

Another problem is the tendency for job search studies to focus on particular outcomes. For example, some studies are mostly concerned with whether a job seeker finds employment (e.g., Wanberg, Watt, & Rumsey, 1996), the earnings obtained from employment (Huffman & Torres, 2001), or the quality of employment obtained (Saks & Ashforth, 2002). Thus, job search studies vary in terms of the criteria used to assess job search effectiveness (Brasher & Chen, 1999).

The main objective of this chapter is to integrate the findings from job search research to develop a coherent and integrative model that includes the different predictors of job search, the various forms of job search behavior, and the different outcomes or criteria of job search success. A second objective is to develop an intervention framework, based on the job search model, to be used for practice to guide those who assist job seekers in finding employment. The basic notion behind the job search intervention framework is that attempts to assist job seekers should be tailored to the needs and goals of a job seeker in terms of specific job search behaviors and outcomes.

The chapter first defines job search as a form of goal-directed behavior. Next, the job search process is described, followed by a review of job search models. This is followed by a review of each of the main variables in models of job search: job search behaviors, predictors of job search, and outcomes of job search. Based on the review, an integrative self-regulatory model of job search predictors, behaviors, and outcomes is presented, followed by a job search intervention framework.

JOB SEARCH AS GOAL-DIRECTED BEHAVIOR

Job search is a process that consists of gathering information about potential job opportunities, generating and evaluating job alternatives, and choosing a job from the alternatives (Barber, Daly, Giannantonio, & Phillips, 1994). These activities determine the type and amount of information that job seekers obtain about job openings as well as the number of job opportunities from which a job seeker may choose.

Kanfer et al. (2001) conceptualized job search as a motivational self-regulatory process that involves "a purposive, volitional pattern of action that begins with the identification and commitment to pursuing an employment goal" (p. 838). Employment goals activate job search behaviors that are intended to lead to the employment goal. Thus, "individuals identify, initiate, and pursue actions for the purpose of obtaining new employment or reemployment" (p. 849). Job search and the self-regulatory process ends when the employment goal has been achieved or is abandoned. Thus, job search can be understood as a form of goal-directed behavior.

Several studies have shown that goals are an important motivator of job search. For example, in a study of unemployed manufacturing workers, Prussia, Fugate, and Kinicki (2001) found that reemployment coping goals (an individual's desired end result that he or she seeks to accomplish in response to a perceived harm/loss or threat such as reemployment in response to job loss) were positively related to job search effort, and job search effort predicted reemployment. Saks and Ashforth (2002) found that career planning, an indicator of career goals, was related to perceptions of preentry person-job (P-J) and person-organization (P-O) fit as well as postentry P-J fit and job attitudes. Wanberg et al. (2002) found that job search clarity (the extent to which unemployed job seekers have clear job search objectives and a clear idea of the type of work desired) was positively related to job-organization fit and lower intention to quit. Thus, goal setting during job search appears to predict job search effort and outcomes and represents a critical factor in the job search process.

THE JOB SEARCH PROCESS

The job search process has been described as a logical sequence of activities. According to Soelberg (1967), job search consists of two phases—planning job search and then job search and choice. Job search begins with an extensive search to gather information and identify job opportunities followed by a more intensive search that involves the acquisition of specific information about jobs and organizations. Similarly, Blau (1993, 1994) distinguished preparatory from active job search behavior. Preparatory job search behavior is an information gathering stage in which job seekers find out about job opportunities through different sources of information. Active job search behavior involves actually applying for positions.

In addition to the *sequential model,* two other models of the job search process have been proposed. According to the *learning model,* job seekers learn more efficient and effective search techniques during the course of their job search. As job seekers gain more experience, they identify those techniques and activities that work best for them and change their behaviors accordingly (Barber et al., 1994). The *emotional response model* asserts that job seekers experience high levels of stress and frustration during the course of their job search, which can lead to avoidance, helplessness, and withdrawal. For some seekers, especially those who experience difficulty in finding employment, the job search process becomes so stressful that they simply abandon their search (Barber et al., 1994).

Several studies have measured the change in job seekers' search behavior. For example, Barber et al. (1994) measured the job search activities of college and vocational-technical school graduates early in the search process, at graduation, and three months following graduation for those who remained unemployed. They found a significant decrease from initial search to late search at graduation in the use of formal job information sources, job search intensity, and information related to obtaining a job. For those who remained unemployed at graduation, they found a significant increase in the use of formal job information sources and intensity three months later. Barber et al. concluded that their results are most consistent with the sequential model of job search.

Saks and Ashforth (2000) studied recent university graduates who had not found a job just before graduation. A follow-up four months later indicated that job seekers increased their active job search behavior, formal job source usage, and search effort, and decreased their job search anxiety. They also found that a change in job search behavior was related to the number of interviews and whether a job seeker obtained employment, and the relationship between change in job search behavior and employment was mediated by the number of job offers that a job seeker received. An increase in job search behavior was related to more job interviews, more job interviews related to more job offers, and more offers related to finding employment.

In summary, job search is a dynamic process that consists of a variety of job search activities and behaviors that change during the course of an individual's job search. Furthermore, changes in job search behavior are associated with job search outcomes.

JOB SEARCH MODELS

Seventeen years ago, Schwab et al. (1987) presented a model of the determinants and consequences of job search intensity. Job search intensity was the only job search behavior variable, and there were two determinants and one consequence. According to the model, self-esteem and financial need predict job search intensity, and job search intensity predicts employment. Employment was defined in terms of whether employment was obtained and the quality of the employment (e.g., wage level, satisfaction with choice, tenure with the new employer).

Since then, additional predictors, job search variables, and outcomes have been investigated, and more complex and expanded job search models have been developed. Most of these models include personal and situational predictors of job search behaviors and consider employment status and the rate or speed of employment as the main outcomes of job search (e.g., see Saks & Ashforth, 1999; Wanberg et al., 1996, 1999).

Two of the most recent models extend existing models in several ways. First, Wanberg et al. (2002) developed a multidisciplinary model of reemployment success that consists of seven major categories of predictors of reemployment success: labor market demand; job seeker human capital (the ability, experience, and personality characteristics the job seeker brings to the job); job seeker social capital (job seeker social networks); job seeker reemployment constraints; job seekers' economic need to work; job seekers' job search intensity, clarity, and quality; and employer discrimination. Reemployment success was conceptualized as consisting of five components: unemployment insurance exhaustion, speed of reemployment, job improvement, and job-organization fit, which in turn predict job attitudes and behavior (e.g., intention to quit).

In another recent model, Saks and Ashforth (2002) focused on P-J and P-O fit perceptions and employment quality. They tested a model in which four job search variables (preparatory job search behavior, active job search behavior, job search effort, and career planning) predict perceptions of P-J and P-O fit, and P-J and P-O fit predict employment quality (i.e., job attitudes and organizational attitudes).

Although there is some overlap between the models in terms of the predictors (e.g., job search self-efficacy, personality variables), job search behaviors (job search intensity), and outcomes (employment status and quality), there is also considerable variability. In the following sections, a review of the research on the predictors and outcomes of job search behaviors is provided and restricted to those variables that have been studied most often and those found to be particularly important. Research on the predictors and outcomes of job search has also varied as a function of sample type. Research has included new entrants to the workforce (e.g., college graduates), employed job seekers, and unemployed job seekers (job losers). College students have been used most often, followed by unemployed job seekers, while reentrants to the workforce have seldom been investigated.

Since the characteristics of these samples differ in terms of experience, motivation, and the use of job search strategies, the predictors and outcomes of job search might differ across studies depending on the nature of the samples used. In fact, in a meta-analysis of the predictors and outcomes of job search by Kanfer et al. (2001), sample type was a significant moderator variable affecting the strength of relationships between the predictors and job search behaviors, and between job search behaviors and employment outcomes. For example, Kanfer et al. found that several of the personality dimensions of the five-factor model (i.e., extraversion, neuroticism, conscientiousness) were more strongly related to job search behavior for new entrants than job losers, whereas several situational predictors (i.e., employment commitment and social support) were more strongly related to job search behaviors among job losers.

JOB SEARCH BEHAVIORS

In their review of the job search literature, Schwab et al. (1987) indicated that employment outcomes are a function of the sources used to acquire information about job openings and the intensity with which an individual pursues such information. While sources and intensity are among the most often studied job search dimensions, job search research has included a number of other dimensions of job search. In this section, the following job search behaviors are described: (1) job information sources, (2) job search intensity, (3) job search effort, (4) assertive job-seeking behavior, and (5) network intensity.

JOB INFORMATION SOURCES

Job information sources are considered to be one of the most important dimensions of job search and are among the most often studied. *Sources* refer to the means by which job seekers learn about job opportunities. Both the recruitment and job search literature has tended to distinguish between formal and informal job information sources. Formal sources involve the use of public intermediaries such as advertisements, employment agencies, and campus placement offices. Informal sources are private intermediaries such as friends, relatives, or persons who are already employed in an organization (Saks & Ashforth, 1997).

Research on job information sources usually asks job applicants to indicate from a list of job sources which ones they used during their job search. The total number of sources indicated is used to create a score for total sources used as well as separate scores for informal and formal sources (Barber et al., 1994; Saks & Ashforth, 2000).

JOB SEARCH INTENSITY

Job search intensity refers to the frequency with which job seekers, during a set period of time, engage in specific job search behaviors or activities such as preparing a resume or contacting an employment agency (Kanfer et al., 2001). Various indicators have been used to measure search intensity, such as the number of employers contacted, the number of hours per week spent searching, and the number of sources used (Barber et al., 1994). However, most measures consist of a list of job search activities, such as "prepared/revised your resume," "telephoned a prospective employer," or "filled out a job application." Respondents indicate how frequently they performed each activity (e.g., 0 times to at least 10 times) over a set time period, such as the past three months.

In response to the failure to distinguish among job search activities at different stages of the job search process as well as the frequent use of single-item measures and dichotomous response scales, Blau (1993, 1994) developed two distinct measures of job search intensity that he called *preparatory job search behavior* and *active job search behavior.* Preparatory job search behavior involves gathering job search information and identifying potential leads during the planning phase of job search. Active job search behavior involves the actual job search and choice process, such as sending out resumes and interviewing with prospective employers. Active job search is conceptualized as reflecting an individual's behavioral commitment to the job search (Blau, 1994).

JOB SEARCH EFFORT

Job search effort refers to the amount of energy, time, and persistence that a job seeker devotes to his or her job search (Kanfer et al., 2001). Unlike measures of job search intensity, measures of job search effort do not focus on specific job search activities or behaviors. Blau (1993, 1994) developed a scale to measure general effort in job search that asks respondents about the time and effort they have devoted to their job search (e.g., "focused my time and effort on job search activities"). Based on confirmatory factor analyses across three diverse samples, Blau (1994) found empirical support that general effort is related to, yet distinguishable from, preparatory and active job search behavior.

ASSERTIVE JOB-SEEKING BEHAVIOR

Assertive job seeking applies the concept of assertiveness to job search and refers to the individual's ability to identify his or her rights and choices during job search and to act on them (Schmit et al., 1993). Specific behaviors include making follow-up calls about the status of a job application and making calls to arrange meetings with organizational representatives to discuss employment opportunities.

Although assertive job-seeking behavior is often recommended in the popular job search literature, only a few studies have actually measured it. Becker (1980) developed a scale to measure assertive job-seeking behavior, called the

Assertive Job-Hunting Survey (AJHS). The measure was found to have good psychometric properties. In one of the few job search studies to use Becker's (1980) scale, Schmit et al. (1993) reported positive relationships between assertive job-seeking behavior and employment among a sample of minimally educated workers.

NETWORKING INTENSITY

In popular job search books, networking is often purported to be one of the most effective job search methods for finding employment, and research has often shown that many people do find jobs by contacting friends, relatives, acquaintances, and contacts (Wanberg et al., 2000).

Networking is a specific job search behavior that involves contacting friends, acquaintances, and referrals to obtain information and leads about job opportunities. More formally, it has been defined as "individual actions directed toward contacting friends, acquaintances, and other people to whom the job seeker has been referred for the main purpose of getting information, leads, or advice on getting a job" (Wanberg et al., 2000, p. 492). A systematic and complete approach to networking as a job search method involves making a list of contacts, informing them that you are looking for employment, asking for job leads and referrals to others who might be able to help, and contacting these leads and referrals (Wanberg et al., 2000).

Although networking activities are often included in job search intensity scales, only one study has investigated the effectiveness of networking as a job search method: Wanberg et al. (2000) examined the predictors and outcomes of networking intensity in a sample of unemployed job seekers. They defined *networking intensity* as the frequency and thoroughness of using networking during a job search. Although networking intensity was related to a greater likelihood of reemployment, it was not a significant predictor after controlling for job search intensity. That is, it did not contribute further to reemployment outcomes beyond job search intensity.

SUMMARY

Research on job search has operationalized job search behavior in several ways. Most research measures job search intensity, or the frequency with which job seekers have performed specific job search activities within a set time period. Blau (1993, 1994) designed separate scales to measure preparatory and active job search behavior, though most studies have not made this distinction when measuring job search intensity. Some studies measure job search effort or general effort and time spent searching for a job rather than performance of specific job search activities. Another stream of research measures use of different formal and informal job information sources. Finally, several studies have examined more specific forms of job search behavior, such as assertive job-seeking behavior and networking intensity. Most studies have measured only one type of job search behavior, and there is some evidence that the relationships between predictors and outcomes of job search behavior vary as a function of the job search measure used (Kanfer et al., 2001).

PREDICTORS OF JOB SEARCH BEHAVIORS

As indicated earlier, models of job search have included a variety of individual and situational predictors of job search behaviors. In fact, research has found that a number of variables consistently predict job search and employment outcomes. For the most part, the main predictors of job search behavior can be classified into three main categories:

1. Biographical variables.
2. Individual difference variables.
3. Situational variables.

The size of the relationships between the predictors and job search behavior has been found to depend on the job search measure and sample type. In their meta-analysis, Kanfer et al. (2001) concluded that a number of the relationships between the predictors and job search behavior were often stronger when measures of job search intensity were used versus job search effort. For some predictors (i.e., extraversion, neuroticism, conscientiousness, education), the relationships were stronger for new entrants, while for other predictors (i.e., self-esteem, employment commitment, social support), the relationships were stronger for unemployed job seekers. In addition, previous job tenure related positively to search behavior for new entrants but related negatively to search behavior for employed and unemployed job seekers. Finally, the relationships between the predictors and search behavior tend to be stronger than the relationships between the predictors and subsequent employment outcomes.

BIOGRAPHICAL VARIABLES

Biographical predictors of job search have usually consisted of gender, age, education, race, and job tenure. In general, biographical variables tend to be only weakly related to job search behavior compared to other predictors. In their meta-analysis, Kanfer et al. (2001) concluded that age, race, gender, education, and tenure were related to job search behavior; that is, older, non-White, female, less educated, and longer tenured individuals engaged in less job search behavior than younger, White, male, more educated, and less tenured individuals.

In a study on gender and job search methods, Huffman and Torres (2001) found some differences between men and women in the use of formal and informal job sources. For example, men were more likely to use informal sources (friends and relatives) and direct applications. Women were more likely to use newspaper ads, help-wanted signs, and temporary employment agencies.

There is also some evidence that biographical variables predict job search outcomes. For example, Kanfer et al. (2001) found that younger, more educated job seekers were more likely to find employment, and more educated and White job seekers experience a shorter period of unemployment. In addition, males were more likely to obtain employment but only if they were new entrants to the labor force.

INDIVIDUAL DIFFERENCE VARIABLES

A number of individual difference or psychological variables have been included in job search research. Various terms have been used to categorize these variables, such as *personality variables* (e.g., self-esteem), *motivational factors* (e.g., self-efficacy), and *attitudes toward employment and work* (e.g., employment commitment). Wanberg et al. (2002) referred to these variables as *job-seeker human capital*, which they defined as "the ability, experience, personality, and other individual difference characteristics of the job seeker" (p. 1102).

Self-Esteem   Self-esteem is among the most common personality variables included in job search research and was originally included in Schwab et al.'s (1987) job search model. Specifically, they suggested that intensity is influenced by job seekers' self-esteem. A number of studies have found that self-esteem predicts job search behavior and outcomes. For example, self-esteem has been found to relate negatively to the use of formal job sources and positively to job search intensity and assertive job-seeking behavior. Higher self-esteem is also associated with a shorter period of unemployment, more job offers received, and greater likelihood of obtaining employment (Ellis & Taylor, 1983; Schmit et al., 1993). In their meta-analysis, Kanfer et al. (2001) found that self-esteem was positively related to job search intensity and job search effort; however, the relationship was stronger for intensity than effort and for job losers compared to new entrants.

Five-Factor Model   There is some evidence that the dimensions of the five-factor model of personality (Digman, 1990) are related to job search behaviors. In fact, Kanfer et al. (2001) organized personality constructs used in job search research on the basis of the five-factor model of personality. They found that extraversion (the extent to which a person is outgoing versus shy) and conscientiousness (the degree to which a person is responsible and achievement oriented) were the strongest positive predictors of job search intensity and effort, followed by openness to experience (the extent to which a person thinks flexibly and is receptive to new ideas) and agreeableness (the extent to which a person is friendly and approachable), which were also significant predictors. Neuroticism (the extent to which a person is prone to experience anxiety, self-doubt, and depression and lacks emotional stability and control) related negatively to job search intensity but not to job search effort. As well, higher levels of extraversion, conscientiousness, openness to experience, and agreeableness were related to a shorter period of unemployment. Conscientiousness was positively related to employment status, and neuroticism was negatively related to the number of job offers and employment status. Kanfer et al. found that some of these relationships were stronger for new entrants than for job losers.

Job Search Self-Efficacy   A cognitive-motivational variable that has received a considerable amount of attention in job search research is job search self-efficacy, which refers to a job seeker's confidence in his or her ability to successfully perform a variety of job search activities (Wanberg et al., 1996, 1999). The results of several studies have demonstrated that job search self-efficacy is one of the best predictors of job search behavior and outcomes. In particular, job search self-efficacy has been found to predict preparatory and active job search behaviors, assertive job search behavior, job source usage, search duration, number of job offers, and employment status (Kanfer & Hulin, 1985; Saks & Ashforth, 1999; Schmit et al., 1993; Wanberg et al., 1999). In their meta-analysis, Kanfer et al. (2001) found that job search self-efficacy was positively related to both job search intensity and job search effort, as well as the number of job offers received and employment status, and negatively related to search duration.

Perceived Control   Another motivational variable is job seekers' perceived control over their job search. Although locus of control (a set of general beliefs about whether their behavior is controlled by internal or external forces) is only weakly related to job search behavior (Kanfer et al., 2001), perceived situational control has been found to relate positively to job search behaviors and employment status. For example, Wanberg (1997) found that unemployed job seekers who had higher levels of perceived situational control (perceived control over their unemployment situation) conducted a more intense job search.

Saks and Ashforth (1999) developed a measure of perceived job search control that asked job seekers about the influence and control they have over the outcomes of their job search. Their results showed that perceived control predicted the employment status of recent university graduates at the time of graduation and four months later.

Ability   Although few studies have included measures of ability, there is some evidence that general cognitive ability might also play a role in job search. For example, the cognitive ability of employed managers has been found to relate positively to job search (Boudreau, Boswell, Judge, & Bretz, 2001). Grade point average, a surrogate measure of cognitive ability, has been found to correlate positively with active and preparatory job search behavior as well as employment status among a sample of recent graduates at graduation and four months post-graduation (Saks & Ashforth, 1999).

Employment Commitment   Employment commitment is an attitudinal variable that reflects the importance and centrality of employment to a job seeker beyond the income that results from being employed. As such, it reflects a general attachment to work (Kanfer et al., 2001). Several studies have found employment commitment to relate positively to job search intensity (Wanberg et al., 1999). Kanfer et al. found that employment commitment predicted job search intensity and effort, and the relationship was stronger for job losers compared to new entrants.

SITUATIONAL VARIABLES

Among situational predictors of job search, financial need and social support have received a considerable amount of attention. Financial need, or hardship, was one of the predictors of job search intensity in the Schwab et al. (1987) model. Several more recent models have included social support as an important predictor of job search behavior (Wanberg et al., 1996).

Financial Need/Hardship   The basic premise behind this predictor is that individuals who have greater financial obligations or who lack adequate financial resources have a greater need and hence a stronger motive to find employment and a greater likelihood of conducting a more intense job search (Wanberg et al., 1999).

Research has generally supported this prediction. Job seekers who have a greater financial need or who are experiencing economic hardship tend to be more intense in their search for employment (Kanfer et al., 2001; Wanberg et al., 1999). Financial need has also been shown to relate positively to both preparatory and active job search behaviors (Blau, 1994). Job seekers with greater unemployment benefits or a longer duration of benefits tend to have lower job search intensity and to remain unemployed for longer periods. Thus, financial need results in a more intense job search and a shorter period of unemployment.

Job-Seeking Social Support   One of the most important situational variables in job search and coping with job loss is social or job-seeking support. *Social support* refers to the network of friends and family who provide counseling, assistance, and encouragement to job seekers. Social support has been shown to be particularly important as a coping resource for individuals following job loss.

Several studies have shown that job-seeking support predicts job search behavior and employment status (Wanberg et al., 1996). In fact, based on the results of their study, Wanberg et al. concluded that "a significant other's support for job seeking plays a crucial role in increasing an unemployed individual's job-seeking behavior and subsequent reemployment" (p. 84). In their meta-analysis, Kanfer et al. (2001) found that social support was positively related to job search intensity and job search effort, and the relationship was stronger for job search intensity and for job losers than new entrants.

SUMMARY

Research over the past 10 years has shown that job search behavior and, to a lesser extent, job search outcomes are predicted by a number of individual and situational variables. Although biographical variables are often included as control variables, they tend to be weak predictors of job search behaviors and outcomes.

Among the personality or psychological variables, self-esteem, extraversion, and conscientiousness have been found to predict job search behavior, and self-esteem and conscientiousness also predict job search outcomes. Two motivational variables, job search self-efficacy and perceived control, have been found to predict job search behavior and outcomes, and job search self-efficacy has been found to be one of the best predictors of job search behavior. A job seeker's commitment to employment has also been shown to predict job search behavior. Among the situational variables, financial hardship and social support predict job search intensity.

Finally, a number of other predictor variables, such as job seeker reemployment constraints (Wanberg et al., 2002), networking comfort (Wanberg et al., 2000), and motivation and emotion control (Wanberg et al., 1999), have also been included as predictor variables in job search research. However, they have not been included in this review either because they have seldom been studied, they are specific to certain kinds of job search behavior (e.g., networking comfort predicts networking intensity), or they have simply not been found to be useful predictors.

OUTCOMES OF JOB SEARCH BEHAVIORS

Job search models include outcomes or consequences of job search. For example, in the Schwab et al. (1987) model, job search intensity predicts whether a job seeker finds employment (employment status) as well as the quality of employment. However, there has been considerable variation in the criteria used to measure job search success. Further, there is little evidence of convergent validity among the various criteria (Brasher & Chen, 1999). Therefore, it is important, for research and practice, to identify the criteria of job search success because the effectiveness of job search will depend on the criteria used to measure success (Brasher & Chen, 1999).

Since Schwab et al. (1987) first proposed their job search model, employment status (i.e., whether a job seeker has obtained employment) has been the most common outcome measure used (Kanfer et al., 2001). Employment quality has only recently been included in job search research. Over the years, a number of other outcomes have also been studied. As a result, the criteria for job search success have become complex and multidimensional (Brasher & Chen, 1999).

Schwab et al.'s (1987) inclusion of employment status and employment quality in their job search model suggested that job search predicts outcomes at different stages of the search process, such as during and after search and subsequent employment. Therefore, a meaningful way to classify job search outcomes is in terms of when they occur in the job search process. For example, some outcomes occur during the job search process itself, such as interviews and job offers. Other outcomes are the result of job search, such as employment status or whether the job seeker has obtained employment, and are usually referred to as *employment outcomes*. A number of outcomes occur only after the job seeker has begun employment, such as job satisfaction and intention to quit, and are usually referred to as *employment quality*. Job search outcomes can also differ in terms of whether they are internal states or external events. For example, some outcomes, such as the number of job offers received, are external to the job seeker; others, such as psychological well-being and job satisfaction, reflect the internal states of the job seeker.

A meaningful way to classify the criteria of job search success, then, is in terms of (1) when they occur during the job search process and (2) their nature (extrinsic versus intrinsic), resulting in the following four categories:

1. Job search outcomes (outcomes that occur during the search process).
2. Employment outcomes (outcomes that are a result of the job search).
3. Employment quality (outcomes that occur during employment or postentry).
4. Psychological well-being (the job seeker's mental health throughout the job search process).

JOB SEARCH OUTCOMES

Job search outcomes are outcomes that occur during the individual's job search. These outcomes can be considered extrinsic to the job seeker and include the number of job interviews and the number of job offers that a job seeker receives during his or her search as well as the speed with which he or she obtains employment or the length of time unemployed.

Number of Job Interviews and Offers   Several studies have found a positive relationship between job search intensity and the number of job interviews and job offers received. For example, Saks and Ashforth (2000) found that (1) preparatory and active job search behavior, job search effort, and formal job sources were positively related to the number of job interviews; and (2) preparatory and active job search behavior, job search effort, and informal job sources were positively related to the number of job offers. Although few studies have investigated the relationships among different outcomes, Saks and Ashforth found not only that the number of job interviews, offers, and employment status all positively correlated, but also that an increase in job search behaviors was related to more job interviews, more job interviews were related to more job offers, and more job offers predicted employment status.

In their meta-analysis, Kanfer et al. (2001) found that both job search intensity and job search effort were positively related to the number of job offers; however, the relationship was stronger for search intensity than search effort.

Speed of Employment   Research has also found that job search intensity is related to the speed of employment or what is also referred to as the *duration* or *amount of time spent searching for employment* (Wanberg et al., 2000, 2002). The basic idea is that job seekers who conduct a more intense search are likely to obtain employment faster. Kanfer et al. (2001) found that job search intensity and job search effort were both negatively related to the duration of unemployment; however, the relationship was stronger for effort measures.

EMPLOYMENT OUTCOMES

Employment outcomes represent the result of an individual's job search and refer to whether a job seeker obtains employment and the nature of that employment in terms of its match or fit.

Employment Status   The most common outcome measure in job search research is employment status. For example, Wanberg et al. (1999) found that higher job search intensity was positively related to reemployment. Saks and Ashforth (1999) found that among recent university graduates, active job search behavior and job search effort predicted employment status at the time of graduation, and preparatory job search behavior predicted employment status four months after graduation. Wanberg et al. (2000) found that networking intensity predicted employment status, but not after controlling for job search intensity.

Although not all studies have found support for a relationship between job search and employment, Kanfer et al. (2001) found that both job search intensity and job search effort were positively related to employment status. The results of moderator analyses indicated that the relationship was stronger for effort measures than measures of intensity. In addition, the relationship between job search behavior and employment status was strongest for employed job seekers, followed by new entrants and unemployed job seekers.

Research on job information sources has also found that job seekers are more likely to obtain employment through the use of informal sources of information (Granovetter, 1995). In particular, friends and personal acquaintances tend to be the main source through which job seekers obtain employment.

Person-Job and Person-Organization Fit   In a study by Allen and Keaveny (1980), graduates who used formal sources were more likely to find jobs that were more closely related to their college training than those who used informal sources. This led Saks and Ashforth (1997) to speculate on the importance of fit in job search. In a study of job information sources and work outcomes, they argued that the criteria of a successful job search should include perceptions of P-J and P-O fit. Their findings indicated that the use of formal job information sources was positively related to preentry perceptions of P-J and P-O fit. Further, these perceptions mediated the relationship among job information sources and postentry job satisfaction, intentions to quit, and actual turnover. Saks and Ashforth (2002) found that job search behavior and career planning were positively related to preentry perceptions of P-J and P-O fit, and career planning was also positively related to postentry P-J fit. Finally, in a recent study by Wanberg et al. (2002), job search clarity (the extent to which job seekers have clear job search objectives) was positively related to a combined measure of perceived job and organization fit.

EMPLOYMENT QUALITY

Employment quality refers to job search outcomes that occur once the job seeker assumes a position and begins employment. The results of several studies, however, have been mixed. For example, although Wanberg et al. (1999) found a significant relationship between job search intensity and reemployment, they did not find a significant relationship between job search intensity and job satisfaction, job improvement, or intentions to turnover. Wanberg et al. (2000) found that neither job search intensity nor networking intensity was related to job satisfaction or intention to turnover. Werbel (2000) also failed to detect a significant relationship between job search intensity and job satisfaction.

Research on involuntary job loss has also failed to find significant relationships between job search and the quality of reemployment (Kinicki, Prussia, & McKee-Ryan, 2000). Wanberg et al. (2002), however, found that job search intensity was related to higher intentions to turnover, perhaps because rapid employment does not always lead to good employment. On the other hand, they found that job search clarity was related to lower intentions to turnover.

Several studies suggest that the relationship between job search behavior and employment quality might be more complex than simple direct relationships between job search behavior and employment outcomes. In particular, both mediation and moderation effects might be involved. For example, as indicated earlier, Saks and Ashforth (1997) found that preentry P-J and P-O fit perceptions mediated the relationship between job information sources and work outcomes. Thus, job search may only be indirectly related to employment quality (Saks & Ashforth, 2002).

In addition to mediation effects, there is also some evidence that the relationship between job search and employment quality might be moderated by certain conditions. For example, Wanberg et al. (2002) found an interaction between job search intensity and economic need to work (financial hardship). Specifically, job search intensity was more strongly related to job improvement for job seekers who scored low on economic hardship, whereas there was no intensity-improvement relationship for individuals who scored high on economic hardship. Wanberg et al. (2002) suggested that job seekers who report low economic hardship and engage in a highly intense search can be more selective in their job choice and choose a better job, while job seekers who report high economic hardship must accept any offer they receive.

PSYCHOLOGICAL WELL-BEING

A major concern in the job search and job loss literature is the psychological well-being of job seekers. This is especially the case in research on job loss, unemployment, and job search interventions. It is well known that the experience of job loss and unemployment is associated with negative physical and psychological effects, including symptoms of psychiatric disorder, distress, and depression (Hanisch, 1999; Wanberg, 1995, 1997). Unlike the other outcomes discussed in this section, psychological well-being is not associated with a particular time during the job search process, but rather is a pervasive, internal experience that can occur throughout the unemployment-job search-reemployment process.

Most research on the mental health of job seekers is concerned with the experience of unemployment and how job seekers cope with it. Several studies have considered the effect of the quality of reemployment on job seekers' mental health and psychological well-being (Wanberg, 1995). Some have suggested that reemployment in an unsatisfying or low-quality job can lead to poor mental health. Wanberg, for example, found that job seekers who were satisfied with their new jobs showed an increase in mental health, while those who remained unemployed or were dissatisfied with their new jobs showed no change.

There is also some evidence that job search is related to job seekers' mental health. That is, job seekers who cope with job loss by engaging in an intense job search are more likely to have improved mental health, especially if they find employment (Wanberg, 1997). On the other hand, a long period of search followed by continued unemployment is likely to lead to decreased mental health. Wanberg also showed that the relationship between job search and mental health was moderated by situational control such that job search was related to improved mental health for job seekers who believed that they had control over the situation. However, job search was related to lower mental health for job seekers with low situational control (i.e., those who believed that they were not likely to find employment even if they conducted an intense job search). This led Wanberg to conclude that a proactive job search might have adverse effects in terms of lower mental health when the situation is perceived as uncontrollable.

SUMMARY

Job search research has used various criteria as indicators of job search success. These criteria can be classified in terms of when they occur during the job search process and whether they involve internal states or external events. In terms of the time frame, job search criteria can be classified as:

- Job search outcomes, or outcomes that occur during an individual's job search, such as the number of job interviews and offers received.
- Employment outcomes, or the outcomes that occur once the job search is complete.
- Employment quality outcomes, or the outcomes that the job seeker experiences on the job.
- Psychological well-being, an internal state that is relevant throughout the job search process.

In summary, job search behaviors have been found to relate to outcomes throughout the job search process. That is, job seekers who engage in a better (i.e., more intense and effortful) job search are more likely to have more interviews and job offers, to obtain employment more rapidly, to obtain a better P-J and P-O fit, and, ultimately, to experience improved psychological well-being. There is also some evidence, although much weaker, that job search is related to employment quality, especially if intensity and effort are complemented by career planning (Saks & Ashforth, 2002). However, not all job search behaviors have been linked to all of the outcomes. Thus, for the time being, we can only conclude that, in general, job search behavior is related to these outcomes, and the strength of the relations varies as a function of the job search measure (e.g., intensity, effort), the sample type (employed job seeker, unemployed job seeker, new entrant), and the outcome (Kanfer et al., 2001).

AN INTEGRATIVE SELF-REGULATORY MODEL OF JOB SEARCH PREDICTORS, BEHAVIORS, AND OUTCOMES

Based on the preceding review, it is possible to develop a job search model that integrates the key variables in the job search process and shows the links among the job search outcomes. This model can be used to guide future job search research and practice.

Figure 7.1 presents an integrative self-regulatory model of the job search process. First, the model shows the main groups of predictors, including biographical

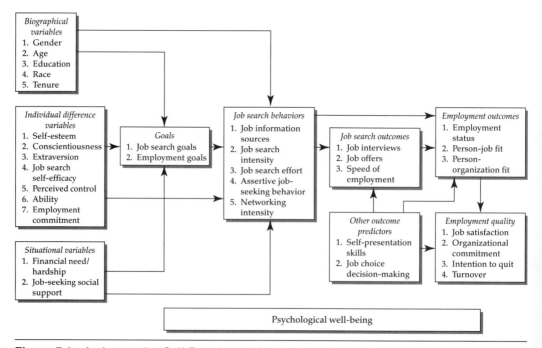

Figure 7.1 An Integrative Self-Regulatory Model of Job Search Predictors, Behaviors, and Outcomes.

variables, individual difference variables, and situational variables. Consistent with the research reviewed earlier, these variables are shown to predict the job search behaviors (job information sources, job search intensity, job search effort, assertive job-seeking behavior, and networking intensity).

Second, the model includes both job search and employment goals. *Job search goals* are more proximal and refer to goals such as sending out a certain number of applications each week or spending a specific amount of time each day searching for employment. *Employment goals* refer to possible outcomes, such as obtaining a specific job or a job in a certain organization. In the model, job search and employment goals are shown to be outcomes of the predictor variables and predictors of the job search behaviors.

The links between the predictors and goals are consistent with Kanfer et al. (2001), who noted that the trait and contextual variables in their meta-analysis "have been shown to affect self-regulatory mechanisms (e.g., goal-setting, self-monitoring, self-reactions) and, in turn, the direction and intensity of goal-directed (i.e., job search) behaviors" (p. 838). Therefore, job search and employment goals are posited to partially mediate the relations between the predictors and job search behaviors. A recent study on personality and the goal-striving process provides some support for the mediating role of goals. In particular, Lee, Sheldon, and Turban (2003) found that several general personality characteristics influence performance and enjoyment of work through goal-striving and self-regulatory processes.

The link between goals and job search behaviors is consistent with Kanfer et al.'s (2001) assertion that employment goals activate search behaviors as well as the motivational effects of goals (Locke & Latham, 2002). Prussia et al.'s (2001) finding that reemployment coping goals predict job search effort also supports the relationship between goals and job search behaviors.

Third, the model shows that the job search behaviors are directly related to job search and employment outcomes and indirectly related to employment quality. As well, the job search outcomes are posited to partially mediate the relationship between job search behaviors and employment outcomes. In other words, job search behaviors are positively related to the number of job interviews and offers, which are in turn related to the probability of employment, and P-J and P-O fit. The model also shows that P-J and P-O fit mediate the relationship between job search behaviors and employment quality (Saks & Ashforth, 1997, 2002). In addition, because goals are strong predictors of performance outcomes (Locke & Latham, 2002), it is likely that job search and employment goals are related to job search and employment outcomes. In the model, job search behaviors are shown to mediate the relationship between goals and job search and employment outcomes. The model also shows the interrelationships among the outcome variables. For example, more interviews and job offers predict employment status as well as P-J and P-O fit, and P-J and P-O fit predict employment quality.

The model includes two other predictors of job search and employment outcomes. Whether job seekers obtain employment and the type of employment obtained are also a function of how they present themselves during the recruitment/selection process as well as their ability to make job choice decisions. Thus, these variables are also shown to have a direct effect on the outcome variables. In particular, presentation skills are shown to have a direct effect on job search and employment outcomes, as well as employment quality. Job choice decision making is predicted to have a direct effect on P-J and P-O fit perceptions and employment quality. In other words, job seekers who are more skilled at making job choice decisions are more likely to choose a job and an organization that are good fits and more likely to obtain quality employment. In addition, both of these variables might also moderate the relationships between job search behaviors and the outcomes, although this is not shown in the model. Finally, psychological well-being is shown in a box at the bottom of the figure to indicate that it is a pervasive outcome of job search that can occur at any time throughout the job search process.

In summary, Figure 7.1 is meant to be an integrative model of the job search process that incorporates goal setting and self-regulatory behaviors. However, not every relationship in the model has received the same amount of attention in previous research. For example, only one study has investigated networking intensity, and only a select number of predictors and outcomes were studied. Further, the role of goals in the job search process has seldom been investigated. Thus, the model is meant to provide a general depiction of what has been the focus of job search research as well as what researchers might focus on in future research. It is unlikely that any single study would be able to test all of the relationships in the model. However, the model can be used to identify specific areas to consider in future research as well as a guide for practice.

JOB SEARCH INTERVENTION FRAMEWORK

In this final section of the chapter, a job search intervention framework is presented as a guide to counselors in the design of job search intervention programs for job seekers. Although the job search model indicates the predictors, behaviors, and outcomes of job search, it needs to be translated into a meaningful guide for practice.

Table 7.1 presents the job search intervention framework. The first step in the framework consists of a job-seeker needs assessment. The idea of a job-seeker needs assessment and feedback tool organized around key variable categories was developed by Wanberg et al. (2002) to help job seekers identify their strengths and weaknesses in skills, motivation, and job search activities. Using the main predictors of job search, a counselor can assess a job seeker on each of the predictors to determine areas that might require improvement. For example, job seekers who have low levels of job search self-efficacy or perceived control will require interventions that are designed to increase them.

Following the job-seeker needs assessment, a counselor can then determine what type of intervention is required. For most job seekers, the first intervention should involve the setting of goals. However, because of the different criteria of job search success, the starting point for goal setting should be a review of the job search success criteria. For example, does the job seeker want to find a job as fast as possible, or does he or she want to take his or her time and obtain a good P-J or P-O fit? Does the job seeker want to find a job with the highest possible wage, or is he or she more interested in the reputation of the organization or perhaps the amount of training and development he or she will receive?

Once a job seeker has identified the success criteria of most importance, two types of goals should be considered. First, employment goals could be set in terms of the type of employment that a job seeker wants to obtain. Employment goals might involve pay, type of employer or organization, type of work, location,

Table 7.1
Job Search Intervention Framework

A. Job-Seeker Needs Analysis
   1. Biographical characteristics
      a. Gender, age, education, race, and tenure
      b. Job search experience and success
   2. Individual difference variables
      a. Self-esteem
      b. Five-factor model
      c. Job search self-efficacy
      d. Perceived control
      e. Ability
      f. Employment commitment
   3. Situational variables
      a. Financial hardship
      b. Job-seeking social support

B. Job Search Success Criteria
   1. Job search outcomes
      a. Number of job interviews
      b. Number of job offers
      c. Speed of (re)employment
   2. Employment outcomes
      a. Employment status
      b. Person-job and person-organization fit
      c. Job and organization attributes (wage, organization reputation, opportunities for advancement, etc.)
   3. Employment quality
      a. Job attitudes (job satisfaction, organizational commitment)
      b. Intent to turnover/expected tenure

C. Employment and Job Search Goal Setting
   1. Employment goals based on job search success criteria
   2. Job search goals based on job search behaviors

D. Job Search Behaviors
   1. Job information sources
      a. Informal sources
      b. Formal sources
   2. Job search intensity
      a. Preparatory job search behaviors
      b. Active job search behaviors
   3. Job search effort
   4. Assertive job search behavior
   5. Networking intensity

E. Job Search Interventions
   1. Goal setting and self-regulation
   2. Job search behaviors and strategies
   3. JOBS intervention
   4. Job finding club
   5. Self-efficacy intervention
   6. Job/organization fit intervention
   7. Presentation skills intervention
   8. Job choice intervention

hours, opportunities for training and advancement, and so on. Employment goals are not only important for motivational reasons, but also they will have some bearing on the nature of the job search. As noted by Kanfer et al. (2001), a job seeker who defines his or her employment goal primarily in terms of pay might engage in a different kind of job search than one whose employment goal is oriented toward the type of employer or location.

A second type of goal that should be part of the goal-setting process focuses on what the job seeker will actually do to obtain the employment goal. Job search goals involve setting goals for the specific job search behaviors, such as sending out resumes, networking, contacting friends and relatives, or making cold calls. At this stage of the intervention, the counselor should review the different job search behaviors and determine those that are necessary for helping the job seeker achieve his or her employment goals and those that the job seeker needs to improve. This might mean increasing the use of formal or informal job information sources, training in preparatory, active, or assertive job search behavior, and so on. The setting of job search goals should be part of a larger self-regulatory process in which job seekers monitor their performance, compare their performance at set periods to their goals, reward themselves for goal achievement, make adjustments to their goals when necessary, and so on. Thus, part of the goal-setting intervention should include instruction on self-regulation.

Once employment and job search goals have been set, an intervention to prepare a job seeker for job search should be provided. This might focus on some of the behaviors listed in Table 7.1, such as preparatory job search behavior, active job search behavior, and so on depending on a job seeker's previous job search experience, needs, and capabilities. In addition, a number of training interventions have been extensively studied in the job search literature and are known to be effective (see Jome & Phillips, Chapter 19, this volume).

For example, research on employment counseling and job loss has found that the Job Club is one of the most effective methods of job search training (Azrin, Philip, Thienes-Hontos, & Besalel, 1980). The Job Club is an intensive, highly structured, group-based behavioral counseling program that emphasizes motivation, maintenance of behavior, feedback and reinforcement, imitation, role playing, and practice activities (Azrin, Flores, & Kaplan, 1975). Participants receive assistance in all areas of job search, including coping with discouragement, preparing resumes, obtaining and pursuing job leads, learning interviewing skills, scheduling time and record keeping, dress and grooming, and using the telephone for making inquiries and contacts.

Job seekers who have attended Job Clubs have been found to be more likely to obtain employment compared to individuals in a control group or those who participated in other types of programs (Azrin & Philip, 1979; Azrin et al., 1975, 1980; Braddy & Gray, 1987; Elksnin & Elksnin, 1991; Rife & Belcher, 1994). Some studies have also found the Job Club to result in higher starting salaries, more work hours, lower depression, greater advancement, and job satisfaction (Azrin et al., 1980; Gray, 1983; Gray & Braddy, 1988; Rife & Belcher, 1994; Stidham & Remley, 1992).

Another extensively studied job search training intervention is JOBS, which is designed to improve job seekers' motivation and skills to engage in job-seeking behavior (Caplan et al., 1989). The intervention includes problem-solving and decision-making processes, inoculation against setbacks, social support, and job-seeking skills similar to those taught in the Job Club. The JOBS intervention has been shown to result in higher rates of reemployment as well as higher quality reemployment in terms of earnings and job satisfaction. Job seekers who have participated in JOBS but remained unemployed reported higher job search motivation and self-efficacy compared to control group participants (Caplan et al., 1989). The benefits of JOBS for reemployment and employment quality have been shown to persist. Individuals who have participated in the JOBS program show higher levels of employment, higher paying jobs, more work hours, and fewer changes in jobs and employers up to two and a half years following the program (Vinokur, van Ryn, Gramlich, & Price, 1991). The JOBS intervention also has a significant effect on the mental health of individuals at high risk for depression (Vinokur, Price, & Schul, 1995).

A third job search intervention that has been shown to be effective is a workshop to improve job seekers' self-efficacy. Eden and Aviram (1993) studied the effects of a behavioral-modeling job search workshop designed to boost the general self-efficacy (GSE) of unemployed vocational workers. Participants who attended the workshop had higher self-efficacy at the end of the workshop and two months later compared to those in a control group. The workshop also increased the job search activity and reemployment of individuals with low initial GSE. Further, the effect of the workshop on reemployment was mediated by job search behaviors.

Another possible intervention might focus on fit-based job search strategies. That is, given the importance of job and organization fit and their relation to employment quality (Saks & Ashforth, 1997, 2002), job seekers might require instruction on what P-J and P-O fit are and how to assess them. This might include instruction on how to identify those factors in themselves and in jobs and organizations that, when matched, will provide them with a good job and organization fit. Current person-environment theories of vocational choice and adjustment (see Dawis, Chapter 1, this volume; Spokane & Cruza-Guet, Chapter 2, this volume) might also be incorporated.

As indicated earlier, job search is not the only factor that can influence job search success. As noted by Kanfer et al. (2001), significant relationships between individual difference variables and job search outcomes suggest that nonmotivational factors, such as the interview-hiring process and self-presentation to employers, also play a role in job search success (Wanberg et al., 2000). Obtaining a job offer requires job applicants to perform well during the selection process and, in particular, during employment interviews. It also depends on the preferences of employers and the employer's perceptions of the applicant's fit to the job and organization. Thus, an effective job search campaign will not result in employment for job seekers who have poor interviewing skills or who are perceived by interviewers as a poor fit. As noted by Kanfer et al. (2001), "how an individual presents himself or herself during the employee selection process may be as important to employment success as job search" (p. 851).

Along these lines, Wanberg et al. (2002) commented: "A person who turns in carefully constructed resumes and job applications and presents him- or herself with ease in a job interview is more likely to be hired than someone who turns in poorly crafted communications and is ineffectual in his or her interviews" (p. 1105). Furthermore, it has been shown that job applicant characteristics, such as nonverbal skills, vocal characteristics, and physical appearance, have an effect on interview outcomes (Wanberg et al., 2000). Unfortunately, job search research has not examined the role of job seekers' interviewing skills although this is clearly a key factor in obtaining employment (Wanberg et al., 1999). Thus, another intervention in the framework is designed to instruct and prepare job seekers on employment interviews and self-presentation skills during the recruitment-selection process.

One area that appears to be especially promising is research on job interview anxiety. In a recent study by McCarthy and Gowan (in press), job applicants completed a self-report measure on their job interview anxiety in five areas of anxiety (communication, appearance, social, performance, and behavioral anxiety) and were interviewed by actual interviewers who evaluated their interview performance. The results indicated that job applicants with higher interview anxiety received lower interview evaluations. This provides a good illustration of how an excellent job search might result in fewer job offers, a longer search period, and continued unemployment for a job seeker who has high interview anxiety. Thus, some job seekers might require more extensive interview training to improve their skills, increase their self-efficacy, and lower their interview anxiety.

A final intervention noted in the framework is on job choice decision making. As noted earlier, the job search process also includes a choice phase in which the job seeker must evaluate job alternatives and make a job choice decision. In fact, in a model of job search and evaluation, Schwab et al. (1987) showed that evaluation follows search and precedes the outcomes. They also noted that evaluation involves content and process dimensions. Content involves a consideration of the importance and attractiveness of job attributes, and process involves mental processes and decision rules used to evaluate job attributes. Thus, a final intervention might focus on those attributes that are most important to a job seeker and the decision rules that will be used to evaluate job offers and to make a job choice.

In summary, the job search intervention framework incorporates the major findings from the job search literature in a manner that will enable counselors to consider the characteristics and needs of job seekers and then to tailor interventions to those characteristics and needs. By considering the main predictors of job search and the criteria for success and then setting employment and job search goals, counselors and job seekers can determine the strategies required to achieve those goals and the interventions that will be most effective for building the capabilities job seekers need to conduct an effective job search.

SUMMARY

During the past 10 years, job search has received a great deal of research attention. Given the large numbers of people searching for work each year, as well as the frequency with which most people today will have to look for work, research on the job search process has real practical value. Research has shown that both individual differences and situational factors influence job search behavior, and job search behavior is related to the probability, speed, and quality of employment that the job seeker obtains. Given that workers today are expected to experience more than a dozen job transitions during the course of their career, the need for individuals to have job search skills is critical for job seekers' continued employment and psychological well-being.

This chapter has reviewed the job search literature to develop an integrative self-regulatory model that brings together the main predictors, behaviors, and outcomes of job search. Thus, it can serve as a guide for both research and practice. A job search intervention framework was developed that incorporates the main variables from the job search model. The job search intervention framework can be used to identify job seekers' needs and to design job search interventions that are tailored to their needs, goals, and desired outcomes.

REFERENCES

Allen, R. E., & Keaveny, T. J. (1980). The relative effectiveness of alternative job sources. *Journal of Vocational Behavior, 1*(16), 18–32.

Azrin, N. H., Flores, T., & Kaplan, S. J. (1975). Job-finding club: A group assisted program for obtaining employment. *Behaviour Research and Therapy, 13,* 17–27.

Azrin, N. H., & Philip, R. A. (1979). The job club method for the job-handicapped: A comparative outcome study. *Rehabilitation Counselling Bulletin, 2*(23), 144–155.

Azrin, N. H., Philip, R. A., Thienes-Hontos, P., & Besalel, V. A. (1980). Comparative evaluation of the job club program with welfare recipients. *Journal of Vocational Behavior, 1*(16), 133–145.

Barber, A. E., Daly, C. L., Giannantonio, C. M., & Phillips, J. M. (1994). Job search activities: An examination of changes over time. *Personnel Psychology, 47,* 739–765.

Becker, H. A. (1980). The Assertive Job-Hunting Survey. *Measurement and Evaluation in Guidance, 1*(13), 43–48.

Blau, G. (1993). Further exploring the relationship between job search and voluntary individual turnover. *Personnel Psychology, 4*(46), 213–330.

Blau, G. (1994). Testing a two-dimensional measure of job search behavior. *Organizational Behavior and Human Decision Processes, 5*(59), 288–312.

Boudreau, J. W., Boswell, W. R., Judge, T. A., & Bretz, R. D., Jr. (2001). Personality and cognitive ability as predictors of job search among employed managers. *Personnel Psychology, 5*(54), 25–50.

Braddy, B. A., & Gray, D. O. (1987). Employment services for older job seekers: A comparison of two client-centered approaches. *Gerontologist, 27,* 565–568.

Brasher, E. E., & Chen, P. Y. (1999). Evaluation of success criteria in job search: A process evaluation. *Journal of Occupational and Organizational Psychology, 72,* 57–70.

Caplan, R. D., Vinokur, A. D., Price, R. H., & van Ryn, M. (1989). Job seeking, re-employment, and mental health: A randomized field experiment in coping with job loss. *Journal of Applied Psychology, 74,* 759–769.

Digman, J. M. (1990). Personality structure: Emergence of the five-factor model. *Annual Review of Psychology, 41,* 417–440.

Eden, D., & Aviram, A. (1993). Self-efficacy training to speed reemployment: Helping people to help themselves. *Journal of Applied Psychology, 78,* 352–360.

Elksnin, L. K., & Elksnin, N. (1991). The school counsellor as job search facilitator: Increasing employment of handicapped students through job clubs. *School Counsellor, 38,* 215–220.

Ellis, R. A., & Taylor, M. S. (1983). Role of self-esteem within the job search process. *Journal of Applied Psychology, 68,* 632–640.

Granovetter, M. S. (1995). *Getting a job* (2nd ed.). Chicago: University of Chicago Press.

Gray, D. O. (1983). A job club for older job seekers: An experimental evaluation. *Journal of Gerontology, 38,* 363–368.

Gray, D. O., & Braddy, B. A. (1988). Experimental social innovation and client-centered job-seeking programs. *American Journal of Community Psychology, 16,* 325–343.

Hanisch, K. A. (1999). Job loss and unemployment research from 1994 to 1998: A review and recommendations for research and intervention. *Journal of Vocational Behavior, 55,* 188–220.

Huffman, M. L., & Torres, L. (2001). Job search methods: Consequences for gender-based earnings inequality. *Journal of Vocational Behavior, 58,* 127–141.

Kanfer, R., & Hulin, C. L. (1985). Individual differences in successful job searches following lay-off. *Personnel Psychology, 38,* 835–847.

Kanfer, R., Wanberg, C. R., & Kantrowitz, T. M. (2001). Job search and employment: A personality-motivational analysis and meta-analytic review. *Journal of Applied Psychology, 86,* 837–855.

Kinicki, A. J., Prussia, G. E., & McKee-Ryan, F. M. (2000). A panel study of coping with involuntary job loss. *Academy of Management Journal, 43,* 90–100.

Lee, F. K., Sheldon, K. M., & Turban, D. B. (2003). Personality and the goal-striving process: The influence of achievement goal patterns, goal level, and mental focus on performance and enjoyment. *Journal of Applied Psychology, 88,* 256–265.

Leicht, K. T., & Marx, J. (1997). The consequences of informal job finding for men and women. *Academy of Management Journal, 40,* 967–987.

Locke, E. A., & Latham, G. P. (2002). Building a practically useful theory of goal setting and task motivation. *American Psychologist, 57*(9), 705–717.

McCarthy, J. M., & Goffin, R. D. (in press). Measuring job interview anxiety: Beyond weak knees and sweaty palms. *Personnel Psychology.*

Prussia, G. E., Fugate, M., & Kinicki, A. (2001). Explication of the coping goal construct: Implications for coping and reemployment. *Journal of Applied Psychology, 86,* 1179–1190.

Rife, J. C., & Belcher, J. R. (1994). Assisting unemployed older workers to become reemployed: An experimental evaluation. *Research on Social Work Practice, 4,* 3–13.

Saks, A. M., & Ashforth, B. E. (1997). A longitudinal investigation of the relationships between job information sources, applicant perceptions of fit, and work outcomes. *Personnel Psychology, 50,* 395–426.

Saks, A. M., & Ashforth, B. E. (1999). Effects of individual differences and job search behaviors on the employment status of recent university graduates. *Journal of Vocational Behavior, 54,* 335–349.

Saks, A. M., & Ashforth, B. E. (2000). Change in job search behaviors and employment outcomes. *Journal of Vocational Behavior, 56,* 277–287.

Saks, A. M., & Ashforth, B. E. (2002). Is job search related to employment quality? It all depends on the fit. *Journal of Applied Psychology, 87,* 646–654.

Schmit, M. J., Amel, E. L., & Ryan, A. M. (1993). Self-reported assertive job-seeking behaviors of minimally educated job hunters. *Personnel Psychology, 46,* 105–124.

Schwab, D. P., Rynes, S. L., & Aldag, R. J. (1987). Theories and research on job search and choice. In K. M. Rowland & G. R. Ferris (Eds.), *Research in personnel and human resources management* (Vol. 5, pp. 129–166). Greenwich, CT: JAI Press.

Soelberg, P. O. (1967). Unprogrammed decision making. *Industrial Management Review, 8,* 19–29.

Stidham, H. H., & Remley, T. P., Jr. (1992). Job club methodology applied in a workfare setting. *Journal of Employment Counselling, 29,* 69–76.

Vinokur, A. D., Price, R. H., & Schul, Y. (1995). Impact of the JOBS intervention on unemployed workers varying in risk for depression. *American Journal of Community Psychology, 232,* 39–74.

Vinokur, A. D., Schul, Y., Vuori, J., & Price, R. H. (2000). Two years after a job loss: Long-term impact of the JOBS program on reemployment and mental health. *Journal of Occupational Health Psychology, 5,* 32–47.

Vinokur, A. D., van Ryn, M., Gramlich, E. M., & Price, R. H. (1991). Long-term follow-up and benefit-cost analysis of the jobs program: A preventive intervention for the unemployed. *Journal of Applied Psychology, 76,* 213–219.

Wanberg, C. R. (1995). A longitudinal study of the effects of unemployment and quality of reemployment. *Journal of Vocational Behavior, 46,* 40–54.

Wanberg, C. R. (1997). Antecedents and outcomes of coping behaviors among unemployed and reemployed individuals. *Journal of Applied Psychology, 82,* 731–744.

Wanberg, C. R., Hough, L. M., & Song, Z. (2002). Predictive validity of a multidisciplinary model of reemployment success. *Journal of Applied Psychology, 87,* 1100–1120.

Wanberg, C. R., Kanfer, R., & Banas, J. T. (2000). Predictors and outcomes of networking intensity among unemployed job seekers. *Journal of Applied Psychology, 85,* 491–503.

Wanberg, C. R., Kanfer, R., & Rotundo, M. (1999). Unemployed individuals: Motives, job-search competencies, and job search constraints as predictors of job seeking and reemployment. *Journal of Applied Psychology, 84,* 897–910.

Wanberg, C. R., Watt, J. D., & Rumsey, D. J. (1996). Individuals without jobs: An empirical study of job-seeking behavior and reemployment. *Journal of Applied Psychology, 81,* 76–87.

Werbel, J. D. (2000). Relationships among career exploration, job search intensity, and job search effectiveness in graduating college students. *Journal of Vocational Behavior, 57,* 379–394.

CHAPTER 8

Theories and Research
on Job Satisfaction

Barbara A. Fritzsche and Tiffany J. Parrish

T HE OLD ADAGE, "A happy worker is a productive worker," pervades American thinking about how to establish and maintain high productivity in organizations. It is widely believed in career development circles that those who experience satisfaction in their work lives also achieve more, have better psychological and physical health, and even experience greater satisfaction in their other life roles. Thus, it is no surprise that job satisfaction is the most widely studied topic in organizational behavior research (Spector, 1997). In fact, our library search of the keyword phrase *job satisfaction* produced almost 5,000 published papers just in the past 10 years (1993 to 2003). It is no wonder that Brief and Weiss (2002) called recent work on the study of affect in the workplace "The Hot 1990s" in their *Annual Review of Psychology* chapter.

Because improvement in job satisfaction is one potential outcome of career counseling, career counseling professionals require knowledge about the theories and empirical research that have shaped our understanding of the job satisfaction construct. This chapter provides an overview of the definition and measurement of job satisfaction, the consequences associated with job satisfaction, and its antecedents. We conclude with concrete ideas for how to apply job satisfaction research specifically to the career counseling process.

DEFINITION AND MEASUREMENT OF
JOB SATISFACTION

Job satisfaction is commonly conceptualized as an affective variable that results from an assessment of an individual's job experiences. Locke (1976) defined job satisfaction as ". . . a pleasurable or positive emotional state resulting from the appraisal of one's job or job experiences" (p. 1300). Cranny, Smith, and Stone (1992) viewed it as "an affective (that is, emotional) reaction to a job, that results from the incumbent's comparison of actual outcomes with those that are desired (expected, deserved, and so on)" (p. 1). In simple terms, job satisfaction is "the extent to which people like their jobs" (Spector, 2000, p. 197).

Brief (1998) argued that commonly accepted definitions of job satisfaction emphasize affect but fail to take into consideration that attitudes also have a cognitive component. In other words, job attitudes are composed of feelings *and* thoughts about work. Even though most *definitions* emphasize the affective nature of job satisfaction, most *measures* of job satisfaction tend to have a strong cognitive, rather than affective, component (Fisher, 2000; Organ & Near, 1985). Typically, measures ask people to evaluate how satisfied they are by comparing their job experience to some standard, such as prior expectations or a reference group of other workers.

Surveys suggest that people generally do like their jobs. A 2003 Gallup Poll found that the vast majority of Americans were generally satisfied with their jobs and with most aspects of their jobs. This finding is consistent with prior Gallup Poll findings such as the 1999 poll report that 90% of employed Americans were generally satisfied with their jobs and the 2001 data indicating that a third of Americans reported that they "loved" their job.

Although job satisfaction tends to be high overall, some people tend to be more satisfied than others. For example, job satisfaction tends to increase with age (Brush, Moch, & Pooyan, 1987; Siu, Spector, Cooper, & Donald, 2001) or has a U-shaped distribution in which new entrants to the workforce and older workers have the highest job satisfaction (Hochwarter, Ferris, Perrewe, Witt, & Kiewitz, 2001). Siu et al. suggested that older workers are more satisfied because they tend to have better coping skills and well-being than do younger workers. It is unclear whether there are sex and racial differences in job satisfaction. On the one hand, research has found that men and women were equally satisfied with their jobs (Brush et al., 1987; Witt & Nye, 1992), and Brush et al. found no evidence for racial differences in job satisfaction. On the other hand, Greenhaus, Parasuraman, and Wormley (1990) and Tuch and Martin (1991) found that Blacks were less satisfied than Whites. Both studies suggest that the lower satisfaction is due to Blacks generally receiving less satisfying jobs (i.e., lower paying, less stable) than Whites. In a study of 3,400 employees, Mor Barak and Levin (2002) found that perceptions of exclusion related to lower job satisfaction and well-being for women and ethnic minorities.

Job satisfaction has been measured using both global and facet measures. Global measures focus on overall feelings about the job and are used to predict behavior such as quitting. Facet measures focus on satisfaction with specific aspects of the job and are used to diagnose strengths and weaknesses at an organization or in a workgroup (Ironson, Smith, Brannick, Gibson, & Paul, 1989). Facets might include satisfaction with coworkers, fringe benefits, job conditions, pay, supervision, or the amount of personal growth offered at work (Spector, 1997).

No theory has been developed to provide guidance for choosing which facets are likely to be most important in different situations or for different people (Brief, 1998). Locke (1976) categorized facets into four main classes: the work itself, rewards, context, and people. However, the number and type of facets measured vary across job satisfaction scales, and little guidance has been offered to help understand the conditions under which different facets are most important to measure (Brief, 1998). Therefore, facet measures of job satisfaction may fail to measure important aspects of job satisfaction for some individuals and may include items that are unimportant to other individuals. As a result, the sum of facet scale scores does not always equal overall job satisfaction (Ironson et al., 1989).

Job satisfaction is most commonly measured via self-report questionnaires. Popular facet measures include the Job Descriptive Index (JDI; Smith, Kendall, & Hulin, 1969), the Job Satisfaction Survey (JSS; Spector, 1985b), the Minnesota Satisfaction Questionnaire (MSQ; D. J. Weiss, Dawis, England, & Lofquist, 1967), and the Job Diagnostic Survey (JDS; Hackman & Oldham, 1975). Global scales, such as the Job in General Scale (JIG; Ironson et al., 1989), the Faces scale (Kunin, 1955), and the Michigan Organizational Assessment Questionnaire satisfaction sub-scale (Cammann, Fichman, Jenkins, & Klesh, 1979), measure general or overall job satisfaction. Several of these measures are described next.

Perhaps the most popular measure of job satisfaction is the Job Descriptive Index (JDI; Smith, Kendall, & Hulin, 1969, 1985). The JDI contains 72 items that assess satisfaction with five facets, including Work, Pay, Promotions, Supervision, and Coworkers. Respondents read adjectives or brief phrases (e.g., "boring," "good") and evaluate whether each describes their job by answering with either a "yes," "no," or "uncertain." Ironson et al. (1989) reported internal consistency reliabilities that range from 0.78 to 0.88, and the validity of the JDI is well established (Brief, 1998).

The Minnesota Satisfaction Questionnaire (MSQ; D. J. Weiss et al., 1967) is another popular facet scale. The scale is available in both long (100 items) and short (20 items) versions. The 20 facets of job satisfaction that the MSQ measures are: Activity, Independence, Variety, Social Status, Supervision (Human Relations), Supervision (Technical), Moral Values, Security, Social Service, Authority, Ability Utilization, Company Policies and Practices, Compensation, Advancement, Responsibility, Creativity, Working Conditions, Coworkers, Recognition, and Achievement. Respondents read each item (e.g., "The feeling of accomplishment I get from this job") and rate that work aspect on a five-point scale from 1 ("I am not satisfied") to 5 ("I am extremely satisfied"). Reasonable reliability (e.g., average test-retest $r = 0.83$) and validity coefficients have been found (Dawis, Pinto, Weitzel, & Nezzer, 1974; Dunham, Smith, & Blackburn, 1977). Some researchers (e.g., Brief, 1998) prefer the MSQ to the JDI because the MSQ measures a much larger set of facets.

One example of a global measure of job satisfaction is the JIG (Ironson et al., 1989). Because the JDI does not include a global measure of job satisfaction, the JIG was designed to be used in conjunction with the JDI when a global measure is desired. It was designed to be ". . . more global, more evaluative, and longer in time frame" (p. 195) than the JDI. It contains 18 items in the form of adjectives or short phrases (items include "better than most," "waste of time"), and respondents use the same response options as on the JDI. Internal consistency estimates ranged from 0.91 to 0.95 across different samples, and the JIG scale correlated 0.66 to 0.80 with other global satisfaction scales (Ironson et al., 1989).

CORRELATES OF JOB SATISFACTION

Not only is having satisfying work an important end in and of itself, but also people who are satisfied with their jobs tend to experience other positive behavioral, affective, and health outcomes. This section summarizes research linking job satisfaction to job performance, counterproductive work behavior, withdrawal behaviors, life satisfaction, and health.

JOB PERFORMANCE

It is intuitively appealing to believe that those who are more satisfied at work are also more productive (Iaffaldano & Muchinsky, 1985). Meta-analyses have found that job satisfaction correlates with performance in the range of 0.17 to 0.18 (Iaffaldano & Muchinsky, 1985; Podsakoff & Williams, 1986) to 0.30 to 0.31 (Judge, Thoresen, Bono, & Patton, 2001; Petty, McGee, & Cavender, 1984). Thus, it is clear that there is a positive relation between satisfaction and job performance, but it is less clear whether the magnitude of the relation is small or moderate. Across individual studies, large variability in the magnitude of the correlation coefficients has been found. In such situations, researchers typically search for important variables that affect the magnitude of the correlation or for methodological problems with certain studies. By directly comparing their results to those of Iaffaldano and Muchinsky (1985), Judge et al. (2001) identified several methodological weaknesses with the Iaffaldano and Muchinsky meta-analysis. The weaknesses indicated their low correlation estimate was likely to be an underestimate of the true relation between the variables. Therefore, the most recent findings suggest a moderate correlation between job satisfaction and job performance.

Some (e.g., Locke, 1976; Porter & Lawler, 1968) have argued that the relationship may be reversed; that is, good performance leads to high satisfaction. When performance is high and leads to valued rewards, such as feelings of success and achievement, promotion, or raises, job attitudes are likely to be positive (Locke, 1976; Podsakoff & Williams, 1986). In fact, stronger correlations have been found between satisfaction and performance for higher level employees, where stronger extrinsic reward contingencies are likely to be found (Petty et al., 1984). Job satisfaction is also likely to result from good performance when the costs associated with attaining high performance are not too high and when achieving high performance does not conflict with other personal values (Locke, 1976). A recent review again emphasized the idea that the performance-leads-to-satisfaction assumption has not been consistently supported in empirical studies and instead proposed that satisfaction and performance mutually influence each other (Judge et al., 2001).

Another approach for understanding the job satisfaction-performance relation has been to examine specific aspects of job performance rather than assuming that attitudes should relate to overall job performance (e.g., Organ, 1988). Job performance is multidimensional (Campbell, McCloy, Oppler, & Sager, 1993), and two main performance dimensions are task and contextual performance (Borman & Motowidlo, 1993). Task performance includes behaviors that form the technical core of a job (such as teaching and conducting research for university professors), whereas contextual performance includes behaviors that support the technical core through improving the organizational, social, and psychological environment in which task performance occurs (such as helping to train a new coworker). Job satisfaction has been shown to relate positively (rs ranged from 0.27 to 0.41) to contextual performance or extra-role behavior (e.g., Bateman & Organ, 1983; Motowidlo, 1984). The correlation between job satisfaction and contextual performance has tended to be higher than that found between job satisfaction and task performance criteria, such as actual sales performance ($r = 0.18$; Puffer, 1987).

Organ (1988) offered a fairness explanation for this finding. He argued that people offer extra-role behavior as long as they maintain a long-term relationship of trust with the organization. When trust is violated and workers become dissatisfied, they discontinue extra-role behavior and offer task performance only in a quid pro quo fashion. Empirical examination of the idea that satisfaction involves an assessment of fairness has received modest support (Farh, Podsakoff, & Organ, 1990; Organ & Konovsky, 1989).

Brief and colleagues (Brief, Butcher, & Roberson, 1995; George & Brief, 1992) offer a "feeling good-doing good" explanation for the link between job satisfaction and extra-role behavior. They suggest that extra-role behavior is determined by experiencing positive mood at work. In a field experiment, Brief et al. demonstrated that even small positive mood-inducing behaviors can influence job satisfaction. Their findings suggest: ". . . an abundance of positive mood inducing events in the workplace might create enduring changes in job satisfaction and, correspondingly, generally higher levels of prosocial behaviors in organizations" (p. 60).

Counterproductive Behavior

Job dissatisfaction has also been associated with counterproductive work behaviors. Counterproductive behaviors are those that hurt the organization, such as sabotage, theft, and aggression against coworkers (Spector, 1997). When people are dissatisfied with their jobs, they become increasingly frustrated and convey their frustration by acting out at work and through physical symptoms (Chen & Spector, 1992; Duffy, Ganster, & Shaw, 1998; Keenan & Newton, 1984). According to Spector, relatively few studies have been done on this topic, but research to date suggests an important link between satisfaction and counterproductive behavior.

Withdrawal Behaviors

It is intuitively appealing to assume that those who are dissatisfied with their jobs are likely to miss work more often than others. However, a meta-analysis of 707 correlations found that the mean correlation between job satisfaction and absenteeism was only −.09 (Hackett & Guion, 1985), suggesting that the two variables are only weakly related. This finding has been echoed in more recent studies (Farrell & Stamm, 1988; Matrunola, 1996).

One alternative explanation for this finding is that the relation between absence and satisfaction may be nonlinear. Thus, the low correlations reported would be due to poor fit between the data and the way that the data were analyzed (e.g., only linear relations have typically been examined). Another possibility is that the distribution of absences may be highly skewed. In other words, most people are absent infrequently, and only a few people are absent often. This violation of the normality assumption will attenuate the correlation coefficient. Finally, Hackett and Guion (1985) argued that personal values are likely to account for more variance in absence behavior than are job attitudes because values are more central to our personality and cognitive makeup and direct more of our behavior choices. Thus, people with the same level of job satisfaction may behave differently (i.e., one may miss work and one may not) when faced with situations in which work and nonwork values conflict.

Using a longitudinal design, Tharenou (1993) examined the causal direction of the absence-satisfaction relationship. She found that uncertified absence (when the absence was not documented as sick leave with a medical certificate, leave for exams, jury duty, military service, bereavement, or worker's compensation) affected job satisfaction rather than the other way around. She argued that the self-explanations that may be required for avoidable absence may reduce job satisfaction. The results also suggest that type of absence (certified or uncertified) may affect the strength of the absence-performance relation.

Hackett and Guion (1985) suggested that the job satisfaction-absence relationship be reconceptualized:

> Rather than continuing to conceptualize absence primarily in terms of a process of *withdrawal* from a negative work environment, which from a managerial perspective conveniently places such behavior under the direct control of organizations, it is likely to prove more fruitful to view absence more in terms of a process in which workers are *drawn out* of the workplace by valued features of their nonwork environments. (p. 375)

Voluntary turnover is another commonly studied withdrawal behavior (e.g., Dickter, Roznowski, & Harrison, 1996; Mitchell, Holtom, Lee, Sablynski, & Erez, 2001). At the individual level, voluntary turnover is the choice to quit the job. Studies have commonly found a link between job dissatisfaction and turnover. In a meta-analysis of 39 correlations, the adjusted mean correlation between satisfaction and turnover was −.26 (Carsten & Spector, 1987), suggesting a small-to-moderate relation between job attitudes and turnover behavior. Carsten and Spector also found that as unemployment rates in the larger economy increased, the job satisfaction-turnover relation decreased. This suggests that people tend to stay at their jobs despite being dissatisfied when alternative job opportunities are limited.

Several models of the turnover process have been offered (e.g., see Hulin, 1991). Most models have conceptualized the relation between job satisfaction and turnover as a process that occurs over time (e.g., see Dickter et al., 1996). Fishbein and Ajzen's (Ajzen & Fishbein, 1977; Fishbein & Ajzen, 1975) general model of the relation among attitudes, behavioral intentions, and behavior has formed the foundation for the more specific turnover models. For example, Mobley, Griffeth, Hand, and Meglino (1979) argued that job satisfaction directly influences intentions to search for alternative employment and intentions to quit the present job. In other words, dissatisfaction in the *present* situation is expected to lead to intentions to seek alternatives. Intentions to search and quit are influenced not only by current job satisfaction but also by an evaluation of *future* expectations. People compare the outcomes they expect to obtain if they continue to stay in the present job with the expected outcomes of possible alternative job opportunities. Thus, likelihood of obtaining alternatives and the rewards that are associated with each alternative are evaluated. Intentions to search for alternatives and quit are then the immediate precursors to turnover behavior. Evaluating possible job alternatives may then cause us to reevaluate our satisfaction with our current job. This model helps to explain why dissatisfaction and turnover do not always go hand-in-hand. For example, if we are dissatisfied, but we perceive that there are no suitable alternatives available, we are likely to stay in the same job, but we may participate in other forms of withdrawal behavior (e.g., absences, daydreaming at work, reducing job inputs). Or, we might stay at a dissatisfying job if we expect that the job will facilitate our future career. Likewise, we might leave a satisfying job if an alternative job is perceived to be even more attractive and attainable.

LIFE SATISFACTION

We have discussed the relationship between job attitudes and job behaviors. This section focuses on the relation between job attitudes and other attitudes. In particular, we focus on how job satisfaction relates to life satisfaction, in general. Many studies have examined this relationship (e.g., Heller, Judge, & Watson, 2002; Iverson & Maguire, 2000; Judge & Watanabe, 1993; Rain, Lane, & Steiner, 1991).

Three main hypotheses have been offered: the spillover, compensation, and segmentation hypotheses (Rain et al., 1991). The spillover hypothesis suggests that the feelings in one area of life affect feelings in other areas of a person's life. In other words, job and life satisfaction should be positively correlated. The compensation hypothesis proposes that people tend to compensate for dissatisfaction in one area of their life with satisfaction in another (e.g., people in dissatisfying job situations will seek more satisfaction and pleasure in their home lives). That is, life and job satisfaction are expected to be negatively correlated. The segmentation hypothesis argues that people compartmentalize their lives and do not allow work and nonwork satisfaction to influence each other. Thus, job and life satisfaction may be unrelated.

Most studies have found a positive relation between job and life satisfaction, providing empirical support for the spillover hypothesis (Rain et al., 1991). In a longitudinal study, Judge and Watanabe (1993) examined the causal direction of this relationship and found that job and life satisfaction were reciprocally related. The relation between job and life satisfaction may be due, in part, to general dispositional tendencies to experience positive mood states (usually called positive affect) or negative mood states (negative affect). Watson and Slack (1993) argued that affective dispositions influence job satisfaction, which may lead to life satisfaction. Then, better life satisfaction leads to better adjustment (i.e., higher positive and lower negative affect). A recent longitudinal study (Heller et al., 2002) found that personality does account for some of the variance in the relationship.

HEALTH

Most popular models of the antecedents and consequences of job stress include job dissatisfaction as an example of a short-term consequence resulting from experiencing stressors in the workplace. Short-term negative consequences, such as job dissatisfaction, then lead to longer term physical and psychological problems (e.g., see Kahn & Byosiere, 1992).

One longer term problem is burnout. *Burnout* has been defined as ". . . a psychological syndrome in response to chronic interpersonal stressors on the job. The three key dimensions of this response are an overwhelming exhaustion, feelings of cynicism and detachment from the job, and a sense of ineffectiveness and lack of accomplishment" (Maslach, Schaufeli, & Leiter, 2001, p. 399). Burnout correlates negatively with job satisfaction, job commitment, and organizational commitment. Those who experience burnout have experienced "chronic mismatches" with their work environment in terms of workload (e.g., when demands exceed capacity), control (e.g., when responsibility outweighs an individual's authority), rewards (e.g., lack of pay or recognition), community (e.g., lack of social support), fairness (e.g., lack of voice), or values (e.g., organizational values that conflict with each other or with the individual's personal values). Burnout is assumed to lead to negative outcomes such as job dissatisfaction and poor job performance (Maslach et al., 2001).

Psychological health (Kirkcaldy, Shephard, & Furnham, 2002; Pearson, 1998) and physical health (Kirkcaldy et al., 2002) have been associated with job satisfaction. Kirkcaldy et al. found that lower job satisfaction and poorer health were associated with having an external locus of control (i.e., the belief that life events are due to forces outside of your control) and a Type A personality (i.e., highly competitive, impatient, restless) compared to those who have an internal locus of control (i.e., the belief that life events are in your control) and a Type B personality (i.e., who have a more laid-back personality).

Although some studies (e.g., DeCotiis & Summers, 1987; Jernigan, Beggs, & Kohut, 2002) have found that job satisfaction predicts organizational commitment, there is also evidence to suggest that commitment to the organization can buffer people from the effects of job stress on job satisfaction (Begley & Czajka, 1993). People who have high organizational commitment care about the fate of their organization, are willing to go above and beyond for the sake of the organization, and feel a sense of attachment to the organization (Mowday, Steers, & Porter, 1979). Commitment may buffer against stress because it helps people attach meaning to their work and connects people more closely to their social networks at work. Begley and Czajka studied commitment and job satisfaction, intentions to quit, and health during a major work consolidation and downsizing effort at one organization. They found that the stress of that event only increased the job displeasure of those who were already low in organizational commitment.

SUMMARY OF RESEARCH ON CORRELATES OF JOB SATISFACTION

Job satisfaction is positively related to work performance, but the two are less closely aligned than might be expected. Job satisfaction also relates to many other personal and work-related outcomes, such as health, life satisfaction, intentions to stay, and contextual performance. As with job performance, the magnitude of the relations between job satisfaction and these other outcomes has typically been small to moderate. It should be less surprising that the correlations are relatively small when considering that the outcomes are complex and influenced by a number of factors. For example, whether people perform well in their jobs depends not only on job satisfaction, but also on their ability, motivation, the organizational context, and so on. Another potential explanation for small correlations is that the distribution of job satisfaction is negatively skewed, which means that people tend to be satisfied with their jobs. People are not randomly assigned to their jobs; instead, we actively seek work environments that are satisfying. This also means that correlations between a skewed distribution of job satisfaction and other criteria will be attenuated. For these reasons, the small-to-moderate correlations found between job satisfaction and outcomes are fairly impressive, and concern about job satisfaction is justifiable from both the individual and organizational perspective (Spector, 1997).

ANTECEDENTS OF JOB SATISFACTION: THEORY AND RESEARCH

In the previous section, we presented evidence suggesting that job satisfaction relates to many other desired individual outcomes. In fact, one longitudinal study found that job satisfaction correlated significantly with longevity in a sample of 268 older volunteers ages 60 to 94 (Palmore, 1969), suggesting that even the length of our lives is related to our happiness at work. At this point, it is logical to ask why some people are more satisfied than others. This section focuses on theories and research about how job attitudes are formed and about commonly studied antecedents of job satisfaction.

There are more job attitude theories than is possible to discuss in one chapter. Instead of providing a comprehensive list of theories, we offer examples of theories and research that exemplify the ideas that job satisfaction is caused by:

1. Comparisons to prior job experiences.
2. The social context of work.
3. Job characteristics.
4. Job stressors.
5. Personal dispositions.
6. Person-environment fit.

For overviews of additional theories not covered here, see Brief (1998), Hulin (1991), and H. M. Weiss and Cropanzano (1996).

THE COGNITIVE JUDGMENT APPROACH

In general, the cognitive judgment approach argues that job satisfaction depends on an evaluation of the difference between an individual's expectations and what he or she actually receives. According to one such theory, Thibaut and Kelley's (1967) theory, people evaluate their current role based on comparisons with their past experience in and observations of others in similar roles. A Comparison Level (CL) is developed and used as a standard against which satisfaction with the current role is evaluated. In essence, the CL is a baseline indicator of what the individual feels that he or she deserves. Roles that exceed the CL will be satisfying, and roles that are judged to be lower than the CL will be dissatisfying.

Thibaut and Kelley also introduced the Comparison Level for Alternatives (CL_{ALT}) as another standard for comparison. The CL_{ALT} represents the outcomes that an individual perceives to be associated with the best possible alternative to the current role. Thus, the CL determines satisfaction with the current role and the CL_{ALT} determines how committed the person feels in the current role. As outcomes in the current role drop relative to the CL_{ALT}, the person will increasingly feel the desire to leave the current role.

Although Thibaut and Kelley's model has been criticized for ignoring the affective or emotional part of job satisfaction and instead focusing on the cognitive components (H. M. Weiss & Cropanzano, 1996), this model adequately accounts for how alternative job opportunities impact job satisfaction and turnover and helps to explain "job hopping" (Hulin, 1991). As individuals change jobs, they gain more information about alternatives. Thus, they may be satisfied in each job but change jobs frequently because of their CL_{ALT}.

SOCIAL INFORMATION PROCESSING THEORY

Social information processing theory (Salancik & Pfeffer, 1978) complements, rather than competes with, the cognitive judgment approach by suggesting that social context influences job attitude formation (H. M. Weiss & Cropanzano, 1996). According to Salancik and Pfeffer, others' evaluations of the job influence our own evaluations, especially when the job is complex or work events are ambiguous. For example, continuous statements from coworkers about how the job is such a bad job can influence a person's own perception of the job. There are two primary ways in which the social context influences attitudes. First, the social context helps people form their attitudes. It provides ". . . guides to socially acceptable beliefs, attitudes and needs, and acceptable reasons for actions" (pp. 226–227). Second, the social context helps people focus attention on attitude-relevant information, ". . . making that information more salient, and provides expectations concerning individual behavior and the logical consequences of such behavior" (pp. 226–227).

THE JOB CHARACTERISTICS APPROACH

The main idea underlying the job characteristics approach is that aspects of the work environment impact work outcomes, such as job satisfaction. This approach offers specific ways in which jobs can be redesigned to be more satisfying. The job characteristics model (Hackman & Oldham, 1976) posits: ". . . an individual experiences positive affect to the extent that he *learns* (knowledge of results) that he *personally* (experienced responsibility) has performed well on a task that he *cares about* (experienced meaningfulness)" (pp. 255–256).

According to Hackman and Oldham (1976), there are five core job dimensions: skill variety (i.e., Do job activities require multiple skills?), task identity (i.e., Do job activities require the completion of a "whole" piece of work?), task significance (i.e., Does the work have influence on others?), autonomy (i.e., Does the job allow independence of thought in determining the way work is completed?), and feedback (i.e., Does the work itself provide performance feedback?). The core job dimensions influence three critical psychological states. Specifically, the dimensions of skill variety, task identity, and task significance influence the degree to which a person experiences the job as *meaningful*. The autonomy dimension influences the degree to which a person feels *personally responsible* for work that is produced. And, the dimension of feedback influences the extent to which a person understands, regularly, *how effectively* he or she is performing. In turn, how meaningful, personally responsible, and effective he or she feels on the job influence motivation, performance, withdrawal behaviors, and job satisfaction. The relation between the five core job dimensions and personal and work outcomes is affected by individual differences in growth need strength. *Growth need strength* is the extent to which a person needs personal growth and development. Positive outcomes are expected when people high in growth need strength are in jobs designed to be high in core job dimensions. However, low growth need strength individuals respond poorly to enriched jobs.

The job characteristics model has been extensively studied. Meta-analyses (e.g., Fried & Ferris, 1987; Loher, Noe, Moeller, & Fitzgerald, 1985; Roberts & Glick, 1981; Spector, 1985a) have found that there is a moderate relation between job characteristics and job satisfaction (e.g., $r = 0.29$), and, as predicted, support has been found for growth need strength as a moderator. A recent study (Morgeson & Campion, 2002) criticized the job characteristics model for focusing on only a narrow set of core job characteristics. There are many ways to redesign work to improve satisfaction and efficiency, and Morgeson and Campion found that the specific job changes made were important only to the extent that they helped achieve the stated goals of the redesign effort.

WORK AND ROLE STRESSORS

A number of other characteristics of the work environment, generally called *workplace and work role stressors,* have been shown to influence job satisfaction (e.g., Fairbrother & Warn, 2003). For example, jobs can be stressful because of poor physical conditions, such as high levels of noise, lack of privacy, and extreme temperatures. Role stressors include role ambiguity (i.e., a lack of clear understanding of role expectations), role overload (i.e., having too much work to do or having overly difficult tasks), and role conflict (i.e., having incompatible role expectations). Other stressors, including underutilization of skills and lack of career development, have also been examined.

According to job stress models (e.g., see Kahn & Byosiere, 1992), job stressors lead to short-term (e.g., job dissatisfaction, boredom) and long-term (e.g., poor physical and psychological health) consequences, typically called *strains.* The job stressor-strain relationship can be buffered by coping mechanisms, such as positive self-care (e.g., exercise) and social support (i.e., providing empathy or tangible help with stressors). Feeling a sense of control over desired outcomes is also an important buffer to the stressor-strain relation.

Studies tend to support the basic idea that stressors are associated with experienced strain. For example, Beehr (1981) found that job satisfaction was related to role ambiguity ($r = -.23$), role overload ($r = -.27$), and underutilization of skills ($r = -.27$). Role ambiguity was found to be especially stressful for managers in low-enriched (rather than in high-enriched) jobs (Abdel-Halim, 1978). Keenan and McBain (1979) found that role ambiguity and satisfaction were more highly related for individuals with Type A personality ($r = -.70$) than those with Type B personality ($r = -.26$). More recently, Yousef (2002) found that role overload-quantitative (i.e., having too much work to do) and role overload-qualitative (i.e., having overly difficult tasks) correlated negatively with job satisfaction ($r = -.17$ and $r = -.31$, respectively). Yousef also found that an important stressor that related to job satisfaction was lack of career development available in the organization ($r = -.45$).

Social support has been associated with greater job satisfaction (e.g., Searle, Bright, & Bochner, 2001; van Emmerik, 2002), but its role in buffering the effects of stressors has received only mixed support (e.g., see Kaufmann & Beehr, 1986;

van Emmerik, 2002). In fact, in Kaufmann and Beehr's study, higher stressor-dissatisfaction correlations were found for those with greater social support. The authors argue that it may be that people seek social support when they are experiencing high levels of stressors and strains. Searle et al. found that how much and what type of social support mattered. People benefited the most from social support when it met their wants and needs. van Emmerik (2002) found that social support and practical assistance from supervisors and colleagues buffered the effects of stressors on job dissatisfaction, but social and practical support from home did not.

Perceived organizational support, the extent to which employees feel that their contributions are valued and that the organization cares about them, is another potential buffer of the stressor-strain relation. For example, Stamper and Johlke (2003) found lower correlations between role ambiguity and job satisfaction for individuals who perceived high organizational support. They stated, "Firms that send signals indicating that they value employee contributions and care about their well-being not only reduce the amount of role stress, but also help workers cope with the expected role stress associated with job tasks" (p. 581).

THE DISPOSITIONAL APPROACH

The dispositional approach maintains that job satisfaction is due to general tendencies to experience positive or negative affect. This approach suggests that certain individuals have dispositions that influence them toward feeling positive generally in their lives and includes being positive about their jobs. Moreover, these general tendencies are assumed to be independent of positive or negative situational characteristics (H. M. Weiss & Cropanzano, 1996). Staw and Ross (1985) were the first to suggest the dispositional approach to job satisfaction. They conducted a longitudinal study of more than 5,000 men and found that job satisfaction was stable over the five-year period in which the study was conducted. Job satisfaction was most stable for participants who remained in the same organization or occupation, but the correlations were still reasonably high even for participants who changed organizations or occupations. In addition, prior job satisfaction was a better predictor of current job satisfaction than were changes in pay and job status. Staw, Bell, and Clausen (1986) reported significant correlations between job satisfaction measures obtained over multiple time points in a longitudinal study that spanned 40 to 50 years. For example, affective dispositions collected during early adolescence correlated 0.37 with overall job satisfaction almost 50 years later. From their results, Staw and Ross (1985) concluded: ". . . it may be easier for organizations to improve the job attitudes of its [*sic*] employees by simply selecting individuals for membership who have positive dispositions than by trying to build positive attitudes through situational changes" (p. 478). This is a premature conclusion because job attitudes were less stable among those who changed jobs, and stability in job satisfaction could be indicative of stable job characteristics rather than dispositions (Gerhart, 1987). Nevertheless, Staw and Ross's study provided the impetus for work that examines potential genetic and personality determinants of job satisfaction.

In a study of genetic determinants of job satisfaction, Arvey, Bouchard, Segal, and Abraham (1989) studied 34 monozygotic twins reared apart (MZA) who were given the Minnesota Satisfaction Questionnaire. They found a heritability estimate of 0.30, suggesting that 30% of the variance in job satisfaction may be due to genetics. Cropanzano and James (1990) strongly criticized the methodology used in Arvey et al.'s study. In a later paper, H. M. Weiss and Cropanzano (1996) stated that it is likely that there is a genetic component to job satisfaction, but knowing that does not really help us to better understand the psychological processes involved.

Most studies that have examined dispositions have focused mainly on the traits of negative affectivity, positive affectivity, and locus of control as predictors of job satisfaction. *Negative affectivity* (NA) is the tendency to experience negative mood states such as distress, hostility, and depression, and *positive affectivity* (PA) is the tendency to experience positive mood states such as being cheerful, confident, and active. It is well documented that individual differences in NA and PA relate to job satisfaction (e.g., Cropanzano, James, & Konovsky, 1993; Duffy et al., 1998; Ilies & Judge, 2002; Watson & Slack, 1993); however, the mechanisms through which this occurs are unclear (Brief & Weiss, 2002). Brief and Weiss suggested that dispositions influence job satisfaction through mood at work and through affecting how an individual interprets objective circumstances of the job.

Locus of control is another widely studied dispositional predictor of job satisfaction (e.g., Lee, Ashford, & Bobko, 1990; Spector, 1982). As stated earlier, those who have an external locus of control tend to attribute the causes of their behavior to outside forces, whereas those who have an internal locus of control tend to view themselves as the causal factor. Job satisfaction has been found to be associated with a high internal locus of control (Spector, 1982). Spector provided four main reasons for this finding:

1. If internals are dissatisfied, they are more likely to quit the job than are externals.
2. Internals may have higher job performance, and when rewards are associated with higher performance, they are likely to be more satisfied.
3. Internals will be more satisfied because they tend to achieve greater advancement than do externals.
4. If internals are dissatisfied but choose not to quit the job, they are likely to cognitively reevaluate their situation in an effort to justify their decision to stay and avoid discrepancies between their attitudes and behavior.

A recent cross-national study conducted across five continents found that the locus of control-job satisfaction relationship is not just a Western finding (Spector et al., 2002). Spector et al. found that locus of control was significantly associated with job satisfaction across all but one of the Eastern and Western nations studied. In the French sample, the correlation was similar in size to the correlations in other countries ($r = -.24$), but the sample size ($n = 61$) was much smaller. In addition, none of the correlations from other countries differed significantly from that of the United States. This suggests that the finding is universal, though small in size.

PERSON-ENVIRONMENT FIT

We have discussed situational variables that influence job satisfaction, such as job characteristics and the social context of work. We have also discussed personal variables, such as locus of control and negative affectivity, which influence job satisfaction. Rather than searching for specific environmental or personality characteristics that contribute to job satisfaction, the person-environment fit (P-E fit) approach posits that job satisfaction is influenced by the extent to which good compatibility exists between people and their work environments. Thus, situational variables interact with personal variables to produce job satisfaction. Two popular P-E fit theories are the theory of work adjustment (TWA; see Dawis, Chapter 1, this volume) and Holland's RIASEC theory (see Spokane & Cruza-Guet, Chapter 2, this volume). Because these theories have been presented in earlier chapters of this book, we discuss only their hypotheses related to job satisfaction.

According to the TWA, work adjustment is, "... the process and the outcome of the interaction between an individual and a work environment that results in mutual satisfaction" (Lofquist & Dawis, 1984, p. 217). Satisfaction is influenced by the fit between the individual's needs and the reinforcers provided by the work environment. In addition, the fit between the ability of the individual and the abilities required by the occupation influences how satisfied the organization is with the individual (called *satisfactoriness*). Satisfaction occurs when organizations meet individuals' needs and when individuals meet organizations' needs. A reciprocal relation between satisfaction and satisfactoriness is also proposed. That is, satisfactoriness influences satisfaction and satisfaction influences satisfactoriness. Empirical support for this theory exists (e.g., see Breeden, 1993; Lofquist & Dawis, 1984).

According to Holland's RIASEC theory, there are six basic personality types (Realistic, Investigative, Artistic, Social, Enterprising, and Conventional) that describe people. Holland (1997) proposed a hexagonal structure for personality, in which each of the six types appears on one point in the hexagon. Personality types that appear closer to each other on the hexagon are more similar or have greater psychological resemblance. The same six basic personality types can describe the personality requirements and structure of work environments. People seek environments that match their personality, and congruence between people and environments is expected to lead to positive outcomes, such as achievement and satisfaction (Holland, 1997). Thus, people view their environments as satisfying when their personality matches the environment in which they work.

Several reviews and meta-analyses have examined the congruence-satisfaction relationship (e.g., Assouline & Meir, 1987; Spokane, 1985; Tranberg, Slane, & Ekeberg, 1993), and results have been mixed. Across 63 studies, Spokane found that congruence was positively correlated with job satisfaction. In contrast, two other meta-analyses found weak-to-moderate correlations (rs = 0.13 to 0.20) between congruence and job satisfaction (Assouline & Meir, 1987; Tranberg et al., 1993). Tranberg et al. noted several methodological weaknesses with some of the studies that were reviewed, such as the use of crude congruence indexes that do not sufficiently capture the essence of Holland's theory. Moreover, they found that Holland type may affect the strength of congruence-satisfaction relations. Specifically, they found the strongest congruence-satisfaction relations for social types (r = 0.33) and the weakest correlations for realistics (r = 0.05). Later studies have found that congruence might better relate to job satisfaction for individuals early in their careers (Tokar & Subich, 1997), possibly because individuals become more congruent and satisfied with their environments over time, and that congruence might better relate to facets of job satisfaction that involve the work itself rather than to facets such as pay or coworkers (Owings & Fritzsche, 2000).

Kristof (1996) argued that vocational fit theories, such as the TWA and Holland's RIASEC theory, focus on fit in the broadest level of the work environment, and, thus, may best predict vocational choice. However, she argued that fit in specific organizations is generally better predicted by person-organization fit (P-O fit). Her model of P-O fit suggests that (1) job satisfaction will result when people bring values, goals, and personality that are similar to those espoused by the organization, and (2) good job performance will result when people bring knowledge, skills, and abilities that are not already available, but needed, at the organization. Thus, supplementary fit (similarity to others) is important in predicting job attitudes, whereas complementary fit (adding what is missing) is important in predicting job performance. People who are high on both types of fit are assumed to have positive work attitudes and to stay with an organization longer. However, Kristof posited that the job satisfaction of people who identify strongly with their vocations will be more influenced by person-vocation fit, such as that proposed by Holland (1997), than by P-O fit.

Empirical support has been found for the relation between P-O fit and job satisfaction (e.g., Saks & Ashforth, 1997). Saks and Ashforth also found support for the relation among a more specific form of person-environment congruence, person-job fit, and job satisfaction. Thus, it appears that person-environment fit, measured on a variety of levels, is important for job satisfaction.

AN INTEGRATED MODEL OF JOB SATISFACTION

Situational influences on job satisfaction (e.g., job characteristics, job stressors) are the focus of bottom-up theories, in which pleasurable and unpleasurable experiences are believed to sum to form satisfaction. In other words, ". . . a happy individual is happy precisely because he or she experiences many happy moments" (Brief, Butcher, George, & Link, 1993, p. 646). Dispositional influences (e.g., negative affectivity) are the focus of top-down theories, in which people are believed to be predisposed to experience pleasure or displeasure. Thus, "Individuals who are happy are happy because they enjoy life's pleasures and not necessarily because they experience more of them in an objective sense" (p. 646).

Brief (1998) offered a model of job satisfaction that acknowledges both the top-down and bottom-up approaches. The model integrates research on the situational and dispositional influences on job satisfaction with some of the ideas about how person-environment fit predicts job satisfaction. His model posits that global internal personality dimensions (e.g., negative affectivity) and objective, external job circumstances (e.g., pay, social cues, status) both combine to influence an individual's interpretations of job circumstances. Interpretations are descriptions of how a person understands the objective aspects of his or her job and are based on what is encoded into memory about the job. Thus, when situational and personal factors interact, the model shifts focus from objective job circumstances to the individual's subjective interpretations of the job (e.g., perceptions of how fairly he or she is paid). Then, job attitudes are formed by cognitively and affectively evaluating his or her interpretations of job circumstances (e.g., What do I think about this fairness of pay? Does this perceived pay fairness feel good or bad?).

Brief (1998) based his integrated model on prior theoretical and empirical work on subjective well-being, but empirical support for the integrated model of job satisfaction has not yet been established. Despite this, the integrated model helps to rectify the seemingly incompatible person and situation approaches to job satisfaction by acknowledging that stable individual differences and characteristics of the situation influence job satisfaction. A key aspect of the theory is the central role that subjective interpretation plays in forming job satisfaction. According to Folger (1986), job satisfaction is "inherently referential." Individuals will be dissatisfied if actual outcomes differ from thoughts about "what might have been," particularly if unfair treatment has caused the discrepancy. As reviewed in this section, salient referent cognitions can be based on personality, comparisons to prior job experiences, perceived alternatives, or relevant others' perceptions.

IMPLICATION FOR CAREER COUNSELORS

Most of the theories and research cited in this chapter come from the industrial and organizational psychology literature. Thus, studies focus on job satisfaction within a work environment rather than on longer term career satisfaction that is more the focus of theory and research in career psychology (Lofquist & Dawis, 1984). However, despite the lack of research on job satisfaction and its promotion in the career literature, career counselors who see adults in their practices undoubtedly have many clients seeking help for issues related to job dissatisfaction. We have attempted in this chapter to review theories and research that seem most useful to helping counselors conceptualize clients' problems with job dissatisfaction and work with them to improve their feelings of satisfaction. This final section provides recommendations for counseling practice that we think derive clearly from prior sections of the chapter.

Not only is job satisfaction an important end goal in and of itself, but also research suggests that job satisfaction is associated with a variety of affective, behavioral, and health outcomes. For these reasons, the broadest implication of job satisfaction research is that career counselors *should* strive to help individuals achieve satisfying careers. Empirical evidence does suggest that there is a grain of truth to commonly held beliefs that individuals who are satisfied at work also tend to lead happier and healthier lives. Research also suggests that job satisfaction is impacted by many situational, personal, and fit factors, and these factors vary in importance for different individuals. Thus, counselors working with job dissatisfied clients need to assess the particular work environment, person, and person-environment fit factors that may be contributing to each client's dissatisfaction.

As reviewed in this chapter, job characteristics (e.g., amount of autonomy) and job stressors (e.g., role ambiguity) can be important contributors to job satisfaction. Some clients may have made appropriate vocational choices for their personalities and abilities, but their current job context may be the cause of the dissatisfaction. Using job characteristics measures such as the Job Diagnostic Survey (JDS; Hackman & Oldham, 1975) or job stress measures such as the Occupational Stress Inventory-Revised (OSI-R; Osipow & Spokane, 1998), counselors can help individuals identify the nature of their job and their experienced psychological states that result from the job characteristics. When problems are identified, clients can be advised on how to determine whether job redesign is likely (or possible) within their current job context, whether coping strategies can be used to buffer the effects of job stressors, or whether and how they should seek a more enriching job.

The dispositional approach suggests that working with a client toward the goal of career satisfaction will not always be brief and uncomplicated; that is, it won't always be straightforward career counseling such as helping the client examine values, skills, and aspirations and then exploring and planning to find a career path that fits these values, skills, and aspirations. Specifically, clients who present with job dissatisfaction and for whom assessment reveals underlying pervasive negative affectivity or certain specific dispositions, such as an external locus of control or Type A style, may need to make major positive changes in disposition to obtain career satisfaction. How exactly this is done will depend on the counselor's theoretical orientation and is beyond the scope of this chapter. As people change jobs, they tend to stay in similar work environments (e.g., see Holland, Fritzsche, & Powell, 1994). Thus, the tendency to experience negative affectivity may be a direct result of a long history of negative employment experiences. Because of the close association between job satisfaction and satisfaction with other life roles and overall life satisfaction, individuals in chronically dissatisfying jobs will likely need more extensive and longer term counseling than other clients to develop and change dispositions.

Assessment may also need to be more extensive with clients presenting with job dissatisfaction concerns. These clients may need not only more extensive job characteristics and personality assessment but also person-environment fit assessments at multiple levels of fit. Assessment of person-vocation fit using measures such as the Self-Directed Search (Holland, Powell, & Fritzsche, 1994) should be accompanied by assessment of person-job and person-organization fit (see Kristof, 1996) to better determine the specific source of the dissatisfaction. In addition, especially for female and ethnic minority clients, counselors should explore whether feelings of exclusion are part of their job dissatisfaction. Some female and minority clients may be able to significantly improve their satisfaction by finding a more inclusive organization in which to work.

Remembering that even Freud said, "Sometimes a cigar is just a cigar," career counselors who are trying to infer motives or meaning from their client's behavior should also keep in mind that, as the cognitive judgment model suggests, job hopping may not always indicate job dissatisfaction. Those who job hop may be gaining more information about alternatives with each job change. Thus, consider that lack of information about alternatives, rather than dissatisfaction, may be the cause of frequent job changes for some individuals. Moreover, absenteeism does not necessarily mean that a client is dissatisfied with his or her job. Instead, a closer exploration of the client's values and life circumstances may help illuminate the cause of the absenteeism as well as assist the counselor in working toward amelioration of absenteeism.

Finally, counselors should keep in mind that job satisfaction and job performance are both important outcomes for individuals, but they are not highly related to each other. Work on one of these areas does not necessarily generalize to, or promote dramatic change in the other, and counselors should educate clients about this as well. Clients, therefore, need to set specific and different goals when desiring change in both of these areas because interventions to maximize each will be different.

SUMMARY

In future years, as the workplace changes due to rapid technological advances, increasing workforce diversity, and global competition, keeping a pulse on individuals' job satisfaction will continue to be an important concern of both researchers and practitioners. Thus, despite an already extensive literature on the topic of job satisfaction, we expect that changes in how work is accomplished and how organizations are structured will create an even greater need to study job satisfaction. Alongside workplace changes, individuals are changing how they prepare for and manage their careers. In the future, career counselors may see more clients who are dissatisfied with their jobs because organizations poorly managed change or because they have not adequately adapted their career strategies to keep up with change. If change is rapid, individuals may also more often find themselves in jobs that have changed in ways that no longer fit their skills or interests and need the assistance of a career counselor to deal with the resulting dissatisfaction. This chapter was designed to provide an introduction to theories and research on job satisfaction so that career counselors are better prepared to assist clients with job dissatisfaction issues.

REFERENCES

Abdel-Halim, A. A. (1978). Employee affective responses to organizational stress: Moderating effects of job characteristics. *Personnel Psychology, 31,* 561–579.

Ajzen, I., & Fishbein, M. (1977). Attitude-behavior relations: A theoretical analysis and review of empirical research. *Psychological Bulletin, 84,* 888–918.

Arvey, R. D., Bouchard, T. J., Segal, N. L., & Abraham, L. M. (1989). Job satisfaction: Environmental and genetic components. *Journal of Applied Psychology, 74,* 187–192.

Assouline, M., & Meir, E. I. (1987). Meta-analysis of the relationship between congruence and well-being measures. *Journal of Vocational Behavior, 31,* 319–332.

Bateman, T. S., & Organ, D. W. (1983). Job satisfaction and the good soldier: The relationship between affect and employee "citizenship." *Academy of Management Journal, 26,* 587–595.

Beehr, T. A. (1981). Work-role stress and attitudes toward co-workers. *Group and Organization Studies, 6,* 201–210.

Begley, T. M., & Czajka, J. M. (1993). Panel analysis of the moderating effects of commitment on job satisfaction, intent to quit, and health following organizational change. *Journal of Applied Psychology, 78,* 552–556.

Borman, W. C., & Motowidlo, S. J. (1993). Expanding the criterion domain to include elements of contextual performance. In I. L. Goldstein (Series Ed.), N. Schmitt, W. C. Borman, & Associates (Vol. Eds.), *Frontiers of industrial and organizational psychology: Vol. 6. Personnel selection in organizations* (pp. 71–98). San Francisco: Jossey-Bass.

Breeden, S. A. (1993). Job and occupational change as a function of occupational correspondence and job satisfaction. *Journal of Vocational Behavior, 43,* 30–45.

Brief, A. P. (1998). *Attitudes in and around organizations.* Thousand Oaks, CA: Sage.

Brief, A. P., Butcher, A. H., George, J. M., & Link, K. E. (1993). Integrating bottom-up and top-down theories of subjective well-being: The case of health. *Journal of Personality and Social Psychology, 64,* 646–653.

Brief, A. P., Butcher, A. H., & Roberson, L. (1995). Cookies, disposition, and job attitudes: The effects of positive mood-inducing events and negative affectivity on job satisfaction in a field experiment. *Organizational Behavior and Human Decision Processes, 62,* 55–62.

Brief, A. P., & Weiss, H. M. (2002). Organizational behavior: Affect in the workplace. *Annual Review of Psychology, 53,* 279–307.

Brush, D. H., Moch, M. K., & Pooyan, A. (1987). Individual demographic differences and job satisfaction. *Journal of Occupational Behavior, 8*(2), 139–155.

Cammann, C., Fichman, M., Jenkins, D., & Klesh, J. (1979). *Michigan Organizational Assessment Questionnaire.* Unpublished manuscript, University of Michigan, Ann Arbor.

Campbell, J. P., McCloy, R. A., Oppler, S. H., & Sager, C. E. (1993). A theory of performance. In I. L. Goldstein (Series Ed.), N. Schmitt, W. C. Borman, & Associates (Vol. Eds.), *Frontiers of industrial and organizational psychology: Vol. 6. Personnel selection in organizations* (pp. 35–70). San Francisco: Jossey-Bass.

Carsten, J. M., & Spector, P. E. (1987). Unemployment, job satisfaction, and employee turnover: A meta-analytic test of the Muchinsky model. *Journal of Applied Psychology, 72,* 374–381.

Chen, P. Y., & Spector, P. E. (1992). Relationships of work stressors with aggression, withdrawal, theft and substance use: An exploratory study. *Journal of Occupational and Organizational Psychology, 65,* 177–184.

Cranny, C. J., Smith, P. C., & Stone, E. F. (Eds.). (1992). *Job satisfaction: How people feel about their jobs and how it affects their performance.* New York: Lexington Books.

Cropanzano, R., & James, K. (1990). Some methodological considerations for the behavioral genetic analysis of work attitudes. *Journal of Applied Psychology, 75,* 433–439.

Cropanzano, R., James, K., & Konovsky, M. A. (1993). Dispositional affectivity as a predictor of work attitudes and job performance. *Journal of Organizational Behavior, 14,* 595–606.

Dawis, R. V., Pinto, P. P., Weitzel, W., & Nezzer, M. (1974). Describing organizations as reinforcer systems: A new use for job satisfaction and employee attitude surveys. *Journal of Vocational Behavior, 4,* 55–66.

DeCotiis, T. A., & Summers, T. P. (1987). A path analysis of a model of the antecedents and consequences of organizational commitment. *Human Relations, 40,* 445–470.

Dickter, D. N., Roznowski, M., & Harrison, D. A. (1996). Temporal tempering: An event history analysis of the process of voluntary turnover. *Journal of Applied Psychology, 81,* 705–716.

Duffy, M. K., Ganster, D. C., & Shaw, J. D. (1998). Positive affectivity and negative outcomes: The role of tenure and job satisfaction. *Journal of Applied Psychology, 83,* 950–959.

Dunham, R. B., Smith, F. J., & Blackburn, R. S. (1977). Validation of the Index of Organizational Reactions with the JDI, the MSQ, and Faces Scales. *Academy of Management Journal, 20,* 420–432.

Fairbrother, K., & Warn, J. (2003). Workplace dimensions, stress and job satisfaction. *Journal of Managerial Psychology, 18,* 8–21.

Farh, J., Podsakoff, P. M., & Organ, D. W. (1990). Accounting for organizational citizenship behavior: Leader fairness and task scope versus satisfaction. *Journal of Management, 16,* 705–721.

Farrell, D., & Stamm, C. L. (1988). Meta-analysis of the correlates of employee absence. *Human Relations, 41,* 211–227.

Fishbein, M., & Ajzen, I. (1975). *Belief, attitude, intention and behavior: An introduction to theory and research.* Reading, MA: Addison-Wesley.

Fisher, C. D. (2000). Mood and emotions while working: Missing pieces of job satisfaction? *Journal of Organizational Behavior, 21,* 185–202.

Folger, R. (1986). Rethinking equity theory: A referent cognitions model. In H. W. Bierhoff, R. C. Cohen, & J. Greenberg (Eds.), *Justice in social relations* (pp. 145–162). New York: Plenum Press.

Fried, Y., & Ferris, G. R. (1987). The validity of the job characteristics model: A review and meta-analysis. *Personnel Psychology, 40,* 287–299.

Gallup Poll. (1999, September). *American workers generally satisfied, but indicate their jobs leave much to be desired.* Retrieved August 31, 2003, from http://gallup.com/subscription/?m=f&c_id=10408.

Gallup Poll. (2001, August). *Most American workers satisfied with their job.* Retrieved August 31, 2003, from http://gallup.com/subscription/?m=f&c_id=10829.

Gallup Poll. (2003, September). *America's employees rate the workplace.* Retrieved August 31, 2003, from http://gallup.com/subscription/?m=f&c_id=13839.

George, J. M., & Brief, A. P. (1992). Feeling good-doing good: A conceptual analysis of the mood at work-organizational spontaneity relationship. *Psychological Bulletin, 112,* 310–329.

Gerhart, B. (1987). How important are dispositional factors as determinants of job satisfaction? Implications for job design and other personnel programs. *Journal of Applied Psychology, 72,* 366–373.

Greenhaus, J. H., Parasuraman, S., & Wormley, W. M. (1990). Effects of race on organizational experiences, job performance evaluations, and career outcomes. *Academy of Management Journal, 33,* 64–86.

Hackett, R. D., & Guion, R. M. (1985). A reevaluation of the absenteeism-job satisfaction relationship. *Organizational Behavior and Human Decision Processes, 35,* 340–381.

Hackman, J. R., & Oldham, G. R. (1975). Development of the Job Diagnostic Survey. *Journal of Applied Psychology, 60,* 159–170.

Hackman, J. R., & Oldham, G. R. (1976). Motivation through the design of work: Test of a theory. *Organizational Behavior and Human Performance, 16,* 250–279.

Heller, D., Judge, T. A., & Watson, D. (2002). The confounding role of personality and trait affectivity in the relationship between job and life satisfaction. *Journal of Organizational Behavior, 23,* 815–835.

Hochwarter, W. A., Ferris, G. R., Perrewe, P. L., Witt, L. A., & Kiewitz, C. (2001). A note on the nonlinearity of the age-job-satisfaction relationship. *Journal of Applied Social Psychology, 31,* 1223–1237.

Holland, J. L. (1997). *Making vocational choices: A theory of careers* (3rd ed.). Odessa, FL: Psychological Assessment Resources.

Holland, J. L., Fritzsche, B. A., & Powell, A. B. (1994). *Self-Directed Search technical manual.* Odessa, FL: Psychological Assessment Resources.

Holland, J. L., Powell, A. B., & Fritzsche, B. A. (1994). *Self-Directed Search professional user's guide.* Odessa, FL: Psychological Assessment Resources.

Hulin, C. L. (1991). Adaptation, persistence, and commitment in organizations. In M. D. Dunnette & L. M. Hough (Eds.), *Handbook of industrial and organizational psychology* (2nd ed., Vol. 2, pp. 445–505). Palo Alto, CA: Consulting Psychologists Press.

Iaffaldano, M. T., & Muchinsky, P. M. (1985). Job satisfaction and job performance: A meta-analysis. *Psychological Bulletin, 97,* 251–273.

Ilies, R., & Judge, T. A. (2002). Understanding the dynamic relationships among personality, mood, and job satisfaction: A field experience sampling study. *Organizational Behavior and Human Decision Processes, 89,* 1119–1139.

Ironson, G. H., Smith, P. C., Brannick, M. T., Gibson, W. M., & Paul, K. B. (1989). Construction of a job in general scale: A comparison of global, composite, and specific measures. *Journal of Applied Psychology, 74,* 193–200.

Iverson, R. D., & Maguire, C. (2000). The relationship between job and life satisfaction: Evidence from a remote mining community. *Human Relations, 53,* 807–839.

Jernigan, I. E., Beggs, J. M., & Kohut, G. F. (2002). Dimensions of work satisfaction as predictors of commitment type. *Journal of Managerial Psychology, 17,* 564–579.

Judge, T. A., Thoresen, C. J., Bono, J. E., & Patton, G. K. (2001). The job satisfaction-job performance relationship: A qualitative and quantitative review. *Psychological Bulletin, 127,* 376–407.

Judge, T. A., & Watanabe, S. (1993). Another look at the job satisfaction life satisfaction relationship. *Journal of Applied Psychology, 78,* 939–948.

Kahn, R. L., & Byosiere, P. (1992). Stress in organizations. In M. D. Dunnette & L. M. Hough (Eds.), *Handbook of industrial and organizational psychology* (2nd ed., Vol. 3, pp. 571–650). Palo Alto, CA: Consulting Psychologists Press.

Kaufmann, G. M., & Beehr, T. A. (1986). Interactions between job stressors and social support: Some counterintuitive results. *Journal of Applied Psychology, 71,* 522–526.

Keenan, A., & McBain, G. D. M. (1979). Effects of Type A behavior, intolerance of ambiguity, and locus of control on the relationship between role stress and work-related outcomes. *Journal of Occupational Psychology, 52,* 277–285.

Keenan, A., & Newton, T. J. (1984). Frustration in organizations: Relationships to role stress, climate, and psychological strain. *Journal of Occupational Psychology, 57,* 57–65.

Kirkcaldy, B. D., Shephard, R. J., & Furnham, A. F. (2002). The influence of Type A behavior and locus of control upon job satisfaction and occupational health. *Personality and Individual Differences, 33,* 1361–1371.

Kristof, A. L. (1996). Person-organization fit: An integrative review of its conceptualizations, measurement, and implications. *Personnel Psychology, 49,* 1–49.

Kunin, T. (1955). The construction of a new type of attitude measure. *Personnel Psychology, 8,* 65–77.

Lee, C. C., Ashford, S. J., & Bobko, P. (1990). Interactive effects of "Type A" behavior and perceived control on worker performance, job satisfaction, and somatic complaints. *Academy of Management Journal, 33,* 870–881.

Locke, E. A. (1976). The nature and causes of job satisfaction. In M. D. Dunnette (Ed.), *Handbook of industrial and organizational psychology* (pp. 1297–1349). Chicago: Rand McNally.

Lofquist, L. H., & Dawis, R. V. (1984). Research on work adjustment and satisfaction: Implications for career counseling. In S. D. Brown & R. W. Lent (Eds.), *Handbook of counseling psychology* (pp. 216–237). New York: Wiley.

Loher, B. L., Noe, R. A., Moeller, N. L., & Fitzgerald, M. P. (1985). A meta-analysis of the relation of job characteristics to job satisfaction. *Journal of Applied Psychology, 70,* 280–289.

Maslach, C., Schaufeli, W. B., & Leiter, M. P. (2001). Job burnout. *Annual Review of Psychology, 52,* 397–422.

Matrunola, P. (1996). Is there a relationship between job satisfaction and absenteeism? *Journal of Advanced Nursing, 23,* 827–834.

Mitchell, T. R., Holtom, B. C., Lee, T. W., Sablynski, C. J., & Erez, M. (2001). Why people stay: Using job embeddedness to predict voluntary turnover. *Academy of Management Journal, 44,* 1102–1121.

Mobley, W. H., Griffeth, R. W., Hand, H. H., & Meglino, B. M. (1979). Review and conceptual analysis of the employee turnover process. *Psychological Bulletin, 86,* 493–522.

Mor Barak, M. E., & Levin, A. (2002). Outside of the corporate mainstream and excluded from the work community: A study of diversity, job satisfaction and well-being. *Community, Work, and Family, 5,* 133–157.

Morgeson, F. P., & Campion, M. A. (2002). Minimizing tradeoffs when redesigning work: Evidence from a longitudinal quasi-experiment. *Personnel Psychology, 55,* 589–612.

Motowidlo, S. J. (1984). Does job satisfaction lead to consideration and personal sensitivity? *Academy of Management Journal, 27,* 910–915.

Mowday, R. T., Steers, R. M., & Porter, L. W. (1979). Measurement of organizational commitment. *Journal of Vocational Behavior, 14,* 224–247.

Organ, D. W. (1988). A restatement of the satisfaction-performance hypothesis. *Journal of Management, 14,* 547–557.

Organ, D. W., & Konovsky, M. (1989). Cognitive versus affective determinants of organizational citizenship behavior. *Journal of Applied Psychology, 74,* 157–164.

Organ, D. W., & Near, J. P. (1985). Cognitive vs. affect measures of job satisfaction. *International Journal Psychology, 20,* 241–254.

Osipow, S. H., & Spokane, A. R. (1998). *Manual for the Occupational Stress Inventory* (Rev. ed.). Odessa, FL: Psychological Assessment Resources.

Owings, S. R., & Fritzsche, B. A. (2000, April). *The relationship between person-environment congruence and job satisfaction.* Poster session presented at the annual meeting of the Society for Industrial and Organizational Psychology, New Orleans, LA.

Palmore, E. (1969). Predicting longevity: A follow-up controlling for age. *Gerontologist Win, 9,* 247–250.

Pearson, Q. N. (1998). Job satisfaction, leisure satisfaction, and psychological health. *Career Development Quarterly, 46,* 416–426.

Petty, M. M., McGee, G. W., & Cavender, J. W. (1984). A meta-analysis of the relationships between individual job satisfaction and individual performance. *Academy of Management Review, 9,* 712–721.

Podsakoff, P. M., & Williams, L. F. (1986). The relationship between job performance and job satisfaction. In E. A. Locke (Ed.), *Generalizing from laboratory to field settings: Research findings from industrial-organizational psychology, organizational behavior, and human resource management* (pp. 207–253). Lexington, MA: Lexington Books.

Porter, L. W., & Lawler, E. E. (1968). What job attitudes tell about motivation. *Harvard Business Review, 46,* 118–126.

Puffer, S. M. (1987). Prosocial behavior, noncompliant behavior, and work performance among commission salespeople. *Journal of Applied Psychology, 72,* 615–621.

Rain, J. S., Lane, I. M., & Steiner, D. D. (1991). A current look at the job satisfaction/life satisfaction relationship: Review and future considerations. *Human Relations, 44,* 287–307.

Roberts, K. H., & Glick, W. (1981). The job characteristics approach to task design: A critical review. *Journal of Applied Psychology, 66,* 193–217.

Saks, A. M., & Ashforth, B. E. (1997). A longitudinal investigation of the relationships between job information sources, applicant perceptions of fit, and work outcomes. *Personnel Psychology, 50,* 395–426.

Salancik, G. R., & Pfeffer, J. (1978). A social information processing approach to job attitudes and task design. *Administrative Science Quarterly, 23,* 224–253.

Searle, B., Bright, J. E. H., & Bochner, S. (2001). Helping people to sort it out: The role of social support in the Job Strain Model. *Work and Stress, 15,* 328–346.

Siu, O., Spector, P. E., Cooper, C. L., & Donald, I. (2001). Age differences in coping and locus of control: A study of managerial stress in Hong Kong. *Psychology and Aging, 16,* 707–710.

Smith, P. C., Kendall, L. M., & Hulin, C. L. (1969). *Measurement of satisfaction in work and retirement: A strategy for the study of attitudes.* Chicago: Rand McNally.

Smith, P. C., Kendall, L. M., & Hulin, C. L. (1985). *The Job Descriptive Index* (Rev. ed.). Bowling Green, OH: Bowling Green State University, Department of Psychology.

Spector, P. E. (1982). Behavior in organizations as a function of employee's locus of control. *Psychological Bulletin, 91,* 482–497.

Spector, P. E. (1985a). Higher-order need strength as a moderator of the job scope—employee relationship: A meta-analysis. *Journal of Occupational Psychology, 58,* 119–127.

Spector, P. E. (1985b). Measurement of human service staff satisfaction: Development of the Job Satisfaction Survey. *American Journal of Community Psychology, 13,* 693–713.

Spector, P. E. (1997). *Job satisfaction: Application, assessment, causes, and consequences.* Thousand Oaks, CA: Sage.

Spector, P. E. (2000). *Industrial and organizational psychology: Research and practice.* New York: Wiley.

Spector, P. E., Cooper, C. L., Sanchez, J. I., O'Driscoll, M., Sparks, K., Bernin, P., et al. (2002). Locus of control and well-being at work: How generalizable are western findings? *Academy of Management Journal, 45,* 453–466.

Spokane, A. R. (1985). A review of research on person-environment congruence in Holland's theory of careers. *Journal of Vocational Behavior, 26,* 306–343.

Stamper, C. L., & Johlke, M. C. (2003). The impact of perceived organizational support on the relationship between boundary spanner role stress and work outcomes. *Journal of Management, 29,* 569–588.

Staw, B. M., Bell, N. E., & Clausen, J. A. (1986). The dispositional approach to job attitudes: A lifetime longitudinal test. *Administrative Science Quarterly, 31,* 56–77.

Staw, B. M., & Ross, J. (1985). Stability in the midst of change: A dispositional approach to job attitudes. *Journal of Applied Psychology, 70,* 469–480.

Tharenou, P. (1993). A test of reciprocal causality for absenteeism. *Journal of Organizational Behavior, 14,* 269–287.

Thibaut, J. W., & Kelley, H. H. (1967). *The social psychology of groups.* New York: Wiley.

Tokar, D. M., & Subich, L. M. (1997). Relative contributions of congruence and personality dimensions to job satisfaction. *Journal of Vocational Behavior, 50,* 482–491.

Tranberg, M., Slane, S., & Ekeberg, S. E. (1993). The relation between interest congruence and satisfaction: A meta-analysis. *Journal of Vocational Behavior, 42,* 253–264.

Tuch, S. A., & Martin, J. K. (1991). Race in the workplace: Black/White differences in the sources of job satisfaction. *Sociological Quarterly, 32,* 13–116.

van Emmerik, I. H. (2002). Gender differences in the effects of coping assistance on the reduction of burnout in academic staff. *Work and Stress, 16,* 251–263.

Watson, D., & Slack, A. K. (1993). General factors of affective temperament and their relation to job satisfaction over time. *Organizational Behavior and Human Decision Processes, 54,* 181–202.

Weiss, D. J., Dawis, R. V., England, G. W., & Lofquist, L. H. (1967). *Manual for the Minnesota Satisfaction Questionnaire* (Minnesota Studies in Vocational Rehabilitation, No. 22). University of Minnesota, Minneapolis.

Weiss, H. M., & Cropanzano, R. (1996). Affective events theory: A theoretical discussion of the structure, causes and consequences of affective experiences at work. In B. M. Staw & L. L. Cummings (Eds.), *Research in organizational behavior: An annual series of analytical essays and critical reviews* (Vol. 18, pp. 1–74). Greenwich, CT: JAI Press.

Witt, L. A., & Nye, L. G. (1992). Gender and the relationship between perceived fairness of pay or promotion and job satisfaction. *Journal of Applied Psychology, 77,* 910–917.

Yousef, D. A. (2002). Job satisfaction as a mediator of the relationship between job stressors and affective, continuance, and normative commitment: A path analytical approach. *International Journal of Stress Management, 9,* 99–112.

CHAPTER 9

Work Performance and Careers

Joyce E. A. Russell

THE BUSINESS ENVIRONMENT is highly turbulent and complex today, and careers are dramatically changing. The traditional psychological contract in which an employee entered a firm, worked hard, performed well, was loyal and committed, and thus received even greater rewards and job security has been replaced by a new contract based on continuous learning and identity change. In short, the organizational career is dead, while the protean career or boundaryless career is alive and flourishing (Arthur & Rousseau, 1996; Hall, 2002; Russell, 2003). Thus, the workplace has changed, and individuals are altering some of their career-related attitudes and behaviors. With a greater interest in career development by individuals and employers, counselors have never before faced so many challenges in meeting the needs of employees.

This chapter takes the perspective that career counselors will want to help facilitate the effective performance of employees. To do this, counselors must understand what is meant by work performance as well as how it is measured. It is also helpful if they are aware of the issues that face employees at various stages in their careers and lives since these issues impact employees' work performance. Throughout the chapter, suggestions are offered for how counselors might be able to assist employees.

DEFINING AND MEASURING WORK PERFORMANCE

Campbell (1991) defined *work performance* as behavior associated with the accomplishment of expected, specified, or formal role requirements on the part of individual organizational members. Thus, work performance includes in-role behavior that can be contingently tied to rewards. One framework that has historically been used to understand the components of performance follows (Steers, Porter, & Bigley, 1996; Vroom, 1964):

$$\text{Performance} = \text{Ability} \times \text{Motivation (Effort)}$$

where:

$$\text{Ability} = \text{Aptitude} \times \text{Training} \times \text{Resources}$$
$$\text{Motivation} = \text{Desire} \times \text{Commitment}$$

Thus, performance is the product of ability multiplied by motivation. Ability is the product of aptitude (physical and mental capabilities a person brings to the job) multiplied by training and resources (technical, personnel, political). Motivation is the product of an employee's desire and commitment (persistence) to perform. Thus, motivation is defined in terms of the direction, intensity, and persistence of individual effort (Campbell & Pritchard, 1976; Kanfer, 1991). The multiplicative nature suggests that all elements are essential for performance to exist. Thus, a person's performance will be limited by his or her ability and motivation (e.g., a person with low motivation yet high ability will not have high performance and vice versa).

Although a person's job performance depends on some combination of ability, effort, and opportunity, it is often measured in terms of outcomes or results produced. Thus, performance has been defined as the record of outcomes produced on a specified job function or activity during a specified time period (Bernardin, Russell, & Kane, 2003). For example, college professors are typically evaluated on three general work functions: research, teaching, and service. Performance in each of these areas is defined with different outcome measures (e.g., research publications, teaching ratings, service awards). Performance on the job as a whole is equal to the sum or average of performance on the job functions or activities.

In recent years, some researchers have also broadened the construct of job performance to indicate effective performance of not only *relevant tasks*, but also contextual performance or *organizational citizenship behaviors* (OCBs; Borman & Motowidlo, 1997). These include extra-role behaviors or prosocial behaviors such as altruism, courtesy, civic virtue, conscientiousness, protecting the organization, and spreading goodwill (Turnley, Bolino, Lester, & Bloodgood, 2003). Today, most researchers agree that performance is due to some combination of individual level factors (e.g., ability, motivation) and system factors (e.g., job design, environmental conditions, raw materials).

CRITERIA USED TO MEASURE PERFORMANCE

In organizations, it is often difficult to measure individual performance since work outcomes are a result of multiple interdependent work processes (Borman, 1991). Consequently, job performance has been conceptualized as an individual's overall performance or task proficiency or as performance on specific dimensions. There are six primary criteria on which the value of performance may be assessed (Bernardin et al., 2003, p. 147; Kane, 1986):

1. *Quality:* The degree to which the process or result of carrying out an activity approaches perfection, in terms of either conforming to some ideal way of performing the activity or fulfilling the activity's intended purpose.
2. *Quantity:* The amount produced, expressed in terms such as dollar value, number of units, or number of completed activity cycles.

3. *Timeliness:* The degree to which an activity is completed, or a result produced, at the earliest time desirable from the standpoints of both coordinating with the outputs of others and maximizing the time available for other activities.
4. *Cost-effectiveness:* The degree to which the use of the organization's resources (e.g., human, monetary, technological, material) is maximized in the sense of getting the highest gain or reduction in loss from each unit or instance of use of a resource.
5. *Need for supervision:* The degree to which a performer can carry out a job function without either having to request supervisory assistance or requiring supervisor intervention to prevent an adverse outcome.
6. *Interpersonal impact:* The degree to which a performer promotes feelings of self-esteem, goodwill, and cooperativeness among coworkers and subordinates.

These six criteria may differ in their relevance to specific job activities. In addition, there may be important interrelationships among the criteria. For example, a manager may push his or her staff to produce as many products as fast as possible (thereby meeting the criteria of quantity) but may end up sacrificing quality. For any job, it is important to conduct a systematic job analysis to identify the critical tasks that must be performed as well as the knowledge, skills, and abilities needed to perform those tasks. This job analysis information can then be used to determine which criteria should be used to appraise an employee's job performance.

In addition to the preceding six criteria, other researchers have suggested that the qualities underlying job performance will change due to changes in the economy and business organizations. For example, Newell (2000) argued that because of the emphasis on "knowledge management" (i.e., the way in which an organization creates, uses, and stores the expertise that underlies its products), sharing knowledge will be a critical component of job performance. Thus, *knowledge sharing* may be considered an important criterion for performance measurement.

TECHNIQUES USED TO APPRAISE OR MEASURE PERFORMANCE

To understand employees' views about their performance, it is important to examine how their performance is being measured in the organization. There are numerous ways to measure performance, but, essentially, either more objective measures (e.g., dollar sales, units produced) or more subjective measures (e.g., ratings or rankings by others) can be used. Both involve some degree of subjectivity and are vulnerable to the effects of contamination (measuring additional irrelevant aspects of performance) and deficiency (not measuring all important aspects of performance). In addition, many of the techniques consider only a person's in-role job performance and typically fail to account for their contextual performance (e.g., organizational citizenship behavior), yet this has been shown to be critical to the success of the firm (Borman & Motowidlo, 1993).

With subjective measures, raters can make either comparisons of ratees' performance (e.g., paired comparisons or ranking employees from best to worst), comparisons among anchors (e.g., forced choice or using a bell-shaped curve such as top 10%, middle 80%, bottom 10%, to assign people into categories), or comparisons of individuals to anchors on a scale (e.g., graphic rating scales, behaviorally anchored rating scales, management by objectives). There is no one best method for rating individuals' performance. All of the approaches have their strengths and problems and can be compared in terms of use for administrative purposes (e.g., promotions), developmental purposes (e.g., feedback), and legal defensibility (e.g., adherence to Title VII of the Civil Rights Act of 1964). (See Bernardin et al., 2003, and Gomez-Mejia, Balkin, & Cardy, 2004, for more details on performance approaches.) There seems to be a g factor of work performance that is analogous to the g (i.e., general intelligence) factor of cognitive ability since about 50% of the variance in performance ratings is common (i.e., due to an overall general perception of the ratee influencing the dimension ratings). Hunter, Schmidt, Rauchenberger, and Jayne (2000) suggested that the g factor in work performance is determined by two characteristics: general mental ability and conscientiousness.

Performance should be evaluated by the most appropriate raters. For example, if most of an employee's work is done at home or at client sites, using clients as raters may be more important than using a traditional supervisor to rate the employee's performance. Managers and supervisors for many of today's workers are often not around or are more removed from day-to-day situations. Thus, they may be less available to answer questions or solve problems for workers. This means that they may not be in the best position to judge an employee's performance. It also means that employees may need to rely on others for more coaching or mentoring on the job. If supervisors are, however, used as raters, once they find performance problems, they should: (1) explore the causes of the problems, (2) provide effective feedback to the employee, and (3) develop an action plan with the employee and empower him or her to reach solutions (Dobbins, Cardy, & Carson, 1991).

Performance should be evaluated at the appropriate level. If an employee works alone, measures of his or her individual performance are important. If, however, he or she works in a team (which is increasingly being done in organizations), performance should be measured at the team level. In other words, individuals should complete peer appraisals whereby they evaluate one another on a number of important dimensions (e.g., effort, attendance, intellectual contributions, cooperation with teammates). Some researchers have suggested that team performance be measured by team members' ratings of one another on actions such as cooperation with others, volunteering for additional work, offering to help others, supporting and encouraging others, taking initiative in group activities, dependability and attendance, and following procedures (Russell & Jacobs, 2003; Werner, 1994). One rating system that has been gaining in popularity has been the use of *360-degree* systems. These involve using ratings by several sources, including an employee's peers, superiors, customers, and self to gain a more thorough picture of the employee's performance (Bernardin et al., 2003). Organizations can also design performance measurement systems that evaluate and reward "organizational performance," such as the firm's overall productivity or efficiency (Lawler, 2000).

EXPLORING THE CAUSES OF POOR PERFORMANCE

Once a supervisor or rater determines that an employee has "poor" performance, it is important that the rater(s) determine the causes of the performance. This is not easy, however. It is possible that the employee is directly responsible for his or her performance. It is also likely, however, that his or her performance is partially due to factors beyond his or her control. In most work situations, observers (raters) tend to attribute the causes of a person's poor performance to the worker, while the actor (worker) attributes his or her poor performance to the situation. This is referred to as the *actor-observer bias* (Carson, Cardy, & Dobbins, 1991; Kelly, 1973) and can cause conflict between the rater (observer) and the worker (actor) if they disagree on what caused the performance problem.

Generally, most performance problems are thought to be due to ability, motivation, or situational factors (Carson et al., 1991). The ability factors include the employee's skills and talents (e.g., job knowledge, intelligence, interpersonal skills). Motivation refers to the effort expended. Situational or system factors include many organizational characteristics that can positively or negatively impact performance, such as these (Gomez-Mejia et al., 2004):

- Poor coordination of work activities among workers.
- Inadequate information or instructions needed to perform a job.
- Low-quality materials.
- Lack of necessary equipment or equipment breakdowns.
- Inability to obtain raw materials, parts, or supplies.
- Inadequate financial resources.
- Poor supervision.
- Uncooperative coworkers and/or poor relations among people.
- Inadequate training.
- Insufficient time to produce the quantity or quality of work required.
- A poor work environment (e.g., cold, hot, noisy, frequent interruptions).

Performance depends on ability, motivation, and situational factors. For each job situation, the rater (typically the manager) should examine (with the help of the employee) the extent to which all three factors influenced the employee's performance (Table 9.1). This is important to help correct performance problems. Once the manager and employee agree on the causes of the performance problems, they can discuss how to eliminate the factors that are negatively affecting the employee's performance (e.g., poor equipment), while increasing the factors that facilitate positive performance. Table 9.1 illustrates what this discussion might look like. As noted, different strategies are needed for different causes of performance; thus, it is critical to first determine the causes of performance. Supervisors are encouraged to play the role of coaches with their employees to ensure that the necessary resources are available to workers and to help them identify an action plan to solve performance problems.

WHY IS PERFORMANCE IMPORTANT?

The measurement of employees' performance is important to individuals and to organizations. For individuals, how their performance is evaluated is often related to the outcomes they receive from work (e.g., future compensation, promotions, selection into training or other developmental programs). These outcomes are then related to employees' satisfaction with their work, which impacts their commitment to the job, absenteeism, turnover, stress, and future effort on the job

Table 9.1
How to Determine and Remedy Performance Problems

Cause	Questions to Ask	Possible Remedies
Ability	Has the worker ever been able to perform the job adequately? Can others perform this job adequately, but not this worker?	Train the employee. Transfer to another job. Redesign the job. Terminate the employee.
Effort	Is the worker's performance level declining? Is performance lower on all tasks?	Clarify linkage between performance and rewards. Recognize good performance.
Situation	Is performance erratic? Are performance problems showing up in all workers, even those who have adequate supplies and equipment?	Streamline work process. Clarify needs to suppliers. Change suppliers. Eliminate conflicting signals or demands. Provide adequate tools.

Source: Modified from "Management Dialogues: Turning on the Marginal Performer," by J. R. Schermerhorn, W. I. Gardner, and T. N. Martin, 1990, *Organizational Dynamics, 18,* pp. 47–59; and "Human Performance Problems and Their Solutions," by G. A. Rummler, 1972, *Human Resource Management, 19,* pp. 2–10.

(Whetten & Cameron, 2002). Thus, performance impacts many aspects of employees' professional lives and career success. See Figure 9.1 for factors related to performance and work outcomes.

For organizations, employee performance is measured in order to assess a team's, department's, or division's productivity. This ultimately provides a measure of the organization's overall productivity.

FACTORS RELATED TO WORK PERFORMANCE

Various models exist for illustrating factors related to task or work performance. In the career literature, Lent, Brown, and Hackett (2002) and Lent (Chapter 5, this volume) suggested that ability (as assessed by achievement, aptitude, or past performance indicators) is seen as affecting performance directly and indirectly through its impact on self-efficacy and outcome expectations. Self-efficacy and

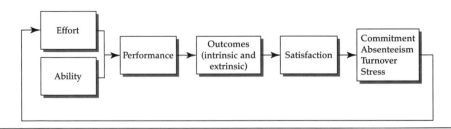

Figure 9.1   Factors Related to Performance and Work Outcomes.

outcome expectations affect the level of performance goals and subgoals that people set for themselves. As they noted, stronger self-efficacy beliefs and more favorable outcome expectations encourage more ambitious goals, which direct and sustain employees' performance. The performance level attained then serves to influence individuals' future development of abilities, self-efficacy, and outcome expectations (i.e., a feedback cycle). Whatever model of work performance is referred to, it is clear that an employee's current performance affects his or her future effort and subsequent performance.

Hall (2002) suggested that two metacompetencies that are related to effective performance are adaptability and identity. Employees who are adaptable demonstrate flexibility, exploration, openness to new and diverse people and ideas, comfort with turbulent change, and an eagerness to accept new challenges. Those with identity learning competencies are involved in self-assessment; they seek feedback, engage in personal development activities, and modify their self-perceptions. He suggested that both are critical for all types of employees. For executives in particular, research has shown that the factors that had the greatest impact on career success or performance were challenging assignments, formal training, education, development, succession planning programs, and developmental relationships (Hall, 2002). Perhaps counselors and employers can assist individuals in enhancing these competencies, thereby improving their performance.

EMPLOYEES AT VARIOUS LIFE AND CAREER STAGES: HOW COUNSELORS CAN FACILITATE EMPLOYEE PERFORMANCE

Not all employees have the same issues that impact their performance. For career counselors to be effective in working with individuals, they need to assess what life and career phase employees are in as well as what issues they are dealing with. For example, at a very basic level, it is important to examine whether an individual is in the early-, middle-, or late-career stage of his or her life and explore the unique issues he or she faces at work. While there is much debate over whether career stages exist, most researchers recognize that individuals do experience a number of common issues as they enter and advance in careers (Feldman, 2002; Hall, 2002). Typically, they go through establishment, advancement, maintenance (which could involve growth or stagnation), and decline periods (as they phase out of organizations). In addition, the type of work that a person does and how it is structured can greatly affect his or her performance. For example, it is important to examine to what extent he or she works in teams or in international assignments. Thus, to better understand a person's work performance, it is important to fully understand the challenges and issues he or she faces on the job.

The following sections describe some issues that employees at the early-, middle-, and late-career stages typically face and some suggestions to assist them. In addition, differences among employees in their values and attitudes due to the generation they grew up in affect their performance. These generational differences are briefly described. Further, issues facing employed spouses and parents, employees working in teams, those working in international assignments, and those who have been terminated or displaced are described. Career counselors who have a better appreciation for the various facets of employees' jobs and lives will have a better understanding of what really impacts their work performance and what can be done to assist them.

Career development interventions can be used to assist most employees regardless of the life or career stage they may be in—self-assessment tools, career-planning workshops, career workbooks (e.g., *What Color Is Your Parachute?* Bolles, 2004), individual counseling, assessment centers, psychological testing, mentoring, job rotation programs, training programs, and other developmental programs (Russell, 2003).

In addition, research suggests several types of career strategies that individuals can use to enhance their work performance and career success and fulfillment (Greenhaus, Callanan, & Godshalk, 2000, p. 85). Not all of these strategies will work in every situation, so employees should evaluate them carefully in line with their career goals. Strategies include:

- Improving competence or developing ability in the current job and acquiring additional work-related skills through education, training, and job experiences.
- Extending work involvement, increasing effort, or devoting considerable time, energy, and emotion to work role.
- Opportunity development or letting others know about career interests and aspirations and taking advantage of opportunities.
- Developing mentoring or other supportive alliances.
- Image building to communicate the appearance of acceptability, success, and potential for success (e.g., accepting and completing high-profile assignments to build reputation in the firm).
- Organizational politics or using flattery, conformity, and trading of favors and influence to attain desired outcomes.

Today, many American workers believe that they have to assume more responsibility for their own career choices and directions because of the turbulent organizational landscape (e.g., restructurings, layoffs, outsourcing). In other words, some workers have accepted more personal responsibility for their careers so they can be more career mobile (Prugh, 1998).

EARLY-CAREER EMPLOYEES

During the early-career period, employees (typically ages 25 to 40) are faced with the tasks of establishment and achievement. They have a number of task needs such as learning the job, understanding the organizational rules and norms, assimilating to the organizational culture, analyzing how they fit into their chosen occupation and firm, increasing their competence, developing specialty and team skills, and pursuing their goals. Essentially, they need to be seen as competent contributors to the organization (Greenhaus et al., 2000; Savickas, 2002). They also have some socio-emotional needs such as the need for support, autonomy, dealing with feelings of competition and rivalries, and developing emotional intelligence (Hall, 2002). Briefly, *emotional intelligence* refers to the development of personal competencies (self-awareness, self-regulation, motivation toward goals) and social competence (empathy, social skills; Goleman, 1995). Goleman (1998) argued that there is a relationship between emotional competencies and effective performance in a variety of work roles and that emotional intelligence is twice as important as pure intellect and expertise in contributing to performance excellence.

One issue that arises during the early-career period is the degree to which the employee's expectations for the job and outcomes (e.g., clear duties, timely feedback, developmental relationships, attractive rewards) is similar to the firms' expectations for the new employee (e.g., competence, loyalty and commitment, capacity to grow, ability to generate and sell ideas; Hall, 2002). Major differences between the expectations of the employee and the firm can cause performance problems and dissatisfaction.

Various programs can assist early-career employees to become more productive, including anticipatory socialization, realistic recruitment or job previews, orientation programs, and mentoring. New employees may want to participate in some or all of these programs to be more effective on the job.

Anticipatory socialization programs (e.g., internships, cooperative education programs) are helpful for individuals to develop accurate, realistic expectations about their chosen career field (Feldman, 2002). By working in the firm part time, individuals can learn about the work and the organization to see if they will be a good fit. They can also gain good information about their performance. The employer can also determine if there is a good fit between the individual and the firm before hiring the employee for full-time work.

Realistic recruitment information can be given to employees before they join the firm so that they have clear expectations of the requirements and duties of the job. If they are told the positive and negative aspects of a job, they may experience less reality shock, dissatisfaction, and turnover. They might also have better performance on the job since they have clearer expectations about what is required (Wanous, 1992).

Once they have joined a firm, *orientation* programs for new employees may help to reduce anxieties and enhance performance. These programs typically provide information on organizational policies, procedures, rules, work requirements, and sources of information. They may also be used to educate employees about any career programs, career paths, and opportunities for advancement in the firm. It is often helpful if new employees get a realistic preview about the requirements of the job so that they have appropriate expectations for their performance. Orientation programs also introduce new employees to the facilities, their peers, and their job duties. This could be an ideal time to pair them up with a mentor.

Typically, *mentoring* refers to a developmental relationship between a more senior employee and a junior employee, although today it is commonly accepted that mentoring can occur in a variety of formats, such as by peers, supervisors, and other high-level managers (Russell, 2003, in press). The mentor provides career-related support (e.g., sponsorship, exposure and visibility, challenging work, coaching, counseling) and psychosocial support (e.g., role modeling, protection, friendship, acceptance, confirmation) to help the protégé grow and develop on the job (Kram, 1985). If successful, mentoring may help reduce a protégé's inflated (unrealistic) expectations about the job, relieve stress associated with a new job, and may improve the protégé's chances for survival and growth in the firm (Dreher & Cox, 1996; Russell, in press). Thus, mentoring can have a strong impact on an employee's performance.

It is also imperative that employees learn the ropes or are *socialized* to how things are done in the organization if they are to be effective performers (Adkins, 1995). Socialization occurs through interactions employees have with their supervisors, peers, and others in the firm. Effective supervisors play the roles of coach, feedback provider, trainer, role model, and protector in an accepting, esteem-building manner (Cascio, 2003). Counselors may also assist new employees by encouraging them to have high career aspirations and by helping them to define their career goals and plans. Research has shown that having higher aspirations often leads to higher performance (Raelin, 1983).

During the early-career period, it is important that new employees be given challenging work early because it has been shown to be related to strong initial performance and to the maintenance of competence and performance throughout a person's career (Northrup & Malin, 1986). It also might ward off some future obsolescence. A newcomer who is exposed to substantial challenges learns that the organization is demanding, it expects people to assume responsibility for decisions, and it holds people accountable for results. In addition, for the employee to have higher performance, he or she needs to receive frequent and constructive feedback. Giving employees challenging assignments can also assist them to be more marketable if they leave the firm in the first few years, which has become more common because of organizational restructurings, technological advances that eliminate jobs, and differing job expectations among employees (e.g., Generation X and Y employees; Scandura, 2002). In addition, as Bobek and Robbins (Chapter 26, this volume) noted, some firms are providing "career pathing" programs to help in recruiting and retaining their workers.

It is especially important to develop strategies for retaining high-potential performers because they are very marketable. Some of these strategies can be carried out by managers or career counselors and might include:

- Holding one-on-one career planning meetings with each employee to record the employee's changing career interests.
- Offering opportunities for on-the-job training and support.
- Encouraging attendance at training to develop employees' technical, supervisory, and communication skills and knowledge.
- Providing mentoring programs.
- Encouraging and supporting them to join professional and technical associations.
- Offering company-paid tuition for completion of courses or programs (Prugh, 1998).

MIDCAREER EMPLOYEES

Once a person has become established in his or her career, the next phase is often called the *maintenance period.* This typically occurs during a person's midcareer period. The major tasks for those typically between 40 and 55 are to reappraise their lives, reaffirm their goals and dreams, and remain productive at work. See Sterns and Subich (2002) for a more detailed review of career progression issues during the midcareer period.

Midcareer is often referred to as the maintenance or management phase because individuals are concerned with managing their self-concept during this tumultuous time. Society expects mature adults to "hold steady" and to remain interested in their work and committed to their organization (Savickas, 2002). This can prove challenging if they are downsized out of their current firm. Many midcareer employees today are finding that they have to update their skills to work for new employers and in new fields (see Griffin & Hesketh, Chapter 20, this volume).

Some midcareer employees may also have to confront a number of midlife issues such as an awareness of advancing age and an awareness of death (e.g., their life is seen as "half over"), an awareness of bodily changes related to aging, a search for new life goals, a marked change in family relationships, a growing sense of obsolescence at work, a change in work relationships from being a novice to a coach, and a feeling of decreased job mobility and increased concern for job security (Bell, 1982). There are individual differences in the extent to which these issues become sources of concern (i.e., for some, these are major concerns; for others, they are less dramatic).

At work, often midcareer employees must deal with growing obsolescence and possible plateauing (i.e., limited future promotions). *Obsolescence* refers to the degree to which employees lack the up-to-date knowledge or skills necessary to maintain effective performance in their current or future roles (Kaufman, 1974). They may also feel bored in their jobs or underutilized. In addition, they may feel less mobile in the job market and thus be more concerned about job security.

Counselors might encourage midcareer employees to participate in life planning and career planning exercises to address their feelings, reexamine their values and life goals, and to set new goals or recommit themselves to previous goals. They might also help them deal with job losses due to organizational restructurings or downsizings. See Bobek and Robbins (Chapter 26, this volume) for more details on job losses.

Counseling sessions can provide midcareer employees with support concerning their midlife experiences and frustrations. It is important to encourage midcareer employees to develop new skills and a broader perspective on their work. The Workforce Investment Act of 1998 provides potential governmental support for worker retraining to provide assistance to those who are unemployed, displaced, or need to have their skills updated. This support might be particularly beneficial for midcareer employees (Werner, 2002).

It is also helpful to train midcareer employees to serve as coaches and mentors to new employees. Thus, the mentor can keep himself or herself up-to-date, and the new employee can learn from the midcareer employee's experiences. To deal with obsolescence, midcareer employees can be encouraged to attend training programs, workshops, and other retooling programs. They can also be given challenging assignments, new projects, and rewards linked to performance (Northrup & Malin, 1986).

LATE-CAREER EMPLOYEES

In the United States, the workforce continues to age. It is estimated that by 2008 the median age of the workforce will be greater than it has ever been (Fullerton, 1999). By 2015, more than one-third of all workers will be 50 and over (Brotherton, 2000). With the elimination of the mandatory retirement age for most jobs by the Age Discrimination in Employment Act (ADEA), more older Americans are working past the traditional retirement age of 65. As the graying of the workforce continues, it is increasingly more important to educate managers, workers, and career counselors about issues facing late-career employees.

Late-career employees are typically considered to be age 55 to retirement. Their major tasks are to remain productive in work, maintain self-esteem, and prepare for effective retirement. This can prove challenging given the negative stereotypes that many individuals have toward older adults and workers. In particular, numerous age stereotypes and myths exist about workers over the age of 55. Some of these myths are that they are absent more often, have higher rates of accidents on jobs, are less productive, are less motivated, are less efficient, and have higher health care costs (see Czaja, 1995, for a review).

Research indicates that these are myths: There is little relationship between age and job performance, and reviews have yielded mixed results (Beehr & Bowling, 2002). Unfortunately, many firms still treat older workers in nonproductive ways (e.g., by not hiring them for jobs, sending them to training, or giving them challenging assignments). These practices are illegal based on the ADEA legislation, which protects workers age 40 and older. It has been noted that age discrimination claims constitute a sizable portion of the Equal Employment Opportunity Commission (EEOC) caseload, comprising 23.6% of the charges in fiscal year 2002 and on the rise since 1993 (Charge Statistics, 2003).

Negative stereotypes and behaviors toward older workers affect the opportunities and performance of older workers. Older workers report that their biggest problems are that people underestimate their skills and that they must often convince managers and peers that they are not feeble or stubborn (Gardenswartz & Rowe, 2000). Managers and counselors can examine the latest research on older workers and help dispel myths about older workers' abilities to facilitate the performance of older workers on the job. Counselors can also communicate to employees the value (e.g., experience, wisdom, institutional memories) that older workers bring to the workplace.

Supervisors and counselors can develop action plans for enhancing the performance of older employees. These plans involve giving older workers more concrete feedback, allowing them to serve as mentors, and providing them with training and cross-training opportunities (i.e., skills development in multiple functional areas). It is also important that managers and counselors help older employees deal with career plateaus so that they can continue to be challenged and productive at work (Allen, Poteet, & Russell, 1998).

At some point, older workers prepare for retirement. It is critical that employers handle retirement issues effectively since they affect not only the preretirees, but also the morale of the remaining staff. Supervisors can be instructed on the changing demographics of the workforce, laws concerning older employees, stereotypes and realities of the aging process, and strategies for dealing with the loss of older employees who retire (i.e., the loss of expertise and skills in their department). These strategies will enable them to be more effective in establishing retirement plans for their older workers.

To assist preretirees, counselors can encourage them to attend workshops to understand the life and career concerns they may face as they prepare for retirement. Topics include health, finances, making the transition from work to retirement status, safety, housing, legal affairs, time utilization, social security, second careers, use of leisure time, and problems of aging. Counselors can offer individual and group workshops to communicate information to them. They can also encourage spouses to attend since many preretirees' decisions will also affect their spouses (e.g., travel, more leisure time). Counselors can provide needed support to help workers establish an identity in activities outside the work role (e.g., involvement in the community). (See Sterns & Subich, Chapter 21, this volume, on counseling for retirement.)

One interesting trend is the increased return of retirees to the workforce. In fact, they are the fastest growing part of the temporary workforce. Many are bored with retirement, have high energy levels, and can maintain flexible schedules (Andrews, 1992). Others need the money and health benefits. Counselors might want to help this returning group readjust to employment after retirement.

GENERATIONAL DIFFERENCES IN EMPLOYEES

In the United States, there are at least five different generations of individuals in the workplace (Cascio, 2003; Fisher, 1996). To understand their work performance, counselors need to be aware of factors that might impact their performance as well as differences in their career interests and behaviors. While there may be differences in values and behaviors among these groups, there are within-group differences as well (e.g., not all generation Xers subscribe to the same beliefs):

- Members of the *swing generation* (born between 1910 and 1929) are mostly retired from the workforce, but some still remain. Having lived through the Great Depression and World War II, they were responsible for building the American economy, which dominated the world for more than 30 years. They are characterized by a set of values that stresses the need for hard work, sacrifice, and toughness.
- The *silent generation* (born between 1930 and 1945) members were smaller in number and, as a result, were in great demand in organizations. Some of them attended some of the best colleges and rose rapidly in organizations. In return, they became the "organization men" by giving their hearts and souls to their employers and receiving jobs of increased responsibility, pay, and benefits. Today, some of them hold positions of power as corporate leaders or members of Congress.
- Members of the *baby-boom generation* (born between 1946 and 1964) currently account for 55% of the workforce. They believe in rights to privacy, due process, and freedom of speech in the workplace. They bring considerable management and leadership expertise and a large base of knowledge and talent to organizations. They believe there is a strong link between hard work and fast promotion up the corporate ladder. Even though times have changed, many in this generation still believe this to some degree and expect other workers to adhere to the same hard work principle.
- *Generation X* or *baby busters* are those born between 1965 and 1977. They comprise one-third of the current workforce. Having grown up in times of rapid change and being witnesses to corporate downsizings, they tend to be independent and may be less likely to expect the security of long-term

employment. They are a computer-literate generation who tend to seek control over their own schedules, opportunities to improve their marketable skills, exposure to decision makers, the chance to put their names on tangible results, and clear areas of responsibility (Labich, 1999).

- *Generation Y* individuals were born between 1977 and 1997 and comprise a very large group of about 80 million members. They are a sophisticated group with respect to technology, having grown up with computers and Internet access. They also appear to be very effective at multitasking numerous projects, but at the same time might have greater needs for stimulation or entertainment and shorter attention spans.

Moses (1999) suggested that those born in the 1960s (now in their 30s and 40s) are caught between the baby-boomer group and the Generation Xers and feel squeezed by both groups. They may feel that the boomers do not respect their needs for independence and time off to care for young children and that workers in their 20s are trying to push them out of their jobs.

There are some similarities in what can be done by employers and counselors to assist both Generation X and Y employees. Several suggestions have been offered for better integrating them into the workforce and enhancing their performance (Munk, 1999): providing full disclosure to them about work activities, creating customized career paths, allowing them to have input into decisions, providing public praise, treating them as sophisticated consumers, encouraging the use of mentors, providing access to innovative technologies, considering new benefits and compensation strategies, and offering them opportunities for community involvement. Moses also suggested that those in their 20s (mostly Generation Yers) could look to increase their experiences, expand their skills portfolio, and shadow (follow around) those employees or managers who are doing work that interests them to learn more about the tasks. They also might want to pursue education at the highest, broadest level, increase their networks, and try to better understand the attitudes of their bosses (many of whom are in their 40s and have different values).

MANAGING MULTIPLE ROLES: WORK AND FAMILY

Today, most adults are part of a "dual-earner" family (Gilbert, 2002). This means that adults have to manage multiple roles. Considerable research has documented the issues associated with work-family conflict and strain (see Betz, Chapter 11, this volume). It is clear that work performance is affected by factors in the work environment (e.g., job design, supervisor's behaviors, and peer group) as well as in other parts of an employee's life (e.g., family, personal). Thus, career counselors must take an employee's entire life into consideration when offering assistance to them. (See also Bobek and Robbins, Chapter 26, this volume, and Betz, Chapter 11, this volume, for more information on dual roles played by adult workers.)

It would be helpful for counselors to work with employees to better understand the priorities they place on their work and nonwork lives. They can do this by exploring careers with them, helping them to set goals, identifying career strategies, and appraising their career progress.

Increasingly, organizations realize that employees may experience role conflict and difficulties dealing with travel, child care, household tasks, job transfers, and relocations. Thus, they have developed more programs to assist their employees who are parents and spouses. Results have indicated that these programs have an impact on the firm's bottom line. They have been shown to increase employees' loyalty, thereby reducing turnover and absenteeism, and increasing organizational productivity (Lawlor, 1996). This often leads to greater performance among employees.

Career counselors could encourage employees to explore whether their firm offers such programs or how they might obtain similar types of assistance, if needed. These programs include:

- Increased use of flexible work arrangements (e.g., flextime, job sharing, part-time work, compressed work weeks, temporary work, telecommuting).
- Flexible career paths (alternatives to the linear or upward career path).
- Child-care and elder-care centers on work sites.
- Financial support for buying homes or paying for child-care costs.
- Paid leaves for fathers and adoptive parents (in addition to maternity leave).
- Relocation assistance for employees and their spouses.
- Relaxed policies on hiring couples.
- Work-family programs to discuss conflict and coping strategies (Russell, 2003).

EMPLOYEES WORKING IN TEAMS

Increasingly, many firms throughout the world are using teams to get work done. As a result, much of an individual's performance may be affected by working with others on project teams. Some of this project work may be done by teams on-site, yet, increasingly, much of it is being done by virtual teams (e.g., teams that work via e-mail, teleconferencing). In either event, individuals have to learn to work effectively with others and to have their performance partially evaluated by others (peer reviews, group goal setting, team awards). They also have to learn to coach and train one another on important job assignments. Career counselors need to be aware of how much of an individual's work is done in teams or alone if they are to understand and counsel them about their performance. They could encourage individuals working in teams to attend team training sessions, learn to deal with conflict, evaluate peers' performance, and provide peers with performance feedback.

EMPLOYEES WORKING IN INTERNATIONAL ASSIGNMENTS

As organizations continue to become more global, employees are faced with the challenges and opportunities of working with employees from other cultures and countries. Whether they physically work overseas or virtually work with those from other cultures, it is important for employees to be able to effectively communicate and interact with others. Many organizations offer training for expatriates to prepare them for overseas assignments. Some also offer training for repatriates to help them make the necessary adjustments once they return to their home country, which is critical because many employees experience shock when traveling to foreign countries or "reentry shock" when returning home to their own country (Stroh, Gregersen, & Black, 1998).

Taking an international assignment has implications for a person's career progress and development in a firm. In some cases, employees cannot move up without international experiences. In other cases, it hurts their career progress because they are away from the corporate headquarters of the firm. What is important is that career counselors understand individuals' career aspirations and have them explore the extent to which international assignments will be in line with those goals. In addition, specialized training could be used to facilitate successful performance in an international assignment or on return to the firm.

COUNSELING EMPLOYEES WHO HAVE BEEN TERMINATED OR DISPLACED

With the increasing number of organizational restructurings and downsizings, many employees have been terminated or displaced. As a result, employers can face morale and work performance problems (Gines, 2001). Bobek and Robbins (Chapter 26, this volume) discuss issues associated with job loss (see also Jome & Phillips, Chapter 19, this volume, and Saks, Chapter 7, this volume, for issues associated with the job search process).

Some organizations offer outplacement programs to assist terminated employees in making the transition to new employment. These programs usually have a human resource professional, psychologist, or counselor provide individual or group counseling to individuals. Issues about being let go, financial concerns, and skills training related to looking for new jobs, developing resumes, and interviewing with prospective employers are often part of the outplacement programs. It is particularly important to provide individual career planning and counseling for older employees who have been let go because they may have been forced into early retirement and may experience some anger, depression, stress, grief, or loss of self-esteem. Counselors can also encourage the use of support groups. Outplacement programs have been shown to benefit employees by helping them to cope with the shock and stress associated with losing a job and by helping them find jobs faster than they could on their own (Russell, 2003).

Displaced employees may have to be redeployed in the firm if the organization has had to change some of its job functions. To help foster the successful redeployment of displaced workers, the following suggestions are offered (London, 1996; see also Saks, Chapter 7, this volume) for use by career counselors as well as managers within the firm to help individuals develop career insight, identity, and resilience:

- Offer assessment and feedback processes to help people better understand their strengths and weaknesses.
- Help individuals develop realistic expectations.
- Encourage them to receive training on job search skills (which can also improve their self-efficacy).
- Teach them to develop networks and to be on the lookout for related job opportunities (see also Jome & Phillips, Chapter 19, this volume, for more research on networking).
- Encourage them to receive training in multiple skills and to use those skills in job assignments (to enhance their own marketability).

- Encourage them to take advantage of job rotation programs to develop a variety of skills.
- Have them participate in mentoring programs to foster work relationships.

COUNSELING EMPLOYEES FOR THE FUTURE

Given the changing views of careers in organizations, what should individuals do to be prepared for future jobs? First, they might want to review statistics on the fastest growing occupations and the education or degrees necessary to be successful in those occupations (*Occupational Outlook Handbook,* 2003). This might provide some perspective on the fields of the future (see also Bobek and Robbins, Chapter 26, this volume, on occupational trends).

Individuals could also make changes in their own characteristics. For example, some research has shown that having a proactive personality (i.e., identifying opportunities and acting on them, showing initiative, persevering until change is achieved) is related to a higher salary, a greater number of promotions, and higher career satisfaction (Callanan & Greenhaus, 1999; Sullivan, Carden, & Martin, 1998). Career counselors can assist individuals to be effective performers, and they can help individuals understand that there are some actions that individuals should take (Russell, 2003).

How Can Career Counselors Assist Individuals?

Career counselors can provide assistance to employees in a number of ways to better prepare them for their future jobs. They can conduct face-to-face counseling, as well as offer online counseling (Boer, 2001). General suggestions include these (see also Griffin & Hesketh, Chapter 20, this volume, for more ideas):

- Help employees to become more marketable and employable. Instead of worrying about holding onto a specific job, individuals need to make sure they have developed the competitive skills to be marketable in the workplace. They need to have portable competencies ("Managing Your Career," 1995).
- Help employees to take more control over their careers and look out for their own best interests. Counselors can help them by encouraging them to take charge of their careers by career planning and working on self-assessments.
- Work with employees to set career goals and clearly define what they are interested in doing.
- Encourage employees to maintain a technical specialty, especially during the early-career period. Thus, they could help employees plan for training courses to enhance their technical skills.
- Encourage employees to invest in reputation building or image enhancement to illustrate success and suitability for jobs (Greenhaus et al., 2000).
- Help employees to develop their collaboration skills because the use of project teams in organizations will continue to increase (Allred, Snow, & Miles, 1996).
- Assist employees in developing multiple networking and peer learning relationships (see Saks, Chapter 7, this volume).

- Encourage employees to be adaptable and flexible to changing job requirements (Callanan & Greenhaus, 1999).
- Help employees to solicit performance feedback and appraise how they are doing relative to their career goals; encourage them to work with their managers to explore the causes of any performance problems.
- Encourage employees to commit to lifelong learning to keep their skills relevant, whether by additional schooling or new assignments.

HOW CAN CAREER COUNSELORS ASSIST EMPLOYERS?

In addition to counseling individual employees, career counselors can offer some suggestions to employers that will enhance their employees' performance, decrease employee turnover, and prevent job burnout and obsolescence. Ideas include the following (Latham & Latham, 2000; Moses, 1999; Russell, 2003, pp. 193–194; also see Griffin & Hesketh, Chapter 20, this volume):

- Provide tools and opportunities for employees to enhance their skills so that the firm has a career-resilient workforce or self-reliant workers who can reinvent themselves to keep up with the fast pace of organizational changes (Waterman, Waterman, & Collard, 1994).
- Create an environment for continuous learning by supporting and rewarding employee development and learning (Callanan & Greenhaus, 1999).
- Provide opportunities for self-assessment and self-directed, continuous learning with career counselors and career centers (London, 2002).
- Encourage the use of Internet-based career services that offer job search tips, relocation information, self-assessment inventories, and networking tips.
- Provide opportunities for additional technical training.
- Have managers trained as coaches to assist employees.
- Develop a formal mentoring program and encourage participation.
- Provide career counseling to help employees deal with stress and career barriers and obstacles and to identify new directions for their careers.
- Assist employees to balance their work and personal lives (e.g., by offering child care, elder care, flexible work arrangements, and benefits).
- Develop a feedback, learning-oriented culture that encourages employees to participate in 360-degree performance appraisals so that they receive feedback about their performance from multiple sources in the organization (e.g., self, peers, clients, supervisors, subordinates).
- Develop performance appraisal and feedback systems that take into consideration the virtual nature of an employee's job (i.e., determine who will be the best raters of an employee's performance if interactions are not on-site but are by e-mails, voice mail, or video or teleconferencing).
- Provide training to employees to learn how to deal with performance feedback and criticism.
- Use reward systems that support the organization's career development strategy.
- Make sure the performance appraisal systems are integrated with other human resource programs (e.g., training, career development, selection, compensation).

- Use retraining of current employees before outplacing them.
- Provide sabbaticals to encourage time off for employees to recharge themselves.
- Allow for project ownership to give employees a stronger sense of entrepreneurial spirit.

SUMMARY

This chapter has been written with the understanding that career counselors will be interested in enhancing employees' work performance. To do this, counselors must understand what is meant by work performance and how it is measured. They must also be aware of the issues facing employees at various stages of their lives and careers since these issues impact employees' job performance. Thus, counselors could tailor their interventions to the specific background and needs of their clients. Today's turbulent business environment requires that counselors be acutely aware of the career issues and challenges facing employees and employers. It is also helpful for career counselors to anticipate the new challenges that will confront employees as the jobs of the future continue to evolve and develop.

REFERENCES

Adkins, C. L. (1995). Previous work experience and organizational socialization: A longitudinal examination. *Academy of Management Journal, 38,* 839–862.

Allen, T. D., Poteet, M. L., & Russell, J. E. A. (1998). Attitudes of managers who are "more or less" career plateaued. *Career Development Quarterly, 47,* 159–172.

Allred, B. B., Snow, C. C., & Miles, R. E. (1996). Characteristics of managerial careers in the 21st century. *Academy of Management Executive, 10*(4), 17–27.

Andrews, E. S. (1992). Expanding opportunities for older workers. *Journal of Labor Research, 13*(1), 55–65.

Arthur, M. B., & Rousseau, D. (1996). A new career lexicon for the 21st century. *Academy of Management Executive, 10*(4), 28–39.

Beehr, T. A., & Bowling, N. A. (2002). Career issues facing older workers. In D. C. Feldman (Ed.), *Work careers: A developmental perspective* (pp. 214–241). San Francisco: Jossey-Bass.

Bell, J. E. (1982, August). Mid-life transition in career men. *AMA Management Digest,* 8–10.

Bernardin, H. J., Russell, J. E. A., & Kane, J. (2003). Performance management and appraisal. In H. J. Bernardin (Ed.), *Human resource management* (pp. 142–162). New York: McGraw-Hill/Irwin.

Boer, P. M. (2001). *Career counseling over the Internet: An emerging model for trusting and responding to online clients.* Mahwah, NJ: Erlbaum.

Bolles, R. N. (2004). *What color is your parachute?* Berkeley, CA: Ten Speed Press.

Borman, W. C. (1991). Job behavior, performance, and effectiveness. In M. D. Dunnette & L. M. Hough (Eds.), *Handbook of industrial and organizational psychology* (Vol. 2, pp. 271–326). Palo Alto, CA: Consulting Psychologists Press.

Borman, W. C., & Motowidlo, S. J. (1993). Expanding the criterion domain to include elements of contextual performance. In N. Schmitt & W. C. Borman (Eds.), *Personnel selection in organizations* (pp. 71–98). San Francisco: Jossey-Bass.

Borman, W. C., & Motowidlo, S. J. (Eds.). (1997). Organizational citizenship behavior and contextual performance. *Human Performance, 10,* 69–192.

Brotherton, P. (2000, March/April). Tapping into an older workforce. *Mosaics, 1,* 4, 5.

Callanan, G. A., & Greenhaus, J. H. (1999). Personal and career development: The best and worst of times. In A. Kraut & A. Korman (Eds.), *Evolving practices in human resource management: Responses to a changing world of work* (pp. 146–171). San Francisco: Jossey-Bass.

Campbell, J. P. (1991). Modeling the performance prediction problem in industrial and organizational psychology. In M. D. Dunnette & L. M. Hough (Eds.), *Handbook of industrial and organizational psychology* (2nd ed., Vol 1, pp. 687–732). Palo Alto, CA: Consulting Psychologists Press.

Campbell, J. P., & Pritchard, R. D. (1976). Motivation theory in industrial and organizational psychology. In M. D. Dunnette (Ed.), *Handbook of industrial and organizational psychology* (pp. 63–130). Chicago: Rand McNally.

Carson, K. P., Cardy, R., & Dobbins, G. H. (1991). Performance appraisal as effective management or deadly management disease: Two empirical investigations. *Group and Organization Studies, 16,* 143–159.

Cascio, W. F. (2003). *Managing human resources: Productivity, quality of work life, profits* (6th ed.). New York: McGraw-Hill/Irwin.

Charge Statistics. (2003, September 25). *For years 1992–2002.* Available from http://www.eeoc.gov/stats/charges.html.

Czaja, S. (1995). Aging and work performance. *Review of Public Personnel Administration, 15*(2), 46–61.

Dobbins, G. H., Cardy, R. L., & Carson, K. P. (1991). Perspectives on human resource management: A contrast of person and system approaches. In G. R. Ferris & K. M. Rowland (Eds.), *Research in personnel and human resources management* (Vol 9). Greenwich, CT: JAI Press.

Dreher, G. F., & Cox, T. H., Jr. (1996). Race, gender, and opportunity: A study of compensation attainment and the establishment of mentoring relationships. *Journal of Applied Psychology, 81,* 297–308.

Feldman, D. C. (Ed.). (2002). *Work careers: A developmental perspective.* San Francisco: Jossey-Bass.

Fisher, A. (1996, September 30). Wanted: Aging baby boomers. *Fortune,* 204.

Fullerton, H. N. (1999). Labor force projections to 2008: Steady growth and changing composition. *Monthly Labor Review, 122,* 19–32.

Gardenswartz, L., & Rowe, A. (2000, March/April). How do we address conflict between employees because of age differences? *Mosaics, 6*(2), 3, 6.

Gilbert, L. A. (2002, August). *Changing roles of work and family.* Paper presented at the meeting of the American Psychological Association, Chicago.

Gines, K. (2001). Motivation and work performance 101. *Incentive, 175*(10), 3–7.

Goleman, D. (1995). *Emotional intelligence: Why it can matter more than IQ.* New York: Bantam Books.

Goleman, D. (1998). *Working with emotional intelligence.* New York: Bantam Books.

Gomez-Mejia, L. R., Balkin, D. B., & Cardy, R. L. (2004). *Managing human resources* (4th ed.). Upper Saddle River, NJ: Prentice-Hall.

Greenhaus, J. H., Callanan, G. A., & Godshalk, V. M. (2000). *Career management* (3rd ed.). New York: Dryden Press.

Hall, D. T. (2002). *Careers in and out of organizations.* Thousand Oaks, CA: Sage.

Hunter, J. E., Schmidt, F. L., Rauchenberger, J. M. R., & Jayne, M. E. A. (2000). Intelligence, motivation, and job performance. In C. L. Cooper & E. A. Locke (Eds.), *Industrial and organizational psychology: Linking theory with practice.* Oxford, England: Blackwell.

Kane, J. S. (1986). Performance distribution assessment. In R. A. Berk (Ed.), *Performance assessment: Methods and applications* (pp. 237–273). Baltimore: Johns Hopkins University Press.

Kanfer, R. (1991). Motivation theory and industrial and organizational psychology. In M. D. Dunnette & L. M. Hough (Eds.), *Handbook of industrial and organizational psychology* (2nd ed., Vol. 1, pp. 75–170). Palo Alto, CA: Consulting Psychologists Press.

Kaufman, H. G. (1974). *Obsolescence and professional career development.* New York: AMACOM.

Kelly, H. H. (1973). The processes of causal attribution. *American Psychologist, 28,* 107–128.

Kram, K. E. (1985). *Mentoring at work.* Glenview, IL: Scott, Foresman.

Labich, K. (1999, September 6). No more crude at Texaco. *Fortune,* 212.

Latham, G., & Latham, S. D. (2000). Overlooking theory and research in performance appraisal at one's peril: Much done, more to do. In C. L. Cooper & E. A. Locke (Eds.), *Industrial and organizational psychology: Linking theory with practice* (pp. 199–215). Malden, MA: Blackwell.

Lawler, E. E., III. (2000). *Rewarding excellence: Pay strategies for the new economy.* San Francisco: Jossey-Bass.

Lawlor, J. (1996, July/August). The bottom line on work-family programs. *Working Women Magazine,* 54–56, 58, 74, 76.

Lent, R. W., Brown, S. D., & Hackett, G. (2002). Social Cognitive Career Theory. In D. Brown & Associates (Eds.), *Career choice and development* (4th ed., pp. 255–311). San Francisco: Jossey-Bass.

London, M. (1996). Redeployment and continuous learning in the 21st century: Hard lessons and positive examples from the downsizing era. *Academy of Management Executive, 10*(4), 67–79.

London, M. (2002). Organizational assistance in career development. In D. C. Feldman (Ed.), *Work careers: A developmental perspective* (pp. 323–345). San Francisco: Jossey-Bass.

Managing your career: Special report. (1995, January 15). *Fortune,* 34–78.

Moses, B. (1999). *The good news about careers: How you'll be working in the next decade.* San Francisco: Jossey-Bass.

Munk, N. (1999, February 1). Finished at forty. *Fortune,* 50–66.

Newell, S. (2000). Selection and assessment in the knowledge era. *International Journal of Selection and Assessment, 8,* 1–6.

Northrup, H. R., & Malin, M. E. (1986). *Personnel policies for engineers and scientists.* Philadelphia: University of Pennsylvania, Wharton School, Industrial Research Unit.

Occupational Outlook Handbook. (2003, September 25). *The fastest growing occupations and occupations projected to have the largest numerical increases in employment between 2000 and 2010, by level of education or training.* Available from http://www.bls.gov/ocotj1.htm#content.

Prugh, C. C. (1998). Managing the career-mobile workforce. *Compensation and Benefits Management, 14*(3), 31–38.

Raelin, J. A. (1983). First-job effects on career development. *Personnel Administrator, 28*(8), 71–76, 92.

Russell, J. E. A. (2003). Career development. In H. J. Bernardin (Ed.), *Human resource management* (pp. 192–212). New York: McGraw-Hill/Irwin.

Russell, J. E. A. (in press). Mentoring. *Encyclopedia of Applied Psychology.*

Russell, J. E. A., & Jacobs, J. D. (2003). Group dynamics, processes, and teamwork. In E. R. Cadotte & H. J. Bernardin (Eds.), *The management of strategy in the marketplace* (pp. 355–375). Mason, OH: SouthWestern/Thompson Learning.

Savickas, M. L. (2002). Career construction: A developmental theory of vocational behavior. In D. Brown & Associates (Ed.), *Career choice and development* (4th ed., pp. 149–205). San Francisco: Jossey-Bass.

Scandura, T. A. (2002). The establishment years: A dependence perspective. In D. C. Feldman (Ed.), *Work careers: A developmental perspective* (pp. 159–185). San Francisco: Jossey-Bass.

Steers, R. M., Porter, L. W., & Bigley, G. A. (1996). *Motivation and leadership at work.* New York: McGraw-Hill.

Sterns, H. L., & Subich, L. M. (2002). Career development in midcareer. In D. C. Feldman (Ed.), *Work careers: A developmental perspective* (pp. 186–213). San Francisco: Jossey-Bass.

Stroh, L. K., Gregersen, H. B., & Black, J. (1998). Closing the gap: Expectations versus reality among repatriates. *Journal of World Business, 33*(2), 111–125.

Sullivan, S. E., Carden, W. A., & Martin, D. F. (1998). Careers in the next millennium: Directions for future research. *Human Resource Management Review, 8*(2), 165–185.

Turnley, W. H., Bolino, M. C., Lester, S. W., & Bloodgood, J. M. (2003). The impact of psychological contract fulfillment on the performance of in-role and organizational citizenship behaviors. *Journal of Management, 29*(2), 187–206.

Vroom, V. (1964). *Work and motivation.* New York: Wiley.

Wanous, J. P. (1992). *Organizational entry: Recruitment, selection, orientation and socialization of newcomers.* Reading, MA: Addison-Wesley.

Waterman, R. H., Waterman, J. A., & Collard, B. A. (1994). Toward a career-resilient work-force. *Harvard Business Review, 72*(4), 87–95.

Werner, J. M. (1994). Dimensions that make a difference: Examining the impact of in-role and extrarole behaviors on supervisory ratings. *Journal of Applied Psychology, 79,* 98–107.

Werner, J. M. (2002). Public policy and the changing legal context of career development. In D. C. Feldman (Ed.), *Work careers: A developmental perspective* (pp. 245–273). San Francisco: Jossey-Bass.

Whetten, D. A., & Cameron, K. S. (2002). *Developing management skills* (5th ed.). Upper Saddle River, NJ: Prentice-Hall.

CHAPTER 10

Career Development in Context: Research with People of Color

Roger L. Worthington, Lisa Y. Flores, and Rachel L. Navarro

C OUNSELING PROFESSIONALS HAVE only relatively recently recognized the importance of addressing issues related to diversity, pluralism, and multiculturalism (American Psychological Association [APA], 2002; D. W. Sue, Arredondo, & McDavis, 1992; D. Sue et al., 1982). Yet, in a short time, multiculturalism has become a vital force throughout psychology (APA, 2002; Pedersen, 1991), which has led scholars, educators, and practitioners to evaluate longstanding assumptions about human nature, psychological knowledge and inquiry, and professional practices. Progress in understanding the roles of gender, race or ethnicity, and sociocultural factors in the career development process has been slow and has generally not been fully integrated conceptually in the vocational literature or given extensive empirical attention within dominant vocational psychology perspectives (Lent, Brown, & Hackett, 1994). Career development psychology has lagged behind the broader multicultural counseling movement (Pope, 2000), publishing its first major volume on the career development of people of color only as recently as 1995 (i.e., Leong, 1995). However, there has been a substantial flow of new research and conceptual scholarship in the past decade concerning the career contexts, choices, decision making, adjustments, and transitions of people of color (Byars & McCubbin, 2001). During this period, some of the original career theories have been updated or expanded, and several new theories have been developed to address issues of diversity (e.g., Gottfredson, 1996; Lent et al., 1994; Super, Savickas, & Super, 1996; Vondracek, Lerner, & Schulenberg, 1986).

The purpose of this chapter is to acquaint readers with the literature on the career development of people of color. To accomplish this goal, we have organized this chapter into two major sections: contextual issues and multicultural vocational psychology research. First, we address the sociocontextual issues that are relevant in the career decision-making process of people of color. Second, we summarize empirical research related to the career development of people of color in the United States over the past decade. We organize our literature review into sections that address the major concepts in career development theories and practice. Due to space limitations, it is impossible for us to fully cover all of the research in this area; thus, we focus primarily on major studies and trends in the literature over the past 10 years.

CONTEXTUAL ISSUES

Before we begin summarizing and reviewing the important career development literature, it is essential to examine the contextual conditions that influence the lives of people of color in the United States. Basic information about the racial-ethnic composition of the population, within-group differences, historical oppression, and employment and educational disparities is essential to our understanding of counseling and career development for people of color. Specifically, we highlight the rapidly changing racial-ethnic demographics in the United States over the past several decades and address differences both between and within racial-ethnic groups. We also discuss the history of oppression toward people of color in the United States and how oppression relates to an ongoing cycle of educational, occupational, and income disparities.

POPULATION DIVERSITY

People of color represent more than 31% of the population in the United States (approximately 90 million people) and include individuals of Hispanic/Latino (12.5%), African American (12.3%), Asian American (3.6%), American Indian/Alaskan Native (0.9%), and multiracial (2.4%) backgrounds (U.S. Census Bureau, 2000a). This constitutes a substantial shift in a relatively short time period, given that non-Hispanic Whites constituted more than 75% of the population just 10 years earlier (U.S. Census Bureau, 1990) and approximately 86% in 1980 (U.S. Census Bureau, 2000b). In the Pacific (Washington, California, Oregon, Alaska, and Hawaii) and West South Central (Arkansas, Oklahoma, Louisiana, and Texas) regions of the country, Whites hold only narrow margins of majority over people of color (53% and 58%, respectively), are on the verge of being outnumbered in Texas (52%), and are already numerical minorities in Hawaii, New Mexico, and California (23%, 45%, and 47%, respectively) as well as in many major metropolitan cities (e.g., Boston, Chicago, Dallas, Detroit, Houston, Los Angeles, Miami, Milwaukee, New York, Philadelphia, San Antonio, San Diego, San Francisco, St. Louis, Washington, DC). The Census Bureau has projected that people of color will be a numerical majority in the United States as a whole some time after 2050.

WITHIN-GROUP DIFFERENCES

Important within-group differences must be considered to fully understand and respond to racial-ethnic diversity in career development and counseling practice. Assumptions about cultural uniformity can be particularly problematic when trying to understand the career development of people of color because overemphasis on between-group differences can result in the perpetuation of stereotypes and oversight about the tremendous complexity contained within diverse human systems. Each of the major racial-ethnic groups in the United

States consists of virtually dozens of discrete subgroups with their own unique sets of characteristics. Furthermore, there are substantial differences among individuals belonging to a particular racial-ethnic group on the basis of generational status, acculturation, racial-cultural identity development, U.S. immigration patterns, and socioeconomic status (SES), among other variables.

For example, Leung (1995) noted that the majority of research studies on the career development of people of color have failed to control for differences in SES. In fact, many studies fail to measure and report the SES of their participants or fail to consider generalizability limitations when samples are selected from (1) more highly educated and affluent college students or (2) members of impoverished communities of very low SES. In addition, many studies on career issues with people of color have used between-group methods and have tended to overemphasize comparisons between Whites and one or more racial-ethnic minority groups, often confounding SES with these between-groups comparisons. Other studies have been criticized in the multicultural literature for using Whites as the expressed or implied normative group to which people of color are compared psychologically. It is critical to recognize important within-group variations, as well as the problems of using Whites as a normative comparison group.

HISTORY OF OPPRESSION

Actual or perceived discrimination has been hypothesized to discourage people of color from pursuing some occupations and may lead to the development of poor or inaccurate vocational self-concepts (Leung, 1995). People of color have a 500-year history of oppression in North America, which includes genocide, displacement, slavery, rape, annexation, repatriation, internment, imprisonment, forced religious conversion, educational inequity, employment discrimination, economic exploitation, political disenfranchisement, police abuse, judicial injustice, cultural ethnocentrism, linguistic intolerance, historical invisibility, intellectual disregard, social marginalization, psychological pathologization, and identity misappropriation (Cushman, 1995; Pinderhughes, 1989; Three Rivers, 1991; W. J. Wilson, 1996; Zinn, 1980). (Readers should become familiar with the preceding forms of oppression; see the cited references for more information.) Efforts to alter the course of historical oppression in the United States have been ongoing since before the Civil War but have only relatively recently gained substantial momentum during the Civil Rights era of the 1960s (Zinn, 1980). Unfortunately, the structural and functional consequences resulting from centuries of racism and discrimination cannot be undone rapidly or easily. As such, historical oppression continues to play a critical role despite more than 40 years of civil rights legislation intended to protect people of color from educational and employment discrimination.

Hotchkiss and Borow (1990) identified economic and sociological processes operating at institutional and societal levels that impede access to the larger opportunity structure for people of color. They identified two complementary segments of the economy, the *core* and the *periphery*, which produce a dual economic structure that limits access to key high-salary and prestigious positions. Individuals who do not match a restricted range of characteristics (e.g., educational background, values, beliefs, gender, and race/ethnicity) encounter barriers to the most desirable opportunities in the labor market. As a result, women and people of color have historically been excluded from core sector jobs in the labor market that provide high wages and prestige. For example, Bertrand and Mullainathan (2003) conducted a particularly well-designed study of potential labor market discrimination. They sent fictitious resumes in response to help-wanted ads in Chicago and Boston newspapers and manipulated perceived race by randomly assigning to the resumes either a very African American-sounding name (e.g., Tamika, Lakisha, Jamal, Tyrone) or a very White-sounding name (e.g., Geoffrey, Todd, Meredith, Carrie). Resumes with White names required about 10 submissions to get one callback, whereas resumes with African American names needed about 15 submissions to get one callback, a 30% advantage for people with White-sounding names. Moreover, when the researchers increased the quality of the resumes, it elicited a corresponding 30% increase in callbacks for White names, but it produced a far smaller increase in callbacks for African American-sounding names. The amount of discrimination was uniform across occupations and industries.

F. D. Wilson, Tienda, and Wu (1995) investigated factors that influence the differences in unemployment between African American and White workers. They found that higher levels of African American unemployment were associated with job discrimination, residential segregation, and employment in occupations with high turnover rates. In addition, Wilson et al. noted that the widest racial difference in unemployment occurred between college-educated African American and White men, thus pointing to the barriers still faced by African Americans despite advancements in education ("education" is often cited as the cause and solution to economic and employment inequities). In another study, Ibarra (1995) examined the informal networks of midlevel managers, especially those with high potential for advancement. She found that high-potential managers of color established both same-race *and* cross-race informal networks and tended to have more cross-race contacts than White managers. However, managers of color had little contact with individuals in higher status positions and had little overlap between their social and instrumental networks when compared to White midlevel managers. These findings illustrate the otherwise invisible systemic influences described earlier by Hotchkiss and Borow (1990) that discriminate between Whites and people of color in providing access to the opportunity structure.

EDUCATIONAL, EMPLOYMENT, AND INCOME DISPARITIES

High school completion rates in the United States (among individuals 25 years and older) have been steadily increasing for all racial-ethnic groups over the past 60 years (U.S. Census, 2003b). In 1940, the high school completion rate for African Americans was less than one-third the rate for Whites—only 7.7% compared to 26.1% for Whites (figures were not kept for Hispanics until 1974, and figures for Asian Americans were reported only for the most recent census). By the time the Civil Rights Act was passed in 1964, the high school graduation rate for African Americans had increased to 25.7%, compared to 50.3% for Whites, narrowing the gap to just over one-half. Census figures for 1974 indicated a 36.5% graduation rate for Hispanics compared to 40.8% for African Americans and 63.3% for Whites; African Americans had closed the gap to nearly two-thirds of the percentage of Whites in only 10 years. The most recent figures indicate that Hispanics continue to lag behind both African Americans and Whites, graduating at less than two-thirds of the rate for Whites, while African Americans' graduation rates are approximately 90% of the rate for Whites (57.0%, 79.2%, and 88.7%, respectively). The high school graduation rate for Asian Americans was 86% in 2000.

College graduation comparisons across racial-ethnic groups yield patterns similar to high school completion rates. Specifically, among individuals 25 years and older, African Americans graduated at a rate of slightly more than one-quarter the rate for Whites in 1940 (1.3% and 4.9%, respectively)—a rate that rose to about 40% of that of Whites by 1964 (3.9% and 9.6%, respectively). Hispanics and African Americans graduated from college at the same rate in 1974 (5.5%), which remained at about 40% of the rate for Whites (14.0%). Although the latest census figures indicate that African Americans have narrowed the college graduation gap to nearly 60% of the rate for Whites (17.2% and 29.4%, respectively), Hispanics continue to lag behind at 11.1%, less than 40% of the rate for Whites. Asian Americans have the highest level of college graduation rates across all groups with 44% having a college degree or more education in 2000. These educational disparities are particularly important when considered along with research on occupational and economic attainment.

According to the Bureau of Labor Statistics (2003), the most frequently held occupational category by Whites was "managerial and professional specialty" (32% of Whites fall into this category compared to 23% of African Americans and 15% of Hispanics). Hispanics and African Americans were overrepresented in "service occupations" (20% and 22%, respectively, compared to 12% of Whites) and "operators, fabricators and laborers" (21% and 18%, respectively, compared to 13% of Whites). Hispanics made up only 6% of "self-employed" agricultural workers (e.g., farm owners) but more than 30% of agricultural "wage and salary" workers (a figure that does not reflect low-wage, undocumented Hispanic agricultural workers who are essential to the competitiveness of U.S. agribusiness). Adults in professional occupations and those holding managerial positions were more likely to have a bachelor's degree (71% and 48%, respectively) than workers in craft, service, farm, and production occupations (8%).

Disparities in employment opportunities and income are the logical result of the continuing lack of educational parity for people of color. For example, full-time workers who did not complete high school earned only $2,000 per month on average in 1996, compared to approximately $7,000 per month on average for workers with professional degrees. People with "some college" (e.g., on average less than one year past high school) earned approximately $340 per month more than high school graduates. Thus, even small amounts of post-secondary education translate into higher earnings. In 2001, the mean income for African American families (across all income groups) was only 59.7% of the average income for non-Hispanic White families; the corresponding figure for families of Hispanic origin was 61.5% of the average income for White families (U.S. Census Bureau, 2003a). Although there is objective evidence of sustained progress, vast inequities in education and employment remain readily apparent, and there are many contributing factors to the achievement gap for people of color.

Swanson and Gore (2000) pointed out that strong relationships among socioeconomic status, educational attainment, and occupational level have led to a "continuous cycle of impoverished, poorly educated, and underemployed [people of color]" (p. 249). For example, Whites are more likely than people of color to:

- Attend schools with smaller class sizes.
- Have access to computers in public schools and at home during schooling.
- Graduate from a four-year college or university.
- Earn higher incomes.
- Retain employment during a recession.
- Have health insurance and gain access to health care.
- Survive some life-threatening illnesses (e.g., cancer).
- Experience better housing conditions (e.g., less crowding, less crime, less litter and deterioration, and fewer problems with public services).
- Spend a smaller proportion of income on housing.
- Have greater access to home mortgage loans and home ownership.
- Invest in the stock market and retirement accounts.
- Gain a substantial net worth (Neville, Worthington, & Spanierman, 2001).

Recognition of the recurrent nature of these types of advantages based on racial group membership has produced efforts to engage in affirmative action as a method of change.

Affirmative action policies were first initiated in the early 1960s to correct many decades of racial discrimination in employment and education, with the first use of the term attributed to President John F. Kennedy in an executive order intended to reduce or eliminate racial discrimination in employment among government contractors. After only a decade of implementation of affirmative action policies, the first two major cases against it were presented to the U.S. Supreme Court (i.e., *DeFunis v. Odegaard*, 1974 and *Regents of the University of California v. Bakke*, 1978), which were followed by a series of additional cases over the course of 20 years. The *Bakke* case against the University of California resulted in a split decision that produced rulings both supporting and limiting affirmative action in educational admissions. More recently, hearing two cases against the University of Michigan simultaneously (*Grutter v. Bollinger*, 2003 and *Gratz v. Bollinger*, 2003), the U.S. Supreme Court issued yet another split decision. In the first decision, the court upheld the policy of the University of Michigan Law School in giving consideration to increasing diversity within the law school and among those in the legal professions by using race as one factor in determining admissions. In the second decision, the court ruled that the University of Michigan admissions policy that awarded points to people of color on the basis of race/ethnicity (along with points awarded for things such as children of alumni, athletes, and men enrolling in nursing programs) was unconstitutional. In writing the majority opinion for *Grutter v. Bollinger*, Justice Sandra Day O'Connor said the Constitution:

> does not prohibit the . . . narrowly tailored use of race in admissions decisions to further a compelling interest in obtaining the educational benefits that flow from a diverse student body. . . . In order to cultivate a set of leaders with legitimacy in the eyes of the citizenry, it is necessary that the path to leadership be visibly open to talented and qualified individuals of every race and ethnicity.

Although the University of Michigan cases were the most important rulings on affirmative action by the U.S. Supreme Court in a generation, there will likely be future cases that continue to test the limits of policies designed to correct long-standing inequities in education and employment for people of color.

SUMMARY

Contextual issues that influence the career development of people of color in the United States are complex and wide ranging. Many career development theories and counseling approaches that focus predominantly or exclusively on personal agency or individual variables as the central determinants of occupational outcomes have been criticized for their lack of attention to the major sociocontextual factors that limit opportunities for people of color. We have attempted to illustrate how historical inequalities are perpetuated via social, political, and economic forces beyond the control of people of color. With these contextual issues in mind, we now turn to the research literature in multicultural vocational psychology.

MULTICULTURAL CAREER DEVELOPMENT THEORY AND RESEARCH

Relative to the origins of vocational psychology in the early 1900s, multicultural career development is a rather recent area of inquiry. Much of this has been the result of the increasing diversity in society and institutional settings such as the workplace, schools, and colleges or universities. In addition, the number of professionals with expressed interest in multicultural issues has increased, and these professionals are among those who have contributed to the developing knowledge base on the career development of people of color.

Notable contributions in the career development of culturally diverse groups have been plentiful in the past two decades. Professional organizations in which career counselors are members (e.g., American Psychological Association [APA], American Counseling Association, National Career Development Association) have recognized the ethical and professional responsibility of their members to demonstrate cross-cultural counseling skills when working with members of culturally diverse groups. In addition, a growing number of studies are addressing the career development of people of color. Although this area of inquiry continues to be relatively small in comparison to the vast domain of career development research conducted each year, reviews have indicated there has been a steady growth in this literature over the past several years (Byars & McCubbin, 2001; Leung, 1995). Special sections within scholarly journals or entire journal issues (e.g., *Journal of Counseling Psychology*, vol. 44, 1997; *Career Development Quarterly*, vol. 39, 1991, and vol. 42, 1993) and textbooks such as *Career Counseling for African Americans* (Walsh, Bingham, Brown, & Ward, 2001) and *Career Development and Vocational Behavior of Racial and Ethnic Minorities* (Leong, 1995) have been devoted to career concerns among diverse U.S. racial and ethnic groups. Career counseling practice models have also been presented to help facilitate the career counseling process with people of color (Bingham & Ward, 1994; Cheatham, 1990; Fouad & Bingham, 1995; Leong & Hartung, 1997). Clearly, multicultural vocational psychology is building a strong theoretical and empirical foundation that has embraced multicultural issues.

There has been substantial disagreement on the extent to which traditional career development theories are valid with persons of color. Many years ago, Warnath (1975) questioned the applicability of career theories to people of color because of their failure to account for contextual and economic disparities that affect the lives of people of color. More recently, Cook, Heppner, and O'Brien (2002) suggested that traditional career counseling reflects male, western European experiences and worldviews about:

1. The separateness of work and family roles.
2. Culturally prescribed values of individualism and autonomy.
3. The centrality of the work role over other life roles.
4. The progressive, linear, logical nature of the processes of career development.
5. The openness of the opportunity structures in the labor force.

In fact, the very foundation of career development as it was established by Parsons in 1909 and extended into mainstream career theories (e.g., Dawis & Lofquist, 1984; Holland, 1959; Krumboltz, 1979; Super, 1953) has been challenged because of its formulation by White scholars (e.g., Fouad & Bingham, 1995) and its basis on research that has historically been limited to a privileged class of primarily college-educated, White, male samples (e.g., D. Brown, 2000; Carter & Cook, 1992; Hackett & Betz, 1981; Osipow & Littlejohn, 1995; Warnath, 1975).

Lent and Worthington (2000) summarized some of the key perspectives that have been offered by various career scholars on the cultural sensitivity of traditional career theories:

- Factors such as racial discrimination, economic and labor forces, and differential opportunities are seen as limiting the applicability of career theories to people of color.
- Generic assumptions that tend to ignore the sociopolitical realities experienced by people of color have been the basis for traditional career theories.
- A comprehensive multicultural theory of career development is needed to supplant traditional career theories.
- Factors such as social class, academic achievement, educational development, and role salience rather than race or ethnicity determine the applicability of career theories to people of color.
- The wholesale dismissal of career theories as irrelevant to people of color is premature given the scarcity of quality research testing their applicability.

Although revisions of the major career development theories indicate that all of the major schools of thought share a set of assumptions about how differing cultural contexts differentially influence work-related variables (e.g., values, skills, interests; Lent & Worthington, 2000), the need for general versus culture-specific career theories continues to be an issue in search of resolution (Leong & Brown, 1995; Osipow & Littlejohn, 1995; Swanson & Gore, 2000).

The multicultural vocational research literature continues to be relatively sparse (compared to other areas of research on career development), and it tends to lack a programmatic quality that is necessary for conclusive judgments to be drawn from the research. Multicultural career research tends to lack linear progression and cohesion and often proceeds in many directions simultaneously without a great deal of organization. In addition, more research has been done with African Americans than other people of color, although there have been recent advances in career research with Hispanics/Latina/os and Asian Americans. There continues to be a paucity of career research with American Indians, and there is little understanding of the issues related to their career development (Juntunen et al., 2001). There also continues to be an overreliance on the use of college student samples when investigating career development issues for people of color. Although there are increasing uses of high school and middle school student samples, the predominance of college student samples clouds the applicability of many findings to a broader range of persons of color.

In the following sections, we address career assessment and career development of people of color. We explore the published literature with respect to the salient issues that need to be addressed in career counseling with people of color. We begin with a discussion of the major issues in testing and assessment within a career context, with particular attention to the concepts of test bias and fairness and the research that addresses career testing applications with people of color.

CAREER ASSESSMENT WITH PEOPLE OF COLOR

According to many career theories, vocational assessment is viewed as a critical component of the career counseling process (Fouad, 1993) and can be used for a variety of purposes, such as clarifying occupational interests, identifying skills and abilities, or examining values and beliefs. A number of scholars have identified critical psychometric issues in career assessment instruments with respect to race and culture (Fouad, 1993; Gainor, 2001; Leong & Hartung, 1997; Leung, 1996; Marsella & Leong, 1995), and others have proposed the interpretation of assessments from a social constructionist perspective and the development of new approaches to assessment using alternative measurement theories (Blustein & Ellis, 2000; Subich, 1996).

Leung (1996) offered a thorough overview of the research related to career assessment with people of color. He urged caution in the use of career assessment with people of color because many career tests were developed from a European American cultural perspective, and many career counselors are not adequately trained to provide multiculturally competent counseling in order to accurately interpret test results on the basis of the client's cultural background. He stated, "differences in scores between Whites and ethnic minorities could be due to biases in testing instruments, and could lead to inaccurate conclusions about the test taker" (p. 477). However, it is impossible to know whether test bias is the cause of group differences in average test scores without additional evaluation of the validity of specific tests with specific groups. The existence of different group means in various studies tells us little or nothing about the talents or characteristics of individual test takers of any racial-ethnic category (Anastasi & Urbina, 1997; Walsh & Betz, 2001).

Test bias is a technical term that refers to deficiencies in a test or the manner in which a test is used that results in different meanings for scores earned by members of different identifiable subgroups (American Educational Research Association

[AERA], APA, & National Council on Measurement in Education [NCME], 1999). Test bias exists when test scores vary systematically in their accuracy according to the type of person being tested—thus, a test is biased if it represents individual differences for some groups of people more accurately than it represents individual differences for other groups (Anastasi & Urbina, 1997). Walsh and Betz (2001) noted that cultural bias in tests could be manifested in three central ways:

1. *Content bias* (e.g., content more familiar to Whites than members of other racial-ethnic groups).
2. *Bias in internal structure* (e.g., items on the test correlate with one another differently when administered to one group versus when given to another group).
3. *Selection bias* (e.g., when a test systematically varies in predictive validity across groups).

There is general consensus that consideration of bias is critical to sound testing practice and that fair treatment of all examinees requires consideration of not only the test itself but also the contexts and purposes of testing and the manner in which test scores are used (AERA, APA, & NCME, 1999).

Fairness is a concept separate but related to *bias* in testing. It refers to the absence of bias *and* equitable treatment of all examinees in the testing process. Unfairness can have individual and collective consequences (AERA, APA, & NCME, 1999). Although it may appear simple and straightforward in the abstract, application of the principle of fairness is much more difficult to accomplish in reality. Psychological testing inherently involves the use of cultural symbols to define and give meaning to the observations we make, such that ultimately the very objects and purposes of testing are culturally defined (Blustein & Ellis, 2000; Marsella & Leong, 1995). *Cultural perspective* can have an enormous influence on the ways in which the purposes, tasks, and outcomes of testing are given meaning and understood. Anastasi and Urbina (1997) noted that the predictive characteristics of test scores are less likely to vary among cultural groups when the test is intrinsically relevant to criterion performance but that culture is still likely to affect test behaviors and interpretations. Thus, the cultural backgrounds of test takers are critical to consider in the selection, administration, and interpretation of career tests (Leung, 1996):

> A full consideration of fairness would explore the many functions of testing in relation to its many goals, including the broad goal of achieving equality of opportunity in our society. . . . It would consider the technical properties of tests, the ways test results are reported, and the factors that are validly or erroneously thought to account for patterns of test performance for groups and individuals. . . . Properly designed and used, tests can and do further societal goals of fairness and equality of opportunity . . . [T]he fairness of testing in any given context must be judged relative to that of feasible test and nontest alternatives. . . . A professional's inferences and reports from test findings may markedly impact the life of the person who is examined. . . . Attention to interpersonal issues is always important, perhaps especially so when examinees . . . differ from the examiner in ethnic, racial . . . or other characteristics. (AERA, APA, NCME, 1999, pp. 73–74)

Only a limited number of studies have been conducted to address the cross-cultural validity of vocational assessment, and most of the published studies have addressed interest inventories (Leung, 1996). In his discussion of the cross-cultural application of career assessment instruments, Leung surveyed the research literature for studies on the cultural validity of vocational assessment, with particular attention to the Strong Interest Inventory (SII), the Self-Directed Search (SDS), the Career Maturity Inventory (CMI), and My Vocational Situation (MVS). He concluded that, although there is a body of research to support the predictive and construct validity of the SII and some evidence for the validity of the SDS, many other career assessment instruments (including the CMI and MVS) have not been adequately researched with people of color. More recently, both the SII and the Campbell Interest and Skill Survey have received research support for their use with persons of color in a national sample of college-educated, employed adults (Lattimore & Borgen, 1999). However, Gainor (2001) continues to recommend caution in using even *accurately* measured interests as the basis for career decisions of people of color because she warns that it is impossible to divorce the social and historical processes (e.g., educational inequities, discrimination, oppression) that affect people's lives from the career interests they express. Thus, consideration must be given to the social and historical reasons for the development of occupational interests among people of color and the potential benefits of considering occupations that may not fall within their expressed range of interests (Gainor, 2001).

Marsella and Leong (1995) also recommended that career assessment instruments be subjected to research on the basis of linguistic, conceptual, scale, and normative equivalencies, yet they acknowledged that test developers cannot be expected to establish these cross-cultural equivalencies for all of the possible cultural groups with whom the instruments might be used. Given these circumstances, we are left with the issue of what to do when cultural differences exist in career testing situations. Table 10.1 provides a nonexhaustive list of strategies for effective management of cultural differences in career assessment. Subich (1996) suggested that traditional models and methods of career assessment require transformation from an overreliance on objective measurement toward more empathic, collaborative assessment strategies that lead to greater understanding of the individual client. Hartung et al. (1998) provided a model to (1) consider cultural identity as a central factor in career development and (2) identify culturally sensitive instruments in the process of assessment and intervention. Blustein and Ellis (2000) have argued that it is not sufficient to simply modify existing instruments to control cultural influences but that test developers need to examine their inferences about constructs of interest in a manner that is "intellectually compelling and affirming of cultural differences" (p. 382).

A paradox is apparent in the development, use, and interpretation of career assessment instruments with people of color—tests have the capacity to increase equitable treatment and fairness, while they simultaneously contain inherent risks of misuse that might serve to perpetuate the status quo of inequity, mistreatment, and discrimination in educational and occupational processes and outcomes. In summary, although there have been many improvements in the past two decades in the development and revision of career assessment instruments to address the needs of people of color, pernicious problems continue

Table 10.1
A Nonexhaustive List of Effective Coping Strategies for
Multicultural Career Assessment

- Understand your own limitations as a competent test user and as a culturally encapsulated individual.
- Obtain formal training in multicultural counseling and career development (Leung, 1996).
- Understand the cultural contexts within which career and vocational problems emerge (e.g., families, workplaces, communities; Leong & Hartung, 1997).
- Recognize and assess the potential influences of culture on perceptions toward assessment and on testing processes and outcomes (Leong & Hartung, 1997).
- Understand the potential for misassessment due to cultural biases in theoretical models or personal training that might lead to culturally inappropriate interventions (Leong & Hartung, 1997).
- Engage in assessment of the cultural background and characteristics of each client (Leung, 1996).
- Select career assessment instruments that are specific to the needs of the client and appropriate for use with members of the client's racial-ethnic, cultural, or linguistic groups (Leung, 1996).
- Actively seek alternative interpretations of the results and interpret their meaning from the cultural context of the test taker (Leong & Hartung, 1997).
- Consider alternatives to testing when cultural factors may impede attainment of the desired outcome (e.g., qualitative assessments, foregoing testing altogether; Subich, 1996).
- Understand and address the potential cultural dynamics that can occur during the communication of test results (Leung, 1996; Leong & Hartung, 1997).
- Use assessment to increase (rather than decrease) clients' perceptions of available options and recognize the potential individual and social consequences involved in using tests to make important, potentially life-altering decisions (Leung, 1996).
- Know when to engage in consultation with, or make a referral to, someone who has competencies to address a given situation more effectively than you can (Marsella & Leong, 1995).

to be identified in the career literature with existing career assessments, including, but not limited to:

- A lack of appropriate norms for specific racial-ethnic groups for many of the most widely used instruments.
- The influence of English language proficiency and the need for appropriate translations of tests into different languages.
- The potential conflicts that may arise when using tests for purposes that may be culturally incongruent for people of color.
- The need for multicultural counseling training to promote appropriate test use and interpretation with people of color.

CAREER DEVELOPMENT OF PEOPLE OF COLOR

In this section, we highlight empirical studies that address the career development processes of people of color in the United States. We pay particular attention to those studies conducted since 1994. For earlier reviews of the literature, see

Byars and McCubbin (2001), Leong (1995), and Leung (1995). We organize our review into sections pertaining to the major concepts arising from the literature on career development theory and practice with people of color.

Racial-Ethnic Identity and Acculturation   Helms and Piper (1994) have cogently argued that race, as a nominal variable in research, is an inappropriate target of study in investigations of career development. They note that studies relying on nominal racial classifications and comparisons (e.g., Whites versus African Americans) are likely to yield inconsistent results and potentially contribute to negative stereotypes about the career behavior and development of people of color. Instead, Helms and Piper recommended that racial identity theory serve as a sociopolitical conceptualization of race within studies of career development and provided a set of hypotheses about how racial identity (1) interacts with the processes and outcomes of career development and (2) influences satisfaction and satisfactoriness in the work environment. Specifically, they proposed the idea that *racial salience* (defined as the extent to which a person believes, correctly or incorrectly, that race significantly defines his or her options in the world of work) will play a moderating role in the career development of people of color. Racial salience is assumed to affect perceptions of access to the opportunity structure and, in turn, educational and career aspirations. In addition, they suggested that African American workers' satisfaction within organizations will likely be a function of racial salience and that satisfactoriness of African American workers within organizations will also be a function of racial attitudes.

Similarly, Leong and Chou (1994) provided an integrative review of the career literature with respect to the role of ethnic identity and acculturation in the vocational behavior of Asian Americans. They hypothesized that ethnic identity and acculturation among Asian Americans are likely to be related to occupational stereotyping and segregation, occupational discrimination, work attitudes, occupational choices and interests, occupational aspirations/expectations, career maturity, and occupational prestige and mobility.

A number of studies have addressed the connections of racial-ethnic identity to various aspects of career development for people of color, which have produced mixed findings generally supporting a relationship. For example, Gloria and Hird (1999) found that college students of color differed from White college students in ethnic identity, trait anxiety, and career decision-making self-efficacy, suggesting that ethnic identity variables are more important for students of color than for Whites. They also found that ethnic identity variables and trait anxiety predicted career decision-making self-efficacy for students of color. However, Carter and Constantine (2000) found that racial identity predicted different aspects of career development based on racial group membership. Specifically, they found significant relationships between African American racial identity attitudes and life role salience but not to career maturity, whereas for Asian Americans, they found significant relationships of racial identity attitudes to career maturity but not to life role salience. C. C. Jackson and Neville (1998) also found mixed results by gender supporting the hypothesis that racial identity is related to vocational identity and confidence in setting goals among African American college students. Racial identity predicted both vocational identity and confidence in setting goals for women, but it only predicted confidence in setting goals for men. Conversely, Evans and Herr (1994) found that racial identity and perceptions of discrimination did not predict the racial traditionality of career aspirations of African American college students.

One explanation of the mixed results concerning the relationships of racial and ethnic identity development to career development may be due to problems identified in the measurement of racial identity development. However, the majority of the findings indicate that racial-ethnic identity is an important variable related to the career development of people of color.

Educational and Career Barriers and Supports   As the field of career psychology expands the scope of inquiry into the experiences and concerns of people of color, there has been increasing attention to understanding and investigating experiences of real and perceived barriers and their influence on career development processes and outcomes. For example, Luzzo (1993) reported that African Americans, Asian Americans, Hispanics, and Filipino Americans were more likely to perceive their racial status as a barrier to career development than were European Americans. Similarly, McWhirter (1997) compared Mexican American and European American high school juniors and seniors with respect to perceived barriers in the formulation and pursuit of educational and career goals. She found that the Mexican American students anticipated more future barriers than Whites did in their pursuit of educational and career goals. Girls also perceived more barriers than did boys. Luzzo and McWhirter (2001) examined perceived educational and career-related barriers and coping self-efficacy. Women and students of color anticipated significantly more career-related barriers, while students of color also exhibited more perceived educational barriers and lower self-efficacy for coping with perceived career-related barriers relative to their European American counterparts. Burlew and Johnson (1992) suggested that barriers to success may be more prominent for people of color in nontraditional careers (e.g., law, engineering, medicine) than for those in more traditional careers.

Given increasing concerns with overcoming barriers to the success of students of color in math and science careers, Catsambis (1994) examined gender differences in learning opportunities, achievement, and choice in mathematics among gender-balanced samples of White, African American, and Latino/a junior high and high school students. Overall, female and male students had similar test scores and grades, but female students tended to have less interest in math and less confidence in their math abilities. Gender differences were the largest among Latino/as and the smallest among African Americans. The major barriers to math achievement for students of color of both sexes were limited learning opportunities and consequent low levels of achievement.

Shifting from a focus solely on barriers to consideration of sources of support, a number of investigators have sought to increase our understanding of how people of color overcome social, institutional, and economic obstacles during the course of career development. For example, Kenny, Blustein, Chaves, Grossman, and Gallagher (2003) investigated the relationship between perceived resources and barriers in two samples of inner-city ninth-grade youth (mostly students of color). Results indicated that perceived general support and kinship support were related to behavioral and attitudinal indexes of school engagement, career aspirations, expectations for attaining career success, and importance of work in the future. Similarly, Chung, Baskin, and Case (1999) attempted to understand the possible effects of fathers, role models, SES, social support, and career intervention programs on the career development of African American men. They used unstructured interviews with African American men of various demographic backgrounds and career paths. Several major themes were evident from these interviews, including:

- The importance of financial support and role-modeling effects of a father.
- Social support, especially parental support, influences the educational and vocational decisions of some individuals.
- School programs that help ethnic minority students to explore various career opportunities seem influential to the development of career aspirations.
- Experiences with racism continue to be a career obstacle for African Americans.

Furthermore, Fisher and Padmawidjaja (1999) examined parental factors that influence career development among African American and Mexican American college students. Their findings indicated that parents influenced their children through encouragement, educational expectations, critical life events, vicarious learning, and work identity. Conversely, Juntunen et al. (2001) found that a lack of support from parents, school personnel, or significant others (particularly for women) were significant career obstacles in their study of a small sample of American Indian adults.

M. A. Jackson and Nutini (2002) conducted a qualitative analysis of interviews with a mixed group of middle school students from low-income families. On the basis of their data, they presented a tentative conceptual model for assessing *contextual barriers and resources* and *psychological barriers and resources*. Contextual barriers included living in a community and attending school in an unsafe environment, discrimination, low income, and negative peer pressure. Psychological barriers included low self-efficacy for academics and perceptions of unequal opportunities for education. Contextual resources included family support, positive role models, cultural support, and school community support. Psychological resources included high coping efficacy for discrimination, bicultural competence, beliefs that racial-ethnic discrimination could be overcome, and coping strategies for managing peer conflict, stress, and pressure.

These findings indicate that educational and career barriers and supports may come from some obvious and some less obvious sources, mostly outside the direct control or influence of individuals. Interventions designed to reduce barriers and establish supports need to be congruent with the cultural backgrounds and expectations of the individuals involved.

Educational Expectations and Persistence   Historical oppression is thought to have subtle, long-lasting influences on many dimensions of the career development of people of color (Gainor, 2001). Studies indicate that there are a number of important variables associated with academic expectations and persistence. Contextual barriers arising from conditions of poverty (e.g., discrimination, community violence, limited learning opportunities, lower parental education) have been shown to be associated with poor educational outcomes for students of color (Catsambis, 1994; Trusty, 2002; Trusty, Ng, & Plata, 2000); and Mau (2003) found that Latino/a students were less likely to persist than White students in science and engineering career aspirations, all other factors being equal. However, of particular importance, various forms of social support were among the most frequently identified factors contributing to high levels of persistence and success (Gloria & Ho, 2003; Gloria & Robinson Kurpius, 2001; Gloria, Robinson Kurpius, Hamilton, & Willson, 1999). Social support from family, peers, and school-community mentorship have been found to be associated with a wide variety of outcomes, including school engagement, aspirations, work role salience, expectations of educational and career success, and academic persistence (Kenny et al., 2003).

There have been mixed findings related to the relative influence of gender and culture on the educational and career expectations of different racial-ethnic groups. For example, Trusty (2002) found that involvement in school, SES, parents' expectations, parental school involvement, and high school behavior differentially predicted African American adolescents' educational expectations among males and females. Specifically, academic reading scores were directly related to African American adolescent women's educational expectations, while math scores and parental involvement contributed to African American adolescent men's educational expectations. Alternatively, McWhirter, Hackett, and Bandalos (1998) provided evidence of the primacy of culture over gender in predicting educational and career expectations of Mexican American girls. Specifically, they found more differences between Mexican American and European American high school girls than they did between boys and girls of Mexican American ancestry.

Academic and career expectations are likely to influence academic and career persistence for people of color, which has been an area of increasing attention in the career literature. Gloria and colleagues (Gloria & Ho, 2003; Gloria & Robinson Kurpius, 2001; Gloria et al., 1999) conducted a series of studies to examine the relation of social support, university comfort, and self-beliefs (i.e., self-esteem and college-related self-efficacy) to the academic persistence decisions of three different racial ethnic groups: African American, Asian American, and American Indian university students. Social support (perceived social support from family and friends; mentoring within the academic setting) was the strongest predictor of academic persistence for all three groups, and positive perceptions of the university environment were particularly important for African Americans and American Indians. Also, differences were found among Asian American subgroups as to the importance of social support, university comfort, and self-beliefs in predicting academic persistence (Gloria & Ho, 2003). In a similar study, Tomlinson-Clarke (1994) followed a group of African American (60%), Hispanic (18%), and White (18%) college students over a three-year period to examine the relationships among academic comfort, occupational orientation, and academic persistence. Tomlinson-Clarke found that relationships between academic comfort and occupational orientation differed by racial group but did not find a relationship between academic comfort and persistence for African American, Hispanic, or White students.

Although there have been some mixed findings in the research concerning academic expectations and persistence, it is clear that factors related to gender, culture, social class, social support, academic environment, self-esteem, and self-efficacy are important. The likely connections between academic expectations and persistence, and the outcomes of both, will continue to be fruitful areas of investigation for years to come as institutions continue to work toward increasing the diversity of students at the upper levels of academic achievement. (See Arbona, Chapter 22, this volume, for a more complete discussion of issues related to educational achievement.)

Educational and Career Aspirations   Career aspirations have often been hypothesized to be important influences on future career choices and behavior, yet they are not always directly tied to career choice outcomes. For example, research has shown that Latino/a and African American youth often have career aspirations that are more prestigious and desirable than the occupations that they actually enter (Arbona, 1990; Arbona & Novy, 1990). Similarly, Qian and Blair (1999) found that (a) while individual educational performance is important for all racial-ethnic groups, human and financial capital have stronger influences on educational aspirations for Whites than for racial-ethnic minority group members, and that (b) parental involvement in school activities has a strong impact on educational aspirations for African Americans and Hispanics. Thus, despite widespread conditions of poverty and discrimination during the career development of people of color, racial-ethnic minority youth tend to develop aspirations that are as high or higher than their White counterparts. Recent research has sought to assist in our understanding of this counterintuitive set of conditions.

King and Multon (1996) found that the career aspirations of African American junior high students were greatly influenced by television role models, particularly those of African American descent. They observed that these students exhibited higher levels of interests in specific careers after viewing television characters' satisfaction with such careers. Given the propensity for stereotypes in popular mass media outlets, the role of television and the types of role models children of color observe (e.g., athletes and rappers) cannot be discounted with respect to their developing educational and career aspirations. Similarly, Tan et al. (2000) found that frequent viewing of American television and positive parental communication led to higher educational aspirations among Hispanic children.

Chung, Loeb, and Gonzo (1996) investigated the factors influencing the educational and career aspirations of African American college freshman on a predominately White university campus. Chung et al. found that African American men had lower educational aspirations than their female counterparts. However, gender differences in educational aspirations did not translate into gender differences in career aspiration. Instead, the most important predictor of higher occupational aspirations was father's occupation, in which higher status fathers tended to be associated with higher aspirations among students. Similarly, Plunkett and Bamaca-Gomez (2003) found that parental educational level, language spoken at home, and gender were predictive of the educational aspirations among a sample of adolescents from Mexican-origin immigrant families. In another study, Reyes, Kobus, and Gillock (1999) found that compared to females aspiring to highly female-dominated careers, females aspiring to highly male-dominated careers were more acculturated, earned higher grade point averages (GPAs), higher achievement scores in science and social studies, and held higher educational aspirations and expectations; a greater number of this group also evidenced a clear understanding of the steps needed to achieve career goals. Finally, Kim, Rendon, and Valadez (1998) found that there were significant differences in the level of educational aspirations among six different groups of Asian American 10th graders (i.e., South Asian, Korean, Japanese, Chinese, Filipino, and Southeast Asian), highlighting the importance of within-group differences in the expression of educational and career aspirations.

These findings make it apparent that (1) racial-ethnic stereotypes might lead some to ignore within-group differences as to aspirations, (2) familial and social role models play an important role in the development of educational and career aspirations, and (3) television and other popular media outlets are likely to play a critical role in shaping the educational and career aspirations of youth.

Career Maturity Super's (1953) concept of career maturity has been the source of some controversy in the career literature with people of color. For example, a number of studies have contrasted African Americans or Hispanics with Whites on measures of career maturity and most often found that Whites tend to be more career mature than their African American or Hispanic counterparts (Fouad & Keeley, 1992; Lundberg, Osborne, & Miner, 1997; Rojewski, 1994; Westbrook & Sanford, 1991). Rojewski's study found that career-immature students were more likely to be African American, educationally disadvantaged, male, and indecisive about their career choice. M. T. Brown (1995) has suggested that research showing lower career maturity of African Americans relative to Whites has often been confounded by SES because lower SES African Americans are often compared to Whites of higher SES. As a result, Leong and Serafica (1995) and M. T. Brown both questioned the applicability of the career maturity concept for people of color because of the unique contextual factors that might be the cause of the differences found in the studies described previously. In addition, Leung (1996) and Brown (1995) have both suggested that there is insufficient evidence to support the use of the Career Maturity Inventory (the most commonly used instrument in research on this topic) with people of color. There is a need for new research in this area with people of color.

Career Values Many career counselors believe that congruence between career values and career choices is critical for optimal career decision making and satisfaction (Yost & Corbishley, 1987). The values important to an individual's culture, career values within groups, and the divergence of career values between groups have been targets of inquiry for career researchers. Vacha-Haase et al. (1994) examined differences in five intrinsic and extrinsic career values with a predominately African American and Hispanic sample of college students. Their findings showed that racial-ethnic minority men tended to place more importance on creativity, aesthetics, altruism, social relations, and lifestyle within their potential careers than did their female counterparts. Given that the instrument used to assess participants' career values was normed with predominately Caucasian women and men, Vacha-Haase and her colleagues suggested that separate gender norms are needed on career values assessments, especially when such instruments are used with people of color.

G. C. Jackson and Healy (1996) surveyed a sample of African American and Latino college freshman as to the relationship among their role salience, career maturity, and socioeconomic status. Despite the fact that African Americans in the sample had higher SES than their Latino/a counterparts, there were no differences by ethnicity or SES, but women were found to place a higher value on their role in the home and family than did men overall. Similarly, Luzzo (1994) investigated differences in students' commitment to work by gender and ethnicity with a large, diverse sample of undergraduate students. Controlling for SES, Luzzo found that women exhibited greater levels of commitment to work than did men, but no significant differences in commitment to work by ethnicity were uncovered.

Although the research in this area continues to be sparse, racial-ethnic differences in career values have not been found. However, gender differences between men and women with respect to role salience appear to be stable across racial-ethnic groups. This continues to be an important area for future study.

Career-Related Self-Efficacy   Hackett and Betz (1981) were the first to describe and investigate the role of self-efficacy, a social cognitive variable, in the career development process. Since its application to vocational psychology, self-efficacy has been the focus of numerous studies investigating the career development of persons of color. A number of studies have found that self-efficacy beliefs are important predictors of educational and vocational outcomes for persons of color (e.g., Bores-Rangel, Church, Szendre, & Reeves, 1990; Gainor & Lent, 1998; Post-Kammer & Smith, 1986; Solberg, O'Brien, Villareal, Kennel, & Davis, 1993). Other researchers have reported that occupational self-efficacy predicted career interests (Post, Stewart, & Smith, 1991) and that students of color may be less likely to develop strong self-efficacy beliefs than other students (Hackett, Betz, Casas, & Rocha-Singh, 1992; Lauver & Jones, 1991).

Three separate studies investigating the career development of African Americans, Mexican Americans, and Asian Americans have found support for the relation between self-efficacy and career choice. Specifically, Gainor and Lent (1998) explored the relationship of racial identity and social cognitive variables to the math-related interests and math-related academic choice intentions of African American college students. Gainor and Lent reported that across levels of racial identity attitudes, self-efficacy and outcome expectations predicted interests, and interests predicted choice intentions. In another study, Flores and O'Brien (2002) examined the relation of several contextual and social cognitive variables to Mexican American adolescent women's career choice prestige, career choice traditionality, and career aspirations. Acculturation and nontraditional career self-efficacy were the strongest predictors of career choice prestige and career choice traditionality. Background contextual variables are hypothesized to indirectly predict self-efficacy through their influences on Bandura's four sources of self-efficacy beliefs; however, the contextual variables of acculturation level, feminist attitudes, mother's education, and mother's career traditionality did not predict nontraditional career self-efficacy. Finally, Tang, Fouad, and Smith (1999) reported that level of acculturation, family involvement, and self-efficacy were important predictors of traditionality of career choices (e.g., Realistic and Investigative) among Asian American college students. It is interesting that the relationship between interest and career choice was not significant for this sample of Asian Americans.

Career decision-making self-efficacy, or an individual's confidence in his or her abilities to make decisions about careers, has also drawn interest among vocational researchers. Recent investigations have provided inconsistent results on career decision-making self-efficacy levels among students of color and their White counterparts. In one study, Chung (2002) reported that African Americans scored higher than Whites on career decision-making self-efficacy and career commitment. On the other hand, Gloria and Hird (1999) found that White students had higher career decision-making self-efficacy and lower ethnic identity and other-group orientation than students of color. These researchers also reported that students who had declared a major tended to also have higher career decision-making self-efficacy and lower trait anxiety than undeclared students. Ethnic identity and other-group orientation were significant predictors of career decision-making self-efficacy for students of color.

There is evidence to suggest that occupational self-efficacy for careers at various levels of status and prestige varies as a function of SES (Hackett et al., 1992; Hannah & Kahn, 1989; Lauver & Jones, 1991), which indicates that racial and ethnic group differences in career self-efficacy may be confounded by social class differences (Arbona, 1995). In addition, scholars have hypothesized that self-efficacy may be a stronger predictor than career interests in the career selection of persons of color.

Overall, the concept of self-efficacy has become a critically important variable in the study of the career development of people of color. It has been tied to educational and vocational outcomes, career interests, and career choice. However, despite findings concerning racial-ethnic differences in self-efficacy in some studies, there continue to be concerns about how these findings should be interpreted given the potential for social class confounds. Nevertheless, career self-efficacy research has contributed substantially to our understanding of the career development of people of color, and it will undoubtedly be a rich topic of investigation for many years to come.

Career Interests   Investigations of Holland's typology theory with people of color have examined endorsement of interest types and the cultural validity of the model with persons of color, and studies have produced mixed outcomes. Researchers have reported that there are some differences in interests by Holland types between racial-ethnic groups (Hansen, Scullard, & Haviland, 2000; Haverkamp, Collins, & Hansen, 1994; Leung, Ivey, & Suzuki, 1994; Park & Harrison, 1995; Swanson, 1992), while others have found that the differences are relatively small or virtually nonexistent (Day & Rounds, 1998; Fouad & Spreda, 1995; Hansen et al., 2000; Haverkamp et al., 1994; Tang, 2002). In a recent study, Armstrong, Hubert, and Rounds (2003) stated that their "results suggest that distinctions made between Holland's types may be less salient for some groups and that additional work is needed to produce interest measures with improved structural validity" (p. 297). Career counselors should be careful to avoid assuming that individuals from various racial-ethnic groups will exclusively endorse certain career interests. Moreover, career counselors need to note that not all clients choose careers based on personal interests, as researchers have found that the congruence between interests and occupational choice may be weaker for persons of color due to both real and perceived employment barriers (M. T. Brown, 1995). It is important for career counselors to consider the relation of cultural variables (e.g., acculturation, parental support) to career interests in persons of color.

Examinations of the cultural validity of the hexagonal model have supported the circular structure of the model across racial-ethnic groups (Day, Rounds, & Swaney, 1998; Fouad & Dancer, 1992; Fouad, Harmon, & Borgen, 1997; Hansen et al., 2000; Ryan, Tracey, & Rounds, 1996) but have failed to support the circumplex model (i.e., equal distances between the Holland types to produce a true hexagon; Fouad & Dancer, 1992; Fouad et al., 1997; Hansen et al., 2000). Research seems to consistently indicate that gender differences in measured interests tend to be larger than racial-ethnic differences (Arbona, 2000), and gender and socioeconomic differences in these validity studies highlight the importance of attending to within-group variability in the career counseling process (Fouad, 2002; Haverkamp et al., 1994; Leung et al., 1994; Park & Harrison, 1995; Ryan et al., 1996).

Career Choice and Decision Making   Decision-making approaches focus on the process that people follow to select a career. The notion of *choice* in career decision making has been one of the most widely criticized concepts in the career development literature when it comes to people of color because the variables that contribute to the decisions people arrive at concerning their career selection are likely to vary from one culture to another, and the influence of oppression in the lives of people of color often limits the number of real and perceived choices they have. For example, some researchers have noted that the decision-making process may differ for people based on whether they come from collectivistic or individualistic cultural backgrounds (e.g., Leong & Chou, 1994). In the former, decisions may be made based on what is best for the family or community and with input from family members. For example, in their study of the career perspectives of American Indians, Juntunen et al. (2001) found that the concept of career was often connected to the contribution made to the community. On the other hand, individuals from individualistic cultures may arrive at their career choice based on personal interests and values.

Researchers have explored factors that may influence the career and educational choices across diverse cultural groups. In one study, Trusty et al. (2000) found that the relationship between educational choice and race/ethnicity was strongest for men at lower SES levels and weakest for women at higher levels of SES. Another study found that African American college women valued flexibility in pursuing career and family concerns as most important when making career decisions (Weathers, Thompson, Robert, & Rodriguez, 1994). Tang et al. (1999) reported that acculturation, family involvement, and self-efficacy predicted selection of traditional careers in a sample of Asian American college students. However, interests and SES were not significant predictors of career choice for these participants. These findings support earlier speculations about the sources of career choice traditionality among Asian Americans. Finally, lack of career information may also limit the career options of people of color. Martin (1991) warned that limited occupational information might adversely impact the career decision making of Native Americans who live on reservations because they have limited exposure to appropriate role models and adequate sources of quality information.

Job Satisfaction   Trait and factor theories posit that job satisfaction, or the fulfillment and happiness individuals experiences in their job, is determined by the correspondence between the work environment and the person. Job satisfaction remains a relatively understudied construct in career research with persons of color. Most studies have examined aspects of the work environment that may be related to job satisfaction among persons of color. A number of these studies have reported negative experiences of African American professionals in their work setting. In a study with African American professionals working in predominantly White employment settings, Holder and Vaux (1998) found that race-related stressors accounted for more variance in workers' job satisfaction than did routine stressors, personal and social resources, and locus of control. Finally, Ibarra (1995) reported that African American managers experienced same-race relationships to be more supportive than their cross-racial relationships at work.

Although job satisfaction has been a central variable in the history of research on career development, there is still a great deal of work to be done concerning the satisfaction of people of color in the workplace. Whereas the majority of research has addressed African Americans, there are rich opportunities to address job satisfaction with other groups as well.

SUMMARY

People of color represent an ever-increasing proportion of the U.S. population and labor force. Although people of color were historically neglected in the career development literature, a substantial amount of new research has been produced within a relatively short time period, reflecting broader trends toward multiculturalism in career counseling and vocational psychology. More often than not, traditional career theories have been found to be valid for people of color (at least in the published literature), yet a number of substantial and pernicious problems exist that limit both research and application. In addition, however, research has demonstrated that there are clear differences between people of color and Whites on a host of important career development variables. Although a number of racial-ethnic group-specific theories of career development have appeared in the literature (e.g., Cheatham, 1990; Fouad & Bingham, 1996; Leong & Hartung, 1997), very little research has been produced on these models. Furthermore, it is readily apparent from data arising from a variety of sources that education, employment, and income disparities have been produced and maintained across time by complexly interacting factors at both micro- and macrolevels of U.S. society. Indeed, although career counselors typically work with clients individually and in small groups, the career development of persons of color is influenced more broadly and substantially by larger historical, cultural, and systemic factors that are often beyond the reach of counseling interventions that target individuals.

REFERENCES

American Educational Research Association, American Psychological Association, & National Council on Measurement in Education. (1999). *Standards for educational and psychological testing.* Washington, DC: Author.

American Psychological Association. (2002). *Guidelines on multicultural education, training, research, practice, and organizational change for psychologists.* Available from American Psychological Association web site, www.apa.org.

Anastasi, A., & Urbina, S. (1997). *Psychological testing* (7th ed.). Upper Saddle River, NJ: Prentice-Hall.

Arbona, C. (1990). Career counseling research and Hispanics: A review of the literature. *Counseling Psychologist, 18,* 300–323.

Arbona, C. (1995). Theory and research on racial and ethnic minorities: Hispanic Americans. In F. T. L. Leong (Ed.), *Career development and vocational behavior of racial ethnic minorities* (pp. 37–66). Mahwah, NJ: Erlbaum.

Arbona, C. (2000). Practice and research in career counseling and development—1999. *Career Development Quarterly, 49,* 98–134.

Arbona, C., & Novy, D. M. (1990). Noncognitive dimensions as predictors of college success among Black, Mexican-American, and White students. *Journal of College Student Development, 31,* 415–422.

Armstrong, P. I., Hubert, L., & Rounds, J. (2003). Circular unidimensional scaling: A new look at group differences in interest structure. *Journal of Counseling Psychology, 50,* 297–308.

Bertrand, M., & Mullainathan, S. (2003). *Are Emily and Greg more employable than Lakisha and Jamal? A field experiment on labor market discrimination.* Manuscript in preparation. Available from http://economics.uchicago.edu/download/_DISCRIMINATION.pdf.

Bingham, R. P., & Ward, C. M. (1994). Career counseling with ethnic minority women. In W. B. Walsh & S. H. Osipow (Eds.), *Career counseling for women: Contemporary topics in vocational psychology* (pp. 165–195). Mahwah, NJ: Erlbaum.

Blustein, D. L., & Ellis, M. V. (2000). The cultural context of career assessment. *Journal of Career Assessment, 8,* 379–390.

Bores-Rangel, E., Church, A. T., Szendre, D., & Reeves, C. (1990). Self-efficacy in relation to occupational consideration and academic performance in high school equivalency students. *Journal of Counseling Psychology, 37,* 407–418.

Brown, D. (2000). Theory and the school-to-work transition: Are the recommendations suitable for cultural minorities? *Career Development Quarterly, 48,* 370–375.

Brown, M. T. (1995). The career development of African Americans: Theoretical and empirical issues. In F. T. L. Leong (Ed.), *Career development and vocational behavior of racial ethnic minorities* (pp. 7–36). Mahwah, NJ: Erlbaum.

Bureau of Labor Statistics. (2003). *Labor force statistics from the current population survey.* Available from Bureau of Labor Statistics web site: http://www.bls.gov/cps/home.htm.

Burlew, A. K., & Johnson, J. L. (1992). Role conflict and career advancement among African American women in nontraditional professions. *Career Development Quarterly, 40,* 302–312.

Byars, A. M., & McCubbin, L. D. (2001). Trends in career development research with racial/ethnic minorities. In J. G. Ponterotto, J. M. Casas, L. A. Suzuki, & C. M. Alexander (Eds.), *Handbook of multicultural counseling* (2nd ed., pp. 633–654). Thousand Oaks, CA: Sage.

Carter, R. T., & Constantine, M. G. (2000). Career maturity, life role salience, and racial/ethnic identity among Black and Asian American college students. *Journal of Career Assessment, 8,* 173–187.

Carter, R. T., & Cook, D. A. (1992). A culturally relevant perspective for understanding the career paths of visible racial/ethnic group people. In H. D. Lea & Z. B. Leibowitz (Eds.), *Adult career development* (pp. 192–217). Alexandria, VA: National Career Development Association.

Catsambis, S. (1994). The path to math: Gender and racial-ethnic differences in mathematics participation from middle school to high school. *Sociology of Education, 67,* 199–215.

Cheatham, H. E. (1990). Africentricity and career development of African Americans. *Career Development Quarterly, 38,* 334–346.

Chung, Y. B. (2002). Career decision-making self-efficacy and career commitment: Gender and ethnic differences among college students. *Journal of Career Development, 28*(4), 277–284.

Chung, Y. B., Baskin, M. L., & Case, A. B. (1999). Career development of black males: Case studies. *Journal of Career Development, 25,* 161–171.

Chung, Y. B., Loeb, J. W., & Gonzo, S. T. (1996). Factors predicting the educational and career aspirations of black college freshman. *Journal of Career Development, 23,* 127–136.

Cook, E. P., Heppner, M. J., & O'Brien, K. M. (2002). Career development of women of color and white women: Assumptions, conceptualizations, and interventions from an ecological perspective. *Career Development Quarterly, 50,* 291–304.

Cushman, P. (1995). *Constructing the self, constructing America.* New York: Addison-Wesley.

Dawis, R. V., & Lofquist, L. H. (1984). *A psychological theory of work adjustment.* Minneapolis: University of Minnesota Press.

Day, S. X., & Rounds, J. (1998). Universality of vocational interest structure among racial and ethnic minorities. *American Psychologist, 53,* 728–736.

Day, S. X., Rounds, J., & Swaney, K. (1998). The structure of vocational interests for diverse racial-ethnic groups. *Psychological Science, 9,* 40–44.

DeFunis v. Odegaard, 416 U.S. 312, 350 (1974).

Evans, K. M., & Herr, E. L. (1994). The influence of racial identity and the perception of discrimination on the career aspirations of African American men and women. *Journal of Vocational Behavior, 44*, 173–184.

Fisher, T. A., & Padmawidjaja, I. (1999). Parental influences on career development perceived by African American and Mexican American college students. *Journal of Multicultural Counseling and Development, 27*, 136–152.

Flores, L. Y., & O'Brien, K. M. (2002). The career development of Mexican American adolescent women: A test of social cognitive career theory. *Journal of Counseling Psychology, 49*, 14–27.

Fouad, N. A. (1993). Cross-cultural vocational assessment. *Career Development Quarterly, 42*, 4–13.

Fouad, N. A. (2002). Cross-cultural differences in vocational interests: Between-groups differences on the Strong Interest Inventory. *Journal of Counseling Psychology, 49*, 283–289.

Fouad, N. A., & Bingham, R. P. (1995). Career counseling with racial ethnic minorities. In W. B. Walsh & S. H. Osipow (Eds.), *Handbook of vocational psychology: Theory, research, and practice* (2nd ed., pp. 331–365). Mahwah, NJ: Erlbaum.

Fouad, N. A., & Dancer, L. S. (1992). Cross-cultural structure of interests: Mexico and the United States. *Journal of Vocational Behavior, 40*, 129–143.

Fouad, N. A., Harmon, L. W., & Borgen, F. H. (1997). Structure of interests in employed male and female members of U.S. racial-ethnic minority and nonminority groups. *Journal of Counseling Psychology, 44*, 339–345.

Fouad, N. A., & Keeley, T. J. (1992). The relationship between attitudinal and behavioral aspects of career maturity. *Career Development Quarterly, 40*, 257–271.

Fouad, N. A., & Spreda, S. L. (1995). Use of interest inventories with special populations: Women and minority groups. *Journal of Career Assessment, 3*, 453–468.

Gainor, K. A. (2001). Vocational assessment with culturally diverse populations. In L. A. Suzuki, J. G. Ponterotto, & P. J. Meller (Eds.), *Handbook of multicultural assessment* (2nd ed., pp. 169–189). San Francisco: Jossey-Bass.

Gainor, K. A., & Lent, R. W. (1998). Social cognitive expectations and racial identity attitudes in predicting the math choice intentions of black college students. *Journal of Counseling Psychology, 45*, 403–413.

Gloria, A. M., & Hird, J. S. (1999). Influences of ethnic and nonethnic variables on the career decision-making self-efficacy of college students. *Career Development Quarterly, 48*, 157–174.

Gloria, A. M., & Ho, T. A. (2003). Environmental, social, and psychological experiences of Asian American undergraduates: Examining issues of academic persistence. *Journal of Counseling and Development, 81*, 93–105.

Gloria, A. M., & Robinson Kurpius, S. E. (2001). Influences of self-beliefs, social support, and comfort in the university environment on the academic nonpersistence decisions of American Indian undergraduates. *Cultural Diversity and Ethnic Minority Psychology, 7*, 88–102.

Gloria, A. M., Robinson Kurpius, S. E., Hamilton, K. D., & Willson, M. S. (1999). African American students' persistence at a predominantly white university: Influence of social support, university comfort, and self-beliefs. *Journal of College Student Development, 40*, 257–268.

Gottfredson, L. S. (1996). Gottfredson's theory of circumscription and compromise. In D. Brown, L. Brooks, & Associates (Eds.), *Career choice and development* (3rd ed., pp. 179–232). San Francisco, Jossey-Bass.

Gratz v. Bollinger et al., 539 U.S. 516 (2003).

Greenhaus, J. H., Parasuraman, S., & Wormley, W. M. (1990). Effects of race on organizational experiences, job performance evaluations, and career outcomes. *Academy of Management Journal, 33*, 64–86.

Grutter v. Bollinger et al., 539 U.S. 241 (2003).

Hackett, G., & Betz, N. E. (1981). A self-efficacy approach to the career development of women. *Journal of Vocational Behavior, 18*, 326–339.

Hackett, G., Betz, N. E., Casas, J. M., & Rocha-Singh, I. A. (1992). Gender, ethnicity, and social cognitive factors predicting the academic achievement of students in engineering. *Journal of Counseling Psychology, 39*, 527–538.

Hannah, J. S., & Kahn, S. E. (1989). The relationship of SES and gender to the occupational choices of grade 12 students. *Journal of Vocational Behavior, 34,* 161–178.

Hansen, J. C., Scullard, M. G., & Haviland, M. G. (2000). The interest structures of Native American college students. *Journal of Career Assessment, 8,* 159–172.

Hartung, P. J., Vandiver, B. J., Leong, F. T., Pope, M., Niles, S. G., & Farrow, B. (1998). Appraising cultural identity in career development assessment and counseling. *Career Development Quarterly, 46,* 276–293.

Haverkamp, B. E., Collins, R. C., & Hansen, J. C. (1994). Structure of interest of Asian-American college students. *Journal of Counseling Psychology, 41,* 256–264.

Helms, J. E., & Piper, R. E. (1994). Implications of racial identity theory for vocational psychology. *Journal of Vocational Behavior, 44,* 124–138.

Holder, J. C., & Vaux, A. (1998). African American professionals: Coping with occupational stress in predominantly white work environments. *Journal of Vocational Behavior, 53,* 315–333.

Holland, J. L. (1959). A theory of vocational choice. *Journal of Counseling Psychology, 6,* 35–45.

Hotchkiss, L., & Borow, H. (1990). Sociological perspectives on career choice and attainment. In D. Brown, L. Brooks & Associates (Eds.), *Career choice and development* (2nd ed., pp. 137–168). San Francisco: Jossey-Bass.

Ibarra, H. (1995). Race, opportunity, and diversity of social circles in managerial networks. *Academy of Management Journal, 38,* 673–703.

Jackson, C. C., & Neville, H. A. (1998). Influence of racial identity attitudes on African American college students' vocational identity and hope. *Journal of Vocational Behavior, 53,* 97–113.

Jackson, G. C., & Healy, C. C. (1996). Career development profiles and interventions for underrepresented college students. *Career Development Quarterly, 44,* 258–269.

Jackson, M. A., & Nutini, C. D. (2002). Hidden resources and barriers in career learning assessment with adolescents vulnerable to discrimination. *Career Development Quarterly, 51*(1), 56–77.

Juntunen, C. L., Barraclough, D. J., Broneck, C. L., Seibel, G. A., Winrow, S. A., & Morin, P. M. (2001). American Indian perspectives on the career journey. *Journal of Counseling Psychology, 48,* 274–285.

Kenny, M. E., Blustein, D. L., Chaves, A., Grossman, J. M., & Gallagher, L. A. (2003). The role of perceived barriers and relational support in the educational and vocational lives of urban high school students. *Journal of Counseling Psychology, 50,* 142–155.

Kim, H., Rendon, L., & Valadez, J. (1998). Student characteristics, school characteristics, and educational aspirations of six Asian American ethnic groups. *Journal of Multicultural Counseling & Development, 26,* 166–176.

King, M. M., & Multon, K. D. (1996). The effects of television role models on the career aspirations of African American junior high school students. *Journal of Career Development, 23,* 111–126.

Krumboltz, J. D. (1979). A social learning theory of career decision making. In A. M. Mitchell, G. B. Jones, & J. D. Krumboltz (Eds.), *Social learning and career decision making.* Cranston, RI: Carroll Press.

Lattimore, R. R., & Borgen, F. H. (1999). Validity of the 1994 Strong Interest Inventory with racial and ethnic groups in the United States. *Journal of Counseling Psychology. 46,* 185–195.

Lauver, P. J., & Jones, R. M. (1991). Factors associated with perceived career options in American Indian, white, and Hispanic rural high school students. *Journal of Counseling Psychology, 38,* 159–166.

Lent, R. W., Brown, S. D., & Hackett, G. (1994). Toward a unifying social cognitive theory of career and academic interest, choice, and performance. *Journal of Vocational Behavior, 45,* 79–122.

Lent, R. W., & Worthington, R. L. (2000). On school-to-work transition, career development theories, and cultural validity. *Career Development Quarterly, 48,* 376–384.

Leong, F. T. (1995). *Career development and vocational behavior of racial and ethnic minorities.* Hillsdale, NJ: Erlbaum.

Leong, F. T., & Brown, M. T. (1995). Theoretical issues in cross-cultural career development: Cultural validity and cultural specificity. In W. B. Walsh & S. H. Osipow (Eds.), *Handbook of vocational psychology* (2nd, pp. 391–426). Mahwah, NJ: Erlbaum.

Leong, F. T., & Chou, E. L. (1994). The role of ethnic identity and acculturation in the vocational behavior of Asian Americans. *Journal of Vocational Behavior, 44,* 155–172.

Leong, F. T., & Hartung, P. J. (1997). Cross-cultural career assessment: Review and prospects for the new millennium. *Journal of Career Assessment, 8,* 391–401.

Leong, F. T., & Serafica, F. C. (1995). Career development of Asian Americans: A research area in need of a good theory. In F. T. L. Leong (Ed.), *Career development and vocational behavior of racial ethnic minorities* (pp. 67–102). Mahwah, NJ: Erlbaum.

Leung, S. A. (1995). Career development and counseling: A multicultural perspective. In J. G. Ponterotto, J. M. Casas, L. A. Suzuki, & C. M. Alexander (Eds.), *Handbook of multicultural counseling* (pp. 549–566). Thousand Oaks, CA: Sage.

Leung, S. A. (1996). Vocational assessment across cultures. In L. A. Susuki, P. J. Meller, & J. G. Ponterotto (Eds.), *Handbook of multicultural assessment* (pp. 475–508). San Francisco: Jossey-Bass.

Leung, S. A., Ivey, D., & Suzuki, L. (1994). Factors affecting the career aspirations of Asian Americans. *Journal of Counseling and Development, 72,* 404–410.

Lundberg, D. J., Osborne, W. L., & Miner, C. U. (1997). Career maturity and personality preferences of Mexican-American and Anglo-American adolescents. *Journal of Career Development, 23,* 203–213.

Luzzo, D. A. (1993). Ethnic differences in college students' perceptions of barriers to career development. *Journal of Multicultural Counseling and Development, 21,* 227–236.

Luzzo, D. A. (1994). An analysis of gender and ethnic differences in college students' commitment to work. *Journal of Employment Counseling, 31,* 38–45.

Luzzo, D. A., & McWhirter, E. H. (2001). Sex and ethnic differences in the perception of educational and career-related barriers and levels of coping efficacy. *Journal of Counseling and Development, 79,* 61–67.

Marsella, A. J., & Leong, F. T. (1995). Cross-cultural issues in personality and career assessment. *Journal of Career Assessment, 3,* 202–218.

Martin, W. E. (1991). Career development and American Indians living on reservations: Cross cultural factors to consider. *Career Development Quarterly, 39,* 273–383.

Mau, W. C. (2003). Factors that influence persistence in science and engineering career aspirations. *Career Development Quarterly, 51,* 234–243.

McWhirter, E. H. (1997). Perceived barriers to education and career: Ethnic and gender differences. *Journal of Vocational Behavior, 50,* 124–140.

McWhirter, E. H., Hackett, G., & Bandalos, D. L. (1998). A causal model of the educational plans and career expectations of Mexican American high school girls. *Journal of Counseling Psychology, 45,* 166–181.

Neville, H. A., Worthington, R. L., & Spanierman, L. B. (2001). Race, power, and multicultural counseling psychology: Understanding white privilege and color-blind racial attitudes. In J. G. Ponterotto, J. M. Casas, L. A. Suzuki, & C. M. Alexander (Eds.), *Handbook of multicultural counseling* (2nd ed., pp. 257–288). Thousand Oaks, CA: Sage.

Osipow, S. H., & Littlejohn, E. M. (1995). Toward a multicultural theory of career development: Prospects and dilemmas. In F. T. Leong (Ed.), *Career development and vocational behavior of racial and ethnic minorities* (pp. 251–261). Hillsdale, NJ: Erlbaum.

Park, S. E., & Harrison, A. A. (1995). Career-related interests and values, perceived control, and acculturation of Asian-American and Caucasian-American college students. *Journal of Applied Social Psychology, 25,* 1184–1203.

Parsons, F. (1909). *Choosing a vocation.* Boston: Houghton Mifflin.

Pedersen, P. B. (1991). Multiculturalism as a generic approach to counseling. *Journal of Counseling and Development, 70,* 6–12.

Pinderhughes, E. (1989). *Understanding race, ethnicity, and power.* New York: Free Press.

Plunkett, S. W., & Bamaca-Gomez, M. Y. (2003). The relationship between parenting, acculturation, and adolescent academics in Mexican-origin immigrant families in Los Angeles. *Hispanic Journal of Behavioral Sciences, 25,* 222–239.

Pope, M. (2000). A brief history of career counseling in the United States. *Career Development Quarterly, 48,* 194–211.

Post, P., Stewart, M. A., & Smith, P. L. (1991). Self-efficacy, interest, and consideration of math/science and non-math/science occupations among black freshmen. *Journal of Vocational Behavior, 38,* 179–186.

Post-Kammer, P., & Smith, P. L. (1986). Sex differences in math and science career self-efficacy among disadvantaged students. *Journal of Vocational Behavior, 29,* 89–101.

Qian, Z., & Blair, S. L. (1999). Racial/ethnic differences in educational aspirations of high school seniors. *Sociological Perspectives, 42,* 605–625.

Reyes, O., Kobus, K., & Gillock, K. (1999). Career aspirations of urban, Mexican American adolescent females. *Hispanic Journal of Behavioral Sciences, 21,* 366–382.

Rojewski, J. W. (1994). Career indecision types for rural adolescents from disadvantaged and nondisadvantaged backgrounds. *Journal of Counseling Psychology, 41,* 356–363.

Ryan, J. M., Tracey, T. J., & Rounds, J. (1996). Generalizability of Holland's structure of vocational interests across ethnicity, gender, and socioeconomic status. *Journal of Counseling Psychology, 43,* 330–337.

Solberg, V. S., O'Brien, K., Villareal, P., Kennel, R., & Davis, B. (1993). Self-efficacy and Hispanic college students: Validation of the College Self-Efficacy Instrument. *Hispanic Journal of Behavioral Sciences, 15,* 80–95.

Subich, L. M. (1996). Addressing diversity in the process of career assessment. In M. L. Savickas & W. B. Walsh (Eds.), *Handbook of career counseling theory and practice* (pp. 277–289). Mahwah, NJ: Erlbaum.

Sue, D., Bernier, J., Durran, A., Feinberg, L., Pedersen, P., Smith, E., et al. (1982). Position paper: Cross cultural counseling competencies. *Counseling Psychologist, 10,* 45–52.

Sue, D. W., Arredondo, P., & McDavis, R. J. (1992). Multicultural counseling competencies and standards: A call to the profession. *Journal of Counseling and Development, 70,* 477–486.

Super, D. E. (1953). A theory of vocational development. *American Psychologist, 8,* 185–190.

Super, D. E., Savickas, M. L., & Super, C. M. (1996). The life-span, life-space approach to careers. In D. Brown, L. Brooks & Associates (Eds.), *Career choice and development* (3rd ed., pp. 121–178). San Francisco: Jossey-Bass.

Swanson, J. L. (1992). The structure of vocational interests for African-American college students. *Journal of Vocational Behavior, 40,* 144–157.

Swanson, J. L., & Gore, P. A. (2000). Advances in vocational psychology: Theory and research. In S. D. Brown & R. W. Lent (Eds.), *Handbook of counseling psychology* (3rd ed., pp. 233–269). New York: Wiley.

Tan, A., Fujioka, Y., Bautista, D., Maldonado, R., Tan, G., & Wright, L. (2000). Influence of television use and parental communication on educational aspirations of Hispanic children. *Howard Journal of Communications, 11,* 107–125.

Tang, M. (2002). A comparison of Asian American, Caucasian American, and Chinese college students: An initial report. *Journal of Multicultural Counseling and Development, 30,* 124–134.

Tang, M., Fouad, N. A., & Smith, P. L. (1999). Asian Americans' career choices: A path model to examine factors influencing their career choices. *Journal of Vocational Behavior, 54,* 142–157.

Three Rivers, A. (1991). *Cultural etiquette.* Indian Valley, VA: Market Wimmin.

Tomlinson-Clarke, S. (1994). A longitudinal study of the relationship between academic comfort, occupational orientation, and persistence among African American, Hispanic, and white college students. *Journal of College Student Development, 35,* 25–28.

Trusty, J. (2002). African American's educational expectations: Longitudinal causal models for women and men. *Journal of Counseling and Development, 80,* 332–345.

Trusty, J., Ng, K., & Plata, M. (2000). Interaction effects of gender, SES and race-ethnicity on postsecondary educational choices of U.S. students. *Career Development Quarterly, 49,* 45–59.

University of California Regents v. Bakke, 438 U.S. 265 (1978).

U.S. Census Bureau. (1990). *Profiles of General Demographic Characteristics for the United States: 1990.* Available from U.S. Census Bureau web site: www.census.gov.

U.S. Census Bureau. (2000a). *Profiles of General Demographic Characteristics: National summary.* Available from U.S. Census Bureau web site: www.census.gov.

U.S. Census Bureau. (2000b). *Statistical Abstracts of the United States.* Available from U.S. Census Bureau web site: www.census.gov.

U.S. Census Bureau. (2003a). *Historical income data.* Available from U.S. Census Bureau web site: www.census.gov.

U.S. Census Bureau. (2003b). *Percent of people 25 years old and over who have completed high school or college, by race, Hispanic origin and sex: Selected years 1940–2002.* Available from U.S. Census Bureau web site: www.census.gov.

Vacha-Haase, T., Walsh, B. D., Kapes, J. T., Dresden, J. H., Thomson, W. A., Ochoa-Shargey, B., et al. (1994). Gender differences on the Values Scale for ethnic minority students. *Journal of Career Assessment, 2,* 408–421.

Vondracek, F. W., Lerner, R. M., & Schulenberg, J. E. (1986). *A life-span contextual approach to career development.* Hillsdale, NJ: Erlbaum.

Walsh, W. B., & Betz, N. E. (2001). *Tests and assessment* (4th ed.). Englewood Cliffs, NJ: Prentice-Hall.

Walsh, W. B., Bingham, R. P., Brown, M. T., & Ward, C. M. (2001). *Career counseling for African Americans.* Mahwah, NJ: Erlbaum.

Warnath, C. F. (1975). Vocational theories: Direction to nowhere. *Personnel and Guidance Journal, 53,* 422–428.

Weathers, P. L., Thompson, C. E., Robert, S., & Rodriguez, J., Jr. (1994). Black college women's career values: A preliminary investigation. *Journal of Multicultural Counseling and Development, 22,* 96–105.

Westbrook, B. W., & Sanford, E. E. (1991). The validity of career maturity attitude measures among black and white high school students. *Career Development Quarterly, 39,* 199–208.

Wilson, F. D., Tienda, M., & Wu, L. (1995). Race and unemployment: Labor Market experiences of black and white men, 1968–1988. *Work and Occupations, 22,* 245–270.

Wilson, W. J. (1996). *When work disappears.* New York: Alfred A. Knopf.

Yost, E. B., & Corbishley, M. A. (1987). *Career counseling: A psychological approach.* San Francisco: Jossey-Bass.

Zinn, H. (1980). *A people's history of the United States.* New York: HarperCollins.

CHAPTER 11

Women's Career Development

Nancy E. Betz

ALTHOUGH IT USED to be assumed that women's careers were not as important as men's because they occupied only short periods of the adult woman's life span, societal changes over the past 40 or 50 years have led to work being a critically important part of most women's lives and, thus, a critically important focus for career psychology and career counseling.

Women now constitute a significant portion of the labor force, and the vast majority of U.S. women work outside the home. In the year 2000, three-fifths of women were employed. Of those ages 25 to 44, 75% were employed. Sixty percent of women with children under the age of 12 months are employed. The odds that a woman will work outside the home during her adult life are more than 90% (U.S. Department of Labor, 2003). What this adds up to is that paid employment (versus work inside the home) is now the rule, not the exception. There is *no* category of women for whom the majority is not employed outside the home (Barnett & Hyde, 2001).

Not surprisingly, the most common family lifestyle today is the "dual-earner" family (Gilbert, 2002). As described by Gilbert and by Barnett and Hyde (2001), we now have "work family role convergence" where both work and family are considered important in the lives of both women and men and where many, if not most, workers prefer the two roles equally. Thus, as career psychologists and counselors, it is now essential to understand the issues facing women at work *and* the reality that both work and family roles are salient in the lives of contemporary women and men.

WHY CAREERS ARE IMPORTANT TO WOMEN

Women, like men, need a variety of major sources of satisfaction in their lives— as once stated by Freud (according to Erikson, 1950), the psychologically well-adjusted human being is able "to love and to work" effectively. Both women and men need the satisfactions of interpersonal relationships, with family and/or friends, but also the satisfaction of achievement in the outside world.

We now have research evidence that women, like men, need to use their talents and abilities and that multiple roles are important for people's psychological well-being.

UTILIZATION OF ABILITIES

Research has shown that the fulfillment of individual potential for achievement is vitally important. Although the roles of homemaker and mother are important and often very satisfying, they do not allow most women to fulfill the development of their unique abilities and talents. These, rather, must be fulfilled through career pursuits or volunteer and avocational activities, just as they are in men. This is not to discount the importance of childrearing but only its insufficiency as a lifelong answer to the issue of self-realization. Even if a woman spends a number of years creatively rearing children, these children inevitably grow up and begin their own lives, lives that must of necessity be increasingly independent from the parental home.

The evidence is strong that homemakers who do not have other outlets for achievement and productivity are highly susceptible to psychological distress, particularly as children grow and leave home. For example, of the women in the Terman studies of gifted children (Terman & Oden, 1959), when followed up in their 60s (Sears & Barbie, 1977), those who reported the highest levels of life satisfaction were the employed women. Least satisfied with their lives were those who had been housewives all of their adult lives. The most psychologically distressed women were those with exceptionally high IQs (above 170) who had not worked outside the home. It seems fairly clear in the Terman study that women with genius-level IQs who had not pursued meaningful careers outside the home have suffered psychological consequences.

There is strong evidence for the beneficial effects of working outside the home on a woman's psychological adjustment, regardless of her marital status. Early research on the relationship between marital status and psychological health concluded that the healthiest individuals were the married men and the single women, whereas married women were at particularly high risk for psychological distress (Bernard, 1971). However, it does not seem to be marriage per se that is detrimental to women's psychological adjustment, but rather the lack of meaningful paid employment. In these studies, the women who were not employed accounted for the more frequent occurrence of psychological distress among the married women.

In a related vein, there is strong evidence that multiple roles, that is, those of both worker and family member, are important to women's mental and physical health (Barnett & Hyde, 2001). Most research finds that even though multiple roles are time consuming and can be stressful, they are protective against depression (Crosby, 1991) and facilitative of positive mental health. There are several hypotheses concerning why multiple roles are beneficial for women (Barnett & Hyde, 2001). First, when more than one role is important in an individual's life, stress or disappointment in one domain can be buffered by success or satisfaction in another role. Second, the added income of a second job/career can reduce the stress of being the sole breadwinner and can in fact provide an economic lifeline when one spouse or partner becomes unemployed. In difficult economic times, characterized by high unemployment and corporate downsizing or collapse, two incomes can be virtually life saving. Third, jobs provide an additional source of social support, which increases well-being (Barnett & Hyde, 2001). For example, Greenberger and O'Neil (1993) found that although men's well-being was related most significantly to social support from their wives, women's well-being was related to support from neighbors, supervisors, and coworkers, as well as from husbands.

There is also evidence to contradict myths that women's career commitment will have a negative effect on her marriage and family. It seems that more equitable sharing of breadwinning may benefit marital satisfaction in both spouses, but especially husbands (Wilke, Ferree, & Ratcliff, 1998). Also interesting is data showing that the two roles are not contradictory but may in fact have a mutually catalytic effect—studies of the relationship between work commitment and family commitment show a positive correlation between the two (Marks & MacDermid, 1996).

In considering women's career development and multiple roles, it should also be noted there are today many lifestyle alternatives. There are 12 million single parents in this country, most of them women (Gilbert, 2002). There is also an increasing number of people who choose to remain single, as well as an increasing number of committed gay and lesbian couples, many of whom are now choosing to have or adopt children. Thus, although the heterosexual dual-career marriage will be the model lifestyle, the options of remaining single or in a committed same-sex or nonmarital partnership should also be considered viable in life planning (see Farmer, 1997). It goes without saying that the issues of combining work and parenthood are different for single people who usually carry sole responsibility for home and parenting and for those in same-sex partnerships for whom there is no obvious assignment of roles and responsibilities based on gender. But regardless of the precise nature of the family unit, helping people to have and manage multiple roles may be beneficial.

PROBLEMS IN WOMEN'S LABOR FORCE PARTICIPATION

Although women now work in overwhelming numbers, their work continues to be focused in traditionally female occupations and to be less well paid than that of men. Even though women have made much progress in entering traditionally male-dominated professions such as medicine and law, where half the entering students are women, the occupational world still has many areas of extreme sex segregation. For example, more than 90% of preschool and kindergarten teachers, dental hygienists, secretaries, child-care workers, cleaners and servants, nurses, occupational and speech therapists, and teachers' aids are women (U.S. Department of Labor, Bureau of Labor Statistics, 2003). Although men were 18% of elementary and middle school teachers in 1981, they are only 9% currently.

In contrast, women remain seriously underrepresented in scientific and technical careers and in high-level positions in business, government, education, and the military. For example, women earn fewer than 20% of the bachelor's degrees in fields such as engineering and physics (National Science Foundation [NSF], 2000) and fewer than 10% of the graduate degrees in engineering (Kuh, 1998). High technology is among the fastest growing and well-paid occupational fields, yet women represent only about 10% of engineers, 30% of computer systems analysts, and 25% of computer programmers (U.S. Department of Labor, 2003). Women account for 8% of physicists and astronomers, 7% of air traffic controllers, 5% of truck drivers, 4% of pilots, and 3% of firefighters. Women remain only a small proportion of workers in the generally well-paid skilled trades and protective service occupations such as police officer and firefighter. Men are nine times as likely as women to be employed in these occupations (U.S. Department of Labor, 2003).

Women continue to be paid less for full-time employment in this country. Overall, women make 73% as much as men, when both are employed full time. Women make most compared to men when they work in the District of Columbia (89%) and least when they work in Wyoming (64%) and Louisiana (65%). The income gap is greater for middle-age and older workers than it is for young workers and is greater for White women compared to African American or Hispanic women. However, women in nontraditional careers earn 150% that of women in traditional careers (U.S. Department of Labor, 2003).

In considering women's lower income, it is essential to note that women cannot ensure they will be taken care of by a husband. Today, the average marriage lasts seven years (Harvey & Pauwels, 1999), and 20% of children live in a single-parent home. As mentioned, there are 12 million single-parent households, most of them headed by women (U.S. Department of Labor, 2003). Women are much more likely to be widowed than men, and women represent 75% of the elderly poor, a percentage much greater than their representation (59%) among the elderly. The odds that a woman will have to care for herself financially during adult life are high, and failure to prepare her for this likelihood with high-quality education and/or training can have tragic consequences.

In summary, career pursuits will play a major role in most women's lives, so it is imperative that we as career counselors help women make career choices that they find fulfilling, satisfying, and economically sufficient. Yet, the data I have described suggest that a substantial number of women are still selecting a smaller range of traditionally female, lower paid careers and are making substantially less money than men, even when employed full time. In the next sections, I discuss barriers to choice and barriers to equity, but following each discussion of barriers, I also discuss supportive factors. This organization follows the distinction of career barriers and supports used in Social Cognitive Career Theory (SCCT; Lent, Brown, & Hackett, 2000; see also Lent, Chapter 5, this volume) and as originated in the writings of Farmer (1976) and Harmon (1977) in their pioneering work on women's career development. Career counselors will be better able to help clients and educators, and parents will be better able to help students if they understand both the barriers to and supports of women's career development.

BARRIERS TO WOMEN'S CAREER CHOICES

Some barriers to career choices are socialized barriers, that is, socialized belief systems or behavior patterns that lead women themselves to avoid certain career fields. Factors discussed herein are math anxiety and avoidance, low self-efficacy and outcome expectations, gender and occupational stereotypes, and a restricted range of vocational interests. Problems with our educational system, the concept of the null educational environment, and multiple role concerns are other barriers to women's career development.

MATH: THE CRITICAL FILTER

The critical importance of a sound mathematics background for entrance to many of the best career opportunities in our society (e.g., engineering, scientific and medical careers, computer science, business, and the skilled trades) is now generally agreed on (Chipman & Wilson, 1985), and a lack of math background constitutes one of the major barriers to women's career development.

The classic study of the importance of math to career options was that of Sells (1973). In a study of freshmen at the University of California at Berkeley, Sells found that only 8% of the women, versus 57% of the men, had taken four years of high school math. Four years of high school math was prerequisite to entering calculus or intermediate statistics courses required in three-fourths of the university's major fields, and the university did not provide remedial courses to allow a student to complete the prerequisites post hoc. Thus, 92% of the freshmen women at Berkeley were prevented by lack of math background from even considering 15 of the 20 major fields. The five remaining "options" were predictable—traditionally female major areas such as education, the humanities, the social sciences, librarianship, and social welfare. Thus, decisions to "choose" these majors may have in many cases been by default, through failure to qualify for any major requiring a math background.

Sells (1982) further elaborated the vital importance of math preparation for both career options and future earnings. Four full years of high school math are vital to surviving the standard freshman calculus course, now required for most undergraduate majors in business administration, economics, agriculture, engineering, forestry, health sciences, nutrition, food sciences, and natural, physical, and computer sciences. Only the arts and humanities do not now require a math background. Further, Sells showed a strong and direct relationship between college calculus background and both starting salaries and employers' willingness to interview students for a given job. Mathematics and science are important even for non-college-degree technical occupations (U.S. Department of Labor, 2000). As so well stated by Sells (1982), "Mastery of mathematics and science has become essential for full participation in the world of employment in an increasingly technological society" (p. 7).

Given the importance of having an adequate math background to career options, females' tendency to avoid math coursework has been one of the most serious barriers to their career development. Further, it is fairly clear now that it is lack of math background, rather than lack of innate ability, that is to blame for females' poorer performance on quantitative aptitude and mathematics achievement tests (e.g., Chipman & Wilson, 1985; Eccles & Jacobs, 1986). Thus, a critical issue is females' avoidance of math. Educational and counseling interventions capable of helping young women to be full participants in an increasingly technological society may be among the most crucial strategies in attempts to broaden women's career choices. These issues are dealt with more extensively in the discussion of counseling implications.

SELF-EFFICACY EXPECTATIONS

Self-efficacy is one of the central concepts of Lent, Brown, and Hackett's (1994, 2000) social cognitive theory (see Lent, Chapter 5, this volume). Self-efficacy expectations (Bandura, 1977, 1997) refer to people's beliefs that they can successfully complete specific tasks or behaviors to reach goals. For example, an individual may perceive herself as able (or unable) to solve algebraic equations, fix a flat tire, or care for an infant.

Self-efficacy expectations are postulated by Bandura (1977, 1997) to have at least three behavioral consequences:

1. Approach versus avoidance behavior.
2. Quality of performance of behaviors in the target domain.
3. Persistence in the face of obstacles or disconfirming experiences.

Thus, low self-efficacy expectations concerning various behavioral domains are postulated to lead to avoidance of those domains, poorer performance in them, and an increased tendency to give up when faced with discouragement or failure. In the context of career development, self-efficacy expectations can influence the types of courses, majors, and careers individuals feel comfortable attempting. They can influence performance on the tests necessary to complete college coursework or the requirements of a job training program. Finally, the postulated effects of self-efficacy on persistence influence long-term pursuit of an individual's goals in the face of obstacles, occasional failures, and dissuading messages from the environment, such as gender or ethnic discrimination or harassment.

There is now more than 20 years of research allowing some generalities about career-related self-efficacy expectations in women (Betz & Hackett, 1981, 1997). In education or job content domains, college women tend to score lower than college men on self-efficacy in domains having to do with math, science, computer science and technology, mechanical activities, and outdoor and physical activities. Women tend to score higher than men on self-efficacy in social domains of activity, for example, teaching and counseling. Note that these differences are consistent with stereotypic patterns of gender socialization. For example, Betz and Hackett (1981) asked college women and men to report whether they felt themselves capable of completing various educational majors. Even though the men and women as a group did not differ in their tested abilities, they differed significantly in their self-efficacy beliefs. These differences were especially striking toward occupations involving mathematics: 59% of college men versus 41% of college women believed themselves able to complete a degree in that field. Seventy-four percent of men, versus 59% of women, believed they could be accountants. Most dramatically, 70% of college men but only 30% of comparably able women believed themselves able to complete a degree in engineering.

Betz and Hackett (1981) also found that self-efficacy was related to the range of career options considered, and self-efficacy for mathematics is linked to choice of a science career (Betz & Hackett, 1983). Other studies have shown that self-efficacy beliefs are related to performance and persistence. For example, Lent, Brown, and Larkin (1984, 1986) showed that efficacy beliefs about the educational requirements of scientific and technical occupations were related to both the performance and persistence (continuing enrollment) of students enrolled in engineering programs.

Thus, low self-efficacy, especially in relationship to male-dominated careers and/or careers requiring mathematical or technical expertise, may reduce the self-perceived career options of women. Also important for women are outcome expectations, the beliefs that desired outcomes will follow from successful behaviors. Given continuing discrimination in the workforce, it would not be surprising if women felt that competent work behavior might not be rewarded or might be disparaged in certain contexts. Women of color may have particularly low outcome, as well as self-efficacy, expectations due to experiences with oppression and racial bias (Byars & Hackett, 1998).

OCCUPATIONAL AND GENDER STEREOTYPES

Gender-related stereotypes detrimentally affect the development of girls and women in at least two ways. First, stereotypes of gender roles may lead girls to believe that they *should* prioritize homemaking and childrearing roles and deemphasize their own educational achievements. One manifestation of this stereotyping is a progressive decrease in the aspirations of girls. Numerous studies suggest that although boys and girls start out with equally high aspirations, girls reduce theirs over time (Farmer, 1997). For example, in the high school valedictorian sample studied by Arnold and Denny (Arnold, 1995), the boys and girls initially aspired to relatively similar levels of career prestige, but as adults the women selected less prestigious majors and ended up in lower level career fields. In Farmer's (1997) longitudinal study of high school students, men's persistence in science was related to high aspirations when young, while for women their youthful high aspirations often faded as they matured (Farmer, 1997). In Arnold and Denny's (Arnold, 1995) sample of high school valedictorians, the girls but not the boys showed steady decrements in aspirations and also in self-esteem after college. The stronger the home/ family priorities, the more precipitous was the decline in both aspirations and self-esteem.

The second way that stereotypes affect women's career choices is through stereotypes about occupations best suited for males and females. Although beliefs that some occupations are more appropriate for men versus women may have lessened, they still exist, as is shown by research. In an illuminating study, for example, Nelson, Acke, and Manis (1996) found that college students assumed that men were majoring in engineering and women in nursing even when contrary information was provided. For example, a 20-year-old male described as having worked in a day-care center was assumed to be majoring in engineering, while a young woman who had had considerable outdoor and mechanical experience was assumed to be majoring in nursing.

Children are susceptible to these stereotypes and begin to use them to guide choice. Early studies (see Betz, 1994, for a review) showed that people consistently rate many occupations as either masculine or feminine. For example, Shinar (1975) showed that miner, federal judge, engineer, physicist, and heavy equipment operator were judged to be highly masculine, while nurse, receptionist, elementary schoolteacher, and dietician were judged to be highly feminine. Children learn these stereotypes at ages as young as 2 to 3 years old and begin to incorporate gender roles into their considerations of careers at ages 6 to 8, grades 1 through 3 (Gottfredson, 1981, Chapter 4, this volume).

RESTRICTED VOCATIONAL INTERESTS

The use of ability and interest measures in career assessment and counseling is derived from the *matching* or trait-factor approach to career counseling (see Dawis, Chapter 1, this volume; Spokane & Cruza-Guet, Chapter 2, this volume). Simply stated, the bases of this approach are:

- Individuals differ in their job-related abilities and interests.
- Job/occupational environments differ in their requirements and in the kinds of interests to which they appeal.
- Congruence or fit between an individual's characteristics and the characteristics of the job is an important consideration in making good career choices.

Among the important variables to be taken into consideration are abilities and aptitudes as included in the Theory of Work Adjustment (Lofquist & Dawis, 1991; Dawis, Chapter 1, this volume) and vocational interests as included in Holland's theory (1997; Spokane & Cruza-Guet, Chapter 2, this volume). From the matching perspective, the purpose of assessment is to assist counselor and client in generating educational or career options that represent a good person-environment fit.

While the *matching model* has been supported by much empirical research, we have also come to realize that this model oversimplifies the career choice process for some groups of people. For example, research has indicated that women tend to underutilize their abilities in selecting careers (Betz & Fitzgerald, 1987). In addition, women's overrepresentation in traditionally female careers and underrepresentation in many male-dominated careers may be due partly to restrictions in how their vocational interests have developed.

Using Holland's (1997) vocational theory as an example, women score lower on Realistic themes and higher on Social themes than men when raw scores are used to measure the Holland types (Lunneborg, 1979). The Realistic theme includes technical, outdoor, and hands-on activities—the kinds of skills often taught in high school shop, electronics, and trades courses or under the tutelage of a parent comfortable with home and automobile repair. The Social theme includes social, interpersonal skills often thought important to teach girls but neglected in the teaching of boys (Tipping, 1997; Yoder, 1999).

There is strong evidence that these interest differences are in part due to stereotypic gender socialization because boys are exposed to different types of learning opportunities growing up than are girls. Because of gender stereotypic socialization, neither gender learns all the skills necessary for adaptive functioning and responding (see Bem, 1974; Stake, 1997). Educational and career options can also be restricted because of restricted learning opportunities (and internalized stereotypes) rather than because of inadequate ability or potential. These restricted learning opportunities can also, however, lead to lower self-efficacy expectations. Thus, narrowed interest development can restrict women's career options.

MULTIPLE ROLE CONCERNS

Fitzgerald, Fassinger, and Betz (1995) noted that "the history of women's traditional roles as homemaker and mother continue to influence every aspect of their career choice and adjustment" (p. 72), typically in the direction of placing limits on what can be achieved. Women today may not be viewing this as an either-or choice, but many *do* plan careers mindful of how they will integrate these with home and family. In contrast, many men plan their careers without needing to sacrifice levels of achievement to accommodate home and families (Farmer, 1997). Spade and Reese (1991) noted that men reconcile the demands of work and family by "reverting to the traditional definition of father as provider" (p. 319).

One unfortunate implication of the perceived overload caused by career and family priorities is that women for whom husband and children are a high priority tend to downscale their career aspirations, relative to other women and to men. (Men, however, may not have had to downscale their career aspirations to have a family.) The research of Arnold and Denney (see Arnold, 1995) following the lives of Illinois valedictorians provided a particularly vivid illustration of how the aspirations of academically gifted women, but not those of similarly gifted men, steadily decreased as they completed college and entered career fields. In her longitudinal study of Midwestern high school students, Farmer (1997) noted that a large number of young women interested in science chose to pursue nursing because they thought it would fit well with having and rearing children or with being a single or divorced head of household. Men in the Farmer study made no such compromises. In Farmer's sample of women (high school students in 1980), career motivation was inversely related to homemaking commitment. As concluded by Gerson (1986) and discussed further by Eccles (1987), women's choices about work continue to be inextricably linked with their decisions about family; thus, family role considerations limit women's investment in the occupational world.

Although we have witnessed tremendous increases in workforce participation among women in all marital and parental categories, the relationship of marital/parental status to career attainment, commitment, and innovation is still very strong. Studies have shown inverse relationships between being married and having children and every measurable criterion of career involvement and achievement (see Betz & Fitzgerald, 1987, for a comprehensive review). This inverse relationship is not true among men. Highly achieving men are at least as likely (if not more so) as their less highly achieving male counterparts to be married and to have one or more children. In other words, men do not have to downscale their aspirations. Women, like men, deserve to have, or at least to try for, "it all."

BARRIERS IN THE EDUCATIONAL SYSTEM

It is probably difficult to overestimate the importance of education to career development and achievement (see Arbona, Chapter 22, this volume; Rojewski, Chapter 6, this volume). The nature and level of obtained education are importantly related to subsequent career achievements and to adult socioeconomic status and lifestyle. An undergraduate degree is now a necessary minimum requirement for the pursuit of many occupations, and graduate or professional education is the only route to careers in many professions. All workers, men and women, earn more with increasing levels of education. For example, Latinos with a college education earn 82% more than do Latinos with a high school diploma (National Center for Education Statistics, 2002). Education is crucial for economic power (Wycott, 1996) and independence (Cardoza, 1991). In short, appropriate educational preparation is a major gateway to occupational entrance. Education creates options, while lack of education closes them; without options, the concept of *choice* itself has no real mean-ing. Thus, the decisions individuals make concerning their education, both in terms of level and major areas of study, will be among the most important career decisions they ever make. Further, success and survival in the educational programs chosen will be critical to the successful implementation of these career decisions.

Studies commissioned by the American Association of University Women (1992, 1999) and a major review done by Sadker and Sadker (1994) document the continuing disadvantaged position of girls in our educational system. Re-searchers concluded that girls receive less attention from teachers than do boys. African American girls receive less attention than do White girls. Gender harass-ment in schools is increasing, and curriculum and texts ignore or marginalize the contributions of girls and women. This research and that by Brody (1997) have also convincingly documented a decline in self-esteem among girls, but not boys, from elementary to middle and high school. For example, 55% of elementary school girls agreed with the statement, "I am good at a lot of things," but this per-centage declined to 29% in middle school and 23% in high school. Girls who pur-sued math and science courses and who participated in sports maintained their self-esteem over this time period (AAUW, 1992). Because of the combination of lack of support with outright discouragement and harassment, Sandler and Hall (1996) described our schools as providing a "chilly educational climate" for girls and women.

By the time girls enter college, they can expect to encounter an educational en-vironment that may continue to be chilly. Sexual harassment, being discouraged from classroom participation, and lack of support and mentoring can affect women in any major, but these and other subtle or direct messages that "she doesn't belong" are particularly true in male-dominated fields, such as engineer-ing and the physical sciences (see the discussion of the experiences of token women in the section on barriers to equity). Ehrhart and Sandler (1987) docu-mented other types of differential treatment of women in higher education such as disparaging women's intellectual capabilities or professional potential, using sexist humor, advising women to lower their academic and career goals, and fo-cusing on marriage and children as a potential barrier to the career development of women but as an advantage for men (Ehrhart & Sandler).

As stated by C. Pearson, Shavlik, and Touchton (1988), "The present record of higher education, in spite of some significant efforts, is not particularly good. Fe-male students, on the whole, still experience a loss of personal and career confi-dence over the period they spend in higher education, even when they make very high grades. For men, the reverse is true."

The Null Educational Environment   One of the most basic and important concepts summarizing the difficulties faced by women in higher education is Freeman's (1979) concept of the *null educational environment*. A null environment, as discussed by Betz (1989) and Freeman (1979), is an environment that neither encourages nor discourages individuals—it simply ignores them. Its effect is to leave the individ-ual at the mercy of whatever environmental or personal resources to which he or she has access. The effects of null environments on women were first postulated by Freeman following her study of students at the University of Chicago. Students were asked to describe the sources and extent of environmental support they received for their educational and career goals. Although both male and female students reported being ignored by faculty (thus experiencing what Freeman called a *null educational environment*), male students reported more encouragement and support from others in their environments, for example, parents, friends, relatives, and significant others.

When added to the greater occurrence of negative messages about women's roles and, in particular, about women's pursuit of careers in fields traditionally dominated by men, the effect of the faculty's simply ignoring women students was a form of passive discrimination—discrimination through failure to act. As stated by Freeman, "An academic situation that neither encourages nor discourages students of either sex is inherently discriminatory against women because it fails to take into account the differentiating external environments from which women and men students come," where *external environments* refer to difference in familial, peer, and societal support for career pursuits (Freeman, 1979, p. 221). In other words, professors do not have to overtly discourage or discriminate against female students. Society has already placed countless negative marks on the female student's ballot, so a passive approach, a laissez-faire attitude, may contribute to her failure. Career-oriented female students, to survive, must do it without much support from their environments (Betz, 1989).

Discrimination can thus result from errors of omission as well as commission, and both have negative effects on females' progress and success in higher education. The critical aspect of this concept for educators, counselors, and parents is that if we are not actively supporting and encouraging women, we are, in effect, leaving them at the mercy of gender role and occupational stereotypes. Eccles (1987) also stated it well when she wrote: "Given the omnipresence of gender-role prescriptions regarding appropriate female life choices, there is little basis for females to develop nontraditional goals if their parents, peers, teachers, and counselors do not encourage them to consider these options" (p. 164). Failure to support her may not be an error of commission, like overt discrimination or sexual harassment, but it is an error of omission because its ultimate effects are the same—limitations in a woman's ability to fully develop and use her abilities and talents in educational and career pursuits. The null environment is a crucial concept to remember in career counseling.

SUPPORTS TO CAREER CHOICES

Among the factors that have been found to facilitate women's career achievements, including perceiving a broader array of career options, are a number of variables which, by their absence, can serve as barriers. Just as unsupportive environments can serve as barriers, supportive environments can be very helpful. One of the most crucial areas of support is that from families, especially parents and older relatives, and this has been found true for women of all racial-ethnic groups. Studies by Fisher and Padmawidjaja (1999), S. M. Pearson and Bieschke (2001), and Juntunen et al. (2001), among others, have found parental support and availability to be very important in the career aspirations and achievements of Mexican American, African American, and Native American as well as White women.

A number of other studies have found maternal employment, particularly in nontraditional career fields, is related to daughters' higher career aspirations (e.g., Selkow, 1984). Gomez et al. (2001) found that although Latino high achievers came from families where traditional gender roles were emphasized, most also had nontraditional female role models—for example, their mothers were nontraditionally employed or, if homemakers, held leadership roles in community organizations. On the other hand, Hackett, Esposito, and O'Halloran (1989) and Weishaar, Green, and Craighead (1981), among others, have reported that the presence of a supportive male family member was important in girls' pursuit of nontraditional career fields. Many women pursuing nontraditional career fields relied heavily on male mentors (Betz, 2002) because no female mentors were available in their environments.

In addition to supportive family and mentors, much previous research has shown the importance of personality factors such as instrumentality, internal locus of control, high self-esteem, and a feminist orientation in women's career achievements (Betz & Fitzgerald, 1987; Fassinger, 1990). *Instrumentality,* one of the critical factors in Farmer's (1997) study, refers to a constellation of traits that were previously called *masculinity* but were seen eventually to reflect a collection of characteristics having to do with independence, self-sufficiency, and the feeling that the individual was in control of his or her life. It has also been described as *agency* and has much in common with self-efficacy (Bandura, 1997).

The possession of instrumental traits does not mean that an individual cannot also possess the most traditionally feminine traits of nurturance and sensitivity to others. These characteristics are now referred to as *expressiveness* or *communion.* Together, instrumentality and expressiveness form the *androgynous* personality style, which is thought to be desirable for both women and men. Thus, positive factors related to support and mentoring from others and a personality characterized by high self-esteem and self-efficacy and a sense of self-sufficiency and instrumentality can help women reach their career goals.

WOMEN OF COLOR: SPECIAL CONCERNS

Before moving to a discussion of barriers to success in the workplace, explicit attention should be paid to the status of women of color in the job market. Although research on women of color is also mentioned where relevant throughout this chapter, a few more general factors should be mentioned.

The disadvantages facing women in the labor force are accentuated for women of color, who have often been described as facing the "double jeopardy" of both gender and race discrimination (Beale, 1970; see also Gomez et al., 2001). Women of color are employed at rates comparable to those of White women but earn less than do White women or minority men. The wage gaps in comparison to White men are as follows: 71%, 64%, and 53% for White, African American, and Latina women (versus 76% and 63% for African American and Latino men, respectively). Lesbians and physically disabled women also earn less than heterosexual White women (Yoder, 1999). It is interesting that this gender gap is much smaller in many Western and African countries—90% in Iceland, France, Australia, and Tanzania.

With reference to specific groups, African American women have achieved higher educational and occupational levels and have had more options than have African American men (DeVaney & Hughey, 2000), but African American women have also often been found in menial jobs such as maids and nannies at a rate exceeding that of White women and still make less money than do both White women and African American men (DeVaney & Hughey, 2000). Since they are the most likely group to be supporting a child or children alone, this can create special hardship.

Latinos currently represent the largest minority group in the United States, 32.8 million or 12.5% of the U.S. population in the 2000 census. The achievement of Latino men and women, both in terms of educational and occupational levels, lags well behind that of other U.S. minorities except for Native Americans (Arbona & Novy, 1991). Mexican American women lag behind other women of Hispanic ethnicity in college completion rates. They also lag behind Latino men who, on the average, earned poorer grades in college.

Asian American women are somewhat more likely than other groups of women to be found in occupations emphasizing math or technology, but they are still predominately found in traditionally female fields and, like other groups of women, earn less money than men. Finally, Native American women, including Native Hawaiians, are almost absent from our literature (Bowman, 1998) and are the most occupationally disadvantaged and the most likely to be unemployed of any group of women. Clearly, the career development needs of women of color must receive more of our attention.

EXTERNAL BARRIERS TO EQUITY

The barriers of discrimination and sexual harassment have long been discussed as crucial in women's attempt to attain equity in the workplace (see Fassinger, 2002; Phillips & Imhoff, 1997). Although outright gender discrimination is against the law, informal discrimination continues to exist (Fitzgerald & Harmon, 2001). For example, although women may be allowed to enter a male-dominated workplace, it may be made clear to them, overtly or more subtly, that they are not welcome. Messages ranging from overt verbal harassment to simply being ignored and receiving no social support from colleagues can make a work environment very unpleasant, and less obvious forms of discrimination in pay, promotions, and perquisites of the job may exist as well (Fitzgerald & Harmon, 2001).

The importance of promotions is related to the continuing existence of the *glass ceiling*, which refers to the very small number of women at top levels of management (Yoder, 1999). The glass ceiling refers to artificial barriers, based on attitudinal or organizational bias, that prevent some groups of people from advancing in an organization. In 1995, the Department of Labor's Federal Glass Ceiling Commission concluded that there still existed a corporate ceiling in that only 3% to 5% of senior corporate leadership positions were held by women, far fewer than their proportionate representation in the labor force. The commission reported that, although the notion of a glass ceiling implies subtlety, the ceiling for women of color is by no means subtle and is better called a "concrete wall" (Federal Glass Ceiling Commission, 1995, pp. 68–69).

Another barrier to women in nontraditional careers is that of being a token. First described by Kanter (1977), tokens are people who in gender or race (or both) constitute less than 15% of their work group. Tokens experience stress, social isolation, heightened visibility, and accusations of role violations ("You don't belong here"). Research on women of color who are double tokens, such as the African American women firefighters studied by Yoder and Aniakudo (1997) and the African American women police officers studied by Martin (1994), shows that these women faced, in both studies, insufficient instruction, coworker hostility, silence, overly close and punitive supervision, lack of support, and stereotyping—an unwavering message of exclusion and a hope that she would fail (Yoder & Aniakudo, 1997). These studies suggest that both race and gender are barriers to these women's satisfaction and success. As one African American firefighter put it, "being a black female—it was like two things needed to be proven" (Yoder & Aniakudo, 1997, p. 336).

Sexual harassment also continues to be a major problem in the workplace, with serious consequences for both women and organizations. Sexual harassment is described in detail by authors such as Fitzgerald (1993), Koss et al. (1994), and Norton (2002). Research now distinguishes two categories of sexual harassment: quid pro quo harassment and hostile environment harassment. *Quid pro quo harassment* refers to situations in which an employee is asked to give in to a supervisor's sexual demands in exchange for pay, a promotion, or continued employment, with the implied threat of loss of raise or promotion, or loss of employment, if the employee refuses to comply. *Hostile environment harassment* refers to instances where the employee is subject to sexual innuendo, sexist or sexually oriented comments, physical touching, or sexually oriented posters or cartoons placed in the work area. The issue here is making women workers sex objects at work. Women are there to make a living and advance their careers, and sexual harassment can seriously interfere with those aims.

Although sexual harassment is not limited to men harassing women—women can harass men, and same-sex harassment can also occur—the vast majority (90%) of complaints involve men harassing women. On the basis of large-scale surveys of working women, Fitzgerald (1993) estimated that one of every two will be harassed during their work lives. Gutek (1985) reported even greater likelihoods of harassment for Hispanic and African American women. Although responses to sexual harassment are beyond the scope of this chapter, sexual harassment is a major barrier to women's equity in the workplace. Research has shown decreases in job satisfaction and organizational commitment, job withdrawal, increased symptoms of anxiety and depression, and higher levels of stress-related illness as responses to sexual harassment (Norton, 2002). These are mental health as well as economic issues and can seriously compromise job performance and job satisfaction.

Another of the persistent conditions affecting women's equity in the workplace and their job satisfaction is that although their workforce participation has increased dramatically, their work at home has not decreased. Although multiple roles are, in general, positive for mental health, the picture becomes more complex when women are expected to shoulder the major burden of homemaking and child care. As well stated by Barnett and Hyde (2001), "there are upper limits to the benefits of multiple roles" (p. 789) when the number of roles becomes too great or the demands of one role become excessive—this would seem to apply to the case where the woman is now expected to cope with two full-time jobs, one outside and the other inside the home. Instead of "having it all," women are "doing it all" (Fitzgerald & Harmon, 2001, p. 215).

Research suggests that few men view parenting and homemaking as their responsibility—they are primarily available to "help out" (Farmer, 1997). Yoder (1999) summarized data showing that, on average, women in married couples do 33 hours of household chores weekly, compared to 14 for their husbands. This constitutes 70% of the workload for women and 30% for men, not including child care. With child care, these women are working a full-time job at home, in addition to what they are doing at work. These figures describe African American and Latina/Latino couples as well. Supreme Court Justice Ruth Bader Ginsburg noted that there could be no equity in the workplace until men assume equal sharing of homemaking and parenting roles (Farmer, 1997).

A related problem is the lack of organizational structures and support systems for employees with families. Subsidized child or elder care, paid family leave, flextime, job sharing, and telecommuting can greatly ease the burdens of managing home, family, and careers, burdens carried mostly by women (Fitzgerald & Harmon, 2001). The United States is still the only developed country in the world without a national child-care policy or a systematic means of addressing the serious problems of elder care (Fitzgerald & Harmon).

SUPPORTS FOR CAREER ADJUSTMENT

The title of Richie et al.'s (1997) study of highly achieving African American and White women—"Persistence, Connection, and Passion" (p. 133)—summarizes some of the supports for women's achievement of their career goals. These might also be viewed as strengths of women, which carry them through or enable them to surmount the barriers they confront. These strengths have also been replicated in a number of studies of highly achieving women (Reddin, 1997; Gomez et al., 2001).

Persistence is critical to succeeding in the face of obstacles, and strong self-efficacy expectations for an individual's career, self-esteem, and a strong sense of purpose are essential to persistence. The characteristics of instrumentality discussed previously—the sense of being in control of your own life and destiny, of being agentic, able to *act* on your own behalf—are also important to persistence.

Related to both self-efficacy and instrumentality is *coping efficacy,* which plays an increasingly important role in Lent et al.'s (2000) Social Cognitive Career Theory. As stated, "when confronted with adverse contextual conditions, persons with a strong sense of coping efficacy (beliefs regarding one's capabilities to negotiate particular environmental obstacles) may be more likely to persevere toward their goals. . . ." (Lent et al., 2000, p. 76). Gomez et al. (2001) found coping strategies especially important to their highly achieving Latinas, as did Richie et al. (1997) with highly achieving African Americans and White women. Gomez et al. list "tenacity and persistence; flexibility; creativity; reframing and redefining challenges, barriers, or mistakes; maintaining a balanced perspective in understanding how racism and sexism may affect career-related behaviors; developing support networks congruent with personal style, values, and culture; and developing bicultural skills where applicable" (p. 298).

Connection refers to the essential part played by familial and peer/friend support in facilitating persistence in the individual's goals. There is ample literature documenting the importance of family, including spouse and children, friends both at work and outside of work, and mentors. This importance has been shown for women of color as well as for White women. For example, Gilbert (1994) and Gomez et al. (2001) discussed the crucial role of a supportive spouse in managing both career and home and family responsibilities; Gomez et al. (2001) reported that supportive families were crucial in maintaining women's career commitment after the birth of children. In addition, Richie et al. (1997) emphasized the importance of interconnectedness with others in the continuing high achievement of both African American and White women. Connection may also be facilitated by a feminist orientation, which gives a woman a sense of community beyond herself. Feminist orientation has consistently been shown to be a facilitative factor in women's career achievements (Fassinger, 1990; Stafford, 1984).

Finally, *passion* is for some women loving what they do and, for others, feeling that they had made a difference in the world (Gomez et al., 2001). For some women, this is the sense of a life's calling. Although not all people are lucky enough to have such a passion in their work, helping people make choices that take their interests and passions into account is a worthy goal of the career counselor.

EDUCATIONAL AND COUNSELING INTERVENTIONS

The preceding sections of this chapter have emphasized the importance to women of successful career development as well as success in their personal relationships, yet have also outlined ways in which women continue to lag behind men in both the variety of career options they consider and the subsequent success in these pursuits. Counselors and educators may be able to help women to close these gaps. In general, suggestions for interventions can be divided into those facilitating the career choice process and those enabling the career adjustment process.

COUNSELING FOR CAREER CHOICE

Because a sexist society and stereotypic socialization have often stood in the way of women's pursuit of a full range of career options, research supports overt attempts to restore options that society has taken away. In other words, counselors and psychologists need to remain aware of the possible impact of sexism and stereotyping in concert with null environments and to accept the role of active options restorers. More specifically, the following guidelines in counseling women in the process of making educational and career decisions are derived from the literature reviewed in the first part of this chapter.

1. Encourage high-quality and extensive education and training. Do not overlook the importance of technical schools, two-year and community colleges, and the military for excellent training and education.
2. Adopt the rule that no one can take too much math. Encourage young women to stay in math coursework as long as possible. Math background opens options and prevents others from being eliminated by default.
3. When in doubt, stress decisions that eliminate the fewest options, such as staying in school and continuing in math.
4. Define the counselor role as a catalyst for the creation of new learning experiences for the client, so that she can fully develop all her capabilities, including those not reinforced by traditional gender stereotyping.

5. Explore the client's outcome expectations and barriers to her goal pursuits, with the idea of helping her to develop coping mechanisms, coping self-efficacy, and barrier-surmounting sources of social support.

6. Remember that all it takes is one supportive counselor, teacher, or parent to enrich the null environment.

7. Assess the role of culture and ethnicity in the client's career planning. Help her to make decisions that, as far as possible, integrate her individual and cultural values.

8. Integrate career theories as appropriate in counseling practice.

USING CAREER THEORIES TO GUIDE PRACTICE

All of the major theories of career development are relevant to career choice counseling with women. For example, Super's (1980, see also Savickas, Chapter 3, this volume) views of lifelong career development and life planning stress a holistic approach to careers and take into account multiple life roles. Gottfredson's theory explicitly incorporates the idea of occupational sex type as a central mechanism in the circumscription of career options. Social cognitive theory supports the idea of continuing growth through the individual's lifetime as a result of new learning experiences and new ideas. More detailed suggestions for the uses of social cognitive and trait-factor theories in career choice counseling with women follow.

Social Cognitive Theory Counselors should informally or formally assess a client's self-efficacy beliefs for career fields. Informal assessment may include general questions about her beliefs in her competence in domains relevant to her career decision making, performance, or advancement. For a young woman, ask questions such as:

- "What would you ideally like to do for a career?"
- "What is holding you back from your ideal?"
- "What career fantasies have you had and what keeps you from pursuing them?"
- "What careers would you pursue if you thought you could do *anything*?"

The purpose of these questions is to identify self-imposed limits on what she can do. It may be that these are realistic limits if the girl or woman does not have the aptitude for that area, but the real contribution of self-efficacy is that it focuses our attention on people who are unrealistically underestimating their capabilities. The evidence is clear that women are particularly prone to underestimate their capabilities and must accordingly have these beliefs challenged. Further probing when a young woman reports herself unable to master a specific domain of behavior should focus on the quality of her background experiences—if she dropped out of math in 10th grade because "math was for boys," then it is no wonder she lacks confidence and competence in math.

Low self-efficacy for career tasks and fields, because it leads to avoidance, can become a self-fulfilling prophecy—we avoid what we fear, so we don't learn it and never become good at it, verifying our perceptions of ourselves as incompetent. Someone, often a counselor, needs to help her break this vicious circle. The counselor should refuse to accept "I can't" for an answer unless and until the client has made a serious attempt to learn it, to master it.

In addition to the informal assessment of self-efficacy, there are now a large number of inventories assessing self-efficacy with respect to career behaviors (see Betz, 2000, for a review). Measures of career decision self-efficacy (Betz, Klein, & Taylor, 1996), math self-efficacy (Lopez, Lent, Brown, & Gore, 1997), career search self-efficacy (Solberg et al., 1994), and self-efficacy for the Holland themes (Betz, Harmon, & Borgen, 1996) are available. A new inventory of self-efficacy with respect to 17 basic domains of vocational activity such as leadership, writing, science, public speaking, and using technology is available (the Expanded Skills Confidence Inventory; Betz et al., 2003).

Self-efficacy measures may also be used jointly with parallel vocational interest measures—for example, the General Occupational Themes of the Strong Interest Inventory measuring the resemblance of the client to each of Holland's six personality types (see Spokane & Cruza-Guet, Chapter 2, this volume) now have parallel self-efficacy measures for the six types in the Skills Confidence Inventory (Betz, Harmon, & Borger, 1996).

Using these two measures jointly, the counselor looks for themes on which the client has both high interests and high self-efficacy—these themes represent good possibilities for career exploration. However, areas of high interest but lower efficacy can be options if efficacy can be increased through interventions based on Bandura's (1997) theory (see Brown & Lent, 1996, for some other suggestions). Self-efficacy interventions are based on Bandura's four sources of efficacy information and should, therefore, ideally include performance accomplishments, vicarious learning or modeling, managing anxiety, and providing support and encouragement. In planning for successful performance accomplishments, opportunities should be sought where success is at first virtually ensured, and only after some success experiences (allowing a moderate degree of self-efficacy to be established) should more difficult challenges be faced. Community or technical colleges offering entry-level or remedial courses, adult education programs, and programmed learning materials may be good sources for such learning.

In using modeling, the counselor would need to locate people who have succeeded in the area in which the client lacks self-efficacy. It is helpful, though not essential, if these models are the same race and gender of the individual, and this may be especially true if the domain of behavior is nontraditional for that person's gender. For example, a woman teaching automobile maintenance and repair or carpentry to other women will provide helpful modeling influences because these are traditionally male domains. Similarly, a man teaching parenting to young men would provide the additional benefit of modeling a nontraditional competency. Models can be in person, on film, television, books, or via other media. For example, a book on the life of a female astronaut or scientist could provide useful modeling for a young girl considering these fields.

The third component of an efficacy-enhancing intervention is anxiety management. Learning new things may be associated with anxiety, particularly if they are gender-nontraditional domains. If a domain such as math has been associated with males and if a woman has internalized a message of "Girls can't do math," anxiety will likely accompany new learning efforts. Thus, teaching anxiety management techniques may also be appropriate. Relaxation training and learning to consciously focus self-talk on the task at hand rather than on the self can be helpful.

Finally, the counselor can serve as the client's cheerleader as she tries new things. This role includes generally encouraging her that she *can* do it and, more specifically, reinforcing her efforts as she tries new things. Helping her set goals, reinforcing her when she achieves them, and helping her to try again when she has temporarily faltered are important. Finally, the counselor can counter beliefs (such as "Girls can't do math") that are getting in her way.

In addition to assessing self-efficacy expectations, outcome expectations should be assessed. This is especially true for women of color, who may expect more barriers to their success than do White women. Similarly, women wishing to pursue traditionally male-dominated occupations may have concerns about the extent to which their efforts will lead to desired rewards and outcomes. Although these concerns may be realistic, helping the client to consider coping strategies and learn about typical organizational/institutional grievance procedures may be helpful. Assertiveness training, learning to seek social support, and externalizing rather than internalizing the causes of discrimination and harassment may be useful.

Using the Matching (Trait-Factor) Model   Trait-factor theories suggest that counselors help young women to fully develop their abilities, talents, and interests. Structured methods of ability and interest assessment have always been a useful part of the assessment of these individuals, but there are a few additional considerations as well.

First, where possible, use within-gender norms to highlight directions in which a female client has developed in spite of gender role socialization. Many aptitude and interest measures now provide same-sex norms (usually within-gender percentiles). For example, the Armed Services Vocational Aptitude Battery and Differential Aptitude Test, two of the most widely used multiple aptitude batteries in career counseling with high school students, provide within-gender percentiles as well as combined group standard scores (see Walsh & Betz, 2001; Ryan Krane & Tirre, Chapter 14, this volume). Most vocational interest inventories, for example, the Strong Interest Inventory (see Hansen, Chapter 12, this volume), also now provide within-gender norms.

As with self-efficacy expectations, counselors should see the client as a work in progress, not a finished product. New learning experiences and opportunities can open the doors in terms of capabilities and interests, and counselors should *always* ask questions enabling them to assess the relative richness versus poverty of a woman's previous educational and experiential background. If she has not had a chance to learn something, then assume she can learn to do it, help her find new learning opportunities, and help convince *her* that she can do it.

CAREER EDUCATION AND EXPANDING OPTIONS

Farmer (1997) noted the crucial importance of career education in the schools. Lack of guidance about how to prepare for higher education and occupations and how to choose a career in the first place characterize many of our schools. Farmer made suggestions for career education that can increase sex equity. For example, girls might be introduced to a wider range of careers and urged to gain information on those in science and engineering. The National Science Foundation funds Project WISE (Brookhaven National Laboratory, Upton, New York), which supports programs that involve high school women in science activities. The project produces a booklet called *The Future is Yours—Get Ready* that describes 250 different occupations in the sciences and engineering (cf. Farmer, 1997). The Girl Scouts of America sponsors a program called Bridging the Gap, designed to help girls become involved in science and engineering (cf. Farmer, 1997). Many colleges and universities now have programs to assist women enrolled in colleges of engineering. Counselors should be aware of these resources and encourage talented girls and women to study them.

COUNSELING FOR CAREER ADJUSTMENT

For employed women, concerns usually fall in the areas of success/performance and satisfaction. As was indicated previously, discrimination, sexual harassment, tokenism, and lack of support represent a few barriers to women's career success and satisfaction. Additionally, the overload that may be experienced from two, rather than one, full-time jobs for women taking full responsibility for family and housework can be a major cause of decrements in *both* performance and satisfaction. A few general guidelines may be useful:

1. Help women at work develop support systems.
2. Help change the system, or help clients change the system as it pertains to flexible work schedules and family leave policies (ideally, which allow leave for adoption as well as childbearing and for elder care, and which assume that men are as willing to be responsible for those they love as are women).
3. Help token women (especially women of color) find support, often by broadening the net that is cast to find support. For example, the lone woman faculty member in chemistry may find support in a group consisting of all the faculty women in the College of Sciences.
4. Teach women to expect full participation in homemaking and childrearing from their husbands or partners. Teach men that it is their responsibility, and also to their benefit, to participate fully in home and family life and work.
5. Help women develop effective cognitive and behavioral coping strategies, as discussed earlier in the section on supports for career adjustment.

For an adult woman considering career change or advancement, the counselor should help her to explore areas of behavior where she feels her skills are holding her back or preventing her from pursuing desired options. In many fields, technical expertise is necessary but not sufficient to the pursuit of managerial or supervisory roles in those areas—if she wishes to make such a move, her self-efficacy beliefs concerning her managerial/leadership skills may be highly relevant to her perceived options. Another assessment question might be, "What new skills would increase your options or satisfaction, and what is stopping you from developing these new skills?" In many cases, the counselor will hear perceived self-efficacy—self-doubts about competence and ability to move in a new direction—and should be prepared to help a woman with such self-doubts to appraise accurately the competencies and abilities she feels she is lacking.

There also may be cases where a woman is in an occupation with poor fit for her abilities or interests. In such cases, going back to the beginning—doing a comprehensive assessment of her abilities, interests, values, and self-perceptions—may be the best place to start.

ORGANIZATIONAL AND STRUCTURAL CHANGE

We in psychology and counseling also have a responsibility to work for organizational, legal, and societal changes that will reduce sexism, stereotyping, discrimination, and harassment and create more flexible and family-friendly workplaces (Meara, 1997). In focusing on women's career development and what is needed to facilitate it, Harmon (1997) also noted that we may have shortchanged the other side of the coin—that is, how to facilitate men's development in homemaking and childrearing roles. For example, as we as counselors provide support for women's working and help them gain self-efficacy for nontraditional careers, we should also support men's pursuits of nurturing roles and help them gain self-efficacy with respect to nurturing and multiple role management. Gilbert (1994) and Harmon (1997) both suggest that it is time to develop theories that conceptualize career development and family life in a more interactive way. Such theory development would increase the satisfaction and well-being of both women and men in multiple life roles.

REFERENCES

American Association of University Women. (1992). *The AAUW Report: How schools short-change girls.* Washington, DC: Author.

American Association of University Women. (1999). *Gender gaps: Where schools still fail our children.* New York: Marlowe.

Arbona, C., & Novy, D. M. (1991). Career aspirations and the expectations of Black, Mexican American, and White students. *Career Development Quarterly, 39,* 231–239.

Arnold, K. D. (1995). *Lives of promise: What becomes of high school valedictorians.* San Francisco: Jossey-Bass.

Bandura, A. (1977). Self-efficacy: Toward a unifying theory of behavioral change. *Psychological Review, 84*(2), 191–215.

Bandura, A. (1997). *Self-efficacy: The exercise of control.* New York: Freeman.

Barnett, R. C., & Hyde, J. S. (2001). Women, men, work, and family: An expansionist theory. *American Psychologist, 56,* 781–796.

Beale, F. (1970). Double jeopardy: To be black and female. In T. Cade (Ed.), *The black woman: An anthology* (pp. 90–100). New York: New American Library.

Bem, S. L. (1974). The measurement of psychological androgyny. *Journal of Consulting and Clinical Psychology, 42,* 155–162.

Bernard, J. (1971). The paradox of the happy marriage. In V. Gornick & B. K. Moran (Eds.), *Women in sexist society* (pp. 145–162). New York: Mentor.

Betz, N. E. (1989). The null environment and women's career development. *Counseling Psychologist, 17,* 136–144.

Betz, N. E. (1994). Basic issues and concepts in career counseling for women. In W. B. Walsh & S. H. Osipow (Eds.), *Career counseling for women* (pp. 1–47). Hillsdale, NJ: Erlbaum.

Betz, N. E. (2000). Self-efficacy theory as a basis for career assessment. *Journal of Career Assessment, 8,* 205–222.

Betz, N. E. (2002). Women's career development: Weaving personal themes and theoretical constructs. *Counseling Psychologist, 30,* 467–481.

Betz, N. E., Borgen, F., Rottinghaus, P., Paulsen, A., Halper, C., & Harmon, L. W. (2003). The Expanded Skills Confidence Inventory. *Journal of Vocational Behavior, 62,* 76–100.

Betz, N. E., & Fitzgerald, L. F. (1987). *The career psychology of women.* New York: Academic Press.

Betz, N. E., & Hackett, G. (1981). The relationship of career-related self-efficacy expectations to perceived career options in college women and men. *Journal of Counseling Psychology, 28,* 399–410.

Betz, N. E., & Hackett, G. (1983). The relationship of mathematics self-efficacy expectations to the selection of science-based college majors. *Journal of Vocational Behavior, 23,* 328–345.

Betz, N. E., & Hackett, G. (1997). Applications of self-efficacy theory to the career assessment of women. *Journal of Career Assessment, 5,* 383–402.

Betz, N., Harmon, L., & Borgen, F. (1996). The relationships of self-efficacy for the Holland themes to gender, occupational group membership, and vocational interests. *Journal of Counsel and Psychology, 43,* 90–98.

Betz, N. E., Klein, K., & Taylor, K. (1996). Evaluation of a short form of the Career Decision Self-Efficacy Scale. *Journal of Career Assessment, 4,* 313–328.

Bowman, S. L. (1998). Minority women and career adjustment. *Journal of Career Assessment, 6,* 417–431.

Brody, J. E. (1997, November 4). Girls and puberty: The crisis years. *New York Times,* p. B8.

Brown, S. D., & Lent, R. W. (1996). A social cognitive framework for career choice counseling. *Career Development Quarterly, 44,* 354–366.

Byars, A., & Hackett, G. (1998). Applications of social cognitive theory to the career development of women of color. *Applied and Preventive Psychology, 7,* 266–267.

Cardoza, D. (1991). College attendance and persistence among Hispanic women: An examination of some contributing factors. *Sex Roles, 24,* 133–147.

Chipman, S. F., & Wilson, D. M. (1985). Understanding mathematics course enrollment and mathematics achievement: A synthesis of the research. In S. F. Chipman, L. R. Brush, & D. M. Wilson (Eds.), *Women and mathematics: Balancing the equation* (pp. 275–328). Hillsdale, NJ: Erlbaum.

Crosby, F. J. (1991). *Juggling: The unexpected advantages of balancing home and family.* New York: Free Press.

DeVaney, S. B., & Hughey, A. W. (2000). Career development of ethnic minority students. In D. A. Luzzo (Ed.), *Career counseling with college students* (pp. 233–252). Washington, DC: American Psychological Association.

Eccles, J. S. (1987). Gender roles and women's achievement-related decisions. *Psychology of Women Quarterly, 11,* 135–172.

Eccles, J. S., & Jacobs, J. (1986). Social forces shape math participation. *Signs, 11,* 367–380.

Ehrhart, J. K., & Sandler, B. R. (1987). *Looking for more than a few good women in traditionally male fields.* Washington, DC: Project on the Status and Education of Women.

Erikson, E. (1950). *Childhood and society.* New York: Norton.

Farmer, H. S. (1976). What inhibits achievement and career motivation in women? *Counseling Psychologist, 6,* 12–14.

Farmer, H. S. (1997). *Diversity and women's career development.* Thousand Oaks, CA: Sage.

Fassinger, R. E. (1990). Causal models of women's career development in two samples of college women. *Journal of Vocational Behavior, 36,* 225–240.

Fassinger, R. E. (2002). Hitting the ceiling: Gendered barriers to occupational entry, advancement, and achievement. In L. Diamant & J. Lee (Eds.), *The psychology of sex, gender, and jobs* (pp. 21–46). Westport, CT: Praeger.

Federal Glass Ceiling Commission. (1995). *Report on the glass ceiling for women.* Washington, DC: U.S. Department of Labor.

Fisher, T. A., & Padmawidjaja, I. (1999). Parental influences on career development perceived by African American and Mexican American college students. *Journal of Multicultural Counseling and Development, 27,* 136–152.

Fitzgerald, L. F. (1993). Sexual harassment: Violence against women in the workplace. *American Psychologist, 48,* 1070–1076.

Fitzgerald, L. F., Fassinger, R. E., & Betz, N. E. (1995). Theoretical advances in the study of women's career development. In W. B. Walsh & S. H. Osipow (Eds.), *Handbook of vocational psychology* (2nd ed., pp. 67–110). Mahwah, NJ: Erlbaum.

Fitzgerald, L. F., & Harmon, L. W. (2001). Women's career development: A postmodern update. In F. L. T. Leong & A. Barak (Eds.), *Contemporary models in vocational psychology* (pp. 207–230). Mahwah, NJ: Erlbaum.

Freeman, J. (1979). How to discriminate against women without really trying. In J. Freeman (Ed.), *Women: A feminist perspective* (2nd ed., pp. 217–232). Palo Alto, CA: Mayfield.

Gerson, K. (1986). *Hard choices: How women decide about work, career, and motherhood.* Berkeley: University of California Press.

Gilbert, L. A. (1994). Current perspectives on dual career families. *Current Directions in Psychological Science, 3,* 101–104.

Gilbert, L. A. (2002, August). *Changing roles of work and family.* Paper presented at the meeting of the American Psychological Association, Chicago.

Gomez, M. J., Fassinger, R. E., Prosser, J., Cooke, K., Mejia, B., & Luna, J. (2001). Voices abriendo caminos (Voices forging paths): A qualitative study of the career development of notable Latinos. *Journal of Counseling Psychology, 48,* 286–300.

Gottfredson, L. S. (1981). Circumscription and compromise: A development theory of occupational aspirations. *Journal of Counseling Psychology, 28,* 545–579.

Greenberger, E., & O'Neil, R. (1993). Spouse, parent, worker: Role commitments and role-related experiences in the construction of adults' well-being. *Developmental Psychology, 29,* 181–197.

Gutek, B. (1985). *Sex and the workplace.* San Francisco: Jossey-Bass.

Hackett, G., Exposito, D., & O'Halloran, M. S. (1989). The relationship of role model influences to the career salience and educational and career plans of college women. *Journal of Vocational Behavior, 35,* 164–180.

Harmon, L. W. (1977). Career counseling of women. In E. Rawlings & D. Carter (Eds.), *Psychotherapy for Women.* Springfield, IL: Charles C Thomas.

Harmon, L. W. (1997). Do gender differences necessitate separate career development theories and measures? *Journal of Career Assessment, 5,* 463–470.

Harvey, J. H., & Pauwels, B. G. (1999). Recent developments in close relationships. *Current Directions in Psychological Science, 8,* 93–95.

Holland, J. L. (1997). *Making vocational choices: A theory of vocational personalities and work environments* (3rd ed.). Odessa, FL: Psychological Assessment Resources.

Juntunen, C. L., Barraclough, D. J., Broneck, C. L., Seibel, G. A., Winrow, S. A., & Morin, P. M. (2001). American Indian perspectives on the career journey. *Journal of Counseling Psychology, 48,* 274–285.

Kanter, R. M. (1977). *Men and women of the corporation.* New York: Basic Books.

Koss, M. P., Goodman, L. A., Browne, A., Fitzgerald, L. F., Keita, G. P., & Russo, N. F. (1994). *No safe haven: Male violence against women.* Washington, DC: American Psychological Association.

Kuh, C. V. (1998). *Data on women doctoral level scientists and universities.* Paper presented at National Invitational Conference on Women in Research Universities, Harvard University and Radcliffe College, Cambridge, MA.

Lent, R. W., Brown, S. D., & Hackett, G. (1994). Toward a unifying social cognitive theory of career and academic interest, choice, and performance. *Journal of Vocational Behavior, 45,* 79–122.

Lent, R. W., Brown, S. D., & Hackett, G. (2000). Contextual supports and barriers to career choice: A social cognitive analysis. *Journal of Counseling Psychology, 47,* 36–59.

Lent, R. W., Brown, S. D., & Larkin, K. C. (1984). Relation of self-efficacy expectations to academic achievement and persistence. *Journal of Counseling Psychology, 31,* 356–362.

Lent, R. W., Brown, S. D., & Larkin, K. C. (1986). Self-efficacy in the prediction of academic performance and perceived career options. *Journal of Counseling Psychology, 33,* 265–269.

Lofquist, L., & Dawis, R. (1991). *Essentials of person-environment correspondence counseling.* Minneapolis: University of Minnesota Press.

Lopez, F. G., Lent, R. W., Brown, S. D., & Gore, P. A., Jr. (1997). Role of social cognitive expectations in high school students' mathematics-related interest and performance. *Journal of Counseling Psychology, 44,* 44–52.

Lunneborg, P. (1979). Service versus technical interest—Biggest sex difference of all? *Vocational Guidance Quarterly, 28,* 146–153.

Marks, S. R., & MacDermid, S. M. (1996). Multiple roles and the self: A theory of role balance. *Journal of Marriage and the Family, 58,* 417–432.

Martin, S. E. (1994). "Outsider within" the station house: The impact of race and gender on black women police. *Social Problems, 41,* 383–400.

Meara, N. M. (1997). Changing the structure of work. *Journal of Career Assessment, 5,* 471–474.

National Center for Education Statistics. (2002). *The condition of education 2002. NCES 2000-025* (U.S. Department of Education). Washington, DC: U.S. Government Printing Office.

National Science Foundation. (2000). *Women, minorities, and persons with disabilities in science and engineering.* Arlington, VA: National Science Foundation.

Nelson, T. E., Acke, M., & Manis, M. (1996). Irrepressible stereotypes. *Journal of Experimental Social Psychology, 32,* 13–38.

Norton, S. (2002). Women exposed: Sexual harassment and female vulnerability. In L. Diamant & J. Lee (Eds.), *The psychology of sex, gender, and jobs* (pp. 82–103). Westport, CT: Praeger.

Pearson, C., Shavlik, D., & Touchton, J. (Eds.). (1988). *Prospectus for educating the majority: How women are changing higher education.* Washington, DC: American Council on Education.

Pearson, S. M., & Bieschke, K. J. (2001). Succeeding against the odds: An examination of familial influences on the career development of professional African American women. *Journal of Counseling Psychology, 48,* 301–309.

Phillips, S., & Imhoff, A. (1997). Women and career development: A decade of research. *Annual Review of Psychology, 48,* 31–59.

Reddin, J. (1997). Highly achieving women: Career development patterns. In H. S. Farmer (Ed.), *Diversity and women's career development* (pp. 95–126). Thousand Oaks, CA: Sage.

Richie, B. S., Fassinger, R. E., Linn, S. G., Johnson, J., Prosser, J., & Robinson, S. (1997). Persistence, connection, and passion: A qualitative study of the career development of highly achieving African American women. *Journal of Counseling Psychology, 44,* 133–148.

Sadker, M., & Sadker, D. (1994). *Failing at fairness: How our schools cheat girls.* New York: Touchstone Books.

Sandler, B. R., & Hall, R. M. (1996). *The chilly classroom climate: A guide to improve the education of women.* Washington, DC: National Association for Women in Education.

Sears, P. S., & Barbie, A. H. (1977). Career and life satisfaction among Terman's gifted women. In J. C. Stanley, W. George, & C. Solano (Eds.), *The gifted and creative: Fifty year perspective* (pp. 72–106). Baltimore: Johns Hopkins University Press.

Selkow, P. (1984). Effects of maternal employment on kindergarten and first-grade children's vocational aspirations. *Sex Roles, 11,* 677–690.

Sells, L. (1973). High school mathematics as the critical filter in the job market. In *Developing opportunities for minorities in graduate education.* Proceedings of the Conference on Minority Graduate Education, University of California, Berkeley.

Sells, L. (1982). Leverage of equal opportunity through mastery of mathematics. In S. M. Humphreys (Ed.), *Women and minorities in science* (pp. 7–26). Boulder, CO: Westview Press.

Shinar, E. H. (1975). Sexual stereotypes of occupations. *Journal of Vocational Behavior, 7,* 99–111.

Solberg, V. S., Good, G. E., Nord, D., Holm, C., Hohner, R., Zima, N., et al. (1994). Assessing career search efficacy expectations. *Journal of Career Assessment, 2,* 111–123.

Spade, J., & Reese, C. (1991). We've come a long way, maybe: College students plans for work and family. *Sex Roles, 24,* 309–321.

Stafford, I. P. (1984). Relation of attitudes towards women's roles and occupational behavior to women's self-esteem. *Journal of Counseling Psychology, 31,* 332–338.

Stake, J. (1997). Integrating expressiveness and instrumentality in real life settings: A new perspective on benefits of androgyny. *Sex Roles, 37,* 541–564.

Super, D. E. (1980). A life-span, life-space approach to career development. *Journal of Vocational Behavior, 16,* 282–298.

Terman, L. M., & Oden, M. H. (1959). *Genetic studies of genius: Vol 5. The gifted group at midlife.* Stanford, CA: Stanford University Press.

Tipping, L. (1997). Work and family roles: Finding a new equilibrium. In H. Farmer (Ed.), *Diversity and women's career development* (pp. 243–270). Thousand Oaks, CA: Sage.

U.S. Department of Labor. (2000). *Occupational outlook handbook.* Washington, DC: U.S. Government Printing Office.

U.S. Department of Labor, Bureau of Labor Statistics. (2003). *Facts on women workers.* Washington, DC: Author.

Walsh, W. B., & Betz, N. E. (2001). *Tests and assessment* (4th ed.). Englewood Cliffs, NJ: Prentice-Hall.

Weishaar, M. E., Green, G. J., & Craighead, L. W. (1981). Primary influences of initial vocational choices for college women. *Journal of Vocational Behavior, 34,* 289–298.

Wilke, J. R., Ferree, M. M., & Ratcliff, K. (1998). Gender and fairness: Marital satisfaction in two-earner couples. *Journal of Marriage and the Family, 60,* 577–594.

Wycott, S. E. M. (1996). Academic performance of Mexican American women: Sources of support that serve as motivating variables. *Journal of Multicultural Counseling and Development, 24,* 146–155.

Yoder, J. (1999). *Women and gender: Transforming psychology.* Upper Saddle River, NJ: Prentice-Hall.

Yoder, J., & Aniakudo, P. (1997). "Outsider within" the firehouse. *Gender and Society, 11,* 324–341.

ASSESSMENT AND OCCUPATIONAL INFORMATION

CHAPTER 12

Assessment of Interests

Jo-Ida C. Hansen

VOCATIONAL INTERESTS ARE one of many variables included in most models of career development and person-environment fit (P-E fit), and assessment of interests is an integral ingredient in career counseling interventions. In fact, vocational interests are the most frequently assessed construct in career counseling. Ironically, then, identifying the origin of interests and developing precise definitions of interests have been elusive tasks. Early in the history of interest measurement, researchers such as E. K. Strong Jr., Leona Tyler, Ralph Berdie, Wilbur Layton, and John Darley and Theda Hagenah all proposed definitions (Berdie, 1944; Darley & Hagenah, 1955; Strong, 1943; Tyler, 1960). Their definitions (and others that have followed them) generally incorporate both *components* of interests and *determinants*. While many components of interests have been proposed, three major components have been identified most often: personality, motivation or drive, and self-concept. The two most widely cited determinants of interests are nurture, which emphasizes socialization and learning and includes numerous environmental and psychological influences that are hypothesized to shape interests; and nature, which emphasizes genetics and the heritability of interests.

Although theorists have made serious efforts to formulate definitions of interests, the construct has become, in many ways, synonymous with scores presented on interest inventory profiles. In other words, interests frequently are regarded simply as "what the test measures." Within the context of interest assessment, then, interests can be defined as a preference for activities expressed as likes or dislikes (e.g., "I like golf" or "I dislike selling things"). Depending on the measure, the activities rated may include school subjects, occupational titles, and other career-relevant stimuli.

INTERESTS AND VOCATIONAL THEORIES

The extent to which interests play a role in theories of career development and P-E fit varies. For example, Super's (1957) theory of vocational development, as expanded by Savickas (Chapter 3, this volume), concentrates on "attitudes, competencies, and behaviors that individuals use in fitting themselves to work that suits them." This career construction theory (Savickas's terminology) acknowledges Holland's typology as an operational definition of vocational personality that incorporates abilities, needs, values, and interests. While Savickas acknowledges that assessing vocational personalities (including interests) can be useful within career counseling, except during the growth stage little attention is paid at the theoretical level to interests or any of the other components of vocational personality in career construction theory (i.e., abilities, values, and needs). (See Savickas, Chapter 3, this volume, for a thorough description of the developmental theory of career construction.)

Social Cognitive Career Theory (SCCT; Lent, Chapter 5, this volume) also emphasizes the impact that external forces (e.g., home, schools, peers) have on the development of interests. However, SCCT places more emphasis on the mechanisms involved in shaping or molding interests than does career construction theory. As individuals try activities and receive feedback on their performance, they develop both self-efficacy and outcome expectations about the activities. If, as a result of feedback or self-evaluation, they view themselves as becoming competent, the "interest in the activity is likely to blossom and endure" (see Lent, Chapter 5, this volume, for a thorough description of the SCCT model).

Gottfredson's Theory of Circumscription and Compromise (L. Gottfredson, 1996), also a developmental model, views social class, sex, and intelligence as influences on a person's self-concept as well as on compromises people face in choosing their careers. Interests are viewed within this theory as just one of several vocationally relevant elements that compose the self-concept. The theory suggests that people often must compromise when they select a job. When asked to choose among sex type (i.e., traditional or nontraditional for the person's own sex), prestige (e.g., high status versus low status), or occupational interests (e.g., a job that matches a person's interests rather than one about which the person feels indifferent) as the sacrificial lamb, the order of compromise will depend on the relative magnitude of the compromise for each. Generally, when trade-offs are small on all three dimensions, interests will be least likely to be sacrificed. When moderate trade-offs among the three are required, people are least likely to sacrifice prestige. If major compromises are required, interests are most likely to be compromised. (For more detail on circumscription and compromise, see L. Gottfredson, Chapter 4, this volume.)

As described by Dawis (Chapter 1, this volume), the theory of work adjustment (TWA; Dawis & Lofquist, 1984) focuses on the way in which a person's abilities and values and their congruence, respectively, with an environment's requirements and reinforcers predicts work outcomes (e.g., satisfaction, performance, and tenure). Although TWA postulates do not specify the role of interests in work adjustment, Dawis and Lofquist, the primary architects of TWA, do acknowledge that vocational interests also predict satisfaction, performance, and tenure. (See Dawis, Chapter 1, this volume, for a thorough description of the theory of work adjustment.)

Among all vocational theories, John Holland's theory of vocational personality types focuses most explicitly on interests (Holland, 1997). He proposes that interest personalities can be summarized as six types—Realistic, Investigative, Artistic, Social, Enterprising, and Conventional (RIASEC). He also postulates that the relationship among these six types can be illustrated as an irregular hexagon with the types adjacent to one another on the hexagon having more characteristics in common than types farther apart on the hexagon. Holland's theory features interests as a reflection of personality. The notion that interests and personality share common variance (i.e., are correlated) has been a popular hypothesis for decades. However, Holland's theory of vocational personality types provides a more comprehensive model of vocational interests and their relationship to career decision making, satisfaction, and performance than those offered by other theorists, and his work has driven much of the research that examines the relationship between interests and personality. His theory has been used to organize the profiles of all major interest inventories and to develop interpretive materials to accompany the profiles; to provide a framework for integrating higher order abilities, personality, values, interests, and needs; and to describe interests relative to people, work environments, and job tasks. (See Spokane & Cruza-Guet, Chapter 2, this volume, for a thorough review of Holland's theory.)

Most career theories, then, focus on the role that nurture plays in shaping and developing interests. While none of the career theories explicitly deny that nature (i.e., genes) plays a role in the origin of a person's interests, they also do not directly address the degree to which interests are determined by heritability of interests. Behavior genetics studies, using twins as well as participants with other kinships, allow research designs that tease apart genetic and nongenetic effects. Especially informative research using twins reared together and apart supports a combination of nature and nurture determinants of interests. One study, which controlled for gender and age and used a large sample that included eight kinships, showed a genetic effect of 36% (Betsworth et al., 1994). This same study identified 9% shared environmental effects (e.g., living in the same home) and an additional 55% nonshared environmental effects (e.g., having different friends) and measurement error. This proportion of genetic and environmental effects is typical of the results reported in other studies. In career counseling, then, it is useful to use a model that incorporates both nature and nurture as important influences on the development and shaping of interests. Such a model is consistent with the early appearance of interest choices in young children and the tremendous stability of interests over the life span; it is also consistent with developmental and learning theories of career development.

INTERESTS AND PERSONALITY

Several attempts have been made to understand the relation of interests and personality. Much of this research has focused on Holland's six types and the five factor model (FFM) of personality, also known as the Big Five (Costa & McCrae, 1992a). Some research also has examined the relationship between Holland's types and Hogan's personality dimensions of sociability and conformity (Hogan, 1983). The general conclusion that can be drawn from this line of research is that there are two or three personality and interest variables that share a modest amount of variance—Openness and Holland's Investigative and Artistic interests; Extraversion and Enterprising and Social interests; and, to a lesser extent, Agreeableness and Holland's Social interests. However, research examining the relations among lower order personality facets (i.e., 30 NEO-PR-I facets; Costa & McCrae, 1992b), Holland's six personality types, and lower order interests (i.e., basic interest scales of the Strong Interest Inventory; Harmon, Hansen, Borgen, & Hammer, 1994) suggests that once the associations between interests and personality facets are accounted for, correlations between higher order personality factors such as the Big Five and interests are negligible (Sullivan & Hansen, under review).

Thus, the vast majority of the relations between interests and personality that have been examined, at both higher order levels (e.g., Holland types and the Big Five) and lower order levels (e.g., basic interest scales and the 30 NEO Personality Inventory facets) are relatively weak, and the evidence leads to the conclusion that, for prediction and career counseling purposes, interests and personality should not be treated as interchangeable constructs.

INTERESTS AND ABILITIES

Early models of career counseling typically attempted to match the abilities of the client with the requirements of the job. Later, vocational assessment was expanded from concentrating on the measurement of abilities to include assessment of interests. For example, E. K. Strong Jr. (1943) suggested that "the relationship among abilities, interests, and achievements may be likened to a motor boat with a motor and a rudder. The motor (abilities) determines how fast the boat can go, the rudder (interests) determines which way the boat goes" (p. 17). More recent work (Achter, Lubinski, Benbow, & Eftekhari-Sanjani, 1999; Lubinski, 2000) has supported Strong's contention that interests add incremental validity beyond ability to the prediction of educational and occupational choices and related outcomes (e.g., satisfaction and success). As Strong (1927a) noted, "The majority of [people] are practically equally fitted to enter a considerable number of occupations" (p. 297), and he later concluded (Strong, 1943):

> Interests supply something that is not disclosed by ability and achievement.
> . . . Counseling that considers both abilities and interests is distinctly superior to
> that based on either alone, for it is in a position to establish both what the [person]
> can do and what [she or he] wants to do. (p. 19)

STABILITY OF INTERESTS

Construct stability is an important prerequisite for any variable incorporated into decision-making exercises such as those used in career counseling. This is especially true for interests since the stability of the construct is intertwined with the reliability of the scores of the tests used to assess interests. If interests are not stable (in other words, if interests are a state rather than a trait), interest inventories have no chance of predicting occupational or educational choices even over short time spans. Based on the early work of E. K. Strong Jr. (1935, 1943) and on decades of research since Strong's early work, we know that interests are very stable over time. In fact, interests may be the most stable of all psychological constructs. We also know that the stability of interests depends on the age at Time 1 testing (the younger the participants, the less stable the interests) and the length of the interval between Time 1 and Time 2 testing (the longer the interval, the less stable the interests).

Typically, the stability of interests is evaluated over set time periods (e.g., 3 years or 12 years or 22 years between Time 1 and Time 2 testing), and the stability is expressed as a correlation between Time 1 and Time 2 scores. This approach looks at the stability of interests for a group, for example, college students tested as freshmen and again as seniors. On average, for example, the stability coefficients for individuals tested at age 18 and again at age 22 (4 years) and age 30 (12 years) are about 0.80 and 0.70, respectively (Hansen & Swanson, 1983; Swanson & Hansen, 1988). For those initially tested at age 33 and retested 12 years later at age 45, the stability coefficient increases to about 0.80 (Johansson & Campbell, 1971). Thus, by age 20 interests are stable even over periods of 5 to 10 years, and by age 25 interests are very stable. This evidence of the stability of interests for individuals, combined with evidence of test-retest reliability for an instrument, allows test users to have confidence in test scores that are used to predict future behaviors such as job or college major choice.

Occasionally, efforts also are made to look at the stability of an *individual's* interests. This approach typically correlates an individual's profile scores for Time 1 with profile scores for Time 2 using either Pearson product-moment correlations or correlations between rank-ordered profiles. The results from these analyses are similar to those for examining the stability of interests of groups of people. Generally, about 50% of individuals have Time 1 and Time 2 interest profiles that are substantially similar, and for many individuals the rank order correlations are in the high 0.90s, over relatively long time periods (e.g., 15 years; Hansen & Swanson, 1983; Lubinski, Benbow, & Ryan, 1995; Swanson & Hansen, 1988). However, these same studies illustrate that individual differences in interest stability do occur. The intraperson correlations for a sample often range from lows in the −.20s to highs in the +0.90s, illustrating that for some individuals dramatic changes in interests do occur over time.

Research also has been conducted to explore the extent to which the interests of occupations change or remain stable over the decades. This knowledge is important for determining the frequency with which interest inventories need to be revised. Even in times of a quickly changing society and technology, studies show that interests of people within a particular occupation (e.g., bankers, lawyers, foresters, psychologists, engineers, reporters) are virtually identical over 40 or 50 years (D. P. Campbell, 1966; Hansen, 1988).

WHY MEASURE INTERESTS?

Within the counseling intervention framework, interests may be assessed for a number of reasons, with the goal of helping individuals to make informed occupational and educational choices. First and foremost, measured interests (reported as scores on interest inventory profiles) can be used by counselors to guide the development of hypotheses about clients. These hypotheses, in turn, may be used to guide career exploration and to provide clients with a fresh perspective and new information. For clients, the profile scores promote self-understanding by various means: identifying previously unknown interests, broadening occupational possibilities for some people and narrowing choices for others, or simply confirming career choices (Hansen, 1994). Although expressed and inventoried interests show similar evidence of predictive validity for occupation and college major choices, many individuals who must make career and educational choices are undecided. For these clients, the scores on interest inventories can serve as powerful stimuli for jump-starting the exploration process and for developing career ideas and possibilities.

Interest inventories also are used in employment settings for selection to help employers determine those job candidates who will be most likely to complete training, to stay with the company, and to be successful (Hansen, 1994). Some employers also use interest inventories to help their workers find the right position within the company. The placement use of interest inventories often occurs when exceptional employees have become dissatisfied with their current positions but wish to remain with the company in another role. Conversely, career counseling that incorporates the use of an interest inventory can be very helpful with displaced employees who have been downsized, terminated, or disabled (Latak & Kaufman, 1988). In summary, career exploration that includes the assessment of interests can be valuable throughout the life span: first for educational and job decisions, then again as people seek more challenging work, then perhaps at some point if they question an initial decision, and once again, if they experience career plateaus or job losses (Hall & Rabinowitz, 1988; Kim & Moen, 2001; Korman, 1988). As people approach retirement, they may repeat the process of exploring their interests, focusing at this time on ways in which to make the transition from actualizing their vocational interests to engaging in activities that reflect their leisure interests (Hansen & Scullard, 2002).

PERSON-ENVIRONMENT INTEREST CONGRUENCE AND SATISFACTION AND PERFORMANCE

Research on job satisfaction has shown that a plethora of variables contribute to the prediction of a satisfied outcome. The role that interests play in job satisfaction usually is studied by examining the congruence or match between an individual's measured interests and the interest requirements of the environment in which she or he works. Typically, these studies look at higher order interests such as Holland's six types. The results from these studies, even those using meta-analysis (a statistical technique that aggregates results from many studies), are mixed, but generally the correlation between person-environment interest congruence and satisfaction is about 0.25 to 0.30 (Assouline & Meir, 1987; Hough, 1988; Tokar & Subich, 1997; Tranberg, Slane, & Ekeberg, 1993).

Intuitively, we expect the correlations between P-E interest congruence and satisfaction to be larger. One popular explanation for the smaller than expected relation is the restricted range (which can decrease correlations) in people's job satisfaction. The fact is that most people (88% according to some surveys) are satisfied with their jobs (Weaver, 1980). Another explanation is that moderator variables, such as occupational level, career stage, Holland type, personality type, values, group importance, job involvement, and career salience, play a role in reducing the correlation (Dawis & Lofquist, 1984; Meir, Keinan, & Segal, 1986; Spokane, Meir, & Catalano, 2000; Stumpf & Rabinowitz, 1981; Tranberg et al., 1993).

A third explanation focuses on the measurement of the satisfaction criterion. Multifactor or facet measures of job satisfaction seem better suited to tease apart the relation between P-E congruence than are global measures. For example, correlations around 0.40 have been found between interest congruence and satisfaction with more specific job facets, such as pay, coworkers, and promotions (Wiener & Klein, 1978). A fourth explanation centers on the level at which interests are assessed in most congruence-satisfaction studies. Often, in studies showing relatively modest correlations, interests are measured and work environments are coded, using Holland's six types, which represent higher order interests. However, studies conducted at a lower order level of interest assessment (e.g., occupational scales) suggest that a large proportion of people (e.g., 70% to 80%), who are satisfied with their jobs, score high on occupational scales that match their chosen occupations or chosen college majors (Hansen & Sackett, 1993; Hansen & Tan, 1992; Holland, 1997; Pendergrass, Hansen, Neuman, & Nutter, 2003). Well-being criteria, other than work satisfaction, that have been shown to be positively related to P-E interest congruence include life satisfaction, self-image, and self-esteem (Hansen & Ton, 2001; Hesketh & Gardner, 1993; Meir & Melamed, 1986). Criteria negatively related to P-E congruence include somatic complaints, burnout, and anxiety (Meir, Melamed, & Abu-Freha, 1990; Meir, Melamed, & Dinur, 1995).

Research also has shown that P-E congruence is related to persistence (i.e., tenure), success, and performance on the job and in school (Henry, 1989; Meir, Esformes, & Friedland, 1994; Richards, 1993; Smart, 1997). However, combining interests and abilities or aptitudes appears to improve predictions of achievement in work and academic settings beyond the levels that can be achieved using either construct alone (McHenry, Hough, Toquam, Hanson, & Ashworth, 1990; Wise, McHenry, & Campbell, 1990). The data support Strong's early contention that people will do well in an occupation if they have both the necessary interest and ability, but that people with only ability and no interest can do well but may not (Strong, 1943). In the same way that the combination of interests and abilities predicts success and performance better than either does alone, incorporating values also can improve the prediction of work outcomes, especially job satisfaction (Rounds, 1990).

METHODS OF INTEREST INVENTORY SCALE CONSTRUCTION

Historically, three approaches or methods have dominated the development of interest inventories: rational/theoretical, the empirical method of contrast groups, and item clustering. In the course of interest inventory development, all three methods or combinations of these methods may ultimately be employed. The rational-theoretical approach begins with a well-defined construct. Ideally, this approach relies on theory for the definition of the construct to be measured and for item development and selection. The definition of the measured construct, the item content, and the use of psychometric data to relate scores to measures of other theoretical constructs contribute to the interpretation of the scales.

The empirical method of contrast groups is based on the assumption that individuals postulated to differ on the construct also will differ in their responses to test items. Items are selected for inclusion in the test because they discriminate significantly between two or more groups hypothesized to differ on a criterion or construct. The empirical method of clustering relies most heavily on statistical analyses (e.g., factor analysis or cluster analysis) to identify underlying dimensions in a large pool of items. The dimensions then become the basis for the scales used to measure the underlying constructs, which in turn contribute to the interpretation of the scores. In practice, the various approaches to test development often are used in a logical sequence. Theory is used initially to generate the item pool. Empirical relationships (i.e., contrast groups or clustering) may then be used to retain, reject, or modify items. Interpretation of scores from the scales derived by this process has the advantage of a theoretical and empirical foundation for the underlying dimensions represented by the test.

POPULAR INTEREST INVENTORIES

Many interest inventories are available for use in career counseling. The Kuder Occupational Interest Survey (KOIS; Kuder & Zytowski, 1991) and the American College Testing Interest Inventory (UNIACT; ACT, 1995) are used most often with high school students. The Career Assessment Inventory (CAI; Johansson, 1986) initially was developed for use with women and men considering nonprofessional career choices. Three of the most frequently used interest inventories are the Self-Directed Search (SDS; Holland, 1971, 1985), Strong Interest Inventory (SII; Harmon et al., 1994), and the Campbell Interest and Skill Survey (CISS; D. P. Campbell, Hyne, & Nilsen, 1992). All three of these instruments include scales to measure Holland's six types. However, the SII and the CISS measure interests at three levels of specificity whereas the SDS focuses only on the broad Holland types. Although the SII and the CISS profiles include sets of scales that resemble one another, the approach for norming and standardizing the instruments differs.

Another notable difference between the SII and the CISS is the inclusion of Skill scales on the CISS that parallel the Interest scales. The Skill scales are designed to provide an estimate of the individual's ability to do tasks related to the interests measured by the Orientations scales, Basic Interest scales, and Occupational scales. The SII does have a companion instrument, the Skills Confidence Inventory (Betz, Borgen, & Harmon, 1996) that provides skill estimates for the six Holland types, but the CISS has Skill scales for all 98 of the interests reported on the CISS profile.

SELF-DIRECTED SEARCH

John Holland developed the Self-Directed Search, first published in 1971, as a vehicle for assessing a person's resemblance to each of his six vocational personality types (Holland, 1971, 1985). Holland selected items for the SDS using his theoretical model, which is based on "voluminous data about people in different jobs" (Holland, 1985, p. 3). The six scales are Realistic (works with things, practical and concrete), Investigative (works with ideas, analytical and scientific), Artistic (works with ideas, creative and imaginative), Social (works with people, empathetic and warm), Enterprising (works with people, ambitious and domineering), and Conventional (works with data, detail oriented and conscientious). Although any combination of types is possible, the closer the types are on the hexagon, the more likely they are to appear together as a person's pattern of interests or as the pattern of activities that occur in a work environment. (For a discussion of Holland's theory of vocational personalities, see Spokane & Cruza-Guet, Chapter 2, this volume.)

The SDS item pool is composed of 228 items dispersed over four sections: work activities (66 items), self-estimated competencies (66 items), occupations (84 items), and self-estimates of abilities that represent each of the six types (12 items). The reading level of the items is estimated to be at the seventh- or eighth-grade level, and a Form Easy (E) is available for individuals who read at about the fourth-grade level (Holland, 1985). The SDS most often is given as a self-administered, self-scored, and even self-interpreted interest inventory. However, a computer-administered and scored version is available. A scoring key is used to compute raw scores on the six scales that can be interpreted directly for a client, or scores can be compared to various norm groups provided in the manual (e.g., high school girls and boys, college women and men). The three highest raw scores are then used to form a summary code, which in turn is used to identify vocational and educational opportunities that incorporate similar interests represented in the individual's summary code. Holland and his colleagues have developed an array of interpretive materials to be used with the inventory results, including a *Dictionary of Holland Occupational Codes* (G. Gottfredson & Holland, 1996) and the *Educational Opportunities Finder* (Rosen, Holmberg, & Holland, 1994), which provide Holland codes for more than 1,000 occupations and for 759 educational programs. These resources are very useful for generalizing from scores on the six broad types to possible occupations and majors for a client to consider.

The SDS has been used extensively in vocational psychology research for the past 30 years. As a result, a wealth of evidence for the validity and reliability of the SDS has been aggregated. Over 4- to 12-week test-retest intervals, the median scale score reliability coefficients range from 0.76 to 0.89, respectively. Studies examining evidence of the concurrent validity of the SDS suggest that adults enter occupations that match their high point code about 60% of the time. The evidence for predictive validity for SDS scores is more variable and depends on the length of time between initial testing and the follow-up assessment, age at initial testing, and educational level. Generally, the studies show that between 40% and 80% of college students and adults are in majors and occupations that match their summary code's first letter (Hansen & Dik, 2004).

STRONG INTEREST INVENTORY

The Strong Interest Inventory (SII) first was published in 1927 under the title Strong Vocational Interest Blank (Strong, 1927b). The item pool for the SII currently includes 317 items divided into six content areas: occupational titles, school subjects, work activities, leisure activities, self characteristics, and preferences in the world of work. The reading level is estimated to be at about the eighth grade (Harmon et al., 1994). The SII is a very comprehensive survey that provides several levels of analysis of an individual's interests. At the highest order and broadest level are the six General Occupational Themes (GOT), developed to measure the six vocational types proposed by Holland (Realistic, Investigative, Artistic, Social, Enterprising, and Conventional). Within career counseling, these scales often are conceptualized as answering the question, "What am I like?"

The GOT were developed using a sequential method of scale construction (D. P. Campbell & Holland, 1972; Hansen & Johansson, 1972). First, items were selected that represented the definitions and descriptions that Holland proposed for each of the six types. Then, item statistics (i.e., intercorrelations) were used to select those items that contributed the most to the homogeneity of the scales. The resulting scales have internal consistencies that range from 0.90 to 0.95 (Hansen & Campbell, 1985) and median test-retest coefficients of 0.86 and 0.81, respectively, over 30-day and three-month intervals (Harmon et al., 1994). Evidence of validity for the GOT scores includes large correlations between same-named scales on the Vocational Preference Inventory (Holland, 1975) and the SII and evidence of the power of the GOT to separate occupational groups over about three standard deviations of scores in a logical way (e.g., engineers and electricians score high, and mental health workers and reporters score low on the Realistic Theme; Hansen & Campbell, 1985).

The 25 Basic Interest scales (BIS) represent the next level of specificity, and scores on these scales help the client to answer the question, "What do I like?" They include scales such as Mechanical Activities, Sales, Medical Science, Applied Arts, Teaching, and Computer Activities. The BIS were developed using the empirical method of clustering. As you would expect based on this method of scale construction, the item content of each scale is homogeneous, with alpha coefficients ranging from 0.77 to 0.96. The test-retest correlations are large, with medians of 0.85 and 0.80 over 30 days and three years, respectively (Harmon et al., 1994). Similar to the GOT, evidence of validity for the BIS scores consists of studies examining the extent to which the scales differentiate occupations in a logical manner (e.g., auto dealers and life insurance agents score high, and psychologists and physicists score low on the Sales BIS; Hansen & Campbell, 1985).

The Occupational scales provide the greatest level of specificity of interest measurement on the SII and answer the question, "Who am I like?" They compare the interests of the respondent directly to those of people employed in the occupation who are satisfied with their work. A total of 109 occupations are represented on the profile; about one-third of the scales represent occupations that typically can be entered without a college degree (e.g., carpenter, beautician, florist, optician, travel agent), and the remainder represent occupations of a more professional nature (e.g., architect, psychologist, nurse, marketing director, social science teacher). The Occupational scales are arranged on the SII profile according to their assigned Holland type (e.g., the Chemist scale and Biologist scale, both coded Investigative, appear on the same section of the profile).

The Occupational scales are constructed using the empirical method of contrast groups. This technique identifies about 50 to 60 items for each Occupational scale that differentiate the likes and dislikes of women or men in the occupation from women in general or men in general. The item content of the Occupational scales is heterogeneous; therefore, internal consistency measures of reliability are not meaningful for Occupational scales. However, because the scales are used to make decisions about college majors and careers, the concept of scale score stability is very important for this set of scales. The median test-retest correlation for the Occupational scales is 0.87 and 0.85, respectively, over 30-day and three-month intervals (Harmon et al., 1994).

Evidence of validity for the Occupational scales was a major research focus of early authors of the SII (e.g., D. P. Campbell, 1971; Hansen & Swanson, 1983; Hansen & Tan, 1992; Strong, 1943). However, much of the evidence of validity for the current version of the SII (Harmon et al., 1994) relies on generalizing from earlier studies. Two studies (Savickas, Taber, & Spokane, 2002; Sullivan & Hansen, in press) have demonstrated that the scores on the SII correlate substantially (convergent validity) with scores on same-named scales on other interest inventories (e.g., the CISS, the SDS, the KOIS, and the UNIACT). These same studies have shown that SII scale scores have small correlations (discriminant validity) with scores on other interest inventory scales that are unrelated. For example, the median correlation reported for same-named, scale scores for the SII and CISS was 0.62 and 0.66 for samples of women and men college students, respectively. For the same samples, the median correlations between nonmatching scales were 0.05 and 0.06 (Sullivan & Hansen, in press).

The extent to which the Occupational scales predict educational and occupational choices is a line of evidence of validity for SII scores that has been developed throughout the history of the inventory. The typical method for examining concurrent and predictive validity (collectively labeled *criterion validity*) involves comparing scores on the Occupational scales to declared choices. In the case of concurrent validity, the research participants complete the SII and provide information about their current occupations or educational choices at the same time. In the case of predictive validity, the research participants complete the SII at Time 1; then at some time in the future (usually after several years have passed), they are contacted to participate in a follow-up study to determine their educational choice or occupation at Time 2.

The summary statistic reported in these studies simply provides the percentage of participants who scored high on Occupational scales that match their choices (e.g., a participant scored high on the Reporter scale and is majoring in journalism or scored high on Personnel Director and works in that field). The results from these studies are stable from one study to the next and from one version of the SII to another. Generally, the concurrent studies show matches for about 75% of the sample, and the predictive studies show matches of about 70% over Time 1-Time 2 intervals of 4 years and about 65% over Time 1-Time 2 intervals of 12 years (Hansen & Sackett, 1993; Hansen & Swanson, 1983; Hansen & Tan, 1992).

The fourth set of scales presented on the SII profile is composed of four Special scales. The Learning Environment (LE) scale measures the extent to which an individual has interests similar to others who persist in academic environments. People who score high on the scale often are interested in learning for learning's sake and often aspire to complete graduate degrees. People with average scores on the LE scale have academic interests similar to people who have completed undergraduate college degrees, and people with low scores are similar to those who do not pursue college degrees. Studies examining evidence of validity for the LE scale indicate that it is not related to ability. Rather, interests of those who score low on the scale tend to reflect an interest in education for the practical knowledge that can be gained and directly applied to the work setting.

The Work Style (WS) scale on the current SII replaces the scale previously named Introversion-Extraversion and reflects interests of those who enjoy spending time with and working with people (high scores) as well as those interested in activities that allow them to work with ideas, data, and things (low scores). For example, child-care providers, flight attendants, and life insurance agents score high; and biologists, computer programmers, and physicists score low on WS. The Leadership Style (LS) scale correlates with introversion-extroversion in the same way that the Work Style scale does. High scores reflect an interest in leading and managing others, whereas low scores reflect the interests of people who prefer to work alone or those who prefer not to take leadership roles. Corporate trainers, public administrators, and school administrators score high while auto mechanics, farmers, and mathematicians score low on LS. The fourth scale is the Risk Taking/Adventure scale, which measures a willingness to try new things and to take social, financial, and physical risks (high scores). Electricians, emergency medical technicians, and police officers score high, and dental assistants, librarians, and mathematicians score low.

The Learning Environment and Work Style scales were developed using the empirical method of contrast groups (the same technique used to construct the Occupational scales), and the Risk Taking/Adventure and Leadership Style scales emerged from cluster and factor analyses. These four scales are normed on a sample of adult women and men drawn from a large number of occupations. The mean for this people-in-general sample is set equal to 50, and the standard deviation is set at 10. Generally, scores on the special scales that are above 55 are considered high, and scores below 45 are considered low. The test-retest reliabilities over 30 days are 0.83, 0.91, 0.85, and 0.87 for Learning Environment, Work Style, Leadership Style, and Risk Taking/Adventure, respectively (Harmon et al., 1994).

CAMPBELL INTEREST AND SKILL SURVEY

The Campbell Interest and Skill Survey (CISS; D. P. Campbell et al., 1992) is a 320-item instrument that assesses vocational interests ($N = 200$ items) as well as self-estimates of skills ($N = 120$ items) that parallel the interests measured by the inventory. Thus, the profile reports two scores (i.e., interest and skill) for each of the 98 scales. Combining self-estimates of interests and skills into one inventory was a unique approach at the time of publication of the CISS in 1992. The reading level is estimated at the sixth-grade level. All of the scales on the CISS are normed and standardized on combined samples of women and men drawn from a large variety of occupations. The mean for this sample is set equal to 50 with a standard deviation of 10. The profile provides interpretive comments, based on the respondent's interest and skill scores on each scale, that advise a course of action for the individual to consider: pursue (high interest and high skill), develop (high interest and low skill), explore (low interest and high skill), and avoid (low interest and low skill).

The types of scales presented on the CISS profile are similar to those on the Strong Interest Inventory. At the most general level, the CISS features seven Orientation scales. Six of the seven scales measure Holland's six types: Producing measures Realistic interests; Analyzing measures Investigative interests; and Creating, Helping, Influencing, and Organizing measure Artistic, Social, Enterprising, and Conventional interests, respectively. The seventh Orientation scale on the CISS is Adventuring, which measures an interest in physical and competitive activities and risk taking. Evidence of construct validity for the Orientation scale scores for both women and men (Sullivan & Hansen, in press) suggests that, with the exception of the Adventuring scale, the Orientation scales are good representatives of Holland's six types. The median correlation between matching CISS and SII GOT scales is about 0.70 for women and for men. For nonmatching scales, the median correlation is about 0.16. The Adventuring scale, relative to the other Orientation scales, does not exhibit convergence with the SII GOT, which measure Holland types (Sullivan & Hansen, in press). However, correlation between the CISS Adventuring and SII Adventure scales is large ($r = 0.65$), indicating that the CISS scale, similar to the SII scale, is a measure of willingness to take risks, to try new activities, and to be spontaneous. Like the SII GOT, the CISS Orientation scales have homogenous item content, large alpha coefficients (ranging from 0.82 to 0.93), and robust test-retest correlations (median $r = 0.87$ for interests and 0.81 for skills over 90 days; D. P. Campbell et al., 1992).

The 29 Basic Interest scales measure more specific interests than do the Orientation scales and include some interests not represented among the BIS on the Strong Interest Inventory, including advertising/marketing, financial service, adult development, child development, international activities, fashion, woodworking, and animal care. Conversely, the SII includes Basic Interest scales that measure interests not represented on the CISS profile: data management and computer activities.

The alpha coefficients for the Basic Interest scales range from 0.69 to 0.92, with a median of 0.86 for the Interest scales, and from 0.62 to 0.87 with a median of 0.79 on the Skill scales. The median test-retest coefficient over a period of 90 days is 0.83 for the Interest scales and 0.79 for the Skill scales (D. P. Campbell et al., 1992).

Evidence of validity for the Basic Interest Scales includes large correlations with SII scales that measure similar interests (e.g., correlations of 0.86 between SII and CISS Science scales and 0.77 between SII Teaching and CISS Adult Development; Sullivan & Hansen, in press) and the ability of the Interest and Skill scales to differentiate samples of people from various occupations in a meaningful way. For example, occupations that have high mean scores on CISS Mechanical Crafts include electricians, airline mechanics, test pilots, military officers, and carpenters; and occupations that have low mean scores include secretaries, social workers, child-care workers, guidance counselors, and nursing administrators (D. P. Campbell et al., 1992).

The 60 Occupational scales on the CISS were constructed using the empirical method of contrast groups that also is used to construct SII Occupational scales. The CISS and SII Occupational scales (OS) do differ in several important ways, however. First, the SII OS are separate sex scales; in other words, for each occupation, one scale was developed based on women in the occupation contrasted with women in general, and another scale was developed based on men in the occupation contrasted with men in general. The CISS scales, on the other hand, are combined-sex scales that used criterion (i.e., occupations) and contrast (i.e., people in general) samples composed of women and men to develop the scales.

Another difference is the way in which the scales are normed and standardized. The SII scales are normed on the occupational criterion sample with the mean set equal to 50. Therefore, a score of 50 on the SII OS indicates strong similarity in interests between the individual taking the inventory and the people in the occupation. However, the OS on the CISS are normed on a people-in-general sample such that a score of 50 indicates little similarity with people in the occupation. Thus, scores on the CISS suggesting strong similarity in interests between the individual and the people in a particular occupation are in the range of 65 to 70.

More evidence of validity has been reported for the CISS Occupational Interest scales than for the Occupational Skill scales. The *CISS Manual* (D. P. Campbell et al., 1992) reports the power of each Interest and Skill scale to discriminate between people in the general population and those in specific occupations. Generally, the mean score for people in general on the Skill scales is about 1.8 standard deviations below the mean score for the occupational criterion samples (range from 0.9 to 3.5 standard deviations). For the Interest scales, the mean for the people in general is about two standard deviations below the mean for people in the occupation (range from 1.2 to 2.9 standard deviations). In addition, two studies demonstrated evidence of convergent and discriminant validity of scores on the Interest scales with Kuder and SII occupational scale scores (Savickas et al., 2002; Sullivan & Hansen, in press).

Only two studies have looked at the concurrent validity of the CISS to predict college majors. The first study examined the use of both the Interest and Skill scales with college students from a variety of majors. The results showed that 69% of the women and 76% of the men scored high on Interest scales that matched their declared college majors. The students also took the SII to provide comparative data; 64% of the women and 73% of the men scored high on SII OS that matched their majors. The hit rates for the Skill scales were slightly lower; 61% of the women and 61% of the men scored high on Skill scales that matched their majors (Hansen & Neuman, 1999).

The second study (Pendergrass et al., 2003) examined the extent to which men student athletes chose college majors that agreed with their measured interests. Among the student athletes in nonrevenue sports (e.g., tennis, golf, cross country, swimming), 74% scored high on Interest scales matching their declared majors. Seventy-one percent of the comparison sample of nonstudent athletes and 63% of the athletes participating in revenue sports (e.g., basketball and football) scored high on Interest scales matching their declared majors.

The final set of scales on the CISS includes the Academic Focus (AF) scale and the Extraversion scale (ES). The AF scale measures interests and skills related to academic pursuits, and the ES measures interests and skills related to social interactions in the workplace. The AF scale was constructed using the empirical method of contrast groups that selected items that differentiated people in general from individuals with high levels of education. The items on the Extraversion scale are ones that have large correlations with a composite extraversion scale from the Campbell Leadership Index (CLI; D. P. Campbell, 1991). The 90-day test-retest coefficients for the AF Interest and Skill scales are 0.87 and 0.77, respectively. For the ES, the stability coefficients are 0.85 for the Interest scale and 0.82 for the Skill scale (D. P. Campbell et al., 1992).

As expected, high-scoring occupations on the Academic Focus Interest and Skill scales include those that require college and graduate degrees and have an interest in science and academic topics such as medical researchers, chemists, physicians, statisticians, and math or science teachers. Low-scoring occupations tend to include those in business fields such as financial planners, advertising executives, insurance agents, bank managers, and realtors. High-scoring occupations on the Extraversion Interest and Skill scales include those who work closely with others such as guidance counselors, school superintendents, and corporate trainers; those scoring low include people who tend to work alone or with things rather than people such as chemists, electricians, and carpenters (D. P. Campbell et al., 1992).

USING INTEREST INVENTORIES IN CAREER COUNSELING

The use of interest inventories in career counseling evolved out of career guidance programs that emerged in the 1930s in an effort to ease unemployment. World War II served as another catalyst as programs were developed, especially through the Veteran's Administration, to help veterans returning from World War II take advantage of educational opportunities offered through the GI Bill and choose new occupations as they were discharged from the military. The University of Minnesota's Department of Psychology, with its emphasis on individual differences, assessment, and applied psychology, became a major research center and counseling center with close ties to the Minneapolis VA Hospital. From this work emerged the trait-and-factor Minnesota point of view of counseling, a model of intervention that is very directive and involves providing clients with information and suggestions to guide them to the best decision. The assessment of abilities and interests was an important ingredient in early applications of trait and factor counseling, and later the assessment of needs, values, and personality also was incorporated into the model. Most current models of career counseling still incorporate assessment of interests as an important component. However, fewer models emphasize the need to objectively measure abilities, values, and personality.

Models of career counseling have been expanded beyond the "test them and tell them" approach of the Minnesota point of view. As counselors needed better intervention skills to deal with both personal and vocational concerns, they turned to Carl Rogers' nondirective approach (1951) for help in working with their clients. More recently, counselors often enrich trait-and-factor interpretation methods with attention to:

1. The counselor-client working relationship.
2. Contextual and cultural factors and individual differences that can have an impact on career decision making.
3. Developmental stages.
4. Economic and social realities.
5. Personal counseling issues.

Although career counseling itself has evolved and changed, the philosophy of the Minnesota point of view—assessment of client strengths and weaknesses and the use of test results to make predictions that will garner satisfaction and success for the client—remains relevant.

Career counseling approaches that incorporate assessment of multiple constructs allow counselors to more fully understand the client than do approaches that incorporate only interest assessment. Comparing results from ability and personality tests and from interest, value, and needs measures allows the counselor to better understand what motivates the client (interests and values), how the client interacts with others (personality), and the level of complexity at which the client is able to function (abilities). In addition, once clients have examined their scores on an interest inventory, they may find it difficult to make a decision because the possibilities, based on interests alone, are many and varied. Clients often find it helpful at this point to have additional information to help them begin to narrow their choices. Having data on abilities, personality, needs, and values provides additional information to determine the best P-E fit for the client. In terms of refining choices, a consideration of the client's abilities helps to determine the level of occupational and educational complexity that the individual will be able to successfully pursue. Understanding personality can provide direction within an organization. For example, a person who scores low on measures of responsibility and assertiveness probably will not make a good manager. In the same way, understanding needs and values can help people understand how they fit into a work environment. A person scoring high on the need for independence may not appreciate a job with close supervision from a superior. A person who values achievement probably will want to work in a job that challenges him or her.

Unfortunately, financial and time constraints often limit assessment to vocational interests. In those instances, counselors will find it useful to use past behaviors to help them understand the client more fully. For example, counselors can gather information on performance in coursework and on achievement tests to estimate abilities. They can inquire about what is important in a job, an employer, and coworkers to estimate values. They can also ask clients to describe ways in which they interact with others on the job, within their family, and with friends and strangers to better understand their clients' personality and the environments in which they excel.

SELECTING AN INTEREST INVENTORY

Which interest inventory to use in career counseling depends to some extent on the age of the client and the resources of the counseling agency. Younger clients (e.g., freshmen and sophomores in high school) may not have interests that are sufficiently well developed to have differentiated scores on occupational scales such as those that appear on the SII or CISS. For younger clients, then, the most useful information probably will come from higher order scales such as those found on Holland's SDS or the Orientation scales of the CISS or General Occupational Themes of the SII. For older high school students, college students, and adults, scales that measure interests relative to specific occupations (i.e., the Occupational scales on the SII and CISS) will be useful.

The SDS is one of the more economical interest inventories available to consumers primarily because the instrument can be self-scored. Instruments such as the CISS and SII, which have a multitude of scores as well as interpretive comments presented on the profile, must be machine scored, which increases the price of these instruments. The trade-off, then, is the reasonable cost of the SDS versus the more detailed information provided by the CISS and SII.

PREPARING TO USE INTEREST INVENTORIES

To prepare to use interest inventories, counselors should study the inventory's manual. Typically, test manuals include information on the purpose of the inventory and provide an overview of the testing materials. Most manuals describe the way in which the scales were constructed, normed, and standardized; report evidence of reliability and validity; note inventory limitations; and offer suggestions for the use and interpretation of the scale scores. The manual also will provide information that helps the counselor to know what the scale names mean and what scores are considered high, average, or low.

ADMINISTERING AN INTEREST INVENTORY

Interest inventories may be administered either individually or in group settings. The most popular method still is the traditional paper-and-pencil format, but computer-administered versions also are available. Regardless of the administration format or setting, a standardized introduction should be given to orient the client to the testing expectations. In addition, for clients who may have difficulty understanding the items, it generally is permissible to provide them with definitions or explanations to ensure that they understand the items.

PREPARING TO INTERPRET AN INTEREST INVENTORY

Before meeting with the client to interpret the test results, it is very useful for the counselor to review the profile. This review should include checking validity indexes that may indicate some problem with the test administration or client's responses and examining the profile for patterns of interests that emerge across various sets of scales. In addition to providing an assessment of work-related interests, interest inventories also often tap leisure interests and preferences for various types of work, recreational activities, and living environments. Therefore, as the counselor prepares for the interpretation session, it is useful to think broadly about the ways in which a client may satisfy the interests that are reported on the interest inventory profile. During the session, clients then can be encouraged to think about ways in which they can integrate their interests into a composite that allows them to satisfy their interests across the many roles in their lives (e.g., worker, family member, leisurite, friend, volunteer; Hansen, 2000).

INTERPRETING AN INTEREST INVENTORY

Interest inventories help clients to identify their interests in an efficient manner, and during the interpretation session the scores are used to stimulate discussion about occupations and activities that match their interests. The results also provide a framework for stimulating discussion about options that clients may not have considered in the past and about ways in which some interests may be better satisfied through leisure or volunteer activities than through the world of work. The client-counselor interaction and exchange, in turn, is used to verify working hypotheses (Watkins, 2000).

While it may be tempting to view test interpretation as a discrete activity within career counseling, research has shown that college student clients tend to recall very little about the specific profile results reported to them one year earlier (Hansen, Kozberg, & Goranson, 1994). Therefore, it is important that test result interpretations are integrated into the overall counseling process.

The counselor needs to be knowledgeable about the meaning of scale scores to provide the client with accurate information about the results and to convey the nuances of the results. Understanding the nuts and bolts of test construction as well as knowing the evidence of reliability and validity for an instrument provides a necessary foundation for proper test interpretation. However, counseling skills also are required for interpreting test results, and common intervention techniques such as establishing rapport, developing a positive working alliance, and providing a safe and supportive atmosphere are just as important during test interpretation as during any other counseling session (V. L. Campbell, 2000). Communication skills also are important. Throughout the process, the counselor is striving to facilitate the client's active involvement in understanding the results and relating them to the goals of counseling. In subsequent counseling sessions, clients often find it useful to return to their profiles to refresh their memory, clarify results, and generally integrate the test scores with the exploration process and their counseling goals.

BASIC STEPS FOR INTERPRETING AN INTEREST INVENTORY

Although counselors will want to develop their own style for interpreting interest inventories—one that blends test interpretation with their theoretical approach to counseling interventions and to career development and decision making—there are several basic steps that can be incorporated into most interpretations. The order of these steps certainly can be changed to individualize the counseling process, but the following steps offer one format frequently used by counselors:

1. Review the purpose for taking the inventory and looking at the results.
2. Ask for any reactions the client may have had to taking the inventory.
3. Remind the client that interest inventories do not measure abilities.

4. Ask if the client can predict two or three high scores—usually for the scales that measure the Holland types.
5. Briefly describe how the scale scores were derived.
6. Explain the way in which the scales are normed and standardized and describe the sample to which the client is being compared.
7. Explain the meaning of numerical scores and interpretive comments.
8. Describe what the scales mean and give an example of one or two items on the scale.
9. Ask the client for reactions to the scores (i.e., How accurate is the picture that the scores paint for the client?).
10. Ask clients to clarify how they satisfy each of their interests (e.g., work, recreation, social activities) and encourage integration of the results with past and current activities to help understand the results.
11. Look for patterns across the profile and ponder ways in which interests in various activities might be combined into a job or career.
12. Identify additional related educational or occupational possibilities not reported on the profile that might also satisfy the client's interests.
13. Develop a plan with the client for the next steps to take in the career exploration process.
14. Ask the client to summarize the results at the end of the session and allow time to discuss any misunderstandings.

RESPONSIBLE USE OF TESTS

Most test publishers require test purchasers to verify their educational background, training, and experience and sell interest inventories only to those who are qualified. Generally, a master's degree, including coursework in psychological testing and measurement, is the minimum requirement. Effective use and interpretation of interest inventories also require training in current testing issues such as the effect of sex differences on interest scores and interpretation; the fair use of interest inventories with diverse racial, ethnic, and cultural groups; and privacy and confidentiality of test results. Most test publishers have made concerted efforts to ensure that the basic elements of interest inventories—the items—are relevant for most test takers. These efforts include revising items so that the wording does not suggest in any way that some activities or occupations are not appropriate for all groups and constructing scales that reflect activities that appeal to multiple groups. In addition, efforts have been made to collect evidence of validity for test scores for diverse populations and to better understand the nature of differences in interests between women and men and among various cultural groups. Nonetheless, counselors still need to be aware that cultural background and contextual variables may have an impact on test results.

Sex Differences in Interests

Sex differences in interests have been studied throughout the history of interest measurement, and the results of these studies have guided inventory development. Women and men do report differential levels of interests in some areas—most notably, women express more Artistic and Social interests, and men express more Realistic and Investigative interests. Some have suggested that the differences in interest between women and men will disappear as the barriers to occupational entry in nontraditional occupations fall. However, studies that have examined sex differences in interests at both the item and scale score level over a 50-year period suggest that gender differences in interests are very stable and robust (Hansen, 1988).

E. K. Strong (1943) was among the first to attempt to develop combined-sex occupational scales. However, he concluded (as have many researchers following in his footsteps) that separate-sex scales were more effective for counseling. This conclusion is especially true for the use of interest inventories with women or men who have interests that are nontraditional for their sex (e.g., women who are interested in farming and men who are interested in clerical work; Hansen, 1982). Nonetheless, some interest inventories do report scores that are based only on combined-sex samples.

Another strategy used by test publishers to reduce sex bias in interest inventories occurs at the item level. Language that infers that a job or activity is appropriate for only one sex or the other has been eliminated from extant inventory items (as well as the interpretive materials). For some interest inventories, new items have been developed that have similar appeal to women and men to replace items that were more stereotypic for one sex or the other. In spite of efforts to develop sex-fair interest inventories, within the broad career counseling context, women and men still may feel restricted in their occupational and educational choices and, therefore, may need support and encouragement from their counselors to explore broadly. (See Betz, Chapter 11, this volume, for a detailed discussion of the role of gender in career development.)

CULTURAL DIFFERENCES IN INTERESTS

The relevance of interests across cultures has been examined most often by looking statistically at the relations among Holland's interest types across racial-ethnic groups. Several large-scale studies using the SII and the UNIACT show that the intercorrelations among the six types fit Holland's circular model for African American, Asian American, Native American, Mexican American, and Caucasian participants (Fouad, Harmon, & Borgen, 1997). This suggests that inventories based on Holland's RIASEC model have validity for diverse populations. Nonetheless, the use of interest inventories with racial, ethnic, and culturally diverse clients may be enhanced if counselors strive to understand the values and attitudes of other cultures and are aware of their own values as well as possible biases and stereotypes. Most of the studies exploring the usefulness of interest inventories with ethnic and racial groups have been concurrent validity studies used to assess the extent to which scores on the profiles predict occupational entry or choice of a college major. Generally, American Indian, African American, Asian American, and Latina/Latino students score high on scales representing the occupations or college majors they have chosen at about the same rate as Anglo American students (about 70%). The Latina/Latino students have the highest match between score and choice (75%), and American Indians have the lowest match (about 56%, which still considerably exceeds chance hit rate expectations of about 28%; Hansen & Haverkamp, 1986; Haviland & Hansen, 1987; Holland, 1997).

One concern with most interest inventories is that the scales are constructed using samples composed primarily of Anglo Americans. Ideally, then, normative data would be made available by the publisher for various racial, ethnic, and cultural groups. The reality, however, is that this goal is rarely achieved. In lieu of these data, good counseling practice is very important. Another concern is that most interest inventories are administered in English. Clients who do not speak English, or for whom English may be a second language, may not understand the meanings or nuances of some items or the labels for some scales. The best practice for counselors is to collaborate with clients to gain an understanding of cultural influences and, at the same time, to be aware of individual differences that may have an impact on the career decision-making process and career choices. (See Worthington, Flores, & Navarro, Chapter 10, this volume, for a detailed discussion of career development of people of color.)

ISSUES OF PRIVACY AND CONFIDENTIALITY

Maintaining client confidentiality is just as important in the use and interpretation of interest inventories as it is in other testing situations or in personal counseling. This means that procedures should be in place for protecting an individual's right to privacy. Test data should not be revealed to others without the written consent of the client or the client's legal guardian. Issues of confidentiality can be especially tricky when the career counselor is employed by the client's employer. Under these circumstances, the counselor needs to discuss issues of privacy with the employer and the client to ascertain in advance (1) how test results will be used, (2) any limits on confidentiality, and (3) the need for informed consent. In addition, systems for receiving test results, especially those that arrive by facsimile or the Internet, should be developed to ensure secure storage with access only by authorized personnel.

SUMMARY

Longitudinal outcome research has shown that students who receive a basic interest inventory interpretation tend to participate more in career exploration activities than do students who have not taken an interest inventory and had it interpreted (Randahl, Hansen, & Haverkamp, 1993). Incorporating interest inventories into career counseling models provides clients and counselors with information that will assist clients to develop their potential. This is true in career counseling as well as in selection and placement uses of interest inventories. Whether the goal is to enhance an individual's satisfaction with the job or the organization's satisfaction with the individual, knowledge of interests as one component in career counseling can help both of these goals to be met.

REFERENCES

Achter, J. A., Lubinski, D., Benbow, C. P., & Eftekhari-Sanjani, H. (1999). Assessing vocational preferences among gifted adolescents adds incremental validity to abilities. *Journal of Educational Psychology, 91,* 777–786.

American College Testing. (1995). *Technical manual: Revised unisex edition of the ACT Interest Inventory (UNIACT).* Iowa City, IA: ACT.

Assouline, M., & Meir, E. I. (1987). Meta-analysis of the relationship between congruence and well-being measures. *Journal of Vocational Behavior, 31,* 319–332.

Berdie, R. F. (1944). Factors related to vocational interests. *Psychological Bulletin, 41,* 137–157.

Betsworth, D. G., Bouchard, T. J., Jr., Cooper, C. R., Grotevant, H. D., Hansen, J. C., Scarr, S., et al. (1994). Genetic and environmental influences on vocational interests assessed using adoptive and biological families and twins reared apart and together. *Journal of Vocational Behavior, 44,* 263–278.

Betz, N. E., Borgen, F. H., & Harmon, L. W. (1996). *Skills Confidence Inventory: Applications and technical guide.* Palo Alto, CA: Consulting Psychologists Press.

Campbell, D. P. (1966). The stability of vocational interests within occupations over long time spans. *Personnel and Guidance Journal, 44,* 1012–1019.

Campbell, D. P. (1971). *Handbook for the Strong vocational interest blank.* Palo Alto, CA: Stanford University Press.

Campbell, D. P. (1991). *Manual for the Campbell Leadership Index.* Minneapolis, MN: National Computer Systems.

Campbell, D. P., & Holland, J. L. (1972). A merger in vocational interest research: Applying Holland's theory to Strong's data. *Journal of Vocational Behavior, 2,* 353–376.

Campbell, D. P., Hyne, S. A., & Nilsen, D. L. (1992). *Manual for the Campbell Interest and Skill Survey.* Minneapolis, MN: National Computer Systems.

Campbell, V. L. (2000). A framework for using tests in counseling. In C. E. Watkins Jr. & V. L. Campbell (Eds.), *Testing and assessment in counseling practice* (pp. 3–11). Mahwah, NJ: Erlbaum.

Costa, P. T., Jr., & McCrae, R. R. (1992a). Four ways five factors are basic. *Personality and Individual Differences, 13,* 653–665.

Costa, P. T., Jr., & McCrae, R. R. (1992b). *NEO-PR-I professional manual.* Odessa, FL: Psychological Assessment Resources.

Darley, J. G., & Hagenah, T. (1955). *Vocational interest measurement.* Minneapolis: University of Minnesota Press.

Dawis, R. V., & Lofquist, L. H. (1984). *A psychological theory of work adjustment.* Minneapolis: University of Minnesota Press.

Fouad, N. A., Harmon, L. W., & Borgen, F. H. (1997). The structure of interests in employed male and female members of U.S. racial/ethnic minority and nonminority groups. *Journal of Counseling Psychology, 44*(4), 339–345.

Gottfredson, G. D., & Holland, J. L. (1996). *Dictionary of Holland occupational codes* (3rd ed.). Odessa, FL: Psychological Assessment Resources.

Gottfredson, L. (1996). Gottfredson's Theory of Circumscription and Compromise. Chapter 5 in D. Brown & L. Brooks (Eds.), *Career choice and development* (3rd ed., pp. 179–232). San Francisco, CA: Jossey-Bass.

Hall, D. T., & Rabinowitz, S. (1988). Maintaining employee involvement in a plateaued career. In M. London & E. M. Mone (Eds.), *Career growth and human resource strategies: The role of the human resource professional in employee development* (pp. 67–80). New York: Qurom Books.

Hansen, J. C. (1982). Sex differences in interests and interpreting opposite-sex scores on the Strong-Campbell Interest Inventory. *Illinois Guidance and Personnel Quarterly, 84,* 5–12.

Hansen, J. C. (1988). Changing interests: Myth or reality? *Applied Psychology: An International Review, 37,* 137–150.

Hansen, J. C. (1994). The measurement of vocational interests. In M. G. Rumsey, C. B. Walker, & J. H. Harris (Eds.), *Personnel selection and classification* (pp. 293–316). Hillsdale, NJ: Erlbaum.

Hansen, J. C. (2000). Interpretation of the Strong interest inventory. In C. E. Watkins Jr. & V. L. Campbell (Eds.), *Testing and assessment in counseling practice* (pp. 227–262). Mahwah, NJ: Erlbaum.

Hansen, J. C., & Campbell, D. P. (1985). *Manual for the SVIB-SCII* (4th ed.). Stanford, CA: Stanford University Press.

Hansen, J. C., & Dik, B. (2004). Measures of career interests. In J. C. Thomas & M. Hersen (Eds.), *Comprehensive handbook of psychological assessment* (Vol. 4, pp. 166–191). New York: Wiley.

Hansen, J. C., & Haverkamp, B. E. (1986). *Concurrent validity of the SCII for American Indian, Asian, Black, and Hispanic college students.* Minneapolis: University of Minnesota, Center for Interest Measurement Research.

Hansen, J. C., & Johansson, C. B. (1972). The application of Holland's vocational theory to the Strong Vocational Interest Blank for Women. *Journal of Vocational Behavior, 2,* 479–493.

Hansen, J. C., Kozberg, J. G., & Goranson, D. (1994). Accuracy of student recall of Strong Interest Inventory results 1 year after interpretation. *Measurement and Evaluation in Counseling and Development, 26,* 235–242.

Hansen, J. C., & Neuman, J. L. (1999). Evidence of concurrent prediction of the Campbell Interest and Skill Survey (CISS) for college major selection. *Journal of Career Assessment, 7,* 239–247.

Hansen, J. C., & Sackett, S. A. (1993). Agreement between college major and vocational interests for female athlete and nonathlete college students. *Journal of Vocational Behavior, 43,* 298–309.

Hansen, J. C., & Scullard, M. G. (2002). Psychometric evidence for the Leisure Interest Questionnaire and analyses of the structure of leisure interests. *Journal of Counseling Psychology, 49,* 331–341.

Hansen, J. C., & Swanson, J. L. (1983). The effect of stability of interests on the predictive and concurrent validity of the SCII for college majors. *Journal of Counseling Psychology, 30,* 194–201.

Hansen, J. C., & Tan, R. (1992). Concurrent validity of the 1985 Strong Interest Inventory for college major selection. *Measurement and Evaluation in Counseling and Development, 25,* 53–57.

Hansen, J. C., & Ton, M. (2001). Using a person-environment fit framework to predict satisfaction and motivation in work and marital roles. *Journal of Career Assessment, 9,* 315–331.

Harmon, L. W., Hansen, J. C., Borgen, F. H., & Hammer, A. L. (1994). *Strong Interest Inventory: Applications and technical guide.* Palo Alto, CA: Consulting Psychologists Press.

Haviland, M. L., & Hansen, J. C. (1987). Criterion validity of the Strong-Campbell Interest Inventory for American Indian college students. *Measurement and Evaluation in Counseling and Development, 19,* 196–201.

Henry, P. (1989). Relationship between academic achievement and measured career interest: Examination of Holland's theory. *Psychological Reports, 64,* 35–40.

Hesketh, B., & Gardner, D. (1993). Person-environment fit models: A reconceptualization and empirical test. *Journal of Vocational Behavior, 42,* 315–332.

Hogan, R. (1983). Socioanalytic theory of personality. In M. M. Page (Ed.), *1982 Nebraska Symposium on Motivation: Personality—current theory and research* (pp. 55–89). Lincoln: University of Nebraska Press.

Holland, J. L. (1971). *The counselor's guide to the Self-Directed Search.* Odessa, FL: Psychological Assessment Resources.

Holland, J. L. (1975). *Manual for the Vocational Preference Inventory.* Palo Alto, CA: Consulting Psychologists Press.

Holland, J. L. (1985). *Self-Directed Search professional manual.* Odessa, FL: Psychological Assessment Resources.

Holland, J. L. (1997). *Making vocational choices: A theory of vocational personalities and work environments* (3rd ed.). Odessa, FL: Psychological Assessment Resources.

Hough, L. M. (Ed.). (1988). *Literature review: Utility of temperament, biodata, and interest assessment for predicting job performance* (ARI Research Note 88-02). Alexandria, VA: U.S. Army Research Institute.

Johansson, C. B. (1986). *Career Assessment Inventory: Enhanced version.* Minneapolis, MN: National Computer Systems.

Johansson, C. B., & Campbell, D. P. (1971). Stability of the SVIB for men. *Journal of Applied Psychology, 55,* 34–36.

Kim, J. E., & Moen, P. (2001). Is retirement good or bad for subjective well-being? *Current Directions in Psychological Science, 10,* 83–86.

Korman, A. K. (1988). Career success and personal failure: Mid-to-late career feelings and events. In M. London & E. M. Mone (Eds.), *Career growth and human resource strategies: The role of the human resource professional in employee development* (pp. 81–94). New York: Quorum Books.

Kuder, F., & Zytowski, D. G. (1991). *Kuder Occupational Interest Survey Form DD general manual.* Adel, IA: National Career Assessment Associates.

Latak, J. C., & Kaufman, H. G. (1988). Termination and outplacement strategies. In M. London & E. M. Mone (Eds.), *Career growth and human resource strategies: The role of the human resource professional in employee development* (pp. 289–313). New York: Quorum Books.

Lubinski, D. (2000). Scientific and social significance of assessing individual differences: "Sinking shafts at a few critical points." In S. T. Fiske (Ed.), *Annual review of psychology* (Vol. 51, pp. 405–444). Palo Alto, CA: Annual Reviews.

Lubinski, D., Benbow, C. P., & Ryan, J. (1995). Stability of vocational interests among the intellectually gifted from adolescence to adulthood: A 15-year longitudinal study. *Journal of Applied Psychology, 80,* 196–200.

McHenry, J. J., Hough, L. M., Toquam, J. L., Hanson, M. A., & Ashworth, S. (1990). Project A validity results: The relationship between predictor and criterion domains. *Personnel Psychology, 43,* 335–354.

Meir, E. I., Esformes, Y., & Friedland, N. (1994). Congruence and differentiation as predictors of worker's occupational stability and job performance. *Journal of Career Assessment, 2,* 40–54.

Meir, E. I., Keinan, G., & Segal, Z. (1986). Group importance as a mediator between personality-environment congruence and satisfaction. *Journal of Vocational Behavior, 28,* 60–69.

Meir, E. I., & Melamed, S. (1986). The accumulation of person-environment congruences and well-being. *Journal of Occupational Behavior, 7,* 315–323.

Meir, E. I., Melamed, S., & Abu-Freha, A. (1990). Vocational, avocational, and skill utilization congruences and their relationship with well-being in two cultures. *Journal of Vocational Behavior, 36,* 153–165.

Meir, E. I., Melamed, S., & Dinur, C. (1995). The benefits of congruence. *Career Development Quarterly, 43,* 257–266.

Pendergrass, L. A., Hansen, J. C., Neuman, J. L., & Nutter, K. J. (2003). Examination of the concurrent validity of the scores from the CISS for student-athlete college major selection: A brief report. *Measurement and Evaluation in Counseling and Development, 35,* 212–218.

Randahl, G. J., Hansen, J. C., & Haverkamp, B. E. (1993). Instrumental behaviors following test administration and interpretation: Exploration validity of the Strong Interest Inventory. *Journal of Counseling and Development, 71,* 435–439.

Richards, J. M. (1993). Career development: A ten year longitudinal study of population scientists. *Journal of Career Assessment, 1,* 181–192.

Rogers, C. (1951). *Client-centered therapy.* Boston: Houghton Mifflin.

Rosen, D., Holmberg, K., & Holland, J. L. (1994). *The educational opportunities finder.* Odessa, FL: Psychological Assessment Resources.

Rounds, J. B. (1990). The comparative and combined utility of work value and interest data in career counseling with adults. *Journal of Vocational Behavior, 37,* 32–45.

Savickas, M. L., Tabor, B. J., & Spokane, A. R. (2002). Convergent and discriminant validity of five interest inventories. *Journal of Vocational Behavior, 61,* 139–184.

Smart, J. C. (1997). Academic subenvironments and differential patterns of self-perceived growth during college: A test of Holland's theory. *Journal of College Student Development, 38,* 68–77.

Spokane, A. R., Meir, E. I., & Catalano, M. (2000). Person-environment congruence and Holland's theory: A review and reconsideration. *Journal of Vocational Behavior, 57,* 137–187.

Strong, E. K., Jr. (1927a). Vocational guidance of engineers. *Industrial Psychology Monthly, 11,* 291–298.

Strong, E. K., Jr. (1927b). *Vocational Interest Blank.* Palo Alto, CA: Stanford University Press.

Strong, E. K., Jr. (1935). Permanence of vocational interests. *Journal of Educational Psychology, 25,* 336–344.

Strong, E. K., Jr. (1943). *Vocational interests of men and women.* Palo Alto, CA: Stanford University Press.

Stumpf, S. A., & Rabinowitz, S. (1981). Career stage as a moderator of performance relationships with facets of job satisfaction and role perceptions. *Journal of Vocational Behavior, 18,* 202–218.

Sullivan, B. A., & Hansen, J. C. (in press). Evidence of construct validity of the interest scales on the Campbell Interest and Skill Survey. *Journal of Vocational Behavior.*

Sullivan, B. A., & Hansen, J. C. (in review). Mapping association between interests and personality: Toward a conceptual understanding of individual differences in vocational behavior. *Journal of Counseling Psychology.*

Super, D. E. (1957). *The psychology of careers.* New York: Harper & Row.

Swanson, J. L., & Hansen, J. C. (1988). Stability of vocational interests over four-year, eight-year, and twelve-year intervals. *Journal of Vocational Behavior, 33,* 185–202.

Tokar, D. M., & Subich, L. M. (1997). Relative contributions of congruence and personality dimensions to job satisfaction. *Journal of Vocational Behavior, 50,* 482–491.

Tranberg, M., Slane, S., & Ekeberg, S. E. (1993). The relation between interest congruence and satisfaction: A meta-analysis. *Journal of Vocational Behavior, 42,* 253–264.

Tyler, L. (1960). The development of interests. In W. L. Layton (Ed.), *The Strong Vocational Interest Blank: Research and uses* (pp. 62–75). Minneapolis: University of Minnesota Press.

Watkins, C. E., Jr. (2000). Some final thoughts about using tests and assessment procedures in counseling. In C. E. Watkins Jr. & V. L. Campbell (Eds.), *Testing and an assessment in counseling practice* (pp. 547–555). Mahwah, NJ: Erlbaum.

Weaver, C. N. (1980). Job satisfaction in the United States in the 1970s. *Journal of Applied Psychology, 65,* 364–367.

Wiener, Y., & Klein, K. L. (1978). The relationship between vocational interests and job satisfaction: Reconciliation of divergent results. *Journal of Vocational Behavior, 13,* 298–304.

Wise, L. L., McHenry, J. J., & Campbell, J. P. (1990). Identifying optimal predictor composites and testing from generalizability across jobs and performance factors. *Personnel Psychology, 43,* 355–366.

CHAPTER 13

Assessment of Needs and Values

James B. Rounds and Patrick Ian Armstrong

WORK VALUES ARE shared interpretations of what people want and expect from work (Nord, Brief, Atieh, & Doherty, 1990). As such, values are central to our understanding of both the meaning of work and the reasons that people work. This shared social reality influences the type of work people design for others to do and how people are socialized for work. Values are central to human motivation and have a long history in psychology. Research on values can be found in many fields in psychology, with much of the theory and research coming from personality and social psychology and the more applied research coming from organizational and counseling psychology. The development of work value measures for career counseling comes from the traditional vocational psychology emphasis on occupational choice and adjustment (Dawis, 1991).

It is generally assumed that values are related to an individual's choice of a career and work behavior outcomes. Values assessment represents an opportunity to frame a client's career-related decisions in the context of underlying motivations. The comparisons between an individual's values and the rewards offered by different occupations can provide information on what kinds of occupations to explore. How well an individual's values fit with an organization has implications for career management strategies. Value-organization fit may influence early career success by contributing to mentoring relations, challenging career assignments, and fast-track promotion ladders (Bretz & Judge, 1994). Values assessments can have benefits for both the individual and organization, as individuals can identify work values that are not sufficiently rewarded and organizations can recruit employees with a close values fit.

Although work values offer potentially important information, value measures have received less research attention than measures of other individual differences characteristics, such as interests. Few papers were published on work values in the 1990s, and the topic of work values in many career development and assessment textbooks is an afterthought. But this situation is not confined to career

We thank Chris Moyer for his comments on a draft of this chapter

305

counseling and vocational psychology. Rohan (2000), in a review of introductory social psychology and personality textbooks, found no discussion of value theory in the 1990s. There are few work value measures commercially available and fewer still with sufficient reliability and validity to be recommended for use with clients. There are several reasons for this state of affairs. Vocational psychology from a counseling psychology perspective has historically focused on vocational choice for high school and college students (Fitzgerald & Rounds, 1989), a population for which the assessment emphasis has been on vocational interests (Rounds, 1990). Work values are considered to be most applicable to individuals who have had some experience in the workplace, an adult clientele who are not frequently seen at college counseling centers. The critical loss of the work value research programs of Super and of Dawis and Lofquist has probably also played an important role in the decline in empirical research.

Several developments may, however, revitalize research on work values. One development is the study of values from a social-cultural approach (Hofstede, 2001; Smith & Schwartz, 1997). A second development has been the Occupational Information Network's (O*NET; Peterson, Mumford, Borman, Jeanneret, & Fleishman, 1999) adoption of the Minnesota work adjustment assessment model for needs and values (Dawis, Chapter 1, this volume; Dawis & Lofquist, 1984; see also Gore & Hitch, Chapter 16, this volume), providing the potential to link need and value scores to the wide range of career-relevant information on all occupations in the U.S. Department of Labor's O*NET database. This chapter highlights these recent developments and focuses on major contributions to the study of values, the development of measures, and the linking of values to important work-related outcomes. We first review the concept of needs and values in detail, laying a conceptual foundation for the application of value measures. Second, we survey and define the content domain of work values. Since work values have typically been studied within a person-environment fit tradition, we then describe the variety of research coming from this tradition that supports the ways that values are applied. We end this chapter with a review of work value measures and their use in career counseling.

CONCEPTUAL ISSUES

Several conceptual distinctions can be made between needs and values, but a close reading of the literature leads us to question some of these distinctions when applied to the practice of career counseling. Similarly, distinctions are made between general or life values and work values, but few studies have examined the relations between these two types of values (Roe & Ester, 1999). This lack of research leaves open a number of important questions. Do work values emerge from general values as individuals interact with work? Alternatively, do work values influence general values? These questions are similar to the issue of multiple roles and values: Do different values become salient as a person moves from one role to another? Should general value measures such as the Study of Values (Allport, Vernon, & Lindzey, 1970) be used in career assessment, or is it best to use work-specific value measures such as the Minnesota Importance Questionnaire? Answers to these questions have practical implications for assessment. Similar questions arise from attempts to distinguish work values and vocational interests. An understanding of the relations between them and their connection to occupations would influence many assessment practices. What is the best way to link the assessment of interests and values? In many cases, the literature has no clear answers to these conceptual and practical concerns.

NEEDS

The concept of psychological needs in modern psychology can be traced to Henry Murray's (1938) person-environment, need-press theory. Murray proposed a list of psychological needs that were important to human behavior. *Needs* refer to how the individual feels, behaves, or reacts. *Press* is defined as what the environment can do to facilitate or hinder the fulfillment of needs. The combination of individual needs and environmental press can be used to explain a wide variety of behaviors. The impact of Murray's theory can be seen on more recent person-environment conceptualizations of needs and values.

Many writers have regarded needs and values as equivalent. For example, Maslow (1954, 1959) viewed needs and values as similar and, at times, he used these terms interchangeably. Rokeach (1973), however, saw needs as biologically derived and values as cognitive representations of those needs subject to influence by social and institutional demands. The need for sex, for example, is cognitively transformed such that love or intimacy is valued as a result. Super (1962, 1995) saw needs as the manifestation of physiological conditions related to survival. Super, like Rokeach (1973), viewed needs as refined through interactions with the environment, leading to the development of values. The resulting values are objectives used to satisfy needs through interest activities. Super (1995) described the needs-value-interests link as such: Valuing material things may lead individuals to seek wealth, and people generally seek wealth through an interest such as managerial and remunerative occupations. In Super's example, value attainment is also linked to occupational choice, as individuals tend to choose occupations that provide opportunities to fulfill values.

Much of the research on needs comes from theories of work motivation in organizational psychology. Work motivation theories attempt to explain the context and processes that account for an individual's energy, direction of effort, and maintenance of that effort in a work setting. One group of work motivation theories is based directly on the concept of needs, appropriately called *need theories*. The need theories that are most prominent in work motivation are Herzberg, Mausner, and Snyderman's (1959) hygienes-motivators theory, Maslow's (1954, 1959) self-actualization theory, and Alderfer's (1969) existence-relatedness-growth theory. Need theories propose that needs energize and direct an individual's behavior toward satisfaction of those needs. Therefore, an assessment of needs may provide important insight into the motivational forces underlying career-related decisions.

An important contribution of need theories is the identification and classification of needs. These need theories are often viewed as taxonomies of motivational variables. For example, Maslow classified needs into five categories: physiological, security, social, self-esteem, and self-actualization. Need theories were popular during the 1960s and 1970s, but interest in these models eventually declined, probably due to a failure to obtain empirical support (see Campbell & Pritchard, 1976). Kanfer (1991) reviewed work-motivation theories placing need and expectancy theories together since intrinsic motives, needs, and values are hypothesized to activate and direct behavior. Expectancy/valence theories introduced a cognitive mediation role for needs and values to explain the process of work motivation. Kanfer criticized these person-centered approaches for "not specifying the mediating processes by which motivational energy is transformed and/or directed toward specific behaviors or patterns of action" (p. 83). These criticisms are also applicable to life value models (e.g., Brown, 1996; Super, 1995).

VALUES

Essential to understanding work values is knowledge of value theory and thought in social psychology. The development of values can be traced to the philosopher Spranger's (1928) six basic types of individuality: theoretical, economic, aesthetic, social, political, and religious. Allport and Vernon's (1931) Study of Values, the first systematic attempt to measure values, was based on Spranger's theory and his six basic values. For Allport, values are "propriate" functioning, meaning that people are motivated to act in a manner that is expressive of the self. A value is "a belief upon which a man [sic] acts by preference" (Allport, 1961, p. 454). Much of the early research and practice used broad value measures such as the Study of Values to assess work-relevant values.

Since Allport, many other researchers have contributed to the broad study of values, including concepts that are important to our current understanding of work values. One such contribution is Rokeach's (1973) theoretical writing and his Value Survey, both of which renewed interest in the study of values. As with Allport, for Rokeach, values are beliefs with some means or end of action that are judged to be desirable or undesirable. Because values are beliefs, they can have cognitive, affective, and behavioral components. Rokeach saw values as enduring but less stable than traits and identified two kinds of values: instrumental and terminal. *Instrumental values* are beliefs concerning desirable modes of conduct (e.g., ambitious, obedient). *Terminal values* are beliefs concerning desirable end states of existence (e.g., comfortable life, equality). The distinction between instrumental and terminal values unites several different approaches to the study of values (e.g., Maslow, 1959).

Rokeach (1973) believed that values are central to understanding behavior. Although not taking such a broad view of values, Brown (1996; Brown & Crace, 1996) proposed a value model to account for human motivation that outlines the function of values in decision making and the impact that values have on the outcome of life choices. Similar to Rokeach, Brown and Crace define values as cognitive representations, transformations of needs, providing standards, orienting people to desired end states, and enduring. Compared to other definitions, they emphasize an internal, cognitive mediated function of values as the basis of human motivation.

Needs and values are rarely the central components of theories in vocational counseling and psychology. An exception is the Theory of Work Adjustment (Dawis, Chapter 1, this volume; Dawis & Lofquist, 1984), which uses needs and values as explanatory constructs. Values in the Theory of Work Adjustment are part of the work personality that also includes abilities and needs. Vocational needs are reinforcing conditions that have been found to be important to job satisfaction. Values are defined in terms of vocational needs as "second-order needs," or "underlying common elements of needs" (see Dawis, 2001; Dawis & Lofquist,

1984, pp. 83–86). Essentially, values are reference dimensions for needs, primarily defined by data reduction techniques such as factor analysis. Values can also be described in terms of work environment reinforcer systems, reflecting the kinds of work reinforcers that are important for an individual.

Super (1995) argued that vocational needs in the Theory of Work Adjustment are similar to his values (see also Macnab & Fitzsimmons, 1987). Operationally, this is true. The measures developed by Super (1970) and Dawis and Lofquist (1984) use similar constructs to describe either needs or values. When examined closely, it is evident that need items in the Minnesota Importance Questionnaire (MIQ; Rounds, Henly, Dawis, Lofquist, & Weiss, 1981) and value items in Work Values Inventory (Super, 1970) both assess the relative importance of work outcomes to the person. The difference in terminology is due to the origins of the Theory of Work Adjustment. Dawis and Lofquist drew their ideas from Schaffer's (1953) research on job satisfaction and the behavioral tradition of Skinner (1938) with its emphasis on reinforcement (Lofquist & Dawis, 1991), whereas Super drew his ideas from the developmental work of Buehler (1933) and Ginzberg, Ginsburg, Axelrad, and Herma (1951).

Schwartz (1992) provides an up-to-date summary of how values have been conceptualized in psychology (see also Rohan, 2000). Schwartz reported that five features of values are frequently discussed in the value literature. Values:

1. Are beliefs.
2. Pertain to desirable end states of behaviors.
3. Guide selection or evaluation of behaviors and events.
4. Remain stable across context and time.
5. Are ordered in terms of relative importance.

Values, therefore, are stable motivational constructs that represent broad goals and, like traits, apply across context and time (Schwartz, 1994). Among value researchers, Schwartz currently has the most active research program. He has studied the structural relations of values across cultures (Schwartz, 1992), the relations of values and behaviors (Bardi & Schwartz, 2003), and has applied his theory of cultural values to work (Schwartz, 1999).

DISTINCTIONS FROM RELATED CONCEPTS

Researchers have grappled with several conceptual issues surrounding the definition of values, the first of which involves the distinction between life values and work values. Research into life values has tended to ignore developments in the field of work values. For example, two attempts to apply Schwartz's model of cultural values to the world of work fall short in their understanding of work values (Ros, Schwartz, & Surkiss, 1999; Schwartz, 1999). Ros et al. (1999) used Schwartz's 10 cultural values to derive only four work values (intrinsic, extrinsic, social, and mixed), a number that is far smaller than what is found in most work value taxonomies.

Work value research, however, has clearly been influenced by mainstream studies on life values (Dawis, 1991; Ronen, 1994). Elizur and Sagie (1999), for example, began with a multifaceted definition of life and work values and then generated both life and work value items. They reported that the structure within work and life domains was similar, but that life and work values occupied two distinct regions in a three-dimensional conical structure. Life values were located at the base of the cone and work values at the top, suggesting that context is important for values assessment. One interesting issue that emerges from this research is the notion of compensatory models: Can fulfillment of a value through work compensate for its nonfulfillment in other life situations, or vice versa? Such value compensation has potentially important implications for career counseling, as clients may choose from different roles and environments to achieve a sense of value fulfillment in their lives. Research that is applicable to the life and work role distinction involves conflicts between work and family demands. Perrewe and Hochwarter (2001), for example, have proposed a model to capture work and family values as they relate to work-family conflict and outcomes. Studies examining the interrelations between work and life values are an emerging area of research, leaving this topic open for additional research and the emergence of new approaches.

The second issue, especially important to career counseling, is how needs, values, and interests are distinct but interrelated concepts. Super (1995) defined interests as preferences for activities in which individuals expect to attain or satisfy their needs and values. An interest, then, is one of the many manifestations of a value. For example, altruism (the value of helping others) leads a person to prefer social occupations (i.e., an interest in work where there will be an opportunity to help others). However, pairing values and interests is rarely this simple because values can often be linked to several different interest areas. For example, the value of achievement can be linked to investigative, artistic, and enterprising interests. A more sophisticated application would link a pattern of values and needs to different interest areas (Armstrong, Day, & Rounds, 2003). Therefore, a critical issue in the use of values and other assessment measures in career counseling is the ability to link together information from different sources to create a multifaceted picture of the individual and relevant career choices.

Dawis (1991) reviewed the conceptual definitions of interest and values and concluded that distinguishing between values and interests is difficult at the conceptual level, leading applied psychologists to prefer operational definitions. From an operational point of view, interests involve liking/disliking, and values involve importance/unimportance. This perspective makes it easy to distinguish between value and interest measures: Value measures ask individuals to rate the importance of items, whereas interest measures ask individuals to rate their liking of items. However, from a counseling standpoint, the lack of a clear conceptual distinction suggests that values and interests may be intertwined for many clients who are making career-related decisions.

CONTENT DOMAIN OF VALUES

A key to the study and assessment of values is to decide what values to measure and how these values are interrelated. To develop a measure of values or to evaluate an existing measure, researchers need to address three questions: What are the substantive contents (definition) of values? How comprehensive is the sample of values generated by the definition? How are the relations among values structured? We review four research programs and describe how these programs address these questions. The research programs reviewed are Dawis and Lofquist (1984), Super (Super & Sverko, 1995), Ronen (1994), and Schwartz (1992).

Dawis and Lofquist's Theory of Work Adjustment

In the theory of work adjustment, the vocational needs measured by the MIQ (Rounds et al., 1981) are grouped into six work values, creating a hierarchical taxonomy (see Table 13.1). In this model, values are conceptualized as reference dimensions and latent variables for the description of needs. Studies of the factor structure of the 20 vocational needs in the MIQ have yielded a six-dimensional structure of work values. The six values can also be described in terms of work rewards that can satisfy the cluster of needs. The work environment descriptions for the six values are:

1. *Achievement:* an environment that encourages accomplishment.
2. *Comfort:* an environment that is comfortable and nonstressful.
3. *Status:* an environment that provides recognition and prestige.
4. *Altruism:* an environment that fosters harmony with and service to others.
5. *Safety:* an environment that is predictable.
6. *Autonomy:* an environment that stimulates initiative.

Table 13.1
6 Work Values and 21 Needs

Work Value	Need	Item
Achievement	Ability utilization	I could do something that makes use of my abilities.
	Achievement	The job could give me a feeling of accomplishment.
Comfort	Activity	I could be busy all the time.
	Independence	I could work alone on the job.
	Variety	I could do something different each day.
	Compensation	My pay would compare well with that of other workers.
	Security	The job could provide for steady employment.
	Working conditions	The job would have good working conditions.
Status	Advancement	The job would provide an opportunity for advancement.
	Recognition	I could get the recognition for the work I do.
	Authority	I could tell people what to do.
	Social status	I could be "somebody" in the community.
Altruism	Co-workers	My coworkers would be easy to make friends with.
	Social service	I could do things for other people.
	Moral values	I could do the work without feeling that it is morally wrong.
Safety	Company policies	The company would administer its policies fairly.
	Supervision-human	My boss would back up the workers with top management.
	Supervision-tech	My boss would train the workers well.
Autonomy	Autonomy	I could plan my work with little supervision.
	Creativity	I could try out some of my own ideas.
	Responsibility	I could make decisions on my own.

Source: A Psychological Theory of Work Adjustment, by R. V. and L. H. Lofquist, 1984, Minneapolis: University of Minnesota Press.

Dawis and Lofquist have also conceptualized three bipolar value dimensions: achievement versus comfort, altruism versus status, and safety versus autonomy. These dimensions are crossed with three types of rewards: self (achievement, autonomy), social (altruism, status), and environment (comfort, safety). The resulting structure graphically represents these opposing sets of values and three major classes of rewards.

This six-value structure was first identified in factor analyses of MIQ data in separate samples of 3,033 employed workers, 1,621 vocational rehabilitation clients, 419 college students, and 285 vocational-technical students (Gay, Weiss, Hendel, Dawis, & Lofquist, 1971). This same six-factor structure was replicated across eight sex-by-age samples of 9,377 vocational rehabilitation clients (Lofquist & Dawis, 1978). The MIQ was revised for the O*NET (see Gore & Hitch, Chapter 16, this volume), producing the Work Importance Profiler and Work Importance Locator (WIP and WIL; McCloy et al., 1999b, 1999c). In the development of the computerized form of the WIP, exploratory and confirmatory factor analyses were conducted to evaluate the six-factor work values model. Results provided moderate support for Dawis and Lofquist's model, although the MIQ and WIP fit a seven-factor model better than the six-factor model. The seven-factor structure is similar to the six-factor structure, with the critical difference being that the comfort value splits into internal comfort (activity, independence, and variety) and external comfort (compensation, security, and working conditions). In practice, the six-factor work value model (with a single comfort value) continues to be used when presenting results to career counseling clients.

Super's Theory of Career Development

Much of Super's final research on work values came from the Work Importance Study (WIS; Super & Sverko, 1995). One objective of the WIS was to investigate the relative importance of work compared to other activities and to study the rewards that youth and adults seek in their major life roles across cultures. In a series of studies (see Ferreira-Marques & Miranda, 1995), decisions were made about the kinds of life and work values to assess and how to assess them. The items composing these values scales, with the exception of the working conditions value scale, had both work- and non-work-related items. The list of values used in the WIS is shown in Table 13.2. As expected, many of the values (e.g., ability utilization, aesthetics, creativity) could be attained in multiple roles and situations. Other values are tied more specifically to work roles (e.g., economics, working conditions, advancement) or to nonwork roles (personal development, lifestyle).

Also shown in Table 13.2 are the five value orientations identified in a principal components analysis of 18,318 participants from 10 countries: Australia, Belgium (Flanders), Canada, Croatia, Italy, Japan, Poland, Portugal, South Africa, and the United States (Sverko, 1995). Many of the participants were students from secondary schools. The five value orientations (Sverko, p. 228) are:

1. *Utilitarian orientation:* the importance of economic conditions and material career progress.
2. *Individualistic orientation:* the importance of an autonomous way of living.
3. *Orientation toward self-actualization:* the importance of inner-oriented goals for personal development and self-realization.

4. *Social orientation:* the importance of social interaction.
5. *Adventurous orientation:* the importance of risk.

In studies of the factor congruence across samples, only the utilitarian and individualistic value orientations showed generalizability. Sverko (1995) speculated that the lack of generalizability for the self-actualization, social, and adventurous orientations may be due to intergroup differences and sampling errors. Another possible reason is that the structure of values may differ across secondary students, college students, and adults.

Table 13.2
5 Value Orientations, 18 Work Values, and Sample Items

Orientation	Value	Sample Item
Utilitarian	Economics	Have a high standard of living.
	Advancement	Get ahead.
	Prestige	Be admired for my knowledge and skills.
	(Authority)	Tell others what to do.
	(Achievement)	Have results which show that I have done well.
Individualistic	Life-Style	Living according to my ideas.
	Autonomy	Act on my own.
	(Creativity)	Discover, develop, or design new things.
	(Variety)	Have every day different in some way from the one before it.
Self-actualization	Ability utilization	Use my skill and knowledge.
	Personal development	Develop as a person.
	(Altruism)	Help people with problems.
	(Achievement)	Have results which show that I have done well.
	Aesthetics	Make life more beautiful.
	(Creativity)	Discover, develop, or design new things.
Social	Social interaction	Do things with other people.
	Social relations	Be with friends.
	(Variety)	Have every day different in some way from the one before it.
	(Altruism)	Help people with problems.
Adventurous	Risk	Do risky things.
	(Physical activity)	Get a lot of exercise.
	(Authority)	Tell others what to do.

Note: Work values in parentheses have salient loadings on more than one orientation or did not load on this orientation for all samples examined. The value of working conditions did not have salient loadings on the orientations. Cultural identity and physical prowess values were not included in the cross-cultural analyses.

Source: "The Structure and Hierarchy of Values Viewed Cross-Nationally," pp. 225–240, by B. Sverko, in *Life Roles, Values, and Careers: International Findings of the Work Importance Study,* D. E. Super and B. Sverko, eds., 1995, San Francisco: Jossey-Bass.

RONEN'S TAXONOMY OF NEEDS

Ronen (1994) has proposed a facet model of values based on Hofstede's (1980) 14 work values linked to major need classifications. These work values, and corresponding items, are shown in Table 13.3. Hofstede's study of work values in 50 nations, with a sample of 117,000 IBM employees, has had a major impact on cross-cultural research, but has received little attention in the area of vocational counseling. Although Hofstede derived four cultural dimensions (power distance, individualism versus collectivism, masculinity versus femininity, and uncertainty avoidance) from his 14 work values, these factors have rarely been replicated (see Smith & Schwartz, 1997; Spector, Cooper, & Sparks, 2001).

Ronen (1994) conducted a series of studies in various countries and cultures that evaluated a common taxonomy of needs. This hierarchical taxonomy linked Hofstede's work values to the need classifications of Maslow (1954), Alderfer (1969), and Herzberg et al. (1959). For example, as shown in Table 13.3, Maslow's physiological and security category contains the work values of working conditions, area,

Table 13.3

14 Work Values and Items Classified According to Maslow's Need Taxonomy

Need	Work Value	Item
Security	Area	Live in an area desirable to you and your family.
	Time	Have a job which leaves you sufficient time for your personal or family life.
	Security	Have the security that you will be able to work for your company as long as you want to.
	Benefits	Have good fringe benefits.
	Physical	Have good physical working conditions (good ventilation and lightening, adequate work space, etc.).
Social	Co-workers	Work with people who cooperate well with one another.
	Manager	Have a good working relationship with your manager.
Ego/Power	Recognition	Get the recognition you deserve when you do a good job.
	Advancement	Have the opportunity for advancement to higher level jobs.
	Earnings	Have an opportunity for high earnings.
Self-actualization	Challenge	Have challenging work to do—work from which you get a personal sense of accomplishment.
	Autonomy	Have considerable freedom to adopt your own approach to the job.
	Skills	Fully use your skills and abilities on the job accomplishment.
	Training	Have training opportunities (to improve your skills or to learn new skills).

Note: Adapted from S. Ronen, "An Underlying Structure of Motivational Need Taxonomies: A Cross-Cultural Confirmation," in *Handbook of Industrial and Organizational Psychology*, vol. 4, H. C. Triandis, M. D. Dunnette, and L. M. Hough, eds., Palo Alto, CA: Consulting Psychologist Press, 1994, pp. 241–270.

Source: Culture's Consequences: International Differences in Work-Related Values, by G. Hofstede, 1980, Beverly Hills, CA: Sage.

personal time, security, benefits, and earnings. The samples included employees from Canada, China, France, Israel, the United Kingdom, Germany, and Japan. These employees rated the importance of Hofstede's (1980) 14 work values. Structural analyses using multidimensional scaling and facet analysis yielded two-dimensions (collectivistic versus individualistic and materialistic versus humanistic) that supported Ronen's hierarchical value-need classification. Overall, Ronen's classification seems robust, having been replicated across countries.

SCHWARTZ'S CIRCUMPLEX MODEL OF VALUES

Schwartz (1992) grouped value types according to common goals, reasoning that basic human values in all cultures would represent biological needs, social interaction, and group functioning. Informed by values identified by previous researchers and discussed in philosophical and religious writing, Schwartz developed and classified values into 10 motivational types, assumed to represent the range of values found across cultures:

1. *Power:* Social status, prestige, control or dominance.
2. *Achievement:* Personal success through competence according to social standards.
3. *Hedonism:* Pleasure or sensuous gratification for self.
4. *Stimulation:* Excitement, novelty, challenge.
5. *Self-direction:* Independence of thought and action, creating, exploring.
6. *Universalism:* Understanding, tolerance, protection of all people and nature.
7. *Benevolence:* Preserving and enhancing the welfare of people.
8. *Tradition:* Respect and commitment to cultural or religious customs.
9. *Conformity:* Restraint of actions and impulses that may upset or harm others or violate social norms.
10. *Security:* Safety and stability of society, relationships, and self.

A key aspect of Schwartz's value theory is the structural relations among values. The 10 values are organized according to the idea that the pursuit of a value has consequences that can be congruent with, or in conflict with, other values. For example, the pursuit of conformity may conflict with the pursuit of self-direction in cases where both values are important to the individual. The values are arranged in a circular fashion, beginning with power and ending with security, portraying the patterns of congruency and conflict. Conflicting values are opposite on the circle, and congruent values are adjacent. Along the perimeter, the distance between any two values is a measure of the similarity of the motivations expressed by the value; those that are closer are more similar in motivation. Schwartz's model, with its emphasis on the properties of a circumplex, is similar to Holland's (1997) vocational interest circle and may eventually have important implications for counseling.

COMPARISON OF VALUE CLASSIFICATIONS

How comprehensive and similar are the value taxonomies? To answer this question, we inspected the need and value definitions and items of three classifications—Dawis and Lofquist, Super, and Ronen—and then matched similar values.

Table 13.4

Comparison of Similar Categories in Dawis and Lofquist's Work Values/Needs, Ronen's Classification of Hofstede's (1980) Work Values, and Super's Work Orientations/Values

Dawis/Lofquist	Hofstede	Super
Achievement	*Self-Actualization*	*Self-Actualization*
Ability utilization	Skills	Ability utilization
Achievement	Challenge	
Autonomy		*Individualistic*
Creativity		Creativity
Responsibility		
Autonomy	Autonomy	Autonomy
	Training	
		Personal development
		Life-Style
		Aesthetics
		Variety
Status	*Ego/Power*	*Utilitarian*
Advancement	Advancement	Advancement
Recognition	Recognition	Achievement
Authority		Authority
Social status		Prestige
		Economics
Altruism	*Social*	*Social*
Co-Workers	Co-Workers	Social relations
Social service		Altruism
Moral values		
	Manager	
		Social interaction
Comfort	*Security*	
Security	Security	
Compensation	Benefits	
Working conditions	Physical	Working conditions
Activity		
Independence		
Variety		
	Area	
	Time	
Safety		
Company policies and practices		
Supervision—human relations		
Supervision—technical		
		Adventurous
		Risk
		Physical activity

Sources: A Psychological Theory of Work Adjustment, by R. V. and L. H. Lofquist, 1984, Minneapolis: University of Minnesota Press; "An Underlying Structure of Motivational Need Taxonomies: A Cross-Cultural Confirmation," pp. 241–270, by S. Ronen, in *Handbook of Industrial and Organizational Psychology,* vol. 4, H. C. Triandis, M. D. Dunnette, and L. M. Hough, eds., 1994, Palo Alto, CA: Consulting Psychologist Press; *Culture's Consequences: International Differences in Work-Related Values,* by G. Hofstede, 1980, Beverly Hills, CA: Sage; and *Life Roles, Values, and Careers: International Findings of the Work Importance Study,* by D. E. Super and B. Sverko, 1995, San Francisco: Jossey-Bass.

The results of this evaluation lead to the taxonomy shown in Table 13.4, which illustrates their similarity to one another. For example, all three classifications have a value that emphasizes the importance of an environment that provides recognition and prestige. Dawis and Lofquist's label for the value is *status,* Super's label is *utilitarian,* and Ronen's label is *ego/power.*

There is considerable overlap among value classifications listed in Table 13.4, with Dawis and Lofquist having the most comprehensive work value system. Neither Super nor Hofstede includes organizational values similar to Dawis and Lofquist's safety value. It is surprising that Super's classification includes only one value—working conditions—in the category that Dawis and Lofquist label *comfort,* and which Ronen calls *security.* Super's classification, however, contains general values (e.g., personal development) that are not necessarily tied to a work setting but that do allow for a values assessment across other environments. But a comparison with Schwartz's model indicates that several life values are missing from Super's system, such as hedonism, universalism, benevolence, tradition, and conformity.

Nord et al. (1990) suggested that models of work values are deficient because they omit several critical elements individuals might want from work. These include spiritual dimensions, the relationship between producers and customers, and the nature of the product relative to its ability to satisfy important human needs. It might be noted, however, that Dawis and Lofquist's moral values, in the altruism category, partially addresses the spiritual dimension and the nature of the product dimension. Super's altruism, contained in the social category, may partially represent the producer and customer relationship dimension. Similarly, several of the values identified by Schwartz (1996) seem to fit in Nord et al.'s omitted categories, including universalism, benevolence, and tradition.

The question of which taxonomy is most representative of the domain of values depends partly on the area of research interest or clinical application. Schwartz (1992) has the most comprehensive set of life values, making this taxonomy an appropriate choice for use in general investigations. Dawis and Lofquist's taxonomy seems to be the best available description of work values and would be the most appropriate for exploring career development issues or other aspects of the world of work. Nevertheless, more study of the domain of work values is required before researchers and practitioners can claim to be measuring the full spectrum of values relevant to people's work lives. Additional research is also needed to clarify the relations between work and life values.

PERSON-ENVIRONMENT PERSPECTIVE

Work value measures are designed to measure the importance of work outcomes expected to be related to satisfaction. It is not surprising that an established finding is that work values predict job satisfaction (for reviews, see Dawis, 1991; Kristof, 1996; Locke, 1976; Ronen, 1994). Work values have also been shown to be related to job choice (Judge & Bretz, 1992), tenure (Bretz & Judge, 1994), commitment and cohesion (Boxx, Odom, & Dunn, 1991), intentions to quit (Chatman, 1991), turnover (O'Reilly, Chatman, & Caldwell, 1991), and self-report ratings of teamwork (Posner, 1992). Research on the value-outcome link has been concerned with how work values and work environments are related to outcomes. These relations are usually studied from a person-environment (P-E) perspective, in which various forms of P-E fit have been studied, including person-vocation, person-job, person-organization, and person-group (for reviews, see Kristof, 1996, and Meglino & Ravlin, 1998). In a special issue on P-E fit, Schneider (2001) identifies two major traditions: individual differences and organizational psychology. These traditions are based on different conceptual models and research approaches.

The individual differences tradition focuses on the person variable (values) first and the environment variable second. Individual outcomes (e.g., satisfaction, attitudes, performance) are studied rather than environmental outcomes (e.g., cooperation, absenteeism, employee turnover). Super (Super & Sverko, 1995), Brown (Brown & Crace, 1996), and Dawis and Lofquist (1984) are examples of research programs in the individual differences tradition. The major difference among them is how environments are conceptualized. Dawis and Lofquist have emphasized work environments almost exclusively. For Super and Brown, environments are roles (e.g., work, family, marital, leisure), the salience of which depends on the values held and the values being satisfied within roles. Lofquist and Dawis (1991) have broadened their theory, now referred to as person-environment-correspondence theory, and expanded their idea of environments to include roles, groups, organizations, and cultures.

Unlike other individual differences models, Dawis and Lofquist (1984) explicitly attempted to assess environments. They developed occupational reinforcer patterns (Stewart et al., 1986) and occupational classifications (Dawis, Dohm, Lofquist, Chartrand, & Due, 1987) to match with clients' value profiles. In contrast, Super (1980; Super & Sverko, 1995) was concerned with the salience of different life roles rather than occupational matching. These approaches lead to different practical research applications. Super's approach aims primarily at value clarification within the context of major life roles, where work is only one such role. Assessment of life values is preferred and is used to promote active consideration of values and how the values relate to roles. Value-role fit is not directly assessed. The client makes the judgment of the value-role fit and implicitly relates that fit to criteria (choice, satisfaction, performance). Lofquist and Dawis, on the other hand, focus on using value data in the work role to identify occupations that may match (reinforce) the individual's values.

A study by Rounds, Dawis, and Lofquist (1987) illustrates the latter approach. They compared career-counseling clients' need and value profiles with occupational reinforcer patterns to determine fit or correspondence. Occupational reinforcer patterns are independent ratings by supervisors or other incumbents of the relative presence of work reinforcers in specific occupations. The correspondence score, a measure of profile similarity between the individual's needs/values and occupational reinforcer patterns, is then correlated with job satisfaction. Correspondence was found to account for between 3% and 30% of the variance in job satisfaction.

Edwards (1991) has criticized the profile similarity approach and has suggested a "variance components" approach to studying person-environment fit. The profile approach does not evaluate the independent contributions of person or environment to work outcomes and may obscure individual variables that make up the profile. Edwards (1991) proposes using a moderated regression by entering the person (e.g., value) and environment (e.g., occupational reinforcer) components before the interaction components in the prediction of work outcomes (e.g., satisfaction).

This assumes that people with certain person characteristics (e.g., values) may be more satisfied than others and that some environmental aspects (e.g., occupational reinforcers) may be more satisfying.

Despite such criticism, the profile similarity methodology is defensible. The primary objective of measuring P-E fit, as applied by vocational or personnel psychologists, is to identify or recommend jobs or occupations that fit the values of the client or job candidate. This is consistent with the individual differences tradition of developing and evaluating the validity of P-E fit indexes and methods that match the unique profile of an individual's characteristics to different jobs or occupations. In comparison, the organizational psychology tradition focuses primarily on the environmental variable (i.e., job characteristics). The primary objective of this approach is to improve job satisfaction and other work-related outcomes (e.g., increase productivity) by modifying characteristics of the work environment. Hackman and Oldham's (1980) job characteristics model is a prototype of this approach in studying job satisfaction (see Fritzsche & Parrish, Chapter 8, this volume).

More recently, the organizational psychology approach has used a variance component approach to study P-E fit. Taris and Feij's (2001) study is an example of the variance components approach to studying interaction. Their study focused on the relationship of values (extrinsic, intrinsic, and social) and organizational supplies (extrinsic, intrinsic, and social) to work outcomes (job satisfaction, intention to leave, and well-being). Supplies are job characteristics that satisfy the individual's work values. The data for all three components were collected from the same person. Edwards' (1991) moderated regression analysis was used to evaluate contribution of main effects and interaction effects for values and supplies simultaneously. Taris and Feij reported that perceived supplies had a greater effect than values on job satisfaction and intentions to leave but that work values moderated the relations of perceived supplies to intention to leave. The moderation effect for intentions to leave occurred among workers who regard the supplies as important, as these workers were more likely to leave a job where supplies were low than were workers who did not regard the supplies as important. Other studies (e.g., Hesketh & Gardner, 1993; Livingstone, Nelson, & Barr, 1997; Meyer, Irving, & Allen, 1998) have also found that work characteristics, when compared to values, account for most of the variance in work outcomes.

The methodology used by Taris and Feij (2001) and others has been criticized (Hesketh & Gardner, 1993; Schneider, 2001) because the person, environment, and outcome components were obtained from the same source. It is not surprising, therefore, that perceived supplies have a greater effect on satisfaction since employees rated the perceived availability of supplies at their job at the same time as they completed a job satisfaction measure. There is a substantial potential to confounding environmental perceptions and satisfaction with this methodology, whereas the value measure was not as closely tied to the work environment. This confounding could increase the contribution of supplies and reduce the contribution of values for predicting satisfaction. Despite these criticisms, we agree with Hesketh and Gardner's (1993) point that more attention should be focused on perceived work environments in career counseling (see also Fritzsche & Parrish, Chapter 8, this volume).

It is clear from this brief review that work values, when studied from a P-E perspective, have considerable power in explaining work- and organizational-related behavior. These effects have been shown using individual differences, organizational psychology, and cross-cultural approaches to studying P-E fit. We next examine work value measures and their use from a career counseling perspective.

APPLICATION OF VALUES MEASURES IN CAREER COUNSELING

We begin with a review of the Dawis and Lofquist's (1984) Minnesota Importance Questionnaire. Next, we discuss the O*NET-based value measures that have been based on the Minnesota Importance Questionnaire. Finally, we examine Super's work value measures (Nevill & Super, 1986a, 1986b). Each of these measures is discussed within the context of career counseling.

THE MINNESOTA IMPORTANCE QUESTIONNAIRE

The Minnesota Importance Questionnaire (MIQ; Gay et al., 1971; Rounds et al., 1981) is a rationally derived measure of 20 vocational needs organized under six work-related values based on the Theory of Work Adjustment (Dawis & Lofquist, 1984). This measure was developed as part of the Work Adjustment Project at the University of Minnesota. The MIQ reflects a P-E fit approach to career counseling (Rounds & Tracey, 1990), which assumes that individuals will seek a work environment that matches their behavioral dispositions, including both needs and abilities. Vocational needs are viewed as a subset of a larger set of personality needs and are especially important for understanding how individuals can identify career choices that will lead to satisfaction through reinforcement. Work-related reinforcers are stimulus conditions that are associated with the performance of work-related behaviors, and vocational needs are preferences for different reinforcers. The purpose of the MIQ is to help individuals identify the relative importance of each reinforcer for themselves and link these preferences to different occupational choices. In a counseling setting, the MIQ can be used to help identify the needs that are most important to the individual and then identify work environments that offer corresponding reinforcers. Comparisons between an individual's needs and the reinforcer patterns of different occupations provide a systematic way to explore the world of work and identify career choices that are most likely to be satisfying.

There are two forms available for the MIQ. One is a 210-item paired-comparison form that includes 190 forced-choice items, where respondents are asked to choose between two need statements, and 20 absolute scale rating items, where respondents are asked to indicate the importance of each of the needs. The other is a multiple rank-order form where the forced-choice items are replaced by a series of items asking respondents to rank the relative importance of sets of five needs. Both versions are pencil-and-paper measures contained in a booklet with a separate answer sheet that is completed by the respondent and sent to the publisher for scoring. As noted in its manual (Rounds et al., 1981), the MIQ has excellent psychometric characteristics, including good internal consistency and test-retest reliability scale scores, which suggests that the MIQ is a reliable measure that assesses individual characteristics that tend to remain stable over time. Data collected as part of the University of Minnesota Work Adjustment Project also demonstrate that MIQ scores are predictive of job satisfaction (see Dawis & Lofquist, 1984).

The Minnesota Importance Questionnaire and Career Counseling   Strategies for using MIQ results in counseling are outlined in the MIQ manual (Rounds et al., 1981). The first step in interpretation is to examine the logically consistent triad (LCT) score, an index of the nonrandomness of the client's response pattern. A number of factors can contribute to random responding, in which case results may reflect the individual's inability to choose among different options or may reflect some problem in the assessment process, including poor understanding of the task, low motivation, carelessness, a response set, or an attempt to fake results. In cases where the LCT score indicates a valid profile, there are a number of interpretation strategies recommended. One method of interpretation is to use the scores on each scale to create an individual's hierarchy of needs and then use this hierarchy as a starting point for exploring career-related options. Minnesota Importance Questionnaire scores can also be interpreted with reference to the norms that have been developed for the measure, and scores can be used to predict satisfaction in different occupations, both at the individual occupation level (Stewart et al., 1986) and based on clusters of occupations from the Minnesota Occupational Classification System (MOCS III; Dawis et al., 1987). Additional strategies include having the client interpret the meaning of each need statement or having the client do a self-estimation of needs.

The MIQ has many characteristics that make it useful for career counseling. Its development is rooted in an empirically supported psychological theory of career development. The MIQ has a hierarchical structure of needs and values that allows for a discussion of results at different levels of specificity to reflect the varying developmental levels of career counseling clients. More specifically, clients who are in the early stages of career development may benefit more from a general discussion of values, whereas clients who are further along in the process of making career-related decisions may benefit more from a more detailed discussion of specific needs. The needs and values measured by the MIQ can be linked to occupational outcomes, although the MIQ offers information on only a limited number of occupations that are not grouped by level of educational requirements. It should be noted that the MIQ, the research data that supported its development, and the information it provides in counseling are becoming progressively more dated. Fortunately, both of these concerns have been addressed by the development of the MIQ-based O*NET value measures.

O*NET-BASED VALUE MEASURES

Two value measures were developed as part of the O*NET that update and expand the information available from the MIQ. Linking results to the O*NET increases the number of occupations that can be matched to an individual's needs and values and allows for the organization of occupations based on Job Zones, a series of hierarchical categories based on the required level of education and training (see Gore & Hitch, Chapter 16, this volume). The Work Importance Profiler (WIP; U.S. Department of Labor, 2000b) is a computerized assessment program that uses the multiple-rank order format from the MIQ. On completion of this measure, a report can be generated that includes a list of occupations from the O*NET database that matches the individual's profile, sorted into categories reflecting different levels of educational requirements. Interpretation of WIP results and their application in career counseling is otherwise the same as for the

MIQ. The Work Importance Locator (WIL; U.S. Department of Labor, 2000a) is a shorter pencil-and-paper measure that uses a card-sorting task to determine the relative importance of the MIQ needs. Value scores are calculated by hand using a workbook that also lists a number of occupations that are associated with each value by Job Zone. Details of the development of these measures are presented in technical reports by McCloy et al. (1999a, 1999b). Overall, the reliability for the computerized WIP is comparable to the reliability for the MIQ, but the reliability for the WIL is less impressive, perhaps reflecting the limitations of using a card-sorting technique.

O*NET-Based Value Measures and Career Counseling   A critical issue with the use of assessment instruments in the career counseling process is being able to link results to occupational choices. In general, the use of a values measure can lead to insights about what is important to the client, serving as a catalyst for personal growth. However, a values measure that can be linked to occupations offers the critical advantage of a second level of discourse—an examination of how values are related to satisfaction. It is this advantage that separates the MIQ and its O*NET offspring from the other value taxonomies and measures discussed in this chapter. The data used to connect O*NET value profiles to occupations are more extensive and up-to-date than what is available for the MIQ. These data and the measures themselves can be downloaded for free at the U.S. Department of Labor's O*NET web site, www.onetcenter.org. The O*NET presents an impressive and unprecedented opportunity to combine different types of information on occupations to create a cohesive picture of how individuals can be matched to work environments. A battery of assessment instruments has been developed for the O*NET, including an ability measure, computerized and pencil-and-paper Holland-based interest measures, and the MIQ-based value measures. Results can be linked to information on the more than 1,000 occupations in the O*NET database, including generalized work activities, work and organizational contexts, skill and ability requirements, knowledge areas and requirements for occupational preparation, and occupational interests and values.

The process of updating occupational reinforcer patterns from the MIQ for the O*NET is detailed in a technical report by McCloy, Campbell, Oswald, Rivkin, and Lewis (1999). Nine nonincumbent raters were trained to generate reinforcer profiles for the occupations in the O*NET. In a pilot study of 30 occupations, it was found that the profiles generated by the nonincumbent raters were similar to data collected from incumbents in each occupation. A group of eight raters was then used to generate profiles for each occupation in the O*NET database. As part of the ongoing process of updating the O*NET database, the original ratings used to assess the level of reinforcement for each occupation will be replaced with information collected from job analyses. Therefore, it is expected that, over time, the O*NET will become an even more effective source of occupational information for use in career counseling. Of the two O*NET-based values measures, the computerized WIP offers more sophisticated methods for matching results to this occupational information and can be used to generate a detailed report for review by the counselor and client. The pencil-and-paper version may be useful in cases where there is limited access to computers or for group administrations.

MEASURES BASED ON SUPER'S THEORY: VALUES SCALE AND SALIENCE INVENTORY

Two values-based measures were developed for the international WIS, the Values Scale (Nevill & Super, 1986b) and the Salience Inventory (Nevill & Super, 1986a). These measures were based on Super's (1980) career development theory and were initially designed in several languages for the cross-cultural study of the career development process, the results of which are detailed in Super and Sverko (1995). Nevill and Kruse (1996) have reviewed the empirical support for the Values Scale and discussed its use in career assessment and counseling, and Nevill and Calvert (1996) have reviewed the empirical support for the Salience Inventory and discussed its use in career assessment and counseling.

The Values Scale is a 105-item instrument measuring the importance of 21 values using 21 five-item scales with a four-point response format. Nevill and Super (1986b) suggest that this assessment method allows for both ipsative and normative interpretations of the results of the Values Survey. By ranking values according to the relative scores obtained on each scale, it is possible to create a values hierarchy for an individual. However, given the social desirability of many values (see Rokeach, 1973), most instrument designers have opted for a forced-choice format to create this type of values hierarchy. With the rating method used in the Values Scale, it is possible for a client who is having difficulty making career-related decisions to indicate that all of the values are "very important" to him or her, making the results meaningless. In other cases, variability in the range of responses may reflect only measurement error instead of substantive differences in the importance of each value. Apart from the values hierarchy, it is possible to provide a normative interpretation of the results, which would compare an individual's scores to a set of norms obtained from a representative sample of the population to which the individual belongs. Unfortunately, such an application is not yet possible. Although the Values Scale was used in the multinational WIS, the data from that project has yet to be presented in a form that would permit this type of normative interpretation.

The Salience Inventory is a 170-item measure designed to assess the importance of five life-career goals: studying, working, community service, home and family, and leisure activities. Items are scored on a four-point Likert-type scale divided into three sets of five measures (50 participation items, 50 commitment items, 70 value expectation items) that assess different aspects of the importance of each role. Participation items ask individuals to rate what they actually do, or have done recently, in each area. Commitment items ask individuals to rate the degree to which they are committed to pursuing each life role. Value expectation items are based on 14 of the values from the Values Scale and ask the individual to rate the degree to which major life satisfactions or values are expected to be found in each role.

Use of the Values Scale and Salience Inventory in Career Counseling   The application of the Values Scale and Salience Inventory in career counseling has been linked to Super's (1983) Career Development Assessment and Counseling (C-DAC) model by Nevill and Kruse (1996) and Nevill and Calvert (1996). In this model, there are three important issues to address. The first issue is to determine the values the client would like to realize through work; second, to assess the relative importance of work to the client relative to other life roles; and third, to assess the client's readiness to make career-related decisions. According to Nevill and Kruse, the Values Scale addresses the first issue by assessing the values of the individual, identifying those that will be important to him or her in the work domain. Understanding the importance of the work role relative to other life roles has important implications for the career counseling process because clients who do not see work as important may not be in the best position to work with the results of career-related assessment measures. The Salience Inventory was developed to measure the relative importance of different life roles and is recommended for assessment of this issue (Nevill & Calvert, 1996). The relative importance of different life roles has implications for the career counseling process. For clients who do not view the work role as being important, Nevill and Kruse recommend using interventions designed to increase awareness of the importance of work, as these clients may not be ready to engage in a detailed analysis of assessment results. In comparison, clients who view the worker role as being important would not need this type of intervention before attempting to make critical educational and career-related decisions.

The primary limitation of using the Values Scale in career counseling is the limited data available linking results to career-related outcomes. The comparison point is the MIQ, the results of which can be linked to meaningful vocational outcomes based on empirical data. For example, if a person scores high on the MIQ measures of achievement or ability utilization, a database of occupational information can be used to identify potential career choices where these values will be reinforced. In comparison, if a person scores high on the Values Scale measures of achievement or ability utilization, there is no equivalent database of information for interpreting results. Furthermore, the Values Scale assesses a limited range of work values, lacking the organizational values measured by the MIQ.

A strength of the Salience Inventory is that it does provide an assessment of an interesting and potentially critical issue to explore with career counseling clients, the relative importance of different life roles. Within the context of the C-DAC model, this issue has important implications for the types of interventions a counselor may want to use with a client (see Nevill & Calvert, 1996). However, the Salience Inventory is a 170-item measure that assesses the relative importance of five life roles. The utility of the measure must be weighed against time constraints, as counselors working within a time-limited treatment model should consider the benefits of other assessment measures that provide a wider range of useful information.

OTHER VALUE MEASURES

In addition to the MIQ, its O*NET-based variations, and the Super-based Values Scale and Salience Inventory, there are a number of values measures available, varying in psychometric robustness, that correspond to the various taxonomies and models previously discussed in this chapter. Included in this category are Rokeach's (1973) classic values measure; Kopelman, Rovenpor, and Guan's (2003) update of the Allport-Vernon-Lindzey Study of Values; the circumplex model of values proposed by Schwartz (1992; see Struch, Schwartz, & van der Kloot, 2002); the values measure used by Hofstede (1980, 2001) in his cross-cultural research; and any number of idiosyncratic value measures developed by researchers in the industrial-organizational area, a review of which is beyond the scope of this chapter. The use of these measures in career counseling could lead to interesting discussions and an increased understanding of the relative importance of different values to a client, but the inability to reliably link these results to occupational outcomes limits the range of their clinical application.

SELECTION OF VALUES MEASURES FOR USE IN CLINICAL AND OTHER APPLIED SETTINGS

Among the measures that represent the different value taxonomies and models presented in this chapter, the O*NET-based WIP offers the best strategy for linking values to occupations. The other values measures we reviewed cannot link results to the range of career-related information available in the O*NET. As the U.S. Department of Labor continues to develop and update the O*NET database, the discrepancy between the range of information available through the WIP and other measures will continue to grow. In short, other value measures may be a starting point for a discussion of what is important to a client but cannot provide an answer to the potentially more interesting question of how to link these values to the world of work. However, in the future it may become possible to apply other values measures as new information and models emerge from research on cross-cultural values and the role of values in the workplace.

A critical issue with career-related assessments with diverse racial-ethnic groups is the interpretation of results in the context of the sociocultural influences that may have an impact on the career development process (Brown, 2002). For example, Eby, Johnson, and Russell (1998) have made important distinctions between the institutional challenges and personal challenges that members of minority groups face in the United States. Institutional challenges include others' stereotypes based on group membership, discrimination in selection practices and organizational practices, hostility from coworkers, and glass ceiling effects. Personal challenges include having your own interests limited or stereotyped based on group membership, problems with self-efficacy and self-confidence, less career exploration, and more career indecision. Flores, Spanierman, and Obasi (2003) outline a career assessment model that emphasizes the importance of infusing cultural sensitivity at all stages in the assessment process, including the choice of assessment instruments, the administration process, and the interpretation of results. Therefore, when linking WIP results to the information in the O*NET database, it is critical to recognize that the values that are important to an individual must also be understood in the context of the individual's culture and other social forces that can influence the range of educational and career-related options being considered.

SUMMARY

Values represent an important source of information that can be used to facilitate the career development process. Ultimately, the use of a values measure in career counseling should be part of an integrative strategy combining different sources of information and perspectives to help individuals make informed career-related decisions. In cases where there is access to a computer and printer, the WIP is recommended for values assessment because it links values to occupational information through the O*NET. Without computer facilities, the pencil-and-paper

WIL provides a useful equivalent to the information provided in the WIP. The primary disadvantage of other values measures is their limited ability to link results directly to occupations in the world of work. The results obtained with other measures may offer some opportunity to discuss career-related issues on a more general level. Therefore, as a values clarification exercise, life value measures may have some utility when working with clients who are in the early stages of career planning. The O*NET-based measures can also be used for general explorations and values clarification, but retain the advantage of having direct linkages to occupational information. Such an advantage should not be overlooked because, irrespective of a client's current state of career development, information linking values to other sources of occupational information will undoubtedly be useful at some point in the career counseling process.

REFERENCES

Alderfer, C. P. (1969). An empirical test of a new theory of human needs. *Organizational Behavior and Human Performance, 4,* 142–175.

Allport, G. W. (1931). *A study of values.* Boston: Houghton Mifflin.

Allport, G. W. (1961). *Pattern and growth in personality.* New York: Holt, Rinehart and Winston.

Allport, G. W., & Vernon, P. E. (1931). A study of values. Cambridge, MA.: Houghton-Mifflin Co.

Allport, G. W., Vernon, P. E., & Lindzey, G. (1970). *Study of values.* (Rev. 3rd ed.). Chicago: Riverside.

Armstrong, P. I., Day, S. X., & Rounds, J. (2003). *A circumplex framework for integrating personality, interests, and abilities.* Poster presented at the annual convention of the American Psychological Association, Toronto, Ontario, Canada.

Bardi, A., & Schwartz, S. H. (2003). Values and behavior: Strength and structure of relations. *Personality and Social Psychology Bulletin, 29,* 1207–1220.

Boxx, W. R., Odem, R. Y., & Dunn, M. G. (1991). Organizational values and value congruency and their impact on satisfaction, commitment, and cohesion. *Public Personnel Management, 20,* 195–205.

Bretz, R. D., Jr., & Judge, T. A. (1994). Person-organization fit and the theory of work adjustment: Implications for satisfaction, tenure, and career success. *Journal of Vocational Behavior, 44,* 32–54.

Brown, D. (1996). Brown's value-based, holistic model of career and life-role choices and satisfaction. In D. Brown, L. Brooks, & Associates (Eds.), *Career choices and development* (3rd ed., pp. 337–372). San Francisco: Jossey-Bass.

Brown, D. (2002). The role of work and cultural values in occupational choice, satisfaction, and success: A theoretical statement. *Journal of Counseling and Development, 80,* 48–56.

Brown, D., & Crace, R. K. (1996). Values in life role choices and outcomes: A conceptual model. *Career Development Quarterly, 44,* 211–224.

Buehler, C. (1933). *Der menschilch lebenslauf als psychologisches problem* [The human life course as a psychological subject]. Leipzig, Germany: Hirzel.

Campbell, J. P., & Pritchard, R. D. (1976). Motivation theory in industrial and organizational psychology. In M. D. Dunnette (Ed.), *Handbook of industrial and organizational psychology* (pp. 63–130). Chicago: Rand McNally.

Chatman, J. (1991). Matching people and organizations: Selection and socialization in public accounting firms. *Administrative Science Quarterly, 36,* 459–484.

Dawis, R. V. (1991). Vocational interests, values, and preferences. In M. D. Dunnette & L. M. Hough (Eds.), *Handbook of industrial and organizational psychology* (2nd ed., Vol. 2, pp. 833–871). Palo Alto, CA: Consulting Psychologists Press.

Dawis, R. V. (2001). Toward a psychology of values. *Counseling Psychologist, 29,* 458–465.

Dawis, R. V., Dohm, T. E., Lofquist, L. H., Chartrand, J. M., & Due, A. M. (1987). *Minnesota Occupational Classification System III: A psychological taxonomy of work.*

Minneapolis: University of Minnesota, Department of Psychology, Vocational Psychology Research.

Dawis, R. V., & Lofquist, L. H. (1984). *A psychological theory of work adjustment*. Minneapolis: University of Minnesota Press.

Eby, L. T., Johnson, C. D., & Russell, J. E. A. (1998). A psychometric review of career assessment tools for use with diverse individuals. *Journal of Career Assessment, 6*, 269–310.

Edwards, J. R. (1991). Person-job fit: A conceptual integration, literature review, and methodological critique. In C. L. Cooper & I. T. Robertson (Eds.), *International review of industrial and organizational psychology* (Vol. 6, pp. 283–357). New York: Wiley.

Elizur, D., & Sagie, A. (1999). Facets of personal values: A structural analysis of life and work values. *Applied Psychology: An International Review, 17*, 503–514.

Ferreira-Marques, J., & Miranda, M. J. (1995). Developing the work importance study. In D. E. Super & B. Sverko (Eds.), *Life roles, values, and careers: International findings of the work importance study* (pp. 62–74). San Francisco: Jossey-Bass.

Fitzgerald, L. F., & Rounds, J. B. (1989). Vocational behavior, 1988: A critical analysis. *Journal of Vocational Behavior, 35*, 105–163.

Flores, L. Y., Spanierman, L. B., & Obasi, E. M. (2003). Ethical and professional issues in career assessment with diverse racial and ethnic groups. *Journal of Career Assessment, 11*, 76–95.

Gay, E. G., Weiss, D. J., Hendel, D. D., Dawis, R. V., & Lofquist, L. H. (1971). Manual for the Minnesota Importance Questionnaire. *Minnesota Studies in Vocational Rehabilitation* (No. XXVIII).

Ginzberg, E., Ginsburg, S. W., Axelrad, S., & Herma, J. (1951). *Occupational choice: An approach to a general theory*. New York: Columbia University Press.

Hackman, J. R., & Oldham, G. R. (1980). *Work redesign*. Reading, MA: Addison-Wesley.

Herzberg, F., Mausner, B., & Snyderman, B. (1959). *The motivation to work* (2nd ed.). New York: Wiley.

Hesketh, B., & Gardner, D. (1993). Person-environment fit models: A reconceptualization and empirical test. *Journal of Vocational Behavior, 42*, 315–332.

Hofstede, G. (1980). *Culture's consequences: International differences in work-related values*. Beverly Hills, CA: Sage.

Hofstede, G. (2001). *Cultural consequences: Comparing values, behaviors, institutions and organizations across nations*. Thousand Oaks, CA: Sage.

Holland, J. L. (1997). *Making vocational choices: A theory of vocational personalities and work environments* (3rd ed.). Odessa, FL: Psychological Assessment Resources.

Judge, T. A., & Bretz, R. D. (1992). Effects of work values on job choice decisions. *Journal of Applied Psychology, 77*, 261–271.

Kanfer, R. (1991). Motivation theory and industrial and organizational psychology. In M. D. Dunnette & L. M. Hough (Eds.), *Handbook of industrial and organizational psychology* (Vol. 1, pp. 75–170). Palo Alto, CA: Consulting Psychologists Press.

Kopelman, R. E., Rovenpor, J. L., & Guan, M. (2003). The study of values: Construction of the fourth edition. *Journal of Vocational Behavior, 62*, 203–220.

Kristof, A. (1996). Person-organization fit: An integrative review of its conceptualizations, measurement, and implications. *Personnel Psychology, 49*, 1–48.

Livingstone, L. P., Nelson, D. L., & Barr, S. H. (1997). Person-environment fit and creativity: An examination of supply-value and demand-ability versions of fit. *Journal of Management, 23*, 119–146.

Locke, E. A. (1976). The nature and causes of job satisfaction. In M. D. Dunnette (Ed.), *Handbook of industrial and organizational psychology* (pp. 1297–1349). Chicago: Rand McNally.

Lofquist, L. H., & Dawis, R. V. (1978). Values as second-order needs in the theory of work adjustment. *Journal of Vocational Behavior, 13*, 12–19.

Lofquist, L. H., & Dawis, R. V. (1991). *Essentials of person environment correspondence counseling*. Minneapolis: University of Minnesota Press.

Macnab, D., & Fitzsimmons, G. W. (1987). A multitrait-multimethod study of work-related needs, values and preferences. *Journal of Vocational Behavior, 30*, 1–15.

Maslow, A. H. (1954). *Motivation and personality*. New York: Harper & Row.

Maslow, A. H. (1959). *New knowledge in human values*. New York: Harper & Row.

McCloy, R., Campbell, J., Oswald, F. L., Rivkin, D., & Lewis, P. (1999). *Linking client assessment profiles to O*NET occupational profiles.* Raleigh, NC: National Center for O*NET Development.

McCloy, R., Waugh, G., Medsker, G., Wall, J., Rivkin, D., & Lewis, P. (1999a). *Determining the occupational reinforcer patterns for O*NET occupational units* (Vols. I & II). Raleigh, NC: National Center for O*NET Development.

McCloy, R., Waugh, G., Medsker, G., Wall, J., Rivkin, D., & Lewis, P. (1999b). *Development of the Computerized Work Importance Profiler.* Raleigh, NC: National Center for O*NET Development.

McCloy, R., Waugh, G., Medsker, G., Wall, J., Rivkin, D., & Lewis, P. (1999c). *Development of the Paper-and-Pencil Work Importance Locator.* Raleigh, NC: National Center for O*NET Development.

Meglino, B. M., & Ravlin, E. C. (1998). Individual values in organizations: Concepts, controversies, and research. *Journal of Management, 24,* 351–389.

Meyer, J. P., Irving, P. G., & Allen, N. J. (1998). Examination of the combined effects of work values and early work experiences on organizational commitment. *Journal of Organizational Behavior, 19,* 29–52.

Murray, H. A. (1938). *Explorations in personality.* New York: Oxford University Press.

Nevill, D. D., & Calvert, P. D. (1996). Career assessment and the salience inventory. *Journal of Career Assessment, 4,* 399–412.

Nevill, D. D., & Kruse, S. J. (1996). Career assessment and the values scale. *Journal of Career Assessment, 4,* 383–397.

Nevill, D. D., & Super, D. E. (1986a). *The Salience Inventory: Theory, application, and research.* Palo Alto, CA: Consulting Psychologists Press.

Nevill, D. D., & Super, D. E. (1986b). *The Value Scale: Theory, application, and research.* Palo Alto, CA: Consulting Psychologists Press.

Nord, W. R., Brief, A. P., Atieh, J. M., & Doherty, E. M. (1990). Studying meaning of work: The case of work values. In A. P. Brief & W. R. Nord (Eds.), *Meanings of occupational work* (pp. 21–64). Lexington, MA: Lexington Books.

O'Reilly, C. A., III, Chatman, J., & Caldwell, D. F. (1991). People and organizational culture: A profile comparison approach to assessing person-organization fit. *Academy of Management Journal, 34,* 487–516.

Perrewe, P. L., & Hochwarter, W. A. (2001). Can we really have it all? The attainment of work and family values. *Current Directions in Psychological Science, 10,* 29–33.

Peterson, N. G., Mumford, M. D., Borman, W. C., Jeanneret, P. R., & Fleishman, E. A. (1999). *An occupational information system for the twenty-first century: The development of the O*NET.* Washington, DC: American Psychological Association.

Posner, B. Z. (1992). Person-organization values congruence: No support for individual differences as a moderating influence. *Human Relations, 45,* 351–361.

Roe, R. A., & Ester, P. (1999). Values and work: Empirical findings and theoretical perspective. *Applied Psychology: An International Review, 48,* 1–21.

Rohan, M. J. (2000). A rose by any name? The values construct. *Personality and Social Psychology Review, 4,* 255–277.

Rokeach, M. (1973). *The nature of human values.* New York: Free Press.

Ronen, S. (1994). An underlying structure of motivational need taxonomies: A cross-cultural confirmation. In H. C. Triandis, M. D. Dunnette, & L. M. Hough (Eds.), *Handbook of industrial and organizational psychology* (Vol. 4, pp. 241–270). Palo Alto, CA: Consulting Psychologists Press.

Ros, M., Schwartz, S. H., & Surkiss, S. (1999). Basic individual values, work values, and the meaning of work. *Applied Psychology: An International Review, 48,* 49–71.

Rounds, J. B. (1990). The comparative and combined utility of work-value and interest data in career counseling with adults. *Journal of Vocational Behavior, 37,* 32–45.

Rounds, J. B., Dawis, R. V., & Lofquist, L. H. (1987). Measurement of person-environment fit and prediction of satisfaction in the theory of work adjustment. *Journal of Vocational Behavior, 31,* 297–318.

Rounds, J. B., Henly, G. A., Dawis, R. V., Lofquist, L. H., & Weiss, D. J. (1981). *Manual for the Minnesota Importance Questionnaire: A measure of needs and values.* Minneapolis: University of Minnesota, Department of Psychology.

Rounds, J. B., & Tracey, T. J. (1990). From trait-and-factor to person-environment fit counseling: Theory and process. In W. B. Walsh & S. H. Osipow (Eds.), *Career counseling* (pp. 1–44). Hillsdale, NJ: Erlbaum.

Schaffer, R. H. (1953). Job satisfaction as related to need satisfaction at work. *Psychological Monographs, 67*(Whole No. 364).

Schneider, B. (2001). Fits about fit. *Journal of Applied Psychology: An International Review, 50,* 141–152.

Schwartz, S. H. (1992). Universals in the content and structure of values: Theoretical advances and empirical tests in 20 countries. In M. P. Zanna (Ed.), *Advances in experimental social psychology* (Vol. 24, pp. 1–65). San Diego, CA: Academic Press.

Schwartz, S. H. (1994). Are there universal aspects in the structure and contents of human values? *Journal of Social Issues, 50,* 19–45.

Schwartz, S. H. (1996). Value priorities and behavior: Applying a theory of integrated value systems. In C. Seligman, J. M. Olson, & M. P. Zanna (Eds.), *Values: The Ontario symposium* (Vol. 8, pp. 1–24). Hillsdale, NJ: Lawrence Erlbaum.

Schwartz, S. H. (1999). A theory of cultural values and some implications for work. *Applied Psychology: An International Review, 48,* 23–47.

Skinner, B. F. (1938). *The behavior of organisms.* New York: Appleton-Century-Crofts.

Smith, P. B., & Schwartz, S. H. (1997). Values. In J. W. Berry, M. H. Segall, & C. Kagitcibasi (Eds.), *Handbook of cross-cultural psychology* (3rd ed., Vol. 3, pp. 97–118). Boston: Allyn & Bacon.

Spector, P. E., Cooper, C. L., & Sparks, K. (2001). An international study of the psychometric properties of the Hofstede Values Survey Module 1994: A comparison of individual and country/province level results. *Applied Psychology: An International Review, 50,* 269–281.

Spranger, E. (1928). *Types of men: The psychology and ethics of personality* (Paul J. W. Pigors, Trans.). Halle, Germany: Max Niemeyer Verlag.

Stewart, E. S., Greenstein, S. M., Holt, N. C., Henly, G. A., Engdahl, B. E., Dawis, R. V., et al. (1986). *Occupational reinforcer patterns.* Minneapolis: University of Minnesota, Department of Psychology, Vocational Psychology Research.

Struch, N., Schwartz, S. H., & van der Kloot, W. A. (2002). Meanings of basic values for women and men: A cross-cultural analysis. *Personality and Social Psychology Bulletin, 28,* 16–28.

Super, D. E. (1962). The structure of work values in relation to status, achievement, interest, and adjustment. *Journal of Applied Psychology, 46,* 227–239.

Super, D. E. (1970). *Work Values Inventory.* Boston: Houghton Mifflin.

Super, D. E. (1980). A life-span, life-space approach to career development. *Journal of Vocational Behavior, 16,* 282–298.

Super, D. E. (1983). Assessment in career guidance: Toward truly developmental counseling. *Personnel and Guidance Journal, 61,* 555–562.

Super, D. E. (1995). Values: Their nature, assessment, and practical use. In D. E. Super & B. Sverko (Eds.), *Life roles, values, and careers: International findings of the work importance study* (pp. 54–61). San Francisco: Jossey-Bass.

Super, D. E., & Sverko, B. (Eds.). (1995). *Life roles, values, and careers: International findings of the work importance study.* San Francisco: Jossey-Bass.

Sverko, B. (1995). The structure and hierarchy of values viewed cross-nationally. In D. E. Super & B. Sverko (Eds.), *Life roles, values, and careers: International findings of the work importance study* (pp. 225–240). San Francisco: Jossey-Bass.

Taris, R., & Feij, J. A. (2001). Longitudinal examination of the relationship between supplies-values fit and work outcomes. *Applied Psychology: An International Review, 50,* 52–80.

U.S. Department of Labor. (2000a). *Work importance locator: User's guide.* Washington, DC: Employment and Training Administration.

U.S. Department of Labor. (2000b). *Work importance profiler: User's guide.* Washington, DC: Employment and Training Administration.

CHAPTER 14

Ability Assessment in Career Counseling

Nancy E. Ryan Krane and William C. Tirre

O NE OF THE best things a career counselor can do is help clients identify current and potential skill strengths and career options that capitalize on them. This chapter focuses on the use of ability assessment in career counseling by:

- Defining the construct of abilities and addressing the importance of abilities to the processes of career choice and adjustment.
- Discussing issues of which a fully informed career practitioner should be aware when assessing abilities.
- Describing various ability assessment strategies and tools.

The net result should be increased knowledge and understanding of appropriate roles and uses of abilities in career work, as well as various approaches to ability measurement.

We provide an overview of the use of both objectively measured abilities and self-estimated abilities. Much has been made of the relative value of objectively measured versus self-estimated abilities in career counseling (e.g., Betz, 1992; Harrington & Schafer, 1996; Lowman & Williams, 1987; Prediger, 1999a, 1999b). We highlight merits and limitations of each, as well as key measurement strategies and tools in both of these areas, to furnish readers with information that may prove helpful in future career work.

ABILITIES: DEFINITIONS

The term *ability* refers to the power to perform a specified act or task, either physical or mental (Snow, 1994). Such powers can be learned or innate, have some kind

The authors wish to thank Kevin A. Field and Peg E. Hendershot for their comments on an earlier version of this chapter.

of neurological basis, and are fairly stable characteristics of the individual. The term *aptitude,* on the other hand, appears to hold at least two meanings in the psychological literature. One general definition of aptitude refers to any attribute or individual differences variable that might be used to predict how likely a person is to succeed in certain environments, such as work environments (e.g., Lubinski & Dawis, 1992; Snow, 1992). A second, more restrictive definition of aptitude is closely aligned with the notion of cognitive ability: "Essentially, aptitude is potential ability or the capacity to learn . . . aptitude tests provide quantitative estimates of a person's potential for learning the knowledge and skills needed for school, training, or career success" (Gregory, 1994, p. 110).

This latter conceptualization of aptitude may prompt the question: What is the difference between aptitude and general intelligence (i.e., *g* or general cognitive ability)? Aptitude differs from intelligence, with intelligence serving as the most general of the abilities because it enters into performance of any task that has some cognitive demand. Tasks and jobs vary in the degree to which they call on this general ability, and information about an individual's intelligence often provides one useful indication of the approximate job level (in terms of training requirements and job complexity) that might be a good fit for him or her. However, such information alone is insufficient for career decisions because occupations within the same job level often vary significantly in the specific aptitudes they emphasize. Kline (2000) nicely illustrated this point, observing that high intelligence levels are necessary to be both a good engineer and a good journalist; however, high spatial ability is also required of the engineer and high verbal ability of the journalist. Along these same lines, Dawis (1996a) stated that multiple-ability tests tend to be especially useful in situations where tests of *g* are not—namely, when trying to differentiate between occupations that reside within the same job level.

In this chapter, we focus on the first (predictive) definition of aptitude as well as ability. Specifically, we focus on tests and other assessment tools (e.g., ability self-estimates) that have the dual purposes of measuring a client's current level of performance on specific tasks (abilities) *and* predicting the types of occupations and jobs in which he or she may succeed in the future (aptitudes).

APPLICATIONS OF ABILITY ASSESSMENT

Ability tests can be routinely and effectively used in two very different applications. The first is in personnel selection and classification; the second is in career assessment and counseling. Other applications, which often require more specialized tests, include educational screening, educational diagnosis, and neuropsychological assessment.

Ability testing in personnel selection is useful in helping organizations identify persons who are likely to succeed on the job. To use a Theory of Work Adjustment (TWA; see Dawis, Chapter 1, this volume) term, the hiring company is concerned with predicting the *satisfactoriness* (i.e., adequacy) of a candidate's job performance.

In career counseling, on the other hand, ability assessments are used to help individuals identify job possibilities in which success is increased rather than to help organizations to identify potentially successful employees. This is done by assessing abilities that can be immediately transferred into job-related skills and by testing aptitudes to predict areas of potential that could be tapped in the future to maximize occupational success.

Career counselors can familiarize themselves with the duties and abilities required of various occupations through counseling experience and through study (e.g., Dawis, Dohm, Lofquist, Chartrand, & Due, 1987; Fleishman & Reilly, 1992; Gore & Hitch, Chapter 16, this volume; Gottfredson, 1986; Lowman, 1991). Furthermore, several useful texts and resources address ability measurement and its applications (e.g., Anastasi & Urbina, 1997; Fleishman & Reilly, 1992; Kline, 2000; Lowman, 1991). By pairing knowledge of a client's aptitudes with knowledge of the basic abilities required of a wide variety of occupations, the career counselor is in a good position to propose career options that capitalize on the client's current and potential strengths and that, thus, may be worthy of exploration. For instance, if a client's aptitude profile reveals strengths in spatial (i.e., 3-D visualization), mechanical, and numerical abilities, fields such as engineering or architecture may merit exploration. Or, if strengths are indicated in clerical (i.e., perceptual speed and accuracy), numerical, memory, and finger-dexterity abilities, fields such as laboratory science or pharmaceutical science/practice might be worth exploring. There is no guarantee of success in these fields, as success is dependent on many factors, including effort, motivation, training, and the availability of support. However, matching persons' aptitudes with the ability requirements of jobs does increase the likelihood of future job success, sufficient for aptitude assessment to be considered a critical aspect of career counseling (see Achter & Lubinski, Chapter 25, this volume; Barrett & Depinet, 1991; Dawis, Chapter 1, this volume; Dawis, 1996b; Prediger, 1989; Russell, Chapter 9, this volume; Spokane & Cruza-Guet, Chapter 2, this volume).

In using ability assessments in career counseling, clients should not, however, be told or led to believe that there is a precise probability of succeeding in a given job or set of jobs. Rather, the message should be that the pattern of results suggests specific work tasks and activities that will currently (ability interpretation) or will likely (aptitude interpretation) come quickly and easily to them, as well as specific work tasks and activities that may not come as easily and, as such, might require more effort, motivation, compensation strategies, or support if they are important to a desired work position. It is legitimate, though, for career counselors to explain to clients that exploring and eventually choosing positions that require current or potential strengths are likely to increase chances of satisfactoriness and job success. Ability assessments will need to be complemented by assessment of other variables (such as work needs, values, interests, and personality) to help direct the client to career possibilities that may additionally yield satisfaction as well as success.

HISTORICAL OVERVIEW OF ABILITY ASSESSMENT IN CAREER COUNSELING

Ability assessment is a time-honored tool in career counseling, and it includes both objective ability assessment as well as ability self-estimation. We turn now to a brief historical overview of each.

OBJECTIVE ASSESSMENT

A milestone in the history of objective ability assessment occurred at the outset of World War I, when a team of leading psychologists in the intelligence testing movement (e.g., Bingham, Goddard, Terman, and Whipple) turned their attention toward the practical problem of recruit selection and classification for the United States military. Chaired by Robert Yerkes, the Committee on the Psychological Examination of Recruits developed the Army Alpha and Beta tests, group-administered intelligence tests that were used to select and classify nearly two million soldiers. The success of this program intensified research on specific vocational aptitudes, which had already been studied by Münsterberg (1913) and Hollingworth (1915) and even earlier by the United States Civil Service Commission. For further historical information, see DuBois (1970).

During this early period, Link (1919) produced aptitude tests for various occupations, including munitions shell inspectors, assemblers, clerks, stenographers, typists, and production machine operators. Additionally, Thurstone (1919a) produced and validated a rhythm test for the selection of telegraphers and a multipart test assessing various aspects of office/clerical jobs (Thurstone, 1919b). Moreover, tests of spatial abilities were developed during the same period, after items requiring spatial ability had served first as nonverbal performance measures of intelligence. For example, Binet and Simon (1916/1980) used a paper-cutting task in one of many tests that they developed to assess intellectual functioning in children. Various other abilities or aptitudes were investigated around this time, including musical aptitude (e.g., C. E. Seashore, 1919), psychomotor/perceptual-motor aptitude (e.g., Fleishman, 1954; R. H. Seashore, 1930), and artistic aptitude (e.g., Meier, 1939). An exhaustive discussion of abilities investigated is available in Carroll (1993).

With the burgeoning number of abilities being investigated by applied psychologists interested in predicting success in school and in various occupations, there became a need for a theoretical and taxonomic categorization of the ability domain. American and British psychologists vied for the lead in this endeavor, representing opposing frameworks; namely, the multiple abilities perspective, championed by Kelley (1928) and Thurstone (1938), and the London school, led by Spearman (1904, 1927), which emphasized *g* above all other abilities.

In contrast to London scholars, North American psychologists found evidence for multiple abilities. Truman Kelley (1928), for example, used an early form of factor analysis to identify several aptitudes, including verbal, numerical, spatial, and memory. Furthermore, Thurstone (1938) proposed seven *primary mental abilities* (PMAs), each uncorrelated with all others (his sample primarily consisted of University of Chicago undergraduates, which we today would recognize as restricted in range on general ability). The PMAs included inductive reasoning, spatial ability, numerical ability, verbal ability, memory, word fluency, and perceptual speed.

According to Dawis (1996a), the groundwork for multiple-ability test batteries and their use in career guidance is thought to have been laid by a classic study of mechanical ability (i.e., Paterson, Elliott, Anderson, Toops, & Heidbreder, 1930) that provided early empirical support for the notion of multiple abilities by establishing that other abilities besides *g* (i.e., mechanical abilities) can serve to explain significant variance in job performance and occupational aptitude.

ABILITY SELF-ESTIMATION

The literature surrounding ability self-estimation is fairly recent in comparison to the literature on objective ability measurement. While ability self-ratings had been employed in career practice and research for some time, it was Mabe and West's (1982) meta-analysis of the validity of ability self-evaluations that seemed to call particular attention to this approach. Specifically, these authors compared ability self-evaluations with objective ability measures and found that for a number of reasons (e.g., person variables, measurement conditions) ability self-evaluations do not tend to correlate strongly with objective ability scores. Since the time of that study, some have championed the use of self-estimated abilities in career counseling (e.g., Harrington & Schafer, 1996; Prediger, 1999a, 1999b), and many such instruments have been developed or refined (two of which are discussed more fully in a later section of this chapter).

Prediger (1999b) discussed the notion of "informed self-estimates" of ability, which draw on first-hand experience (including past ability test results if available) as well as vicarious experience. Given the roots that ability self-estimation shares with two of four of Bandura's (1977, 1986) sources of efficacy information (i.e., past performance and vicarious learning/modeling; see Lent, Chapter 5, this volume) and the conceptual overlap between ability self-estimates and self-efficacy perceptions, you might naturally question the distinction between these two constructs. One important difference between the two is that the approach often taken with ability self-estimation is to have individuals rate themselves as compared to others rather than rate their perceived competence in an absolute sense, as is typically done with self-efficacy measures (Tracey & Hopkins, 2001). Additionally, self-efficacy belief measures tend to inquire about future performance capabilities, whereas ability self-estimates generally ask people to make contemporaneous judgments (see Brown, Lent, & Gore, 2000). Brown et al. (2000) investigated the empirical distinction between these two constructs and found that while occupational self-efficacy beliefs and self-estimated abilities do indeed overlap, they are empirically distinguishable from one another.

DIMENSIONALITY OF WORK-RELEVANT ABILITIES

Highly influential contributions to our understanding of the content and organization of cognitive abilities have been made in recent decades. For instance, the structure of intellect model (e.g., Guilford, 1956, 1967; Guilford & Hoepfner, 1971) provided a theoretical framework of the abilities literature that was exceptionally descriptive in nature. In this model, Guilford proposed 120 distinct cognitive abilities and organized them in a three-dimensional cube according to the type of content (figural, symbolic, semantic, and behavioral), the type of operation performed (cognition, memory, divergent production, convergent production, and evaluation), and the resulting product (unit, class, relation, system, transformation, and implication) involved in the deployment of each ability.

Another example is Carroll's (1993) empirical efforts, which resulted in what is considered by many to be the most comprehensive factor-analytic investigation of abilities ever performed. Moreover, this model nicely illustrates the nature of modern hierarchical ability models (Murphy, 1996). Carroll reanalyzed as much of the existing factor-analytic research as he could (467 datasets), collecting studies spanning several decades. His efforts resulted in a three-level, hierarchical structure of cognitive abilities that ranges from a lowest level of very specific abilities to a highest level of g or general ability (see Figure 14.1). Specifically, the lowest level of Carroll's hierarchy is entitled Stratum I, which represents 68 very specific abilities

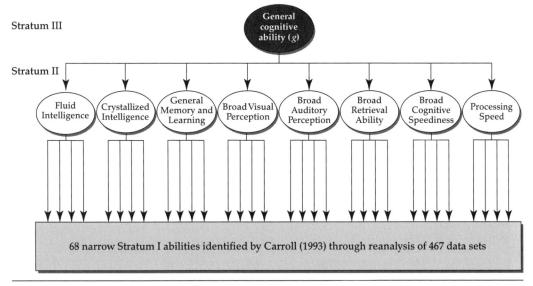

Figure 14.1 Carroll's (1993) Structure of Cognitive Abilities: Strata 2 and 3. [From *Human Cognitive Abilities: A Survey of Factor-Analytic Studies*, by J. B. Carroll, 1993, New York: Cambridge University Press. Copyright 1993 by Cambridge University Press. Adapted with the permission of Cambridge University Press.]

such as reading speed and simple reaction time. The next highest and more general level is Stratum II, composed of eight broad ability factors: Fluid Intelligence, Crystallized Intelligence, General Memory and Learning, Broad Visual Perception, Broad Auditory Perception, Broad Retrieval Ability, Broad Cognitive Speediness, and Processing Speed. Finally, the highest and most general level is Stratum III, represented by g (i.e., General Intelligence or general cognitive ability).

Inspection of the second level (stratum) in this model suggests that Thurstone's PMAs were not far from the truth, at least as best could be discerned in 1993. Induction falls under fluid intelligence, verbal comprehension falls under crystallized intelligence, memory falls under general memory and learning, spatial ability falls under broad visual perception, word fluency falls under broad retrieval ability, and perceptual speed falls under broad visual perception and broad cognitive speediness. Numerical facility also falls under broad cognitive speediness, but the tests indicating this factor involve simple numerical operations. Thurstone (1938; Thurstone & Thurstone, 1941) had in mind a level factor indicating power rather than speed of processing.

Taken together, the abilities that have been reliably identified across studies and that tend to appear on most multiaptitude test batteries today are generally reflective of Thurstone's PMAs: inductive reasoning, spatial ability, numerical ability, verbal ability, memory, word fluency, and perceptual speed. Furthermore, objective and self-estimated ability measures often measure psychomotor ability, which is important to many occupations that involve working with things and objects (e.g., building, repairing, assembling, organizing, writing). Some multiaptitude test batteries measure technical knowledge areas (e.g., auto and shop information) in addition to the PMAs, and self-estimated ability instruments

Table 14.1

Number of Subtests Measuring Ability Categories in
Selected Ability Assessment Instruments

Ability Category	Self-Estimated		Objectively Estimated				
	CDM-R 2000	IWRA	ASVAB	Ability Profiler	DAT	CAPS	BAB (Classic)
Reasoning	0	0	0[a]	0[a]	2[a]	1	2[a]
Spatial	2	2	1	1	2	2	2
Numerical	2	1	3	2	1	1	2
Verbal	1	2	2	1	2	2	1
Memory	0	0	0	0	0	0	2
Creativity	2	2	0	0	0	0	2
Perceptual Speed	1	1	1	2[b]	1	1	1
Psychomotor	1	1	0	3	0	1	3
Other or Technical	5	6	3	0	0	0	1

Note: ASVAB = Armed Services Vocational Aptitude Battery; BAB = Ball Aptitude Battery; CAPS = Career Ability Placement Survey; CDM-R 2000 = Harrington-O'Shea Career Decision-Making System Revised-2000; DAT = Differential Aptitude Test; IWRA = Inventory of Work-Relevant Abilities. Rows represent broad ability categories; tests within rows are similar in purpose and content to varying degrees. Mechanical comprehension, mechanical reasoning, and technical/mechanical tests appear under *Spatial*. Word fluency and artistic (e.g., musical) tests appear under *Creativity*. Reading, language usage, word knowledge, paragraph comprehension, and spelling tests appear under *Verbal*. Verbal reasoning test(s) appear under *Reasoning*. Scientific or general science tests appear under *Other or Technical*, as do social/meeting people tests.
[a]Mathematical reasoning and arithmetic reasoning tests appear under *Numerical*.
[b]Form Perception appears under *Perceptual Speed*.

often assess additional work-relevant abilities (e.g., social, leadership) in addition to the PMAs. Table 14.1 provides an overview of the number of subtests measuring the PMAs, psychomotor, and *other or technical* ability categories in selected ability assessment instruments. More specific (e.g., subtest) information about these instruments is provided later in the chapter.

STABILITY OF WORK-RELEVANT ABILITIES

Cognitive abilities (especially more general versus specific abilities) are considered to be rather stable over time (Carroll, 1993; Schaie & Hertzog, 1986; see also Gottfredson, 2003). Research also suggests that the structure of cognitive abilities and an individual's standing relative to peers on abilities tends to reach a fairly high level of stability by early adolescence (Carroll, 1993; Dawis, Goldman, & Sung, 1992; Dixon, Kramer, & Baltes, 1985), though there is room at that age and beyond for further cognitive change (Dixon et al., 1985). Taken together, the consensus seems to be that there is more room for malleability in the more specific and fine-tuned abilities than at the more general level. Gottfredson (2003) presented an incisive summary of these findings and incorporated them into a useful framework for determining which cognitive abilities should be considered in career exploration and guidance, as well as how they might be considered. In so doing, she suggests that because the broader abilities represented by Strata II and III in Carroll's model are more stable and nonmalleable than Carroll's specific Stratum I abilities, a sound approach in working with career clients is to help them consider and explore a list of best-bet career options that are a good match on the broader abilities and then help them to fine-tune such choices on the basis of specific Stratum I abilities that are already possessed by the client or that might be more easily trained due to the increased malleability associated with them.

The Seattle Longitudinal Study (SLS; Schaie, 1994; Schaie & Hertzog, 1986) examined specific ability changes over time among adults. This program of research involved the assessment of mental abilities in more than 5,000 adults over a period of some 35 years. Schaie (1994) summarized this research, reporting modest increases from young adulthood to age 60 in inductive reasoning, spatial orientation, verbal ability, and verbal memory, and notable declines during this age period in numeric skill and perceptual speed. Between the ages of 25 and 88, declines were found in inductive reasoning, verbal memory, spatial orientation, numeric ability, and perceptual speed. Schaie (1994) also reported that while reliable average decreases are found for all abilities by age 67, the decline is modest until the 80s, and it occurs for most individuals in a stair-step (rather than linear) fashion. Furthermore, Schaie (1994) noted that much of the observed late-life decline in abilities is attributable to the slowing of processing and response speed and that when age changes in perceptual speed are removed from the other abilities, their amount of age decline is significantly reduced. Variables identified through the SLS to reduce the risk of cognitive decline in old age include the absence of cardiovascular or other chronic diseases, favorable environmental circumstances such as those associated with a high SES, extensive involvement in complex and intellectually stimulating activities, a flexible personality style, and higher life satisfaction (Schaie, 1994).

Taken together, it seems that while there is malleability in some more specific abilities, individuals over time tend to hold a similar standing on tests of ability relative to an age cohort (Carroll, 1993; Schaie, 1994). Although some practitioners may be disappointed that abilities are not more malleable, the demonstrable stability of abilities has a decided advantage for career counseling—ability assessments can be used to forecast into the future the types of work experiences and jobs in which an individual might be successful, since ability levels assessed at one time are likely to be present in the future as well. Thus, we can be reasonably comfortable that knowledge about abilities can be used in educational and career decision making from adolescence through adulthood.

INCORPORATING ABILITY ASSESSMENT INTO CAREER COUNSELING

Several factors warrant consideration when using ability assessment in career counseling. They include assessor training, criteria for evaluating ability assessment instruments, ways to apply ability assessment to specific career concerns, and the consideration of sex, ethnicity, and disability factors in ability assessment. We discuss each of these matters in turn.

ASSESSOR TRAINING

Users of psychological tests (be they tests of ability or other constructs) require formal training in psychological measurement and assessment, in addition to training and experience with the specific instruments they plan to employ. Assessors need also to understand and comply with the information and guidelines set forth in the manuals that accompany tests and be knowledgeable as to existing guidelines and criteria for the responsible and ethical use of assessment instruments (e.g., American Educational Research Association [AERA], American Psychological Association [APA], & National Council on Measurement in Education [NCME], 1999). Kapes and Whitfield (2001) have a handy appendix containing codes and standards for psychological test use.

Garfield and Krieshok (2001) provide a useful checklist for counselors to evaluate their basic assessment and counseling competencies. The three domains tapped by this checklist are:

1. Counseling skills (e.g., rapport establishment, sensitivity to diversity, knowledge of career theories).
2. Assessment skills (e.g., knowledge of statistics used in testing and test manuals, knowledge of types of assessment instruments, knowledge of score-reporting procedures, knowledge of standardization, reliability, and validity).
3. Responsibilities/competencies (preparing for test use, administration and scoring, and test interpretation).

EVALUATING ABILITY ASSESSMENT INSTRUMENTS

Lowman (1991) highlights six useful criteria for career counselors to use in the selection of ability measures:

1. Validity (e.g., Is there convincing support for the construct and predictive validity of the ability?).
2. Reliability (e.g., Does the test measure the ability consistently?).
3. Norms (e.g., How recent, extensive, and age-appropriate are the normative data for the measure?).
4. Commercial availability (i.e., Is the test readily available?).
5. Clarity of measurement (e.g., Is it clear which ability constructs or subconstructs are being measured by the test?).
6. Occupational applications (e.g., Are the proposed occupational applications clear and compelling, and does the test show a differential validity pattern for a variety of occupational groups?).

To this list, we add comprehensiveness, ease of administration and scoring, and usefulness of the resultant report. A brief overview of these three factors follows.

Comprehensiveness An ability assessment instrument to be used in career counseling should be evaluated for its comprehensiveness (i.e., the diversity of abilities that is measured). The measurement of a diverse set of abilities is desirable because a good match between a person and an occupation depends on a thoughtful consideration of the multidimensional natures of people and work. The optimal level of comprehensiveness is something that the counselor must decide on a case-by-case basis. Lowman (1991) provides a useful conceptual background on abilities and their use in career assessment and counseling, as well as a thoughtful discussion of various issues associated with the measurement of abilities. In so doing, he focuses on occupationally relevant ability variables, integrates relevant literature in his explanation of each ability construct, and cites commercially available measures of each. In addition, Fleishman and Reilly (1992) provide an accessible and informative description of 52 different abilities that highlights the job tasks and titles that call on each ability. This resource also provides a sampling of tests for each. However, both Lowman (1991) and Fleishman and Reilly (1992) tend to focus on the specific-ability level (rather than the multiple-ability level) in their discussions of ability construct and measurement issues.

Ease of Administration and Scoring and Usefulness of Report   Computer administration or self-administration via audio CD is becoming an option for the career practitioner who does not have time for test administration. Furthermore, the resultant test report should, at a minimum, include an ability profile along with examples of occupations that make use of the abilities or the overall ability profile. Better still is a report that integrates ability and interest data and that uses these data to make career recommendations. Some reports also include interpretive sections that help the client understand the implications of scores and score profiles for career choice and work adjustment.

APPLYING ABILITY ASSESSMENT TO SPECIFIC CAREER CONCERNS

Ability assessment can be effectively employed to address a wide array of career counseling concerns. We highlight four: expanding career options, narrowing options, confirming a career choice, and enhancing job performance.

Expanding Options   For the client with too few career options, ability assessment can help generate a broad array of realistic recommendations. When working with such clients, it may seem logical to first consider a set of occupations on the basis of interests and then find a subset of occupations that fall into a realistic ability range for the individual. While many interest areas offer a multitude of occupations that are differentiated on the basis of the aptitudes required of them, a disadvantage of such an approach is that the client may not have yet had the opportunity to develop interest in an occupational area due to limited exposure to the world of work, inaccurate outcome expectations, or the erroneous belief that he or she does not have the required aptitude(s) (see Brown & Lent, 1996; Lent, Brown, & Hackett, 1994). As such, occupational areas with the potential to be a good fit with both interests and abilities may not be fully considered. Ability assessment can, therefore, be used to identify a variety of congruent occupational titles, work groups, or activities that can be subsequently narrowed on the basis of interests, values, and other motivations.

Narrowing Options   For the client with a need to narrow a set of career options, ability assessment can be used to identify a subset of alternatives that plays to particular strengths the person currently has or that requires skills that the individual is likely to acquire quickly and easily. Such positions would offer a higher likelihood of success than positions chosen on the basis of other factors. This subset of occupations can be further narrowed in light of other important characteristics (e.g., interests, values, personality).

Confirming a Career Choice   For individuals seeking to confirm a career choice, both multiple and specific ability assessment can be employed in a more fine-tuned way by discussing the results in the context of the educational, training, and job requirements of the career in question. This can serve as powerful information in confirming a client's choice. It can also promote important discussions about motivation and choice realism. For instance, if it appears as though there is congruence in the approximate level of the occupation (in terms of training requirements and cognitive complexity) but there is a mismatch between the abilities of the individual and the abilities required of the career in question, two things should be kept in mind. First, while self-ratings of ability are clearly estimates of ability, so are objective ability assessments. Such tools are fallible and subject to measurement error, including error associated with conditions such as fatigue, preoccupation, lack of motivation, or lack of familiarity with such tests. For these reasons and others (there are many variables in addition to ability that directly affect career success), objective assessment results should always be corroborated with other materials (e.g., self-reports, school grades), and career clients should never be left with the impression that "the tests say that I cannot do what I want to do." Furthermore, if the majority (or entirety) of a client's self-estimated abilities are in the low range, there is an opening to discuss the possibility of ability underestimation. Second, should the mismatched (objective or self-estimated) ability results be corroborated, it is critical to discuss issues of effort, motivation, opportunity, and supports concerning the development of the requisite skills. If the mismatch occurs in abilities that are not as amenable to training or education (e.g., spatial abilities), it is important to convey to the client that the results suggest that he or she may need to work longer and harder than coworkers to achieve the same level of performance, and, realistically, there may be some work tasks that may never be mastered at a peak level of performance.

Gottfredson (2003) states that while already-mature individuals cannot expect to increase their broad abilities, there are other proactive ways to increase competitiveness in a desired field, including emphasizing relevant noncognitive traits such as conscientiousness or integrity, as well as developing necessary knowledge areas and skills (Gottfredson's examples include learning a computer program, finding a tutor or mentor, and preparing more fully for interviews). According to Gottfredson, these noncognitive attributes will not substitute for the needed cognitive abilities, but they could make the difference when broad abilities are near the margin for what is required.

Enhancing Work Performance   Finally, for the client seeking to enhance performance on the job, ability assessment can be used to help identify possible reasons for current difficulty on the job. For example, a low score in one of the speed and accuracy or memory aptitudes (i.e., clerical, writing speed, associative memory, and auditory memory span) can sometimes provide an explanation for an otherwise puzzling difficulty in completing job training or certain job tasks. Once identified, certain compensation strategies can be taught (e.g., taking extra time to attend to detail, having others double-check your work, learning how to use shorthand and/or mnemonic strategies). Furthermore, ability assessment can be used to identify areas of currently untapped potential (e.g., creativity, reasoning, mathematical, spatial) that can be explored and capitalized on in the workplace.

CONSIDERING SEX, ETHNICITY, AND DISABILITY FACTORS IN ABILITY ASSESSMENT

Counselors need to be sensitive to the ways in which characteristics such as age, sex, ethnicity, linguistic background, and educational and work history might affect an individual's response to career assessment and feedback. Counselors are also encouraged to use ability results to identify relative strengths and weaknesses within the individual rather than comparing one individual to another or one group to another. Although there are some small but consistent between-group differences in test score means on some (but not all) ability subtests, there are always substantial within-group differences. You cannot make meaningful or responsible generalizations from the group to the individual (Neisser et al., 1996). We next provide a brief overview of group-based findings in ability assessment research.

Sex   The overall equivalence that has been found between the sexes on intelligence measures does not imply equal performance on every individual ability; in fact, large differences favoring males appear in visual-spatial tasks such as mental rotation and spatiotemporal tasks such as tracking a moving object through space, while females tend to score significantly higher than males on tests of some verbal abilities including synonym generation and verbal fluency (Neisser et al., 1996). Furthermore, there is consistent evidence of sex differences on some quantitative abilities, with females scoring higher on quantitative tasks in the early years of school and with this trend reversing before puberty and males demonstrating superior performance into old age (Neisser et al., 1996). Further, while women tend to score higher on tasks including fine motor skills and perceptual speed, men tend to score higher on tasks including spatiotemporal responding and fluid reasoning (Sternberg, 1997). According to Sternberg (1997), the best available evidence is that biological and social factors work together to produce such differences.

Ethnicity   Much of the study in ethnic group differences in ability has occurred at the level of g (see Neisser et al., 1996, for a comprehensive coverage of the associated findings and an insightful analysis of possible explanations). Although there are some differences among ethnic groups in the levels and profiles of scores on conventional intelligence and ability tests (Sternberg, 1997), ability test scores do not generally show differential predictive validity in studies of selection bias (Betz, 1992). In other words, test scores tend to be equally predictive of educational and occupational outcomes (such as grades and performance ratings), regardless of examinee ethnicity. However, because many tests and self-estimates of ability involve abilities (e.g., verbal, numerical) that are more or less heavily influenced by education and training, it is important to take into account the quality of the client's educational background. This is especially salient when working with ethnically or culturally diverse clientele because African Americans and other minorities are more likely than Whites to be socioeconomically disadvantaged, which may expose them to poorer school systems and the associated dearth of educational opportunities that would facilitate performance on standardized tests (Betz, 1992). Furthermore, while not totally explaining group differences in test scores, socioeconomic factors also tend to play a role in that the poor nutrition, prenatal care, and intellectual resources associated with lower socioeconomic status are likely to have negative effects on cognitive development (Neisser et al., 1996).

Disability   Individuals with disabilities are defined as possessing a physical, mental, or developmental impairment that substantially limits their engagement in one or more of their major life activities (AERA, et al., 1999). The *Standards for Educational and Psychological Testing* (AERA, et al., 1999) encourages test users to familiarize themselves with federal, state, and local laws or court rulings that regulate the assessment of individuals with disabilities. This reference also provides helpful information about the rights of test takers with disabilities, the appropriateness and responsible use of test accommodations and modifications, the reporting of scores on modified tests, and professional standards for testing, interpreting, and communicating the results of tests to individuals with disabilities. Test users should also consult test manuals, accompanying materials, and/or the test publisher if necessary about the appropriate deployment of test modifications or accommodations.

Two key issues to be especially attuned to when assessing individuals with disabilities include the purpose for which the test was designed and validated, as well as the norm data on which the test scores are interpreted (see also Fabian & Liesener, Chapter 23, this volume). If a test is not designed and validated to diagnose special needs or disabilities, it is not valid to use the test for such a purpose. Furthermore, it is important to determine whether the norm data that are used to interpret scores on the test include samples of populations with special needs or disabilities. If not, the use of the existing norm data will provide information only about the test taker's ability levels relative to the general population, rather than a population of individuals with a specific type or degree of disability.

Counselors must use manual guidelines as well as their best judgment concerning test modifications or accommodations, keeping in mind that test modifications may impair the validity of test interpretations. The ultimate goal is to provide the individual with reliable self-knowledge to use in career development and career decision making.

ABILITY MEASUREMENT: MAJOR STRATEGIES AND ASSESSMENT TOOLS

We turn now to a discussion of two major strategies of ability measurement (self-estimation and objective assessment), as well as advantages and disadvantages associated with each strategy. In so doing, we also present a brief overview of selected self-estimate and objective ability measures on the market. Our purpose is not exhaustiveness, but rather to provide a sampling of the types of tools available to career counselors. The following criteria helped to guide our selection of the highlighted tools:

- The instrument needs to have ability assessment as a primary purpose.
- It must be designed for and used in career counseling.
- It must possess solid psychometric backing in terms of reliability and validity estimate data (and it's helpful if reviews or objective write-ups are available on the instrument).
- It must be fairly easy for counselors to access information about the instrument.

While most of the instruments selected are widely used, we've also aimed to include lesser known, yet high-quality and useful instruments. We provide more samples of objectively estimated versus self-estimated ability assessment instruments because the number of instruments from which to draw examples that meet the criteria outlined previously is larger for objectively estimated than for self-estimated abilities.

SELF-ESTIMATED ABILITIES: ADVANTAGES, DISADVANTAGES, AND ASSESSMENT TOOLS

Many career professionals believe that people can adequately and accurately estimate their own abilities. This is a point of contention in the field. In this section we will look at ability self-estimation in some detail.

Advantages A key advantage of ability self-estimation is that it allows for the measurement of abilities (e.g., leadership, teaching, helping others) not commonly assessed by traditional multiaptitude test batteries (Harrington & Schafer, 1996; Prediger, 1999a). Prediger (1999a) provided a succinct presentation of eight work-relevant abilities that are not commonly assessed by objective paper-and-pencil tests (i.e., meeting people, helping others, sales, leadership-management, organization, creative-literary, creative-artistic, and manual dexterity). These abilities are clearly work-world relevant and are thus important to assess and consider in career counseling.

Other advantages of self-estimated abilities include ease of administration and scoring and lower cost relative to objective ability instruments. Furthermore, there is evidence of correspondence between self-estimated ability factors and specific work task dimensions underlying Holland's (1997) hexagonal model of interest and occupational types (Prediger, 1999a). This could aid the counselor and client's ability to identify and explore occupational options that are congruent both with ability self-estimates and the work task dimensions underlying occupational interests (Prediger, 1999a). Finally, self-estimates of ability take into account the powerful roles of self-concept and the individual's understanding of his or her abilities built on years of experience and feedback (American College Testing [ACT], 2001).

We have found that self-ratings (formal or informal) can be an especially valuable tool when used in combination with objective test results because working with a person to compare the two can yield helpful insights into self-ratings that significantly under- or overestimate ability. Such a pairing of ability assessment information can prompt rich discussions about occupational areas in which interest may have been prematurely truncated because of ability underestimation and occupational areas that would likely require more effort, motivation, or training than previously assumed due to ability overestimation (see also Brown & Lent, 1996).

Disadvantages Betz (1992), however, urges caution in the use of ability self-estimates because of research findings that suggest that self-estimates of ability vary substantially from measured ability. As Prediger (1999a) stated, when ability test and self-estimates results do not agree, both could be problematic in that accuracy depends in part on how the results are obtained. However, when Maurer (1997) examined the accuracy of self-estimated abilities and employed several measures of self-estimation accuracy to compensate for the limitations of the measures used, he found that most participants were poor estimators of their own abilities on all measures of accuracy. Intelligence was significantly correlated with all measures of accuracy (i.e., more intelligent people were more accurate), and sex differences were also found, with women tending to underestimate their abilities and men tending to overestimate theirs. Additional evidence (e.g., Betsworth, 1999) suggests that women are significantly more likely to underestimate rather than overestimate their abilities, and females in general tend to underuse their abilities in educational and occupational pursuits (Betz, 1992). Furthermore, data (Betsworth, 1999; Handschin, 1996) suggest that when there exists inconsistency between tested and self-estimated abilities, people are more likely to choose occupations that are consistent with their own self-estimates (see Brown & Ryan Krane, 2000). The problem is that when doing so, such people may not have considered the widest possible range of potentially rewarding and satisfying career choices (Brown & Ryan Krane, 2000). These data suggest the importance of helping individuals to become fully cognizant of their objectively measured abilities (in addition to their ability self-estimations).

Finally, the ability self-estimate assessment approach is reliant on individuals' ability to report accurately their standing on various abilities compared to (in most cases) an age cohort. Given the social-psychological importance of reference groups (see Festinger, 1954; Kruglanski & Mayseless, 1990), it stands to reason that a restriction of range in ability in the individual's primary reference group (either at the low or high end of the ability spectrum) could conceivably serve to impair that individual's ability to appraise accurately his or her standing relative to a more general (and appropriate) norm group. For instance, if the individual's primary reference group is at the high end of the ability spectrum, the given individual may tend to underestimate his or her abilities as compared to others in general. On the other hand, if the individual's primary reference group is at the low end of the ability spectrum, the individual in question may tend to overestimate his or her abilities as compared to others in general (for related research, see Dunning, Johnson, Ehrlinger, & Kruger, 2003).

Assessment Tools   Several ability self-estimate measures exist on the market. Detailed information about each of these instruments can be found in their associated technical, user's, and/or administrator's manuals, and some are described and reviewed in the fourth edition of *A Counselor's Guide to Career Assessment Instruments*, fourth edition (Kapes & Whitfield, 2001).

The Harrington-O'Shea Career Decision-Making System Revised-2000 (CDM-R 2000; Harrington & O'Shea, 2000) is a comprehensive career assessment instrument that measures self-reported abilities in addition to other factors, including interests, career choices, school subjects, work values, and training plans. The system uses this multidimensional information to suggest career options for further exploration (Kapes & Whitfield, 2001). According to Campbell and Raiff (2001), the CDM-R 2000 relies largely on the psychometric information from the 1991 revision and the original 1981 version, and its psychometric characteristics compare favorably to similar instruments. In the CDM-R, participants are instructed to select their four strongest abilities from a list of 14: Artistic, Clerical, Computational, Language, Leadership, Manual, Mathematical, Mechanical, Musical, Persuasive, Scientific, Social, Spatial, and Teaching. Hand-scored editions of the CDM-R 2000 are available in English and Spanish for Levels 1 (middle school and low-level readers) and Level 2 (high school through adult); the computer-scored edition is available in English for Level 2 (Kapes & Whitfield, 2001).

The Inventory of Work-Relevant Abilities (IWRA; ACT, 2001) is a component of ACT's Discover and Career Planning Survey programs. The IWRA contains 15 abilities rooted in the four basic work tasks of data, ideas, things, and people that were chosen on the basis of their practical relevance to career counseling applications rather than to exhaust the pool of abilities relevant to the work world (Prediger, 1999a): Reading, Numerical, Language Usage, Spatial Perception, Clerical, Mechanical, Scientific, Creative/Literary, Creative/Artistic, Manual Dexterity, Meeting People, Helping Others, Sales, Leadership (Management), and Organization. Prediger (1999a) noted that the 15 abilities are work-world comprehensive in that they address each of Holland's six interest/personality types. The IWRA asks respondents to estimate each ability compared to age peers on a five-point scale, after which respondents are asked to review and compare their estimates as a whole and make revisions if so desired. The resulting report allows users to see how their work-relevant abilities relate to a wide variety of career options.

OBJECTIVELY ESTIMATED ABILITIES: ADVANTAGES, DISADVANTAGES, AND ASSESSMENT TOOLS

Objective ability assessment has a rich history in the field of career counseling. In this section, we discuss this assessment approach in more detail.

Advantages The primary advantage of objective ability measurement centers on validity. A large body of literature exists that indicates objectively measured abilities predict success in a variety of work endeavors (Dawis, 1996b). The same cannot be said of ability self-estimates. While most of this research evidence has been attributed to the predictive power of g (see Ree & Earles, 1991; Ree, Earles, & Teachout, 1994), there is reason to believe that the emphasis given to g is misguided (Dawis, 1996a; Murphy, 1996). Because many or most cognitive abilities seem to be related to g, it is just as logical to consider substantively important abilities (e.g., verbal, spatial) first in the prediction of performance and ask what g adds to them as the other way around (Murphy, 1996). In short, and as suggested by Murphy, the purpose underlying cognitive assessment is paramount. If the purpose is to gain an understanding of a person's ability to perform above average on a wide range of work tasks, then g is helpful. If a deeper purpose is to understand the nature and content of the work tasks that are likely to come quickly and easily to the individual (as in career counseling), examination of individual abilities is also very useful.

Another compelling argument for the use of objective ability assessment in career counseling is the opportunity it creates for career clients to uncover or highlight untapped areas of potential and thus consider a wider range of career options. As previously mentioned, people have been known to underestimate their potential in various areas, thereby limiting the number and types of occupations that they consider. Aptitude assessment provides objective information or evidence that can sometimes be used to counter or challenge such erroneous beliefs in the service of helping the individual to explore and consider a wider array of career options (see Brown & Lent, 1996).

Disadvantages   Disadvantages of objective ability tests include the fact that they do not assess the full range of work-relevant abilities that are relevant to performance in a variety of work settings (Harrington & Schafer, 1996; Prediger, 1999a, 1999b). There are many reasons that an occupationally relevant ability might not be included in an objective ability test. The main reason might be that such a test simply does not exist. For example, no major test publisher offers an aptitude test for aircraft piloting, though the capability exists (e.g., Tirre, 1997; Tirre & Raouf, 1998). Other reasons might include the fact that the test would be too time-consuming, require individual administration and considerable expertise for administration or scoring, or it might be too narrow or specialized for broad application. It is not clear, however, that self-estimated abilities would be a valid substitute.

Another disadvantage of objective ability testing is that it may sometimes be perceived as threatening to clients. Although efforts can be made to reduce clients' test anxiety, the specter of testing may be enough to keep some from seeking the help they may need or would find useful.

Assessment Tools   Several multiaptitude batteries, which vary considerably in purpose, content, and quality, are available. We now turn to a discussion of five.

The Armed Services Vocational Aptitude Battery (ASVAB; U.S. Department of Defense [DOD], 1995a) is distinguished by superior norms, a thorough investigation of test fairness, and unsurpassed criterion-related validity data. It is best known for its use in military recruitment and use with students, and ASVAB 18/19 (DOD, 1995b) is part of a comprehensive career exploration program for high school sophomores, juniors, seniors, and postsecondary students (see Kapes & Whitfield, 2001, for additional information). Separately timed subtests of the ASVAB 18/19 include General Science, Arithmetic Reasoning, Word Knowledge, Paragraph Comprehension, Numerical Operations, Coding Speed, Auto and Shop Information, Mathematical Knowledge, Mechanical Comprehension, and Electronics Information (Kapes & Whitfield, 2001). Factor analysis of an earlier form of the ASVAB suggests that it measures general cognitive ability, a verbal-math ability, clerical speed, and technical knowledge (Ree & Carretta, 1994). The ASVAB is heavily g-saturated, which makes differential prediction (which is the basis for occupational classification and recommendation) difficult. Roberts et al. (2000) suggest that the g in the ASVAB is actually Gc (crystallized ability), reflecting acculturated learning. To be more useful as a multiple abilities battery, these authors suggest additional tests for fluid ability and learning and memory that could be incorporated into counseling with the ASVAB.

The Occupational Information Network (O*NET) *Ability Profiler* (U.S. Department of Labor, 2003; see www.onetcenter.org) serves as the final component of O*NET career exploration, counseling, and planning tools (see Gore & Hitch, Chapter 16, this volume). The O*NET Ability Profiler is a latter-day version of the General Aptitude Test Battery (GATB; U.S. Department of Labor, 1970). This instrument is administered to participants and includes both paper-pencil and optional apparatus sections. The nine job-relevant abilities assessed by the Ability Profiler are Verbal Ability, Arithmetic Reasoning, Computation, Spatial Ability, Form Perception, Clerical Perception, Motor Coordination, Manual Dexterity, and Finger Dexterity. On completion of the O*NET Ability Profiler, participants receive a computer-generated score report that, when paired with O*NET data and related occupational information, allows individuals to compare their abilities to the abilities required by different occupations.

Another venerable multiaptitude battery is the Differential Aptitude Tests (DAT, 5th ed.; Bennett, Seashore, & Wesman, 1990), designed for educational and vocational guidance with individuals in middle school through adulthood. The DAT includes a Total Scholastic Aptitude test as well as eight subtests: Spelling, Language Usage, Numerical Reasoning, Space Relations, Mechanical Reasoning, Abstract Reasoning, Verbal Reasoning, and Perceptual Speed and Accuracy. Unlike the ASVAB and GATB, for which occupational validity data are abundantly available, evidence for the DAT's validity is generally limited to (1) correlations with other tests purporting to measure the same or similar constructs and (2) studies demonstrating its utility as a predictor of academic achievement. The DAT is, however, distinguished by superior norms, thorough attention to test fairness issues, and excellent reliability data.

The Career Ability Placement Survey (CAPS; Knapp, Knapp, & Knapp-Lee, 1992) is primarily intended for the same market as the DAT. It includes eight subtests: Mechanical Reasoning, Spatial Relations, Verbal Reasoning, Numerical Ability, Language Usage, Word Knowledge, Perceptual Speed and Accuracy, and Manual Speed and Dexterity. Confirmatory factor analysis of the CAPS based on 422 students in the 10th grade indicates that four primary factors are measured: general cognitive ability (word knowledge, verbal reasoning), verbal ability (language usage), spatial (mechanical reasoning, spatial relations), and perceptual-motor speed (clerical speed and accuracy, numerical ability, manual speed and dexterity; Tirre, 2002). The CAPS is part of a system that also includes a vocational interest survey (Career Occupational Preference System, COPS) and a work values survey (Career Orientation Placement and Evaluation Survey, COPES).

The Ball Aptitude Battery (BAB; Ball Foundation, 1993, 2002) is another example of a multiaptitude test battery designed for use with adolescent and adult clients, and it stands out in terms of aptitude coverage and in quality of reports. The BAB is used by private practitioners, high schools, and colleges, as well as within the Ball Foundation's own career consulting service called Career Vision. The BAB can also be made available for research. The BAB can be traced back to pioneering work by Johnson O'Connor (e.g., O'Connor, 1940, 1943, 1948), and it exists in three formats (paper-pencil and apparatus combined [aka the Classic BAB], a short-form paper-and-pencil [aka BAB, Form M], and a computerized version [aka the BABc]). The subtests of the Classic BAB include Clerical, Inductive Reasoning, Writing Speed, Paper Folding, Vocabulary, Idea Generation, Numerical Computation, Numerical Reasoning, Associative Memory, Auditory Memory Span, Analytical Reasoning, Idea Fluency, Finger Dexterity (left and right hand), Grip Strength (left and right hand), Shape Assembly, and Word Association. Validity data for the BAB include correlations with similar subtests in different aptitude batteries and confirmatory factor analyses that include other batteries such as the ASVAB and the GATB (Tirre & Field, 2002). An occupational supplement to a technical manual (Ball Foundation, 1995) also lists criterion-related validity data for more than a dozen occupations.

Confirmatory factor analysis of the BAB indicates that in addition to g, it measures verbal (vocabulary), reasoning (analytical reasoning), perceptual-motor speed (writing speed, clerical speed), memory (auditory memory span), creativity/broad retrieval (idea fluency), and numerical (numerical computation) abilities

(Tirre & Field, 2002). This research also indicates that there are factors that are unique to the Classic BAB (i.e., that are not measured by the GATB or ASVAB), including Broad Retrieval Ability, Creativity, Memory, and Grip Strength (Tirre & Field, 2002). The BAB Classic and Form M versions possess adequate reliability evidence (both internal consistency and stability). Stability (test-retest) reliability evidence has not yet been collected for the BABc, which is still under development.

Many multiple aptitude batteries are available to the career counselor. For detailed test reviews and information, see Kapes and Whitfield (2001), Sweetland and Keyser (1991), and the *Mental Measurements Yearbook* series.

RECENT DEVELOPMENTS IN ABILITY ASSESSMENT

Ability testing has become increasingly automated in the past decade with several multiple abilities test batteries now available in computer-administered versions, including the Ball Aptitude Battery (BAB), Multidimensional Aptitude Battery (MAB; Jackson, 1998), CareerScope (Vocational Research Institute; www.VRI.org), Bridges Career Aptitude Survey (CAS; www.bridges.com), Mindcue (www.intellicue.com), and Aviator (www.valparint.com). Computer-administered tests offer a variety of advantages over traditional paper-and-pencil tests. On the practical side, computer-administered tests are largely self-administering, reduce testing time for many examinees, and free up counselor time. Tailored assessment is also easier to achieve because counselors can choose tests most appropriate for the client from a menu of tests. The next step in this trend is Web-based testing, which should make aptitude testing and objective self-knowledge available to millions of otherwise unreached persons who need help in making career decisions.

The advantages promised by computer-administered testing extend beyond convenience. The keywords are *control* and *flexibility*. The personal computer (PC) allows precise control over the timing and events of test presentation and makes measurement of solution time possible. Animation and simulation are also possible with PCs. Together, these features may enable us to measure aptitudes that have never been testable with printed tests (see Kyllonen, 1993). And perhaps no less important, these features make testing more interactive and game-like and, therefore, more engaging experiences. Readers wishing to learn more about a host of topics relating to computer-based career assessment may consult Sampson, Lumsden, and Carr (2001) and Oliver and Chartrand (2000).

Finally, the newly developed O*NET offers the promise of linking ability test results with a wide and representative range of occupational possibilities. The O*NET (see Gore & Hitch, Chapter 16, this volume) provides a comprehensive system to describe occupations and organizes information about jobs in a way that links job task characteristics with the abilities required for effective performance on the job (Peterson et al., 2001). Furthermore, recent research based on the O*NET database has resulted in an empirical method of generating occupational options that match clients' aptitudes. Specifically, Converse, Oswald, Gillespie, Field, and Bizot (2004) developed profile-matching algorithms that match individuals' BAB score profiles to occupations' predicted aptitude profiles on the O*NET. The matching process involves comparison of the aptitude profile to O*NET occupational requirements. The end result for practitioners and clients using the BAB is a report that provides a set of empirically based occupational suggestions that can be supplemented and refined on the basis of other nonaptitude career assessment information.

SUMMARY

Rapid technological, economic, and labor market changes have resulted in an increased responsibility on the part of workers to identify and construct their own career paths through an often-confusing array of possibilities (Hesketh, 2000). Knowledge of an individual's own ability patterns, along with the ability requirements of a broad range of occupations, provides individuals with a vocabulary with which to describe themselves and work environments that may offer a good fit for them. Embedded within an overall framework of career exploration and decision-making skills, this information can be employed by individuals not just in the short-term, but throughout their working lives as well.

REFERENCES

American College Testing. (2001). *Career Planning Survey technical manual.* Iowa City, IA: Author.

American College Testing. (2001). *Research support for discover assessment components.* Iowa City, IA: Author.

American Educational Research Association, American Psychological Association, & National Council on Measurement in Education. (1999). *Standards for Educational and Psychological Testing.* Washington, DC: Author.

Anastasi, A., & Urbina, S. (1997). *Psychological testing* (7th ed.). Upper Saddle River, NJ: Prentice-Hall.

Ball Foundation. (1993). *Ball Aptitude Battery technical manual.* Glen Ellyn, IL: Author.

Ball Foundation. (1995). *Ball Aptitude Battery technical manual* (Rev. ed.). Glen Ellyn, IL: Author.

Ball Foundation. (2002). *Ball Career System technical manual.* Glen Ellyn, IL: Author.

Bandura, A. (1977). Self-efficacy: Toward a unifying theory of behavioral change. *Psychological Review, 84*(2), 191–215.

Bandura, A. (1986). *Social foundations of thought and action: A social-cognitive theory.* Englewood Cliffs, NJ: Prentice-Hall.

Barrett, G. V., & Depinet, R. L. (1991). A reconsideration of testing for competence rather than for intelligence. *American Psychologist, 46*(10), 1012–1024.

Bennett, G. K., Seashore, H. G., & Wesman, A. G. (1990). *Differential Aptitude Tests* (5th ed.). San Antonio, TX: Psychological Corporation.

Betsworth, D. G. (1999). Accuracy of self-estimated abilities and the relationship between self-estimated abilities and realism for women. *Journal of Career Assessment, 7*(1), 35–43.

Betz, N. E. (1992). Career assessment: A review of critical issues. In S. D. Brown & R. W. Lent (Eds.), *Handbook of counseling psychology* (2nd ed., pp. 453–484). New York: Wiley.

Binet, A., & Simon, T. (1980). *The development of intelligence in children* (E. S. Kite, Trans.). Nashville, TN: Williams Printing. (Original work translated 1905, published 1916)

Brown, S. D., & Lent, R. W. (1996). A social cognitive framework for career choice counseling. *Career Development Quarterly, 44,* 354–366.

Brown, S. D., Lent, R. W., & Gore, P. A., Jr. (2000). Self-rated abilities and self-efficacy beliefs: Are they empirically distinct? *Journal of Career Assessment, 8*(3), 223–235.

Brown, S. D., & Ryan Krane, N. E. (2000). Four (or five) sessions and a cloud of dust: Old assumptions and new observations about career counseling. In S. D. Brown & R. W. Lent (Eds.), *Handbook of counseling psychology* (3rd ed., pp. 740–766). New York: Wiley.

Campbell, V. L., & Raiff, G. W. (2001). Harrington-O'Shea Career Decision Making System, Revised (CDM) (Test Review). In J. T. Kapes & E. A. Whitfield (Eds.), *A counselor's guide to career assessment instruments* (4th ed., pp. 230–234). Columbus, OH: National Career Development Association.

Carroll, J. B. (1993). *Human cognitive abilities: A survey of factor-analytic studies.* New York: Cambridge University Press.

Converse, P. D., Oswald, F. L., Gillespie, M. A., Field, K. A., & Bizot, E. B. (2004). Matching individuals to occupations using abilities and the O*NET: Issues and an application in career guidance. *Personnel Psychology, 57,* 451–487.

Dawis, R. V. (1996a). Vocational psychology, vocational adjustment, and the workforce: Some familiar and unanticipated consequences. *Psychology, Public Policy, and Law, 2*(2), 229–248.

Dawis, R. V. (1996b). The theory of work adjustment and person-environment-correspondence counseling. In D. Brown, L. Brooks, & Associates (Eds.), *Career choice and development* (3rd ed., pp. 75–120). San Francisco: Jossey-Bass.

Dawis, R. V., Dohm, T. E., Lofquist, L. H., Chartrand, J. M., & Due, A. M. (1987). *Minnesota Occupational Classification System III: A psychological taxonomy of work*. Minneapolis: University of Minnesota, Department of Psychology, Vocational Psychology Research.

Dawis, R. V., Goldman, S. H., & Sung, Y. H. (1992). Stability and change in abilities for a sample of young adults. *Educational and Psychological Measurement, 52*, 457–465.

Dixon, R. A., Kramer, D. A., & Baltes, P. B. (1985). Intelligence: A life-span developmental perspective. In B. B. Wolman (Ed.), *Handbook of intelligence: Theories, measurements, and applications* (pp. 301–350). New York: Wiley.

Dubois, P. H. (1970). *A history of psychological testing*. Boston: Allyn & Bacon.

Dunning, D., Johnson, K., Ehrlinger, J., & Kruger, J. (2003). Why people fail to recognize their own incompetence. *Current Directions in Psychological Science, 12*(3), 83–87.

Festinger, L. (1954). A theory of social comparison processes. *Human Relations, 7*, 117–140.

Fleishman, E. A. (1954). Dimensional analysis of psychomotor abilities. *Journal of Experimental Psychology, 48*(6), 437–454.

Fleishman, E. A., & Reilly, M. E. (1992). *Handbook of human abilities: Definitions, measurements, and job task requirements*. Palo Alto, CA: Consulting Psychologists Press.

Garfield, N. J., & Krieshok, T. S. (2001). Assessment and counseling competencies and responsibilities: A checklist for counselors. In J. T. Kapes & E. A. Whitfield (Eds.), *A counselor's guide to career assessment instruments* (4th ed., pp. 65–72). Columbus, OH: National Career Development Association.

Gottfredson, L. S. (1986). Occupational Aptitude Patterns Map: Development and implications for a theory of job aptitude requirements [Monograph]. *Journal of Vocational Behavior, 29*, 254–291.

Gottfredson, L. S. (2003). The challenge and promise of cognitive career assessment. *Journal of Career Assessment, 11*(2), 115–135.

Gregory, R. J. (1994). Aptitude tests. In R. J. Sternberg (Ed.), *Encyclopedia of human intelligence* (Vol. 1, pp. 110–117). New York: Macmillan.

Guilford, J. P. (1956). The structure of intellect. *Psychological Bulletin, 53*(4), 267–293.

Guilford, J. P. (1967). *The nature of human intelligence*. New York: McGraw-Hill.

Guilford, J. P., & Hoepfner, R. (1971). *The analysis of intelligence*. New York: McGraw-Hill.

Handschin, B. (1996). *The role of self-estimated and tested abilities in vocational choice in adults at four time periods postcounseling*. Unpublished doctoral dissertation, University of Minnesota, Minneapolis.

Harrington, T. F., & O'Shea, A. J. (2000). *Harrington-O'Shea Career Decision-Making System-Revised*. Circle Pines, MN: American Guidance Service.

Harrington, T. F., & Schafer, W. D. (1996). A comparison of self-reported abilities and occupational ability patterns across occupations. *Measurement and Evaluation in Counseling and Development, 28*, 180–190.

Hesketh, B. (2000). Prevention and development in the workplace. In S. D. Brown & R. W. Lent (Eds.), *Handbook of counseling psychology* (3rd ed., pp. 471–498). New York: Wiley.

Holland, J. L. (1997). *Making vocational choices: A theory of vocational personalities and work environments* (3rd ed.). Odessa, FL: Psychological Assessment Resources.

Hollingworth, H. L. (1915). Specialized vocational tests and methods. *School and Society, 1*(26), 918–922.

Jackson, D. N. (1998). *Multidimensional Aptitude Battery—II*. Port Huron, MI: Sigma Assessment Systems.

Kapes, J. T., & Whitfield, E. A. (Eds.). (2001). *A counselor's guide to career assessment instruments* (4th ed.). Columbus, OH: National Career Development Association.

Kelley, T. L. (1928). *Crossroads in the mind of man: A study of differentiable mental abilities*. Stanford, CA: Stanford University Press.

Kline, P. (2000). *Handbook of psychological testing* (2nd ed.). London: Routledge.

Knapp, L., Knapp, R. R., & Knapp-Lee, L. (1992). *Technical manual: CAPS (Career Ability Placement Survey)*. San Diego, CA: Edits Publishers.

Kruglanski, A. W., & Mayseless, O. (1990). Classic and current social comparison research: Expanding the perspective. *Psychological Bulletin, 108*(2), 195–208.

Kyllonen, P. C. (1993). Aptitude testing inspired by information processing: A test of the four-sources model. *Journal of General Psychology, 120*(3), 375–405.

Lent, R. W., Brown, S. D., & Hackett, G. (1994). Toward a unifying social cognitive theory of career and academic interest, choice, and performance [Monograph]. *Journal of Vocational Behavior, 45*, 79–122.

Link, H. C. (1919). *Employment psychology*. New York: Macmillan.

Lowman, R. L. (1991). *The clinical practice of career assessment: Interests, abilities, and personality*. Washington, DC: American Psychological Association.

Lowman, R. L., & Williams, R. E. (1987). Validity of self-ratings of abilities and competencies. *Journal of Vocational Behavior, 31*, 1–13.

Lubinski, D., & Dawis, R. V. (1992). Aptitudes, skills, and proficiencies. In M. D. Dunnette & L. M. Hough (Eds.), *Handbook of industrial and organizational psychology* (2nd ed., Vol. 3, pp. 1–59). Palo Alto, CA: Consulting Psychologists Press.

Mabe, P. A., III., & West, S. G. (1982). Validity of self-evaluation of ability: A review and meta-analysis. *Journal of Applied Psychology, 67*(3), 280–296.

Maurer, S. T. (1997). *Work needs, work values, personality traits, and other factors related to the accuracy of self-estimated abilities*. Unpublished doctoral dissertation, University of Minnesota, Minneapolis.

Meier, N. C. (1939). Factors in artistic aptitude: Final summary of a ten-year study of a special ability. *Psychological Monographs, 51*(5), 140–158.

Münsterberg, H. (1913). *Psychology and industrial efficiency*. Boston: Houghton Mifflin.

Murphy, K. R. (1996). Individual differences and behavior in organizations: Much more than *g*. In K. R. Murphy (Ed.), *Individual differences and behavior in organizations* (pp. 3–30). San Francisco: Jossey-Bass.

Neisser, U., Boodoo, G., Bouchard, T. J., Boykin, A. W., Brody, N., Ceci, S. J., et al. (1996). Intelligence: Knowns and unknowns. *American Psychologist, 51*(2), 77–101.

O'Connor, J. (1940). *Unsolved business problems*. Boston: Human Engineering Laboratory.

O'Connor, J. (1943). *Structural visualization*. Boston: Human Engineering Laboratory.

O'Connor, J. (1948). *The unique individual*. Boston: Human Engineering Laboratory.

Oliver, L. W., & Chartrand, J. M. (Eds.). (2000). Career assessment and the Internet [Special issue]. *Journal of Career Assessment, 8*(1).

Paterson, D. G., Elliott, R. M., Anderson, L. D., Toops, H. A., & Heidbreder, E. (1930). *Minnesota mechanical ability tests*. Minneapolis: University of Minnesota Press.

Peterson, N. G., Mumford, M. D., Borman, W. C., Jeanneret, P. R., Fleishman, E. A., Levin, K. Y., et al. (2001). Understanding work using the Occupational Information Network (O*NET): Implications for practice and research. *Personnel Psychology, 54*, 451–492.

Prediger, D. J. (1989). Ability differences across occupations: More than *g*. *Journal of Vocational Behavior, 34*, 1–27.

Prediger, D. J. (1999a). Basic structure of work-relevant abilities. *Journal of Counseling Psychology, 46*(2), 173–184.

Prediger, D. J. (1999b). Integrating interests and abilities for career exploration: General considerations. In M. L. Savickas & A. R. Spokane (Eds.), *Vocational interests: Meaning, measurement, and counseling use* (pp. 295–325). Palo Alto, CA: Davies-Black.

Ree, M. J., & Carretta, T. R. (1994). Factor analysis of the ASVAB: Confirming a Vernon-like structure. *Educational and Psychological Measurement, 54*(2), 459–463.

Ree, M. J., & Earles, J. A. (1991). Predicting training success: Not much more than *g*. *Personnel Psychology, 44*(2), 321–332.

Ree, M. J., Earles, J. A., & Teachout, M. S. (1994). Predicting job performance: Not much more than *g*. *Journal of Applied Psychology, 79*(4), 518–524.

Roberts, R. D., Goff, G. N., Anjoul, F., Kyllonen, P. C., Pallier, G., & Stankov, L. (2000). The Armed Services Vocational Aptitude Battery (ASVAB): Little more than acculturated learning (Gc)!? *Learning and Individual Differences, 12*(1), 81–103.

Sampson, J. P., Jr., Lumsden, J. A., & Carr, D. L. (2001). Computer-assisted career assessment. In J. T. Kapes & E. A. Whitfield (Eds.), *A counselor's guide to career assessment instruments* (4th ed., pp. 47–63). Columbus, OH: National Career Development Association.

Schaie, K. W. (1994). The course of adult intellectual development. *American Psychologist, 49*(4), 304–313.

Schaie, K. W., & Hertzog, C. (1986). Toward a comprehensive model of adult intellectual development: Contributions of the Seattle Longitudinal Study. In R. J. Sternberg (Ed.), *Advances in the psychology of human intelligence* (Vol. 3, pp. 79–118). Hillsdale, NJ: Erlbaum.

Seashore, C. E. (1919). *The psychology of musical talent.* Boston: Silver & Burdett.

Seashore, R. H. (1930). Individual differences in motor skills. *Journal of General Psychology, 3,* 38–66.

Snow, R. E. (1992). Aptitude theory: Yesterday, today, and tomorrow. *Educational Psychologist, 27*(1), 5–32.

Snow, R. E. (1994). Abilities and aptitudes. In R. J. Sternberg (Ed.), *Encyclopedia of human intelligence* (Vol. 1, pp. 3–5). New York: Macmillan.

Spearman, C. (1904). "General intelligence," objectively determined and measured. *American Journal of Psychology, 15*(2), 201–293.

Spearman, C. (1927). *The abilities of man.* New York: Macmillan.

Sternberg, R. J. (1997). Intelligence and lifelong learning: What's new and how can we use it? *American Psychologist, 52*(10), 1134–1139.

Sweetland, R. C., & Keyser, D. J. (Eds.). (1991). *Tests: A comprehensive reference for assessments in psychology, education, and business* (3rd ed.). Austin, TX: ProEd.

Thurstone, L. L. (1919a). Mental tests for prospective telegraphers: A study of the diagnostic value of mental tests for predicting ability to learn telegraphy. *Journal of Applied Psychology, 3*(2), 110–117.

Thurstone, L. L. (1919b). A standardized test for office clerks. *Journal of Applied Psychology, 3*(3), 248–251.

Thurstone, L. L. (1938). *Primary mental abilities* (Psychometric Monograph No. 1). Chicago: University of Chicago Press.

Thurstone, L. L., & Thurstone, T. (1941). *Factorial studies of intelligence.* Chicago: University of Chicago Press.

Tirre, W. C. (1997). Steps toward an improved pilot selection battery. In R. F. Dillon (Ed.), *Handbook on testing* (pp. 220–255). Westport, CT: Greenwood Press.

Tirre, W. C. (2002). *Confirmatory factor analyses of published multiple aptitude test batteries.* Unpublished report, The Ball Foundation, Glen Ellyn, IL.

Tirre, W. C., & Field, K. A. (2002). Structural models of abilities measured by the Ball Aptitude Battery. *Educational and Psychological Measurement, 62*(5), 830–856.

Tirre, W. C., & Raouf, K. K. (1998). Structural models of cognitive and perceptual-motor abilities. *Personality and Individual Differences, 24*(5), 603–614.

Tracey, T. J., & Hopkins, N. (2001). Correspondence of interests and abilities with occupational choice. *Journal of Counseling Psychology, 48*(2), 178–189.

U.S. Department of Defense. (1995a). *Armed Services Vocational Aptitude Battery.* Seaside, CA: Author, Defense Manpower Data Center.

U.S. Department of Defense. (1995b). *ASVAB 18/19 counselor manual: The ASVAB career exploration program.* North Chicago: United States Military Entrance Processing Command.

U.S. Department of Labor. (1970). *Manual for the USES General Aptitude Test Battery* (Section 3: Development). Washington, DC: U.S. Department of Labor, Manpower Administration.

CHAPTER 15

Beyond Interests, Needs/Values, and Abilities: Assessing Other Important Career Constructs over the Life Span

Jane L. Swanson and Catalina D'Achiardi

A SSESSMENT IN CAREER development and counseling has had a long history. The *Big Three* constructs typically deemed central to career choice—interests, needs/values, and abilities—were the first to be assessed objectively via standardized instruments, spurred on by Parsons' (1909) articulation of "self-knowledge." These three constructs continue to be the most frequently assessed within career counseling (Watkins, Campbell, & Nieberding, 1994), with measures that are psychometrically sound and sophisticated interpretative materials that frequently are individually tailored. Further, these three constructs have been thoroughly discussed in the preceding three chapters of this text. Yet, we would be remiss to conclude that interests, needs/values, and abilities are the *only* important constructs to consider in counseling for career choice, adjustment, and change, and career counseling professionals do address constructs beyond the Big Three (Watkins et al., 1994). Moreover, all theories of career development incorporate factors in addition to interests, needs/values, and abilities.

CONSTRUCTS BEYOND THE BIG THREE

In this introductory section, we define the range of other important constructs to consider in career counseling, as well as outline the life span background that serves as the structure for this chapter (see Table 15.1). We present two categories of constructs—process-oriented and outcome—as particularly relevant to individuals' careers. These categories represent constructs beyond the Big Three in that interests, needs/values, and abilities form the *content* of individuals' career decisions (Savickas, 2000). In contrast, the constructs that we focus on in this chapter form the *process* and *outcome* of individuals' career decisions.

Table 15.1
Important Process-Oriented and Outcome Constructs over the Life Span

	Process	Outcome
Career exploration	Career maturity Career salience Career beliefs and thoughts Career decision making –Decision-making style –Career indecision –Decision-making self-efficacy Personality Perceived barriers Interpersonal supports Self-efficacy beliefs Outcome expectations Circumscription and compromise	*Intermediate:* –Self-efficacy beliefs –Outcome expectations –Career maturity –Occupational information *Target:* –Career decision
Career choice and implementation	Career decision making – Decision-making style – Career indecision – Decision making self-efficacy Career beliefs and thoughts Personality Perceived barriers Interpersonal supports	*Intermediate:* –Self-efficacy beliefs –Outcome expectations *Target:* –Choice certainty –Choice satisfaction
Adjustment or change	Career adaptability Career salience Personality Perceived barriers Interpersonal supports Workplace supports	*Intermediate:* –Career adaptability –Self-efficacy beliefs *Target:* –Career satisfaction –Job performance

Process-oriented constructs deal with *how* clients make career decisions or the circumstances surrounding those decisions. These constructs include career maturity and career adaptability, career salience, decision-making styles and processes, self-efficacy about decision making, career beliefs and myths, and personality. Clients' standing on these constructs will influence their level of decidedness or indecision, the specific way in which they make decisions, their preferences for how to make decisions, and the interaction between counselor and client. Some additional constructs address contextual factors that also influence the process by which clients make career decisions, such as interpersonal and workplace supports, self-efficacy, and processes of circumscription and compromise. These latter constructs were brought to the forefront via two influential theories: Social Cognitive Career Theory (SCCT; Lent, Brown, & Hackett, 1994; Lent, Chapter 5, this volume) and Gottfredson's Theory of Circumscription and Compromise (Gottfredson, 1981, 1996, 2002, Chapter 4, this volume).

Outcome constructs frequently have been the focus of research endeavors, as they include the *results* of career interventions; some constructs in this category overlap with those in the process-oriented category because they serve both purposes. Further, these outcome constructs may be divided into two subcategories based on temporal considerations: the *target outcomes,* which are perhaps most salient to recipients of career counseling, and *intermediate outcomes,* which facilitate the attainment of the target outcomes. Target outcome constructs include certainty of choice, satisfaction with choice, career satisfaction, job performance, and other organizational outcomes—tangible results of career counseling and other interventions. Intermediate outcomes include self-efficacy, outcome expectations, career maturity and adaptability, and acquisition of occupational information—changes in clients' behavior or attitudes that will serve them well in attaining target outcomes. Considerable research has demonstrated the overall effectiveness of career interventions, including individual career counseling, workshops, classes, and computer-assisted interventions, as well as comparative efficiency and effectiveness of differential types of interventions (S. D. Brown & Ryan Krane, 2000; S. D. Brown et al., 2003; Oliver & Spokane, 1988; Spokane & Oliver, 1983; Whiston, Brecheisen, & Stephens, 2003; Whiston, Sexton, & Lasoff, 1998). In this chapter, we focus on the ways in which career counseling professionals might assess outcomes of their own career interventions with individuals or groups.

As we discuss later, Whiston (2001) proposed a division of outcomes, along a dimension of time, into short-term and long-term outcomes. While Whiston's classification bears some similarity to the one we use in this chapter, we see one important difference: *Short term* and *long term* imply a quantitative distinction by some specific period of elapsed time, whereas *intermediate* and *target* suggest a qualitative distinction in terms of what has been accomplished.

CAREER COUNSELING ISSUES OVER THE LIFE SPAN

As implied in the previous discussion, important constructs related to process and outcome vary somewhat over the life span. Thus, to address these constructs in a systematic fashion, we consider how these constructs may be manifested at three stages of the life span: career exploration, initial career choice, and career adjustment and/or change. *Career exploration* is most likely to occur in adolescence and early adulthood, during which time individuals learn about themselves and the world of work and make some initial decisions about education and career directions (such as entering the labor force versus pursuing further education). *Career choice* entails a narrowing of options identified during exploration, so that an individual makes and implements a specific choice and begins the process of establishment and adjustment. *Career adjustment and/or change* implies some type of career transition or difficulty, such as poor fit, dissatisfaction, poor performance, or transition to a new job or career or unemployment. Career change may be voluntary or involuntary, anticipated or unanticipated, positive or negative.

We recognize that these are not necessarily discrete steps or stages in individuals' lives. Further, we are aware that placing the constructs into each specific cell of Table 15.1 is done at the risk of overcompartmentalization. Our intention is to provide a useful way to organize the tasks or challenges individuals are likely to confront at different junctures in life and to highlight the types of assessments that career counselors might use in working with such individuals. Further, the stages of exploration and choice might be encountered anew during career adjustment or change later in life.

Conceptualizing career assessments salient to these three stages highlights two intriguing features of the field of vocational psychology and the practice of career counseling. First, career counselors and vocational psychologists have focused on issues related to exploration and initial choice and have left much of the later stages to other specialties, such as organizational behavior, industrial/ organizational psychology, management, and occupational psychology (Swanson, 1992, 2003). Moreover, organizational perspectives on career development (more likely referred to as career *management*) are different from individual perspectives proffered by career counseling and vocational psychology (see Griffin & Hesketh, Chapter 20, this volume).

Second, the availability of career counseling services is uneven throughout the life span (Swanson, 2003; Watts, 1996). However, if vocational choices are viewed as a series of "good fit" decisions throughout the life span (Super, 1983), career counseling services should be available at the times that individuals face decisions. Services have most often been built into the system at natural transition points, such as entering and exiting college or other training, yet transition points may occur at any time in individuals' lives.

CAVEATS

Before addressing specific process-oriented and outcome constructs, we offer three caveats about the material included in this chapter. These caveats are intended to frame our decisions about what to cover, including the constructs and instruments we selected and the psychometric variability of available instruments, as well as the ultimate goal of integrating these constructs with the career choice content represented by the Big Three.

Constructs versus Instruments   Despite our use of life span stages to organize this chapter, we remain construct driven in our discussion of the myriad constructs and associated instruments available to career counseling practitioners. As a result, we discuss some instruments in more than one place in the chapter. For example, the Myers-Briggs Type Indicator (MBTI) is perhaps the most frequently used measure of personality in career counseling and thus is discussed in the section on personality. However, it also may be used to discuss a client's decision-making style; thus, it is also mentioned in the section on decision making. Further, some instruments contain a heterogeneous set of subscales spanning a variety of constructs, such as the Career Beliefs Inventory; thus, they necessitate discussion in multiple sections of this chapter.

A second consequence of being construct driven is that some instruments included in other textbooks are not in this chapter. We began by identifying important constructs—other than interests, abilities, needs/values—and then searched for measures and methods of assessing these constructs. There are a plethora of other instruments available, particularly as researchers and practitioners become more interested in the process of career decision making and the process of career counseling. However, we chose to focus on the constructs as an organizing framework and thus have neglected some instruments that have been developed to measure constructs that are not included in this chapter (e.g., My Vocational Situation; Holland, Daiger, & Power, 1980).

Formal versus Informal Assessment A third consequence of being construct driven is reflected in the varying degrees of attention to psychometric development of the instruments and measures discussed in this chapter. In the three previous chapters, the primary inventories that measure interests, needs/values, and abilities are well developed with appropriate reliability, validity, and normative data. In contrast, measures of the constructs covered in this chapter often are less psychometrically grounded, partly because attention to these constructs does not have as long a history within career counseling as measures of the Big Three constructs. We discuss specific measures in this chapter only if there is adequate reliability and validity information available; then we discuss more informal methods of assessing these constructs within counseling because the constructs seem important to a thorough and integrated delivery of career counseling services. In the hands of competent career counseling professionals, many of these instruments and methods can raise important issues to discuss with clients in a fashion similar to qualitative assessment such as card sorts (see Lent, Chapter 5, this volume, for a description of one such card sort procedure).

Thus, the psychometric formality of the instruments described in this chapter varies across constructs. For some measures, no normative data exist at all, or at least not in a form that is readily available to the career counseling practitioner. For other measures, the amount of psychometric data rivals that of instruments to measure the Big Three constructs. In all cases, however, we chose to include these instruments because they focus on important process and outcome variables and may yield insight that would be missed by an exclusive focus on the Big Three. In other words, these instruments are worthy of further consideration even though they may not have yet received desired psychometric investigation.

Traditional views of validity emphasize the relation of inventory scores to the constructs they are intended to measure. Thus, for example, showing that a new measure of artistic interests correlates highly with another more well-established measure of artistic interests provides evidence of the validity of the former. Similarly, showing that the new measure correlates as it should with choice of, or satisfaction with, artistic pursuits also is critical to establishing whether artistic interests are being measured with the new scale. Two additional views of validity—consequential validity and exploration validity—may be particularly important within the context of career counseling. *Consequential validity* requires an evaluation of the consequences of inventory use, including both the intended and unintended consequences of test interpretation and test use (Messick, 1995) and both positive and negative consequences. For example, Fouad (1999) noted that positive consequences of interest inventories may include greater exploration of options, whereas negative consequences may include inappropriate restriction of options for a particular group of individuals. *Exploration validity* refers to the power of an inventory to facilitate career exploration activities, including instrumental behaviors such as talking to professionals and seeking occupational information (Randahl, Hansen, & Haverkamp, 1993; Tittle, 1978). Primary reasons for using assessment in career counseling are to enhance clients' self-knowledge and stimulate exploration, so these two types of validity are important because they reflect whether clients act on that newly gained knowledge.

Integrating These Constructs with the Big Three   The purpose of this chapter is to discuss assessment of constructs other than the Big Three (interests, needs/values, abilities). However, our ultimate goal is to encourage the systematic and integrated assessment of constructs relevant to every client's concerns. In other words, career assessment should, for most clients, encompass all or most of the constructs discussed in this and the preceding three chapters. Further, competent career counselors attend to the themes and discrepancies revealed in clients' assessment and interview data. Several authors have outlined how counselors might generate and test hypotheses based on clients' assessment results, with particular attention to points of convergence and divergence across domains (Lowman, 1991; Swanson & Fouad, 1999).

ASSESSMENT OF PROCESS-ORIENTED CONSTRUCTS

Examining the *process* surrounding career decisions explicitly acknowledges the unique styles and circumstances that clients bring to career counseling. Attention to these process constructs complements attention to the content and outcome of career counseling, allowing a richer and more complete career counseling experience. Important process constructs include career maturity and career adaptability, career salience, career beliefs and thoughts, career decision making, personality, perceived barriers, interpersonal supports, self-efficacy beliefs, outcome expectations, and circumscription and compromise.

CAREER MATURITY AND CAREER ADAPTABILITY

The concept of *career maturity* has been used to describe both the process by which individuals make career choices appropriate to their age and stage of development and their ability to successfully resolve and transition through the specific tasks of each of these stages. In considering career maturity during career exploration, it is important to attend to the multidimensionality of the concept. Crites (1976) described career maturity as having attitudinal and cognitive dimensions. The former refers to individuals' attitudes and feelings about making an effective vocational choice and whether they continue to pursue their career choice as they enter the workforce. On the other hand, the cognitive dimension usually refers to clients' awareness of a need to make a career decision and to their understanding about their vocational preferences. Cognitive competencies needed to make a good career decision include adequate knowledge about the world of work and personal abilities and skills. Moreover, Savickas (2002) argues that the cognitive dimension is important to assess because it is cognitive competencies that lead a client into action.

Career maturity is considered to be a particularly important variable to assess during career exploration with adolescents because, at this life stage, they often have to make important career decisions that they are not developmentally ready to make. Many adolescents fail to integrate their interests, skills, and abilities and are unable to focus toward a particular career goal, which is the main task of the exploration stage in Super's (1980) theory of career development. Therefore, assessing the obstacles that have hindered adolescents' development and helping them establish ways to overcome those obstacles may be an important initial goal of career counseling with individuals at this stage of development (i.e., exploration). However, career maturity may also be useful to consider at stages other than exploration. As noted in the definition, career maturity implies that the client is able to accomplish tasks that are appropriate for his or her age and stage of development. Therefore, career maturity can also be assessed with all career counseling clients (Super, Savickas, & Super, 1996).

Even though career maturity has been researched for more than 40 years and many measures have been developed to assess this variable, there has been much controversy about its definition and exactly what career maturity inventories measure. It has been argued that many of the measures of career maturity assess clients' intellectual ability and not necessarily their readiness to negotiate the tasks and transitions in their particular developmental stage (Chartrand & Camp, 1991; Seligman, 1994). To address this argument, Super (1983) suggested that a more appropriate term to refer to career maturity after adolescence is *career adaptability*. According to Super, career adaptability includes five elements:

1. The ability to learn from experiences and anticipate the future (i.e., *planfulness*).
2. The ability to ask questions and collect information and the ability to interact in the community, at school, and with family members (i.e., *exploration*).
3. The ability to gather information about the world of work (i.e., *information gathering*).
4. The ability to make choices based on knowledge of career decision-making principles (i.e., *decision making*).
5. The ability to develop self-awareness, self-knowledge, and establish realistic options that are consistent with preferences (i.e., *reality orientation*).

Savickas (2002) suggested that after assessing the career concerns in the client's particular stage of development, the counselor may use a structured interview to assess career adaptability. He suggests that four categories of questions be included in this interview:

1. The client's career salience (i.e., importance of the work role vis-à-vis other life roles) and readiness for career counseling.
2. Experiences with decision-making strategies and career control (e.g., self-determination beliefs, decisiveness and compromise, decisional competence).
3. Coping strategies for career concerns, career convictions, and decisional style.
4. Assessment of the client's problem-solving skills and career confidence.

Some instruments have also been developed to assess clients' career maturity/ adaptability. Unfortunately, many of the psychometric properties of these measures are problematic, and a few others are no longer commercially available (Chartrand & Camp, 1991). However, we mention two instruments that are still available and may be useful tools in the career counseling process because they facilitate communication between counselors and clients: the Career Maturity Inventory (CMI; Crites, 1973; Crites & Savickas, 1995) and the Adult Career Concerns Inventory (ACCI; Super, Thompson, & Lindeman, 1984).

CAREER SALIENCE

Savickas (2002) described *career salience* as one of the major components of career adaptability. The concept of career salience has received significant attention in the career literature, particularly in the career development of women. *Career salience* has been defined as the value and preference that an individual places on his or her career and work roles in comparison to other life roles. Moreover, the value and preference for each role may change over time (Greenhaus, 1971). This construct has been primarily incorporated into career counseling with clients who have already made a career choice but are having trouble committing to their chosen occupation. Career salience has also been examined to a lesser extent with women who are struggling to manage dual roles of family and work. It is often used to assess the relative importance that these women place on each of these roles to help them make relevant decisions.

As with the measures of career maturity, the instruments developed to measure career salience do not have well-established psychometric properties. However, counselors can assess clients' career salience by asking questions related to:

- Perceived importance of work and career in their lives.
- Commitment and values in different roles (i.e., studying, working, community service, home, and family).
- Actual time that clients spend in each of these roles relative to their values and preferences.
- Attitudes, thoughts, and degree of planning toward career and other vocationally relevant roles.
- Job involvement (e.g., work as a life interest, active job participation, work performance as it relates to self-esteem and self-concept).

CAREER BELIEFS AND THOUGHTS

Zunker (2002) presents "unearthing career beliefs" as one of eight goals of assessment in career counseling and defines them as "clients' beliefs about careers, decision-making styles, identity issues, maladaptive behaviors, degrees of anxiety, fear of failure, and reasons why people are undecided" (p. 212). Krumboltz, in his Social Learning Theory of career development (Mitchell & Krumboltz, 1996), further suggested that career beliefs are, in essence, faulty assumptions or ideas that interfere with career decision making and later career progress. For example, a client may believe that her choices today entail a lifelong commitment to a specific career path, putting undue (and perhaps debilitating) pressure on her to make the "right" decision. Krumboltz identified ways in which career counselors can identify, assess, and counter career beliefs or faulty assumptions:

1. Examining the origin of the content of clients' self-observation and generalization ideas.
2. Providing and reinforcing problem-solving tasks.
3. Using traditional cognitive restructuring techniques to modify the dysfunctional or generalization beliefs.
4. Identifying assumptions that have been previously established by clients that block them from achieving their own career goals.

CAREER DECISION MAKING

Research on career decision making is also extensive in the vocational psychology literature. *Career decision making*, the process by which individuals make career

and educational decisions, has been described by some authors as the main assessment task of career counseling (Crites, 1974; Savickas, 2000; Super, 1983). More
specifically, it examines *how* people make career decisions (*decision-making style*);
the precursors that may influence or impede career choice (*career indecision*); and,
more recently, individuals' beliefs that they can successfully accomplish behaviors that will lead to desired outcomes (*decision-making self-efficacy beliefs*). In the
following paragraphs, these constructs are discussed in more detail, as well as the
most common ways of assessing each of them.

Career decision making is an important variable to assess in the career counseling process because not all clients are similarly skilled at, or confident about,
making a career choice even after exploring their interests, skills/abilities, and
values. It is the process of arriving at an occupational or educational choice that
some clients find difficult (Savickas, 2002). This is not to say that making a career
or educational choice should be the bottom-line outcome of all career counseling.
What this does suggest, however, is that counselors need to attend particularly to
decision-making issues with clients who are still struggling, or seem more confused, after the content-oriented constructs have been explored. Counseling may
then involve helping these clients develop the skills and confidence to make career decisions in addition to making a specific career choice.

Career decision-making style is a cognitive construct, which, as described earlier,
is the process by which individuals regularly make career decisions. Decision-
making styles have been most frequently categorized as:

1. Rational—decisions are made intentionally and logically.
2. Intuitive—decisions are made based on feelings and emotional responses.
3. Dependent—decisions are made by others' opinions (Harren, 1979).

In addition, Harren (1979) proposed that the most useful style for career decision
making was the rational style although research has been inconclusive on this
proposition (e.g., Blustein & Phillips, 1990; Mau, 1995) and the dependent style
has frequently been found to be the least adaptive of the three. Harren's Assessment of Career Decision-Making inventory (ACDM; Harren, 1979) was developed
to assess the degree to which clients adhere to these three styles. Another taxonomy also has been commonly used in career counseling to assess clients' decision-
making style; that is, Jung's four dimensions represented in the Myers-Briggs
Type Indicator (MBTI), which, in addition to being a personality measure, is used
in career counseling for the purpose of helping clients understand their own
decision-making style.

A number of researchers have examined the construct of *career indecision*,
most recently in explicating its connection to other core constructs in career development. Kelly and Lee (2002), for example, noted the lack of attention to career indecision within contemporary career development theories. They
conducted a factor analysis of assessment instruments that measure career indecision with the dual purpose of clarifying the different domains of the construct and identifying its internal structure. Seven unique factors emerged from
their analysis:

1. Trait indecision, defined as a "pervasive and enduring form of indecision
that does not abate as information is acquired" (p. 307).

2. Lack of information, reflecting lack of knowledge about the career decision-making process, lack of knowledge about self, and lack of knowledge about career information.
3. Choice anxiety, reflecting emotional distress related to having to make a career decision.
4. Identity diffusion, defined as "an inability to adequately crystallize one's career relevant characteristics or to see how one's personal characteristics can be implemented in careers" (p. 319).
5. Disagreement with others, reflecting problems that emerge after a career decision has been reached due to objections from significant others.
6. Positive choice conflict, representing the indecision of choosing one career from a number of attractive alternatives.
7. Need for information, reflecting similar deficits to those in the "lack of information" factor but also not recognizing the necessity of seeking information.

Based on these seven factors, Kelly and Lee (2002) proposed that career indecision (i.e., the inability to specify an educational or occupational choice) may be due to three specific problems:

1. Problems occurring before decision making, such as information deficit and identity diffusion.
2. The cognitive experience of trait indecision or the affective experience of choice anxiety.
3. Disagreements with others that inhibit the implementation of a career choice.

The seven factors and three client types that Kelly and Lee (2002) found should help counselors better understand why their clients are seeking career help and even aid in tailoring interventions to clients' unique needs. For example, indecisive and/or anxious clients may need more intensive and individualized counseling than those with primarily informational needs, while those experiencing external conflicts may need help in negotiating with significant others (see also S. D. Brown & McPartland, in press). Some instruments that may be used to facilitate assessment of career indecision include the Career Decision Scale (Osipow, Carney, Winer, Yanico, & Koschier, 1987), the Career Factors Inventory (Chartrand & Robbins, 1997), and the Career Decision Difficulties Questionnaire (Gati, Osipow, Krausz, & Saka, 2000).

The last component of career decision making is *career decision-making self-efficacy beliefs.* Taylor and Betz (1983) adapted Bandura's (1977) construct of self-efficacy specifically to refer to an individual's confidence in his or her ability to effectively complete career decision-making tasks. They developed the Career Decision Making Self Efficacy Scale (CDMSE), which is also available in a short form (CDMSE-SF; Betz & Taylor, 1994). The measure can be used to assess clients' feelings of competency in their abilities to self-appraise, gather occupational information, select career goals, engage in career planning, and problem solve when difficulties are encountered, although this five-factor (i.e., subscale) structure of the CDMSE has not been completely supported by research (Betz, Klein, & Taylor, 1996).

Personality

Personality is included in this section on process-oriented constructs because it seems relevant to *how* clients make career decisions; however, it also could be conceptualized as a construct relevant to the content of career counseling (in addition to the Big Three). Personality influences the way an individual behaves across many situations and across time and, thus, plays a pervasive role in career choice and development.

The role of *personality* in career development and career counseling presents an interesting paradox. On one hand, personality plays a central role in many career development theories, and the links between personality and other career variables such as vocational interests have captured the attention of researchers (see Hansen, Chapter 12, this volume). However, within the context of career counseling, the assessment of personality often plays a lesser role than other types of assessment. As noted by Zunker and Osborn (2002), counselors could use personality inventories to measure clients' social traits, motivational drives and needs, attitudes, and adjustment—all of which are important to career exploration and choice. Yet, Zunker (2002) also noted that while the case for using personality inventories in career counseling is well established, there is little evidence that such inventories are widely used.

Nonetheless, personality assessment has a place in career counseling, particularly to supplement information gathered from ability, need, and interest assessments (Costa, McCrae, & Kay, 1995; McCaulley & Martin, 1995). For example, Costa et al. (1995) suggest that personality information can help in understanding the client's strengths and weaknesses and result in more appropriate and realistic career choices. For example, a client with a high level of extraversion may do well to consider career options that encourage and value verbal skill and gregariousness. Several personality inventories are available in interpretive packages with other career-related instruments (e.g., the Strong Interest Inventory and the Myers-Briggs Type Indicator) or have interpretive report options that address career issues (e.g., the 16 PF or the NEO-PI).

Personality assessment when used in career counseling typically focuses on "normal" personality traits rather than maladaptive or pathological traits. The most frequently used framework to conceptualize normal personality is the *Big Five* or five-factor model of personality (Digman, 1990), which suggests that normal personality can be comprehensively understood by five broad human traits: extraversion (quantity and intensity of interpersonal interaction), emotional stability (emotional adjustment and self-confidence), openness to experience (willingness to entertain new ideas and values), agreeableness (cooperation and interpersonal warmth), and conscientiousness (planning, organizing, and carrying out tasks). The Big Five model has been used extensively to examine job performance and other work behavior (see Saks, Chapter 7, this volume; Fritzsche & Parrish, Chapter 8, this volume; Russell, Chapter 9, this volume). Accumulated research indicates that conscientiousness and emotional stability are the dimensions most predictive of overall job performance across occupations (Hurtz & Donovan, 2000; Russell, Chapter 9, this volume; Salgado, 1997), while emotional stability also predicts job satisfaction (Fritzsche & Parrish, Chapter 8, this volume). Both conscientiousness and extraversion have been implicated as important predictors of job search success (Saks, Chapter 7, this volume). Other dimensions predict specific types of career-relevant constructs or other adjustment criteria, such as extraversion with leadership behavior, conscientiousness and emotional stability with performance motivation and career success (Judge, Bono, Ilies, & Gerhardt, 2002; Judge, Heller, & Mount, 2002; Judge, Higgins, Thoresen, & Barrick, 1999; Judge & Ilies, 2002).

In addition to the Big Five, other personality characteristics have demonstrated associations with career-related behavior, such as achievement orientation, locus of control, instrumentality, expressiveness, anxiety, optimism, risk-taking, collectivism, and shyness (Lowman, 1991; Tokar, Fischer, & Subich, 1998). These personality characteristics are relevant to the process and content of individuals' career decisions but are rarely formally assessed in career counseling. Rather, counselors are likely to infer clients' standing on these characteristics via other information as reported by clients or observed in counseling.

Recent work has focused on the overlap of the Big Five personality dimensions with vocational interests. A number of studies, now summarized via meta-analyses, suggest that the link between personality and interests is stronger for some dimensions than for others. Namely, substantial connections exist between artistic and investigative interests and openness to experience, between enterprising and social interests and extraversion, and between social interests and agreeableness. Realistic interests do not appear to overlap directly with any aspects of personality (Barrick, Mount, & Gupta, 2003; Hansen, Chapter 12, this volume; Larson, Rottinghaus, & Borgen, 2002).

The most typical methods of personality assessment are well-established, formal instruments, including the NEO Personality Inventory (NEO-PI-R), the Myers-Briggs Type Indicator (MBTI), the Edwards Personal Preference Schedule (EPPS), and the 16PF. In contrast to other constructs, personality is not likely to be assessed via informal methods, although as noted earlier, it may be inferred from other aspects of clients' behavior and self-report.

The NEO Personality Inventory (NEO-PI-R; Costa & McCrae, 1992) is available in two forms: a 60-item version that provides scores on the Big Five personality traits (extraversion, emotional stability, openness, agreeableness, conscientiousness), as well as a 240-item version that adds scores on 30 facet scales (six facets per Big Five dimension; Costa et al., 1995). One of the available scoring options is a Professional Development Report that may be particularly useful for personality assessment related to career adjustment or change because it includes interpretive information about problem-solving skills; planning, organizing, and implementation skills; style of relating to others; personal style; and a summary of an individual's "most distinctive characteristics."

The MBTI (Myers, McCaulley, Quenk, & Hammer, 1998) presents scores on four dimensions derived from Jung's types: extroversion-introversion, sensing-intuition, thinking-feeling, and judging-perceiving. As noted earlier, the MBTI is available in a package with the Strong Interest Inventory (see Hansen, Chapter 12, this volume), and a career report is available for the MBTI alone or in combination with Strong. In addition, a work styles report is available for the MBTI, which includes interpretive information on clients' communication, information-gathering, decision-making, and project management styles. The MBTI has many potential applications in career counseling, including serving as a framework for analyzing job/career activities, increasing self-understanding, integrating other assessment data, understanding decision-making styles, structuring information-gathering activities, engaging the client in planning and taking action, and enhancing the client-counselor relationship and the process of career counseling (McCaulley & Martin, 1995).

Other measures may provide useful information but are not as widely used, such as the EPPS and the 16PF. The EPPS (Edwards, 1959) measures 15 personality variables based on the manifest needs proposed by Murray (1938): achievement, deference, order, exhibition, autonomy, affiliation, intraception, succorance, dominance, abasement, nurturance, change, endurance, heterosexuality, and aggression. The Sixteen Personality Factor Questionnaire (16PF; Cattell, 1989) includes bipolar scales measuring warmth, reasoning, emotional stability, dominance, liveliness, rule-consciousness, social boldness, sensitivity, vigilance, abstractedness, privateness, apprehension, openness to change, self-reliance, perfectionism, and tension. In addition, scores are available on five global factor scales that correspond to the Big Five personality factors. Although early work on the 16PF focused on vocational personality patterns, current versions of the instrument do not contain explicit information related to vocational choice. However, a Personal Career Development Profile report is available that relates the 16PF characteristics to a wide variety of work-related issues.

Personality assessment during initial career exploration is most likely to be used to enhance client self-understanding and to examine the match between an individual's strengths and career options. As with any type of assessment, examining personality characteristics may serve as a springboard for discussion between counselor and client. For example, a client who is uncomfortable with highly structured environments would benefit from considering how this preference might impact a career choice. Personality assessment, thus, may be included as part of a thorough, integrated assessment package, including interests, personality, values, and skills. During career choice and entry, personality assessment also may be used as a screening device for entry into specific careers or placement within organizations. A human resources department may use results of personality assessment such as the MBTI to address fit of individual employees with the existing styles of different operational units. In terms of career adjustment, assessment of personality may be used when individuals are dissatisfied with their career/job choice, are performing at less-than-satisfactory levels, or have been terminated from employment (Pickman, 1994). An individual's strong need for dominance, for example, may contribute to maladjustment or dissatisfaction within a specific organizational setting.

PERCEIVED BARRIERS

Discussion of barriers to making and implementing career choices originated in the literature related to the career psychology of women as a way to explain the gap between women's abilities and their achievements (Betz & Fitzgerald, 1987; Fitzgerald & Crites, 1980). Attention to perceived career barriers has increased substantially in the past decade, particularly in light of the development of Social Cognitive Career Theory (SCCT; Lent et al., 1994; Lent, Brown, & Hackett 2000; Lent, Chapter 5, this volume). Perceived barriers and interpersonal supports are intertwined and may be best considered as a pair of related constructs to assess in counseling. These constructs are widely viewed as important to address in career counseling, yet the instruments available to assess the constructs are more informal in nature (i.e., relatively little normative information is available). We present alternative ways to examine these variables in counseling.

Perceived barriers have been defined in a number of ways, but generally involve clients' perceptions of negative conditions that might interfere with career progress (e.g., discrimination, multiple-role conflict, or lack of opportunities). In the context of research, the assessment of perceived barriers has been approached through several different methods, many of which may be adapted for counseling use. The simplest is using a thought-listing technique, such as requesting clients to list any potential barriers to their educational or career progress (Luzzo, 1995; Luzzo & Hutcheson, 1996; Swanson & Tokar, 1991a).

Researchers also have used traditional psychometric methods to develop instruments measuring perceived barriers. At least three measures exist to assess a range of barriers to educational and career goals: the Perceptions of Barriers Scale (POB; McWhirter, Hackett, & Bandalos, 1998), the Perceptions of Educational Barriers measure (PEB; McWhirter, Rasheed, & Crothers, 2000), and the Career Barriers Inventory (CBI; Swanson, Daniels, & Tokar, 1996; Swanson & Tokar, 1991b). The POB measures barriers related to gender and racial job discrimination and to attending and progressing in college, and the PEB measures barriers specific to postsecondary education. These two measures were designed for use with high school students. The CBI covers a range of potential barriers and was designed for use with college students. None of these measures, however, offer normative information but may provide a useful springboard for discussion within career counseling.

In addition to these research-based methods of assessing perceived barriers, several authors have suggested ways to address barriers in career counseling (S. D. Brown & Lent, 1996; Swanson & Woitke, 1997). First, counselors could use traditional assessment tools such as interest inventories and card sorts as opportunities to examine clients' perceptions of career barriers. For example, counselors might observe and discuss clients' choices as they complete assessment; measured or expressed interests might reflect the influence of perceived barriers. Any discrepancies between interests and measures of abilities or skills might also suggest perceived barriers (S. D. Brown & Lent, 1996; Lent, Chapter 5, this volume).

Second, as part of the decision-making process, counselors could help clients examine perceived negative consequences of different options as a source of barrier information (S. D. Brown & Lent, 1996; Lent, Chapter 5, this volume). Third, counselors could directly ask clients about perceived barriers, whether past, present, or future. Another approach is to ask clients to list every career option they have considered and the reasons for their current interest or lack of interest (Swanson & Woitke, 1997). Given the range of potential barriers identified in previous research, it is important for counselors to probe thoroughly for different types of barriers. Items included in the POB, PEB, and CBI provide a comprehensive set of potential barriers that counselors might use to ensure that they have helped clients explore barriers as thoroughly as possible.

INTERPERSONAL SUPPORTS

The importance of career supports has long been recognized, yet, until recently, has received little research attention (Lent et al., 2000). Within SCCT, supports are environmental variables that facilitate the formation and pursuit of career choices, such as encouragement, financial resources, and role models, and have a logical and complementary link to perceived barriers. Engaging clients' social support networks is one of the five ingredients identified by S. D. Brown and Ryan Krane (2000) as critical to enhancing career counseling outcomes. Further, S. D. Brown et al. (2003) hypothesized that the positive effects of engaging support will be increased if clients examine support for the different career options they are considering, if they learn how to marshal support, and if they do these activities in writing.

Although several measures of social support are available, informal assessment of a client's social support would provide a direct and more flexible method within career counseling. Counselors might use methods similar to those proposed earlier concerning perceived barriers. For example, counselors could use other types of assessment as opportunities to examine the amount of social support clients perceive for their various options. Interpretation of interest inventories or card sorts present openings for discussion of how clients might garner additional support for their choices (Lent, Chapter 5, this volume). Counselors could also directly and explicitly ask clients about perceived support from important people in their lives.

SELF-EFFICACY BELIEFS

Self-efficacy is defined as "people's judgments of their capabilities to organize and execute courses of action required to attain designated types of performances" (Bandura, 1986, p. 391), or "Can I do this?" As with social support, self-efficacy may be viewed as a complementary variable to perceived barriers. If a barrier impedes career progress, both self-efficacy and social support are mechanisms for overcoming a barrier. *Support* may be conceptualized as an external mechanism, whereas *self-efficacy* is an internal mechanism.

In the context of career development, self-efficacy has been studied relative to specific occupational areas, gender-nontraditional occupations, mathematics performance, and by Holland type (Betz & Hackett, 1997). Self-efficacy also has been related to other important constructs, most notably, interests (Lent, Chapter 5, this volume; Rottinghaus, Larson, & Borgen, 2003). For example, Betz (1999) discussed helping clients act on their interests by considering self-efficacy as a mediator to implementing vocational interests. A specific form of self-efficacy, career decision-making self-efficacy, was discussed earlier in this chapter.

Measures of self-efficacy typically have been developed to focus on specific tasks, such as the Mathematics Self-Efficacy Scale (MSES; Betz & Hackett, 1983) or the Career Decision-Making Self-Efficacy Scale (CDMSE; Taylor & Betz, 1983). Some measures of generalized self-efficacy are available; however, one conceptual issue is that self-efficacy, by definition, contains a degree of specificity (e.g., "I am able to learn math").

Integrated assessment of interests and self-efficacy also is available via the Skills Confidence Inventory (SCI; Betz, Borgen, & Harmon, 1996) as part of the Strong Interest Inventory. This measure provides a parallel assessment of interests and self-efficacy within the same domain (Holland types), allowing counselors to directly link these two constructs in their work with clients.

Self-efficacy also could be assessed via informal methods during career counseling (see Lent, Chapter 5, this volume). As with the two previous constructs (perceived barriers and social support), opportunities to examine a client's self-efficacy may arise during other types of assessment, such as interests. Self-efficacy also could be assessed directly by discussing clients' beliefs about their abilities to achieve specific tasks or goals necessary for various career options under consideration or their ability to overcome identified barriers.

OUTCOME EXPECTATIONS

The construct of outcome expectations is also central to SCCT, yet it has received considerably less attention from researchers (Lent et al., 2000; Swanson & Gore, 2000). *Outcome expectations* refer to beliefs about the consequences about performing specific behaviors—"If I do this, what will happen?" (Lent et al., 1994)—and provide a conceptual link between self-efficacy and actions. In other words, having self-efficacy for a set of career behaviors (i.e., a specific occupational choice) does not guarantee that a person will pursue a career direction unless he or she also believes that the behaviors will lead to certain outcomes and that he or she values those outcomes. Thus, outcome expectations complete the SCCT picture of how career choices are made and implemented.

Unfortunately, few measures exist for outcome expectations, although there are some promising new instruments. As with other constructs, outcome expectations could be assessed informally during career counseling, through focused attention to how clients talk about the consequences of specific career choices (see Lent, Chapter 5, this volume). Implicit outcome expectations may alter the way clients view other factors in career choice, such as interests. For example, clients' responses to interest inventory items may be tinged with negative outcome expectations (wherein the activity is of interest, but the eventual outcome of performing that activity is undesirable). Outcome expectations also might color clients' self-efficacy about tasks; in other words, a client's low self-efficacy about math classes may be influenced by her concern about how strong math performance would be perceived by others.

CIRCUMSCRIPTION AND COMPROMISE

In Gottfredson's theory (1981, 1996, Chapter 4, this volume), *circumscription* refers to the process by which children narrow their "zone of acceptable alternatives" by progressive and irreversible elimination of unacceptable alternatives. The narrowing of acceptable alternatives occurs in age-graded stages. Stages 1 to 3 (beginning at age 3 and extending into early adolescence) parallel children's increasing cognitive ability to think abstractly, and occupations are conceptualized in terms of their sex-appropriateness, social prestige, and perceived abilities. In Stage 4, the process of *compromise* becomes salient: Circumscription in the previous stages entails rejecting unacceptable alternatives, whereas compromise focuses on identifying which of the acceptable alternatives are most preferred.

In the life span scheme featured throughout this chapter, career counselors are most likely to enter clients' lives in the compromise stage of Gottfredson's theory (age 14 and above). However, although clients are most likely to be actively working with the compromise portion of Gottfredson's theory, they will have previously progressed through the various stages of circumscription. The pertinent question thus becomes how to assess the degree to which clients have circumscribed their occupational alternatives in ways that may not be beneficial to them.

Gottfredson (2002) argued that counselors ought to encourage clients to think as realistically as possible about their career alternatives. She suggested several criteria for determining whether clients are adequately dealing with reality, including clients' ability to name occupational alternatives, the match of their interests and abilities to their chosen occupation, whether they are satisfied with their choice, and whether they have unnecessarily restricted their options.

Although there are no established measures for assessing Gottfredson's main constructs of circumscription and compromise (other than techniques used in research), counselors can attend to these processes through informal assessment with their clients. In addition, Gottfredson and Lapan (1997) proposed an assessment activity called Mapping Vocational Challenges (MVC), in which different occupations are mapped onto a three-dimensional grid. In the initial two-dimensional grid, clients place 42 occupations (7 per Holland type) into 15 boxes defined by prestige along one axis and sex type along the other axis. Clients next mark occupations according to interests. Subsequent steps include marking occupations according to self-efficacy and parental support. S. D. Brown and Lent (1996) also offer some suggestions about how career options that might have been previously circumscribed could be reconsidered by clients (see Lent, Chapter 5, this volume).

ASSESSMENT OF OUTCOME CONSTRUCTS

Assessment of outcome shifts our focus to the *results* of career counseling. Considerable research has demonstrated the effectiveness of a variety of modalities of career choice, although research attention to outcome may be waning (Whiston et al., 2003). In the past two decades, a series of increasingly refined meta-analyses have focused on the outcomes of career choice (S. D. Brown & Ryan Krane, 2000; S. D. Brown et al., 2003; Oliver & Spokane, 1988; N. E. Ryan, 1999; Spokane & Oliver, 1983; Whiston et al., 2003; Whiston et al., 1998). In addition to documenting the positive effects of career interventions, these meta-analyses also have highlighted important conceptual and methodological problems in determining outcome. Our goals in this section are to discuss ways to conceptualize the range of potential outcome constructs, clarify how intermediate and target outcome constructs are connected to one another, and suggest how career counseling practitioners can assess outcomes with their own clients.

CONCEPTUALIZING OUTCOME CRITERIA

The first challenge in addressing the outcome of career counseling is to describe and classify the range of outcome criteria of interest to researchers and practitioners. In response to the "chaotic approach to outcome selections" (Whiston et al., 2003, p. 406), Whiston (2001) developed an organizational scheme to guide the choice of outcome measures in career counseling (and other interventions). The four major domains are content, source, focus, and time orientation. *Content* includes four subcategories drawn from Fretz (1981): career knowledge and skills, career behaviors, sentiments and beliefs, and effective role functioning. The *source* domain includes the variety of perspectives from which change might be measured, including client, counselor, trained observer, relevant other, and institutional/archival sources of information. *Focus* is either general (such as using a measure of career maturity to indicate global improvement) or specific (an outcome measure tied explicitly to the goals of the intervention, such as goal attainment scaling) and *time orientation* includes macro-outcomes (long term) and micro-outcomes (short term). As Whiston (2001) noted, in an ideal world, a practitioner or researcher would choose an instrument in each category of each domain; however, the organizational scheme also may be used to choose the most comprehensive measure given constraints of the real world.

Further, Whiston (2001) presented general guidelines for selecting outcome measures. First and foremost, given the complexity of career counseling, the purpose of the career intervention must be considered. In other words, do the outcome measures directly connect to the initial goals of the intervention? The second guideline addresses the developmental level of the clients; selected measures must be age- and stage-appropriate. Other guidelines include selecting measures that are reliable and valid and that provide meaningful results, and conducting follow-up assessment (in addition to posttreatment assessment).

Several authors have raised the issue of what constitutes an appropriate outcome (Fretz, 1981; Heppner & Heppner, 2003; Phillips, 1992; Swanson, 1995; Whiston et al., 2003). The basic issue is that effective career counseling may lead to a wide variety of "appropriate" outcomes for a given individual. Heppner and Heppner (2003) noted that it is "imperative to examine whether the outcomes researchers determine are important to assess, actually lead to a better quality of life for the individual in the months after counseling (p. 443)." For example, a client may make a career decision at the conclusion of career counseling, which would typically be deemed a good outcome. However, does the client implement his or her decision? Does the decision lead to a better quality of life for the client? (Phillips, 1992).

Another example is that of an increased number of career options under consideration. Whiston et al. (2003) reported that this was a frequently used measure of outcome in career intervention studies, yet, for many clients, a *decrease* in career options under consideration may be a more appropriate outcome (see also Brown & McPartland, in press). Thus, researchers and practitioners may want to use more individually tailored measures of outcome, such as goal attainment scaling (Kiresuk & Sherman, 1968), that address questions such as: What were the client's initial goals for career counseling? Were these goals reformulated after discussion with the counselor? Did clients meet their initial or modified goals for counseling?

In the remainder of this section, we discuss outcome constructs and measures across the life span. Some of these constructs, however, already have been discussed in earlier portions of the chapter and thus are mentioned only briefly. For example, career maturity may be relevant to how a client approaches career counseling and decision making; therefore, it may be considered a process-oriented construct. However, we might also expect career maturity to increase as a result of career counseling; thus, it also may be considered an intermediate outcome that enhances achievement of an ultimate outcome. In other words, increased career maturity may smooth the process of making a career choice.

What are important outcomes to assess during career exploration, initial choice, and entry? In a comparison of treatment modalities, Whiston et al. (2003) reported that the three most commonly used outcome variables were information seeking, career maturity, and increased career choice options. Information seeking is typically considered an instrumental behavior (that is, something that the client *does*), career maturity an attitudinal variable, and increased options a cognitive variable.

Additional outcome variables during career exploration and initial choice may be classified according to Oliver's (1979) categories. The first category, career decision making, includes accuracy of self-knowledge, appropriateness of career choice, instrumental behaviors (career information seeking, getting hired, decision-making skills), attitudes toward career choice (degree of certainty, the presence of a career decision), the number of options under considerations, and traditionality of choice. Oliver's second category is effective role functioning, including performance variables (career-related knowledge and skills such as interviewing and writing) and adjustment variables (career maturity, self-concept change, attitude change, locus of control, cognitive complexity, anxiety, and identity). The third category is an evaluation of the counseling itself, including general evaluation, satisfaction, effectiveness, and helpfulness. Other variables not explicitly mentioned by Oliver include satisfaction with career decisions, self-efficacy beliefs, and outcome expectations.

Much of the previous research concerning outcomes of career counseling has focused on the earlier stages of exploration and initial choice. All of the previous outcomes may continue to be relevant at later life span stages. For example, an individual entering career counseling to contemplate a substantive career change may desire and achieve the same outcomes as an individual earlier in the career development process. We follow the schema outlined in Table 15.1, however, to discuss the range of outcome constructs across the life span.

INTERMEDIATE VERSUS TARGET OUTCOMES

Target outcomes are *ultimate* outcomes, or those that clients probably enter career counseling to achieve, such as making an initial career decision, achieving greater career choice certainty and satisfaction, or improving career satisfaction and job performance. These constructs frequently are discrete behaviors or events, rather than attitudes or beliefs. For example, "making a career choice" is a common endpoint of career counseling: Clients come to counseling for assistance in making a career decision and feel better and choose to discontinue counseling when they have accomplished that goal. As an outcome variable, this is a dichotomous, categorical variable that does not need extensive inventory development to assess. Similarly, a client's level of certainty about a career decision may be readily determined in counseling, without use of an inventory.

On the other hand, job or career satisfaction and job performance are multidimensional constructs that might require more complex assessments, depending on the purpose of the assessment (Fritzsche & Parrish, Chapter 8, this volume; Russell, Chapter 9, this volume). Moreover, target outcomes may not occur until well after the completion of counseling or other interventions, yet are still relevant to what occurs in counseling. It might be, for example, premature to assess career satisfaction immediately after counseling, but it would certainly be important to assess at longer term follow-up intervals.

Intermediate outcomes can be viewed as important in their own right, but also helpful in attaining later target outcomes (e.g., the amount of information searching engaged in by clients is an important intermediate outcome because it relates to clients' ultimate ability to make a satisfying career decision). As noted in Table 15.1, the intermediate outcomes are similar across the three life span stages, although some constructs may be more salient within specific stages. Self-efficacy beliefs and outcome expectations are likely to be important intermediate outcomes across all stages due to the central role they are hypothesized to play in forming choice actions and goals and in attaining desired levels of educational or work performance. Likewise, career maturity and career adaptability are important intermediate outcomes across the life span. Searching for and acquiring occupational information is perhaps most relevant during the early stage of career exploration, although it may resurface as an important intermediate outcome in later stages. Most of these constructs were discussed earlier in the section on process-oriented constructs. The exception is occupational information, also discussed by Gore and Hitch (Chapter 16, this volume).

Organizationally Relevant Target Outcomes

In addition to these individually oriented outcomes, there also are relevant organizationally-oriented outcomes. In other words, examining outcomes related to career adjustment/maladjustment or career change/transition must include a perspective other than the individual himself or herself, namely, the perspective of the employing organization.

Only one traditional vocational psychology theory addresses work adjustment issues from both individual and organizational perspectives, the Theory of Work Adjustment (TWA; Dawis, 1996; Chapter 1, this volume; Dawis & Lofquist, 1984). According to TWA, individuals have certain requirements for their work environments (work needs) and offer their work environments a set of skills and abilities. Work environments, in turn, have certain requirements of their employees (ability requirements) and can meet certain worker needs (reinforcement systems). Correspondence between a worker's abilities and the work environment's ability requirements predicts *satisfactoriness,* which is a perception of satisfaction from the perspective of the employing organization. Correspondence between a worker's needs and the work environment's reinforcement system predicts *satisfaction,* which is a perception of satisfaction from the perspective of the employee. Taken together, satisfactoriness and satisfaction are hypothesized to predict tenure of an individual within an organization.

What outcomes are important to an employing organization? Salient outcomes can be divided into attitudes and behaviors. The two attitudes most frequently studied by organizational psychologists are job satisfaction and organizational commitment. Behaviors include work withdrawal behaviors such as absenteeism and voluntary turnover (or turnover intentions), job performance, organizational citizenship behaviors, and involuntary turnover (unsatisfactoriness).

Job satisfaction has received an enormous amount of attention from industrial/ organizational psychologists (see Fritzsche & Parrish, Chapter 8, this volume) and is conceptualized either as *global* or *facet* satisfaction (such as satisfaction with pay). Attention to the attitude of organizational commitment is more recent and is conceptualized as consisting of three components: affective commitment (emotional attachment to an organization), continuance commitment (perceived costs associated with leaving an organization), and normative commitment (perceived obligation to remain in an organization; Meyer & Allen, 1997).

Each of these outcomes also may become an impetus for entering career counseling or other forms of career intervention. For example, poor job performance may lead to corrective measures or to involuntary turnover (being fired), both of which may result in services such as outplacement counseling. An individual also may seek services because of perceived stress and strain or voluntary turnover (quitting his or her job).

A full discussion of issues relevant to measuring job performance is far beyond the scope of this chapter (see Russell, Chapter 9, this volume). Because evaluation of job performance is used to make decisions about so many other aspects of organizational functioning (selection, promotion, reward delivery systems, firing), the measurement aspects of performance ratings are particularly important.

From the perspective of career counseling practitioners, job performance and satisfactoriness are most likely to be determined via a client's self-report. And, as with many other aspects of client self-report, these evaluations are fraught with the positive and negative biases that make self-evaluations less than accurate. For example, a client may be performing adequately (or even exceptionally) on the job, yet present a negative self-evaluation because of dissatisfaction with the job, depression, inaccurate self-efficacy, low self-esteem, or other mental health issues. In contrast, a client truly may be performing poorly, yet attribute negative performance evaluations to office politics, personality conflicts with superiors, or a need to save face.

Practitioners who work within organizational settings may have access to more "objective" information other than client self-report and, may, in fact, be providing services to clients because they have been referred due to poor performance evaluations or other work-related difficulties.

CULTURAL CONSIDERATIONS IN CAREER ASSESSMENT

The career development of diverse populations is complex and, therefore, difficult to describe in a few paragraphs (see Betz, Chapter 11, this volume; Worthington, Flores, & Navarro, Chapter 10, this volume). However, our purpose with this section is to remind the reader that many of the constructs and associated measures cited in this chapter have been normed and developed with European Americans and, therefore, do not always fit the worldviews, career decision-making processes, and other influential factors of career counseling with minority group individuals. We hope that this brief review illustrates why career assessment with diverse populations is indeed complex and that career counselors ought not homogenize career clients in assessment and treatment.

Examination of the cultural validity of mainstream career theories and constructs has been one of the predominant areas of research in vocational psychology in the past decade (e.g., Morrow, Gore, & Campbell, 1996; J. M. Ryan, Tracey, & Rounds, 1996). Moreover, models that incorporate some of these cultural considerations have been developed (e.g., Peterson, Sampson, & Reardon, 1991; Spokane, 1991; Spokane, Fouad, & Swanson, 2003; Yost & Corbishley, 1987). One of the most commonly cited models was developed by Fouad and Bingham (1995). They proposed attending to both culturally specific and culturally general considerations in every phase of the career counseling process. In their model, the assessment phase of career counseling includes a comprehensive account of variables that may impact career counseling. Fouad and Bingham proposed that there are five spheres of influence in the assessment of the effects of cultural variables:

1. The core unit or the individual.
2. Gender (e.g., role expectations).
3. Family (e.g., definitions, expectations, and values).
4. Racial or ethnic group (e.g., cultural factors, racial-identity development, worldview).
5. Dominant (majority) group (e.g., structural factors including perceptions, barriers, definitions, and expectations).

Incorporating assessment of these spheres of influence is, we suggest, an important component of effective career counseling to guard against assuming that clients are all alike. Career counseling that considers cultural and contextual variables is effective for *all* clients (Swanson & Fouad, 1999).

Another model for intervention with racial-ethnic minorities was proposed by Leung (1995), who suggested a number of personal, cultural, and economic issues that should be assessed. This model was designed to better guide the mode in which counselors approach career counseling and the expected outcomes of interventions. Leung's model separates career-related outcomes and education-related outcomes, reasoning that educational attainment is an important factor for most racial-ethnic minority groups and should, therefore, be considered in assessment. The model also proposed three modes of intervention:

1. A system intervention, which is community based and could benefit populations that are at risk.
2. A group counseling intervention, which may be more helpful for individuals who come from collectivist cultures.
3. A one-to-one intervention approach, which is obviously the mode of intervention that has been addressed most frequently in the vocational literature and which can facilitate the attainment of both educational and career-related outcomes.

An extension of Leung's (1995) model was later proposed by Leong and Hartung (1997) in which they considered not only career interventions and the use of assessment but also the process by which clients arrive at the awareness or recognition that they could benefit from seeking career counseling. The latter factor is important because clients' cultural backgrounds may affect their attitudes toward seeking professional help.

Comas-Diaz and Greiner (1998) wrote specifically about the importance of conducting what they referred to as an "ethnocultural assessment" in career counseling, which they argued is crucial in planning other forms of assessment and in developing treatment plans for clients. Their suggestions for this ethnocultural assessment evolved from previous work by Comas-Diaz (1996), which entailed one of the most comprehensive lists of contextual assessment areas that has been proposed. While counselors are unlikely to assess all of these factors with most clients, the list serves as a reminder of the relevant factors that might be salient to clients:

1. Ethnocultural heritage.
2. Racial and ethnocultural identities.
3. Gender and sexual orientation.
4. Socioeconomic status.
5. Physical appearance, ability, or disability.
6. Religion when being raised and what the individual is now practicing, spiritual beliefs.
7. Biological factors (e.g., genetic predispositions).
8. Historical era, age cohort.
9. Marital status, sexual history.
10. History of (im)migration.
11. Acculturation and transculturation levels.
12. Family of origin and multigenerational history.
13. Family scripts (roles of women and men, prescriptions for success or failure).
14. Individual and family life cycle development and stages.
15. Client's languages and those spoken by family of origin.
16. History of individual abuse and trauma (physical, emotional, sexual, and political including torture, oppression, and repression).
17. History of collective trauma (slavery, colonization, Holocaust).
18. Gender-specific issues, such as battered wife syndrome.
19. Recreations and hobbies, avocations, and special social roles.
20. Historical and geopolitical reality of ethnic group and relationship with dominant group (including wars and political conflict; Comas-Diaz, 1996).

What are other cultural, economic, gender, and individual differences in the career development of clients that may influence the process of assessment? Farmer and her colleagues (1997) discussed many diversity and women's issues in career development from adolescence to adulthood. Moreover, the career development of many diverse groups has been studied, including members of racial-ethnic groups, lesbian women and gay men, and youth with disabilities (Sue & Sue, 1999; Swanson & Gore, 2000). Collectively, these articles suggest that there is still much work to do in this area. Career development theories and career counseling practice have not fully integrated factors that affect the career behavior of diverse groups.

How can counselors meet the needs of the wide range of clients who seek services? S. D. Brown and Ryan Krane (2000) reviewed a number of studies and concluded that there are three main types of clients in career counseling:

1. Those who need additional information about the world of work and different occupations.
2. Those who are mainly anxious about making career choices.
3. Those who present with a variety of career decision-making and developmental issues.

But these are not the only differences to consider at the time of assessment and intervention. Heppner and Heppner (2003) described client differences based on cultural background. They concluded that there are a number of questions still unanswered and that the little amount of information that we know is related to the negative attitudes that racial-ethnic minority clients have toward seeking and persisting in counseling services. They hypothesized that these negative attitudes are possibly due to clients' experiences with counselors who lack interest in the cultural context variables that influence these clients' career choice and development and to counselors' implementation of biased interventions.

In conducting career counseling assessment with culturally different clients, then, counselors need to acknowledge the value that each client places on each of the variables that are traditionally assessed and those that are relevant to his or her cultural background. Moreover, assessing clients' cultural variables should facilitate building a therapeutic alliance and, ideally, allowing clients to have more positive attitudes toward career counseling.

SUMMARY

The primary focus of career assessment on the Big Three constructs of interests, needs/values, and abilities reflects the origins of career counseling, particularly the trait-and-factor approach that dominated the delivery of career services through the majority of the twentieth century. However, subsequent theories of career development—such as developmental, social cognitive, and social learning theories—emphasized additional constructs that are relevant to a comprehensive approach to career choice. Moreover, attention to cultural considerations in career development and interventions has introduced important constructs to address with clients.

In this chapter, we focused on process-oriented constructs dealing with how clients make career decisions and the circumstances surrounding those decisions, and outcome constructs dealing with the results of career interventions, whether target outcomes of particular interest to clients or intermediate outcomes that facilitate attainment of target outcomes. These constructs, in conjunction with the Big Three, offer a rich, contextualized approach to counseling that ultimately will improve quality of the career services that clients receive and the career choices they make.

REFERENCES

Bandura, A. (1977). Self-efficacy: Toward a unifying theory of behavioral change. *Psychology Review, 84*, 191–215.

Bandura, A. (1986). *Social foundations of thought and action. A social-cognitive theory.* Englewood Cliffs, NJ: Prentice-Hall.

Barrick, M. R., Mount, M. K., & Gupta, R. (2003). Meta-analysis of the relationship between the five-factor model of personality and Holland's occupational types. *Personnel Psychology, 56*, 45–74.

Betz, N. E. (1999). Getting clients to act on their interests: Self-efficacy as a mediator of the implementation of vocational interests. In M. L. Savickas & A. R. Spokane (Eds.), *Vocational interests: Their meaning, measurement, and counseling use* (pp. 327–344). Palo Alto, CA: Davies-Black.

Betz, N. E., Borgen, F. H., & Harmon, L. W. (1996). *Skills Confidence Inventory: Applications and technical guide.* Palo Alto, CA: Consulting Psychologists Press.

Betz, N. E., & Fitzgerald, L. F. (1987). *The career psychology of women.* Orlando, FL: Academic Press.

Betz, N. E., & Hackett, G. (1983). The relationship of mathematics self-efficacy expectations to the selection of science-based college majors. *Journal of Vocational Behavior, 23*, 329–345.

Betz, N. E., & Hackett, G. (1997). Applications of self-efficacy theory to the career assessment of women. *Journal of Career Assessment, 5,* 383–402.

Betz, N. E., Klein, K. L., & Taylor, K. M. (1996). Evaluation of a short form of the Career Decision-Making Self-Efficacy Scale. *Journal of Career Assessment, 4,* 47–57.

Betz, N. E., & Taylor, K. M. (1994). *Career Decision-Making Self-Efficacy Scale manual.* Columbus: Ohio State University, Department of Psychology.

Blustein, D. L., & Phillips, S. D. (1990). Relation between ego identity status and decision-making styles. *Journal of Vocational Behavior, 30,* 61–67.

Brown, D., Brooks, L., & Associates. (1996). *Career choice and development* (3rd ed.). San Francisco: Jossey-Bass.

Brown, S. D., & Lent, R. W. (1996). A social cognitive framework for career choice counseling. *Career Development Quarterly, 44,* 354–366.

Brown, S. D., & McPartland, E. B. (in press). Career interventions: Current status and future directions. In W. B. Walsh & M. L. Savickas (Eds.), *Handbook of vocational psychology* (3rd ed.). Mahweh, NJ: Erlbaum.

Brown, S. D., & Ryan Krane, N. E. R. (2000). Four (or five) sessions and a cloud of dust: Old assumptions and new observations about career counseling. In S. D. Brown & R. W. Lent (Eds.), *Handbook of counseling psychology* (3rd ed., pp. 740–766). New York: Wiley.

Brown, S. D., Ryan Krane, N. E., Brecheisen, J., Castelino, P., Budisin, I., Miller, M., et al. (2003). Critical ingredients of career choice interventions: More analyses and new hypotheses. *Journal of Vocational Behavior, 62,* 411–428.

Cattell, H. B. (1989). *The 16PF: Personality in depth.* Champaign, IL: Institute for Personality and Ability Testing.

Chartrand, J. M., & Camp, C. C. (1991). Advances in the measurement of career development constructs: A 20-year review. *Journal of Vocational Behavior, 39,* 1–39.

Chartrand, J. M., & Robbins, S. B. (1997). *Career Factors Inventory: Applications and technical guide.* Palo Alto, CA: Consulting Psychologists Press.

Comas-Diaz, L. (1996). Cultural considerations in diagnosis. In F. W. Kaslow (Ed.), *Handbook on relational diagnosis and dysfunctional family patterns* (pp. 159–160). New York: Wiley.

Comas-Diaz, L., & Greiner, J. R. (1998). Migration and acculturation. In J. Sandoval, C. L. Frisby, K. F. Geisinger, J. D. Scheuneman, & J. R. Greiner (Eds.), *Test interpretation and diversity* (pp. 213–241). Washington, DC: American Psychological Association.

Costa, P. T., & McCrae, R. R. (1992). *Revised NEO-Personality Inventory (NEO-PI-R) and NEO Five Factor Inventory (NEO-FFI): Professional manual.* Odessa, FL: Psychological Assessment Resources.

Costa, P. T., McCrae, R. R., & Kay, G. G. (1995). Persons, places, and personality: Career assessment using the Revised NEO-Personality Inventory. *Journal of Career Assessment, 3,* 123–139.

Crites, J. O. (1973). *Career Maturity Inventory.* Monterey, CA: CTB/McGraw-Hill.

Crites, J. O. (1974). Problems in the measurement of vocational maturity. *Journal of Vocational Behavior, 4,* 25–31.

Crites, J. O. (1976). A comprehensive model of career development in early adulthood. *Journal of Vocational Behavior, 9,* 105–118.

Crites, J. O., & Savickas, M. L. (1995). *Revised Form Attitude Scale and Competence Test CMI Sourcebook.* Oroville, WA: Bridges.com (Careerware).

Dawis, R. V. (1996). The theory of work adjustment and person-environment-correspondence counseling. In D. Brown, L. Brooks, & Associates, *Career choice and development* (3rd ed., pp. 75–120). San Francisco: Jossey-Bass.

Dawis, R. V., & Lofquist, L. H. (1984). *A psychological theory of work adjustment.* Minneapolis: University of Minnesota Press.

Digman, J. M. (1990). Personality structure: Emergence of the five-factor model. *Annual Review of Psychology, 41,* 417–440.

Edwards, A. L. (1959). *Edwards Personal Preference Schedule (2nd ed).* New York: Psychological Corporation.

Farmer, H. S., & Associates. (1997). *Diversity and women's career development.* Thousand Oaks, CA: Sage.

Fitzgerald, L. F., & Crites, J. O. (1980). Toward a career psychology of women: What do we know? What do we need to know? *Journal of Counseling Psychology, 27,* 44–62.

Fouad, N. A. (1999). Validity evidence for interest inventories. In M. L. Savickas & A. R. Spokane (Eds.), *Vocational interests: Their meaning, measurement, and counseling use* (pp. 193–209). Palo Alto, CA: Davies-Black.

Fouad, N. A., & Bingham, R. P. (1995). Career counseling with ethnic/racial minorities. In W. B. Walsh & S. H. Osipow (Eds.), *Handbook of vocational psychology* (2nd ed., pp. 331–366). Hillsdale, NJ: Erlbaum.

Fretz, B. R. (1981). Evaluating the effectiveness of career interventions. *Journal of Counseling Psychology, 29,* 77–90.

Gati, I., Osipow, S. H., Krausz, M., & Saka, N. (2000). Validity of the Career Decision-Making Difficulties Questionnaire: Counselee versus career counselor perceptions. *Journal of Vocational Behavior, 56,* 99–113.

Gottfredson, L. S. (1981). Circumscription and compromise: A developmental theory of occupational aspirations. *Journal of Counseling Psychology, 28,* 545–579.

Gottfredson, L. S. (1996). Gottfredson's Theory of Circumscription and Compromise. In D. Brown, L. Brooks, & Associates, *Career choice and development* (3rd ed., pp. 179–232). San Francisco: Jossey-Bass.

Gottfredson, L. S. (2002). Gottfredson's theory of circumscription, compromise, and self-creation. In D. Brown & Associates, *Career choice and development* (4th ed., pp. 85–148). San Francisco: Jossey-Bass.

Gottfredson, L. S., & Lapan, R. T. (1997). Assessing gender-based circumscription of occupational aspirations. *Journal of Career Assessment, 5,* 419–441.

Greenhaus, J. H. (1971). An investigation of the role of career salience in vocational behavior. *Journal of Vocational Behavior, 1,* 209–216.

Harren, V. A. (1979). A model of career decision making for college students. *Journal of Vocational Behavior, 14,* 119–133.

Heppner, M. J., & Heppner, P. P. (2003). Identifying process variables in career counseling: A research agenda. *Journal of Vocational Behavior, 62,* 429–452.

Holland, J. L. (1999). Why interest inventories are also personality inventories. In M. L. Holland, J. L., Daiger, D. C., & Power, P. G. (1980). *My Vocational Situation.* Palo Alto, CA: Consulting Psychologists Press.

Hurtz, G. M., & Donovan, J. J. (2000). Personality and job performance: The big five revisited. *Journal of Applied Psychology, 85,* 869–879.

Judge, T. A., Bono, J. E., Ilies, R., & Gerhardt, M. W. (2002). Personality and leadership: A qualitative and quantitative review. *Journal of Applied Psychology, 87,* 765–780.

Judge, T. A., Heller, D., & Mount, M. K. (2002). Five-factor model of personality and job satisfaction: A meta-analysis. *Journal of Applied Psychology, 87,* 530–541.

Judge, T. A., Higgins, C. A., Thoresen, C. J., & Barrick, M. R. (1999). The Big Five personality traits, general mental ability, and career success across the life span. *Personnel Psychology, 52,* 621–652.

Judge, T. A., & Ilies, R. (2002). Relationship of personality to performance motivation: A meta-analytic review. *Journal of Applied Psychology, 87,* 797–807.

Kelly, K. R., & Lee, W. C. (2002). Mapping the domain of career decision problems. *Journal of Vocational Behavior, 61,* 302–326.

Kiresuk, D. J., & Sherman, R. E. (1968). Goal attainment scaling: A general method of evaluating comprehensive community mental health programs. *Community Mental Health Journal, 4,* 443–453.

Larson, L. M., Rottinghaus, P. J., & Borgen, F. H. (2002). Meta-analyses of Big Six interests and Big Five personality factors. *Journal of Vocational Behavior, 61,* 217–239.

Lent, R. W., Brown, S. D., & Hackett, G. (1994). Toward a unifying social cognitive theory of career and academic interest, choice and performance. *Journal of Vocational Behavior, 45,* 79–122.

Lent, R. W., Brown, S. D., & Hackett, G. (2000). Contextual supports and barriers to career choice: A social cognitive analysis. *Journal of Counseling Psychology, 47,* 36–49.

Lent, R. W., Brown, S. D., Talleyrand, R., McPartland, E. B., Davis, T., Chopra, S. B., et al. (2002). Career choice barriers, supports, and coping strategies: College students' experiences. *Journal of Vocational Behavior, 60,* 61–72.

Leong, F. T., & Hartung, P. J. (1997). Career assessment with culturally different clients: Proposing an integrative-sequential conceptual framework for cross-cultural career counseling research and practice. *Journal of Career Assessment, 5,* 183–201.

Leung, S. A. (1995). Career development and counseling: A multicultural perspective. In J. G. Ponterotto, J. M. Casas, L. A. Suzuki, & C. M. Alexander (Eds.), *Handbook of multicultural counseling* (pp. 549–566). Thousand Oaks, CA: Sage.

Lowman, R. L. (1991). *The clinical practice of career assessment: Interests, abilities, and personality.* Washington, DC: American Psychological Association.

Luzzo, D. A. (1995). Gender differences in college students' career maturity and perceived barriers in career development. *Journal of Career Development, 73,* 319–322.

Luzzo, D. A., & Hutcheson, K. G. (1996). Causal attributions and sex differences associated with perceptions of occupational barriers. *Journal of Counseling and Development, 75,* 124–130.

Mau, W. C. (1995). Decision-making styles as a predictor of career decision status and treatment gains. *Journal of Career Assessment, 3,* 90–101.

McCaulley, M. H., & Martin, C. R. (1995). Career assessment and the Myers-Briggs Type Indicator. *Journal of Career Assessment, 3,* 219–239.

McWhirter, E. H., Hackett, G., & Bandalos, D. L. (1998). A causal model of the educational plans and career expectations of Mexican American high school girls. *Journal of Counseling Psychology, 45,* 166–181.

McWhirter, E. H., Rasheed, S., & Crothers, M. (2000). The effects of high school career education on social-cognitive variables. *Journal of Counseling Psychology, 47,* 330–341.

Messick, S. (1995). Validity of psychological assessment: Validation of references from persons' responses and performances on scientific inquiry into score meaning. *American Psychologist, 50,* 741–749.

Meyer, J. P., & Allen, N. J. (1997). *Commitment in the workplace: Theory, research, and application.* Thousand Oaks, CA: Sage.

Mitchell, L. K., & Krumboltz, J. D. (1996). Krumboltz's learning theory of career choice and counseling. In D. Brown, L. Brooks, & Associates, *Career choice and development* (3rd ed., pp. 233–280). San Francisco: Jossey-Bass.

Morrow, S. L., Gore, P. A., & Campbell, B. W. (1996). The application of a sociocognitive framework to the career development of lesbian women and gay men. *Journal of Vocational Behavior, 48,* 136–148.

Murray, H. A. (1938). *Exploration in personality.* New York: Oxford University Press.

Myers, I. B., McCaulley, M. H., Quenk, N. L., & Hammer, A. L. (1998). *Manual for the Myers-Briggs Type Indicator* (3rd ed.). Palo Alto, CA: Consulting Psychologists Press.

Oliver, L. W. (1979). Outcome measurement in career counseling research. *Journal of Counseling Psychology, 26,* 217–226.

Oliver, L. W., & Spokane, A. R. (1988). Career-intervention outcome: What contributes to client gain? *Journal of Counseling Psychology, 35,* 447–462.

Osipow, S. H., Carney, C. G., Winer, J. L., Yanico, B. J., & Koschier, M. (1987). The Career Decision Scale. Odessa, FL: Psychological Assessment Resources.

Parsons, F. (1909). *Choosing a vocation.* Boston: Houghton Mifflin.

Peterson, G. W., Sampson, J. P., Jr., & Reardon, R. C. (1991). *Career development and services: A cognitive approach.* Pacific Grove, CA: Brooks/Cole.

Phillips, S. D. (1992). Career counseling: Choice and implementation. In S. D. Brown & R. W. Lent (Eds.), *Handbook of counseling psychology* (2nd ed., pp. 513–547). New York: Wiley.

Pickman, A. J. (1994). *The complete guide to outplacement counseling.* Mahweh, NJ: Erlbaum.

Randahl, G. J., Hansen, J. C., & Haverkamp, B. E. (1993). Instrument behaviors following test administration and interpretation: Exploration validity of the Strong Interest Inventory. *Journal of Counseling and Development, 71,* 435–439.

Rottinghaus, P. J., Larson, L. M., & Borgen, F. H. (2003). The relation of self-efficacy and interests: A meta-analysis of 60 samples. *Journal of Vocational Behavior, 62,* 221–236.

Ryan, J. M., Tracey, T. J., & Rounds, J. (1996). Generalizability of Holland's structure of vocational interests across ethnicity, gender, and socioeconomic status. *Journal of Counseling Psychology, 43,* 330–337.

Ryan, N. E. (1999). *Career counseling and career choice goal attainment: A meta-analytically derived model for career counseling practice.* Unpublished doctoral dissertation, Loyola University, Chicago.

Salgado, J. F. (1997). The five-factor model of personality and job performance in the European community. *Journal of Applied Psychology, 82,* 30–43.

Savickas, M. L. (2000). Assessing career decision making. In C. E. Watkins & V. Campbell (Eds.), *Testing and assessment in counseling practice* (pp. 429–477). Mahweh, NJ: Erlbaum.

Savickas, M. L. (2002). Career construction: A developmental theory of vocational behavior. In D. Brown & Associates, *Career choice and development* (4th ed., pp. 149–205). San Francisco: Jossey-Bass.

Seligman, L. (1994). *Developmental career counseling and assessment* (2nd ed.). Thousand Oaks, CA: Sage.

Spokane, A. R. (1991). *Career intervention.* Englewood Cliffs, NJ: Prentice-Hall.

Spokane, A. R., Fouad, N. A., & Swanson, J. L. (2003). Culture-centered career intervention. *Journal of Vocational Behavior, 62,* 453–458.

Spokane, A. R., & Oliver, L. W. (1983). Outcomes of vocational intervention. In S. H. Osipow & W. B. Walsh (Eds.), *Handbook of vocational psychology* (pp. 99–136). Mahweh, NJ: Erlbaum.

Sue, D. W., & Sue, D. (1999). *Counseling the culturally different: Theory and practice* (3rd ed.). New York: Wiley.

Super, D. E. (1983). Assessment in career guidance: Toward truly developmental counseling. *Personnel and Guidance Journal, 61,* 555–562.

Super, D. E., Savickas, M. L., & Super, C. M. (1996). The life-span, life-space approach to careers. In D. Brown, L. Brooks, & Associates, *Career choice and development* (3rd ed., pp. 121–178). San Francisco: Jossey-Bass.

Super, D. E., Thompson, A. S., & Lindeman, R. H. (1984). *The Adult Career Concerns Inventory.* Palo Alto, CA: Consulting Psychologists Press.

Swanson, J. L. (1992). Vocational behavior, 1989–1991: Life-span career development and reciprocal interaction of work and nonwork. *Journal of Vocational Behavior, 41,* 101–161.

Swanson, J. L. (1995). Process and outcome research in career counseling. In W. B. Walsh & S. H. Osipow (Eds.), *Handbook of vocational psychology* (2nd ed., pp. 217–259). Hillsdale, NJ: Erlbaum.

Swanson, J. L. (2003). Understanding midcareer development: From whose perspective? *Counseling Psychologist, 31,* 212–220.

Swanson, J. L., Daniels, K. K., & Tokar, D. M. (1996). Assessing perceptions of career-related barriers: The Career Barriers Inventory. *Journal of Career Assessment, 4,* 219–244.

Swanson, J. L., & Fouad, N. A. (1999). *Career theory and practice.* Thousand Oaks, CA: Sage.

Swanson, J. L., & Gore, P. A. (2000). Advances in vocational psychology: Theory and research. In S. D. Brown & R. W. Lent (Eds.), *Handbook of counseling psychology* (3rd ed., pp. 233–269). New York: Wiley.

Swanson, J. L., & Tokar, D. M. (1991a). College students' perceptions of barriers to career development. *Journal of Vocational Behavior, 38,* 92–106.

Swanson, J. L., & Tokar, D. M. (1991b). Development and initial validation of the Career Barriers Inventory. *Journal of Vocational Behavior, 39,* 344–361.

Swanson, J. L., & Woitke, M. B. (1997). Theory into practice in career assessment: Assessing women's career barriers. *Journal of Career Assessment, 5,* 443–462.

Taylor, K. M., & Betz, N. E. (1983). Application of self-efficacy theory to the understanding and treatment of career indecision. *Journal of Vocational Behavior, 22,* 63–81.

Tittle, C. K. (1978). Implications of recent developments for future research in career interest measurement. In C. K. Tittle & D. G. Zytowski (Eds.), *Sex fair interest measurement: Research and implications* (pp. 123–128). Washington, DC: National Institute of Education.

Tokar, D. M., Fischer, L. R., & Subich, L. M. (1998). Personality and vocational behavior: A selective review of the literature, 1993–1997. *Journal of Vocational Behavior, 53,* 115–153.

Watkins, C. E., Campbell, V. L., & Nieberding, R. (1994). The practice of vocational assessment by counseling psychologists. *Counseling Psychologist, 22,* 115–128.

Watts, A. G. (1996). The changing concept of career: Implications for career counseling. In R. Feller & G. Walz (Eds.), *Career transitions in turbulent times* (pp. 229–235). Greensboro, NC: ERIC/CASS Publications.

Whiston, S. C. (2001). Selecting career outcome assessments: An organizational scheme. *Journal of Career Assessment, 9,* 215–228.

Whiston, S. C., Brecheisen, B. K., & Stephens, J. (2003). Does treatment modality affect career counseling effectiveness? *Journal of Vocational Behavior, 62,* 390–410.

Whiston, S. C., Sexton, T. L., & Lasoff, D. L. (1998). Career-intervention outcome: A replication and extension of Oliver and Spokane (1988). *Journal of Counseling Psychology, 45,* 150–165.

Yost, E. B., & Corbishley, M. A. (1987). *Career counseling: A psychological approach.* San Francisco: Jossey-Bass.

Zunker, V. G. (2002). *Career counseling: Applied concepts of life planning* (6th ed.). Pacific Grove, CA: Brooks/Cole.

Zunker, V. G., & Osborn, D. S. (2002). *Using assessment results for career development* (6th ed.). Pacific Grove, CA: Brooks/Cole.

CHAPTER 16

Occupational Classification and Sources of Occupational Information

Paul A. Gore Jr. and Jorie L. Hitch

NDIVIDUALS TODAY ARE faced with an overwhelming number of educational and occupational choices. Emerging industries, rapidly changing technologies, and the globalization of economies are just a few of the changes that make career choices more complicated than ever. Individuals faced with a daunting array of educational and career choices can benefit from accurate and up-to-date information. The importance of providing career counseling clients with accurate career information has been recognized since Parsons proposed the first organized theory of career guidance in 1909 (Parsons, 1909). In Parsons' system, self- and occupational information formed the foundation for making a rational career decision. In spite of the changes that have occurred since Parsons' time, having accurate information about self and the world of work continues to be a fundamental component of most current career theories. Recent research on the effectiveness of career counseling strongly supports the importance of providing clients with accurate academic and career information (Brown et al., 2003).

The nature of career information has undergone dramatic changes since the beginning of the twentieth century. Whereas Parsons and his colleagues struggled to find any educational or occupational information, the overwhelming volume and availability of this information today present a new set of challenges. Boyce and Rainie (2002) estimated that one of every five Americans has searched online for information about work or careers and that more than four million users do so every day. Today, anyone with a computer and Internet connection can access large volumes of unedited educational and occupational information. Modern career counselors need to be skilled not only in the use of well-established career information resources but also in the critical evaluation of new sources of occupational information—especially electronic sources.

This chapter (1) provides an overview of current systems used to classify occupations and (2) reviews several of the many resources that can be used to assist career clients in gathering occupational information. Less than 50 years ago, a chapter such as this one could have offered a comprehensive overview of the systems of occupational classification and the sources of occupational information. Today, career guidance self-help books are housed in their own section of our local bookstores, and Internet sites that number in the thousands offer services ranging from online career assessment to person-job matching. Given the proliferation of occupational information and the pace with which information changes, our coverage of these resources is limited. Specifically, we limit our coverage of occupational classification systems to those systems currently in widespread use by career counselors or vocational specialists, such as the Standard Occupational Classification System and Holland's classification system. Further, because of the sheer number of resources that are currently available, we do not cover occupational field-specific books, book series, or career self-help books.

Finally, we have intentionally limited our review of career-related Internet sites. Although we have included web page addresses for well-established sites, the sheer number of sites and their transient nature make any thorough review of these resources futile. Instead of simply listing career-related Internet sites, we have chosen to review two widely used Internet-based career guidance programs. Users seeking a critical review of career-related web sites are referred elsewhere (Harris-Bowlsbey, Dikel, & Sampson, 2002). We believe that one of the biggest challenges faced by career counselors today is effectively evaluating career-related Internet sites before recommending them to clients. As such, we briefly review some of the major ethical issues involved in using electronic career guidance and information resources.

OCCUPATIONAL CLASSIFICATION

There are many reasons for developing an occupational classification system. The order imposed by a classification system allows us to work more efficiently with a large set of events or items. Specifically, classification allows us to explore or describe the similarities and differences among items. It is important to remember that the rules that are applied to generate a classification system dictate the nature of the characteristics shared by members of a category. As such, different classification systems emphasize certain relations and ignore others. For example, as discussed in this chapter, the Standard Occupational Classification System organizes occupations according to the work performed, the skills used, and the education or training required for the job. In contrast, an occupational classification system derived from the Minnesota Theory of Work Adjustment (Dawis, Chapter 1, this volume) classifies occupations according to the reinforcement system that is present in the environment and the skills that are required on the job (Dawis, Dohm, Lofquist, Chartrand, & Due, 1987). In short, classification allows us to communicate with our clients more efficiently about occupations that share common characteristics. More importantly, classification systems can be taught to, and used by, clients in an effort to assist them in their career exploration.

Individuals vary greatly in their reasons for seeking career counseling. Not surprisingly, a career counselor may employ different classification systems with different clients or even with the same client at different times during the counseling process. For example, a counselor may help a client understand the relations between her interests and the interest patterns of people employed in various occupations using a system that classifies occupations based on the patterns of likes and dislikes of job incumbents. Later, when this client has identified a short list of possible careers, she might be introduced to the U.S. government's system of occupational classification in an attempt to help her narrow her list to include only those occupations that allow her to use her unique skills. Counselors skilled in the use of multiple classification systems and knowledgeable about when to use them will be better prepared to provide for the varied needs of their clients.

In addition to facilitating the work of career counselors, occupational classification systems may also be used by employers for personnel, marketing, or organizational planning purposes or by economists, sociologists, or public policy workers. For example, there currently exist several government agencies that collect and use occupational data for different purposes. The Bureau of Labor Statistics gathers annual wage and salary information in order to describe the conditions of the workforce and workplace to the American public, the Congress, and other federal agencies. The Bureau of the Census collects both decennial and monthly data on the U.S. population and publishes data about workers in approximately 500 different occupations. A standard classification system allows these two agencies to share and compare their data more efficiently. The users of occupational classification and information systems might be grouped as micro-users and macro-users. Micro-users require information to structure jobs, to assist in the development of career plans, or to recruit workers. Macro-users, on the other hand, require occupational information to develop models in an effort to understand and predict the performance of the economy or to promote economic development.

History of Occupational Classification

Employment classification in the United States began almost 200 years ago with the administration of several censuses (e.g., Census of Manufactures, Census of Mining, Census of Fisheries). These early attempts at describing the U.S. workforce were industry driven and included brief descriptions of each company and a summary of the number of employees. Industry-based classification systems continue to play a key role in our modern economy. The Standard Industrial Classification (SIC) system, for example, was developed after the great depression in an attempt to homogenize industry-based data collection in the United States. This system was recently superceded when the passage of the North American Free Trade Agreement (NAFTA) mandated an industry classification system that could accommodate the economies of the United States, Canada, and Mexico. The North American Industry Classification System (NAICS; U.S. Office of Management & Budget, 1999) allows direct comparison of industrial production statistics collected and published in the three NAFTA countries.

Efforts to classify occupations paralleled those designed to classify industries. Occupational classification in this country began in 1850 with the publication of the U.S. Census. Consistent with the industry-based focus of the time, the 300 occupations listed in this census were tied to specific industries. For example, glass manufacturers, clock makers, and looking glass makers were treated as distinct occupations even though the tasks they performed were similar. The classification of occupations was further advanced in 1933 with the passage of the Wagner-Peyser Act. This act established federal and state employment security programs and led to the development of a national occupational-information research program. Regional employment offices throughout the United States, together with organizations such as the Minnesota Employment Stabilization Research Institute, gathered detailed information on thousands of different occupations (Crites, 1969). Their efforts resulted in the publication of the first edition of the *Dictionary of Occupational Titles* (DOT; U.S. Department of Labor [USDOL], 1939). Although revisions to the DOT reflected changes in the occupational matrix of our society, the classification system offered by this reference was not widely adopted by federal and state agencies. The growing disparities among federal classification systems led to the formation of the Interagency Occupational Classification Committee. This committee was responsible for developing and revising the occupational classification system that is currently used by all U.S. government agencies (Standard Occupational Classification System; USDOL, 1999).

OCCUPATIONAL CLASSIFICATION SYSTEMS

Occupational classification systems are themselves subject to classification. For example, we might compare systems developed by public (government) agencies to those developed in the private sector. Alternatively, we might compare classification systems that are developed atheoretically to those developed from career theory. We discuss four occupational classification systems in this chapter (Standard Occupational Classification System, Holland's hexagon, the World of Work Map, and the Minnesota Occupational Classification System). These systems were chosen either because career counselors frequently use them or because they are used as organizing schemes in popular occupational information products. The Standard Occupational Classification System is an example of an atheoretical system, whereas the others are examples of classification systems developed from career theory. Some readers may notice the absence of the *Dictionary of Occupational Titles* in the section that follows. This historically important resource is still available in many libraries but is being replaced by the Standard Occupational Classification System and the O*NET—both of which are covered in the following discussion.

We have chosen the occupation of childcare worker to use in all subsequent examples. By using a single occupation, we hope that the reader will be better able to make comparisons between occupational classification systems and sources of occupational information.

The Standard Occupational Classification System   The Standard Occupational Classification (SOC) System was developed to unify the language used by federal and state employment agencies to communicate about occupations and jobs. This system classifies occupations based on the nature of the work and on the occupational skill, education, and training requirements for the job. The SOC system was intended to replace older classification systems such as the *Dictionary of Occupational Titles*, the Occupational Employment Statistics system, and the Census occupational classification system. Unfortunately, early versions of the SOC system suffered from budgetary setbacks and neglect. The most recent revision of the SOC system has received a more favorable reception. Counselors should become familiar with the SOC system because it has been adopted by all federal agencies that collect and publish occupational data and will likely be adopted by state and local agencies in the near future.

The SOC system includes all occupations in which work is performed for pay or profit but does not include occupations that are unique to volunteers. The system classifies occupations at four levels of specificity: (1) major group, (2) minor group, (3) broad occupation, and (4) detailed occupation. Currently, the system includes 23 major groups, 96 minor groups, 449 broad occupations, and 821 detailed occupations. Table 16.1 contains a complete listing of the major groups and an expanded listing of the Personal Care and Service group (the group containing the occupation of Childcare Workers). In the SOC system, a six-digit number is assigned to each occupation. The first two numbers are used to classify the major group to which the occupation belongs. The third digit describes the minor group that is associated with an occupation. The fourth and fifth digits are used to designate a broad occupational group, and the sixth digit is used to identify unique occupations. Data collection agencies wanting more detailed classification may create subclassifications for an occupation by adding digits after the decimal point. Thus, by including multiple levels of specificity, the SOC system can be used by agencies or organizations with differing needs or capabilities with respect to data collection and analysis.

Let's look at an example. The occupation of Childcare Worker is classified in the Personal Care and Service Occupations major group (**39**-0000), the Other Personal Care and Service Workers minor group (39-**9**000), and the broad occupation group of Childcare Workers (39-9**01**0). The last digit of the SOC code for Childcare Worker (39-901**1**) designates the actual occupation within the broad occupational group. In this case, Childcare Worker is the only occupation within the broad occupational group of the same name. In contrast, the broad occupational group Recreation and Fitness Workers (39-9030) contains two specific occupations: Fitness Trainers and Aerobic Instructors (39-903**1**) and Recreation Workers (39-903**2**). If an organization wanted to further classify the occupation of Childcare Worker, it could do so by including additional numbers after the decimal point (e.g., 39-9011.**01**—Childcare Workers, Infant and Toddler; 39-9011.**02**—Childcare Workers, Primary School Age). The SOC system also includes a brief description for each occupation. The following is the job description for Childcare Workers:

> Attend to children at schools, businesses, private households, and child care institutions. Perform a variety of tasks, such as dressing, feeding, bathing, and overseeing play. Exclude "Preschool Teachers" (25-2011) and "Teacher Assistants" (25-9041).

Residual categories in the SOC system are indicated by the use of the number 9 and are used at three levels of classification (minor group, broad occupation, and occupational group levels). Residual categories are also identified by the use of the terms *other, all other,* or *miscellaneous.* Childcare Worker is a good example of the use of residual categories. This occupation resides in a residual minor group (Other Personal Care and Service Workers). Other broad occupations that are included in this residual category include Personal and Home Care Aides, Recreation and Fitness Workers, Residential Advisors, and Miscellaneous Personal Care and Service Workers (a residual category at the broad occupational level).

In addition to being used by government agencies for the purposes of data collection and analysis, the SOC system can be accessed by counselors or clients for

Table 16.1

The Standard Occupational Classification System (SOC)

Major Group-Level Classification	Detailed Classification of 39-0000
11-0000 Management Occupations	39-0000 Personal Care and Service Occupations
13-0000 Business and Financial Operations Occupations	39-1000 Supervisors, Personal Care and Service Workers
15-0000 Computer and Mathematical Occupations	39-2000 Animal Care and Service Workers
17-0000 Architecture and Engineering Occupations	39-3000 Entertainment Attendants and Related Workers
19-0000 Life, Physical, and Social Science Occupations	39-4000 Funeral Service Workers
21-0000 Community and Social Services Occupations	39-5000 Personal Appearance Workers
23-0000 Legal Occupations	39-6000 Transportation, Tourism, and Lodging Attendants
25-0000 Education, Training, and Library Occupations	39-9000 Other Personal Care and Service Workers
27-0000 Arts, Design, Entertainment, Sports, and Media Occupations	39-9010 Childcare Workers
29-0000 Healthcare Practitioners and Technical Occupations	39-9011 Childcare Workers
31-0000 Healthcare Support Occupations	39-9020 Personal and Home Care Aides
33-0000 Protective Service Occupations	39-9021 Personal and Home Care Aides
35-0000 Food Preparation and Serving Related Occupations	39-9030 Recreation and Fitness Workers
37-0000 Building and Grounds Cleaning and Maintenance Occupations	39-9031 Fitness Trainers and Aerobic Instructors
39-0000 Personal Care and Service Occupations	39-9032 Recreation Workers
41-0000 Sales and Related Occupations	39-9040 Residential Advisors
43-0000 Office and Administrative Support Occupations	39-9041 Residential Advisors
45-0000 Farming, Fishing, and Forestry Occupations	39-9090 Miscellaneous Personal Care and Service Workers
47-0000 Construction and Extraction Occupations	39-9099 Personal Care and Service Workers, All
49-0000 Installation, Maintenance, and Repair Occupations	
51-0000 Production Occupations	
53-0000 Transportation and Material Moving Occupations	
55-0000 Military Specific Occupations	

the purpose of researching occupations. Because the system clusters occupations that are similar with respect to the work performed and the skills and training required, a user who enters the SOC system to gather information about the occupation of Home Health Aide (31-1011) will have easy access to information about related occupations such as Occupational Therapist Assistant (31-2010) and Dental Assistant (31-9091). Career counselors and clients can access the SOC system via the Internet at http://stats.bls.gov/soc. Users can browse the system or search occupational titles and job descriptions using keywords. The SOC system is now used as the classification system to organize occupations in the O*NET and will be used to organize information in subsequent editions of the *Occupational Outlook Handbook* (USDOL, 2002c).

For an example of an innovative use of the SOC system, explore the Internet web site http://clickonmycareer.com developed by the Cedar Rapids and Iowa City Chambers of Commerce, the Iowa Workforce Development Office, and the Workplace Learning Connection. This site includes a database of local businesses that hire individuals in various occupations. This database is organized using the first three levels of the SOC system. Users can browse through occupations using SOC categories, or they can search occupational descriptions and titles using keywords. At the occupation level, users are presented with a job description, the educational level expected for entry-level work, the regional salary range, and the name and web address of local employers who hire individuals in this occupation.

In summary, the SOC system is the occupational classification system used by federal agencies to collect, share, analyze, and communicate with one another about employment-related data. In the future, consumers of occupational information, such as career counselors and their clients, will benefit from the compatibility of resources that will result from the widespread implementation of this system. The SOC system is dynamic in that it can accommodate the occupational consolidation that results from technological changes just as easily as it can respond to the growth and development of new occupations.

Holland's Hexagon   Spokane and Cruza-Guet (Chapter 2, this volume) provide a comprehensive overview of John Holland's theory of career choice (Holland, 1997). One of Holland's fundamental hypotheses is that job satisfaction is a function of the degree of congruence between an individual's work personality and the characteristics of the occupation in which he or she is employed. According to Holland's theory, work personalities can be described using six primary dimensions: Realistic, Investigative, Artistic, Social, Enterprising, and Conventional. An individual's work personality is composed of preferences, skills, attitudes, and values. Although a person's work personality has components of each of the six types, Holland believes that most individuals have work personalities that come to primarily resemble a subset of the six types. According to Holland, the strongest personality dimensions are the most potent determinants of vocational behavior.

In addition to describing work personalities, Holland believes that the six dimensions can be used to characterize work environments. Characteristics of the work environment can be assessed either through a detailed analysis of job functions or by measuring the work personalities of job incumbents. Like work personalities, most work environments can be described using a subset of the six dimensions. A basic premise of Holland's theory is that individuals will find satisfaction to the extent that their work personalities are congruent with the characteristics of their work environment.

Holland's theory has enjoyed widespread attention from both practitioners and researchers. A number of different interest inventories use Holland's typology as their primary organizing schema. For example, the Self-Directed Search (SDS; Holland, 1987) can assist career counselors in assessing the work personalities of their clients. This instrument provides users with scores on each of Holland's six personality dimensions. Supplemental materials such as the Educational Opportunities Finder (Rosen, Holmberg, & Holland, 1994), the Leisure Activities Finder (Holmberg, Rosen, & Holland, 1990), and the Career Options Finder (Holland, 2001) can be used to encourage clients in postassessment career exploration. A parallel instrument, the SDS Career Explorer (Holland & Powell, 1996), has been developed for assessing the career interests of middle school students. Several additional career assessment instruments, such as the Strong Interest Inventory (Harmon, Hansen, Borgen, & Hammer, 1994) and the Skills Confidence Inventory (Betz, Borgen, & Harmon, 1996), provide users with information using Holland's six types as their organizing scheme.

A comprehensive list of occupational titles organized by Holland types is available in the *Dictionary of Holland Occupational Codes* (DHOC; Gottfredson & Holland, 1996). Three-letter Holland codes are provided for more than 12,000 occupational titles, and users can convert from Holland code to DOT code or look up Holland codes in an alphabetized occupational title list. Additionally, the DHOC includes listings of college majors by Holland code and Classification of Instructional Programs (CIP) codes. Career counselors can use the DHOC in a number of different ways. For example, the DHOC can be used as a simple reference with clients looking up Holland codes for particular occupations. Alternatively, a client who knows his or her Holland code can use the DHOC to generate an expanded list of occupational alternatives.

In addition to being widely used in practice, Holland's person-environment typology has been the subject of extensive research. For example, research consistently reveals relations between person-environment congruence and levels of academic major or occupational satisfaction (see Spokane & Cruza-Guet, Chapter 2, this volume). Further, evidence is accumulating supporting the relations between Holland's six work personalities and theoretically consistent measures of nonwork personality such as the NEO-PI (Larson et al., 2002), the 16PF (Bolton, 1985), and the Myers-Briggs Type Indicator (Martin & Bartol, 1986). Other research has shown that the structure of interests is remarkably invariant across gender and racial-ethnic groups (Anderson, Tracey, & Rounds, 1997; Day & Rounds, 1998; Day, Rounds, & Swaney, 1998; Spokane & Cruza-Guet, Chapter 2, this volume).

Holland's typology permeates career counseling theory, research, and practice. This simple and intuitive classification system offers career counselors a structure for discussing interests, abilities, or the world of work. The fact that Holland's system has been so widely adopted is a testament to its utility and simplicity.

World-of-Work Map   ACT, Inc. released an occupational classification system in 1973 called the World-of-Work Map (WWM). This map was the result of research suggesting that two bipolar and bisecting work task dimensions (Data/Ideas and Things/People) underlie Holland's hexagon (Prediger, 1976, 1982; Rounds, 1995). The WWM can be used to suggest occupations to users who enter the map with a set of attribute scores, or it can be used to locate persons on the map based on the degree to which they express an interest in working with data, ideas, people, and things. The position of occupations on the WWM is based on the degree to which they involve working with data, ideas, people, and things.

From an environment perspective, the data dimension includes occupations that require working with facts, records, files, and the use of systematic, concrete procedures. Occupations such as accountant, financial analyst, and medical records administrator are examples of data-intensive occupations. In contrast, the ideas dimension includes occupations such as writer, economist, and psychologist that require the use of abstract theories or that reinforce expression, creativity, and novelty. When overlaid on Holland's hexagon, the Data/Ideas dimension bisects the Enterprising/Conventional and Artistic/Investigative vectors. The Things/People dimension is synonymous with Holland's Realistic and Social themes, respectively. Occupations that map on the Things end of this dimension involve the use of machines, tools, and materials (e.g., construction work and skilled trades). Occupations in the social or educational services sector, on the other hand, map closer to the People end of this dimension.

Two versions of the WWM are commonly encountered (counselor and student versions). The counselor version (Figure 16.1) differs from the student version in that it includes six career clusters corresponding to Holland's six dimensions. The WWM contains 26 career areas. Career areas contain occupations that are relatively homogenous with respect to the work tasks that are required. For example, Career Area Z (Personal Services) contains the occupation Childcare Worker (Domestic). Individuals in this occupation work closely with children, books, toys, games, art materials, personal hygiene products, and food and drink. Other occupations in this career area include Travel Guide and Gaming Occupations Worker. The WWM is also divided into 12 career regions that are primarily used to provide directional interest information to students or clients. For example, a client interested in mechanical activities might be encouraged to explore all occupations in Region 7 (e.g., explore occupations in Career Areas K, L, M, and N).

The WWM can be found in a range of academic and career-related products. It is used as an interpretive device in conjunction with products that contain the Unisex Edition of the ACT Interest Inventory (UNIACT; Swaney, 1995) such as DISCOVER, the Career Planning Survey, EXPLORE, PLAN, and the ACT Assessment. Counselors can use a client's UNIACT scores to suggest career areas that a client might want to explore more thoroughly. Prediger (2002) described how the WWM could also be used to integrate results obtained from other vocational interest inventories, ability self-estimate measures, and measures of work-relevant values. DISCOVER, a computer-based career guidance program, is an excellent example of how assessment results from these three sources can be combined to encourage focused occupational exploration.

The WWM was originally developed using data on more than 13,000 occupations and interest scores for more than 110,000 persons in 570 different occupational groups. The map was revised in 2000 using data from three independent sources:

1. Expert ratings on Holland's six work environments for each of 1,122 occupations in the O*NET database (Rounds, Smith, Hubert, Lewis, & Rivkin, 1998).
2. Job analysis data used in the 1999 electronic *Dictionary of Occupational Titles* database.

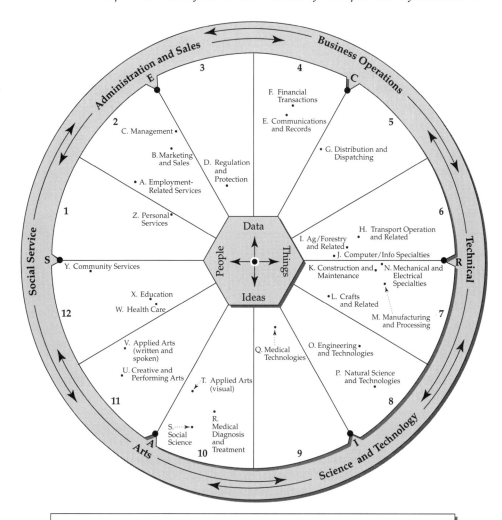

About the Map

- The World-of-Work Map arranges 26 career areas (groups of similar jobs) into 12 regions. Together, the career areas cover all U.S. jobs. Most jobs in a career area are located near the point shown. However, some may be in adjacent Map regions.
- A career area's location is based on its primary work tasks. The four primary work tasks are working with—

  DATA:　Facts, numbers, files, accounts, business procedures.

  IDEAS:　Insights, theories, new ways of saying or doing something—for example, with words, equations, or music.

  PEOPLE:　People you help, serve, inform, care for, or sell things.

  THINGS:　Machines, tools, living things, and materials such as food, wood, or metal.

- Six general types of work ("career clusters") and related Holland types (RIASEC) are shown around the edge of the Map.
  The overlapping career cluster arrows indicate overlap in the occupational content of adjacent career clusters.
- Because they are more strongly oriented to People than Things, the following two career areas in the Science and Technology clusters are located toward the left side of the Map (Region 10): Medical Diagnosis and Treatment and Social Science.

Figure 16.1　ACT's World-of-Work Map (Counselor Version). [Copyright 2000 by ACT, Inc. all rights reserved. Reproduced with permission.]

3. Interest inventory scores (from four different interest inventories) for persons pursuing more than 600 different occupations.

The WWM is a well-researched, user-friendly occupational classification system. Because the UNIACT is a component in other popular products, it is presented to more than five million individuals each year.

The Minnesota Occupational Classification System　The Minnesota Occupational Classification System (MOCS III) (Dawis et al., 1987) was developed to support applications of the Minnesota Theory of Work Adjustment (TWA; see Dawis, Chapter 1, this volume). According to TWA, individuals will experience longevity on the job to the extent to which (1) their needs are being met by the reinforcement system in the work environment and (2) their skills correspond to the work requirements of the job. Career counselors can use the MOCS III to assist their clients with issues that relate to career choice, work adjustment, or job dislocation. Consistent with its theoretical underpinnings, the MOCS III classifies occupations according to the abilities that are required for successful performance in the occupation as well as the reinforcer patterns that are commonly experienced in the work environment. Two previous versions (MOCS, Dawis, & Lofquist, 1974; MOCS II, Dawis, Lofquist, Henly, & Rounds, 1982) were of limited use in that they included a relatively small number of occupations. In contrast, the MOCS III classifies the 1,769 occupational titles present in the 1977 edition of the *Dictionary of Occupational Titles* (USDOL, 1977). The MOCS III organizes occupations by taxons as described next.

The authors of the MOCS III suggest that the ability requirements of an occupation can be divided into 64 categories based on the levels of perceptual (e.g., spatial), cognitive (e.g., verbal), and motor (e.g., manual dexterity) skills needed to perform successfully on the job. In this system, occupations are classified based on whether they require a high, average, or nonsignificant level of these three skills. This ability classification was aided by the use of Occupational Aptitude Patterns (OAPs) derived from the General Aptitude Test Battery (GATB) data (USDOL, 1979) and from job analysts' estimates of ability requirements using GATB nomenclature. Thus, a taxon captures the differential patterns of skills that are required for successful performance in an occupation. For example, an individual working as a loan counselor (Taxon 302) will need average perceptual, high cognitive, and insignificant motor skills to be successful at work. In contrast, a furniture assembler (Taxon 687) relies more heavily on motor skills (average) but may not require highly developed cognitive or perceptual skills.

In addition to capturing the ability requirements of an occupation, taxons group occupations according to the pattern of reinforcers that are typically available in the work environment. Classification based on reinforcer patterns stems from research that identified three underlying reinforcer dimensions (Shubsachs, Rounds, Dawis, & Lofquist, 1978). Internal reinforcers provide for individuals' needs for ability utilization, achievement, creativity, responsibility, autonomy, advancement, recognition, authority, and social status. In contrast, social reinforcers provide for individuals' needs for coworkers, social service activities, and the fulfillment of moral values. Finally, occupations that provide environmental reinforcers will satisfy individuals' needs for supervision, independence, variety, compensation, security, and good working conditions. Occupations in the

MOCS III are classified according to whether they provide a high, average, or nonsignificant level of each of the three classes of reinforcers. When the 27 possible reinforcer patterns are combined with the 27 possible ability requirement patterns, a total of 729 possible taxons exist.

Table 16.2 presents Taxon 617, which includes the occupation of Childcare Attendant. According to the MOCS III, this occupation requires an average level of cognitive abilities, but nonsignificant levels of perceptual and motor abilities. A person working as a Childcare Attendant can expect a high level of reinforcement for social needs but only an average level of reinforcement for his or her internal needs. A summary of the ability requirements and reinforcement system for each taxon is captured in the upper-right corner as the Level code. The numbers 0, 1, and 2 (nonsignificant, average, and high) are used to describe the ability requirements for perceptual, cognitive, and motor abilities and the reinforcer availability for internal, social, and environmental needs, respectively. As is evident from this table, the MOCS III provides a great deal of additional information. For example, data in the DPT column provides information about the degree to which workers must work with data, people, and things, and the FX column gives estimates of the degree to which the work environment tolerates deviations from its ability requirements (i.e., the environment's flexibility—see Dawis, Chapter 1, this volume). Unfortunately, because the MOCS III has not been revised since 1987, some of the other information contained in the taxons is now outdated.

One of the benefits of the MOCS III is that it provides clients with a tool that can assist them in matching their values to occupations that are likely to reinforce those values while simultaneously suggesting the degree to which their skills will match the ability requirements of the job. To use the MOCS III effectively, counselors should be familiar with the instruments that are used in conjunction with this resource (e.g., Minnesota Importance Questionnaire [MIQ] and GATB). One of the main drawbacks of this system is that much of the data used to develop the MOCS III is now dated. Fortunately, much of the work initiated by Dawis and his colleagues 40 years ago (Dawis, England, & Lofquist, 1964) is being updated to serve the career development and counseling needs of O*NET (described next) users. For example, Occupational Reinforcer Patterns (ORPs) have been developed for more than 1,000 occupational units contained in the O*NET (McCloy, Waugh, Medsker, Wall, Rivkin, et al., 1999a), and the Work Importance Profiler was developed to provide clients with an understanding of their work-related needs and values (McCloy, Waugh, Medsker, Wall, Rivkin, et al., 1999b).

OCCUPATIONAL INFORMATION

Once an individual has located a set of occupations using one of the classification systems described above, he or she may be interested in gathering specific information about those occupations. For example, a student might be interested in knowing the starting salary of an occupation that she is considering entering upon graduation. Alternatively, a worker might be interested in researching the training requirements for advancement in his field. Counselors may encourage their clients to use a range of sources of occupational information. Popular sources of information include personal interviews with job encumbents, trade magazines, printed reference materials, or computer-delivered occupational information. A description of widely used occupational information resources follows.

Table 16.2
Taxon 617 from the MOCS III

OCCUPATIONAL REQUIREMENTS

Perceptual Abilities S, P, Q Not Significant	DOT Code			Cognitive Abilities G, V, N Average DOT Profile			Job Des		FX	PR	Motor Abilities K, F, M Not Significant Additional Data				
DOT Title	GRP	DPT	EC	INT	TMP	PHY	DOT	OOH	FX	PR	OAP	SCH	ORP	ORC	INV
Ambulance Attendant	355	374	10	429	589	LM4 5	241	193	MOD	MOD	51	V	NO		
Childcare Attendant, School	355	674	10	429	589	LM4 5	241	323	MOD	MOD	51	V	NO	F	
Psychiatric Aide (1) Assistant therapy aide Asylum attendant Charge attendant Psychiatric attendant	355	377	14	429	589	LM4 5	241	000	MOD	MOD	00	V	NO		
Psychiatric Aide (2) Ward attendant	355	377	14	429	589	LM4 5	241	000	MOD	MOD	00	V	NO		
Teacher, Preschool	092	227	18	429	589	LM4 5	68	000	MOD	MOD	50	V	NO	A	

Internal	ACH AUT STA	AVERAGE	
Social	ALT	HIGH	
Environment	SAF COM	NOT SIGNIFICANT	

OCCUPATIONAL REINFORCERS

GRP: Occupational Group; DPT: Worker function code for data people, things; EC: Extended code (from Dictionary of Occupational Titles) (DOT; USDOL, 1977). INT: Interests; TMP: Temperaments; PHY: Physical demands from DOT (USDOL, 1965). DOT: Page number for occupational description in the DOT (USDOL, 1977). OOH: Page number of occupation in the Occupational Outlook Handbook (USDOL, 1986). FX: Estimated flexibility of the work environment; PR: Occupational prestige level; OAP: Occupational aptitude pattern (where available); SCH: Schedule of reinforcement; ORP: Availability of occupational reinforcer pattern; ORC: Occupational reinforcer cluster (where available); INV: Interest inventory containing occupational scale (where available). © 1987 by Vocational Psychology Research, University of Minnesota. Reproduced with permission.

THE OCCUPATIONAL INFORMATION NETWORK

In 1998, the U.S. Department of Labor introduced the Occupational Information Network (O*NET) as a replacement for the long-established *Dictionary of Occupational Titles* (DOT; USDOL, 1991). The O*NET is a comprehensive system for organizing, describing, distributing, and collecting data on occupations and the workforce. Contrary to popular belief, the O*NET is not just a database of occupational and workforce information. Rather, it is a network of products, databases, services, and projects designed to enhance the availability and usability of occupation and workforce information. As the nation's primary source of occupational information, the O*NET is being developed for multiple audiences and applications. For example, the O*NET may be used by employers to develop job descriptions or to forecast future human resource needs. Alternatively, the O*NET might be used to supplement existing performance evaluation procedures or to establish employee training and development programs. Further, unlike many previous information resources, the O*NET is being developed with the needs of career counselors and their clients in mind.

The O*NET database is available in a number of formats. The format most useful for career counselors and their clients is the O*NET online (http://online.onetcenter.org). On this site, users can search for occupational information using a number of search criteria including keywords, titles, DOT codes, SOC number, or SOC category name. Additionally, users can conduct searches based on the skills required for the occupation. Although the O*NET database contains information about the interests of occupational incumbents and the values and needs that are likely to be met in different occupations, there is currently no way to search for occupations based on this information using the O*NET online. It is hoped that this functionality will be considered for future versions of the O*NET online.

The content model that describes the organizational structure of the O*NET database is presented in Figure 16.2 and can be used as a general guide to the types of information contained in the O*NET database. This model includes both the characteristics of occupations and the people who inhabit those occupations. The content model is organized into six major domains (Occupation Requirements, Occupation Specific Information, Occupation Characteristics, Worker Requirements, Worker Characteristics, and Experience Requirements). Because the content model and its respective domains are so integral to the organization, collection, and dissemination of O*NET occupational and workforce information, we briefly describe each of them here. Additionally, to help the reader understand how the content model is translated into end-user information, we offer examples of how the O*NET online provides information based on the content model.

Occupation Requirements include a set of typical activities that might be experienced by people inhabiting a set of closely related occupations. Several example activities for the occupation of Childcare Workers are shown in Table 16.3 (e.g., Assisting and Caring for Others). This general information is supplemented by Occupation Specific Information, such as the knowledge, skills, and abilities that are required for the occupation, and specific tasks that may be performed on a regular basis. For example, in Table 16.3 we can see that Childcare Workers need to have knowledge of human behavior and performance in addition to knowledge of the principles and methods of training and instruction. Childcare Workers

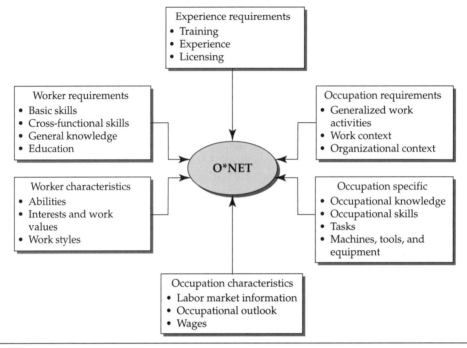

Figure 16.2   O*NET Content Model.

should possess skills in speaking and listening and should be able to interpret other people's reactions. Further, Childcare Workers may care for children in various settings and be expected to organize and participate in recreational or educational activities. Because occupations exist in the context of larger organizations, industries, and economies, the O*NET provides users with helpful information about the industry in which an occupation exists. This information, which includes wage and employment outlook data, is captured in the Occupation Characteristics domain of the content model. This information is provided as a result of collaborative efforts with the Bureau of Labor Statistics, the Department of Commerce, America's Job Bank, and other state and federal employment organizations. When accessing the O*NET database via the Web interface, Occupation Characteristics information is available via a hyperlink to America's Career InfoNet (http://www.acinet.org).

The Worker Requirements domain of the content model includes work-related attributes that may be acquired through the processes of experience or education. This domain complements the job-oriented domain of Occupation Specific Information and defines the knowledge, skills, and educational requirements necessary for an individual to succeed in an occupation. Users are provided with information on the level of experience, training, or education required for an occupation through the use of job zones. Each occupation is classified into one of five zones depending on the level of preparation needed to enter the occupation. Zone 1 describes occupations that require little or no preparation, whereas occupations in Zone 5 require extensive experience and/or extended postsecondary education. The job zone description for the occupation of Childcare Workers is presented in

Table 16.3

Abridged Information Describing the Occupation of
Childcare Worker from the O*NET Online

39-9011.00: Childcare Workers

Attend to children at schools, businesses, private households, and childcare institutions. Perform a variety of tasks, such as dressing, feeding, bathing, and overseeing play.

Tasks:
• Cares for children in institutional settings, such as group homes, nursery schools, private businesses, or schools for the handicapped.
• Organizes and participates in recreational activities.
• Disciplines children and recommends or initiates other measures to control behavior.

Importance	Work Activities	Work Activities Definitions
83	Assisting and caring for others	Providing personal assistance, medical attention, emotional support, or other personal care to others such as coworkers, customers, or patients.
75	Performing general physical activities	Performing physical activities that require considerable use of your arms and legs and moving your whole body, such as climbing, lifting, balancing, walking, stooping, and handling of materials.

Importance	Work Context	Work Context Definitions
100	Contact with others	How much does this job require the worker to be in contact with others (face to face, by telephone, or otherwise) in order to perform it?
70	Indoors, environmentally controlled	How often does this job require working indoors in environmentally controlled conditions?
70	Spend time standing	How much does this job require standing?

Importance	Knowledge	Knowledge Definitions
92	Customer and personal service	Knowledge of principles and processes for providing customer and personal services. This includes customer needs assessment, and meeting quality standards for services.
63	Psychology	Knowledge of human behavior and performance; individual differences in ability, personality, and interests; learning and motivation; psychological research methods; and the assessment and treatment of behavioral and affective disorders.
50	Education and training	Knowledge of principles and methods for curriculum and training design, teaching and instruction for individuals and groups, and the measurement of training effects.

Importance	Abilities	Abilities Definitions
92	Oral expression	The ability to communicate information and ideas in speaking so others will understand.

(continued)

Table 16.3 *(Continued)*

Importance	Abilities	Abilities Definitions
63	Oral comprehension	The ability to listen and understand information and ideas presented through spoken words and sentences.
50	Problem sensitivity	The ability to tell when something is wrong or is likely to go wrong. It does not involve solving the problem, only recognizing there is a problem.

Job Zone Component	Job Zone Component Definitions
Title	Job Zone One: Little or No Preparation Needed
Overall experience	No previous work-related skill, knowledge, or experience is needed for these occupations. For example, a person can become a general office clerk even if he/she has never worked in an office before.
Job training	Employees in these occupations need anywhere from a few days to a few months of training. Usually, an experienced worker could show you how to do the job.
Job zone examples	These occupations involve following instructions and helping others. Examples include bus drivers, forest and conservation workers, general office clerks, home health aides, and waiters/waitresses.
SVP range	(Below 4.0)
Education	These occupations may require a high school diploma or GED certificate. Some may require a formal training course to obtain a license.

Interest	Interests	Interests Definitions
94	Social	Working with, communicating with, and teaching people. These occupations often involve helping or providing service to others.
44	Artistic	Working with forms, designs and patterns. They often require self-expression and the work can be done without following a clear set of rules.
33	Realistic	Work activities that include practical, hands-on problems and solutions. They often deal with plants, animals, and real-world materials like wood, tools, and machinery. Some require working outside, and do not involve a lot of paperwork or working closely with others.
28	Investigative	Working with ideas, and require an extensive amount of thinking. These occupations can involve searching for facts and figuring out problems mentally.
28	Enterprising	Starting up and carrying out projects. These occupations can involve leading people and making many decisions. Sometimes they require risk taking and often deal with business.
28	Conventional	Following set procedures and routines. These occupations can include working with data and details more than with ideas. Usually there is a clear line of authority to follow.

Table 16.3 *(Continued)*

Extent	Work Values	Work Values Definitions
70	Relationships	Occupations that satisfy this work value allow employees to provide service to others and work with coworkers in a friendly noncompetitive environment. Corresponding needs are Coworkers, Moral Values, and Social Service.
52	Working conditions	Occupations that satisfy this work value offer job security and good working conditions. Corresponding needs are Activity, Compensation, Independence, Security, Variety, and Working Conditions.
48	Independence	Occupations that satisfy this work value allow employees to work on their own and make decisions. Corresponding needs are Creativity, Responsibility, and Autonomy.
47	Achievement	Occupations that satisfy this work value are results oriented and allow employees to use their strongest abilities, giving them a feeling of accomplishment. Corresponding needs are Ability Utilization and Achievement.

Extent	Work Needs	Work Needs Definition
94	Social service	Workers on this job have work where they do things for other people.
69	Activity	Workers on this job are busy all the time.
63	Security	Workers on this job have steady employment.
59	Moral values	Workers on this job are never pressured to do things that go against their sense of right and wrong.
56	Company policies and practices	Workers on this job are treated fairly by the company.
56	Working conditions	Workers on this job have good working conditions.

Importance	Skills	Skills Definitions
92	Speaking	Talking to others to convey information effectively.
63	Social perceptiveness	Being aware of others' reactions and understanding why they react as they do.
50	Active listening	Giving full attention to what other people are saying, taking time to understand the points being made, asking questions as appropriate, and not interrupting at inappropriate times.

Note: Importance, extent, and interest ratings in O*NET are measured on different scales. To provide users with more intuitive scores, ratings are standardized to a scale ranging from 0 to 100. Higher values reflect more importance

Table 16.3. Work as Childcare Workers requires little or no preparation, and training typically occurs on the job. It is important to remember that job zone descriptions are designed to capture the experiential and educational requirements of a broad class of occupations. Clients should be encouraged to seek more specific information about the requirements of occupations that they are considering.

The Worker Characteristics domain of the content model describes the enduring characteristics that might influence individuals' performance on the job and their capacity to acquire additional knowledge and skills to advance. Enduring characteristics might include abilities, values, interests, or work styles. Table 16.3 includes a summary of the interest patterns, global work values, and specific work needs of individuals in the field of Childcare. Finally, the Experience Requirements domain of the content model generates information about the typical experiential background of workers in the occupation and the need for licensure or certification.

The data that drive the O*NET database have been collected using at least four separate sources. The primary source of data is job incumbents. Job incumbents completed surveys describing their typical work activities, their work environment, and the skills and knowledge areas that are required for successful performance on the job. Additional data are provided by trained job analysts and organizational representatives. Finally, economic data in the O*NET database are provided by existing databases maintained by the Departments of Commerce, Education, and Labor Statistics.

As mentioned previously, the O*NET was developed with career counselors and their clients in mind. To this end, the O*NET development project has produced a number of career assessment instruments to assist clients in understanding their interests, values, and abilities. The Ability Profiler (USDOL, 2002a; see also Ryan Krane & Tirre, Chapter 14, this volume) is a paper-and-pencil instrument that can be used to assess skills in nine areas (e.g., verbal ability, spatial ability, clerical perception, and manual dexterity). Computer-generated scores can be used to link clients with skill requirements for more than 950 different O*NET occupations. A training manual is available for test administrators, and other documents are provided to aid counselors and clients with interpreting score profiles.

The O*NET Interest Profiler (Lewis & Rivkin, 1999; USDOL, 2000a) is an interest inventory that provides clients with scores on Holland's six work personality dimensions. Like the Self-Directed Search, this instrument can be self-administered and self-scored. The score report booklet includes activities for generating a list of occupational alternatives and orients clients to the concept of job zones (ratings of the degree of preparation or training required for job entry). A personal computer version of the Interest Profiler is now available for downloading at no cost. An added benefit of using the personal computer version of the Interest Profiler is that the score report automatically generates a list of occupations whose occupational interest profiles correlate highly with the interest profile of the client. Finally, a paper-and-pencil version (O*NET Work Importance Locator; USDOL, 2000b) and a personal computer version (O*NET Work Importance Profiler; USDOL, 2002b; McCloy et al., 1999b) of a values clarification exercise are now available. These card sorting exercises are modeled after the MIQ (Rounds, Henly, Dawis, Lofquist, & Weiss, 1981) and can be used to assist clients with understanding their work-related needs and values and how those needs and values correspond to O*NET occupations. Although electronic versions of both the interest and values instruments are currently available, these versions are stand-alone products. As such, clients are not currently able to use their interest or values results to search for occupations using the online version of the O*NET.

In summary, the O*NET is a comprehensive occupational and career guidance network developed and maintained by the National Center for O*NET Development. The O*NET has the potential to provide valuable links between comprehensive occupational information and both new and existing career guidance assessment resources. Like any resource, however, the O*NET has several limitations (N. G. Peterson, Mumford, Borman, Jeanneret, Fleishman, et al., 2001). For example, these authors point out the low response rates that were obtained during initial attempts at securing data from job incumbents. Occupational information provided by incumbents is currently available for only a small subset of the almost 1,000 occupations available on the O*NET. Thus, the current O*NET provides occupational information that combines job incumbent and analyst ratings. Research is needed to assess the relations between incumbent and analyst ratings and to increase incumbent participation rates if the O*NET is to realize its full potential. For the time being, counselors are encouraged to familiarize themselves with the O*NET but to use it cautiously and in combination with other extant sources of career information.

OCCUPATIONAL OUTLOOK HANDBOOK

For more than 50 years, the *Occupational Outlook Handbook* (OOH) has provided individuals with accurate and detailed occupational information (USDOL, 2002c). The OOH includes information about the nature of the work, working conditions, the number and distribution of workers, training required for occupational entry and advancement, and the average earnings of job incumbents in a large number of occupations. What makes the OOH unique among sources of occupational information is the fact that it provides readers with projected five- to seven-year employment outlooks. A recent report (Alpert & Auyer, 2003) suggested that the employment projections provided by the OOH are remarkably accurate. A review of the 1988 to 2000 employment projections found that the direction of change was accurate in more than 70% of cases. The OOH is revised biennially and includes information on more than 250 distinct jobs. Because the OOH includes a detailed narrative for each occupation, related occupations are often grouped together. For example, the OOH contains a single entry for biological and medical scientists even though at least eight separate occupations are covered in the narrative. According to the Bureau of Labor Statistics, the occupations described in the OOH represent approximately 90% of the U.S. workforce.

The OOH is currently available in both print and electronic versions. The Internet version of the OOH (http://www.bls.gov/oco) allows users to browse occupations by occupational clusters or conduct keyword searches. The OOH also includes general information that may be helpful to job seekers or prospective students. For example, the OOH includes a section that outlines strategies for gathering career information and job opportunities from friends and families, societies and professional organizations, and counselors. Additional sections of the OOH provide information on student financial aid and state employment security agencies. Finally, an online version of the OOH has been developed for use with younger children (http://stats.bls.gov/k12/html/edu_over.htm). There are nine sections included for each occupation covered in the OOH: Significant Points; Nature of the Work; Working Conditions; Employment; Training, Other Qualifications, and Advancement; Job Outlook; Earnings; Related Occupations; and Sources of Additional Information. Table 16.4 contains an abridged version of the OOH entry for Childcare Workers.

The Significant Points section serves as an executive summary of noteworthy occupational characteristics and contains only information that is presented in more depth in subsequent sections. The Nature of the Work section provides a snapshot of general work tasks as well as tasks performed by specialists within the discipline. The Working Conditions section includes a description of the physical work environment and the nature of the workweek. This section also includes information related to occupational health risks, unusual physical demands, and special equipment that may be associated with an occupation. The Employment section includes data on the current number of U.S. job incumbents and the distribution of employment across industries or work settings. This section may also include information about full- versus part-time employment and geographic trends observed in the employment statistics. The Training, Other Qualifications, and Advancement section describes the nature and amount of training required for occupational entry, in addition to the nature of training required for advancement in the field. This section also includes information related to certification or licensure of employees.

The Job Outlook section provides readers with detailed information on the future job market for an occupation or set of occupations. This section includes a discussion of factors that may influence occupational growth or decline in the next decade. For example, high rates of turnover in the field of childcare suggest that there will be a continued need for entry-level workers; personal and home care aides are expected to be in great demand as the number of elderly people in our population rises. This section may also support employment projections based on economic trends, projected industry growth or decline, technological changes, or trends in trade relations.

The Earnings section describes typical wage and compensation data such as salaries, commissions, hourly wages, piece rates, tips, or bonuses. The range of earnings is presented to account for differences due to experience, tenure, performance, responsibility, and geographic location. Benefits, such as paid vacation, insurance, childcare, and sick leave are not discussed as thoroughly due to organizational variability. The next section, Related Occupations, includes a list of occupations that are similar with respect to interests, skills, duties, education, and training. Finally, the Sources of Additional Information section includes a list of addresses, phone numbers, and Internet URLs for government agencies, unions, associations, and other organizations related to the occupation.

In addition to providing information about specific occupations, the OOH includes sections devoted to overall trends in the labor force, finding a job and evaluating a job offer, and alternative resources for gathering career and occupational information. The Internet version of the OOH includes links to the Bureau of Labor Statistics and to the *Occupational Outlook Quarterly* (OOQ; http://www.bls.gov/opub/ooq/ooqhome.htm). The OOQ includes articles that may be of interest to career counselors and their clients. Each issue of the OOQ includes an essay detailing a single occupation and a collection of shorter essays on career development

Table 16.4
Abridged Description of the Occupation Childcare Workers
from the *Occupational Outlook Handbook*

Significant Points

- About 2 out of 5 childcare workers are self-employed; most of these are family childcare providers.
- A high school diploma and little or no experience are adequate for many jobs, but training requirements vary from a high school diploma to a college degree.
- High turnover should create good job opportunities.

Nature of the Work

Childcare workers nurture and teach children of all ages in childcare centers, nursery schools, preschools, public schools, private households, family childcare homes, and before- and after-school programs. These workers play an important role in a child's development by caring for the child when parents are at work or away for other reasons. Some parents enroll their children in nursery schools or childcare centers primarily to provide them with the opportunity to interact with other children. In addition to attending to children's basic needs, these workers organize activities that stimulate the children's physical, emotional, intellectual, and social growth. They help children explore their interests, develop their talents and independence, build self-esteem, and learn how to behave with others.

Working Conditions

Preschool or childcare facilities include private homes, schools, religious institutions, workplaces in which employers provide care for employees' children, and private buildings. Individuals who provide care in their own homes generally are called family childcare providers.

Employment

Childcare workers held about 1.2 million jobs in 2000. Many worked part time. About 2 out of 5 childcare workers are self-employed; most of these are family childcare providers.

Training, Other Qualifications, and Advancement

The training and qualifications required of childcare workers vary widely. Each state has its own licensing requirements that regulate caregiver training, ranging from a high school diploma, to community college courses, to a college degree in child development or early-childhood education. Many states require continuing education for workers in this field. However, state requirements often are minimal. Childcare workers generally can obtain employment with a high school diploma and little or no experience. Local governments, private firms, and publicly funded programs may have more demanding training and education requirements.

Job Outlook

High turnover should create good job opportunities for childcare workers. Many childcare workers leave the occupation each year to take other jobs, to meet family responsibilities, or for other reasons. Qualified persons who are interested in this work should have little trouble finding and keeping a job. Opportunities for nannies should be especially good, as many workers prefer not to work in other people's homes.

(continued)

Table 16.4 *(Continued)*

Earnings

Pay depends on the educational attainment of the worker and the type of establishment. Although the pay generally is very low, more education usually means higher earnings. Median hourly earnings of wage and salary childcare workers were $7.43 in 2000. The middle 50 percent earned between $6.30 and $9.09. The lowest 10 percent earned less than $5.68, and the highest 10 percent earned more than $10.71. Median hourly earnings in the industries employing the largest numbers of childcare workers in 2000 were as follows:

Residential care	$8.71
Elementary and secondary schools	8.52
Civic and social associations	6.98
Child daycare services	6.74
Miscellaneous amusement and recreation services	6.65

Related Occupations

Childcare work requires patience; creativity; an ability to nurture, motivate, teach, and influence children; and leadership, organizational, and administrative skills. Others who work with children and need these qualities and skills include teacher assistants; teachers—preschool, kindergarten, elementary, middle, and secondary; and special education teachers.

Sources of Additional Information

For eligibility requirements and a description of the Child Development Associate credential, contact:

• Council for Professional Recognition, 2460 16th St. NW., Washington, DC 20009-3575.
Internet: http://www.cdacouncil.org

For eligibility requirements and a description of the Certified Childcare Professional designation, contact:

• National Childcare Association, 1016 Rosser St., Conyers, GA 30012.
Internet: http://www.nccanet.org

State Departments of Human Services or Social Services can supply state regulations and training requirements for childcare workers.

Source: Occupational Outlook Handbook

programs, college majors, employment trends, and other topics that would be useful to the practicing career counselor. In short, the OOH is one of the most widely available and widely used occupational information resources in the United States.

USING COMPUTERS TO ACCESS CAREER INFORMATION

Computers have been a part of career counseling and guidance for more than 30 years. In the 1960s, for example, the U.S. Department of Labor funded a project to develop a mainframe computer program that could provide up-to-date information about the state labor market and state educational opportunities. In the 1970s, computer-assisted career guidance systems (CACGS) such as SIGI (http://www.ets.org/sigi) and DISCOVER (http://www.act.org/discover) were developed. These guidance systems can administer and score inventories and provide clients with an explanation of their results. More comprehensive systems integrate results from multiple career assessment devices to suggest academic and occupational alternatives. Additionally, these systems may provide common psychoeducational content such as descriptions of effective job search strategies or decision-making skills. Research clearly documents the beneficial effects of computer-assisted guidance products on a range of outcomes (Oliver & Spokane, 1988; Whiston, Sexton, & Lasoff, 1998).

The rapid growth of communication technologies such as the Internet has changed both the nature of work (Gore, Leuwerke, & Krumboltz, 2002; Grantham, 2000) and the practice of career guidance and counseling (Chartrand & Oliver, 2000; Gore & Leuwerke, 2000). A recent GOOGLE search of the term *career counseling,* for example, revealed more than 250,000 web sites. Given the difficulty of reviewing such a massive amount of information and the transient nature of many sites, we limit our discussion to two computer-assisted guidance systems that are currently available on the Internet (SIGI Plus and DISCOVER).

SIGI Plus   SIGI Plus (http://www.ets.org/sigi) represents the most recent version of a system that was originally developed by Martin Katz (1963). Katz's System for Interactive Guidance Information (SIGI) was developed to help students identify occupations based on an assessment of their work values and skills. SIGI Plus continues to provide career clients with up-to-date career information that is integrated with results from self-assessment of work values, skills, and interests.

SIGI Plus is organized into nine sections. In the Introduction section, users are provided with an overview of the program. Through an orientation to the different functions of the program, users can identify which functions apply to their current career development needs. In the Self-Assessment section, clients can complete inventories to help them clarify their work values, interests, and skill confidence. Users can then search for occupational titles based on the results of these inventories or by selecting a two- or four-year college major. Clients can also view detailed occupational information in the Information section of the program. In the Skills section, clients are able to rate the degree to which they believe they have the specific skills required for occupations covered by SIGI Plus. This section also contains a management skills self-appraisal survey. Students can identify typical paths for preparing for any of SIGI Plus's occupations in the Preparing section. This section also provides individuals with an opportunity to consider factors that relate to preparing for work (e.g., finding time and money, staying motivated). A section on Coping helps students or clients to consider issues related to preparing for, or changing, a career, such as arranging for childcare or relocating.

One of the strengths of SIGI Plus lies in the Deciding section of the program. In this section, students are able to rate the degree to which they believe an occupation will provide them with the rewards they find desirable and will allow them to engage in activities in which they are interested. Additionally, users are asked to rate the degree to which they believe they have the skills necessary to be successful on the job and to rate their overall chances of completing the educational requirements and successfully securing a job offer. Users can conduct this self-appraisal/estimation for multiple occupations for a side-by-side comparison. Finally, SIGI Plus includes a Next Steps section in which users consider issues such as getting more information, developing a resume, or applying for jobs. As with most computerized career guidance applications, users' assessment information is saved in a database for use during subsequent visits.

Research generally supports the efficacy of stand-alone personal computer versions of the SIGI Plus system, and users have favorable ratings of their experience with the program (Kivlighan, Johnston, Hogan, & Mauer, 1994; G. W. Peterson, Ryan-Jones, Sampson, Reardon, & Shahnasarian, 1994). Research is needed, however, to assess the benefits of using newer Internet-based CACGSs in general and SIGI Plus in particular. SIGI Plus includes several limitations. Very little documentation exists on the development or psychometric properties of the instruments used to assess interests, values, or skills. This is particularly concerning since some of the inventories are short. Additionally, there is no documentation describing the computer algorithms that are used to make recommendations (e.g., recommended occupations or majors) to users based on their career assessment results.

DISCOVER   The Internet version of DISCOVER (http://www.act.org/discover) is the modern-day incarnation of JoAnn Harris-Bowlsbey's Computer Vocational Information System (CVIS; Harris, 1970). Like SIGI Plus, DISCOVER includes self-assessment inventories, searchable academic and occupational databases, and information to assist a client who is actively searching for employment. The anchor self-assessment instrument in DISCOVER is the Unisex Edition of the ACT Interest Inventory (UNIACT; Swaney, 1995). This instrument measures interests using the six Holland types and ACT's World-of-Work Map. Extensive norms are available, allowing this inventory to be used by high school students, college students, and adults. Additional instruments available in DISCOVER include the Inventory of Work-Relevant Abilities (IWRA; ACT, 2001) and the Inventory of Work-Relevant Values (Prediger & Staples, 1996). An added advantage of DISCOVER is that users can utilize the search capabilities of the program by entering assessment scores from non-ACT inventories, such as the Strong Interest Inventory (Harmon et al., 1994) or the Career Ability Placement Survey (Knapp, Knapp, & Michael, 1977).

DISCOVER has seven primary modules: Home (which provides orientation and planning information), Inventories, Occupations, Majors, Schools, Job Search, and My Portfolio. In addition to orienting the user to the program, the Home section includes the Plan My Path pages that offer suggested DISCOVER paths in response to users' self-assessment of their current career development needs. As mentioned previously, the Inventories section allows users to complete interest, values, or skills self-estimate inventories or to enter results from other skills or interest inventories. Comprehensive search algorithms in the Occupations module allow users to search for occupations based on assessment results, the WWM, or a host of other characteristics such as keyword, academic major, income, or educational level. Equally comprehensive searches are possible in the Majors and Schools modules of the program. The Job Search module is populated primarily by static educational content that provides information on topics such as preparing a resume, preparing for an interview, and securing apprenticeships. The My Portfolio module allows users to manage and modify information they have saved during visits to DISCOVER.

An Internet version of DISCOVER for middle school students may also be of interest to career counselors who plan to work in a school system. Users can complete middle school versions of the UNIACT and the IWRA and can explore occupations based on results from those inventories. With counselor and parent involvement, students can establish a course plan for high school and can gain an understanding of the relations among their goals, high school course work, and occupations.

One of the main advantages of DISCOVER is the extensive documentation that exists to assist clients, counselors, counselors in training, and DISCOVER site administrators. For example, counselor aids include printed versions of the assessment instruments available in DISCOVER and exercises to assist clients at various levels of career choice and implementation (e.g., practice job application, action plan exercise). Additionally, counselors or clients can download complete printed copies of lists of occupations, majors, and schools for review off-line.

There is a growing body of literature that supports the beneficial effects of personal computer versions of DISCOVER. For example, DISCOVER is associated with increases in occupational decidedness and certainty (Fukuyama, Robert, Neimeyer, Nevill, & Metzler, 1988) and career maturity (Langley & Schepers, 1990; Luzzo & Pierce, 1996). Findings from other studies suggest that the use of computer-assisted guidance systems in general can be enhanced if their use is combined with individual or group career counseling, leading some authors to discourage their use in isolation (Barnes & Herr, 1998; Brown et al., 2003). Evidence suggests that the effects of computer use on outcomes may depend on variables such as Holland type (Lenz, Reardon, & Sampson, 1993) or presenting concern (Gati, Saka, & Krausz, 2001; Peterson et al., 1994). For example, Lenz and his colleagues discovered that clients who scored high on the Social and Enterprising Holland (people-oriented) dimensions rated computer-based career interventions as less useful compared to clients who scored low on these Holland dimensions. Further, results from a study by Peterson and his colleagues suggest that computers may be more useful helping clients identify career alternatives if those clients express a need for information and are in the early stages of career decision making. Taken together, these data suggest that although computer guidance systems can be an integral and effective component of career counseling practice, they should not be used indiscriminately or in isolation. As with SIGI Plus, research investigating the Internet version of DISCOVER is lacking.

ETHICAL ISSUES IN THE USE OF COMPUTERS IN CAREER COUNSELING

Recently, a great deal of attention has been focused on the use of the Internet in career counseling. Gore and Leuwerke (2000), among others (Herr, 1996; Lent, 1996; Watts, 1996), encourage counselors to fashion novel services that take advantage of advances in computer and communication technologies, and a growing number of career counselors are heeding that call (e.g., see Clark, Horan, Tompkins-Bjorkman, Kovalski, & Hackett, 2000; Walz & Reedy, 2000). Other authors have focused on how computers and the Internet have changed the landscape of career assessment (Chartrand & Oliver, 2000; Gati & Saka, 2001; Tinsley,

2000; Wall, 2000). Web applications of career counseling may range from formal online assessment, to information-only pages that educate users about a specific topic, to real-time digital audio/video career counseling. Fortunately, the increased use of the Internet for career and personal counseling purposes has been accompanied by thoughtful guides, critical evaluations, and discussions of the ethical issues that are unique to these practices (Bloom, 1998; DuMez, 2000; Harris-Bowlsbey et al., 2002).

The use of the Internet and other computer-enhanced technologies (e.g., teleconferencing) to provide career counseling and career-information services gives rise to unique legal and ethical questions. For example, most state counselor and psychologist licensure laws restrict or limit out-of-state practice. Are licensed career counselors eligible to provide services via the Internet to clients who do not reside in their practice jurisdiction? Alternatively, can career counselors guarantee the confidentiality of information transmitted electronically? Is a career counselor responsible for the quality or accuracy of information provided on linked web pages? Are electronically administered career assessment devices as valid for the same uses as are the paper-and-pencil versions? The professional associations that govern the practice of counseling and psychology have made concerted efforts to begin to address these issues in revisions of their ethics codes. The ethics codes of the American Counseling Association (ACA, 1999), the National Board for Certified Counselors (NBCC, 1997), the National Career Development Association (NCDA, 1997), and the American Psychological Association (APA, 1997, 2003) should be consulted by career counselors intending to use technology in their practice.

Robinson and his colleagues (Robinson, Meyer, Prince, McLean, & Low, 2000) outlined both the advantages and disadvantages of providing career information on the Internet. Advantages include having easy access to the information, having a variety of sources to choose from, and having access to sources of information that are easily updated. Unfortunately, there are an equal number of disadvantages to accessing career information on the Internet. Perhaps the most serious concern has to do with the quality of the information being provided. Whereas printed documents typically undergo an editorial or peer review process, anyone is permitted to publish materials on the Internet without regard to their accuracy. It is up to career counselors to evaluate the quality and appropriateness of the information resources they use with their clients. Counselors are encouraged to consult the standards developed by the Association of Computer-based Systems for Career Information (ACSCI). This organization was founded in 1978 to advance the use and quality of career information available through electronic means. Stressing core values such as accuracy, relevancy, bias, and user support, ACSCI strives to ensure that counselors and clients have access to the highest quality and most accurate career information and services available. In addition to the ACSCI standards, counselors using Internet-based career information resources are encouraged to review the NCDA's statement on using the Internet for the provision of career information (NCDA, 1997).

USING CAREER INFORMATION IN COUNSELING

Beginning career counselors may find themselves relying too heavily on the use of formal career assessment instruments and sources of occupational information. These structured psychoeducational processes ease the stress associated with having to "fill the counseling hour." Too often, however, assessment and career information is included in the counseling process without a systematic appraisal of the client's needs. Providing too much information at the wrong time might overwhelm a client. Moreover, relying solely on formal assessment and sources of career information oversimplifies the complex process of career decision making. Gysbers and his colleagues (Gysbers, Heppner, & Johnston, 2003) offer several excellent suggestions for evaluating the client's need for information within the career counseling session. These authors aptly note that many career clients request specific information or experiences. For example, in some career counseling centers, it is not uncommon for clients to come in specifically asking to "take the test." Alternatively, many clients present because of a perceived need for specific career information. Gysbers and his colleagues suggest that career counselors must acquire knowledge of the type of information that is available and how, when, and in what form to provide it. For example, these authors encourage counselors to seek continuing education to remain knowledgeable of new sources of occupational information. Additionally, these authors highlight the important role professional organizations (e.g., NCDA) and journals (e.g., *Career Development Quarterly*) play in making professionals aware of new resources.

How and when career counselors choose to introduce career information into the counseling process will depend on many factors, including the counselor's theoretical orientation, the developmental level of the client, the client's presenting concern, the stage of counseling, and the availability of information. Gysbers and his colleagues (Gysbers et al., 2003) encourage counselors to consider why they are introducing career information. For example, information may be introduced to stimulate further exploration, to motivate a client to action, or to provide confirmation of what the client already suspects is true. Further, these authors suggest that it is important to consider timing issues when considering the use of career information in counseling. Assessing the client's level of need for information throughout the counseling process will help counselors avoid the potentially negative consequences of providing a client who is in information overload with even more information.

SUMMARY

Occupational classification provides structure to the diverse world of work. Career counselors who are familiar with a number of different classification systems will be able to select from among those systems when working with clients with different needs and expectations. Counselors are encouraged to effectively teach their clients the meaning and uses of occupational classification systems, when appropriate, to promote career development and exploration. Systematic occupational classification also allows us to provide clients with organized sources of occupational information such as the OOH and the O*NET. Broadly speaking, career information can take the form of self-assessment interpretation, printed or electronic occupational information, portrayal of occupations in the media, job availability data, or information acquired through discussions with friends, family, or job incumbents. Career counselors today are faced with an overwhelming amount of career information that describes a rapidly changing world of work. Moreover, career counselors now find themselves working with technologically sophisticated clients who are adept at accessing information online but who are not necessarily skilled at evaluating the quality of that information. Career counselors must be skilled in knowing where to access academic and career-related information, how to evaluate its quality, and whether or when to introduce it into the counseling process.

REFERENCES

ACT. (2001). *Career Planning Survey: Technical manual.* Iowa City, IA: Author.

Alpert, A., & Auyer, J. (2003, Spring). The 1988–2000 employment projects: How accurate were they? *Occupational Outlook Quarterly,* 2–21.

American Counseling Association. (1999). *Ethical standards for Internet on-line counseling.* Alexandria, VA: Author.

American Psychological Association. (1997). *APA statement on services by telephone, teleconferencing, and internet.* Washington, DC: Author.

American Psychological Association. (2003). *Ethical principles of psychologists and code of conduct.* Washington, DC: Author.

Anderson, M. Z., Tracey, T. J., & Rounds, J. (1997). Examining the invariance of Holland's vocational interest model across gender. *Journal of Vocational Behavior, 50,* 349–364.

Barnes, J. A., & Herr, E. L. (1998). The effects of interventions on career progress. *Journal of Career Development, 24,* 179–193.

Betz, N. E., Borgen, F. H., & Harmon, L. W. (1996). *Skills Confidence Inventory: Applications and technical guide.* Palo Alto, CA: Consulting Psychologists Press.

Bloom, J. W. (1998). The ethical practice of Web Counseling. *British Journal of Guidance and Counseling, 26,* 53–59.

Bolton, B. (1985). Discriminant analysis of Holland's occupational types using the Sixteen Personality Factor Questionnaire. *Journal of Vocational Behavior, 27,* 210–217.

Boyce, A., & Rainie, L. (2002, July). *Online job hunting. Pew Internet project data memo.* Retrieved April 15, 2003, from http://www.pewinternet.org/reports.

Brown, S. D., Ryan Krane, N. E., Brecheisen, J., Castelino, P., Budisin, I., Miller, M., et al. (2003). Critical ingredients of career choice interventions: More analyses and new hypotheses. *Journal of Vocational Behavior, 62,* 411–428.

Chartrand, J. M., & Oliver, L. W. (2000). Introduction to the special issue: Career assessment and the Internet. *Journal of Career Assessment, 8,* 1–2.

Clark, G., Horan, J. J., Tompkins-Bjorkman, A., Kovalski, T., & Hackett, G. (2000). Interactive career counseling on the Internet. *Journal of Career Assessment, 8,* 85–94.

Crites, J. O. (1969). *Vocational psychology: The study of vocational behavior and development.* New York: McGraw-Hill.

Dawis, R. V., Dohm, T. E., Lofquist, L. H., Chartrand, J. M., & Due, A. M. (1987). *Minnesota occupational classification system III.* Minneapolis: University of Minnesota, Vocational Psychology Research.

Dawis, R. V., England, G. W., & Lofquist, L. H. (1964). *A Theory of Work Adjustment. Minnesota Studies in Vocational Rehabilitation* (No. XV, 1–27). Minneapolis: Industrial Relations Center.

Dawis, R. V., & Lofquist, L. H. (1974). *Minnesota occupational classification system.* Minneapolis: University of Minnesota, Vocational Psychology Research.

Dawis, R. V., Lofquist, L. H., Henly, G. A., & Rounds, J. B., Jr. (1982). *Minnesota occupational classification system* (II). Minneapolis: University of Minnesota, Vocational Psychology Research.

Day, S. X., & Rounds, J. (1998). Universality of vocational interest structure among racial and ethnic minorities. *American Psychologist, 53,* 728–736.

Day, S. X., Rounds, J., & Swaney, K. (1998). The structure of vocational interest structure among racial and ethnic minorities. *American Psychologist, 53,* 728–736.

DuMez, E. (2000). Cyberpaths to ethical competence. In J. W. Bloom & G. R. Walz (Eds.), *Cybercounseling and cyberlearning: Strategies and resources for the millennium* (pp. 379–401). Alexandria, VA: American Counseling Association.

Fukuyama, M. A., Robert, B. S., Neimeyer, G. J., Nevill, D. D., & Metzler, M. A. (1988). Effects of DISCOVER on career self-efficacy and decision-making of undergraduates. *Career Development Quarterly, 37,* 56–62.

Gati, I., & Saka, N. (2001). Internet-based versus paper-and-pencil assessment: Measuring career decision-making difficulties. *Journal of Career Assessment, 9,* 397–416.

Gati, I., Saka, N., & Krausz, M. (2001). "Should I use a computer-assisted career guidance system?" It depends on where your career decision-making difficulties lie. *British Journal of Guidance and Counseling, 29,* 301–321.

Gore, P. A., Jr., & Leuwerke, W. C. (2000). Information technology for career assessment on the Internet. *Journal of Career Assessment, 8,* 3–20.

Gore, P. A., Jr., Leuwerke, W. C., & Krumboltz, J. D. (2002). Technologically enriched and boundaryless lives: Time for a paradigm upgrade. *Counseling Psychologist, 30,* 847–857.

Gottfredson, G. D., & Holland, J. L. (1996). *Dictionary of Holland occupational codes* (3rd ed.). Odessa, FL: Psychological Assessment Resources.

Grantham, C. (2000). *The future of work: The promise of the new digital work society.* New York: McGraw-Hill.

Gysbers, N. C., Heppner, M. J., & Johnston, J. A. (2003). *Career counseling: Processes, issues, and techniques.* New York: Allyn & Bacon.

Harmon, L. W., Hansen, J. C., Borgen, F. H., & Hammer, A. L. (1994). *Strong Interest Inventory: Applications and technical guide.* Palo Alto, CA: Consulting Psychologists Press.

Harris, J. (1970). The computerization of vocational information. In D. E. Super (Ed.), *Computer-assisted counseling* (pp. 46–59). New York: Columbia University, Teachers College.

Harris-Bowlsbey, J. H., Dikel, M. R., & Sampson, J. P., Jr. (2002). *The Internet: A tool for career planning. A guide to using the Internet in career planning.* Tulsa, OK: National Career Development Association.

Herr, E. L. (1996). Perspectives on ecological context, social policy, and career guidance. *Career Development Quarterly, 45,* 5–19.

Holland, J. L. (1987). *The Self-Directed Search professional manual.* Odessa, FL: Psychological Assessment Resources.

Holland, J. L. (1997). *Making vocational choices:: A theory of vocational personalities and work environments* (3rd ed.). Odessa, FL: Psychological Assessment Resources.

Holland, J. L. (2001). *Career options finder.* Odessa, FL: Psychological Assessment Resources.

Holland, J. L., & Powell, A. B. (1996). *SDS career explorer.* Odessa, FL: Psychological Assessment Resources.

Holmberg, K., Rosen, D., & Holland, J. L. (1990). *The leisure activities finder.* Odessa, FL: Psychological Assessment Resources.

Katz, M. R. (1963). *Decisions and values.* New York: College Entrance Examination Board.

Kivlighan, D. J., Jr., Johnston, J. A., Hogan, R. S., & Mauer, E. (1994). Who benefits from computerized career counseling? *Journal of Counseling and Development, 72,* 289–292.

Knapp, R. R., Knapp, L., & Michael, W. B. (1977). Stability and concurrent validity of the Career Placement Survey (CAPS) against the DAT and the GATB. *Educational and Psychological Measurement, 37,* 1081–1085.

Langley, R., & Schepers, J. M. (1990). Computerized career guidance: An evaluation of the DISCOVER system. *South African Journal of Psychology, 20,* 287–293.

Larson, L. M., Rottinghaus, P. J., & Borgen, F. H. (2002). Meta-analyses of Big Six and Big Five personality factors. *Journal of Vocational Behavior, 61,* 217–239.

Lent, R. W. (1996). Career counseling, science, and policy: Revitalizing our paradigms and roles. *Career Development Quarterly, 45,* 58–64.

Lenz, J. G., Reardon, R. C., & Sampson, J. P. (1993). Holland's theory and effective use of computer-assisted career guidance systems. *Journal of Career Development, 19,* 245–253.

Lewis, P., & Rivkin, D. (1999). *Development of the O*NET Interest Profiler.* Raleigh, NC: National Center for O*NET Development.

Luzzo, D. A., & Pierce, G. (1996). Effects of DISCOVER on the career maturity of middle school students. *Career Development Quarterly, 45,* 170–172.

Martin, D. C., & Bartol, K. M. (1986). Holland's Vocational Preference Inventory and the Myers-Briggs Type Indicator as predictors of vocational choice among master's of business administration. *Journal of Vocational Behavior, 29,* 51–65.

McCloy, R., Waugh, G., Medsker, G., Wall, J., Rivkin, D., & Lewis, P. (1999a). *Determining the occupational reinforcer patterns for O*NET occupational units.* Raleigh, NC: National Center for O*NET Development Employment Security Commission.

McCloy, R., Waugh, G., Medsker, G., Wall, J., Rivkin, D., & Lewis, P. (1999b). *Development of the O*NET paper-and-pencil Work Importance Locator.* Raleigh, NC: National Center for O*NET Development Employment Security Commission.

National Board of Certified Counselors. (1997). *Standards for the ethical practice of Web-Counseling.* Greensboro, NC: Author.

National Career Development Association. (1997). *NCDA guidelines for the use of the Internet for provision of career information and planning services.* Columbus, OH: Author.

Oliver, L. W., & Spokane, A. R. (1988). Career intervention outcome: What contributes to client gain? *Journal of Counseling Psychology, 35,* 447–462.

Parsons, F. (1909). *Choosing your vocation.* Boston: Houghton Mifflin.

Peterson, G. W., Ryan-Jones, R. E., Sampson, J. P., Jr., Reardon, R. C., & Shahnasarian, M. (1994). A comparison of the effectiveness of three computer-assisted career guidance systems: DISCOVER, SIGI, and SIGI PLUS. *Computers in Human Behavior, 10,* 189–198.

Peterson, N. G., Mumford, M. D., Borman, W. C., Jeanneret, P. R., Fleishman, E. A., Levin, K. Y., et al. (2001). Understanding work using the Occupational Information Network (O*NET). *Personnel Psychology, 54,* 451–492.

Prediger, D. J. (1976). A world-of-work map for career exploration. *Vocational Guidance Quarterly, 24,* 198–208.

Prediger, D. J. (1982). Dimensions underlying Holland's hexagon. Missing link between interests and occupations? *Journal of Vocational Behavior, 21,* 259–287.

Prediger, D. J. (2002). Abilities, interests, and values: Their assessment and their integration via the World-of-Work Map. *Journal of Career Assessment, 10,* 209–232.

Prediger, D. J., & Staples, J. G. (1996). *Linking occupational attribute preferences to occupations. ACT Research Report Series (96-3).* Iowa City, IA: American College Testing.

Robinson, N. K., Meyer, D., Prince, J. P., McLean, C., & Low, R. (2000). Mining the Internet for career information: A model approach for college students. *Journal of Career Assessment, 8,* 37–54.

Rosen, D., Holmberg, K., & Holland, J. L. (1994). *The Educational Opportunities Finder.* Odessa, FL: Psychological Assessment Resources.

Rounds, J. B. (1995). Vocational interests: Evaluating structural hypotheses. In D. J. Lubinski & R. V. Dawis (Eds.), *Assessing individual differences in human behavior: New concepts, methods, and findings* (pp. 177–232). Palo Alto, CA: Consulting Psychologists Press.

Rounds, J. B., Henly, G. A., Dawis, R. V., Lofquist, L. H., & Weiss, D. J. (1981). *Manual for the Minnesota Importance Questionnaire: A measure of vocational needs and values.* Minneapolis: University of Minnesota, Department of Psychology.

Rounds, J. B., Smith, T., Hubert, L., Lewis, P., & Rivkin, D. (1998). *Development of occupational interest profiles (OIPs) for the O*NET.* Raleigh: Southern Assessment Research and Development Center, Employment Security Commission of North Carolina.

Shubsachs, A. P. W., Rounds, J. B., Dawis, R. V., & Lofquist, L. H. (1978). Perceptions of work reinforcer systems: Factor structure. *Journal of Vocational Behavior, 13,* 54–62.

Swaney, K. B. (1995). *Technical manual: Revised UNISEX edition of the ACT interest inventory (UNIACT).* Iowa City, IA: American College Testing.

Tinsley, H. E. A. (2000). Technological magic, social change, and counseling rituals: The future of career assessment. *Journal of Career Assessment, 8,* 339–350.

U.S. Department of Labor. (1939). *Dictionary of occupational titles* (1st ed.). Washington, DC: U.S. Government Printing Office.

U.S. Department of Labor. (1977). *Dictionary of occupational titles* (3rd ed.). Washington, DC: U.S. Government Printing Office.

U.S. Department of Labor. (1979). *Manual of the general aptitude test battery.* Washington, DC: U.S. Government Printing Office.

U.S. Department of Labor. (1991). *Dictionary of occupational titles* (4th ed. rev.). Washington, DC: U.S. Government Printing Office.

U.S. Department of Labor. (1999). *Revising the Standard Occupational Classification System* (Report No. 929). Washington, DC: U.S. Government Printing Office.

U.S. Department of Labor. (2000a). *Interest profiler: Users guide.* Washington, DC: U.S. Government Printing Office.

U.S. Department of Labor. (2000b). *Work importance locator: Users guide.* Washington, DC: U.S. Government Printing Office.

U.S. Department of Labor. (2002a). *Ability profiler: Administration manual.* Washington, DC: U.S. Government Printing Office.

U.S. Department of Labor. (2002b). *Work importance profiler: Users guide.* Washington, DC: U.S. Government Printing Office.

U.S. Department of Labor. (2002c). *Occupational outlook handbook.* (2002–2003 ed.). Indianapolis, IN: JIST Works.

U.S. Office of Management & Budget. (1999). *North American Industry Classification System.* Indianapolis, IN: JIST Works.

Wall, J. E. (2000). Technology-delivered assessment: Power, problems, and promise. In J. W. Bloom & G. R. Walz (Eds.), *Cybercounseling and cyberlearning: Strategies and resources for the millennium* (pp. 237–251). Alexandria, VA: American Counseling Association.

Walz, G. R., & Reedy, L. S. (2000). The international career development library: The use of virtual libraries to promote counselor learning. In J. W. Bloom & C. G. Walz (Eds.), *Cybercounseling and cyberlearning: Strategies and resources for the millennium* (pp. 143–160). Alexandria, VA: American Counseling Association.

Watts, A. G. (1996). Toward a policy for lifelong career development: A transatlantic perspective. *Career Development Quarterly, 45,* 41–53.

Whiston, S. C., Sexton, T. L., & Lasoff, D. L. (1998). Career-intervention outcome: A replication and extension of Oliver and Spokane (1988). *Journal of Counseling Psychology, 45,* 150–165.

CAREER INTERVENTIONS ACROSS THE LIFE SPAN

CHAPTER 17

Promoting Career Development and Aspirations in School-Age Youth

Sherri L. Turner and Richard T. Lapan

T
HE PRIMARY GOAL of this chapter is to discuss how professional school counselors, career counselors, career educators, and psychologists can support
the career development and aspirations of K-12 students so that the students are in a more advantageous position to create satisfying, productive, and
self-fulfilling adult lives. While limited research exists concerning the career development of young children, relationships among personality variables, vocational interests, vocational aspirations, and career orientations have been found
in children as young as 8 years old (Whiston & Brecheisen, 2002). Several studies
have yielded evidence supporting the hypothesized relationships among personality and career variables in adolescence as well (Creed, Patton, & Bartrum, 2002;
L. M. Larson & Borgen, 2002). The results of these and other investigations (see
Rojewski, Chapter 6, this volume) have led researchers and practitioners toward
the goal of more thoroughly understanding the career development needs of this
population and toward establishing the underpinnings of empirically supported
career interventions.

Career development, as the word suggests, is a developmental learning process
that evolves throughout our lives (McDaniels & Gysbers, 1992). The term also pertains to the interventions used by practitioners to facilitate age- and situation-
appropriate career behaviors across a person's lifetime (Herr, 2001). We contend
that both aspects of career development need to be considered when preparing
school-age youth to creatively and proactively manage the significant challenges
they face. School-age youth need to learn a set of skills that will assist them in
their efforts to establish satisfying life structures across their life spans (Super,
Savickas, & Super, 1996).

At the heart of providing career development services to children and adolescents is the recognition of their need to develop more adaptive, resilient, and
proactive approaches to their present situations and possible future career
selves (Markus & Nurius, 1986; Savickas, 1997). Lapan (2004) argued that youth

are more likely to develop such an approach to the present and future if they can accomplish the following separate, but interrelated, tasks:

1. Develop positive career-related self-efficacy expectations and attributional styles (Albert & Luzzo, 1999; Lent, Brown, & Hackett, 1994, 2000).
2. Form a vocational identity by engaging in more self-directed career exploration and planning activities, setting effective educational and career goals, and making a commitment to reach these goals (Flum & Blustein, 2000).
3. Learn effective social, prosocial, and work readiness skills and behaviors (Bloch, 1996).
4. Construct a better understanding of self, the world of work, and how to best fit in the work world (Parsons, 1909).
5. Crystallize personally valued vocational interests (Strong, 1927).
6. Be empowered to achieve academically and become self-regulated learners (Arbona, Chapter 22, this volume; Lapan, Kardash, & Turner, 2002).

Although drawn from different theoretical perspectives, young people who accomplish these tasks gain adaptive advantages as they enter a world of work characterized by rapid and unpredictable changes (Savickas, 1995), a high demand for personal responsibility and self-determination (Watts, 1996), and an expectation that people should be both agentic and adapt flexibly to new challenges without losing their core identities (Flum & Blustein, 2000).

CAREER DEVELOPMENT TASKS

In the following sections, research supporting each of these career developmental tasks is briefly reviewed and summarized. Then, career interventions that can be used to promote the career development of K-12 youth are reviewed. These interventions can offer a basis for providing contextually responsive career counseling for all young people (Lapan, 2004; Lee, 2001).

DEVELOPING POSITIVE CAREER-RELATED SELF-EFFICACY EXPECTATIONS AND ATTRIBUTIONAL STYLES

Self-efficacy expectations refer to "beliefs concerning one's ability to successfully perform a given behavior" (Betz, 1994, p. 35). Self-efficacy is task-specific; in the context of this chapter, self-efficacy refers to a person's belief that he or she can successfully engage in academic or career-related tasks (Bandura, 1977). Self-efficacy expectations have been shown to be predictive of both academic and career outcomes among children and adolescents. For example, self-efficacy has been associated with subject matter interests, such as in math, science, and English (Lopez, Lent, Brown, & Gore, 1997; P. L. Smith & Fouad, 1999). Self-efficacy expectations have been positively linked to intermediate career developmental tasks, such as career planning and exploration, and overcoming personal challenges in academic and occupational settings (Lapan, Gysbers, Multon, & Pike, 1997; O'Brien, Dukstein, Jackson, Tomlinson, & Kamatuka, 1999). Self-efficacy has been found to be correlated with both majority and minority youths' interests, aspirations, expectations, goals, career pursuits, and career trajectories (Bandura,

Barbaranelli, Vittorio-Caprara, & Pastorelli, 2001). Moreover, self-efficacy is theoretically associated with personal agency, which may be more fundamental than the actual skills and circumstances that encompass young people's career development in that self-efficacy can "motivate people to create opportunities and acquire capabilities they do not yet possess" (Ford, 1992, p. 124).

As to academic and career-related self-efficacy, researchers have given us clues about how to develop these expectations among K-12 youth. In four empirical studies, Bandura's (1977) four learning sources of efficacy information (performance accomplishments, vicarious learning, the management of emotional arousal, and social persuasion; see Lent, Chapter 5, this volume) have been significantly associated with the development of social (Anderson & Betz, 2001), academic (Chin & Kameoka, 2002), math (Lopez & Lent, 1992), and career-related (Turner, Alliman-Brissett, Lapan, Udipi, & Ergun, 2003) self-efficacy. In the Turner, Alliman-Brissett, et al. study, parents' provision of efficacy information along each of these learning source dimensions (i.e., parents' instrumental assistance to facilitate their adolescents' performance accomplishments, parents' career-related role modeling to facilitate their adolescents' vicarious learning, parents' emotional support to facilitate their adolescents' management of emotions, and parents' social persuasion in the form of verbal encouragement) was positively related to adolescents' efficacy to engage in academic and career planning, knowledge of self and others in career and academic contexts, understanding of the relationships between academic achievement and occupational opportunities, and early career decision making. The results of this study led Turner, Alliman-Brissett, et al. to recommend further investigations into how extended families, teachers, and school and career counselors can provide opportunities for adolescents to continue to develop career-related self-efficacy beliefs using Bandura's schema to focus their efforts.

Research on attributional styles also offers potential implications for the development of self-efficacy and related psychological variables (Luzzo, Funk, & Strang, 1996). Positive self-attributional styles refer to young people's confidence that their own skills, abilities, and efforts will determine the bulk of their life experiences, including their educational and career success. More specifically, people with positive attributional styles attribute their successes to themselves, while people with negative attributional styles attribute their failures to themselves. Positive attributional styles have been related to a decrease in the perceptions of career barriers among children and adolescents (Albert & Luzzo, 1999). Among high school adolescents, significant positive relationships were found between optimistic attributional styles and career maturity (i.e., vocationally mature attitudes, behavior, and knowledge that characterize adaptive career development during late adolescence and early adulthood; Powell & Luzzo, 1998). Among African American adolescents, positive attributions and work salience were shown to partly mediate the relations of sex, socioeconomic status, and educational level to career maturity (Naidoo, Bowman, & Gerstein, 1998). Among British final-year school leavers, self-attributions for employment success were found to relate to use of positive job search strategies (Furnham & Rawles, 1996).

One study examined the effects of attributional retraining on the self-attributions of college students (Luzzo, James, & Luna, 1996). After viewing an eight-minute video presentation designed to foster internal, controllable attributes for career decision making and to challenge faulty attributional beliefs, experimental group participants displayed more positive career beliefs and attributional styles and exhibited significantly more career exploratory behaviors than did control group participants. While this type of training has not yet been evaluated among K-12 students, we suggest that developmentally appropriate attributional style training may positively affect the career development of this population as well.

FORMING A VOCATIONAL IDENTITY

Vocational identity refers to the integration and crystallization of an individual's energy, aptitudes, and opportunities into a consistent sense of the uniqueness of himself or herself and fit into the vocational world. An adolescent's vocational identity gives clarity and stability to his or her current and future career goals (Holland, 1997) and sets forth the career direction he or she will pursue. Vocational identity is related to the concept of ego identity (Erikson, 1968) and is achieved through the same cognitive processes as ego identity (i.e., exploration, observation, reflection, commitment). Vocational identity has been shown to be clearly achieved before ideological, political, or religious identity (Skorikov & Vondracek, 1998). This finding is indicative of the leading role that vocational development plays in adolescent identity formation.

Significant associations between vocational identity and many desirable career outcomes in adolescents have been demonstrated. For example, higher levels of vocational identity have been associated with more congruent college major choices among gifted high school students (Leung, 1998) and with greater career certainty and career choice commitment among high school adolescents (Ladany, Melincoff, Constantine, & Love, 1997; Schulenberg, Vondracek, & Kim, 1993). The achievement of vocational identity in adolescents has also been associated with the strengthening and solidifying of reality-based vocational aspirations (Sarriera, Silva, Kabbas, & Lopes, 2001); vocational choice orientation, planning about preferred occupations, and formation of success-creating work attitudes (Wallace-Broscious, Serafica, & Osipow, 1994); and positive mental health indicators, including self-esteem and psychological adjustment (De Goede, Spruijt, Iedema, & Meeus, 1999; W. W. Munson, 1992; Skorikov & Moore, 2001).

An intensive review of the research literature revealed only one reported career intervention designed to increase adolescents' vocational identity (Schmidt & Callan, 1992). In this study, high school students were assigned to receive individual career counseling, personal counseling, or career counseling combined with career information. Compared with controls, students in all three treatment conditions demonstrated a significant increase in their level of vocational identity from pretest to posttest, suggesting that personal counseling, career counseling, and career information can each be useful ways to assist adolescents in the successful achievement of their vocational identity.

LEARNING EFFECTIVE SOCIAL, PROSOCIAL, AND WORK READINESS SKILLS

Work readiness skills are composed of general employability skills (e.g., the ability to accept responsibility and make sound decisions), social competency skills (e.g., the ability to appropriately initiate conversations and appropriately regulate emotions), and prosocial skills (i.e., voluntary behavior intended to benefit another; Eisenberg & Fabes, 1992; Lapan, 2004). Intuitively, one might think that learning these skills is a natural function of the socialization process. Yet in today's complex world, with understaffed schools, fluctuating economies, increasing family and educational transitions, increased residential mobility, and increasing demographic and cultural diversity, counselors concerned with the career development of children and adolescents may need to take a deliberate and proactive stance in the development of these career-related competencies.

Both career researchers and governmental policymakers have recommended a number of work readiness skills (Bloch, 1996; see Juntunen, Chapter 24, this volume). For example, the Job Training Partnership Act of 1982 identified those work readiness skills believed to be necessary in the retraining of displaced workers. These skills include maintaining regular attendance, being punctual, displaying positive work attitudes and behaviors, completing tasks effectively, presenting an appropriate appearance, and demonstrating good interpersonal relationship skills. Lapan (2004) outlined a comprehensive set of skills to help children and adolescents maximize their career potential, including:

1. Social competence (i.e., the ability to build effective relationships).
2. Diversity (i.e., the ability and flexibility to successfully interact with coworkers, clients, customers, or students from different cultures).
3. Positive work habits (including sound judgment, responsibility, dependability, punctuality, attendance, life-planning and management skills, and recognition of and adherence to the legal and ethical standards that govern your profession).
4. Personal management skills (including positive self-attitudes, cleanliness, appropriate dress, both verbal and nonverbal communication skills).
5. Entrepreneurship (including leadership, creativity, desire, motivation, and openness to opportunity).

Research has shown that adult workers who possess adequate work readiness skills experience greater work satisfaction (Meir, Melamed, & Abu-Freha, 1990). Other investigators have found that greater work readiness skills lead to more integration into the work environment (Ashford & Black, 1996), a stronger commitment to the organization in which the individual is employed (Fisher, 1985), more successful job performance (Ashford & Black, 1996), fewer job turnovers, and greater workplace rewards (Wanberg & Kammeyer-Mueller, 2000).

A small body of literature suggests that work readiness skills are developed within family and classroom environments. For example, Naimark and Pearce (1985) hypothesized that children learn skills within the family that can be transferred to the workplace, such as goal setting, decision making, scheduling, budgeting, leading, nurturing, and communicating. Harkins (2001) suggested that work readiness skills can be learned through direct instruction and should be infused into classroom curriculum. H. L. Munson and Rubenstein (1992) suggested that school personnel, such as school counselors and career educators, are in an ideal position to contribute to a student's sense of work, work values, work habits, and work behaviors.

A more extensive body of literature suggests that work readiness skills are developed through children's friendships and peer group interactions. For example, researchers have shown that, within peer groups, children have opportunities to learn (1) social skills, such as successfully exchanging information, being clear in communication with others, and engaging in appropriate self-disclosure

(Gottman, 1983) and (2) prosocial skills, such as empathy and treating others with justice and kindness (Youniss, 1980). Gaining these social and prosocial skills can facilitate greater workplace stamina and adjustment (Ladd & Kochenderfer, 1996) by promoting such worker characteristics as stability, resilience, self-esteem, self-efficacy, and adaptability (Rigby & Slee, 1993). We maintain that psychologists, counselors, and career educators can help shape children's family, school, and community contexts in ways that promote the growth of those critical work readiness skills that are the foundation for a wide range of work readiness behaviors in adulthood (Lapan, 2004).

CONSTRUCTING A BETTER UNDERSTANDING OF ONE'S SELF, THE WORLD OF WORK, AND ONE'S FIT IN THE WORK WORLD

Constructing a better understanding of oneself, the world of work, and how one best fits into the world of work has been the foundation of vocational psychology since Frank Parsons (1909) first introduced these concepts. Since then, both career development researchers and counselors have focused on helping career clients understand their own abilities, interests, values, and personality styles; the specifics of current labor market information; and how to make better and more satisfying career decisions. However, in the past several years, researchers have noted that children and adolescents experience special challenges in constructing their career pathways. Three of these challenges, discussed in this section, are gender-based circumscription of vocational aspirations, career decision-making readiness, and school-to-school/school-to-work transitioning.

Gender-Based Circumscription of Vocational Aspirations   Gottfredson's Theory of Circumscription and Compromise (Gottfredson, 1981, Chapter 4, this volume) has generated more than 50 research reports, dissertations, and published discussions. These studies generally have shown that children and adolescents tend to circumscribe their vocational interests, self-efficacy expectations, outcome expectations, and prestige expectations according to their social valuation of occupations as gender inappropriate (Gottfredson & Lapan, 1997; Lapan, Hinkelman, Adams, & Turner, 1999). This process of circumscription (i.e., continual narrowing of occupations an individual will consider) and compromise (i.e., eliminating the most preferred options for less compatible ones) can result in young people sacrificing the fulfillment of their "internal unique selves" by choosing occupations that they perceive to be more socially acceptable (Gottfredson, 2002). Circumscription of vocational aspirations has been shown to begin in early childhood (Henderson, Hesketh, & Tuffin, 1988), with children identifying segments of the occupational world as unattainable. The process continues throughout middle and later adolescence, during which time adolescents make vocational preparation decisions that can affect their ability to enter into more prestigious, lucrative, or congruent occupations (Leung & Harmon, 1990; Mendez & Crawford, 2002). One of the most disturbing outcomes of the circumscription process is young women's frequent avoidance of the more highly paid and higher prestige math, science, and technology-based careers (Lapan & Jingeleski, 1992).

Career Decision-Making Readiness   Piaget (1977) theorized that sometime during early adolescence (approximately age 12), young people undergo a fundamental shift in the way they view the world by moving away from concrete thinking toward more abstract, logical thinking. During this stage of cognitive development, adolescents begin to think more scientifically, design and test multiple hypotheses, and manipulate objects, operations, and future outcomes in their minds. Physical maturation, experience, and socialization allow young adolescents to envision not only what they will be like in the future, but also how they will implement what they conceive themselves to be.

Building on Piaget, information processing theorists have argued that cognitive development can be strongly influenced through cognitive interventions (e.g., information sharing, knowledge construction, learning critical thinking skills; e.g., Case, 1991; Siegler, 1991; Vygotsky, 1978). Career theorists who adhere to an information processing approach advocate sequential training in problem solving as a prerequisite to adolescent career decision making. For example, Sampson, Peterson, Lenz, and Reardon (1992) proposed that adolescents be trained in the cycle of information processing skills used in career decision making, which consists of:

1. Problem identification.
2. Analyzing the causes of the problem and the relationships among the problem components.
3. Synthesizing possible courses of action through elaboration and crystallization.
4. Evaluating each course of action.
5. Implementing and executing a plan of action.

They also argued that adolescents should be assessed as to their career decision-making readiness before career counseling as a way to improve the value of service delivery to them (Sampson, Peterson, Reardon, & Lenz, 2000). Although there is disagreement in the research literature about when adolescents attain the cognitive maturity to make career decisions, there is general agreement about the value of improving students' problem-solving and career decision-making competencies (Patton & Creed, 2001).

School-to-School/School-to-Work Transitioning Helping children and adolescents know how to best fit into the world of work also is accomplished through facilitating their school-to-school/school-to-work transitioning. Transitioning has been described as a prolonged and increasingly complex process for young persons (Bynner, Chisholm, & Furlong, 1997; Jones & Wallace, 1992). Transitioning is typically characterized by few institutional supports, the prolongation of education, and a multitude of options that combine school, work, and family in unique ways (Mortimer, Zimmer-Gembeck, Holmes, & Shanahan, 2002). Although the literature is sparse in this area, researchers have shown that transitioning can be accompanied by negative thoughts and emotions that may diminish children's and adolescents' ability to achieve, explore, and plan at the level of their abilities, especially for students who are already vulnerable. For example, transitioning from grade school to junior high school has been associated with decreases in self-esteem in ethnically diverse adolescents living in poverty (Seidman, Lambert, Allen, & Aber, 2003). Transitioning from primary to secondary school was shown to be accompanied by fears of bullying, getting lost, increased workload, and more challenging peer relationships in a British sample (Zeedyk et al., 2003).

Among young adults, the deployment of maladaptive strategies, such as passive avoidance and external control attributions (i.e., a sense that one's personal destiny is controlled by others rather than oneself), was associated with increased difficulties in dealing with school-to-work transitions (Maeaettae, Nurmi, & Majava, 2002). This avoidance behavior could arguably be said to begin in childhood, which suggests that earlier interventions might provide young people with the cognitive-behavioral strategies to more successfully pursue school-to-school and school-to-work transitioning.

Researchers and theorists have suggested ways to help children and adolescents engage in school-to-school and school-to-work transitioning (see Juntunen & Wettersten, Chapter 24, this volume). For example, Phillips, Blustein, Jobin-Davis, and Finkelberg White (2002) argued that the use of resources in an adolescent's environment (e.g., supportive available adults, siblings, peers) is associated with clearer transitional plans. Lapan, Tucker, Kim, and Kosciulek (2003) found that the career development activities recommended by the School-to-Work Opportunities Act—school-based learning, work-based learning, connecting activities (e.g., job shadowing), and stakeholder support (e.g., from teachers, counselors, parents)—predicted grades, interests, expectations, goals/actions, and person-environment fit among high school students. Shanahan, Mortimer, and Krueger (2002) proposed that helping adolescents recognize connections between school and work might assist them in preparing for school-to-work transitions. Worth (2002) suggested that assisting adolescents to enhance their flexibility in decision making might help them to better adapt to more precarious employment situations and to increase their opportunities in a quickly changing labor market.

CRYSTALLIZING PERSONALLY VALUED VOCATIONAL INTERESTS

Many theorists have highlighted the importance of interests in young people's career development (Holland, 1997; Super et al., 1996). Additionally, researchers have noted the strength of young people's career interests in predicting their subsequent career behavior (Hansen, Chapter 12, this volume). Deci and Ryan (1985; Deci, 1992) argued that career interests provide intrinsic motivation, are related to self-determination, and are very closely tied to the career actions that adolescents take. The foundation of career interests is hypothesized to be based on such factors as young people's self-exploration of their own abilities, self-efficacy expectations, and values (Holland, 1997; Lent et al., 1994, 2000; Super et al., 1996).

The crystallization of interests implies the formation of young people's career interests into a defined and somewhat permanent structure. Career interests are developed and clarified by related experiences (Hansen & Swanson, 1983), and often crystallize at the point of educational and vocational transitions (Mortimer et al., 2002). The crystallization of interests occurs when adolescents recognize that they must make choices about how to fit into a complex world (Sharf, 2002). At the point of crystallization, adolescents begin to weigh their values, for instance, choosing occupations that are altruistic, or ones that are expressive of their personal moral views. The crystallization of interests involves a clarification of vocational goals and implies a commitment to preparing for and pursuing specific occupations. During subsequent developmental stages, this initial commitment is reanalyzed with continuing reflection on the value of previous occupational choices (Cochran, 1997).

Researchers have suggested that not all children and adolescents have the opportunity to crystallize personally valued vocational interests (Hackett & Byars, 1996). Social forces, such as uneven educational opportunities, uneven environmental supports, discrimination, and cultural and gender-based valuing of various careers (see Gottfredson, Chapter 4, this volume) may seriously hinder the crystallization of personally valued interests. Indeed, recent research has shown that the value systems underlying young people's vocational interests are systematically tied to social origin and early experiences, are highly influenced by the social manifestations of race and gender, and change the most when adolescents come to terms with the limits of their opportunities (M. K. Johnson, 2002). We suggest that career counselors are in key positions to help all young people crystallize personally valued interests (1) by designing strategies to help them explore the underlying dimensions of their interests and expand their awareness of vocational possibilities; and (2) by working for community awareness, social justice, and advocacy for children and adolescents who may be disadvantaged in the marketplace because of their race, socioeconomic status, or gender.

EMPOWERING ALL STUDENTS TO ACHIEVE ACADEMICALLY AND BECOME SELF-REGULATED LEARNERS

Self-regulated learning is defined as an active, constructive process whereby learners set goals for their learning and then attempt to monitor, regulate, and control their cognitions, motivations, and behavior (Pintrich, 2000). Zimmerman (2000) construed self-regulated learning as the monitoring of the individual's own planning, performance, and the expected and real outcomes of any learning activity, whether interesting or uninteresting. Self-regulated learning promotes both academic achievement and lifelong learning (Lapan, Kardash, et al., 2002).

Researchers have shown that self-regulation promotes goal motivation and direction (McWhaw & Abrami, 2001), effort intensity and task performance (Boekaerts, 1997), academic performance and achievement (Pintrich & de Groot, 1990; Wolters, 1999), and positive self- and other-expectations (Zimmerman, 2000). Further, schools, families, and communities can work together to promote and enhance self-regulated learning in K-12 youth through identifying programs that effectively promote academic achievement, instituting mutual accountability structures and practices, and supporting the learning of children from different social contexts (Lapan & Kosciulek, 2001). Researchers have provided initial data and strategies outlining how career professionals can work with community/career partnerships (e.g., Lapan & Kosciulek, 2001; Lapan, Osana, Tucker, & Kosciulek, 2002), as well as provide other types of career interventions, to enhance the career development of all students. It is to these topics that we turn next.

INTERVENTIONS THAT FACILITATE THE CAREER DEVELOPMENT OF CHILDREN AND ADOLESCENTS

As can be seen from the previous section, there are many junctures at which career professionals can intervene to promote children's and adolescents' career development and many key points on which to focus. In this section, we discuss the relative value of various types of interventions, and then describe in detail selected examples of the interventions that we believe to be particularly promising, including individual career counseling; group career counseling, classroom-based career curricula, and career education; parent involvement in career interventions; computer assessment and guidance programs (e.g., Web-based programs); community/career partnerships; and self-directed activities.

THE VALUE OF CAREER INTERVENTIONS

Regardless of age or educational level, career counseling interventions have been shown to be effective in assisting individuals whose primary concern is either to make or remake a career choice (Brown & Ryan Krane, 2000; see Miller & Brown, Chapter 18, this volume). Based on the results of two meta-analyses of more than 60 studies, Spokane and Oliver (1983; Oliver & Spokane, 1988) concluded that group- and classroom-based interventions were somewhat more effective than individual or alternative interventions. Based on the results of meta-analyses of 47 and 57 studies, respectively, Whiston and colleagues (Whiston, Brecheisen, & Stephens, 2003; Whiston, Sexton, & Lasoff, 1998) argued that there are substantial differences in the effectiveness of various modes of career interventions, with counselor-led interventions being considerably more effective than self-directed interventions overall. In addition, they found that individual career counseling was the most effective but not the most cost-effective method of intervention, followed by group counseling, computer-assisted interventions, career development workshops, career class interventions, and, finally, self-directed career interventions. While these two groups of researchers' results were somewhat conflicting, they did agree that career clients made significant positive gains regardless of the type of career intervention used.

INDIVIDUAL CAREER COUNSELING

Individual career counseling is one of the most traditional methods of providing career services to students (Williamson, 1939). However, new and innovative methods have been developed that we believe have increased the versatility of this form of career counseling when working with children and adolescents. In this section, we briefly examine two new approaches career counselors can use to enhance their individual career work with young people: the Structured Career Development Interview (SCDI; Lapan, 2003) and Possible Selves Mapping (Shepard & Marshall, 1999).

The Structured Career Development Interview   The SCDI (Lapan, 2003) is a recently developed instrument designed to assess adolescents':

1. Academic achievement.
2. Self-efficacy beliefs and attributions.
3. Person-environment fit (self-exploration of abilities, talents, values, and interests; career exploration and planning skills; and school-to-work transitioning skills).
4. Vocational goals.
5. Work-readiness skills and behaviors.
6. Proactivity (assertiveness, commitment, active preparation, awareness of opportunities, initiative).
7. The emotional and instrumental support they receive from significant others.

Career counselors engage young people in an exploration of these issues through a series of open-ended questions. SCDI interviews take approximately 30 to 45 minutes to complete. After interviews are scored, individual profiles are constructed so that counselees can have a visual representation of those career development areas in which they are strong (e.g., are better prepared or have more skills) and those areas they may want to improve on. Profiles can be used to design career interventions that are specific to the needs of individual counselees.

Structured interviews, such as the SCDI, have many advantages. First, in a relatively brief period, structured interviews can be used to focus the attention of clients and counselors on constructs found by researchers to be of critical psychological importance. Second, young people can be engaged in a relatively nonthreatening method of exploring self in relation to the world of work in a supportive and caring environment. Third, young people who have difficulty reading may benefit more from this type of interview than from traditional paper-and-pencil-based assessments (Sattler, 1992).

In an initial study of the SCDI among middle-school students at risk for dropping out of school (Turner, Lapan, Yang, Trotter, Alliman-Brissett, et al., 2003), career counselors found that they could use the interview as an entry point to discuss a wide range of personal, family, and developmental issues that confront these adolescents. Career counselors further reported that by using the structured interview, they were in a much better position to recommend further career interventions as needed. In addition, young people reported that they valued and were interested in focusing on those career issues they perceived as being important in preparing for their futures.

Possible Selves Mapping   Possible Selves Mapping (Shepard & Marshall, 1999) is based on Kelly's (1955) constructivist view of counseling. Constructivist counselors help clients understand what the relationships are among events in their lives, how they impose order on their problems, and how they derive meanings from their experiences. Constructivist counselors typically use a narrative method (i.e., asking clients to tell their story) to accomplish these purposes.

Kelly (1955) extended constructivist theory to career counseling through his view that a person's career is a major means of providing clarity and meaning to his or her life. Subsequently, Markus and Nurius (1986) introduced possible selves narration to help career clients describe their past, present, and "imagined" future career selves. For children and adolescents, the use of this form of career counseling may be especially valuable in that helping them focus on their career story can assist them in expressing their beliefs, desires, values, emotions, and experiences (Shepard & Marshall, 1999).

In a particularly creative application of the possible selves narrative, Possible Selves Mapping, Shepard and Marshall (1999) ask young persons to identify on index cards as many hoped-for selves and feared selves as possible. Hoped-for selves (e.g., a competent professional, an airplane pilot) are the positive selves that a person could become, and feared selves (e.g., homeless, depressed) are the negative selves that a person could become (Markus & Nurius, 1986). The young people are then asked to rank order their hoped-for selves in order of importance. Next, their most important possible selves are displayed on a map showing relationships and distances between their hoped-for and feared selves. Then, adolescents are asked a series of questions, such as: Describe the way you imagine your life would be if you attained your most important possible selves, and what actions could you engage in to help you bring about your most important possible selves? These questions are designed to help adolescents see the connections between their actions (e.g., finish high school, find out more about careers in which they are interested) and the selves they hope to become.

Shepard and Marshall (1999) evaluated this intervention with 42 adolescents (ages 11 to 13 years). They found that hoped-for selves were expressed more frequently than feared selves. Based on a qualitative analysis of their interviewees' responses, they suggested that by exploring their possible selves, clients have a better understanding of the occupations they aspire to, their career-related hopes and fears, and their multifaceted self-concepts.

GROUP CAREER COUNSELING, CLASSROOM-BASED CAREER CURRICULUM, AND CAREER EDUCATION

Group career counseling includes career-based classroom guidance, integrated career counseling and academic instruction, and career education, as well as other innovative career counseling strategies. Group interventions consistently have been shown to be effective in promoting a wide range of career outcomes for children and adolescents (Spokane & Oliver, 1983). Group strategies have the advantage of maximizing benefits to individuals while lowering the cost of career counseling interventions (Spokane & Oliver, 1983). They allow career counseling to be brought into the classroom and to be integrated with academics. Group strategies allow children and adolescents to provide one another with support and encouragement, as well as bring fresh viewpoints into situations with which others are struggling. Several group interventions, along with the results of group career counseling with K-12 youth, are described next.

In an eight-week joint program offered by language arts teachers and high school counselors, increases were reported in both the career development and academic achievement of 166 high school juniors (Lapan, Gysbers, Hughey, & Arni, 1993). In this joint program, school counselors presented extensive in-class career exploration exercises (e.g., opportunities for adolescents to understand their own goals, interests, personalities, and talents; to gather information about the world of work through computer-assisted and other reference materials; and to reflect on how to create more career support for other students within their immediate peer group), while the language arts teachers worked with students on composing a research paper that addressed their post-high school transition plans. After statistically controlling for prior academic achievement, gains in the students' career development competencies (e.g., career planning and exploration, understanding how being male or female relates to jobs and careers, understanding how education and careers are related) significantly predicted higher earned grades on their papers.

McWhirter, Crothers, and Rasheed (2000) evaluated a nine-week career education class conducted with high school sophomores. The class met for 50 minutes each day over a nine-week period. The students were engaged in a variety of hands-on activities, small group experiences, lectures, and exposure to guest speakers. Curriculum objectives included learning how to locate and use world of work information, developing a budget, learning about the expectations of employers, conducting explorations of postsecondary educational and career options, learning how to write a resume and interview for a job, and locating sources of financial support for their post-high school plans. Students were expected to participate actively in the class. An effort was made to make certain parts of the class (e.g., developing and adhering to a budget) closely related to the realities of the world students would find themselves in after leaving high school. At the end of the nine weeks, students completed inventories assessing their abilities, interests, and personalities. The career education class was found to increase students' career-related self-efficacy and outcome expectations and assist them with their career decision making.

Spokane and Oliver (1983) found that a structured group career intervention (Thoresen & Hamilton, 1972), which was based on peer social modeling, produced one of the largest effect sizes in their initial meta-analysis of 40 studies. In this experiment, 11th-grade students were randomly assigned to one of five groups: (1) a written stimulus materials group, (2) a peer social modeling group, (3) a combined written stimulus materials and peer social modeling group, (4) an attention-placebo control group, and (5) a wait list no-treatment group. The stimulus materials were pamphlets of career exploration activities, titled "Planning My Career." Peer social modeling was provided in the form of videotapes showing other adolescents engaged in career exploration activities. Each experimental group participated in four 50-minute treatment sessions. Subsequent to each treatment session, experimental group participants discussed personally relevant information about their career planning and exploration, their goals and preferences, how they would acquire information about preferred careers, and tentative decisions about their future plans. Results demonstrated that the peer social modeling and combined treatments were more effective than no treatment with respect to knowing how to obtain and use relevant career information. However, the materials treatment alone was not significantly more effective than no treatment on these knowledge outcomes. They concluded that peer social modeling is an intervention strategy that can be used to assist students to:

1. Seek needed world of work information.
2. Actually use that information.
3. Make initial and tentative decisions on what they would do next.
4. Change their plans, if necessary.

These are just a few examples of the many group career interventions that can be used with children and adolescents. Overall, analyses of such group-based interventions have shown that they are related to positive changes in such psychological constructs as vocational identity (Remer, O'Neill, & Gohs, 1984), career maturity (Whiston et al., 1998), reduced career indecision (D. C. Johnson & Smouse, 1993; Quinn & Lewis, 1989; Whiston et al., 1998), and greater psychosocial development (Stonewater & Daniels, 1983). Further, research has shown that students who participate in career education programs across the K-12 years do slightly better academically than students who do not participate (Evans & Burck, 1992). The latter authors suggested that the positive influence of career education on academic achievement is strengthened if:

1. The career education program is integrated with the mathematics or language arts curriculum.
2. The intervention is intensive.
3. The intervention is in at least its second year of implementation with the same cohort.

Parent Involvement in Career Interventions

The research literature is replete with findings about the benefits of parental support for children's and adolescents' career development. For example, Bandura et al. (2001) found that parents' self-efficacy to promote their children's academic endeavors was positively associated with their children's self-efficacy related to a broad variety of careers. Marjoribanks (2002) demonstrated that parents' perceived aspirations for their adolescent children have medium to large associations with the adolescents' educational aspirations and small but significant associations with the adolescents' occupational aspirations (see Rojewski, Chapter 6, this volume). F. M. Smith and Hausafus (1998) showed that middle school minority students had higher test scores in math when their parents helped them to see the importance of taking advanced math courses, emphasized the importance of math for today's careers, and supported their children's participation in extracurricular math/science activities. Hoyt (2001) argued that because there will be less opportunity in the labor market for young people with four-year or graduate school degrees (only 30% of the newly created jobs in the next 10 years are predicted to require a bachelor's or graduate school degree), parents should be enlisted to help adolescents explore a wide variety of educational options in order to choose those that are best suited to their needs. Practical strategies to help counselors work with families have been empirically examined, and suggestions have been made to help parents become more productively involved in promoting their children's career futures. Two of these strategies are discussed next.

Mother-Daughter Dyads   In a study examining the support of mothers for their daughters' career development, African American mothers and their teenage daughters both completed a possible selves intervention in which both described the daughters' "possible selves" (Kerpelman, Shoffner, & Ross-Griffin, 2002). They also completed a possible selves card-sort focusing on the personal attributes, roles, and life circumstances that might be expected for the daughters' futures. Findings from the card-sort data indicated two distinctive mother-daughter groups, with one group emphasizing the daughters' personal attributes (e.g., organization, helpfulness, creativity, intelligence), and the other group emphasizing the daughters' future occupations (e.g., business owner, religious leader, lawyer) and life circumstances (e.g., rich, famous). By analyzing the qualitative responses of these two groups, Kerpelman et al. concluded that adolescents have very different support needs depending on their personal characteristics, and their personal, environmental, and developmental resources. These researchers further suggested that by using possible selves interventions with mothers and daughters, young women's differential needs can be uncovered so that mothers will be in a more advantageous position to assist in their daughters' academic and career development.

The Partners Program (Cochran, 1985)   This program was designed to help parents help their adolescents develop a sense of agency about a career. In this program, parents offer career guidance to their sons and daughters using (1) a career exploration workbook that identifies interests, strengths, and values; (2) a career grid workbook that facilitates deliberation on viable options and tentative career decisions; and (3) a career planning workbook that encourages educational planning toward a vocational goal. Parents are given information about the importance of parental support in the career development of children and adolescents and about how to interact with their adolescents around the Partners materials. Parents also are taught microcounseling skills and attitudes, such as warmth, reciprocity, mutual balance of power, and attentiveness. Finally, parents are provided support and guidance in the form of phone calls and discussion groups with other parents, as they work individually with their adolescents through the Partners materials.

Two studies examined the effectiveness of the Partners Program with high school students. Palmer and Cochran (1988) found that adolescents reported increased career orientation, and a strengthening of parental bonding. Kush and Cochran (1993) found that, compared to the control group, experimental group adolescents reported more certainty in their career directions, less career indecision, greater career confidence, and more career motivation.

COMPUTER ASSESSMENT AND GUIDANCE PROGRAMS (INCLUDING WEB-BASED PROGRAMS)

Computer assessment and guidance programs are typically welcomed by K-12 youth. As children growing up in the information age, these students are often computer savvy and are able to receive maximum benefit from using this medium. Two computer programs and their uses are briefly reviewed here: DISCOVER (American College Testing, 2003) and Mapping Vocational Challenges (Lapan & Turner, 1997, 2000).

DISCOVER The DISCOVER program is a widely administered career guidance and assessment program designed for middle school and high school students. (An online version is now available from ACT.) Children and adolescents who use the DISCOVER program can explore educational and occupational options, including types of occupations available in the world of work, major programs of study offered by various post-high school institutions, financial aid information, and job-seeking skills information. Embedded in DISCOVER is the Unisex ACT Interest Inventory, which predicts adolescents' Holland theme codes and future career interests by asking them to rate their attraction to current school and extracurricular activities. Students also are able to use DISCOVER to develop a career plan that is digitally stored and can be reaccessed. The individual assessment reports generated by DISCOVER can be used by career counselors to assist young people in their career planning and exploration. Evaluation studies testing the effectiveness of this career development system have shown that, subsequent to program use, middle school students demonstrate significant gains in career maturity (Luzzo & Pierce, 1996), and high school students demonstrate significant increases in the specificity of their educational and vocational plans (Rayman, Bryson, & Bowlsbey, 1978).

Mapping Vocational Challenges (MVC) The MVC is a computerized career intervention based on Holland's theory (1997; Spokane & Cruza-Guet, Chapter 2, this volume), Gottfredson's Theory of Circumscription and Compromise (1981; Gottfredson, Chapter 4, this volume), and Social Cognitive Career Theory (Lent et al., 1994; Lent, Chapter 5, this volume). Using this program, middle school adolescents explore information (summarized from the Occupational Outlook Handbook; Bureau of Labor Statistics, 2002–2003) that is related to specific careers, such as associated work activities, recommended high school classes, post-high school training requirements, salary levels, and geographic availability. They then complete a career assessment in which they explore their career interests, efficacy for pursuing various occupations, perceived parent support for pursuing various occupations, valuing of various occupations, and perceived gender-typing of various occupations. Assessments are computer scored, and an interpretive report is computer generated. Evaluation of the MVC (Turner & Lapan, in press), in which career counselors used interpretive report results to challenge middle school adolescents' gender-traditional career interests, demonstrated that program use increased career planning and exploration efficacy, educational and vocational development efficacy, and career interests in both traditional and nontraditional occupations.

Community/Career Partnerships

Communities can create situations in which it will be much more likely for young people to successfully engage in career development tasks. A growing body of research suggests that structured community-based experiences are critical developmental pathways through which young people can become self-directed, socially competent, caring, and successful young adults (R. W. Larson, 2000). Structured activities such as service and civic activities, Girl Scouts, Cub Scouts, and sports have been shown to help young people develop initiative, responsibility, and follow-through (Lapan, 2004). Community/career partnerships that provide career development opportunities for young people, such as work-based learning, service learning, internships, and apprenticeships, are likely to engage K-12 youth in the exploration of broader career pathways. They can guide young people in planning high school coursework around their career goals and in using elective courses to meet avocational goals. Well-established and maintained community-based partnerships can enable career counselors to meet more effectively the career development needs and challenges of children and adolescents (Lapan, Osana, et al., 2002).

One example of a community/career partnership for which some data are available is the mentoring program described by Terry (1999). In this program, community partners mentored 7- to 11-year-old children. Through interviewing both the mentors and their mentees, Terry found that the children enjoyed spending time with their mentors, learned about the world of work, and participated in a variety of experiences. Mentors enjoyed the relationships with their mentees and believed that their mentees learned many things from them, including problem-solving techniques and information about potential careers and higher education.

Another example of community/career partnerships is the offering of summer camps for primarily low-income or first-generation potential college students. These camps are typically hosted by universities and funded by consortiums of government and community agencies (e.g., U.S. Department of Education, United Way). The camps typically focus on specific career programs, such as math and science, basic engineering and robotics, computer science, business and entrepreneurship, or precollege exploration. The programs are advertised under such names as Bridges to Medicine, American Indian Science and Engineering programs, Upward Bound, and TRIO. Program information is usually mailed to high school and middle school guidance offices. Alternatively, this information can be found on individual university web sites. Although most data on summer camps are anecdotal, one study was conducted on the effectiveness of a two-week summer science exploration camp (Gibson & Chase, 2002). Results indicated that program participants maintained a more positive attitude toward science and a higher interest in science-based careers than did the comparison group of students who applied to the program but were not selected. However, the internal validity of this study's design was compromised by selection bias (i.e., possible preexisting differences between program participants and nonparticipants).

Other examples of community/career partnerships are the work-based learning classes funded by many urban school districts designed to serve the needs of students who are at risk for academic failure (Juntunen & Wettersten, Chapter 24, this volume). These community/career partnerships allow students as young as 15 years old to hold part-time jobs during part of their school day, while under the supervision of both their career education instructor and their employer. In their career education classes, they learn job and life skills such as interviewing and job acquisition techniques (e.g., using labor market information to find jobs, preparing a resume, filling out job applications, interviewing for a job), managing personal resources (e.g., balancing a checking account, saving money, credit use), and self-sufficient living (e.g., preparing a budget, renting an apartment, buying a car). While at work, they practice the interpersonal skills, basic literacy skills (e.g., writing, math, and English language skills), and the job skills required to become successful full-time employees.

These types of community/career partnerships take advantage of the current research on work-based learning, which shows that training young people in basic work-related and job-specific skills is very effective when it takes place on the job or in a job-like setting, and that the more this training is linked to work, the better the results (Mikulecky, 1989). Basic skills are often easier to learn when they are integrated into a training program that is specific to the context of a particular job (Mikulecky). Employer-provided training may also have more motivated trainees, more effective tutorial learning methods, and more appropriate training materials and equipment (Bishop, 1994).

Lapan and Kosciulek (2001) developed a framework that career development specialists can use to evaluate the impact of community-based career partnerships. They suggested that outcomes should be organized around three themes: benefits to students, benefits to employers, and benefits to the community. Evaluations of community/career partnerships organized around these three themes have shown positive initial results. For example, in a program review submitted to Congress, Hershey, Silverberg, Haimson, Hudis, and Jackson (1999) demonstrated that both college-bound and non-college-bound students were equally likely to participate in partnership activities; young women, especially African American women, had become much more involved in school- and workplace-related learning opportunities; and secondary students were now enrolled in more academic classes that focused on their career interests. Based on their review of these initial outcome studies, Lapan and Kosciulek suggested that community partnerships can dramatically improve the career development of an increasingly diverse K-12 youth population.

SELF-DIRECTED ACTIVITIES

Counselor-free career interventions are widespread and will likely become increasingly popular choices for career clients in the future. One of the most popular and well-researched counselor-free interventions is the Self-Directed Search (SDS; Holland, 2001). Two of the more user-friendly Self-Directed Search versions are the online version, which can be located at www.self-directed-search.com, and the self-scoring version, which can be purchased inexpensively from the publisher. SDS respondents list their occupational daydreams, and then rate their attraction to various career-related activities, their self-perceived job-related competencies, their interests in various occupations, and their self-estimated abilities. By scoring the SDS (the online version is automatically scored), respondents learn their Holland occupational theme codes, and then use these codes to locate and explore corresponding occupational information. The online version provides a personal report that includes both Holland theme scores and corresponding occupational information. (Note that other computer-based guidance systems also can be used as counselor-free interventions.)

Self-directed career activities can also take the form of part-time and summer jobs. While some researchers have shown that working too many hours leads to problems in academic achievement among adolescents (Quirk, Keith, & Quirk, 2001), other researchers have shown that there are a variety of positive outcomes for adolescents who work a few hours each week (Mortimer, 2003; Mortimer & Johnson, 1999). For example, high school students who work fewer than 12 hours per week demonstrate greater academic achievement than those students who are not employed (Quirk et al., 2001). Having part-time jobs can increase high school adolescents' confidence, cultivate time management skills, promote vocational exploration, and increase subsequent academic success (Mortimer, 2003). In addition, the wider social circle of adults that teens meet through their jobs can buffer the effects of family problems, and some skills young people learn on the job can give them an advantage in their later work life (Mortimer).

SUMMARY

In this chapter, we have examined how career development professionals can assist K-12 youth to develop more adaptive approaches to their present and possible career futures. We have argued that counselors who actively engage young people in career planning and exploration can provide substantial help to them by teaching them the skills needed to live more effective and satisfying adult lives. We have demonstrated that career interventions should be consistently and intentionally provided for all children and adolescents, according to their individual needs and circumstances. Further, we have suggested that career development activities begun earlier in children's lives can provide a foundation for later successful career development in young adulthood.

With respect to the types of interventions that are most effective, we suggest that a variety of methods can be used, depending on the needs of the child and the expertise of the counselor. Counselor-directed methods appear to be more effective than self-directed methods. However, both may be important as adolescents individuate and take more responsibility for their career directions. In addition, the inclusion of family and community support can strengthen the impact of career counseling with K-12 children. Finally, we hope that this chapter has acquainted the reader with the positive results that career interventions can offer all children and adolescents. Promoting the aspirations and career development of school-age youth is a rich and fruitful area for further empirical study. Providing skillful and informed career services to school-age youth can meaningfully assist them in establishing more satisfying, productive, and fulfilling adult lives.

REFERENCES

Albert, K. A., & Luzzo, D. A. (1999). The role of perceived barriers in career development: A social cognitive perspective. *Journal of Counseling and Development, 77,* 431–436.

American College Testing. (2003). *DISCOVER.* Iowa City, IA: Author.

Anderson, S. L., & Betz, N. E. (2001). Sources of social self-efficacy expectations: Their measurement and relation to career development. *Journal of Vocational Behavior, 58,* 98–117.

Ashford, S. J., & Black, J. S. (1996). Proactivity during organizational entry: The role of desire for control. *Journal of Applied Psychology, 81,* 199–214.

Bandura, A. (1977). Self-efficacy: Toward a unifying theory of behavioral change. *Psychological Review, 84*(2), 191–215.

Bandura, A., Barbaranelli, C., Vittorio-Caprara, G., & Pastorelli, C. (2001). Self-efficacy beliefs as shapers of children's aspirations and career trajectories. *Child Development, 72,* 187–206.

Betz, N. E. (1994). Basic issues and concepts in career counseling for women. In W. B. Walsh & S. H. Osipow (Eds.), *Career counseling for women: Contemporary topics in vocational psychology* (pp. 1–41). Hillsdale, NJ: Erlbaum.

Bishop, J. (1994). *The incidence and payoff to employer training: A review of the literature.* Ithaca, NY: Cornell University School of Industrial and Labor Relations. Retrieved May 29, 2003, from http://www.doleta.gov/documents/bestpractice/reportbp.htm.

Bloch, D. T. (1996). Career development and workforce preparation: Educational policy versus school practice. *Career Development Quarterly, 45,* 20–40.

Boekaerts, M. (1997). Self-regulated learning: A new concept embraced by researchers, policy makers, educators, teachers, and students. *Learning and Instruction, 7,* 161–186.

Brown, S. D., & Ryan Krane, N. E. (2000). Four (or five) sessions and a cloud of dust: Old assumptions and new observations about career counseling. In S. D. Brown & R. W. Lent (Eds.), *Handbook of counseling psychology* (3rd ed., pp. 740–766). New York: Wiley.

Bureau of Labor Statistics. (2002–2003). *Occupational outlook handbook.* Retrieved May 29, 2003, from http://www.bls.gov/oco.

Bynner, J., Chisholm, L., & Furlong, A. (1997). *Youth, citizenship, and social change in a European context.* Brookfield, VT: Ashgate/Aldershot.

Case, R. (1991). *The mind's staircase: Exploring the conceptual underpinnings of children's thought and knowledge.* Hillsdale, NJ: Erlbaum.

Chin, D., & Kameoka, V. A. (2002). Psychosocial and contextual predictors of educational and occupational self-efficacy among Hispanic inner-city adolescents. *Hispanic Journal of Behavioral Sciences, 24,* 448–464.

Cochran, L. (1985). *Parent career guidance manual.* Richmond, VA: Buchanan-Kells.

Cochran, L. (1997). *Career counseling: A narrative approach.* Thousand Oaks, CA: Sage.

Creed, P. A., Patton, W., & Bartrum, D. (2002). Multidimensional properties of the LOT-R: Effects of optimism and pessimism on career and well-being related variables in adolescents. *Journal of Career Assessment, 10,* 42–61.

Deci, E. L. (1992). The relation of interest to the motivation of behavior: A self-determination perspective. In K. A. Reengineer, S. Hide, & A. Knapp (Eds.), *The role of interest in learning and development* (pp. 43–70). Hillsdale, NJ: Erlbaum.

Deci, E. L., & Ryan, R. M. (1985). *Intrinsic motivation and self-determination in human development.* New York: Plenum Press.

De Goede, M., Spruijt, E., Iedema, J., & Meeus, W. (1999). How do vocational and relationship stressors and identity formation affect adolescent mental health? *Journal of Adolescent Health, 25,* 14–20.

Eisenberg, N., & Fabes, R. A. (1992). Emotion, regulation, and the development of social competence. In M. S. Clark (Ed.), *Emotion and social behavior: Vol. 14. Review of personality and social psychology* (pp. 119–150). London: Sage.

Erikson, E. (1968). *Identity: Youth and crisis.* New York: Norton.

Evans, J. H., & Burck, H. D. (1992). The effects of career education interventions on academic achievement: A meta-analysis. *Journal of Counseling and Development, 71,* 63–68.

Fisher, C. D. (1985). Social support and adjustment to work: A longitudinal study. *Journal of Management, 11,* 39–53.

Flum, H., & Blustein, D. L. (2000). Reinvigorating the study of vocational exploration: A framework for research. *Journal of Vocational Behavior, 56,* 380–404.

Ford, M. E. (1992). *Human motivation: Goals, emotions, and personal agency beliefs.* Newbury Park, CA: Sage.

Furnham, A., & Rawles, R. (1996). Job search strategies, attitudes to school and attributions about unemployment. *Journal of Adolescence, 19,* 355–369.

Gibson, H. L., & Chase, C. (2002). Longitudinal impact of an inquiry-based science program on middle school students' attitudes toward science. *Science Education, 86,* 693–705.

Gottfredson, L. S. (1981). Circumscription and compromise: A developmental theory of occupational aspirations [Monograph]. *Journal of Counseling Psychology, 28,* 545–579.

Gottfredson, L. S. (2002). Gottfredson's theory of circumscription, compromise, and self-creation. In D. Brown & Associates (Ed.), *Career choice and development* (4th ed., pp. 85–148). San Francisco: Jossey-Bass.

Gottfredson, L. S., & Lapan, R. T. (1997). Assessing gender-based circumscription of occupational aspirations. *Journal of Career Assessment, 5,* 419–441.

Gottman, J. M. (1983). How children become friends. *Monographs of the Society for Research in Child Development, 48*(86, No. 201).

Hackett, G., & Byars, A. M. (1996). Social cognitive theory and the career development of African American women. *Career Development Quarterly, 44,* 322–340.

Hansen, J. C., & Swanson, J. L. (1983). The effect of stability of interests and the predictive and concurrent validity of the 1981 SCII for college majors. *Journal of Counseling Psychology, 30,* 194–201.

Harkins, M. A. (2001). Developmentally appropriate career guidance: Building concepts to last a lifetime. *Early Childhood Education Journal, 28,* 169–174.

Henderson, S., Hesketh, B., & Tuffin, K. (1988). A test of Gottfredson's theory of circumscription. *Journal of Vocational Behavior, 32,* 37–48.

Herr, E. L. (2001). The impact of national policies, economics and school reform on comprehensive guidance programs. *Professional School Counseling, 4,* 236–245.

Hershey, A. M., Silverberg, M. K., Haimson, J., Hudis, P., & Jackson, R. (1999). *Expanding options for students: Report to Congress on the National Evaluation of School-to-Work Implementation.* Princeton, NJ: Mathematica Policy Research.

Holland, J. L. (1997). *Making vocational choices: A theory of vocational personalities and work environments* (3rd ed.). Odessa, FL: Psychological Assessment Resources.

Holland, J. L. (2001). *Self-directed search.* Lutz, FL: Psychological Assessment Resources.

Hoyt, K. B. (2001). Helping high school students broaden their knowledge of postsecondary education options. *Professional School Counseling, 5,* 6–12.

Johnson, D. C., & Smouse, A. D. (1993). Assessing a career-planning course: A multidimensional approach. *Journal of College Student Development, 34,* 145–147.

Johnson, M. K. (2002). Social origins, adolescent experiences, and work value trajectories during the transition to adulthood. *Social Forces, 80,* 1307–1341.

Jones, G., & Wallace, C. (1992). *Youth, family and citizenship.* Buckingham, England: Open University Press.

Kelly, G. A. (1955). *The psychology of personal constructs.* New York: Norton.

Kerpelman, J. L., Shoffner, M. F., & Ross-Griffin, S. (2002). African American mothers' and daughters' beliefs about possible selves and their strategies for reaching the adolescents' future academic and career goals. *Journal of Youth & Adolescence, 31,* 289–302.

Kush, K., & Cochran, L. (1993). Enhancing a sense of agency through career planning. *Journal of Counseling Psychology, 40,* 434–439.

Ladany, N., Melincoff, D. S., Constantine, M. G., & Love, R. (1997). At-risk urban high school students' commitment to career choices. *Journal of Counseling and Development, 76,* 45–52.

Ladd, G. W., & Kochenderfer, B. J. (1996). Linkages between friendship and adjustment during early school transitions. In W. M. Bukowski, M. William, A. F. Newcomb, et al. (Eds.), *The company they keep: Friendship in childhood and adolescence. Cambridge studies in social and emotional development* (pp. 322–345). New York: Cambridge University Press.

Lapan, R. T. (2003). *The Structured Career Development Interview.* All rights reserved.

Lapan, R. T. (2004). *Career development across the K-16 years: Bridging the present to satisfying and successful futures.* Alexandria, VA: American Counseling Association.

Lapan, R. T., Gysbers, N., Hughey, K., & Arni, T. J. (1993). Evaluating a guidance and language arts unit for high school juniors. *Journal of Counseling and Development, 71,* 444–451.

Lapan, R. T., Gysbers, N., Multon, K. D., & Pike, G. R. (1997). Developing guidance competency self-efficacy scales for high school and middle school students. *Measurement & Evaluation in Counseling & Development, 30,* 4–16.

Lapan, R. T., Hinkelman, J. M., Adams, A., & Turner, S. (1999). Understanding rural adolescents' interests, values, and efficacy expectations. *Journal of Career Development, 26,* 107–124.

Lapan, R. T., & Jingeleski, J. (1992). Circumscribing vocational aspirations in junior high school. *Journal of Counseling Psychology, 39,* 81–90.

Lapan, R. T., Kardash, C. A. M., & Turner, S. L. (2002). Empowering students to become self-regulated learners. *Professional School Counseling, 5,* 257–265.

Lapan, R. T., & Kosciulek, J. F. (2001). Toward a community career system program evaluation framework. *Journal of Counseling and Development, 79,* 3–15.

Lapan, R. T., Osana, H. P., Tucker, B., & Kosciulek, J. F. (2002). Challenges for creating community career partnerships: Perspectives from practitioners. *Career Development Quarterly, 51,* 172–190.

Lapan, R. T., Tucker, B., Kim, S., & Kosciulek, J. F. (2003). Preparing rural adolescents for post-high school transitions. *Journal of Counseling and Development, 81,* 329–342.

Lapan, R. T., & Turner, S. L. (1997, 2000). *Mapping vocational challenges.* All rights reserved.

Larson, L. M., & Borgen, F. H. (2002). Convergence of vocational interests and personality: Examples in an adolescent gifted sample. *Journal of Vocational Behavior, 60,* 91–112.

Larson, R. W. (2000). Toward a psychology of positive youth development. *American Psychologist, 55,* 170–183.

Lee, C. C. (2001). Culturally responsive school counselors and programs: Addressing the needs of all students. *Professional School Counseling, 4*(4), 257–261.

Lent, R. W., Brown, S. D., & Hackett, G. (1994). Toward a unifying social cognitive theory of career and academic interest, choice, and performance. *Journal of Vocational Behavior, 45,* 79–122.

Lent, R. W., Brown, S. D., & Hackett, G. (2000). Contextual supports and barriers to career choice: A social cognitive analysis. *Journal of Counseling Psychology, 47,* 36–49.

Leung, S. A. (1998). Vocational identity and career choice congruence of gifted and talented high school students. *Counselling Psychology Quarterly, 11,* 325–335.

Leung, S. A., & Harmon, L. W. (1990). Individual and sex differences in the zone of acceptable alternatives. *Journal of Counseling Psychology, 37,* 153–159.

Lopez, F. G., & Lent, R. W. (1992). Sources of mathematics self-efficacy in high school students. *Career Development Quarterly, 41,* 3–12.

Lopez, F. G., Lent, R. W., Brown, S. D., & Gore, P. A. (1997). Role of social-cognitive expectations in high school students' mathematics-related interest and performance. *Journal of Counseling Psychology, 44,* 44–52.

Luzzo, D. A., Funk, D. P., & Strang, J. (1996). Attributional retraining increases career decision-making self-efficacy. *Career Development Quarterly, 44,* 378–386.

Luzzo, D. A., James, T., & Luna, M. (1996). Effects of attributional retraining on the career beliefs and career exploration behavior of college students. *Journal of Counseling Psychology, 43,* 415–422.

Luzzo, D. A., & Pierce, G. (1996). Effects of DISCOVER on the career maturity of middle school students. *Career Development Quarterly, 45,* 170–172.

Maeaettae, S., Nurmi, J. E., & Majava, E. M. (2002). Young adults' achievement and attributional strategies in the transition from school to work: Antecedents and consequences. *European Journal of Personality, 16,* 295–312.

Marjoribanks, K. (2002). Family contexts, individual characteristics, proximal settings, and adolescents' aspirations. *Psychological Reports, 91*(3, Pt. 1), 769–779.

Markus, H., & Nurius, P. (1986). Possible selves. *American Psychologist, 41,* 954–969.

McDaniels, C., & Gysbers, N. C. (1992). *Counseling for career development: Theories, resources, and practice.* San Francisco: Jossey-Bass.

McWhaw, K., & Abrami, P. C. (2001). Student goal orientation and interest: Effects on students' use of self-regulated learning strategies. *Contemporary Educational Psychology, 26,* 311–329.

McWhirter, E. H., Crothers, M., & Rasheed, S. (2000). The effects of high school career education on social-cognitive variables. *Journal of Counseling Psychology, 47,* 330–341.

Meir, E. I., Melamed, S., & Abu-Freha, A. (1990). Vocational, avocational, and skill utilization congruences and their relationship with well-being in two cultures. *Journal of Vocational Behavior, 36,* 153–165.

Mendez, L. M. R., & Crawford, K. M. (2002). Gender-role stereotyping and career aspirations: A comparison of gifted early adolescent boys and girls. *Journal of Secondary Gifted Education, 13,* 96–107.

Mikulecky, L. (1989). *Second chance basic skills education. Investing in people: Background papers of the commission on workforce quality and labor market efficiency, Investing in people: A strategy to address America's workforce crisis* (Vol. 1). Washington, DC: U.S. Department of Labor.

Mortimer, J. T. (2003). *Working and growing up in America.* Cambridge, MA: Harvard University Press.

Mortimer, J. T., & Johnson, M. K. (1999). Adolescent part-time work and postsecondary transition pathways in the United States. In W. R. Heinz & R. Walter (Eds.), *From education to work: Cross-national perspectives* (pp. 111–148). New York, NY: Cambridge University Press.

Mortimer, J. T., Zimmer-Gembeck, M. J., Holmes, M., & Shanahan, M. J. (2002). The process of occupational decision making: Patterns during the transition to adulthood. *Journal of Vocational Behavior, 61,* 439–465.

Munson, H. L., & Rubenstein, B. J. (1992). School IS work: Work task learning in the classroom. *Journal of Career Development, 18,* 289–297.

Munson, W. W. (1992). Self-esteem, vocational identity, and career salience in high school students. *Career Development Quarterly, 40,* 361–368.

Naidoo, A. V., Bowman, S. L., & Gerstein, L. H. (1998). Demographics, causality, work salience, and the career maturity of African-American students: A causal model. *Journal of Vocational Behavior, 53,* 15–27.

Naimark, H., & Pearce, S. (1985). Transferable skills: One link between work and family. *Journal of Career Development, 12,* 48–54.

O'Brien, K. M., Dukstein, R. D., Jackson, S. L., Tomlinson, M. J., & Kamatuka, N. A. (1999). Broadening career horizons for students in at-risk environments. *Career Development Quarterly, 47,* 215–229.

Oliver, L. W., & Spokane, A. R. (1988). Career-intervention outcome: What contributes to client gain? *Journal of Counseling Psychology, 35,* 447–462.

Palmer, S., & Cochran, L. (1988). Parents as agents of career development. *Journal of Counseling Psychology, 35,* 71–76.

Parsons, F. (1909). *Choosing a vocation.* Boston: Houghton Mifflin.

Patton, W., & Creed, P. A. (2001). Developmental issues in career maturity and career decision status. *Career Development Quarterly, 49,* 336–351.

Phillips, S. D., Blustein, D. L., Jobin-Davis, K., & Finkelberg White, S. (2002). Preparations for the school-to-work transition: The views of high school students. *Journal of Vocational Behavior, 61,* 202–216.

Piaget, J. (1977). *The development of thought: Equilibration of cognitive structures.* New York: Viking Press.

Pintrich, P. R. (2000). The role of goal orientation in self-regulated learning. In M. Boekaerts, P. R. Pintrich, & M. Zeidner (Eds.), *Handbook of self-regulation* (pp. 452–502). New York: Academic Press.

Pintrich, P. R., & de Groot, E. V. (1990). Motivational and self-regulated learning components of classroom academic performance. *Journal of Educational Psychology, 82,* 33–40.

Powell, D. F., & Luzzo, D. A. (1998). Evaluating factors associated with the career maturity of high school students. *Career Development Quarterly, 47,* 145–158.

Quinn, M. T., & Lewis, R. J. (1989). An attempt to measure a career-planning intervention in a traditional course. *Journal of College Student Development, 30,* 371–372.

Quirk, K. J., Keith, T. Z., & Quirk, J. T. (2001). Employment during high school and student achievement: Longitudinal analysis of national data. *Journal of Educational Research, 95,* 4–10.

Rayman, J. R., Bryson, D. L., & Bowlsbey, J. H. (1978). The field trial of DISCOVER: A new computerized interactive guidance system. *Vocational Guidance Quarterly, 26,* 349–360.

Remer, P., O'Neill, C. D., & Gohs, D. E. (1984). Multiple outcome evaluation of a life-career development course. *Journal of Counseling Psychology, 31,* 532–540.

Rigby, K., & Slee, P. T. (1993). Dimensions of interpersonal relations among Australian school children and their implications for psychological well-being. *Journal of Social Psychology, 133,* 33–42.

Sampson, J. P., Peterson, G. W., Lenz, J., & Reardon, R. C. (1992). A cognitive approach to career services: Translating concepts into practice. *Career Development Quarterly, 41,* 67–74.

Sampson, J. P., Jr., Peterson, G. W., Reardon, R. C., & Lenz, J. G. (2000). Using readiness assessment to improve career services: A cognitive information-processing approach. *Career Development Quarterly, 49,* 146–174.

Sarriera, J. C., Silva, M. A., Kabbas, C. P., & Lopes, V. B. (2001). Occupational identity formation in adolescents. *Estudos de Psicologia [Studies in Psychology], 6,* 27–32.

Sattler, J. M. (1992). *Assessment of children* (3rd ed.). San Diego, CA: Jerome Sattler.

Savickas, M. L. (1995). Current theoretical issues in vocational psychology: Convergence, divergence, and schism. In W. B. Walsh & S. H. Osipow (Eds.), *Handbook of vocational psychology* (2nd ed., pp. 1–34). Mahwah, NJ: Erlbaum.

Savickas, M. L. (1997). Career adaptability: An integrative construct for Life-Span, Life-Space Theory. *Career Development Quarterly, 45,* 247–259.

Schmidt, A. M., & Callan, V. J. (1992). Evaluating the effectiveness of a career intervention. *Australian Psychologist, 27,* 123–126.

Schulenberg, J., Vondracek, F. W., & Kim, J. (1993). Career certainty and short-term changes in work values during adolescence. *Career Development Quarterly, 41,* 268–284.

Seidman, E., Lambert, L. E., Allen, L., & Aber, J. L. (2003). Urban adolescents' transition to junior high school and protective family transactions. *Journal of Early Adolescence, 23,* 166–193.

Shanahan, M. J., Mortimer, J. T., & Krueger, H. (2002). Adolescence and adult work in the twenty-first century. *Journal of Research on Adolescence, 12,* 99–120.

Sharf, R. S. (2002). *Applying career development theory to counseling* (3rd ed.). Belmont, CA: Brooks/Cole.

Shepard, B., & Marshall, A. (1999). Possible selves mapping: Life-career exploration with young adolescents. *Canadian Journal of Counselling, 33,* 37–54.

Siegler, R. S. (1991). *Children's thinking.* Englewood Cliffs, NJ: Prentice-Hall.

Skorikov, V., & Moore, S. (2001, August). *Relationships between career development and mental health: Implications of research.* Paper presented at the 109th annual convention of the American Psychological Association, San Francisco.

Skorikov, V., & Vondracek, F. W. (1998). Vocational identity development: Its relationship to other identity domains and to overall identity development. *Journal of Career Assessment, 6,* 13–35.

Smith, F. M., & Hausafus, C. O. (1998). Relationship of family support and ethnic minority students' achievement in science and mathematics. *Science Education, 82,* 111–125.

Smith, P. L., & Fouad, N. A. (1999). Subject-matter specificity of self-efficacy, outcome expectancies, interests, and goals: Implications for the social-cognitive model. *Journal of Counseling Psychology, 46,* 461–471.

Spokane, A. R., & Oliver, L. W. (1983). The outcomes of vocational interventions. In S. H. Osipow & W. B. Walsh (Eds.), *Handbook of vocational psychology* (Vol. 2, pp. 99–136). Hillsdale, NJ: Erlbaum.

Stonewater, J. K., & Daniels, M. H. (1983). Psychosocial and cognitive development in a career decision-making course. *Journal of College Student Personnel, 24*, 403–410.

Strong, E. K., Jr. (1927). *Vocational interest blank.* Palo Alto, CA: Stanford University Press.

Super, D. E., Savickas, M. L., & Super, C. M. (1996). The life-span life-space approach to careers. In D. Brown, L. Brooks, & Associates (Eds.), *Career choice and development* (3rd ed., pp. 121–178). San Francisco: Jossey-Bass.

Terry, J. (1999). A community/school mentoring program for elementary students. *Professional School Counseling, 2*, 237–240.

Thoresen, C. E., & Hamilton, J. A. (1972). Peer social modeling in promoting career behaviors. *Vocational Guidance Quarterly, 20*, 210–216.

Turner, S. L., Alliman-Brissett, A. E., Lapan, R. T., Udipi, S., & Ergun, D. (2003). The Career-Related Parent Support Scale. *Measurement and Evaluation in Counseling and Development, 56*, 83–94.

Turner, S. L., & Lapan, R. T. (in press). Evaluation of an intervention to increase nontraditional career interests and career-related self-efficacy among middle-school adolescents. *Journal of Vocational Behavior.*

Turner, S. L., Lapan, R. T., Yang, P., Trotter, M., Alliman-Brissett, A. E., & Czajka, K. (2003). *Using a structured career development interview with at-risk adolescents.* Manuscript in preparation.

Vygotsky, L. (1978). *Mind in society: The development of higher psychological processes.* Cambridge, MA: Harvard University Press.

Wallace-Broscious, A., Serafica, F. C., & Osipow, S. H. (1994). Adolescent career development: Relationships to self-concept and identity status. *Journal of Research on Adolescence, 4*, 127–149.

Wanberg, C. R., & Kammeyer-Mueller, J. D. (2000). Predictors and outcomes of proactivity in the socialization process. *Journal of Applied Psychology, 85*, 373–385.

Watts, A. G. (1996). Toward a policy for lifelong career development: A transatlantic perspective. *Career Development Quarterly, 45*, 41–53.

Whiston, S. C., & Brecheisen, B. K. (2002). Practice and research in career counseling and development—2001. *Career Development Quarterly, 51*, 98–154.

Whiston, S. C., Brecheisen, B. K., & Stephens, J. (2003). Does treatment modality effect career counseling effectiveness? *Journal of Vocational Behavior, 62*, 390–410.

Whiston, S. C., Sexton, T. L., & Lasoff, D. L. (1998). Career-intervention outcome: A replication and extension of Oliver and Spokane (1988). *Journal of Counseling Psychology, 45*, 150–165.

Williamson, E. G. (1939). *How to counsel students.* New York: McGraw-Hill.

Wolters, C. A. (1999). The relation between high school students' motivational regulation and their use of learning strategies, effort, and classroom performance. *Learning and Individual Differences, 11*, 281–299.

Worth, S. (2002). Education and employability: School leavers' attitudes to the prospect of non-standard work. *Journal of Education and Work, 15*, 163–180.

Youniss, J. (1980). *Parents and peers in social development.* Chicago: University of Chicago Press.

Zeedyk, M. S., Gallacher, J., Henderson, M., Hope, G., Husband, B., & Lindsay, K. (2003). Negotiating the transition from primary to secondary school: Perceptions of pupils, parents and teachers. *School Psychology International, 24*, 67–79.

Zimmerman, B. J. (2000). Attaining self-regulation: A social cognitive perspective. In M. Boekaerts, P. R. Pintrich, & M. Zeidner (Eds.), *Handbook of self-regulation* (pp. 13–39). New York: Academic Press.

CHAPTER 18

Counseling for Career Choice: Implications for Improving Interventions and Working with Diverse Populations

Matthew J. Miller and Steven D. Brown

ALMOST ALL PERSONS in the modern world arrive at a point when they must make (and sometimes remake) decisions about work. For some, this choice comes freely, naturally, and easily. However, for others, the choice-making process is much more constrained and difficult, often seeming as though there is no choice at all. Although a variety of factors may create problems in the choice-making process and limit an individual's ability to find satisfying work, a substantial body of research has accumulated since at least the early 1950s that provides important insights, guidelines, and prescriptions for working with people experiencing difficulties in deciding on the type of work that they want to pursue. One purpose of this chapter is to summarize this research and draw some specific suggestions for counselors working with such persons.

Despite the cumulative wisdom that has been generated through some 50 years of research on career counseling process and outcome, there are still serious gaps in our knowledge base. Foremost among these has been the tendency of researchers to treat all clients in studies of career interventions as if they are alike—as if the reasons for their indecision are similar and their goals for counseling identical. A second purpose of this chapter, therefore, is to provide some suggestions, based on our counseling experiences and the writings of others, about how career counseling might be differentially tailored to meet the needs of the widest array of clients.

Much has also been written about the unique issues and potentially career-limiting experiences that persons bring with them to counseling on the basis of their gender, race/ethnicity, and sexual orientation that need to be attended to by counselors to effectively facilitate the choice making of diverse clientele. Although, as we later discuss, this writing has yet to be incorporated fully into research on career interventions, it is a literature that counselors must know so they can provide effective career service in today's diverse society. Thus, a third purpose of this chapter is to highlight important implications for choice-focused counseling that are derivable from research and theory on gender, race/ethnicity, and sexual orientation and the career development process.

We also have a fourth purpose in this chapter—to highlight within each section important questions that still need research attention. In the end, therefore, we hope that the chapter serves not only as a practical guidebook for those providing, or preparing to provide, career choice counseling services, but also as a road map for those who want now, or in the future, to contribute to the research literature in the field in a way that not only advances knowledge but also fosters greater equality, justice, success, and happiness for all people—even for those who may feel now that their lives provide them with no choices at all.

WHAT DO WE KNOW ABOUT COUNSELING FOR CAREER CHOICE?

This section will discuss the effectiveness of career choice interventions and highlight how they might be improved. Suggestions for improvement will include ensuring that interventions are based more fully on empirically supported theories and that they are designed to take into account the unique goals and circumstances that clients bring with them to counseling.

HOW EFFECTIVE ARE CAREER CHOICE INTERVENTIONS?

Most of the suggestions and guidelines that we provide in this section are derived from meta-analyses of the career intervention outcome literature. Meta-analysis is a systematic statistical approach to synthesizing the results of numerous studies to arrive at empirically derived conclusions from a body of literature. The primary difference between meta-analysis and other approaches to research is that data are pooled across studies rather than individuals and then analyzed to address important research questions that might not have even been addressed in the primary studies that went into the meta-analysis itself. In relation to the career intervention outcome literature, some of the most important questions that have been addressed are:

- How effective are career interventions for choice-making difficulties?
- Does intervention effectiveness vary as a function of client characteristics (e.g., Are interventions more effective for men than for women?)?
- Does intervention effectiveness vary as a function of intervention characteristics (e.g., Are more sessions better than fewer sessions? Is individual counseling better than group counseling?)?
- Does intervention effectiveness vary as a function of counseling strategies or techniques (e.g., Is counseling outcome improved if interest inventories are given?)?

The first question is usually addressed by calculating across all studies an average estimate of the magnitude of effect of the intervention (called an *effect size* or *effect size estimate*). The other questions are typically addressed by comparing effect sizes. For example, to address the question of whether individual interventions are better than group interventions, the average effect size for studies that employed individual counseling interventions can be compared to the average effect size of studies that tested group interventions. Alternatively, when possible (see Whiston, Brecheisen, & Stephens, 2003), effect sizes can be calculated directly from studies that compared one form of intervention (e.g., individual) to another (e.g., group).

Although there are a variety of effect size estimates, the one that is most frequently employed in meta-analyses of career interventions is the standardized mean difference (usually symbolized as d). This effect size is interpreted as the difference, in standard deviations, between treatment and control or comparison group outcomes. Thus, for example, a d of 1.00 means that the average person in one group improved a standard deviation more than the average person in the other group on the relevant outcome. If the comparison was between individual and group interventions and the outcome was level of decidedness, a d of this magnitude would suggest that clients who received individual counseling became, on the average, one standard deviation more decided about their career directions than clients who received group counseling. If the comparison was between receiving any type of career choice intervention and no treatment, a d of 1.00 would suggest that the average counseled client became one standard deviation more decided than the average uncounseled person. A d of 0.00 would mean that the outcomes of the interventions being compared were essentially the same (the average person in one group improved no standard deviations more than the average person in the other group), while a negative d value would suggest an effect in the opposite direction (e.g., untreated persons improved more than counseled clients). The larger the value of d, the larger the differences between conditions and, therefore, the more potent the treatment effect.

The findings across four major meta-analyses of the career intervention outcome literature published between 1983 and 2000 suggest that career interventions in general are effective (S. D. Brown & Ryan Krane, 2000; Oliver & Spokane, 1988; Spokane & Oliver, 1983; Whitson, Sexton, & Lasoff, 1998), and those designed specifically for clients with choice-making difficulties yield an average overall effect size (d) of about 0.34 (S. D. Brown & Ryan Krane, 2000). Thus, it appears that the average client who receives help in the career choice-making process is, at the end of the intervention, about a third of a standard deviation more decided, satisfied, certain, and mature about his or her choices and efficacious about his or her decision-making skills than persons who received no career help. Although guidelines established to interpret effect sizes in the social sciences (Cohen, 1988) would suggest that this effect is modest (i.e., ds of 0.30, 0.50., and 0.70 are considered to be small, medium, and large, respectively), the meta-analyses have also yielded some important suggestions about how intervention effectiveness might be enhanced. It is to these suggestions that we turn next after briefly summarizing the focus and content of "typical" career choice interventions (see also S. D. Brown & McPartland, in press, for a discussion of how effect sizes of even this seemingly modest magnitude translate into socially and practically meaningful effects).

How Can Career Choice Interventions Be Improved?

Although career choice interventions that have been tested in the research literature are varied (e.g., they range from single, one-hour test interpretation sessions to semester-long career classes; are sometimes wholly self-directed or involve interactions with a computerized career guidance system with varying levels of counselor involvement), most seem to be built around Parsons' (1909) three-stage model of vocational guidance (diagnosis, information, and true reasoning) and are directed largely by prominent trait-factor theories—usually Holland's (1997; Spokane & Cruza-Guet, Chapter 2, this volume) theory of career choice. For example, of the 62 studies employed in the S. D. Brown and Ryan Krane (2000) meta-analysis, nearly all assisted clients in understanding their work personalities through standardized self-report inventories (62%), values clarification exercises (30%), card sorts (8%), and/or a "learning about self" module in computer-assisted guidance systems (26%)—see Gore and Hitch (Chapter 16, this volume) for a description of the two most widely used of these systems. The most frequent targets for self-understanding were clients' vocational interests and, to a lesser extent, work and life values. Objective ability tests, on the other hand, were never employed, and self-rated ability estimates were used to increase self-understanding or generate occupational possibilities in only 30% of the studies, most of which were via "learning about self" modules in computer guidance systems. Thus, it appears that clients in extant research-based career interventions are helped systematically to learn about their vocational interests and RIASEC codes and, although somewhat less frequently, their needs and values. They are virtually never helped to consider their abilities in a systematic way unless they are exposed to a computer-assisted guidance system as part of the intervention, and, even then, ability assessment is always by self-report.

In relation to Parsons' information stage, clients were also exposed to occupational information in 35% of the studies and were introduced to occupational information sources and encouraged to use them outside of regularly scheduled sessions in an additional 18% of the studies. Finally, direct assistance or instruction in decision making (true reasoning?) was provided to clients in 55% of the studies.

Thus, it appears that extant interventions that have appeared in the research literature, although ostensibly based on a long-standing model and well-developed theories, have not fully implemented either the model or the theories. Our first suggestion to improve current career interventions, therefore, is to incorporate the theories on which the interventions seem to be based more fully, especially by focusing on constructs that are suggested by the Theory of Work Adjustment (Dawis, Chapter 1, this volume) as intensively as interests and RIASEC personality types. Rounds (1990), for example, showed convincingly that a combination of interest congruence and need-reinforcer correspondence did a much better job of predicting clients' future levels of work satisfaction than did either congruence or correspondence alone. Thus, since one goal of most choice-based interventions is to help clients forecast and ultimately choose occupations that will give them satisfaction, there is both theoretical and empirical support for using both interest and vocational need/value data to generate occupational possibilities for clients—not just, as seems to be commonly the case, to engage in values clarification exercises to facilitate self-understanding of the latter.

Further, as Achter and Lubinski have so eloquently demonstrated in Chapter 25 of this volume, ability assessment is critical to facilitating the choice-making of the intellectually talented. We would also hypothesize that all clients, as suggested by the Theory of Work Adjustment (Dawis, Chapter 1, this volume), would benefit more fully if ability assessments, beyond self-reports, were incorporated into interventions. We would, in fact, go so far as to hypothesize that such assessments might be most critical for those whose ability perceptions may have been compromised because of the experiences that they have had growing up poor or as a woman and/or racial-ethnic minority in today's society, especially if accompanied by instructions that would reduce the negative influence of stereotype threats (e.g., Steele, 1997) on ability assessment results. Our goal should be to help people identify talents, overcome career-limiting influences, and reach as high as their talents can take them using the best methods available rather than to avoid such methods by assuming, without empirical evidence, that tests of intellectual competence and abilities will necessarily limit rather than expand possibilities.

In addition to incorporating more fully extant trait-factor theories into career choice interventions, it may be helpful to consider how other theories might inform practice. For example, as summarized by S. D. Brown and McPartland (in press), both Social Cognitive Career Theory and Gottfredson's Theory of Circumscription and Compromise suggest that some people (perhaps many) may prematurely eliminate viable career options from consideration because of inaccurate self-efficacy beliefs, incomplete occupational information (see Lent, Chapter 5, this volume), or through sex role socialization and other experiences of childhood (see Gottfredson, Chapter 4, this volume). Both theories also indicate that it is important to help people during counseling to identify and reconsider these possibilities, and both theories also provide some strategies to help in this process (see Gottfredson, Chapter 4, this volume; Lent, Chapter 5, this volume). Thus, we would also suggest that career choice intervention effectiveness might be further enhanced by incorporating such strategies into counseling, especially for those whose experiences are likely to have caused them to seriously truncate their possibilities and potentials.

As another example, Savickas (2002; Chapter 3, this volume) advocates that counselors help clients gain a fuller understanding of the personal salience of the work role vis-à-vis other life roles (role salience), their readiness to make a career decision (career adaptability), and the career themes that provide them with self-definition in order to make fully informed career decisions. These suggestions, as well as those provided by Gottfredson (Chapter 4, this volume) and Lent (Chapter 5, this volume), certainly also deserve to be tested in future career intervention research to see if they add to career choice counseling outcome beyond what can be obtained from fully implemented, nontruncated (Williamson, 1965; Achter & Lubinski, Chapter 25, this volume) trait-factor-based counseling.

Finally, the meta-analytic research has also suggested some ways that career choice counseling outcomes can be improved. S. D. Brown and Ryan Krane (2000), for example, identified five strategies that, when employed in career choice interventions, seemed to be critically related to improved counseling outcome across different types of clients and interventions. These five strategies, called *critical ingredients* by Brown and Ryan Krane, are:

1. Having clients establish in writing goals for future career work.
2. Talking with clients individually (in group, classroom, and computer-guided interventions) about their future written goals and difficult-to-interpret assessment results.

3. Exposing clients to models of effective decision making.
4. Providing time in session to engage in occupational information searches and promoting greater use of information sources between sessions.
5. Helping clients attend to, identify, and (if necessary) build support for their preferred career plans (see S. D. Brown et al., 2003, for a fuller discussion of these ingredients and how they might be implemented).

More importantly, Brown and Ryan Krane also found that interventions that employed any combination of three of these five critical ingredients, regardless of how otherwise theoretically truncated the interventions might have been, yielded large ($d = 0.99$), rather than small, overall effect sizes. Thus, we also suggest that, whatever else they do, counselors build these critical ingredients into their interventions.

Another important meta-analysis (Whiston et al., 2003) that compared directly the effects of different intervention formats (e.g., group, individual, computer, self-directed) has also yielded some important insights into how career choice interventions might be improved. The potentially most important of these insights, as summarized by S. D. Brown and McPartland (in press), included these:

- Totally self-directed and stand-alone computer interventions were substantially less effective than all other intervention formats.
- The effects of computer-directed interventions were improved considerably (effect size increase of 0.37) if a counselor was involved at some point during computer use.
- Structured groups were more effective (effect size difference of 0.34) than less structured groups and, perhaps, other forms of intervention—except that the comparative effects of individual counseling had been studied so infrequently that the relative benefit of this form of intervention could not be ascertained relative to other formats.

Thus, it seems that totally self-directed interventions, including self-directed computer-guided interventions, should be avoided unless no other alternative is available, and some degree of counselor involvement may improve the effectiveness of computer-guided systems (and perhaps other forms of self-directed interventions as well), especially if that involvement includes helping clients decipher difficult-to-interpret information and assisting them in establishing future career goals (see S. D. Brown et al., 2003). These data also suggest that structured group experiences may be the most empirically and cost-effective interventions for many clients.

SUMMARY AND CONCLUSIONS

The research discussed in this section provides some important data on the effectiveness of career choice interventions and some equally important insights about how they might be structured to maximize their benefits. First, it is clear that career interventions for choice-making difficulties are demonstrably effective. Second, however, it is also clear that their effectiveness, although currently somewhat modest, might be improved (perhaps substantially) in several important ways:

- Ensuring that they are embedded more firmly and comprehensively than they currently seem to be in the well-established trait-factor traditions in vocational psychology.
- Incorporating more fully the insights and strategies provided by other empirically supported theories of career choice and development.
- Building into them as many of the critical ingredients identified in the meta-analytic research as possible.
- In the case of computer-directed guidance systems, incorporating counselor involvement in ways that will maximize the effectiveness of these systems.

It is also, however, clear that each of these more general suggestions as well as the more specific ones outlined in this section (e.g., the hypothesized added benefits of ability and need assessments, the importance of critical ingredients to outcome, and the necessity of identifying prematurely eliminated possibilities) requires concerted research attention in the future. They thus provide a rich source of ideas for those who are interested in contributing, now or in the future, to the knowledge base of the field and to providing an empirical basis for helping people reach their full career potentials and achieve more satisfying work (and, ideally, personal) lives.

TAILORING INTERVENTIONS TO CLIENT NEEDS AND GOALS

Although research over the past half-century and more recent meta-analyses have yielded valuable insights into how people can be helped to make more satisfying vocational choices, there is still much more that we need to know to provide maximally effective career service to the widest array of clientele. The final two sections of this chapter focus on how we might tailor interventions more effectively on the basis of client presenting concerns and goals (this section) and social/cultural experiences (next section). In both cases, our suggestions and conclusions are much more speculative and clinically based than in the first section simply because career intervention research has not yet made sufficient use of available theoretical and empirical knowledge on these topics. The meta-analyses have also not been able to identify client characteristics that might suggest differential treatments because clients are not described with sufficient precision in the primary studies that are included in the meta-analyses to enable the types of analyses that would shed empirical light on these issues. These sections should, therefore, provide a rich set of ideas for those readers interested in a research career in the field as well as some ideas that practitioners may want (if they have not already done so) to attempt to implement in their practices.

VOCATIONAL PROBLEM DIAGNOSTICS

There is, for example, a large body of research that suggests that clients' choice-making difficulties may have different underlying causes, some of which may require different, and perhaps more intensive, forms of intervention than we described in the previous section. A host of factors that might contribute to a client's feeling undecided have been studied over the years—for example, lack of knowledge, anxiety, vocational identity, career maturity, goal stability, and career decision-making self-efficacy beliefs. More recent research has begun successfully to suggest a diagnostic scheme that might be usefully employed in counseling (and instruments that can aid in the diagnostic process—see, for example, Chartrand and Robbins' [1997] Career Factors Inventory described in Chapter 15). Specifically, cluster analytic studies (Chartrand et al., 1994; Kelly & Lee, 2002; Larson, Heppner, Ham, & Dugan, 1988; Larson & Majors, 1998; Lucas, 1993; Lucas & Epperson, 1990; Multon, Heppner, & Lapan, 1995), which have attempted to identify homogeneous sets of clients on the basis of presenting characteristics, have consistently identified at least two somewhat distinct client types: (1) those expressing a need for more self- and occupational knowledge and (2) those presenting with more pervasive problems. The latter clients, who have typically been labeled as chronically indecisive, tend to report more long-standing problems in making a variety of decisions that are accompanied, in some combination, by high levels of anxiety proneness (trait anxiety) and negative affectivity; a tendency to focus on, and ruminate about, what will go wrong with different choice options (i.e., fear of commitment); and low levels of perceived problem-solving abilities, career decision-making self-efficacy beliefs, and goal stability.

While the former (developmentally undecided) clients may respond very well to the types of career choice interventions that we described in the first section of this chapter, the more chronically indecisive client may, as has been frequently suggested (S. D. Brown & McPartland, in press; Peterson, Sampson, Lenz, & Reardon, 2002; Salomone, 1982; Savickas, 1996), require more intensive, longer term counseling. For example, although Whiston et al.'s (2003) meta-analysis suggested that structured groups may in general be the preferred form of intervention for many clients, this may not be true for the chronically indecisive. They may, rather, require individual counseling that focuses not only on helping them identify, and decide among, viable career options on the basis of their interests, needs, and abilities, but also on managing their anxiety, fears of commitment, and less than adequate confidence in their abilities to make important decisions. Further, although the S. D. Brown and Ryan Krane (2000) meta-analysis also found that maximum benefit for clients may be achieved after four to five sessions of career help, this finding may hold primarily for the developmentally undecided—more indecisive clients may require not only individual counseling but also substantially more than four to five sessions to be able to arrive at a decision to which they can commit.

The cluster analytic research has also, albeit less consistently, found at least two other client subtypes—those experiencing heightened anxiety that is focused only on their current career decision (due, perhaps, to its growing imminence—see Chartrand & Robbins, 1997) and those feeling stuck because of conflicts with significant others about their preferred career choices (Kelly & Lee, 2002). The former clients may need help managing their current feelings of anxiety in addition to finding a viable career direction, while the latter may not really need help identifying viable options (they may have already done that), but rather assistance in managing conflict with their significant others, garnering support for their plans, and (if necessary) considering compromise options.

Counseling Goals

There are other data to suggest not only that clients' indecision may have different underlying causes, but also that people come to counseling with different goals for what they want to accomplish. The counseling outcome research literature, unfortunately, treats all clients not only as if they are developmentally undecided but also as if they have only one goal, namely, to increase their career options. Although many clients do, in fact, want to expand their options, research has found that other clients seek counseling because they are confused by an overwhelming number of options (e.g., Gati, Krausz, & Osipow, 1996), while still others seem to need help deciding between, or among, a few viable options (e.g., Shimizu, Vondracek, Schulenberg, & Hostetler, 1988). Some even seek help to confirm, and receive assurance about, an already chosen option before they commit to it fully and attempt to implement it (Chartrand et al., 1994).

Again, although we have no data to support our clinical hunches and experiences, we would suggest that counseling should be tailored to the goals that clients bring with them to counseling. Those, for example, needing fewer rather than more options might benefit from focused, in-depth information searches over already identified options rather than broad information searches designed to uncover options. They may also benefit more from activities designed to help them prioritize their needs, interests, and abilities (i.e., identify core requirements) than from activities designed to help them broaden their self-understanding (see Gati, Fassa, & Houminer, 1995, for additional suggestions).

Likewise, clients who come to counseling for help in choosing among viable options are really not looking for more possibilities, but instead for help in making a tentative choice. Activities designed to assist them with the decision that they want to make are, therefore, clearly called for and may include help in considering the consequences for different decision alternatives. For example, a large body of research on Janis and Mann's (1977) conflict model of decision making has shown consistently that the thoroughness with which people consider both positive and negative consequences for the options they are considering is positively related to their postdecisional satisfaction and tenure and negatively related to feelings of postdecisional regret (Colton & Janis, 1982; Hoyt & Janis, 1975; Janis & La Flamme, 1982; Mann, 1972). One theoretical mechanism that appears to account for these results is that by considering potential consequences as completely as possible, people are inoculated against postdecisional setbacks if anticipated negative consequences materialize—they have had an opportunity to anticipate, and even prepare for, them.

However, it is also true that people may have preferred methods of making decisions that may or may not correspond to the somewhat rational approach advocated by the Janis and Mann (1977) model. Harren (1979), for example, suggested, and subsequent research has confirmed (Mau, 1995, 2000), the existence of at least three decision-making styles that represent people's preferred methods of making decisions across different types of decision-making situations—rational, intuitive, and dependent. Those who prefer to make decisions rationally tend to try carefully to consider their options and the likely consequences of each and ultimately choose the option that minimizes negative and maximizes likely positive consequences. Intuitive decision makers, on the other hand, tend to rely on emotions more than cognitions and tend to choose that decisional option that "feels right," regardless of the balance or positive and negative consequences associated with it. Finally, those who use a predominantly dependent style rely more on the input, expectations, and suggestions of others (and may defer to family or peer preferences) than on their emotional reactions to, or cognitive analyses of, possible options.

Research on the relative effectiveness of these decision-making styles in terms of their relations to postdecisional satisfaction has been both consistent and inconsistent—the dependent style has been shown consistently to be the least effective style, while the evidence is mixed on the relative superiority of the other two styles (see Mau, 1995). These data might, at first glance, suggest that we counsel dependent decision makers to adopt one of the other, apparently more adaptive, styles. Such a strategy might, however, be culturally insensitive and multiculturally inappropriate when working with clients from collectivist cultures in which the input from others, especially the family, are of paramount importance. Tang, Fouad, and Smith (1999), for example, found in a test of Social Cognitive Career Theory's choice model (see Lent, Chapter 5, this volume) in a sample of Asian American college students that the strongest predictors of these students' choices were their self-efficacy beliefs and their family preferences rather than their interests—students' choices were not based so much on their interests but rather on what their families wanted them to do and whether they felt capable in their family-preferred choices. This effect was also more pronounced for less acculturated students—those who more strongly adhered to traditional rather than Western values.

These streams of research, therefore, create a bit of a counseling conundrum—how do we remain true to the data but, at the same time, culturally aware and appropriate? One possibility that we have used is first to help clients, following the Janis and Mann (1977) strategy, to consider carefully the pros and cons of each decisional alternative, but then to encourage them to use their personally and/or culturally preferred strategy in arriving at a tentative choice and supporting them in their choice. Although the cross-cultural viability and effectiveness of this strategy needs research attention, it does have the potential advantages of inoculating clients against postdecisional setbacks while remaining true to their personal preferences and cultural dictates.

SUMMARY AND CONCLUSIONS

Clients would benefit greatly if counselors attended more closely to the conditions that might underlie their clients' choice-making difficulties and their goals for counseling rather than taking, as is the case in the research literature, a one-size-fits-all intervention approach. There are rich literatures that can be called on to direct such counseling efforts and to provide testable ideas and questions for subsequent research.

Some of the most clinically important questions for future research include:

- Are the types of well-developed, theoretically sound, and empirically based interventions that we advocated in the first section of this chapter as effective for chronically indecisive and choice-anxious clients, and those who are experiencing significant conflict with their families, as with more developmentally undecided (i.e., information-needing) clients?
- Are the interventions also equally effective for clients with goals of expanding, reducing, or deciding among options?

If the ultimate answers to either or both of these questions are, as we obviously expect them to be, negative, we need research that tests out in the counseling arena the effectiveness of interventions that are built specifically to address the needs of clients with differing presenting concerns and goals.

Such interventions, whether generic or specifically tailored, also need to attend to the unique career-limiting and inhibiting influences that clients may bring with them to counseling on the basis of their gender, race/ethnicity, or sexual orientation. It is to these that we turn next.

IMPROVING CAREER CHOICE INTERVENTIONS WITH DIVERSE POPULATIONS

The outcome research on career choice interventions seems to treat all clients, regardless of presenting concerns and goals, not only as if they are alike but also as if clients' gender, race/ethnicity, and sexual orientation have inconsequential influences on their responsiveness to counseling or the outcomes that they might attain. In fact, except for gender, we know little about the race/ethnicity and sexual orientations of participants in the intervention research. For example, in the 62 studies employed by S. D. Brown and Ryan Krane (2000) in their meta-analysis of the career choice counseling outcome literature, only 19% ($n = 12$) provided data on the racial-ethnic composition of their samples and none provided sexual orientation data.

Further, although it is often assumed that extant interventions may not be as effective for these clients as for others, there has been little research of which we are aware that has compared directly the effects and effectiveness of extant interventions with people of different races and ethnicities or sexual orientations. Finally, although some comprehensive models for directing career counseling with these groups have been developed (e.g., Cook, Heppner, & O'Brien, 2002; Fouad & Bingham, 1995; Leong & Brown, 1995), these models have not yet to any consistent extent been subject to direct empirical testing. All of this is somewhat surprising and very disconcerting given that professional guidelines have been developed that provide recommendations for responsible multicultural counseling (American Psychological Association [APA], 2003) and rich literatures exist on the career development experiences of women; people of color; and lesbian, gay, bisexual, and transgendered (LGBT) individuals. In the remainder of this section, we review the latter literatures to provide some suggestions for working with culturally diverse clientele and for directing future research.

CAREER CHOICE COUNSELING WITH WOMEN

The career development of women has become one of the most investigated topics in vocational psychology over the past 20 or so years. Although this research has revealed that the career development of men and women is similar in a number of respects, it has also identified some unique experiences that women may encounter that make their development somewhat more complex and their decision making more challenging and complicated than men's (Betz & Fitzgerald, 1987; Fassinger, 2000; Fitzgerald, Fassinger, & Betz, 1995; Flores & Heppner, 2002). Three somewhat unique issues that have been identified in the literature that make women's career decision making and success challenging are:

1. Dealing with multiple role relationships.
2. Coping with and overcoming gender-related barriers.

3. Managing the reentry process (see Betz, Chapter 11, this volume, for a more detailed discussion of these and other issues pertaining to women's career development and choices).

Multiple Role Relationships   One unique aspect of women's career development is the societal, familial, and individual expectation that a woman manage household responsibilities *in addition* to her career. While multiple role responsibilities (e.g., wife, partner, worker, parent, and homemaker) rarely affect the career development of men, women often must choose a career that simultaneously allows them the time and flexibility necessary to manage these extra-work roles. The effect of having to manage multiple roles may be to limit the number of viable career choices available to women; that is, women may choose (freely or not) to trade their career aspirations for work that accommodates multiple role responsibilities. Counselors, however, must also realize that not every woman seeking choice counseling desires to maintain household or familial responsibilities. Ultimately, career counselors must pay attention to how their clients assign meaning and importance to career and family and tailor career choice interventions appropriately.

Sex-Related Internal and External Barriers   Internal (e.g., work-family stress) and external barriers (e.g., discrimination, lack of support systems) can also reduce or restrict the range of acceptable occupational choices women consider. For example, the presence of barriers often results in women making traditional, stereotypic, female choices (Betz & Fitzgerald, 1987). Therefore, career counselors need also to take intentional steps to attend to and help clients identify potential barriers to their preferred choices and to other options they might have ruled out. Counselors can also help clients consider how barriers may be prevented or surmounted, including how support systems might be built as an aid in overcoming barriers (Richie et al., 1997).

Reentry   A number of women reenter the workforce after an extended period of absence (Padula, 1994). This population of women typically took a leave from the workforce due to multiple role responsibilities, including parenthood and familial responsibilities (Morgan & Foster, 1999). Reentry women are typically in their 30s or 40s, choose social or helping occupations, exhibit higher levels of self-reported career indecision and lower levels of self-reported assertiveness and autonomy, and tend to use the rational career decision-making style (MacKinnon-Slaney, Barber, & Slaney, 1988; Morgan & Foster, 1999; Pickering & Galvin-Schaefers, 1988; Slaney, Stafford, & Russell, 1981). Two other seemingly consistent findings from research with reentry women is that they have lower career aspirations and tend to choose lower level occupations than other women (Chae, 2002; Pickering & Galvin-Schaefers, 1988). While this may reflect the necessity of reentry women finding occupations that accommodate multiple role responsibilities, career counselors must also be cognizant of the fact that many reentry women aspire to occupations that underutilize their talents (Chae, 2002; Pickering & Galvin-Schaefers, 1988). Although standardized interest measures (e.g., Strong Interest Inventory) and card sort techniques (e.g., Vocational Card Sort) have been shown to reduce the career indecision of reentry women (Slaney & Lewis, 1986), counselors might also consider strategies provided by Social Cognitive Career Theory (Lent, Chapter 5, this volume) and other emerging theories (e.g., Cook et al., 2002) to help their reentry clients identify prematurely eliminated career options.

Some reentry women also face increased stress and conflict stemming from the accumulation of work and family demands. In addition, the reentry client must often face the barriers experienced by all women in the workforce (e.g., discrimination based on sex or age). Given the increase in mental and physical energy required as a partner, worker, and parent, in addition to possible sex and age discrimination found in the workplace, reentry women have been found to be at increased risk for emotional, physical, and psychological distress (Chae, 2002; Morgan & Foster, 1999). In sum, in working with reentry women, counselors may need to attend to and help clients manage or reduce any or all of the following factors in addition to those already discussed in relation to choice counseling in general:

- Work-family conflict.
- Multiple role demands.
- Age and sex discrimination in the hiring and advancement process.

Additionally, it may be important to assess the realism of clients' aspirations and help clients counter aspirations that seem to be unrealistically low (see Cook et al., 2002; Lent, Chapter 5, this volume).

CHOICE COUNSELING WITH LESBIAN, GAY, BISEXUAL, AND TRANSGENDERED INDIVIDUALS

While research on the vocational development of lesbian, gay, bisexual, and transgendered (LGBT) populations has been sparse (Chung, 1995; Lonborg & Phillips, 1996; Pope, 1995), more theoretically oriented writing has consistently highlighted some factors that may relate to choice-making difficulties that LGBT clients might experience, including (1) sexual identity development, (2) barriers related to sexual orientation, and (3) sexual identity management.

Sexual Identity Salient aspects of sexual identity development (see Troiden, 1989, for a review) typically occur during adolescence (Morrow, Gore, & Campbell, 1996). Given the stigmatization often associated with a nonheterosexual identity, it is possible that sexual identity development can be a traumatic and stressful experience for many LGBT individuals. Because sexual identity development typically occurs during the same period when academic and career interests crystallize (i.e., adolescence), LGBT individuals may not consider fully their career possibilities, may abandon potentially acceptable career choices due to stress and turmoil associated with an LGBT sexual identity development, and may even present with a very limited set of career options or no options at all (Fassinger, 1996; Morrow et al., 1996; Prince, 1995).

Barriers Related to Sexual Orientation Morrow et al. (1996) and Chung (1995) suggested that career choices of LGBT individuals may also be directly limited by external barriers related to sexual orientation (e.g., discrimination, lack of social support), which serve to hinder their ability to choose appropriate and satisfying careers. Lesbian, gay, bisexual, and transgendered populations have a long history of being discriminated against and oppressed in work and educational environments. Discrimination may cause LGBT clients to rule out otherwise gratifying and acceptable career alternatives; therefore, it restricts ultimate choices (Chung,

1995; Elliot, 1993). Discrimination in the workplace may make safety (as opposed to interest) the primary influence on career choice for LGBT individuals, limiting their career choices to occupations that they perceive as LGBT-friendly (Fassinger, 1996; Morrow et al., 1996). Assisting clients to explore nondiscrimination policies of different work environments may also facilitate the career choice-making process of LGBT clients (Rostosky & Riggle, 2002).

Sexual Identity Management   Sexual identity management is the way in which LGBT individuals handle self-disclosure of their sexual orientation (De Montefloers, 1986; Prince, 1995). Many LGBT individuals may choose to "pass" as heterosexual, while others may disclose their sexual orientation in the workplace. While the strategy of passing may eliminate the barriers associated with an LGBT orientation (e.g., discrimination, oppression), it may be detrimental to the overall well-being of the individual in the long run (Prince, 1995). Unfortunately, disclosing an LGBT orientation can have serious (and typically negative) repercussions on the individual's career advancement. It, therefore, seems important for career counselors to discuss the implications of sexual orientation disclosure with their clients (Elliot, 1993).

Pope (1995) summarized the major issues faced by many LGBT individuals and suggested that career counselors need to learn models of sexual identity development and be aware of their own personal biases and attitudes. Additionally, Pope suggested that counselors may need to:

1. Openly discuss disclosure of sexual orientation and discrimination in the workplace.
2. Assist clients in identifying and resolving internalized negative stereotypes about LGBT issues.
3. Identify, support, encourage, and use LGBT professionals as role models for clients.

Degges-White and Schoffner (2002) added that it is important to acknowledge (as opposed to minimize or discount) barriers, assist clients in weighing the costs and benefits of disclosure of sexual orientation, encourage the exploration of a wide variety of occupations, and use local LGBT resources, publications, and community centers when working with this population. Elliot (1993) also suggested that career counselors provide workshops that specifically address LGBT issues in the workplace.

CHOICE COUNSELING WITH RACIAL MINORITIES

It is estimated that by 2006 approximately 30% of the workforce in the United States will consist of persons from racial minority groups (U.S. Bureau of Labor Statistics, 2001). Career counselors need to be familiar with the unique sociopolitical history of the client's racial and cultural group and take steps to learn the values, norms, religion, tradition, and other aspects of the culture relevant to the career development of the client (APA, 2003; D. Brown, 2003; Sue & Sue, 1999). In addition to understanding group differences, the culturally informed career counselor should also realize that individual differences exist within each cultural and racial group and that variables of interest in career counseling may vary in salience across culture and race (Fouad & Bingham, 1995). In this section, we review salient issues for major racial groups in the United States (see

Worthington, Flores, & Navarro, Chapter 10, this volume, for a more detailed discussion of these and other important issues).

Hispanic Americans Hispanics are the fastest growing (Arbona, 1995; Lucero-Miller & Newman, 1999) and currently the largest numerical minority group in the United States (U.S. Census Bureau, 2000). Mexican, Puerto Rican, and Cuban are the first-, second-, and third-largest Hispanic subgroups, respectively (Arbona, 1995; Herr & Cramer, 1996). It is important to note that the term *Hispanic* is not universally accepted. Instead, some have suggested that *Latino* be used as a designation for this population (Calderon, 1992; L. Gomez, 1992).

Despite the fact that there are currently more than 35 million Hispanics in the United States (U.S. Census Bureau, 2000), research on the career development of this population is sparse (M. Gomez et al., 2001). What we do know from the literature is that, whereas Hispanics are a diverse group, they:

1. Are, in general, less well off than the general population.
2. Are underrepresented at all levels of education.
3. Are concentrated in the lower paid, less skilled occupations.
4. Have staggering drop-out rates from school, with many of them not finishing the 10th grade.
5. Are overrepresented among the poor and unemployed (Flores & O'Brien, 2002; Herr & Cramer, 1996; Miranda & Umhoefer, 1998; Sue & Sue, 1999).

Limited educational attainment as well as constricted knowledge and exposure to occupations may restrict the range of perceived or real occupational choices for many Hispanics (Herr & Cramer, 1996).

Cultural values may also influence the career development of Hispanics and the choices they make. While not exhaustive, some of the important Hispanic cultural values to consider are *allocentricism, familismo, simpatia, respeto,* and *machismo* (Fouad, 1995; Lucero-Miller & Newman, 1999). *Allocentricism* is the value that group goals come before individual goals (D. Brown, 2003; Marin & Marin, 1991). Similarly, *familismo* represents the strong familial relationships in the Hispanic culture. *Allocentricism* and *familismo,* when taken together, may mean that a Hispanic client seeking assistance for a career choice may be influenced more by family or community concerns than by personal interests. *Simpatia* and *respeto* refer to the desire to avoid conflict and deference to authority, respectively. *Machismo* is a term used to indicate the freedom, power, and authority of men in the culture. Career counselors, therefore, must realize that when working with Hispanic clients, desire for group welfare, deference in hierarchical relationships, and traditional sex roles may be present and will need to be considered in the decision-making process.

English proficiency and acculturation are two more factors to consider in counseling Hispanic clients. For many Hispanic individuals, their language of choice may be their native language rather than English. Preferred language (i.e., English versus culture of origin language) may best differentiate Hispanic and other minority groups in the United States (Herr & Cramer, 1996). Sue and Sue (1999) reported that Spanish is the primary language in more than 50% of the Hispanic households in the United States. Thus, limited English language proficiency for some Hispanics may represent a real barrier in the choice-making process.

Acculturation, which can be described as the degree to which the values of the dominant culture are adopted, accounts for much of the within-group variance among Hispanic individuals (Lucero-Miller & Newman, 1999). Lucero-Miller and Newman found that highly acculturated Hispanics were similar in career behavior to Caucasians, but that career behaviors, attitudes, and choice influences were different for less acculturated individuals. The latter seemed to be more influenced by *allocentricism, familismo, simpatia, respeto,* and *machismo* than the former.

Miranda and Umhoefer (1998) found that high levels of acculturation and English language proficiency were predictive of more positive career self-efficacy beliefs, regardless of the educational and personal history of respondents. Thus, it might be that less acculturated, Spanish-speaking individuals feel less competent in their ability to choose and obtain a desired occupation. Collectively, these results suggest that when working with Hispanic clients engaging in the career decision-making process, it may be necessary to assess the degree to which low educational attainment, limited English proficiency, and issues of acculturation are limiting their choices. Helping to foster greater educational attainment among Hispanic youth may be a particularly potent way to expand their ultimate choices and their later work satisfaction and achievement (see Arbona, Chapter 22, this volume).

African Americans   African Americans are the second-largest ethnic minority group in the United States with more than 34 million people (U.S. Census Bureau, 2000) and are the most researched racial minority group (Bowman, 1995). Previous data showed poverty rates for this group three times higher and unemployment rates twice as high as Caucasians (Bowman, 1995; Sue & Sue, 1999). Furthermore, they were underrepresented in higher education and overrepresented in low-level occupations that offered little room for professional growth and development (Herr & Cramer, 1996). However, more recent data suggest substantial educational and professional gains for African Americans (Sue & Sue, 1999). Part of this may be due to the role of parental influence on academic and career aspirations of African American adolescents. Fisher and Padmawidjaja (1999), for example, reported that African American students with college-educated parents were likely to aspire to vocational levels similar to those of their parents. Given the increased educational and occupational attainment experienced by many African Americans in recent history, it is not surprising that more than one-third of the African American population is middle class or higher, and more than 1.5 million work in executive and managerial positions (Herr & Cramer, 1996). Career counselors may be able to help facilitate the continued career development of African American clients by helping foster greater educational achievement for those from families where educational attainment has been limited (see Arbona, Chapter 22, this volume) and by attending to issues of racial identity, discrimination, and cultural values.

Racial identity refers to persons' beliefs and attitudes and acknowledgment of membership in their own racial group (Helms, 1990). Helms's (1995) Black Racial Identity model proposed five fluid statuses for African Americans: contact, dissonance, immersion/emersion, internationalization, and integrative awareness. Individuals in the *contact* status tend to prefer Caucasian standards and minimize the salience of race. The hallmark of the *dissonance* status is feelings of ambivalence toward the African racial group, typically due to an event that challenges the person's previously held worldview, which ultimately results in the search for racial identity (McCowan & Alston, 1998). At this point, a person may feel torn between preference for, and commitment to, Caucasian and African groups. *Immersion/emersion* is characterized by idealizing the African racial group and forsaking all things Caucasian. Individuals in the *internalization* status maintain a positive commitment to their racial group and are able to take a more objective perspective on the strengths and weaknesses of both racial groups. The *integrative awareness* status is marked by a person's "capacity to value one's own collective identities as well as empathize and collaborate with members of other oppressed groups" (Helms, 1995, p. 185). Helms conceptualized racial identity development as dynamic and complex, not a step-by-step process. Therefore, African Americans may experience one or more statuses at the same time and may move among or between them throughout their lives. Many writers have suggested that when assisting African Americans with career issues, it is imperative to assess the status of the client's racial identification and understand that it can impact the choice-making process.

Another important factor to consider in the career development of African Americans is the racism and discrimination they may have experienced. The racism and discrimination that many African Americans experience may serve to hinder their career development and restrict their vocational choices (McCollum, 1998). For example, research suggests that many African Americans seek out occupations they perceive to be racially friendly (McCollum, 1998). Career counselors must, therefore, take into consideration that an African American client's career choice may not be solely based on his or her career interests, but may be limited by barriers of racism and discrimination and a desire to find racially friendly work environments. It is possible that African American clients will not choose occupations for which they are well-suited and would likely be successful and satisfied because of these external factors. As with all diverse clients, career counselors should take care to understand the context and phenomenological experience of the individual.

African American cultural values tend to be group-focused rather than individualistic (Bowman, 1995; McCollum, 1998; Sue & Sue, 1999). Research has shown that family support and strong parental expectations facilitate career development of African Americans (Pearson & Bieschke, 2001). Therefore, it is important to consider family and community resources when assisting in the choice process. For example, providing role models from families and the African American community may facilitate the career choice-making of African American clients (McCollum, 1998).

In summary, to increase the efficacy of choice interventions with African American clients, counselors may need to attend to their clients' racial identity development, experiences with discrimination, and their cultural values. Also, the use of role models (either family or community) has been suggested as a powerful and positive way to shape career development and especially broaden the range of viable alternatives that are perceived as acceptable by African American clients (Bowman, 1995).

Asian Americans   More than 40 distinct subgroups make up the Asian American population (Sue & Sue, 1999). Demographers have estimated the Asian population in the United States will be between 50 million and 60 million by the year 2050 (Sue, 1994). Research on the career development of Asian Americans has been scant until recently.

Available investigations, however, have revealed that Asian Americans:

- Tend to underuse mental health services (but to use less stigmatized career counseling services somewhat more frequently).
- Have a low tolerance for ambiguity.
- Desire direct and structured career counseling interventions with nonconfrontational communication.
- Are less autonomous.
- Prefer a dependent decision-making style.
- Desire more prestigious occupations than other groups (Leong, 1985; Leong, 1991; Leong & Gim-Chung, 1995; Leung, Ivey, & Suzuki, 1994; Mau, 2000; Tracey, Leong, & Glidden, 1986).

The data also suggest that attending to cultural values and acculturation may increase the effectiveness of career choice interventions with Asian American individuals.

Traditional Asian values are strikingly different from Western values. For example, the valuing of collectivism means that Asian Americans seek input on career choices from others and do not rely solely on self-interest in the career decision-making process. Tang et al. (1999), as discussed earlier in this chapter, found that family influences and self-efficacy beliefs had the strongest impact on the choice-making of Asian Americans, whereas the influence of interests was virtually nil. These and other data (Leong & Chou, 1994) suggest not only that family expectations strongly influence many Asian Americans' choices but also that parents frequently expect their children to select prestigious and financially rewarding occupations and to avoid occupations that may expose them to prejudice and discrimination (Leung et al., 1994). In contrast to Caucasian Americans, Asian Americans may view making a career choice as a practical (e.g., How can I best provide for my family?) rather than identity-enhancing (e.g., What do I want from a career?) task (Leong, 1991). Therefore, the career choice process for Asian Americans may be pragmatic and not based on personal interest or preference.

Acculturation is one of the leading variables in Asian American research and appears to be a dominant moderator variable in the career development of this population (Leong, 2001). Leong and Chou (1994) suggested that Asian Americans with low levels of acculturation (i.e., oriented toward traditional Asian culture) tend to choose science and engineering occupations, whereas highly acculturated (i.e., equal orientation toward Asian and Western culture or oriented toward Western culture) individuals tend to consider a wider range of occupational choices. Leong (2001) also found that levels of acculturation were positively related to job satisfaction, overall well-being, and supervisor performance ratings. These data suggest that less acculturated Asian Americans, many who tend to make choices for reasons other than interest, may not be as satisfied with their occupational choices; may experience higher levels of psychological, interpersonal, and physical strain; and may even receive poorer performance ratings than their more acculturated counterparts.

When counseling for career choice with Asian Americans, it, therefore, seems imperative to assess the degree to which the client is acculturated to Western culture. For clients with low levels of acculturation, providing highly acculturated role models who can educate the client on possible workplace dynamics may assist them in making career choices (Leong, 2001). Leong also suggested that counselors might teach bicultural competencies to individuals with low levels of acculturation to facilitate a consideration of more nontraditional occupations. We outlined earlier in the chapter how a rational model of career decision making can be implemented in such a way that the client's ultimate decision is determined by her or his preferred decision-making style (i.e., dependent in the case of less acculturated Asian Americans). Such a strategy might be beneficial in aiding less acculturated individuals' decision making by helping them consider more fully the consequences of various occupational alternatives while not changing their culturally preferred method of decision making.

Native Americans   There are approximately 2.5 million Native Americans in the United States, a number that will almost double by 2050 (Sue & Sue, 1999; U.S. Bureau of the Census, 2000). While the smallest of minority groups, Native Americans are probably the most diverse of all cultural and racial groups in the United States (D. Brown, 2003). There are currently more than 450 (with some sources citing as many as 562) federally registered and distinct tribes encompassing more than 200 languages within the Native American population (Herring, 1992; Johnson, Swartz, & Martin, 1995; Martin & Farris, 1994; Sue & Sue, 1999). Historically, Native Americans, when compared to non-Native Americans, have been shown to have lower high school graduation rates, lower income levels, and poverty rates three times higher than the national average (Herr & Cramer, 1996; Johnson et al., 1995; Martin, 1991; Martin & Farris, 1994; Sue & Sue, 1999).

While theoretical and conceptual explorations of factors affecting Native American career choice and development exist, little is known about the career development of this population (Juntunen et al., 2001). Native Americans have been shown to have a limited knowledge of the world of work and to possess a narrow range of occupational possibilities (Martin, 1991). To develop and implement effective choice interventions with this population, it is important to understand some of the unique influences on Native Americans' career development, including family and community, cultural orientation, orientation to time, and language proficiency.

While there are between-group differences among the different tribes, Native Americans generally see family as a source of identity and worth (Garrett & Garrett, 1994), which is frequently more important than career (Martin, 1991). In fact, Native Americans typically defer personal (career) choices to family needs. The family is often seen as a resource for problem solving, thus making it difficult for many Native Americans to seek outside career counseling help (Martin, 1991). In addition to family, Native Americans may also have a strong sense of connectedness with their tribal community. Many Native Americans view tribal community as primary and career as secondary (Martin, 1991). Native Americans "perceive themselves as parts of the greater whole rather than as a whole consisting of individual parts" (Garrett & Garrett, 1994, p. 4). Native Americans are likely to choose occupations that simultaneously do not detract from familial and community relationship and benefit the family and community systems. Furthermore, Native Americans are often motivated to make choices that benefit the family or tribe (Garrett & Garrett, 1994). It, therefore, seems necessary for career counselors to understand the degree to which a client's family and community involvement is important to his or her career choice.

It is also important to realize the great cost of choosing a career that will require moving from family and relinquishing community support. Approximately two-thirds of the Native American population has moved from rural areas and reservations to urban areas in search of job opportunities (Martin & Farris, 1994). Many of these individuals continue to return to their rural communities or reservations on weekends to maintain familial and community ties. Given the increase in Native Americans migrating to urban centers for better occupational opportunities, it is important for career counselors to discuss the implications of leaving familial and community support systems. Counselors may also need to help clients weigh positives and negatives of leaving or staying and develop ways to alleviate the stress of leaving (e.g., help schedule and plan return visits to family and community) for those who choose to leave.

Similar to other minority groups, Native Americans must negotiate living in two cultural worlds. LaFromboise, Trimble, and Mohatt (1990) suggested that Native Americans' experiences in two cultures result in one of five acculturation statuses: traditional, transitional, marginal, assimilated, or bicultural. *Traditionalists* adhere to their culture of origin and typically do not accept mainstream culture. *Transitionalists* begin to accept some of the mainstream culture and loosen adherence to culture of origin. *Marginalists* do not adhere to either culture and are typically the least adjusted. *Assimilationists* adhere to mainstream culture, and the *bicultural* individual is competent and comfortable in both cultures.

LaFromboise et al. (1990) also suggested that traditionalists and transitionalists may place more emphasis on their families and communities when making career decisions, whereas assimilationists and marginalists may be more likely to consider other factors (e.g., personal interest). Bicultural clients might need help deciding in which cultural setting to seek employment or in finding opportunities to combine both cultures in their choice of careers (Martin & Farris, 1994).

Native Americans tend also to be present, rather than future, oriented and tend not to rely on clocks and calendars to monitor time (D. Brown, 2003; Sue & Sue, 1999). Therefore, chronological flexibility may need to be considered when choosing among occupations, especially for the less assimilated and more traditional Native Americans. Also, the number of proficient native language speakers is diminishing in Native American populations. The focus on English proficiency in Native American schools and poor modeling of English usage have resulted in many Native Americans who use both languages but are proficient in neither (Martin & Farris, 1994). Depending on the language proficiency of the client, the counselor may need to help expand choices by exploring occupations that use both native and English language skills.

In summary, it is important when working with Native Americans to be aware of the individual's:

- Relationship with family and community.
- Orientation to native and mainstream culture.
- Orientation to time.
- Language proficiency.

Career counselors should take intentional steps to learn about the tribe and reservation with which his or her Native American client is associated (Martin, 1995). Given the pervasive lack of knowledge of the world of work and restricted range of occupations that many Native Americans hold, choice interventions with this population could be improved by exposing clients to print and Web-based sources of occupational information as well as to successful Native American role models in nontraditional occupations. The latter (role models) may be particularly beneficial by helping clients learn how others have dealt with salient issues in the workplace.

SUMMARY

While career choice interventions have proven effective, their effectiveness might be increased further if counselors not only attend to the suggestions that we outlined earlier in this chapter but also ensure that their interventions are more multiculturally informed. We have attempted in the previous section of the chapter to note and discuss many (but certainly not all) of the unique issues that clients may bring with them to counseling as a function of their gender, race/ethnicity, and sexual orientations. We hope that our discussion of these issues, as well as the more complete treatments of them provided in other chapters in this book (see, for example, Chapters 10, 11, 22, and 26), will improve future services that diverse clientele receive and stimulate research that will ensure that what we do as counselors with diverse clients is as empirically based as possible.

Our ultimate goal in working with diverse clients, we think, should be helping them identify occupational options that make full use of their talents, interests, and personal and cultural values, including occupational paths that they might not have previously considered as viable because of their life experiences. But this is the goal we should have with all clients—to help them aspire to, and ultimately choose, occupations that are as high as their talents will take them, that fit as seamlessly as possible with other characteristics and roles that they value, and that will, therefore, ultimately provide them with a life of happiness, satisfaction, and fulfillment. A tall order to be sure, but one that is central to creating a more just society. We can think of no more professionally rewarding and socially important way to spend a professional career. We hope that readers agree.

REFERENCES

American Psychological Association. (2003). Guidelines on multicultural education, training, research, practice, and organizational change for psychologists. *American Psychologist, 58*, 377–402.

Arbona, C. (1995). Theory and research on racial and ethnic minorities: Hispanic Americans. In F. T. L. Leong (Ed.), *Career development and vocational behavior of racial and ethnic minorities* (pp. 37–66). Mahwah, NJ: Erlbaum.

Betz, N. E., & Fitzgerald, L. F. (1987). *The career psychology of women.* San Diego, CA: Academic Press.

Bowman, S. L. (1995). Career intervention strategies and assessment issues for African Americans. In F. T. L. Leong (Ed.), *Career development and vocational behavior of racial and ethnic minorities* (pp. 137–164). Mahwah, NJ: Erlbaum.

Brown, D. (2003). *Career information, career counseling, and career development* (8th ed.). New York: Allyn & Bacon.

Brown, S. D., & McPartland, E. B. (in press). Career interventions: Current status and future directions. In W. B. Walsh & M. L. Savickas (Eds.), *Handbook of vocational psychology* (3rd ed.). Hillsdale, NJ: Erlbaum.

Brown, S. D., & Ryan Krane, N. E. (2000). Four (or five) sessions and a cloud of dust: Old assumptions and new observations about career counseling. In S. D. Brown & R. W. Lent (Eds.), *Handbook of counseling psychology* (3rd ed., pp. 740–766). New York: Wiley.

Brown, S. D., Ryan Krane, N. E., Brecheisen, J., Castelino, P., Budisin, I., Miller, M., et al. (2003). Critical ingredients of career choice interventions: More analyses and new hypotheses. *Journal of Vocational Behavior, 62,* 411–428.

Calderon, J. (1992). "Hispanic" and "Latino": The visibility of categories for panethnic unity. *Latin American Perspectives, 19,* 37–44.

Chae, M. H. (2002). Counseling reentry women: An overview. *Journal of Employment Counseling, 39,* 146–152.

Chartrand, J. M., Martin, W. F., Robbins, S. B., McAuliffe, G. J., Pickering, J. W., & Calliotte, J. A. (1994). Testing a level versus interactional view of career indecision. *Journal of Career Assessment, 2,* 55–69.

Chartrand, J. M., & Robbins, S. B. (1997). *Career Factors Inventory: Applications and technical guide.* Palo Alto, CA: Consulting Psychologists Press.

Chung, Y. B. (1995). Career decision making of lesbian, gay, and bisexual individuals. *Career Development Quarterly, 44,* 178–190.

Cohen, J. (1988). *Statistical power analysis for the behavioral sciences* (2nd ed.). Hillsdale, NJ: Erlbaum.

Cook, E. P., Heppner, M. J., & O'Brien, K. M. (2002). Career development of women of color and white women: Assumptions, conceptualization, and interventions from an ecological perspective. *Career Development Quarterly, 50,* 291–305.

Colton, M. E., & Janis, I. L. (1982). Effects of moderate self-disclosure and the balance sheet procedure. In I. L. Janis (Ed.), *Counseling on personal decisions* (pp. 159–172). New Haven, CT: Yale University Press.

Degges-White, S., & Schoffner, M. F. (2002). Career counseling with lesbian clients: Using the Theory of Work Adjustment as a framework. *Career Development Quarterly, 51,* 87–96.

De Montefloers, C. (1986). Notes on the management of differences. In T. S. Stein & C. J. Cohen (Eds.), *Contemporary perspectives on psychotherapy with lesbians and gay men* (pp. 73–101). New York: Plenum Press.

Elliot, J. E. (1993). Career development with lesbian and gay clients. *Career Development Quarterly, 41,* 210–226.

Fassinger, R. E. (1996). Notes from the margins: Integrating lesbian experience into the vocational psychology of women. *Journal of Vocational Behavior, 48,* 160–175.

Fassinger, R. E. (2000). Gender and sexuality in human development: Implications for prevention and advocacy in counseling psychology. In S. D. Brown & R. W. Lent (Eds.), *Handbook of counseling psychology* (3rd ed., pp. 346–378). New York: Wiley.

Fisher, T. A., & Padmawidjaja, I. (1999). Parental influences on career development perceived by African American and Mexican American college students. *Journal of Multicultural Counseling and Development, 27,* 136–152.

Fitzgerald, L. F., Fassinger, R. E., & Betz, N. E. (1995). Theoretical advances in the study of women's career development. In W. B. Walsh & S. H. Osipow (Eds.), *Handbook of vocational psychology* (2nd ed., pp 67–110). Hillsdale, NJ: Erlbaum.

Flores, L. Y., & Heppner, M. J. (2002). Multicultural career counseling: Ten essentials for training. *Journal of Career Development, 28,* 181–202.

Flores, L. Y., & O'Brien, K. M. (2002). The career development of Mexican American adolescent women: A test of Social Cognitive Career Theory. *Journal of Counseling Psychology, 49,* 14–27.

Fouad, N. A. (1995). Career behavior of Hispanics: Assessment and career intervention. In F. T. L. Leong (Ed.), *Career development and vocational behavior of racial and ethnic minorities* (pp. 165–192). Mahwah, NJ: Erlbaum.

Fouad, N. A., & Bingham, R. P. (1995). Career counseling with racial and ethnic minorities. In W. B. Walsh & S. H. Osipow (Eds.), *Handbook of vocational psychology* (2nd ed., pp. 331–366). Hillsdale, NJ: Erlbaum.

Garrett, J. T., & Garrett, M. W. (1994). The path of good medicine: Understanding and counseling Native Americans. *Journal of Multicultural Counseling and Development, 22,* 134–144.

Gati, I., Fassa, N., & Houminer, D. (1995). Applying decision theory to career counseling practice: The sequential elimination approach. *Career Development Quarterly, 43,* 211–220.

Gati, I., Krausz, M., & Osipow, S. H. (1996). A taxonomy of difficulties in career decision making. *Journal of Counseling Psychology, 43,* 510–526.

Gomez, L. (1992). The birth of the "Hispanic" generation: Attitudes of Mexican-American political elites toward the Hispanic label. *Latin American Perspectives, 19,* 45–58.

Gomez, M. J., Fassinger, R. E., Prosser, J., Cooke, K., Mejia, B., & Luna, J. (2001). Voces abriendo caminos (voices foraging paths): A qualitative study of the career development of notable Latinas. *Journal of Counseling Psychology, 48,* 286–300.

Harren, V. A. (1979). A model of career decision-making for college students. *Journal of Vocational Behavior, 14,* 119–133.

Helms, J. E. (1990). *Black and white racial identity: Theory, research, and practice.* Westport, CT: Greenwood Press.

Helms, J. E. (1995). An update of Helms's white and people of color racial identity models. In J. G. Ponterotto, J. M. Casas, L. A. Suzuki, & C. M. Alexander (Eds.), *Handbook of multicultural counseling* (pp. 181–191). Thousand Oaks, CA: Sage.

Herr, E. L., & Cramer, S. H. (1996). *Career guidance and counseling through the lifespan: Systematic approaches* (5th ed.). New York: HarperCollins.

Herring, R. D. (1992). Seeking a new paradigm: Counseling Native Americans. *Journal of Multicultural Counseling and Development, 20,* 35–43.

Holland, J. L. (1997). *Making vocational choices: A theory of vocational personalities and work environments* (3rd ed.). Odessa, FL: Psychological Assessment Resources.

Hoyt, M. F., & Janis, I. L. (1975). Increasing adherence to stressful decisions via the balance sheet procedure: A field experiment on attendance at an exercise class. *Journal of Personality and Social Psychology, 31,* 833–839.

Janis, I. L., & La Flamme, D. M. (1982). Effects of outcome psychodrama as a supplementary technique in marital and career counseling. In I. L. Janis (Ed.), *Counseling on personal decisions* (pp. 305–323). New Haven, CT: Yale University Press.

Janis, I. L., & Mann, L. (1977). *Decision making: A psychological analysis of conflict, choice, and commitment.* New York: Free Press.

Johnson, M. J., Swartz, J. L., & Martin, W. E. (1995). Applications of psychological theories for career development with Native Americans. In F. T. L. Leong (Ed.), *Career development and vocational behavior of racial and ethnic minorities* (pp. 103–136). Mahwah, NJ: Erlbaum.

Juntunen, C. L., Barraclough, D. J., Broneck, C. L., Seibel, G. A., Winrow, S. A., & Morin, P. M. (2001). American Indian perspectives on the career journey. *Journal of Counseling Psychology, 48,* 274–285.

Kelly, K. R., & Lee, W. C. (2002). Mapping the domain of career decision problems. *Journal of Vocational Behavior, 61,* 302–326.

LaFromboise, T. D., Trimble, J. E., & Mohatt, G. V. (1990). Counseling intervention and American Indian tradition: An integrative approach. *Counseling Psychologist, 18,* 628–654.

Larson, L. M., Heppner, P. P., Ham, T., & Dugan, K. (1988). Investigating multiple subtypes of career indecision through cluster analysis. *Journal of Counseling Psychology, 35,* 439–446.

Larson, L. M., & Majors, M. S. (1998). Applications of the Coping with Career Indecision instrument with adolescents. *Journal of Career Assessment, 6,* 163–179.

Leong, F. T. (1985). Career development of Asian Americans. *Journal of College Student Personnel, 26,* 539–546.

Leong, F. T. (1991). Career development attributes and occupational values of Asian American and white American college students. *Career Development Quarterly, 39,* 221–230.

Leong, F. T. (2001). The role of acculturation in the career adjustment of Asian American workers: A test of Leong and Chou's (1994). Formulations. *Cultural Diversity and Ethnic Minority Psychology, 7,* 262–273.

Leong, F. T., & Brown, M. T. (1995). Theoretical issues in cross-cultural career development. In W. B. Walsh & S. H. Osipow (Eds.), *Handbook of vocational psychology* (2nd ed., pp. 143–180). Mahwah, NJ: Erlbaum.

Leong, F. T., & Chou, E. L. (1994). The role of ethnic identity and acculturation in the vocational behavior of Asian Americans: An integrative review. *Journal of Vocational Behavior, 44,* 155–172.

Leong, F. T., & Gim-Chung, R. H. (1995). Career assessment and intervention with Asian Americans. In F. T. L. Leong (Ed.), *Career development and vocational behavior of racial and ethnic minorities* (pp. 193–226). Mahwah, NJ: Erlbaum.

Leung, S. A., Ivey, D., & Suzuki, L. (1994). Factors affecting the career aspirations of Asian Americans. *Journal of Counseling and Development, 72,* 404–410.

Lonborg, S. D., & Phillips, J. M. (1996). Investigating the career development of gay, lesbian, and bisexual people: Methodological considerations and recommendations. *Journal of Vocational Behavior, 48,* 176–194.

Lucas, M. S. (1993). A validation of types of career indecision at a counseling center. *Journal of Counseling Psychology, 40,* 440–446.

Lucas, M. S., & Epperson, D. L. (1990). Types of vocational undecidedness: A replication and refinement. *Journal of Counseling Psychology, 37,* 382–388.

Lucero-Miller, D., & Newman, J. L. (1999). Predicting acculturation using career, family, and demographic variables in a sample of Mexican American students. *Journal of Multicultural Counseling and Development, 27,* 75–92.

MacKinnon-Slaney, F., Barber, S. L., & Slaney, R. B. (1988). Marital status as a mediating factor on the career aspirations of re-entry female students. *Journal of College Student Development, 29,* 327–334.

Mann, L. (1972). Use of a "balance sheet" procedure to improve the quality of personal decision making. *Journal of Vocational Behavior, 2,* 291–300.

Marin, G., & Marin, B. V. (1991). *Research with Hispanic populations: Applied Social Research Methods Series* (Vol. 23). Newbury Park, CA: Sage.

Martin, W. E. (1991). Career development and American Indians living on reservations: Cross-cultural factors to consider. *Career Development Quarterly, 39,* 273–283.

Martin, W. E. (1995). Career development assessment and intervention strategies with American Indians. In F. T. L. Leong (Ed.), *Career development and vocational behavior of racial and ethnic minorities* (pp. 227–251). Mahwah, NJ: Erlbaum.

Martin, W. E., & Farris, K. K. (1994). A cultural and contextual decision path approach to career assessment with Native Americans: A psychological perspective. *Journal of Career Assessment, 2,* 258–275.

Mau, W. C. (1995). Decision-making style as a predictor of career decision-making status and treatment gains. *Journal of Career Assessment, 3,* 89–99.

Mau, W. C. (2000). Cultural differences in career decision-making styles and self-efficacy. *Journal of Vocational Behavior, 57,* 365–378.

McCollum, V. J. C. (1998). Career development issues and strategies for counseling African Americans. *Journal of Career Development, 25,* 41–52.

McCowan, C. J., & Alston, R. J. (1998). Racial identity, African self-consciousness, and career decision making in African American college women. *Journal of Multicultural Counseling and Development, 26,* 28–38.

Miranda, A. O., & Umhoefer, D. L. (1998). Acculturation, language use, and demographic variables as predictors of the career self-efficacy of Latino career counseling clients. *Journal of Multicultural Counseling and Development, 26,* 39–51.

Morgan, B., & Foster, V. (1999). Career counseling for reentry dual career women: A cognitive developmental approach. *Journal of Career Development, 26,* 125–136.

Morrow, S. L., Gore, P. A., & Campbell, B. W. (1996). The application of a sociocognitive framework to the career development of lesbian women and gay men. *Journal of Vocational Behavior, 48,* 136–148.

Multon, K. D., Heppner, M. J., & Lapan, R. T. (1995). An empirical derivation of career decision subtypes in a high school sample. *Journal of Vocational Behavior, 47,* 76–92.

Oliver, L. W., & Spokane, A. R. (1988). Career intervention outcome: What contributes to client gain? *Journal of Counseling Psychology, 35,* 447–462.

Padula, M. A. (1994). Reentry women: A literature review with recommendations for counseling and research. *Journal of Counseling and Development, 73,* 10–16.

Parsons, F. (1909). *Choosing a vocation.* Boston: Houghton Mifflin.

Pearson, S. M., & Bieschke, K. J. (2001). Succeeding against the odds: An examination of familial influences on the career development of professional African American women. *Journal of Counseling Psychology, 48,* 301–309.

Peterson, G. W., Sampson, J. P., Jr., Lenz, J. G., & Reardon, R. C. (2002). A cognitive information processing approach to career problem solving and decision making. In

D. Brown & Associates (Ed.), *Career choice and development* (4th ed., pp. 312–369). San Francisco: Jossey-Bass.

Pickering, G. S., & Galvin-Schaefers, K. (1988). An empirical study of reentry women. *Journal of Counseling Psychology, 35,* 298–303.

Pope, M. (1995). Career interventions for gay and lesbian clients: A synopsis of practice knowledge and research. *Career Development Quarterly, 44,* 191–203.

Prince, J. P. (1995). Influences on the career development of gay men. *Career Development Quarterly, 44,* 168–177.

Richie, B. S., Fassinger, R. E., Linn, S. G., Johnson, J., Posser, J., & Robinson, S. (1997). Persistence, connection, and passion: A qualitative study of the career development of highly achieving black and white women. *Journal of Counseling Psychology, 44,* 133–148.

Rostosky, S. S., & Riggle, E. D. B. (2002). "Out" at work: The relation of actor and partner workplace policy and internalized homophobia to disclosure status. *Journal of Counseling Psychology, 49,* 411–419.

Rounds, J. B. (1990). The comparative and combined utility of work value and interest data in career counseling with adults. *Journal of Vocational Behavior, 37,* 32–45.

Salomone, P. R. (1982). Difficult cases in career counseling: II. The indecisive client. *Personnel and Guidance Journal, 60,* 496–499.

Savickas, M. L. (1996). A framework for linking career theory and practice. In M. L. Savickas & W. B. Walsh (Eds.), *Handbook of career counseling theory and practice* (pp. 191–208). Palo Alto, CA: Davies-Black.

Savickas, M. L. (2002). A developmental theory of vocational behavior. In D. Brown & Associates (Ed.), *Career choice and development* (4th ed., pp. 149–205). San Francisco: Jossey-Bass.

Shimizu, K., Vondracek, F. W., Schulenberg, J. E., & Hostetler, M. (1988). The factor structure of the Career Decision Scale: Similarities across selected studies. *Journal of Vocational Behavior, 32,* 213–255.

Slaney, R. B., & Lewis, E. T. (1986). Effects of career exploration on career undecided reentry women: An intervention and follow-up study. *Journal of Vocational Behavior, 28,* 97–109.

Slaney, R. B., Stafford, M. J., & Russell, J. E. A. (1981). Career indecision in adult women: A comparative and descriptive study. *Journal of Vocational Behavior, 19,* 335–362.

Spokane, A. R., & Oliver, L. W. (1983). The outcomes of vocational interventions. In W. B. Walsh & S. H. Osipow (Eds.), *Handbook of vocational psychology* (pp. 99–116). Hillsdale, NJ: Erlbaum.

Steele, C. M. (1997). A threat in the air: How stereotypes shape intellectual identity and performance. *American Psychologist, 52,* 613–629.

Sue, D. W. (1994). Asian-American mental health and help-seeking behavior: Comment on Solberg et al. (1994), Tata and Leong (1994), and Lin (1994). *Journal of Counseling Psychology, 41,* 292–295.

Sue, D. W., & Sue, D. (1999). *Counseling the culturally different: Theory and practice* (3rd ed.). New York: Wiley.

Tang, M., Fouad, N. A., & Smith, P. L. (1999). Asian Americans' career choices: A path model to examine factors influencing their career choices. *Journal of Vocational Behavior, 54,* 142–157.

Tracey, T. J., Leong, F. T., & Glidden, C. (1986). Help seeking and problem perception among Asian Americans. *Journal of Counseling Psychology, 33,* 331–336.

Troiden, R. R. (1989). The formation of homosexual identities. *Journal of Homosexuality, 17,* 43–73.

U.S. Bureau of the Census. (2000). *Census 2000: United States profile.* Washington, DC: U.S. Government Printing Office.

U.S. Bureau of Labor Statistics. (2001). *News: United States Department of Labor.* Washington, DC: Author.

Whiston, S. C., Brecheisen, B. K., & Stephens, J. (2003). Does treatment modality affect career counseling effectiveness? *Journal of Vocational Behavior, 62,* 390–410.

Whiston, S. C., Sexton, T. L., & Lasoff, D. L. (1998). Career intervention outcome: A replication and extension of Oliver and Spokane (1988). *Journal of Counseling Psychology, 45,* 150–165.

Williamson, E. G. (1965). *Vocational counseling: Some historical, philosophical, and theoretical perspectives.* New York: McGraw-Hill.

CHAPTER 19

Counseling for Choice Implementation

LaRae M. Jome and Susan D. Phillips

H AVING ARRIVED AT a promising vocational direction, the next task in the career development process is to implement that choice. Toward that end, counselors may be called on to assist clients in identifying opportunities and help them develop the skills to successfully present themselves to potential employers. What does the literature have to offer to assist counselors in guiding their clients through the implementation process?

Approaching the literature with this question in mind, we focus here on the strategies and interventions the literature provides for helping individuals to implement their vocational choices. The chapter is organized around two implementation processes—search and persuasion—that occur after an individual has chosen an occupational direction. The search section is focused on how individuals seek out—or create—opportunities to implement their choices, while the persuasion section focuses on how individuals convince others to allow them to pursue those opportunities. The literature from a broad range of fields (i.e., industrial/ organizational psychology, social work, rehabilitation counseling) published in the past 15 years was consulted concerning an array of transitions in which choices are implemented (e.g., finding a first job or seeking work after a job loss). Findings from intervention studies designed to increase individuals' success in the implementation process and findings from research designed to broaden knowledge about the implementation process are synthesized to provide counselors with guidelines for helping individuals through search and persuasion processes.

SEARCH

How do individuals approach the task of identifying—or creating—career and job-related opportunities? This section explores the literature related to how individuals search for career-related opportunities in their environments, specifically focusing on factors that facilitate or hinder the search process (see Saks, Chapter 7, this volume, for a comprehensive review of this literature and a model for organizing it). Synthesizing the extant research on the search process, we provide a picture of the characteristics of successful seekers of career-related opportunities. In addition, current research on searcher strategies and behaviors is explored, as well as research on interventions that offer guidelines for a successful search process. The section ends with conclusions about how counselors can guide job seekers through the process of searching for employment opportunities.

IDENTIFYING CAREER OPPORTUNITIES

We start with consideration of the individuals who have chosen a specific career direction. Having reached this point, their next step is to implement that choice by gaining access to (or re-entrance into) the workforce in their chosen field. To engage in this implementation process, they must seek out and identify information that will lead to career-related opportunities. It is generally agreed that the process of searching for information occurs both internally and externally; that is, individuals must seek knowledge of themselves concerning their preferences and competencies as well as seek occupational information from other individuals in their social network or other external sources (Steffy, Shaw, & Noe, 1989; Stumpf, Colarelli, & Hartman, 1983). The former (self-knowledge) enables persons to identify occupations they will like, while the latter aids them in finding these more quickly (see Saks, Chapter 7, this volume). There is some empirical evidence for a two-phase model of successful searching whereby the searcher engages in an initial, preparatory period of information gathering and exploration of self and environment, followed by an active, intense information- or job-seeking phase (Blau, 1994; Linnehan & Blau, 1998; Werbel, 2000). This process requires at least a minimal level of individual effort as well as the internal motivation to take action. However, even in an actively searching phase, the intensity with which individuals search (i.e., how often they seek information, how much information they seek, and from which individuals they seek information) can vary greatly. Further, the search process can unfold through both formal and informal mechanisms, and the degree of social isolation or support with which the search process unfolds also varies considerably. Indeed, it has been noted that the process of job searching can be a potentially difficult and uninformed process, especially for American youth, because there seem to be few formal mechanisms for guiding work-bound youth through the choice implementation process into the workforce (Mortimer, Zimmer-Gembeck, Holmes, & Shanahan, 2002; Orfield, 1997).

Within these general parameters, we turn to the literature to examine what is known about factors that assist—or hinder—the process of identifying opportunities. As summarized next, the literature suggests three perspectives on this issue:

1. Personality or social-cognitive characteristics of the individual that play an important role in the search process.
2. The behaviors or strategies that individuals might use in the course of searching (Saks, Chapter 7, this volume).
3. Intervention efforts that have been undertaken to help individuals achieve a more successful search.

CHARACTERISTICS OF INDIVIDUALS WHO SUCCESSFULLY IDENTIFY CAREER OPPORTUNITIES

As Saks's chapter (Chapter 7) reveals, the literature on the searching process sheds light on the characteristics of individuals that facilitate or hinder the degree to which they are successful in identifying career opportunities. Successful searchers seem to be oriented to the world of work and are psychologically ready and internally motivated to engage in this process (Borgen, 1999; Phillips, Blustein, Jobin-Davis, & White, 2002). Beyond this basic orientation, the research has yielded a profile of the personality and social-cognitive characteristics of individuals who achieve greater success in identifying career opportunities. One consistent theme emerging from this literature is that being extraverted and conscientious is distinctly advantageous in various aspects of the search process. Greater extraversion and conscientiousness are related to greater job-search effort and intensity (Kanfer, Wanberg, & Kantrowitz, 2001; Wanberg, Kanfer, & Banas, 2000; Wanberg, Watt, & Rumsey, 1996). Further, the more extraversion, conscientiousness, and positive affect individuals exhibit, the more they rely on the more successful social or relational search strategies (such as networking) in identifying career opportunities (Burger & Caldwell, 2000; Linnehan & Blau, 1998; Wanberg et al., 2000). More introverted individuals, however, tend to prefer more impersonal or formal approaches to searching, such as using want ads or mailing résumés (Linnehan & Blau, 1998).

While gregariousness (extraversion) and attention to detail (conscientiousness) facilitate the search process, especially in ease of interacting with others to obtain career-related information, some evidence suggests that excessive anxiety and other neurotic qualities can impede the process. More anxious job seekers tended to engage in less effective searching, such that they report great effort in the process, but engage in fewer actual search behaviors (Kanfer et al., 2001). Other studies have suggested that an optimal or manageable level of anxiety may facilitate the search process. For example, Phillips et al. (2002) found that a healthy level of anxiety facilitated the process by which work-bound youth searched for resources in their environment. Similarly, in a longitudinal study of the antecedents and consequences of job-search behavior, undergraduate students who reported higher Type A behavior engaged in a more focused search (Steffy et al., 1989).

Other individual characteristics related to successfully identifying career opportunities are self-esteem and (especially) self-efficacy expectations, with job-search self-efficacy being one of the strongest predictors of search behaviors. Blau (1994) found that global self-esteem was not related to either exploratory or active job-search phases; however, the more job-searching self-efficacy, the more likely individuals were to move from a preparatory to an actively searching phase. Saks and Ashforth (1999) found that only job-search self-efficacy—and not self-esteem—was related to job-search behaviors and employment outcomes.

Career or job-search self-efficacy has become a popular variable of study in the search literature, and it has shown promising links to employment outcomes. Solberg et al. (1994) delineated four dimensions of career search self-efficacy concerning the belief in an individual's ability to (1) engage in the job search, (2) to network, (3) to interview successfully, and (4) to explore himself or herself. Individuals with greater self-efficacy for engaging in the job-search process tended to report greater job-searching behaviors, more intensive searching, and greater success in obtaining employment (Kanfer et al., 2001; Saks & Ashforth, 1999; Wanberg, Kanfer, & Rotundo, 1999).

In addition, Kanfer et al. (2001) found that job-search self-efficacy and employment commitment were more strongly related to job-search behavior among unemployed job seekers than new job entrants, perhaps illustrating how job loss may affect an individual's self-evaluation.

BEHAVIORS AND STRATEGIES OF SUCCESSFUL SEARCHERS

In addition to the role of personality and social-cognitive characteristics of the individual, a number of specific behaviors or strategies are characteristic of successful searchers. Foremost among these is the intensity with which the search is undertaken. Specifically, the research evidence suggests that the more intense the job search, the more successful the outcome. That is, the harder individuals look for a job, the more quickly they will find one (Kanfer et al., 2001; Saks & Ashforth, 1999; Schmit, Amel, & Ryan, 1993; Wanberg et al., 1999). Further, this conclusion would seem to hold true for a range of individual circumstances. For example, for undergraduate students searching for a job, the more active and intense the job search, the more likely they will obtain employment soon after graduation (Saks & Ashforth, 1999). The same principle is evident for unemployed older adults, where those who engaged in a more intense search tended to have less depressive symptoms and were unemployed for shorter time periods (Rife & Belcher, 1993).

The intensity of the search—usually measured as the degree of time and effort put into searching for career opportunities—is associated with a number of other search-related variables. For example, Werbel (2000) found that the more intensive their job search, the higher paying, more satisfying jobs individuals obtained. In addition, job-search intensity seems to be facilitated by commitment to work, financial difficulties, and confidence in job-search abilities (Wanberg et al., 1999).

Recognizing that searching for career opportunities may well occur over an extended time period, several researchers have examined how searcher behaviors and strategies might evolve over time. Barber, Daly, Giannantonio, and Phillips (1994), for example, found that job-search behaviors change over time, such that as the search continues, college and vocational-technical student seekers become less intense in their search (i.e., use fewer sources, actively search for fewer hours, expend less effort), use fewer formal job-search sources, and seek less information related to obtaining a job. For searchers who had not obtained employment three months after graduation, however, the pattern reversed in that they increased their use of more formal sources and again engaged in a more extensive search process. Given that a long or unsuccessful search process can take an emotional toll on searchers, advice from college graduates who have successfully traversed the job-search process includes beginning the job-search process early (i.e., before graduation), coping with frustration if active searching does not result in immediate job offers, and being flexible (e.g., willing to take a temporary position; Crozier & Grassick, 1996).

In the face of an extended search process, some findings suggest that a negative relationship exists between perceived control over the job-search process and job-search behaviors. Specifically, Saks and Ashforth (1999) suggested that the less control individuals perceive, the more intensely they search. In a similar vein, Wanberg et al. (1999) found that motivational control, and not search self-efficacy, was related to job-searching intensity for individuals who had been unemployed for at least three months. These findings imply that when individuals have been searching unsuccessfully, their ability to stay cognitively focused on activities such as goal setting and planning will be more helpful in maintaining an active search than will their confidence in their ability to search.

Apart from the intensity of the search process, several investigators have focused on specific search strategies. Common search strategies include networking, sending résumés, perusing want ads, using recruitment services or employment agencies, taking internships, and cold calling (Crozier & Grassick, 1996; Green, Tigges, & Diaz, 1999; Mau & Kopischke, 2001; Montoya & Atkinson, 1996). Some research has focused on the search strategies considered important by adolescents for the purpose of facilitating the school-to-work transition. Furnham and Rawles (1996), for example, found that the job-search strategies of British adolescents were related to their attributions and attitudes toward school and employment. Those with more internal attributions, who liked school more, were more open to career advice, and those who sought more intrinsically satisfying jobs believed in the importance of using self-effort job-search strategies (i.e., strategies that involved taking initiative such as cold calling, asking for advice, and actively gathering information). Similarly, Heaven (1995) found that Australian high school students held different views of the merits of self-effort strategies that required individual action versus external strategies that involved seeking help from others or registering with employment agencies. It was found that stronger work ethic beliefs were related to greater belief in the importance of self-effort strategies. Further, it was found that the greater the students' need for a job, the more useful they saw external strategies. In contrast, the higher the status of the job being sought, the more important the self-effort strategies were seen.

One of the most popular job-search strategies reported by job seekers is an informal job-search strategy that entails networking with people in an individual's social environment, such as family, friends, coworkers, and neighbors (Schwab, Rynes, & Aldag, 1987; Villar, Juan, Corominas, & Capell, 2000; Wanberg et al., 2000). Granovetter (1973, 1995) distinguished between "strong" ties (networking with close social network of family and friends) and "weak" ties (networking with professional acquaintances). Studying these differential strategies, research has indicated that those using weak ties in searching tended to obtain jobs with higher incomes, were more satisfied with their jobs, and were more likely to be working within their field of study compared to individuals who used strong ties or formal job strategies (D. W. Brown & Konrad, 2001; Villar et al., 2000).

Although there is good evidence about the generally successful nature of networking (D. W. Brown & Konrad, 2001; Granovetter, 1995; Villar et al., 2000; Wanberg et al., 2000), not all searchers are comparably successful in applying this tool. Many searchers, especially those with less work experience and more barriers in the search process, may underestimate the importance of networking (Montoya & Atkinson, 1996). In addition, it has been noted that introverted individuals may be at a disadvantage in their searches because they may be less inclined to network and may have fewer social contacts (Wanberg et al., 2000). Comfort with networking has been related to networking intensity above and beyond personality factors, and the more confidence or self-efficacy with networking that individuals reported, the more they relied on that search strategy (Villar et al., 2000; Wanberg et al., 2000). Although greater use of social networking does not increase the speed of obtaining employment, the use of the strategy does seem to be related to greater possibility of securing a position (Wanberg et al., 2000). Overall, the findings related to social networking point to the importance of increasing networking comfort for those seeking employment.

Given the popularity of networking strategies and their links to successful employment outcomes, gender and racial-ethnic group differences concerning using others in the search process have important implications. Although some research found no gender differences in use of networking (Mau & Kopischke, 2001; Villar et al., 2000), other findings report that men tend to use networking strategies more than women (Frazee, 1997; Straits, 1998). Further exploration of networking strategies reveals that job searchers tend to network with same-race (Green et al., 1999) and same-sex (Straits, 1998) others. One potential disadvantage of networking within an individual's race or gender is the perpetuation of sex segregation in the workplace as well as channeling racial-ethnic minorities into lower paying jobs (Green et al., 1999; Huffman & Torres, 2002; Straits, 1998).

SEARCH INTERVENTIONS

Interventions for increasing the search behavior of job seekers have largely employed a structured group model that relies on social learning principles in teaching and reinforcing job-search skills. The two most popular of these group interventions are the Job Club (Azrin & Besalel, 1980; Azrin, Flores, & Kaplan, 1975) and JOBS (Caplan, Vinokur, Price, & van Ryn, 1989), and evidence of the efficacy of these intervention programs has been accumulated since the early 1980s (S. D. Brown & McPartland, in press).

These group interventions have been linked to a variety of positive outcomes for different populations. For example, Rife (1997) described a job-search club for unemployed older women, based on social learning and self-efficacy principles. Participants showed decreased levels of depression as well as increased job-searching self-efficacy following the group. Similarly, Rife and Belcher (1994) reported that older adults participating in a 12-week job club were more likely to be employed, less depressed, and making more money and working more hours than those in the control group. P. W. Corrigan, Reedy, Thadani, and Ganet (1995) found that adults with severe mental illness who completed a job club improved in their quality of life, reported fewer negative psychological symptoms, and showed greater job interviewing skills after the club, compared to individuals who dropped out. Those with poorer quality of life were more likely to complete the group. Admunson and Borgen (1988) found that unemployed adults reported largely helpful, positive effects from participating in a job club. Further evidence for the benefits of employment support groups was found by Borgen (1999), who reported that unemployed adults evaluated their life situations more positively after the support program and found the program very empowering.

Recent research has focused on understanding the mechanisms underlying the efficacy of job-searching clubs, namely, their ability to enhance searchers' self-efficacy in their job-search skills. Eden and Aviram (1993) designed a self-efficacy training workshop for unemployed adults that used modeling, role playing, feedback, and positive reinforcement to enhance participants' self-efficacy for job-searching behaviors. The workshop was associated with increased global self-efficacy for unemployed adults, energizing them to continue with the job search. Specifically, those who had high general self-efficacy before beginning the intervention were more likely to increase their job-searching activities, after which they were more likely to obtain employment. The authors concluded that job seekers with high self-efficacy in general have the confidence in their ability to engage in the job-search process on their own, but interventions that boost confidence in job-seeking skills are especially helpful for those individuals with lower general self-efficacy. In a related intervention, van Ryn and Vinokur (1992) found that a job skills training program for unemployed adults increased participants' confidence in job searching; job-search self-efficacy influenced job-search behaviors by increasing participants' intentions and attitudes concerning searching for career opportunities. At a four-month follow-up, the treatment also showed direct effects on job-search behaviors. Finally, welfare recipients participating in a job club showed increased career search self-efficacy at posttest but no change in global self-esteem; all participants were employed at a 90-day follow-up (Sterrett, 1998).

Another focus of the intervention research is on the social support embedded within the job club model. Here, there is considerable evidence about the power of interacting with, and gaining support from, similar others through the search process, especially in boosting a positive outlook about the job situation and receiving support through a stressful situation (Admunson & Borgen, 1988). Wenzel (1993) found that for financially disadvantaged and homeless individuals participating in employment training, the more social support they received, specifically in the form of validating their personal worth and inherent skills, the more their self-efficacy for finding a job increased. Unemployed older adults who received more support from others engaged in more intense job-search activities (Rife & Belcher, 1993). Wanberg et al. (1996) found that job-seeking support was related to greater job-seeking behavior. The social support that seemed most influential for this group was positive messages from unemployed peers, where messages from employed family and friends were perceived as less supportive.

The literature provides descriptions of some search interventions and programs that do not necessarily stem from a job-finding club model, but sound promising and need to be evaluated for their effectiveness. For example, one creative intervention includes a collaborative program between university counseling centers and libraries to provide students with job-searching skills and job-related information (DeHart, 1996). Other programs focus on providing students with work-related experiences to better prepare them to engage in the job-search process in the future. For example, there are programs focused on linking school and businesses to help keep at-risk youth in school (Gendron, 1997), preparing college students for a career in law enforcement (Dale, 1996), preparing high school students for technical careers (Kate, 1994), increasing communication skills and job-search self-efficacy among college students with disabilities (M. J. Corrigan, Jones, & McWhirter, 2001), and emphasizing importance of internships for their exposure to corporate culture (Jones, 1995; Rimby & Davis, 1993). While many of the described programs would seem innovative and promising, the evidence about their usefulness in the search process remains to be established.

CONCLUSIONS

For counselors seeking to aid individuals in searching for career opportunities, the literature offers a number of suggestions. First, counselors need to be aware of the influential role that personality and social-cognitive characteristics appear to play in the search process. Those searchers for whom interpersonal interactions do not come easily may be at a disadvantage, and counselors may seek to provide social support and identify ways to enhance comfort with the highly social nature of the search process. Second, counselors can foster the use of successful search strategies and behaviors by encouraging searchers to maintain an active, intense, concentrated search that is continually vigilant about networking with individuals in the client's environment. This idea coincides with the popular notion that job seekers must make job searching an active, full-time job. Third, counselors can seek to enhance individuals' searching self-efficacy, as well as ensure that the search process is accompanied by individual or group support. Finally, counselors' efforts to evaluate innovative search interventions and report program effectiveness would greatly contribute to knowledge about the effectiveness of job-search interventions.

PERSUASION

Once individuals have successfully searched out career opportunities in their environment, the next task of implementation involves persuading others to allow them to pursue those desired opportunities. In this process, individuals wrestle with issues of how to present themselves to make them optimally attractive to prospective employers and how to negotiate the terms of their prospective employment. Correspondingly, the literature in this area focuses on building interviewing and communication skills (whether in writing or in person) and increasing competencies in negotiation. In this section, we focus on research and interventions designed to help individuals to navigate the process of obtaining actual entry into the work world. The characteristics of individuals who are successful in this persuasion process are explored, in addition to the research on effective interventions for enhancing persuasion skills. Finally, implications for counselors helping individuals through the persuasion process are explored.

CHARACTERISTICS OF PEOPLE WHO SUCCESSFULLY PERSUADE

Paralleling the findings in the section on searching, certain personality characteristics seem to provide advantages in persuasion-related activities. Greater extraversion, conscientiousness, and positive affect are linked to greater interview success, such that more extraverted individuals were found to receive multiple offers for interviews and jobs (Burger & Caldwell, 2000; Caldwell & Burger, 1998). In addition, more extraverted individuals were more likely to prepare for interviews by interacting with other people, and this use of social job-searching strategies was also related to greater success in interviewing (Burger & Caldwell, 2000). Beyond personality traits, other individual differences show links to successfully implementing an individual's career choices. A Finnish study revealed that youth who tended to use more avoidant strategies (such as being passive and having expectations that they will fail) were less likely to find employment within a few months (Määtä, Nurmi, & Majava, 2002).

Successful persuasion also seems connected to success in the search process itself in that the more job-search behaviors engaged in by individuals, the more interviews they report receiving (Mau & Kopischke, 2001). On the other hand,

Steffy et al. (1989) found that job-search behaviors were only somewhat related to interviewing activities and number of job offers. However, the more confidence undergraduate students demonstrated in obtaining a job, the better their interview and placement outcomes, thus highlighting the importance of self-efficacy throughout the implementation process.

Finally, participating in a work experience outside school may give individuals an advantage when it comes to success in entering the workforce. A Swedish study (Gustafusson, 2002) explored the differences between youth who had participated in "school-arranged workplace training" (i.e., cooperative education) and those who had engaged in "market-governed workplace training" (i.e., students who were employed in jobs outside school). Youth who had held part-time extracurricular jobs while in high school were nearly three times as likely to avoid being unemployed later and showed more positive attitudes about their personal chances of success in the labor market compared to those who had participated in school-arranged workplace training.

ENHANCING PERSUASION SKILLS

Given the importance of the job-seeking process, it is not surprising that job seekers may lack confidence in their persuasion skills and that they need further assistance with cover letter and résumé writing and interviewing (Montoya & Atkinson, 1996; Thompson & Dickey, 1994). It is interesting that strategies to enhance these persuasion skills seem to be more prevalent in the popular press than in the professional literature. With respect to written persuasion (résumé writing, in particular), popular job-search books tout the virtues of a good résumé, and some evidence suggests that college graduates largely obtain jobs by simply submitting their résumés (Mau & Kopischke, 2001). However, little evidence is available on what résumé characteristics may be more advantageous in the persuasion process or how best to teach individuals to develop résumé writing skills.

There is some evidence that conciseness and brevity are essential in résumé formation in that one-page résumés were seen as more attractive by interviewers compared to longer résumés or narrative-style résumés and qualitative briefs (Helwig, 1985; Thoms, McMasters, Roberts, & Dombkowski, 1999). Ryland and Rosen (1987) found that personnel professionals rated a nontraditional, functional résumé (which included a brief employment history but mainly focused on the individual's skills and accomplishments) more highly than a traditional-style résumé that emphasized a chronological listing of previous employment experiences. Providing a clear, specific objective statement, mentioning grade-point average—especially if it is high—and listing relevant coursework and accomplishments may also make the résumé more attractive to interviewers, especially for applicants with less work experience (Thoms et al., 1999). Highlighting relevant job and educational experiences is beneficial (Knouse, 1994), but embellishing the résumé with exaggerated adjectives may be perceived negatively (Knouse, Giacalone, & Pollard, 1988).

In addition to exploring the components that increase or decrease the attractiveness of a résumé, research has focused on career outcomes for those receiving résumé preparation assistance. The process of developing a résumé with a skilled counselor may increase confidence in career activities. For example, Krieshok, Ulven, Hecox, and Wettersten (2000) found that vocational rehabilitation clients who participated in one or two sessions of résumé therapy that focused on identifying client strengths using narrative and solution-focused therapeutic techniques showed increased career decision-making self-efficacy. The most popular intervention in the current persuasion literature focuses on increasing interpersonal skills—especially in the context of the interview situation. There is some evidence that personnel professionals consider oral communication more important than written credentials (i.e., résumé and cover letter) in the interview situation (Ugbah & Evuleocha, 1992). This emphasis on the importance of communication skills has been demonstrated in several early studies in which individuals were specifically taught components of effective communication (i.e., eye contact, assertiveness, enthusiasm, clear explanation of skills) through didactic instruction, modeling, and role-play practice and feedback. Using interventions focusing on these elements, researchers have been able to demonstrate positive outcomes in terms of enhanced assertiveness and interview performance for first-generation college students (Austin & Grant, 1981), enhanced probability of hire for prerelease inmates (Speas, 1979), and interview proficiency for college students (Harrison et al., 1983) and disabled adults (Mathews, 1984).

In the more contemporary literature, these general strategies continue to be employed, although there is a greater awareness of the multicultural context in which vocational behavior occurs. For example, Jung and Jason (1998) reported a case study of three Asian immigrants and found that a six-day job-interviewing skills training program that focused on teaching Western interpersonal behavior (e.g., the importance of direct eye contact, shaking hands, being assertive) improved participants' interpersonal and interviewing skills (as judged according to Western standards). In addition, participants reported feeling more confident and comfortable in their ability to interview for jobs. High school students participating in didactic instruction in cross-cultural interpersonal job skills showed greater interpersonal skills after training compared to a control group (Barker, 2002).

Other intervention studies have found increased interview skill acquisition for various populations following behavioral interview skills training. For example, a study of behavioral interview training for developmentally disabled individuals found that using verbal prompting, feedback, modeling, and praise significantly improved the quality of participants' responses to interview questions (Mozingo, Ackley, & Bailey, 1994). After participating in interview skills training involving group discussion, modeling, and role-play practice, high school students in Northern Ireland demonstrated lower levels of worry about job interviews compared to a control group (Tourish, Hargie, & Curtis, 2001). Finally, Dunn, Thomas, and Engdahl (1992) found that participating in a two-hour interview skills workshop, which included didactic presentation, discussion, and role-play practice, improved male recovering alcoholics' interview skills. At a three-month follow-up, 66% of the treatment group reported obtaining employment compared to 47% of the control group.

Other intervention studies have sought to evaluate the effectiveness of strategies for teaching interviewing skills. For example, Maurer, Solamon, Andrews, and Troxtel (2001) found that job candidates who volunteered to participate in an interview coaching session (consisting of didactic instruction about the interview procedures and knowledge requirements, role-play interview, and discussion) demonstrated greater use of interview preparation strategies compared to candidates who did not receive the coaching. Greater use of interview preparation strategies was related to better interview performance. Another study demonstrated that both peer-directed and teacher-directed instruction in responding to employment interview questions increased the accuracy of two developmentally delayed individuals' interview responses (Schloss, Santoro, Wood, & Bedner, 1988). Using an intervention designed to help college students improve their job interviewing skills, it was found that students preferred an instructor-interview format compared to a peer-interview format. Students rated the instructor-facilitated interview as more realistic, valuable, and as more highly increasing their confidence in interviewing; however, students rated both interview formats highly (Ralston, 1995). In a different example, Hutchinson, Freeman, and Quick (1996) found that a cognitively focused intervention using teacher modeling and peer interaction increased high school students' job problem-solving skills.

Despite the importance of effective persuasion skills, much of the literature in this area remains descriptive, with little evaluative data on effectiveness. Some creative and promising interventions have been reported together with some preliminary evaluative data. For example, Fortson (1997) conducted a college retention program for male African American students that focused on career planning, job interviewing, and résumé writing skills. The intervention was not associated with increased academic self-concept as hypothesized, and it is unknown if the intervention improved students' persuasion-related skills. A program focused on providing adult mentors for low-income teen moms showed some evidence that mentors influenced the teen mother's career plans by increasing their focus on education and providing advice on vocational issues, such as job and school applications, financial aid, interviews, and résumé preparation (Zippay, 1995). Etters (2002) described a program for incarcerated inmates focused on building self-esteem and self-efficacy through workshops on goal setting, résumé writing, interviewing, and transitioning to the workplace. Etters noted that completion of the workshops has been linked to less recidivism.

Other programs are simply reported without evaluative information. For example, seeking to facilitate transition to work, Beale (1988) described a behaviorally focused group program in which recovering substance abusers were videotaped in simulated interview sessions. Modeling, role playing, and didactic instruction were also provided. Focusing on interpersonal skills needed in today's workplace, Davis and Miller (1996) described a group project model used in college business courses to teach group interaction. Crawford, Henry, and Dineen (2001) noted the need for accounting students to develop interviewing and listening skills in addition to the technical skills they learn in college. They developed a unique, discipline-specific, interactive computer program that used a case study format (i.e., consulting on an accounting problem in a business setting) to teach effective interviewing skills to accounting majors.

Targeting workforce preparation more broadly, Barthorpe and Hall (2000) described a college program focused on increasing the workforce preparation skills of engineering students. Internship coordinators and career counselors collaborated to provide workshops focused on job preparation skills such as searching, résumé writing, and interviewing. Also linking the intervention to eventual workforce participation, Schroth, Pankake, and Gates (1999) tried a number of pedagogical approaches to increase education administration students' ability to make connections between their learning and their future job effectiveness. They reported that the students rated the activities that were most clearly related to their future employment, such as résumé preparation and mock interviews, as valuable and enjoyable. Taken together, these represent a variety of promising intervention programs and would benefit from further evaluative scrutiny.

Finally, in an innovative newer line of research, O'Neil and colleagues (1977) have focused on interventions to enhance negotiation skills. Arguing that novice job seekers may not have competent skills to successfully negotiate a job offer, O'Neil, Allred, and Dennis (1997a, 1997b, 1997c) validated a computer simulation for assessing job negotiation skills. Some preliminary evidence suggests that experts demonstrate superior negotiation skills compared to novices—experts obtained higher counteroffers than novices—and may show fewer cognitive biases during the job negotiation process; however, further research is needed to validate these findings. Although the simulation was designed to assess the current level of job negotiation skills, rather than teach or improve these skills, the simulation represents a method that has potential to be used to increase the job negotiation skills of job seekers.

CONCLUSIONS

The literature on successfully navigating the process of entering the workforce offers some guidelines for counselors. Clients whose personality characteristics orient them toward the social, detail-oriented nature of the job-search process would seem likely to fare better. Enhancing communication and interpersonal skills, whether by reducing it to its behavioral components or by providing examples and practice, would appear to be effective, at least as it relates to interviewing performance. Less is known about the process of facilitating résumé writing skills; however, simply working with clients on this concrete task can increase their confidence in the job-search process. Newer research on developing negotiation skills seems promising and perhaps reflects a new essential skill in the implementation of career choices. Finally, we echo the need for more partnerships between practitioners and researchers to provide information about intervention efforts.

SUMMARY

Reflecting on the literature on choice implementation processes that we reviewed, we conclude that there are some useful guidelines for counselors. However, much remains to be learned about how best to assist individuals as they seek career opportunities and attempt to enter their chosen fields. The first observation that we offer about this literature is that, relative to other areas of career development, questions about implementation of choices are understudied. While research in some areas is strong, such as the efficacy of job-finding clubs and individual characteristics that enhance the search process, more research is needed on the processes of persuasion as well as intervention research that seeks to establish the best ways to help people implement their vocational choices. While there are clearly a number of innovative and promising interventions being offered, there is also a large need for evaluative data that will provide further information about the ways—and for whom—these programs are most effective. Taken together, the available literature provides only some very broad-brush ways to construct a picture of the best implementation process.

Second, in the interest of moving this literature forward, we offer a best-case model of the implementation process derived from the existing literature. That model would begin by noting that there are certain traits, behaviors, and contextual factors that may contribute to a more effective search and persuasion process. The most successful searchers and persuaders would seem to be the extraverted and conscientious individuals who seem comfortable interacting with others and possess confidence in their abilities to engage and be successful in the implementation process. As they enter the implementation process, they engage in more intense searching behaviors (including, but not limited to, networking), exhibit solid written and oral communication skills, and are familiar with the finer nuances of Western communication style and interpersonal interaction. The best-case model also suggests that the social environment surrounding the implementation process provides rich support, and the potentially constricting role of demographic characteristics such as race/ethnicity, gender, and age is minimized. Counselors, if present in the implementation process, have worked to enhance search self-efficacy, offered programs to provide support, and facilitated the searcher's communication skills.

Third, in reflecting on this best-case model of the implementation process, we find a rather large number of unanswered questions ready for future research. For example, given the apparent importance of personality characteristics in both search and persuasion activities, we wonder how counselors might be able to encourage successful implementation activities in those individuals who lack these qualities. Might there need to be implementation-specific interventions designed to enhance the social interaction comfort and skill of these individuals? From a different angle, although it is clear that having social support is advantageous, we do not know when in the implementation process it is most beneficial nor for whom it may be most essential.

Placing the implementation process in the larger context of career development, we know little about how the factors that help or hinder in other phases of career development might help or hinder in the implementation process. We know, for example, that anxiety can be paralytic in the career decision-making process (Newman, Fuqua, & Seaworth, 1989); what happens when that anxious person comes to implement the choice that was finally made? What might the search and persuasion processes look like for a person who might be characterized as indecisive? In a related example, does the more introverted individual avoid career choices that would require him or her to engage in more extraverted search and persuasion activities? Similarly, at what point in a long search process might an individual decide that he or she needs to recycle the earlier decision-making process and select a different career direction? And, ultimately, what connection is there between the search and persuasion processes and eventual career success and satisfaction?

If we place this model and literature into an even broader context, it is heartening to note that the existing literature has begun to attend to contextual and multicultural issues. Research exploring the role of race and gender in the search process provides useful information that can be used to broaden the scope of an individual's search, and there is now explicit recognition of the interview process being one that may require a particular set of cultural traditions. However, the literature that we consider here reflects an implicit assumption that career opportunities are readily available to those who search successfully. How might these processes work differently for those who experience disabling circumstances in even becoming ready to identify opportunities or who experience a discriminatory environment as they set out in the implementation process? In these circumstances, the focus of career implementation efforts and assistance may be less on identifying opportunities than on creating career opportunities by (1) enhancing individuals' readiness for work and (2) reducing the external barriers that may prevent them from accessing their desired fields.

Finally, it is clear that there is a rather large agenda for future study. Given the critical role that implementation plays in an individual's career development, we call for an increased attention to the questions outlined on the part of both researchers and practitioners. And, in an area that is rich with opportunities for collaboration between practitioners and researchers, we advance with considerable optimism the conclusion that such partnerships will extend the very promising progress that has been made in this literature.

REFERENCES

Admunson, N. E., & Borgen, W. A. (1988). Factors that help and hinder in group employment counseling. *Journal of Employment Counseling, 25,* 104–114.

Austin, M. F., & Grant, T. N. (1981). Interview training for college students disadvantaged in the labor market: Comparison of five instructional techniques. *Journal of Counseling Psychology, 28,* 72–75.

Azrin, N. H., & Besalel, V. A. (1980). *Job club counselor's manual: A behavioral approach to vocational counseling.* Baltimore: University Park Press.

Azrin, N. H., Flores, R., & Kaplan, S. J. (1975). Job-finding club: A group assisted program for obtaining employment. *Behavior Research and Therapy, 13,* 17–27.

Barber, A. E., Daly, D. L., Giannantonio, C. M., & Phillips, J. M. (1994). Job search activities: An examination of changes over time. *Personnel Psychology, 47,* 739–766.

Barker, S. A. (2002). Utilizing cross-cultural curricula to improve interpersonal job skills training. *Journal of European Industrial Training, 26,* 38–52.

Barthorpe, S., & Hall, M. (2000). A collaborative approach to placement preparation and career planning for university students: A case study. *Journal of Education and Training, 52,* 165–175.

Beale, A. V. (1988). A replicable program for teaching job interview skills to recovering substance abusers. *Journal of Applied Rehabilitation Counseling, 19,* 47–49.

Blau, G. (1994). Testing a two-dimensional model of job search behavior. *Organizational Behavior and Human Decisions Processes, 59,* 288–312.

Borgen, W. A. (1999). Implementing "starting points": A follow-up study. *Journal of Employment Counseling, 36,* 98–114.

Brown, D. W., & Konrad, A. M. (2001). Granovetter was right: The importance of weak ties to a contemporary job search. *Group and Organizational Management, 26,* 434–462.

Brown, S. D., & McPartland, E. B. (in press). Career interventions: Current status and future directions. In W. B. Walsh & M. L. Savickas (Eds.), *Handbook of vocational psychology* (3rd ed.). Mahwah, NJ: Erlbaum.

Burger, J. M., & Caldwell, D. F. (2000). Personality, social activities, job-search behavior and interview success: Distinguishing between PANAS trait positive affect and NEO extraversion. *Motivation and Emotion, 24,* 51–62.

Caldwell, D. F., & Burger, J. M. (1998). Personality characteristics of job applicants and success in screening interviews. *Personnel Psychology, 51,* 119–136.

Caplan, R. D., Vinokur, A. D., Price, R. H., & van Ryn, M. (1989). Job seeking, reemployment, and mental health: A randomized field experiment in coping with job loss. *Journal of Applied Psychology, 74,* 759–769.

Corrigan, M. J., Jones, C. A., & McWhirter, J. J. (2001). College students with disabilities: An access employment group. *Journalists for Specialists in Group Work, 26,* 339–349.

Corrigan, P. W., Reedy, P., Thadani, D., & Ganet, M. (1995). Correlates of participation and completion in a job club for clients with psychiatric disability. *Rehabilitation Counseling Bulletin, 39,* 42–53.

Crawford, M., Henry, W., & Dineen, F. (2001). Developing interviewing skills of accounting students on the Web—a case study approach. *Accounting Education, 10,* 207–218.

Crozier, S. D., & Grassick, P. (1996). I love my BA: The employment experience of successful bachelor of arts graduates. *Guidance and Counseling, 11,* 19–26.

Dale, K. W. (1996). College internship program. *FBI Law Enforcement Bulletin, 65,* 21–24.

Davis, B. D., & Miller, T. R. (1996). Job preparation for the 21st century: A group project learning model to teach basic workplace skills. *Journal of Education for Business, 72,* 69–73.

DeHart, B. (1996). Job search strategies: Library instruction collaborates with university career services. *Reference Librarian, 55,* 73–81.

Dunn, G. E., Thomas, A. H., & Engdahl, B. E. (1992). Teaching job interview skills to alcoholics: Implications for future employment rates. *Journal of Employment Counseling, 29,* 14–21.

Eden, D., & Aviram, A. (1993). Self-efficacy training to speed reemployment: Helping people to help themselves. *Journal of Applied Psychology, 78,* 352–360.

Etters, K. (2002). Job-readiness training program at the Wayne County jail. *Corrections Today, 64,* 112–115.

Fortson, S. B. (1997). An evaluation of a program to influence academic self-concept among African American male college students. *Journal of Employment Counseling, 34,* 104–107.

Frazee, V. (1997). Study reveals a gender difference in job-search strategies. *Workforce, 76,* 26.

Furnham, A., & Rawles, R. (1996). Job search strategies, attitudes to school and attributions about unemployment. *Journal of Adolescence, 19,* 355–369.

Gendron, B. (1997). The implementation of local initiative complementary training programmes in post-secondary education. *European Journal of Education, 32,* 303–318.

Granovetter, M. S. (1973). The strength of weak ties. *American Journal of Sociology, 78,* 1360–1380.

Granovetter, M. S. (1995). *Getting a job* (2nd ed.). Chicago: University of Chicago Press.

Green, G. P., Tigges, L. M., & Diaz, D. (1999). Racial and ethnic differences in job-search strategies in Atlanta, Boston, and Los Angeles. *Social Science Quarterly, 80,* 263–278.

Gustafusson, U. A. (2002). School-arranged or market-governed workplace training? A labour market perspective. *Journal of Education and Work, 15,* 219–236.

Harrison, R. P., Horan, J. J., Torretti, W., Gamble, K., Terzella, J., & Weir, E. (1983). Separate and combined effects of a cognitive map and a symbolic code in the learning of a modeled social skill (job interviewing). *Journal of Counseling Psychology, 30,* 499–505.

Heaven, P. C. L. (1995). Job-search strategies among teenagers: Attributions, work beliefs, and gender. *Journal of Adolescence, 18,* 217–228.

Helwig, A. A. (1985). Corporate recruiter preferences for three résumé styles. *Vocational Guidance Quarterly, 34,* 99–105.

Huffman, M. L., & Torres, L. (2002). It's not only "who you know" that matters: Gender, personal contacts, and job lead quality. *Gender and Society, 16,* 793–813.

Hutchinson, N. L., Freeman, J. G., & Quick, V. E. (1996). Group counseling intervention for solving problems on the job. *Journal of Employment Counseling, 33,* 2–19.

Jones, J. (1995). Applied learning: Giving African-American students an edge in the job market. *Black Collegian, 26,* 78–81.

Jung, R. S., & Jason, L. A. (1998). Job interview social skills training for Asian-American immigrants. *Journal of Human Behavior in the Social Environment, 1,* 11–25.

Kanfer, R., Wanberg, C. R., & Kantrowitz, T. M. (2001). Job search and employment: A personality-motivational analysis and meta-analytic review. *Journal of Applied Psychology, 86,* 837–855.

Kate, N. T. (1994). Job training that works. *American Demographics, 16,* 47.

Knouse, S. B. (1994). Impressions of the résumé: The effects of applicant education, experience, and impression management. *Journal of Business and Psychology, 9,* 33–45.

Knouse, S. B., Giacalone, R. A., & Pollard, H. (1988). Impression management in the résumé and its cover letter. *Journal of Business and Psychology, 3,* 242–249.

Krieshok, T. S., Ulven, J. C., Hecox, J. L., & Wettersten, K. (2000). Résumé therapy and vocational test feedback: Tailoring interventions to self-efficacy outcomes. *Journal of Career Assessment, 8,* 267–281.

Linnehan, F., & Blau, G. (1998). Exploring the emotional side of job search behavior for younger workforce entrants. *Journal of Employment Counseling, 35,* 98–113.

Määtä, S., Nurmi, J., & Majava, E. (2002). Young adults' achievement and attributional strategies in the transition from school to work: Antecedents and consequences. *European Journal of Personality, 16,* 295–311.

Mathews, R. M. (1984). Teaching employment interview skills to unemployed adults. *Journal of Employment Counseling, 21,* 156–161.

Mau, W. C., & Kopischke, A. (2001). Job search methods, job search outcomes, and job satisfaction of college graduates: A comparison of race and sex. *Journal of Employment Counseling, 38,* 141–149.

Maurer, T. J., Solamon, J. M., Andrews, K. D., & Troxel, D. D. (2001). Interviewee coaching, preparation strategies, and response strategies in relation to performance in situational employment interviews: An extension of Maurer, Solamon, and Troxel. (1998). *Journal of Applied Psychology, 86,* 709–717.

Montoya, I. D., & Atkinson, J. (1996). Economic perceptions and expectations of out-of-treatment drug users. *American Journal of Alcohol Abuse, 22,* 299–311.

Mortimer, J. T., Zimmer-Gembeck, M. J., Holmes, M., & Shanahan, M. J. (2002). The process of occupational decision making: Patterns during the transition to adulthood. *Journal of Vocational Behavior, 61,* 439–465.

Mozingo, D., Ackley, G. B. E., & Bailey, J. S. (1994). Training quality job interviews with adults with developmental disabilities. *Research in Developmental Disabilities, 15,* 389–410.

Newman, J., Fuqua, D., & Seaworth, T. (1989). The role of anxiety in career indecision: Implications for diagnosis and treatment. *Career Development Quarterly, 37,* 221–231.

O'Neil, H. F., Jr., Allred, K., & Dennis, R. A. (1997a). Review of workforce readiness theoretical frameworks. In H. F. O'Neil Jr. (Ed.), *Workforce readiness: Competencies and assessment* (pp. 3–25). Mahwah, NJ: Erlbaum.

O'Neil, H. F., Jr., Allred, K., & Dennis, R. A. (1997b). Use of computer simulation for assessing the interpersonal skill of negotiation. In H. F. O'Neil Jr. (Ed.), *Workforce readiness: Competencies and assessment* (pp. 205–228). Mahwah, NJ: Erlbaum.

O'Neil, H. F., Jr., Allred, K., & Dennis, R. A. (1997c). Validation of a computer simulation for assessment of interpersonal skills. In H. F. O'Neil Jr. (Ed.), *Workforce readiness: Competencies and assessment* (pp. 229–254). Mahwah, NJ: Erlbaum.

Orfield, G. (1997). Going to work: Weak preparation, little help. In K. W. Wong (Ed.), *The Indiana Youth Opportunity Study: A symposium, Advances in Educational Policy* (Vol. 3, pp. 3–31). Greenwich, CT: JAI Press.

Phillips, S. D., Blustein, D. L., Jobin-Davis, K., & White, S. F. (2002). Preparation for the school-to-work transition: The views of high school students. *Journal of Vocational Behavior, 61,* 202–216.

Ralston, S. M. (1995). Teaching interviewees employment interviewing skills. *Journal of Business and Technical Communication, 9,* 362–369.

Rife, J. C. (1997). Group counseling model for helping older women secure employment. *Clinical Gerontologist, 18,* 43–47.

Rife, J. C., & Belcher, J. R. (1993). Social support and job search intensity among older unemployed workers: Implications for employment counselors. *Journal of Employment Counseling, 30,* 98–107.

Rife, J. C., & Belcher, J. R. (1994). Assisting unemployed older workers to become reemployed: An experimental evaluation. *Research on Social Work Practice, 4,* 3–13.

Rimby, J. N., & Davis, C. L. (1993). Linking cooperative education with scholarship awards to advance specific disciplines. *Journal of Cooperative Education, 29,* 80–85.

Ryland, E. K., & Rosen, B. (1987). Personnel professionals' reactions to chronological and functional résumé formats. *Career Development Quarterly, 35,* 228–238.

Saks, A. M., & Ashforth, B. E. (1999). Effects of individual differences and job search behaviors on the employment status of recent university graduates. *Journal of Vocational Behavior, 54,* 335–349.

Schloss, P. J., Santoro, C., Wood, C. E., & Bedner, M. J. (1988). A comparison of peer-directed and teacher-directed employment interview training for mentally retarded adults. *Journal of Applied Behavior Analysis, 21,* 97–102.

Schmit, M. J., Amel, E. L., & Ryan, A. M. (1993). Self-reported assertive job-seeking behaviors of minimally educated job hunters. *Personnel Psychology, 46,* 105–124.

Schroth, G., Pankake, A., & Gates, G. (1999). A comparison of pedagogical approaches to teaching graduate students in educational administration. *Journal of Instructional Psychology, 26,* 238–249.

Schwab, D. P., Rynes, S. L., & Aldag, R. J. (1987). Theories and research on job search and choice. In K. M. Rowland & G. R. Ferris (Eds.), *Research in personnel and human resources management* (Vol. 5, pp. 129–166). Greenwich, CT: JAI Press.

Solberg, V. S., Good, G. E., Nord, D., Holm, C., Hohner, R., Zima, N., et al. (1994). Assessing career search expectations: Development and validation of the career search self efficacy scale. *Journal of Career Assessment, 2,* 111–123.

Speas, C. M. (1979). Job-seeking interview skills training: A comparison of four instructional techniques. *Journal of Counseling Psychology, 26,* 405–412.

Steffy, B. D., Shaw, K. N., & Noe, A. W. (1989). Antecedents and consequences of job search behaviors. *Journal of Vocational Behavior, 35,* 254–269.

Sterrett, E. A. (1998). Use of a job club to increase self-efficacy: A case study of return to work. *Journal of Employment Counseling, 35,* 69–78.

Straits, B. C. (1998). Occupational sex segregation: The role of personal ties. *Journal of Vocational Behavior, 52,* 191–207.

Stumpf, S. A., Colarelli, S. M., & Hartman, K. (1983). Development of the Career Exploration Survey (CES). *Journal of Vocational Behavior, 22,* 191–226.

Thompson, A. R., & Dickey, K. D. (1994). Self-perceived job search skills of college students with disabilities. *Rehabilitation Counseling Bulletin, 94,* 358–370.

Thoms, P., McMasters, R., Roberts, M. R., & Dombkowski, D. A. (1999). Résumé characteristics as predictors of an invitation to interview. *Journal of Business and Psychology, 13,* 339–356.

Tourish, D., Hargie, O. D. W., & Curtis, L. (2001). Preparing adolescents for selection interviews: The impact of a training intervention on levels of worry and local of control. *International Journal of Adolescence and Youth, 9,* 273–291.

Ugbah, S. D., & Evuleocha, S. U. (1992). The importance of written, verbal, and nonverbal communication factors in employment interview decisions. *Journal of Employment Counseling, 29,* 128–137.

van Ryn, M., & Vinokur, A. D. (1992). How did it work? An examination of the mechanisms through which an intervention for the unemployed promoted job-search behavior. *American Journal of Community Psychology, 20,* 577–597.

Villar, E., Juan, J., Corominas, E., & Capell, D. (2000). What kind of networking strategy advice should career counsellors offer university graduates searching for a job? *British Journal of Guidance and Counselling, 28,* 389–409.

Wanberg, C. R., Kanfer, R., & Banas, J. T. (2000). Predictors and outcomes of networking intensity among unemployed job seekers. *Journal of Applied Psychology, 85,* 491–503.

Wanberg, C. R., Kanfer, R., & Rotundo, M. (1999). Unemployed individuals: Motives, job-search competencies, and job-search constraints as predictors of job seeking and reemployment. *Journal of Applied Psychology, 84,* 897–910.

Wanberg, C. R., Watt, J. D., & Rumsey, D. J. (1996). Individuals without jobs: An empirical study of job-seeking behavior and reemployment. *Journal of Applied Psychology, 81,* 76–87.

Wenzel, S. L. (1993). The relationship of psychological resources and social support to job procurement self-efficacy in the disadvantaged. *Journal of Applied Psychology, 23,* 1471–1497.

Werbel, J. D. (2000). Relationships among career exploration, job search intensity, and job search effectiveness in graduating college students. *Journal of Vocational Behavior, 57,* 379–394.

Zippay, A. (1995). Expanding employment skills and social networks among teen mothers: Case study of a mentor program. *Child and Adolescent Social Work Journal, 12,* 51–69.

CHAPTER 20

Counseling for Work Adjustment

Barbara Griffin and Beryl Hesketh

ANY ADULT CLIENTS come to counseling seeking help with problems of work adjustment. There are a variety of theories (e.g., Dawis & Lofquist, 1984; Holland, 1997; Schneider, 1997) and much research (see Fritzsche & Parrish, Chapter 8, this volume; Russell, Chapter 9, this volume) that can help counselors conceptualize clients' problems and intervene to promote better work adjustment. Although the theories and research have much to offer counselors working with clients with work adjustment difficulties, changes in the nature of work in contemporary society suggest that the definitions of adjustment need to be expanded to include issues associated with adaptability.

We briefly summarize current theories of work adjustment (focusing specifically on Dawis and Lofquist's, 1984, theory of work adjustment) in terms of how work adjustment has been conceptualized and how it can be promoted. This initial section of the chapter is intended to complement other chapters in this text that also focus on issues of work adjustment (Dawis, Chapter 1; Spokane & Cruza-Guet, Chapter 2; Fritzsche & Parrish, Chapter 8; Russell, Chapter 9). We then provide a structure for the sorts of counselor-assisted interventions that may help twenty-first century clients with difficulties in work adjustment.

DEFINITION OF WORK ADJUSTMENT

The term *work adjustment* is seen by contemporary person-environment (P-E) fit theorists as the result of an interaction between an individual's characteristics (e.g., needs and abilities) and commensurate attributes of the work environment (e.g., reinforcer systems and ability requirements). A good fit between the two, often referred to as *correspondence* (Dawis & Lofquist, 1984) or *congruence* (Holland, 1997), leads to better work adjustment, as indicated by satisfaction, satisfactory performance, and tenure.

Two P-E fit theories that have been a major influence on career development are the Theory of Work Adjustment (TWA; Dawis & Lofquist, 1984) and Holland's (1997) theory. Dawis (Chapter 1, this volume) provides an excellent overview of

TWA, while Spokane and Cruza-Guet (Chapter 2, this volume) do the same for Holland's approach. A major difference in these two fit models relates to the comprehensiveness of TWA, which deals separately with the extent to which (1) skills and abilities match the requirements of the work environment and (2) the environment supplies outlets for the needs, interests, and values of the individual. As shown in Dawis (Chapter 1, this volume), skill-ability requirement matches lead to satisfactory performance, while the extent to which an environment supplies outlets for the person's interests, needs, and values relates to satisfaction. Together, satisfaction and performance account for the length (or tenure) of the interaction between the two parties. Holland's theory takes a more generic and less detailed approach, relying heavily on the concepts of occupational stereotypes.

We contend that the specificity of the matching factors offered through TWA provides a more helpful framework for the development of approaches to work adjustment counseling and other interventions. Furthermore, TWA provides a set of concepts that are aimed at the dynamic responsiveness of individuals and work organizations striving to achieve a better fit. These constructs, also outlined by Dawis (Chapter 1, the volume), highlight the styles that may be used to achieve work adjustment and provide a basis for expanding the types of interventions that might be used, as well as measuring and assessing the potential of both individuals and environments to be responsive to the needs of the other. These are the constructs that form the major focus of this chapter, although we also draw on related ideas and measures from the field of industrial and organizational psychology.

A number of other perspectives on work adjustment provide ideas for interventions in the workplace. These perspectives include Schneider's (1997) attraction, selection, attrition (ASA) model, which highlights the importance of fit as part of what attracts people to apply for a position and influences employers during the selection process. According to this model, turnover occurs when good individual fit is not obtained. Research addressing the issue of newcomer socialization (e.g., Ashford & Black, 1996; Lance, Vandenberg, & Self, 2000) deals more specifically with the processes of adjustment that occur for new employees shortly after appointment when there is the most need for adjustment on the part of both the employer and employees. In this chapter, we draw on these and related ideas from the organizational psychology literature to supplement the general framework offered by TWA.

ASSESSING WORK ADJUSTMENT

In the context of the TWA (Dawis & Lofquist, 1984), performance and satisfaction, together with tenure, are the major criteria used to assess fit and the effectiveness of work adjustment counseling. We provide a brief overview of the original perspective provided by TWA but place more emphasis on developments that better address the global, dynamic, and security-conscious world of today.

Specifically, we draw attention to the Campbell (1990) model of performance, which attempts to highlight the antecedents of performance using cognitive constructs, while also reviewing recent developments in partitioning the performance domain into task, contextual, and adaptive performance. The Theory of Work Adjustment argues that satisfaction arises as a result of the person's needs being met by reinforcing aspects of the environment. The reinforcing aspects can be grouped into three categories, namely, those that emerge from (1) the physical environment, (2) other people, and (3) the self. It is interesting that these three categories can be related to the groupings that emerge from Alderfer's (1972) theory of work satisfaction where satisfaction follows when needs relating to energy (the physical environment), relatedness (other people), and growth (self) are met. Missing from TWA and many other theories of work adjustment is a consideration of mental health and well-being as important work adjustment outcomes. However, in light of the changing nature of work in contemporary society, mental health and well-being should, as we later discuss, be included as outcomes of work adjustment counseling.

PERFORMANCE

Although many approaches to work adjustment and career development have tended to emphasize the individual's perspective, TWA has also incorporated the employer's perspective by including the construct of satisfactoriness, or satisfactory performance. Job performance is an important construct in much of industrial/organizational psychology, being the cornerstone variable by which many organizational activities and interventions are evaluated. Performance is also important for the individual worker. Not only can good performance lead to a sense of satisfaction (Sonnentag & Frese, 2002), but also to promotion and better career opportunities (Van Scotter, Motowidlo, & Cross, 2000).

From the organization's perspective, performance is behavior that can be evaluated in terms of how effective it is in achieving goals of the organization or individual (Campbell, McCloy, Oppler, & Sager, 1993). Until the early 1990s, job performance was treated as a unitary factor. However, Campbell's (1990) seminal work introduced the concept that performance is multidimensional in nature. He proposed an eight-factor model that is embedded in a broader, causal theory of performance. Campbell's eight factors, or dimensions, of performance are:

1. Demonstrating effort.
2. Maintaining personal discipline.
3. Non-job-specific task proficiency.
4. Written and oral communication.
5. Facilitating peer and team performance.
6 Supervision/leadership.
7. Management/administration.
8. Job-specific task proficiency.

These components of performance are defined in Table 20.1.

Campbell's (1990) model also distinguishes performance components in terms of the extent to which they are unique or common to jobs, resulting in three categories:

1. Components that all jobs share (e.g., demonstrating effort and maintaining personal discipline).
2. Components that are shared within an organization (e.g., non-job-specific tasks).

Table 20.1
Models of Performance

Borman and Motowidlo (1993) Factors	Campbell (1990) Factors	Description of Factors
Task performance	Non-job-specific task proficiency	Performance on tasks that are shared with other jobs in the same organization.
	Written and oral communication	Making formal written and oral presentations.
	Supervision/ leadership	Influencing subordinates' performance including training, rewarding, disciplining, counseling.
	Management/ administration	Developing and facilitating organizational goals including planning, problem solving, decision making, allocating resources, monitoring progress.
	Job-specific task proficiency	Performance on tasks and responsibilities for a particular job.
Contextual performance	Demonstrating effort	Showing the willingness to consistently expend effort under normal and adverse conditions.
	Maintaining personal discipline	Avoidance of behaviors that disrupt performance or are against the rules and regulations.
	Facilitating peer and team performance	Support given to coworkers and commitment to group goals.

Source: "Expanding the Criterion Domain to Include Elements of Contextual Performance," by W. C. Borman and S. J. Motowidlo, in *Personnel Selection in Organizations*, N. Schmitt, W. C. Borman, and Associates, (Eds.), 1993, San Francisco: Jossey-Bass.

3. Components that might be shared across several, but not all, jobs (e.g., supervision/leadership).

Campbell's model and the grouping according to generalizability provide a guide for counselors. When assisting clients who lack the confidence required to change jobs, it is worth emphasizing those aspects of performance that are common across jobs, such as demonstrating effort and maintaining personal discipline.

An alternative and more parsimonious model, which has been extensively examined in empirical studies, is Borman and Motowidlo's (1993) division of performance into task and contextual performance. *Task performance* refers to the technical aspects of a job, involving either executing the technical processes or maintaining and servicing the technical requirements (Borman & Motowidlo, 1997). *Contextual performance* refers to activities that contribute to maintaining the broader organizational, social, or psychological environment. Examples include helping coworkers, cooperating, following rules, supporting the organization's goals, and volunteering for additional tasks (Borman & Motowidlo, 1993).

As shown in Table 20.1, the task/contextual model can be considered a broader or higher level approach than Campbell's (1990) model. Borman and Motowidlo (1993) argued that the components of task performance vary among jobs whereas the components of contextual performance are likely to be relatively similar across jobs.

These two models, considered either separately or together, can be used to help clients understand that performance appraisals at work are dependent on more than just an individual's task performance and that contextual performance indicators are also important (Conway, 1999). These models can also be used to help counselors identify sources of a client's performance difficulties so that intervention can be more specifically targeted. In context of the need to change jobs, use of these models can encourage clients to understand that contextual skills are transferable.

According to the TWA, performance results from a good match between the person and his or her environment, implying that performance is not a stable construct. Studies show that performance initially increases with time spent doing the job but then plateaus (Quinones, Ford, & Teachout, 1995). Murphy (1989) described this trajectory in terms of two stages of performance: transition and maintenance. The transition stage occurs when individuals are new to the job or when tasks are novel. This is a time when counseling interventions to facilitate newcomer socialization can be applied (Lance et al., 2000). The maintenance stage occurs once task accomplishment becomes automatic. Frequent and rapid changes common to today's workplace mean that many employees cycle between the transition and maintenance stages continually, not just when they are new to a job. This demand to keep adjusting to new conditions is not adequately accounted for in the traditional models of performance described here. Therefore, Allworth and Hesketh (Allworth, 1997; Allworth & Hesketh, 1999) developed the concept of adaptive performance, which is described in more detail later in this chapter.

SATISFACTION AND MENTAL HEALTH

Job satisfaction is a person's psychological response to his or her job and includes cognitive, affective, and behavioral components (Hulin & Judge, 2003). Distinctions are made between a broad summary response, referred to as *overall job satisfaction*, and responses to particular job features, such as working conditions, pay, or independence in decision making, referred to as *facet-specific satisfactions* (Fritzsche & Parrish, Chapter 8, this volume).

Satisfaction is a function of correspondence between the reinforcer system of the work environment and an individual's needs. Person-environment fit research consistently supports this proposal. For example, Lauver and Kristof-Brown (2001) found that subjective estimates of person-job fit and person-organization fit both predicted job satisfaction. Likewise, Cable and Scott De Rue (2002) showed that perceived needs-supplies fit was a significant predictor of job and career satisfaction. Counselors often have to help clients reconsider their expectations of work because it is not always possible to find an exact fit.

Other research shows that both the component parts of the fit (i.e., person factors and environment factors) independently affect satisfaction. Examples of the independent influence of the environment include investigations stemming from Hackman and Oldham's (1976) job characteristics model, which show that characteristics of the work itself, such as the degree of autonomy and feedback provided, are related to satisfaction and motivation (e.g., Frye, 1996). Similarly, research examining dispositional influences on job satisfaction recognizes the importance of person factors. Most recently, Judge and Bono (2001) conducted a meta-analysis of correlations between core self-evaluation traits—self-esteem, generalized self-efficacy, locus of control, and emotional stability—and job satisfaction. A composite of all four traits correlated 0.37 with job satisfaction.

As discussed more fully in Hesketh and Myors (1997), valuable information is lost if you do not examine the person and environment characteristics in addition to their interaction (fit). From a practical view, the preceding results illustrate the importance of independently assessing the individual and the environment, as well as the fit between the two, when planning interventions.

Originally, TWA gave primary attention to satisfactoriness and satisfaction as the indicators of work adjustment. Others have since expanded these criteria to include related concepts such as organizational commitment and job involvement (Tziner & Meir, 1997) and mental health and well-being (Warr, 1991). Warr suggested that job satisfaction is a specific aspect of job-related well-being, which in turn is a component of mental health. Aspects of the work environment thought to be significantly associated with well-being include level of control, opportunity for skill use, variety, and workload (Warr, 1990). Because stable individual difference factors, such as neuroticism, affect well-being (Judge & Bono, 2001), it is not clear to what extent job design initiatives alone can improve mental health.

TENURE

In TWA, tenure is used to indicate the length of the relationship between employee and employer. Tenure can be terminated as the result of voluntary departure by the individual or by termination of employment by the employer. The probability that an organization will terminate a person's employment is inversely related to satisfactory performance, and the probability that an individual will chose to leave is inversely related to satisfaction. A significant body of research supports these two propositions (Hesketh & Griffin, in press).

At least two additional factors are likely to affect voluntary departure. First, the current focus on self-managed career advancement may result in individuals proactively moving elsewhere to better position their future prospects, explaining why apparently satisfied employees choose to leave. Second, lack of job alternatives (particularly in times of economic downturn) will keep dissatisfied individuals employed in the job (Hulin, 1991). It is often these clients who seek counseling, and interventions may well aim to adjust expectations, while maintaining output.

Tenure, along with turnover and retirement intentions, is a manifestation of a group of behaviors labeled *job withdrawal*. A second group of behaviors, labeled *work withdrawal* (i.e., remaining in the job but disengaging from work tasks), includes absenteeism, lateness, and intentional misbehavior (Hanisch & Hulin, 1991). These withdrawal behaviors might be a more likely manifestation of poor work adjustment in employees who have limited job options. Dissatisfied workers who stay because of a lack of alternatives show increases in work withdrawal behaviors (Krausz, Koslowsky, & Eiser, 1998), and the counseling challenge is to discourage such withdrawal. Tziner and Meir (1997), therefore, extended the TWA to include work withdrawal behaviors in addition to job withdrawal behaviors.

CHANGES IN THE WORKPLACE

About a decade ago, many writers started drawing attention to the pace of change that was occurring in the workplace. At that time, the specific issues related to the impact of information and communication technologies, globalization, and large-scale mergers and acquisitions. More recently, concepts associated with security, terrorism, and public health have dominated as causes of disruption and change. For example, the combination of increasing travel and globalization of business and trade has opened the world to threats arising from diseases such as SARS. These issues will continue to dominate for many years and will be joined over the next decades by challenges associated with local transportation, deteriorating infrastructures, aging populations, and environmental issues.

When thinking about these changes and their possible impact on careers, it is valuable to engage in exercises that facilitate planning over a longer time frame. In Table 20.2, we provide a primer for a brainstorming exercise that can be useful in

Table 20.2
Change Exercise

Year	Major Development
1975	Mainframe computers for accounting, data management, and analysis.
1980	Desktop and portable computers, computer-controlled machining.
1985	Computerized manufacturing—shift from hand-eye coordination to cognitive skills required.
1990	World Wide Web—and capacity to process information off-line.
1995	Enterprisewide information technology systems radically altering job requirements.
2000	Mobile communications, wireless networks, palms, short message service (SMS), genomic developments leading to the sequencing of the human genome.
2005	Visualization and virtual worlds and grid computing. Security consciousness, reduced travel requirements. Solar power, photonic communication (very high-speed communication). Medical interventions targeted to genetic structure.
2010	Environmental requirements faced by industry, construction, town planning. Scientific possibility of using genetic information in workplace selection—social issues unresolved.
2015	Secure environments.
2020	Self-driven non-gas-powered vehicles.
2025	Biomimetic approaches where technology and work organizations mimic what has been learned by biological systems through centuries of evolution.

encouraging clients to think back over the sorts of events that have caused major change in the workplace and attempt to anticipate future changes with implications for the nature of work and careers. For this exercise, we have identified major developments that have radically altered the nature of work, hence, the skills required in work over the past 25 years. The examples we have chosen tend to relate to information and communication technologies, but readers may wish to include different areas. The timing of the events listed in Table 20.2 is not precise and may differ slightly in different countries and organizations, but the basic idea is worth considering. We have also listed changes that might affect work over the next 25 years. These are more speculative, as it is easier to look back and recognize change than it is to predict the major drivers of future changes. An awareness of the context of change should help clients to maintain the skills and attitudes needed to cope with change. These skills and attitudes are discussed next.

AN UPDATED VERSION OF THE THEORY OF WORK ADJUSTMENT

The nature and pace of change in today's workplace have created a situation where adaptability is a competency increasingly recognized as important, and possibly even essential, for survival and success (Hannigan, 1990). However, despite this widespread recognition of the need for people to be able to adapt to changing conditions in order to operate effectively, adaptability remains a poorly understood construct. Researchers in the fields of both selection and training have connected work adjustment to adaptability, adopting a P-E fit approach to understanding the process of adaptation. Chan (2000, p. 4) provides the following definition: "Individual adaptation refers to the process by which an individual achieves some degree of fit between his or her behaviors and the new work demands created by the novel and often ill-defined problems resulting from changing and uncertain work situations."

In this section, we discuss how the traditional concepts used in work adjustment counseling can be updated to better meet the needs of those facing the demands of changing, uncertain work environments.

ADAPTIVE PERFORMANCE

Extant models of performance, which we reviewed earlier, tend to view jobs as stable across time and, therefore, do not account for changing task demands (Hesketh & Allworth, 1997; Landis, Fogli, & Goldberg, 1998). To address this gap in the performance domain, Allworth and Hesketh (Allworth, 1997; Allworth & Hesketh, 1999) extended Borman and Motowidlo's (1993) dichotomous model of task and contextual performance to include a third dimension, that of adaptive performance, referring to those aspects of performance related to coping with change. Allworth and Hesketh demonstrated the uniqueness of adaptive performance by showing that it could be distinguished from task and contextual performance using factor analysis and differential prediction.

Building on the concept of adaptive performance, Pulakos, Arad, Donovan, and Plamondon (2000) developed a taxonomy of the domain based on an extensive literature review and an analysis of a large set of critical incidents collected from incumbents employed in a cross-section of jobs. They proposed that adaptive performance includes eight separate dimensions:

1. Solving novel or complex problems.
2. Dealing with emergencies or crises.
3. New learning (of tasks, technologies, and procedures).
4. Demonstrating interpersonal adaptability.
5. Demonstrating cultural adaptability.
6. Demonstrating physically oriented adaptability.
7. Coping with work stress.
8. Coping with uncertain or ambiguous work situations.

Table 20.3 provides definitions for these dimensions.

Table 20.3
Taxonomy of Adaptive Performance

Dimension Title	Dimension Definition
Solving novel or complex problems	Generating new ideas, looking for new approaches to solve problems, entertaining wide-ranging options, and developing innovative methods of using resources.
Dealing with emergencies and crises	Reacting appropriately, analyzing options quickly, remaining clear and focused in thinking, and maintaining emotional control.
New learning	Showing enthusiasm for learning new approaches and technologies, keeping knowledge and skills current, learning new skills quickly, adjusting to new work processes, anticipating changes in work demands, and participating in training/assignments that will prepare self for change.
Demonstrating interpersonal adaptability	Being flexible and open-minded, listening to others' views, being open to criticism, developing effective relationships with diverse personalities, demonstrating insight into others' behavior, and tailoring own behavior to influence and work effectively with others.
Demonstrating cultural adaptability	Learning about others' needs/values/beliefs, adjusting behavior to comply with others' customs, and understanding the implications of your actions.
Demonstrating physically oriented adaptability	Adjusting to heat/cold/dirtiness, pushing self physically, and adjusting physical fitness for the requirements of the job.
Coping with work stress	Remaining calm in difficult circumstances, demonstrating resilience, and acting as a calming influence for others.
Coping with uncertainty and ambiguity	Taking effective action without needing to have all the facts at hand; adjusting plans, goals, and priorities; imposing structure to focus as much as possible; not being paralyzed by uncertainty.

Source: "Adaptability in the Workplace," by E. D. Pulakos, S. Arad, M. S. Donovan, and K. E. Plamondon, 2000, *Journal of Applied Psychology, 85,* pp. 612–624.

Pulakos et al.'s (2000) research found that although jobs differed in the extent and mix of adaptive behavior requirements, such requirements are more likely to generalize across jobs. As Herr (1993) argues, the skills necessary for adaptive behavior are not only more likely to transfer across jobs but also less likely to become obsolete than the job-specific skills typical of task performance. Therefore, work adjustment counseling that includes enhancing adaptive skills as well as task and contextual skills has potential long-term benefit for clients.

Although this eight-dimension taxonomy can facilitate counseling by clarifying and elaborating the content of adaptive performance, the possibility remains that the taxonomy is not a comprehensive list and that other dimensions might be identified. For example, Pratzner and Ashley (1985) added transfer skills (i.e., those enabling a person to adjust previous learning and experience to different situations), and Ashford (1986) included feedback seeking. Furthermore, the taxonomy is not based on an underlying theory that might explain how or why the behaviors are adaptive. We, therefore, provide an organizing framework for these eight adaptive performance dimensions based on the TWA, which not only allows us to identify and classify additional adaptive behaviors but also explains the process by which they result in adjustment.

In the context of the environmental change experienced by many modern organizations, it is likely that a person's skills, knowledge, and abilities that originally fit the requirements of the prechange job no longer correspond to the new requirements of the changed environment. Likewise, in light of the trend for employees to manage their own career trajectories, it is possible that the incentives and other reinforcers provided by an organization may no longer fit the changing requirements of the person employed in that organization. In both cases, a state of mismatch (discorrespondence) results, which, according to the TWA, causes a decline in performance and satisfaction. As outlined by Dawis (Chapter 1, this volume), improved correspondence between a person and his or her environment is achieved through one of several different styles of adjustment. Taken from the individual's perspective, active adjustment involves changing the environment to achieve a better fit, reactive adjustment occurs when the individual changes himself or herself to improve fit, and flexibility is tolerating a mismatch. Adjusting terms slightly, we propose that the behaviors within the adaptive performance domain be defined as:

1. *Proactive behavior:* person-initiated actions to change the environment.
2. *Reactive behavior:* changing or modifying self to better suit the new environment.
3. *Tolerant behavior:* being able to continue functioning despite changed circumstances and when either proactive or reactive behavior may not be appropriate.

The Pulakos et al. (2000) dimensions can be summarized into this framework. Thus, proactive behavior would include *solving novel problems* and *dealing with crises. New learning, interpersonal, cultural,* and *physically-oriented adaptability* would be reactive behaviors. Tolerant behavior would include *coping with stress* and *coping with uncertainty.* Griffin (2003) provided support for this classification using exploratory and confirmatory factor analyses.

The proposed framework easily incorporates research on proactivity in organizational settings (e.g., Bateman & Crant, 1993; Chan & Schmitt, 2000; Crant, 2000; Parker, 2000; Wanberg & Kammeyer-Mueller, 2000). For example, the context of organizational entry has been described as an example of an individual adaptation process (Chan & Schmitt, 2000), and recent emphasis has been on the proactive behaviors enacted by new hires that facilitate adaptation. *Proactivity* is described as workers actively taking steps to change their environment to increase person-environment fit (Wanberg & Kammeyer-Mueller, 2000). It involves taking initiative and actively creating environmental change (Bateman & Crant, 1993). The parallels with the TWA description of active mode of adjustment are obvious.

The inclusion of both proactive and reactive behaviors in the adaptive performance domain is further supported by the considerable comment across a broad spectrum of research suggesting that adaptability involves not only reacting to the environment but also being assertive and creative in forming it (Ashford & Taylor, 1990; Chown, 1959; De Leeuw & Volberda, 1996; Kirton, 1985; Pratzner & Ashley, 1985; Sternberg, 1997). The distinction between these types of behaviors has implications for counseling, coaching, and training clients to adjust to change.

Further, although the focus in career counseling is most often on the individual, the TWA alerts us to the possibility that the organization can also adjust in proactive, reactive, and tolerant ways to maximize fit with an employee. Maintaining an organizational perspective extends the choice of interventions that might be used and, as discussed later, highlights the importance of "learning" organizations to facilitate adaptation.

SATISFACTION WITH CHANGE

Over the past decade, a major challenge for organizations was the resistance to change on the part of employees. From both the organizational and the individual perspective, it would be more advantageous if employees could enjoy the challenge of change and see it as an opportunity to add to their skill repertoire. We, therefore, suggest traditional outcome measures assessing job satisfaction be updated to include a *satisfaction with change* dimension.

PERSON FACTORS

Having suggested that the indicators of work adjustment should include adaptive performance and satisfaction with change, we, therefore, need to identify the person factors that might relate to an individual's being likely to have high adaptive performance and satisfaction with change.

Cognitive Factors It is well established that general cognitive ability is a good predictor of performance (Arvey, 1986; Hunter, 1986; Schmidt & Hunter, 1998). However, the finding that cognitive ability predicts performance best when the tasks are complex or novel (Murphy, 1989) suggests that it may be particularly important for adaptive performance. Indeed, Hesketh and Allworth (1997) and Pulakos et al. (2002) found that popular tests of cognitive ability were good predictors of adaptive performance, and LePine, Colquitt, and Erez (2000) showed that cognitive ability was more highly correlated with postchange (adaptive) performance than prechange (task) performance.

Stankov (1988) argued that it is the fluid intelligence (Gf) component of general cognitive ability that relates most closely to problem solving and verbal reasoning. Therefore, measures of Gf may be more useful than general ability measures in identifying a person's capacity for adaptive performance. An even more specific component of Gf, cognitive flexibility, maps most closely onto the construct of adaptability (Griffin & Hesketh, 2003). Griffin (2003) reported the predictive validity of cognitive flexibility in several studies. For example, cognitive flexibility predicted the adaptive performance of insurance industry employees and of new hires within the public service.

Another individual difference factor that is cognitive in emphasis is flexible role orientation (FRO; Parker, 2000). Those with high FRO recognize the importance of taking on broader responsibilities, being proactive, and using initiative, while those with low FRO have a "that's not my job" mentality to their work (Parker, Wall, & Jackson, 1997). Parker (2000) reports that FRO predicted employee initiative and good performance in autonomous teamwork situations. It was also related to, but distinct from, job satisfaction and organizational commitment.

Personality Factors   Meta-analytic findings over the past decade have shown that personality variables are important in enhancing positive work adjustment. In particular, two of the Big Five factors, conscientiousness and emotional stability, have been identified as being significant predictors of satisfactory performance (Barrick, Mount, & Judge, 2001). However, much of the research examining these two factors has focused on the outcomes of overall job performance and satisfaction in relatively stable work environments. In fact, a growing body of research indicates that the dependability facets of conscientiousness (order, dutifulness, and deliberation), while having a positive influence on normal task and contextual behavior, may not be beneficial for adaptive performance (LePine et al., 2000). Griffin (2003; Griffin & Hesketh, 2001) showed that the dependability facets were either not related or negatively related to adaptability, whereas the achievement facets of conscientiousness (achievement-striving, competence, and self-discipline) were related to adaptability. We, therefore, suggest that other personality factors will be important for employees working in fluid, changing contexts.

Openness to experience appears to be the most relevant of the five factors to adaptability. In fact, Caligiuri, Jacobs, and Farr (2000) summarized the construct as "flexibility of one's attitudes and behaviors" (p. 29). Individuals high in openness are described as being inquisitive, flexible, and tolerant (McCrae & Costa, 1997). They seek new and varied experiences, are tolerant of alternative viewpoints, and are likely to cope with diversity and cross-cultural differences (Chan, 2001; McCrae & Costa, 1997). Its consistent relationship with training performance suggests that openness is involved in both learning new tasks and being willing to participate in learning experiences (Judge & Barrick, 2001). Hesketh and Allworth (1997) showed that openness to experience predicted adaptive performance (but not task or contextual performance), and it was significantly correlated with postchange (but not prechange) performance in a dynamic laboratory task (LePine et al., 2000). Other adjustment outcomes relating to openness to experience include problem solving (Ferguson & Patterson, 1998), managerial creativity (Scratchley & Hakstian, 2001), and coping with organizational change (Judge, Thoresen, Pucik, & Welbourne, 1999).

   Lower order personality traits that also relate to adaptability include change receptiveness (Parker, 2000), tolerance of ambiguity (Judge et al., 1999), and proactivity (Bateman & Crant, 1993). A counselor might discuss a more detailed personality profile with the client, highlighting areas where the client may need to take special care in maintaining flexibility.

Motivation Factors   People's interests, values, and needs are factors that motivate their engagement in work. The traditional measures of these factors (see Hansen, Chapter 12, this volume; Rounds & Armstrong, Chapter 13, this volume) can be updated to include change constructs such as interest in change, interest in variety, value of changing environments, and value of opportunities for new learning. Those who value learning and are self-directed learners are thought to be particularly valuable in the modern workplace (London & Mone, 1999).

   A further motivational factor, self-efficacy, has been identified as an important predictor of work adjustment. Self-efficacy is the individual's belief that he or she can perform certain behaviors (see Lent, Chapter 5, this volume). It is not what the person actually does, but rather what he or she feels capable of doing (Parker, 1998), and it is specific to a particular domain or task. A number of authors (e.g., Ashford & Taylor, 1990; Fay & Frese, 2001; Martin & Rubin, 1995) argue for self-efficacy as an essential component of adjustment because adaptive behavior is unlikely to occur unless an individual first has the confidence to perform such behavior. Here we are referring to self-efficacy for adjusting to, and coping with, change.

   According to Bandura's (1986) social cognitive theory, self-efficacy is not a generalized trait but a motivational construct that relates to a specific task. Bandura, Adams, and Beyer (1977), therefore, argued that measures should be tailored to the domain of interest. In frequently changing work environments, this would mean measuring self-efficacy for behaving adaptively. For example, Parker's (1998) "role breadth self-efficacy" assesses the extent to which employees feel confident in carrying out an extended and more proactive role than would be expected in a traditional job requirements situation.

   There is increasing evidence that self-efficacy relates to adjustment outcomes: It has predicted coping with the introduction of new technology (Hill, Smith, & Mann, 1987), adjustment to organizational settings by a group of newcomers (Saks, 1995), change acceptance in the face of major restructuring (Wanberg & Banas, 2000), and finding reemployment after job loss (Caplan, Vinokur, Price, & van Ryn, 1989). Hesketh and Allworth (1997) showed that self-efficacy for change predicted supervisor ratings of adaptive performance in a large sample of public servants, and Ford, Quinones, Sego, and Sorra (1992) found that it affected the breadth of experience gained and type of tasks performed. Furthermore, Major and Kozlowski (1997) found that self-efficacious new hires adopted more innovative role orientations compared to the traditional roles preferred by those low in self-efficacy.

ENVIRONMENT FACTORS

Just as individual factors specific to coping with change are needed for a new conceptualization of work adjustment, so environmental factors that affect adaptability need to be identified. We have already discussed the changing requirements of the modern workplace and will later address the possibility that individuals who self-manage their own careers will have a new set of needs and values around continuous learning to which organizations must respond to remain competitive. London and Mone (1999) outlined the resources and support that promote continuous learning, such as supervisor support, human resource policies, programs, and rewards for development. Assessment of the environment, therefore, needs to include a measure of the organization's values and norms for knowledge sharing, quality improvement, innovation, and competitiveness.

Other environmental factors that affect the adaptability of employees include task complexity and management support. Ford et al. (1992) suggested that workers are more likely to feel comfortable performing new behaviors in the presence of highly supportive managers. This view was endorsed by their finding that trainee airmen assigned to supportive supervisors and workgroups performed more complex and different tasks than their colleagues assigned to less supportive teams. Managers with a positive attitude toward change have also been found to impact the degree of employee innovation (Oldham & Cummings, 1996).

Task complexity implies the presence of multifaceted challenging task demands that have higher requirements for information processing. Smith, Ford, and Kozlowski (1997) contended that experience in complex and challenging environments builds complex metacognitive skills that enhance performance. An alternative explanation is that complexity has a more immediate motivating influence on employees because people rise to challenge and complexity but become bored and unproductive when tasks are simple and routine.

COACHING AND COUNSELING FOR WORK ADJUSTMENT

One of the pitfalls for counselors working in organizational contexts relates to the tendency to attribute problems to individuals and, hence, to seek a solution at an individual level. This bias is understandable because most counselor training places an emphasis on the individual and may not include organizational theory and interventions. In a climate of change, there is obviously much that can be done at an individual level to give clients the skills to adjust to and cope with change. However, the role of the organization in creating a climate and support is just as important. A similar point can be made in relation to the role of selection in achieving P-E fit. Selection cannot be approached in isolation without taking into account the role of training and development on the job, which requires management support and a learning climate in an organization. These issues underline the importance of interventions that are addressed at the organizational leadership and management level as well as those where the focus is on change and adjustment on the part of the individual. In the following sections we therefore examine how to counsel for proactive, reactive, and tolerant behaviors by both the individual and the organization.

Historically, vocational counseling has come under the auspices of career or vocational counselors and psychologists. Over the past decade, businesses have shown an increasing interest in coaching, especially for managers and senior leaders, often conducted by human relations professionals or clinical and organizational psychologists. Traditional counseling approaches fit well with coaching, and we suggest that counselors consult Grant and Greene (2001). Although there is currently little empirical data on the efficacy of such coaching, we include coaching here because of its pervasive use throughout organizations and its focus on coping with change. Kampa-Kokesch and Anderson (2001) argued that the popularity of coaching is due to the pressure to improve performance, the need for continued development, and the lack of training opportunities for executives.

Promoting Proactive Behaviors by the Individual

Although some theorists regard proactivity as an individual characteristic (e.g., Bateman & Crant, 1993) and, therefore, less amenable to change, others (e.g., those researching proactive socialization) have found very few individual difference effects. Nevertheless, there has been little investigation into the effectiveness of training and other interventions in increasing proactive behaviors. Here we outline the types of proactive behaviors that have been associated with positive work adjustment, with the aim of providing coaches and counselors with information to assist clients in broadening their behavioral repertoire.

As to the Pulakos et al. (2000, 2002) taxonomy, dealing with crises and solving novel or complex problems come under the category of proactive behavior. The process of problem recognition and the generation of novel or adapted ideas and solutions is part of a process of innovation. Kanter (1988) defined *innovation* as the production, adoption, and implementation of useful ideas, including adapting products or processes from outside the organization. Innovation, together with socialization, feedback seeking, issue selling (calling attention to and influencing senior management's understanding of an issue), and career management are the context-specific proactive behaviors identified by Crant (2000) in his review of the proactivity literature.

The proactive components of newcomer socialization include seeking out information, building social networks, and negotiating job changes. According to Ashford and Black (1996), these behaviors are associated with work adjustment outcomes such as satisfaction, performance, role clarity, and social integration. Networking and negotiation skills not only assist in initial work adjustment but also have an ongoing effect on career advancement. Proactive feedback seeking occurs when clients ask directly for information on their performance or infer it by monitoring their environment (Crant, 2000). While Ashford and Northcraft (1992) found that supervisors are impressed with high-performing individuals who seek feedback, soliciting feedback may diminish other's perceptions of an individual's managerial effectiveness (Ashford & Tsui, 1991). Therefore, clients need to be made aware of situational cues that indicate the appropriateness of feedback-seeking behaviors. Likewise, issue selling can have both positive and negative outcomes. It is generally thought to be a management-level behavior, and learning to assess the favorability of the context is important for success (Dutton, Ashford, O'Neill, Hayes, & Wierba, 1997). Appropriate conditions include senior management's willingness to listen, competitive pressures, ongoing change, supportive culture, and knowing when organizational norms will not be violated.

As previously mentioned, changes in traditional work have created a situation where employees need to take a proactive approach to their own career development rather than passively rely on their employer to take responsibility. Hesketh and Considine (1998, p. 406) suggested employing a "Me Incorporated" metaphor, where "people think about themselves as a mini company." Investment in self-directed learning and skill development, consultation for advice and help from experts, and career planning must be carried out to maintain flexibility and employability. Accumulating social capital through networking and the development of a diverse array of social contacts is also an important feature (Langford, 1997). "Me Inc." clients can be assisted in analyzing the factors within their current environment (required knowledge, skills, and abilities; work environment reinforcers) and the external factors (e.g., market trends, opportunities) to assess any change necessary to maintain their future marketability. Information obtained is then used to develop an effective set of immediate and longer term actions to achieve their goals.

PROMOTING PROACTIVE BEHAVIORS BY THE ORGANIZATION

Organizations can act proactively by developing a *learning* culture, which involves a management culture that allows individuals to be responsive to their environment, recognizes the value of investment in staff and their flexible skill set for the future, and develops feed-forward and feed-back systems to permit hypothesis testing. This is no simple task and would draw on the approaches used in organizational development and change. Senge (1992) highlighted key features of a learning organization such as the importance of personal mastery, shared mental models, vision, and team learning for members of the organization. Organizations that are able to provide development opportunities and a climate that fosters learning have an advantage in both attracting staff and in ensuring that new staff are able to adjust to their new roles and adapt to the workplace. A key feature of such organizations is the acceptance that staff may need to have opportunities to learn from errors (Ivancic & Hesketh, 1995).

PROMOTING REACTIVE BEHAVIORS BY THE INDIVIDUAL

The Pulakos et al. (2000) dimensions identified reactive behavior as including adapting to the requirement for new skills and use of technology and interpersonal and cross-cultural adaptability.

Training employees to update their knowledge and skill base is a well-researched option for encouraging reactive behavior in the individual. Here the organization takes the initiative to provide training, rather than the individual proactively seeking to update skills (as described earlier). Historically, transfer of knowledge and skills—the outcome of interest in training theory and research—has been defined as the ability to reproduce and maintain skills across environments. More recently, this perspective has shifted to include *generalization,* which is the ability to adapt trained knowledge and skills to new and more complex situations (Kozlowski et al., 2001). A dilemma exists, however, because traditional training designs, while useful when trainees are required to reproduce exact behaviors, are often counterproductive in the face of changing task demands and the need for adaptive expertise (Smith et al., 1997). Much of the current research is, therefore, aimed at discovering and examining strategies that build adaptive expertise such as guided discovery, error-based training, metacognitive instruction, and mastery-oriented learning. Students are referred to Hesketh and Ivancic (2002) for a detailed discussion of training methods.

Interpersonal adaptability and cross-cultural adaptability have been identified as specific reactive behaviors required by employees in modern, change-oriented organizations. This is particularly so for individuals who are required to work in international settings. Parker and Axtell (2000) recognized the relevance of perspective taking in enhancing an individual's ability to interact with others who have different worldviews and ways of seeing things. They suggested that perspective taking includes empathy toward and positive attribution about the other person and that being given opportunity for interaction is one important intervention that increases the likelihood of an employee's taking the perspective of a coworker, customer, or supplier. Likewise, frequency of interaction with host nationals, together with family support and training programs, was found to be a significant predictor of adjustment to cross-cultural assignment in a recent meta-analysis of the expatriate adjustment literature (Hechanova, Beehr, & Christiansen, 2003).

PROMOTING REACTIVE BEHAVIORS BY THE ORGANIZATION

Perhaps the best way to help individuals adjust to and cope with change is to design work environments in a manner that supports such coping. *Work design* refers to the way an organization structures its physical, mental, and interpersonal job tasks and the way those tasks are grouped together and supervised (Parker & Turner, 2002). As indicated throughout this chapter, *re*designing work has an impact on employee adjustment. Two of the major ways that organizations can redesign work is by job enlargement (i.e., increasing job variety by including additional tasks) and by increasing workers' autonomy (i.e., the extent to which employees are free to behave independently). Provision of supportive management is a third way that companies can improve the character of their work environment.

PROMOTING TOLERANT BEHAVIORS BY THE INDIVIDUAL

The Pulakos et al. (2000, 2002) taxonomy identifies coping with stress and coping with ambiguity as dimensions of adaptive performance. We have categorized these as tolerant behaviors.

Stress management refers to interventions designed to reduce stress symptoms such as anxiety, depression, and exhaustion through the enhancement of the person's coping ability. Volumes have been written on different techniques that come under the rubric of stress management training (e.g., Everly & Lating, 2002), and space does not permit an adequate review of these. Briefly, emotion-focused methods attempt to help people handle their negative feelings, whereas problem-focused methods aim to teach the individual how to change unpleasant work conditions and how to communicate with difficult people. Gist and Mitchell (1992) also recommend the use of vicarious training or modeling, which involves observation of others using self-control techniques, coping with anxiety, and persisting despite difficulty. Research suggests that individual training is more effective than group training.

PROMOTING TOLERANT BEHAVIORS BY THE ORGANIZATION

Specific needs of an aging workforce and working parents create situations in which organizations are required to be tolerant to retain their best talent. Examples include the need to provide flexible hours of work, part-time and casual positions, parental leave, caregiver leave (e.g., time off work to care for ailing relatives), and telecommuting. The implications of tolerant behavior on the part of employers have not been well researched (Murphy, 1999), and this is an area that does require more attention.

ENHANCING SELF-EFFICACY

According to social cognitive theory, self-efficacy is a malleable construct (Bandura, 1986). In light of its significant effect on work adjustment outcomes, facilitation of an increased sense of efficacy, therefore, represents a potentially influential intervention at the disposal of counselors. Bandura (1997) suggested that self-efficacy can be enhanced by means of four different information cues: enactive mastery, modeling, verbal persuasion, and judgment of affective and physiological states (see Lent, Chapter 5, this volume, for a discussion of approaches to enhancing self-efficacy).

The most influential information comes from active mastery, or repeated performance success, which Gist (1987, p. 473) described as being facilitated "when gradual accomplishments build the skills, coping abilities, and exposure needed for task performance." However, care should be exercised in counseling clients to engage in adaptive behaviors where there is insufficient support because failure to perform successfully can decrease self-efficacy, and some individuals will avoid performance opportunities because of a fear of failure. In situations where it is inappropriate for a client to perform a challenging task, vicarious experience (modeling) through observing another person perform the task is beneficial (Bandura, 1997). This method of enhancing self-efficacy is most effective when the model is similar to the client in terms of personal characteristics such as age and ability (Bandura, 1997) and when success comes after perceived effort (Gist, 1987).

Persuading or convincing clients about their capability to adjust to changing conditions is also thought to influence efficacy perceptions, although the empirical support for this form of intervention (e.g., training and feedback seeking) comes from studies that examine self-efficacy for a specific task. Conversely, Parker (1998) showed that training was not effective for increasing role breadth self-efficacy, that is, efficacy for a range of tasks. It is also important that characteristics of the *persuader,* such as expertise, credibility, trustworthiness, and prestige, will affect outcome (Bandura, 1997).

Finally, information from internal cues, such as positive and negative arousal states and beliefs about the malleability of an individual's skills and abilities, is used to establish self-efficacy levels. For example, clients who interpret arousal as acute fear of the task ahead will be more likely to feel vulnerable to failure (Gist, 1987). Counselors, therefore, need to attend to factors, such as personality (e.g., neuroticism, trait anxiety) and current mood or state anxiety, that affect psychological arousal, remembering that nonwork issues related to factors such as family and health will affect mood and anxiety.

SUMMARY

We have approached the subject of work adjustment from the perspective of P-E fit theories, with a particular emphasis on the Minnesota Theory of Work

Adjustment (Dawis & Lofquist, 1984). We showed that pervasive and significant changes have created a modern workplace that demands constant adjustment and adaptability by its workers. To better understand the implications of these adjustment requirements, we updated the traditional work adjustment variables to include adaptive performance, satisfaction with change, and well-being in the midst of change. We also suggested a new conceptualization of the individual and environmental variables that affect those adaptive outcomes. We argued that counseling for work adjustment in today's changing, fluid environment effectively means assisting clients to cope with, adjust to, and enjoy change. Therefore, intervention ideas based on this type of counseling were then presented under the categories of promoting proactive, reactive, and tolerant behaviors in both the individual and the organization.

REFERENCES

Alderfer, C. P. (1972). *Existence, relatedness, and growth: Human needs in organizational settings.* New York: Free Press.

Allworth, E. (1997, June). *Cognitive ability, biodata and personality: Incremental and differential validity in a training context.* Paper presented at the 2nd Australian Industrial and Organizational Psychology Conference, Melbourne.

Allworth, E., & Hesketh, B. (1999). Construct-oriented biodata: Capturing change-related and contextually relevant future performance. *International Journal of Selection and Assessment, 7*(2), 97–111.

Arvey, R. (1986). General ability in employment. *Journal of Vocational Behavior, 29,* 415–420.

Ashford, S. J. (1986). Feedback-seeking in individual adaptation: A resource perspective. *Academy of Management Journal, 29*(3), 465–487.

Ashford, S. J., & Black, J. S. (1996). Proactivity during organizational entry: The role of desire for control. *Journal of Applied Psychology, 81,* 199–214.

Ashford, S. J., & Northcraft, G. B. (1992). Conveying more (or less) than we realize: The role of impression management in feedback-seeking. *Organizational Behavior and Human Decision Processes, 53,* 310–334.

Ashford, S. J., & Taylor, M. S. (1990). Adaptation to work transitions: An integrative approach. In G. R. Ferris & K. M. Rowland (Eds.), *Research in personnel and human resource management* (Vol. 8, pp. 1–39). Greenwich, CT: JAI Press.

Ashford, S. J., & Tsui, A. S. (1991). Self-regulation for managerial effectiveness: The role of active feedback seeking. *Academy of Management Journal, 34*(2), 251–280.

Bandura, A. (1986). *Social foundations of thought and action: A social-cognitive view.* Englewood Cliffs, NJ: Prentice-Hall.

Bandura, A. (1997). *Self-efficacy: The exercise of control.* New York: Freeman.

Bandura, A., Adams, N. E., & Beyer, J. (1977). Cognitive processes mediating behavioral change. *Journal of Personality and Social Psychology, 35*(3), 125–139.

Barrick, M. R., Mount, M. K., & Judge, T. A. (2001). Personality and performance at the beginning of the new millennium: What do we know and where do we go next? *International Journal of Selection and Assessment, 9*(1/2), 9–30.

Bateman, T. S., & Crant, J. M. (1993). The proactive component of organizational behavior: A measure and correlates. *Journal of Organizational Behavior, 14,* 103–118.

Bonino, S., & Cattelino, E. (1999). The relationship between cognitive abilities and social abilities in childhood: A research on flexibility in thinking and co-operation with peers. *International Journal of Behavioural Development, 23*(1), 19–36.

Borman, W. C., & Motowidlo, S. J. (1993). Expanding the criterion domain to include elements of contextual performance. In N. Schmitt, W. C. Borman, & Associates (Eds.), *Personnel selection in organizations.* San Francisco: Jossey-Bass.

Borman, W. C., & Motowidlo, S. J. (1997). Task performance and contextual performance: The meaning for personnel selection research. *Human Performance, 10*(2), 99–109.

Cable, D. M., & Scott De Rue, D. (2002). The convergent and discriminant validity of subjective fit perceptions. *Journal of Applied Psychology, 87,* 875–884.

Caligiuri, P. M., Jacobs, R. R., & Farr, J. L. (2000). The Attitudinal and Behavioral Openness Scale: Scale development and construct validation. *International Journal of Intercultural Relations, 24,* 27–46.

Campbell, J. P. (1990). Modeling performance prediction problem in industrial and organizational psychology. In M. D. Dunnette & L. M. Hough (Eds.), *Handbook of industrial and organizational psychology* (2nd ed., pp. 687–732). Palo Alto, CA: Consulting Psychologists Press.

Campbell, J. P., McCloy, R. A., Oppler, S. H., & Sager, C. E. (1993). A theory of performance. In N. Schmitt & W. C. Borman (Eds.), *Personnel selection in organisations* (pp. 35–70). San Francisco: Jossey-Bass.

Caplan, R. D., Vinokur, A. D., Price, R. H., & van Ryn, M. (1989). Job seeking, reemployment, and mental health: A randomized field experiment in coping with job loss. *Journal of Applied Psychology, 74,* 759–769.

Chan, D. (2000). Understanding adaptation to changes in the work environment: Integrating individual difference and learning perspectives. *Research in Personnel and Human Resources Management, 18,* 1–42.

Chan, D. (2001). *Practical intelligence and job performance.* Paper presented at the 16th annual conference of the Society for Industrial and Organizational Psychology, San Diego, CA.

Chan, D., & Schmitt, N. (2000). Interindividual differences in intraindividual changes in proactivity during organizational entry: A latent growth modeling approach to understanding newcomer adaptation. *Journal of Applied Psychology, 85*(2), 190–210.

Chown, S. M. (1959). Rigidity—a flexible concept. *Psychological Bulletin, 56,* 196–223.

Chown, S. M. (1972). The effect of flexibility-rigidity and age on adaptability in job performance. *Industrial Gerontology, 13,* 105–121.

Clark, J. M. (1996). Contributions of inhibitory mechanisms to unified psychological theory in neuroscience and psychology. *Brain and Cognition, 30,* 127–152.

Conway, J. (1999). Distinguishing contextual performance from task performance for managerial jobs. *Journal of Applied Psychology, 84*(1), 3–13.

Crant, J. M. (2000). Proactive behavior in organizations. *Journal of Management, 26*(3), 435–462.

Dawis, R. V., & Lofquist, L. H. (1984). *A psychological theory of work adjustment.* Minneapolis: University of Minnesota Press.

De Leeuw, A., & Volberda, H. (1996). On the concept of flexibility: A dual control perspective. *International Journal of Management Science, 24*(2), 121–139.

Dutton, J. E., Ashford, S. J., O'Neill, R. M., Hayes, E., & Wierba, R. R. (1997). Reading the wind: How middle managers assess the context for selling issues to top managers. *Strategic Management Journal, 18,* 407–425.

Everly, G. S., & Lating, J. M. (2002). *A clinical guide to the treatment of the human stress response* (2nd ed.). New York: Kluwer Academic/Plenum Press.

Fay, D., & Frese, M. (2001). The concept of personal initiative: An overview of validity studies. *Human Performance, 14*(1), 97–124.

Ferguson, E., & Patterson, F. (1998). The five factor model of personality: Openness a distinct but related construct. *Personality and Individual Differences, 24*(6), 789–796.

Ford, J. K., Quinones, M. A., Sego, D. J., & Sorra, J. (1992). Factors affecting the opportunity to perform trained tasks on the job. *Personnel Psychology, 45,* 511–527.

Frye, C. M. (1996). *New evidence for the Job Characteristics Model: A meta-analysis of the job characteristics-job satisfaction relationship using composite correlations.* Paper presented at the 11th annual meeting of the Society for Industrial and Organizational Psychology, San Diego, CA.

Gist, M. E. (1987). Self-efficacy: Implications for organizational behavior and human resource management. *Academy of Management Review, 12*(3), 472–485.

Gist, M. E., & Mitchell, T. R. (1992). Self-efficacy: A theoretical analysis of its determinants and malleability. *Academy of Management Review, 17*(2), 183–212.

Grant, A. M., & Greene, J. (2001). *Coach yourself: Make real change in your life.* London: Momentum Press.

Griffin, B. (2003). *A construct-oriented model of adaptability for use in selection contexts.* Unpublished doctoral thesis, the University of Sydney, Sydney, Australia.

Griffin, B., & Hesketh, B. (2001). *Some questions about the relationship between conscientious-ness and performance.* Paper presented at the 16th annual conference of the Society of Industrial and Organizational Psychology, San Diego, CA.

Griffin, B., & Hesketh, B. (2003). Adaptable behaviours for successful work and career adjustment. *Australian Journal of Psychology, 55*(2).

Hackman, J. R., & Oldham, G. R. (1976). Motivation through the design of work: Test of a theory. *Organizational Behavior and Human Performance, 16,* 250–279.

Hanisch, K. A., & Hulin, C. L. (1991). General attitudes and organizational withdrawal: An evaluation of a causal model. *Journal of Vocational Behavior, 39,* 110–128.

Hannigan, T. P. (1990). Traits, attitudes, and skills that are related to intercultural effectiveness and their implications for cross-cultural training: A review of the literature. *International Journal of Intercultural Relations, 14,* 89–111.

Hechanova, R., Beehr, T. A., & Christiansen, N. D. (2003). Antecedents and consequences of employees' adjustment to overseas assignment: A meta-analytic review. *Applied Psychology, 52*(2), 213–236.

Herr, E. L. (1993). Contexts and influences on the need for personal flexibility for the 21st century. *Canadian Journal of Counselling, 27*(3), 148–164.

Hesketh, B., & Allworth, E. (1997). *Adaptive performance: Updating the criterion to cope with change.* Paper presented at the 2nd Australian Industrial and Organizational Psychology Conference, Melbourne, Australia.

Hesketh, B., & Considine, G. (1998). Integrating individual and organizational perspectives for career development and change. *European Journal of Work and Organizational Psychology, 7*(3), 405–481.

Hesketh, B., & Griffin, B. (in press). Work adjustment. In W. B. Walsh & M. L. Savickas (Eds.), *Handbook of vocational psychology* (Vol. 3). Hillsdale, NJ: Erlbaum.

Hesketh, B., & Ivancic, K. (2002). Enhancing performance through training. In S. Sonnentag (Ed.), *The psychological management of individual performance in organisation.* London: Sage.

Hesketh, B., & Myors, B. (1997). How should we measure fit in organisational psychology: Or should we? *Australian Psychologist, 32,* 71–76.

Hill, T., Smith, N. D., & Mann, M. F. (1987). Role of efficacy expectations in predicting the decision to use advanced technologies. *Journal of Applied Psychology, 72,* 307–314.

Holland, J. L. (1997). *Making vocational choices: A theory of vocational personalities and work environments.* Englewood Cliffs, NJ: Prentice-Hall.

Hulin, C. L. (1991). Adaptation, persistence, and commitment in organizations. In M. D. Dunnette & L. M. Hough (Eds.), *Handbook of industrial and organizational psychology* (Vol. 2, pp. 445–505). Palo Alto, CA: Consulting Psychologists Press.

Hulin, C. L., & Judge, T. A. (2003). Job attitudes. In W. C. Borman, D. R. Ilgen, & R. Klimoski (Eds.), *Handbook of psychology: Industrial and organizational psychology* (Vol. 12, pp. 255–276). New York: Wiley.

Hunter, J. E. (1986). Cognitive ability, cognitive aptitudes, job knowledge and job performance. *Journal of Vocational Behavior, 29,* 340–362.

Ivancic, K., & Hesketh, B. (1995). Making the best of errors during training. *Training Research Journal: The Science and Practice of Training, 1,* 103–126.

Jausovec, N. (1994). *Flexible thinking: An explanation for individual differences in ability.* Cresskill, NJ: Hampton Press.

Judge, T. A., & Barrick, M. R. (2001). *Personality and work.* Paper presented at the 16th annual conference of the Society for Industrial and Organizational Psychology, San Diego, CA.

Judge, T. A., & Bono, J. E. (2001). Relationship of core self-evaluations traits—self-esteem, generalized self-efficacy, locus of control, and emotional stability—with job satisfaction and job performance: A meta-analysis. *Journal of Applied Psychology, 86*(1), 80–92.

Judge, T. A., Thoresen, C. J., Pucik, V., & Welbourne, T. M. (1999). Managerial coping with organizational change: A dispositional perspective. *Journal of Applied Psychology, 84*(1), 107–122.

Kampa-Kokesch, S., & Anderson, M. Z. (2001). Executive coaching: A comprehensive review. *Consulting Psychology Journal: Practice and Research, 53*(4), 205–228.

Kanter, R. (1988). When a thousand flowers bloom: Structural, collective, and social conditions for innovation in organizations. In B. M. Staw & L. L. Cummings (Eds.), *Research in organizational behavior* (Vol. 10, pp. 169–211). Greenwich, CT: JAI Press.

Kirton, M. J. (1985). Adapters, innovators, and paradigm consistency. *Psychological Reports, 57,* 487–490.

Kozlowski, S. W. J., Gully, S. M., Brown, K. G., Salas, E., Smith, E. M., & Nason, E. R. (2001). Effects of training goals and goal orientation traits on multidimensional training outcomes and performance adaptability. *Organizational Behavior and Human Decision Processes, 85*(1), 1–31.

Krausz, M., Koslowsky, M. Y., & Eiser, A. (1998). Distal and proximal influences on turnover intentions and satisfaction: Support for a withdrawal progression theory. *Journal of Vocational Behavior, 52,* 59–71.

Lance, C. E., Vandenberg, R. J., & Self, R. M. (2000). Latent growth models of individual change: The case of newcomer adjustment. *Organizational Behavior and Human Decision Processes, 83*(1), 107–140.

Landis, R. S., Fogli, L., & Goldberg, E. (1998). Future-oriented job analysis: A description of the process and its organizational implications. *International Journal of Selection and Assessment, 6*(3), 192–197.

Langford, P. (1997). *The role of networking, referent power, and social support in career success.* Paper presented at the 2nd Australian Industrial and Organizational Psychology conference, Melbourne, Australia.

Lauver, K. J., & Kristof-Brown, A. (2001). Distinguishing between employees' perceptions of person-job and person-organization fit. *Journal of Vocational Behavior, 59,* 454–470.

LePine, J. A., Colquitt, J. A., & Erez, A. (2000). Adaptability to changing task contexts: Effects of general cognitive ability, conscientiousness, and openness to experience. *Personnel Psychology, 53*(3), 563–593.

London, M., & Mone, E. M. (1999). Continuous learning. In D. R. Ilgen & E. D. Pulakos (Eds.), *The changing nature of performance.* San Francisco: Jossey-Bass.

Major, D. A., & Kozlowski, S. W. J. (1997). Newcomer information seeking: Individual and contextual influences. *International Journal of Selection and Assessment, 5*(1), 16–28.

Martin, M. M., & Rubin, R. B. (1995). A new measure of cognitive flexibility. *Psychological Reports, 76*(2), 623–626.

McCrae, R. R., & Costa, P. T. (1997). Conceptions and correlates of openness to experience. In R. Hogan, R. Johnson, & S. Briggs (Eds.), *Handbook of personality psychology* (pp. 825–847). San Diego, CA: Academic Press.

Murphy, K. R. (1989). Is the relationship between cognitive ability and job performance stable over time? *Human Performance, 2,* 183–200.

Murphy, K. R. (1999). The challenge of staffing a postindustrial workplace. In D. R. Ilgen & E. D. Pulakos (Eds.), *The changing nature of performance.* San Francisco: Jossey-Bass.

Oldham, G., & Cummings, A. (1996). Employee creativity: Personal and contextual factors at work. *Academy of Management Journal, 39*(3), 607–625.

Parker, S. K. (1998). Enhancing role breadth self-efficacy: The roles of job enrichment and other organizational interventions. *Journal of Applied Psychology, 83*(6), 835–852.

Parker, S. K. (2000). From passive to proactive motivation: The importance of Flexible Role Orientations and Role Breadth Self-Efficacy. *Applied Psychology: An International Review, 49*(3), 447–469.

Parker, S. K., & Axtell, C. M. (2000). Seeing another view point: Antecedents and outcomes of employee perspective taking activity. *Academy of Management Journal, 44*(6), 1085–1100.

Parker, S. K., & Turner, N. (2002). Work design and individual performance: Research findings and an agenda for future inquiry. In S. Sonnentag (Ed.), *Psychological management of individual performance* (pp. 69–93). Chichester, England: Wiley.

Parker, S. K., Wall, T. D., & Jackson, P. R. (1997). "That's not my job": Developing flexible employee work orientations. *Academy of Management Journal, 40*(4), 899–929.

Pratzner, F. C., & Ashley, W. L. (1985). Adults and the changing workplace. *1985 Yearbook of the American Vocational Association,* 13–22.

Pulakos, E. D., Arad, S., Donovan, M. S., & Plamondon, K. E. (2000). Adaptability in the workplace: Development of a taxonomy of adaptive performance. *Journal of Applied Psychology, 85,* 612–624.

Pulakos, E. D., Schmitt, N., Dorsey, D. W., Arad, S., Hedge, J. W., & Borman, W. C. (2002). Predicting adaptive performance: Further tests of a model of adaptability. *Human Performance, 15*(4), 299–323.

Quinones, M. A., Ford, J. K., & Teachout, M. S. (1995). The relationship between work experience and job performance: A conceptual and meta-analytic review. *Personnel Psychology, 48*(4), 887–910.

Reder, L. M., & Schunn, C. D. (1999). Bringing together the psychometric and strategy worlds: Predicting adaptivity in a dynamic task. In D. Gopher & A. Koriat (Eds.), *Attention and performance XVII: Cognitive regulation of performance. Interaction of theory and application* (pp. 315–342). Cambridge, MA: MIT Press.

Rende, B. (2000). Cognitive flexibility: Theory, assessment, and treatment. *Seminars in Speech and Language, 21*(2), 121–133.

Runco, M. A., & Okuda, S. M. (1991). The instructional enhancement of the flexibility and originality scores of divergent thinking tests. *Applied Cognitive Psychology, 5*(5), 435–441.

Saks, A. M. (1995). Longitudinal field investigation of the moderating and mediating effects of self-efficacy on the relationship between training and newcomer adjustment. *Journal of Applied Psychology, 80*(2), 211–225.

Schmidt, F. L., & Hunter, J. E. (1998). The validity and utility of selection methods in personnel psychology: Practical and theoretical implications of 85 years of research findings. *Psychological Bulletin, 124*(2), 262–274.

Schneider, B. (1997). People make the place. *Personnel Psychology, 40*, 437–454.

Schunn, C. D., & Reder, L. M. (2001). Another source of individual differences: Strategy adaptivity to changing rates of success. *Journal of Experimental Psychology: General.*

Scratchley, L. S., & Hakstian, A. R. (2001). The measurement and prediction of managerial creativity. *Creativity Research Journal, 13*(3/4), 367–384.

Senge, P. (1992). *The Fifth Discipline: The art and practice of the learning organization.* Sydney: Random House Australia.

Smith, E. M., Ford, J. K., & Kozlowski, S. W. J. (1997). Building adaptive expertise: Implications for training design strategy. In M. A. Quinones & A. Ehrenstein (Eds.), *Training for a rapidly changing workplace* (pp. 89–118). Washington, DC: American Psychological Association.

Sonnentag, S., & Frese, M. (2002). Performance concepts and performance theory. In S. Sonnentag (Ed.), *Psychological management of individual performance* (pp. 3–25). Chichester, West Sussex, England: Wiley.

Stankov, L. (1988). Aging, attention, and intelligence. *Psychology and Aging, 3*(1), 59–74.

Sternberg, R. J. (1997). The concept of intelligence and its role in lifelong learning and success. *American Psychologist, 52*, 1030–1045.

Tziner, A., & Meir, E. I. (1997). Work adjustment: Extension of the theoretical framework. In C. I. Cooper & I. T. Robertson (Eds.), *International review of industrial and organizational psychology* (Vol 12). Chichester, England: Wiley.

Van Scotter, J. R., Motowidlo, S. J., & Cross, T. C. (2000). Effects of task performance and contextual performance on systemic rewards. *Journal of Applied Psychology, 85*(4), 526–535.

Wanberg, C. R., & Banas, J. T. (2000). Predictors and outcomes of openness to changes in a reorganized workplace. *Journal of Applied Psychology, 85*(1), 132–142.

Wanberg, C. R., & Kammeyer-Mueller, J. D. (2000). Predictors and outcomes of proactivity in the socialization process. *Journal of Applied Psychology, 85*(3), 373–385.

Warr, P. B. (1990). The measurement of well-being and other aspects of mental health. *Journal of Occupational Psychology, 63*(3), 193–210.

Warr, P. B. (1991). Mental health, well-being and job satisfaction. In B. Hesketh & A. Adams (Eds.), *Psychological perspectives on occupational health and rehabilitation* (pp. 143–165). Sydney, Australia: Harcourt Brace Jovanovich.

CHAPTER 21

Counseling for Retirement

Harvey L. Sterns and Linda Mezydlo Subich

T
HE DECISION TO retire or continue working reflects a complex array of factors, including economic well-being, personal preference, subjective health, attitudes about leisure, and the desire to continue work. Satisfaction with current work and ability to continue work reflect normative aging, generational differences, and unique life events of the older adult worker. Intervention in the workplace in areas such as wellness promotion, training and retraining, and human resources management may make work-life extension a more frequent choice. The ultimate responsibility for maintaining professional competence rests on the individual employee. At the same time, an organization can foster competence by providing updating opportunities, challenging work assignments, and interaction with coworkers and management. Nonetheless, retirement is an option that most older workers consider at some time in their work lives. Older workers often make this choice on their own; however, many are forced to make the choice because of downsizing, early buyouts, and business closings. Many people may want to continue to work and seek so-called bridge jobs before retirement (Beehr & Bowling, 2002; Kim & Moen, 2001; Shultz, 2003; Sterns & Gray, 1999; Sterns & Huyck, 2001; Sterns & Subich, 2002).

Research on retirement indicates that in the 2000s we will need to carefully weigh the importance of voluntary and involuntary decisions to retire and relevant factors related to work satisfaction. For more than 30 years, a major emphasis has been on the positive aspects and normalcy of retirement and approaches to facilitate the transition to retirement (Schlossberg, 2004). At the same time, the United States stands as one of a small number of countries in its advocacy for the rights of older adult workers to continue to work if they are capable and able.

There are multiple definitions of *an older worker* (i.e., chronological/legal, functional, psychosocial, organizational, life span). Psychosocial and life-span definitions of older workers are especially relevant for counseling applications. Psychosocial definitions (Sterns & Doverspike, 1989) are based on social perceptions, including age typing of occupations, perceptions of the older worker, and the aging of knowledge, skill, and ability sets. The individual's self-perception is also considered. How individuals perceive themselves and their careers at a given age may be congruent or incongruent with societal image. Relatively little research has addressed the basic question of how we know when workers will perceive themselves, or be perceived by others, as old. Life-span definitions (Sterns & Doverspike, 1989) emphasize that behavioral change can occur at any point in the life cycle.

Another important influence in individual decision making about retirement is the perception of timing norms. Timing norms are discussed as prescriptions about when and how an individual retires, influenced by level of commitment to the work organization, modes and styles of exiting, and pension incentives. Timing norms become the bearer of societal, firm level, or reference group preferences for retirement (Ekerdt, 1998). Ekerdt's analysis of the *Health and Refinement Study* 1992 baseline wave (ages 51 to 61) reveals support for the concept of a usual age for retirement, which may vary in different work settings and occupational categories. Plan incentives influence timing of retirement behavior, and 85% of workers reported that they planned to leave at or before the local, usual age for retirement. In addition, more than 80% of respondents did not plan to work beyond the usual age.

A GENERAL MODEL OF RETIREMENT COUNSELING

A prominent model of retirement counseling is that of Richardson (1993). This model served as the foundation for her classic book titled *Retirement Counseling*, and it is composed of three phases: listening, assessment, and intervention. In the listening phase, the counselor works to develop rapport with the client. Developing trust, being nonjudgmental, and aiding clients to reflect on their expectations for, or experience of, retirement are some of the tasks of this first phase. Richardson highlighted the importance of attentive listening, genuineness, and acceptance by the counselor. She also emphasized the importance of identifying the "precipitating problem" that led the client to seek assistance.

In the assessment phase, the magnitude of the retirement problem is assessed. This includes determining the history of the issue, the client's perception of its severity, and the affect associated with the problem. In addition, Richardson recommended that the counselor obtain information about how the client is behaving and what coping attempts are being made. The assessment must take into consideration the client's retirement phase; Richardson (1993) delineated three critical phases of retirement: preretirement, retirement decision-making, and adjustment. These phases were deemed times when individuals face critical decisions with implications for their future functioning, and different issues may be more relevant to assess at each phase. Implicit in the assessment phase is that a goal for change emerges from it.

Finally, Richardson (1993) described three distinct approaches to the intervention phase of retirement counseling: nondirective, collaborative, and directive. In the nondirective approach, the counselor is supportive and relies on the client's strengths and resources. This approach is recommended for mild concerns and focuses on clients' exploring and initiating action to resolve their issues. The collaborative approach is described as one where the counselor takes a more active role in aiding clients to resolve their issues, often because clients' concerns are more serious. The counselor may actively educate clients, help brainstorm solutions, and guide them in their process of coming to a solution to the problem. In cases where a client is extremely dysfunctional (e.g., severely depressed, suicidal, psychotic), Richardson recommended a directive approach to keep the client safe and functioning adequately.

This model of retirement counseling seems consistent with many traditional approaches to counseling (e.g., Corey & Corey, 1998; Egan, 1990; C. E. Hill & O'Brien, 1999; Ivey, 2002). Its focus, like that of Hill and O'Brien or Ivey, for example, is on connecting with the client and using the therapeutic relationship to assist the client in setting and acting on a goal. With all but the most disturbed or dysfunctional clients, the counselor relies on the client's strengths and acts to empower him or her to resolve the issue at hand. As such, Richardson's (1993) model is both well-connected to a body of research that supports the effectiveness of relationship-based counseling and flexible enough to serve as a foundation for varied retirement interventions.

PRERETIREMENT COUNSELING

One important determinant of what sort of intervention is needed by a client is the person's retirement phase. The initial phase of retirement, preretirement, is described as generally occurring in midlife (Richardson, 1993), although the exact timing of it varies widely across individuals. At that point, individuals recognize their future disengagement from the workforce and may begin thinking about, talking about, or planning for this future point. Preretirement counseling is most often described in terms of processing of client attitudes (e.g., Ferguson & Koder, 1998; Geist, 1988; Waters, 1984) and aiding with client planning behavior (e.g., Kalt & Kohn, 1975; Richardson, 1993). It most typically occurs in a group setting and is likely to involve a strong educational component and a weaker focus on the individual's affective experience (Geist, 1988; Richardson, 1993).

Countless authors have outlined the preferred and actual topical content of preretirement counseling programs (e.g., Dennis, 1984, 1986; Glass & Flynn, 2000; Hunter, 1976; Kalt & Kohn, 1975; Pyron, 1969; Richardson, 1993; Tinsley & Bigler, 2002). Most typically, such programs are described as including a focus on pension benefit information, health care information, and financial planning. These topics also are reported as most strongly preferred by program consumers. Less typical and less often requested is coverage of housing options, legal issues, leisure activities, and emerging marital or relationship issues. These latter issues, however, are deemed by many retirement specialists as critical to consider in retirement planning (Dennis, 2002; Hunter, 1976). Together, these content domains comprise the educational component of most programs and often are covered straightforwardly in a group format.

The lesser focus on clients' affective experiences in most preretirement programs may be in part a function of their typical group format. Richardson (1993) and others (e.g., Ferguson & Koder, 1998) have noted, however, the value of individual preretirement counseling in certain instances and emphasized the need to provide clients with a comfortable forum in which to share feelings and fears about this life transition. Although data from Ferguson and Koder suggested that the majority of their older adult sample had optimistic views of the future, a sizable minority (16%) held a more negative view. Comparable data emerged from work by Kimmel, Price, and Walker (1978), who found such views to predict subsequent retirement satisfaction. Individuals with negative retirement attitudes, then, might be most likely to benefit from individual counseling sessions. This idea is consistent with recommendations of many authors (e.g., Ferguson & Koder, 1998; Richardson, 1993; Sterns, Weis, & Perkins, 1984). Indeed, Ferguson and Koder suggested that more intensive individual preretirement counseling be targeted specifically toward at-risk adults. Risk status may be indicated by characteristics such as being in ill health, having a low income, facing involuntary retirement, or lacking in social supports (Taylor & Doverspike, 2003).

The typically greater educative focus and lesser affective focus of preretirement counseling may come together in that negative affect surrounding retirement may be a reflection of the person's lack of knowledge and consequent anticipatory anxiety. Indeed, Schlossberg, Troll, and Leibowitz (1978) suggested that role ambiguity may underlie many preretirement concerns. Relatedly, Fretz, Kluge, Ossana, Jones, and Merikangas (1989) found that preretirement worry correlated with inadequate information as well as with lesser retirement adjustment self-efficacy, planfulness, and social support. Taking a social cognitive perspective, as did Fretz et al., these correlates of retirement-related negative affect all are amenable to intervention. We might follow Bandura's (1986) general suggestions concerning the use of information provision (vicarious modeling, verbal persuasion), skill development (mastery experiences), and anxiety reduction to help clients build self-efficacy, facilitate goal-directed behaviors, and attain desired outcomes in preretirement interventions.

General support for the value of preretirement counseling can be drawn from Sterns and Gray (1999) as well as from Taylor and Doverspike (2003); both sets of authors concluded that the research literature supports the notion that those who plan for major life transitions are more successful at them. More specifically, Sterns, Junkins, and Bayer (2001) reported that those who engaged in preretirement programs gained more positive attitudes about retirement, improved in their knowledge and planning, and were more satisfied subsequently with retirement. Richardson (1993) summarized a variety of outcome research on preretirement counseling and reported that modalities that incorporated both information provision and time for processing that information resulted in the most positive outcomes (e.g., more planning behavior, feeling prepared). She warned that negative outcomes seemed most likely when participants were not given an opportunity to voice questions and concerns.

Taylor and Doverspike (2003) took a social cognitive perspective and suggested that the observed positive relation between retirement planning behavior and later retirement adjustment may reflect that, in planning, the individual develops realistic expectations and goals for retirement. They noted that those expectations and goals in turn facilitate and guide the retirement process, and they urged wider use of preretirement counseling to foster planning.

Indeed, one of the major goals of retirement education is the development of key issues of retirement. Much of the emphasis is on consciousness-raising, values clarification, getting in touch with personal feelings, and awareness of viewpoints held by significant others. Staudinger (1999) and Smith (1996) both have presented important work on the development of planning capability, wisdom concerning life events, and the development of an approach to the art of living.

The literature and recommendations concerning preretirement counseling seem consistent with the concept of the self-managed career (see Griffin & Hesketh, Chapter 20, this volume). Career self-management is carefully discussed by Hall and Mirvis (1996) in their presentation of the protean career. A protean career is directed by the individual rather than the employing organization. Greater responsibility for learning, skill mastery, and reskilling is also placed on the individual (Hall & Mirvis, 1995). The individual is in charge, in control, and able to change the shape of his or her career at will—similar to a free agent in sports (Hall & Mirvis, 1996). This perspective and the goals of this type of career (e.g., psychological success, identity expansion, and learning) also recognize the artificiality of the distinction between work and nonwork life. Personal roles and career roles are highly interrelated and the boundaries between these roles tend to be fuzzy rather than clearcut (Hall & Mirvis, 1995). One disadvantage of protean careers is that an individual's identity is not likely to be tied to any one organization; problems of self-definition may result in that an individual's personal identity is not connected to a formal organizational work role.

This newer self-management perspective recalls, however, Jacobson's conclusion in 1974 that among his sample of British adults, no amount of preretirement counseling could compensate for a lifelong pattern of poor/unhealthy personal and financial habits. Similarly, Pellicano (1973) stated three decades ago: "To be effective . . . retirement counseling must begin years before the employee actually retires" (p. 616). It seems that part of our challenge is to sensitize and to involve persons in thinking about retirement at an early age.

RETIREMENT DECISION COUNSELING

Richardson's (1993) second phase of retirement involves making the decision to retire. Retirement decisions have been suggested to be influenced most strongly by health concerns, financial resources, and attitudinal variables (Sterns & Gray, 1999). In addition, August and Quintero (2001) provided a detailed discussion of how limited work opportunity structures for retired adults may affect the decision to retire. Sterns and Gray cautioned, however, that the manner in which each of these domains influences decisions is complex and may depend on individual circumstances. Richardson (1993) also generated an expansive list of issues that may drive a decision to retire including finances, health, family circumstances, attitudes about work and retirement, and personality variables. Her inclusion of psychosocial variables such as dual-earner relationship status and extent of social support network is an especially notable contribution to the literature; it is consistent with newer models of career decision-making (Phillips, 1997; Phillips, Christopher-Sisk, & Gravino, 2001; Schultheiss, Kress, Manzi, & Glasscock, 2001) and with research on critical factors in career counseling (Brown & Ryan Krane, 2000).

Focusing more specifically on the decision to retire early, Feldman (1994) suggested that individual differences (e.g., health status, attitude toward work), opportunity structures (e.g., age-related performance decrements), organizational factors (e.g., pension, flexible policies), and external environmental factors (e.g., tax laws, inflation) should be considered in analyses of retirement decisions. His comprehensive and contextually grounded view highlighted some factors not typically seen in psychological considerations of retirement decision-making.

Feldman's factors seem equally applicable to normative retirement decisions, and his review of the literature concerning each one may be informative for counselors working with adults who are grappling with the decision of when to retire.

Knowing *what* clients may be considering in their decisions is one part of effective intervention at this retirement phase, but knowing *how* they are processing the information seems important as well. Richardson (1993) noted that such decision-making often encompasses formal as well as informal planning processes and is affected by issues of timing and the control the person has concerning the decision to retire. Indeed, she outlined as one of her two primary goals of retirement decision counseling aiding the client to feel in control of the process. Her second goal was facilitating the client's making the best decision possible. Richardson's focus on empowering clients as they grapple with the decision of whether and when to retire seems consistent with her general model of retirement counseling as well as social cognitive and self-management approaches to conceptualizing retirement.

More specifically, Richardson (1993) suggested that the counselor be attentive to client affect in retirement decision counseling because transition states such as retirement may elicit strong feelings of confusion, anger, depression, or anxiety. Listening and fully exploring these feelings were recommended. Subsequent to these activities, Richardson recommended a more cognitive focus to aid the client in arriving at a decision. This focus on cognition is maintained as the client moves to implementing the decision. Although Richardson acknowledged the affective components of the retirement decision-making process, she emphasized a rational approach. More recent thinking in the realm of career decision-making may augment her perspective in that authors such as Phillips (1997) have suggested considering alternative styles of adaptive decision-making. Phillips noted that emotional or intuitive styles may be adaptive depending on the person and situation. Counselors may need to assess, and be open to working from, the decision-making perspective that works best for a particular client (see Miller & Brown, Chapter 18, this volume).

RETIREMENT ADJUSTMENT COUNSELING

The final phase of retirement delineated by Richardson (1993) is retirement adjustment. Predictors of adjustment following retirement have been heavily researched and include health, finances, and social support (Taylor & Doverspike, 2003). Better health, adequate finances, and social supports that meet the person's needs all predict better postretirement adjustment. Sterns and Gray (1999), however, observed that the retirement adjustment process is dynamic, and satisfaction with retirement may wax and wane as a result of personal and environmental changes. That variability suggests the importance of retiree flexibility to adapt to change. Indeed, Trepanier, Lapierre, and Baillargeon (2001) found that in their sample of recent retirees, retiree flexibility when confronted with impediments to personal goals best predicted psychological well-being (i.e., depression, life satisfaction, self-esteem) in retirement.

Carter and Cook (1995) also highlighted the importance of adaptability for retirement adjustment. They proposed a model in which the effects of social and work roles on retirement adjustment are mediated by locus of control and self-efficacy. As social and work roles change later in life, adjustment is affected as well unless the individual is able to adapt to the changes. Carter and Cook's model is significant in that it places in a prominent position the personality variable of locus of control and the social cognitive variable of self-efficacy for retirement. This placement is consistent with emphases on self-efficacy, personal control, and personality found in other retirement literature (e.g., Kimmel et al., 1978; Richardson, 1993; Taylor & Doverspike, 2003). That Carter and Cook and others have suggested that these variables have direct effects on retirement adjustment implies that they warrant counselors' attention in assessment and intervention.

Similarly, Reis and Gold (1993) proposed a model in which the retiree's personality and environmental context contribute to adjustment through interrelated cognitions, emotions, and behaviors. These mediators (i.e., cognitions, emotions, and behaviors) reflect the manner in which the person appraises and copes with the stresses and strains of retirement. Using their model as a guide, Reis and Gold recommended both careful assessment of personality and contextual influences in retirement counseling as well as intervention at the level of the mediating factors (with an eye to how personality may contribute to these factors). Their model seems a useful approach that capitalizes on constructs and processes that are consistent with two current and well-regarded psychological theories—the five factor model of personality (McCrae & Costa, 1990) and social cognitive theory (Bandura, 1986).

Also addressing constructs consistent with a social cognitive approach, Payne, Robbins, and Dougherty (1991) and Robbins, Lee, and Wan (1994) focused on how goals and personal orientations toward goal setting related to the adjustment of older adult retirees. Payne et al. reported that retirees who were able to set goals and maintain their direction toward them were more optimistic, persistent, resourceful, and connected to social support systems. Their data suggested greater risk status for adjustment problems for retirees who were less able to set and maintain a goal direction, and they recommended intervention to assist these retirees with the retirement transition and to enhance their social supports. Robbins et al. extended the work of Payne et al. by examining how social support, health, and socioeconomic status (SES) contributed to retirement adjustment along with the ability to set and act on goals. Specifically, they found that greater support, better health, and higher SES contributed to retirees' goal-setting ability, which, in turn, fostered better retirement adjustment. These studies' findings underscore the value of attending to goal setting in retirement counseling—a focus that is also consistent with Richardson's counseling model.

Few specific models for retirement adjustment counseling, however, exist in the literature, perhaps because interventions most often take the form of the particular adjustment issue. Richardson (1993) enumerated the following as common retirement adjustment issues: anxiety reactions, depressive reactions, marital/relationship problems, occupational problems, health problems, economic problems, social deprivation, and identity problems. She also suggested assessment and intervention approaches for each of them, with most recommendations derived from treatment strategies that are used commonly with varied adult populations (e.g., cognitive or pharmacological treatment for depression).

Although retirement adjustment counseling interventions may look similar to interventions for comparable problems with other populations, the underlying origin of the concerns may differ. Awareness of the unique stresses of retirement may facilitate the counselor's work with a retiree and enhance the counselor-client relationship. For example, Tinsley and Schwendener-Holt (1992) highlighted how negative social stereotypes about retirement and later adulthood can adversely affect retirees and contribute to depression and low self-esteem. They suggested, too, that changes in roles and time spent with partners may contribute to stress and, relatedly, retirees may need assistance structuring their time. Exploration of part-time work, community service, and leisure activities are themes relevant to retirement counseling that are raised by numerous authors (e.g., August & Quintero, 2001; Entine, 1977; Schlossberg, 2004; Sinick, 1976; Sterns & Gray, 1999; Sterns & Kaplan, 2003; Taylor & Doverspike, 2003; Tinsley & Schwendener-Holt, 1992).

Tinsley and Schwendener-Holt (1992) mentioned two additional challenges faced by older adults and retirees: relationship losses and spiritual development. Similarly, Richardson (1993) suggested that the loss of important others through death, or loss of life direction and meaning through spiritual or existential confusion, are important factors contributing to depression among retirees. Loss of income and occupational status may contribute to depression and anxiety reactions as well and be important areas for assessment and processing in counseling (Richardson, 1993; Sinick, 1976; Tinsley & Bigler, 2002).

DIVERSITY AND RETIREMENT COUNSELING

Any discussion of retirement and retirement counseling must address the issue of individual differences in views, plans, and reactions to retirement and retirement interventions. Richardson (1993) devoted multiple chapters of her classic text to how gender and ethnicity are important to consider in retirement interventions. Similarly, Tinsley and Schwendener-Holt (1992) enumerated gender and ethnic differences in how retirement is perceived and enacted. Both Tinsley and Bigler (2002) and Taylor and Doverspike (2003) specifically addressed how the retirement planning needs of women and members of diverse ethnic groups may differ from those of Caucasian men.

Common themes found in the preceding sources include the need to attend to women's lesser incomes and greater caregiving responsibilities; the former may contribute to women having inadequate financial resources, and the latter may contribute to stress and strain. The lower incomes and lesser (or nonexistent) pensions of members of many ethnic minority groups are mentioned often as influencing the decision to retire and contributing to stress and strain after retirement. Special health problems are associated with membership in some ethnic groups and may contribute to poorer retirement adjustment as health consistently predicts both the decision to retire and postretirement adjustment. Cultural tradition concerning the role of the elderly person in the community is yet another issue to consider in counseling.

Finally, Taylor and Doverspike (2003) contributed to the literature by delineating how generational influences may shape retirement attitudes, behaviors, and reactions. They suggested that the better health of upcoming retirees may require longer term planning to ensure adequate financial resources. They also recognized that little information exists in the literature on the retirement needs and issues of members of diverse groups and called for more intensive study of individual differences in this important life transition. Despite the currently limited literature base, it seems clear that retirement interventions must be undertaken with sensitivity to cultural and contextual influences.

A MODEL FOR SELF-MANAGEMENT OF CAREER AND RETIREMENT

A model that brings together many of the themes in the theoretical and empirical literature on older adulthood and retirement is that of Sterns and Kaplan (2003). Their model focuses on four major areas of consideration in retirement: self, work, family and friends, and community. This model for conceptualizing the many influences on the older adult may be used in conjunction with Richardson's (1993) counseling approach to guide the practitioner in assisting the individual who presents for retirement counseling. Careful exploration, assessment, and evaluation of the four domains, and the influences contributing to each, may lead to more informed and comprehensive interventions.

The first domain is that of the self, and Sterns and Kaplan (2003) emphasize that a person's self-concept is influenced by many factors relative to retirement issues (see Figure 21.1). First, there is the understanding of our past selves and what values, preferences, and desires are based in our past. Examples are returning to our hometown in retirement after living in another community for many years, maintaining close contact with old friends, or making use of a family summer home in retirement. This is countered and complemented by our future selves, such as the possibility of new lifestyles, new living environments, new friends, and new actions, or the decision to live in the same community but with a new set of life activities outside work.

Three factors are important here. One is the understanding of change and an awareness of the passage of time. How we view change in others and ourselves over time and how we see and understand the implications of time in the future are major aspects of personal cognitive integration leading to increased self-understanding. The second factor influencing self-concept is the perceived control that we have of our lives at the personal level, in relation to significant others

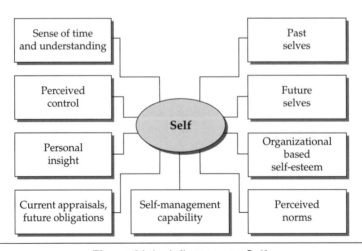

Figure 21.1   Influences on Self.

and in our work and career environments. We may feel in control based on financial resources, position held, or seniority, or we may feel extremely vulnerable based on the current financial situation and business climate. In the past few years, we have gone from the highest level of employment to a sense of great vulnerability, and many potential early retirees have had to come to terms with the fact that they will have to work longer based on the decline of their investments. In many cases, people in retirement have had to change lifestyle or return to working for pay to maintain desired lifestyles.

The third factor is personal insight—how well we understand ourselves, our motivations, our personal desires, our work approaches, and our relations to family, friends, and organizations. Self-study, education, and counseling may aid this process. Relatedly, organizational-based self-esteem (OBSE) is the bridge to the world of work. How valued an individual feels, how an individual feels in relation to his or her fellow workers, and the feeling of contribution that the individual gets from his or her work are all part of OBSE. Another important area is how an individual perceives the work and retirement norms in his or her environment. An individual's personal social clock, a set of internalized norms or timetable for when life's tasks are to be accomplished, and his or her understanding of social norms will influence self-perceptions and actions to be taken (Neugarten & Neugarten, 1987; Papalia, Sterns, Feldman, & Camp, 2002).

The orchestration of all of these influences on self and the needed interpretation, planning, sophistication, and wisdom are all part of retirement self-management capability. An important continuing area of research will focus on people's ability to self-manage their planning and execution of retirement decision making. Some persons may require more assistance and support to take action effectively.

Figure 21.2 focuses on the demands of the work environment and how they influence the decision to continue to work full time or part time or to retire. Briefly, individuals are concerned here with their self-evaluation of the employment situation. Part of this relates to their appraisal of the current situation, including how they believe they are viewed by supervisors, the outcomes of performance appraisals, perceived growth opportunities within the organization, and observations of treatment received by other later career employees. Part of this is an understanding of personal strengths and weaknesses as well as self-knowledge of their approach to meeting assignments and deadlines.

Employment-based appraisal refers to the formal and informal feedback that an individual receives from supervisors—outcomes of performance appraisal, salary increases, and involvement in organization planning and policy. *Work opportunities* refer to future plans within the work context and potential opportunities over time. New work opportunities may be an important incentive to continue to work as a bridge to retirement. Other bridge opportunities may provide a gradual change in responsibilities to part-time employment. A major dimension is an individual's activities in continuous learning and maintaining professional competence. Remaining competitive with up-to-date skills may make the individual valuable to the organization.

Relationships to coworkers may be extremely important in continued employment. How people feel about their work situation is highly influenced by coworker interactions in many cases. Middle-age and older workers value relationships on the job. A negative relationship with coworkers may lead a valuable older worker

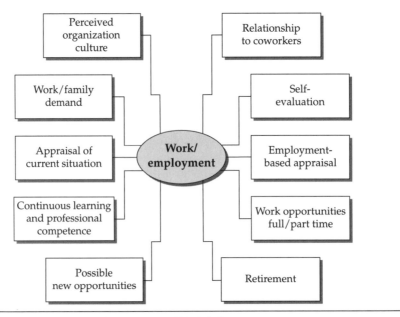

Figure 21.2   Work Influences.

to take retirement. Supervisors may want the employee to stay but may not be aware of interaction difficulties. On the other hand, older employees who feel the need to work longer than they really wanted to because of financial reasons may be a challenge for coworkers and supervisors.

Perceived organizational culture is another dimension that provides important messages to current employees. Choices made by current organization leadership and how these are transmitted to current employees provide important general information. Middle-age and older employees are usually very aware of changing climate and how long-term employees are being treated.

Another dimension is possible new opportunities—looking for new employment opportunities within or outside the individual's organization. This can be planful in terms of second- or third-career education and training or may be related to chance encounters or in response to a corporate recruiter. In those cases where the individual is self-managing and no longer desires to continue in his or her employment, the decision to retire may be the decision of choice. Often, middle-age and older employees may not be in a position to choose when to retire.

Figure 21.3 focuses on marriage and other significant relationships as major influences in decisions about work and retirement. One of the benefits of formal retirement education is that husbands and wives or significant others can engage in planning exercises that often are awareness-creating. Caregiving responsibilities for parents may be a major concern for many people. Corporate elder-care services have been available for more than two decades to assist employees who have care responsibilities. In many cases, an employee may choose or feel forced to retire to provide care to loved ones. Many people did not expect their retirement to become a major caregiving experience to parents or spouse. Family relationships may become more important and become a major influence in self-management of retirement, and these relationship changes may precipitate distress or conflict that may lead the individuals or families to counseling.

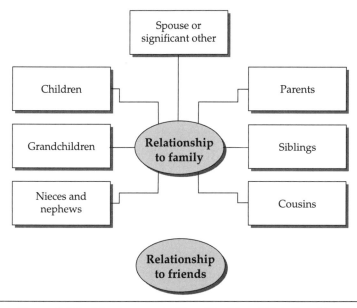

Figure 21.3   Marriage and Other Significant Relationships.

Choosing to be near children, grandchildren, or other important family members may be a reason to retire from a current job, move, and reestablish a household in a new location. New part-time or full-time employment may be a choice after such a move. Migration research tells us that approximately 80% of older adults choose to stay in their home communities to be near family and friends. This does not preclude new and exciting choices as part of a new life period.

Probably the most complex ties are the intergenerational ones (Sterns & Huyck, 2001). Some 90% of adults ages 35 to 64 are parents. According to a review of some of the research, "no single trajectory is characteristic of all or even most families during the middle years of parenthood" (Seltzer & Ryff, 1994). It is, thus, impossible to generalize neatly about the "midlife family" given the changes in timing of births, marriage, divorce and remarriage, and blended families. Instead, parenting experiences vary by social class, gender, life events and transitions, and psychological functioning in both parent and child generations. Generally, Whites, married couples, and unmarried fathers have more material resources than do minority group parents, unmarried parents, and single mothers. Divorced parents report more strain in and less support from parenting and are generally less satisfied with parenting during these years. The majority of parents need to attend both to work and parenting: 81% of the fathers and 64% of mothers ages 35 to 44 have children at home and are employed (Seltzer & Ryff, 1994).

Grandparenting is a relationship with many meanings and varied enactments (Robertson, 1977). In contrast to the stereotyped images of sedentary, cookie-making or fishing grandparents, many grandparents now are very involved in vigorous, complex lives of their own. With the rise in unwed maternity, divorce, and substance abuse, more grandparents—especially grandmothers—have found themselves playing an active parental role with grandchildren, and many grandparents have fought for legal recognition of grandparent's rights. While some grandparents have little contact with their grandchildren, others are thrust into responsibilities they thought they had left behind (Hayslip & Goldberg-Glen, 2000).

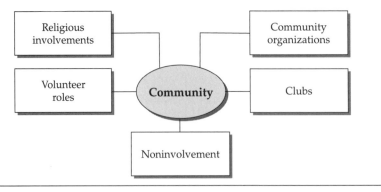

Figure 21.4 Community Influences.

Many middle-age children have living parents, and the wish and/or the need to be involved in their lives can pose another balancing challenge. For comparison, in 1800, a 60-year-old woman had only a 3% chance of having a living parent; by 1980, that had risen to 60% (Watkins, Menekn, & Bongaarts, 1987). The increased longevity of elders means that four- and five-generation families are increasingly common. As mentioned, many of the elders are still involved in nurturing younger generations. However, the increased longevity, the relatively low fertility of women who are now elderly, and changes in the health care system mean that families are providing more care and more difficult care over longer periods of time than ever before in history (Brody, 1990; Sterns et al., 1984).

Elaine Brody (1990) described the situation of "women in the middle," with the recognition that "women" included others who provide care. A 1992 Harris survey of adults over 55 found that 29% of men and 29% of women are caregivers for spouses, parents, other relatives, friends, and neighbors (The Commonwealth Fund, 1993). The heroic balancing efforts of family caregivers have been well documented. Many caregivers feel pulled among spouse, children, parents, and employment. Work may be, in such cases, a relief from otherwise relentless pressures. Some women, however, find they must reduce work to part time or withdraw altogether.

Finally, Figure 21.4 relates to what keeps people in their home communities or what aspects of community may be important in providing a meaningful context and sense of belonging. Much of the classical retirement literature has focused on these dimensions of community. What is important here is how these dimensions relate to our self-concept and how this influences our decisions to continue to work or to retire. Some individuals feel alienated by their community relationships and wish to reestablish themselves in a new community context. Others may have more than one residence and move back and forth between the new and the old, empowered by both locations. Yet others totally enjoy being a part of roles and involvements that are longstanding (Schlossberg, 2004). What is critical is our ability to bridge from the individual level to the broader work and societal context.

SUMMARY

The Sterns and Kaplan (2003) model provides the practitioner with an initial approach to organizing what may otherwise be an overwhelming array of issues. It also echoes themes noted by R. D. Hill, Thorn, and Packard (2000) in their chapter on counseling older adults. Hill et al.'s emphasis on continuity and change in later life development and the importance of meaning-making seems consistent with Sterns and Kaplan and much of the other literature overviewed in this chapter. Individuals' decisions about when and how to retire likely are mediated by personal history and longstanding coping mechanisms. The ability to be reflective about this life transition and to consider concomitantly the many facets of their life is critical if people are to make meaning out of their personal history; many people need assistance with these tasks.

Practitioners, then, would do well to heed the call of R. D. Hill et al. (2000) to provide educative, preventative, and remedial counseling services to older adults, and especially those grappling with retirement-related issues. Indeed, from a life-span approach, prevention may be the most critical mode of intervention; raising awareness about the multifaceted nature of retirement issues at the beginning of adulthood could avert some subsequent problems. Young adults would be well served by life planning services that might be offered through community outreach or educational programs or perhaps their employer. Currently, retirement planning programs often are offered too late to be effective.

Thus, there is much for us to do to assist persons to manage effectively their careers and retirement. The issues raised in this chapter identify themes and recommendations of earlier literature and may serve to guide future research and practice. Considering the dramatic increase in the number of middle-age and older people, counseling practitioners need to be prepared to provide services to their clients of all ages and backgrounds. Knowledge about life-span development and the many aspects of aging in our society is critical if the practitioner is to assess and intervene thoughtfully and appropriately (R. D. Hill et al., 2000).

REFERENCES

August, R. A., & Quintero, V. C. (2001). The role of opportunity structures in older women workers' careers. *Journal of Employment Counseling, 38,* 62–81.

Bandura, A. (1986). *Social foundations of thought and action: A social-cognitive theory.* Englewood Cliffs, NJ: Prentice-Hall.

Beehr, T. A., & Bowling, N. A. (2002). Career issues facing older workers. In D. C. Feldman (Ed.), *Work careers: A developmental perspective* (pp. 214–241). San Francisco: Jossey-Bass.

Brody, E. M. (1990). *Women in the middle: Their parent-care years.* New York: Springer.

Brown, S. D., & Ryan Krane, N. E. (2000). Four (or five) sessions and a cloud of dust: Old assumptions and new observations about career counseling. In S. D. Brown & R. W. Lent (Eds.), *Handbook of counseling psychology* (3rd ed., pp. 740–766). New York: Wiley.

Carter, M. A. T., & Cook, K. (1995). Adaptation to retirement: Role changes and psychological resources. *Career Development Quarterly, 44,* 67–82.

The Commonwealth Fund. (1993). *The untapped resource: The final report of Americans over 55 at work program.* New York: Author.

Corey, M. S., & Corey, G. (1998). *Becoming a helper.* Pacific Grove, CA: Brooks/Cole.

Dennis, H. (Ed.). (1984). *Retirement preparation: What retirement specialists need to know.* Lexington, MA. Lexington Books.

Dennis, H. (1986). Retirement preparation programs: Issues in planning and selection. *Journal of Career Development, 13,* 30–38.

Dennis, H. (2002, Summer). The retirement planning specialty. *Generations, 26,* 55–60.

Egan, G. (1990). *The skilled helper: A systematic approach to effective helping.* Pacific Grove, CA: Brooks/Cole.

Ekerdt, D. J. (1998). Workplace norms for the timing of retirement. In K. W. Schaie & C. Schooler (Eds.), *Impact of work on older adults* (pp. 101–123). New York: Springer.

Entine, A. D. (1977). Counseling for mid-life and beyond. *Vocational Guidance Quarterly,* *25,* 332–336.

Feldman, D. C. (1994). The decision to retire early: A review and conceptualization. *Academy of Management Review, 19,* 285–311.

Ferguson, S. J., & Koder, D. A. (1998). Geropsychology: Some potential growth areas in psychological research and practice. *Australian Psychologist, 33,* 187–192.

Fretz, B. R., Kluge, N. A., Ossana, S. M., Jones, S. M., & Merikangas, M. W. (1989). Intervention targets for reducing preretirement anxiety and depression. *Journal of Counseling Psychology, 36,* 301–307.

Geist, H. (1988). *Manual for retirement counselors.* San Diego, CA: Libra.

Glass, J. C., & Flynn, D. K. (2000). Retirement needs and preparation of rural middle-aged persons. *Educational Gerontology, 26,* 109–134.

Hall, D. T., & Mirvis, P. H. (1995). Careers as lifelong learning. In A. Howard (Ed.), *The changing nature of work* (pp. 323–361). San Francisco: Jossey-Bass.

Hall, D. T., & Mirvis, P. H. (1996). The new protean career: Psychological success and the path with a heart. In D. T. Hall & Associates (Eds.), *The career is dead: Long live the career: A relational approach to careers.* San Francisco: Jossey-Bass.

Hayslip, B., & Goldberg-Glen, R. (Eds.). (2000). *Grandparents raising grandchildren: Theoretical, empirical and clinical perspectives.* New York: Springer.

Hill, C. E., & O'Brien, K. M. (1999). *Helping skills: Facilitating exploration, insight, and action.* Washington, DC: American Psychological Association.

Hill, R. D., Thorn, B. L., & Packard, T. (2000). Counseling older adults: Theoretical and empirical issues in prevention and intervention. In S. D. Brown & R. W. Lent (Eds.), *Handbook of counseling psychology* (3rd ed., pp. 499–531). New York: Wiley.

Hunter, W. W. (1976). *Preparation for retirement.* Ann Arbor: University of Michigan.

Ivey, A. E. (2002). *Intentional interviewing and counseling.* New York: Wadsworth.

Jacobson, D. (1974). Planning for retirement and anticipatory attitudes towards withdrawal from work. *British Journal of Guidance and Counselling, 2,* 72–83.

Kalt, N. C., & Kohn, M. H. (1975). Pre-retirement counseling: Characteristics of programs and preferences of retirees. *Gerontologist, 15,* 179–181.

Kim, J. E., & Moen, P. (2001). Moving into retirement: Preparation and transitions in late midlife. In M. E. Lachman (Ed.), *Handbook of midlife development* (pp. 487–527). New York: Wiley.

Kimmel, D. C., Price, K. F., & Walker, J. W. (1978). Retirement choice and retirement satisfaction. *Journal of Gerontology, 33,* 575–585.

McCrae, R. R., & Costa, P. T., Jr. (1990). *Personality in adulthood.* New York: Guilford Press.

Neugarten, B. L., & Neugarten, D. A. (1987, May). The changing meanings of age. *Psychology Today,* 29–33.

Papalia, D. E., Sterns, H. L., Fledman, R. D., & Camp, C. J. (2002). *Adult development and aging* (2nd ed.). Boston: McGraw-Hill.

Payne, E. C., Robbins, S. B., & Dougherty, L. (1991). Goal directedness and older-adult adjustment. *Journal of Counseling Psychology, 38,* 302–308.

Pellicano, D. (1973). Retirement counseling. *Personnel Journal, 52,* 614–618.

Phillips, S. D. (1997). Toward an expanded definition of adaptive decision-making. *Career Development Quarterly, 45,* 275–287.

Phillips, S. D., Christopher-Sisk, E. K., & Gravino, K. L. (2001). Making career decisions in a relational context. *Counseling Psychologist, 29,* 193–213.

Pyron, H. C. (1969). Preparing employees for retirement. *Personnel Journal, 48,* 722–727.

Reis, M., & Gold, D. P. (1993). Retirement, personality, and life satisfaction: A review and two models. *Journal of Applied Gerontology, 12,* 261–282.

Richardson, V. E. (1993). *Retirement counseling: A handbook for gerontology practitioners.* New York: Springer.

Robbins, S., Lee, R., & Wan, T. (1994). Goal continuity as a mediator of early retirement adjustment: Testing a multidimensional model. *Journal of Counseling Psychology, 41,* 18–26.

Robertson, J. F. (1977). Grandmotherhood: A study of role concepts. *Journal of Marriage and the Family, 39,* 165–174.

Schlossberg, N. K. (2004). *Retire smart retire happy: Finding your true path in life.* Washington, DC: American Psychological Association.

Schlossberg, N. K., Troll, L. E., & Leibowitz, Z. (1978). *Perspectives on counseling adults: Issues and skills.* Monterey, CA: Brooks/Cole.

Schultheiss, D. P., Kress, H. M., Manzi, A. J., & Glasscock, J. M. J. (2001). Relational influences in career development: A qualitative inquiry. *Counseling Psychologist, 29,* 214–239.

Seltzer, M. M., & Ryff, C. D. (1994). Parenting across the life span: The normative and non-normative cases. In D. L. Featherman, R. M. Lerner, & M. Perlmutter (Eds.), *Life-span development and behavior* (Vol. 12, pp. 1–40). Hillsdale, NJ: Erlbaum.

Shultz, K. S. (2003). Bridge employment: Work after retirement. In G. A. Adams & T. A. Beehr (Eds.), *Retirement: Reasons, processes, and results* (pp. 214–241). New York: Springer.

Sinick, D. (1976). Counseling older persons: Career change and retirement. *Vocational Guidance Quarterly, 25,* 18–25.

Smith, J. (1996). Planning about life: A social-interactive and life-span perspective. In P. Baltes & U. M. Staudinger (Eds.), *Interactive minds: Life-span perspectives on the social foundation of cognition* (pp. 242–272). Hillsdale, NJ: Erlbaum.

Staudinger, U. M. (1999). Social cognition and a psychological approach to an art of life. In T. M. Hess & F. Blanchard-Fields (Eds.), *Social cognition and aging* (pp. 343–375). San Diego, CA: Academic Press.

Sterns, H. L., & Doverspike, D. (1989). Aging and the training and learning process in organizations. In I. Goldstein & R. Katzell (Eds.), *Training and development in work organizations* (pp. 299–332). San Francisco: Jossey-Bass.

Sterns, H. L., & Gray, J. H. (1999). Work, leisure, and retirement. In J. C. Cavanaugh & S. K. Whitbourne (Eds.), *Gerontology: An interdisciplinary perspective* (pp. 355–389). New York: Oxford University Press.

Sterns, H. L., & Huyck, M. H. (2001). Midlife and work. In M. E. Lachman (Ed.), *Handbook of midlife development* (pp. 447–486). New York: Wiley.

Sterns, H. L., Junkins, M. P., & Bayer, J. G. (2001). Work and retirement. In B. R. Bonder & M. B. Wagner (Eds.), *Functional performance in older adults* (pp. 148–164). Philadelphia: Davis.

Sterns, H. L., & Kaplan, J. (2003). Self-management of career and retirement. In G. A. Adams & T. A. Beehr (Eds.), *Retirement: Reasons, processes, and results* (pp. 188–213). New York: Springer.

Sterns, H. L., & Subich, L. M. (2002). Career development in midcareer. In D. C. Feldman (Ed.), *Work careers: A developmental perspective* (pp. 186–213). San Francisco: Jossey-Bass.

Sterns, H. L., Weis, D. M., & Perkins, S. E. (1984). A conceptual approach to counseling older adults and their families. *Counseling Psychologist, 12,* 55–62.

Taylor, M. A., & Doverspike, D. D. (2003). Retirement planning and preparation. In G. A. Adams & T. A. Beehr (Eds.), *Retirement: Reasons, processes, and results* (pp. 53–82). New York: Springer.

Tinsley, D. J., & Bigler, M. (2002). Facilitating transitions in retirement. In C. L. Juntunen & D. R. Atkinson (Eds.), *Counseling across the lifespan: Prevention and treatment* (pp. 375–397). Thousand Oaks, CA: Sage.

Tinsley, D. J., & Schwendener-Holt, M. J. (1992). Retirement and leisure. In S. D. Brown & R. W. Lent (Eds.), *Handbook of counseling psychology* (2nd ed., pp. 627–662). New York: Wiley.

Trepanier, L., Lapierre, S., & Baillargeon, J. (2001). Ténacité et flexibilité dans la pursuite do projets personnels: Impact sur le bien-être à la retraite. *Canadian Journal on Aging, 20,* 557–576.

Waters, E. B. (1984). Building on what you know: Techniques for individual and group counseling with older adults. *Counseling Psychologist, 12,* 63–74.

Watkins, S. C., Menekn, J. A., & Bongaarts, J. (1987). Demographic foundations of family change. *American Sociological Review, 52,* 346–358.

SPECIAL NEEDS AND APPLICATIONS

CHAPTER 22

Promoting the Career Development and Academic Achievement of At-Risk Youth: College Access Programs

Consuelo Arbona

IN THE UNITED STATES, opportunities for career development and choice are closely related to level of academic attainment. As several authors have noted, the concept of career choice has the most meaning for individuals with levels of academic attainment that lead to occupations that allow for progressive opportunities over time (Fitzgerald & Betz, 1994; Richardson, 1993). In the current labor market, where most of the fastest growing occupations require high levels of technical skills, jobs that provide opportunities for advancement, professional autonomy, and personal fulfillment require at least a college degree (U.S. Department of Labor, 2002).

Educational attainment is also closely related to the opportunities and rewards people experience in the labor market. For example, in the year 2000, among people 25 years and older, 1.7% of those with a bachelor's degree or higher were unemployed while the same was true for 3.5% of high school graduates and 6.4% of high school dropouts. Similarly, those with higher levels of education garner better incomes. In 1999, the median annual income (in 2001 dollars) for year-round full-time male workers was about $25,000 for high school dropouts, $33,000 for high school graduates, and $53,000 for college graduates (the median incomes for women were, $17,000, $23,000, and $38,000, respectively). Overall, a college graduate is estimated to earn $1 million more in income and benefits over a lifetime than a high school graduate (National Center for Educational Statistics, 2001).

In his theory of career development, Super conceptualized occupational aspirations and choice primarily as a stage-wise process in which individuals seek careers that are congruent with their self-concepts (Super, Savickas, & Super, 1996). Traditional developmental theories have been criticized for neglecting to take into account the environments in which children, adolescents, and young adults make the myriad choices that result in specific career trajectories in adulthood (Arbona,

1996; Gottfredson, 1981; Vondracek, Lerner, & Schulenberg, 1986). In contrast, contextual developmental and social cognitive approaches, which emphasize the reciprocal interaction between individuals and their contexts, propose that occupational aspirations and choices are often facilitated or constrained by adolescents' perceptions of their academic potential, gender role stereotypes, and opportunities in their environment (Gottfredson, 1981; Lent, Brown, & Hackett, 1994; Vondracek et al., 1986). In other words, for many individuals, vocational outcomes are influenced at least as much by opportunities and constraints in the environment as they are by personal, purposive choices. Social class appears to be an important aspect of the opportunity structure. Research conducted during the past 30 years has consistently shown that parental income and education are among the strongest predictors of educational achievement and occupational attainment (Berkner & Chavez, 1997; Choy, 2002; Sewell, Haller, & Ohlendorf, 1970).

Overall, members of ethnic and racial minority groups in the United States, particularly African Americans and Hispanics, have lower educational and income levels than their White counterparts (U.S. Census Bureau, 1998). Not surprisingly, and despite the fact that ethnic minority parents consistently report high academic aspirations for their children (Delgado-Gaitán, 1990; Steinberg, 1996), ethnic minority adolescents and young adults show lower academic achievement and attainment than their White peers. For example, the percentage of 25 to 29 year olds with at least a bachelor's degree in 2000 was higher for Whites (34%) as compared to African Americans (18%) or Hispanics (10%; National Center for Educational Statistics, 2002).

Research findings suggest that the various ecological contexts in which children and adolescents are embedded, including the family and the school, contribute to the lower academic attainment of low-income and minority youth. In contrast to middle-class White parents, low-income minority parents often lack the necessary knowledge and social networks to successfully support their children's academic achievement and attainment (Steinberg, 1996). In addition, the learning environment and resources available in schools that serve primarily White and middle-class students tend to be better than in schools that primarily serve students from low-income and ethnic minority backgrounds. Teachers and principals in low-income schools report more problems with parent involvement and support, teacher morale and absenteeism, students' negative attitude, and gang activity than in schools in more affluent areas, which tend to have stronger teachers and offer more demanding curricula (National Center for Educational Statistics, 2002).

Another important resource, the quality and quantity of school counselors, differs by income level and education of parents. In most inner-city public high schools, large student case loads (ranging from 300 to 700 students per counselor) and substantial administrative responsibilities leave counselors with little time to help students develop career exploration and decision-making skills, plan their academic programs, and take the necessary steps to pursue postsecondary education. These limited counselor resources are often dedicated to students with the highest academic achievement, leaving a large proportion of students with college potential without much guidance (Lee & Ekstrom, 1987; Rosenbaum, Miller, & Krei, 1996). To compensate for the lack of career counseling and guidance offered in schools, middle-class parents have access to private college counselors whose advice on effective college application strategies facilitate the access of high-achieving students to competitive colleges and help even mediocre students find colleges that meet their needs (McDonough, Korn, & Yamasaki, 1997).

Many governmental and private efforts have been directed to help low-income and minority students improve their academic achievement, graduate from high school, and increase their odds of pursuing a college degree (Arbona, 1994; Cunningham, Redmond, & Meritosis, 2003; Gándara, 2001; James, Jurich, & Estes, 2001). The purpose of this chapter is to provide an overview of college access programs and review the program evaluation literature to examine to what extent these programs have been successful in promoting access to a college education for at-risk students. To place the efforts of these programs in context, recent research findings on the predictors of college attendance and completion among at-risk students is presented first, together with a brief overview of how researchers have defined the characteristics of at-risk students.

PREDICTORS OF COLLEGE ATTENDANCE AMONG AT-RISK YOUTH

Researchers in the social sciences and education have extensively examined the predictors of school success and college attendance among socioeconomically advantaged and disadvantaged children and youth (see Arbona, 1994; Baker & Velez, 1996, for reviews of this literature). More recently, researchers have examined the high school and college trajectories of American youth using information gathered as part of the National Education Longitudinal Study started in 1988 (Choy, 2002). Data for this study, known as the NELS: 88, were first collected from a nationally representative sample of eighth graders (26,432 students across the United States) in the spring of 1988, and follow-up surveys were conducted in 1990, 1992, 1994, and 2000. The data gathered included interviews with students, teachers, and parents as well as students' high school and postsecondary school transcripts (Ingels et al., 2002). This section provides an overview of the major findings on the predictors of college attendance and graduation among at-risk students obtained primarily from longitudinal studies conducted with data from the NELS:88.

DEFINITION OF AT-RISK STUDENTS IN THE NELS:88.

The factors most commonly used to identify children at risk academically have been low socioeconomic background and membership in racial or ethnic minority groups. Based on these demographic factors, entire groups of children have been labeled *at risk,* even though many students from low-income households and racial and ethnic minority groups do well academically (Borman & Rachuba, 2001; National Center for Educational Statistics, 2002). Other researchers have, therefore, attempted to refine the at-risk category by examining family and school factors that, independent of family income and racial/ethnic group membership, distinguish students who do and do not achieve well academically.

Using data from the NELS:88, Chen and Kaufman (1997) identified five factors that increased the odds of students dropping out of high school when socioeconomic status and membership in racial or ethnic minority groups were controlled for. These factors included being from a single-parent family, having an older sibling who dropped out of high school, changing schools two or more times from first to eighth grade, low grades (C or lower) from sixth to eighth grade, and repeating a grade between first and eighth grade. Students were considered at low risk academically if they showed only one factor, at moderate risk if they showed two factors, and at high risk if they showed three or more factors. Follow-up studies with the NELS:88 data have shown that students considered at moderate and high risk in eighth grade were less likely to complete high school, attend college, and obtain a college degree as compared to students at low or no risk (Ingels et al., 2002). These risk factors were associated with dropping out of school regardless of the student's family income or racial-ethnic group membership. However, students at moderate- or high-risk status were more likely than students at lower risk to be African American or Hispanic and to have parents with lower levels of education (Chen & Kaufman, 1997; Horn & Chen, 1998). Close to 58% of the 1992 high school graduates in the NELS:88 cohort had at least one risk factor (33% had one factor, 16% had two factors, and 9% had three or more risk factors).

Another group of students considered at risk for educational achievement is first-generation college students, those whose parents did not continue their education past high school. About 27% of the 1992 high school graduates in the NELS:88 cohort were first-generation college students. Similar to at-risk students as defined by Chen and Kaufman (1997), first-generation college students were more likely than students who had at least one parent with a college degree to come from low-income families and to be Hispanic or African American (Horn, Nuñez, & Bobbitt, 2000). Even though first-generation college students are less likely to obtain a college degree than students with college-degreed parents (Choy, 2002; Horn et al., 2000), the occupational outcomes for both groups tend to be similar. A study using data from the 1989/1990 Beginning Postsecondary Longitudinal Study (BPS:90/94) revealed that in 1994, five years after enrolling in college, first-generation students who had attained a bachelor's or an associate's degree were as likely to be employed, earn comparable salaries, and work in similar occupations as their non-first-generation peers with similar degrees (Nuñez & Caroll, 1998). These findings suggest that obtaining a postsecondary degree serves to equalize the playing field for students from different socioeconomic and educational backgrounds.

One of the most often cited explanations for the underrepresentation of minority and low-income students in higher education is the high incidence of school dropouts among this population. For example, in 2000 the school dropout rates among 16- to 24-years-olds was much higher for African Americans (13%) and Hispanics (28%) than for their White (7%) counterparts (National Center for Educational Statistics, 2002). Researchers have identified a long and consistent list of social (e.g., race/ethnicity, family income, parental education, family structure) and academic factors (e.g., test scores, grades, held back in school) associated with dropping out of school (Arbona, 1994; Chen & Kaufman, 1997; Dryfoos, 1990). Studies based on the NELS:88 have confirmed these findings. Compared to their peers who in eighth grade showed none of the risk factors (single-parent household, a high school dropout sibling, frequent school changes, low grades, and repeating a grade) identified by Chen and Kaufman, four years later students at low risk (only one risk factor) were four times more likely to have dropped out of school. Meanwhile, students at moderate (two risk factors) and high risk (three or more factors) were, respectively, 13 and 30 times more likely to have left school without a degree than their no-risk peers.

Nevertheless, some at-risk students beat the odds and succeed academically. Approximately 60% of students in the NELS:88 who showed multiple risk factors as eighth graders graduated from high school in 1992. Chen and Kaufman (1997) found that several family, individual, and peer factors differentiated the resilient high-risk students from their peers who did not obtain a high school diploma. A positive school attitude, a cohesive family, parental support for schooling, and having friends engaged in school played a protective role in reducing the impact of risk on the resilient students. Previous studies also have found that school engagement and parental involvement are associated with academic persistence among at-risk high school students (Dryfoos, 1990; Finn, 1993). Data from the NELS:88 have allowed researchers to examine longitudinally factors that predict college attendance and completion among different types of at-risk students who beat the odds and graduate from high school (e.g., Berkner & Chavez, 1997; Horn, 1997; Horn et al., 2000).

PREDICTORS OF COLLEGE ATTENDANCE AMONG AT-RISK STUDENTS

The pathway to college includes five sequential steps starting with students' aspirations to continue their education beyond high school and culminating with matriculation in a four-year college. Obtaining academic skills, completing college entrance exams, and submitting college applications are the necessary intermediate steps to go from aspirations to college enrollment (Horn, 1997). Results of logistic regression analyses show that when controlling for parental education, family income, and completion of the five steps in the college pipeline, similar proportions of White, Asian, Black, and Hispanic high school graduates in the NELS:88 cohort enrolled in four-year colleges. Small but statistically significant differences in college enrollment related to parental income and education persisted even when controlling for students' academic qualifications and preparation for college (Berkner & Chavez, 1997).

Findings from the NELS:88 cohort indicated that at-risk students face difficulties in completing most of the steps in the college pipeline (Berkner & Chavez, 1997). College aspirations, the first step in the pipeline, were less prevalent among low-income eighth-grade students (58%), compared to their middle income (76%) and high income (92%) peers. A large proportion of at-risk high school graduates also lacked the academic preparation necessary to gain admission to four-year colleges. Berkner and Chavez developed a composite index of academic qualifications for college that considered students' high school GPA, senior class rank, scores in aptitude standardized tests, and rigor of the high school curriculum. According to this index, close to 65% of the 1992 high school graduates from the NELS:88 cohort were at least minimally qualified to attend college. However, most of these academically qualified students came from high-income families (86%) and had college-educated parents (82%). Similarly, among academically qualified students, those whose parents were college graduates were more likely than their peers with nondegreed parents (90% versus 60%) to complete steps two and three in the college pathway: taking entrance exams and submitting college applications (Berkner & Chavez, 1997).

Researchers (Horn, 1997; Horn & Chen, 1998) have identified several parent, peer, and school engagement factors that increased the odds of attending college among academically qualified high school graduates in the NELS:88 cohort who, as eighth graders, had exhibited two or more of the at-risk characteristics identified by Chen and Kaufman (1997). The two factors that most strongly predicted attendance at a four-year college among at-risk students, when controlling for standardized academic achievement in eighth grade and highest level of math taken in high school, were:

1. Having parents who reported speaking frequently with their children (when they were in the tenth grade) about school-related issues.
2. Students' reports that their friends planned to attend college (Horn, 1997).

Friends seemed to have the strongest influence; at-risk students who had reported during their sophomore high school year that most or all of their friends planned to attend college were four times more likely to have enrolled in college two years after high school graduation than their at-risk peers with similar academic qualifications but who had reported that none of their friends planned to attend college (Horn & Chen, 1998). Participating in high school outreach programs, receiving help with college applications from school staff or counselors, and preparing for entrance exams also increased the odds of at-risk high school graduates' attending four-year colleges (Horn, 1997; Horn & Chen, 1998). Similar factors predicted college attendance among first-generation college students (Horn et al., 2000).

The parent, peer, and school factors that had a positive influence on the chances of at-risk students attending a four-year college did not seem to have much effect on increasing the odds of their persisting in college once they enrolled (Horn, 1997). Access to college is important because it is the first step toward obtaining a college degree. However, it is obtaining the degree, and not just college attendance, that may open doors to career choices and opportunities. Adelman (1999) examined variables that predicted college completion among a nationally representative group of high school students (High School and Beyond sophomore cohort of 1,980 tenth graders), who, at some point in the 11 years after high school graduation, had attended a four-year college. He found that the strongest predictors of bachelor's degree attainment were continuous enrollment in college and the academic resources students brought from high school, measured in terms of quality and intensity of high school curriculum, standardized test scores, and class rank. Of these three academic indexes, the intensity and quality of the high school curriculum were the academic factors most strongly related to college completion among ethnic minority students (Adelman, 1999). Unfortunately, not all secondary schools provide students access to a rigorous curriculum that includes advanced mathematics beyond Algebra 2, the three basic laboratory sciences, foreign languages, and advanced placement courses (Spade, Columba, & Vanfossen, 1997). Furthermore, low-income and ethnic minority students generally have less access to advanced curricula, even in schools where such opportunities exist (Monk & Haller, 1993).

Results of longitudinal studies with the NELS:88 data confirm the generalized perception that a large proportion of high school graduates from low-income backgrounds lack the academic skills necessary to gain admissions to four-year colleges. Furthermore, many at-risk students with adequate academic credentials fail to complete two important steps for college admissions: taking college entrance exams and submitting college applications. In sum, research findings consistently point to several barriers or impediments to college access faced by at-risk students, including lack of aspirations, inadequate academic preparation, peers who are not engaged in school, parents who are not involved in students' schooling or knowledgeable about college planning, and lack of financial resources. Fortunately, interventions provided by school counselors and outreach programs seem to increase the chances of at-risk students attending a four-year college. Only a small proportion of at-risk high school graduates (5%) in the NELS:88 study survey indicated that they had participated in college outreach programs; however, these students were twice as likely to attend a four-year college than their peers who had not participated in these programs (Horn, 1997). These findings underscore the need for outreach programs to facilitate the academic development and college access of low-income and at-risk children and youth.

TYPICAL FEATURES OF COLLEGE ACCESS PROGRAMS

Since the 1980s, a large number of programs have been implemented to help low-income and ethnic minority students achieve academically, graduate from high school, and attend college. College access programs vary along several dimensions, including sources of funds, type of agency that implements the program, characteristics of program participants, services offered, and strategies used to evaluate program outcomes. In this section, findings from several reviews that have identified the typical features of these programs are first summarized (Arbona, 1994; Cunningham et al., 2003; Gándara, 2001; Swail, 2000). Then, eight programs that exemplify specific program features are described.

Results of an extensive survey of all types of precollege outreach programs in the United Stares and its territories conducted by the College Board in 1999/2000 (Swail, 2000) indicated that more than half (54%) of the 1,100 programs that responded to the survey were funded by the federal government. Other sources of funds included state governments (15%), universities (9%), and corporations and foundations (20%). These outreach programs were sponsored and implemented by diverse institutions including colleges and universities (57%), schools (16%), community-based organizations (13%), and other private nonprofit entities such as foundations or corporations (14%).

For the most part, precollege outreach programs recruit low-income, minority, and first-generation students offering services to individual students, entire classrooms, or whole schools (Arbona, 1994; Gándara, 2001; Swail, 2000). About 10% of the programs in the College Board's national survey (Swail, 2000) served students younger than middle school, and about half of the programs targeted only high school students. Interventions provided by college outreach programs primarily focus on college and career awareness, social support, and academic enrichment. The most common components included in these programs are counseling, academic enrichment, parental interventions, social and cultural enrichment, mentoring, college scholarships, and evaluation of program's activities (Arbona, 1994; Cunningham et al., 2003; Gándara, 2001; Swail, 2000).

Counseling In most outreach programs, counseling services, offered individually and in small groups, emphasize the dissemination of college information and advising. Specific services include career planning and decision making, academic advising, social skills development, study skills training, college fairs and career days, and assistance with the completion of college and financial aid applications. In some programs, counselors also provide personal emotional counseling.

Academic Enrichment   Academic enrichment activities are provided to increase students' school retention, graduation rates, and preparedness for college. Academic interventions include tutoring, SAT test preparation workshops, and the opportunity to take college-level courses while in high school. Some programs offer extensive courses to complement the school's curriculum in areas such as reading, writing, and analytical skills, whereas other programs attempt comprehensive changes in the content and delivery of the school curriculum, with the intent of offering most students access to rigorous college preparatory coursework. Academic enrichment activities are offered during regular school hours, after school, and during the summer.

Parental Intervention   Research findings as well as field experiences indicate that parental involvement is a critical factor in students' academic achievement. Swail (2000) reported that about two-thirds of college access programs offered a parental component and, in about one-fifth of the programs, parents were required to actively participate in program activities. Services specifically provided for parents include orientation sessions about the program, information sessions on college requirements, college and financial aid applications workshops, and psychoeducational interventions. These interventions emphasize adolescent development and how to help students succeed in school, including communication, discipline, and monitoring homework. Some programs also recruit parents as volunteers and members of school teams and advisory committees.

Social and Cultural Enrichment   Social and cultural enrichment activities are designed to help students become more knowledgeable of the world around them and to develop a network of peers that promotes and supports a culture of "college-going." In some cases, graduates of the programs are recruited to serve as tutors and counselors for the younger cohorts. Social and cultural enrichment activities organized by programs include leadership development, goal-setting, and confidence-building workshops, community service activities, cultural activities connected to the arts, visits to college campuses, and field trips to recreational and cultural sites. It is expected that these experiences will help students to develop a positive sense of self and motivate them to pursue their academic and career goals.

Mentoring   Formal mentoring programs pair participants with volunteers who provide one-to-one friendship, guidance, and support to students. Mentors usually are older peers, university or school staff and faculty, volunteers from the community, corporate personnel, and professionals. It is expected that the mentoring relationship will improve students' academic performance indirectly by improving their attitudes about school and raising their personal goals and motivation. Mentors also support youth during times of personal or social stress and help in decision making. In career mentoring programs, students are paired with adults employed in the student's field of interest who are willing to help students become familiar with the world of work in general along with the requirements of their specific occupational field.

College Scholarships   Scholarship programs usually promise middle and high school students money to cover college tuition costs as a way to motivate them to pursue the necessary steps to attend college. *Last-dollar scholarships* provide funds to cover the difference between all other scholarships and aid a student receives and the actual college costs. Statewide scholarship programs generally provide full tuition waivers for public institutions to students who meet academic performance eligibility requirements (Southern Regional Education Board, 2000). Other programs offer college money only for students pursuing specific fields or careers.

Program Evaluation   Descriptions of educational programs for at-risk youth abound in the literature; however, rigorous evaluations of such programs are scarce. Most rigorous evaluations use an experimental design where applicants who meet eligibility criteria for the program are randomly assigned to either an experimental group, who is given the opportunity to participate in the program, or to a control group of nonparticipants. Because it is expected that randomization distributes unmeasured characteristics of students equally between the two groups, outcomes observed in the control group are a good estimate of what would have happened without the program's intervention. Less rigorous empirical program evaluation designs use for comparison purposes information obtained from national and local data or from groups of students in the same or other schools who share participants' sociodemographic characteristics.

As part of their evaluation efforts, most programs keep track of the percentage of participants who complete the program, graduate from high school, and enroll in college (Swail, 2000). Few programs use pre-post designs to compare students' behaviors before and after receiving the program's intervention or compare outcomes observed in participants to a control group of similar students not exposed to the program (Arbona, 1994; Cunningham et al., 2003; Gándara, 2001). Nevertheless, studies that carefully examine programs' outcomes, even if they do not rigorously assess programs' impacts, provide valuable information to policymakers and program managers.

DESCRIPTION OF COLLEGE ACCESS PROGRAMS FOR AT-RISK STUDENTS

In this section, eight college access programs that exemplify different approaches to service delivery, selection of participants, and evaluation of program outcomes are briefly described. These eight programs are meant to serve as examples of types of programs and not as a representative sample of all the types of programs that have been documented in the literature. In recent years, the American Youth Policy Forum has published several comprehensive compendiums of school and youth programs that have documented outcomes across a wide range of academic achievement indicators (James, 1997, 1999; James et al., 2001; Jurich & Estes, 2000). Other publications have provided detailed descriptions of a wide variety of college access programs (e.g., Cunningham et al., 2003; Gándara, 2001; Southern Regional Education Board, 2000). Interested readers may consult these resources.

The eight programs described here have been implemented in more than one site and have reported a behavioral outcome evaluation by either comparing students' behaviors before and after the program's intervention or by comparing program participants to a similar group of nonparticipants. Programs differed in the population of students they served. Most programs work with high school students by offering services to individual students or to specific cohorts of students within a high school. Other programs target students before they reach high school. In some cases, programs have attempted to institute school-wide changes at the middle school level. College sponsorship programs have attempted to motivate entire classrooms of middle school students by guaranteeing college scholarships to students who persevere and graduate from high school.

HIGH SCHOOL PROGRAMS THAT SERVE INDIVIDUAL STUDENTS

Two programs, Upward Bound and Career Beginnings, served high school students individually and reported the most rigorous outcome evaluations.

Upward Bound   Upward Bound is a federally funded program established in 1965 to help low-income, first-generation college students enroll and succeed in college. Currently, there are 563 regular Upward Bound projects across the country serving approximately 44,000 students. Most of these projects are sponsored by two- and four-year colleges, although some projects are hosted by high schools and community-based organizations. Projects provide a wide variety of services to high school students (freshmen to seniors) during the school year and the summer, including formal instruction in high school subjects (e.g., English, math, science), tutoring, mentoring, counseling, career planning, cultural and recreational field trips, visits to college campuses, and college planning activities (e.g., workshops on completing financial aid and college applications). In most programs, the summer session includes an intensive instructional program and a residential component on a college campus. Services in Upward Bound are primarily directed at individual students who tend to be educationally motivated, have few behavioral or disciplinary problems, and earn mostly Bs or Cs in school (Moore, 1997; Upward Bound Program, n.d.).

Upward Bound is undergoing a six-year longitudinal evaluation commissioned by the Planning and Evaluation Service of the U.S. Department of Education (Myers & Schirm, 1999). Of students who were eligible applicants to a nationally representative sample of 67 Upward Bound programs from 1992 to 1994, the evaluators randomly assigned 1,524 to Upward Bound and 1,320 to a control group of nonparticipants. Myers and Schirm (1999) reported that retention in Upward Bound tends to be low; typically, participants remained in the program for about 19 months. Upward Bound students had slightly higher educational expectations and had earned a few more high school credits in math and social studies than did students in the control group. The two groups did not differ in other high school outcomes associated with college-going, including participation in school activities, talking with parents about school, or parental involvement at school. Furthermore, a similar number of students in the treatment and control groups attended two- and four-year colleges. However, students who entered Upward Bound as 10th graders and remained in the program for 13 to 24 months were more likely than their counterparts in the control group to attend a four-year college, indicating that longer exposure to the program led to stronger effects. Once in college, Upward Bound students earned more nonremedial credits from four-year colleges, were more likely to receive financial aid (loans, grants, and work study appointments), and reported more informal contacts with advisors and faculty and greater participation with peers in study groups and school clubs. The outcomes related to postsecondary education must be interpreted with caution because the last published report of the evaluation included data gathered when most students were in their last years of high school, and only about one-fourth of them had entered college (Myers & Schirm, 1999).

Even though Upward Bound seems to have limited impact on students' academic behaviors during high school, it shows stronger effects once students enroll in college. Upward Bound also seemed to have a larger impact on more disadvantaged students. Among students with lower educational expectations (less than a college degree) and lower academic performance, students who participated in Upper Bound completed more high school credits, were less likely to drop out of school, and were more likely to attend college than their counterparts in the control group. Similarly, Upward Bound had stronger impact on high school retention and course taking among low-income students.

Career Beginnings Career Beginnings brings together high schools, colleges, and businesses in working partnerships to facilitate college attendance among low-income high school juniors and seniors of average academic achievement. Students participate in structured workshops on career awareness and college readiness topics, remedial classes in basic academic skills, entry-level summer jobs, and mentoring relationships with adults from the business or professional community. A rigorous evaluation of the program implemented in seven sites (of 24) across the country was conducted by the Manpower Demonstration Research Corporation (MDRC; Cave & Quint, 1990). Eligible applicants to the program in each of the seven sites were randomly assigned in equal numbers either to the program or to a nonparticipant control group. The evaluation of the program's impact is based on the experiences of 1,233 youth who responded to two follow-up interviews (78% response rate) conducted one and two years after random assignment.

In terms of college attendance, Career Beginnings did not lead to an overall increase in access to postsecondary education. However, a larger proportion of students who had participated in the program (53%) attended a four-year college as compared to students in the control group (48%). In contrast to the results reported for Upward Bound, students with greater academic or economic barriers to college attendance were not helped more by Career Beginnings. Cave and Quint (1990) concluded that receiving more services was, however, associated with college-going and that mentoring seemed to serve as a catalyst that increased the effectiveness of other services. Attending three types of services— college entrance exam preparation classes, college fairs and college information sessions, and job-readiness workshops—was related to college enrollment, though participating in tutoring, remedial courses, and workshops in study-skill and test-taking strategies were not. Because the characteristics of students who participated in the different types of activities were not controlled for, these findings must be interpreted with caution. It is possible that students with better academic skills were more likely to attend college and that, because they did not need academic remediation, they chose to attend more college preparatory activities than their peers.

HIGH SCHOOL PROGRAMS THAT SERVE COHORTS OF STUDENTS

Three programs, AVID, Puente Project, and Gateway to Higher Education, offered college preparatory classes during the school year to cohorts of high school students.

Advancement via Individual Determination (AVID)   The AVID program was created in 1980 by a high school English teacher in San Diego, California, to counteract the common school practice of tracking low-income and ethnic minority students into general and vocational education classes. The program has been implemented by more than 1,500 schools in 21 states (AVID, n.d.). Eligibility criteria for participation in AVID include average to high scores in standardized achievement tests of basic skills, C-level grades, regular school attendance, good self-discipline, and parental support for program participation. The AVID program places underachieving, academically capable low-income and ethnic minority middle school and high school students (seventh through twelfth grade) with their high-achieving peers in college preparatory classes and provides them with social and academic support services. The cornerstone of these support services is an AVID elective class that students take every day from seventh to twelfth grade that focuses on reading comprehension and abstract thinking, test-taking skills, and essay writing. The program also offers tutorial assistance, committed teachers who meet with parents and students before and after school hours, field trips, college visits, and guest speakers.

In the earliest published evaluation of AVID (Mehan, Villanueva, Hubbard, & Lintz, 1996), researchers located 248 of 1,053 students who had participated in AVID for three years in eight San Diego schools. Forty-eight percent of these students reported enrolling in a four-year college right after high school graduation whereas 37% of students in the local school system had enrolled in four-year colleges. The program seemed to have its greatest effects among ethnic minority students. Forty-three percent of Hispanic and 55% of African American AVID graduates enrolled in four-year colleges compared to 25% and 38% general enrollment rates, respectively, for Hispanic and African American students in the San Diego schools. A more recent survey of 100 AVID participants from California high schools indicated that one and two years after finishing high school, 95% of survey respondents were enrolled in a postsecondary institution, 77% were attending four-year colleges, and almost 80% had been enrolled in college continuously since leaving high school (Guthrie & Guthrie, 2000). These impressive results must be interpreted cautiously because it is not known to what extent AVID students attending college were overrepresented among respondents to the surveys.

Watt, Yanez, and Cossio (2002–2003) examined the implementation of AVID in 26 Texas junior high and high schools during two academic years (1999 to 2001). Findings showed that during this time, AVID students increased their participation in rigorous coursework (92% were placed in the school's college preparatory track), outperformed the general school population on state-mandated standardized achievement tests (e.g., algebra and biology), and earned high grade-point averages (above the 80th percentile) in rigorous coursework. Because AVID students were compared to the general school population, it is not possible to determine to what extent the program interventions or the characteristics of students selected for the program were most responsible for students' outcomes.

Puente Project The Puente Project (from the word *bridge* in Spanish) started in San Diego in 1993 to help Hispanic students navigate the transition from high school to college. Puente currently operates in 36 schools in California where it recruits motivated ninth-grade students of different academic achievement levels (GPAs ranging from 1.4 to 3.5) whose parents agree to participate in the program's activities (Puente Project, n.d.). Each Puente class has about 25 to 30 students. The program emphasizes three major components: a two-year English college preparatory class that substitutes for students' English requirements in ninth and tenth grades, intensive college preparatory counseling, and assignment to a mentor. Students also participate in college visits, field trips, and other social activities. To help infuse the program with cultural sensitivity, the two-year English class incorporates community-based writing and Hispanic-authored literature into the college preparatory curriculum. In addition, the program's staff (English teacher, counselor, and community liaison) and mentors are recruited from the Hispanic community.

A four-year longitudinal evaluation compared 75 Puente students from three schools with a control group of 75 non-Puente students from the same schools matched on age, ethnicity, sex, eighth-grade GPA, and reading scores (Gándara, Mejorado, Gutiérrez, & Molina, 1998). Students were followed up from the beginning of high school to the end of their senior year. Findings revealed that even though by the end of the twelfth grade the two groups did not differ in high school retention, school grades, or enrollment in college preparatory courses, a larger proportion of Puente (84%) than control students (75%) attended a postsecondary institution right after high school. Puente students were also more likely to enroll in a four-year college than their peers in the control group (43% versus 24%). Consistent with their higher college enrollment rates, while in high school Puente students reported more knowledge about and active involvement in the college preparation process than students in the control group; twice as many Puente students reported being knowledgeable about the college application process in the eleventh grade (75% versus 36%) and had taken the SAT exam by the twelfth grade (72% versus 34%). Gándara et al. (1998) concluded that Puente students were able to exploit their academic potential better than students with similar academic profiles who did not benefit from the network of supportive adults and peers and other services offered by the program.

Gateway to Higher Education Started in 1986 and administered by the City University of New York, Gateway operates in 11 schools in New York City with the purpose of preparing primarily African American and Latino high school students for careers in science, medicine, and technology. From 1986 to 2000, Gateway served 3,500 students (Slater & Iler, 2000). To be eligible for the program, students must have scored at least in the 50th percentile in the seventh-grade standardized math and reading achievement tests given in New York, have regular school attendance, and a grade-point average of at least 80/100. Gateway provides cohorts of students with four years of intensive instruction in math and science, after-school tutoring, and summer academic enrichment programs.

Other Gateway services include counseling, internships, college visits, cultural activities, SAT preparation workshops, and participation in advanced placement courses.

To assess the impact of Gateway, evaluators compared outcomes for 136 Gateway students who expected to graduate from high school in 1993/1994 to a control group of 136 nonparticipant students matched according to gender, race/ethnicity, math and reading scores, and family income (Campbell et al., 1997). Compared to the control group, Gateway students were more likely to graduate from high school (93% versus 73%) and to take the SAT test (93% versus 15%). In 1992, Gateway students were much more likely than high school graduates in general to have taken advanced courses in math (98% versus 52%), chemistry (97% versus 56%), and physics (83% versus 25%). In 1993, 92% of Gateway graduates went to college, with 51% of them attending competitive four-year institutions (Campbell et al., 1997). Findings from an internal report of the program (Slater & Iler, 2000) revealed that in the academic year 1999/2000, the average math SAT score of Gateway students was higher than the national SAT means for African American (520 versus 426) and Latino (530 versus 460) students and similar to the mean for White students (530). By the spring of 2000, 97% of Gateway graduates had been accepted to four-year colleges (25% of them into highly selective schools). These findings indicate that most Gateway participants complete the steps in the college pathway and enroll in college.

PROGRAMS THAT INSTITUTE SCHOOLWIDE CHANGES

Two programs, Dare to Dream and Project GRAD, instituted school wide changes to increase college access among all students.

Dare to Dream: Educational Guidance for Excellence   The Dare to Dream program uses educational counseling as the lever for school change. It brings together administrators, teachers, counselors, students, parents, and local college and community representatives to develop school-specific strategic plans to strengthen counseling services with the goal of increasing academic success and college access among low-income and at-risk students. Funded by the Lilly Endowment and the Jesse Ball DuPont Foundations, Dare to Dream programs have been implemented in more than 50 schools across the United States.

The evaluation of Dare to Dream consisted of intensive case studies of seven sites (six high schools and one middle school) that had implemented the program successfully. In these schools, educational guidance services were taken out of the counselor's offices and incorporated into all school activities. In addition, centers with information about higher education were installed in different school locations, and academic tracks were made less rigid so that at-risk students were mixed in classrooms with their higher achieving peers (Snyder, Morrison, & Smith, 1996). Results indicated that within two years of program implementation, African American high school students substantially increased their participation in advanced placement courses and in freshman and senior college preparatory English classes, and Hispanic students almost doubled their enrollment in precalculus and calculus classes. Two schools experienced an increase in college-going rates. In one school, the rates increased from 50% in 1986 to 72% in 1994. In a high school located in an Appalachian community, the percentage of students attending a four-year college increased from 31% in 1989 to 53% in 1996. Finally, from 1990 to 1992, students from the only middle school included in the evaluation nearly doubled their enrollment in freshman algebra. In sum, in implementing the Dare to Dream program, counselors used educational and college counseling as the lever for school change to provide greater postsecondary options to at-risk students.

Project GRAD   The purpose of Project GRAD is to change the school climate and academic achievement patterns of school systems that serve low-achieving inner-city children, with the ultimate goal of increasing high school graduation and college enrollment rates for all students. The program is implemented across a feeder pattern of schools, that is, a high school and the middle and elementary schools that feed into it. Project GRAD started in Houston schools in 1993 and by the close of the 2001/2002 school year, it was serving more than 130,000 students in 10 urban school districts in seven states (Project GRAD USA, n.d.). At the elementary and middle school level, Project GRAD implements several research-based educational reform initiatives designed to improve reading and math achievement, classroom management and discipline, and parent and community involvement. To facilitate college access among high school students, Project GRAD works with schools in enriching the academic curriculum and provides students tutoring services and preparation classes for college entrance examinations. In addition, the program guarantees college scholarships ranging from $4,000 to $6,000 to all high school graduates who have completed three years of math coursework (beginning with Algebra I), have at least a 2.5 grade-point average, have completed two university-based summer academic institutes offered by the program, and have graduated from high school within four years of freshman enrollment.

An evaluation of Project GRAD in the two school systems where the program was first implemented in 1994 and 1996 revealed that by 1999 students in both feeder systems had increased their passing rate on the Texas Assessment of Academic Skills (TAAS; Opuni, 1999). Students who had started kindergarten in one of the systems in 1994 outperformed their peers from other Houston schools with similar demographics in math and reading standardized achievement scores. By 1999, disciplinary referrals were reduced by 74% and by 22% in the two systems, respectively. From 1989 (when Project GRAD scholarships were first offered) to 1999, college enrollment among graduates from one of the high schools increased from 12% to 50%. The Manpower Demonstration Research Corporation is currently undertaking a five-year evaluation of Project GRAD in Newark, New Jersey, examining the program's impact on school functioning and student achievement (Ham, Doolittle, Holton, Ventura, & Jackson, 2000).

COLLEGE SPONSORSHIP PROGRAMS

The I Have a Dream program is built around guaranteed college scholarships offered to an entire class of middle school students to motivate them to stay in school and to complete the steps in the college pipeline.

I Have a Dream (IHAD)   One of the trends in preventing school failure and dropout rates among younger adolescents is privately funded programs that combine a financial aid guarantee for postsecondary education, one-on-one mentoring, and intensive academic enrichment activities. The best known of these initiatives is Eugene Lang's I Have a Dream program started in New York City in 1981 and now replicated nationally. There are more than 180 I Have a Dream Projects in 27 states and 64 cities, serving more than 13,000 students (I Have a Dream Foundation, n.d.). In the IHAD model, an individual or group sponsor guarantees college tuition funding (usually last-dollar scholarships) for an entire class of randomly selected at-risk sixth or seventh graders. Funds are also provided for support services including tutoring, counseling, summer programs, field trips, and hiring a project coordinator, who takes on a mentoring and case management role with the students from their initial participation in the program until they graduate from high school (Higgins, Furano, Toso, & Branch, 1991).

Kahne and Bailey (1999) conducted a two-and-a-half-year study of two IHAD programs in Chicago that served primarily low-income Hispanic and African American students who had started the program in sixth grade. Researchers followed the students from the eleventh grade until their high school graduation and initial college enrollment. Results revealed impressive outcomes. IHAD participants showed twice the graduation rate of students from previous sixth-grade classes at the same school (approximately 70% versus 35%). About 65% of the IHAD students attended a postsecondary institution (approximately 78% of them enrolled in four-year colleges), three times the average enrollment for African American and Hispanic students in the Chicago public schools (about 19%).

Kahne and Bailey (1999) noted unique features of the implementation of the IHAD program in these two Chicago sites that may have contributed to their success. In both sites, the project coordinators had remained in the program for its entire duration, whereas in other IHAD programs in the Chicago area, the average duration of the program coordinator was about two years. In addition, about half of the IHAD students in the two sites had been placed by the program's staff in parochial schools. This practice, which was not as common in other IHAD programs, makes it difficult to disentangle the effects of the other program's activities from those of the parochial schools that students attended. For example, enrollment in four-year colleges versus two-year colleges was more than four times higher among the IHAD graduates who attended private schools than among their peers who remained in the public schools.

LESSONS LEARNED FROM PROGRAM EVALUATION EFFORTS

For the most part, evaluations of college access programs have examined the impact of program participation versus nonparticipation on the following outcomes: academic achievement in reading and math, school retention and high school graduation, enrollment in college preparatory high school courses, changes in career and educational goals, rates of college admissions and enrollment, and receipt of financial aid. In most cases, evaluators have not followed students long enough to determine the program's impact on college persistence and graduation. Because most college access programs provide a combination of interventions and do not carefully track each student's level of participation in each intervention, the relation of specific program components to students' outcomes is not known. Nevertheless, reviewers of evaluations of college access programs have drawn conclusions about effective practices and challenges faced by these programs (Arbona, 1994; Cunningham et al., 2003; Dryfoos, 1990; Gándara, 2001; James, 1997, 1999; James et al., 2001; Swail, 2000). Results of these reviews, summarized next, are organized in four areas: (1) program structure and services, (2) intensity and length of interventions, (3) eligibility criteria for participants, and (4) program evaluation strategies.

PROGRAM STRUCTURE AND SERVICES

Research findings and field experiences suggest that comprehensive services are needed to increase college attendance and persistence among low-income and at-risk students. Even though lack of information and college costs represent two significant barriers to attending four-year colleges for these students, just providing college-related information or offering college scholarships does not seem to be enough to increase at-risk students' attendance and persistence in four-year colleges. Three types of services have emerged as crucial in helping at-risk students pursue postsecondary education: (1) adult support and mentorship, (2) academic enrichment, and (3) career counseling and college advising.

Adult Support   Effective youth programs connect students with knowledgeable and caring adults who serve as role models and provide advisement, mentorship, and encouragement. The experience of many programs with middle school and high school students suggests that the effectiveness of other services is enhanced by a one-on-one mentoring experience. Even though there is little evidence that mentoring improves academic performance directly, it seems to have beneficial effects on school attendance, educational aspirations, and college attendance (Flaxman, 1992). Several reviewers of intervention programs for underrepresented youth have concluded that an important feature of effective programs is a close, caring relationship with an adult (program director, teacher, counselor, or mentor) who monitors the student's progress over time (Dryfoos, 1990; Gándara, 2001; Kahne & Bailey, 1999). However, it is not clear who is better able to provide this kind of long-term relationship, paid program staff or volunteer mentors. In any case, for a mentorship program to be successful, carefully selected and properly trained mentors need to be consistently available to students for an extended time period.

Parents are also important adults in students' lives. As described earlier, at-risk high school graduates in the NELS:88 study whose parents reported speaking frequently with them about school issues were more likely than their peers with less involved parents to attend a four-year college (Horn, 1997). Therefore, it is crucial to help parents understand early on the steps their children need to complete to attend college. However, many programs report that involving parents of low-income, at-risk adolescents in activities and workshops related to their children's career development is very difficult. Two approaches that have shown success with low-income parents are home visits and recruiting them for meaningful roles within the program. Project GRAD, for example, implements a community outreach program called Walk for Success where program's staff and volunteers visit families in their homes to raise awareness of the program. Parents are also recruited to participate in Project GRAD's decision-making committees that manage the project in the feeder schools.

Academic Enrichment   Completing a challenging high school college preparatory curriculum that includes high-level math courses is among the strongest predictors of college access and attainment among at-risk and first-generation students (Adelman, 1999; Warburton, Bugarin, & Nuñez, 2001); therefore, a strong academic component is an essential feature of effective college access programs. Evaluation efforts show that successful programs, rather than watering down standards to accommodate at-risk students, maintain high expectations for academic achievement and behavior at the same time that they provide a strong support system to facilitate students' success. Strategies to provide academic support for students include smaller classes, creating small learning communities of program participants, one-on-one tutoring, and extended learning time during longer school hours and Saturday and summer courses. Programs such as Upward Bound and AVID have shown more significant academic improvements among high school students with lower academic achievement and educational expectations, whereas results of more selective programs, such as Gateway to Higher Education and Puente Project, indicate that academically capable students with average achievement can be challenged to perform at still higher levels.

Career Counseling and College Advising   Researchers have concluded that low-income and at-risk students need help in dealing with the career development tasks appropriate for their age. Even though most students express high academic and occupational aspirations, often they are not aware of the training requirements for their preferred occupations or of the importance of high school grades and curriculum choices to their probabilities of attending college and attaining their occupational aspirations in the future (Arbona, 1994; Ingels et al., 2002). High school students whose parents have not attended college also need guidance in completing the necessary steps in the college pipeline (Berkner & Chavez, 1997; Horn et al., 2000).

Practically all the high school college access programs that have been evaluated implement activities to disseminate information and provide advising concerning the college-going process. In some cases, such as Gateway to Higher Education, activities focus on careers in specific fields such as science and engineering whereas most programs provide a broader focus. College advising activities engaged in by most programs include individual consultations with students to help them plan their high school curriculum, speaker events where college representatives and students talk about college opportunities and campus life, and assistance with college and financial aid applications. Some programs also offer career counseling to help students acquire occupational information and identify careers of interest. As part of the career counseling process, students complete interest inventories, participate in career fairs, attend speaker events with representatives from various occupational fields, and participate in internship programs with corporate sponsors. (See Turner & Lapan, Chapter 17, this volume, for information on interventions designed to promote the career development and aspirations of school-age youth.)

To help students deal with life stressors that may interfere with their academic achievement, some programs offer personal counseling as well as referrals to social service agencies in the community. Programs that work with middle school students provide extensive personal and social counseling to facilitate students' retention. For example, in the I Have a Dream program, the project's director and the program's paid mentor assigned to each participant closely coordinate students' access to personal counseling and social services. Project GRAD brings to the schools the extensive counseling, community outreach, and family case management services provided by Communities in Schools (CIS), a social services agency that places full-time social workers in schools.

INTENSITY AND LENGTH OF INTERVENTIONS

To be most effective, college access programs need to carefully select the types of needs they will address and plan the intensity of services accordingly. Because programs have limited resources to serve a population with great needs, providers face a dilemma about the range and intensity of services offered. Practitioners must choose between offering less extensive services to more students versus providing more intensive, long-term services to fewer students. Program evaluation efforts have consistently shown that participants who receive more services for longer time periods tend to show better outcomes than their less active peers (e.g., Upward Bound, Career Beginnings). Therefore, it is very likely that short interventions will not be very effective even if they reach large numbers of students.

Research findings have indicated that by the sixth grade most disadvantaged students require individualized attention and intensive instruction to improve their academic performance (Levin, 1986). The literature on prevention efforts also suggests that early interventions without follow-up are not very effective in helping high-risk children succeed as adolescents and young adults (Dryfoos, 1990). Therefore, to enhance the academic achievement and school persistence of younger adolescents, comprehensive and long-term academic and personal support services, such as those provided by Project GRAD and I Have a Dream, are needed. Relatively intensive services and continuity of support, as offered by Upward Bound and the Puente Project, are also necessary to significantly increase college attendance among low-income high school students who show satisfactory school adjustment.

ELIGIBILITY CRITERIA FOR PARTICIPANTS

Practitioners must identify eligibility criteria for program participation such as students' age and level of academic achievement. Programs that work with at-risk students in middle schools, such as Project GRAD and I Have a Dream, tend not to be selective, offering their services to entire classrooms. On the other hand, most college-access high school programs primarily recruit students with either average (e.g., Career Beginnings, AVID) or above-average academic achievement levels (e.g., Puente Project, Gateway to Higher Education). None of the college-oriented high school programs found in the evaluation literature targeted the most educationally disadvantaged at-risk students; therefore, no conclusions may be reached about the effectiveness of these programs in increasing college attendance among students showing very low academic achievement or high rates of school absenteeism.

The research literature suggests that attempts to remediate low academic achievement in the high school years are for the most part unsuccessful (Dryfoos, 1990; Levin, 1986). At the same time, the greater the needs of participants, the more difficult it is to demonstrate significant program effects. It seems that to show better outcomes, high school college access programs tend to recruit at-risk students whose academic records and motivational dispositions suggest a stronger college potential versus casting a broader net to capture students whose potential may be less certain. While such practices increase the programs' chances of success, they probably do not substantially increase the pool of potential college students among the most disadvantaged low-income and at-risk youth. Prevention efforts in the preschool and early school years may be needed before it is too late to reach the most at-risk children. Evaluations of early developmental programs such as Head Start and Child Parent Centers in Chicago have yielded encouraging results. Compared to control groups, low-income children who attend early childhood enrichment programs are more likely to remain in school, complete more years of education, and are less likely to attend special education (James et al., 2001).

PROGRAM EVALUATION STRATEGIES

The literature on program evaluation suggests that even though many college access programs are able to demonstrate positive outcomes, documenting the net impact of these outcomes is difficult (Gándara, 2001; Swail, 2000). Most rigorous evaluations employ an experimental random-group design like the one exemplified by Upward Bound and Career Beginnings. However, evaluation efforts that include random assignment of eligible applicants to the program and to a nonparticipant control group are complex and difficult to conduct. The idea of denying services to a group of eligible applicants, which is required in true randomization, is distasteful to many practitioners. Another problem with experimental designs is that eligible applicants denied participation in the program often seek similar services elsewhere. In the evaluation of both Upward Bound and Career Beginnings, a large number of students in the control group reported receiving services such as counseling, college advising, tutoring, and help with college admissions and financial aid applications from other sources. Therefore, results of these rigorous evaluations indicate the incremental effect of the program over and above other available services in the community and not the impact of the intervention versus no treatment at all.

Many program evaluations used for comparison purposes an existing group of students considered similar to the treatment group but who did not attend the program. To ensure the comparability of the groups, it is necessary to carefully match students in the treatment and control group on demographics, socioeconomic status, and prior academic performance. This strategy was used by the evaluators for Puente Project and Gateway to Higher Education. Another common strategy is to compare program outcomes with normative student information obtained from national, state, or local databases as was done in the evaluations of AVID, Project GRAD, and I Have a Dream.

IMPLICATIONS FOR COUNSELORS

Promoting the career development of at-risk youth and facilitating their access to a college education is a complex task that requires comprehensive and extensive services. Even though career counselors are key players in this endeavor, they cannot do it alone. Practically all college access programs provide the typical career counseling and advising interventions (e.g., career interest assessment, academic planning counseling) offered to students in American high schools as described in the taxonomy of career development interventions developed by Dykeman et al. (2001). (See Juntunen & Wettersten, Chapter 24, this volume, for a detailed description of this taxonomy.) However, reaching at-risk students and engaging them in college advising and career development activities presents several challenges.

Because at-risk youth often lack adult role models who provide them guidance and encouragement concerning higher education, many of them may not aspire to college or be aware of the necessary steps in preparing themselves to succeed in four-year institutions. Rather than waiting for students to come to their office, career counselors need to reach out to youth in school or community settings to encourage and facilitate their development of college aspirations, the first step in the college pipeline. Turner and Lapan (Chapter 17, this volume) provide examples of interventions designed to help school-age youth develop positive career-related self-efficacy expectations and attribution styles that may be useful with at-risk students. Early on in the career counseling process, it will be important to provide low-income students and their parents with information about financial aid opportunities for college to help them start visualizing college as a real possibility. To reach out to parents of at-risk students, counselors need to take a proactive stance. The experience of several college access programs indicates that calling parents at home and involving them in meaningful activities, such as volunteer work in the counselor's office and as members of school teams and advising committees, are useful in increasing the participation of parents of at-risk children in school activities.

Networking and coordinating services with other resources in the school and community will increase the effectiveness of career counselors in reaching at-risk youth. For example, counselors may collaborate with teachers in offering classroom-based introductory career interventions, such as guidance lessons on academic planning, exploration of the world of work, and identification of career interests (Dykeman et al., 2001). Some of these introductory career interventions can be integrated with academic subjects such as language arts or social studies. Reaching out to the local business community will allow counselors to develop internship programs and partnerships with corporate sponsors who can provide volunteers to mentor students.

Access to a challenging curriculum in high school has emerged as one of the strongest predictors of college attendance and graduation. Counselors, who in many schools are the gatekeepers of students' academic schedules, can play a very important role in encouraging and placing at-risk students in college preparatory and advanced placement classes. However, to achieve this goal, counselors may need to enlist the collaboration of other professionals in the school. Results obtained by the Dare to Dream program, described earlier, show the pivotal role that professional counselors can play in fostering schoolwide changes to provide greater access to a college preparatory curriculum for traditionally underserved students. In the schools where the program was implemented successfully, changes were made in the curriculum so that students considered at risk, and those who were not, participated in the same rigorous academic courses. Counselors can also promote the academic achievement of students by facilitating their access to services, such as tutoring and college entrance preparation workshops, that may be provided in the school or in other agencies in the community.

Attending to the personal and social well-being of at-risk students is another important aspect of their career development. Facilitating students' access to social and cultural enrichment activities (e.g., workshops in leadership development and confidence building, recreational and cultural field trips, community service) is one way to help them develop a positive sense of self and to motivate them to improve their academic achievement. Student participation in these activities will facilitate the development of peer groups that support academic and career aspirations, another important predictor of college attendance. Career counselors may also need to offer personal emotional counseling to students who experience specific stressors or refer these students to counseling and social services in the community.

In sum, the program evaluation literature indicates that to increase at-risk students' access to college, counselors will need to add to their career counseling efforts the support and collaboration of school administrations, teachers, parents, local businesses, and social service agencies. College-access programs, like the ones described here, exist in many communities. Career counselors working in schools may establish partnerships with community agencies or institutions of higher education to seek funding to implement college access programs on their campuses.

SUMMARY

Research findings consistently show that parental income and education are among the strongest predictors of academic achievement at any point in the child's life and of career attainment in adulthood. At the same time, students who complete an academically rigorous high school curriculum are much more likely than their peers to attend college and obtain a degree. These findings suggest that parents transmit the advantages of higher education and income, at least in part, through the educational decisions they make for their children early on in their school careers. Highly educated parents tend to maximize the opportunities of exposing their children to demanding curricula, which in turn, translate into substantial academic advantages as the children attend higher grades (Schanabel, Alfeld, Eccles, Koller, & Baumert, 2002). While low-income parents may lack the educational resources to effectively monitor their children's academic development and successfully coach them in the process of getting ready for college, schools in low-income areas often lack the resources needed to compensate for the students' lack of individual guidance and coaching at home.

Fortunately, researchers have identified protective factors associated with high school graduation and college enrollment among low-income and at-risk students. Adolescents who have a positive attitude toward school, a cohesive family, and who report parental and peer support for schooling are more likely to graduate from high school than their peers who lack these characteristics. Similarly, friends seem to exert a strong influence on the chances of actual college enrollment among at-risk students who graduate from high school. Academically successful at-risk students who report that most or all of their friends plan to attend college are more likely to enroll in college than their peers whose friends do not have similar plans. Other factors that increase the odds of attending a four-year college among at-risk high school graduates include participating in high school outreach programs, receiving help with college applications from school staff or counselors, and preparing for college entrance exams. Once in college, the factors most strongly related to degree completion include continuous enrollment and the quality and intensity of the student's high school academic curriculum.

Numerous public and private initiatives have been implemented to promote the academic achievement of at-risk and low-income students. College access programs specifically help students acquire occupational information, identify careers of interest, increase their academic skills, enroll in college preparatory high school classes, and complete the steps in the college pipeline. Evaluations of these programs suggest that even though they are not very effective in dramatically increasing students' school grades or scores on standardized achievement tests, college access programs do help students better use the skills that they have and increase their enrollment in college. These efforts are important in reducing the educational and occupational attainment gap experienced by low-income populations because the at-risk youth of today who beat the odds and obtain a college degree will tomorrow be able to offer their children a great advantage: college-educated parents.

REFERENCES

Adelman, C. (1999). *Answers in the toolbox: Academic intensity, attendance patterns, and bachelor's degree attainment.* Washington, DC: U.S. Department of Education, Office of Educational Research and Improvement.

Advancement via Individual Determination. (n.d.). *About us. 2002–2003 AVID Program overview.* Retrieved June 30, 2003, from http://www.avidonline.org/info/?ID=286.

Arbona, C. (1994). *First generation college students: A review of needs and effective interventions.* Washington, DC: U.S. Department of Education, Office of Planning and Evaluation.

Arbona, C. (1996). Career theory and practice in a multicultural context. In M. Savickas & B. Walsh (Eds.), *Integrating career theory and practice* (pp. 45–54). Palo Alto, CA: Davies-Black Publishing Press.

Baker, T., & Velez, W. (1996). Access to and opportunity in postsecondary education in the United States: A review. *Sociology of Education* [extra issue], 82–101.

Berkner, L., & Chavez, L. (1997). *Access to postsecondary education for the 1992 high school graduates* (NCES 98–105). Washington, DC: U.S. Department of Education, National Center for Education Statistics.

Borman, G. D., & Rachuba, L. T. (2001). *Academic success among poor and minority students: An analysis of competing models of school effects* (Report No. 52). Baltimore: Johns Hopkins University Center for Research on the Education of Students Placed At Risk (CRESPAR).

Campbell, P. B., Wahl, E., Slater, M., Iler, E., Moeller, B., Ba, H., et al. (1997). *Make it possible for students to succeed and they will: An evaluation of the Gateway to Higher Education program.* New York: Education Development Center.

Cave, G., & Quit, J. (1990). *Career Beginnings impact evaluation: Findings from a program for disadvantaged high school students.* New York: Manpower Demonstration Research Corporation.

Chen, X., & Kaufman, P. (1997). *Risk and resilience: The effects of dropping out of school.* Paper presented at the American Association of Education Research annual meeting, Chicago.

Choy, S. P. (2002). *Access and persistence: Findings from 10 years of longitudinal research on students.* Washington, DC: American Council on Education.

Cunningham, A., Redmond, C., & Meritosis, J. (2003). *Investing early: Intervention programs in selected U.S. states.* Montreal: Canada Millennium Scholarship Foundation.

Delgado-Gaitán, C. (1990). *Literacy for empowerment: The role of parents in children's education.* London: Falmer Press.

Dryfoos, J. G. (1990). *Adolescents at risk: Prevalence and prevention.* New York: Oxford University Press.

Dykeman, C., Herr, E. L., Ingram, M., Pehrsson, D., Wood, C., & Charles, S. (2001). *A taxonomy of career development interventions that occur in US secondary schools.* Columbus, OH: National Dissemination Center for Career and Technical Education.

Finn, S. J. (1993). *School engagement and students' at risk.* Washington, DC: U.S. Department of Education, National Center for Education Statistics.

Fitzgerald, L. F., & Betz, N. E. (1994). Career development in cultural context: The role of gender, race, class, and sexual orientation. In M. L. Savickas & R. Lent (Eds.), *Convergence in theories of career development* (pp. 103–108). Palo Alto, CA: Consulting Psychologists Press.

Flaxman, E. (1992). Evaluating mentoring programs. *Institute for Urban and Minority Education (IUME) Briefs, 1,* 1–4.

Gándara, P. (2001). *Paving the way to postsecondary education: K-12 intervention programs for underrepresented youth* (Report of the National Postsecondary Education Cooperative Working Group on Access to Postsecondary Education). Washington, DC: U.S. Department of Education, National Center for Education Statistics.

Gándara, P., Mejorado, M., Gutiérrez, D., & Molina, M. (1998). *Final report of the evaluation of High School Puente: 1994–1998.* New York: Carnegie Corporation of New York.

Gottfredson, L. S. (1981). Circumscription and compromise: A developmental theory of occupational aspiration. *Journal of Counseling Psychology, 28,* 545–579.

Guthrie, L. F., & Guthrie, G. P. (2000). *Longitudinal research on AVID 1999–2000: Final report.* Burlingame, CA: Center for Research, Evaluation, and Training in Education (CREATE).

Ham, S., Doolittle, F. C., Holton, G. I., Ventura, A. M., & Jackson, R. (2000). *Project GRAD Newark. Building the foundation for improved student performance: The pre-curricular phase of Project Grad.* New York: Manpower Demonstration Research Corporation.

Higgins, C., Furano, K., Toso, C., & Branch, A. Y. (1991). *I Have a Dream in Washington, DC: Initial report.* Chicago: Public/Private Ventures. (ERIC Document Reproduction Service No. ED 337 523).

Horn, L. (1997). *Confronting the odds: Students at risk and the pipeline to higher education* (NCES 98-094). Washington, DC: U.S. Department of Education, National Center for Education Statistics.

Horn, L., & Chen, X. (1998). *Toward resiliency: At risk students who make it to college.* Washington, DC: U.S. Department of Education, Office of Educational Research and Improvement.

Horn, L., Nuñez, A., & Bobbitt, L. (2000). *Mapping the road to college: First-generation students' math track, planning strategies, and context of support (NCES 2000-153).* Washington, DC: U.S. Department of Education, Office of Educational Research and Improvement.

I Have a Dream Foundation. (n.d.). The "I Have a Dream" Foundation. Retrieved June 30, 2003, from http://www.ihad.org.

Ingels, S. J., Curtin, T. R., Kaufman, P., Alt, M. N., Chen, X., & Owings, J. A. (2002). *Coming of age in the 1990s: The eighth-grade class of 1988 12 years later* (NCES 2002-321). Washington, DC: U.S. Department of Education, National Center for Education Statistics.

James, D. W. (1997). *Some things DO make a difference for youth.* Washington, DC: American Youth Policy Forum. Retrieved June 30, 2003, from http://www.aypf.org /compendium/index.html.

James, D. W. (1999). *More things that DO make a difference for youth.* Washington, DC: American Youth Policy Forum. Retrieved June 30, 2003, from http://www.aypf.org /compendium/index.html.

James, D. W., Jurich, S., & Estes, S. (2001). *Raising minority academic achievement: A compendium of education programs and practices.* Washington, DC: American Youth Policy Forum. Retrieved June 30, 2003, from http://www.aypf.org/rmaa/index.html.

Jurich, S., & Estes, S. (2000). *Raising academic achievement: A study of 20 successful programs.* Washington, DC: American Youth Policy Forum. Retrieved June 30, 2003, from http://www.aypf.org/RAA/index.htm.

Kahne, J., & Bailey, K. (1999). The role of social capital in youth development: The case of I Have a Dream. *Educational Evaluation and Policy Analysis, 21,* 321–343.

Lee, V. E., & Ekstrom, R. B. (1987). Student access to guidance counseling in high school. *American Educational Research Journal, 24,* 287–310.

Lent, R. W., Brown, S. D., & Hackett, G. (1994). Toward a unifying social cognitive theory of career and academic interests, choice, and performance. *Journal of Vocational Behavior, 45,* 79–122.

Levin, H. (1986). *Educational reform for disadvantaged students: An emerging crises.* West Haven, CT: National Education Association.

McDonough, P. M., Korn, J. S., & Yamasaki, E. (1997). Access, equity, and the privatization of college counseling. *Review of Higher Education, 20,* 297–317.

Mehan, H., Villanueva, I., Hubbard, L., & Lintz, A. (1996). *Constructing school success: The consequences of untracking low-achieving students.* New York: Cambridge University Press.

Monk, D. H., & Haller, E. J. (1993). Predictors of high school academic course offerings: The role of school size. *American Educational Research Journal, 30,* 3–21.

Moore, M. T. (1997). *A 1990's view of Upward Bound: Programs offered, students served, and operational issues.* Washington, DC: U.S. Department of Education, Planning and Evaluation Service.

Myers, D. E., & Schirm, A. (1999). *The impacts of Upward Bound: Final report for phase I of the national evaluation.* Washington, DC: U.S. Department of Education, Planning and Evaluation Service.

National Center for Educational Statistics. (2001). *Digest of Education Statistics* (NCES 2002-130). Washington, DC: U.S. Department of Education, Office of Educational Research and Improvement.

National Center for Educational Statistics. (2002). *The condition of education 2002.* (NCES 2002-025). Washington, DC: U.S. Department of Education, Office of Educational Research and Improvement.

Nuñez, A., & Caroll, C. D. (1998). *First-generation students: Undergraduates whose parents never enrolled in postsecondary education* (NCES 98-082). Washington, DC: U.S. Department of Education, National Center for Education Statistics.

Opuni, K. A. (1999). *Project GRAD: Program evaluation report: 1998–1999.* Houston, TX: University of Houston.

Project GRAD, USA. (n.d.). What is Project GRAD? Retrieved June 30, 2003, from http://www.projectgrad.org.

Puente Project. (n.d.). *Welcome to the Puente Project!* Retrieved June 30, 2003, from http://www.puente.net/index.html.

Richardson, M. S. (1993). Work in people's lives: A location for counseling psychologists. *Journal of Counseling Psychology, 40,* 425–433.

Rosenbaum, J. E., Miller, S. R., & Krei, M. S. (1996). Gatekeeping in an era of more open gates: High school counselors' views of their influence on students' college plans. *American Journal of Education, 104*(4), 257–279.

Schanabel, K. U., Alfeld, C., Eccles, J. S., Koller, O., & Baumert, J. (2002). Parental influence on students' educational choices in the United States and Germany: Different ramifications—same effect. *Journal of Vocational Behavior, 60,* 178–198.

Sewell, W. H., Haller, A. O., & Ohlendorf, G. W. (1970). The educational and early occupational status attainment process: Replication and revision. *American Sociological Review, 35,* 1014–1027.

Slater, M., & Iler, E. (2000). *Science and Technology Entry Program: 1999–2000 final report.* New York: City University of New York Medical School.

Snyder, J., Morrison, G., & Smith, C. (1996). *Dare to Dream: Educational guidance for excellence.* Indianapolis, IN: Lilly Endowment.

Southern Regional Education Board. (2000). *State-funded merit-based scholarship programs: Why are they popular? Can they increase participation in higher education?* Retrieved June 30, 2003, from http://www.sreb.org/main/publications/meritbased/meritbasedscholarship.asp.

Spade, J. Z., Columba, L., & Vanfossen, B. E. (1997). Tracking in mathematics and science: Courses and course-selection procedures. *Sociology of Education, 70,* 108–127.

Steinberg, L. (1996). *Beyond the classroom: Why school reform has failed and what parents need to do.* New York: Simon & Schuster.

Super, D. E., Savickas, M. L., & Super, C. M. (1996). The life-span, life-space approach to careers. In D. Brown, L. Brooks, & Associates (Eds.), *Career choice and development* (3rd ed., pp. 121–178). San Francisco, Jossey-Bass.

Swail, W. S. (2000). Preparing America's disadvantaged for college: Programs that increase college opportunity. *New Directions for Institutional Research, 107,* 85–101.

Upward Bound Program. (n.d.). *Federal trio programs: Upward Bound.* Retrieved June 30,
2003, from http://www.ed.gov/offices/OPE/HEP/trio/upbound.html.

U.S. Census Bureau. (1998). *Population profile of the United States: 1997* (Current Population
Reports, Series P23-194). Washington, DC: U.S. Government Printing Office.

U.S. Department of Labor. (2002). *Occupational outlook handbook, 2002-03.* Washington, DC:
Bureau of Labor Statistics, Office of Occupational Statistics and Employment.

Vondracek, F. W., Lerner, R. M., & Schulenberg, J. E. (1986). *Career development: A life-span
developmental approach.* Hillsdale, NJ: Erlbaum.

Warburton, E., Bugarin, R., & Nuñez, A. (2001). *Bridging the gap: Academic preparation and
postsecondary success of first-generation students* (NCES 2001-153). Washington, DC: U.S.
Department of Education, National Center for Education Statistics.

Watt, K. M., Yanez, D., & Cossio, G. (2002–2003). AVID: A comprehensive school reform
model for Texas. *National Forum of Educational Administration and Supervision Journal, 19,*
43–59.

CHAPTER 23

Promoting the Career Potential of Youth with Disabilities

Ellen S. Fabian and James J. Liesener

UNDERSTANDING THE CAREER development of youth and young adults with disabilities requires knowledge of both individual and environmental factors. One of the challenges of trying to conceptualize the impact of disability on career development is the enormous heterogeneity among individuals with disabilities, suggesting that no theory can be fully applicable or nonapplicable to this group (Szymanski, Hershenson, Enright, & Ettinger, 1996). As a result, disability is best viewed not as a static construct that has a similar effect on all individuals, but as a socially defined construct that can be a risk factor to the achievement of career and social participation (Pledger, 2003). From this perspective, we can understand that while the career development of individuals with disabilities follows the same processes and is impacted by the same factors as the career development of nondisabled individuals, having a disability exposes the individual to unique experiences that influence their career development.

Despite decades of advances in special education and rehabilitation legislation and policy, the postschool outcomes for many youth with disabilities exiting from special education programs remain dismal (Benz, Yovanoff, & Doren, 1997; National Council on Disability [NCD], 2000). This state of affairs not only limits opportunities to these youth but also guarantees that the financial and social costs of their unfulfilled potential will be ones that the entire country continues to pay well into this century. For example, information from the Social Security Administration (SSA) indicates that about 350,000 youth ages 18 to 25 are receiving social security income supports rather than working. This alone costs taxpayers more than $10 billion annually (NCD, 2000).

School reform initiatives popularized at the turn of the current century may have limited impact on the more than 5.6 million special education students in America, where, for example, less than 30% of them earn a high school diploma (Wittenburg & Stapleton, 2000). In general, students who receive special education certificates are more likely to be unemployed, more likely to earn less money when they eventually secure work, and more likely to receive public assistance than they would if they had obtained a high school diploma (Wagner, Blackorby, Cameto, Hebbeler, & Newman, 1993; Yelin & Katz, 1994).

Unfortunately, the bleak future encountered by these youth is not improved upon their entry to adulthood. The economic and labor force achievements associated with working age adults with disabilities significantly lag behind that of adults without disabilities in America. Census data indicate that just over 30% of individuals with work-related disabilities were in the labor force in 1998, compared to the labor force participation of 82% of the general population. Of those 30% who were attached to the labor force, meaning that they were employed, receiving unemployment, or actively seeking a job, only 26% were working, compared to 78% of their nondisabled peers (U.S. Census Bureau, 2000). The National Longitudinal Transition Study (NLTS), the largest study of school-to-adult-life transition of students leaving secondary special education programs, found that only 20% of these students achieved what they considered successful adult adjustment by five years after graduation. Successful adult adjustment was defined as independent functioning in three domains: (1) employment, (2) residential, and (3) social activities (Wagner et al., 1993).

The barriers to work participation for youth and young adults with disabilities have been addressed by federal legislation, policy initiatives, and vocational program advances. Still, employment and educational data associated with this group suggest that they continue to fare worse than any other group in America. The purpose of this chapter is to review the context and issues confronted by youth and young adults with disabilities as they manage their careers and work lives. Specifically, we describe characteristics of the population, review significant legislative and policy issues that influence career and employment, summarize effective programmatic interventions, and recommend best practices.

DEFINITIONS OF DISABILITY

The U.S. Census (2000) reported that approximately 49.7 million Americans report some type of disability. It requires little imagination to see the enormous heterogeneity of abilities, limitations, and experiences that exist within this large group. There are multiple types of disabilities (e.g., spinal cord injuries, developmental disabilities, psychiatric disorders, sensory disorders, AIDS), all of which exist along a continuum of severity in terms of their impact on the functional capacities of the individual. In addition, myriad factors influence an individual's reaction to disability, such as personality, age, intelligence, educational level, family factors, gender, and exposure to discrimination and prejudice. All of these factors, in turn, influence careers and employment (Patterson, DeLaGarza, & Schaller, 1997). Given these factors, any definition of disability needs to be broad enough to encompass them and to take into account the interaction of disability and its functional attributes with the environment.

Although there is no one accepted or universal definition of disability, today disability is understood as a multifaceted experience representing an interaction of the person and the environment. Older definitions of disability equated the idea of having an impairment, or a pathology, with having a handicap (Hahn, 1993). There was a presumed medical model assumption within this definition in the sense that the problems and barriers the individual with a disability encountered could all be attributed to the impairment. The medical model solution to vocational training was either to change the person by ameliorating the condition to the extent possible or, where not possible, to compensate for the disability by training the person to function in an alternative way.

Disability advocates in the 1960s argued against this medical model assumption, proposing that disability could be understood as a barrier in the environment, not in the individual, and removing obstacles meant modifying the physical and the social environment, not changing the person. The person-in-environment construct that has emerged today not only reflects federal definitions of disability but also provides a framework for rehabilitation and career interventions (Nagi, 1979). Recently, definitions describing disability as a positive attribute have emerged (Swain & French, 2000). These new definitions (1) challenge the idea that persons need to develop the skills and have opportunities to succeed *despite* their disability and (2) present the possibility that persons can succeed *with and because of* their disability, if the social/political environment is changed.

Being aware of emerging disability definitions is important because they affect the attitudes and behaviors of both persons with disabilities and professionals who provide services to them (Hershenson, 1996). Understanding the meaning of disability to the individual is crucial to understanding the impact of the disability on his or her career development (Beveridge, Craddock, Liesener, Stapleton, & Hershenson, 2002). Understanding how professionals define disability facilitates the selection of interventions that do not unintentionally impede career and social participation outcomes of youth and young adults with disabilities. Although there is consensus today about the multifaceted approach to understanding disability, there are still more than 20 different federal definitions of disability written into various laws (National Institute on Disability and Rehabilitation Research, 1995). The most relevant laws, and those that would encompass the majority of youth and young adults, include special education, vocational rehabilitation, and the Americans with Disabilities Act (ADA).

The definition of disability within special education is codified in the Individuals with Disabilities Education Act of 1997 (IDEA; PL 105-17). IDEA defines a child with a disability as a child:

> with mental retardation, hearing impairments (including deafness), speech or language impairments, visual impairments (including blindness), serious emotional disturbance (hereinafter referred to as emotional disturbance), orthopedic impairments, autism, traumatic brain injury, other health impairments, or specific learning disabilities, and who, by reason thereof, needs special education and related services.

The definition of disability under IDEA does not presume that the nature or extent of the disability needs to interfere with functioning in a life domain, as stipulated in other laws, such as those that authorize adult services through the public vocational rehabilitation services program. This situation can create difficulties and confusion for many students as they leave school and come under the adult system of services.

The federal vocational rehabilitation program (codified in the Workforce Investment Act of 1998) defines disability as a physical, mental, or emotional impairment that needs to present a "substantial impediment to employment." Similarly, the ADA(PL 101-336) definition of disability includes a physical, mental, or emotional impairment that substantially limits functioning in a major life activity, such as walking, learning, or working. Finally, disability is defined by the SSA as a physical or mental condition that is "marked and severe" and that can be expected to last not less than 12 months or that may result in death. While the SSA does not provide services, it does provide income to some 8.1 million beneficiaries under its disability income support programs (Social Security Administration [SSA], 2002).

To an extent, the various definitions of disability have created confusion for people with disabilities and their families. For example, there are about 5.6 million children who meet the special education definition of disability, with the largest disability category being learning disability (about 41%). However, not all of these children meet the vocational rehabilitation definition of disability, a status that limits their eligibility for certain types of services. This situation has created aging-out phenomena for youth with disabilities who graduate or leave secondary schools (where they have qualified for special services) and then enter an adult system where their condition no longer meets more stringent requirements (Wagner & Blackorby, 1996).

The person-in-environment approach, as reflected in some federal definitions, has important implications for career planning and vocational interventions. First, it is equally important for counselors to have knowledge of working and work environments as it is to have knowledge about specific disabilities. This means that counselors must pay attention to how the physical and attitudinal environment creates career barriers for persons with disabilities. Second, it provides a foundation for considering that impairments or the associated symptoms of impairments are not as relevant to vocational planning as are the functional manifestations of them in a specific environmental context. For example, the fact that an individual has schizophrenia with its characteristic symptoms is less important than how these symptoms are functionally relevant (such as attenuated concentration) in a particular job context. Functional definitions of impairments enable counselors and clients to develop strategies that reduce their effect on performance. A final implication of this approach is that it emphasizes the importance of counselor knowledge about disability law and policy issues in order to effectively assist youth and young adults in preparing for and securing jobs.

BARRIERS TO WORK

In American culture, work is understood to encompass both a sense of identity and the primary means of attaining the economic and social benefits that contribute to overall quality of life. Thus, employment has traditionally been among the most critical measures of the status and progress of various groups in American society, including, for example, women, ethnic minorities, and people with disabilities. It has also provided a general yardstick against which the quality of various systems, whether educational, vocational, or social in nature, has been measured.

For people with disabilities in America, employment has long represented a significant challenge to full participation in society. For example, national polls of individuals with disabilities consistently find that even though two-thirds of working age people with disabilities are not employed, most want to work (Hountenville, 2000). It is interesting that these discrepancies in employment participation tend to persist even in the face of more positive economic indicators and higher employment rates in the general population (Schwochau & Blanck, 1999), as well as positive changes in the social and legislative climate for persons with disabilities over the past decade or so. The persistent lack of employment among individuals with disabilities suggests a complex array of factors, both intrinsic and extrinsic, that contribute to this generally bleak picture. It is important for career counselors to be familiar with the common obstacles to employment, and those that have received the most attention in the literature are described next.

FEDERAL POLICY CONCERNING DISABILITY BENEFITS AND ACCESS TO HEALTH INSURANCE

People with disabilities who qualify for income support programs through the SSA (some eight million adults and 880,000 children) may be discouraged from considering employment because of fear of loss of benefits, particularly health insurance (SSA, 2002). This issue has been cited as one of the most severe in terms of discouraging people with disabilities to return to work or to leave benefits rolls and enter employment (Hennessey, 1997).

EMPLOYER ATTITUDES AND DISCRIMINATION

Despite the more positive media depiction of individuals with disabilities and despite legislative advances such as the ADA, there have been only modest improvements noted in the attitudes and practices of employers (Unger, 2001). This is a particularly salient barrier for individuals with certain highly stigmatized conditions—such as emotional and mental disabilities, as well as chronic diseases such as HIV/AIDS. These negative employment attitudes influence the hiring as well as tenure and promotion of persons with disabilities (Schwochau & Blanck, 1999). More important, negative social attitudes, or stigma, may affect vocational identity development for youth, thus interfering with several important career processes described later.

LACK OF ADEQUATE PREPARATION FOR THE WORKPLACE

The majority of young people with disabilities continue to lag behind their peers in postsecondary school training and education (Wagner & Blackorby, 1996). Young people with severe disabilities, such as mental and emotional disabilities, or multiple ones, tend to receive inadequate preparation for jobs or leave school before attaining employment (Benz et al., 1997). Inadequate preparation also affects persons with mild disabilities. For example, the results of studies on the career development of adolescents with disabilities found that they experienced:

1. Limitations in early career exploratory experiences.
2. Limited opportunities to develop decision-making abilities.
3. A negative self-concept resulting from societal attitudes toward persons with disabilities (Conte, 1983; Ochs & Roessler, 2001).

LACK OF POSTSECONDARY EDUCATION AND VOCATIONAL TRAINING

In today's workforce, "the two new dominant labor groups are knowledge workers and service workers" (Szymanski, Ryan, Merz, Trevino, & Johnston-Rodriguez, 1996, p. 18). As a result, there are new requirements for education and the ability to manage complexity in almost every occupation (Coates, Jarrat, & Mahaffie, 1991). These new requirements have increased the importance of postsecondary education for the success of anyone entering the workforce. After reviewing the literature on the current status and trends of the workforce and the employment rates and trends of people with disabilities, Szymanski, Hershenson, et al. (1996) recommended that "education should be a consideration in assisting people with disabilities in entering and retaining value in the labor force" (p. 33). However, research on the experiences of people with disabilities in postsecondary education indicates that they have a significantly lower probability of graduating (Hurst & Smerdon, 2000) and are likely to face discrimination and social isolation (Loewen, 1993; Wiseman, Emry, & Morgan, 1988). Furthermore, the majority of college students with disabilities who graduate do so from majors outside the science and technology fields (National Science Foundation, 1999)—the fields showing the most growth in the changing economy—and possess few marketable occupational skills (Roessler, 1987).

Lack of Available Community Employment Services

Although special education services for children with disabilities is a federal mandate, there is no such universal program for young adults after they leave school. Available programs are generally funded through public monies, so they are susceptible to downsizing in state and federal budgets. The federal Workforce Investment Act of 1998 (PL 105-220) was enacted partially to address the issue of inadequate community-based services through the establishment of career and employment One Stop Centers, offering an array of information, resources, and referrals to youth and young adults with disabilities, among other groups. However, implementation of the One Stop concept has been inconsistent across state and local jurisdictions, and the issue of how well such generic services provide preparation and assistance to individuals with disabilities has not been ascertained.

Professional Attitudes toward Employment

People with disabilities who need services the most are frequently the least likely to be served because of the perceived difficulties in providing these services, as well as the intensity and duration of services required (Mank, 1994). Moreover, people with severe disabilities are not often provided with career or vocational choices; instead, they are frequently placed in entry-level jobs that they leave because of lack of interest and choice in the matter (Fabian, 1992). According to Szymanski and Trueba (1994), "at least some of the difficulties faced by persons with disabilities are not the result of functional impairments, but rather are the result of a castification process embedded in societal institutions for rehabilitation and education and enforced by well-meaning professionals" (p. 195).

LEGISLATION AND DISABILITY

A long federal tradition of laws has provided access to educational and vocational opportunities for people with disabilities. Knowledge of federal legislation that affects disability benefits and services is a critical matter for those who provide career services to people with disabilities. This section describes the major disability-related legislation, with particular relevance to practice and to the specific barriers to employment described earlier. These laws include the Individuals with Disabilities Education Act, the Americans with Disabilities Act, the Ticket to Work and Work Incentives Improvement Act, and the Workforce Investment Act of 1998.

THE INDIVIDUALS WITH DISABILITIES EDUCATION ACT (PL 101-476)

The IDEA establishes specific federal regulations for youth with disabilities who are transitioning from school to adult life. Although special education legislation has existed since the landmark 1976 Education of All Handicapped Children (EAHC) Act, it was not until this act was amended in 1990 and 1997 and renamed the Individuals with Disabilities Education Act that it addressed the issue of special education youth as they prepare to leave secondary school for adult life. Specifically, IDEA requires schools to develop transition plans that stipulate services and outcomes each special education student requires to make a successful transition. The transition objectives covered under IDEA include:

1. Postsecondary education and vocational training.
2. Employment.
3. Independent living.
4. Social and community participation.

As a result of IDEA, sweeping changes in both programs and policies have been seen over the past two decades (Stodden & Dowrick, 2000). In some cases, these changes have positively affected postschool situations for individuals with disabilities, particularly those with more severe disabilities, such as mental retardation and mental health conditions. Although there has been an uneven implementation of transition practices across the country and almost 50% of the transition-age population does not qualify for services from adult systems (Hayward & Schmidt-Davis, 2000), a plethora of models and practices have been described and, to an extent, validated in the literature. These programs are discussed later in the chapter.

AMERICANS WITH DISABILITIES ACT (PL 101-336)

The ADA, enacted in 1990, represented a major thrust forward for disability policy in America (Miller, 2000). Its provisions prohibit discrimination against people with disabilities in all facets of life: employment, public services, private businesses, telecommunications, and transportation. For career and employment-related counselors, the major interest is in two key areas of the ADA: (1) Title I, which covers employment, and (2) the definition of the protected individual (i.e., Who is an individual with a disability?).

The latter issue has received a great deal of attention in policy and legal circles since the act first passed. The ADA defines disability as a "physical, mental or emotional impairment" that substantially limits functioning in a major life activity. Major life activities are defined broadly and include walking, speaking, breathing, seeing, learning, caring for self, and working, among others. Generally, the courts have increasingly limited the definition of disability under the act, for example, determining that a disability is no longer covered when it can be mitigated by devices or equipment (such as eyeglasses) or medication (such as antidepressants; NCD, 2003). Although such a change may seem minor, it has major implications for employees who, for example, may have a psychiatric condition that is controlled by medication but who still would benefit from accommodations in the workplace that would otherwise be offered under the protections of the act.

Another key area under Title I, the employment provision of the ADA, is the idea of reasonable accommodations. The law states that employers must provide "reasonable accommodations" that would enable a qualified individual with a disability to perform the essential functions of a job. What is important here is the legal word *qualified,* meaning that an applicant or employee must have the requisite background, credentials, education, or experience to perform the essential functions of the job with or without an accommodation. Thus, a clerical employee who demonstrates requisite typing speed and accuracy and who uses a wheelchair might need a computer keyboard hand rest that would allow him or her to type more easily. Typically, reasonable accommodations are modifications to the physical space, equipment, procedures, policies, or practices.

TICKET TO WORK AND WORK INCENTIVES IMPROVEMENT ACT OF 1999 (PL 106-170)

This legislation was enacted in an attempt to dismantle the work disincentives in the SSA's income support programs for people with disabilities. These programs had served as employment barriers because they limited the amount of monthly and annual income that beneficiaries could earn without jeopardizing their benefits, including access to federal health care insurance. Many studies of the effect of SSA on work-related decisions of people with disabilities cited the fear of loss of health insurance (Medicaid or Medicare) as a primary reason for refusing to work or return to work (Burkhauser & Wittenburg, 1996).

In 1999, Congress enacted the Ticket to Work and Work Incentives Improvement Act (TWIIA) to encourage states to expand health care coverage to working individuals with disabilities by extending the insurance time limits for covered individuals as they reenter the workplace. The "ticket" portion of the act puts the decision about seeking a vocational service provider into the hands of the client by providing him or her with a voucher that can be used to purchase these services from private providers. Similar to managed care systems in mental health, service providers are paid by SSA based on vocational outcomes. Although the voucher system represents a sweeping policy shift in service provision, it is too soon to measure the impact of its implementation.

WORKFORCE INVESTMENT ACT OF 1998 (PL 105-220)

The Workforce Investment Act (WIA) of 1998 was enacted to consolidate and improve employment, training, literacy, and vocational rehabilitation programs in the United States. Under this act, states are required to write workforce development plans that specifically address how the state will meet the vocational and employment-related needs of diverse populations requiring services, including transitioning youth, adults with disabilities, unemployed and underemployed workers, and various other constituents with unmet needs. Although states vary in how they implement the WIA, most have established One Stop Centers, where people who require various services to support employment, such as vocational rehabilitation, counseling, or employment training, can access them in one setting.

Title IV of the WIA covers the reauthorization of the Rehabilitation Act of 1973. Important provisions have implications for career planning for persons with disabilities. For example, self-determination and vocational choice have been mandated within the Act, insofar as its provisions apply to the state/federal system of services. This aspect of the Act reflects the changes in laws over the past several decades that have emphasized equitable education and treatment for individuals with disabilities.

FACTORS INFLUENCING VOCATIONAL BEHAVIOR

For individuals with disabilities, careers are influenced by external issues and barriers, such as social policy and laws, as well as internal factors, such as functional capacities and psychosocial factors.

FUNCTIONAL CAPACITIES AND WORK

Although federal definitions of disability vary and may create confusion within systems of disability services, it is now a widely accepted assumption that disability should be defined within an environmental or ecological context. This approach means shifting the focus from a symptom or impairment orientation to a functional one. In other words, a condition or impairment is a disability only to the extent that it affects an individual's functioning in one or more environments, such as employment. This represents a biopsychosocial approach to conceptualizing disability where, for example, there is a physical or biological condition that may alter awareness, perception, or adjustment and is influenced by and, in turn, influences social behavior and interpersonal functioning. To the extent that the environment does influence perceptions and behavior, a functional understanding of disability incorporates a reciprocal interaction perspective. For example, negative social attitudes or stigma can cause stress reactions, thus exacerbating medical or psychological conditions. This is particularly true for youth and young adults with psychiatric or learning disabilities, who may be particularly vulnerable to social attitudes.

There are several important assumptions underlying a functional or functional capacities approach to exploring the influence of impairments or conditions on vocational performance. First, functional capacities are to a great extent situationally specific (MacDonald-Wilson, Rogers, & Anthony, 2001). A person who is totally blind, for example, may experience minimal or no limitations within her own home, or even neighborhood, but may be significantly limited in a new setting. A person who has schizophrenia may not be able to maintain social relationships but may be able to function well in certain jobs. As early research in the field suggested, functioning in one environment is not predictive of functioning in another (Neff, 1967).

Second, it is more important to modify or shape the physical and even social environment than to change or modify the individual. This assumption is what gave rise to the disability rights movement in the 1960s and the ADA. The World Health Organization (WHO) recently broadened its definition of disability to include the unique interaction among the person, the health condition, and the environment in a model that emphasizes functioning. A classification system based on this model was approved by the World Health Assembly and is called the International Classification of Functioning, Disability and Health (WHO, 2001).

A third important assumption implicit in the functional shift was the need to conduct vocational and career assessments that emphasize a person-in-environment perspective. For example, knowing that one of the symptoms of schizophrenia may be auditory hallucinations matters less in planning for employment than does figuring out how this particular symptom compromises or interferes with functioning in an environmental context. Or identifying that a youth has a specific learning disability such as dyslexia means figuring out, again, how this presents a functional limitation in a specific environmental context.

The manner in which functional capacities affect work performance has always attracted a great deal of attention in the rehabilitation/career-related literature. Of particular importance have been functional capacities that directly affect performance, as well as the perceived effect they have on coworkers and supervisors. For example, the literature has suggested that employers tend to rely on stereotypes of disability and thus exaggerate the extent to which a functional impairment may interfere with vocational performance (Feurstein & Thebarge, 1991; Unger, 2001). The ADA has discouraged the use of stereotypes by employers in arbitrarily ruling out classes of individuals with disabilities based on stereotypes, but certain stereotypes tend to persist (Unger, 2001). The effect that these attitudes continue to have on an individual's perception of his or her own capacities and the psychological issues that arise from disability are discussed in the next section.

PSYCHOSOCIAL ISSUES

Understanding disability as an interplay of personal and environmental factors provides a framework for assessing individual abilities within a specific situational context. It also provides a basis for exploring the manner in which psychological attributes interact with social setting factors to influence individual perceptions about vocational choice and performance (Lent, Brown, & Hackett, 1994).

In terms of social attitudes, empirical research indicates that employer attitudes toward individuals with disabilities, although improved since the passage of the ADA, remain moderately negative, particularly toward certain disability groups (Unger, 2001). For example, negative stereotypes about people with psychiatric conditions have contributed to the particularly poor employment rates associated with this group (Diksa & Rogers, 1996). Other surveys of attitudes have identified employer concern about the work performance of workers with mental and other disabilities (Blanck, 1998).

Less often considered within the rehabilitation literature is the effect that negative attitudes have on decreasing work-related self-efficacy and depressing future work expectations (Fabian, 2000), thereby eroding the work motivation of people with disabilities (Baron, 2000). Similar processes have been described in relation to certain minority groups (M. T. Brown, 1995; Hackett & Betz, 1981; Hackett, Betz, Casas, & Rocha-Singh, 1992; Hackett & Byars, 1996). For people with disabilities, some of whom may have little experience with competitive employment, self-perceptions of work capacity may thus be severely limited, constraining vocational exploration as well as choice. These factors are taken into account in the career practices described later.

Another significant psychosocial area to be addressed emerges from the individualistic adjustment perspective on disability, which holds that reactions to disability depend on a range of individual attributes and circumstances, such as personal history of depression, family background and support, educational attainment, work-related aspirations, and age. These individual factors, together with environmental supports and available services, are associated with work entry and work retention across a variety of disability groups, including, for example, individuals with psychiatric conditions (Wewiorski & Fabian, 2004), spinal cord injuries (Krause & Anson, 1997), and mental retardation (Westbrook, Legge, & Pennay, 1993).

CAREER ISSUES FOR INDIVIDUALS WITH DISABILITIES

Career counseling and career development are relatively new concepts in disability studies, even though vocational rehabilitation programs have existed for 100 years. Early conceptions of disability that focused on individual deficits tended to severely limit, if not disregard, career choice activities. For example, early conceptions of mental retardation emphasized only the negative attributes of the individual, labeling people as "defective" or "simple minded" (Trent, 1994). Construing mental retardation as an untreatable cognitive deficit essentially relegated most of these individuals either to institutions or to "sheltered workshops," performing repetitive tasks in segregated facilities (Olshansky, 1976). As discussed earlier, as the perception of disability shifted from a problem-in-the-person perspective to a problem in the environment, the realm of potential job possibilities enlarged, as community-based employment became a viable option, along with the provision of sufficient supports and resources (Wehman, West, & Kregel, 1999). Enlarging career or employment opportunities meant that people had a choice in the type of job or career that they might select.

Another event contributing to an increased emphasis on career choice was changes in laws, starting with the EAHC, which mandated including children and youth with disabilities in general education programs, rather than segregating them in special classrooms or schools. As a result, children with disabilities were exposed to general education curricula in the schools, as well as school guidance services that emphasized post-high school achievement, such as enrolling in colleges or preparing for a job. In this way, laws that mandated inclusive education paved the way for equal opportunity and set the stage for encouraging professionals, families, and youth to think in new ways about career goals.

In fact, later amendments to special education legislation, culminating in the IDEA discussed earlier, mandated post-high school planning by requiring that all special education students have a transition plan by the time they turned 16. The requirement for transition planning and the parallel need to provide vocational and career intervention services necessary to achieve it resulted in a great deal of national attention toward school-to-work and school-to-adult-life programs for students with disabilities.

TRANSITION TO ADULT LIFE PROGRAMS

The concept of school-to-work transition programs was popularized in the mid-1980s (Will, 1984) and codified in subsequent federal legislation. The purpose of these programs was to assist youth with disabilities to identify career and life goals before their exit from high school to have sufficient time to prepare to achieve those goals. The aim of these programs is to mitigate the poor postschool outcomes that were reported for youth with disabilities, such as high unemployment, delinquency, and poverty (Wagner & Blackorby, 1996). Studies over the past several decades have identified effective transition programs and practices, which include vocational training, paid employment before school exit, community-based instruction, and service coordination between educational and other personnel, such as rehabilitation counselors, mental health professionals, and social services staffs (Kohler & Chapman, 1999).

That these programs are achieving some measure of success is reflected in some of the positive indicators that may be attributed to them. For example, data from the National Council on Disability (2000) indicated that about 50% of young adults with disabilities (ages 20 to 29) who expressed a desire to work are working, while enrollment of disabled students in postsecondary institutions rose from 2.3% in 1978 to 9.8% in 1998 (Henderson, 1999). While these figures are heartening, they also illustrate the progress that still needs to be made. Many issues and policies will affect how much progress will be made by youth with disabilities in realizing equal employment and educational opportunities, many of which have to do with external barriers described earlier, such as work disincentives, employment discrimination, and lack of available community services. However, the emerging success of school-to-adult-life transition programs has stimulated interest in developing career interventions that help students to manage these barriers, as well as provide skills that help them to maximize career choice. The next section describes career theory and practice issues for youth with disabilities.

THE CONTEXT OF CAREERS FOR PEOPLE WITH DISABILITIES

However unfortunate it is, there is little doubt that disability itself plays a significant role in shaping employment prospects for youth and young adults. Several studies have shown that type and severity of disability are significant determinants of employment outcome, with research concluding that postschool employment is highest among young adults with learning disabilities and lowest among those with multiple or severe impairments, such as mental retardation (Wagner & Blackorby, 1996). Similar to general population findings, employment rates are also higher for young men than women and higher among Caucasians than other ethnic groups (Research Triangle International, 2003).

It is certainly consistent with career theory to describe disability or impairment in terms of the specific challenges or barriers it imposes on choice and performance (Szymanski, Enright, Hershenson, & Ettinger, 2003). Some of the barriers that arise from disability have been described earlier and include social stigma (e.g., Stone, Stone, & Dipboye, 1992), employment discrimination (Unger, 2001), inadequate vocational training and preparation (e.g., Ochs & Roessler, 2001), and social security disincentives (e.g., Noble, 1998). Generally, these external barriers interact with individual attributes, such as poor self-efficacy and lowered career aspirations, to hamper the career development process. Thus, disability or impairment may be viewed from the same perspective as are other status conditions, such as age or race, in understanding career-related behavior and developing interventions to promote it.

Within this context, disability is not seen as the fundamental attribute around which vocational development proceeds, but rather as an individual risk factor that can interfere with the career planning and development sequence (Szymanski, 1999). For example, children with disabilities in special education may lack exposure to career role models that foster the development of vocational exploration via occupational daydreaming and role playing (Benz & Halpern, 1993). Thus, disability might yield inadequate career education resulting from segregated classrooms, lack of adequately trained personnel, and other school-based factors (Turnball, 1990). Children in special education with inadequate career preparation, then, may develop a diminished sense of career self-efficacy, one of the most potent attributes linked to career choice and vocational outcome (see Anderson & Brown, 1997; Lent, Chapter 5, this volume). Even though best practices in career development would suggest the need to include career education for all students, the uneven and inconsistent implementation of these practices in special education and transition planning unfortunately remains the norm (Ochs & Roessler, 2001).

Another important consideration in career interventions for youth with disabilities is the surprising dearth of theory-building studies that would help explain and eventually improve career education outcomes. Szymanski et al. (2003) attributed the lack of studies in this area to a number of factors, such as the heterogeneity of the population and the lack of psychometrically sound instruments for measuring constructs for individuals with disabilities. Another factor limiting theory-based research has been the traditional focus in transition and rehabilitation programs on initial employment as the ultimate outcome, rather than encouraging a perspective on the process of career development. This outcome-oriented focus is one result of federal initiatives and funding regulations that emphasize getting a job and encourage program evaluation studies that divorce theory from practice. Finally, a relative lack of attention to persons with disabilities in the general career development and research literature may reflect general stereotypes and social stigma toward individuals with disabilities.

THEORY-BASED CONSTRUCTS

There have been a number of papers in the disability literature describing how extant career theories relate to people with disabilities, but relatively few empirical studies of how theoretical constructs could be validated with this population (Shahnasarian, 2001). However, some career constructs, notably those emerging from Social Cognitive Career Theory (Lent et al., 1994), have been applied to the career behavior of different groups of individuals with disabilities.

Self-Efficacy and Outcome Expectancies Interest in self-efficacy as a useful construct in explaining career behavior emerges from studies that have examined the utility of this construct in various special populations, including women (Hackett & Betz, 1981) and racial-ethnic minorities (Hackett & Byars, 1996). In the disability literature, self-efficacy has also been studied as a predictor of work status among samples of individuals with a variety of impairments. For example, several authors have examined the relation of self-efficacy beliefs to career interests and behavior of students with learning and emotional disabilities, suggesting that not only do such students have lower efficacy beliefs than their nondisabled peers (Ochs & Roessler, 2001; Slemon & Shafir, 1997) but also self-efficacy beliefs played an important role in understanding their career choice and interests. Paganos and DuBois (1999) investigated the relationship between self-efficacy beliefs and career interests in high school students with learning disabilities and found that self-efficacy was the strongest contributor to career interests for these students, well beyond the contribution of outcome expectancies. Similarly, Ochs and Roessler found significantly lower career self-efficacy beliefs among high school students with learning disabilities when compared to their nondisabled peers. In a study of students with serious emotional disturbance (SED), Willis (2002) found self-efficacy beliefs to be a significant predictor of postschool employment.

Studies have also examined the utility of social cognitive predictors of employment outcomes for other disabled groups. For example, Regenold, Sherman, and Fenzel (1999) found that higher self-efficacy beliefs predicted employment status for a sample of individuals with psychiatric disorders. In another study of predictors of vocational outcome among adults with psychiatric disorders, Mowbray, Bybee, Harris, and McCrohan (1995) identified positive outcome expectations concerning return to work to be most strongly associated with work status in a supported employment program. Altmaier, Russell, Kao, Lehmann, and Weinstein (1993) found self-efficacy related to rehabilitation outcome for clients with low back pain. Barlow, Wright, and Cullen (2002) found that higher self-efficacy beliefs were associated with the ability to manage disability issues during job interviews among a heterogeneous group of people with disabilities.

Efficacy beliefs have also been the targets of intervention studies. Conyers and Szymanski (1998) found that a brief career intervention was effective in improving career self-efficacy for college students with and without disabilities. Enright (1997) evaluated a short-term career intervention designed to improve career decision-making efficacy and self-esteem among a heterogeneous group of adults with disabilities. Although the experimental group did not indicate higher levels of career decision-making self-efficacy, she did find an increase in what she called life decision-making self-efficacy.

Career Maturity   Career maturity, a construct emerging from Super's career development model (Super, Savickas, & Super, 1996), has also been addressed in the disability literature. In this research, the timing of the disability during a person's career development is important to consider, and three subgroups of persons with disabilities have been identified and hypothesized to undergo different career development processes: those with precareer-onset disabilities, those with midcareer-onset disabilities, and those with progressive or episodic disabilities (Beveridge et al., 2002).

Persons with precareer disabilities enter and progress through their career development with a disability. The information on the lack of adequate preparation for the workplace best applies to these individuals, for example, youth with developmental or learning disabilities severe enough to warrant special education services. Individuals with midcareer disabilities acquire or are diagnosed as having a disability at some point after their career entry. According to Hershenson

(1996), if the impairments or perceived impairments associated with the disability affect the person's work competencies, it will result in subsequent changes in work personality and work goals. Super et al. (1996) referred to this as a "minicycle," involving the recycling of new growth, reexploration, and reestablishment. Depending on the age of initial onset or diagnosis, the effects of progressive or episodic disabilities can be similar to those of pre- or midcareer disabilities. An important difference is that each significant functional change in an individual's disability has the potential to have a similar effect to that of acquiring a midcareer disability, as well as a potential cumulative effect. It is necessary to understand the effect of each episode or change in functional abilities on the individual's attitudes about both work and disability.

Lindstrom and Benz (2002) identified three distinct phases of career maturity among a small sample of young women with learning disabilities: (1) unsettled, (2) exploratory, and (3) focused. Several studies have indicated that individuals with disabilities manifest lower levels of career maturity when compared to their nondisabled peers (e.g., Hitchings, Luzzo, Retish, Horvbath, & Ristow, 1998). Mori (1982) found that special education students were significantly less knowledgeable about job duties than were general education students. Rojewski (1993) found that learning-disabled high school students scored lower on the career maturity index than did their nondisabled counterparts. Ochs and Roessler (2001) similarly found lower levels of career maturity and career information among disabled high school students. Although the number of studies exploring career maturity and other developmental constructs among youth and young adults with disabilities is small, there is emerging empirical support for their utility in the disability context (Lindstrom & Benz, 2002).

IMPLICATIONS FOR CAREER COUNSELING

As noted earlier, traditional career counseling approaches for individuals with disabilities have relied on matching strategies—where the emphasis was on matching capacities to job demands. Although there is nothing inherently wrong with this trait and factor approach, the manner in which practices evolved proved problematic in terms of assisting individuals with disabilities to secure chosen jobs. First is the issue described earlier, where vocational evaluations emphasized deficits, not strengths—a process that tended to severely constrain choice. Second, even within a strengths-based assessment approach, various problems have been noted in the application of standardized tests and instruments for people with disabilities (Parker & Schaller, 2003), raising questions about their predictive utility with several disabled populations (Anthony & Jansen, 1984; Caston & Watson, 1990; Jones, 1995). Such problems include nonrepresentative norms, inexperienced test takers, inappropriate and/or inadequate modifications to standardization protocols, and poorly trained examiners (Anastasi, 1976; Parker & Schaller, 2003).

One result of the challenge to traditional career assessment has been to modify assessment approaches. These modifications include incorporating more informal interviews and observational techniques into assessment (Power, 2000), having family members or significant others participate in helping the individual identify interests and skills (Hagner & DiLeo, 1993), and relying more on contextual assessment methods, where observations and ratings occur in a specific environmental context. In this manner, career assessment is an important intervention, particularly from a strengths-based approach that helps motivate the individual toward an employment orientation.

Another career intervention that has received some attention in the literature (described earlier) is improving career self-efficacy. It is particularly important that individuals with disabilities tend to have lower efficacy beliefs and lower outcome expectations when compared to their nondisabled peers. This finding is not surprising because they may have less exposure to the types of experiences and activities that contribute to efficacy-building, such as volunteer and work experiences, exposure to role models, and reinforcing feedback (Benz & Halpern, 1993). In addressing these barriers, it is important that the few studies that have used interventions to improve career self-efficacy beliefs have shown positive results in terms of mitigating negative feedback or environmental inadequacies that have limited vocational development (Conyers & Szymanski, 1998). This suggests that career counselors might need to assess—either formally or informally—the efficacy beliefs and outcome expectations of their clients with disabilities, being aware of how these beliefs may have compromised their interests, goals, and future expectations. Direct interventions designed to bolster self-efficacy can be incorporated into career counseling programs using strategies that help clients to anticipate and shape a vocational future (Fabian, 2000). Counselors can ensure that clients are exposed to a diverse array of vocational options, as well as peers who have achieved success in different jobs and settings. Social cognitive career counseling would also suggest an explicit focus on (1) anticipating, analyzing, and preparing to deal with contextual barriers and (2) building support systems (e.g., see S. D. Brown & Lent, 1996). Providing more intensive coaching or support—both individually and in groups—may assist clients with disabilities to persist in achieving their goals. These types of interventions would apply to individuals at all stages of career development.

Because young adults with disabilities have been found to exhibit lower levels of career maturity when compared to their peers, counselors may need to incorporate developmentally oriented strategies as much as possible into career education programs. For example, one of the strongest predictors of successful postsecondary adjustment for youth with disabilities is having a paid employment experience before leaving high school (Luecking & Fabian, 2000). Unlike their nondisabled counterparts, these youth may not have had the types of volunteer and entry-level job experiences (such as babysitting or delivering newspapers) that assist in developing work attitudes and interests. Helping high school students to acquire paid work experiences, similar to their nondisabled peers, promotes the development of a vocational self-concept because these experiences provide opportunities for exploration, as well as personal feedback about vocational preferences and aptitudes. At the same time, paid work experiences set the stage for identifying longer term career goals.

The purpose of career counseling activities is to help the individual to identify and pursue career goals. The shift in disability policy from a deficit model to an empowerment one has also affected rehabilitation planning and goal setting by encouraging individuals to consider a wider array of vocational choices (Kosciulek, 1998). At the same time, the ADA affected goal setting by reducing environmental barriers that may have circumscribed career goals. Reasonable accommodations that are mandated under the ADA enable individuals with disabilities to perform a much wider variety of jobs than were possible before its enactment, for example, allowing hearing-impaired young adults to have interpreters on the job or mobility-impaired individuals to request adaptive equipment. There is less discussion of how to discourage people with disabilities from pursuing "unrealistic" goals and more examples of how to use any type of stated occupational preference as a potential motivator (Hagner & DiLeo, 1993). Performance motivation and outcome expectations are particularly important for individuals with disabilities, where a paucity of previous experience, lack of access to role models, and negative social attitudes may have severely impeded career goal setting. This suggests that to encourage choice processes in identifying vocational goals, counselors may have to assist individuals with disabilities to acquire a vision of a vocational future, a necessary first step to career aspirations (Savickas, 1990). Intervention strategies designed to bolster vocational self-efficacy, such as participating in paid work experiences or exposure to potential peer role models, may be basic prerequisites toward developing a capacity to develop future goals or aspirations.

Another important consideration is that the issue of the meaning that work has in an individual's life plays a pivotal role in career development. Counselors may need to alter their assumptions about work as a primary life activity to viewing work as an option that clients may or may not incorporate into their life planning. In other words, during certain life stages, clients may need to focus their energies on managing their disabilities, allowing vocational or prevocational activities to play a secondary role (Baron, 2000). Career counselors may need to regard long-term attachment to the labor market as a necessary and sufficient goal for many, but not all, individuals, encouraging people to map a vocational future that allows for individual differences in the amount of energy expended toward work. This is a particularly important stance for young adults with remitting/relapsing disabilities (e.g., depression, diabetes, AIDS, multiple sclerosis). For example, a young woman who experiences severe depressive episodes and wants a career in health care administration may need to look at occupational alternatives that more easily accommodate rapid reentry to the job market if she requires time off. Even persons with more stable disabilities may need to reflect on the meaning and value of work in their lives, as well as prepare to cope with the types of barriers described earlier.

Generally, career counseling tends to taper off when counselor and client have identified career goals and specific steps to achieve them. However, career counselors may need to be more actively engaged in the job search and adjustment process when working with individuals with disabilities, based on the issues raised earlier in the chapter, such as employer stereotypes, negative social attitudes, and fear of loss of insurance benefits. In the rehabilitation field, job search and subsequent job placement have received a great deal of attention—more so than in the general career development or career counseling field (see Jome & Phillips, Chapter 19, this volume; Saks, Chapter 7, this volume). As a result, there are a number of different approaches described in the literature toward helping an individual secure a job, including job-seeking skills groups (Azrin, Flores, & Kaplan, 1975), supported employment (Wehman et al., 1999), and marketing applicants to employers through a variety of different job development approaches (Gilbride, Stensrud, & Johnson, 1994). Although the details are well beyond the scope of this chapter, the fundamental practices across all of these approaches are similar. They include careful preparation of individuals with disabilities for job interviews (including legal rights and disclosure of disability), developing and using job connections and networks as the most likely source of job leads and referrals, assisting employers after the placement as to workplace accommodations, and encouraging work retention support groups (either virtual or face to face; Hagner, 2003). Work retention or job support groups help employees to manage possible negative attitudes, deal with issues concerning loss of social security benefits, and provide connections for future employment. Some of these services, such as job placement, postemployment support, or benefits counseling, may be provided through various federal and state groups, including the state's vocational rehabilitation agency, One Stop Career Centers, and SSA field offices. Career counselors may want to maintain linkages with all of these resources in their local communities.

A final implication concerning career counseling practices for individuals with disabilities is to argue that taking into account disability is frequently no different from taking into account other client variables, such as race, sex, or age in devising effective strategies. Mainstream career development theorists and researchers have tended to ignore the application of concepts and services to people with disabilities, even while the research in applying these same constructs to other diverse groups continued to grow. This was further compounded by traditional practices in vocational rehabilitation that focused on individual impairments and deficits, rather than on the individual's career-related attributes or the environment. As the shift from deficit model to empowerment continues to grow, we expect that more attention will be directed toward understanding the career behavior of, and career practices for, individuals with disabilities. Additional research studies that would assist in extending career theories and practices to individuals with disabilities are clearly needed.

REFERENCES

Altmaier, E. G., Russell, D. W., Kao, C. F., Lehmann, T. R., & Weinstein, J. N. (1993). Role of self-efficacy in rehabilitation outcome among chronic low back pain patients. *Journal of Counseling Psychology, 40,* 335–339.

Anastasi, A. (1976). *Psychological testing* (4th ed.). New York: Macmillan.

Anderson, S., & Brown, C. (1997). Self-efficacy as determinant of career maturity in urban and rural high school seniors. *Journal of Career Assessment, 5,* 305–315.

Anthony, W. A., & Jansen, M. (1984). Predicting the vocational capacity of the chronically mentally ill. *American Psychologist, 39,* 537–544.

Azrin, N., Flores, T., & Kaplan, S. (1975). Job finding club: A group-assisted program of obtaining employment. *Behavioral Research and Therapy, 13*(1), 17–27.

Barlow, J., Wright, C., & Cullen, L. (2002). A job-seeking self-efficacy scale for people with physical disabilities: Preliminary development and psychometric testing. *British Journal of Guidance and Counseling, 30,* 37–53.

Baron, R. C. (2000). *The past and future career patterns of people with serious mental illness: A qualitative inquiry* [Monograph]. Washington, DC: National Institute of Disability and Rehabilitation Research (H133F980011).

Benz, M. R., & Halpern, A. S. (1993). Vocational and transition services needed and received by students with disabilities during their last year of high school. *Career Development for Exceptional Individuals, 16,* 197–211.

Benz, M. R., Yovanoff, P., & Doren, B. (1997). School-to-Work components that predict postschool success for students with and without disabilities. *Exceptional Children, 63,* 151–165.

Beveridge, S., Craddock, S., Liesener, J., Stapleton, M., & Hershenson, D. (2002). INCOME: A framework for conceptualizing the career development of persons with disabilities. *Rehabilitation Counseling Bulletin, 45,* 195–206.

Blanck, P. D. (1998). *The Americans with Disabilities Act and the emerging workforce.* Washington, DC: American Association on Mental Retardation.

Brown, M. T. (1995). The career development of African Americans: Theoretical and empirical issues. In F. T. Leong (Ed.), *Career development and vocational behavior of racial and ethnic minorities (pp. 7–36).* Mahwah, NJ: Erlbaum.

Brown, S. D., & Lent, R. W. (1996). A social cognitive framework for career choice counseling. *Career Development Quarterly, 44,* 354–366.

Burkhauser, R., & Wittenburg, D. (1996). How current disability transfer policies discourage work: Analysis from the 1990 SIPP. *Journal of Vocational Rehabilitation, 7,* 9–27.

Caston, H. L., & Watson, A. L. (1990). Vocational assessment and rehabilitation outcomes. *Rehabilitation Counseling Bulletin, 34,* 34, 61–67.

Coates, J. F., Jarrat, J., & Mahaffie, J. B. (1991). Future work. *The Futurist, 25*(3), 9–19.

Conte, L. (1983). Vocational development theories and the disabled person: Oversight or deliberate omission? *Rehabilitation Counseling Bulletin, 26,* 316–328.

Conyers, L., & Szymanski, E. M. (1998). The effectiveness of an integrated career intervention on college students with and without disabilities. *Journal of Postsecondary Education and Disability, 13*(1), 23–34.

Diksa, E., & Rogers, S. E. (1996). Employer concerns about hiring persons with Psychiatric disability: Results of employer attitudes questionnaire. *Rehabilitation Counseling Bulletin, 40,* 31–44.

Enright, M. S. (1997). The impact of short-term career development program on people with disabilities. *Rehabilitation Counseling Bulletin, 40,* 285–301.

Fabian, E. (1992). Longitudinal outcomes in supported employment: A survival analysis. *Rehabilitation Psychology, 37*(1), 23–25.

Fabian, E. (2000). Social cognitive theory of careers and individuals with serious mental health disorders: Implications for psychiatric rehabilitation practice. *Psychiatric Rehabilitation Journal, 23,* 262–269.

Feurstein, M., & Thebarge, R. (1991). Perceptions of disability and occupational stress as discriminators of work disability in patients with chronic pain. *Journal of Occupational Rehabilitation, 1,* 185–195.

Gilbride, D. D., Stensrud, R., & Johnson, M. (1994). Current models of job placement and employer development: Research, competencies and educational considerations. *Rehabilitation Education, 7,* 215–239.

Hackett, G., & Betz, N. E. (1981). A self-efficacy approach to the career development of women. *Journal of Vocational Behavior, 18,* 326–339.

Hackett, G., Betz, N. E., Casas, J. M., & Rocha-Singh, I. A. (1992). Gender, ethnicity, and social cognitive factors predicting the academic achievement of students in engineering. *Journal of Counseling Psychology, 39,* 527–538.

Hackett, G., & Byars, A. M. (1996). Social cognitive theory and the career development of African American women. *Career Development Quarterly, 44,* 322–340.

Hagner, D. (2003). Job development and job search assistance. In E. Szymanski & R. M. Parker (Eds.), *Work and disability: Issues and strategies in career development and job placement* (2nd ed., pp. 343–372). Austin, TX: ProEd.

Hagner, D., & DiLeo, D. (1993). *Working together: Workplace culture, supported employment, and persons with disabilities.* Cambridge, MA: Brookline.

Hahn, H. (1993). The political implications of disability definitions and data. *Journal of Disability Policy Studies, 4,* 41–52.

Hayward, B., & Schmidt-Davis, H. (2000). *Fourth interim report: Characteristics and outcomes of transitional youth in VRA longitudinal study of the vocational rehabilitation program* (Submitted by the Research Triangle Institute to the Rehabilitation Services Administration of the U.S. Department of Education). Retrieved June 23, 2002, from: http://www.als.uiuc.edu/dri.

Henderson, C. (1999). *College freshmen with disabilities: Statistical year 1998.* Washington, DC: American Council on Education.

Hennessey, J. C. (1997). Factors affecting the work efforts of disabled-worker beneficiaries. *Social Security Bulletin, 60,* 3–19.

Hershenson, D. B. (1996). Work adjustment: A neglected area in career counseling. *Journal of Counseling and Development, 74,* 442–446.

Hitchings, W. E., Luzzo, D. A., Retish, P., Horvbath, M., & Ristow, R. S. (1998). Identifying the career development needs of college students with disabilities. *Journal of College Student Development, 39*(1), 23–32.

Hountenville, A. (2000). *Economics of disability research report #2: Estimates of employment rates for persons with disabilities in the United States by state, 1980–1998.* Ithaca, NY: Cornell University, Research and Rehabilitation Training Center for Economic Research on Employment Policy for Persons with Disabilities.

Hurst, D., & Smerdon, B. (2000). *Postsecondary students with disabilities: Enrollment, services, and persistence. Status in brief.* Washington, DC: National Center for Educational Statistics.

Jones, P. W. (1995). Holland vocational personality codes and people with visual disabilities: A need for caution. *Review, 27,* 53–63. Retrieved August 10, 2003, from http://www.search.epnet.com.

Kosciulek, J. (1998). Empowering the life choices of people with disabilities through career counseling. In N. C. Gysbers, M. J. Heppner, & J. A. Johnson (Eds.), *Career counseling: Process, issues and techniques* (pp. 109–121). Needham Heights, MA: Allyn & Bacon.

Kohler, P., & Chapman, S. (1999). *Literature review on school-to-work transition.* Retrieved July 10, 2003, from http://www.ed.uiuc.edu/sped/tri/stwpurpose.htm.

Krause, J. S., & Anson, C. A. (1997). Adjustment after spinal cord injury: Relationship to participation in employment or educational activities. *Rehabilitation Counseling Bulletin, 40,* 202–214.

Lent, R. W., Brown, S. D., & Hackett, G. (1994). Toward a unifying social cognitive theory of career and academic interest, choice and performance. *Journal of Vocational Behavior, 45,* 79–122.

Lindstrom, L. E., & Benz, M. R. (2002). Phases of career development: Case studies of young women with learning disabilities. *Exceptional Children, 69*(1), 67–83.

Loewen, G. (1993). Improving access to post-secondary education. *Psychosocial Rehabilitation Journal, 17,* 151–153.

Luecking, R., & Fabian, E. (2000). Paid internships and employment success for youth in transition. *Career Development for Exceptional Individuals, 23,* 205–221.

MacDonald-Wilson, K., Rogers, S. E., & Anthony, W. A. (2001). Unique issues in assessing work function among individuals with psychiatric disabilities. *Journal of Occupational Rehabilitation, 11,* 217–232.

Mank, D. M. (1994). The underachievement of supported employment: A call for reinvestment. *Journal of Disability Policy Studies, 5*(2), 1–24.

Miller, P. S. (2000). The evolving ADA. In P. D. Blanck (Ed.), *Employment, disability, and the Americans with Disabilities Act* (pp. 3–18). Evanston, IL: Northwestern University Press.

Mori, A. A. (1982). Career attitudes and job knowledge among junior high school regular, special, and academically talented students. *Career Development for Exceptional Individuals, 5,* 62–69.

Mowbray, C. T., Bybee, D., Harris, S. N., & McCrohan, N. (1995). Predictors of work status and future work orientation in people with psychiatric disability. *Psychiatric Rehabilitation Journal, 53,* 31–42.

Nagi, S. Z. (1979). The concept and measurement of disability. In E. D. Berkowitz (Ed.), *Disability policies and government programs* (pp. 1–15). New York: Praeger.

National Council on Disability. (2000). *2000 N.O.D./Harris survey of Americans with disabilities.* Washington, DC: Louis Harris & Associates.

National Council on Disability. (2003). *The Americans with Disabilities Act Policy Brief: Righting the ADA.* Retrieved June 27, 2003, from http://www.ncd.gov/newsroom/publications/extentoflimiations.html.

National Institute on Disability and Rehabilitation Research. (1995). *Federal statutory definitions of disability.* Falls Church, VA: Conwal Inc. (ERIC Document Reproduction Service No. ED 427 472).

National Science Foundation. (1999). *Women, minorities, and persons with disabilities in science and engineering.* Washington, DC: Author.

Neff, W. (1967). *Work and human behavior.* New York: Atherton Press.

Noble, J. H. (1998). Policy reform dilemmas in promoting employment of persons with severe mental illnesses. *Psychiatric Services, 49,* 775–781.

Ochs, L. A., & Roessler, R. T. (2001). Students with disabilities: How ready are they for the 21st century? *Rehabilitation Counseling Bulletin, 44,* 170–176.

Olshansky, S. (1976). Counseling, state vocational rehabilitation agencies, and related matters. *Rehabilitation Literature, 37, 9,* 263–267.

Paganos, R. J., & DuBois, D. C. (1999). Career self-efficacy development and students with learning disabilities. *Learning Disabilities Research and Practice, 4*(1), 25–34.

Parker, R., & Schaller, J. L. (2003). Vocational assessment and disability. In E. M. Szymanski & R. M. Parker (Eds.), *Work and disability: Issues and strategies in career development and job placement* (2nd ed., pp. 155–200). Austin, TX: ProEd.

Patterson, J., DeLaGarza, D., & Schaller, J. (1997). Rehabilitation counseling practice: Considerations and interventions. In R. Parker & E. Szymanski (Eds.), *Rehabilitation counseling: Basics and beyond* (3rd ed., pp. 269–302), Austin, TX: ProEd.

Pledger, C. (2003). Discourse on disability and rehabilitation issues: Opportunities for psychology. *American Psychologist, 58,* 279–285.

Power, P. (2000). *A guide to vocational assessment* (3rd ed.). Austin, TX: ProEd.

Regenold, M., Sherman, M. F., & Fenzel, M. (1999). Getting back to work: Self efficacy as a predictor of employment outcome. *Psychiatric Rehabilitation Journal, 22,* 361–367.

Research Triangle International. (2003). *Longitudinal Study of the Vocational Rehabilitation Services Program.* Retrieved June 23, 2003, from http://www.als.uiuc.edu/dri.

Roessler, R. T. (1987). Work, disability, and the future: Promoting employment for people with disabilities. *Journal of Counseling and Development, 66,* 188–190.

Rojewski, J. W. (1993). Theoretical structure of career maturity for rural adolescents with learning disabilities. *Career Development for Exceptional Individuals, 16,* 39–52.

Savickas, M. L. (1990, January). *Career interventions that create hope.* Paper presented at the annual meeting of the National Career Development Association, Scottsdale, AZ.

Schwochau, S., & Blanck, P. D. (1999). The economics of the Americans with Disabilities Act: Part III: Does the ADA disable the disabled? *Berkeley Journal of Employment and Labor Law, 21,* 271–313.

Shahnasarian, M. (2001). Career rehabilitation: Integration of vocational rehabilitation and career development in the twenty-first century. *Career Development Quarterly, 49,* 275–283.

Slemon, J. C., & Shafir, U. (1997, March). *Academic self-efficacy of post-secondary students with and without learning disabilities.* Paper presented at the annual meeting of the American Educational Research Association, Chicago.

Social Security Administration. (2002). *Annual statistical report on the Social Security Disability Insurance policy, 2001.* Retrieved July 23, 2003, from http://www.ssa.gov/policy/docs/statcomps/di_asr/2001/index.html#editions.

Stodden, R. A., & Dowrick, P. W. (2000). Postsecondary education and employment of adults with disabilities. *American Rehabilitation, 24*(3), 23–24.

Stone, E. F., Stone, D. L., & Dipboye, R. L. (1992). Stigmas in organizations: Race, handicaps, and physical unattractiveness. In K. Kelly (Ed.), *Issues, theory and research in industrial and organizational psychology* (pp. 385–457). New York: Elsevier Science.

Super, D. E., Savickas, M. L., & Super, C. M. (1996). A life-span, life-space approach to careers development. In D. Brown, L. Brooks, & Associates (Eds.), *Career choice and development* (3rd ed., pp. 121–178). San Francisco: Jossey-Bass.

Swain, J., & French, S. (2000). Towards an affirmation model of disability. *Disability and Society, 15,* 569–582.

Szymanski, E. M. (1999). Disability, job stress, the changing nature of careers, and the career resilience portfolio. *Rehabilitation Counseling Bulletin, 42,* 279–289.

Szymanski, E. M., Enright, M. S., Hershenson, D. B., & Ettinger, J. M. (2003). Career development theories, constructs and research: Implications for people with disabilities. In E. M. Szymanski & R. M. Parker (Eds.), *Work and disability: Issues and strategies in career development and job placement* (2nd ed., pp. 91–153). Austin, TX: ProEd.

Szymanski, E. M., Hershenson, D. B., Enright, M. S., & Ettinger, J. M. (1996). Career development theories, constructs, and research: Implications for people with disabilities.

In E. M. Szymanski & R. M. Parker (Eds.), *Work and disability: Issues and strategies in career development and job placement* (pp. 79–126). Austin, TX: ProEd.

Szymanski, E. M., Ryan, C., Merz, M. A., Trevino, B., & Johnston-Rodriguez, S. (1996). Psychosocial and economic aspects of work: Implications for people with disabilities. In E. M. Szymanski & R. M. Parker (Eds.), *Work and disability: Issues and strategies in career development and job placement* (pp. 9–31). Austin, TX: ProEd.

Szymanski, E. M., & Trueba, H. (1994). Castification of people with disabilities: Potential disempowering aspects of castification in disability services. *Journal of Rehabilitation, 60,* 12–20.

Trent, J. W. (1994). *Inventing the feeble mind: A history of mental retardation the United States.* Berkeley: University of California Press.

Turnball, R. H. (1990). *Free appropriate public education: The law and children with disabilities.* Denver, CO: Love.

Unger, D. D. (2001). *Employer's attitudes toward people with disabilities in the workforce: Myths or realities* (In Employers views of workplace supports: Virginia Commonwealth University Charter Business Round Tables' National Study of Employer's Experience with Workers with Disabilities). Retrieved June 16, 2003, from http://www.worksupport.com.

United States Census Bureau. (2000). *Disability data.* Retrieved July 2, 2003, from http://www.census.gov/hhes/www/disable/disabstat2k.html.

Wagner, M., & Blackorby, J. (1996). Transition from high school to work or college: How special education student's fare. *Special Education for Students with Disabilities, 6*(1), 103–120.

Wagner, M., Blackorby, J., Cameto, R., Hebbeler, K., & Newman, L. (1993). *The transition experiences of young people with disabilities: A summary of findings from the National Longitudinal Study of Special Education Students.* Menlo Park, CA: SRI International.

Wehman, P., West, M., & Kregel, J. (1999). Supported employment program development and research needs: Looking ahead to the Year 2000. *Education and Training in Mental Retardation and Development Disabilities, 34*(1), 3–19.

Westbrook, M. T., Legge, V., & Pennay, M. (1993). Attitudes towards disabilities in a multicultural society. *Social Science and Medicine, 36,* 615–623.

Wewiorski, N., & Fabian, E. (2004). Association between demographic and diagnostic factors and employment outcomes for people with psychiatric disabilities: A synthesis of recent research. *Mental Health Services Research, 6*(1), 9–21.

Will, M. (1984, June). Bridges from school to working life. *Interchange,* 2–6.

Willis, S. (2002). *The relationship of social cognitive variables to outcomes among young adults with emotional disturbance.* Unpublished doctoral dissertation, University of Maryland, College Park.

Wiseman, R. L., Emry, R. A., & Morgan, D. (1988). Predicting academic success for disabled students in higher education. *Research in Higher Education, 28,* 255–269.

Wittenburg, D., & Stapleton, D. (2000). *Review of longitudinal data on the school to work transition for youth with disabilities* (Final report submitted to the Department of Education, National Institute on Disability and Rehabilitation). Retrieved July 23, 2003, from http://www.ilr.cornell.edu/rrtc/papers.html.

World Health Organization. (2001). *International classification of functioning, disability and health* (Final draft). Retrieved July 25, 2003, from: http://www.who.int/icidh.

Yelin, E., & Katz, P. (1994). Labor force trends of persons with and without disabilities. *Monthly Quarterly, 72,* 593–620.

CHAPTER 24

Broadening Our Understanding of Work-Bound Youth: A Challenge for Career Counseling

Cindy L. Juntunen and Kara Brita Wettersten

Tᴏ TRANSITION FROM school to work (STW) has been a focus of American society since its inception, with founding fathers such as Thomas Jefferson and Benjamin Franklin writing on the importance of training citizenry for employment (Herr, 1997). Career development and counseling, as distinct professional foci, can also trace their roots to the school-to-work reformer Frank Parsons (1909), who at the beginning of the twentieth century sought to understand how young people could find the best match between their aptitudes/interests and employment opportunities. Despite these influential markers in our history, numerous writers in the past two decades have commented on the substantial lack of policy, programs, and research in the area of school-to-work transitions (Blustein, Juntunen, & Worthington, 2000; Lent & Worthington, 1999), particularly in comparison to the school-to-college transition. Blustein et al. wrote, "Although the United States has some of the finest university training in the world, our educational preparation for those who move into the workforce directly after high school is far less systematic, empowering, and equitable" (p. 435).

In response to a growing recognition of need, Congress passed the School-to-Work Opportunities Act (STWOA) in 1994. The act had as its chief aim the provision of services to prepare students (from kindergarten through grade 12) for employment after high school. As such, STWOA had three main elements:

1. School-based learning activities that directly relate to work preparation.
2. Work-based (i.e., on-the-job) learning activities that provide students with relevant and specific work experiences.
3. Connecting activities that link school activities to work activities and work activities to school activities.

The passing of STWOA was intended to provide needed programs for thousands of students who were not college bound. However, school-to-work programs were plagued with difficulties, including sparse implementation across the country; lack of employer, parent, and teacher involvement; and lack of effective and multiculturally sensitive assessments to measure success or failure (Blustein et al., 2000). Additionally, STWOA funding ended in 2001, leaving well-intended programs to flounder at the starting gates.

Despite the end of the School-to-Work Opportunities Act, the movement to recognize and meet the needs of work-bound (or non-college-bound) youth continues to grow (e.g., Fouad, 1997; Phillips, Blustein, Jobin-Davis, & White, 2002; Worthington & Juntunen, 1997). For example, in 1999, the American Psychological Association (APA) formed a multidisciplinary task force that reported on the characteristics and needs of youth who are making school-to-work transitions and on the policies and programs that assist in that transition (APA School-to-Work Task Force, 1999). Researchers specific to the fields of career counseling and vocational psychology have also made gains in examining, implementing, and evaluating specific factors related to the needs of work-bound youth (Fouad, 1997; Phillips et al., 2002).

While the concerns of youth making the school-to-work transition have gained scholarly and clinical momentum (Blustein, Phillips, Jobin-Davis, Finkelberg, & Roarke, 1997; Worthington & Juntunen, 1997), the plight of work-bound but out-of-school youth has not (Herr, 1995). This lack of attention is disappointing, especially in light of strong indications that this population is underserved and underresourced. For example, a recent General Accounting Office (GAO) document indicates that even though 30% of the funding meant to facilitate youth employment is required to go to out-of-school youth, providers of those services have a difficult time utilizing that funding because they cannot reach the individuals who make up this component of the work-bound youth population (GAO, 2002).

Further evidence of the need to assist out-of-school youth is provided by a quick survey of dropout rates and unemployment statistics. Like the general population of work-bound youth, out-of-school work-bound youth make up a diverse group of people. However, for the sake of description, this population may be divided into two groups: those with high school degrees and those without. As to those without, the Bureau of Labor Statistics (BLS) reported that in the year between fall 2000 and fall 2001, roughly half a million youth dropped out of secondary school, and the unemployment rate for these youth was approximately 36% (BLS, 2002).

Given the changing political and economic landscapes—and increasing knowledge base—related to work-bound youth, this chapter has three primary goals:

1. To provide an overview of work-bound youth, including definitions, characteristics, and statistics.
2. To examine the current multidisciplinary knowledge concerning the school-to-work transition.
3. To explore the issues and concerns of out-of-school work-bound youth, including youth who are participants in the juvenile justice system, are welfare recipients, or are victims of domestic violence.

Throughout this chapter is an implicit message about the need for counselors and psychologists to take on the challenge first posed by Parsons (1909): to better assist our nation's youth in their process of finding meaningful employment and satisfying lives.

OVERVIEW OF THE WORK-BOUND YOUTH POPULATION

Work-bound youth have typically been described as those individuals who intend to enter the labor market after they leave high school (Herr, 1997; Worthington & Juntunen, 1997). Herr (1995) noted that individuals who make up the work-bound population are heterogeneous in terms of race, ethnicity, gender, and intellectual ability. We concur that diversity is an essential aspect of work-bound youth and that diversity awareness must be kept in the forefront of interventions targeting this population. We also seek to expand that definition to include those individuals between the ages of 16 and 24 who seek to enter the labor force and, whether in some type of school or not, neither have nor currently intend to seek their bachelor's degree. In contrast to the first definition, this second definition includes both those who are making the school-to-work transition and those youth who may have been out of school or work but are now seeking employment (i.e., the out-of-school-to-work transition).

STUDENTS AND RECENT HIGH SCHOOL GRADUATES

It is eye opening to consider the number of individuals who do not seek a college education after leaving high school. In a BLS publication titled *College Enrollment and Work Activity of Year 2001 High School Graduates* (2002), approximately 900,000 individuals—39% of the total graduating population—were non-college bound. Approximately 80% of those high school graduates who were not enrolled in college entered the labor force. Of those individuals, 21% were unemployed. In our expanded definition of work-bound youth, it is also worthwhile to consider those individuals who start college and do not finish. According to the Education Trust (2000), roughly 25% of those who start college at a four-year school do not make it to their sophomore year, and this figure is roughly 50% for students in two-year colleges.

Census data collected in 2001 suggest that gender and race/ethnicity differences in unemployment exist for high school graduates (with no college) between 18 and 24 years of age. For example, 15% of males in this population are unemployed, and 12% of females are unemployed. The unemployment rate for 18- to 24-year-old African Americans with high school diplomas (and no college coursework) is approximately 23%. For Hispanics, this same statistic is 11%; for Asians and Pacific Islanders, 13%; and for Whites, 12%. Employment opportunities for this cohort appear to be largely in the areas of service, administrative support, and sales (U.S. Census Bureau, 2002).

OUT-OF-SCHOOL YOUTH

As to 16- to 24-year-olds who are not engaged in formal educational activities, more men (89%) than women (76%) are in the labor force (BLS, 2002). Differences were also noted in terms of race/ethnicity. For example, African Americans had the lowest labor force participation (76%) followed by Hispanics (80%) and Whites (84%). Racial-ethnic differences in unemployment were also noted by the BLS, with out-of-school African Americans facing the highest unemployment rate (22%), followed by Hispanics (12%) and Whites (10%; BLS, 2002).

When specifically looking at high school dropouts, these numbers show even wider divergence. As already noted, the unemployment rate for high school dropouts is 36% (BLS, 2002). Roughly 24% of women and 18% of men who drop out of high school are unemployed (BLS, 2002). This difference may indicate that men and women drop out of high school under different circumstances. According to the BLS (2000), employment is the goal for both men and women who leave high school and enter the labor force. However, women additionally face the responsibilities of child care and parenting more often than the men in this same sample.

The Education Trust (2000) reported that dropout rates also vary significantly by race and socioeconomic status (SES). Specifically, approximately 3% of Whites, 5% of African Americans, and 10% of Latinos drop out of high school annually. Native American statistics are not reported by either the BLS or the Education Trust, but Northern Arizona University (2003) reported Native American dropout rates to be approximately 30%. The dropout rate in the 1990s ranged between 9% and 12% for individuals from a low SES group and between 1% and 3% for people in a high SES bracket.

SOCIAL AND FAMILIAL CHARACTERISTICS OF WORK-BOUND YOUTH

Work-bound youth make up some of the primary infrastructure of our country (Herr, 1995). Despite the lack of resources we make available to them to fulfill their roles, as a society, it is clear that we cannot operate without their presence. Herr (1997) stated that "employment-bound students constitute such an important proportion of the labor force, certainly of the technical, skilled, clerical, retailing, and distribution system of the nation, that their needs must be given national, state, and local priority" (p. 5). To meet the needs of work-bound youth, we must understand some of the possible characteristics (beyond demographic information) that make up success and failure within this population.

For example, Kenny, Blustein, Chaves, Grossman, and Gallagher (2003) looked at a series of variables believed to predict school engagement, career aspirations, and work role salience among inner-city school youth. The variables of social support, familial (kinship) support, and perceived barriers were shown to statistically predict the three dependent variables. Kenny et al.'s study looked at perceived barriers as they relate to school and career. A common theme in the school-to-work literature is barriers related to discrimination, gender, and parenthood. Discrimination can take the form of racial or ethnic discrimination, both real (Wilson, 1996) and perceived (Flores & O'Brien, 2002; McWhirter, 1997). Similar issues are present with real and perceived gender discrimination (Flores & O'Brien, 2002; Maynard, 1995) and the perceived discrimination and actual poverty of single young parents. For example, Maynard found that even five years after giving birth to a child, 43% of teenage mothers and their children were living at or below the poverty line. Maynard also found that approximately 30% of teenage parents drop out of high school.

Finally, all work-bound youth share one characteristic: their youth—a factor that might work against them with many employers. A passage in the seminal report, *The Forgotten Half: Non-College Youth in America,* reads:

> The basic truth faced by too many youth is that regardless of how well schools do their job and regardless of how well high school graduates learn basic skills, most large, established employers seldom hire recent high school graduates for career-ladder positions, even at the entry-level. (William T. Grant, 1988, p. 26)

The APA's (1999) *Report of the School-to-Work Task Force* noted that another barrier that needs to be addressed within the school-to-work transition is related to the nature of jobs available in our economy. Specifically, they noted that the largest growth areas in employment are in jobs dealing with computers and technology. However, the degree to which schools teach these skills, and more directly addressed by the APA, the degree to which *girls* gain skills in computers and technology, impacts the success of the school-to-work transition.

The APA task force on school-to-work transition is not the first to discuss a model of school-to-work that includes the impact of perceived employment opportunities on school achievement and meaningful employment of youth. In fact, the rocky relationship among the three variables has often been discussed (Bellair & Roscigno, 2000; Blustein et al., 1997; Hartnagel, 1998). In a qualitative study of students making a school-to-work transition, Blustein et al. found that students who are seeking work after leaving high school perceive that their coursework is not relevant to gainful employment. Bellair and his colleagues have also consistently made a link between perception of a lack of employment opportunities and delinquency in adolescence (Bellair & Roscigno, 2000; Bellair, Roscigno, & McNulty, 2003; see also Baron & Hartnagel, 1997; Crutchfield & Pitchford, 1997; Hartnagel, 1998).

Finally, it is important to discuss youth who have immigrated to the United States from other countries. According to the BLS report titled *Trends in Youth Employment: Data from the Current Population Survey* (2000), youth born outside the United States are less likely to be employed. Indeed, immigrant youth face a range of general and country-specific barriers. General barriers can include ESL difficulties, discrimination, lack of (U.S.-based) job search skills, and lack of community contacts to assist with employment networking. There is a surprising lack of research and programs offered by governmental agencies concerning the career paths of immigrant youth.

THE TRANSITION FROM SCHOOL TO WORK

According to Ray Marshall, former U.S. Secretary of Labor, "America has the worst school-to-work transition process of any industrialized nation (reported in Wilson, 1996, p. 216)." There are few systematic services in place to help high school students and graduates make the transition to work. Further, many American employers are reluctant to hire youth until they have had some work experience, particularly for jobs that are accompanied by benefits, adequate salaries, and advancement opportunities. Wilson argued that this delay in hiring work-bound youth has several negative consequences for both youth and the U.S. labor force. Specifically, it hampers the ability of employers to influence new workers during their earliest years of work, it eliminates the connection employers have to schools that would allow them to communicate about the changing needs of the workplace, and it separates school achievement from workplace achievement, undermining at least some of the incentive for academic success (Wilson, 1996).

Historically, the field of career counseling has contributed to the emphasis on the work transition of college-bound youth, demonstrated by the extensive attention paid to the career development experience of college students throughout the applied and empirical literature base. However, efforts by numerous authors (Blustein et al., 2000; Lent, O'Brien, & Fassinger, 1998; Solberg, Howard, Blustein, & Close, 2002; Worthington & Juntunen, 1997) have sought to remedy this bias, and the result is a growing understanding of the school-to-work transition and increased potential to provide valuable interventions for work-bound youth. Of particular importance are the contributions of vocational psychology to the theoretical understanding of the school-to-work transition. A 1999 special issue of the *Career Development Quarterly* (Lent & Worthington, 1999) is an essential contribution to this topic. The volume highlights the several ways career counseling can both inform and be informed by school-to-work issues. Certainly, the authors make it clear that there is a role for vocational psychology within school-to-work efforts. Yet, as the following discussion demonstrates, that role has not been easy to define or claim.

SCHOOL-TO-WORK POLICY: ECONOMIC AND PROGRAM DEVELOPMENT IMPLICATIONS

The transition from school to work is a developmental process experienced by most youth, and counselors are typically focused on what is most likely to assist a given individual in making a successful transition. This may occur within a formal school-to-work (STW) program or on an as-needed basis within or outside the school setting. Nonetheless, it is important to recognize that the STW transition, as a social rather than personal experience, exists within a political and economic context.

Economic Implications   As an educational reform effort, the STW transition has been addressed through numerous acts of legislative and federal appropriations, relying on various programs and interventions, beginning with the Smith-Hughes Act of 1917, which mandated the first federal support for vocational education in the United States. The Vocational Education Act of 1963 (and expansions in 1968 and 1976), the Carl D. Perkins Vocational Education Act of 1984 (renewed in 1990 and 1998), and the School-to-Work Opportunities Act (STWOA) of 1994 have all had a significant effect on the structure of vocational education (Rojewski, 2002), now widely referred to as career and technical education (CTE). For additional information on these policy initiatives, see Blustein et al. (2000), Rojewski (2002), and Worthington and Juntunen (1997). Currently, the Workforce Investment Act (WIA) of 1998 mandates three separate streams of funding to streamline employment and training services: youth, adults, and displaced workers. At least 30% of funding from the youth stream must be allocated to non-school youth, but the remaining 70% can be used to support in-school youth in employment training, with an emphasis on at-risk youth.

The nature of work has changed, from farms and factories to technology that spans international boundaries. But the emphasis of the STWOA, Perkins III, and the WIA echo the 1917 Smith-Hughes Act by mandating secondary education programs designed to better prepare youth to be effective members of the labor force. It is important to remember that the motivation behind these initiatives is largely economic; even with an emphasis on reaching all students and serving the underserved, the goal is to better prepare workers for the labor force, not necessarily to make the labor force more accessible or responsible to workers.

To meet that economic goal, each of these government programs has been accompanied by significant federal, state, and local funds. However, the resources dedicated to support work-bound youth are still less than 10% of the resources afforded those who complete college (Worthington & Juntunen, 1997). Based on information published by the United States General Accounting Office (GAO, 2003a, 2003b), federal support of approximately $950 per student is available for each work-bound student, compared to approximately $11,744 for each college student (of which roughly 75% is from federal loans that will likely be repaid in the future). Further, a comparison of allocations between 1999 and 2003 demonstrates only a nominal increase, and in some cases a decrease, in funding each year (GAO, 2003a).

Implications for Program Development   Several common guiding principles exist within the aforementioned collection of STW policies and initiatives. In one way or another, each called for an integration of academic and career education, a strategy for coordinating the STW transition, training in skills that meet the labor force needs of the day, and revisions in programming to accommodate changing workforce demographics (Rojewski, 2002). However, the initiatives themselves did not identify the specific skills that youth would need to be successful contributors to the workforce.

Those skills were identified by the Secretary's Commission for Achieving Necessary Skills (SCANS), which produced a set of five competencies and a three-part foundation of skills deemed necessary for successful job performance, even though they are not generally part of the traditional curriculum leading to a high school diploma (SCANS, 1992). The five competencies, which are considered essential workplace know-how, are the ability to productively use (1) resources, (2) interpersonal skills, (3) information, (4) systems, and (5) technology. The three foundation skills that must be achieved are (1) basic skills, such as reading, writing, mathematics, and listening; (2) thinking skills, such as the ability to learn, reason, and solve problems; and (3) personal qualities, including responsibility, self-esteem, and integrity.

The recommendations gathered from the SCANS (1992) report reflect an important change in focus for educational reform (Blustein et al., 2000). Although supporting the responsibility of schools to prepare youth for work, the SCANS report also provided specific recommendations for industry. Employers were explicitly encouraged to change their approach to human resource development. Instead of considering only which individual was the best applicant for a given position, emphasis was placed on the responsibility of employers to develop human resources in the firm, the community, and the nation.

With the common goals of educational reform initiatives and an articulated set of skills addressing the roles of both schools and employers, the basic principles of coordinating the STW transition would appear to be in place. However, the differing emphases of government and educational reform initiatives have, not surprisingly, generated a broad array of specific programs designed to facilitate the transition from school to work. Further, these programs vary on the basis of the needs of individual communities and school districts.

Nonetheless, seven contemporary models of career and technical education have been identified by Blustein et al. (2000) and Rojewski (2002): tech prep, career academies, youth apprenticeships, school-based enterprises, cooperative education (noted only by Rojewski, 2002), career pathways (described in Blustein et al., 2000, as occupation-academic cluster programs), and integrated vocational and academic education.

Also known as 2 + 2 programs, *tech prep* programs emphasize technology-related instruction and occupations, generally by linking the last two years of high school with the first two years of community college. This leads to an associate degree or certificate in the specific career area. Math, science, technology, and communications are the common academic core and are seen as being relevant for all career areas. This experience combines academic rigor with applied instruction and prepares students for continuing education to the baccalaureate degree as well.

Career academies are school-within-a-school programs that focus on a specific industry, wherein a small number of students move as a cohort through most coursework and on-the-job training in the industry. A team of educators that stays with them throughout their education teaches the cohort, and employers provide ongoing training specific to the workplace. The emphasis on career fields provides some flexibility for students, and there is an assumption that the career focus might increase retention of at-risk students.

A variation on career academies, *occupation-academic cluster programs* are larger programs that allow all students in a given high school to take courses that are linked to a cluster of occupations. Students take introductory, career-related courses and then pursue work-based learning. Career pathways are mandated in several states (Castellano, Stringfield, & Stone, 2002). They result in a high school curriculum that is organized around a cluster of occupations that require similar skills and knowledge but may differ in terms of required education and training (e.g., engineering, manufacturing, and industrial technology can prepare a student for a job as an engineer or a machinist).

Youth apprenticeship programs use the workplace as a learning environment and link students to a mentor in the workplace. Classroom instruction emphasizes the integration of academic and vocational learning, and the product is a certificate or diploma demonstrating that the student has the knowledge and skills required by a specific workplace. This arrangement requires that employers make significant changes in the workplace, as mentoring and collaboration with the school are essential.

In a *school-based enterprise,* students essentially operate a business and are in charge of producing goods or services for sale to customers. This provides the application of academic knowledge to work and helps students gain an understanding of business. Generally, instructors maintain control of instructional activity, but the tasks of the business are largely completed by the students.

Work-based learning is the key component of *cooperative education,* which involves a written training agreement among the student, school, and employer. The work experience is typically paid, supervised, and worth academic credit. Often, this model is used by employers as a screening device to select new employees, an issue that can be viewed as a boon for the students' job search but a problem if the employer is putting workplace needs ahead of the students' training. This model typically follows a less formal or structured cooperation between academic and work-based learning.

As the name implies, *integrated vocational and academic education* balances theory with application and blends work-based and academic learning. This model requires increased communication and coordination among academic teachers, vocational teachers, and counselors. The key issue in this approach is for involved school professionals and community members to adapt school organization and philosophy to make the integrated education program appropriate for all students.

EVALUATING SCHOOL-TO-WORK PROGRAMS

Research on the effectiveness of school-to-work transition programs remains in the early stages, in part because of the wide variety of STW models. As was noted by Blustein et al. (2000), there remains a considerable need for more comprehensive program review and more specific research questions. Future research should particularly attend to the differential effectiveness of STW interventions across gender, cultural, socioeconomic, and age groups. However, a growing body of work is considering adolescent work experience, career education, and the school-to-work transition, and these efforts can inform school-to-work implementation. Selections from each of these areas are presented next.

Adolescent Employment   Because youth who work are less likely to be unemployed during early adulthood (Carr, Wright, & Brody, 1996), early employment may be particularly important for work-bound youth (Schoenhals, Tienda, & Schneider, 1998). However, there is some debate about whether work has a positive or negative effect on long-term outcomes, including education (Barling & Kelloway, 1999; Carr et al., 1996; Schoenhals et al., 1998). For example, Carr et al. analyzed data from a subset (including 2,716 youth) of the National Longitudinal Survey of Youth (NLSY) to address the long-term effects of youth employment. They found that working during high school was positively and significantly related to labor force participation, employment, and income, but negatively related to educational attainment, particularly for males. The authors concluded that the positive effect of work on earnings and employment outweighed the possible negative effect of less education, but also acknowledged that the latter could have a greater impact as time out of high school increased.

One factor that has been addressed in the debate about the value of adolescent work is the number of hours a student works each week. Some research has suggested that working a few hours a week can provide benefits in terms of academic achievement, improved work-related skills, and self-confidence (Mortimer, 2003; Quirk, Keith, & Quirk, 2001). These authors caution that employment is helpful when limited to fewer than 12 hours per week and that more hours in employment can contribute to academic problems (Quirk et al., 2001).

However, Schoenhals et al. (1998) analyzed the impact of employment on more than 15,000 10th-grade students and concluded that the consequences of adolescent employment were generally positive, even for students who worked substantially more hours each week. The employed students did demonstrate increased absenteeism from school, missing up to 1.3 days more each semester than students who were not working. However, students demonstrated no decrease in grades, time spent on homework, or time spent in leisure reading when they worked up to 20 hours per week. Those who worked more than 31 hours per week did reduce the time spent in leisure reading but not the other categories. The biggest change was noted in television viewing; all employed students spent less time watching television than nonemployed students. The authors stated "confidently that no serious adverse consequences of youth employment are operating through the outcomes" (p. 750) that they observed, at least through 10th grade.

Career Education   Plank (2001) determined that students at risk for noncompletion were less likely to drop out of high school when the ratio of career and technical education credits to academic credits was 3 to 4. Ratios either higher or lower than that were associated with increased likelihood of dropping out. Further, the author suggested that a balance of academic and CTE experiences might result in increased options after high school. However, the CTE-academic balance was also correlated with a slight reduction in standardized test scores in the core academic areas. Plank argued that the increased graduation rates for at-risk youth are worth this slight decrease. However, presently, the emphasis on standardized testing through the "No Child Left Behind" model of educational reform might dissuade some school administrators from embracing that idea. In fact, for one school included in another study (Castellano et al., 2002), the very existence of the school depended on the ability of students to pass a test. For such a school, the tradeoff of emphasizing increased graduation rates but with possibly lower test scores might be too high.

In a review of at-risk youth enrolled in career academies, Kemple and Snipes (2000) reported a decrease in dropout rates and increased attendance and graduation achievement among academy students, compared to nonacademy students. They attribute this, at least in part, to the interpersonal and academic support that career academies can provide. Interpersonal support, which is typified by the cohort model of career academies wherein students and a team of teachers work together over several years, requires a substantial investment by the school and may be beyond the resources of many institutions. These authors also suggested that the students should be drawn from a heterogeneous population of students, arguing that at-risk students are more likely to benefit if they work alongside more engaged students. Thus, interpersonal support might be provided by peers, making this emphasis more feasible for some schools.

School-to-Work Activities   Several studies have considered the effect of specific STW models. Because of space constraints, a comprehensive review of these models cannot be presented here, but several reviews can be easily accessed online. Examples of successful programs have been collected by the Manpower Demonstration Research Corporation (www.mdrc.org/sps/swish.cgi), the National Center for Research in Vocational Education, and the National Research and Dissemination Centers for Career and Technical Education (both archived at www.nccte.com). Far fewer examples of specific STW interventions are available in the counseling literature, although Blustein et al. (2000) identified several successful program components. In one example, Solberg et al. (2002) reported positive outcomes for a school-to-work-to-life (STWL) intervention implemented in the Milwaukee school system. The STWL curriculum was based on developmental-contextualism theory and included four linked components that empower youth to make their own decisions and shape their own career development. In a sample of 131 ninth-grade students involved in this program, students demonstrated improved grades, increased credits earned, improved passing rates, and greater attendance.

Due to the variety of STW models and the various ways in which they are implemented across communities and school districts, caution must be applied in the interpretation of individual evaluation findings. This is exemplified in one evaluation of Tech Prep programs (Hershey, Silverberg, Owens, & Hulsey, 1998), in which very few of the included Tech Prep programs included all of the prescribed Tech Prep components at the same time. Hershey et al. found that both students and parents resisted the lock-step sequence of courses that Tech Prep employs to prepare students to move into the local community or other two-year college. In fact, because the sequence was viewed as making preparation for a four-year college less likely, only 10% of the Tech Prep programs included in the study followed such a rigid structure. In another study (Bragg, 2001), the significant differences in execution across eight programs resulted in the conclusion that anywhere from 17% to 75% of students went to two-year colleges after graduation, and anywhere from 5% to 53% went to four-year colleges. These two studies illustrate a conundrum in the evaluation of STW programs: The very flexibility that is necessary to ensure that programs can deliver needed services to students in a given community creates significant challenges for comprehensive, rigorous evaluation.

A three-part evaluation study series, the National Evaluation of School-to-Work Implementation, reported on the impact of the School-to-Work Opportunities Act (STWOA; 1994). All three reports (Haimson & Bellotti, 2001; Hershey, Hudis, Silverberg, & Haimson, 1997; Hershey, Silverberg, Haimson, Hudis, & Jackson, 1999) concluded that only a limited number of students had participated in multiple career development activities that were meaningfully linked to one another. The most common activities were those that focused on increasing career awareness, such as interest inventories, presentations by various employers, and job shadowing opportunities, rather than the more intensive, paid internships or apprenticeships envisioned by the STWOA.

The work-based learning aspect of the STW effort presented several challenges. Although local partnerships were very enthusiastic about work-based learning, it was difficult to identify or develop employment activities that provided paid work experiences for more than a small percentage of students. However, on a more positive note, 16% of students did report having some kind of activity that linked work-based and school-based learning. In addition, by the time of the second report (Hershey et al., 1999), participation in career-related activities had doubled among work-bound students, helping to narrow the training gap with college-bound students.

The final report (Haimson & Bellotti, 2001) highlighted the challenges of establishing intensive work-based experiences, noting three contributing factors:

1. Workplace learning requires significant support (and expense) from school staff.
2. Employers can incur substantial costs and may not benefit directly because many students leave the employer upon graduation.
3. Tension exists between workplace activities and academic success.

Implications of the Evaluation Findings   Individual adolescents and young adults respond differently to the challenge of integrating school- and work-based learning activities, and gender, age, and cultural differences must be considered in both the development and effectiveness of such learning activities. However, the preceding research does demonstrate that, as a group, youth can receive benefits from working while in school, and these benefits may be particularly important for work-bound youth. Further, school-arranged work experiences, which are linked to academic activities, are more likely to help youth clarify their own work expectations, provide more valuable work-based learning, and increase school attendance and graduation rates among youth at risk for dropping out. However, implementing STW activities presents several challenges. Creating partnerships with local constituents (including schools, employers, parents, and students) is essential to meet local employment and labor force needs. Yet establishing and maintaining these partnerships is difficult. Counteracting stereotypes about vocational education and STW activities continues to be difficult, and convincing employers to participate is also challenging. Finally, the inconsistency in program funding and the absence of high-level support for STW initiatives leave local initiatives with limited support.

What Counselors Can Do

The turbulent history of STW initiatives suggests that many counselors will be unlikely to work directly within formal STW programs. However, most counselors and career development professionals *will* work with clients, either individually or in groups, who are experiencing the transition from school to work. Therefore, it is critical that career professionals develop the tools necessary to facilitate that transition or simply recognize the applicability of commonly used interventions to issues encountered by work-bound youth. These interventions can be organized into three broad categories: student-centered career exploration interventions, work-based interventions, and curriculum-based interventions.

Student-Centered Career Exploration Interventions   Student-based interventions focus on both identifying and developing the attributes of the individual, with the intention of fostering a successful match to the expectations of a workplace or multiple workplaces. As such, many interventions within this category are consistent with person-environment fit career theories. The value of person-environment strategies in the school-to-work transition has been highlighted by Swanson and Fouad (1999), who suggested several strategies for the school-to-work transition:

1. Provide sufficient opportunities and time for students to engage in exploration leading to self-knowledge.
2. Teach the basic components of self-knowledge, occupational knowledge, and the steps in decision making.
3. Focus adequate attention on the decision-making process and the implications of those decisions.
4. Evaluate the interventions and students' decisions periodically throughout the school-to-work transition.
5. Recognize that work-bound youth need particular knowledge of self and work and how to fit the two together, because they have fewer opportunities for trial and error than do college-attending youth.

Dykeman et al. (2001) have identified two large categories of interventions used by career counselors and other school professionals to foster individual career exploration: introductory interventions and advisory interventions. Introductory interventions are brief interventions designed to "awaken a student's interest in their own personal and professional growth" (p. 18). Interventions include career fairs and field trips, culturally sensitive aptitude assessments, bringing community members into the classroom, and providing guidance lessons on personal/social development, career development, and academic planning. Activities of this nature are designed to increase student awareness of opportunities and the diverse array of career options. Krumboltz and Worthington (1999) have suggested that counselors need to help students expand their interests and abilities, rather than focus on work that matches already existing interests. Introductory interventions support that goal, with the objective of increasing the individual student's field of perceived options.

Advising interventions can be defined as "the class of interventions designed to provide direction, resolve impediments, or sustain planfulness in students about their goals for the future" (Dykeman et al., 2001, p. 18). When working with work-bound students, the most relevant activities include career counseling and assessments, assistance with recruiting and interview skills, maintenance of a career library or resource center, and job-hunting preparation. Culturally appropriate assessments can be used to further student learning about both the self and the world of work, rather than simply providing information about possible matches between work and personal characteristics (Krumboltz & Worthington, 1999; Swanson & Fouad, 1999). In addition, both assessment information and developing plans to meet future goals can help students prepare for a world of work in which they are likely to change their jobs and occupations numerous times (Krumboltz & Worthington, 1999; Lent, Hackett, & Brown, 1999; Savickas, 1999, 2003). Encouraging youth to commit to a given occupation may be both "unrealistic and self-defeating" (Krumboltz & Worthington, 1999, p. 317) given current social trends. Instead, counselors can better assist youth by preparing them to see occupational change as normative, rather than problematic (Lent et al., 1999), and by fostering their problem-solving and adaptation skills.

Work-Based Interventions   Work-based interventions have been defined as a "class of interventions designed to promote both career and academic self-efficacy and motivation through sustained and meaningful interactions with work sites in the community" (Dykeman et al., 2001, p. 18). Many of the interventions in this category were included in the STW models previously described, as they include work placements such as cooperative education, internship, service learning, work-study, and youth apprenticeships.

Numerous activities that can occur outside formal STW programs are also included here. Counselors can assist students in gaining experience through numerous work preparation activities that require less structure than those previously listed, for example, job shadowing, mentorship programs, and work-based learning projects. Students who have the opportunity to visit a workplace for a short time period might be assigned to one worker to shadow that worker and better understand the actual responsibilities of a given job. An information interview can also be integrated into job shadowing or another learning project. In this activity, students interview one or more persons in one or more occupations to better understand their experience of the work and their strategies for obtaining the work. Involving students with a mentorship program, such as meeting for one-on-one guidance with an adult or slightly advanced peer in a certain career or education area, may foster a student's belief in his or her own abilities to achieve a similar goal. Mentors who have characteristics or experiences similar to the student (i.e., similar gender or cultural background, similar barriers) may be the most effective for increasing self-efficacy (Lent et al., 1999).

The goal of work-based interventions is to expose youth to the work environment, preferably with sufficient depth and duration of experience. This exposure can help students prepare themselves for an environment that is substantially different from the school environment from which they are emerging (Savickas, 1999, 2003). In fact, Savickas (2003) has identified 11 characteristics on which schools and work differ: membership, status, interpersonal relationships, morality, goals, success, means to advance, supervisory authority, punishment, movement, and schedule. While work-based interventions will not necessarily prepare students for all of these changes, opportunities to become even a bit more familiar with the work environment will contribute to a "quicker and better adaptation" (Savickas, 2003, p. 3).

Curriculum-Based Interventions   The interventions in this category are long-term activities that serve as school-based complements to the work-based interventions. Defined as "the class of interventions designed to promote career and academic knowledge and skills through means and content relevant to the world of work" (Dykeman et al., 2001, p. 18), sample activities include career/technical education courses, career skills and information infused into the curriculum, career academy and career magnet schools, school-based enterprise programs, student clubs, and tech prep or 2 + 2 curriculum. Several formal STW models are included in this category of interventions, but interventions that can be infused into the curriculum, and perhaps developed and delivered by both teachers and counselors, are also of importance.

The infusion of career education into the school curriculum is particularly important when thinking about the numerous transitions students must make throughout their school career. Several authors, representing developmental (Savickas, 1999, 2003), social cognitive (Lent et al., 1999), and person-environment fit (Swanson & Fouad, 1999) theories of career development, have pointed out that the STW transition is a process, rather than a single event. Although emphasis is often placed on the actual point of moving from school to work at an individual's first job, the transition itself begins much earlier and extends well past attainment of an initial position. Career development professionals can use the knowledge of developmental issues and adjustment to ease key transition points. The transition from school to work is one obvious point for work-bound youth. It may, in fact, be a critical period of identity transformation for some (Cohen-Scali, 2003). Another is the transition from middle school to high school (Castellano et al., 2002). Many students begin to disengage from the school experience during the middle school years, and the precursors for high school achievement appear during middle school as well. Career interventions beginning at the high school level may simply be too late (Castellano et al., 2002; Worthington & Juntunen, 1997). Instead, career and school counselors need to seek opportunities to make career exploration and other activities a key aspect of middle school at the very latest. Ideally, a consistent offering of career development activities throughout elementary, middle, and high school would be available for all students.

The integration of career exploration activities into the curriculum may be challenging in many settings, perhaps, at least partially, because of negative perceptions that counselors and career education advocates appear to have of one another. For example, within much of the career and technical education literature reviewed in this chapter, the emphasis for delivering services to youth is placed on vocational instructors, with counselors not even included as essential members of the CTE effort in high schools (Lewis, 2001; Rojewski, 2002). In fact, participants in Lewis's (2001) analysis of the needs for career and technical education tended to view counselors as a barrier to program success or at least to a positive image of CTE.

Nonetheless, counselors must address this challenge and work with other school professionals to integrate career exploration into coursework. Savickas (1999) suggested that role rehearsal, through the use of problem-based classroom instructional techniques, can be one valuable strategy for helping students prepare for the problem-solving required in work situations. Identifying interests and skills can begin in early elementary school, by linking basic skills such as spelling, reading, mathematics, and developing interpersonal skills (including multicultural awareness) to work-related content. Numerous individual interventions can be included here, and many examples for curriculum-based learning are available in the CTE literature. Perhaps the key issue is that counselors and other school personnel need to work together as a team to effectively implement such interventions. One framework for attaining that goal is provided by the comprehensive guidance program model (Gysbers & Henderson, 2000), which constructs essential counselor roles around critical student outcomes (American School Counselors Association, 1997). Proponents argue that this model offers results-based accountability for the effectiveness of school counseling to meet the needs of all youth (Lapan, 2001).

CONCLUDING COMMENTS ON THE SCHOOL-TO-WORK TRANSITION

Extensive efforts in educational reform, legislative activity, program design, and evaluation research have contributed valuable knowledge and understanding about the transition of work-bound youth from school to the workplace. The good news is that innovative programs are being developed, and work-bound youth in some school districts have improved access to integrated activities that help them understand and make a successful transition from school to work. Yet these efforts lack the comprehensive focus necessary to assist work-bound youth throughout the nation. The diverse concerns of parties involved in both educational reform and vocational education, the changing funding priorities of federal and state governments, and the challenges of conducting thorough evaluation research all contribute to a system that remains fractured and allows too many work-bound youth to fall between the cracks.

Career development professionals do, however, have numerous resources that can be used to "catch" those youth and facilitate a successful transition. Culturally relevant interventions that are consistent with and have been developed through career development theory can be applied to the transition needs of work-bound youth with thoughtful modification. Further, the growing vocational psychology research on the school-to-work transition is providing alternative views of the transition process, along with calls to consider whether new theory development might be necessary (Blustein, 1999; Phillips et al., 2002). These developments will continue to increase both an understanding of the complexity of the school-to-work transition and the ability of career development professionals to effectively support work-bound youth.

THE TRANSITION FROM NONSCHOOL SITUATIONS TO WORK

As disjointed as services for the school-to-work transition can be, youth who are work-bound but not in school have access to even fewer resources. For youth who do not complete high school, employment and income opportunities are particularly bleak. To provide some context, the U.S. Bureau of the Census (2002) reported that the mean annual income of workers over 18 years of age who have completed a college degree or higher is $56,376 (median = $41,648). The mean annual income of high school graduates (including GED completers) 18 years and older is $24,885 (median = $19,900). In contrast, workers 18 years and older who did not complete high school have mean annual earnings of $16,234 (median = $11,864), or approximately 65% of the income earned by high school graduates. A closer look at this group shows, not surprisingly, significant disparities across sex and race, with women (across all ages) earning less than men, and African American non-Hispanic workers earning less than White or Hispanic workers.

In this section, we discuss some of the issues encountered by youth in three nonschool situations: criminal justice settings, social assistance (welfare) programs, and domestic violence counseling. Although out-of-school youth may be involved in situations beyond these three, the various issues encountered by these examples highlight the diversity of experiences and concerns for which a counselor must be prepared when working with nonstudent work-bound youth.

CRIMINAL JUSTICE SETTINGS

There exists substantial evidence that employment has an inverse relationship with criminal activity among youth. In a series of qualitative interviews with homeless youth, Baron (2001) shed some light on the experience of criminal behavior among youth. The youths' own reports reflected that negative work experiences left them vulnerable to criminal behavior: As they failed to find better employment and as even poor employment became inaccessible, they became further estranged from the labor market. This estrangement, in turn, contributed to a belief that negative circumstances would not change, and the youth subsequently moved toward illegal resources for survival. Further, on a seemingly more pragmatic, yet poignant note, these youth reported that crime simply added structure to the day. In a way, it may have helped them cope with the depression and listlessness of having nothing to do.

Working with a large diverse sample ($N = 8,127$) of participants 18 years of age and older from the National Longitudinal Survey of Youth data, Crutchfield and Pitchford (1997) determined that the stability of good work, as much or more than income, serves to inhibit criminal activity. Marginal employment and time out of the labor force, as well as unemployment, stimulate greater criminality. Bellair and Roscigno (2000) found unemployment to be a significant contributor to both fighting behavior and drug use, even after controlling for family well-being and attachment. School attachment, however, did reduce fighting and limited the negative effects of low family income and nonsupportive family structure. Hartnagel (1998) suggested that education and school involvement may mediate the relationship between unemployment and crime. In particular, he noted that unemployment and job instability during the school-to-work transition of high school graduates did not contribute to increased criminal behavior. In contrast, Baron and Hartnagel (1997) demonstrated that among street youth and high school dropouts, employment instability was related to increased criminal behavior.

Three important conclusions about the development of adolescent delinquency and criminal behavior were drawn by Bellair et al. (2003). First, relying on a large sample from the National Longitudinal Study of Adolescent Health ($N > 14,000$), they stated that "low-wage service sector concentration has a persistent effect on adolescent violence" (p. 25), even after controlling for prior violence and other factors. They suggested that adolescents realize that when employment prospects appear bleak, they cannot rely on legitimate employment, placing them at greater risk for delinquency. Second, they concluded that in-school processes might contribute to delinquency. Specifically, they asserted that disparate assignment of lower SES adolescents to non-college preparatory classes not only depresses their achievement but also supports rebellion against traditional control structures. Their third conclusion was that the roots of adult offending behaviors take hold during adolescence, and delinquency has a long-term negative effect on education and employment opportunities. This conclusion is supported by a longitudinal follow-up of National Longitudinal Survey of Youth data (Tanner, Davies, & O'Grady, 1999), which found that adolescent delinquency "yielded a negative dividend and reduces educational and occupational attainment in young adulthood" (p. 269), particularly for males.

What Counselors Can Do   Despite the obvious connections between successful employment and crime and the possible preventive effects of educational attainment and attachment, very little work in career counseling or vocational psychology has addressed the needs of youth who are involved in the criminal justice system. One exception is INTUIT: Work and Career (Shivy, 2002), which is tailored to prepare offenders for integration back into the workplace using several career development activities and vocational interventions. This is a new program, with limited evaluation data. However, it builds on a program called Project PROVE (Chartrand & Rose, 1996), which was supported for six years by the Virginia Department of Correctional Education. Participants in Project PROVE demonstrated increased self-efficacy for work and life skills and career decision making. Participants also experienced an increase in career-related anxiety, which program administrators felt increased the motivational aspects of their participation in career development.

Both INTUIT and PROVE are based on Social Cognitive Career Theory (SCCT; Lent, Brown, & Hackett, 1994). Chartrand and Rose argued that SCCT is particularly helpful for at-risk populations because it takes into account both limitations in environmental resources and opportunities, as well as individual perceptions (or beliefs) about those same resources and opportunities. INTUIT was specifically created to be more culturally sensitive than its predecessor. Shivy (2002) discussed six specific components that make up INTUIT:

1. A reflective (written) exercise that outlines relevant life and/or job experiences, which may take the form of a timeline task.
2. Individualized test interpretations of the Self-Directed Search (Holland, 1994) and the NEO Five Factor Inventory (Costa & McCrae, 1992).
3. A component composed of teaching prisoners how to access up-to-date information on the world of work (e.g., O*NET Online).
4. The opportunity to interact with individuals who are INTUIT program success stories (i.e., successful models).
5. Focused attention on evaluating and building support networks that facilitate the transition from prisoner to being a successful (and crime-free) worker.
6. As part of its group format, a hypothetical case of a prisoner engaged in a prison-to-work transition, with the goal of facilitating discussion about the decision points in that prisoner's life.

Alternative sentencing programs can also play a role in the transition to work. *Alternative sentencing* refers to a process of placing nonviolent offenders in non-prison programs, such as treatment or an employment program, or combining daytime out-of-prison activities with nighttime incarceration. If the offender successfully completes this program, he or she will not serve a regular prison sentence. Evaluation data for such programs are not currently available, but this is a promising area for future work. There is also a need for programs that can provide more academic and career education programs for juvenile offenders: Preliminary data indicate that youth in juvenile justice education programs are, on average, a full two to three academic years behind their same-age peers (Major, Chester, McEntier, Waldo, & Blomberg, 2002).

To develop viable interventions, career counselors and psychologists will need to become familiar with the literature, customs, and processes of the criminal justice system. This is a daunting task, likely to be much more difficult than creating partnerships with schools, challenging as that has been. Nonetheless, taking on this task can provide numerous opportunities for innovative program development, new approaches to evaluation, and improved service to a seriously under-resourced and neglected population.

WORK-BOUND YOUTH RECEIVING SOCIAL ASSISTANCE

Welfare reform was enacted by the Personal Responsibility and Work Opportunity Reconciliation Act (PRWORA; U.S. Congress, 1996). The primary changes to welfare after 1996 include time limits on assistance (a switch from permanent Aid to Families with Dependent Children [AFDC] to *Temporary* Assistance for Needy Families [TANF]), an emphasis on marriage and parenthood, work requirements to receive aid, and special requirements for teen parents.

Poverty indicators in the United States were bleak before welfare reform. In a study of eight industrialized nations (Rainwater & Smeeding, 1995), the United States ranked last in the percentage of working families living at or below the poverty level. Initial indicators suggested that PRWORA was indeed successful at moving people off the welfare roles. In fact, the caseloads for welfare recipients nationally dropped by almost 50% by the year 2000 (Loprest, 2001). However, follow-up studies suggested that the picture was not quite as bright as it first appeared. Specifically, 40% of families were moving from welfare to poverty, and more than 20% returned to welfare (Loprest, 2001).

Youth are an identified special emphasis group within the government's welfare appropriations. Provisions of PRWORA related to youth include prevention of teen pregnancy, funding for abstinence education, a requirement that minor teen parents live in adult-supervised settings to receive TANF benefits, required education participation for minor teen parents to receive TANF benefits, 60-month lifetime time limit for receipt of TANF for teen parents, the option for states to terminate Medicaid to teen parents who are head of household, and bonuses to states that demonstrate decreased rates of "illegitimacy" and abortion (Center for Law and Social Policy, 2001).

Certainly, parenthood and pregnancy are key issues for youth receiving welfare. Maynard (1995) reported that teen parents consume a disproportionate share of welfare funding, and teen parenthood contributes to the transfer of poverty across generations. For individual teen parents, the transition to work (or education) involves planning for the best interest of dependents and obtaining good child care, in addition to the already stressful developmental transition to work. Given that some are forced to stay in nonsupportive home environments (by the adult supervision requirement of the PRWORA), the stressors quickly multiply for teens dealing with these complex concerns.

But parenthood is not the only issue of concern when working with youth in the social welfare system. One overarching concern is that there are weak links between youth services and the adult service system (Lehman, Clark, Bullis, Rinkin, & Castellanos, 2002), in which TANF and other welfare services are firmly entrenched. Even with mandated youth programs built into legislation, the service centers and service providers tend to be adult-oriented. A case manager approaching a 17-year-old parent receiving TANF with the same expectations as he or she would approach a 30-year-old parent is likely to be unprepared to address salient developmental concerns. Lack of preparation for those developmental differences can lead to a breakdown in service and a youth who feels lost in the bureaucracy of social services. To address this, some employment programs are trying to implement youth-oriented One Stop Service Centers, where all activities and staff are specifically oriented toward youth issues (GAO, 2002), but that is too costly for many states and communities.

Youth in the welfare system also encounter the dilemmas that are common across welfare-to-work populations: lack of transportation, low self-efficacy for work skills, less-than-optimal housing situations, limited opportunities for career development, and the need to develop interpersonal communication and problem-solving skills (Juntunen, 2002). All of these must be addressed to facilitate the transition to work, a potentially overwhelming task.

What Counselors Can Do   Creating partnerships with multiple service providers can help to meet the multiple needs of youth (Juntunen, Cavett, Clow, Olson, & Reed, 2001). For example, in one youth employment program in North Dakota, the local Jobs Service, Housing and Urban Development, and Parks District offices, as well as a university-based welfare-to-work career preparation program called Project HOPE (Juntunen, 2002), have joined to provide multiple services to youth in a relatively comprehensive fashion. Among the four agencies, youth participants are involved in a work experience, job search skills, life skills planning, and career development activities. Initial analyses suggested that the program contributes to decreased depression, increased vocational identity, and increased employment outcomes (e.g., enrollment in educational programs, job attainment, and work for higher wages; Juntunen, 2002).

Individual interventions, such as those described earlier in the work-based and student-based interventions within the school-to-work transition, can certainly help youth who are making the transition from welfare to work. However, greater emphasis needs to be placed on comprehensive services that attempt to address the multiple concerns of this population. In addition, increasing pressure must be applied to improve access to the labor force for youth who are often motivated to work and get out of the welfare system, yet find satisfactory employment unattainable.

WORK-BOUND YOUTH AND DOMESTIC VIOLENCE

While many issues (substance abuse, child care, mental health) impact the career development of work-bound youth, one issue that is frequently ignored is domestic violence. Women ages 16 to 24 report more experience with intimate violence than any other category of women, with an estimated 20 per 1,000 women experiencing domestic violence (Department of Justice, 2000). Prevalence of domestic violence among female welfare recipients is consistently found to be approximately 14% (Lloyd & Taluc, 1999; Tolman & Rosen, 2001). Despite these estimates, little work has been done to investigate the impact of domestic violence on young men's and women's working lives, and even less work has been done to identify interventions that are effective in overcoming that impact.

Extant research suggests that domestic violence may impact a woman's ability to remain employed over time (Browne, Salomon, & Bassuk, 1999), but not her ability to be employed (Tolman & Rosen, 2001). However, Lloyd and Taluc (1999) found that low-income women experiencing intimate partner violence had not only more job turnover but also more periods of unemployment and lower income.

The process by which domestic violence impacts employment is only beginning to be addressed. In a reanalysis of data from women in a low-income area of Chicago, Lloyd (1997) reported that 8% of women indicated that a partner had prevented them from going to school, and 16% indicated that a partner controlled their finances (e.g., took their money, withheld common money). Women in this sample who reported domestic violence were also more likely to experience mental and physical health concerns that impacted their employability or their job performance.

Three studies done with women in shelter from intimate partner violence also addressed the impact of domestic violence on the employment of work-bound youth. In one study, Riger, Ahrens, and Blickenstaff (2000) found that 46% of women who worked while in an abusive relationship were forbidden by their abusive partner to get a job, 85% reported missing work due to the actual abuse, and 52% reported losing a job due to the abuse. Similar to Riger et al., Wettersten et al.'s (2002) qualitative analysis indicated that women who worked while in domestically violent relationships reported job loss, job absenteeism, and lost work opportunities. Wettersten et al. additionally found that women generally reported concentration difficulties at work, mixed messages about the appropriateness of their working, harassment (at work) by their intimate partners, intimate partner jealousy over their (alleged) work relationships, and loss of economic control. On the positive side, a large percentage of women in their study also indicated that work was a safe place to escape from their abusive partners. Finally, Brown, Reedy, Fountain, Johnson, and Dichiser (2000) reported that women in shelter identified the main barriers to their career goals as discrimination, insufficient career preparation, and lack of career satisfaction.

What Counselors Can Do   Counselors encounter work-bound youth who are also survivors of domestic violence in a variety of situations, including crisis centers, community mental health centers, job service/TANF programs, hospitals, schools, and other counseling agencies. Several authors have made recommendations for working with survivors of domestic violence, and many of those recommendations involve a stage model approach, often based in self-efficacy theory (Bandura, 1977; Betz, 1992) and Social Cognitive Career Theory (Lent et al., 1994; see, e.g., Chronister & McWhirter, 2003). Ibrahim and Herr (1987) recommended taking a developmental approach to working with women who experience domestic violence (and we would argue for its use with male survivors as well). They argued that women who are victims of intimate partner violence are likely to have a narrow vocational self-concept, and taking a developmental perspective allows for the growth of that self-concept. Ibrahim and Herr divided their developmental approach into eight phases:

1. Inner preparation (dealing with relationship loss and fears).
2. Intensive family involvement (working with remaining family members to build family life-career goals).
3. Vocational experimentation (using fantasy and role play to imagine new occupations roles).
4. Vocational planning (self-appraisal and realistic decision making).
5. Vocational implementation (dealing with the fears of moving forward with the vocational plan).
6. Vocational analysis (reviewing life-career choices and their success).
7. Vocational resynthesis (adjusting and solidifying goals).
8. Vocational development resources (becoming a resource for others).

Gianakos (1999) followed Salomone's (1988, 1993) five stages of career counseling:

1. *Understanding the self:* Gianakos expands this stage to include being aware of safety issues (leaving a relationship is not always the safest option) and providing information about domestic violence. In this stage, the counselor also works to identify the negative cognitive distortions that relate to self-concept and self-efficacy, both generally and career specific. Client autonomy and self-determination, especially within the counseling relationship, are a primary concern during this stage.
2. *Understanding the world of work and the survivor's potential within that world:* During this stage, Gianakos indicated the importance of encouraging women to look closely into a number of different job interests, given that the social isolation frequently associated with domestic violence often leads to a lack of awareness about the outside world.
3. *Understanding the decision-making process:* In this stage, survivors both come to understand and act on the steps required to make a career decision (such as Krumboltz & Hamel's, 1977, DECIDES model), while simultaneously dealing

with the potential fear of making major decisions that were previously made by an abusive partner.

4. *Implementing educational and vocational decisions:* According to Gianakos, this stage may increase the home-life tension of survivors who are still living with or are in contact with an abusive partner. Consequently, care must be given to a survivor's safety concerns and self-determination, always keeping in mind the survivor's well-being in any given decision.

5. *Work or school adjustment:* In this stage, women work with the counselor to adjust not only to a new work or school situation but also to the impact that domestic violence (past or present) has on that new situation. The role of the counselor is supportive as survivors navigate a different set of social rules than those found at home.

In one of the few experimental intervention studies conducted in the area, Chronister and McWhirter (2004) sought to increase the career search self-efficacy of women who experience domestic violence. Chronister and McWhirter found that their SCCT-based intervention raised both career search self-efficacy and awareness of the impact that domestic violence had in the lives of the participants.

SUMMARY

Getting involved in services for work-bound youth is not always an easy task for career counselors. Nonetheless, the needs of work-bound youth present a challenge that career counselors and psychologists cannot ignore. There is much work to be done, many avenues to follow in pursuit of that work, and several barriers to overcome along the way.

First, it is important for career counselors to be aware of biases toward college attendance that they may hold. It is consistent with counselor training to think of each person as having the potential to meet whatever goals they set, and our bias may be to assume that more education is the best goal, particularly given the perspective of a person who has completed substantial professional training. That perspective can result, intentionally or otherwise, in our dismissal of the needs of work-bound youth or a devaluation of plans that are noncollege in nature.

Counselors also need to become more familiar and involved with vocational education. We often rely too heavily on the literature of our own discipline and fail to look at the work being done by others. Combining the knowledge and perspectives of vocational education, career counseling, and vocational psychology will strengthen transition-to-work interventions for work-bound youth and facilitate greater communication among professionals.

Both in and outside the school setting, counselors can become involved in, and even initiate, community partnerships. Partnerships composed of youth, parents, teachers, employers, service providers, and job placement employees can become powerful agents of local change, creating awareness about the needs of work-bound youth and generating resources beyond what an individual provider could secure.

Finally, one of the largest challenges presented by the needs of work-bound youth in the United States is the call to change public policy, bringing work-bound youth and the concerns they regularly encounter to the forefront of American awareness. Industry and government will need to offer much more significant support to make successful work transitions accessible to all youth. The theoretical and empirical knowledge of career counselors and vocational psychology can provide program development and evaluation with the goal of helping work-bound youth find meaningful employment and satisfying lives.

REFERENCES

American School Counselors Association. (1997). *Executive summary: The national standards for school counseling programs.* Alexandria, VA: Author.

APA School-to-Work Task Force. (June, 1999). *Report of the School-to-Work Task Force: How psychology can contribute to the School-to-Work Opportunities Movement.* Retrieved May 26, 2003, from www.apa.org/pubinfo/school/page16.html.

Bandura, A. (1977). *Social learning theory.* Englewood Cliffs, NJ: Prentice-Hall.

Barling, J., & Kelloway, E. K. (1999). *Young workers: Varieties of experience.* Washington, DC: American Psychological Association.

Baron, S. W. (2001). Street youth labour market experiences and crime. *Canadian Review of Sociology and Anthropology, 38,* 189–215.

Baron, S. W., & Hartnagel, T. F. (1997). Attributions, affect and crime. *Criminology, 35,* 409–439.

Bellair, P. E., & Roscigno, V. J. (2000). Local labor-market opportunity and adolescent delinquency. *Social Forces, 78,* 1509–1538.

Bellair, P. E., Roscigno, V. J., & McNulty, T. L. (2003). Linking local labor market opportunity to violent adolescent delinquency. *Journal of Research in Crime and Delinquency, 40,* 6–33.

Betz, N. E. (1992). Counseling uses of career self-efficacy theory. *Career Development Quarterly, 41,* 22–26.

Blustein, D. L. (1999). A match made in heaven? Career development theories and the school-to-work transition. *Career Development Quarterly, 47,* 348–352.

Blustein, D. L., Juntunen, C. L., & Worthington, R. L. (2000). The school-to-work transition: Adjustment challenges of the forgotten half. In S. D. Brown & R. W. Lent (Eds.), *Handbook of Counseling Psychology* (pp. 435–470). New York: Wiley.

Blustein, D. L., Phillips, S. D., Jobin-Davis, K., Finkelberg, S. L., & Roarke, A. E. (1997). A theory building investigation of the school-to-work transition. *Counseling Psychologist, 25,* 364–402.

Bragg, D. D. (2001). *Promising outcomes for Tech Prep participants in eight local consortia: A summary of initial results.* Columbus, OH: National Dissemination Center for Career and Technical Education.

Brown, C., Reedy, D., Fountain, J., Johnson, A., & Dichiser, T. (2000). Battered women's career decision-making self-efficacy: Further insights and contributing factors. *Journal of Career Assessment, 8*(3), 251–265.

Browne, A., Salomon, A., & Bassuk, S. S. (1999). The impact of recent partner violence on poor women's capacity to maintain work. *Violence Against Women, 5*(4), 393–426.

Carr, R. V., Wright, J. D., & Brody, C. J. (1996). Effects of high school work experience a decade later: Evidence from the National Longitudinal Survey. *Sociology of Education, 69,* 66–81.

Castellano, M., Stringfield, S., & Stone, J. R., III. (2002). *Helping disadvantaged youth succeed in school: Second-year findings from a longitudinal study of CTE-based whole-school reforms.* Columbus, OH: National Dissemination Center for Career and Technical Education.

Center for Law and Social Policy. (2001, November). *List of key provisions in PRWORA related to teens and to family formation.* Retrieved June 3, 2003, from www.clasp.org/DMS/DMS/Documents/1012502653.3/list_of_key_provisions.pdf.

Chartrand, J. M., & Rose, M. L. (1996). Career interventions for at-risk populations: Incorporating social cognitive influences. *Career Development Quarterly, 44,* 341–353.

Chronister, K. M., & McWhirter, E. H. (2003). Applying Social Cognitive Career Theory to the empowerment of battered women. *Journal of Counseling and Development, 81,* 418–425.

Chronister, K. M., & McWhirter, E. H. (2004). *An experimental examination of two career intervention programs for battered women.* Manuscript submitted for publication.

Cohen-Scali, V. (2003). The influence of family, social, and work socialization on the construction of the professional identity of young adults. *Journal of Career Development, 29,* 237–249.

Costa, P. T., & McCrae, R. R. (1992). Normal personality assessment in clinical practice: The NEO Personality Inventory. *Psychological Assessment, 4,* 5–13.

Crutchfield, R. D., & Pitchford, S. R. (1997). Work and crime: The effects of labor stratification. *Social Forces, 76,* 93–118.

Dykeman, C., Herr, E. L., Ingram, M., Pehrsson, D., Wood, C., & Charles, S. (2001). *A taxonomy of career development interventions that occur in US secondary schools.* Columbus, OH: National Dissemination Center for Career and Technical Education.

The Education Trust, Inc. (2000). *Youth at the crossroads: Facing high school and beyond.* Retrieved June 2, 2003, from www.commissiononthesenioryear.org/hsreportfinal.pdf.

Flores, L. Y., & O'Brien, K. M. (2002). The career development of Mexican American adolescent women: A test of Social Cognitive Career Theory. *Journal of Counseling Psychology, 49,* 14–27.

Fouad, N. A. (1997). School-to-work transition: Voice from an implementer. *Counseling Psychologist, 25*(3), 403–412.

Gianakos, I. (1999). Career counseling with battered women. *Journal of Mental Health Counseling, 21,* 1–14.

Gysbers, N. C., & Henderson, P. (2000). *Developing and managing your school guidance program* (3rd ed.). Alexandria, VA: American Counseling Association.

Haimson, J., & Bellotti, J. (2001). *Schooling in the workplace: Increasing the scale and quality of work-based learning. Final report* (MPR No. 8292). Princeton, NJ: Mathematica Policy Research.

Hartnagel, T. F. (1998). Labour-market problems and crime in the transition from school to work. *Canadian Review of Sociology and Anthropology, 35,* 435–459.

Herr, E. (1995). *Counseling employment-bound youth.* Greensboro, NC: ERIC Clearinghouse on Counseling and Student Services No. ED 1.310/2:382899.

Herr, E. (1997). *Career development and work-bound youth.* Greensboro, NC: ERIC Clearinghouse on Counseling and Student Services.

Hershey, A. M., Hudis, P., Silverberh, M., & Haimson, J. (1997). *Partners in progress: Early steps in creating school-to-work systems.* Princeton, NJ: Mathematica Policy Research.

Hershey, A. M., Silverberg, M. K., Haimson, J., Hudis, P., & Jackson, R. (1999). *Expanding options for students: Report to Congress on the national evaluation of the school-to-work implementation* (MPR No. 8292–660). Princeton, NJ: Mathematica Policy Research.

Hershey, A. M., Silverberg, M. K., Owens, T., & Hulsey, L. K. (1998). *Focus for the Future: The final report of the National Tech-Prep evaluation* (MPR No. 8087–220). Princeton, NJ: Mathematica Policy Research.

Holland, J. L. (1994). *Self-directed search.* Odessa, FL: Psychological Assessment Resources.

Ibrahim, F. A., & Herr, E. (1987). Battered women: A developmental life-career counseling perspective. *Journal of Counseling and Development, 65,* 244–248.

Juntunen, C. L. (2002, August). Welfare to work transition: Evaluating a vocational intervention. In K. Wettersten (Chair), *Community, work, and social justice—Integrating vocational interventions and research.* Paper presented at the 110th annual convention of the American Psychological Association, Chicago.

Juntunen, C. L., Cavett, A. M., Clow, R. B., Olson, P., & Reed, M. (2001, August). Making connections with community partners: Working together for welfare recipients. In J. Swanson (Chair), *Vocational psychology in the trenches.* Symposium conducted at the 109th annual convention of the American Psychological Association, San Francisco.

Kemple, J. J., & Snipes, J. C. (2000). *Career academies: Impacts on students' engagement and performance in high school.* New York: Manpower Demonstration Research Corporation.

Kenny, M. E., Blustein, D. L., Chaves, A., Grossman, J. M., & Gallagher, L. A. (2003). The role of perceived barriers and relational support in the educational and vocational lives of urban high school students. *Journal of Counseling Psychology, 50*(2), 142–155.

Krumboltz, J. D., & Hamel, D. A. (1977). *Guide to career decision-making skills.* New York: College Entrance Examination Board.

Krumboltz, J. D., & Worthington, R. L. (1999). The school-to-work transition from a learning perspective. *Career Development Quarterly, 47,* 312–325.

Lapan, R. T. (2001). Results-based comprehensive guidance and counseling programs: A framework for planning and evaluation. *Professional School Counseling, 4,* 289–299.

Lehman, C. M., Clark, H. B., Bullis, M., Rinkin, J., & Castellanos, L. A. (2002). Transition from school to adult life: Empowering youth through community ownership and accountability. *Journal of Child and Family Studies, 11,* 127–141.

Lent, R. W., Brown, S. D., & Hackett, G. (1994). Toward a unifying social cognitive theory of career and academic interests, choice, and performance [Monograph]. *Journal of Vocational Behaviors, 45,* 79–122.

Lent, R. W., Hackett, G., & Brown, S. D. (1999). A social cognitive view of school-to-work transition. *Career Development Quarterly, 47,* 297–311.

Lent, R. W., O'Brien, K. M., & Fassinger, R. E. (1998). School-to-work transition and counseling psychology. *Counseling Psychologist, 26,* 489–494.

Lent, R. W., & Worthington, R. L. (1999). Introduction: Applying career development theories to the school-to-work transition process. *Career Development Quarterly, 47,* 291–296.

Lewis, M. V. (2001). *Major needs of career and technical education in the year 2000: Views from the field.* Columbus, OH: National Dissemination Center for Career and Technical Education.

Lloyd, S. (1997). The effects of domestic violence on women's employment. *Law and Policy, 19,* 139–167.

Lloyd, S., & Taluc, N. (1999). The effects of male violence on female employment. *Violence Against Women, 5*(4), 370–392.

Loprest, P. (2001, April). How are families that left welfare doing? A comparison of early and recent welfare leavers (Urban Institute Series, "New Federalism: National Survey of America's Families," Number B-36). Retrieved May 10, 2004, from www.urban.org /Template.cfm?Section=ByAuthor&NavMenuID=63&template=/TaggedContent /ViewPublication.cfm&PublicationID=7249.

Major, A. K., Chester, D. R., McEntire, R., Waldo, G. P., & Blomberg, T. G. (2002). Pre-, post-, and longitudinal evaluation of juvenile justice education. *Evaluation Review, 26,* 301–321.

Maynard, R. (1995). Teenage childbearing and welfare reform: Lessons from a decade of demonstration and evaluation research. *Children and Youth Services Review, 17,* 309–332.

McWhirter, E. H. (1997). Perceived barriers to education and career: Ethnic and gender differences. *Journal of Vocational Behavior, 50,* 124–140.

Mortimer, J. T. (2003). *Working and growing up in America.* Cambridge, MA: Harvard University Press.

Northern Arizona University. (2003). *American Indian school dropouts and pushouts.* Retrieved August 30, 2003, from jan.ucc.nau.edu/~jar/AIE/Dropouts.html.

Parsons, F. (1909). *Choosing a vocation.* Boston: Houghton Mifflin.

Phillips, S. D., Blustein, D. L., Jobin-Davis, K., & White, S. F. (2002). Preparation for the school-to-work transition: The views of high school students. *Journal of Vocational Behavior, 61,* 202–216.

Plank, S. (2001). *Career and technical education in the balance: An analysis of high school persistence, academic achievement, and postsecondary destinations.* Columbus, OH: National Dissemination Center for Career and Technical Education.

Quirk, K. J., Keith, T. Z., & Quirk, J. T. (2001). Employment during high school and student achievement: Longitudinal analysis of national data. *Journal of Educational Research, 95,* 4–10.

Rainwater, L., & Smeeding, T. M. (1995, August). *Doing poorly: The real income of American children in a comparative perspective* (Luxembourg Income Study, Working Paper No. 127). Retrieved May 10, 2004 from www.lisproject.org/publications/liswps/127.pdf.

Riger, S., Ahrens, C., & Blickenstaff, A. M. (2000). Measuring interference with employment and education reported by women with abusive partners: Preliminary data. *Violence and Victims, 15*(2), 161–172.

Rojewski, J. W. (2002). *Preparing the workforce of tomorrow: A conceptual framework for career and technical education.* Columbus, OH: National Dissemination Center for Career and Technical Education.

Salomone, P. R. (1988). Career counseling: Steps and stages beyond Parsons. *Career Development Quarterly, 36,* 218–221.

Salomone, P. R. (1993). Annual review: Practice and research in career counseling and development, 1993. *Career Development Quarterly, 42,* 99–128.

Savickas, M. L. (1999). The transition from school to work: A developmental perspective. *Career Development Quarterly, 47,* 326–336.

Savickas, M. L. (2003, June). *Contextual parameters of the school-to-work transition.* Paper presented at the 6th biannual meeting of the Society of Vocational Psychology, Coimbra, Portugal.

Schoenhals, M., Tienda, M., & Schneider, B. (1998). The educational and personal consequences of adolescent employment. *Social Forces, 77,* 723–762.

School-to-Work Opportunities Act of 1994. Pub. L. No. 103–239. (1994).

Secretary's Commission on Achieving Necessary Skills (SCANS). (1992). *Learning a living: A blueprint for high performance.* Washington, DC: U.S. Department of Labor.

Shivy, V. A. (2002, August). Assisting offenders with career reentry and development. In K. Wettersten (Chair), *Community, work, and social justice—Integrating vocational interventions and research.* Paper presented at the 110th Annual Convention of the American Psychological Association, Chicago.

Solberg, V. S., Howard, K. A., Blustein, D. L., & Close, W. (2002). Career development in the schools: Connecting school-to-work-to-life. *Counseling Psychologist, 30,* 705–725.

Swanson, J. L., & Fouad, N. A. (1999). Applying theories of person-environment fit to the transition from school to work. *Career Development Quarterly, 47,* 337–347.

Tanner, J., Davies, S., & O'Grady, B. (1999). Whatever happened to yesterday's rebels? Longitudinal effects of youth delinquency on education and employment. *Social Problems, 46,* 250–274.

Tolman, R. M., & Rosen, D. (2001). Domestic violence in the lives of women receiving welfare: Mental health, substance dependence, and economic well-being. *Violence Against Women, 7*(2), 141–158.

U.S. Bureau of Labor Statistics. (November 2000). *Trends in Youth Employment: Data from the Current Population Survey.* Retrieved June 1, 2003, from www.bls.gov/opub/rylf/pdf/chapter4.pdf.

U.S. Bureau of Labor Statistics. (May 2002). *College enrollment and work activity of year 2001 high school graduates.* Retrieved June 1, 2003, from www.bls.gov/news.release/hsgec.nr0.htm.

U.S. Census Bureau. (March 2002). *Educational Attainment in the United States: March 2002 Detailed Tables (PPL-169).* Retrieved June 2, 2003, from www. census.gov/population/www/socdemo/education/ppl-169.html.

U.S. Congress. (August 1996). *Personal Responsibility and Work Opportunities Reconciliation Act (PL 104-193).* Retrieved May 31, 2003, from frwebgat.access.gpo.gov/cgi-bin/getdoc.cgi?dbname=104_cong_public_laws&docid=f:publ193.104.pdf.

U.S. Department of Justice. (2000). *Full report of the prevalence, incidence, and consequences of violence against women: Findings from the national violence against women survey.* Retrieved May 1, 2003, from www.ojp.usdoj.gov/vawo/statistics.htm.

U.S. General Accounting Office. (2002, April). *Work Initiative Act: Youth provisions promote new service strategies, but additional guidance would enhance program development* (US GAO Report No. GAO-02-413). Washington, DC: Author. Retrieved June 1, 2003, from www.gao.gov/newitems/d02413.

U.S. General Accounting Office. (2003a, April). *Multiple employment and training programs: Funding and performance measures for major programs* (US GAO Report No. GAO-03-589). Washington, DC: Author. Retrieved June 1, 2003, from www.gao.gov/newitems/d03589.

U.S. General Accounting Office. (2003b, April). *Student financial aid: Monitoring aid greater than federally defined need could help address student loan indebtedness* (US GAO Report No. GAO-03-508). Washington, DC: Author. Retrieved June 1, 2003, from www.gao.gov/newitems/d03508.

Wettersten, K. B., Rudolph, S. E., Slocombe, K., Trangsrud, H., Gallagher, K., Adams, K., et al. (2002, August). Freedom through self-sufficiency: Vocational interventions for female survivors of domestic violence. In K. Wettersten (Chair), *Community, work, and social justice—Integrating vocational interventions and research.* Paper presented at the 110th annual convention of the American Psychological Association, Chicago.

William T. Grant Foundation Commission on Work, Family, and Citizenship. (1988). *The forgotten half: Non-college youth in America.* Washington, DC: Author.

Wilson, W. J. (1996). *When work disappears: The world of the new urban poor.* New York: Vintage Books.

Worthington, R. L., & Juntunen, C. L. (1997). The vocational development of non-college-bound youth: Counseling psychology and the school-to-work transition movement. *Counseling Psychologist, 25,* 323–363.

CHAPTER 25

Blending Promise with Passion: Best Practices for Counseling Intellectually Talented Youth

John A. Achter and David Lubinski

Despite the American myth, I cannot be or do whatever I desire—a truism, to be sure, but a truism we often defy. . . . Like organisms in an ecosystem, there are some roles and relationships in which we thrive, and others in which we wither and die. (Palmer, 2000, *Let Your Life Speak: Listening for the Voice of Vocation*, p. 44)

W̲E̲ ̲O̲P̲E̲N̲ ̲W̲I̲T̲H̲ this quote from educator and writer Parker Palmer as a way of capturing parts of both the challenge and essence of career counseling with intellectually talented individuals. One of the challenges is highlighted by the message that we can "be or do whatever we desire," which is pervasive in Western society and can become particularly poignant for the intellectually talented, as they attempt to journey toward finding success and satisfaction in work and life. An important part of the essence of career counseling with this special population is captured by the latter part of the quote. That is, we believe there exist particular applications of each individual's unique set of talents, interests, and ambitions—that is, their intellectual promise and personal passion—which will allow them to differentially thrive in some niches relative to others. Even those with abundantly diverse gifts will find they are better suited for, and more fulfilled by, certain environments than others.

Isolating the subset of environments that individuals are best suited for is an important first step that career counselors and psychologists are uniquely positioned to facilitate. Just as problem definition is an important first step in issue resolution, identifying personal assets and relative liabilities is a critical first step

This chapter was supported by a Templeton Award for Positive Psychology, NICHD Grant P30HD15052 to the John F. Kennedy Center at Vanderbilt University and a Cattell Sabbatical Award.

in talent development. We believe it is our obligation as counselors to use the best that modern science has to offer to assist intellectually talented students in finding environments in which they are most likely to thrive. Doing so requires that we begin by focusing at early ages on determinants that enhance positive development (Achter & Lubinski, 2003), a process counseling psychologist and gifted student advocate Sidney Pressey (1955) referred to as "furtherance."

Contributing to this volume is a privilege, and with this opportunity we hope to impart to readers—whether budding career counselors or seasoned veterans wishing to expand or update their knowledge about intellectually talented students—the essential ideas and tools for providing effective career counseling to intellectually talented populations. Our aim is to present findings (especially longitudinal findings) in a fashion that logically flows into practice. Some of the perceived roadblocks to successful counseling with this special population are addressed, in particular, multipotentiality; and we summarize research that reframes issues surrounding multipotentiality and draws links to counseling contexts. The broad framework guiding our approach is familiar to those versed in person-environment approaches to vocational psychology. We begin with some background, drawn from pioneers in gifted education and leaders of the individual differences approach to counseling psychology (e.g., Dawis, 1992; Tyler, 1974, 1992; Williamson, 1965).

FOCUSING ON YOUTH

Readers might ask why our focus is on youth or, more specifically, adolescents. A brief perusal of work over the past 100 years provides the answer. Modern approaches to identifying and working with intellectually talented students began in the early 1900s, with notable educators and scientists such as Leta Hollingworth (1926, 1942) and Lewis Terman (1954; Terman & Oden, 1947). Both of these pioneers recognized that those with high general intelligence (which was how the gifted were exclusively identified in those days) needed special attention if they were to develop their gifts and avoid becoming bored or underachieving. In addition, they, along with other eminent psychologists throughout the twentieth century (e.g., Paterson, 1957; Pressey, 1946, 1955, 1967; Seashore, 1922; Stanley, 1974, 1996; Tyler, 1974, 1992; Williamson, 1965), believed that the early detection of intellectual giftedness was the first step in facilitating truly exceptional talent development.

Within gifted populations, by definition, intellectual abilities exist at extraordinary levels. The emergence of superior intellectual abilities in children and adolescents, as measured by various standardized tests, is best conceptualized in terms of precocity (Benbow, 1991; Jackson & Butterfield, 1986; Sternberg & Davidson, 1985). The precocity explanation asserts not that intellectually talented children differ qualitatively in terms of reasoning or cognitive functioning, but rather that they are ahead of their time—that is, functioning at an intellectual level indicative of persons a few to several years older (Benbow, 1991; Dark & Benbow, 1993). In this view, preadolescent children who perform highly on tests such as the Scholastic Aptitude Test (SAT) are believed to be reasoning at a level characteristic of students three to five years older. This was the guiding principle driving the inception of the Study of Mathematically Precocious Youth (SMPY; Stanley, 1974, 1996; Stanley & Benbow, 1986), a longitudinal study of more than 6,000 intellectually gifted individuals, now in its fourth decade, which has expanded identification of the gifted beyond general intelligence to specific abilities. Much of the data presented in this chapter has been drawn from this ongoing study.

In addition to their precocious intellectual development, it has also been observed that the intellectually talented tend to begin at an earlier age to think about their career possibilities (Milne, 1979; Willings, 1986). If a seventh grader is capable of reasoning mathematically or verbally at or above the twelfth-grade level, the thinking goes, maybe he or she is also thinking ahead to college majors in architecture, math/science, or philosophy, for example, or perhaps even to a career in one of these fields. Much evidence exists to suggest that advanced thinking about educational possibilities and careers is present in many gifted youth, as an outgrowth of their advanced cognitive development (Shoffner & Newsome, 2001; Silverman, 1993). In fact, Willings (1986) suggested that most gifted students begin thinking seriously about their work futures by the age of 9. Typically, however, structured career search programs in schools are not implemented until the senior high years, when they may be developmentally mistimed for gifted students (Kerr, 1981; Willings, 1986).

As we hope to make clear from available empirical evidence, early adolescence is a time when it is both possible and reasonable to begin applying tools intended for older students (e.g., college entrance exams and interest inventories) to help the intellectually talented: (1) come to a better personal understanding of their unique talents and interests, (2) consider the relevance of these attributes for education and the world of work, and (3) begin to think about how nurturing these characteristics could contribute toward their future development. Against this historical and conceptual backdrop, we now move to addressing effective foundations for educational and vocational counseling with the intellectually talented. For the reasons just outlined, our approach to working with these students begins with the assumption that traditional theories and tools of vocational psychology are well suited to this task.

APPLICATIONS OF PERSON-ENVIRONMENT FIT THEORIES: A MODEL FOR BLENDING PROMISE WITH PASSION

Fredrick Beuchner (1993) defined *vocation* as "the place where your deep gladness meets the world's deep need" (p. 119). This language, from outside the realm of vocational psychology, eloquently captures the essence of the person-environment (P-E) fit approach to the vocational decision-making process. That is, a person's "deep gladness" reflects an internal state that is likely to be achieved when the combination of his or her unique abilities, interests, and values (both intellectual "promise" and personal "passion") match the "world's deep need."

For more than a decade, the Study of Mathematically Precocious Youth (SMPY) has used the Theory of Work Adjustment (TWA; Dawis & Lofquist, 1984; Lofquist & Dawis, 1991; see also Dawis, Chapter 1, this volume), a modern-day P-E fit theory, as the overarching framework for understanding and studying talent development over the life span (Lubinski & Benbow, 2000). Within this theory, the critical areas of abilities and preferences are given greater specificity through the application of two empirically validated organizational systems:

1. Snow's (Snow, Kyllonen, & Marshalek, 1984; Snow & Lohman, 1989) radex scaling application for organizing the hierarchical structure of cognitive

abilities (a general factor supported by three major group factors—verbal-linguistic, mathematical-numerical, and spatial-mechanical).
2. Holland's (1985, 1996) hexagon structure for six general educational-vocational interest themes (i.e., Realistic, Investigative, Artistic, Social, Enterprising, and Conventional).

Figure 25.1 depicts an integration of the radex and RIASEC models with TWA, a broader theoretical framework for conceptualizing educational-vocational adjustment as well as talent development (Lubinski & Benbow, 2000). For more specific details on cognitive abilities, see Carroll (1993), Jensen (1998), Lubinski (2004), and Ryan Krane and Tirre (Chapter 14, this volume); and, for interest dimensions, see Holland (1985, 1996), Prediger (1982), and Spokane and Cruza-Guet (Chapter 2, this volume). For a more complete theoretical treatment for how these models, organized around TWA, have been extended to intellectually gifted youth, see Lubinski and Benbow (2000). Additional extensions to applied practice in gifted education are found in Benbow and Lubinski (1997) and Lubinski and Benbow (1995).

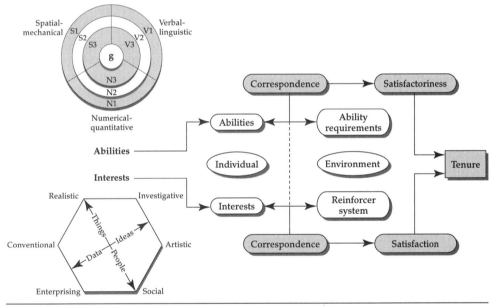

Figure 25.1 The Theory of Work Adjustment (Right) Combined with the Radex Scaling of Cognitive Abilities (Upper Left) and the RIASEC Hexagon of Interests (Lower Left) for Conceptualizing Personal Attributes Relevant to Learning and Work (Lubinski & Benbow, 2000). [*Note:* The letters in the cognitive ability arrangement denote different regions of concentration, whereas their accompanying numbers increase as a function of complexity. Contained within the RIASEC is a simplification of this hexagon. Following Prediger (1982), it amounts to a two-dimensional structure of independent dimensions: people/things and data/ideas, which underlie RIASEC. The dotted line running down the individual and environment sectors of TWA illustrates that TWA places equal emphasis on assessing the personal attributes (abilities and interests) and assessing the environment (abilities requirements and reward structure).]

According to TWA, optimal learning and work environments are defined by the co-occurrence of two broad dimensions of correspondence: (1) *satisfactoriness* (a match between ability and ability requirements) and (2) *satisfaction* (a match between preferences such as interests and values and the rewards typical of contrasting learning and work environments). The Theory of Work Adjustment places equal emphasis on matching these two and, subsequently, aligning these broad dimensions of correspondence with the unique ambitions and energies of individual clients, students, and workers.

It is important to highlight the dual emphasis on abilities and preferences when working with the intellectually talented. They are not a categorical type, and cognitive ability and preference assessments are helpful in uncovering the magnitude of their individuality. Whereas the field of vocational counseling more generally has shifted its focus away from ability assessment in recent decades (Gottfredson, 2003), accurate measurement of abilities remains a critical component that cannot be neglected when working with any population; indeed, doing so was referred to as a "truncated" view of vocational psychology by Williamson (1965). Parsons (1909), Paterson (1957), and Tyler (1974) said much the same (cf. Lubinski, 1996, 2001). Strong's (1943) concern that much "time and money are often wasted trying to prepare youths for careers which they or their parents desire today but not tomorrow, and for which too often the young people have no ability" (p. vii) is useful to keep in mind.

Following these ideas, Gottfredson (2003) published a modern treatment of this point of view, which makes a compelling case that cognitive abilities are at least as important as interests for vocational counseling. This point needs to be stressed because many theoretical frameworks of vocational development do not incorporate cognitive abilities (cf. Gottfredson, 2003) and, because of this, are misspecified or underdetermined models (Lubinski, 2000; Lubinski & Humphreys, 1997). F. L. Schmidt and Hunter's (1998) meta-analysis of 85 years of personnel research makes this omission scientifically indefensible, as it empirically documents the critical influence of abilities in several work-related performance outcomes (for further details, see Drazgow, 2002; Gottfredson, 1997; Humphreys, Lubinski, & Yao, 1993; Hunt, 1995; Lubinski, 2004; Shea, Lubinski, & Benbow, 2001; Visweswaran & Ones, 2002; Webb, Lubinski, & Benbow, 2002; Wilk, Desmarais, & Sackett, 1995; Wilk & Sackett, 1996).

ABOVE-LEVEL ABILITY ASSESSMENTS

Beginning with Julian Stanley and his SMPY research and service program initiated at Johns Hopkins University (and now located at Vanderbilt University), the use of above-level testing (i.e., using tests developed for older students) for identifying and nurturing intellectual precocity among gifted adolescents (Keating & Stanley, 1972; Stanley, 1977) has gained widespread use and acceptance. Stanley and his colleagues were the first to systematically use college entrance exams—the SAT and, later, the ACT (Benbow, 1991), tests typically taken by college-bound high school juniors and seniors—to differentiate levels of ability in both math and verbal domains for gifted adolescents (ages 12 to 14) who scored in the top 1% to 3% on grade-level achievement tests. By raising the ceiling of test difficulty, above-level ability testing has the benefit of spreading out high-ability students and distinguishing the able from the exceptionally able. Over the past 30 years, literally millions of seventh and eighth graders have taken these college entrance exams through annual talent searches throughout the United States (Benbow & Stanley, 1996). Currently, around 200,000 young adolescents do so annually.

The assessment of gifted youth at ages 12 or 13 using above-level tests such as SAT-Math and SAT-Verbal produces an ability profile that is beneficially diagnostic (Benbow & Lubinski, 1996; Benbow & Stanley, 1996; Stanley, 2000). For example, researchers at SMPY have observed that many intellectually talented individuals exhibit differential (rather than uniform—as was once assumed) strengths in either mathematical or verbal reasoning in adolescence (Achter, Lubinski, & Benbow, 1996). Over time, these differential areas of strength forecast the selection of contrasting educational and career paths (Achter, Lubinski, Benbow, & Eftekhari-Sanjani, 1999; Lubinski & Benbow, 2000; Lubinski, Benbow, Shea, Eftekhari-Sanjani, & Halvorson, 2001; Lubinski, Webb, Morelock, & Benbow, 2001). This information can meaningfully influence practice. Equipped with this specific ability information, educators, counselors, parents, and students can work together to differentially plan educational programs that are developmentally appropriate for bright youth (as we detail later in the section on interventions).

As is true for all adolescents (Humphreys et al., 1993), both ability *level* and ability *pattern* harbor practical importance in the lives of the intellectually talented (Achter et al., 1996, 1999; Shea et al., 2001; Webb et al., 2002). Consider first the importance of ability level. The range of individual differences in human abilities is huge, and the magnitude of these differences is sometimes underappreciated. Consider, for example, general intelligence. In terms of IQ points, scores within the top 1% on general intellectual ability range from approximately 137 to well over 200, a tremendous amount of quantitative variation among an already highly select group. The same is true for specific abilities, which in part is why persons considered gifted do not represent a categorical type. But the question often asked is whether these ability differences make a difference over the course of a person's life. Recent longitudinal reports unequivocally reveal that they do.

Building on a study of quantitative differences in educational and career outcomes between gifted individuals in the top versus the bottom quartiles of the top 1% in mathematical ability (Benbow, 1992), Lubinski, Webb, et al. (2001) studied a sample of 320 profoundly gifted individuals, identified for their exceptional (i.e., top 1 in 10,000) mathematical or verbal reasoning ability at age 13 (mean estimated IQ > 180). By age 23, 93% of this group had obtained bachelor's degrees, 31% had earned master's degrees, and 12% had completed doctoral degrees. Furthermore, fully 56% of this select group expressed intentions to pursue doctorates, a number more than 50 times the base rate expectation (i.e., 1% in the general population, U.S. Department of Education, 1997). By comparison, studies of persons in the highly able, but less select, top 1% (i.e., top 1 in 100) of cognitive ability have revealed pursuit of doctoral degrees at 25 times base rate expectations (Benbow, Lubinski, Shea, & Eftekhari-Sanjani, 2000)—which is truly remarkable, yet *only* half the rate observed among the top 1 in 10,000.

As impressive as this difference is, there is more to the story on the magnitude of achievement in the profoundly talented group. For example, among those pursuing doctorates in the top 1 in 10,000 study (Lubinski, Webb, et al., 2001), 42% were doing so at universities ranked within the top 10 in the United States, another indication of the extraordinary promise of this group. By comparison, only 21% of the top 1 in 100 (Benbow et al., 2000) were pursuing doctorates at universities ranked in the top 10, again half the rate of the higher ability group. It certainly appears that increased ability level translates into increased achievement among those at different segments of the top 1% (or the top one-third of the ability range), just as they do in the general population (Lubinski, 2004; Murray, 1998).

It is important to note that ability *pattern* also proved psychologically significant among these profoundly gifted individuals, by foreshadowing qualitatively distinct types of achievements. To demonstrate this, Lubinski, Webb, et al. (2001) categorized favorite courses (high school and college) and the age 23 accomplishments attained by the top 1 in 10,000 group, into Sciences & Technology, Humanities & Arts, and Other clusters. They then assessed whether these three clusters contained different proportions of members from the three distinct ability groups in their sample:

1. Those who had one standard deviation more mathematical, relative to verbal, ability (High-Math).
2. Those who had one standard deviation more verbal, relative to mathematical, ability (High-Verbal).
3. Those whose math and verbal abilities were more uniform and within one standard deviation of each other (High-Flat).

As for favorite courses, the High-Math group consistently preferred math/science courses relative to the humanities, whereas the inverse was true for the High-Verbal group; the High-Flat group showed more balanced course preferences overall (see Figure 25.2). The differential course preferences among these three groups in high school and college also coincided with qualitative differences in age 23 accomplishments (see Table 25.1). Of those listing achievements in science and technology, three-fourths were in the High-Math group. By comparison, two-thirds of those listing accomplishments in the humanities and arts were in the High-Verbal group. High-Flat participants reported similar numbers of accomplishments in both the sciences and humanities clusters. It is evident that ability patterns emerging in early adolescence among the intellectually talented relate to the types of activities to which these individuals devoted time and effort.

Other investigations on the longitudinal significance of ability pattern have generated even more refined predictions by adding the assessment of spatial abilities to the equation. For example, Shea et al. (2001) tracked a group of 563 intellectually precocious participants (393 boys, 170 girls) at three time points over a 20-year interval. At age 13, participants were in the top 1% of their age mates in general intellectual ability; at this time, they were assessed on quantitative, spatial, and verbal reasoning measures. At ages 18, 23, and 33, individual differences in their mathematical, spatial, and verbal abilities assessed in early adolescence were related in distinct ways to preferences for contrasting disciplines and ultimate educational and occupational group membership.

The four developmentally sequenced panels of Figure 25.3 visually depict these patterns. Specifically, panels A and B, respectively, show whether participants' favorite and least favorite high school courses were in math/science or the humanities/social sciences. Panels C and D, respectively, reflect college major at age 23 and occupation at age 33. All four panels represent a three-dimensional view of how mathematical (X), verbal (Y), and spatial (Z) ability factor into educational-vocational preferences and choice. For all four panels, all three abilities are standardized in z-score units (A and B are within sex; C and D are combined across sex). For each labeled group within each panel, the direction of the

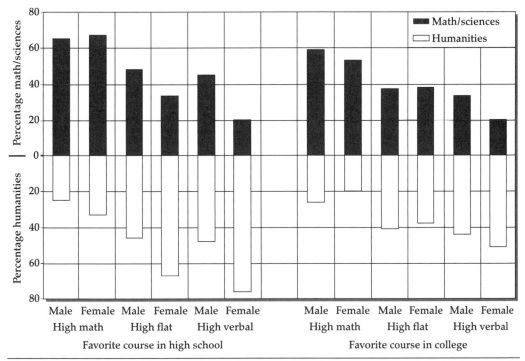

Figure 25.2   Participants' Favorite Course in High School and in College (Lubinski, Webb, et al., 2001). [*Note:* Percentages in a given column do not necessarily sum to 100% because only participants indicating either math/sciences or humanities courses are displayed. Significance tests for differences among groups for favorite course are as follows: high school math/science χ^2 (2, $N = 320$) = 20.7, $p < .0001$; college math/science χ^2 (2, $N = 320$) = 18.2, $p < .0001$; high school humanities χ^2 (2, $N = 320$) = 36.6, $p < .0001$; and college humanities $\chi^2 >$ (2, $N = 320$) = 30.2, $p < .0001$.]

arrows represents whether spatial ability (Z-axis) was above (right) or below (left) the grand mean for spatial ability. These arrows were scaled in the same units of measurement as the SAT (math and verbal) scores, so you can envision how far apart these groups are in three-dimensional space in standard deviation units as a function of these three abilities.

In summary, these findings suggested that higher levels of math, relative to verbal abilities, characterized group membership in engineering and math/computer science areas. The engineering and math/computer science groups also demonstrated higher levels of spatial abilities. The natural and physical sciences stood alone in being characterized by higher levels of all three abilities: math, spatial, and verbal. More balanced verbal and math profiles and generally lower levels of spatial abilities characterized fields such as medicine, law, and business. These findings were highly consistent for other outcome criteria as well, such as graduate field of study (Shea et al., 2001). In addition, it is important to note that across all time points, all three abilities achieved a statistically significant degree of *incremental validity* (Sechrest, 1963) relative to the other two in predicting group membership in the educational-vocational groups.

Table 25.1
Awards and Special Accomplishments of the Top 1 in 10,000
in Mathematical or Verbal Reasoning Ability

Sciences and Technology	Humanities and Arts	Other
Scientific publications (11)	Creative writing (7)	Phi Beta Kappa (71)
Software development (8)	Creation of art or music (6)	Tau Beta Pi (30)
Inventions (4)	Fulbright award (2)	Phi Kappa Phi (14)
National Science Foundation fellowship (2)	Wrote proposal for a novel voting system for new South African Constitution	Entrepreneurial enterprises (2)
Designed image correlation system for navigation for Mars Landing Program	Solo violin debut (age 13) Cincinnati Symphony Orchestra	Omicron Delta Kappa
The American Physical Society's Apker Award	Mellon Fellow in the Humanities	Olympiad Silver Medal
Graduated from Massachusetts Institute of Technology in three years at age 19 (entered at 16) with perfect (5.0) grade point average and graduated from Harvard Medical School with MD at age 23	Presidential Scholar for Creative Writing	Finished bachelor's and master's in four years
	Hopwood writing award	Received private pilot's license in one month
	Creative Anachronisms Award of Arms	
Teaching award for "Order of Magnitude Physics"	First place in midreal-medieval poetry	
	Foreign language study fellowship	
	International predissertation award	

Group	Sciences and Technology	Humanities and Arts
High-Math	16	5
High-Flat	6	6
High-Verbal	7	13

Note: Numbers in parentheses represent the number of participants indicating each accomplishment. All other entries represent a single individual.

Source: From "Top 1 in 10,000: A 10-Year Follow-Up of the Profoundly Gifted," by D. Lubinski, R. M. Webb, M. J. Morelock, and C. P. Benbow, 2001, *Journal of Applied Psychology*, 86, pp. 718–729.

ABOVE-LEVEL ASSESSMENT OF PREFERENCES

While the systematic application of above-level assessment of specific abilities now enjoys more than a 30-year history of documented applied utility, what was not known until more recently was the extent to which preference dimensions could be assessed in a reliable and valid manner at early ages to address the satisfaction dimension of TWA with intellectually talented youth. Is it possible, for instance, to think about the presence of precocity among the intellectually talented in the vocational preference domain, conceptualized as early crystallization of interests and values? If so, perhaps such assessments might offer clues about what these bright young students are likely to be passionate about later in

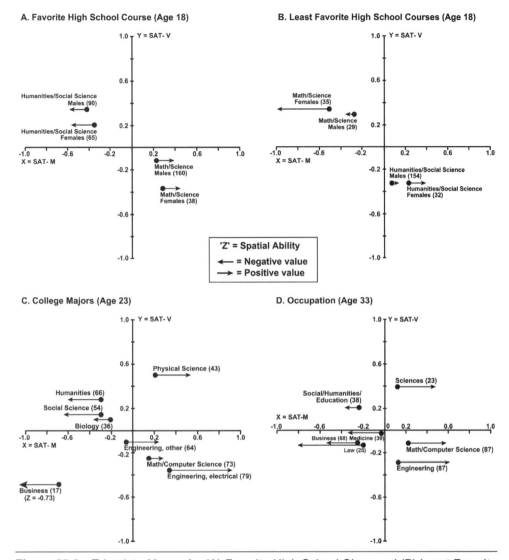

Figure 25.3 Trivariate Means for (A) Favorite High School Class and (B) Least Favorite Class at Age 18, (C) Conferred Bachelor's Degree at Age 23, and (D) Occupation at Age 33. [*Note:* Group *ns* are in parenthesis. SAT-V = Verbal subtest of the Scholastic Assessment Test; SAT-M = Mathematical subtest of the Scholastic Assessment Test; and Spatial Ability = A composite of two subtests of the Differential Aptitude Test (space relations + mechanical reasoning). Panels A and B are standardized within sexes, panels C and D between sexes. The large arrowhead in panel C indicates that this group's relative weakness in spatial ability is actually twice as great as that indicated by the displayed length. *Source:* Adapted from Shea et al. (2001).]

life. Roe (1956) asserted that, on average, interests tend to crystallize by approximately age 18 in the general population. This general finding guided the development of vocational preference instruments, which typically target persons from high school age and above. Among the intellectually gifted, however, crystallization may occur at an earlier age and could be combined with ability assessment to aid advanced educational and early career planning.

Several pieces of evidence support this line of thinking. As noted previously, many career educators and teachers of the gifted have asserted that interests, values, and other preferences appear to crystallize earlier in this special population (Milne, 1979). In earlier empirical studies, Flanagan and Cooley (1966) found that gifted students tended to have more developed interests and a better understanding of their personal values and attitudes than students not identified as gifted. Terman (1954) noted that childhood interests of gifted individuals discriminated several years later between scientists and nonscientists and that the Strong Vocational Interest Blank (now Strong Interest Inventory) could usefully differentiate between interests in intellectually gifted samples.

More recent studies from SMPY have provided further validation to the early application of conventional preference questionnaires initially designed for adults. First, in a study among intellectually precocious young adolescents, Achter et al. (1996) showed that both the Strong Interest Inventory and the Study of Values revealed marked individual differences in this population; that is, between 72% and 77% of gifted adolescents had interest and value profiles that showed clear differentiation between themes.

A second pair of studies highlighted the temporal stability of preferences assessed at an early age in this population. The first, by Lubinski, Benbow, and Ryan (1995), provided support for the general stability of vocational interest patterns in 162 gifted individuals over a 15-year period from adolescence to adulthood (age 13 to age 28). Specifically, the dominant theme for any individual at age 13 was significantly more likely than chance to be either dominant or adjacent to the dominant theme at age 28 (following the hexagonal organization of RIASEC; Holland, 1985). In a constructive replication (Lykken, 1968) of the aforementioned study, Lubinski, Schmidt, and Benbow (1996) assessed the temporal stability of the Study of Values (SOV; Allport, Vernon, & Lindzey, 1970) among an independent sample of 202 intellectually gifted participants over a 20-year period from age 13 to age 33. Consistent with results of the first study, the dominant SOV theme at age 13 was significantly more likely than chance to be dominant or adjacent to the dominant theme at age 33 (see Lubinski et al., 1996, for definition of adjacency). In addition, a comprehensive evaluation of the construct validity of the Strong and SOV for intellectually precocious 12- to 14-year-olds (D. B. Schmidt, Lubinski, & Benbow, 1998) found that using these instruments on this special population generated psychometric properties parallel to those of young adults.

To solidify the generalization that vocational preferences tend to crystallize early among the intellectually talented, Achter et al. (1999) set out to examine whether preferences identified in adolescence were predictive of temporally remote educational outcomes and, importantly, to ascertain whether preference assessments added to predictions that already had been established by abilities as assessed by the SAT. To do so, the researchers followed a group of 432 intellectually precocious young adolescents over 10 years, from the time they took the SAT and Study of Values (SOV) at age 13, until approximately age 23, when they had secured college degrees. Results showed that age 13 assessments on preference dimensions added incremental validity to age 13 assessments of mathematical and verbal abilities in predicting broad categories of college majors (i.e., Math-Science, Humanities, and Other; the same broad categories used by the ability studies reviewed earlier). Specifically, of the 23% of total variance accounted for by the SAT and SOV across all three groups of college majors (which is excellent given the heterogeneity within each of these groups), the SOV accounted for an additional 13% of the variance between groups over and above the SAT scales, which accounted for 10%.

Discriminant analysis in the Achter et al. (1999) study revealed that high math ability and theoretical values, combined with lower social and religious values, were most predictive of completing math-science majors. High verbal ability and aesthetic values were most predictive of completing majors in the humanities. Majors categorized as "Other" (e.g., social sciences, business) were predicted by high social and religious values and low mathematical abilities and aesthetic values. Figure 25.4 summarizes results obtained from the discriminant analysis in this study. Overall, this collection of findings supports the notion that educationally and vocationally relevant preferences tend to crystallize early among the intellectually talented and that their applied use for this special population is warranted.

A final note to make about early emerging abilities and preferences is that they reveal how commensurate occupational success and satisfaction later in life are achieved in different ways—as TWA would forecast and as established with ability and preference measures in older populations (Dawis & Lofquist, 1984;

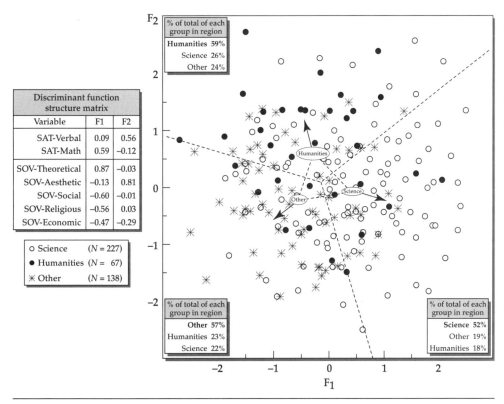

Figure 25.4 Group Centroids and a Discriminant-Structure Matrix (Achter et al., 1999). [*Note:* The bivariate group centroids for the total sample were (Function 1, followed by Function 2): math-science (.43, −.05); humanities (−.29, .60); and other (−.57, −.21). To make the scatter plot less cluttered, each bivariate point represents an average of two participants' discriminant scores (most typically, the closest geometrically). Percentages were computed using all individual data points. SOV = Study of Values; SAT = Scholastic Aptitude Test; F1 = Function 1; F2 = Function 2.]

Lofquist & Dawis, 1991). For instance, Benbow et al. (2000) reported that mathematically gifted 33-year-olds, first identified as gifted 20 years prior at age 13, overwhelmingly described themselves as both successful and satisfied with the direction of their careers. Across two different cohorts (total $N = 1,975$), roughly two-thirds of these individuals described themselves as "successful" or "very successful" and "satisfied" or "very satisfied" with their careers. These data on success and satisfaction showed no statistically significant sex differences, despite the fact that the males and females were differentially represented in various occupations (e.g., greater proportions of male math/computer scientists and engineers; greater proportions of female medical doctors, health care workers, and homemakers). This is likely due to the differential male-female ability/preference profiles among the intellectually talented (Lubinski & Benbow, 1992; Webb et al., 2002), which we address further in a subsequent section on gender differences and similarities.

After reviewing these modern findings, it should seem fairly clear that comprehensive ability and preference assessment among the intellectually talented, at an early age, is useful in predicting educational/vocational choice, level of success/achievement, and satisfaction. The contemporary research supports and extends the work of pioneers dating to Terman, Hollingworth, and many individual differences psychologists throughout the past century, highlighting the utility of early identification, attention to both general and specific abilities, and the importance of nonintellective factors such as preferences (i.e., interests and values).

These robust empirical findings provide a helpful backdrop for addressing two topics that have received much attention in the literature pertaining to the education and counseling of intellectually talented youth: multipotentiality and gender differences.

Addressing Perceptions of Multipotentiality

Implied in the preceding findings is that the assessment of abilities and preferences among the intellectually talented can be practiced at early ages and has significant applied psychological utility over the life span. Yet, this empirical evidence runs counter to an enduring perception among many who work with the gifted; that is, that most intellectually talented individuals can thrive in almost any vocation or career because of their multitude of high-level abilities and interests, a condition termed *multipotentiality* in the gifted literature (cf. Achter, Benbow, & Lubinski, 1997). Critiques and empirical findings notwithstanding (e.g., Achter et al., 1996; Kidner, 1997; Milgram & Hong, 1999; Sajjadi, Rejskind, & Shore, 2001), the perception of multipotentiality continues to be discussed as a critical barrier in career counseling with the intellectually talented (Kerr & Fisher, 1997; Rysiew, Shore, & Leeb, 1999). Because the concept of multipotentiality is likely to be encountered by those working with this special population, we feel compelled to further address it.

Operationally, multipotentiality has been said to be present in individuals who earn uniformly high scores across ability and achievement tests and exhibit multiple interests at equal intensities on interest inventories (Sanborn, 1979a, 1979b). Given such high-flat ability *and* interest profiles, multipotentiality is believed to lead to the reasonable consideration of multiple career options and difficulty with career choice (Fredrickson, 1986; Kerr & Ghrist-Priebe, 1988). But these high-flat profiles are found only with age-based instruments, if at all. When developmentally appropriate (i.e., above-level) assessment tools are used with this special population, a different picture emerges.

As we have reviewed, abilities and preference patterns among gifted adolescents are found to be differentiated when measures with enough "ceiling" or "top" are used. The first explicit demonstration of this, by Achter et al. (1996), was summarized earlier; and it has now been replicated at least twice. The first replication, by Kidner (1997), sampled gifted students (average age 15.9 years) from a residential, early college entrance program and found that the proportion of ability and preference profiles considered multipotential decreased when cognitively appropriate (i.e., above-level) ability (SAT), interest (Self-Directed Search), and values (Study of Values) measures were used. The second study, by Milgram and Hong (1999), used the top 5% of a slightly older (high school) sample of Israeli students who were first identified by a general ability measure used for military assignment. Through subsequent administration of math, verbal, and mechanical ability tests, they found that only between 20% and 23% produced the high-flat ability profile consistent with the concept of multipotentiality. Further, through codifying leisure activities to assess interest themes, the number of combined flat ability and interest profiles declined to 5.5%. Milgram and Hong reported one additional finding that runs counter to the notion of multipotentiality: Even among those with flat interest profiles, more of them were low-flat (no discernable interest) than high-flat (multiple interests).

These are the only three studies we are aware of that addressed multipotentiality empirically, and they are uniform in their findings. They also square well with what is known about correlations among the major ability areas (e.g., mathematical, verbal, spatial-mechanical) for individuals at different intellectual levels, namely, that more highly intelligent individuals are more likely to have jagged, or differentiated, ability profiles (Gottfredson, 2003; Lubinski, 2004).

Researchers who have identified multipotentiality among the intellectually talented through self-reported broad abilities and interests (e.g., Sajjadi et al., 2001; Shute, 2000), rather than using standardized ability and interest measures, reported a much higher incidence of multipotentiality (e.g., 84% of university honors students in Shute, 2000)—supporting the notion that many gifted persons perceive themselves as having diverse talents and interests. However, as the researchers examined other aspects of their participants' career perceptions, they discovered that the students did not, as was expected, report high levels of difficulty with career decision making (Shute, 2000), satisfaction, or general well-being (Sajjadi et al., 2001). In fact, those who perceived themselves as multipotential possessed greater than average confidence in finding a satisfying career (Sajjadi et al., 2001).

We believe the primary reason the notion of multipotentiality persists, in spite of the weight of available empirical evidence to the contrary, is that it is consistent with surface observations. This sentiment was echoed by Rysiew et al. (1999), who stated, "the *anecdotal and clinical reports* of counselors and psychologists who work closely with highly able adolescents and young adults continues to support the existence of a characteristic such as multipotentiality with both ability and interest dimensions" (p. 428, emphasis added). Even if their ability and interest profiles would show differentiation (which can only be determined through proper assessment), school performance and grade-level achievement test scores of the intellectually talented are typically well above average in several areas, and these students tend to possess greater interest in academic topics in general. To others, and even to talented students themselves (Sajjadi et al., 2001; Shute, 2000), this creates the perception of multipotentiality. By extension, these surface appearances make it seem evident that the intellectually talented have many more opportunities open to them than others (i.e., by virtue of their high abilities, they meet or exceed the *minimum* requirements of many occupations). While this may be true in purely numerical terms, it ignores the fact that, like for persons of all ability ranges, the unique combinations of abilities, preferences, and energies make any intellectually talented person *optimally* suited for only a subset of career areas.

The scientific evidence speaking to the issue of multipotentiality is important for helping us recognize that, despite outward appearances, we cannot assume that the gifted have undifferentiated, or flat, abilities and interests—in fact, most do not. It further informs us that even for those intellectually talented students who perceive themselves as having multiple and uniformly high abilities and interests, this perception will not necessarily create problems in educational/career decision making or ultimate satisfaction (Sajjadi et al., 2001). We understand how perceptions of multipotentiality arise and how they may even contribute to internal and external expectations that pull intellectually talented persons in multiple directions. However, we believe the robust empirical findings about stable educationally and vocationally relevant personal information offer a constructive reframing of these surface perceptions and open the door to a more helpful approach for assisting the intellectually talented in their personal development. This special population needs valid personal information about their abilities and preferences, at least as a starting point for meaningful conversation about their academic and career development. To be sure, clinical experiences can attenuate accurate perceptions in many ways (Dawes, 1994; Grove & Meehl, 1996; Meehl, 1986); but ultimately, conclusions should be based on the best empirical evidence.

GENDER DIFFERENCES AND SIMILARITIES

Much is often made of the differential educational needs of intellectually talented males and females. In the context of the individual differences model described in this chapter and elsewhere (Tyler, 1974), we believe there are two important statements to make about the influence of gender on identifying and nurturing intellectual talent. First, there are indeed some stable individual differences observed between the ability and preference profiles of gifted males and females. Although males and females do not differ in general intellectual ability, they do differ, on average, in certain specific cognitive abilities. Females show slightly greater verbal abilities in some areas than males, whereas males, on average, show greater mathematical and spatial abilities (Halpern, 2000; Kimura, 1999). On preference measures, males and females differ by more than one standard deviation on interest in working with people versus working with things (Lippa, 1998; Lubinski, 2000, p. 421); females as a group are more attracted to opportunities and environments involving the former, males the latter. Furthermore, males tend to show greater differentiation among preference domains, with females showing more breadth across preference themes (Achter et al., 1996, 1999; Lubinski & Benbow, 1992). In samples of highly talented male students, the most common Holland interest theme is Investigative and the most common value theme (using the Study of Values) is Theoretical; for highly talented female students, on the other hand, Investigative, Artistic, and Social interest themes are often found to be at comparable levels, as are their Theoretical, Aesthetic, and Social values on the SOV (Achter et al., 1999).

The second important statement is that the gender differences just described are equally predictive of outcomes (e.g., choice, success, and satisfaction) for both males and females, just as TWA would suggest. For instance, more females than males are likely to gravitate toward humanities, medicine, law, and social sciences, consistent with their higher verbal abilities and more balanced ability and interest profiles (Lubinski, Webb, et al., 2001; Webb et al., 2002). And more males than females are likely to gravitate toward physical and applied science areas, consistent with higher mathematical abilities and dominant Investigative interests, on average. It is important to note, as previously mentioned, that both males and females with high intellectual talent report similarly high levels of success and satisfaction with their educational and career choices over time. This even holds for the occupational classification of homemaker, which more talented women choose relative to similarly talented men (Benbow et al., 2000).

Another way to investigate the predictive equality of individual differences measures across genders was examined by Lubinski, Benbow, et al. (2001). Rather than selecting gifted students based on specific math and verbal abilities and following them over time, they instead compared the attributes of 368 males and 346 females who had already earned admission to prestigious math-science graduate programs. What they found among these males and females were many more similarities than differences. Specifically, both males and females in this sample were characterized by very high mathematical abilities, relatively weaker verbal abilities, and strong scientific preferences (i.e., dominant Investigative interests and Theoretical values) relative to all other preference domains. And mathematics tended to be their favorite course in high school. There were other salient similarities as well (see Lubinski, Benbow, et al., 2001, for details). While more males than females fit this ability-preference profile combination overall, in both the general population and among the intellectually talented, it appears to be the prototypic ability-preference profile, irrespective of gender, that fits highly select math/science environments. Most important for our purposes, these studies support the veracity of the individual differences model for identification and intervention with both male and female students with high intellectual talent.

FRAMING EDUCATIONAL/VOCATIONAL COUNSELING: INTERVENTIONS TO FOSTER FURTHERANCE

Given the longitudinal research summarized thus far, we are confident in making the best practice recommendation that counselors keep their focus on optimal development of intellectual talent by providing accurate, cognitively appropriate (e.g., above-level) information concerning students' abilities (mathematical, verbal, spatial-mechanical) and preferences (interests and values)—manifestations of their intellectual promise and personal passions. This information is useful in helping students make informed choices about where they might be *most* successful or *most* satisfied and, therefore, likely have the *most* positive personal and societal impact over time. It also foreshadows the likelihood of navigating successfully through the learning or training hurdles leading toward fulfilling and productive careers (Gottfredson, 2003).

Developmental theorist Sandra Scarr helps us to further conceptualize counseling interventions with the intellectually talented, giving theoretical substance to Pressey's (1955) idea of furtherance. Scarr (1996) asserted that the primary objective of human development is for individuals to become (more) uniquely themselves. Rather than being passive recipients of exclusively environmental determinants, Scarr emphasized that individuals play an active role in choosing, creating, and experiencing their environments based on their individuality—their unique personalities, interests, and talents—and this active role increases from childhood to adolescence to adulthood. The goal, then, for anyone, including counselors, trying to assist individuals in building on strength is to (1) identify and capitalize on their salient abilities and interests (nurturing their potential and finding their passion) and (2) encourage them to focus their energies on opportunities that align with their distinctive potential.

Lubinski (1996) noted that the individual differences tradition in psychology, into which TWA and other person-environment fit models clearly fall, dovetails nicely with Scarr's explication of development in its focus on facilitating psychological growth through the careful measurement of personal characteristics, followed by counseling to assist in planning developmentally appropriate courses of action (e.g., educational, mentoring, and training opportunities). This tradition emphasizes giving information and skills to individuals to enable them to take active roles in their own development (Pressey, 1955; Tyler, 1992; Williamson, 1965). As Lubinski stated, "optimal development occurs when opportunities are tailored to an individual's readiness to profit from opportunities" (p. 191). "Readiness" can be reliably evaluated through the systematic assessment of abilities and preferences organized around the TWA concepts of satisfaction (fulfillment) and satisfactoriness (competence).

An efficient way for counselors to help intellectually talented adolescents to obtain above-level ability testing is through participation in one of the four regional talent searches in the United States (hosted by Johns Hopkins University, Duke University, Northwestern University, University of Denver). These programs coordinate testing and supply interpretative materials to help talented students and their counselors make educational decisions based on test scores. Unfortunately, the talent searches typically do not offer preference or spatial ability assessments. However, counselors can easily add this component by administering one of the many instruments that assess spatial visualization (Humphreys et al., 1993; Humphreys & Lubinski, 1996; Lohman, 1988; Lubinski, 2003; Shea et al., 2001) and one of the number of inventories available designed to assess Holland's (1996) six themes of vocational interests. Note the special significance of spatial ability for identifying women likely not only to have interests in and commitment to the math/sciences but also to succeed in these areas with distinction (Figure 25.3, Panels A & B).

When combined, *comprehensive* ability and interest information will offer a more refined portrait of educational paths that are most likely to lead to genuine success and satisfaction. The next step, then, is to recommend developmentally appropriate opportunities in the educational environment. Essentially, the same counseling principles routinely applied to college-going high school seniors can be generalized to this special population. But instead of using ability and interest information to help in focusing considerations about college majors, the goal would be to use this information to discuss how developmentally appropriate learning opportunities might be structured. For adolescents, the decisions being made are more general and tentative in nature (e.g., what classes to take next semester) than choosing an occupation or career. These early decisions are nonetheless significant and have important implications for subsequent educational and career decisions of intellectually talented students because they typically choose careers requiring much advanced educational preparation (Benbow et al., 2000; Lubinski, Benbow et al., 2001).

RESOURCE NEEDS

The institutional modifications necessary to support the model we have been espousing are relatively minimal, yet they can pay large dividends over time in the lives of intellectually talented students (Benbow & Stanley, 1996; Bleske-Rechek, Lubinski, & Benbow, 2004; Stanley, 2000). What is required in most cases is the flexible use of currently available educational resources, not significant additions in personnel or budget. For starters, this would include making available career counseling services and resources to intellectually talented middle school students. The more individualized these services could be, the better, with a baseline of facilitating talent search participation and making available valid career interest inventories. A next step in the schools would be allowing younger students to take courses when the assessment data suggests they are ready for them, rather than when they are offered to all students at a particular grade level (Colangelo & Davis, 2003; National Research Counsel, 2002, annex 6-1, pp. 11–14; Southern, Jones, & Stanley, 1993). While simple in concept, these modifications are not implemented without controversy and challenge in many places. For a thorough discussion of the sociopolitical landscape contributing to these challenges and a data-driven response, see Benbow and Stanley (1996).

Although thorough discussion of specific forms of educational interventions is beyond the scope of this chapter, a brief mention of some of the more common options is in order. In keeping with our focus on optimal development, we advocate most strongly for educational options that fall under the broad category of acceleration—educational practices that might more accurately be labeled "curricular flexibility" or "appropriate developmental placement" and which have long-standing and widespread empirical support for helping the intellectually talented without negatively affecting other students (Benbow & Stanley, 1996). Options that fit under this rubric and could be applied at various points during educational development include early admittance to school, grade skipping, entering college early, attending residential high schools tailored for gifted students, single (or multiple) subject acceleration, taking college courses while in high school, taking special fast-paced classes during the summer or academic year, taking advanced placement (AP) courses and exams, individual tutoring, and mentoring (excellent resources for further reading on these topics is found in Colangelo & Davis, 2003; National Research Council, 2002, annex 6-1, pp. 11–14; Southern et al., 1993).

The application of any of these options should consider that "learning is optimized, as is growth in achievement motivation, when the individual is presented with tasks that match or slightly exceed [current] capabilities" (Benbow & Stanley,

1996, p. 274). Counselors need also to remain vigilant that the educational environments secured by highly motivated and intellectually talented students are of high quality. Just as psychotherapeutic interventions with the same label can vary widely in their application (Dawes, 1994), programs designed for intellectually able students can represent a great deal of heterogeneity as well (Bleske-Rechek et al., 2004). For these reasons, counselors are also encouraged to monitor the reactions of their students to ensure that their educational needs are being met. Longitudinal findings from intellectually precocious youth now in adulthood have found overwhelmingly positive subjective reactions (Benbow et al., 2000; Benbow, Lubinski, & Suchy, 1996; Lubinski, Webb, et al., 2001) as well as better objective outcomes (Bleske-Rechek et al., 2004; Cronbach, 1996) resulting from accelerative learning opportunities.

LIMITATIONS AND FUTURE DIRECTIONS

While the model presented here represents a time-tested, empirically validated approach to educational/career counseling with talented youth, there still remain important gaps to be addressed in the future. First, despite the reliability and validity supporting the use of above-level ability and preference assessments for educational counseling, they still provide only rough guideposts for facilitating educational and career planning. Indeed, periodic reassessment of these personal attributes over the course of an individual's adolescence is advisable. Abilities and interests can and do change for some individuals, and assessing the magnitude of such changes is helpful for making informed educational and career choices.

Second, the talent search model that most systematically applies the above-level testing model we espouse currently fails to systematically incorporate measures of spatial abilities. As we strive not to miss those students who might usefully contribute to our increasingly technological society, identifying spatially talented individuals is one of the current critical challenges in the field. Indeed, using normal curve theory (Shea et al., 2001), it is estimated that approximately half of the top 1% in spatial visualization are not identified by modern talent search procedures that focus only on mathematical and verbal talent. These students will not necessarily find their own way if their exceptional spatial talents are not recognized and nurtured (Gohm, Humphreys, & Yao, 1998).

Finally, it is clear from studies drawing on SMPY samples that success and satisfaction are also based on other personal determinants not adequately captured by assessing conventional abilities and interests. Our studies have revealed, for instance, that even among individuals who possess comparable ability and preference profiles and who have been given similar opportunities, sizable individual differences in achievement are routinely observed. Counselors need to be aware of the individual differences in energy and time that people invest in developing their careers (e.g., Lubinski & Benbow, 2000, p. 143; Figure 25.2). While we do not know all the causal determinants relevant to modeling individual differences in achievement, creativity, and work performance, we believe that the conative factors (i.e., mental characteristics contributing to purposeful action) are critical elements begging for valid methods of measurement and subsequent research (Jensen, 1996; Lubinski, 2004). These include attributes variously referred to as capacity to work, industriousness, persistence, zeal, energy, and psychological tempo—characteristics that have been highlighted since the time of Aristotle, extending to modern theoreticians studying art, athletics, business, the military, politics, and science, among others (Ericsson, 1996; Eysenck, 1995; Gardner, 1993; Lubinski & Benbow, 2000; Simonton, 1988). Some persons seem to have great mental ability (e.g., high IQ), but appear to lack the energy needed to fully actualize their intellectual potential. Indeed, it is likely that under- and overachievers are distinguished, in part, by this set of attributes. Like all special populations, intellectually talented kids are not a categorical type.

SUMMARY

Our deepest calling is to grow into our own authentic self-hood. . . . As we do so, we will not only find the joy that every human being seeks—we will also find our path of authentic service in the world. (Palmer, 2000, p. 16)

Like students at all ability levels, intellectually talented students are faced with a range of opportunities and challenges as they seek to understand, develop, integrate, and, ultimately, apply their intellectual promise and their personal passions—or, as Palmer (2000) would put it, to grow into "authentic self-hood" and find both "joy" (satisfaction) and "authentic service in the world" (success). We submit that the early application of vocational assessment methods for measuring abilities and preferences can be used confidently by counselors to provide windows into authentic self-hood. We might also say that they afford insight into barriers to personal authenticity. They are incomplete and imperfect windows, to be sure, but they are nonetheless useful and represent the most accurate and objective tools we have at the present time. They can be especially helpful in clarifying choices in the face of potentially conflicting views from family, peers, teachers, and self on how best to structure an individual's educational, vocational, and personal development (Lubinski & Benbow, 2001). Indeed, a cogent case could be made that failing to employ these construct-valid measures—or, practicing a "truncated view of vocational counseling"—contributes to "educational and occupational maladjustment," which, years ago, Paterson (1957) called on applied psychologists to alleviate with practice based on science.

We hope that counselors choosing to work with the most talented students find merit in the idea that a scientifically valid place to start is early assessment of personal characteristics relevant to educational and career environments, followed by access, support, and encouragement to pursue developmentally appropriate opportunities. These two connected, and seemingly simple, steps will have profound impact on facilitating the optimal development of intellectual talent and propelling talented youth toward achieving rewarding and socially valued lives. In light of this, our charge as counselors with this special population has been succinctly put by Benbow and Stanley (1996): "If we want talented individuals to be well prepared when society needs them, we need to be there for them when they need us" (p. 279). May we respond enthusiastically to this charge.

REFERENCES

Achter, J. A., Benbow, C. P., & Lubinski, D. (1997). Rethinking multipotentiality among the intellectually gifted: A critical review and recommendations. *Gifted Child Quarterly, 41,* 5–15.

Achter, J. A., & Lubinski, D. (2003). Fostering exceptional development in intellectually talented populations. In W. B. Walsh (Ed.), *Counseling psychology and optimal human functioning* (pp. 25–54). Mahwah, NJ: Erlbaum.

Achter, J. A., Lubinski, D., & Benbow, C. P. (1996). Multipotentiality among the intellectually gifted: It was never there and already it's vanishing. *Journal of Counseling Psychology, 43,* 65–76.

Achter, J. A., Lubinski, D., Benbow, C. P., & Eftekhari-Sanjani, H. (1999). Assessing vocational preferences among gifted adolescents adds incremental validity to abilities. *Journal of Educational Psychology, 91,* 777–786.

Allport, G. W., Vernon, P. E., & Lindzey, G. (1970). *Manual: Study of values.* Cambridge, MA: Houghton Mifflin.

Benbow, C. P. (1991). Mathematically talented children: Can acceleration meet their educational needs. In N. Colangelo & G. A. Davis (Eds.), *Handbook of gifted education* (pp. 154–165). Boston: Allyn & Bacon.

Benbow, C. P. (1992). Academic achievement in mathematics and science between ages 13 and 23: Are there differences among students in the top one percent of mathematical ability? *Journal of Educational Psychology, 84,* 51–61.

Benbow, C. P., & Lubinski, D. (1996). *Intellectual talent: Psychometric and social issues.* Baltimore: Johns Hopkins University Press.

Benbow, C. P., & Lubinski, D. (1997). Intellectually talented children: How can we best meet their needs? In N. Colangelo & G. A. Davis (Eds.), *Handbook of gifted education* (2nd ed., pp. 155–169). Boston: Allyn & Bacon.

Benbow, C. P., Lubinski, D., Shea, D. L., & Eftekhari-Sanjani, H. (2000). Sex differences in mathematical reasoning ability at age 13: Their status 20 years later. *Psychological Science, 11,* 474–480.

Benbow, C. P., Lubinski, D., & Suchy, B. (1996). Impact of the SMPY model and programs from the perspective of the participant. In C. P. Benbow & D. Lubinski (Eds.), *Intellectual talent: Psychometric and social issues* (pp. 266–300). Baltimore: Johns Hopkins University Press.

Benbow, C. P., & Stanley, J. C. (1996). Inequity in equity: How "equity" can lead to inequity for high-potential students. *Psychology, Public Policy, and Law, 2,* 249–292.

Beuchner, F. (1993). *Wishful thinking: A theological ABC.* San Francisco: Harper & Row.

Bleske-Rechek, A., Lubinski, D., & Benbow, C. P. (2004). Meeting the educational needs of special populations: Advanced placement's role in developing exceptional human capital. *Psychological Science, 15,* 217–224.

Carroll, J. B. (1993). *Human cognitive abilities: A survey of factor-analytic studies.* New York: Cambridge University Press.

Colangelo, N., & Davis, G. A. (2003). *Handbook of gifted education* (3rd ed.). Boston: Allyn & Bacon.

Cronbach, L. J. (1996). Acceleration among the Terman males: Correlates in midlife and after. In C. P. Benbow & D. Lubinski (Eds.), *Intellectual talent: Psychometric and social issues* (pp. 179–191). Baltimore: Johns Hopkins University Press.

Dark, V. J., & Benbow, C. P. (1993). Cognitive differences among the gifted: A review and new data. In D. K. Detterman (Ed.), *Current topics in human intelligence* (Vol. 3, pp. 85–120). New York: Ablex.

Dawes, R. M. (1994). *House of cards: Psychology and psychotherapy built on a myth.* New York: Free Press.

Dawis, R. V. (1992). The individual differences tradition in counseling psychology. *Journal of Counseling Psychology, 39,* 7–19.

Dawis, R. V., & Lofquist, L. H. (1984). *A psychological theory of work adjustment.* Minneapolis: University of Minnesota Press.

Drazgow, F. (2002). Intelligence and the workplace. In W. C. Borman, D. R. Ilgen, & R. J. Klimoski (Eds.), *Handbook of psychology, industrial and organizational psychology* (Vol. 12, pp. 107–130). New York: Wiley.

Ericsson, K. A. (1996). *The road to excellence.* Mahwah, NJ: Erlbaum.

Eysenck, H. J. (1995). *Genius: The natural history of creativity.* Cambridge, England: Cambridge University Press.

Flanagan, J. C., & Cooley, W. W. (1966). *Project Talent one-year follow-up studies.* Pittsburgh, PA: University of Pittsburgh.

Fredrickson, R. H. (1986). Preparing gifted and talented students for the world of work. *Journal of Counseling and Development, 64,* 556–557.

Gardner, H. (1993). *Multiple intelligences: The theory in practice.* New York: HarperCollins.

Gohm, C. L., Humphreys, L. G., & Yao, G. (1998). Underachievement among spatially gifted students. *American Educational Research Journal, 35,* 515–531.

Gottfredson, L. S. (1997). Intelligence and social policy [special issue]. *Intelligence, 24*(1, Whole issue).

Gottfredson, L. S. (2003). The challenge and promise of cognitive career assessment. *Journal of Career Assessment, 11,* 115–135.

Grove, W. M., & Meehl, P. E. (1996). Comparative efficiency of informal (subjective, impressionistic) and formal (mechanical, algorithmic) prediction procedures: The clinical-statistical controversy. *Psychology, Public Policy, and Law, 2,* 293–323.

Halpern, D. F. (2000). *Sex differences in cognitive abilities (3rd ed.).* Mahwah, NJ: Lawrence Erlbaum.

Holland, J. L. (1985). *Making vocational choices* (2nd ed.). Englewood Cliffs, NJ: Prentice-Hall.

Holland, J. L. (1996). Exploring careers with a typology: What we have learned and some new directions. *American Psychologist, 51,* 397–406.

Hollingworth, L. S. (1926). *Gifted children: Their nature and nurture.* New York: Macmillan.

Hollingworth, L. S. (1942). *Children above 180 IQ.* New York: World Books.

Humphreys, L. G., & Lubinski, D. (1996). Brief history and psychological significance of spatial-visualization abilities. In C. P. Benbow & D. Lubinski (Eds.), *Intellectual talent: Psychometric and social issues* (pp. 116–140). Baltimore: Johns Hopkins University Press.

Humphreys, L. G., Lubinski, D., & Yao, G. (1993). Utility of predicting group membership and the role of spatial visualization in becoming an engineer, physical scientist, or artist. *Journal of Applied Psychology, 78,* 250–261.

Hunt, E. (1995). *Will we be smart enough? A cognitive analysis of the coming workforce.* New York: Russell Sage Foundation.

Jackson, N. E., & Butterfield, E. C. (1986). A conception of giftedness designed to promote research. In R. J. Sternberg & J. E. Davidson (Eds.), *Conceptions of giftedness* (pp. 151–181). New York: Cambridge University Press.

Jensen, A. R. (1996). Giftedness and genius: Crucial differences. In C. P. Benbow & D. Lubinski (Eds.), *Intellectual talent: Psychometric and social issues* (pp. 393–411). Baltimore: Johns Hopkins University Press.

Jensen, A. R. (1998). *The g factor.* Westport, CT: Praeger.

Keating, D. P., & Stanley, J. C. (1972). Extreme measures for the exceptionally gifted in mathematics and science. *Educational Researcher, 1,* 3–7.

Kerr, B. A. (1981). Career education strategies for the gifted. *Journal of Career Education, 7,* 318–324.

Kerr, B. A., & Fisher, T. (1997). Career assessment with gifted and talented students. *Journal of Career Assessment, 5,* 239–251.

Kerr, B. A., & Ghrist-Priebe, S. L. (1988). Intervention for multipotentiality: Effects of a career counseling laboratory for gifted high school students. *Journal of Counseling and Development, 66,* 366–369.

Kidner, C. L. (1997). *Increasing differentiation on vocational assessments among gifted high school students.* Unpublished doctoral dissertation, University of North Texas, Denton.

Kimura, D. (1999). *Sex and cognition.* Cambridge, MA: Massachusetts Institute of Technology.

Lippa, R. (1998). Gender-related individual differences and the structure of vocational interests: The importance of the people-things dimension. *Journal of Personality and Social Psychology, 74,* 996–1009.

Lofquist, L. H., & Dawis, R. V. (1991). *Essentials of person-environment-correspondence counseling.* Minneapolis: University of Minnesota Press.

Lohman, D. F. (1988). Spatial abilities as traits, processes, and knowledge. In R. J. Sternberg (Ed.), *Advances in the psychology of human intelligence* (Vol. 4, pp. 181–248). Hillsdale, NJ: Erlbaum.

Lubinski, D. (1996). Applied individual differences research and its quantitative methods. *Psychology, Public Policy, and Law, 2,* 187–203.

Lubinski, D. (2000). Scientific and social significance of assessing individual differences: "Sinking shafts at a few critical points." *Annual Review of Psychology, 51,* 405–444.

Lubinski, D. (2001). Interests: A critical domain of psychological diversity: Review of M. L. Savickas & A. R., Spokane (Eds.), *Vocational interests: Meaning, measurement, and counseling use.* In *Contemporary Psychology, 46,* 82–86.

Lubinski, D. (2003). Exceptional spatial abilities. In N. Colangelo & G. A. Davis (Eds.), *Handbook of gifted education* (3rd ed., pp. 521–532). Boston: Allyn and Bacon.

Lubinski, D. (2004). Introduction to the special section on cognitive abilities: 100 years after Spearman's (1904) "'General intelligence,' objectively determined and measured." *Journal of Personality and Social Psychology, 86,* 96–111.

Lubinski, D., & Benbow, C. P. (1992). Gender differences in abilities and preferences among the gifted. *Current Directions in Psychological Science, 1,* 61–66.

Lubinski, D., & Benbow, C. P. (1995). Optimal development of talent: Respond educationally to individual differences in personality. *Educational Forum, 59,* 381–392.

Lubinski, D., & Benbow, C. P. (2000). States of excellence. *American Psychologist, 55,* 137–150.

Lubinski, D., & Benbow, C. P. (2001). Choosing excellence. *American Psychologist, 56,* 76–77.

Lubinski, D., Benbow, C. P., & Ryan, J. (1995). Stability of vocational interests among the intellectually gifted from adolescence to adulthood: A 15-year longitudinal study. *Journal of Applied Psychology, 80,* 196–200.

Lubinski, D., Benbow, C. P., Shea, D. L., Eftekhari-Sanjani, H., & Halvorson, M. B. J. (2001). Men and woman at promise for scientific excellence: Similarity not dissimilarity. *Psychological Science, 12,* 309–317.

Lubinski, D., & Humphreys, L. G. (1997). Incorporating general intelligence into epidemiology and the social sciences. *Intelligence, 24,* 159–201.

Lubinski, D., Schmidt, D. B., & Benbow, C. P. (1996). A 20-year stability analysis of the Study of Values for intellectually gifted individuals from adolescence to adulthood. *Journal of Applied Psychology, 81,* 443–451.

Lubinski, D., Webb, R. M., Morelock, M. J., & Benbow, C. P. (2001). Top 1 in 10, 000: A 10-year follow-up of the profoundly gifted. *Journal of Applied Psychology, 86,* 718–729.

Lykken, D. T. (1968). Statistical significance in psychological research. *Psychological Bulletin, 70,* 151–159.

Meehl, P. E. (1986). Causes and effects of my disturbing little book. *Journal of Personality Assessment, 50,* 370–375.

Milgram, R. M., & Hong, E. (1999). Multipotential abilities and vocational interests in gifted adolescents: Fact or fiction? *International Journal of Psychology, 34,* 81–93.

Milne, B. G. (1979). Career education. In A. H. Passow (Ed.), *The gifted and talented: Their education and development* (pp. 246–254). Chicago: University of Chicago Press.

Murray, C. (1998). *Income, inequality, and IQ.* Washington, DC: American Enterprise Institute.

National Research Council. (2002). *Learning and understanding: Improving advanced study of mathematics and science in U.S. high schools.* Washington, DC: National Academy Press.

Palmer, P. J. (2000). *Let your life speak: Listening for the voice of vocation.* San Francisco: Jossey Bass.

Parsons, F. (1909). *Choosing a vocation.* Boston: Houghton Mifflin.

Paterson, D. G. (1957). The conservation of human talent. *American Psychologist, 12,* 134–144.

Prediger, D. J. (1982). Dimensions underlying Holland's hexagon: Missing link between interests and occupations? *Journal of Vocational Behavior, 21,* 259–287.

Pressey, S. L. (1946). Acceleration: Disgrace or challenge? *Science, 104,* 215–219.

Pressey, S. L. (1955). Concerning the nature and nurture of genius. *Scientific Monthly, 81,* 123–129.

Pressey, S. L. (1967). "Fordling" accelerates ten years after. *Journal of Counseling Psychology, 14,* 73–80.

Roe, A. (1956). *The psychology of occupations.* New York: Wiley.

Rysiew, K. J., Shore, B. M., & Leeb, R. T. (1999). Multipotentiality, giftedness, and career choice: A review. *Journal of Counseling and Development, 77,* 423–430.

Sajjadi, S. H., Rejskind, F. G., & Shore, B. M. (2001). Is multipotentiality a problem or not? A new look at the data. *High Ability Studies, 12,* 27–43.

Sanborn, M. P. (1979a). Career development: Problems of gifted and talented students. In N. Colangelo & R. T. Zaffrann (Eds.), *New voices in counseling the gifted* (pp. 284–300). Dubuque, IA: Kendall/Hunt.

Sanborn, M. P. (1979b). Counseling and guidance needs of the gifted and talented. In A. H. Passow (Ed.), *The gifted and talented: Their education and development* (pp. 424–428). The seventy-eighth yearbook of the national society for the study of education. Chicago: University of Chicago Press.

Scarr, S. (1996). How people make their own environments: Implications for parents and policy makers. *Psychology, Public Policy, and Law, 2*, 204–228.

Schmidt, D. B., Lubinski, D., & Benbow, C. P. (1998). Validity of assessing educational-vocational preference dimensions among intellectually talented 13-year olds. *Journal of Counseling Psychology, 45*, 436–453.

Schmidt, F. L., & Hunter, J. E. (1998). The validity and utility of selection methods in personnel psychology: Practical and theoretical implications of 85 years of research findings. *Psychological Bulletin, 124*, 262–274.

Seashore, C. E. (1922). The gifted student and research. *Science, 56*, 641–648.

Sechrest, L. (1963). Incremental validity: A recommendation. *Educational and Psychological Measurement, 23*, 153–158.

Shea, D. L., Lubinski, D., & Benbow, C. P. (2001). Importance of assessing spatial ability in intellectually talented young adolescents: A 20-year longitudinal study. *Journal of Educational Psychology, 93*, 604–614.

Shoffner, M. F., & Newsome, D. W. (2001). Identity development of gifted female adolescents: The influence of career development, age, and life-role salience. *Journal of Secondary Gifted Education, 12*, 201–211.

Shute, L. D. (2000). *An investigation of multipotentiality among university honors students.* Unpublished doctoral dissertation. University of Connecticut.

Silverman, L. K. (1993). Career counseling. In L. K. Silverman (Ed.), *Counseling the gifted and talented* (pp. 215–238). Denver, CO: Love.

Simonton, D. K. (1988). *Scientific genius.* Cambridge, England: Cambridge University Press.

Snow, R. E., Kyllonen, P. C., & Marshalek, B. (1984). The topography of ability and learning correlates. In R. J. Sternberg (Ed.), *Advances in the psychology of human intelligence* (Vol. 2, pp. 47–104). Hillsdale, NJ: Erlbaum.

Snow, R. E., & Lohman, D. F. (1989). Implications of cognitive psychology for educational measurement. In R. L. Linn (Ed.), *Educational measurement* (3rd ed., pp. 263–331). New York: Collier.

Southern, W. T., Jones, E. D., & Stanley, J. C. (1993). Acceleration and enrichment: The context and development of program options. In K. A. Heller, F. J. Monks, & A. H. Passow (Eds.), *International handbook for research on giftedness and talent* (pp. 387–410). Oxford, England: Pergamon Press.

Stanley, J. C. (1974). Intellectual precocity. In J. C. Stanley, D. P. Keating, & L. H. Fox (Eds.), *Mathematical talent: Discovery, description, and development* (pp. 1–22). Baltimore: Johns Hopkins University Press.

Stanley, J. C. (1977). Rationale of the Study of Mathematically Precocious Youth (SMPY) during its first five years of promoting educational acceleration. In J. C. Stanley, W. C. George, & C. H. Salano (Eds.), *The gifted and the creative: A fifty year perspective* (pp. 73–112). Baltimore: Johns Hopkins University Press.

Stanley, J. C. (1996). SMPY in the beginning. In C. P. Benbow & D. Lubinski (Eds.), *Intellectual talent: Psychometric and social issues* (pp. 225–235). Baltimore: Johns Hopkins University Press.

Stanley, J. C. (2000). Helping students learn only what they don't already know. *Psychology, Public Policy, and Law, 6*, 216–222.

Stanley, J. C., & Benbow, C. P. (1986). Youths who reason exceptionally well mathematically. In R. J. Sternberg & J. E. Davidson (Eds.), *Conceptions of giftedness* (pp. 361–387). New York: Cambridge University Press.

Sternberg, R. J., & Davidson, J. E. (1985). Cognitive development in the gifted and talented. In F. D. Horowitz & M. O'Brien (Eds.), *The gifted and talented: Developmental perspectives* (pp. 37–74). Washington, DC: American Psychological Association.

Strong, E. K., Jr. (1943). *Vocational interests of men and women.* Palo Alto, CA: Stanford University Press.

Terman, L. M. (1954). The discovery and encouragement of exceptional talent. *American Psychologist, 9*, 221–230.

Terman, L. M., & Oden, M. H. (1947). *Genetic studies of genius: Vol. 4. The gifted child grows up*. Stanford, CA: Stanford University Press.

Tyler, L. E. (1974). *Individual differences*. Englewood Cliffs: Prentice-Hall.

Tyler, L. E. (1992). Counseling psychology—Why? *Professional Psychology: Research and Practice, 23*, 342–344.

U.S. Department of Education. (1997). *Digest of Education Statistics, 1997* (NCES 98–015). Washington, DC: U.S. Department of Education, National Center for Education Statistics.

Viswesvaran, C., & Ones, D. S. (2002). The role of general mental ability in industrial, work, and organizational psychology [Special issue]. *Human Performance, 15*, 1–231.

Webb, R. M., Lubinski, D., & Benbow, C. P. (2002). Mathematically facile adolescents with math/science aspirations: New perspectives on their educational and vocational development. *Journal of Educational Psychology, 94*, 785–794.

Wilk, S. L., Desmarais, L. B., & Sackett, P. R. (1995). Gravitation to jobs commensurate with ability: Longitudinal and cross-sectional tests. *Journal of Applied Psychology, 80*, 79–85.

Wilk, S. L., & Sackett, P. R. (1996). Longitudinal analysis of ability-job complexity fit and job change. *Personnel Psychology, 49*, 937–967.

Williamson, E. G. (1965). *Vocational counseling: Some historical, philosophical, and theoretical perspectives*. New York: McGraw-Hill.

Willings, D. (1986). Enriched career search. *Roeper Review, 9*, 95–100.

CHAPTER 26

Counseling for Career Transition: Career Pathing, Job Loss, and Reentry

Becky L. Bobek and Steven B. Robbins

IN THE UNITED STATES, occupational and economic upheavals are challenging mature adult workers to adjust to more frequent and varied career transitions. Effectively counseling mature adult workers involves applying appropriate interventions in view of client circumstances and theoretical, empirical, and practical perspectives that guide the adult career counseling process. In this chapter, the following sections relevant to counseling mature adult workers are presented:

- Worker demographics, work context, societal pressure and change, and likely career transitions.
- Theoretical and practical perspectives on mature adult concerns (e.g., loss of identity, finances).
- Elements of successful career counseling.
- Case vignettes illustrating counseling approaches to three mature adult career transitions.

CAREER TRANSITIONS AND THE MATURE ADULT WORKER ARE HERE TO STAY

In this chapter, *mature adult workers* are defined as individuals ages 40 and older, the bulk of whom are from the baby boom generation (born between 1946 and 1964). We selected this age range, which could be viewed as arbitrary, because workers ages 40 and older comprise a major and influential cohort in the labor force, have developed a history of work and life experiences, and may confront career transition issues (e.g., health concerns, age discrimination) that differ from younger workers. This is not to say that some of the issues in this chapter are less relevant to persons under the age of 40 because they may contend with similar life context issues and need assistance with career transition issues. At the same time, mature adults have generally settled into certain lifestyle patterns, having undertaken a host of roles (e.g., spouse, parent, worker, volunteer), along with their requisite obligations, which increase the complexity of career transition decisions. Mature adults represent a majority of the paid workers participating in the labor force, which will be an ongoing trend over the next 20 years (U.S. Bureau of Labor Statistics, 2001). In addition, a larger proportion of these workers have completed some college or have attained two-year degrees or four-year degrees, than any other age group of working adults (U.S. Bureau of the Census, 2001).

We also know from the retirement literature (cf. Robbins, Lee, & Wan, 1994) that health and finance are key factors for mature adults and may take on increasing importance during career transitions. Financially, median incomes for mature adult males working full time range from $42,404 to $48,687, while median incomes for mature adult females working full time range from $31,323 to $35,494 (U.S. Bureau of the Census, 2001). The trends indicate that males continue to earn more money than females and mature adult workers increase their income with age (experience and tenure on the job). Despite income increases over time, two-thirds of mature adults worry about their financial future (Russell, 1998). Health status among mature working adults varies, being influenced by education, income, and lifestyle choices, to name a few. A majority of these adults are overweight, with dramatic increases in obesity (U.S. Centers for Disease Control, 2000). These individuals are at increased risk of physical ailments and psychological disorders, which increases work absences and health care costs. Disability rates have also increased among mature adult workers, which can alter their ability to function to the capacity required by some occupations and place additional demands on the health care system. With increased life expectancy and uncertainties surrounding financial security throughout retirement, mature adults are expected to remain active participants in the labor force. At the same time, it should be recognized that with these trends, these labor force participants may be confronted with physical and financial limitations.

CHANGING NATURE OF WORK

Counselors also need to consider the changing nature of work as they counsel mature adults in the midst of career transitions. Structurally, a rising service sector and corresponding declines in manufacturing are concentrating the labor force in service occupations and providing the most employment opportunities. This shift to a service-producing labor sector has prompted the growth of part-time and temporary workers. These individuals work in an uncertain economy, with few, if any, benefits and limited wages.

At one time, the fastest growing occupations were in the computer industry, with software engineers, support specialists, and network systems/database administrators at or near the top of the list of high-growth occupations. Since the rapid economic upheaval of the late 1990s and early 2000s, the job market has changed again. Currently, there is a high demand for personal care and home health aides, medical assistants, other health care assistants, and social and human service assistants. These occupations vary by earnings potential and educational requirements. The computer-related occupations all require postsecondary education and pay the highest wages. The health care and human service assistants generally receive on-the-job training and earn from $7.76 to $10.88 an hour. These, along with other jobs that require on-the-job training (e.g., administrative support personnel, laborers, service workers), are projected to account for the most occupational growth.

Advancing technologies contribute to ever-changing and continuous forms of production. Technology is able to pace and monitor production 24 hours a day. Many work environments are fast paced, and workers are being asked to increase their productivity. In some instances, personnel are already obsolete and may become more so. In other cases, these advances require workers to upgrade skills or move across occupational sectors for continued employment. There are flatter organizational structures among the various sectors of the labor market, which translate into fewer career ladders for people to move up in a company. The workplace is also more heterogeneous, requiring multicultural competency among workers if they are to interact effectively with coworkers and achieve the goals of the organization. It is clear that continual change and uncertainty, where job competency and hard work no longer secure a person's position, mark the job scene. Given these work characteristics, mature adult workers who are not highly adaptable may confront additional challenges during career transitions.

SOCIETAL PRESSURES AND PERSONAL CHANGE

The life context of mature adult workers grows more complex as societal pressures and the nature of personal change are incorporated into the counseling process. One situation confronting the general public involves an aging population working longer. At one time, the natural course of events was for people to have long productive work lives, retire at 65, and be replaced by a new crop of young, motivated labor to follow the same path as their elders. Now people are working into their late 60s and 70s and trying to compete with younger cohorts for a limited number of jobs. At the same time, mature adults may want to seek fulfillment in a variety of life roles, one of which includes their jobs. A desire to stay productive, economic instability, and rising health care costs are motivating many mature adults to remain in the workforce.

Mature adult workers are also being confronted with a unique set of dual role demands as caregivers. Referred to as the "sandwich generation," mature adults are "being squeezed between the demands of their children and the responsibility they feel to assist their aging parents" (Anderson, 1999). They must cope with the stresses and pressures of increased caregiving responsibilities. Many mature adults are providing financial, psychological, and/or physical support to a number of relatives, which can strain their resources and influence their work lives.

On top of societal changes, a changing labor market, health, and life role considerations, it is important to consider the process of change or transition per se. A career transition is the "period during which an individual is either changing roles (taking on a different objective role) or changing orientation to a role already held (altering a subjective state)" (Louis, 1981, p. 57). In other words, people who either take on the tasks and behaviors of a new job or shift their internal view of a current job would be in career transition. The duration of time it takes to make a career transition varies, depending, in part, on the type of transition and the degree of familiarity between old and new situations. For example, a person faced with unanticipated involuntary unemployment may have little immediate opportunity to find a new job that satisfies financial and psychological needs. The duration of this person's career transition may be longer and more difficult than the person experiencing a planned exit from one job and subsequent entrance into another.

As Hesketh (2000) noted, "Effective transition management leads to improved posttransition adjustment, and this in turn feeds into appropriate anticipatory behaviors and attitudes in the next preparation stage" (p. 477). Similarly, the experience surrounding each transition influences "one's future experience of transitions" (Nicholson, 1990, p. 87). This is critical for counselors to understand given that career transitions are more frequent and of different types. The more different they are from one time to the next, the more difficult the transition experience may be for mature adult workers. The more frequent, the more complex additional transitions become as these experiences build on each other to influence mature adult thoughts and behaviors.

Another way to view change is akin to loss. Changes that involve the experience of loss bring with them a host of responses. Typical stages of response to loss provide a useful guide to understanding individuals' reactions to their experiences. These stages are denial, anger, bargaining, depression, and acceptance (Kübler-Ross, 1969). Not everyone proceeds through every stage in the same order or at the same pace. People move back and forth between stages. In the section on job loss, these stages are incorporated as a framework for discussing responses to this type of career transition.

MATURE ADULT TRANSITIONS: CAREER PATHING, JOB LOSS, AND REENTRY

The transition process is more complex than can be described in this chapter. To obtain diverse perspectives on this process, refer to models posited by Bridges (1980), Nicholson (1990), and Schlossberg, Waters, and Goodman (1995). The transitions considered here are career-related and relevant to mature adults. Mature adults experience various career transition alternatives, which can include (1) shifting their career path (moving up, down, across, or enriching the status quo); (2) responding to the loss of a job; or (3) reentering the labor market after having concentrated their energies in other life roles.

Career Pathing   With organizations constantly responding to the changing forces of supply and demand, a shrinking labor pool with strong qualifications, and a variety of career direction alternatives confronting workers, companies have designed *career pathing* programs to aid their recruitment (Bejian & Salomone, 1995) and to increase productivity by helping workers to transition into occupations that would best suit them. Specifically, career pathing involves developing and implementing processes and resources designed to continually help individuals to make their most significant and satisfying contributions throughout their career (Davis, n.d.). At the individual level, career pathing takes into account the planned and unplanned sequence of a worker's occupational positions over time.

The career pathing flowchart (Figure 26.1) was developed by ACT to create a model career pathing solution as part of its workforce development agenda. The figure presents the elements necessary for helping mature adult workers to make career changes. The first element is to identify the goal. Does the individual desire a lateral or vertical career move? Does the person recognize that a high stress, high profile position is too demanding and want to explore his or her options for moving down the career ladder? Does the person want to maintain a current

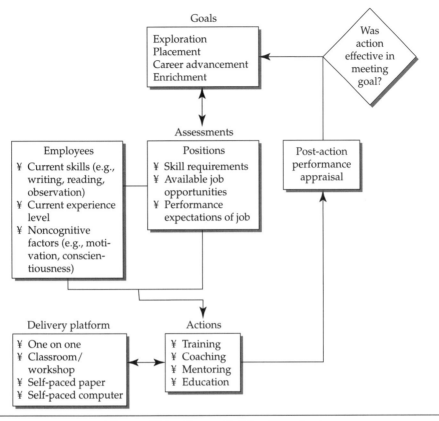

Figure 26.1   Career Pathing Flowchart.

position but is seeking to enrich his or her experience of it? Has a person been recently notified that his or her employment is being terminated, and does he or she want to quickly find another position? The answers to these types of questions clarify the type of career goal under consideration. Following goal identification, an assessment of skills, experience, and factors such as motivation and energy level are used to help establish a realistic self-appraisal of the individual. On the occupational side, a survey of available job opportunities, their skill requirements, and performance expectations is used to compare with what a mature adult brings to the employment table. For mature adults who may have a wide range of experiences but limited skills or energy to compete with a 20-something salesperson for commissions, it is critical to obtain a complete assessment to more fully consider with the client whether certain career alternatives are realistic options.

The next steps are to determine what actions and appropriate delivery platform(s) would serve to effectively meet the stated goal. A variety of actions and delivery platform(s) are necessary given the need to be creative about how information is delivered on demand in business and industry. Counselors can avail themselves of these options, recognizing that the business and industry context supports both traditional education activities and alternative approaches to advancing the professional development of employees. For individuals in career transition, the selection of actions and subsequent delivery platforms suited to their individual and occupational needs makes the most of available options and enhances a successful transition. Counselors must be cognizant of issues that may limit the effectiveness of specific actions or modes of delivery when working with mature adults. For example, some mature adults may be uncomfortable using self-paced computer programs to learn new skills. Others may be less likely to opt for a full-scale education program requiring four years of college because it is too time-intensive. Over time, individuals can revisit the career pathing elements as needed. There may be a need to redefine goals or reassess skill set depending on the situation and on voluntary or involuntary career shifts.

Job Loss   Arguably, the career transition that may have the most severe consequences is the loss of a job. Organizational merging, downsizing, or restructuring, economic downturns, and individual illness or disability are all potential contributors to job loss. With declines in product demand and profits, companies are laying off hundreds of workers for indefinite time periods. Recently, job loss has affected thousands of workers in both blue- and white-collar labor sectors due to a sluggish and uncertain U.S. economy. Disabilities contribute to job loss when individuals are no longer able to function in the capacity required by a specific job. For example, a bulldozer operator who is blinded in an accident would not be able to effectively function in this position and would, therefore, lose his or her job.

Job loss and ongoing unemployment can have serious repercussions for mature adults. When they seek work, it takes them longer to obtain employment than younger workers. For mature adults with low education levels, it is even more difficult to find another position (Kinicki, 1989). For those who have advanced within the corporate structure, these middle-age adults are "faced with the prospect of being unable to find a position of comparable status and may not be ready to retire" (Aiken, 1998, p. 274). Job opportunities become more limited for mature adults, and those opportunities that are available may be incompatible with these individuals' education or experience. (See chapters on job search research and implementation strategies by, respectively, Saks, Chapter 7, & Jome & Phillips, Chapter 19, this volume.)

Job loss can also lead to compromised physical and psychological health. Job loss is associated with increased anxiety, depression, feelings of isolation, feelings of failure and rejection, as well as lowered confidence and self-esteem and stress-related somatic complaints (DeFrank & Ivancevich, 1986; Eby & Buch, 1994; Kelvin & Jarrett, 1985). Further, job loss increases the likelihood of marital difficulties and financial problems. There are a host of adverse effects resulting from job loss. To offset these effects, a counselor might naturally want to engage the mature adult client in job search activities. But, according to Eby and Buch, an "effective job search process cannot commence until an individual has adequately dealt with the psychological issues related to their job loss" (p. 71). At the same time, some individuals may not have the supports in place (e.g., adequate savings, access to counseling) to delay their job search. Other individuals may be able to mount an effective job search despite their psychological distress. Still others might slip further into despair and depression if they did not have the structure of the job search process. It behooves counselors to consider both individual differences in response to job loss and variations in the contextual resources to which individuals have access as appropriate interventions for mature adults are determined.

Responses to job loss can be framed within the loss/grief stages referred to earlier in this chapter. In the denial stage, a person first informed of impending unemployment may be stunned and think, "I cannot believe this is happening to me." He or she may go through a period of confusion, panic, fear, or guilt over the situation. After people realize their jobs are ending, they may become angry and feel deceived, cheated by the employer, rejected, and frustrated. This represents the anger stage. Mature adults may take their anger out on family and friends during this stage. During the bargaining stage, individuals want to buy more time. They may ask for divine intervention and have unrealistic hope about maintaining employment. Then, the reality of the situation hits, and people may experience sadness and hopelessness as part of the depression stage. If the depression is severe enough, normal functioning may be inhibited. There may be decreased contact with others and an inability to make decisions. Finally, people in the acceptance stage face up to the realities of the situation and start to engage in constructive thinking and action. Although there may be continuing reservation and concern, there is increased hope and excitement about what lies ahead. By understanding these responses, counselors are better equipped to help clients work through their reactions to the job loss transition.

Reentry Labor market reentry is the final career transition alternative considered here. This alternative applies to individuals who have focused their time (usually a number of years) and energy on roles other than that of paid worker. Although both men and women may prepare for reentry, it is primarily women who experience this career transition alternative. Those who consider reentry may be single heads of households, displaced homemakers, empty-nesters, or those married with children but seeking other venues (Padula, 1994). Reentry may be motivated by vocational, family, or financial factors (Padula, 1994). There may be a desire to have a career and become self-supporting.

Many women "continue to delay establishing their vocational role until after 35 years of age when they have established their family roles" (Padula, 1994, p. 10). Once children enter school or grow up and leave home, women may want to concentrate their energies on reentering the labor force. A reason for reentry among homemakers who have primarily worked without remuneration to care for home and family is that they become financially responsible for themselves due to disability, divorce, death, or other circumstances related to their spouses (Moss & Baugh, 1983). Referred to as *displaced homemakers*, these women may never have anticipated working outside the home, think they lack marketable skills, and be unsure how and where to seek help (Moss & Baugh, 1983).

Reentry women often have multiple responsibilities that include caring for children, maintaining a home, and volunteering in the community. They may experience role conflict and emotional distress as they attempt to balance family demands and work obligations (see Vetter, Hull, Putzstuck, & Dean, 1986, for a more complete discussion). Other common difficulties include low self-concept, underconfidence about abilities, and relatively lower autonomy and assertiveness than women already engaged in careers. To effectively counsel reentry women, counselors must take into account such factors. Counselors must also consider the theoretical and empirical perspectives that can enhance their understanding of mature adult workers and guide the process by which they assist them in career transition. These perspectives are discussed next.

MATURE ADULT CONCERNS:
THEORETICAL AND PRACTICAL PERSPECTIVES

Career counselors assume that clients will inevitably face transition points in their lives, whether voluntary or involuntary. These points may be the result of job loss, change of life circumstance, or natural career progression. In this chapter, we call these transition alternatives *job loss, reentry,* and *career pathing.* The counselor's first major task is to organize the complex, multifaceted information being presented to them by the client. Once this information is organized, it must be put into a conceptual framework that identifies the salient issues, desired outcomes, and plan of action. At this point, the counselor and client must enter into a shared agreement and commitment to pursue these agreed-on actions.

Put another way, we believe that theory serves as the linchpin by which counselors implicitly or explicitly organize information, create an explanation for the client's expressed and implied difficulties or desires, and determine action steps (Robbins, 1989). Given the potential complexity of mature adult issues, it is imperative that we have a coherent conceptualization of the salient or defining constructs of interest in our clients' lives. These constructs frequently require both a career and personal focus, with implications for expected outcomes. In shaping a counselor's approach, career and adult development theories help to:

1. Surface the critical connection between a counselor's worldview and the actions taken to assist clients.
2. Reinforce the need for conceptual and practical consistency in action.
3. Integrate career and personal issues when addressing the needs of mature adults.

The four career development theories we chose for inclusion are well-established and supported approaches to understanding career development. The first two represent person-environment (P-E) fit models, with an emphasis on the assessment and exploration of personal and work environment attributes, and their corresponding congruence or fit. The third is a developmental approach to career development, and the fourth has its roots in social learning theory. The two adult development theories were selected because of their robustness and relevance to issues of concern to mature adults. Regardless of the context in which these theories were developed, they all lend themselves to identifying both career and personal issues and to establishing clear, measurable client outcomes. We briefly discuss each theory and then return to the typical issues brought into counseling by mature adults experiencing a career transition.

A Person-Environment Fit Perspective   Both the Minnesota Theory of Work Adjustment (see Dawis, Chapter 1, this volume; Hesketh, 2000) and Holland's (Spokane & Cruza-Guet, Chapter 2, this volume) theory of vocational types focus on the interrelationships between personal and work environment characteristics that affect career satisfaction and work productivity. Counselors have historically used assessment to identify and match key constructs with the intent of ensuring proper placement and training, resulting in both satisfaction and productivity outcomes.

As with any client, the P-E fit perspective would suggest that the mature adult focus on identifying and matching key abilities, values, and interests with potential work settings and occupations. A critical issue in this process is the notion of *transfer of skills,* or the generalization of past work and life experiences to novel or alternative settings. This is critical to the success of adult workers who face the pressure of obtaining a new job after experiencing job loss, a dramatic revision of their career path, or reentry into the workforce. As we have discussed, personal reactions may impede the systematic analysis and execution of a career search plan using a P-E fit approach: The experience of reduced self-esteem due to job and personal losses and indecision and anxiety about an uncertain future must be acknowledged and overcome. Ultimately, the P-E approach assumes that work attainment and satisfaction are the positive outcomes and indicators of success.

Super's Career Development Theory   An alternative approach to understanding the issues facing the adult worker is found in Super's (Super, Savickas, & Super, 1996) lifespan/lifespace career development theory. Within this conception, understanding the life stages and roles of individuals is critical to helping them frame their needs and expectations. Identification and elaboration of work self-concept, an individual's personal values and goals at this stage of life, and level of career maturity are central to career counseling. Career concerns include the establishment of clear work goals and skills necessary to compete with others and the identification of desired work. Personal concerns include the individual's accepting his or her limitations, understanding multiple role demands and fulfillment at this stage of life, and grappling with the potential loss of job security. Vocational choices are viewed as embedded within a broader model of life satisfaction and adjustment, and the actual *process* of finding a job is seen as leading to increased self-concept development.

Social Cognitive Career Theory   Contemporary models of career development have drawn heavily on social learning theory (see Krumboltz & Henderson, 2002). More specifically, social cognitive theory (see Lent, Chapter 5, this volume), a considerable updating, extension, and recasting of social learning theory, emphasizes motivational factors such as self-efficacy beliefs and outcome expectations to explain the career development process. These salient constructs are viewed as central to an individual's ability to marshal his or her internal and external resources when identifying, choosing, and acting on a career plan. Problems in the career planning and job search process are attributed to self-defeating and faulty career choice beliefs, unrealistic appraisals, and impaired decision-making ability. Personal issues for an adult client may center around financial and performance anxiety and on concerns about lack of abilities, negative outcome expectations, environmental barriers, and support systems.

Adult Development Theories   Our discussion of the conceptual underpinnings of career counseling for mature adult clients can also be embedded in the broader adult development theoretical literature. Two of the prevailing theories that address potential career and personal issues are Baltes' (1997) selective optimization with compensation theory and Atchley's (1989) continuity theory. Baltes' theory holds that people demonstrate considerable plasticity or compensatory behavior to accommodate as they age. In a sense, this theory highlights the importance of realistic appraisal and creative adaptive strategies to take full advantage of (i.e., optimize) current and past skills within the context of changing task demands. Emotionally, this requires acceptance of gradually diminishing internal resources while maintaining a sense of personal agency or control. Vondracek and Porfeli (2002) have integrated the selective optimization model with Super's (Super et al., 1996) developmental theory to provide a "developmental-contextual" perspective on adult career development. More specifically, they elaborate a life span development perspective by emphasizing environmental and social influences on the developmental process. From this perspective, key factors include selection pressures, adaptive processes, and enhanced functioning outcomes. These key factors are a direct consequence of, and interaction with, the environment.

Atchley's (1989) continuity theory reflects the strong emphasis in the adult development literature on maintaining a sense of life purpose or meaning across important middle-age, young-old, and old-old life transition points (cf. Robbins, Lee, et al., 1994). Making adaptive or realistic choices is a matter of connecting past work with future work within the context of internal and external changes. At a personal level, this requires both emotional risk and social (e.g., peer and family) support. As Robbins, Lee, et al. found, goal continuity, or the ability to maintain a sense of equilibrium or balance as evidenced by an inner sense of goal direction, life meaning, and purpose, was a critical mediator of adjustment as middle-age adults moved into early retirement and alternative work settings from their primary careers or jobs. They found that the ability to use financial, health, and social resources was dependent on a person's ability to access them. Conversely, a sense of discontinuity, or an inability to create and sustain goal-directed behavior, is viewed as a significant indicator of maladaptation. The implications for career counseling are clear: Clients demonstrating an inability to sustain purpose and direction during times of transition will not be able to access available resources or to use them in achieving a career plan. They will also demonstrate decreased personal and interpersonal satisfaction.

COMMONLY OBSERVED ISSUES

Although the mature adult population represents a heterogeneous group of individuals with varied needs and issues, the adult career counseling literature (Kerka, 1995; Newman, 1995; Rife & Belcher, 1993) suggests some commonalities in the career transition issues mature adults present to counselors. These issues may include establishing a realistic self-appraisal of current skills and abilities; dealing with financial loss and anxiety; loss of job security, colleagues, and identity; lack of confidence and self-esteem; fear of failure; and age as a liability. The effects of these issues depend on a person's ability to access and use internal and external resources, given the circumstances.

One issue that may confront mature adults is developing a realistic self-appraisal of their skills and abilities. After working many years in specific careers, the day-to-day tasks people carry out become second nature. They do not stop and think about the skills needed to complete those tasks. For example, homemakers with numerous responsibilities may be unable to see how their skills generalize to job requirements in the workplace. Counselors can assist mature adults by obtaining a complete and detailed history that charts the assortment of skills and abilities used along the way. Throughout this process, clients are positively recognized for their activities and accomplishments, while at the same time considering whether they need to upgrade their skills or whether their current abilities would enable them to successfully perform in certain jobs.

Finances may be a critical issue for mature adults, especially among individuals who have lost jobs or are reentering the workforce. Decreases in income can have significant financial and personal consequences. Many mature adults do not have a sizeable nest egg to sustain them during periods of unemployment. Without financial security, these individuals experience considerable stress over paying monthly expenses, affording health insurance, retaining their homes, and providing for the needs of family members. Financial problems are a major reason for family conflict and marital discord. People feel powerless when they struggle with finances because they have little control over their options. For mature adults, it can be extremely disconcerting if they had stable lifestyles and steady incomes before career transition. In addition, some mature adults are not comfortable discussing their financial situation and may be embarrassed to divulge their limited resources. Counselors must be sensitive to their clients' financial circumstances while at the same time working with them to offset the potential consequences of economic insecurity.

During times of career transition, the loss of job security, colleagues, and identity may become more acute and intensely experienced among mature adults. These individuals may have a well-established career identity, which is forfeited. This commonly encountered concern is less relevant for workforce reentrants than for career pathers or those experiencing job loss. The loss of work translates into the loss of a self-defining characteristic (Holm & Hovland, 1999). Leaving or changing a job also means leaving colleagues and regular social relationships. Career transitions alter people's daily habits and activities. As described by Kelvin (1981), "the need to work, and the work itself, provide a structure to life through specifying the time, place, and patterns of many of one's activities—including patterns of social relationships imposed by the interdependence of people in their working situation" (p. 8). The loss of social supports and daily routines may compromise an individual's ability to mobilize psychological resources. These losses limit coping and problem-solving abilities and diminish life satisfaction.

A lack of confidence and self-esteem and a fear of failure may also be experienced by mature adults during career transition. With the loss of a job, people lose their sense of worth and feel devalued as less productive members of society. For people who have worked comfortably in a certain job for years or are reentering the workforce, the prospect of entering a completely new position can inspire fear of failure because they are unsure of their ability to adjust and perform different tasks. Level of confidence and self-esteem may be compromised during any of the three career transition alternatives discussed in this chapter. For counselors working with mature adults, the need for support, encouragement, and active preparation is crucial to their adjustment and success. Lent and Brown's (2002) social cognitive theory comprehensively details the role of self-efficacy and outcome expectations in response to life transitions.

Mature adults may view age as a liability, which is reinforced by our youth-oriented culture. Employers view mature adults in the context of increasing pension and health insurance costs and a perceived lack of mobility (Newman, 1995). Potential employers "may wonder if the investment of time, money, and training is warranted in the case of the older career changer" (p. 65), given that these individuals will not be in the labor force as long as younger workers. According to Eby and Buch (1995), "It is well documented that older workers experience longer periods of unemployment, are less likely to be retrained at another job, and face the very real possibility of age discrimination" (p. 27).

How then can counselors respond to mature adult clients concerned about their age? Counselors can help clients identify mature workers' assets, such as valuable life experience, demonstrated responsibility, stability, and demonstrated interpersonal skills (Newman, 1995). Other potential positive characteristics include a stronger work ethic, lower absenteeism, higher productivity, more patience, willingness to learn new skills, and greater likelihood of remaining on the job than younger workers (Bird, 1992). These qualities are selling points for mature adults, and counselors can encourage their clients to present them as such to employers.

ELEMENTS CONTRIBUTING TO EFFECTIVE COUNSELING WITH MATURE ADULTS

What is unique and what is common to the general counseling process when serving mature adults? In the preceding section, we highlighted commonly observed issues presented by mature adults. How do we place these issues into context so critical elements are in place for counseling success? We highlight four key elements:

1. The importance of client history and baseline behavior.
2. Understanding the personality and intellectual resources available using appropriate assessments and clinical interviewing.
3. Selecting appropriate activities and modes of delivery.
4. Understanding the sociocultural context of the mature adult, especially for those clients experiencing involuntary transitions.

CLIENT HISTORY AND BASELINE BEHAVIOR

The adage "Past behavior is the best predictor of future behavior" is partly accurate for assessing the needs and concerns of mature adults. Taking a careful work, social, and educational history is critical to any counseling, but is especially important for adults grappling with the stress and strain of career change, reentry, or job loss. For example, the client's response to the request, "Give me examples of how you responded at other times in your life when stressed," may reveal considerable information about how the individual approaches task demands and adaptation processes. Theoretical perspective will influence what the counselor listens for and how the client's self-report of information is framed. The interpretation of career and personal issues is somewhat theory dependent.

From another angle, a careful history helps to identify a set of skills and experiences that can be generalized or transferred to new situations. An upbeat but realistic assessment of internal and external resources is critical to negotiating and executing a career plan of action. Several key internal factors are associated with mature adult worker adjustment, especially concerning life transition or life stress events (Hesketh, 2000). One cluster of factors is related to a sense of agency, optimism, and positive coping (Lightsey, 1996). A second relates to clear and realistic planning and to identifying opportunities (cf. Peterson, Lumsden, Sampson, Reardon, & Lenz, 2002). A third relates to the sense of continuity, purpose, and direction found to be critical as a mediator of older adult adjustment (cf. Robbins, Lee, et al., 1994). What we are suggesting is that the psychological ability to reach out and access available external resources, whether family support, a job club/coach, or a career counselor, is central to adjustment—called the *psychological resource hypothesis* (Riley & Eckenrode, 1986).

Personality and Intellectual Resources

All the theories we highlighted assume interplay between individual difference and environmental factors. Mature adults have well-formed and consistent personality characteristics and traits (cf. Crites & Taber, 2002; Hill, Thorn, & Packard, 2000). Depending on the trait, this can be both a strength and weakness when new situations require novel responding or when there are significant personal detriments to positive action. Is there a role for formal personality assessment? Our recommendation is that the solicitation of a history and clinical interview is a wise approach before determining whether to use formal psychological testing. Even then, we would recommend using those instruments geared toward adaptive behavior and functioning relevant to the workplace, such as the California Psychological Inventory (CPI; Gough, 1995), the 16 Personality Factor Inventory (16PF; Schuerger & Watterson, 1998), or the Revised NEO Personality Inventory (NEO-PI-R; Costa & McCrae, 1992) rather than a test focused on psychopathology.

Assessment of intellectual resources is in some ways more complicated because of the natural fears and realities of the aging process. Many middle-age adults express concern with their general recall of information (cf. Crites & Taber, 2002), but this does not necessarily point to a diminishment of intellectual resources. Use of formal testing such as the Wechsler Adult Intelligence Scales (WAIS; Wechsler, 1997) should be reserved for when there is a serious concern raised by either the counselor or clients that they are experiencing a serious decline in intellectual ability or that they have prolonged doubts about their capabilities. The alternative approach is to take a detailed work history in which the counselor examines exactly the kinds of task demands that are encountered and the individual's ability to address them.

Appropriate Activities and Modes of Delivery

Mature adults with a positive history of undergoing stress and strain due to job burnout, job loss, or job reentry are prime candidates for action-oriented rather than insight-oriented career counseling (Maslach, Schaufeli, & Leiter, 2001; Washington, 1993). As seasoned consumers, they are likely to rely on rational decision-making approaches that incorporate self-assessment and exploration activities aimed at removing self-defeating or inhibiting barriers (e.g., see American Association for Retired Persons [AARP] "Think of Your Work Future" program, 1991). All the theories we have highlighted are consistent with a prosocial or positive health approach. For example, a social cognitive approach would highlight the importance of appropriate and positive self-efficacy beliefs and outcome expectations that are commensurate with the client's skills and current job market realities. A life span developmental approach would use an educational approach to help clients understand their career goals within the context of multiple life roles as a middle-age adult. It would encourage them to make decisions based on values clarification of competing life roles.

Peer support is a potentially powerful tool for mature adults (Schlossberg et al., 1995), as evidenced by the tradition of job clubs and support groups within vocational and career rehabilitation (e.g., see www.fortyplus.org). The use of adjunctive interventions is an important and appropriate strategy for encouraging and mobilizing mature adults. While traditional one-on-one career counseling may be what *counselors* are comfortable with, extensive experience with peer support strategies should not be discounted. The AARP has developed outstanding materials and a local network of support groups throughout the country (see www.aarp.org/career for more information). Robbins, Chartrand, McFadden, and Lee (1994) carefully evaluated the AARP program, finding it was highly regarded and resulted in knowledge and behavior change across both self-directed and peer group conditions.

UNDERSTANDING THE SOCIETAL CONTEXT

Cultures differ, and our cultural frame affects our perceptions of life stress events and our responses to them. This is particularly important for involuntary transitions, where an increased sense of lack of control, fear and anxiety, and uncertainty can magnify perceived threats. Within the African American community, institutional racism is a reality, and during a poor economic climate, it is ethnic and racial minority groups that are more likely to undergo involuntary work transitions. It is incumbent on the counselor to be familiar with and comfortable responding to differences in cultural values and social class. It is not simply a matter of promoting the key factors associated with adaptive transitions (e.g., agency, optimism, clear and realistic planning, and perceived opportunity), but rather embedding these factors within the cultural and social frame of the client.

Côté's (2000, 2002) seminal work on identity capital development highlights the importance of viewing perceptions of and reaction to the world within a cultural and social frame. He proposed that navigation of life transitions is dependent on a combination of tangible (e.g., parent's social class, gender, and other structural factors) and intangible (e.g., agentic personality, psychosocial and intellectual development, and past experience) resources. The acquisition of identity capital reflects the ability to incorporate agentic and structural or environmental factors to achieve positive personal and occupational outcomes. Côté (2000) argued that an individual's ability to "know when I am grown up" and understand "models of maturity" is contingent as much on societal influences such as mass marketing and peer pressure as it is on internal forces of psychological development. We mention this theory because it reinforces the importance of contextual or social factors when understanding mature adult development. It is critical for counselors to understand how institutional and organizational variations in culture influence clients.

STATUS OF CAREER INTERVENTIONS FOR MATURE ADULTS

There is a striking absence of research on the efficacy of career interventions for mature adult workers, with most articles geared toward practice concerns without an evaluation component (cf. Kerka, 1995; Washington, 1993; Whiston & Brecheisen, 2002). This is surprising, given the increasing number of Americans working in later years and the importance of the topic. What we do know is that career counselors can help clients deal with job loss and other stressful transitions by encouraging coping strategies, fostering realistic work expectations, and responding to individual needs (Eby & Buch, 1994). We also know that midlife career renewal (Bejian & Salomone, 1995), or what we have called career pathing, requires acknowledgment of and sensitivity to mature adult worker reevaluation and renewal.

As Schlossberg (1981, 1991) noted, biological, social, environmental, and cognitive changes are inevitable for mature adults. She proposed that career counseling interventions must incorporate three sets of factors when understanding reactions to job change and loss:

1. The individual's perception of the transition (e.g., voluntary versus involuntary, anticipated versus unanticipated).
2. Characteristics of pre- and postchange environments (e.g., financial, social, health changes).
3. Internal resources and adaptive capacity.

While the research literature remains unsettled about the efficacy of adult-based career interventions, the conceptual underpinnings addressed by Schlossberg and other adult theorists remain compelling.

Olson and Robbins (1986) echoed Schlossberg's call for theoretically consistent approaches when they stipulated guidelines for the development and evaluation of career services for older adults. They further argued that career services must be comprehensive enough to acknowledge the unique characteristics and circumstances of mature adults from individual difference and sociocultural perspectives. A range of career intervention strategies geared toward mature and older adults are highlighted in a book edited by Niles (2002), which provides a comprehensive review of traditional and nontraditional services for adults, focusing on the strategies, resources, and methods aimed toward the mature adult worker.

Fretz (1981) called for research on career interventions that incorporated individual differences, using an attribute by treatment interaction model. Olson and Robbins (1986) similarly urged individuals and agencies providing career intervention services to not only evaluate the efficacy of their efforts but also ask the more basic question: "*Which* interventions produce the desired results for *what types* of individuals . . ." (p. 68). Robbins, Chartrand, et al. (1994) examined this question when comparing leader-led and self-directed career workshops for middle-age and older adults undergoing a career transition. They used the well-developed career and life-planning guides produced by AARP (1991). The program was developed as a leader-led, group-oriented, seven-week program using a combination of minilectures, in-class group exercises, and homework assignments. Straw (1988, 1989) found it to be a highly informative and robust career development program for older adults. Robbins, Chartrand, et al. modified the program as a self-directed and self-paced program and compared the differential effects of leader-led and self-directed programs. They also stratified participants by goal-directedness and sociability attributes. They found that career and life-planning workshops were positively received, regardless of format and participant attribute.

CONCEPTUALIZING CAREER INTERVENTION FOR MATURE ADULTS

We have highlighted the commonly encountered concerns of mature adult workers in career transition and the theoretical models available to help synthesize information and plan action. Only a few career textbooks are geared primarily toward adult career counseling (e.g., Niles, 2002; Vetter et al., 1986). What they hold in common are the notions of (1) distinguishing between personal and career concerns and outcomes, (2) assigning appropriate career intervention strategies, and (3) embedding career interventions within human development, sociocultural, and work contexts.

Patton and Meara's (1992) counseling textbook is a helpful guide to thinking about the issues confronting mature adults because it emphasizes organizing client information around what they term the "condition for which help is needed," referring to the causal statements a counselor would make to describe the underlying causes or reasons for clients' presenting complaints. The goals of treatment and expected success criteria follow suit. While Patton and Meara relied on a contemporary psychoanalytic perspective, any of the theories highlighted in this chapter can be used to organize both career and personal interventions for the commonly observed complaints and task demands of mature adult workers.

At the same time, any career intervention is best understood within a "phase-of-treatment model" commonly proposed in most career counseling models (e.g., Swanson, 1995; Swanson & Fouad, 1999). Spokane's (1991) career intervention model, for example, highlights the beginning, activation, and completion stages of individual and group career interventions. We propose a simple career process intervention model that incorporates four phases: assessment, conceptualization and agreement, intervention and action, and evaluation and reassessment. In essence, successful intervention with mature adults requires putting together the various elements we have covered:

1. Theoretical approach to guide the collection and organization of information.
2. Identification of central issues and treatment planning.
3. Execution and evaluation of treatment.

COUNSELING FOR SPECIFIC
MATURE ADULT TRANSITIONS: CASE EXAMPLES

We present three different case vignettes that, in turn, highlight the adult transition issues of career pathing, job loss, and reentry into the workforce.

CASE 1: IS IT TIME TO CHANGE MY CAREER? THE CASE OF BENNY

Benny is a 51-year-old adult who is dissatisfied with his current position as an auditor with a large public agency. He wants to make a career change but is not certain where to begin. He does not want his agency to know about his dissatisfaction, so he has contacted a local career counselor/executive coach. Benny called because he was upset about a recent financial audit that he did where people in the agency being audited were terminated for fiscal mismanagement. The career counselor interviewed Benny for an hour. Benny was articulate and clear about his dissatisfaction at work.

Benny has held various positions in the same agency for 25 years, all within the comptroller's office. Benny has an undergraduate degree in business finance, with a specialization in accounting. He never took the CPA exam but has become a certified public auditor. Benny feels stifled by his work, which is routine and predictable. He also intensely dislikes confrontation and being responsible for auditing financial irregularities. He enjoys being with people, but other than a few office colleagues, interacts with others at work only when there are financial questions or audit discrepancies.

Benny is married with two children who are completing college. He is financially comfortable but does worry about long-term security. On the other hand, he and his wife have managed to launch their children into and out of college. His wife is a nurse, who is satisfied with her job but would like to retire by the time she is 50. They are active in their diocese of the Catholic Church and volunteer with refugees entering the United States from Mexico and Central America. Benny is a first-generation Hispanic American. His parents were migrant workers who pushed Benny to excel in school. Accounting was a secure and important job and, given Benny's strengths in math, an "obvious choice."

Determining the Condition for Which Help Is Needed The recent precipitating event for Benny to seek help was the audit that resulted in employee termination. Benny expressed considerable conflict and unhappiness with his role as "accuser." It is clear that Benny feels both tired of accounting and trapped within a narrowly defined job within the public sector. Benny has difficulty fantasizing about other career options and seems puzzled when asked how he chose accounting. It is also clear that Benny is beginning to anticipate a new phase of his life, as his children move into adulthood.

The career counselor combines elements of Super's developmental theory with trait and factor approaches. Specializing in mature adults, she finds this combination especially salient for the presenting problems and needs of her clients. She views Benny's recent complaints within the context of shifting developmental stages. He is anticipating the change in family structure and is beginning to evaluate what is important to him. At the same time, he has never fully explored career options based on interests and values due to strong early parental pressure and to prematurely choosing a career field where his natural strengths in math would be a good fit. Benny's recent crisis has opened the door for him to reevaluate his professional and personal life goals. This is an opportunity to proactively plan for the next stage(s) of his life. From a career pathing perspective, Benny is interested in enrichment rather than career advancement. He has not explored alternative career options, nor has he fully matched his current skills and experiences with career options apart from his current position.

Treating Benny The career counselor contracted to meet with Benny three times. She explored her initial clinical impressions from the first interview in her second interview. At the third interview, the counselor presented to Benny her initial impressions by summarizing her beliefs of the underlying developmental and career fit issues driving Benny's dissatisfaction and restlessness. The counselor offered Benny two options. The first was to contract with her to complete a series of career assessments/transfer of skill exercises to help Benny assess, explore, and plan alternative career options. She would also explore with him the meaning of his shifting professional and personal roles. The second option was for Benny to purchase and use a self-directed career planning guidebook (AARP, 1991) to help him plan a new career choice. Benny chose the second option. The counselor strongly encouraged Benny to schedule a follow-up meeting to review his progress and to help answer Benny's questions.

Follow-Up   Benny reported having completed the workbook. He realized that he has strong "social and clerical" interests, which seem a little incompatible to him. He also realized that he was not sure how to proceed. The counselor contracted to meet with Benny for three additional sessions. She reviewed with Benny how to creatively explore career options, including interviewing current workers in positions he found interesting. She also asked him to create a life map and to share it with his wife and children. The life map is a technique used by Super (Super et al., 1996) to help individuals plot their life course, tasks associated with each step, and the multiple roles assumed in this process. Finally, she asked Benny to list his fears about making a career change. Benny returned with three items: fear of losing job security, fear of being unfulfilled, and fear of disappointing his parents. The counselor explored each fear with him. She suggested that if he had difficulty acting on his plans, they should reevaluate the degree to which these fears were barriers.

Benny returned in two months. He had interviewed several people in the public and private sector who had accounting backgrounds. He really liked a financial consultant who had helped a range of clients with their financial planning. He determined that by taking two courses, he could become a certified financial planner. He also found several sites that would hire him either as a contract worker or as a salaried worker. Benny felt confident he could build a caseload of clients. He believed this work would help satisfy his social needs. Benny also stated that he and his wife have begun talking about "life without children." This was difficult, and they both realized they were avoiding thinking about it. His wife ended up filling out her own life map, and they shared notes. Benny's plan is to take the courses at night and on weekends and to gradually prepare for a major change in employment. His goal is to leave the agency within a year.

Evaluating Outcomes   Benny was able to complete the self-directed career guidance program, but several fears inhibited his ability to take action. He recontracted with the counselor and was able to identify and address several fears limiting his ability to take action. At the same time, his combined social and clerical interests surprised Benny but helped him to select several people to interview. He was able to create a career plan that built on his strengths while moving him into work that fulfilled his social needs. Benny also benefited by confronting his changing life roles and exploring the implications with his wife.

The counselor was pleased with this outcome. She did not believe Benny was interested in, or needed, psychological counseling to address either early parental pressure or changing life roles. She also knew he was self-motivated and independent-minded and was best served by giving him ample opportunity for self-exploration and guidance, with counselor assistance as needed.

CASE 2:   WHAT IF I'M NOT READY TO RETIRE? THE CASE OF FRANK

Frank is a 53-year-old European American man with a high school education who has worked as a machine repairer for a textile manufacturing plant for 30 years. Two weeks ago, he was summoned to the manager's office and told that the plant was closing. Frank was commended for his years of hard work, but the company could no longer employ him. Unfortunately, Frank cannot take advantage of the company's early retirement package because the minimum age requirement is 55. Besides, he does not want to retire but wants to continue working and supporting his family. Frank has saved some money but not nearly enough for a secure future.

Frank is anxious about his prospects. The town he lives in had three manufacturing plants, and all of them have already closed or will be closing in the near future. He is angry that all his years of service were being rewarded by a sudden and unanticipated dismissal. The company did provide employees with exit counseling, which focused on updating his resume, developing a job search network, and surfing the Internet for job possibilities. After the counseling session, Frank was discouraged, remarking, "All my buddies are in the same boat as me," and "I do not know the first thing about surfing, on water or on the computer." Frank grew more frustrated as he talked the situation over with his wife.

Frank and his wife (a homemaker) have four children. Two are on their own, one just completed college but lives at home because he cannot find a job, and the youngest will graduate from high school this year. Frank spends most of his time after work socializing with friends from work down at the local pub. He does have a workshop in the garage where he putters around, fixing old lawnmowers (the local neighbors have even brought their nonstarting mowers by for his help) and small appliances. Recently, Frank has been spending more time alone out in the workshop and less time with his buddies. His wife encouraged him to go to the counselor recommended by one of his friends and Frank agreed.

Determining the Condition for Which Help Is Needed   The precipitating event for Frank to seek help was his impending dismissal. He is anxious and discouraged about the future. He does not recognize any career options at this point. Frank is concerned about financially providing for his family. Frank's identity was closely aligned with his work, and now he has lost that self-defining part of himself.

The career counselor has worked with numerous mature adult men who lost jobs at the manufacturing plants. He uses Atchley's continuity theory to frame the way in which he counsels his clients. He views Frank's situation in the context of a sudden life disruption—unanticipated loss of a job. With 30 years on the job, Frank had a clearly established identity that allowed him to maintain his internal continuity. Frank's self-concept was also reinforced in the provision of financial support to his family. It is expected that Frank's internal structures, which aid adaptation, are compromised. His external structures are also in question since most of his social relationships involved friends from work and activities that took place after work.

Treating Frank   After the first interview, the career counselor and Frank agreed to meet once a week for a month. During this interview, the counselor established an early rapport with Frank because the counselor had also worked in manufacturing years ago. Frank felt comfortable describing his situation and thought the counselor could help him find another job. The counselor acknowledged Frank's anger at losing his job after 30 years, believing that this would have to be worked through before Frank could move forward.

It was during the second interview that the career counselor probed for the different elements that helped Frank to maintain his internal and external structures during his career at the plant. The counselor recognized that the bulk of Frank's life revolved around work. With pride, Frank told the counselor that he always showed up for work early and put in extra hours whenever necessary. After work, the guys always sat at their table in the pub and had some beers. Frank was also proud that he earned a good enough living to support a wife, who never had to work, and four children. Frank's work behaviors, the reinforcement received from his buddies, and the monetary rewards from his work all contributed to his identity development and self-worth. Now that Frank has lost his job, spends less time with his buddies, and does not bring home a paycheck, his identity is compromised and he has diminished self-worth. To aid Frank's internal continuity, the counselor reinforces his ability to fix appliances and motorized equipment. The counselor connects Frank's past work (fixing machines) with current activities. This presents an opportunity for Frank to make a list of all the different skills he used on the job. The counselor starts the process by giving Frank a booklet that lists and describes a number of skills used in the manufacturing industry. Frank's first task is to go through and mark those skills that apply to him. Then, he can add ones that are not already listed. After Frank thinks about skills as they relate to his job, his task is to write down any skills he has related to all other life experiences.

To aid external continuity, the counselor reminds Frank of how he must be a great help to his neighbors when they are having mechanical troubles that he is able to fix. The counselor also encourages him to stay in contact with his buddies because they can help to maintain some stability for Frank, reinforce his self-worth, and provide an established network of friends when seeking a new position. The neighbors who stop by with their lawnmowers are also potential job contacts, and Frank can let them know he is looking for a new job.

Once Frank and the counselor have worked through his job loss reactions and considered how Frank might identify with something concrete in his life, they move on to connecting past experience and skills with future possibilities. They discuss how Frank's set of skills might be applied in other settings. The counselor encourages Frank to explore career options by selecting five occupations that interest him and offers to help him set up job-shadowing opportunities.

Evaluating Outcomes   Frank had considerable difficulty overcoming his anger and felt rejected after 30 years of loyalty and hard work. Exploring his anxiety surfaced fears over his inability to support his family and to obtain employment at the age of 53. As Frank worked through the skills exercise, he began to realize how much he knew and what he could present to potential employers as strengths. His past activities could be used to support new endeavors.

Frank also started meeting with his buddies again. This social support helped Frank to feel less isolated and more valued. Such positive social reinforcement can enhance self-esteem, communicate belongingness, and help inoculate the person against setbacks as he or she engages in job-seeking behavior (Caplan, Vinokur, Price, & van Ryn, 1989). It has also been reported that for older workers, positive social support is related to higher job search intensity (Rife & Belcher, 1993).

Frank enjoyed going out to job shadow, talking with people in related jobs, and understanding how his skills might apply in these settings. He knew that he wanted to stay in the same field, had no desire to go back to school, and accepted that he would have to commute to his next job. While looking for a position, Frank decided, with encouragement and support from his family, to place an advertisement for fixing mowers and appliances, charging a nominal fee. Although difficult at first, Frank's job loss presented a new opportunity for him.

The counselor was somewhat surprised by Frank's resilience. In many cases, the men who define themselves primarily in terms of their careers may experience prolonged anxiety and depression until they are able to find new careers on which to rebuild their identities. Fortunately, Frank was able to connect his past work skills with current and potential future endeavors. As a result of viewing his job loss as a turning point and with the support of his family and friends, Frank was able to sustain his internal continuity. The outcome of Frank's situation was mixed, at least in the short run, in that he had preserved his identity and was able to work through his job loss reactions, though he had not yet obtained a satisfactory new job that would allow him to financially support his family.

CASE 3: HOW DO I WORK FOR A LIVING? THE CASE OF SYLVIA

Sylvia is a 41-year-old Caucasian female with two school-age children whose husband divorced her six months ago. He has a new life and no interest in Sylvia or the children. She was shocked to find herself with no husband, no job, and two kids to raise by herself. Sylvia has never held a full-time paid job (she married right out of high school), and her husband had been a good provider so she never anticipated that she would need to work in the labor force. Sylvia was used to taking care of the kids, cooking, cleaning the house, and managing the finances. She is highly organized. Unfortunately, the money in her bank account has been dwindling and will run out within the next few months. Sylvia received one small check for child support, but that was five months ago. Sylvia is starting to panic because she has diminishing funds and does not have a clue about how to find a job, let alone what jobs might be available. She wonders who would hire her anyway because she believes she cannot do anything. Sylvia keeps telling the children that everything will be fine but cries herself to sleep every night because she is sad and afraid.

Sylvia completed two years of college after high school (liberal arts education courses) but did not earn a degree. She remembers being an average student. Sylvia describes herself as a friendly and outgoing person who could talk to anybody. She has always enjoyed helping other people. She volunteers to help with school and church bake sales and to chaperone children on field trips. She also helps raise money to support the local firefighters and the community hospital. Sylvia relies heavily for support on her Sunday worship group, who encourage her and make themselves available whenever she needs them. Sylvia decides to visit a counselor at the local community college.

Determining the Condition for Which Help Is Needed   The precipitating event for Sylvia to seek help was the divorce, resulting in a loss of funds and the need to work to provide for her children and herself. Sylvia is not only confronted by financial need but also lacks information about the world of work and job search skills. She has some education but not a degree. Sylvia does not feel marketable, wondering why someone would employ her. She has anticipated her need to enter the labor force as she seeks help before all her resources evaporate.

The career counselor determined that her approach with Sylvia would be guided by social cognitive career theory. As a mature adult without much labor force experience, Sylvia may foreclose on occupational options because she has faulty self-efficacy percepts and outcome expectations. The counselor identified low self-efficacy and limited cultivation of interests as areas for treatment. She also wants Sylvia to be cognizant of how job choice can be constrained by economic need, making occupational interest a secondary consideration. Although Sylvia's past environmental context and personal beliefs may have weakened her personal agency in career decision making, the counselor believes that, with self-efficacy modifications and her current supports, she will be able to establish positive outcome expectations and personal goals that can be translated into action.

Treating Sylvia   During the initial interview, Sylvia and the career counselor agreed to meet six times with the option of meeting additional times as needed. The counselor clarified presenting information in the second interview and proceeded to review with Sylvia her accomplishments, examining whether she felt successful after these experiences. Sylvia's perception was that she had been successful in taking care of her children and the house. She was also proud of the fact that her community fund-raising efforts were well received and met annual goals. Sylvia's homework was to acquire a new success experience; she was to do something where she felt she would be successful and perceive her actions as successful. This effort was designed to influence Sylvia's self-efficacy beliefs as she mastered new experiences and expanded her skill set.

The third counseling session entailed assessing Sylvia's interests, abilities, values, and self-efficacy. Sylvia's homework after this session was to read about five occupations that she had thought about at some time in her life. She could look through any of the materials in the counseling office. The idea here was to get Sylvia to start exploring occupations in general. The assessment results were then used in the fourth meeting to analyze discrepancies between Sylvia's self-efficacy beliefs and skills as well as outcome expectations and suggested occupations.

The fifth session was devoted to exploring occupational options. Given Sylvia's assessment results and subsequent discussion with the career counselor, a card sort procedure was implemented to examine the compatibility between Sylvia's attributes and possible occupations. Once a list of possible occupations was identified, the sixth counseling session involved an examination of potential barriers to occupational choice-making and setting personal goals. For Sylvia, finances were a major barrier. She had to find a job before her resources were depleted, and she could not afford to go to school. The counselor helped Sylvia compare her interests and skills to the identified occupations, taking into consideration possible barriers, and together they determined that she would explore the occupation of fundraiser at local nonprofit organizations, charities, and museums. Compatible with her self-efficacy beliefs, interests, skills, and positive outcome expectations, Sylvia was enthusiastic and excited about setting the personal goal of obtaining this type of position.

The plan to jumpstart Sylvia on her occupational trek is augmented with job search information during the seventh counseling session. The counselor and Sylvia discussed resume writing, cover letter writing, interviews, and the importance of networking. The counselor reminded Sylvia that she has already established a number of contacts through her community activities, reflecting additional effort to increase self-efficacy.

Evaluating Outcomes Sylvia made considerable progress throughout counseling. By recognizing her accomplishments and experiencing new success, she was able to alter her self-efficacy beliefs and outcome expectations. By having a more positive view of her efficaciousness and the possible results of her actions, Sylvia was able to set realistic personal goals and select an occupational option that was compatible with her interests, skills, educational level, and financial constraints.

The counselor was pleased that foreclosed occupational options were allowed to resurface and that Sylvia was willing to explore a broad range of occupations without allowing potential barriers to inhibit her consideration of them. Sylvia and the counselor agreed to meet one more time to discuss Sylvia's resume and cover letter and engage in a mock interview. Sylvia actively searched for a position and continued to make progress in the context of highly supportive conditions.

SUMMARY

The mature adult worker is the dominant group in the United States labor force, yet little career development research or empirically derived interventions are specifically devoted to the mature adult clients of career counselors. The only constant for these workers is change. We have highlighted the continuing economic upheavals, occupational shifts, and changes in the workplace itself. Placed within a life span developmental context, mature adult workers are challenged by the need to cope with multiple role demands, physical and cognitive changes, and an increasingly unpredictable economy.

We strongly believe that career and adult development theory must remain our guide for effective career counseling. Despite limited research on career interventions for mature adults, we contend that all counseling requires a well-grounded theory of both the person and the treatment hour (cf. Robbins, 1989). Our synopsis of four prevailing career and two prevailing adult development theories should stimulate thinking and provide a framework for generating effective interventions that take into account the personal and career dimensions of mature adults. We approached three very different cases using this theoretical framework: Benny, Frank, and Sylvia experienced a career transition, career loss, and career reentry, respectively. Their presenting issues and task demands were different, challenging the counselor to prescribe and evaluate interventions uniquely suited to each individual within his or her social context.

Our chapter was aimed toward counselor interventions that aid mature adult career clients experiencing change and loss. What about mature adults who have not yet been confronted with an immediate or impending career crisis? Can our ideas about theory and practice help inform how to prepare adults for coping with the changing nature of work? In addition, are there nontraditional counseling resources that would help to inoculate or assist the mature adult? Hill et al.'s (2000) and Hesketh's (2000) discussions of older adults and prevention and development in the workplace, respectively, highlight how mature adult workers can proactively manage their own career and life development. Teaching mature workers about the importance of planning and goal setting, in addition to anticipating life stress, is critical for coping with change. Individuals, as well as businesses and organizations, can avail themselves of strategies for coping and strategies for accessing and using resources, which can be provided by career counselors. Teaching personnel in organizations to facilitate workplace development through career resource libraries and coaches is also crucial.

For the mature adult undergoing considerable stress and upheaval, using a range of adjunctive resources, whether job clubs and peer support groups or self-directed learning guides and materials, can help facilitate the change process. As Hesketh (2000) argued, the goal is to help mature workers "take control of their own career management" (p. 471). (Also see Griffin & Hesketh, Chapter 20, this volume.) Whether using a social cognitive, life span development, or P-E fit model, the premium must be on teaching workers how to realistically appraise their life circumstances, to respond adaptively and flexibly to these life demands, and to effectively engage those around them to aid in this process.

REFERENCES

Aiken, L. R. (1998). *Human development in adulthood.* New York: Plenum Press.

American Association for Retired Persons. (1991). *Think of your work future.* Washington, DC: Author.

Anderson, T. (1999, November). Taking a bite out of the sandwich generation (caring for elderly parents and children at the same time). *USA Today.* Retrieved February 24, 2003, from http://www.findarticles.com/cf_dls/m1272/2654_128/57564071/print.jhtml.

Atchley, R. (1989). A continuity theory of normal aging. *Gerontologist, 29,* 183–190.

Baltes, P. (1997). On the incomplete architecture of human ontogeny. *American Psychologist, 52,* 366–380.

Bejian, D., & Salomone, P. R. (1995). Understanding midlife career renewal: Implications for counseling. *Career Development Quarterly, 44*(1), 52–63.

Bird, C. (1992). *Second careers: New ways to work after 50.* Boston: Little, Brown.

Bridges, W. (1980). *Transitions: Making sense of life's changes.* New York: Addison-Wesley.

Caplan, R. D., Vinokur, A. D., Price, R. H., & van Ryn, M. (1989). Job seeking, reemployment, and mental health: A randomized field experiment in coping with job loss. *Journal of Applied Psychology, 74,* 759–769.

Costa, P. T., & McCrae, R. R. (1992). *Professional manual: Revised NEO Personality Inventory (NEO-PI-R) and NEO Five-Factor Inventory (NEO-FFI).* Odessa, FL: Psychological Assessment Resources.

Côté, J. E. (2000). *Arrested adulthood: The changing nature of maturity and identity.* New York: New York University Press.

Côté, J. E. (2002). The role of identity capital in the transition to adulthood: The individualization thesis examined. *Journal of Youth Studies, 5*(2), 117–134.

Crites, J., & Taber, B. (2002). Appraising adults' career capabilities: Ability, interest and personality. In S. Niles (Ed.), *Adult career development: Concepts, issues and practices* (pp. 120–138). Tulsa, OK: National Career Development Association.

Davis, B. (n.d.). *Career pathing: A practical strategy and process for developing leadership and performance throughout your organization.* LMA Consulting Group. Retrieved December 10, 2002, from http://www.lmasystems.com/Articles/LMACareerPathing.htm.

DeFrank, R., & Ivancevich, J. M. (1986). Job loss: An individual level review and model. *Journal of Vocational Behavior, 19,* 1–20.

Eby, L. T., & Buch, K. (1994). The effect of job search method, sex, activity level, and emotional acceptance on new job characteristics: Implications for counseling unemployed professionals. *Journal of Employment Counseling, 31,* 69–82.

Eby, L. T., & Buch, K. (1995). Job loss as career growth: Responses to involuntary career transitions. *Career Development Quarterly, 44,* 26–42.

Fretz, B. R. (1981). Evaluating the effectiveness of career interventions. *Journal of Counseling Psychology, 28,* 77–90.

Gough, H. (1995). *California Psychological Inventory* (3rd ed.). Palo Alto, CA: Consulting Psychologists Press.

Hesketh, B. (2000). Prevention and development in the workplace. In S. D. Brown & R. W. Lent (Eds.), *Handbook of counseling psychology* (3rd ed., pp. 471–498). New York: Wiley.

Hill, R., Thorn, B. L., & Packard, T. (2000). Counseling older adults: Theoretical and empirical issues in prevention and intervention. In S. D. Brown & R. W. Lent (Eds.), *Handbook of counseling psychology* (3rd ed., pp. 499–531). New York: Wiley.

Holm, S., & Hovland, J. (1999). Waiting for the other shoe to drop: Help for the job-insecure employee. *Journal of Employment Counseling, 36,* 156–166.

Kelvin, P. (1981). Work as a source of identity: The implications of unemployment. *British Journal of Guidance and Counselling, 9,* 2–11.

Kelvin, P., & Jarrett, J. A. (1985). *Unemployment: Its social and psychological effects.* Cambridge, England: Cambridge University Press.

Kerka, S. (1995). *Adult career counseling in a new age* (ERIC Digest No. 167). Columbus, OH: ERIC Clearinghouse on Adult, Career, and Vocational Education. (ERIC Document Reproduction Service No. ED389881).

Kinicki, A. J. (1989). Predicting occupational role choices after involuntary job loss. *Journal of Vocational Behavior, 35,* 204–218.

Krumboltz, J., & Henderson, S. (2002). A learning theory for career counselors. In S. Niles (Ed.), *Adult career development: Concepts, issues and practices* (pp. 39–56). Tulsa, OK: National Career Development Association.

Kübler-Ross, E. (1969). *On death and dying.* New York: Macmillan.

Lent, R. W., & Brown, S. D. (2002). Social cognitive career theory and adult career development. In S. Niles (Ed.), *Adult career development: Concepts, issues and practices* (pp. 76–97). Tulsa, OK: National Career Development Association.

Lightsey, O. R., Jr. (1996). What leads to wellness? The role of psychological resources in well-being. *Counseling Psychologist, 24,* 589–759.

Louis, M. R. (1981). Career transitions: Varieties and commonalities. In R. E. Hill, E. L. Miller, & M. A. Lowther (Eds.), *Adult career transitions: Current research perspectives* (pp. 55–73). Ann Arbor: University of Michigan.

Maslach, C., Schaufeli, W. B., & Leiter, M. P. (2001). Job burnout. *Annual Review of Psychology, 52,* 397–422.

Moss, W., & Baugh, J. (1983, July). Displaced homemakers: An overlooked extension audience. *Journal of Extension, 21*(4). Retrieved March 5, 2003, from http://www.joe.org/joe/1983july/a3.html.

Newman, B. (1995). Career change for those over 40: Critical issues and insights. *Career Development Quarterly, 44,* 64–66.

Nicholson, N. (1990). The transition cycle: Causes, outcomes, processes, and forms. In S. Fisher & C. Cooper (Eds.), *On the move: The psychology of change and transition* (pp. 83–108). Chichester, West Sussex, England: Wiley.

Niles, S. G. (Ed.). (2002). *Adult career development: Concepts, issues, and practices.* Tulsa, OK: National Career Development Association.

Olson, S., & Robbins, S. (1986). Guidelines for the development and evaluation of career services for the older adult. *Journal of Career Development, 13*(2), 63–73.

Padula, M. (1994). Reentry women: A literature review with recommendations for counseling and research. *Journal of Counseling and Development, 73,* 10–16.

Patton, M., & Meara, N. (1992). *A textbook of psychoanalytic counseling.* New York: Wiley.

Peterson, G. W., Lumsden, J. A., Sampson, J. P., Reardon, R. C., & Lenz, J. G. (2002). Using a cognitive information processing approach in career counseling with adults. In S. G. Niles (Ed.), *Adult career development: Concepts, issues and practices* (pp. 98–117). Tulsa, OK: National Career Development Association.

Rife, J. C., & Belcher, J. R. (1993). Social support and job search intensity among older unemployed workers: Implications for employment counselors. *Journal of Employment Counseling, 30,* 98–107.

Riley, D., & Eckenrode, J. (1986). Social ties: Subgroup differences in costs and benefits. *Journal of Personality and Social Psychology, 51,* 770–778.

Robbins, S. (1989). The role of contemporary psychoanalysis in counseling psychology. *Journal of Counseling Psychology, 36,* 267–278.

Robbins, S., Chartrand, J., McFadden, K., & Lee, R. (1994). Efficacy of leader-led and self-directed career workshops for middle-aged and older adults. *Journal of Counseling Psychology, 41*, 83–90.

Robbins, S., Lee, R., & Wan, T. (1994). Goal continuity as a mediator of early retirement adjustment: Testing a multidimensional model. *Journal of Counseling Psychology, 41*, 18–26.

Russell, C. (1998, August). Boomers may go bust. *American Demographics, 20*(8), 14, 16–17.

Schlossberg, N. K. (1981). A model for analyzing human adaptation to transition. *Counseling Psychologist, 9*(2), 2–18.

Schlossberg, N. K. (1991). *Overwhelmed: Coping with life's ups and downs.* Lexington, MA: Lexington Books.

Schlossberg, N. K., Waters, E. B., & Goodman, J. (1995). *Counseling adults in transition: Linking practice with theory* (2nd ed.). New York: Springer.

Schuerger, L., & Watterson, D. (1998). *Occupational interpretation of the 16 personality factor questionnaire.* Cleveland, OH: Author.

Spokane, A. R. (1991). *Career intervention.* Englewood Cliffs, NJ: Prentice-Hall.

Straw, M. K. (1988). *Evaluation of the AARP WORKS pilot program* [Reprint]. Washington, DC: American Association for Retired Persons, Research and Data Resources Department.

Straw, M. K. (1989). *AARP WORKS: Summary of the evaluation of the 1987 and 1988 pilot programs* [Reprint]. Washington, DC: American Association for Retired Persons, Research and Data Resources Department.

Super, D. E., Savickas, M. L., & Super, C. M. (1996). The life-span, life-space approach to careers. In D. Brown & L. Brooks (Eds.), *Career choice and development* (3rd ed., pp. 121–178). San Francisco: Brown, Brooks, and Associates.

Swanson, J. L. (1995). The process and outcome of career counseling. In W. B. Walsh & S. H. Osipow (Eds.), *Handbook of vocational psychology: Theory, research, and practice* (2nd ed., pp. 217–259). Mahwah, NJ: Erlbaum.

Swanson, J. L., & Fouad, N. (1999). *Career theory and practice: Learning through case studies.* Thousand Oaks, CA: Sage.

U.S. Bureau of the Census. (2001). *Statistical abstract of the United States: 2001.* Washington, DC: U.S. Government Printing Office.

U.S. Bureau of Labor Statistics. (2001, Winter). Charting the projections: 1998–2008 [Electronic version]. *Occupational Outlook Quarterly, 45*(4), 1–6.

U.S. Centers for Disease Control. (2000, September). *CDC Fact Book 2000/2001.* Washington, DC: U.S. Centers for Disease Control.

Vetter, L., Hull, W., Putzstuck, C., & Dean, G. (1986). *Adult career counseling: Resources for program planning and development.* Bloomington, IL: Meridian Education Corporation.

Vondracek, F., & Porfeli, E. (2002). Life-span developmental perspectives on adult career development: Recent advances. In S. Niles (Ed.), *Adult career development: Concepts, issues and practices* (pp. 20–38). Tulsa, OK: National Career Development Association.

Washington, T. (1993). Career counseling the experienced client. *Journal of Career Planning and Employment, 53*(2), 37–39, 67–68.

Wechsler, D. (1997). *Wechsler Adult Intelligence Scale* (3rd ed.). San Antonio, TX: Psychological Corporation.

Whiston, S. C., & Brecheisen, B. K. (2002). Evaluating the effectiveness of adult career development programs. In S. Niles (Ed.), *Adult career development: Concepts, issues and practices* (pp. 370–388). Tulsa, OK: National Career Development Association.

Author Index

Subject Index